# THE AMERICAN
# REPUBLIC

*Through Reconstruction*

THE

REP

RICHARD HOFSTADTER

Columbia University

WILLIAM MILLER

DANIEL AARON

Smith College

VOLUME ONE

PRENTICE-HALL, INC.

*Englewood Cliffs, New Jersey*

# AMERICAN

# UBLIC

**THROUGH RECONSTRUCTION,** Second Edition

THE AMERICAN REPUBLIC

Volume One, THROUGH RECONSTRUCTION

Second Edition

Hofstadter, Miller, and Aaron

Copyright 1959, 1970 by Prentice-Hall, Inc.,
Englewood Cliffs, New Jersey.

Library of Congress Catalog Card No.:73–98456
Printed in the United States of America.
Maps by Hagstrom Company, Inc.
Design by Walter Behnke.

PRENTICE-HALL INTERNATIONAL, INC., London
PRENTICE-HALL OF AUSTRALIA, PTY., LTD., Sydney
PRENTICE-HALL OF CANADA, LTD., Toronto
PRENTICE-HALL OF INDIA PVT. LTD., New Delhi
PRENTICE-HALL OF JAPAN, INC., Tokyo

Current printing (last digit):

15 14 13 12 11 10 9 8 7 6 5 4 3 2 1

0–13–029173–0

# PREFACE

The first edition of *The American Republic* has had a gratifyingly large and loyal following, and in this Second Edition the authors have been careful to retain and strengthen those features of style, interpretation, contemporary detail, and extensive contemporary quotations in the context of the narrative, which readers have taken the trouble to commend. They also have aimed to preserve and improve those qualities of readability and design in layout, type, maps, and illustrations which won the first edition publishing-industry awards.

At the same time, this new edition is in many respects a new book. Each generation, as it approaches maturity, rewrites the history of the past. Its vantage point has become different from that of earlier generations. Its perspective has been altered by its own experience. Its hopes have changed shape because of frustrations in some areas, fulfillment in others. This edition of *The American Republic* has been largely rewritten to provide a synthesis of American History for students of the 1970s.

Those teachers who used *The American Republic* in the past, we believe, will discover on a mere perusal of this Second Edition the freshness of the entire work. The first three chapters present a thoroughly reconsidered approach to the age of discovery, the aboriginal peoples, the epoch of colonization, and the maturation of the English colonies with their large non-English populations, white and black alike. The last chapter, on Reconstruction after the Civil War, by carrying the analysis of the South well beyond 1877, gives meaning to recent happenings in American society. A more detailed examination of these and the intervening chapters, we feel certain, will only deepen the impression made by a quick look.

It is to the new student more than to the experienced teacher, nevertheless, that this Second Edition is most directly addressed. The authors are aware of how often college students may have encountered courses in American History in their earlier school work. It is their hope and intention in this book to open up the subject of American History even for such students and not to close it, as so many textbooks do.

Throughout this book the authors have sought to keep clear their awareness that America is and always has been part of the world and a force in it, that our national experience may most illuminatingly be viewed in the context of Western Civilization and its world-wide impact. We have enlarged and we hope strengthened all sections on foreign relations, and in particular those covering Latin America and Canada. Immigration, voluntary and forced, can profitably be seen as part of American relations with the rest of the world; and the place of "ethnic groups" in American life, from the first arrival of large numbers of Germans and Scotch-Irish in the eighteenth century, is newly elaborated. The condition and role of the Negro in America pervades the history of the country from the start, and it pervades our book. A special feature of the new edition is the consideration given to the lasting impact at home and abroad of such living documents as the Declaration of Independence, the Constitution, and the Emancipation Proclamation.

The authors believe that history is more than politics and public policy. This edition, like the first, gives extended consideration to those aspects of life and action that emerge from intellectual tradition, aesthetic experience, and human values. In this edition, chapters on economic and social organization, like those on literature, philosophy, and art, have been somewhat more closely integrated with the main thread of political narrative and analysis. But we have tried not to neglect the reverse relationship as well: Historians today study politics with perceptions sharpened and awareness deepened by knowledge of the economy and social structure, and by familiarity with the religion, philosophy, and creative arts by which a people and a nation strive for self-realization.

In writing this revised edition the authors have not hesitated to draw upon their own other works to enhance the presentation. At the same time, this edition contains much new detail and interpretation to help convey a feeling for the past, some insight into its mean-

ing, and an appreciation of historical personages.

All the maps in this edition have been redrawn for clarity and simplicity and to make the most advantageous use of color. Many of the maps, like many of the illustrations, are new.

The suggested Readings at the end of each chapter, and the General Readings at the end of the book, have been rewritten to reflect here, as in the text itself, significant advances in American scholarship. But important older books have not been neglected.

The authors wish to thank all those who took the trouble to call attention to errors in the first edition. These they have made every effort to correct. They also wish to acknowledge the helpful comments they received from those asked to review the first edition with the new edition in view. Professor Arthur R. Dudden has supplied a most helpful teacher's manual and student guide.

It is a pleasure to be able to acknowledge publicly the unfailing enthusiasm and helpfulness of our editor at Prentice-Hall, Robert Fenyo, and of his assistant, Barbara Van Osten. For the most patient consideration, sometimes under the most trying conditions, we are once again deeply obligated to the Project Planning Division of Prentice-Hall, directed by Ronald Nelson. To him and to Marjorie Graham we are especially indebted. This book, like all our Prentice-Hall publications, has been designed by Walter Behnke, to our and to our readers' lasting good fortune. Prentice-Hall itself has stinted nothing in the planning and production of this volume.

R.H.    W.M.    D.A.

# CONTENTS

# MAPS

# THE AMERICAN REPUBLIC

*Through Reconstruction*

# ONE

At about a quarter to five in the morning, a half hour before dawn on Friday, August 3, 1492, the pull of the moon began to draw the waters of the Atlantic Ocean back from their crest on the Rio Tinto at the little port of Palos in Andalusia in Spain.

As the tide ran out to sea that morning, it carried from the security of Palos harbor three fated ships, *Niña, Pinta,* and *Santa Maria.* Aboard *Santa Maria,* flagship of this fleet, sailed the "Captain-General" in command, long-faced, hawk-nosed Christopher Columbus, an aging mariner many thought mad. His destination was "the lands of India," a storied realm of wealth and power somewhere to the east of the Mohammedan world that sorely menaced Christendom. "I should not go by land, the usual way, to the Orient," Columbus the Genoese told his royal backers, King Ferdinand and Queen Isabella of Spain, but by water, westward, "by the route to the Occident, by which no one to this day knows for sure that anyone has gone."

His ships, Columbus said himself, were "well furnished with much provision and many seamen." The season was sounder than he knew for an ocean voyage on the course he proposed to follow. The morning of departure his sails hung limp in the windless air, but by eight o'clock the river tide had floated his small ships to open water where they caught "a strong sea breeze."

By sunset on the first day officers and men lost sight, over the curving rim of the earth, of dear, familiar shores, visible havens from the unknown terrors of the deep that claimed so many of the seagoing clans. But Columbus's mariners, seasoned in ocean navigation, knew, or thought they knew, something of what lay ahead and did not worry yet.

# THE DISCOVERY
# OF AMERICA
# BY EUROPEANS

Six days out, 660 miles "South and by West" of Palos, the little fleet reached the Canary Islands, already owned and settled by Spain for nearly a hundred years. These islands cluster just off Africa's turbulent western coast at 28° north latitude, the very parallel, Columbus believed, on which lay Cipangu—Japan—the richest part, according to the information he trusted most, of "the lands of India" he sought.

Columbus and his men rested in the Canaries for a month while their ships underwent needed repairs and supplies were replenished. The Captain-General fell in love with the lady ruler of the island of Gomera, Doña Beatriz de Peraza. But Columbus loved his mission more than his mistress, and in the early hours of the morning of September 6, his prayers said and his vessels bulging with fresh wood and water, wine, biscuit, and cheese, he weighed anchor at San Sebastián, Doña Beatriz's pleasant port.

For nearly 48 hours Columbus's fleet stood becalmed off the island of Tenerife, its fiery 12,000-foot volcano the tallest in the Canaries. Then, at 3 A.M. Saturday, September 8, as the commander recorded, "the wind come fair" from the northeast, and he set his bold new course: *"Oeste: Nada del noroeste, nada del sudoeste"*—"West: nothing to the northward, nothing to the southward."

The next day he did something bolder still. What this was he put down in the privacy of his Journal, in the third person, as was his practice: "he decided to reckon less than he made," to doctor the log, that is, "so that if the voyage were long the people," as he called the crew, "would not be frightened and dismayed." The people, that Sunday morning and afternoon, still could see the westernmost of the Canaries, the island of Ferro, and lofty Tenerife breathing smoke. By dusk, each last point of land had faded out. By nightfall, the three small ships bobbed alone on the uncharted sea, their crews, mostly Spanish, restive under a foreign captain they did not fully trust.

Thirty days out, on October 10, having doubled all known records for ocean sailing beyond sight of the shore, *Santa Maria*'s people mutinied. The very uneventfulness of the lengthening voyage had overstrained the nerves of sailors made idle by the easy passage. Only Columbus's promise to turn back if no land were raised in three days quieted the crew. Then, just past 2 A.M. on October 12, the deadline nearing, *Pinta*'s lookout called, *"Tierra! Tierra!"*

4

After three false landfalls on recent days, this cry in the night awakened mixed feelings in the men. But a light on an island in the Bahamas had indeed been sighted six miles off. As soon as daylight made debarkation safe on this engaging gateway to the New World—"all is so green that it is a pleasure to gaze upon it," wrote the Captain-General in his Journal—the momentous "Landing of Columbus" took place.

"To the first island which I found," Columbus later wrote home to his sovereigns, "I gave the name 'San Salvador,' in remembrance of the Divine Majesty, Who had marvellously bestowed all this; the Indians call it 'Guanahaní.'" Today a British possession, this island is officially and perhaps more appropriately known as Watling's Island after the English buccaneer who settled there in the seventeenth century.

Soon, "I found very many [other] islands," Columbus added in his letter to Ferdinand and Isabella, "filled with innumerable people, and I have taken possession of them all for their Highnesses, done by proclamation and with the royal standard unfurled, and no opposition was offered to me."

Columbus's hosts, during his first few weeks of exploration, were the mild Arawaks, as pleasing to gaze upon as the land itself and "so guileless and so generous with all that they possess, that no one would believe it who has not seen it. They refuse nothing . . . if it be asked of them; on the contrary, they invite any one to share it and display as much love as if they would give their hearts."

Columbus was quick, on this first contact, to return native kindness with aggression: "As soon as I arrived in the Indies, in the first island which I found, I took some of the natives by force, in order that they might learn and might give information of whatever there is in these parts." When he then mended his manners, it was not without ulterior motives of enduring consequence: "I gave them a thousand handsome good things, which I had brought, in order that they might conceive affection for us and, more than that, might become Christian and be inclined to the love and service of Your Highnesses and of the whole Castilian nation, and strive to collect and give us of the things which they have in abundance and which are necessary to us."

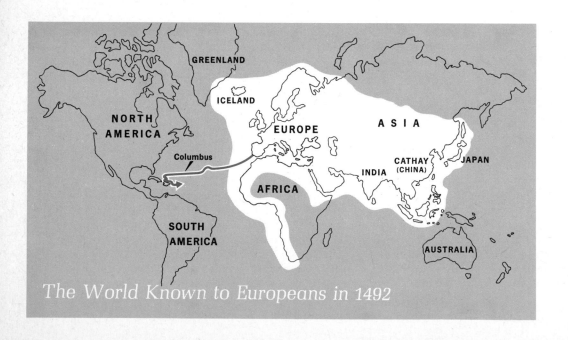

*The World Known to Europeans in 1492*

*An impression, dating from 1590, by the Flemish artist Theodor de Bry, of Columbus, Ferdinand, and Isabella at Palos Harbor as the explorer is about to embark on his first trans-Atlantic voyage in 1492 to "the Indies." (Theodor de Bry, America, Part IV.)*

## 1   *The New World before Columbus*

### THE CHALLENGE OF INDIAN CULTURE

When we say, "Columbus discovered America," we mean only that his voyage across the Atlantic Ocean in 1492 first opened the New World to permanent occupation by people from Europe, itself a complex and challenging term perhaps most usefully defined by the geographer Derwent Whittlesey as "the habitat of western civilization, a dynamic society not paralleled in any other part of the earth, until Europeans carried their expansive mode of life overseas."

Before Columbus charted the course followed by his ambitious rivals in the age of Europe's Renaissance, "America" certainly had been discovered two or three times and may have been discovered many more. The most recent estimates place the arrival of the earliest-known settlers—Columbus was the first to name these tawny Mongoloids "Indians"—between 40,000 and 20,000 years ago. These people, or more properly this mixture of peoples, having moved eastward across Asia over thousands of years (while others somehow differently mixed and grown fatefully fair in complexion, were moving into European lands), apparently crossed from Siberia to Alaska by way of the ancient land bridge, now 300 feet beneath Bering Strait, whose long existence modern science recently established. With the conspicuous exception of the late-arriving Eskimos, the newcomers gradually spread southward in pursuit of the big game on which they chiefly lived. Some settled permanently on the high plains of what is now the arid Southwest of the United States. Here, until a great climatic change occurred about 8000 B.C., a lush forest afforded ample greenery on which mammoths, wild bison, antelopes, and mountain goats fed. This fare thinned out farther west where a "desert culture" developed. For thousands of years small desert groups, occasionally finding shelter in

5

6

the mountain caves where their traces have been preserved, eked out the big game with smaller carnivores such as coyotes, gophers, bobcats, and rats, and, more significantly, with plant food. After 8000 B.C., with the forests of the high plains dying because of the dwindling water supply, the plains Indians also turned to scrub plants for their principal food supply. Some 2000 years later they were successfully gathering, preserving, and planting seeds, and cultivating regular crops with crude tools of wood and stone.

As early, according to recent findings, as 12,000 B.C., husbandry had also begun in the "valley of Mexico," where the largest numbers of Indians had settled down after the southward trek. The stable society husbandry made possible turned Mexico, and neighboring Guatemala and Honduras, into the "heartland of Middle America." Here and in Peru, during the early centuries of the Christian era in Europe, which we call the Dark Ages, Indian culture flowered.

Widespread if disconnected disasters—earthquakes and epidemics, prolonged droughts and dynastic civil wars—seem to have disrupted many areas of Indian life in the century or two before the catastrophic European invasion and helped prepare the ground for the Europeans' success among the dark worshipers of the Sun in Heaven, who innocently welcomed white men coming from the direction of the Sun's rising as the true children of the Gods. Yet, even in the years of their decline, when they first were encountered by the Spanish *conquistadores* (see p. 19), the Aztecs of Mexico, the Incas of Peru, the Mayas of Guatemala and Yucatán astonished the newcomers with their wealth and artistry; and to this day their accomplishments, and those attributed to predecessor peoples they themselves had mastered, challenge the mind and heart.

Bernal Díaz del Castillo, who fought with Cortez in all his campaigns and wrote the best account of *The Discovery and Conquest of Mexico,* conveys the characteristic wonder of his countrymen on their first triumphant march across the American mainland:

During the morning, we arrived at a broad Causeway and continued our march towards Iztapalapa, and when we saw so many cities and villages built in the water and other great towns on dry land and that straight and level Causeway going towards Mexico [City], we were amazed and said that it was like the enchantments they tell of in the legend of Amadis [the most popular chivalric romance of the age], on account of the great towers and temples and buildings rising from the water, and all built of masonry. And some of our soldiers even asked whether the things that we saw were not a dream. . . .

And then when we entered the city of Iztapalapa, the appearance of the palaces in which they lodged us! How spacious and well built they were, of beautiful stone work and cedar wood, and the wood of other sweet scented trees, with great rooms and courts, wonderful to behold, covered with awnings of cotton cloth.

When we had looked well at all this, we went to the orchard and garden, which was such a wonderful thing to see and walk in. . . . Then the birds of many kinds and breeds which came into the pond. I say again that I stood looking at it and thought that never in the world would there be discovered other lands such as these. . . . Of all these wonders that I then beheld today all is overthrown and lost, nothing left standing.

Even Bernal Díaz's English editor in the 1950s shared the white man's tendency to discredit the achievements of "savages," to which Cortez's companions' own eyes testified: "It could not have failed to make a vivid impression on the Spaniards, who, it must be remembered, . . . had seen nothing better during the twenty-five years of exploration of America than the houses of poles and thatch of Indian tribes, none of whom had risen above the state of barbarism." Yet, when Albrecht Dürer, the great German artist, saw the trophies sent from Mexico by Cortez for the coronation at Aix-la-Chapelle in 1520 of

Charles I of Spain as Holy Roman Emperor, his enchantment matched that of Bernal Díaz del Castillo, and he wrote in his diary:

Also did I see the things which one brought to the King out of the new Golden Land: . . . all sorts of marvelous objects for human use which are much more beautiful to behold than things spoken of in fairy tales. . . . In all the days of my life I have seen nothing which so rejoiced my heart as these things, . . . and I marveled over the subtle genius of these men in strange countries.

For all the stunning beauty of their environment—the sturdy causeways, for example, and the enchanting ponds and lakes and canals of Mexico were man-made parts of intricate irrigation systems—the Aztecs were a brutal and terrifying people, much given to human sacrifice. And yet the desolation Bernal Díaz mentions was wrought by the Spanish not the savages, by the Christians and not the children of darkness.

The Incas of Peru, inheritors, like the Aztecs, of an earlier advanced culture, were at least the Aztecs' equal in building and design.

*(Left) Stone carving, 30½ inches, representing Xipe Totec, the flayed-skin god, 1507, from the Valley of Mexico. This Aztec deity was worshipped in rites celebrating the Spring earth-renewal. (Center) Modeled-clay whistle, 9¼ inches, in the form of a standing female Maya figure, c. 800, from Campeche, Mexico. (Right) Gold female figurine, 9½ inches, c. 1500, from the Inca culture, coastal Peru. Spectacular for its size and grace, this figure is one of the few to escape the Spanish melting pot. (Photographs courtesy of Museum of the American Indian. Heye Foundation.)*

In imperial and social organization and administration, they were far ahead. At the time of the Spanish invasion, the Inca empire stretched along the western coast of South America from 2° north to 37° south latitude and included much of modern Ecuador, Peru, Bolivia, and Chile, all bound together by roads and runners the Romans would have admired. Nor were their rulers lacking in the consciousness of power. When urged by Pizarro's chaplain, on his way to the conquest of Cuzco, the glittering Inca capital, to accept Christ as his Lord, the Pope as his master, and Emperor Charles as his monarch, the reigning Inca sovereign, Atahuallpa, replied:

I will be no man's tributary. . . . Your emperor may be a great prince; I do not doubt it, when I see that he has sent his subjects so far across the waters; and I am willing to hold him as a brother. As for the Pope of whom you speak, he must be crazy to talk of giving away countries which do not belong to him. For my faith, I will not change it. Your own God, as you say, was put to death by the very men whom he created. But mine, my God still lives in the heavens and looks down upon his children.

In the "classic age" of their "Theocratic Period," which seems to have ended catastrophically about 900 A.D., the Mayas, possessors of the third great Indian culture, were the uncontested masters of the science of the sky. Their gods were many and were associated with the peaceful pursuit of husbandry. Their efficiency in cultivation supplied the wherewithal for the support of priestly learning, and especially the learning that had to do with the weather, the seasons, the round of the year. Mayan priests specialized in astronomy, to which mathematics was the key. Abstract thought itself was the key to mathematics. The Mayas' brilliant achievements along all these lines culminated, before the end of the seventh century A.D., in their extraordinary 365-day calendar, one better than Europeans generally would have for a thousand years. The quality of Mayan thinking has prompted Western historians to think of them as the Greeks, as they think of the imperial Incas as the Romans, and the marauding Aztecs as the Assyrians, of pre-Columbian America. Mayan triumphs in art serve only to underscore the Grecian theme. Only nowadays are pre-Columbian art objects being transferred from natural history museums, where they were preserved mainly as artifacts, to the galleries that house the aesthetic treasures of civilization.

This Grecian theme—in fact, it is but a metaphor of European-oriented men—can easily be overdone. The Indians of Mexico and Peru had a high civilization all their own. The Aztecs are said to have known of the wheel, yet to have used it for no productive purpose. They and others also practiced metallurgy, but only for ornaments, not arms. The Mayas in particular probably had many of what we call advanced ways and ideas, including a system of written notation which we have as yet only partially translated. Invading Spanish soldiers, fearful of retribution, destroyed Mayan cities as they destroyed those of Mexico and Peru. So also, in the 1560s, intrusive Spanish missionaries, fearful of the Devil's words, burned almost all the Mayan books. Such desecration heightens the challenge to our understanding of Indian culture, while revealing some of the barbarism in Europe's own.

Indian Mexico and Peru, at their peak, held a population (possibly 30 million) almost as great as that of western Europe at the time of the Renaissance; and their principal cities, despite much controversy over their precise size, far outdistanced contemporary Paris and London. The simple fact that such populations and urban concentrations were adequately fed for centuries testifies to the technological standards and political stability of what we may appropriately call the old New World.

From Mexico and Peru, long before the white man's arrival, aboriginal peoples had spread once more far into the temperate zones, north and south. The farther they moved from their great heartland, like Europeans from

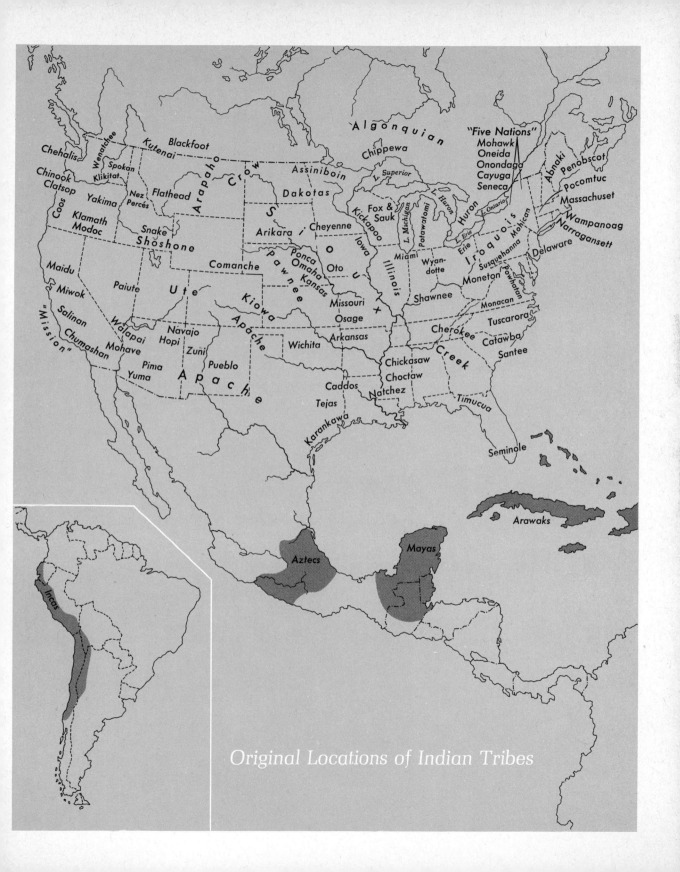

Original Locations of Indian Tribes

10

their Mediterranean havens, generally speaking the cruder and harsher their culture seems to have become.

Yet, even as far north as the St. Lawrence River Valley the earliest explorers from overseas marveled at the cities they encountered. One such was Hochelaga, the site of modern Montreal, of which the French explorer Cartier reported to his king in 1535 how impressed he was by "the immense numbers of peoples living there" and "their kindness and peacefulness." Ralph H. Brown, in his *Historical Geography of the United States,* remarks that "it has often been suggested, among other explanations, that originally the name 'Canada' signified a place of large Indian lodges." Brown goes on to describe the "underestimation of the extent to which the Indians had been engaged in agriculture," the frequency of Indian towns farther south, and the "Indian old fields" so commonly encountered and so zealously coveted for their open spaces by the first English settlers in what was to become the eastern United States.

Of the Indians in the rest of the future United States something new is being discovered almost every day as archaeological remains in the great river basins are exposed by the rush to develop hydroelectric power and establish flood control. And most of what is being discovered tends to undermine the myth of Indian savagery by which the first white settlers, on each new advance into fresh territory, comforted themselves and assuaged their guilt.

Of these same Indians, John Collier, a former Commissioner of Indian Affairs, wrote in 1947: "At the time of the discovery, the region that is now the United States contained some one million Indians, . . . formed within more than six hundred distinct societies. . . . These societies existed in perfect ecological balance with the forest, the plain, the desert, the waters, and the animal life. . . . At the time of the white arrival there was no square mile unoccupied or unused."

By their step-by-step resistance to encroachment for almost 300 years these Indians are said by some to have hardened the fighting qualities in the American character. Their more peaceful contributions to the American civilization include the canoe and the snowshoe, the tobacco leaf that was to become the first staple of the English mainland colonies, and Indian corn, that remarkable man-made hybrid, which remains to this day the staple of much of the Middle West.

## CONTACTS THAT FAILED TO ENDURE

While America was developing in isolation a still mystifying civilization, other parts of the world were themselves much more restless than our casual inattention to them suggests. Only now are we beginning to gain some knowledge of the internal history of Africa south of the Sahara and west of the Nile, the source of one of the earliest and eventually one of the largest, though involuntary, migrations of people to the New World. Rather better known, but still subject to conjecture and debate, are certain older contacts that somehow failed to endure, especially those from the Far East of Asia and the far north of Europe.

For hundreds of years, while Europe slumbered, China developed the most advanced civilization on earth and was to bequeath to the West such basic instrumentalities for its own later expansion as the compass, gunpowder, and printing. One climax of Chinese achievement was reached in the opening decades of the fifteenth century when seven tremendous seagoing expeditions, each of fifty huge junks manned by some 25,000 hands, sailed westward to India, Siam, the Persian Gulf and the Red Sea, and even visited East Africa. These expeditions dwarfed the pitiful little Portuguese ventures which at the same time were so painfully seeking the way around West Africa in search of the fabled East (see p. 16).

Why, with their infinite resources and virtuosity, did these Chinese fail to press on into the vast unknown, while the impoverished Europeans of the same period would be

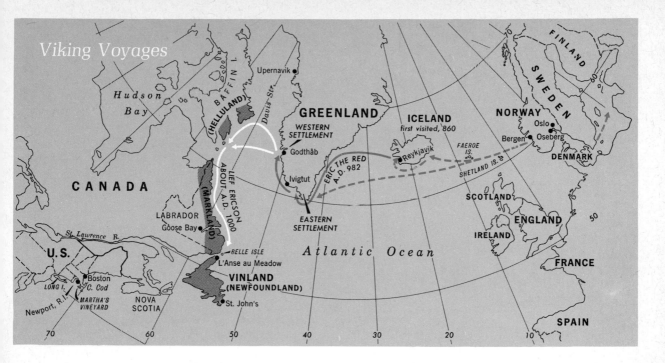

stopped by nothing in their unprecedented expansive thrust? No doubt the fact that Europe in the fifteenth century was "on the make," as we say, while China felt it "had it made," suggests some part but hardly all of the explanation. At any rate, centuries before these awesome excursions of the Ming emperors, and far in advance of the white man, modest Chinese and Japanese fishermen, swarming on the north Pacific, may easily have been blown by the prevailing west winds to British Columbia, Oregon, or California. In the mid-1960s strong evidence was uncovered of Japanese presence as far south as modern Ecuador as early as 3000 B.C.

The white man may have reached the Atlantic shores of North America by the ninth century A.D., when the Irish Christian hermit sect that had lived perhaps for a century in Iceland fled before the pagan Viking invasion beginning about 860. Little is known of these Celtic saints beyond their religious zeal, their navigational skill, and their seaworthy craft, all three contributing simply to the possibility that in their quest for a new haven they reached the New World island of Greenland and even Labrador.

More is known of their Viking oppressors, especially the Norwegians who, while the Swedes staked out large holdings in the Baltic and the Danes moved into Engand, themselves monopolized the *vestervegen* (the "westward way") to Iceland and beyond. Soon after they dislodged the Irish Christians, the Norwegians had developed a flourishing Icelandic settlement and turned their eyes to Greenland. Only 200 miles beyond Greenland lay the outermost reaches of modern Canada. Greenland won its name late in the tenth century when Erik the Red, a wily Norseman expelled from the Iceland republic for disrupting the peace, tried to lure settlers to its barren wastes. His deception worked well. Greenland was settled from Iceland in 986 and became a colony of Norway in the thirteenth century, when its population had reached a peak of about 4000. For reasons still hidden, white men in Greenland lost all contact with Europe fifty years or more before 1492. When John Davis visited the great island in 1585 and gave his name to the strait that separates it from Baffin Island, he found the white man extinct. Not until the eighteenth century did white settlers return.

11

12

Around the year 1000, Leif Ericsson, son of Erik the Red, set out from Greenland to explore the American mainland coast he had learned of some years earlier from a less enterprising Norse captain, Bjarni Herjulfsson, who had missed his Greenland anchorage and probably sighted Labrador before turning back. Leif may have sailed as far south as Massachusetts, but modern evidence makes that doubtful. The land he first sighted probably was Baffin Island, which he named Helluland, land of flat stones. Sailing southward, he next sighted forested Labrador, which he called Markland, or woodland. Sailing southward still another two days, he and his companions came ashore at last at the place they called Vinland, "in accordance with the good things they found in it."

Vinland, for centuries, sorely tried the historian's imagination. Thought to have been a vine land, a land of grapes, its location was pressed as far south as an historian's patriotic impulse might dictate. In 1964, however, its most likely location was fixed. Not a land of grapes, but a land of grass, as its Norse etymology indicates, "Vinland the Good" was named by thankful Greenlanders for its lovely grazing lands. Leif and his company remained there from ten to twelve months, and left artifacts that have been dug up in recent years. These voyagers were followed by Leif's brother, Thorvald, who first encountered the hostile natives, whom he called Skraelings, or screechers, and died at their hands. Next came Thorfinn Karlsefni, at the head of an expedition of three ships with 160 settlers and livestock and tools. For three years Karlsefni struggled to establish a colony, but the Skraelings far outnumbered them and eventually drove them back to Greenland. The place was the little fishing village known today as L'Anse au Meadow, the bay of the meadow, at the northernmost tip of the island of Newfoundland.

By the time of Columbus even this certain discovery and attempted settlement of America by Europeans had been lost to memory— except simply as one more strand in the richly embroidered tales of other worlds by which the medieval imagination was possessed.

## FORESHADOWINGS IN MIND AND SPIRIT

These tales of other worlds, and certain morsels of truth which they contained, went back to the Old Testament story of the Garden of Eden and to pagan Homer and the classic Greeks. As part of the mythology and learning of Western culture, they were more important in motivating Columbus and his successors than the hazy discoveries of the more recent past.

Almost 2500 years before Columbus, the poet Homer, in the story of Odysseus, placed the Elysian Fields—the *earthly* paradise—on the river Oceanus, "at the world's end where all existence is a dream of ease." Thereafter, successive Mediterranean civilizations took heart from visions of new Edens across the western ocean, visions that materialized at last in the United States.

Four hundred years after Homer, the philosopher Plato wrote of the lost island of Atlantis, once the site, he said, of an ideal commonwealth just beyond the Strait of Gibraltar. For a full millennium and more, few would sail beyond this Strait, "where Hercules his landmarks set as signals," as Dante wrote in the thirteenth century, "that no man farther onward should adventure." As long as men failed to disprove the existence of Atlantis, Plato's pleasing myth or invention grew ever more real to the European mind.

During the Middle Ages, imaginary Atlantic lands multiplied, and two in particular exercised an enduring spell. One was St. Brendan's isle of contentment, the discovery and domicile of a sixth-century Irish monk, which adorned even the most authentic maps of the ocean until the middle of the eighteenth century. The second was the Island of the Seven Cities, also known in Columbus's time as Antilia, where each of seven Christian bishops, fleeing the Mohammedan invasion of Spain in the eighth century, was said to have built a gilded town, one more lovely than another. From it comes the name Antilles, given derisively to the Caribbean islands by some of Columbus's own mariners, skeptical that they were in fact in the *Indies,* as their captain claimed.

The peak of medieval misdirection was reached in that popular fourteenth-century phantasmagoria, *The Travels of Sir John Mandeville,* which Columbus and his men knew well. Replete with fables of ants the size of hounds guarding hills of gold, and of monstrous chameleons that fed on air, this work also described, and described truly for all one knew, an "Indian" archipelago of no less than 5000 islands strung out from Asia almost to the western sea. "And man may well prove by experience and subtle compassment of it," wrote the author of *The Travels of Mandeville,* "that a man might go by ship all about the world above and beneath . . . and turn again to his country. . . . And always he should find men, lands and isles," while circumnavigating the globe.

## THE REACH
## OF GEOGRAPHIC SPECULATION

The morsels of "experience and wit" in *Mandeville* and similar medieval concoctions derived largely from the geographical learning of antiquity which the Arabs preserved and enlarged. This learning Europe began to regain in Columbus's early years, when it was given greater currency than ever before by the spread of printing and by the growing secular interests of scholars and scientists upon which the printers fed.

As early as the fourth century B.C., Aristotle's mathematical proofs had caused most learned Greeks to agree that the earth was more or less a sphere. By then, too, commerce and war with neighboring Mediterranean lands had familiarized even ordinary Greeks with the nearest borders of three continents— Europe, Asia, and Africa. In 327–325 B.C. Alexander the Great's armies crossed northern India almost to Tibet. This exploit pushed Greek knowledge of the inhabited world well over 1500 miles eastward and opened up more distant vistas of Oriental marvels which thereafter held the minds of Europeans enthralled.

The Greeks called familiar territory the *oekumene,* or the known world, or the "Old World," the name which itself gave rise to the use of "New World" for Columbus's discoveries. The farther the *oekumene* was extended, the more interested did the Greeks become in the size of the whole sphere and the extent of its watery parts. The principle of symmetry, or balance, the first general principle in the history of geographical science, dominated their thinking.

Aristotle himself argued from the occurrence of elephants in both Africa and India, and from the assumed difficulty of carrying them by sea from one place to the other, that the watery surface of the sphere was limited and the ocean passage from the western bulge of Africa to the eastern extremity of Asia was short. This conclusion sailed through the ages on Aristotle's immense authority as a seer and was quoted often and energetically by Columbus.

Since most Greeks agreed that land was heavier than water, and that these elements must nevertheless balance one another by weight, it followed from the belief in a small watery surface that the heavier land surface of the sphere must be smaller still. By such reasoning Aristotle reached a second long-lived geographical conclusion: that the short ocean passage from Africa to Asia was uncluttered by islands. The land mass known to the Greeks in Europe, Africa, and Asia, he said, was ample to balance all the water on the sphere.

For all his authority, Aristotle's reasoning about the occurrence of elephants and the absence of islands did not go unchallenged even in his own time. Some Greeks held that since there was a habitable land mass on the one surface of the sphere known to them, there must be at least its antipode on the opposite side, there must be at least that "world above" balanced by the "world beneath" which *Mandeville* in fact recalled. And indeed, said some, there may be a number of unknown lands, each in balance with one another, and hence a very much larger ocean than Aristotle spoke of with water enough to balance all.

13

14

The principle of balance also led certain Greeks to divide the sphere latitudinally into five climatic zones—two frigid zones balancing each other at the poles; a broad torrid zone girdling the center; and between the torrid zone and each frigid zone, two temperate zones in balance in the northern and southern latitudes. These Greeks and most of their followers for almost 2000 years held that the frigid zones were too cold and that the torrid zone was too hot to sustain life even if there were land. But about the familiar north temperate zone they were willing to make bold non-Aristotelian predictions. Eratosthenes, who lived and wrote in Alexandria during the third century B.C., was responsible for one of the most remarkable of these:

If the extent of the Atlantic Ocean were not an obstacle, we might easily sail from Iberia [Spain] to India, on the same parallel. . . . It is quite possible that within the same temperate zone there may be two or even more inhabited earths.

Eratosthenes was a brilliant mathematician who calculated the circumference of the sphere at 25,000 miles, almost precisely right. A successor of his in Alexandria in the second century B.C., Hipparchus by name, was the first to divide the sphere by parallels of latitude and meridians of longitude and to attempt to locate habitable points on it in terms of degrees. A third Alexandrian, known to us as Ptolemy, who lived in the second century A.D., made what may have been the very first atlas of the world employing the method Hipparchus developed.

Ptolemy's atlas accompanied his work on world geography, which reflected much of the ancient Greek tradition, corrected, as he thought, by all the evidence he could gather from the itineraries of sailors and the reports of travelers. But many of Ptolemy's corrections proved to be erroneous. Most significant for the future was his espousal of the idea of a sphere much smaller than that of Eratosthenes. This led him to calculate each of the sphere's 360 degrees as itself much smaller

than it was in reality. Ptolemy also brought west Africa and east Asia far too close to each other.

These errors, embalmed in the geographical writings he absorbed while preparing for his "enterprise of the Indies," were to prove irresistible to Columbus. Indeed, so possessed was he by his notion of finding a short sea route to the Orient that he even improved on Ptolemy. He was encouraged to take this step by a more recent source to whose accuracy on virtually every point modern scholarship has testified except the one point on which Columbus most relied. This source was Marco Polo's *Travels*.

On his return to his native Venice in 1298, after nearly 30 years in China in the service of the Great Khan, Polo published his famous book only to be scoffed at by his countrymen for the Oriental wonders he reported. Numerous handwritten copies of Polo's work, no two alike, circulated among the learned in Europe before it was printed for the first time in 1477. Thereafter, all aspiring ocean navigators devoured it, Columbus's own copy with his marginal markings dating from 1485. Polo reserved his choicest language for the wonders of Japan, which he never actually visited and of whose extent his knowledge remained vague.

By indefensible manipulations of fanciful Arabic evidence, Columbus compulsively shrank each short Ptolemaic degree by 10 per cent. And on the basis of Polo's second- and third-hand information, he stretched Asia no less than 30 degrees nearer West Africa, so that, as S.E. Morison writes, "Japan almost kissed the Azores." Columbus's calculations, in fact, placed Japan almost precisely where he made his Bahamas landfall.

## II  *The Expansion of Europe*

### THE MENACE OF MOHAMMEDANISM

Columbus was about 30 years old, a veteran Atlantic sailor and ship captain in Portuguese service, when he first sought the support of the Portuguese king early in the 1480s for his westward voyage to the East. Columbus was in the right place at the right time for the promotion of this enterprise. Vast historical changes had already assured the Atlantic primacy over the Mediterranean in Europe's future, and Portugal, at land's end, primacy over Europe's other maritime nations in Atlantic navigation. At the heart of these historical changes lay the menace of Mohammedanism, or Islam, to Christianity.

Spain, of which Portugal was long a part, had been the first Christian country to succumb to the Mohammedan invasion of Europe from North Africa in the eighth century. Thereafter, although checked in western Europe by Charles Martel of France in the memorable battle of Tours in 732, Mohammedanism quickly spread to Mediterranean islands, Adriatic and Aegean lands, the entire Middle East, and ever farther south in Africa, ever father east in Asia. Tolerant of captives willing to join the easy brotherhood of Islam, Mohammedanism gradually absorbed the legends, lore, and learning of the world from Persians, Hindus, Jews, Egyptians, Greeks, and others.

"The old legend that Islam was born of the desert," writes Sir Hamilton Gibb in his brilliant account of Mohammedan culture, "is taking a long time to die," but the desert "had no creative part in it. . . . Islam had grown up within the framework of an urban civilization." Within the vast expanse of Islam by the end of the tenth century lay most of the great cities known to man: Cairo and Alexandria, Baghdad, Damascus, and Antioch, Tabriz, Samarkand, and Jerusalem. In such cities of the Levant, or the land of the rising sun, were to be found the luxuries of the yet more distant East, whence they would be distributed more deeply into Islam and poorer Christendom.

The Christian reaction began early in the eleventh century when, with the encouragement of the Pope, the Italian republic of Pisa expelled the Mohammedans from the island of Sardinia. The Christian offensive gained its strongest momentum with the start of the Crusades in 1096, and reached a peak three years later when holy Jerusalem was regained.

The Crusades solidified the authority of the Roman popes in Christendom and solidified the leadership of the Italian city-states in the Mediterranean trade. Pisa, Genoa, and Venice in particular profited from carrying pilgrims eastward from Europe to Jerusalem and from carrying westward from the Levant the spices, silks, gems, tapestries, and other exotic wares which Europe's upper classes had learned to love.

By the thirteenth century, however, Christianity's crusading spirit had spent itself. Jerusalem had once again fallen to the Mohammedans, and the onslaught of Islam on Europe from the east had taken on renewed force under Turkish leadership. The Levantine trade was so hard hit by this reversal of fortune that Pisa, Genoa, and Venice engaged in suicidal wars among themselves in their efforts to hold on to a worthwhile share of it. And the rest of Europe, with prices of Oriental goods soaring because of the disruption of the traditional lines of supply, began to yearn for new routes to the Indies which would somehow circumvent the formidable Turkish strongholds.

### PORTUGAL TAKES THE LEAD

As early as 1291 two brothers, Ugolino and Vadino Vivaldo of Columbus's native Genoa, embarked on what may have been the first deliberate effort to reach the East by sailing west. They appear to have perished on the voyage. Early in the next century, other Italians, and Spaniards and Frenchmen, beginning to explore the western coast of Africa, discovered and occupied the Canaries, the somewhat more westerly Madeiras, and ultimately the still more westerly Azores. But it remained for the Portuguese, after 1415, to begin that systematic collection of geographic information which dissipated ancient fears of the "green sea of gloom," as the Arabs described the Atlantic, and transformed that ocean into a great path of adventure and com-

16

merce, not least commerce in enslaved blacks whom the Portuguese first brought to Europe in 1442.

Portugal had freed herself from Spain in 1140 and in 1249 had rid herself of the last Mohammedan enclave while retaining much of the ancient learning that the Mohammedans had preserved. Thereafter, while consolidating their territory at home, her rulers prepared to pursue the Mohammedans in Africa itself. The legend of Prester (that is, Priest) John, which began to spread through beleaguered Europe late in the twelfth century, emboldened the Portuguese. Prester John was said to be a mighty Christian potentate somewhere in the heart of Islam who had withstood Mohammedan expansion and might help the Europeans subdue the infidel. The Portuguese quest for Prester John was intensified when the House of Avis took the throne in 1385 and gained still greater momentum

*Henry the Navigator, a fifteenth-century portrait. (Bibliothèque Nationale, Paris.)*

after 1415 when the Portuguese forces invaded Africa and took the Moroccan port of Ceuta, opposite Gibraltar, from the Mohammedans.

Thenceforth, Prince Henry, son of King John I and famous in history as Henry the Navigator, gave African exploration a tremendous impetus. In 1488, many years after Prince Henry's death, of course, and after Prester John had proved to be nothing more than an Abyssinian native chieftain, Bartholomeu Diaz at last rounded *Cabo Tormentoso,* the Cape of Storms, at the southernmost tip of Africa and thereby opened the first all-water route from Europe to the Indies. So impressed was the king of Portugal with the prospects afforded by this feat that he promptly renamed the treacherous neck of land "Cape of Good Hope."

Nine years after Diaz's voyage a flotilla of four Portuguese ships under Vasco da Gama sailed for Calicut from Lisbon and returned in 1499 laden with spices and jewels. Da Gama's voyage marked the end of Levantine supremacy in the Oriental trade, the eclipse of the Italian merchants, and the decline of the Mediterranean. The Portuguese, moreover, soon drove the Mohammedan merchants from the Indian Ocean itself, destroyed their navy, and reduced their strongholds at the sources of supply for Oriental goods.

In 1500, on a voyage to the Orient, a Portuguese captain, Pedro Alvarez Cabral, finding himself on the New World shore, promptly claimed it for his native land under the name of "Terra de Vera Cruz," and proceeded on his journey. Cabral's men had discovered on the land a tree with bright red wood similar to the "brazil" wood long imported from the Far East for the making of red dye, and soon the place he found became known as Brazil, and brazilwood became its principal product. But Portuguese interest in the New World languished until, half a century later, other European nations showed a growing interest in Brazil. It was in the Orient that the Portuguese made their major effort and created an empire that lasted, at least in fragments, to our own day.

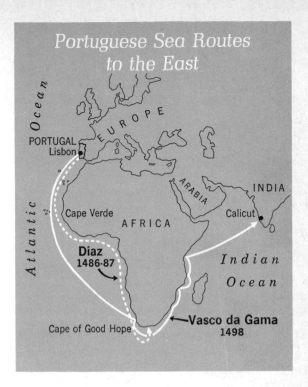

Portuguese Sea Routes to the East

If Columbus was in the right place at the right time when he first broached his enterprise of the Indies in Portugal, he offered all the wrong reasons for his daring idea. Portugal's mariners, by the 1480s, simply by their own venturesomeness, had long since proven Ptolemy wrong on so many points that her maritime experts had discarded him along with all other Greek authorities. Marco Polo, moreover, had no standing whatever with them. Guided by these experts, Portuguese officials promptly laughed Columbus's proposition out of court, and by persisting in offering it he gradually won the reputation for madness that henceforth clung to him.

Columbus left Portugal in 1485 to try his luck in Spain, but here he found King Ferdinand and Queen Isabella wholly engaged in ridding their own country, after 700 years, of the last Mohammedan strongholds in Granada. Columbus had returned to Portugal when the news of Diaz's success reached Lisbon and killed what little interest might have lingered there in his own bolder scheme. He next tried the kings of England and France without success, and finally the rulers of Spain once more, where, as in Portugal, the royal experts in 1490 judged his plan "impossible and vain and worthy of rejection."

When Ferdinand and Isabella succeeded at last, in January 1492, in expelling Islam from Granada, they moved immediately to wipe out all other non-Catholic elements in the Spanish population, including the Jews who had helped immensely in financing the long wars. The rulers' instrument was the Spanish Inquisition; its penalties, execution or expulsion. Driven thus to dissolve in blood and misery the sources of their wealth and power at home, Ferdinand and Isabella were now prepared to view more favorably Columbus's project for converting the "princess and people" of "the Indies" to the holy faith and attracting their fabled wealth to Spain's purposes. In April 1492 they capitulated to the importunings of Columbus's influential friends, granted him his coveted title, "Admiral of the Ocean Sea," and began to equip his fleet.

Every ship carrying refugee Jews had been ordered by Ferdinand and Isabella to leave Spain by August 2, 1492. S.E. Morison, in his admirable biography of Columbus, suggests that he may have on this account put off his own departure until the following day to set sail under a brighter omen. Even so, the same tide that carried Niña, Pinta, and Santa Maria so hopefully toward such golden isles as the Admiral might "discover and acquire by his labor and industry," also bore the last of some hundreds of thousands of Spanish Jews toward Italy and other hostile refuges, whence many of them eventually moved to eastern Europe.

We know now what Columbus found. After a few months spent exploring in the Caribbean, where the climate constantly reminded the Admiral of "spring in Andalusia," he left some of his men behind in Hispaniola, modern Haiti, and set out for Spain with a

17

18

few gold nuggets and a few red Indians to prove the success of his venture. None of the Indians survived the voyage. In September 1493 Columbus set sail once more with 1500 settlers for his islands in the Ocean Sea and for further exploratory work. Columbus made two later voyages to America, in 1498 and again in 1502, only four years before his death. His search, on these visits, was for a passage through the tantalizing barrier just beyond which, he remained certain, must lie Japan, his goal.

Naturally, Columbus found no passage. Not until Magellan's men circumnavigated the globe in the service of Spain in 1519–1522 did the truth become known about how enormously long was the westward passage to the East—as Eratosthenes and other Greeks had foretold. But Columbus, nevertheless, had his compensations. When he was assailed by doubts that he had in fact reached Japan (as

he was, indeed, from his very first sight of the naked island natives who, as he wrote, "were a people very deficient in everything"), his faith in the Lord's apparently altered purpose continued firm. During his third visit in 1500 Columbus wrote from America: "God made me the messenger of the new heaven and the new earth of which He spoke in the Apocalypse by St. John, after having spoken of it by the mouth of Isaiah, and He showed me the spot where to find it." During the same visit he also referred to "those lands which I have recently discovered, and where I believe in my soul the earthly paradise is situated."

So little trust did Ferdinand and Isabella place in the Admiral's claims to have found Japan, that in 1493 they had the Pope, himself a Spaniard, divide the world beyond the *oekumene* between themselves and the Portuguese. The next year, in the Treaty of Tordesillas,

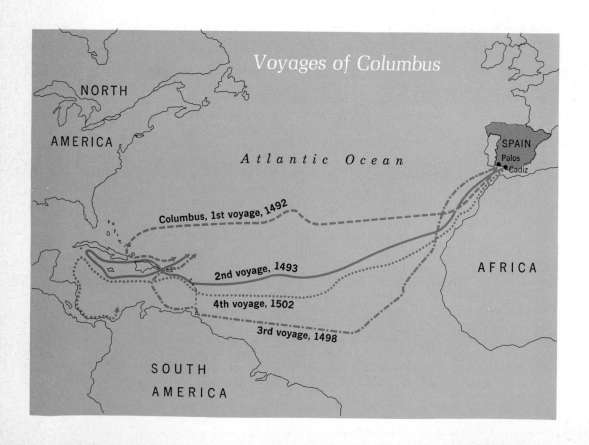

### Voyages of Columbus

NORTH
AMERICA

*Atlantic Ocean*

SPAIN
Palos
Cadiz

AFRICA

Columbus, 1st voyage, 1492

2nd voyage, 1493

4th voyage, 1502

3rd voyage, 1498

SOUTH
AMERICA

Spain and Portugal agreed on the specific boundary separating their portions of the sphere. Portugal, in effect, received the Orient and Spain the New World, except for the region that became Brazil. Spain soon encouraged others besides Columbus to occupy her claim, to search out its limits, convert its inhabitants, and uncover its wealth.

One of the first to sail under her colors was a Florentine, Amerigo Vespucci, who in 1497 began a series of voyages on which he explored the American coastline southeast from Mexico all the way to Brazil. Historians now feel that he well earned the fame that attached to his name ever since a German geographer, in 1507, first called the New World "America."

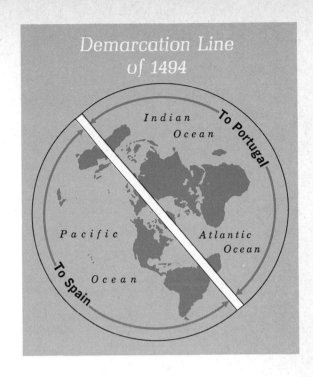

## SPANISH ASCENDANCY IN THE NEW WORLD

More useful to Spain than the navigators who followed Columbus under her flag in seeking the passage to India were many of her old *conquistadores*. Freed now from fighting the Mohammedan at home, they boldly crossed the sea to establish Spain's ascendancy over the Indian and the land in the New World.

Very soon after Columbus's first discoveries, these rough opportunists lorded it over Hispaniola. From this base they extended their grasp to Jamaica in 1509, Cuba in 1511, and Puerto Rico in 1512, thereby completing Spain's occupation of the Greater Antilles. By then rumors of immense wealth on the mainland had begun to exert their charm, and the *conquistadores,* disappointed with their rewards in the islands, left the Lesser Antilles to later adventurers and embarked on the conquest of Central America, Mexico, and Peru.

The first Spanish settlement on the American mainland was made in Panama in 1508 by Alonzo de Ojeda. In 1513 Vasco Nuñez de Balboa worked his way across the Panama isthmus to sight the Pacific, and Ponce de Léon began his quest for the fountain of youth in Florida. But the two greatest exploits

were yet to come. The first was the conquest of the Aztecs of Mexico, beginning in 1519, by Hernando Cortez and his mighty horsemen. The second, beginning in 1528, was the yet more cruel conquest of the Incas of Peru by the brutal Francisco Pizarro. Here, at last, was the wealth Spain sought, stored up in hoards more manificent than any European could imagine, and at hand for her superior arms to claim.

From Mexico and Peru, their appetites sharpened by the finds of their superiors, other *conquistadores* set out to discover hoards of their own, but with little success. Tough Hernando de Soto led his men on a fruitless search through the gloomy forests from Florida to the Mississippi River, which he discovered in 1541 only to die of fever on its banks. In the same year Francisco de Coronado, seeking the mythical Seven Cities of Cibola and the gold they held, began his broad explorations of the American Southwest which he disgustedly called the "great American desert," a description which helped retard settlement there for 300 years. On the water, moreover, Spanish ship captains, by 1600, had

19

ranged as far south as Chile and Argentina and as far north and west as the shores of upper California.

Long before other Atlantic nations challenged her in the New World, Spain had established a vast empire in the West Indies and on the Spanish Main. The Spanish regime was in many respects inflexible and harsh. The papal bull of 1493, which had confirmed Spain's right to most of the New World (see p. 18), stated explicitly that the sole purpose of the grant was the propagation of Christianity among the people there. At the same time, Spain's own purpose was the extraction of gold and silver. Her obligation to the Pope worked sufficiently on the consciences of her rulers for them to send active missionaries overseas; and these missionaries themselves sometimes proved to be humanitarians. Most notable among them was Bartolomé de Las Casas, who devoted his life to combating the enslavement and extermination of the Indians. But other missionaries soon fell themselves into the ways of the *con-*

*quistadores,* and like them disdained both the scruples of the Crown and the censure of the Church. Indeed, the priesthood itself became one of the most exploitive of the Spanish castes and eventually controlled more than half the land of the empire.

The principal instrument of early Spanish exploitation was the *encomienda,* which Columbus himself introduced into Hispaniola and which still colors the land and labor practices of many Latin American countries. Under this system each deserving conqueror was entrusted with a given number of Indians whose work he could command in exchange for his care of their souls. Under a supplementary system, the *repartimiento,* the Indians could be gathered up in one section and transported to another. Both the *encomienda* and the *repartimiento* became in fact deadly systems of enslavement on lordly fiefs run by men who cared little enough for their own souls not to be hampered by concern for the souls of natives.

It is true that many Indians, like the fierce

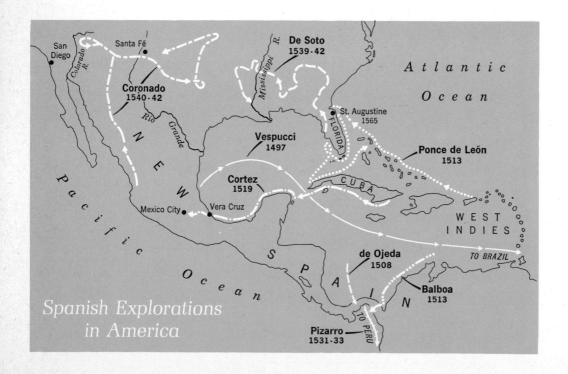

Spanish Explorations in America

*Contemporary Mexican drawing of Cortez's invasion of Mexico City. This scene, from the Codex Azcatitlan, includes Cortez, his Indian guide, and natives carrying supplies. (Bibliothèque Nationale.)*

Caribs whom Columbus himself encountered on West Indian islands he visited on his later voyages, as well as mainland Aztecs, Incas, and Mayas, resisted and sometimes withstood enslavement, just as did many fierce tribes of blacks who scared off the slave trade's Iberian minions in Africa. But it is also true that other Africans were first introduced into the New World by *conquistadores* who, having literally depopulated entire islands (they called them "useless," for their lack of gold) by carrying off the aborigines as short-lived bondsmen, required a continually replenished labor supply to "strive to collect and give us" as Columbus said, "the things which . . . are necessary to us."

One of the lasting myths of the Negro's past is that he took docilely to enslavement, a myth fed largely by the contrasting myth of the Indian's brave preference for extinction. But in those tropical regions where they were most numerous, millions of Indians were extinguished (and additional millions and their descendants were repressed) *by* enslavement; and in the same regions many of those blacks who were successfully carried into slavery chilled their captors with the menace of servile revolts.

By the 1540s the reign of the *conquistadores* was drawing to a close. In the islands the precious metals they sought never were found in quantity. When they turned to the land itself for wealth, first in ranching and then in staple agriculture, their unfitness as managers left poor and discontented those who did not take off for the mainland. On the mainland, in turn, *conquistadores* became rich on the hoards they captured, but most of them failed in their efforts to augment their finds by organizing systematic production in the mines from which the hoards had come. These failures hastened the more thoroughgoing intervention of the Crown in the New World. The Crown had thought of intervening even earlier, when mariners of rival nations began to pirate Spanish ships that were carrying the royal share of New World treasure on the high seas.

Under the reorganized official regime, the great gold and silver mines of Mexico and Peru began to add some $30 million a year to the currency of world trade. Yet commercial cattle-raising, especially for the production of hides, and commercial agriculture, especially sugar- and tobacco-growing, soon challenged mining as the major source of wealth and

21

22

eventually surpassed it. In each of these activities the *encomienda* system lasted almost to the close of the eighteenth century, its frightful abuses in no way mitigated by the aristocrats and bureaucrats in the mother country under whose dominion it had fallen, nor by the Spanish-born officials who ran things in the New World.

These officials quickly imposed their own cultural institutions in America. In 1544 the first New World printing press was set up in Mexico City. Its initial publication was a *Compendium of Christian Doctrine*, *"en lengua Mexicana y Castellana."* In 1551, the first New World universities were opened in Mexico City and Lima. Shortly thereafter imposing cathedrals were to be found in important coastal cities, while all over the land hundreds of monasteries plied their business of saving souls. Still, the progress of Europeanizing, if discernible at all, was slow. In 1595, for example, the Viceroy of New Spain, Luis de Velasco II, wrote for the benefit of his suc-

cessor: "The two Republics, of Spaniards and Indians, of which this Kingdom consists are so repugant to each other . . . that it seems that the conservation of the former always means the oppression and destruction of the latter."

## III  *National Rivalry in America*

### THE RELIGIOUS TRANSFORMATION IN EUROPE

If the menace of Islam underlay the extension of Portuguese and Spanish power to the most distant habitable regions of the globe, a religious revolution within Christendom itself fostered the *permanent settlement* of Europeans in the New World, and especially in its northern parts.

This religious revolution, which we call the Protestant Reformation, had been fed for gen-

The Indians, when given the opportunity, acted brutally toward the Spaniards. In this scene by de Bry (1590), the Indians are testing the "immortality" of the Spaniards by immersing them in water to see if they suffocate. (Theodor de Bry, America, Part IV.)

erations by the corruption of the Roman Church and the worldly aspirations of Church leaders before it broke into the open in 1517. In that year, the deeply troubled German monk and teacher Martin Luther posted his famous 95 "theses" on the church door in Wittenberg denouncing in particular the "deception" practiced on "the greater part of the people" by the "indiscriminate" sale of "pardons" for sins. Men, Luther asserted, were not saved by such "good works" (by which he

*Martin Luther, 1520, by Lucas Cranach the Elder. (The Bettmann Archive.)*

meant largely these and similar contributions to Church coffers forcibly exacted by heartless clergymen from easily frightened believers), but by a deep and abiding faith that came directly from God. Christians, he added, should learn about religion not through priestly intermediaries, themselves often ignorant and unprincipled, but directly from the Bible, the word of God, and he translated the Bible into magnificent vernacular German.

Luther aimed at a drastic reformation of the Church, not its abolition, but his doctrine pointed toward the radical notion of the priesthood of all believers—"all Christians are truly of the spiritual estate," he argued in 1520—and it soon became clear that his views were inconsistent with the very structure of the Roman Catholic establishment. After the Pope excommunicated Luther in 1521, the monk gained the support of many German princes and Scandinavian rulers who had their own quarrels with Rome (see p. 26) and in 1529 "protested" the Pope's efforts to crush the reform movement. Luther, in turn, acknowledged that the state might dominate his church the better to insure, as he said, that "the glorious Teutonic people should cease to be the puppet of the Roman pontiff."

In 1536, almost 20 years after the posting of Luther's "theses," John Calvin, harried from his native France to Geneva, published his *Institutes of the Christian Religion,* which lifted the arguments of the Protestant Reformation from their German and Scandinavian setting and made them more fully international. Calvin shared many of Luther's convictions, including the belief in justification by faith rather than by works. But there were significant differences too, the most important being Calvin's greater emphasis on "predestination." Only a few choice spirits, the "visible elect," Calvin maintained, were preordained by God to enjoy the "Covenant of Grace." Only these few vessels of Christ, he said, were endowed with the requisite faith to rule the world, God's creation. The rest were doomed to eternal damnation for their inescapable "original" sin.

It may seem odd that a faith so paralyzing in its implications, a faith that saved the few and forever damned the rest, making eternal bliss dependent upon the arbitrary act of God, should prove so satisfying for so many. Yet this stern Protestant creed unleashed a special kind of energy. Calvinists strove to lead the kind of disciplined and saintly lives that would give them, or at least give others, reason to believe they were recipients of God's

24

grace. Convinced that they alone possessed the true faith and a divine mission, that the Almighty was on their side, they displayed a militant confidence that distinguished them throughout Europe. Later Calvinists pursued the business of this world with the same passionate intensity that the medieval saints had shown in contemplating the next, and thereby gave religious significance even to the economic virtues of thrift, abstinence, and frugality.

The religious revolution begun by Luther and Calvin spawned a number of sects throughout Europe—sects led by men who believed themselves to be in direct communication with God. Made up of mystics and perfectionists, such sects often carried reformation to the extreme and excited the anger of Calvinist and Catholic alike. Unlike Luther, Calvin rejected the idea that the state should be supreme over religion. He proposed instead that the self-governing church be made strong enough to influence, indeed to Christianize, the state. In Geneva, where Calvin himself promptly took over the government, he afforded his zealous followers elsewhere in Europe a model of a purified or "puritan" regime in which Calvinism permeated all civic activities. Here non-Calvinists, sectarians as well as papists, even if good Christians, were harshly persecuted.

Although in practice as in theory Calvinism was undemocratic, it nevertheless furthered the cause of individual freedom by insisting on a learned clergy and a literate citizenry, by making all "callings" honorable however humble, by giving laymen a vital role in church government, and by teaching that the authority of the state was limited by a higher, divine law concerned with the individual soul.

On religious grounds Calvinism became as much a menace to the papacy as Lutheranism. On political grounds it became far more of a menace than Lutheranism to those monarchs who remained, in the Calvinists' estimation, impure and Godless men even though the Pope had given them his blessing. Chief among these monarchs was Charles I, who became King of Spain in 1516. Three years later Charles also was named Holy Roman Emperor, and thereby suzerain of all the German princes and chief protector of the Roman popes. Charles also became the principal enemy of France, whose territory his Spanish and German holdings virtually hemmed in and many of whose great nobles would soon become "Huguenots," or "confederates" of Calvin.

As early as 1521, when the Pope excommunicated Luther, Charles swore that in undertaking to crush the German's heresy he would not spare his "dominions, friends, body, blood, life, and soul." The next year he began to impose the Spanish Inquisition on his subjects in non-Spanish lands. In 1534 Charles approved the creation, by the Spanish monk Ignatius Loyola, of the Society of Jesus, whose task it became to help reclaim Europeans to Catholicism and convert the heathen masses overseas to the old religion. The Jesuits, the members of this Society, zealously pursued their mission; and yet, Protestantism—in the form of Lutheranism, Calvinism, and other rising sects—spread far in Europe. Outside of Germany and France, most irritating to Charles was the infection of his Dutch subjects in the Spanish Netherlands with the most virulent brand of Calvinism, and the infection of England with Anglicanism, a local form of Protestantism declared to be the state religion in 1534 after Henry VIII, in defiance of the Pope, annulled his marriage to Charles's aunt, Catherine of Aragon, and was excommunicated.

In 1556, worn out in the service of the popes, Charles retired to a monastery and left the immense burden of his crusade against the Reformation to his son, who ruled Spain and the other extensive Hapsburg holdings as Philip II. Philip also claimed to be King of England, for in 1554 he had married Queen Mary, the Catholic daughter of Henry VIII and Catherine. Between them, Philip and Mary restored Catholicism in England, the Queen earning notoriety as "Bloody Mary" for executing some 300 Protestants. When

Mary died in 1558, Philip sought to marry her successor, her half-sister Elizabeth, but the new queen rejected both Philip and his faith.

In 1563 Elizabeth strengthened the position of Anglicanism in England by subscribing to the Thirty-nine Articles of religion, which made clearer and more specific the differences between the new Church of England and the old Church of Rome. By taking this step, however, she severed the attachment of the many remaining English Catholics to the throne and also weakened the loyalty of the growing numbers of English Calvinists who wished to go much farther than the Thirty-nine Articles in eliminating the last vestiges of Romanism in English belief and worship.

These religious divisions in her island—which were profound enough to lead eventually to civil war—tempered Elizabeth's policies in many ways. And yet having declared unequivocally for her own brand of Protestanism at home, she soon offered to aid anti-Catholics elsewhere in Europe. Elizabeth especially aided the Dutch, who had revolted against Philip in 1568. In 1570, the Pope excommunicated her and absolved English Catholics of allegiance to the throne.

Spain and England now became more bitter enemies than ever, and the "scepter'd isle" at last turned her attention to mastery of the seas. The principal lures on the seas were the Spanish galleys carrying the wealth of Mexico and Peru to Philip's treasury for the support of his Catholic armies. The Elizabethan "sea dogges" pursued these galleys unremittingly, Francis Drake in *Golden Hind* bringing home the most magnificent catch of all. Weighing anchor in 1577, Drake spent the next three years on the water raiding the Atlantic and Pacific coasts of the Spanish Main, the Spanish New World islands, and Spanish shipping on the two great oceans. He returned to England in 1580 with £1,500,000 in American gold and silver, a blow to Philip made all the more pointed by Elizabeth's promptly and publicly knighting the sailor.

The final insult came in 1587, when Eliza-

beth, impelled by the urging of her council, her Parliament, and most of her people, ordered the execution of her Catholic cousin, Mary, Queen of Scots. Twenty years earlier, when Mary had been forced by the Calvinists in her own country to abdicate, she found a refuge in England, where she repaid Elizabeth's calculated hospitality—the better to keep an eye on Mary—by conspiring constantly with Philip's English friends to help him grasp the throne. As English relations with Spain worsened, the menace of Mary's presence—and her machinations—grew until she had to be dispatched.

Philip now declared open war on England, sending out in 1588 the grand Armada with which he hoped to destroy Elizabeth, proceed to victory over the Dutch, and assist the Catholic party in France to crush the Huguenots. The Armada's defeat by Sir Francis Drake and the bold Dutch "water beggars" who sailed down to join the battle, frustrated Philip's plans and initiated his decline. In 1589 the wars between Catholic and Protestant forces in France ended in victory for the Huguenot Henry of Navarre, who as Henry IV became the first Bourbon king. To placate the French Catholics, Henry returned to the Roman Church in 1593. But this was a political not a religious step. In 1598 Henry issued the famous Edict of Nantes offering an exceptional degree of religious liberty to the Huguenots with whom his heart remained. Along with the Protestant English and Calvinist Dutch, he was soon to establish his own claims to New World lands in defiance of Catholic Spain's monopoly.

### ECONOMIC AND POLITICAL NATIONALISM

Protestantism so rapidly transformed so much of sixteenth-century Europe largely because Catholicism had fallen on evil days. The failure of the late Crusades against Islam had placed the papacy at once in debt and on the defensive. As calls for funds on Catholic rulers grew more frequent and burdensome, their resistance to paying matched in ingenuity and intensity the popes' importunities. One reason why the Reformation began in Germany was that the popes were forced increasingly to seek their funds from the German people on whom, as subjects of the Holy Roman Empire, they had the most direct claim. Methods so crude and corrupt were used to wring money from the Germans that they became profoundly disenchanted with the materialism of their priests and their religion. This widespread popular discontent with Rome made all the more practical the lust of the German princes themselves for the vast lands of the Church, and for control of Church offices and income. For similar reasons the spark of the German Reformation quickly inflamed much of the rest of Europe.

As sides were drawn, other always volatile elements—ancient feudal family rivalries, dynastic ambitions of rising clans, greed for commercial monopolies—fed the blaze. The very nature of European civilization was altered with extraordinary speed. Great new nations emerged out of the searing chaos of contending principalities. New national armies incurred heavy costs not only in establishing the new monarchs but also in protecting and extending their authority. To meet these costs the monarchs sought new national taxes and loans. These, in turn, could be most effectively obtained by abating the old Church doctrine against high profits and interest.

One of the most obvious sources of high profits in still largely agricultural communities was improved land use. Such improvement often entailed the dislodging of many small husbandmen and the combination of their fields into extensive estates producing cash crops. Then, as later, the removal of families from the land supplied many new hands for commercial and industrial enterprises, for the growing national armies and navies, and for settlement in colonial outposts overseas. Improved land use and commerce in cash crops, in turn, made available the wherewithal for heavy-interest loans to royalty, and also for investment in colonial enterprises.

Naturally these enterprises were usually promoted and manned in newly Protestant countries by those in revolt against Roman Catholic ideas and institutions. In England especially, during the early decades of Elizabeth's reign, a strong new impulse was given to the modernization of society. In keeping with emerging "mercantilist" theories of national competition (see p. 74), the commercialization of agriculture, the development of mining and manufacturing, the improvement of facilities for domestic commerce all were speeded up. The object was to make the Protestant Queen "a prince of power" by promoting English self-sufficiency to the extent that nature and improved technology permitted. At the same time, every national advantage was sought in extending foreign trade.

Much else, of course, in what we may justly call the New World of Europe fostered the development of the New World in America. With the resurgence of interest during the Renaissance in classical society and the imperial grandeur of Rome, the very idea of empire grew more attractive even in Catholic lands. The attack of Protestant thinkers on the mysticism, not to say the superstition, of the old Church strengthened the rising spirit of secularism and science, including the science of discovery. Discovery itself raised profound questions about the origins of strange beasts and people which the Bible inadequately accounted for. Such questions culminated centuries later in the Darwinian theories of evolution and the science of anthropology. The concern with empire, secular thought, and scientific study spread across Europe after the fifteenth century; but it most deeply altered life in the new maritime (as against the old Mediterranean) nations of the north, especially France, the Netherlands, and England.

### THE WAY OF THE FRENCH

The French launched their activities in the New World as early as 1520 when their vessels began probing the coasts of Brazil and putting men ashore to cut up cargoes of brazil-wood. Soon they were landing missionaries as well. But the main result of their labors here was the heightening of Portuguese antagonism toward all foreign interlopers, a policy to which the French succumbed in 1615, when Portugal evicted them from Brazil.

The French had better luck against the Spanish. As early as 1523, more than half a century before Drake in *Golden Hind* (see p. 25), a French corsair, Jean Fleury, intercepted Spanish galleys carrying the gold and silver of the New World to the treasury of Charles V. The next year, Francis I of France

sent Giovanni Verrazano to North America in search of the northwest passage to the Indies. Verrazano explored the coast from Newfoundland to North Carolina, to which Dutch mapmakers, mocking Spanish claims to the whole New World, soon gave the name "New France." In 1534 Jacques Cartier, on a mission similar to Verrazano's, began the exploration of the Gulf and River of St. Lawrence and thereby strengthened French claims to the sites of future Quebec and Montreal.

Soon after Cartier's expedition, France was ravaged by religious wars, and exploration ceased for almost 75 years. But free-lance

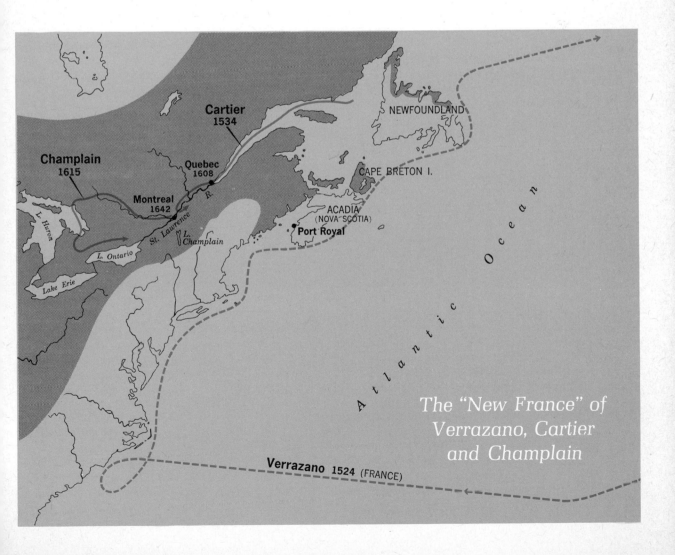

The "New France" of Verrazano, Cartier and Champlain

28

French corsairs continued so to harass Spanish shipping from the New World that Spain, in 1565, was forced to set up a base at St. Augustine, Florida, from which to combat the marauders. This was the first European settlement on land that was to become part of the continental United States. Far to the north other Frenchmen on fishing voyages to Newfoundland had begun exchanging precious bits of metal for the rich pelts the native red men would bring to the shore. The trade in fur (soon enlarged by the exchange of brandy and guns as well as scraps of iron) became the staple of New France after exploration and settlement were resumed under the leadership of Samuel de Champlain.

Champlain's voyages to America were supported by private French capitalists who hoped to make a good thing of the fur trade. Champlain himself was more interested in discovery than in business. In 1603 he made his first visit to the area of Cartier's explorations and ascended the St. Lawrence River to the Lachine (or China) rapids. From 1604 until its abandonment in 1607, Champlain was the leading figure in the little colony established at modern Annapolis Royal, Nova Scotia. During these years he accurately charted the Atlantic Coast as far south as future Plymouth harbor and Cape Cod. But Champlain yearned to return to the St. Lawrence region, and there, in 1608, he built a fort at Quebec, the foundation of the first permanent French colony in North America. The next year, in company with friendly Huron Indians, he ascended the Richelieu River to the lovely lake in New York State which bears his name. Here, French arms helped the Hurons defeat their bitter enemy, the Iroquois; but the victory cost the French the undying enmity of these formidable New York tribes which so vitally affected later French history in the New World (see p. 148). By 1615, Champlain had penetrated westward to Lake Huron. Thereafter, he sent out other pathfinders, and when he died in 1635, the French were in a position to dominate the entire Great Lakes area.

Until near the end of Champlain's life there had never been more than a hundred white men in New France at any one time, and while most of them roamed the country, Quebec itself constantly threatened to go the way of Annapolis Royal. In 1627, soon after taking over responsibility for French colonial affairs, Cardinal Richelieu tried to infuse New France with vitality and purpose by withdrawing the charters of the old trading companies and substituting in their place a single government-sponsored enterprise known as the "Company of the One Hundred Associates," or the Company of New France. Under its direction he dispatched some 300 new settlers to America. But this venture was mortally injured at the outset. In the spring of 1628, English privateers operating off Quebec captured a fleet of supply ships sent out to the colony, thereby depleting most of the Company's capital, and that July the English occupied Quebec itself, holding it for three years.

Catastrophic Indian wars in the following decades (see p. 148) so weakened New France that Louis XIV, in 1663, took personal charge of overseas activity, but to little avail. Under this regime a semifeudal society slowly took form in New France, with *seigneurs* pretending to live the life of large land-holders at home and *habitants,* or peasants, serving as their vassals. But it was all sham. A French visitor reported in the 1670s that the *seigneurs* "spend most of their time in hunting and fishing. As their requirements in food and clothing are greater than those of the simple 'habitants,' they mix themselves up in trade, run into debt on all hands, incite the young habitants to range the woods, and send their own children there to trade for furs." The *seigneur's* manor house for a long time was likely to be nothing more than a two-room log cabin. As for the *habitants,* many of them quickly succumbed to the easy lures of the wilderness to become virtual Indians.

The French Protestants, or Huguenots, were the only dissidents in France who might have made good settlers, for they were mostly artisans with the skills and aptitudes useful in a new country. But the Jesuits, whom Richelieu introduced into New France in 1625, saw to it that Huguenots already there were promptly deported and that thereafter none were to be admitted. The Jesuits, moreover, along with other representatives of the Crown soon subjected the ordinary Frenchmen in the colony to the same suspicious scrutiny that the King imposed on *them* from Versailles, so that such initiative as the people and their local rulers may have shown was paralyzed.

And yet New France became a great New World power and the Jesuits, to whom Richelieu had early vouchsafed the monopoly of American inland exploration and exchange as part of his policy of central control, proved to be the spearheads of its advance, following Champlain's lead (see Chapter Five). Under their suzerainty, in the words of Francis Parkman, it became "the nature of French colonization to seize upon detached strategic points, and hold them by bayonet, forming no agricultural base, but attracting the Indians by trade and holding them by conversion. A musket, a rosary, and a pack of beaver skins may serve to represent it, and in fact it consisted in little else."

### THE WAY OF THE DUTCH

Although the French corsairs led the way in attacking Spain, the Dutch far outdid them in pirating Spanish gold. The Dutch had other capabilities as well. Many Jews who had been exiled from Spain in 1492 found opportunities in Holland to use their industrial, commercial, and financial skills. Strengthened by these versatile capitalists, the Dutch developed their own manufactures, fisheries, trade centers, and banks. Splendidly situated between booming Scandinavia, which was supplying Europe with much of its timber and naval stores, and booming France and England, which were exporting wines, woolens, and coal, the Dutch became the middlemen on the northern, as the Italians once had been on the southern water routes.

Once the Portuguese had opened their direct trade with the Orient, moreover, the Dutch worked out an agreement with them to meet their ships at sea in order to pick up and speed the delivery of Oriental wares to the northern countries. They also were licensed to serve as carriers between Lisbon and Brazil. Portugal fell to Spain once more in 1580,

*Trading vessels in Amsterdam harbor, 1619. (William L. Clements Library.)*

30

when the Dutch were engaged in their own successful revolt against their Spanish rulers. The Dutch promptly included Portugal among their enemies and soon supplanted her in the Oriental and Brazilian trade.

In 1602 the Dutch created the Dutch East India Company to consolidate their Oriental interests. Its record of dividend payments is probably the most spectacular in business annals, and it endowed the nation, in addition, with a Far Eastern empire that remained intact until 1949.

In 1609 the Dutch East India Company sent Henry Hudson in *Half Moon* to make its own futile search for the elusive northwest passage. Hudson entered the river which now bears his name by way of New York harbor, and, finding it salt, proceeded hopefully northward. His search failed; but while anchored in the vicinity of modern Albany he entertained a band of Mohawks of the great Iroquois nation and made them gifts of "firewater" and firearms. The friendship of the Iroquois helped the Dutch in their contest with the French, which began in 1614 when another Dutch party established Holland's first fur-trading post near Albany. The English inherited Iroquois good will when they ousted the Dutch from North America (see p. 71). In April 1610, this time employed by English adventurers, Hudson set forth on his last voyage, on which he discovered Hudson Bay.

On the model of the East India Company, the Dutch, in 1621, also created a West India Company to extend their grip on Portuguese Brazil and break the Spanish Caribbean monopoly. The Dutch gained their first successes in Brazil in 1630 and by 1637 controlled 1200 miles of coastal lands, on which they grew brazilwood, tobacco, and above all, sugar cane. When, in 1640, Portugal rewon her independence from Spain, Brazilian Catholics were shocked by a Portuguese-Dutch agreement recognizing Dutch holdings. They revolted against both the Portuguese and the Dutch, and by 1654, faced with crises elsewhere, the Dutch completed their withdrawal, taking with them their slaves, their tools, and their

invaluable knowledge of sugar production.

By 1630 the Dutch West India Company had also smashed Spanish shipping in the Caribbean and largely taken charge of the carrying trade there themselves. They also had begun their occupation of islands in the Lesser Antilles, with Curaçao as their main base. Dutch victories over the Spanish permitted the English and the French to grasp Lesser Antilles islands too, the British making their earliest settlements on St. Christopher, Barbados, and Nevis, the French theirs on Martinique and Guadeloupe as well as on St. Christopher, which they shared with the British until 1713.

The attraction of these and neighboring islands lay initially in their value as bases for smuggling and piracy; but the English settlers on the islands soon tried to make a go of it by growing tobacco for the European market. The Virginia variety, however, had already proved of higher quality (see p. 51). The Dutch watched the islanders' losing struggle with concern, and in order to keep full the holds of their own vessels in the Caribbean trade they began, as early as 1637, to teach the English and the French the intricacies of sugar-growing and manufacture. The Dutch also supplied them with capital and equipment and with the enslaved Africans who soon displaced the white workers and laid the foundation for the heavy black concentration in the population of these islands to this day. After 1650 sugar produced by slave labor on large plantations made the islands in the Lesser Antilles the most precious of New World colonies.

In 1626 the Dutch West India Company purchased Manhattan Island from the local braves as a base for its own fur-trade operations and changed its name to New Amsterdam. The Company next extended its claims up the Hudson Valley and outward to Hartford on the Connecticut River, to Camden on the Delaware, and to Long Island. In 1629 it made its first immense grants of land along the Hudson to the patroons who were expected to bring in permanent tenants. In 1638 the first Scandinavians in America established New Sweden in the vicinity of the Delaware, and the Dutch Company for a few years made no move to dislodge them.

In 1638, flouting mercantilist theory (see p. 74), the Dutch opened New Amsterdam to mariners of all nations. This step alone showed that the Dutch, a nation of a mere 2.5 million souls, had begun to overreach themselves; but long after they surrendered New Amsterdam to the English in 1664 they remained a power to reckon with elsewhere.

### THE WAY OF THE ENGLISH

The French and the Dutch exposed the weakness of Spain's hold on America, but it was England that most effectively contested Spanish claims and most successfully colonized the northern hemisphere.

In 1497 Henry VII, the first of the Tudor line, who established the modern national monarchy in England by his victory in the War of the Roses 12 years earlier, sent out John Cabot, a naturalized Venetian, to seek the fabled northwest passage to Asia. Upon Cabot's single visit to Labrador, England's New World claim long rested. Almost a century later, in 1576, the Cathay Company, formed to develop English trade with China, sent Martin Frobisher on the first of three voyages duplicating Cabot's quest, but nothing came of them except reinforcement of English reluctance to chase this will-o'-the-wisp any

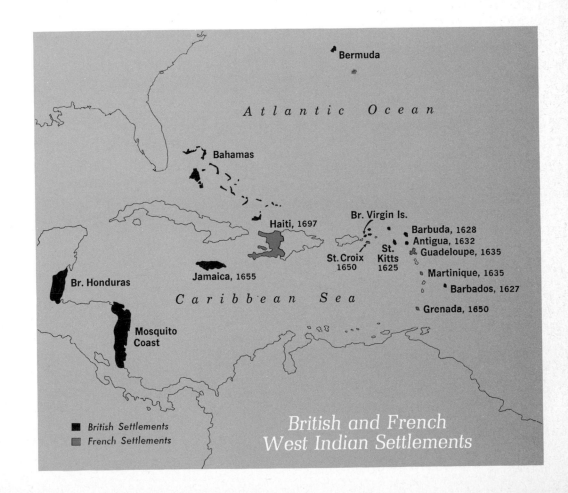

British and French West Indian Settlements

32

longer. Drake's voyage in *Golden Hind* in 1577 (see p. 25) confirmed the greater value of chasing Spanish galleys.

While Elizabethan sailors were scourging the seas, Elizabethan soldiers dreamed their own dreams of adventure and wealth. Walter Ralegh was the greatest of them, but it was his half-brother, Humphrey Gilbert, who in 1578 obtained from Elizabeth the first charter for a North American settlement. Gilbert was not without ambitions to emulate Drake; nor had the lure of the northwest passage altogether died in him. His path-breaking goal was a permanent North American base for his endeavors.

The outcome of Gilbert's first voyage in

*Sir Walter Ralegh at age 44, artist unknown. (National Gallery of Ireland.)*

1578–1579 remains a mystery. In June 1583 he embarked on his second voyage in command of five ships and 260 men with the aim of establishing a settlement in Newfoundland. Insubordination and foul weather plagued the enterprise from the start, and most of the participants, including Gilbert, perished in the sea on the voyage home. Only one of his ships made it back to England, with nothing to show for the project. Ralegh then took up the mission, only to exhaust his fortune on three profitless expeditions. On the first of these, in 1584, his captains made their landfall in the vicinity of Roanoke Island, to which, on their return with enchanting reports, Ralegh gave the name Virginia for the virgin queen, Elizabeth. Ralegh's second expedition in 1585 included a group of intended settlers who sailed home after one year, having found neither gold nor the "South Sea." Ralegh's third effort, his most serious attempt at colonization, was launched in 1587, when he sent 120 persons to Virginia under the leadership of John White. Once he had landed his passengers and selected the site for their settlement, White sailed home for supplies. On his return to Virginia in 1590 he found the settlement deserted. No one, to this day, knows its fate.

In later years, in a desperate effort to recoup his personal fortune at Spain's expense. Ralegh abandoned North America for the Spanish Main where he vainly sought gold in "Guinea." His and Gilbert's work, meanwhile, was taken up by their friend Richard Hakluyt the younger, who, beginning in 1589, promoted the establishment of permanent colonies overseas as the way to relieve the growing economic crisis in England, especially the mounting unemployment, following the outbreak of the Spanish war two years earlier.

Hakluyt's *Voyages,* numerous publications in which he gathered every scrap of information he could find about foreign lands, revealed much of the outside world to his insular countrymen. Hakluyt argued persuasively for a North American settlement as a source of raw materials for English industry, a market for English goods, and an attraction for the "able men" who "pestered" English prisons. When Hakluyt wrote, the English statute books listed some 400 capital crimes. Many felons in the sixteenth century—given the choice of deportation or death—preferred the perils of the newly discovered world to the mysteries of that "undiscovered country" from which (as Shakespeare reminded them) no travelers returned.

But not all Englishmen who eventually left for the New World acted from such desperate motives. Some dutifully followed the clerical injunction to "marry this land, a pure virgin, to thy kingly son Christ Jesus." For others less concerned with converting the heathen, "a Land more like the Garden of Eden than any part else of all the earth" offered another congenial challenge. Reports of exotic animals and plants, variations in climate, unusual customs, and rare "objects for contemplation" also whetted the appetite for adventure. Prospects of new Inca and Aztec hoards, moreover, continued to sharpen the greed of "right worthy"

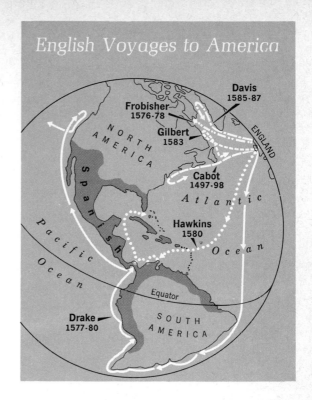

English Voyages to America

promoters as well as the avarice of the settlers they sent out.

## READINGS*

W.H. McNeill, *The Rise of the West* (1963), offers a stimulating study of the emergence of Western civilization against the background of world history. The new world of Europe, from which emerged the impulse to seek new worlds overseas, is the subject of R.L. Reynolds, *Europe Emerges: Transition Toward an Industrial World-Wide Society 600–1750* (1961). On this theme see also Derwent Whittlesey, *Environmental Foundations of European History* (1949). More conventional are two books by E.P. Cheyney: *The European Background of American History 1300–1600* (1904) and *The Dawn of a New Era 1250–1453* (1936).

* So many scholarly books are now published only in paperbacks, or are published in paperbacks simultaneously with or very shortly after hard-cover editions, that we have given up identifying paperback titles as a practice too rapidly dated. Instead, we recommend to our readers the use of *Paperbound Books in Print,* published quarterly (with monthly supplements) by the R.R. Bowker Company, a comprehensive listing of such books by title, by author, and by subject. Current issues should be available in every college and school library.

Digging into the earth for archeological survivals is going on as actively as the exploration of space. New findings are often presented in authoritative fashion in such magazines as *Scientific American* and *National Geographic*. Examples from the first include W.C. Haag, "The Bering Strait Land Bridge" (January 1962), and R.S. MacNeish, "The Origins of New World Civilization" (November 1964). Of special interest in the second is Helge Ingstad, "Viking Ruins Prove Vikings Found the New World" (November 1964), a study elaborated in detail in Ingstad's *Westward to Vinland* (1969). Background for the discovery and settlement of Vinland is perhaps best supplied in two books by Gwyn Jones: *The Norse Atlantic Saga* (1964) and *A History of the Vikings* (1968). R.A. Skelton, T.E. Marston, and G.D. Painter, *The Vinland Map and the Tartar Relation* (1965), adds useful information.

G.R. Willey, *An Introduction to American Archaeology* (vol. 1, 1966), and George Kubler, *The Art and Architecture of Ancient America* (1962), are authoritative. Excellent on the Aztecs and Mayas is M.D. Coe, *Mexico* (1962), and on the Incas, J.A. Mason, *The Ancient Civilizations of Peru* (1961). Still valuable on pre-Columbian culture are the American classics by W.H. Prescott and Francis Parkman. Most germane here are Prescott's *History of the Conquest of Mexico* (3 vols., 1843), and *History of the Conquest of Peru* (2 vols., 1847), both abbreviated in paperback editions, and Parkman's Introduction on "Native Tribes" in his *The Jesuits in North America in the Seventeenth Century* (2 vols., 1867). This Introduction is reproduced in the excellent one-volume edition of selections from Parkman, *The Parkman Reader* (1955), edited by S.E. Morison. A contemporary classic on the Spanish invasion of the American mainland is Bernal Díaz del Castillo, *The Discovery and Conquest of Mexico*, edited in a satisfactory one-volume edition by I.A. Leonard (1956). Cortez's own dispatches from Mexico are available in I.R. Blacker and H.M. Rosen, *Conquest* (1962). Of unusual interest are M. Leon-Portilla, *The Broken Spears, the Aztec Account of the Conquest of Mexico* (1962), and R.C. Padden, *The Hummingbird and the Hawk, Conquest and Sovereignty in the Valley of Mexico 1503–1541* (1967). Of the many general works on the Indians, the following three offer varied fare: John Collier, *Indians of the Americas* (1947); R.M. Underhill, *Red Man's America* (1953); and A.M. Josephy, Jr., *The Indian Heritage of America* (1968), with an up-to-date bibliography. W.E. Washburn, *The Indian and the White Man* (1964) is an invaluable anthology.

J.E. Gillespie, *A History of Geographical Discovery 1400–1800* (1933), is a good short introduction. Rhys Carpenter, *Beyond The Pillars of Hercules* (1966), is outstanding on classical exploration and geographic thought. A.P. Newton, ed., *Travel and Travellers of the Middle Ages* (1930), and Boies Penrose, *Travel and Discovery in the Renaissance 1420–1620* (1960), are excellent on the background for Columbus's adventure. Sir Henry Yule and Henri Cordier, eds., *The Book of Ser Marco Polo* (2 vols., 1921), is the best edition of the famous travels. M.C. Seymour, ed., *Mandeville's Travels* (1968), is a modern English version of that book. C.E. Nowell, *The Great Discoveries and the First Colonial Empires* (1954), is a short, authoritative survey. Roland and Caroline Oliver, *Africa in the Days of Exploration* (1965), and J.J. Saunders, *The Muslim World on the Eve of Europe's Expansion* (1966), afford scholarly short anthologies. The outstanding biography of Columbus is S.E. Morison, *Admiral of the Ocean Sea* (2 vols., 1942). The best edition of Columbus's own writings and related materials is S.E. Morison, ed., *Journals and Other Documents on the Life and Voyages of Christopher Columbus* (1963). E.P. Hanson, ed., *South from the Spanish Main* (1967), provides revealing material on, as its subtitle says, "South America Seen through the Eyes of its Discoverers." J.B. Brebner, *The Explorers of North America 1492–1806* (1933), is indispensable for the opening of that continent. R.H. Brown,

*Historical Geography of the United States* (1948), is excellent on the character and use of the land.

On Portugal and her empire, useful introductions are supplied in C.E. Nowell, *A History of Portugal* (1952); Elaine Sanceau, *Henry the Navigator* (1947); and two short works by C.R. Boxer: *Four Centuries of Portuguese Expansion 1415–1825* (1961) and *Race Relations in the Portuguese Colonial Empire 1415–1825* (1963). On the Spanish empire, besides Prescott, see J.H. Parry, *The Spanish Seaborne Empire* (1966); F.A. Kirkpatrick, *The Spanish Conquistadores* (1934); and L.B. Simpson, *The Encomienda in New Spain* (1950). A.P. Newton, *The European Nations in the West Indies 1493–1688* (1933), is invaluable for Spain and her rivals. On the great event of 1588, see Garrett Mattingly, *The Armada* (1959). On France in the New World, in addition to Parkman, see W.B. Munro, *Crusaders of New France* (1920), and G.M. Wrong, *The Rise and Fall of New France* (2 vols., 1928). On the expansion of Holland, see C.R. Boxer, *The Dutch Seaborne Empire: 1600–1800* (1965) and George Masselman, *The Cradle of Colonialism* (1963).

The background for English expansion is presented in numerous works by J.A. Williamson, such as *Maritime Enterprise 1485–1558* (1913) and *The Age of Drake* (1938). K.R. Andrews, *Drake's Voyages* (1967), is an authoritative modern interpretation. Extracts from Richard Hakluyt's twelve volumes of *Voyages* are presented in the excellent one-volume World's Classics edition by Janet Hampden (1958). *The England of Elizabeth* (1951) and *The Expansion of Elizabethan England* (1955) by A.L. Rowse capture the spirit of the age. Rowse's *The Elizabethans and America* (1959) is excellent on the early attempts at colonization. His *Sir Walter Ralegh, His Family and Private Life* (1962) is an illuminating biography.

# TWO

In July 1603, a few months after James I became King of England, Sir Walter Ralegh was locked up in the Tower of London for treason. His personal fortunes had sunk as low as the fortunes of his colonial enterprises in North America almost 20 years earlier, but he still clung to his old hopes for Virginia which he expressed as late as 1602: "I shall yet live to see it an English nation."

When in 1618 Ralegh at last was executed under his old sentence, Virginia had indeed become an English colony. But the English *nation* Ralegh had in mind was a far grander enterprise than the feeble settlement that had been planted at Jamestown in 1607. This settlement, which tried in every way to emulate the Spanish *conquistadores,* was to be a disastrous failure for a generation. Ralegh's idea had been not to emulate but to evict the Spanish. He would so develop the economy of his territory that the "shipping, victual, munition, and transporting of five or six thousand soldiers may be defrayed." With this force he would march on and conquer New Spain. Ralegh's Virginia was to be nothing less than the New World itself, unshared, unpartitioned, a mighty imperial accession for the English.

Ralegh, as we know, failed in his grand design. New Spain prospered, and fragments of the New World were to remain under Spanish rule until the eve of the twentieth century. New France, in turn, continued to occupy most of the northern part of North America until the English took it in 1763. A mere 20 years later, the English themselves were driven out of what was to prove the gateway to the richest region of the Western Hemisphere by the rebellious inhabitants of

# AN ENGLISH NATION

their own "plantations," assisted by the French, who were eager to return.

And yet Ralegh's hopes for Virginia were not altogether unfulfilled. Although surrounded by foreign enemies and inhabited by many foreign peoples, the American colonies became an "English nation" in language, law, and tradition. Indeed, they quickly became more English than the English in those very qualities which helped distinguish the English from their continental rivals other than the Dutch—nonconformism in religion, representative government, economic and social opportunity for the common man. For a generation before the permanent settlement of America, these social aspirations were bitterly fought in England, a situation which impelled people more strongly to migrate overseas. Certain old obstacles to social advancement were carried to America, and new ones appeared here. Yet, virtually from the start of mainland settlement, Englishmen in America began to demand individual liberty, self-government, and equality with their betters, and gradually attained these objectives. They took such pride in their new "system," as they came to call it, that as late as the 1890s, Ralegh's vision of the New World with "but one flag and one country" continued to animate America's expansive policy.

## 1  The English at Home

### THE CHALLENGE OF THE UNDERWORLD

In the English nation under the Tudors, royal power had been built on the breakup of feudal institutions (see p. 26). The cause of the Crown was advanced by self-serving commoners like Wolsey and Thomas Cromwell under Henry VIII and Walsingham and the Cecils under Elizabeth, men who by sheer ability dominated the Privy Council. In keeping with the spirit of the times, these men seized opportunities arising from their closeness to the monarch to feather their nests and those of their own sycophants out of the new royal offices and emoluments.

Many others besides the Crown, its councillors, and its favorites at Court profited from the modernization of English society; but the circumstances of most people steadily worsened until, in Elizabeth's time, destitution stalked the land. Respectable farmers dislodged by the enclosure movement, rural tenants and laborers, village artisans and shopkeepers often grew so weak from want that before they could stand up to be whipped for

37

38

begging without a license, "they had need to be relieved with foode." Their ranks were swelled by monks and friars evicted from fallen monasteries and mendicant orders, by clowns and players from broken baronies, by poor university students deprived of church support. Drilled to a degree by military personnel cast off from great houses and mariners and fighters discharged armed but penniless in port after overseas campaigns, this "rowsey rabblement of rakehells" became "a nation within a nation," often holding respectable elements at bay.

On one occasion at least, [writes A. V. Judges in his fine anthology of tracts and ballads, *The Elizabethan Underworld,*] London was threatened with something like a siege. . . . The returning soldiery was landed on the south coast. Each man kept his arms and uniform, and these he was expected to sell to make up the deficit in his pay. When large numbers of them drifted up to London, and a band of five hundred threatened to loot Bartholomew Fair, martial law was proclaimed. Two thousand city militiamen were called out on one occasion to scatter a horde which was menacing the capital. A proclamation of 24 August [1589] threatened all mariners, soldiers and masterless men who did not procure passports to their homes within two days with summary execution. It was at least six months before the panic abated.

Under enactments of the 1560s and 1570s, known collectively as the Elizabethan Poor Laws, anyone without property, aged 14 or older, on being caught in "the roguish trade of life" and refusing to work for the parish as punishment at lawful wages, was to be "grievously whipped and burnt through the gristle of the right ear with a hot iron." For a third offense he could be put to death. In later years the scope and severity of these laws were increased. Yet "the roguish nation" multiplied until it became the gravest social concern of the kingdom. Children were born into it as the only life they would ever know, "to take the basest and most poorest shape," as Shakespeare wrote in *King Lear,* "that ever penury, in contempt of man, brought near to beast." Laws were also enacted to force such children to train for useful employment and to serve long apprenticeships from which there was no legal escape. But many refused to be bound to labor.

Thousands of boys and beggars eventually were transported to Virginia and other colonies, along with English laws explicitly re-enacted in America for their control. But

*"The manner of crying things in London," about 1600. (The Henry E. Huntington Library, San Marino, California.)*

Some broken Breade and meate for y poore prisnors for the lords sake pittey the poore

Buy a steele or a Tinder Box

I haue fresh Cheese and Creame I haue fresh

*English soldiers on the march to put down the rebellious Irish. Efforts to establish English colonies in Ireland in the late 1560s and the 1570s kept alive the idea of colonies overseas. (Derrick,* The Image of Ireland, *1581.)*

bound labor short of outright slavery proved even harder to manage and constrain in a free and open land.

### THE MIRROR OF IRELAND

Besides the unnerving challenge of the underworld and the spread of want, the shadow of Spanish power, the menace of Catholic ambition, continued to hang over Elizabeth's island like an eternal London fog. For a generation the Queen's self-made soldiers of fortune—Hawkins, Drake, Gilbert, Ralegh—had dazzled the populace with daring exploits. Beyond the treasure they brought from their Spanish victims on the sea (and from others under any flag, including their own, if the truth be told), they had buoyed up the throne which knew well the value of heroes in holding the hearts of the people. Yet final victory eluded them and their Queen before they died, soured, or retired. Worse, for all the booty of its most sensational prizes, privateering—and piracy—paid the Queen and her captains, on the average, little more than the cost of fitting out and putting to sea, and the growing distress in the kingdom was aggravated by rising wartime taxes, untimely harvest failures, and the hazards to trade of privateering itself. The drain on Elizabeth's funds for her last disastrous wars in Ireland, which broke out in 1598, forced her to call parliaments to extract yet additional "subsidies" from subjects sick of fighting and yearning for her end.

For 30 years now, mainly because the Queen had so arbitrarily opposed all efforts to bring about Calvinist religious reforms by means of legislation, Parliament had been nourishing its own independence and developing aggressive tactics. Among these tactics was that of trying to force the Queen to bargain for funds by yielding on other issues. Because of official apprehension over the people's temper, the Parliament of 1601 in particular was more carefully packed than usual with the Queen's minions, yet the mounting rebelliousness that was soon to decide the Stuarts' fate (see p. 47) was apparent from the start. A provocative issue this time was that of "patents" of monopoly bestowed by the Queen and her councillors on their favorites, who thereby pushed up the people's cost of living and closed the door of opportunity to ordinary entrepreneurs, most of them now of the Puritan persuasion. The right of the Queen to grant these patents independently of Parliament was also questioned, thereby lifting the curtain once again on the fateful constitutional issue, whether men or laws were supreme.

39

40

As the monopolies granted since the last session were being read off in the House, a crowd was found milling about the lobby and the stairs in an unheard-of demonstration to bring pressure on the members to withstand the Queen's "prerogative." Elizabeth eventually was voted her subsidies for continuing the Irish war, but not before she promised "her careful reformation," in accordance with which no new monopolies "should be . . . put into execution but such as should have a trial according to the law for the good of her people."

Ireland, as so often in English history, soon disclosed more about the character of the reign. Gleaming on England's open flank to the sea, the Emerald Isle for centuries loomed as a temptation both to England and her enemies. In Elizabeth's time, the government persistently tried to plant Protestant colonies there, as in America, to relieve land hunger and unemployment at home and to strengthen the throne abroad. These attempts, combined with rash programs of conversion, had led only to grim guerrilla warfare, with occasional wild uprisings ferociously put down (by Gilbert, Ralegh, and perhaps even John Smith of Virginia fame), when the full-scale rebellion of 1598 broke out, inviting Spanish intervention and conquest. The young Earl of Essex, the Queen's newest favorite, was sent to crush the Irish in time-honored fashion. He proceeded to botch the mission in a way that aroused the Queen's suspicions and mistrust. Soon after his recall, seething with her reproaches and stripped of his lucrative offices and especially of his monopoly of sweet wines, Essex led a mad revolt against Elizabeth in London's streets, which cost him his head in 1601 and the Queen her reason for living. When Lord Mountjoy finally suppressed the Irish rebellion in the spring of 1603, Elizabeth was dead.

Mountjoy proceeded to impose on the Irish countryside the "peace of the grave," dislodging and dismembering the people with the traditional malignity that made the English approach to the Indians of North America al-

most seem humane. "It has been said," writes G. M. Trevelyan, in his *History of England,* "that the Elizabethan eagles flew to the Spanish Main while the vultures swooped down on Ireland; but they were in many cases one and the same bird. . . . They saw in America and Ireland two new fields of equal importance and attraction, where private fortunes could be made, public service rendered to their royal mistress, and the cause of true religion upheld against Pope and Spaniard."

### "THE PRINCE'S POWER AND THE FREEDOM OF ENGLISHMEN"

Much is often made of "the English birthright," of the "Liberties, Franchises, and Immunities," as the first Virginia charter put it in 1606, of English subjects living under the rule of law and not of men. That these are more than mere phrases history attests. Yet we are not to confuse them, or even the aspirations they suggest, with the egalitarian concepts of our own day, however liberal the tradition they inspired, especially in America.

The reign of the Tudors, brought to a close by Elizabeth's death, remained a despotism with a long roll of martyrs to conscience, to conviction, and to convenience. Many troublesome books were burned publicly, their possessors executed, their authors expelled from the country. Freedom of expression meant no more than the Commons' right to introduce legislation not proposed by the Crown, and it usually was denied. Freedom of assembly and of petition were considered seditious goals. Religious dissidents were persecuted mainly on political grounds, the numerous Catholics (except under "Bloody Mary") as agents of a foreign foe, the growing number of Puritans as enemies of monarchy; but these were grounds enough to kill the bloom of toleration.

Toward the end of her reign, Elizabeth herself conducted a virtual reign of terror against Catholics, no doubt in self-defense against heightened Spanish intrigue. In 1583, with her appointment of John Whitgift as Archbishop of Canterbury, the head of the Church of England, she also set in motion what became a perpetual "Romish Inquisition" against Puritan "traitors," which frightened her own Privy Council. The more determined Puritans now were driven underground—both the Presbyterians, who still clung to their hope of obtaining reforms *within* the Church of England; and the Separatists, the more radical minority, who broke away from the Church and its control to meet in independent congregations, "as near the primitive pattern of the first churches [as] the light of the gospel" revealed it.

The Tudors, moreover, created and freely employed exceptional agencies of administration whose potentiality for repression the Stuarts were only the more cavalierly to explore. The Tudors also tried to undermine popular forums which, by exercising their capacity for resistance, were to grow strong enough to throw the unfortunate Stuarts out.

Henry VII, beginning as early as 1497, became the first English ruler to make a formal instrument of authority of the "Court of Star Chamber," where torture could be used in secret hearings to wring confessions from political challengers, and cruel punishments were imposed without indictments, juries, or cross-examination. Henry VIII extended Star Chamber proceedings to offenders against his proclamations, to which his malleable parliaments gave statutory standing after 1540. Attempting to influence juries in England was "accounted very violent, tyrannical, and contrary to the liberty and custom of the realm." Yet, country juries misbehaving under Elizabeth "were many times commanded to appear in star chamber, or before the privy council for the matter," where their ignorance or prejudice was corrected. From her own first Parliament in 1559, Elizabeth also extracted the establishment of the Court of High Commission, with secret inquisitorial and judicial powers in religious cases equivalent to those of Star Chamber in political ones. Whitgift made this court almost as brutal a weapon

against nonconformists as the notorious Laud later did under Charles I (see p. 48). In 1566 Elizabeth told the French ambassador that the three parliaments she had already called were sufficient for any reign. The nagging need for money compelled her to summon ten more sessions, but these were fewer and shorter than England had grown accustomed to even under earlier Tudor monarchs.

By and large, among Englishmen still habituated to doffing the cap, bending the knee, and prostrating themselves in supplication, the Tudors' was a popular despotism satisfying, however imperfectly, the deep yearning for domestic peace. It may fairly be said of Elizabeth in particular—comely, gracious, clever, confident—that she ruled more by "progresses" than by "prerogative." Elizabeth owned numerous palaces, rallying points of national pride. And she was constantly on the move across the country from one palace to another, her living presence filling such pride to overflowing. Each of her "progresses" was an act of state, meticulously well thought out. No one knew better than the Tudors, as a contemporary of Elizabeth said, that "in pompous ceremonies a secret of government doth much consist." To the people, she said herself, "no music is so sweet as the affability of their prince." Yet even Elizabeth wore out her welcome, especially among Puritans who never tasted "the affability of their prince" and who hated "pompous ceremonies."

Near the end of Elizabeth's reign, Puritans probably made up a majority of the kingdom. With their friends in the Commons, mainly lawyers and justices of the peace aroused to the defense—really, the revolutionary extension—of their privileges by the Queen's intransigence in religious matters, they certainly commanded an overwhelming majority of Parliament. When the drive for a Presbyterian order was at its height in 1593 and her own repressive measures were most vicious, Elizabeth told the Commons: "I see many overbold with God Almighty, making too many subtle scannings of His blessed will, as lawyers do with human instruments. . . . If I were not

42

certain that mine were the true way to God's will, God forbid that I should live to prescribe it to you." Such sentiments sat very poorly even with her own carefully selected members of the House.

By the time of Elizabeth's death, Parliament had fashioned itself into a well-tempered instrument of opposition to all pretensions to absolutism. Above all, the frequency of its meetings within a short span of time toward the end of the reign had brought many of the same members together again and again. They developed an *esprit de corps*, an institutional self-consciousness, a realization of their role as the voice of the popular will. This deepening

*Elizabeth I in her old age. Painting by an unknown artist. (The Bettmann Archive.)*

appreciation of their character strengthened the members' determination to gain the initiative in legislation. For this purpose they extended and refined the practice of submitting the Crown's proposals to committees, a powerful device by which members could gather free of Crown surveillance and examine independently not only what the Queen asked but alternative proposals of their own. The Speaker of the House, nominally elected by the members, was in fact a Crown designee with responsibility so to run the sessions that the Queen's business won full and swift approval and nothing else came up. The committee system made the Speaker's position increasingly difficult until the House gained the power freely to choose its own Speaker, one responsive to the members, not the Crown. But that step lay in the future when Elizabeth's heirs, her Stuart cousins, foreigners to England and with strong leanings toward absolutist Spain and France, turned English despotism into tyranny. When that happened, Parliament twice cut them down.

### THE STUART SUCCESSION

When Elizabeth succeeded "Bloody Mary" on the English throne in 1558, no question agitated Englishmen more deeply than that of the new Queen's marriage, so that she might soon give birth to a legitimate Protestant heir. Indeed, the momentous issue of freedom of speech in Parliament arose largely over the right of the members to remind the Queen of her obligation in this respect, especially from the religious point of view, and her determination to forbid their interference. Once Elizabeth had passed the age of child-bearing, the succession gnawed all the more painfully at England's heart. Once she had grown old, even her closest councillors sharpened their watchfulness, their eyes cocked on one another and on the likely successor to the throne.

Elizabeth's secret choice was James VI of Scotland, son of Mary, Queen of Scots, whom she herself had ordered executed (see p. 25).

To prepare James, Elizabeth had long engaged in secret correspondence with him, tutoring him in English ways. In one letter she observed, "There is risen a sect of perilous consequences, who would have no kings but a presbytery. . . . Suppose you I can tolerate such scandals!" No one had had a harder time at the hands of presbyteries than James himself, who came to the throne of Scotland at the age of one in 1567, when his mother, amidst scenes of murder, abduction, attempted flight, imprisonment, and escape, was forced to abdicate by the followers of John Knox (see p. 25). James's own early years were spent in terror of warring Protestant groups; and while he was well trained in Calvinism as befitted a Scottish king, he disavowed with the full fervor of his soul that part of the doctrine stated by Knox himself to Mary: "If . . . princes exceed their bounds, Madam, they may be resisted and even deposed."

Whatever else Elizabeth attempted to teach James about England seems never to have taken hold. James's Calvinism commended him the more readily to many Puritans who, having grown sick of combating a woman's wiles, were eager to have a king. Catholics, on the other hand, despaired. It was a strange Catholic plot, the Bye Plot, to capture and dispose of James in 1603, that somehow implicated Ralegh and got him thrust into the Tower by James for treason. Yet Puritans, as it turned out, had as much to fear from James as Catholics, and England more to fear than both. Still, the Stuarts did have a chance to win English hearts.

It is difficult to grasp today the ecstasy of relief in monarchies when the succession was effected peaceably, especially in time of war with no direct heir available; and the surge of love for a new ruler, fed by awe for the Crown and the quieting of anxiety. On his own royal progress from Scotland to take the throne Elizabeth had held too long, thousands all along the way greeted James with adulation. His own repulsive countenance, build, gear, and gait gave a twinge to those accustomed to Tudor beauty in kings and queens. When

guards caught a purse-snatcher working the crowds, James ordered him instantly hanged without a trial, an awful augury. Yet only the most amiable demonstrations floated him and his entourage to London.

James's peaceful accession brought a welcome lull in the bitter border wars with Scotland which ravaged the northern frontier. When his assumption of the throne was followed in 1604 by his making peace at last with Spain, and this peace was followed with new commercial treaties, the reign enjoyed an unprecedented expansion of trade which further gilded its prospects.

During the great surge of economic expansion in the early years of Elizabeth's reign (see p. 26), the joint-stock company, a device borrowed from the Dutch especially for distant trading, had come into general use in England. Joint-stock companies, by selling shares to those rising on the economic scale and accustoming themselves to the long-term risks of far-off ventures, could quickly amass far larger capital funds than most individuals had at their disposal. Anyone with money could subscribe to company stock, participate in the profits, and even gain a voice in management —features that favorably distinguished joint-stock enterprises from the traditional trading gilds with their prohibitive fees and tests, and the hated monopolies by which court favorites ate out the substance of the country.

In the early decades of Elizabeth's reign, joint-stock companies had extended English commerce to Russia, Scandinavia, and the Levant, even to Africa and the Orient. America still remained too formidably Spanish, too hazily exotic, to attract any but the most adventurous soldiers and sailors; yet even Gilbert and Ralegh, once they had run through the private funds available to them, had each bartered certain commercial privileges in their patents to experienced joint-stock promoters in London who undertook to raise new funds and fresh supplies for another try. This try was long deferred because of Elizabeth's interminable Spanish war. James's peace with Spain in 1604 led to its spectacular revival.

### THE RESUMPTION
### OF THE AMERICAN ENTERPRISE

Joint-stock undertakings in America fol-lowed directly upon the voyage to the Maine coast in 1605 of Captain George Waymouth in search of a refuge for Catholics who had already aroused James's ire (see p. 45). In Maine, Waymouth kidnapped five Indians, an act local tribes were to hold against all later white visitors, and when he displayed them in London on his return, having trained them to talk of the wonders of their native land, they caused a sensation. Sir Ferdinando Gorges, one of the organizers of the Virginia Company of Plymouth late in 1605 or early the next year (the records are lacking), de-clared that "this accident" of the red men's arrival "must be acknowledged the means un-der God of putting on foot and giving life to all our plantations."

One of those to whom Ralegh had bartered commercial privileges in Virginia in 1589 was Thomas Smith, probably the leading mer-chant in London. In 1600, on the organization of the great joint-stock enterprise, the English East India Company, Smith was elected its first governor. Sir Thomas, as he became on being knighted in 1603, almost certainly was one of the promoters of the second Virginia Company chartered in 1605 or 1606, the Vir-ginia Company of London. In any case he quickly assumed a leading role in its direction. The possibility of finding a short route to China by way of Virginia rivers, an objective dear to his East India Company, no doubt con-tributed to his enthusiasm for the venture.

The Virginia Company of Plymouth never fulfilled its promise (see p. 49). The Virginia Company of London, having got Jamestown started in 1607, was thoroughly reorganized under a new charter in 1609. Despite Sir Thomas Smith's heroic efforts at home and those of Captain John Smith in America, it also failed (see p. 52). But before its demise in 1624, the Virginia Company of 1609 had done more than establish the English perma-nently in the New World. Its joint-stock orga-nization set the pattern for self-government in all future English "corporate" colonies. The joint-stock company governor was the proto-type of the provincial governor, the directors the prototypes of his "assistants" or council, the shareholders or "freemen" the prototypes, in the aggregate, of the "General Court" or "assemblie." Self-government in the "proprie-tary" colonies to be established on princely grants to royal favorites was more closely de-rived from the example of Parliament, espe-cially as it increasingly asserted its indepen-dence of the Stuart kings, the prototypes of the colonial proprietors.

### THE IMPULSE TO LEAVE ENGLAND

The release of mercantile energies during the early years of James's reign was fostered by the Privy Council under the leadership of Robert Cecil, Elizabeth's able Secretary of State who had helped smooth the way for James's accession and was retained in his post until his death in 1612. Cecil's revival of expansive mercantilism promoted what may be called the *colonizing* activity of the na-tion, the staking out in many parts of the world, of English outposts like the one Ralegh first intended a generation earlier in America. James himself, and Charles after him, un-wittingly secured the permanence and profit-ability of colonies, particularly in America, by promoting the *settlement*—the flight, really—of large numbers of Englishmen over-seas. The Stuarts accomplished this by for-feiting every good hope for their reign almost from their first contact with the people.

James believed in the divine right of kings, a convenient belief for Protestant rulers after breaks such as Henry VIII had had with the Pope. Elizabeth, as we have seen (p. 41), said that she knew God's will better than any-one and could be trusted to carry it out. But she also acknowledged the scope of the law and the dangers of overstepping it. James was a logician who thought divine right could admit of no ifs or buts.

Even in the midst of James's first "progress" from Scotland to London, spokesmen for a thousand reform clergymen placed in his hand the "Millenary Petition" requesting alterations in Church of England doctrine and worship far milder than those which had driven Elizabeth to extremities. In January 1604 James yielded sufficiently to call a conference at Hampton Court to consider the petition and, as was his wont, he argued patiently with the members before smiting them with the full fury of his wrath. "If you aim at a Scottish Presbytery," he cried, "it agreeth as well with monarchy, as God with the Devil." The reformers had expressed no such aim, but grasping his hat to signalize the end of the conference, James shouted: "If this be all your party hath to say, I will make them conform themselves or else harry them out of the land."

Shortly thereafter, hundreds of reform clergymen were evicted from their livings, and thousands more, for conscience' sake, embraced the Puritan position. The radical Separatists recognized the bleakness of their plight and began preparations for their exodus to Holland and eventually to a haven in the New World (see p. 59). At the same time, the royalist clergy took to announcing their own divinity and infallibility, a position sustained by the ecclesiastical courts, including the Court of High Commission. Royalist judges, in turn, assented to ecclesiastical court encroachments on the jurisdiction of the common-law courts. In self-defense, common-law lawyers were impelled ever more strongly toward nonconformist ranks.

James spent as little time dallying with the Catholics as he had with the Protestant reformers. Under Elizabeth, the Catholics had been the hunted pariahs of the realm. James's own goal in the Spanish peace was to bring an end to Spanish subversion of the Catholic underground in England. This accomplished, he even restored diplomatic relations with the Pope and gave other signs of toleration. Having thus drawn Catholics out of hiding, he promptly conjured up the old blood-curdling fears among all Protestants, to which, indeed, Catholic leaders had quickly given some substance. As early as February 1604 the royal reaction began, and Catholics found themselves worse off than ever. Certain Catholic leaders now worked out the elaborate Gunpowder Plot in which Guy Fawkes and others planned to blow up both the King and Parliament, initiate a civil war, and call Spain in to restore order. The great explosion was planned for December 1605, but the plot was uncovered in November, when Fawkes and his co-conspirators were arrested and soon tried, convicted, and hanged.

For 15 years, Catholics knew no more peace in England; and like the radical Protestants, they turned their eyes to refuges abroad. The official condition of the English Catholics improved after the outbreak of the Thirty Years' War on the Continent in 1618, when James, by an elaborate exercise in king-craft, tried to save Protestant regimes, including that of his son-in-law in Germany, from Spanish aggression by pushing the marriage of his son Charles to the Spanish Infanta. To give James's plan a better odor, English royalty and its friends began to cultivate eminent Catholics again and to conciliate others. The rest of the country, however, saw through James's scheme. The projected family tie with Spain could only result in the resumption of Spanish power in England. Popular detestation of this policy was manifested by heightened violence against Catholics all across the land and in the deepening hostility of Protestant subjects to the King.

James realized that England's safety could not be left to the marriage project alone; to put the country on a war footing he was forced to call on Parliament for funds. The session that opened in January 1621 was the first formal one in ten years, and it soon made James sorry that he had not tried to govern another ten years without it. Although England did not engage in the Thirty Years' War, the conflict brought a halt to the great period of trade expansion. The depression that followed intensified the impulse to leave England even among those not irreversibly impelled to go by defeat in the struggle for law and liberty.

### THE VICTORY OF LAW DEFERRED

Elizabeth's successive parliaments had gained their strength from the growing strength of their members. As Tudor society became more complex, the scope of legislation broadened, and the responsibilities of justices of the peace, in particular, were gradually extended to include the administration of many new laws. Numerous justices resisted the new responsibilities and "went to grass." But others, especially those who were elected to Parliament and who helped make the new laws, gained greater respect and even reverence for the whole legal tradition of the community. The great difference between Elizabeth's parliaments and those under James and Charles was the strengthening of this tradition by the common-law lawyers and judges, whose own work gained in force from contending against Stuart claims to absolutism.

The greatest of the common-law lawyers and judges was Sir Edward Coke, royalist enough to serve both Elizabeth and James, but legalist enough to combat both. The tenor of Coke's lifelong thinking is evident in his report of a case in 1605, when he was James's Attorney-General. The King had justified his interference with a lay court that had been reluctant to yield the case to an ecclesiastical court, as the King desired. "Then," writes Coke:

the king said that he thought the law was founded upon reason, and that he and others had reason as well as the judges. To which it was answered by me that . . . His Majesty was not learned in the laws of his realm of England and causes which concern the life or inheritance or goods or fortunes of his subjects; they are not to be decided by natural reason, but by the artificial reason and judgement of the law, which law is an art which requires long study and experience before that a man can attain cognizance of it; and that the law was the

golden . . . measure to try the causes of his subjects. . . . With which the king . . . said that then he should be under the law, which was treason to affirm.

Without Coke's own "long study and experience" it is doubtful that the English common law could have been carried to America. Much of the strength of the common law lay in its antiquity, which went back at least to the reign of Henry II in· the twelfth century. Its weakness lay in the inconsistencies that had accumulated in the precedents over the centuries and in the many localities in which the common-law courts functioned. In 1600, Coke started publishing the 13 volumes of his *Reports* of common-law cases, taken down "while the matter was . . . almost yet sounding in the ear," and yet buttressed by precedents "beyond the memory or register of any beginning." These *Reports*, like Coke's own influential decisions, teem with references to ancient statutes and rulings painfully dug up. They made the common law viable just when America was on the verge of settlement. Coke's *Institutes*, which he began to publish in 1628, went even deeper. In them, for the first time, the great documents from Magna Carta on were exhumed and printed in full or extensively excerpted. Coke's tendentious glosses upon them underscored the supremacy of the law and the majesty of its tradition as against the willfulness of chance holders of the throne, especially such as James and Charles.

James had inherited large war debts from Elizabeth. He also came to the throne with obligations to many backers. Insecure in his new eminence, he sought, furthermore, to enlist the support of many courtiers with lavish grants. His hunger for funds had forced James in his early years as King to call session after session of Parliament; but the members would yield little without the certainty that their growing lists of grievances, especially on religious and legal issues, would be corrected. In the meantime, they added new institutional devices, such as sitting as the "committee of the whole house," the better to develop their own programs without interference from Speaker or Clerk. The first such committee assembled in 1607. Smaller special committees also were set up to unearth precedents, like Coke's own, to support Parliament's increasingly radical tendency.

The struggle between Crown and Commons deepened when James, and Charles after him, deprived of funds by the House, began to reach out for other sources of revenue. Among the tastiest of these were the "impositions," or duties, on imported goods, which had grown greatly in value during the economic boom. James, moreover, frequently raised the duties by proclamation, and those who protested too strongly were haled before the Court of Star Chamber and might have an ear cut off for their impudence. The Commons, in 1610, reminding James that "without advice or counsel of Parliament" he had "in time of peace set both greater impositions and more in number than any of your noble ancestors did ever in time of war," went on to assert its own power of the purse. It asked that "a law be made to declare that all impositions set upon your people . . . save only by common consent in parliament, . . . shall be void." This House also asked for restraints on the Court of High Commission and other ecclesiastical courts.

In a rage, James dissolved this Parliament in 1611. When a new Parliament in 1614 presented even stronger religious and legal demands in exchange for "supplies" for the King, James not only dissolved it immediately, but sent four of its leading members to the Tower. With his new chief minister, George Villiers, whom he made Duke of Buckingham, James now ruled without restraint until the wartime Parliament of 1621. Impositions soared; peerages were sold for huge sums; new monopolies were granted to the rich. At the same time, economies so ruined the navy that Turkish pirates enslaved English seamen in the Channel itself, while the Dutch captured much of London's trade.

Never had England suffered under a more corrupt regime, and when Parliament met in 1621 it made its first order of business the punishment of those responsible. A fifteenth-century law had been found empowering the Commons to impeach offenders against the commonwealth for trial in the Lords. Parliament now reached for the most conspicuous of the officers of state, the Lord Chancellor, Sir Francis Bacon. Bacon spent no time preparing a defense: "I do plainly and ingenuously confess that I am guilty of corruption." He had, in fact, been thrown to the wolves by the even more corrupt men around the King, and on conviction was let off with light punishment.

Having stretched its power in domestic affairs, the Parliament of 1621 reached for power in foreign affairs as well. It denounced the Spanish marriage proposal and petitioned for war with Spain and the guarantee of a Protestant marriage for Prince Charles. James received the petition with threats of imprisonment for its bearers. The Commons then resolved:

That the liberties, franchises, privileges and jurisdictions of Parliament are the ancient and undoubted birthright and inheritance of the subjects of England; and that the arduous and urgent affairs concerning the King, state, and defence of the realm, and of the Church of England, . . . are proper subjects and matter of council and debate in Parliament. And that in the handling and proceeding of those businesses every member of the House hath, and of right ought to have, freedom of speech to propound, treat, reason, and bring to conclusion the same.

The King demanded the Journal of the House, ripped out the resolution, and dissolved the session.

When Charles I succeeded James in 1625, Buckingham embarked on military and maritime adventures to regain mercantile support. But these were such costly failures that the Crown itself was brought into ever worse repute and Parliament into outright rebellion. Parliament's refusal to vote money for further adventures like Buckingham's brought Charles at last to the policy of "forced loans," refusal to lend carrying with it the penalty of imprisonment without trial. A compliant clergy attempted to aid Charles by declaring nonpayment of taxes and loans a sin. This reminder of papal corruption completed the mortification of the Puritans who had already become alarmed by the sincere efforts of Charles's new Archbishop, William Laud, to reform the Church of England. Unfortunately, Laud's reforms went directly opposite to those the Puritans themselves demanded, bringing in many Roman innovations to attract worshippers who did not in fact have Christ in their hearts. Laud, at the same time, intensified the persecution of nonconformists.

In 1629, Parliament, with Sir John Eliot showing the way, proposed the famous "Three Resolutions" to Charles, demanding that the King declare "as a capital enemy to this kingdom and commonwealth" not only him who lays and him who pays taxes "not being granted by Parliament," but him also who "shall bring in innovation in religion." Charles rejected the Resolutions. When Parliament voted them despite his opposition, Charles dissolved the body, not to recall it until April 1640, when he again needed funds to suppress an uprising of Scotch Presbyterians. This "Short Parliament" was immediately dissolved when it insisted on reforms first. By then no less than 70,000 Englishmen had migrated to the West Indies and North America.

A settlement with the Scots committed Charles to still further outlays, and in November 1640 he called the fateful "Long Parliament," which resisted his demands, raised its own army, touched off the Civil War, and paved the way for the dictatorship of Oliver Cromwell. Before any of these events, the "Long Parliament," in May 1641, passed two revolutionary measures. One required the convening of Parliament every three years even without a call from the Crown. The second forbade the dissolution of this Parliament without its consent.

The "Long Parliament" held office until the Restoration in 1660. During its turbulent career, Cromwell welded his army of "Roundheads" into an irresistible force. Soon after Parliament ordered the beheading of the King in 1649, Cromwell became Lord Protector of the Commonwealth, as the kingdom came to be called. In the Commonwealth period, the flow of dissenters to America slackened, and only a few royalists were prepared to leave England, joyless and austere though the land now seemed, for the uncertainties of the New World.

## II  *The Rude Beginnings on the Chesapeake*

### SURVIVAL IN VIRGINIA

The petition of the promoters of the two Virginia companies seeking a royal patent for the renewal of the Virginia enterprise (see p. 44) was submitted to King James in September 1605. Thereafter, it received the careful attention of the Privy Council which worked out the details for "so noble a Work," as they said, sometimes in consultation with the petitioners. Before the King's great seal was affixed to the final draft of the charter in April 1606, it was studied by the Attorney-General, Sir Edward Coke himself, who is credited with having seen to it that the "Liberties, Franchises, and Immunities" of Englishmen at home were expressly to be carried with them overseas; and likewise, that the limitations and obligations of the law were not to be evaded there. Coke may also have been largely responsible for the charter provision creating a royal council of 13 appointed by the King and responsible only to him to oversee the whole enterprise. The charter also provided that each of the two distinct colonies it projected should have its own council of 13 to see to details of administration.

Under the charter of 1606, the Virginia Company of London obtained the right to settle at any point between 34° and 41° north latitude; the Virginia Company of Plymouth at any point between 38° and 45°, the Crown considering this region "either appertaining to us, or . . . not now actually possessed by any *Christian* Prince or People." The borders of the two companies overlapped, but they were required to make their first "Plantations and Habitations" at least 100 miles from one another. Each was granted the land 50 miles north and south of its first settlement, extending 100 miles inland and 100 miles out to sea.

The merchants of Plymouth outdid their rivals in getting underway. Their first expedition set sail in August 1606, only to fall prey to Spaniards in the West Indies. In May and June 1607 Sir Ferdinando Gorges dispatched two ships, one of them carrying Waymouth's pilot, to the region of Waymouth's visit (see p. 44), and there, on the Sagadohoc River, the lower Kennebec today, the Plymouth Company's first and only colony endured one "extreme, unseasonable and frosty" winter and quit. Thereafter, fishermen from all expansionist nations of Europe regularly visited the Maine coast but established no lasting bases.

In December 1606, meanwhile, *Susan Constant, Godspeed,* and *Discovery,* with 160 men, all under the command of Captain Christopher Newport, an experienced West Indian buccaneer, had quietly weighed anchor for the London Company, and on April 26, 1607, sighted "the Bay of Chesupiac," or Chesapeake. Landing amidst "faire meddows and goodly tall Trees," a scouting party under Newport immediately fell into a skirmish with the Indians. A few days later, the expedition sailed some 50 miles up the river they named the James and chose a site they named Jamestown, one well situated for defense. The settlers had been warned not to "plant in a low or moist place, because it will prove unhealthfull." But, fearing an assault from the sea more than malaria and bad water, they ignored the warning and suffered the consequences. When Newport returned to England after two months in Virginia, he took many of his original passengers

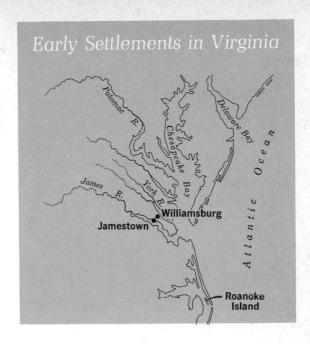

## Early Settlements in Virginia

back with him. Of the 104 or 105 who remained to make the settlement, more than half perished during the first summer, most of them the victims of fluxes and fevers.

Following its plan to settle Virginia gradually, the company sent Newport out again in October 1607 with 120 more settlers, and still again the next year with 70, but their fate was no kinder than that of the first contingent. In 1610 only 60 persons lived in Jamestown, and Virginia was on the verge of going the way of Sagadohoc. Indeed, in June 1610 the despairing bitter-enders, one of their numbers having been tortured and executed for cannibalism, were afloat toward the sea hoping for some fishing craft to pick them up and take them home to England. Then the heralds of a substantial fleet under Thomas West, Lord De la Warr, suddenly appeared on the James. The refugees were ordered back to Jamestown, "which appeared," as one of the newcomers observed, "rather than as the ruins of some ancient fortification, than that any people living might now inhabit it."

Virginia's plight had many causes, the basic ones being confusion of purpose and igno-

50

rance of conditions other than climate and terrain. Sir Thomas Smith and his colleagues in London hoped that the Virginia settlers might discover the elusive route to China, establish trade with the Indians, and develop gold, copper, and iron mines. But none of these grandiose hopes was realized. During the bleak winter of 1608–09, the "starving time," only the efforts of Captain John Smith had held the colony together. Smith was as interested in gold and China as anyone, but he also had an appreciation of the necessity of hard work that escaped his superiors in London and most of the "decayed gentlemen" they sent out. Work meant building shelters, planting food, seeing to fortifications, before the quest for metallic and commercial wealth could begin. It meant trying to befriend the Indian, elicit his assistance, implement his recommendations. For all his exertions and

*Captain John Smith, 1616. (William L. Clements Library.)*

example, Smith failed to arouse his fellow-settlers even to look to their survival.

The company's policies helped as little as its goals. The company, for example, held on to all the land itself and required the settlers to work it for the common store. This system probably was essential to security during the precarious first years in a strange country, but it also helped to kill incentive. The London council, furthermore, provided that Virginia should be run by a council of seven there, with a president at its head. But the president had no power except to preside at meetings. Thus authority, sorely needed if only to keep order, was wholly lacking. Smith took authority upon himself; but the gentlemen of early Virginia looked down their noses at the rough soldier. When Smith was injured in 1609 and left Virginia for good, the "starving time" grew worse than ever. His explorations in search of the river to the South Sea, moreover, had aroused the suspicions even of the most helpful Indians, who realized that the English had come not only to trade metal for corn, but to take their land as well. "It is true," said De la Warr's emissary in 1610, that the Indian was "as fast killing without as the famine and pestilence within."

The Virginia Company council in London gradually learned of Virginia's travail from those who fled home with Newport after his successive visits and by other means. They knew, as one said, that "the eyes of all Europe are looking upon our endeavours to . . . plant an English nation there, . . . to the end that we may thereby be secured from being eaten out of all profits of trade by our more industrious neighbours." As the first step in their "great effort" to improve their enterprise, the London Company applied successfully for a new charter in 1609, terminating their association with the Plymouth Company, abolishing the royal council overseeing their activities, and setting up as a thoroughgoing joint-stock enterprise with the right and power to govern as well as to trade. The new charter also greatly enlarged the company's boundaries north and south and extended its grant

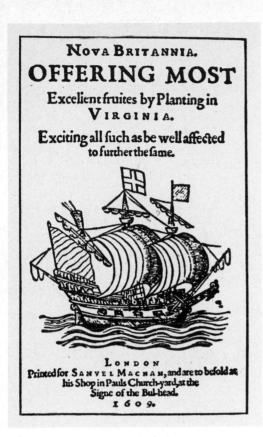

*Title page of a London Company pamphlet of 1609, issued to promote colonization of Virginia. (The Bettmann Archive.)*

across the entire continent however large it might prove to be.

Armed with this new patent, the company immediately launched a strong promotional campaign for subscribers to the stock which quickly brought it almost 700 shareholders, including some of the richest and most ancient companies in London as well as 650 individuals. It also launched the biggest expedition to America before the "great migration" to Massachusetts Bay (see p. 61). This expedition of six ships with some 800 passengers, again under Captain Newport, set forth on May 15, 1609. The new governor, De la Warr, was to leave shortly after. Difficulties delayed his arrival in Virginia for almost two years, and it was the group under his deputy, Sir Thomas Gates, that reached the vicinity of Jamestown in time to turn back the last desperate refugees. In place of the wrangling council in Virginia, the company now gave the new governor the absolute power of a military commander over settlers, who were treated like prisoners. This was another mistake, however justified it may have seemed. The "starving time" did not end under the new regime, for the colonists were to suffer privations for another decade. But Virginia's economic future was assured between 1612 and 1614 when the settlers discovered a new cash crop—tobacco, a variety imported from Trinidad proving more satisfactory than the bitter native plant. John Rolfe is credited with being the first to experiment with commercial tobacco in Virginia. The momentous consequences of his discoveries were deepened after 1619, when the first black Africans accidently were landed in the colony by a Dutch privateer just when its hunger for field hands was sharpened. In 1618, Virginia sent 30,000 pounds of tobacco to England. By 1627, she was shipping 500,000 pounds a year.

Until 1619, the Virginia Company paid little attention to the comforts and desires of the colonists. Soon after the arrival of a new governor in 1619, however, a proclamation declared "that those cruel lawes by which we had soe longe been governed were now abrogated," and that the settlers would henceforth be governed "by those free lawes" under which the king's subjects lived in England. The company parceled out land to the "ancient planters" (those who had arrived before 1616) and to later settlers who had paid their own way. This policy, declared John Rolfe,

giveth all greate content, for now knowing their owne landes, they strive and are prepared to build houses & to cleer their groundes ready to plant, which giveth . . . them greate incouragement, and the greatest hope to make the Colony florrish that ever yet happened to them.

Under the "head-right" system, introduced at this time, the company turned over 50 acres of land to any person who transported himself to the colony and stuck it out for three years. Later, the head of a family could claim an additional 50 acres for any dependent or servant he brought with him. Some men made a business of importing colonists, and acquired large tracts of land in this way.

On the model of the company government in England the directors now also "granted a general assemblie should be helde yearly once, whereat were to be present the Gov^r and Counsell with two Burgesses from each plantation freely to be elected by the inhabitants thereof; this assembly to have the power to make and ordaine whatsoever lawes and orders should by them be thought good and proffittable for our subsistance." This liberal policy was carried out on July 30, 1619, when the New World's first representative assembly (later known as the House of Burgesses) met at Jamestown.

Despite these political and social improvements, the Virginia enterprise continued its decline. A frightful Indian massacre in 1622 dissipated much of the hope inspired by the discovery of the tobacco staple and the liberalized administration of the colony. The difficulties in America only aggravated the problems of the managers in London. A royal investigation of the company in 1623 revealed some melancholy statistics: Of the 6000 colonists carried to America since 1606, about 4000 had died. Virginia was a financial failure as well, the £200,000 investors had put into the company returning not a shilling.

The plight of the colony and the company prompted the Crown to take up the charter in 1624 and make Virginia the first royal colony, a change that imperiled the new governmental system. A royal governor was sent to rule the people and no further meetings of the assembly were held until 1628. Not before 1639 did the king accept the assembly's right to permanent existence under the governor and council. Under the administration of Sir William Berkeley, beginning in 1642, life in Virginia improved, at least for white landholders. Berkeley's suppression of an Indian uprising in 1644 was followed by almost 30 years of peaceful Indian relations.

### THE MARYLAND REFUGE

Maryland, first settled in 1634, was truly a "sprout from Virginia," but an unwanted and unwelcome one of entirely different parentage.

Maryland's founder, Sir George Calvert, had long nourished great ambitions for his family, ambitions which were encouraged by James I, who knighted him in 1617. Following Elizabethan precedents, James, for services rendered, also granted Calvert vast domains wrung from the Irish and in 1625 made him an Irish peer as Baron Baltimore of Baltimore. Calvert's interest in America went back at least as far as the chartering of the Virginia Company, to whose shares he had subscribed. In 1622 James granted him the whole of Newfoundland virtually with regal powers there, and in 1625, after he acknowledged his conversion to Catholicism, Calvert attempted to make the settlement already underway in the province a refuge for his coreligionists.

Calvert hated the Newfoundland weather, and in 1629, after his northern enterprise had foundered, he visited Jamestown where he was suspected of having characteristically grand designs on the land. In any case, his religion supplied ample excuse for his being ordered out of the settlement. When, in 1632, Calvert was indeed granted land in their region, the Virginians felt their suspicions sufficiently confirmed to make the most resolute protests to Charles I, now king. Charles yielded to the extent of moving Calvert's grant north of the Potomac, whence it extended all the way to the fortieth parallel. Calvert named his new holding Maryland, after Charles's Queen, Henrietta Maria. When he died later in the year, his charter was reconfirmed to his son, the second Lord Baltimore. For years, Virginians carried on a private war to regain Maryland and on one occasion, in 1644, temporarily drove out the governor.

Cecilius Calvert, the second Lord Baltimore, began the settlement of Maryland in November 1633, when he sent out his brother, Leonard, and 300 persons in *Ark* and *Dove*. Their instructions were to deal fairly with the Indians, and soon after their arrival at the mouth of the Potomac in March 1634, they purchased from them a healthful and accessible tract which they named St. Mary's. Their consideration for the red men spared the newcomers the terrors of war during the critical early period; orders from the Crown to the governor of Virginia to supply the new colony with grain, along with supplies brought in by Plymouth and Massachusetts traders (see p. 67), also spared Maryland the terrors of starvation. Once they had looked to their own subsistence, most of the colonists began to raise tobacco in competition with Virginia and soon enjoyed a modest prosperity.

Maryland was the first of the so-called "proprietary" colonies among the English mainland settlements. The others all came after the restoration of the Stuarts to the throne in 1660 (see p. 68) and reflected, as did the establishment of Maryland itself, the persistence of feudal as against commercial motivations for colonization among aristocrats to whom the Stuarts were indebted.

As the proprietor's charter required, Leonard Calvert laid out the new colony in manors of from 1000 to 3000 acres, each under a manor lord, usually a Catholic. The lords were themselves privileged to "subinfeud" their land to lesser vassals. Both small and large landholders, to be "quit" of traditional feudal obligations to the proprietor, were obliged to pay him annually a "quit-rent" in money, amounting to two shillings per hundred acres. The manors were expected to be self-sufficient in traditional feudal ways, with local government taken care of by traditional baronial courts. But manors, in fact, seldom

were set up on this basis, and only the quit-rent provision survived.

Calvert's charter, like his father's earlier ones in Ireland and Newfoundland, gave the proprietor "free, full and absolute power" to make laws that even a king could not review. At the same time it required that he act "with the advice, assent and approbation of the Freeman of the . . . Province," who were to be assembled from time to time by the proprietor or his heirs, "in such sort and form as to him or them shall be best." The first Mary-

**Early Settlements in Maryland**

BALTIMORE'S CHARTER BOUNDARY OF 1632

land assembly met in 1635, but no record remains of its proceedings. Later assemblies found it increasingly difficult to give their "assent and approbation" to certain of the proprietor's notions. At the same time, the proprietor, endowed personally with all military, judicial, and executive prerogatives, and with a council like the Privy Council in England to assist him in his work, found it difficult to heed the assembly's "advice." In the first assembly for which there is a record of the proceedings, that of 1637, freemen and council sat together and only the council's proposals were taken up. But Parliament's own recent gains in initiative and independence served as models to colonial delegates in Maryland as elsewhere. The assembly insisted on proposing and adopting its own measures. By 1650, the elected house was separated from the council and Maryland had a bicameral legislature which gradually asserted its superior authority.

The Baltimores realized from the start that most English Catholics fleeing persecution at home would seek refuge in Catholic countries in Europe and that in Maryland, as elsewhere in America, most settlers would be Protestants. Thus, although Catholics were offered a place to go to freely if they wished, the proprietors warned them from the outset that "no scandall nor offence" be given to Protestants. The Baltimores' great hope was to create an atmosphere of toleration which, by avoiding the grim example of religious conflict in Europe, would foster peace and prosperity in America. This hope was realized for some years. When Virginia's loyalty to the Crown in the 1640s led to increasing harassment of Puritans in that colony, however, Maryland, in 1648 invited hundreds of them to come to her. Rightly fearful of Puritan tyranny now, against the Catholic minority in Maryland, the reigning Lord Baltimore, in 1649, sent over his "Act Concerning Religion," justly famous as his "Toleration Act," which the Maryland assembly promptly approved. Under this act, anyone who used reproachful epithets like "heretic," "popish priest," or "Puritan" was to be severely punished. Although the Toleration Act made the denial of the Trinity a capital offense, it nonetheless advanced the cause of conscience by requiring the hostile Christian denominations to suffer one another peacefully.

Despite attempts to negotiate with the Puritan rulers in England after 1649, the Baltimores lost control of their colony. From 1650 to 1657, the Puritan element managed Maryland's affairs. In 1654, the assembly repealed the Toleration Act, and in 1655 a force of 200 men under the proprietor's deputy-governor was routed by a troop of Puritan planters during a brief civil war. But the antiproprietary group exercised authority for only a few years, and by 1657 Baltimore had regained his privileges. The Calverts ruled unchecked until 1691, when Maryland became a royal colony, to remain so until returned to the Calverts in 1715.

### ESTABLISHING THE PLANTATION SYSTEM

The early settlements in Virginia and Maryland, whatever their political and legal differences, were drawn into an economic unit by Chesapeake Bay. Together, these settlements provided the English with their first firm foothold on America's "moving frontier."

The marshy coastal plain that became known as the tidewater region of the Chesapeake settlements was threaded by countless navigable streams along which the first "planters" extended their estates. Ocean-going vessels could sail right up to plantation wharves, making it unnecessary for the planters to send their tobacco to export centers. This geographic circumstance helps account for the development of a society of independent plantations and smaller farms more or less sufficient to themselves, often uncooperative with public authorities and difficult to administer. For more than a century Chesapeake society did not "have any one place of Cohabitation . . . that may reasonably bear the Name of a Town."

While subsistence farms remained common in the Chesapeake region, and beaver and other fur-bearing game continued to be trapped or shot, the basic unit of production by 1650 had become the independent tobacco plantation. Before the end of the seventeenth century, many large cash-crop plantations were found even in the interior, their owners established as the dominant class and as models for the ambitious. The spread of such plantations forced those who had not gradu-

*Seventeenth-century English impression of a Virginia tobacco plantation. Barrels filled with tobacco leaves are being rolled to ships waiting in the harbor. (Arents Collection, New York Public Library.)*

ated to planter status ever deeper inland where hunting and subsistence agriculture remained the principal occupations.

The extraordinary rapidity with which tobacco, unlike sugar, for example, wore out the soil, combined with "the Ambition each Man had of being Lord of a vast, tho' unimproved Territory," led the more far-sighted tidewater planters themselves to reach out westward for more land. The very laws designed to check them, moreover, merely improved their opportunities. Theoretically, the "head-right" system (see p. 52) should have peopled the wilderness with small landholders; actually, it played into the hands of the speculative planters and colonial officials, many of whom obtained head-right lands by the baldest frauds. The head-right law required that land granted under it be put into cultivation within three years, a proviso conveniently ignored. Since land taxes were hard to collect on the frontier, those who had grasped the land could easily afford to hold it

off the market as long as they liked while its value grew.

Most of the newcomers to the Chesapeake country once the plantation system got under way were Englishmen sent over as indentured servants or contract laborers. In the typical contract made with company or planter agents before sailing, each person agreed to work for a fixed period (usually five to seven years) in payment for his passage. During this time he was forbidden to marry, and violation of this and other restrictions might lengthen his term of service. As the demand for labor grew, convicts were impressed for shipment overseas, along with beggars and rogues kidnapped in English slums, and child apprentices often coerced into leaving for America by poor-law administrators. As this traffic grew, conditions on the transport vessels worsened and many died at sea. Among those who survived the hideous ordeal of the Atlantic crossing and the hard years of servitude that followed, a few became rich and re-

55

spected citizens. Runaways, moreover, were numerous. Drawn by the abundance of free land on the frontier to strike out for themselves, many did so successfully.

After 1660 the widely held theory that England was overpopulated was abandoned and the flow of servants from the home country declined until, by 1689, there were few new arrivals. This change only worsened the situation on the plantations where the need for labor was always greater than the supply. It also strikingly raised the demand for Negro hands. As late as 1670, Virginia counted only 2000 blacks in a population of 40,000, and in Maryland the ratio was even smaller. During the next 30 years the number of blacks in the Chesapeake settlements multiplied five or six times, much faster than the number of whites, and conditions in the slave ships, always brutal, grew deadly for the many in chains. Maryland legislation, almost from the start of settlement, made invidious distinctions between white servants and Negro slaves. In Virginia, Negroes at first were subject to the same laws as white servants, more severely enforced; but legal differentiations began to be made explicit in 1630, and by 1661 Virginia recognized slavery for life. After 1669 strict laws were passed controlling Negro activities. In 1671 Virginia law lumped the slave with "sheep, horses and cattle" as property, his body freely subject to the master's whip, his life to the master's whim. Slave-owning itself, as much as land-owning, became the mark of aristocratic standing and conceit.

Tobacco brought wealth to Chesapeake planters after the West Indies gave up tobacco for sugar-growing in the middle of the seventeenth century. But Chesapeake prosperity throughout the colonial period remained subject to all the hazards of unregulated one-crop systems, especially those dependent for markets on ocean shipping which was likely to be disrupted by war. One of the worst hazards was overproduction, which periodically glutted the market and depressed prices. At a low point in 1661, the

Virginia assembly forbade tobacco planting for one year. But many Virginians refused to bow to dictation. Those, moreover, who did hold their tobacco off the market found Marylanders taking advantage of this fortuitous scarcity to "pour into England all they can make, both good and bad without Distinction," thereby giving Chesapeake tobacco a bad name in the bargain. Governor Berkeley tried to wean the planters over to such varied crops as hemp and silk and grapes, and to the manufacture of cloth and wine. He even sent expeditions once more "to make Discoveries . . . amongst the Indians" of ways to diversify Virginia's economy, but to no avail. When the assembly's ban ran out, "All the people relaps'd again into the Disease of planting Tobacco."

## BACON'S REBELLION

The commitment of the Chesapeake planters to this one-crop system, which was so demanding in land for expansion, so vulnerable to distant contingencies, and so inviting to undesirable controls, brought into focus all the grievances that culminated in Bacon's Rebellion in Virginia in 1676.

Until the 1670s, the Virginia frontier had been pushed only some 50 miles inland, a shallow and slow penetration which for 30 years had helped keep the general peace with the Indians of the region, who served as buffers between the colony and unfriendly tribes deeper in the interior. Yet the pressure on all the red men mounted. Their territory had already been infiltrated by unwelcome refugees from broken tribes in the North and East fleeing before the Englishman's well-known land hunger. Then, in 1671 and again in 1673 expeditions sent out by the most influential Virginia fur traders and land speculators pierced the Appalachian barrier for the first time. These explorations greatly enlarged the Virginians' vision of empire; but they also sent a quiver of dismay through the Indian nations whose country they trespassed upon. Meanwhile, the day-to-day encroachment of tobacco planters on Indian towns and farms close to white settlements, as well as the enslavement of Indian captives, was making the tribesmen wild with frustration and fear. Hardened Virginians, in turn, had already learned to shoot first, "it matters not whether they be Friends or Foes Soe they be Indians."

In Maryland, in this period, the Susquehannocks, far up at the head of Chesapeake Bay, had played a role similar to that of the friendly tribes of Virginia, guarding the northern reaches of the colony from the aggressive Iroquois League (see p. 146). By 1674, however, Maryland had made grants of land to planters deep in the Susquehanna Valley and, in anticipation of the spread of settlement, had signed a treaty with the Senecas, members of the Iroquois League most hostile to the Susquehannocks just south of them. Protected by this treaty from English reprisals, the Senecas promptly made war on the betrayed Susquehannocks and forced them southward toward the older settlements where they met the usual hostile reception not only from the white men but also from the local braves who were, like the tribes in Virginia, now in an exceptionally excitable state.

Food shortages soon drove the Susquehannocks and other Indians to raid frontier plantations in Maryland, with accompanying atrocities. In September 1675, a combined force of Maryland and Virginia militia failed in an attempt to wipe out the Susquehannocks, who then poured across the Potomac in wild roving bands that became the scourge of the Virginia frontier as far south as the James River. Frontier planters, flying eastward, demanded that Governor Berkeley send a new force sufficiently strong to destroy all the rampaging braves. Berkeley at first agreed to do so. When he then countermanded his orders, the frontiersmen's own anger, well warmed by many older grievances, took fire.

These grievances arose out of rising taxes levied in a manner discriminatory toward the inland settlers for purposes against which they were strongly opposed. One such purpose was the development of Jamestown into a city suitable for the effective administration of the navigation acts regulating the tobacco trade and other English laws (see p. 75). There were, at the same time, policies which inland settlers strongly favored, such as protection against the Indians, about which little was ever done. Well-founded suspicions that public funds were being misappropriated by the self-serving elite further soured the spirit of the times; and since this elite was beholden to the proud Governor for its place and privileges, the mounting dissatisfaction soon focused on Berkeley himself. He had in fact failed to call a single election of Burgesses since 1661 and ruled with his congenial friends of long standing, "the very persons our complaints do accuse," said one embittered frontier leader.

Berkeley's failure to enlist a force sufficiently powerful to check the unprecedented Indian violence was the last straw. The Governor's defense was that the militia could never find the Susquehannocks, who melted into the forest, and that any serious attempt to do so must only stir the more distant tribes to unite to drive the white man once and for all into the sea, as other tribes had almost succeeded in doing in New England only a few months earlier (see p. 66). Berkeley tried instead to conciliate Virginia's traditionally friendly nearby braves, a policy with which the assembly, meeting in March 1676, most reluctantly complied. Berkeley's shilly-shallying gave the firebrand, Nathaniel Bacon, his chance.

A young aristocrat with a short, shady past, Bacon was in his twenties when he arrived in Virginia as recently as 1674 and set himself up on more than 1000 acres of fine land in the interior up the James. Berkeley, 40 years his senior, was his cousin by marriage, and within a year of Bacon's arrival had given him a coveted seat on the Governor's Council. Bacon, however, was not won over to the Governor's side. The country, he said, wanted dead, not friendly, Indians; and he demanded that Berkeley grant him a military commission to do the job against the red men that the

Governor had mishandled. When Berkeley angrily refused, Bacon set himself up as the leader of the anti-Berkeley party, collected a force of willing volunteers, and led them in successful raids. For his pains, the Governor formally branded him a "rebel."

When Bacon arrived in Jamestown to take his seat in the House of Burgesses after an election which Berkeley had called in order to seek a vote of confidence for himself, Berkeley had him arrested and placed under parole. When the Governor again refused Bacon's request for a military commission, the rebel rallied 500 men and terrorized Berkeley into granting it. This was in June 1676. The House of Burgesses itself, at that time, with no assistance from the firebrand himself, proceeded to enact what became known as "Bacon's Laws," which aimed at liberalizing suffrage and office-holding requirements, equalizing the tax burden, and righting other wrongs, real and alleged.

When Bacon, commissioned, again left Jamestown to suppress a new Indian outbreak on the frontier, Berkeley once more branded him a traitor subject to being hanged, and tried with little success to raise an army against him. A further attempt by the Governor to regain control brought Bacon back to Jamestown in September, when he captured and burned the capital. When Bacon died suddenly of dysentery in October 1676, the rebel force disintegrated. Berkeley regained control, and before King Charles's commissioners arrived to relieve him of his office he had executed 23 of Bacon's followers.

Bacon was not the "Torchbearer of the Revolution," as he has been painted. If his rebellion did in fact hasten the Revolution, which, it must be recalled, did not begin for another hundred years, it could only be because of the impetus it gave to the tightening of English control on colonial expansiveness. When news of the uprising first reached England in September 1676, 1100 soldiers under Colonel Herbert Jeffreys were promptly shipped out to Virginia to restore order. Jeffreys himself was to take over as Lieutenant-Gov-

ernor. This military force, one of the very first sent to America, with a military man placed in charge of the colony, showed the determination of the Stuarts to bring the far-off freemen to book. The policy in relation to the Indians, henceforth, was to keep the Americans away from them, the land the settlers already held, it was said in 1677, "being more than they either will or can cultivate to profitt." Beyond that, the hope of peaceful relations was surrendered, the goal of conversion to Christianity abandoned, the policy of swift extermination rejected as too costly in money and men. Indian and white man both knew that the aborigines' hold on the land was sure to be broken. In 1682, when Jeffreys' force was recalled after the Virginia assembly refused to bear the cost of it, the formal policy was adopted that was to be followed along the whole course of the moving frontier: It was acknowledged that the Indians would never yield peacefully; to reduce the hazards of retaliation to the minimum, the system of frontier rangers was initiated. These rangers, armed and mounted at their own expense, rode regular patrols to learn of menacing Indian movements and to warn the settlers to prepare for attacks.

## III  *The Puritan Colonies of New England*

### THE PILGRIMS OF PLYMOUTH

While the first English settlers were struggling at Jamestown and the first French at Quebec, the country between these outposts engaged the active attention of adventurers from the New World and the Old. In 1614 Captain John Smith, in the employ of London merchants still in quest of gold and copper mines, sailed to the northern reaches of Virginia, brought back fish and furs instead, and a map from which, in 1616, the name New England first was given to the region.

Although New England was to become a

land of family farms, Congregational villages, and town-meeting government, the most grandiose early schemes for it, like those in Maryland, were feudal in character. The leading spirit behind these schemes was Sir Ferdinando Gorges of the Plymouth Company (see p. 44), who in 1620, along with some 40 aristocrats, petitioned the king for a charter for the Council of New England to supplant the Company. They also sought a new land grant reaching from present-day Philadelphia to Newfoundland and from the Atlantic westward to land's end. The plan to divide this empire into fiefs for the aristocratic subscribers never materialized, but after 1622 Sir Ferdinando himself was busy laying out vast estates between the Merrimack and Kennebec rivers.

Almost on the very day in November 1620 that the Council of New England won its charter, a much more homely group, bound for Virginia in the ship *Mayflower,* accidentally made their landfall off the Council's shores at Cape Cod. They were a mixed group of 102 persons, 35 of them from among the most dedicated of Separatists who had fled from persecution in England in 1608 and 1609 to a refuge granted them in the Netherlands. By 1617 they had grown disenchanted with life in a foreign country and had decided that their best hope "was to live as a distinct body by themselves" on the virgin land of the New World.

Three years of the most disheartening haggling passed before the Pilgrims could set out for America. When they did, it was with the financial backing of a group of London merchants who had obtained a grant from the Virginia Company for a colony of their own. These merchants sent out with the Pilgrims a rough company of some 60 "strangers"— artisans, indentured servants, and soldiers, including John Alden and Captain Miles Standish. In return for their backing and for their promise to continue to send out supplies, the settlers agreed to work together for seven years for the promoters. At the end of this period such profits as had been made were to be divided equally between the Londoners and the American community.

The mainstay of the Pilgrim group during the voyage and their first governor after they landed was the deacon, John Carver. Only second to him was William Bradford, his successor as governor on Carver's death from overwork in 1621. On finding themselves off Cape Cod in November 1620, Carver and his colleagues decided to forego Virginia and to seek a suitable site in the region where God had led them. This decision made, they felt the urgency to form "a combination . . . before they came ashore, being the first foundation of their government in this place." Why they did this is well told by Bradford in his *Of Plymouth Plantation.* This "combination," Bradford writes, was

occasioned partly by the discontented & mutinous speeches that some of the strangers amongst them had let fall from them in the ship—That when they came ashore, they would use their own liberty; for none had power to command them, the patent they had being for Virginia, and not for Newengland, which belonged to another Government. . . . And partly that such an act by them done . . . might be as firm as any patent, and in some respects more sure.

This "combination" was the memorable Mayflower Compact, the autonomous instrument of government by which the 41 members of the expedition who signed it on November 11,

do by these presents solemnly and mutually in the presence of God and one of another, Covenant and Combine ourselves together into a Civil Body Politic, for our better ordering and preservation . . . ; and by virtue hereof to enact, constitute and frame such just and equal laws, . . . as shall be thought most meet and convenient for the general good of the Colony.

It was December 11 before the voyagers' searching party under Carver found Plymouth harbor, already so named by John Smith, "and marched into the land and found divers cornfields and little running brooks." On December 25, Christmas day to many but not to the Pilgrims who denounced Christmas as another Romish "corruption" since men did not know when Christ was born, the main body "began to erect the first house for common use." That first winter half the colonists died, and only the friendship and tutelage of Squanto and his Indian friends, "a spetiall instrument sent by God for their good," preserved the remainder for another year. The Indians' own strength for possible resistance had been depleted by a plague three years before that destroyed a third of their number, a visitation, the newcomers said, by which "divine providence made way for the quiet and peaceable settlement of the English in those nations." In November 1621 the ship *Fortune* came with provisions to augment the first crops. Her arrival inspired the first Thanksgiving feast, a celebration which reduced supplies once more.

The Pilgrims by 1626 felt sufficiently well established to buy out the London investors who themselves had made no profit from the venture. This step severed all effective connection with the mother country, and the specific means by which the purchase was completed in effect established the colony as a joint-stock corporation. Those who subscribed to the purchase price, 53 men in the settlement and five friends in England, became freemen of the corporation and the colony. In 1628, when there were still fewer than 300 persons in Plymouth, each head of a family among the freemen received 20 acres of cleared land as his share. When Massachusetts Bay was settled in 1630 (see p. 61), the Council of New England confirmed Plymouth's right to its own territory, whose boundaries were now set for the first time.

In 1636, when new towns had been added to Plymouth and problems of government had grown more complex, the colony adopted the "Great Fundamentals," the first basic system of laws originating in the English colonies. These "Fundamentals" instituted a system of representative government in place of the arbitrary, informal rule of the Pilgrim found-ers. They prescribed the formation of a general court or unicameral legislature to which the freemen of each town might elect two deputies from among themselves, who would sit with the governor and his assistants. In Plymouth, as elsewhere in the corporate colonies, the rank of freeman was gradually extended to nonshareholders. In Plymouth, as in Massachusetts Bay, those aspiring to this rank had to survive the strictest examination by the divines, and those found "insufficient or troublesome" were rejected.

Until 1691, when it was absorbed into Massachusetts Bay, the Pilgrim community led an austere but independent existence, sustained chiefly by trade in fish and fur. "Let it not be grievous to you," one of their friends wrote from England, that "you have been but the instruments to break the ice for others; the honor shall be your's till the world's end."

### THE COMMONWEALTH OF MASSACHUSETTS

The Pilgrims of Plymouth made up only a small minority of the Separatist exiles from England early in the seventeenth century. The Separatists themselves made up only a small minority of the whole body of Puritans, most of whom remained, in their own estimation, the only loyal members both of the Kingdom and the Church of England. But even these Puritans felt by 1629, in the words of the lawyer, John Winthrop, that God was "turning the Cup toward us also, & because we are the last our portion must be, to drink the very dregs that remain." The following March, under Winthrop's direction, the Great Migration "to inhabit and continue in New England" began.

The Puritans had been anticipated in New England not only by the Pilgrim Fathers but also by a group of settlers on Cape Ann sent out in 1624 by promoters from Dorchester. When the promoters abandoned the project in 1626, 40 or 50 of the newcomers, led by Roger Conant, established a settlement of their own at Naumkeag, soon renamed Salem. In 1628 a number of Puritan merchants and others, organized as the New England Company, obtained the rights of the Dorchester promoters and sent to Salem a vanguard of 40 Puritan settlers under John Endecott, who became governor there. They strengthened their title to the land by obtaining a patent from the Council of New England for the territory between the Charles and the Merrimack rivers. In 1629 the New England Company was reorganized as the Massachusetts Bay Company with a new charter from the king confirming its land title, which included the Salem settlement.

This company's charter resembled those granted to other trading companies. The colony was to be administered by a governor, a deputy-governor, and a council of assistants elected by the freemen sitting as its general court or "assemblie." It neglected, however, to specify the company's official residence or to declare that the colony must be administered from England. Winthrop, named governor of the company, and his colleagues hungrily seized upon this oversight to transfer the whole enterprise to Massachusetts, where, as Cotton Mather later explained, "we would have our posterity settled under the pure and full dispensation of the gospel; defended by rulers who should be ourselves." By winter 1630 a thousand picked settlers had been landed in Massachusetts, and radiating from Boston, the Puritan capital, seven other towns were laid out. Within a decade, 25,000 persons had journeyed to the commonwealth. Winthrop and his colleagues, however, struggled manfully to keep control in the godly minority he headed.

This minority was so small at the start that when Winthrop, in October 1630, ordered the government of the commonwealth to be set up, it was found that the provision of the charter requiring *eighteen* assistants, all of whom must be freemen, could not be met, for there were as yet not that many shareholders of the company in the colony. In order to

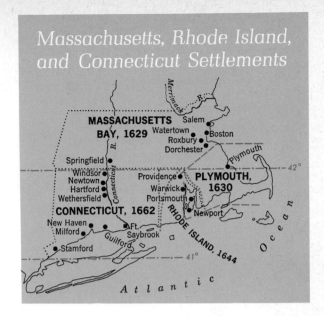

Massachusetts, Rhode Island, and Connecticut Settlements

proceed, some who were not freemen promptly were named assistants, and this tiny group constituted the full general court as well. Since the general court alone was empowered by the charter to make others freemen, the self-perpetuating nature of the oligarchy was obvious from the outset.

Before the end of the year, popular pressure compelled the general court to enlarge the number of freemen. At the same time, however, contrary to the charter, which required quarterly meetings of the court, the assistants limited its meetings to one a year. They also restricted the general court's duties to electing the governor and assistants, who would then exercise all the powers of government, including the laying and collecting of taxes and the distribution of undivided land. In 1631 the assistants declared that no one could become a freeman who was not a member of a Puritan church—a difficult position to attain here as in Plymouth. Three years later the assistants ruled that no new church could be started without their consent.

These regulations were so harsh that petitioners demanded that Winthrop show them the charter under which they were imposed. Winthrop knew his administration had gone

61

62

beyond its charter rights, and after unlocking and displaying the document, he acknowledged the privileges and powers of the general court set forth in it. At the same time, rather than permit all the new freemen to sit in the general court, where they would easily outvote the freemen who served as assistants, the latter made the court a representative body composed of themselves and two or three deputies elected by the freemen of each town. By 1644, the number of deputies even under this system had become too large for the assistants. They now divided the court into two houses, one

*Governor John Winthrop, after portrait by Van Dyck. (The Fogg Art Museum.)*

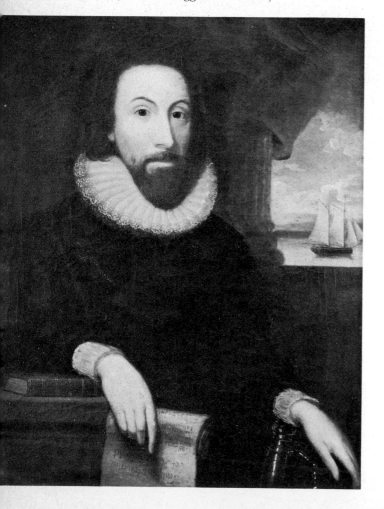

of deputies and one of assistants, each with power to veto the acts of the other, a power the deputies in fact already had by their majority in the old court.

By an act of 1635, the general court adopted the historic measure giving the freemen of the separate towns unprecedented freedom in town government. This act inaugurated the general town meeting at which, to this day in many small communities, the entire body of voters acts directly on such important matters as schools, roads, water supply, and police. But here, too, there was a catch. Since only Puritan church members could be freemen under the law of 1631 (see p. 61), this measure in effect extended the power of the oligarchy over localities, and did not mitigate at all the growing conflict for control of the Bible Commonwealth between the self-perpetuating "visible elect" and the less religious visibly successful.

As early as May 1635, the visibly successful also began to press Winthrop to prepare and publish an explicit code of laws, "whereby," as the general court put it later, "we may manifest our utter disaffection to arbitrary government." The oligarchy managed to withstand the petitioners for 13 years. When at last in 1648, the general court published the great "Book of the General Lawes and Libertyes concerning the Inhabitants of the Massachusets," it acknowledged that public laws made by self-governing freemen were to take precedence over the Mosaic code and other laws of God. Even so, the court said, "we had opportunity put into our hands . . . to frame our civil Polities, and Laws according to the rules of his most holy word whereby each do help and strengthen other (the Churches the civil Authoritie, and the civil Authoritie the Churches)" and the opportunity was not missed.

The year 1648 saw another momentous event in the running conflict between the "elect" and the others, with the elect again having their way. This event was the promulgation of the Cambridge Platform. On learning that Oliver Cromwell in England had received Baptists, Quakers, and members of other radical sects into his "New Model" Army, the general court of Massachusetts that year called a synod, or general court of Puritan clergymen, to meet at Cambridge expressly to sever all remaining ties with Presbyterianism at home. Lest Cromwell's "pernicious errors" seep into Massachusetts, the synod went on to confirm the unity of church and state in the commonwealth and to make the secular government the explicit agent for enforcing the religious and moral decrees of the Puritan—now the Congregational—clergy. The "dictatorship of the visible elect," in Perry Miller's phrase, soon became known as "the New England Way."

The appeal to the power of the state seemed gradually to diminish Puritanism's moral strength. When the Anglican Church was re-established in England on the restoration of the Stuarts in 1660, and thus enjoyed a revival in America as well, those tired of Puritan engrossment found a welcome escape within the Anglican structure. Aware of this competition, and fearful of an English investigation of their "tyranny" under the New England Way, the Massachusetts general court and the Congregational general synod in 1662 agreed to the "Half-Way Covenant," under which those who preferred not to run the rigors of seeking membership in the Congregational Church might now become freemen and participate equally with the elect in civic affairs. They might also have their children baptized into the Covenant of Grace.

Winthrop warned that New England's marked material success (see p. 66) would make the colonists "fall to embrace this present world and prosecute our carnall intentions." Yet Yankee merchants quickly came to the support of churches which, of course, were built in Massachusetts from the first. They also supported the college that was organized in 1636 to train the "learned clergy" of the future, and gentlemen as well. In 1638, John Harvard, no stranger to wealth as it was judged at the time, bequeathed the new college his library and half his estate, and since

*Boston's first Town-house. A drawing constructed from the original specifications of 1657. (The Bostonian Society.)*

then it has borne his name. In 1642 and again in 1647, noting that "one chief point of that old deluder, Satan, [was] to keep men from a knowledge of the Scriptures . . . by keeping them in an unknown tongue," the general court adopted legislation to further public education to insure that all might read and even "to fit youths for the university." This legislation proved ineffective (see p. 136); but it established the principle of compulsory public education, new to the English-speaking world, and served as an inspiration to other New England settlements.

### THE RADICALS OF RHODE ISLAND

Concessions like the legal code of 1648 and the Half-Way Covenant of 1662 had come hard to the leaders of Massachusetts Bay. In earlier times they used harsher means to deal

63

64

with what Winthrop once called, "the seditious and undermining practices of hereticall false brethren."

Among the first of the "false" was Roger Williams, the founder of Rhode Island, "a man," to quote Bradford, "having very many precious parts, but very unsettled in judgment." Williams, of a well-to-do London family and a protege of Sir Edward Coke, who supervised his education, was a Separatist chaplain who arrived in Massachusetts in 1631 after having encountered the wrath of Archbishop Laud at home. In Massachusetts he promptly raised embarrassing issues—by asserting, for example, that the Bay Colony had no just claim to Indian lands. He also denied that the Puritan rulers, or any others, had the right to compel men to engage in religious observances.

The magistrates insisted that "the powers that be are ordained by God . . . and they that resist shall receive to themselves damnation." Williams repudiated this doctrine not as a secular liberal but simply as a deeply religious man who doubted that "Judges are God upon earthe." The Puritan leaders recognized the dangerous undercurrent of his thinking and decided he would have to leave. Threatened with banishment to England, Williams in the winter of 1635 fled to the region of Narragansett Bay. The following spring, having been joined by some of his sympathizers, he established his own community there, which he called Providence, the foundation of later Rhode Island.

Three years later a second Rhode Island community was started by another refugee from Massachusetts, Anne Hutchinson. The sharp-witted wife of a mild Puritan merchant, Mrs. Hutchinson had moved from practical discussions of midwifery in Boston to more touchy analyses of sermons she heard on Sundays. Her incautious speculations soon split the town. Behind the jargon of Puritan theology lay an all-important question: Was it possible for a person to know that he had received the grace of God directly and to bypass scripture, ministerial authority, or logic? Anne

Hutchinson insisted that it was. Her enemies in Boston believed that Satan, not God, was the source of her inspiration, and the more she talked, the more certain they grew that she was "deluded by the Devil." In 1638 the magistrates ordered her expelled. Early the following year, on being excommunicated, she left Massachusetts for Rhode Island with her husband and children, and there founded a town, later called Portsmouth. On her husband's death in 1642 she moved to New York, near present-day New Rochelle, where Indians massacred her and her household in 1643.

By then, four loosely federated settlements existed in Rhode Island, and to insure their title to the land Williams sought a charter from Parliament, which he received in 1644. Under this charter, Rhode Island established a corporate government similar to that of Massachusetts, with the privilege of electing its own governor. When a new charter was obtained from Charles II in 1663 and Rhode Island became a royal colony, it still retained its old governmental autonomy.

For many years Rhode Island was the only colony in which all Christian sects enjoyed "liberty in religious concernments," as the charter put it, including the liberty to vote, whether a church member or not. Perhaps such libertarianism lay behind the attitude of the other New England colonies, which continued to regard Rhode Island as "Rogues' Island"—"the receptacle of all sorts of riffraff people, and . . . nothing else than the latrina of New England."

## THE EXPANSION OF NEW ENGLAND

By 1643, Puritan settlements had spread beyond Rhode Island, westward to the Connecticut River, southward to Long Island Sound, and northward to New Hampshire and Maine. The Moses of the exodus into the fertile Connecticut River Valley in the late 1630s was the Reverend Thomas Hooker, whose congregation had grown dissatisfied with the poor land around the village of Newtown (Cambridge), Massachusetts. Hooker himself was too powerful and ambitious a man to be content with a subordinate role in Massachusetts affairs. Moreover, he was among those disturbed by the absence in Massachusetts of a codified body of law, a situation not rectified until 1648 (see p. 62).

The Fundamental Orders of Connecticut, drawn up in 1639 by delegates from the newly established towns of Hartford, Wethersfield, and Windsor, has been hailed as "the first written constitution of modern democracy." Actually, it was not democratic in our sense of the word, and it followed rather closely the Puritan theory of civil government and the implementation of the theory in the corporate charter of Massachusetts Bay.

The Fundamental Orders dispensed with religious qualifications for citizenship so long as the candidate was "acceptable," but in effect all but good Puritans were excluded. A general assembly or court was provided for, to which each town might send four deputies. The general assembly was to choose a new governor each year, consecutive terms being forbidden. It was also to elect a group of assistants to function as an upper house with the right (after 1645) to veto assembly legislation. Similar governments ruled in the New Haven settlement on Long Island Sound, founded by the Reverend John Davenport and Theophilus Eaton in 1638, and in the neighboring towns that soon affiliated themselves with New Haven (1643–56). In all of them Puritan orthodoxy persisted, and only church members could vote.

Connecticut emerged as a separate colony in 1662, when, like Rhode Island the next year, it obtained a charter from the Crown which joined New Haven with the river towns to the north. Like Rhode Island, although it now became a royal colony, Connecticut retained the right to elect its own governor.

The colonies of New Hampshire and Maine began as illegal settlements on the tracts of Captain John Mason and Sir Ferdinando Gorges, who between them owned all the land between the Merrimack and Kennebec rivers. Even though the two proprietors neglected to do anything substantial to develop their holdings, small settlements began to spring up here and there across the countryside. The gradual occupation of the New Hampshire area by Massachusetts emigrants foreshadowed its absorption into the Bay Colony in 1644. Charles II detached it again in 1679 and made New Hampshire a royal province. The penetration of Maine proceeded along the same lines as in New Hampshire, and after the death of Gorges in 1668 Maine was formally annexed to Massachusetts.

The Puritans in Massachusetts, like the Pilgrims in Plymouth, had at first encountered the smallest and least thickly settled Indian tribes of the entire eastern seaboard, their numbers, as we have seen (p. 60), having been sorely reduced by the fierce plague of 1616–17 from about 25,000 to 16,000. Although these tribes, mainly of the Algonquian culture, had had many unhappy experiences with English fishermen and traders, and with other white men, before the Puritan settlements were established, they now seemed content to be friendly with the newcomers and, as in Virginia, first looked upon them as possible allies in their rivalry with other red men.

The rivalry among the New England tribes had grown more intense after 1620 when the French and the Dutch, as well as the English, began to compete with one another for Indian allies in the fur trade. The rapid expansion of New England settlements and encroachments in the 1630s, however, soon gave the tribes a common grievance. The Puritans usually acquired Indian territory by fair purchase treaties, but the Indians, with no knowledge of private property or its laws, failed to understand what they had surrendered. Soon Indian raids on white frontier settlements changed the Puritan attitude from one of peaceful attempts to convert the red men to fearful retaliation, which in turn was reciprocated by the tribes.

The most important of the early Indian wars in New England saw the extermination of the

Pequots, who dominated the Rhode Island and Connecticut areas around Long Island Sound. The Pequots were "Mohicans," not Algonquians. Their name, in fact, meant "destroyer" in the Algonquian tongue. In July 1636 some Pequot braves murdered a New England trader in their area, and the next spring a Connecticut force sought revenge. The colonists routed the tribesmen, burned their main camp near present-day Stonington, Connecticut, and chased the survivors to the vicinity of New Haven, where settlers converging from Plymouth, Massachusetts Bay, and northern Connecticut slaughtered them.

After describing the "stink and stench" of the Pequots burning, Bradford writes: "But the victory seemed a sweet sacrifice and they (the English) gave praise thereof to God." They also saw that the Indian menace as well as that of the French and Dutch was greater than they had realized and that their attacks on the Pequots, successful though they proved, were poorly coordinated. In an effort to strengthen resistance to the common danger, and also to promote common interests, Massachusetts Bay, Plymouth, Connecticut, and New Haven joined together in 1643 to form "The Confederation of the United Colonies of New England," the first of a series of colonial efforts to work together without thinking to consult the mother country. The Confederation boycotted Rhode Island, whose lands the members coveted as strongly as they detested her principles. Maine's petition for entrance also was rejected. According to the agreement, each of the four member colonies were to elect two representatives who together would determine Indian policy, negotiate with foreign powers, and arbitrate differences among themselves.

Although the Confederation had languished by the middle 1660s, its sternest test lay ahead. In June 1675 a number of revived local tribes, organized in a confederation of their own under the Wampanoag chieftain, King Philip, attacked settlements around Plymouth. Soon a full-scale war was in progress between the braves and the New England Confederation and other New England colonies. In this war, which lasted a full year, more than 40 English towns were pillaged and burned, and about 500 colonists died. At least 1000 Indians also perished, while the survivors escaped to Canada where they soon joined the French in further bedeviling northern New England.

In 1684 the Confederation finally broke up. Massachusetts's overbearing behavior and her refusal on occasion to submit to majority rule may have speeded its end.

## NEW ENGLAND'S MATERIAL FOUNDATIONS

With the exception of the Connecticut and Merrimack valleys, the New England countryside was a rough land, less fertile than the Chesapeake region, and less inviting to large-scale farming. As the years passed, small farms and compact villages grew up among the New England hills. When a group of settlers wished to establish a new town (for, unlike the Virginians, the New Englanders sought to plan their expansion on an orderly model), they usually asked permission from the general court to settle a block of land of approximately six square miles adjoining an established one. The settlers then laid out the main street, the village green, the central church, the school, the town lots, and the outlying fields. All freemen were eligible to draw for the town lots and to make use of the undistributed woods and meadows. The richer settlers sometimes acquired additional lots, but even the most favored rarely received more than two or three times as much land as the poorest.

This system of establishing new towns carried with it certain disadvantages. The original proprietors, for example, by retaining control over the future distribution of undivided land, could discriminate against late-comers, who in fact soon formed a disgruntled majority along with landless and voteless tenants and laborers. Disputes between the old settlers and the new often ended with the newcomers moving west or north to areas beyond the regime's control, and gradually the old New

England system of planned expansion broke down. Late in the seventeenth century, in New England as well as in the colonies farther south, townships were being sold to speculators instead of family communities. During most of the seventeenth century, however, the New England plan worked effectively, and the culture of the region was carried to new frontiers more or less intact.

About 85 per cent of New England settlers during this period engaged in subsistence agriculture and home industry, both pursued by all grown members of the family with little hired help or bound labor. As early as 1644 iron was being smelted commercially in Massachusetts, while rum distilled from West Indian molasses and cider pressed from local fruits had become available for sale locally and overseas. New England craftsmen also made many of the commodities needed in the colony, such as furniture, silverware, pottery, hardware, and tools, articles which the Puritans, who did not have a big export staple such as the southerners had in tobacco, could not easily pay for abroad.

While most New Englanders clung to the soil or serviced the farm families, a more enterprising 15 per cent or so, finding the land intractable, had turned to the water. Fishing off the banks of Newfoundland became so important in the Massachusetts economy that the cod was placed on the commonwealth's coat of arms. Enough fish were caught for export to the West Indies and elsewhere, along with foodstuffs, timber, and even captive Indians to be sold as slaves. This trade nurtured a class of Puritan merchants as sharp and self-important as any in the world. Commerce, like fishing, greatly stimulated shipbuilding; and New England vessels proved at once so seaworthy and so cheap that they soon were being built for foreign as well as domestic merchants and captains.

Verner W. Crane, in *The Southern Frontier,* writes that, "Yankee merchants and masters, before they became great purveyors of blacks from Guinea to the plantation colonies, had made acquaintance with the slave-trade in their trafficking [in Indian slaves] from Carolina to Boston and Newport." But the Puritan business in black slaves began long before Carolina itself was settled. In 1638 the Salem ship *Desire* brought home the first blacks from Barbados in the West Indies. Thereafter in the seventeenth century blacks were landed only spasmodically in New England; yet by 1700 it was estimated that the region's population of 90,000 included 1000 colored people, most of them slaves. It was the traffic *to* the West Indies, not from it, that soon dominated the New England slave trade. Early in the 1640s, Puritan captains began visiting the main slave marts on West Africa's Guinea coast where their shooting wars in their efforts to fill up their holds with black cargoes quickly earned them Massachusetts indictments for murder, "these acts and outrages being committed where there was noe civill government which might call them to accompt." It was English, Dutch, French, and Portuguese competition, nevertheless, rather than Massachusetts views of "the haynos and crying sinn of man stealing," that at first drove the Puritans from the Guinea coast, forcing them to seek their black cargoes in Madagascar and other *east* coast islands heavily frequented by pirates. But the Puritans were not to be intimidated for long, and before the end of the century, Massachusetts and Rhode Island merchants in particular had become heavily engaged in the Guinea trade, their main customers being found in the Caribbean islands. Gradually they won larger markets in the mainland tobacco colonies as well, where the English slave traders predominated.

Once on the sea, of course, Puritan ships, like those of other maritime nations, sought out all kinds of cargoes and sailed to every beckoning port, legal or illicit, to make a trade. When they reached home at last they might land goods from around the world along with the profits from frequent distant exchanges. As early as 1675, Boston was described as, "a magazine both of all American and European commodityes for the furnishing and supplying of seaverall countreys." Al-

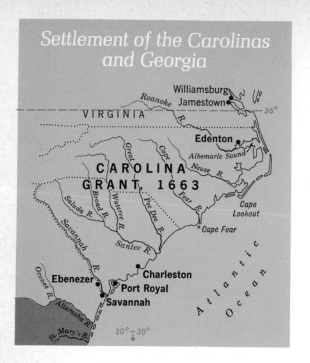

## Settlement of the Carolinas and Georgia

*(Map labels:)*

Roanoke R.
Williamsburg
Jamestown
VIRGINIA — 36°
Edenton
Albemarle Sound
Great R.
Cape Fear R.
Neuse R.
CAROLINA GRANT 1663
Saluda R.
Broad R.
Wateree R.
Pee Dee R.
Fear R.
Cape Lookout
Cape Fear
Santee R.
Savannah R.
Oconee R.
Ebenezer
Altamaha R.
Charleston
Port Royal
Savannah
St. Mary's R.
Atlantic Ocean
30° — 30°

ready the leading mainland American port, it was to keep its primacy for generations.

## IV  *The Completion of Mainland Colonization*

### THE CAROLINAS AND GEORGIA

While England was torn by civil war and problems of the Cromwellian Protectorate from 1640 to 1660 (see p. 48), emigration to America practically ceased. With the restoration of the Stuarts in the person of Charles II in 1660, new men came into power with claims on the new king and designs on the New World. During the following three-quarters of a century seven new colonies, most of them established by such men, and all growing from proprietary grants, completed the roster of those that first formed the United States.

The earliest of the Restoration colonies was called Carolina and extended from the southern boundary of Virginia to the borders of Spanish Florida and westward as far as the continent itself. This princely domain was granted by Charles II in 1663 to eight of his friends who had been instrumental in placing him on the throne. Among them were rich men who had made their fortunes in sugar-growing in Barbados. Since England, as we have seen (p. 56), had by this time altered its views about excess population at home, and indeed, in 1660, explicitly forbade the migration of skilled artisans, these men proposed to people their land in America with tenants from the West Indies and elsewhere in the New World. On the model of the similar proprietorship in Maryland, they also expected further to enrich themselves by collecting quit-rents from such tenants.

As early as 1653, Virginia had permitted some of her own more intractable settlers to occupy the northern part of the Carolina grant around Albemarle Sound as buffers against the Spanish and the Indians. In 1664 the new proprietors named a governor for this area. Albemarle, as it was now formally called, continued to draw Virginia malcontents who resisted control as successfully as their soil resisted cultivation. Limited access to the sea also contrived to keep the settlers poor. As in Virginia, their main crop was tobacco, for which they found their principal markets in the Old Dominion itself. When, in 1679, Virginia forbade any further importation of the Albemarle leaf, the growers began to dispose of it to bold New England traders who carried it directly to the European continent in defiance of the English navigation acts then in force (see p. 76).

In addition to attracting such smugglers, Albemarle became the haunt of pirates who preyed on Spanish shipping, defaulting debtors, and other discreditable persons, as well as runaway slaves. After 1691, when it acquired the name of North Carolina, this region was looked upon by the aristocrats of Virginia and South Carolina as a "lubberland," the home of paper-money agitation and other economic heresies as well as distasteful political equality and religious toleration.

The Carolina "Lord Proprietors" began the settlement of the more southerly part of their domain around the Cape Fear River in 1665 when they brought in the first contingent of Barbadians from among those who had been squeezed off the land by the growth of great sugar plantations on the island. The proprietors provided these settlers with a government under liberal "Concessions and Agreements," which granted them liberty of conscience and generous representation in a one-house legislature. Within two years this experiment failed; many of the Barbadians returned to the island, the rest scattered elsewhere.

Sir Anthony Ashley Cooper, who had emerged as the leader among the proprietors, persuaded the famous philosopher John Locke, in 1668, to become secretary of the group and devise a framework of government deliberately designed to "avoid erecting a numerous democracy." The result was the remarkable document known as "The Fundamental Constitutions of Carolina," which made the Maryland manorial plan seem a model of practical wisdom. How much Locke himself contributed to the provisions for a hereditary nobility of "seignors," each endowed with 12,000 acres, and lesser "landgraves," "caciques," and "lords of the manor," is debatable. The Fundamental Constitutions also provided for a governor to be appointed by the proprietors in England, and a one-house legislature made up of the great landholders and of deputies (owners of at least 500 acres) elected by freeholders (owning at least 50 acres).

In the succeeding years, about 50 great estates actually were set up, few of them, however, on a hereditary basis. As settlement proceeded, the Fundamental Constitutions gradually were liberalized, a bicameral legislature was established, and the lower house, here as elsewhere in the English colonies, assumed ever greater powers. By the end of the century, the Fundamental Constitutions had been wholly superseded in practice. In 1721 South Carolina was proclaimed a royal colony and

in 1729, when the proprietors at last yielded their charter to the Crown, North Carolina also became a royal colony. In South Carolina, the aristocratic spirit of the Fundamental Constitutions persisted. Property qualifications for office-holding and voting, for example, were among the highest in the British mainland empire.

The first settlement under the Fundamental Constitutions was begun in March 1670, off Port Royal Sound, with the arrival of an expedition of Englishmen augmented by Barbadians and other West Indians picked up on the way. Fear of the Spanish this far south prompted a northward move a month later to the Ashley River. Twenty-five miles up the river Charles Towne was begun. In 1680, the town was moved to its present site where the Ashley and Cooper rivers meet. A successful war in 1671 against the Kusso Indians, thought to be conspiring with the Spanish against the settlement, led to the enslavement of captured braves, an experiment soon followed by new assaults on the Indians simply to provide more captives for this slave trade (see p. 67). By 1680 South Carolina traders had spread as far south as the Savannah River. A war that year with the Westos of the region convinced the red men that they had better cooperate with the Charles Towne adventurers by supplying furs, deer hides, and other skins, as well as more captive Indians. This traffic rapidly made Charles Towne a flourishing commercial community whose population grew even more cosmopolitan after 1685 when Louis XIV resumed persecution of the Huguenots and French Protestant refugees poured in.

In the 1690s, as rice became South Carolina's export staple, the plantation system spread. Negro slavery, with many harsh aspects more characteristic of the West Indies than the mainland, became common, and here as in Virginia it fed the sense of superiority among the masters. The large landholders held firm to the reins of government in South Carolina from their Charles Towne homes, a situation that gradually embittered politics in

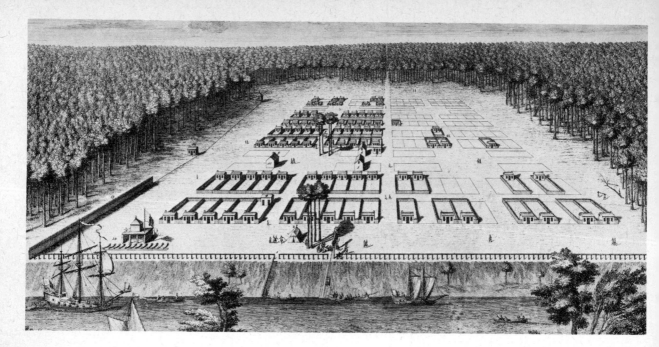

*A view of Savannah in 1734—the earliest known to exist. This plan probably was issued with a pamphlet published to secure settlers. George Oglethorpe made his headquarters in the tent pitched in the shadow of the four tall pines in the foreground. (Stokes Collection, New York Public Library.)*

the colony as settlers pushing the frontier westward saw their problems ignored and themselves imposed upon like the frontiersmen in Virginia earlier (see p. 57).

Spain, outraged by the formation of South Carolina on her borders, grew furious when in 1732 George II of England granted the unsettled southernmost part of Carolina, reclaimed by the Crown in 1729, to a group of philanthropists whose spokesman was the reformer James Oglethorpe. The next year, Oglethorpe landed the first hundred settlers of Georgia, as he called his grant, above the mouth of the Savannah River where they established the town of Savannah.

The Crown regarded Georgia as a military outpost; the proprietors hoped to make it an asylum for Englishmen imprisoned for debt; Oglethorpe himself envisioned a community of small farmers who might also constitute a yeoman militia. No person, the trustees ruled, could own more than 500 acres, and the land could be passed on only to male heirs. The importation of rum and brandy was banned, while for both humanitarian and strategic reasons slavery was prohibited. Believing that enslaved blacks susceptible to Spanish inducements to revolt against their masters might prove a military hazard, the trustees unrealistically planned an economy based on the production of wine and silk, neither of which required slave labor.

These regulations did not sit well with the mixed group of Welsh, Scots, English, and Germans who had come to Georgia to improve their fortunes. These Georgians found active supporters among the South Carolinians who gradually infiltrated the colony and soon made it their satellite. The ban on the importation of rum was removed in 1742, and after 1749 slavery was permitted and rice-planting spread. Three years later Georgia became a royal colony. By then Parliament itself had appropriated more than £135,000 to further Georgia's humanitarian and imperialistic future. The humanitarian phase now passed. Spain herself never conceded Georgia's existence, and not until the United States purchased Florida from Spain in 1819 was the incendiary southern border of Georgia defined.

## NEW YORK AND NEW JERSEY

While the expansion of New England encroached on New France in the north and the establishment of the Carolinas encroached on New Spain in the south, England's principal maritime rival, the Dutch, with their colony of New Netherland, split England's growing mainland empire in two. New Netherland, with forts at Albany and Kingston and the thriving town of nearly 10,000 at New Amsterdam on Manhattan Island, dominated the whole range of the Hudson Valley. Her allies, the Iroquois, moreover, dominated the country west of the Hudson, radiating from the Mohawk Valley (see p. 149), so that together they controlled the first great gateway to the West south of the St. Lawrence River. New Netherland also extended east of the Hudson to the Connecticut River and southwest to the Delaware, but the Dutch did little to develop the distant reaches of their claim. In 1655 they extinguished the settlement of New Sweden on the Delaware, but otherwise evicted few squatters.

The English in the later seventeenth century certainly coveted the expanse of Dutch territory. Yet their main quarrel with the Dutch in America, as in Europe and Asia, arose from the latter's free-wheeling infringement upon the sea-going traffic the English now tried increasingly to keep for themselves. Dutch ships, like England's own and those of the upstart Puritans of Massachusetts, sailed everywhere for cargo and markets. They were as active as any in the slave trade and New Netherland itself, as late as 1650, numbered more Negroes than any other mainland colony, many of them having been brought in from Brazil as well as from the Caribbean islands, East Africa, and other lands where Dutch ships touched. To check Dutch traffic on American waters, the English, in 1664, decided to expel the Dutch from America.

In March 1664, with Parliament's consent, Charles II granted to his brother James, Duke of York, all the territory between the Connecticut and the Delaware rivers. In April, the Duke commissioned Colonel Richard Nicolls, with a force of four frigates, to secure the grant. Nicolls reached New Amsterdam at the end of August, and within ten days, without resistance, Governor Peter Stuyvesant capitulated. The Dutch at home retaliated by declaring war on England. When they made peace in 1667 they acknowledged the loss of New Amsterdam, but during the renewal of the war they recaptured New York, as New Amsterdam had been renamed, in 1673. When the new war ended the next year, the Dutch finally gave up the town for good.

Four new English colonies were carved from the Dutch mainland empire—New York, New Jersey, Pennsylvania, and Delaware. Until 1683, New York was ruled as the Dutch had ruled it, with an absolute governor and council, and with the same unfortunate results. In 1683 a new governor, Colonel Thomas Dongan, arrived in New York with instructions to create an elected assembly privileged to meet every three years and to impose provincial taxes. By the time this assembly held its first meeting in 1686, the Duke of York had ascended the throne as James II and had made New York a royal colony. When the assembly's legislative efforts reached him for approval, he rejected them, restored the absolute rule of governor and council, and ordered the assembly dissolved.

New York had to wait a few years yet, and to endure a violent rebellion in the bargain, before it joined the other colonies in enjoying a representative government (see p. 78). Not until well into the eighteenth century, moreover, did New York begin to take advantage of its unparalleled harbor and rich inland soil to develop its economy.

In 1664 Colonel Nicolls, who had become James's governor in New York for four years following the capitulation of Peter Stuyvesant, tried to strengthen the colony by inviting English Puritans from eastern Long Island to

72

settle in its southeasterly portion between the Hudson and the Delaware. To make his invitation more appealing, Nicolls offered them their own representative assembly. Many Long Islanders accepted the invitation and thereby offset the preponderance of Netherlanders already living in the northwesterly part of this region.

Unbeknown to Nicolls, James in 1664 had granted the whole region from the Hudson to the Delaware to two of his aristocratic friends,

Settlements in Pennsylvania, Delaware, and New Jersey

Sir George Carteret and John, Lord Berkeley, who proceeded to name it New Jersey, after the Isle of Jersey where Carteret had once served as governor. All James had granted them was the soil and the right to quit-rents from it; but on no greater authority than Nicolls's own, Carteret and Berkeley in 1665 offered their settlers a set of "Concessions and Agreements" modeled on the liberal ones issued that same year in Carolina (see page 69). They also named Philip Carteret, a relative of Sir George, as governor. The Dutch in the

northwesterly section accepted the new proprietors and their government; the Puritans in the southeasterly section resisted them.

In 1674 Berkeley and Carteret divided their holdings, Berkeley taking the northwesterly portion which he promptly sold to a group of Quakers. In 1676 this division was formalized by the creation of West New Jersey (Berkeley's portion), and East New Jersey (Carteret's). On Carteret's death in 1680, a second group of Quaker proprietors bought East New Jersey from his estate, and under their liberal control the Jerseys became a haven for the persecuted. The Puritans continued to resist Quaker rule until the Crown reunited East and West New Jersey in 1702, giving it one representative assembly under the governor of New York. New Jersey did not have a royal governor of its own until 1738.

### PENNSYLVANIA AND DELAWARE

In 1681, William Penn, who had been largely responsible for the liberal government of West New Jersey, acquired a charter from Charles II that enabled him to found a colony of his own. The son of an aristocratic and wealthy British admiral, Penn, at this time 37 years old, had been infected with Quaker ideas as a boy. Despite the attempts of his angry father to make him renounce the principles of what was then a despised sect, he held onto them doggedly throughout his life.

Like other dissenters, the Quakers rejected the ritual and hierarchical organization of the Anglican Church, but they also rejected the Calvinism of the Puritans. George Fox, the founder in the early 1650s of the Religious Society of Friends, as the Quakers called themselves, was a mystic who felt himself divinely commissioned to preach the new creed: that man's love for God could best be shown by man's love for man, and that salvation was possible for all. Every Quaker regarded himself as a member of the priesthood, since all men possessed the "inner light" that enabled them to "hear" God's voice. The radical egalitarianism of the Quakers—their refusal to swear oaths, to fight wars, to accept class distinctions—seemed a threat to the existing order, and they were savagely persecuted both in Europe and America. And yet they prospered through their diligence and frugality.

After his father's death, Penn set out to fulfill his dream of providing a refuge for his persecuted brethren. In exchange for a debt Charles II had owed his father, Penn in 1681 obtained a grant to a large area in the Delaware region north of Maryland that had once been part of New Netherland but that lay outside the Duke of York's original proprietorship. To "Sylvania"—Penn's name for his forest-covered province—the King attached the prefix "Penn" in honor of his old friend, the Admiral.

The terms of Penn's charter did not give him the sweeping powers enjoyed by the early proprietors, for British officials had begun to check colonial pretensions to self-rule. Nevertheless, Penn laid down a plan of government that was certainly the most liberal in the colonies and perhaps in the world. It called for a two-chambered parliament, both houses to be elected by the freemen. The upper house would propose legislation; the lower house would ratify or reject it. Since the ownership of a small amount of land or the payment of taxes entitled a man to vote, suffrage was widely held. Only the Rhode Islanders could claim so liberal a franchise.

Even though Penn's government and humane legal code proved attractive to settlers, non-Quakers in the colony fought his administration from the start. Moreover, boundary disputes with New York and Maryland, together with charges in 1692 that he favored the cause of the exiled James II (see p. 77), made his position insecure. In 1692, he in fact lost his charter, and his colony was directed for the next two years by the governor of New York. In 1694, the Crown restored the proprietorship, but Penn remained in England until 1699. Though disgusted with his enemies in the colony, Penn in 1701 liberalized his government even further, the "Charter of Privileges" granted that year reducing proprietary authority to a minimum. This "Charter" made the Assembly the real law-making body, although subject to vetoes by the governor. It also officially detached from Pennsylvania the so-called "lower counties" west of the Delaware that once belonged to the Swedes but had been granted to Penn in 1682, and gave them their own legislature. This body first met in 1704. The "lower counties," eventually known as Delaware, remained under the jurisdiction of the governor of Pennsylvania until they became a separate state in 1776.

The immediate success and extraordinary progress of Pennsylvania indicate how much practical wisdom the colonists had accumulated since the days of Jamestown and Plymouth. Penn carefully selected the site for Philadelphia before the first settlers had even arrived, and he laid out his city with foresight. That his province turned out to be fertile and that its beginnings happened to coincide with religious persecutions on the Continent, were, of course, accidental. But Penn skillfully took advantage of his opportunities. He circulated a prospectus for his colony in England and on the Continent and persuaded hundreds of German sectarians from the Rhineland to migrate. Colonists of all faiths were attracted by Penn's guarantee of complete religious toleration for anyone who worshiped God. By 1689, there were 12,000 settlers in Pennsylvania, including about 250 Negroes. As in New England, a flourishing trade quickly sprang up with the West Indies, where Pennsylvania pork, beef, wheat, and flour were in great demand. Pennsylvania ship captains also engaged in the slave traffic, although Quaker scruples in this early period seemed stronger than Puritan ones in keeping their number small.

William Penn's colony soon became the richest in North America, but the proprietor did not share in its good fortune. After returning to England in 1701 to keep the

74

Crown's grasp off his charter, Penn met financial difficulties and even spent a short time in the debtor's prison. He died in 1718.

## v  *Consolidation of the Imperial System*

### THE SPIRIT OF MERCANTILISM

The permanent settlement of the mainland colonies, their economic growth, political maturity, and strategic expansion, all occurred within the framework of the emerging British mercantilist system. Of course, many of the colonists went largely untouched by this system. Perhaps as many as nine out of every ten mainland families lived on subsistence farms. On these farms they grew their own corn and grain, raised their own meat, wove their own cloth, built much of their own furniture, and made many of their own tools. If they had surplus crops to dispose of, they often bartered them locally for such commodities as salt, iron, and ammunition, which they could not make at home. Thus the vast majority of Americans in all sections shared an independence of the market, of the fluctuating value of money, of the ups and downs of international trade. From time to time, however, even the most isolated were caught up in the problems of government, war, and rebellion.

Under the mercantilist system, economic activity was organized and controlled—insofar as organization and control could be applied—for the advantage not of the individual but of the rising national state. Spain, Portugal, France, the Netherlands, and England all lived under some sort of mercantilist system from the fifteenth to the nineteenth century. Such a system, indeed, was the means by which each of these states mobilized its economic resources behind its national aims. Since these aims usually were in conflict and often led to war, one of the fundamental goals of the mercantilist system was to preserve and enlarge a nation's gold supply by which armies and navies were supported. The rush to America in the sixteenth and seventeenth centuries was strongly motivated, as we have seen, by the quest for gold hoards and gold mines.

Where there was little or no gold, as in the English mainland colonies, bullion was sought through the regulation of trade. Stated simply, colonies were useful for selling raw materials cheaply to the mother country and buying her

*London, about 1650. (Prints Division, New York Public Library.)*

manufactures dearly, thereby giving the mother country a favorable edge in the exchange which, by further exchange elsewhere, she could convert into gold. An important corollary of this mode of exchange, lest gold be paid out to foreigners for services, was the requirement that commodities going in either direction be carried in national or colonial ships. Lest gold also be paid to foreigners for goods, another corollary of the mercantilist system was the granting of bounties to colonial settlers to encourage the production of critical commodities. The British, for example, paid Americans bounties for producing hemp for ships' ropes, for refining tar for pitch, for cutting timber for ships' masts, and for growing indigo for the manufacture of dyes.

The mercantilist system worked best in connection with overseas colonies that produced great agricultural staples—such as the tobacco of Virginia and Maryland and the sugar of the West Indian islands. The planters of these staples found a protected market for their products in the mother country. They were also granted extensive credit for the manufactures they bought. British exporters, assured of payment in marketable crops each year, encouraged the colonial planters to live well, indeed beyond their means.

The mercantilist system had fewer attrac-

tions to the merchants of the Middle colonies and fewest of all to those of New England who had to roam the world in their ships to get sufficiently ahead in their transactions to earn money for the good life. Earn it they did, but in ways that brought little benefit to the mother country.

### ADMINISTRATION OF THE NAVIGATION ACTS

As early as 1620 the English ordered Virginia tobacco to be exported exclusively to England in English ships even though its principal users were on the Continent. Subsequent "navigation acts" placed additional colonial products under similar mercantilist restrictions. The system was enlarged under Cromwell in the early 1650s, when Dutch carriers took advantage of English internal conflicts to encroach on English overseas trade. After the restoration of the Stuarts in 1660, the Crown was urged to tighten the reins on its New World settlements in order to improve the revenues of the kingdom. Heretofore, only occasional parliamentary committees were charged with the responsibility for administering the navigation acts, and little real attention had been paid to their enforcement. Early in the 1660s, Charles II created a "civil list" of

Crown employees to give full time to colonial regulation, while Parliament stiffened the navigation code.

One of Parliament's new measures was the Navigation Act of 1660, re-enacted by the first regular Restoration Parliament in 1661. This act provided that no goods or commodities could be brought to or sent from any English colony except in ships owned by Englishmen, operated by English masters, and manned by crews at least three-fourths English. These requirements worked no hardship on the colonials, because the term "English" was always understood to include them as English subjects.

The 1660/1661 Act also required that certain "enumerated articles"—chiefly sugar, tobacco, indigo, and cotton-wool—that were grown or manufactured in the colonies be sold only to England or to another colony. Among the first enumerated articles only tobacco was of major importance, but other items were added from time to time. This measure was intended primarily to keep other countries from obtaining colonial commodities, but the mother country had no intention of harming colonial trade itself. To assure the colonials the full benefit of the English market, the act forbade both tobacco growing in England and English importation of foreign tobacco.

In 1663 Parliament passed another Navigation Act giving English merchants a monopoly of colonial trade, and this one affected the colonists more seriously. With a few exceptions, the new act required that all European goods destined for the colonies be shipped by way of English ports on English ships. Import and export duties were charged on landing and reloading such goods, but a system of rebates enabled the colonists to buy foreign goods coming by way of England about as cheaply as Englishmen could buy them at home. The colonial merchants, nonetheless, complained that the required stopover in England sometimes added an extra leg to the return voyage from the Continent. They now began to violate the Act of 1660/1661

by shipping enumerated articles directly to European ports, and to violate the Act of 1663 by carrying foreign goods directly home.

To close up some of the loopholes in these early measures, Parliament passed a third Navigation Act, which became effective in 1673. Colonial captains, for example, would pretend that they were carrying enumerated articles simply to another colonial port, but after having cleared that port they would strike out for Europe with their illegal cargoes. To stop this practice, the Act of 1673 assessed duties on colonial products *at the port of clearance,* unless the captain would bind himself to take the cargo to England. To collect these new export duties, a staff of officials was set up in America and friction quickly developed between them and the colonists.

After the Restoration in 1660, much of the authority to make recommendations on colonial policy and colonial trade had been granted to the Committee for Trade and Plantations of the Privy Council, more commonly known as the Lords of Trade. As early as 1664, this Committee had sent a royal commission to America to bring the colonists up to date on their obligations to the restored Crown and to investigate and arbitrarily correct any deviations from them. The commission succeeded in most of the provinces, but the Puritan Commonwealth of Massachusetts proved exceedingly reluctant to surrender her "independency for government" in religious and political as well as in economic affairs. Her reluctance stumped the commissioners, who returned home in 1665 with a very negative report.

Following the Navigation Act of 1673, the Lords of Trade made a new effort to bring the Puritans to book. Their instrument this time was Edward Randolph, who arrived on his first visit in 1676 and thereafter, for a generation, proved so tireless in searching out infractions that he rose to be "surveyor-general" of His Majesty's customs in all of British America. Hateful to the Puritan merchants, Randolph made Massachusetts so hateful to the Crown that Charles II annulled her charter in 1684. The next year, on succeeding Charles, James II began to consolidate all the northern colonies into one administrative unit, called the "Territory and Dominion of New England." This "Dominion" included all the New England colonies, together with New York and East and West New Jersey—an unwieldy realm administered from Boston by the dictatorial Sir Edmund Andros, James's governor.

Andros abolished the colonial assemblies and even tried to force the colonists to worship in the Anglican Church. No one could have reconciled Massachusetts to these steps, but Andros made matters even worse by the insolence with which he offended Yankee sentiments. Everyone felt threatened by his policies, especially by his attempt to undermine the validity of the Massachusetts land titles. In 1687 Massachusetts sent her leading minister, Increase Mather, to England to try to retrieve the charter and effect Andros's recall. Mather failed to do either while James held the throne. After the "Glorious Revolution" of 1688, Massachusetts at least regained its identity as a distinct colony.

## THE GLORIOUS REVOLUTION IN ENGLAND AND AMERICA

Edward Randolph and Sir Edmund Andros were not the only members of the Stuart "civil list" to incite the Americans. Both Charles II and James II filled colonial offices with indigent court favorites to help them make or recoup their fortunes at the Americans' expense. Others sent over were royal zealots, inquisitors who boldly overrode not only colonial liberties but also those of English merchants engaged in the colonial trade. Before long, such merchants so tired of James's administrators and of the King himself that they joined with others in forcing James to abandon the throne and flee to France in 1688. Most of these others had been aroused by James's militant Catholicism. On taking the throne in 1685, James was forced to put

down a Puritan revolt under the Duke of Monmouth, after which he suppressed dissenters with such zeal that Anglicans too took fright. By placing many Catholics in positions of power, James also flouted the Test Act of 1673, which prohibited all but Anglicans from holding public office in England. Such measures shook even royalist Tories who believed in the doctrine of the divine right of kings. When James fathered a son in June 1688, the dire menace of a new Catholic succession chilled the English soul, and Tories and Whigs together drove James out.

A parlimentary committee itself now boldly invited William of Orange, the Dutch Protestant husband of James's daughter Mary, to England. After some months devoted, as one historian has put it, to "decently covering up the unpleasant rents in the fabric of the constitution," the reign of William and Mary, or of William III, began in February 1689. At that time, Parliament also adopted the "Bill of Rights," opening with an array of accusations against James II foreshadowing those arrayed against George III by the Americans in July 1776. The famous "Bill" then proceeded to set forth the rights of Englishmen under the law. No Catholic could henceforth occupy the throne. Dissenters might worship openly as they pleased, but public office remained closed to them and to others not subscribing to the communion of the Church of England.

Such was the peaceful "Glorious Revolution," which, at least for English constitutional theory during the life of the new rulers, seemed to give the elected representatives of the "people" superiority over their "elected" king. As elaborated by John Locke (see p. 139), this theory became one of the pillars of the colonists' own argument later, that since they did not participate in the election of parliamentary representatives in England, their allegiance must be only to their own local "parliaments" and the king *these* parliaments chose to recognize.

On learning of James's abdication, the Puritans of Massachusetts, even before news of the Glorious Revolution reached America, conducted a bloodless revolution of their own. In April 1689, an armed band of Boston citizens led by young Cotton Mather, son of Increase, marched against Andros, forced him to seek refuge in a fort, and aroused the public to such a high pitch of feeling against him that he capitulated and went to jail. An ad hoc "council" of the general court ruled Massachusetts until the Commonwealth was brought under a new royal charter in 1691. This charter reflected the failure of Increase Mather's mission. No longer would Massachusetts elect its own governor. Henceforth, he would be appointed by the Crown. His council would be elected by the general court, subject to the governor's veto. General court legislation itself was to be subject to review in England. The new charter also ended Plymouth's independent existence. Along with Maine it was incorporated in Massachusetts Bay. Andros's downfall in Massachusetts had prompted Connecticut and Rhode Island to resume their old regimes, which they were now permitted to continue.

In New York, meanwhile, Andros's deputy, Francis Nicholson, resigned on learning of his superior's plight. In May 1689, Jacob Leisler, a German trader in Manhattan since its Dutch days, took advantage of Nicholson's absence to call upon neighboring counties and towns to set up a representative government for the first time. Backed by dissident elements who were alarmed by rumors of a French invasion and a Catholic conspiracy, Leisler managed civil affairs vigorously and efficiently for several months. But by disregarding a message he had intercepted from the Crown ordering Nicholson to conduct colonial affairs until new authorities took over, he gave support to the charges of his enemies that he was a revolutionist and a usurper. When in March 1691 Leisler resisted the deputy sent by William III, he was captured and soon tried and sentenced to death along with seven of his men. Leisler and his son-in-law, his closest follower, were hanged in May. The others were pardoned by the Crown, which pro-

ceeded to establish royal and representative government in New York.

### THE ENGLISH SYSTEM AFTER 1696

William III brought with him to England his traditional continental rivalry with the Catholic French, which was only intensified by Louis XIV's hospitality to the ousted James II. As early as 1689, this rivalry flared up in the War of the League of Augsburg, the opening conflict in the world wars of the eighteenth century over the domination of North America as well as other regions (see Chapter Five). To bolster his position at home, William III undertook to strengthen the Anglican establishment. To bolster his position in the New World he enlarged, as we have seen, the number of royal colonies and in other ways strengthened the position of the royal governors. Starting in 1696, he also revamped the administration and extended the reach of the navigation system.

As the Crown's chief representative in the colonies, the royal governor came to possess broad powers. He could summon and dissolve assemblies, veto their legislation, appoint minor officials. The upper house, or council, served as his advisory board, with executive, legislative, and judicial functions. Except in Massachusetts, this house was chosen from among leading colonials by the Board of Trade in England. But since the governor's recommendations influenced the Board in its choice of council members, his friendship counted for much among wealthy and capable colonials who sought his favors. With all his dignity and authority, however, the governor found himself caught between colonial and royal crossfire. As the symbol and spokesman of the Crown, he was expected to follow instructions from England that reflected the rigid policies of British officialdom, the interests of British merchants, and decisions of the Board of Trade which were made thousands of miles away from the scene of their application. Yet at the same time he had to respect the needs of the colony and keep from offending its leaders, among whom he had to live. The job called for remarkable tact, a genius for knowing when to compromise and when to stand firm, but even the best of governors gradually lost their primacy to the colonial assemblies (see p. 116).

The changes in the navigation system after 1696 did little to improve the governors' prospects of good relations with the Americans. In May, that year, the Stuarts' old administrative agency, the Lords of Trade (see p. 76), was supplanted by the Lords Commissioners of Trade and Plantations, commonly known as the Board of Trade. With the Privy council, it administered colonial relations until the Revolution. New parliamentary navigation acts then strengthened the board's hand.

Under the new legislation, new customs offices were to be set up in each colony, with customs officials given the same powers as those in England, including access to "writs of assistance" by which they could invoke constabulary aid in forcing their way into suspect private premises. Offenders against the new navigation code were henceforth to be tried in new admiralty courts. Manned by royal, not provincial, judges, these courts could try colonial merchants without juries. The admiralty courts became one of the most detested of all English institutions. The navigation code itself also was strengthened by the "enumeration" of more commodities which had to be shipped exclusively to England. Parliament also began to ban the exportation to England of colonial wheat, flour, and fish which competed with England's own. Starting with the Wool Act of 1699, moreover, colonial craftsmen were forbidden to export and later even to make many manufactured goods in which English merchants were thus given a monopoly.

And yet the colonies prospered. The modern reader may easily imagine that English regulation of American affairs was more burdensome to the colonies than it actually was. Smuggling and other modes of evasion went largely unpunished. American as well as English merchants, moreover, benefited from the exclusion of the Dutch and others from the imperial trade and from protection against enemies on the sea. To draw up a balance sheet of the gains and losses of American membership in the Empire would be difficult. What seems certain, however, is that the apparatus of colonial regulation and control schooled the Americans first in the arts of evasion and then in the defiance of authority. Although on principle they accepted most of the regulations of the old colonial system, in practice they were extremely uneasy about conforming with the demands of any external authority. These demands grew harsher as Britain's costly wars with the French approached their showdown phase, and the friction engendered by mounting British pressure on the colonies went far to rekindle the spirit of independence that had been so marked in the early settlements.

# READINGS

The books by A.L. Rowse cited at the end of the Readings for Chapter One afford a stirring introduction to the English background of American settlement. S.T. Bindoff, *Tudor England* (1950), and G.M. Trevelyan, *England under the Stuarts* (1904), are scholarly general accounts, updated but not outdated by Roger Lockyer, *Tudor and Stuart Britain 1471–1714* (1964), and H.R. Trevor-Roper, *The Crisis of the Seventeenth-Century* (1968). J.E. Neale, *Queen Elizabeth* (1934), probably is the best biography. Neale,

*Elizabeth I and Her Parliaments* (2 vols., 1958), is excellent on legislative development. C.D. Bowen, *The Lion and the Throne, The Life and Times of Sir Edward Coke 1552–1634* (1957), helps carry this story through early Stuart years.

C.H. and Katherine George, *The Protestant Mind of the English Reformation 1570–1640* (1961), and William Haller, *The Rise of Puritanism* (1938), are good introductions to the religious controversy. M. St. Clare Byrne, *Elizabethan Life in Town and Country* (rev. ed., 1961), is illuminating on social conditions. A.V. Judges, ed., *The Elizabethan Underworld* (1930), is a scholarly anthology of Tudor and early Stuart tracts and ballads. Wallace Notestein, *The English People on the Eve of Colonization* (1954), affords a useful summary but must be supplemented, especially for the history of the common people, by Carl Bridenbaugh, *Vexed and Troubled Englishmen 1590–1642* (1968), and for the elite by Lawrence Stone, *The Crisis of the Aristocracy 1558–1641* (1965).

The first three volumes of C.M. Andrews, *The Colonial Period of American History* (4 vols., 1934–1938), offer the most satisfactory extended account of American settlement. The fourth volume is excellent on Britain's commercial and colonial policy. The standard single-volume account of the colonial period is C.P. Nettels, *The Roots of American Civilization* (1938). Three books by T.J. Wertenbaker cover the social history of the early colonial period under the general title, *The Founding of American Civilization*. These are *The Old South* (1942); *The Middle Colonies* (1938); and *The Puritan Oligarchy* (1947).

W.F. Craven, *The Southern Colonies in the Seventeenth Century 1607–1689* (1949), is outstanding on Virginia and her neighbors. P.L. Barbour, *The Three Worlds of Captain John Smith* (1964), is the best biography. G.F. Willison, *Behold Virginia* (1952), is an informal but scholarly narrative. See also the essays by Mildred Campbell and Bernard Bailyn in the exceptional collection, J.M. Smith, ed., *Seventeenth Century America, Essays on Colonial History* (1959). L.B. Wright's modern edition (1947) of Robert Beverley, *The History and Present State of Virginia* (first published in 1705), affords an invaluable early account, especially of Indian relations. W.E. Washburn, *The Governor and the Rebel: A History of Bacon's Rebellion in Virginia* (1957), stresses the importance of these relations. A.E. Smith, *Colonists in Bondage: White Servitude and Convict Labor in America 1607–1776* (1947), is the standard study. V.W. Crane, *The Southern Frontier 1670–1732* (1929), is excellent on early Carolina history, for which see also Readings for Chapter Three.

William Bradford, *Of Plymouth Plantation 1620–1647* (in the S.E. Morison edition, 1952), is the best work on its subject. George Langdon, *Pilgrim Colony: A History of New Plymouth 1620–1691* (1966), is the outstanding modern account. Of Perry Miller's many indispensable works on Massachusetts Bay and its satellites, the following may be noted: *The New England Mind: The Seventeenth Century* (1939); *The New England Mind: From Colony to Province* (1953); and *Orthodoxy in Massachusetts 1630–1650* (1933). Perry Miller and T.H. Johnson, eds., *The Puritans* (1938), is an excellent anthology of Puritan writings, as is E.S. Morgan, ed., *Puritan Political Ideas* (1965). J.T. Adams, *The Founding of New England* (1921), is strongly anti-Puritan. Its biases may be corrected in S.E. Morison, *Builders of the Bay Colony* (1930). E.S. Morgan, *The Puritan Dilemma: The Story of John Winthrop* (1958), is a somewhat disenchanted biography. See also D.B. Rutman, *Winthrop's Boston: A Portrait of a Puritan Town 1630–1649* (1965). O.E. Winslow, *Master Roger Williams* (1957), and Emery Battis, *Saints and Sectaries* (1962), on Anne Hutchinson, are good on the religious malcontents.

A.T. Vaughan, *New England Frontier, Puritans and Indians 1620–1675* (1965), is a well-written study of Puritan attitudes and actions. G.L. Haskins, *Law and Authority in Early Massachusetts* (1960), affords an excellent introduction to the American legal tradition. Bernard Bailyn, *The New England Merchants in the Seventeenth Century* (1955), is a useful supplement to the still valuable older study by W.B. Weeden, *Economic and Social History of New England 1620–1789* (2 vols., 1890). Richard Pares, *Yankees and Creoles, the Trade between North America and the West Indies before the American Revolution* (1956), is illuminating for this period and later ones. Land policy in early New England and elsewhere in the English colonies is analyzed authoritatively in Marshall Harris, *Origin of the Land Tenure System in the United States* (1953). S.C. Powell, *Puritan Village, The Formation of a New England Town* (1963), is full of insight and evidence.

Two special studies help broaden the picture of early New York: J.R. Reich, *Leisler's Rebellion, A Study of Democracy in New York 1664–1720* (1953), and A.W. Trelease, *Indian Affairs in Colonial New York, the Seventeenth Century* (1960). E.D. Bronner, *William Penn's "Holy Experiment," the Founding of Pennsylvania 1681–1701* (1962), is a sound, straightforward account. F. B. Tolles, *Meeting House and Counting House, The Quaker Merchants of Colonial Philadelphia 1682–1763* (1948), is outstanding on God and Mammon in Pennsylvania. C.O. Peare, *William Penn* (1957), is a useful biography. F.B. Tolles and E.G. Alderfer, eds., *The Witness of William Penn* (1957), is an anthology of Penn's writings. J.E. Pomfret, *The Province of West New Jersey* (1956) and *The Province of East New Jersey* (1962), unravel early Jersey history.

On British colonial regulation, in addition to C.M. Andrews, cited at the head of these Readings, the standard older works are those by G.L. Beer, *The Origins of the British Colonial System 1578–1660* (1908) and *The Old Colonial System* (2 vols., 1912). L.H. Gipson, *The British Empire before the American Revolution* (13 vols., 1936–1967), is a monumental modern account. Special studies of importance include L.A. Harper, *The English Navigation Laws, A Seventeenth Century Experiment in Social Engineering* (1939), and M.G. Hall, *Edward Randolph and the American Colonies 1676–1703* (1960), a valuable study of the most presistent British inquisitor. M.G. Hall, L.H. Leder, and M.G. Kammen, *The Glorious Revolution in America, Documents on the Colonial Crisis of 1689* (1964), is an illuminating anthology.

# THREE

In 1614 Captain John Smith had written of North America:

As for the goodness and fine substance of the land, we are for the most part yet altogether ignorant of them, but only here and there where we have touched or seen a little, the edges of these large dominions which do stretch themselves into the main, God doth know how many thousand miles.

By the time Georgia was settled in 1733 as the last of the mainland colonies originating overseas (see p. 70), the English and their rivals had gained a better if still imperfect grasp of America's dimensions and a deeper yet still incomplete understanding of how to live within them.

The earliest English settlers had approached the shores of the New World pitifully ill-equipped for its rigors. We have spoken of the agonies of Jamestown and of the "humorous ignorances" of the Pilgrims of Plymouth, to quote John Smith once more, which "caused them for more than a year to endure a wonderful deal of misery with infinite patience . . . thinking to find things better than I advised them." During the next century and a half, strengthened toward the end of this period by a pouring in of strangers from other lands of the British Isles, the European continent, Africa, and the West Indies, the English clinched their hold on 1200 miles of Atlantic seaboard. For all its turbulence and dangers, the Atlantic formed a bridge to the culture and commodities of the Old World. It also provided a path of communication among the settlements of the New World from Labrador to the Caribbean islands and the Spanish Main. In the eigh-

# COLONIAL

# AMERICANS

teenth century, the English seaboard merchants became the principal organizers of this New World unity, with even New France and the Caribbean islands dependent for their very food and materials for shelter, as well as for their trade, largely upon Yankee, Yorker, and Quaker coasting vessels, irregular though their sailings were.

Well to the west of this first range of established English settlements, the rivers then known to most colonials began their course to the sea. Beyond the "fall line" of these rivers, where cataracts 200 feet high dramatically signalled a halt to upstream navigation, the Susquehanna Valley in Pennsylvania and the "Great (Shenandoah) Valley" of Virginia tied the "back parts" of the English colonies together (see map, p. 85). In the eighteenth century, along with English frontiersmen and functionaries, thousands of the non-English immigrants settled in these valleys each year, gradually penetrating farther south and southwest. By the 1750s, issues of Indian relations and runaway slaves and servants, as well as of church administration, participation in politics, law enforcement, and commercial growth all dictated the need for easier intercourse between this hinterland and the tidewater plantations and cities and har-

bors of the seaboard. Forward-looking seaboard leaders like the Washingtons and Jeffersons of Virginia, the Norrises, Morrises, and Franklins of Pennsylvania, had begun to press for east-west roads and bridges to link up the natural north-south routes.

In North America, then, east of the Appalachian mountains, a new land had arisen among the settled regions of the earth, one clearly marked off by natural boundaries and occupied by a new people, a million and a half strong, with regional differences in "constitutions and complexions, air and government," as one observer put it, yet most of them sharing a common official language, a common legal tradition, a common Protestant heritage. To these new "Americans" of the eighteenth century, the country beyond the Appalachians still loomed as a trackless wilderness so densely wooded that the sun seldom penetrated the foliage beneath whose cover lurked wild brave and beast and terrifying creatures of the mind. When the war for this North American wilderness finally was fought out between Britain and France (see Chapter Five), the British mainland settlement, constituting a new nation despite their differences, were to play an American rather than a British role.

84

## 1 *The New American Population*

### EXTRAORDINARY GROWTH AND SPREAD

Britain's ultimate success against France in North America sprang largely from the astonishing growth of her mainland colonies, the vigor of whose people already gave European rulers cause for wonder and alarm. After 1700, the population of these colonies almost doubled every 25 years. In round numbers, the 200,000 settlers in 1688 had grown to about 1,600,000 in 1760. At that time there were but 65,000 Europeans in New France.

The most heavily populated mainland colonies lay in the South, which in 1760 num-

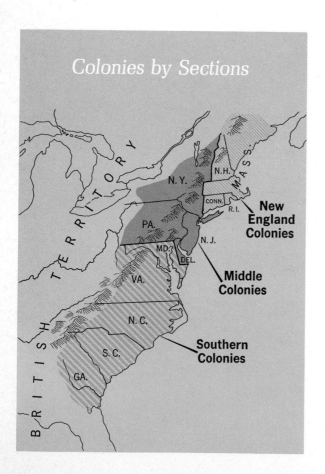

Colonies by Sections

bered some 700,000 inhabitants. Of these no less than 300,000 were Negroes, all but a few of them slaves. Approximately 500,000 people, 12,700 of them black, lived in New England at this time, and some 400,000, almost 30,000 of them Negroes, in the Middle colonies, which were growing most rapidly. In all but the lower New England commonwealths, Indians, although unenumerated, continued to make their presence felt.

Among the white colonials an extraordinarily high birth rate accounted in large part for the remarkable rise in population—it has been estimated that the average colonial family increased by one child every two years. The large immigration from the British Isles and elsewhere helped swell the total. Less is known of the birth rate among the blacks, boasts of their fertility as evidence of good care distorting the sketchy figures; but their death rate was enormous, those who survived the terrors of the ocean passage to America often succumbing to grief as well as to disease, violence, malnutrition, and overwork.

During most of the seventeenth century, the English mainland settlers had remained hostile to newcomers of other nationalities. Even Protestant Welsh, Scots, and Irish, near neighbors of the English in the Old World, received the coolest of welcomes, sometimes indeed because they were too well known. Yet these peoples, and Swedes, Finns, Germans and Walloons, French Huguenots and Spanish and Portuguese Jews, with a sprinkling of more exotic races, black as well as white, together with the Dutch on land once their own, all lived among the English in America. In the eighteenth century, the overpowering need for workers and fighters in the rapidly growing settlements induced the English colonials to alter their policies if not their attitudes. At the same time, social conditions in northern Ireland and western Germany conspired to create a large pool of discontented persons willing if not eager to migrate overseas, many of them inured like the Israelites of old to uprooting their families for religious and other reasons. The "Scotch-

Irish," as those from the province of Ulster in northern Ireland came to be called, and the "Palatines," the name Americans carelessly bestowed upon most Germans, even those from principalities other than the Palatinate, made up by far the largest contingents of white eighteenth-century newcomers. The most numerous group of all in this century were the black Africans who, carried here involuntarily, were not classed as immigrants, though the thousands of whites also transported to America involuntarily were so counted.

In the early years of the eighteenth century, especially on the southern frontier, slaves and free Negroes sometimes were enlisted in the militia along with whites to fight the Indians

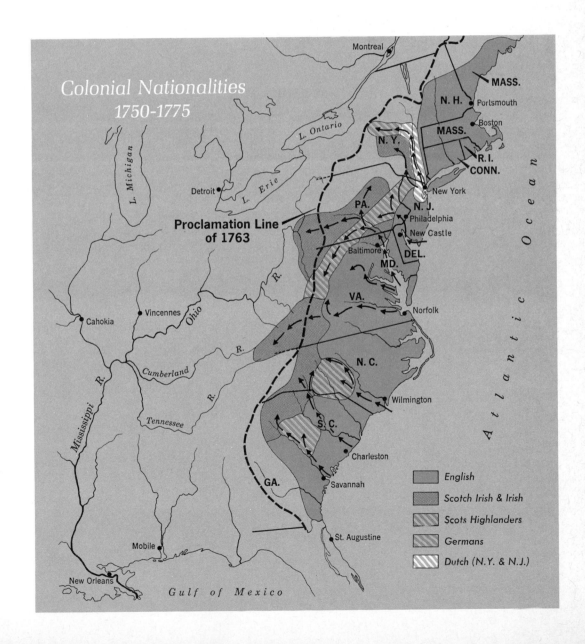

Colonial Nationalities
1750-1775

Proclamation Line
of 1763

English

Scotch Irish & Irish

Scots Highlanders

Germans

Dutch (N.Y. & N.J.)

and the Spanish; but as the number of slave workers grew, their restiveness and rebelliousness persuaded their masters no longer to arm them. Indeed, in most southern colonies, however exigent the planters became for slave labor, their "great fear and terror" of slave revolts soon induced them to place heavy provincial duties on Negroes to discourage their further importation. The proceeds of such duties, in turn, helped defray the cost of bounties and land grants, and of agents overseas, used to lure white foreigners to America to offset the growing disproportion of blacks and to police and suppress them as well as to fight the Spaniard and the brave.

In northern and southern, older and newer colonies alike, the dominant English also compelled white immigrants who came in more conventional ways to serve as "frontier guards." Boston's leaders, for example, gave a most inhospitable reception to the advance body of Scots from Ulster who landed in 1718. "These confounded [Scotch-]Irish," complained the surveyor-general of customs, "will eat us all up, provisions being most extravagantly dear, and scarce of all sorts." They and others who soon followed were directed 50 miles west to Worcester, where recent English attempts at settlement on the rich land had been frustrated by Indian resistance.

In Pennsylvania, besides the lure of the land, writes F.R. Diffenderffer in his account of the German migration to that colony,

the traditional policy of the Proprietary Government also pushed [the newcomers] to the frontiers—the places of danger. . . . It is the boast of the historian that so mild and generous was the dealing of the Quaker with the aborigines that "not a drop of Quaker blood was ever shed by an Indian." Shall I tell you why? It was because the belt of Quaker settlement was enclosed in a circumference described by a radius of fifty miles from Penn's city on the Delaware. Beyond that point came the sturdy Germans . . . whose settlements effectually prevented the savages from spilling Quaker blood. Instead, the tomahawk and scalping knife found sheath in the bodies of the . . . children of the Palatinate.

Among those Scotch-Irish, in turn, who had moved from Pennsylvania by the 1750s to help subdue the Great Valley of Virginia, Indian warfare, it is said, took such a toll of heads of families that the apprenticeship of orphans became one of the most acute social problems.

Benjamin Franklin detested the Pennsylvania Germans as heartily as any colonial worthy. He held them to be "the most stupid of their own nation," and was especially concerned about their unwillingness to abandon their native tongue. "I am not without apprehensions," he wrote to a friend in England in 1753, "that through their indiscretion or ours, or both, great disorders may one day arise among us. . . . Unless the stream of importation could be turned from this to other colonies, . . . they will soon outnumber us," and we will "be not able to preserve our language, and even our government will become precarious." In Virginia somewhat later, Charles Lee deplored the "Mac-ocracy" reigning there, "a banditti of low Scotch-Irish whose names usually begin with Mac—and who are either the sons of imported servants, or themselves imported servants," and now "Lords Paramount."

One of the persistent complaints against the newcomers, as James Logan, the secretary and advisor of Penn's heirs, stated it as early as 1725, was that they "resolutely set down [on the proprietors' land] and improved it without any right to it. . . . They say the Proprietor invited People to come & settle his Countrey, that they are come for that end, & must live." "In doing this by force," he added a few years later, "they alleged that it was against the laws of God and nature, that so much land should be idle, while so many Christians wanted it to labor on, and to raise their bread." As the pressure of newcomers on the land increased, the older leaders accused them more sharply of stirring up rather than restraining the Indians. Despite the insatiable appetite even among successful newcomers themselves for servants or for slaves to help work the land, mid-century provincial legislatures tried as hard to diminish the flow of troublesome whites as southern legislatures had tried earlier to curtail that of troublesome blacks, but to as little effect.

A powerful influence in swelling the tide of both blacks and whites were the merchants and shipowners, English, Irish, Dutch, and colonial in particular, whose concern for their immortal souls scarcely tempered their determination to pack their vessels with human cargoes beyond the tolerance of sanity and life itself. Much is rightly made of the violence and warfare by which Africans were rounded up, chained together, and driven aboard noxious vessels in the slave trade. The role of "spirits," "crimps," "soul-sellers," and "new-landers" in kidnaping or cozening poor and ignorant Europeans in order to sell their labor in America is not as fully known nor is the number of their victims. Yet this trade became as systematic as the slave trade, the capture, voyage, sale, and "seasoning" of its white victims sometimes differing little from that of the blacks.

According to A. E. Smith, in his authoritative study of *Colonists in Bondage,* most contemporary observers agreed that the "new-landers" who returned to their native lands sporting gold watch chains and other finery presumably earned in America, and spouting fine words about the quick fortunes to be made there in order to dupe the poor, "were the principal influences stimulating the large annual movement from Germany and Switzerland to the colonies." In these countries as in Ireland, "such agents were paid by ship captains, merchants, or proprietors, generally at a fixed rate per head for all recruits whom they produced ready for transportation. Their activities," Smith concludes, "were at the root of all emigration during colonial times except in those periods when a true 'fever' was running its course."

And yet, Smith writes, "the 'spirits' were not only man-stealers but were also the hope and refuge of all persons who wished to fly the country for any reason whatever." Others acknowledged that the indenture system, in

the eighteenth as in the seventeenth century (see p. 55), afforded many of the poor abroad the same opportunity that the rich could afford unaided for a new life in the New World. It would be a mistake to underestimate the sacrifice and heartbreak of this life, or to excuse the brutality of the experience simply as a reflection of the spirit of the age or the custom of the times. Emigration, even if voluntary, said an eighteenth-century witness, "is never produced . . . without great pangs and struggles." Another, early in the nineteenth century, observed that "emigration is a form of suicide because it separates a person from all that life gives except the material wants of simple animal existence." Many leaders in Germany and Ireland and elsewhere in the eighteenth century who knew immigrant life in America at first hand denounced the "spirits" and "newlanders" and implored their ill-prepared countrymen to remain at home. At the same time, it would be a mistake to underestimate the genuineness of the opportunity for those persuaded and even abducted to risk the adventure and who survived it. Even among Negroes in thralldom, many withstood debasement and devoted themselves to ameliorating the terror and trials of their fellow blacks. Others gained the full confidence and respect of their masters to whom they chose to remain loyal all their lives. And still others obtained their freedom and improved it with their plantation training, becoming landholders and even slaveholders themselves.

## THE GERMAN SECTARIANS

Although the older ports of Boston, New York, Baltimore, and Charleston received sizable numbers of white immigrants in the eighteenth century, William Penn's Philadelphia, "a community of God in the spirit," became the haven or at least the destination of most of the European newcomers after its dedication in 1682. Penn appeared to have provided in the New World a final resting place before the world's end for his fellow

88

pietists and mystics. But more than that, the rich Pennsylvania land attracted the worldly as well as the unworldly and converted many of the radical followers of the "inner light" from their otherworldly preoccupations.

After the Reformation, the politically established Protestant churches (see p. 23) grew more intolerant of otherworldly Christians than the Catholic church itself, and pietists and mystics, chafing under their constraints, multiplied most rapidly where such churches were most numerous—in the independent Protestant principalities of Germany and the neighboring German-speaking cantons of Switzerland. Here, persecution by petty political tyrants often accompanied that by the church dominies, driving the radical believers to huddle the more closely in their spiritual enclaves, their *ecclesiolae in ecclesia* ("little churches within Christianity") until forced like Jews to seek consolation together in repeated exoduses.

The first German pietist exodus to Pennsylvania was a small one. In April 1683 a group of well-to-do Friends in Frankfurt-on-Main in Hesse organized the Frankfurt Company to purchase land from William Penn as a refuge for their co-religionists. They appointed as their agent the learned lawyer, Francis Daniel Pastorius, who completed negotiations with Penn in Philadelphia in August and in October welcomed the initial 13 German Quaker families to the village of Germantown, which he had by then laid out adjacent to Penn's capital. For 36 years until his death in 1720, Pastorius reigned as Germantown's chief citizen. He is perhaps best remembered for having led the first organized religious protest in the English mainland colonies against the practice of keeping slaves, at least by Quakers. This protest, drawn up and signed by Pastorius and other members of the Germantown Monthly Meeting in 1688, said:

There is a liberty of conscience here which is right and reasonable, and there ought to be likewise liberty of the body, except for evil-doers, which is another case. But to bring men hither, or to rob and sell them against their will, we stand against.

The Germantown Quakers sent this declaration to the Irish Quaker Meeting that by then had been established in Pennsylvania at Lower Dublin, and they forwarded it to others who unceremoniously administered its last rites. Yet as slavery became more profoundly institutionalized in the colonies, Quakers stood in the forefront of the opposition to it.

Pastorius, although a leader of the Quaker Meeting in Germantown, never lost his attraction to adult baptism and other tenets of the sixteenth-century Catholic priest Menno Simons, whose Anabaptist followers in Switzerland and Germany later took the name Mennonites. They were admitted to Germantown by the Quakers almost from the start, and proceeded to live apart from the other settlers until doctrinal conflicts among themselves fragmented their spiritual unity. Some Mennonites left Germantown in 1702 to establish a new community at Skippack Creek 30 miles away. Others migrated some 50 miles west to the frontier settlement in future Lancaster county in the Susquehanna Valley where, in 1709, German-speaking lowland Swiss refugees from Bern had planted the most enduring Mennonite community. What helped Lancaster and neighboring counties retain even to this day some of their early character was the arrival in the region about 1727 of the first of the Amish Mennonites, upland Germanic Swiss followers of Jacob Ammon, who took even more literally than the others the New Testament injunction (Romans, xii, 2), "be not conformed to this world." They proved worldly enough, nevertheless, to become recognized as among the best farmers in Pennsylvania by obeying the Old Testament injunction to till the earth with reverence for the soil.

In 1719 the Germantown Mennonites were further distressed by the coming of their Anabaptist rivals, the Dunkers of the Church of the Brethren, who, under leaders like those of other sects, "wise in their own conceit," soon split into discordant groups. One of these, on becoming a celibate monastic order, moved to Lancaster county in 1728. Here, at Ephrata, they built their cloister, a self-sustaining community famous for its music and printing press, where all property was held in common.

Still another sect found its way to the Susquehanna Valley in this period, the Moravians of the United Brethren. Presumably descendants of Germans who had fled south to Moravia in eastern Bohemia in the fifteenth century, they were forced to seek asylum in Saxony once more for their conscientious objection to military service following the outbreak of the Thirty Years' War in 1618. Among the last of the sects to migrate to America, the Moravians first landed in Savannah, Georgia, in 1736 where they joined the Lutheran colony of Salzburgers in the village of Ebenezer. But when asked there to take up arms against the Spanish, they made their exodus to Pennsylvania. Here, in 1741, in "a barren wooded region" in the Lehigh valley on Philadelphia's northern frontier, they built their first community and called it Bethlehem. A second settlement followed a few years later, farther north at Nazareth.

As their name, United Brethren, suggests, the Moravians sought to bring unity to German Protestantism, and for this purpose their patron and leader, Count Zinzendorf, called a grand conference in Germantown in 1742. Henry Antes, a recent convert from Lutheranism to the United Brethren and known as "king of the Germans" for his own determined campaign to unify German-Americans, presided at this "Congregation of God in the Spirit"; but even he failed to soften the sectarians' spirit of independence, and the unity movement came to nothing. The Moravians also were devoted missionaries and soon embarked on their strikingly successful efforts to Christianize rather than kill off the Indians. Education, especially for girls neglected by ordinary schools, was another of their objectives; and one of the best of their numerous ladies' seminaries, Linden Hall, still functions in their Lancaster county community of Lititz.

89

## THE GREAT GERMAN INFLUX

All of the German sects were profoundly anti-Erastian, that is, opposed to domination of the church by the state, a position that took its most radical form among others as well as the Moravians in the refusal of their members to bear arms. Their refusal to swear oaths also made them thorns in the flesh to British administrators of the navigation acts and to other political and judicial functionaries (see p. 75). Yet, along with the sects, intensely Erastian German Lutherans and German Reformed (the established church of those principalities that went Calvinist) were also permitted to settle in Germantown early in the eighteenth century. These denominations, since they were official state religions, numbered by far most of the Protestants in Germany, with Lutherans predominant among them; and they numbered by far most of the German-speaking immigrants to America. As members of the established denominations these immigrants are usually called "church people," but on the whole they were less devoted to their faith than the sectarians, and partly on that account succumbed more rapidly to the frontier's stripping them of the vestiges of belief and of other aspects of their Old World culture.

Widely quoted sectarian letters home from Philadelphia, Germantown, and other communities, praising Pennsylvania for easy availability of land and the high quality of the soil as much as for its liberties, exerted as strong a pull on the church people in Germany as on the pietists and mystics. But the push exerted by the world wars of the eighteenth century, beginning with King William's War in 1689 (see p. 158) and continuing right up to the onset of the American revolutionary movement itself, was even more instrumental in their migration. The Palatinate and the more southerly principalities on the Rhine, scarcely recovered from the Thirty Years' War which by 1648 had reduced their populations in some instances by an almost incredible 75 per cent, were repeatedly invaded and brutishly pillaged during the eighteenth-century wars by conquerors harsher even than their own petty tyrants. Their life thus made almost unendurable at home, thousands of German church people each year fled down the Rhine to Rotterdam in the Netherlands, itself a costly journey of many weeks. Here they took passage, increasingly vile, for Philadelphia and in much smaller numbers for such other ports as Baltimore and Charleston.

The pressure of these newcomers in the Pennsylvania capital reached such an alarming level by 1727 that careful records of arrivals began to be kept, and two years later a tax of 40 shillings per head was levied to discourage the traffic, a forerunner of similar taxes in later years here and in other colonies. By 1727 probably 20,000 Germans lived in Pennsylvania, a few thousand more in neighboring New York, New Jersey, and Maryland, with others scattered southward. During the next half century, despite the restrictive measures, the number of Germans in Pennsylvania multiplied about six times, mainly by immigration but also by reproduction, and on the eve of the Revolution they made up no less than a third of the colony's white population. With the Germans in other colonies, they constituted nearly 10 per cent of the white population of English mainland America.

While the sectarians had come to Pennsylvania almost uniformly in groups under specific leadership, most of the church people set out initially as distinct families and eventually as unattached indviduals, mainly youthful males. Those who had money often spent all their savings on the journey or were robbed of them in European and American ports. "The Palatines pretend they would pay," the Penns' secretary, Logan, complained as early as 1727, "but not one in twenty has anything to pay with." As has been said (p. 86), characteristically they simply claimed and cleared the proprietors' land and defended their hard-earned homesteads at gun point.

The fact that the Penns' affairs were so disturbed in this period that the land office in the colony remained virtually inoperative from the time of William Penn's death in 1718 until 1732 made squatting easier. But it was no less distasteful on that account to the proprietors' representatives.

At least half, according to some estimates as many as two-thirds, of the church people set out from Germany with no money at all. To pay for their passage they would deliver themselves into the hands of the soul-brokers and other middlemen at home who bore the cost of the trip to Rotterdam or lesser ports. Here, the emigrant, at his middleman's direction, would sign an indenture or contract similar to that the English poor signed in the seventeenth century (see p. 55). Usually written in English he could not comprehend, this contract obliged the poor German to redeem his current debt, and the price of the impending ocean voyage in the bargain, by agreeing to work in America for a stipulated period for the purchaser of this contract when offered for sale by the "redemptioner's" ship captain or his agent. It was upon such poor people that the unscrupulous "newlanders" preyed in order to deliver a cargo to the carrier for as much as $7.00 a head. In the 1740s as many as 130 newlanders plied their trade in villages up and down the Rhine.

It is believed that on the average a third of the redemptioners, and a much higher proportion of their children, died at sea. On one ship arriving in Philadelphia in 1745, only 40 of 400 passengers had survived; on another in 1752, a mere 19 of 200 lived. Such a fatality rate forced shipowners to improve conditions if only to insure the financial success of the voyage; but on some Atlantic crossings, unnerving calms as well as storms delayed the overladen vessels for as much as six desperate months, while starvation and epidemic diseases ravaged the travelers. On landing, unwanted sick men sometimes were forced to sell off their wives, and mothers their surviving children, to meet their debt for the journey; others, to compensate for family members lost at sea, were obliged grossly to extend their own period of servitude.

The servant's normal obligation ran from five to seven years, during which he might, in effect, be bought and sold, his indenture being freely negotiable by his master. Laws forbidding the cudgeling of servants, or other mistreatment usually reserved for convicts and slaves, themselves offer evidence of the widespread harshness of servant life. At the expiration of his term the servant was to receive "freedom dues" according to "the custom of the country." In the seventeenth century this had meant 50 acres of land, tools, and clothing, and perhaps a bit of cash to get started on. During the eighteenth century, the land stipulation became converted into a cash equivalent, which when paid (the evidence suggests that masters often withheld these dues) was usually soon spent. On the other hand, many servants ran away before the end of their terms, and their color making it easier for them than for blacks, they more often went unapprehended. Sometimes they became squatters themselves, staking out farms in the woods.

Late in the 1720s the church people began to move through recently discovered "gaps" in the Appalachians to the Shenandoah Valley in Virginia and farther south to the Carolina Piedmont, some of them selling their Pennsylvania farms for a profit to break cheaper land on a new frontier (a reverse flow of Maryland, Virginia, and Carolina farmers from slavery north to freer Pennsylvania also developed at this time). Before the southward migration gained momentum, the church people of Pennsylvania had already inundated the sectarian communities of the Susquehanna and Lehigh valleys and the surrounding countryside. That they do so was Philadelphia policy: In 1729 John, Thomas, and Richard Penn, William's sons and heirs, wrote to Logan from London: "As to the Palatines [who] had Lately arrived in greater Quantities than may be consistent with the welfare of the Country, . . . THEY SHOULD BE OBLIG'D TO SETTLE, EITHER BACKWARDS TO SUSQUEHANNAH OR NORTH IN YE COUNTRY BEYOND THE OTHER SETTLEMENTS." Professional people, shopkeepers, artisans, and laborers among them, nevertheless, also swelled the population of Philadelphia and Germantown, to the discomfort of the Quaker oligarchy.

The most tenacious enemies of the sects at home, the church people by sheer numbers now completed the breakdown of their communal refuges in America. Even before the Palatine invasion reached its peak, the sects, including the original English Quakers whose experience in this respect resembled that of the Pilgrims and Puritans of Massachusetts, had found it increasingly difficult to hold young people to the beliefs of their fathers. The forces that in Europe had driven their members so desperately to cleave to one another and each group to its distinct, even precious, path to God and the hereafter, simply vanished in America, and the more rapidly since new forces, such as manifestly unlimited economic opportunity, exerted an almost irresistible centrifugal, and worldly, energy. In Pennsylvania in particular, with the Penns themselves providing an example of worldly grasping of the land, the rewards of farming and of commerce, manufacturing, the professions, and politics simply dissolved the communal religious spirit, which yielded the more swiftly for having grown more doctrinaire in self-defense. The new barbarians, or so they seemed even to their own clergymen belatedly arrived from Europe in the 1740s to reclaim them for church and civilization, thus fell upon much weakened citadels of the spirit and overcame them.

By mid-century, the town of Lancaster, first laid out in 1730, had become the largest inland city in the colonies, with the most unworldly Amish almost alone clinging to their nonconforming ways in the countryside. Germantown, a manufacturing as well as a trading center, had become cosmopolitan enough at the time of the Revolution to aspire to be named the new nation's capital. And Philadelphia, the true capital, grown so rapidly into

*Inside the Old Lutheran Church, York, Pennsylvania, late eighteenth century, by Lewis Miller. Details of everyday life among Pennsylvanians were recorded by Miller, a carpenter by trade and artist by avocation. (Historical Society of York County, York, Pennsylvania.)*

the largest of all colonial cities, had been transformed, in the words of its historian, S.B. Warner, Jr., from a liberal spiritual community, a "holy experiment," into "a community of private money makers."

The community ideal, overrun by the advance of colonial capitalism, enjoyed a revival in the next century in response to the cruelties of early industrialization (see Chapter Fourteen); but it proved no more successful then than before. At the same time, in the eighteenth as in the nineteenth century, it provided a useful heritage. While many of the German church people who stayed on in Pennsylvania strove, to the dismay of their leaders, to become more English than the English, others held tenaciously to their frontier homesteads and national traditions. As the open space filled up around them, the village if not the communal example of the sects re-

vived, and the love of the soil, so profound among the Godly, entered others as well. In a nation notorious for using up the land, the Pennsylvania Germans became celebrated throughout the country for their rich gardens and orchards, their stout barns and well-tended livestock, their sturdy self-sufficiency. Many skilled craftsmen, both German and Swiss, had settled in the Pennsylvania interior, where they introduced their techniques of knitting, weaving, shoemaking, and carving. German artisans developed the famous long rifle, first manufactured in Lancaster and later adopted and improved by frontiersmen everywhere. Equally important innovations were the iron stove and the Conestoga wagon, the stove a vast improvement over the heat-wasting open hearth of the English-style dwelling, the wagon a durable, efficient vehicle for carrying commodities and persons over the roughest of frontier roads.

On the spiritual side, the desiccation of the sects and the deprivation of the church people created a hunger for religious experience soon to be satisfied by the Great Awakening. An international movement with many ramifications, this religious revival was first preached by the topmost clergymen of the mid-eighteenth century, but it soon engaged the hearts of tens of thousands of the lowly (see Chapter Four). The German Protestant unity movement of Zinzendorf and Antes (p. 89), although a failure itself, helped prepare the stage for the Great Awakening in Pennsylvania. It also gave impetus to the tendency of Germans of all persuasions to rally to the support of one another in a single ethnic group in the increasingly kaleidoscopic American population.

### ULSTERMEN FROM NORTHERN IRELAND

Alarmingly numerous though they became, the German immigrants in the English colonies were exceeded in numbers by the so-called Scotch-Irish, who grew as disconcertingly visible to the English (and the Indians) only shortly after the great flow of "Palatines" began. The record of the Scotch-Irish in America is at once simpler and more profound than that of most other immigrant nationalities. It is simpler in that by and large they came (those who came voluntarily) for the single purpose of bettering themselves; more often than others, they arrived not even as families, but as individuals who eventually married and bore large numbers of children to improve their chances of success. Their record is more profound in that their readiness to penetrate ever deeper across the Indian frontier formed them and their descendants into the characteristic American type, the model of those who, with eye turned from the sea and the Old World, looked westward toward America's continental destiny. As with the Germans, the harsh wilderness life the first Scotch-Irish immigrants encountered here was not what they had been led to expect at home. At the same time, they had become inured to moving onward in their quest. "To them," writes R.J. Dickson, a leading student of the Scotch-Irish in Ireland, "the tie of their adopted country was weak and the tradition of emigration strong. . . . Their sojourn there appear[s] as but a resting place on the journey to the land of promise." In the New World, they were to persevere on this journey generation after generation.

Lowland Scotch Presbyterians, the forebears of the Scotch-Irish, began to cross the North Channel for Ulster at the urging of James I early in the seventeenth century. They were dispatched to strengthen Protestantism there, at least by numbers, after the Tudors' tragic failures (see p. 39). The men found for this mission naturally were those with least to lose at home. They were, James said himself, "maisterles men and vagabondis wanting a lawfull trade, calling and industrie." They were "set forward that way," declared another of their detractors, by "poverty, scandalous lives, or, at best, adventurous seeking after better accomodations."

However they began, the Scots in Ulster prospered sufficiently as farmers and manufacturers to draw thousands of their countrymen in their wake. Success, however, only made them chafe the more under the burdens of tenancy on the land and taxes levied to support the hostile Anglican establishment while Presbyterianism fell into disfavor. The Puritan Revolution in England relieved some of the Presbyterian discontents in Ireland, but not for long. The restoration of the Stuarts in 1660 brought both the "renewal of episcopal aggression" and new economic burdens, while stricter enforcement of newly discriminatory navigation acts here as in America after the Glorious Revolution of 1688, deepened economic distress (see p. 78). To protect English farmers and textile interests, for example, Parliament excluded Ulster meat and dairy products, woolens and linens from English and American markets. The final blow came when British absentee landlords, around 1717, demanded practically double the rents the Scotch-Irish had long been paying for the renewal of leases that expired that year and the next. This calamity struck simultaneously with certain natural visitations such as animal diseases and prolonged drought which drove up the cost of food beyond most people's means and by the mid-'twenties confronted them with famine.

Poverty in Ulster never reached the grim universality prevailing in the Catholic south of Ireland at this time, as later; but it did inspire the Scotch-Irish, heretofore leaving in hundreds, to begin to move from the north in thousands. No doubt many "mere Irish," that is Catholic Irish passers, stole out along with them, and their number surely would have been larger were they not explicitly excluded from America as "papists," even by colonies avidly seeking white immigrants to police the red men and the black.

One of the earliest sizable Scotch-Irish migrations to America took place in 1716 following the offer by South Carolina of grants of 300 to 400 acres, with payments deferred for four years, to newcomers who would immediately occupy the so-called Yamasee lands. The year 1716 saw the South Carolina militia break the back of Indian resistance in the frightfully costly Yamasee war and drive the Yamasee braves into Florida. Creeks, Cherokees, and other tribes, however, continued on

94

the warpath, and the proprietary government sought instant white reinforcements. About 500 Scotch-Irish grasped the land offer and soon occupied their grants, only to have the proprietors and their resident secretary retrieve title three years later and dispossess them without more ado.

After 1729, when Britain allowed Carolina rice to be sold direct to continental markets (see p. 102), the colony embarked on a long period of prosperity marred only by new pressure on Indian lands and rising restiveness among fresh slave recruits. From time to time, henceforth, South Carolina offered white immigrants outright land bounties in new frontier townships. Such offers drew many Ulster vessels once more to Charleston harbor laden with Scotch-Irish. For two decades before the Revolution the available statistics show Charleston third only to New York and Philadelphia as the principal destination of vessels leaving Ulster's five active ports for America.

Poverty in Ireland as in England helped fill the prisons as well as the ranks of the poor. In time of war, whatever happened to female offenders, males often were thrust into the army; but when poverty spread during periods of peace, as it did during some of the 25 years following the Peace of Utrecht, 1713 (see p. 159), new expedients were needed to relieve the jails besides the common penalties of "burning in the hand and whipping." The transportation of convicts had a long history in England, and it has been reliably estimated that during the eighteenth century somewhat more than 20,000 English felons were shipped to Maryland and Virginia to work in the tobacco fields. Most of them arrived after 1717 when Parliament greatly enlarged the list of crimes subject to the penalty of transportation while other London authorities disallowed colonial laws, old and new, denying criminals admittance however strong the demand for labor. A Treasury decision in 1716 to pay merchants liberally for carrying felons overseas, meanwhile, created a powerful special interest behind the perpetuation of the practice. The first shipload of English convicts under this ruling reached Maryland in 1718.

Transportation of convicts, or at least their banishment, had been practiced in Ireland for some time before being formally sanctioned there in 1703. In 1719 and in the 1720s the Irish Parliament enacted transportation laws based on the English law of 1717 and extended to Irish merchants the privilege of carrying the victims on terms as attractive as those in England. About 10,000 persons appear to have been shipped involuntarily from Ireland to the American mainland "plantations" in the eighteenth century, at least half of them felons, the rest vagabonds and derelicts. Estimates of the number of Scotch-Irish among them vary, but merchant records and other evidence, such as the frequent complaints of paying passengers on having to share ship facilities with such "wicked villains" after having been assured that none such would be loaded, indicate that convict-carrying became an active if unadvertised business.

Scotch-Irish paying passengers probably accounted for no more than one in ten of the free Ulster immigrants. The rest, like most of the Germans, obtained their passage by signing indentures before sailing similar in virtually all respects to those signed by the "Palatines" and disposable to the highest bidder by ship captains or their "assigns" in American ports of entry. Convicts also were disposed of in this manner by the merchant carriers, the principal difference in the terms of their servitude being their legal susceptibility to corporal "correction" for misbehavior.

No part of northeast Ireland is more than 40 miles from one of the five ports engaged in the American traffic, so that the Scotch-Irish were spared the Germans' usual harsh journey to Rotterdam before going to sea. Each of these ports had its own hinterland where the shipowner or his agent, like the newlanders of the Rhine Valley, advertised the advantages of America and of his own vessel to people who could not tell truth from fancy. Crimps and spirits abducting the young and homeless as they did in England and Germany to fill out a cargo appear to have been few in Ulster, the merchants there leaving it to misery and deception to supplement the frequently genuine urge to leave. There are few Scotch-Irish jeremiads to match the German descriptions of the horrors of the Atlantic crossing; yet at a time when the capacity of vessels was judged to be equal to their tonnage, it is known that Ulster merchants often grossly overstated tonnage in their advertisements, leading to severe overcrowding with the usual fatal consequences, especially when calms and storms unfortunately drew out a voyage.

While many of the paying passengers among the Scotch-Irish debarked in Charleston and the convicts in the Chesapeake colonies, most of the servants, and of others as well, landed in the Middle colonies. New York attracted the successors of those who fled their distressing experience in New England in 1718 (p. 86) to seek land in the Cherry and Mohawk valleys west of the large estates on the Hudson. Most of the Scotch-Irish landed in Philadelphia or in nearby Newcastle, Delaware. Quickly marked as "bold and indigent strangers" by the authorities, as they spread from the port to the country they incurred all the strictures the German church people endured for clearing land not their own and resisting the proprietors' quit-rent collectors with guns. Their situation was worsened by their having to face the wrath of the Germans already on the best land as well as that of the English whose land it was. Their "Irish" origins also raised the specter of a "papist" invasion among those who could not or would not distinguish Scots from Celts. The convict taint, moreover, marked even the most law-abiding, Logan, for example, exclaiming in 1729 of the great Ulster influx then fully underway in Pennsylvania, "few besides convicts are imported thither," although, in fact, such few as there may have been would be lost in the swarms of servants.

As newcomers continued to arrive by the thousands each year and indentures expired, the Scotch-Irish penetrated beyond the Germans on Philadelphia's northern frontier, becoming especially numerous in this region in the Delaware Valley. They also moved across the Susquehanna to the Cumberland Valley, where the town of Chambersburg was laid out in 1730. From here, the mountain passes led naturally southwestward to Maryland, western Virginia, and North Carolina, and two events in the 1730s speeded the Ulstermen's determination to take nature's course. One was the revitalization of the Pennsylvania proprietors' management of their domains. This led promptly to demands for higher prices for land and for higher annual quit-rents, archaic feudal survivals now growing intolerable. There was also the likelihood that stronger measures would be taken against squatters, especially such greedy ones as drove the Indians to the warpath in self-defense. The second event was the successful visit in 1738 of Philadelphia Presbyterian leaders to Virginia and North Carolina, where they obtained assurances of religious liberty for their followers from the governor in each province. Only after the main stream of the Scotch-Irish penetration had moved southwesterly all the way to the Carolinas, on the outer rim of the Germans who had earlier moved in the same direction, did the Ulstermen resume their push westward in Pennsylvania. This course took them first along the "west branch" of the Susquehanna, or the Juniata River, in the 1760s, from where they soon pressed across the Allegheny River beyond present-day Pittsburgh.

Many Ulstermen and their families died early on the frontiers from incessant toil with worn-out tools and implements, constant exposure to the harsh elements, unattended illness, epidemic disease, and violent engagements with white and red men alike. Fierce drinking and fierce brawling accompanied the fierce tasks they undertook, privation in the New World as in the Old honing both their appetites and their determination. Runaways and hence castaways were more numerous among them than among the Germans. Those who triumphed over every frontier trial clung the more tenaciously to the rewards and methods of their success, permitting no cessation in the defense and enlargement of their property. Others, having found constraint unbearable, sometimes refused to constrain their fellowmen.

In both characters the Scotch-Irish encountered familiar models among the English gentry with whom they quarreled over religion and politics as well as property. By the time of the revolutionary movement, such quarrels had added to the Ulstermen's ingrained hatred of Britain a misanthropic hostility toward Britain's more genteel enemies in the increasingly rebellious English colonies. After the Revolution, many Ulstermen mingled with the gentry as soldiers and speculators, but also as distinguished ministers, lawyers, orators, and political leaders. With no lingering loyalties to some Old Country abroad, they fell the more readily into the American grain.

### BLACKS AMONG WHITES

The severity of language in which the fortune of the average eighteenth-century white immigrant to America is described, reflecting the severity of his life, is outdone even in the most abstract and objective accounts of the fate of the black African. "It is difficult to write [of this subject] with restraint," said Frank Tannenbaum in *Slave and Citizen* (1947). In *Capitalism and Slavery* (1944), a "strictly economic study" of the connection of Negro slavery with the industrial revolution, Eric Williams speaks of this labor system as the "odious resource": "Negroes . . . were stolen in Africa to work the lands stolen from the Indians in America." Elizabeth Donnan, the compiler of four volumes of *Documents Illustrative of the History of the Slave Trade to America* (1930–1935), says of her subject that by the end of the eighteenth century the humanitarian revolt it inspired, "from feeble beginnings grew to power sufficient to convince the world that this traffic was not business but crime, and crime of so intolerable a nature that it must be outlawed by civilization."

More recently, W.D. Jordan, in *White Over Black* (1968), described the fully developed slave codes of the eighteenth century as the means employed by popularly elected legislatures to "coerce" the "slaveholding gentry . . . as individuals . . . toward maintenance of a private tyranny which was conceived to be in the community interest." Let a slave offer "violent resistance to the authority of white persons," he says, and "the reaction was likely to be swift and often vicious even by eighteenth-century standards." Jordan quotes another scholar who said of slaves apprehended in New York in 1708 for murders they may or may not have committed, that they were "put to death with all the torment possible for terror to others."

Certain writers have suggested that, "counting those killed in wars and raids in Africa and in the horrors of the Middle Passage [across the sea], the transatlantic slave trade might easily have cost Africa . . . 50,000,000 people." The awesome implications of this total appear in "the very conservative guess" that no more than 15,000,000 Africans reached the New World in the 350 years of this trade. Almost half of them arrived in the eighteenth century after Britain had supplanted Holland and France as the leading slave carrier. Approximately half of the remainder reached the Americas during the first 60 years of the nineteenth century, many of them smuggled into Brazil, Cuba, and the southern states of the United States after Britain and others had outlawed the slave trade early in the century and slavery itself in most parts of the Western world as the century wore on.

In 1698 the British Crown terminated the slave traffic monopoly held since 1660 by the Company of Royal Adventurers into Africa and its successor, the Royal African Company. This step formally opened the Dark Continent in the eighteenth century to the competition of aggressive independent British merchants, heretofore limited to illegal interloping. Merchants in the American mainland colonies also gained legitimate commercial access to West Africa at this time and made the most of it.

In 1713, at the end of the War of the Spanish Succession (see p. 159), Britain supplanted France as the holder of the *asiento,* the contract by which Spain had earlier bestowed upon the Portuguese and the Dutch the exclusive right to supply the Spanish Indies with African slaves. Although this contract limited Britain to *delivering* no more than 4800 slaves per year for 30 years, or 144,000 in all, scholars agree that the British South Sea Company, for whom alone the Crown had negotiated the contract, grossly exceeded this number as the demand for slaves soared. The South Sea Company's monopoly in the Spanish-American market, moreover, like that of the Royal African Company in the West African slave sources earlier, was flagrantly invaded by swarms of independent carriers of all slave-trading nations and their receivers. Following termination of the *asiento* in mid-

century, the ranks of the independents swelled; the rapid enlargement, at the same time, of the Chesapeake, Carolina, and Georgia markets lifted the slave trade to its zenith.

Whether or not the eighteenth-century slave trade proved profitable over-all remains an unanswered and probably an unanswerable question. There is no doubt, at the same time, that large personal fortunes were made in it, in England and New England, and that a formidable political interest developed in Parliament to promote and perpetuate it. The absentee sugar growers marshaled behind the slave traders the fortunes they made in the British Caribbean islands from slave labor. The ranks were further augmented by the shipbuilders and their workers who constructed, outfitted, and maintained the hun-

*Diagram of the holds of an eighteenth-century slave ship demonstrating their cargo capacity. (Schomburg Collection, New York Public Library.)*

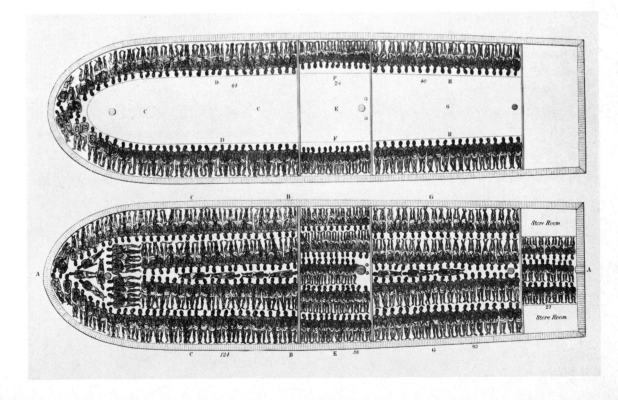

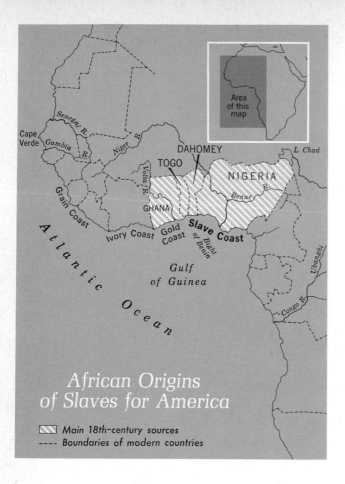

**African Origins
of Slaves for America**

▨ Main 18th-century sources
---- Boundaries of modern countries

Beyond the momentum the slave trade and the personal fortunes made in it gave to the eighteenth-century industrial revolution in the Western world, by enlarging the dependence of African rulers on European goods and weakening their resistance to European power, it also gave momentum to nineteenth-century Western imperialism. The slave trade of the eighteenth century brought the prodigious labor supply of Africa to the capital of Europe and the land of America. The imperialism of the nineteenth century brought the prodigious capital supply of Europe to the natural resources and the labor of Africa, and of Asia as well.

Between the opening of the European slave trade by the Portuguese in the fifteenth century and the closing of the trade by the major slaving powers in the nineteenth century, Negroes were collected over a vast 4000 miles of African coastline ranging from the mouth of the Senegal River in the north to Angola in the south. The trade spread along this coastline gradually; at its eighteenth-century peak it was largely concentrated on the "Slave Coast" of modern Ghana, Togo, Dahomey, and Nigeria where the Volta and Niger rivers empty into the Bight of Benin and the Gulf of Guinea. Here the African sellers ruled; by and large the white buyers kept to their shoreline forts and factories where slaves collected in the interior were brought to them by local merchants permitted by king or chieftain to engage in the traffic for a price.

Africans, like others from time immemorial, had enslaved enemies taken alive in war. As the European slave trade grew, wars simply for the capture of millions of the likely young men most desired by the buyers (as in the wars for Indian slaves early in colonial history; see p. 69) became the major means of supply. In these wars, European firearms played an increasingly determinate role, at once extending the range of a favored ruler's hinterland and narrowing his freedom from white domination. As friction within Africa mounted, a steady supply of European fire-

dreds of vessels engaged in the trade, and by the industrialists and their workers who manufactured the goods used in the direct dickering with the African middleman to raise a cargo. Rhode Island's particularly heavy concentration on distilling rum for slave trading was exceptional. Although other American colonies and Britain herself employed distilled spirits in the bargaining, Britain counted much more heavily on the attraction of iron bars, brass basins and rings (for collars and bracelets), beads, colored cloth, cutlasses, and above all, firearms and gunpowder. The production of such commodities gave a lasting impetus to Britain's metallurgical, textile, and chemical industries, each strengthened further by the spiraling demand for clothing and tools used by the slaves at their dire destinations.

arms became the foundation of a ruler's might; thus the slave trader's hunger for Negro captives was supplemented by the African's urgency to supply them. The entire process grew monstrously destructive of African society while the individual African victim often killed himself rather than succumb to bondage.

The cruelty of slavery began at the very instant of capture (or of kidnaping, a secondary source of supply) and during the marches, often hundreds of miles, from the scene of defeat to the shore. Here, for those who survived the trek, chained imprisonment, branding, flogging, and even murder on sufficient provocation despite the Negro's value now as property, characteristically preceded the voyage, the bestiality of which knew no limits. Despite the careful organization of the trade at its maturity, vessels engaged in it frequently sat idle in ports for weeks before acquiring a full load or finding a favorable wind. Slaves mutined more often during these periods than on the high seas, some even, on becoming unfettered, throwing themselves into the shark-infested waters in seeking to regain their liberty.

Britain was one of the last of the Western powers to enter the African slave trade on a commercial basis and only gradually enlarged her interest in it. Britain's mainland colonies, at the same time, only gradually fell prey to the "peculiar institution" as a labor system (see p. 56). In the eighteenth century as in the seventeenth, many of the slaves in these colonies had been "seasoned" in the Caribbean sugar islands before coming to the mainland staple plantations. The majority of eighteenth-century mainland slaves, however, landed straight from Africa, a situation that deepened the planters' fear and terror of their blacks, as yet unbroken to plantation discipline and the constraints of the "quarter." This circumstance also heightened, as we have said, the planters' determination to secure white immigrants whom they could arm in their defense.

The spread of slavery, however, soon expropriated the white immigrant's opportunities. A Carolina merchant in 1740 made clear what was to become a distressingly persistent southern condition: "Where there are Negroes," he said, "a white man despises to work, saying, *what, will you have me a Slave and work like a Negro?*" Six years earlier, a petition to the Crown signed by the President and Speaker of the South Carolina Council stated that,

*Artist's conception of the inspection and sale of a Negro on Africa's "Slave Coast." (Schomburg Collection, New York Public Library.)*

many Negroes are now train'd up to be Handicraft Tradesmen, to the great discouragement of Your Majestys white Subjects, who come here to settle with a View of Employment in their several Occupations, but must often give way to a People in Slavery: which we daily discover to be a great Obstruction to the Settlement of this Frontier with white People.

If Negro gang labor turned whites from work in the fields, white legislation soon discouraged Negroes from seeking work off the fields. The fully developed slave codes and related ordinances of the early eighteenth century barred slaves and free Negroes alike from many occupations reserved for whites. This became true in northern as well as southern colonies. The latter, moreover, as the slave system matured and its danger grew, closed in on Negro life in numerous other ways. W.D. Jordan summarizes the tendency:

In the last quarter of the seventeenth century the trend was to treat Negroes more like property and less like men, to send them to the fields at younger ages, to deny them automatic existence as inherent members of the community, to tighten the bonds on their personal and civil freedom, and correspondingly to loosen the traditional restraints on the master's freedom to deal with his humanity as he saw fit. In 1705 Virginia gathered up the random statutes of a whole generation and baled them into a "slave code" which would not have been out of place in the nineteenth century.

The Negro's response to this trend became apparent in the number of runaways and the groundswell of resistance and revolt. No one phrased the pervasive psychology of the slaveholder in mid-century better than William Byrd of Virginia in a private letter in 1736:

We have already at least 10,000 men of these descendants of Ham, fit to bear Arms, and these numbers increase every day, as well by birth, as by Importation. And in case there should arise a Man of desperate courage amongst us, exasperated by a desperate fortune, he might with more advantage than Cataline kindle a Servile War. Such a man might be dreadfully mischievous before any opposition could be formed against him, and tinge our Rivers as wide as they are with blood.

Roughly a generation later, in the 1760s, the proportion of blacks in the American population reached its highest level ever, about 21 per cent. In the South generally it reached nearly 50 per cent; in parts of the South it may have soared above 80 per cent. All the talk in the revolutionary period about liberty and equality made certain whites increasingly aware, by contrast, of the systematic submersion and suppression of the blacks, of the institution of slavery that had matured in their midst. Awareness made some sensitive to criticism and studious in slavery's defense. Others set forth on the long road toward ameliorating the slave's condition.

## II  *The Mature Southern Colonies*

### THE TIDEWATER

While the white immigrant of the eighteenth century helped guard the frontier from the Indian, and the slave worked the protected plantations, the gentry assuaged their fear of the red man and the black by pretensions to aristocratic living and self-indulgence. Some of them saw through their own pretensions, but enjoyed life nonetheless; others took them for reality and suffered for their mistake.

In colonial times, as later, the American South differed profoundly enough from the North for each section to flaunt and nourish its distinctive culture. Yet the South, like the North, by the eighteenth century, had itself become a land of social contrasts among which that between white and black, master and slave, was only the most far-reaching.

Throughout the colonial period, most of the white population of the Chesapeake region, of tidewater Virginia and Maryland and adjacent parts of North Carolina, remained of English extraction. Here, although grain and other food crops continued to be widely grown in the eighteenth century, the production and export of tobacco, as we have seen (p. 54), gave the strongest impulse to economic expansion, with land speculation offering a hedge against the uncertainties of staple agriculture for distant and fluctuating markets. The Carolina low country, extending southward to the Savannah River and inland about 60 miles, was settled later than the Chesapeake region by people more mixed in their origins (see p. 69). For reasons of climate and terrain they specialized in the cultivation of rice until indigo was introduced in the middle of the eighteenth century.

The Chesapeake planters, led by a small elite group, kept close ties with the mother country and aped the manners of the English aristocracy. The Carters, Lees, Byrds, Randolphs, and Fitzhughs of Virginia, and the Carrolls, Dulanys, and Galloways of Maryland, families of political power as well as economic substance, lived in Georgian mansions far grander than the seventeenth-century farmhouses of their grandfathers. They filled the well-proportioned rooms with the finest imported furniture, or hired able artisans to carry out the designs of foreign cabinetmakers. The evidence of colonial craftsmanship may be seen today in the Byrd mansion, "Westover," and in the stylish town houses of Annapolis.

We can detect the aspirations of these planters in their portraits, which show them and their families in all their imported finery. Although contemporary artists presented the Chesapeake gentry as an idealized colonial nobility, their middle-class American expressions are not altogether obliterated. We see them for what they were: shrewd, down-to-earth members of a planter oligarchy. Some of them boasted large libraries with books in a number of languages. Yet those devoted to cultural interests were exceptional.

"Few Men of Fortune" in Virginia, wrote

*King William County Courthouse, Virginia. Built in the 1730s, this is one of the oldest courthouses in America. (Virginia State Chamber of Commerce.)*

*Robert Carter (1708–1804) of Nomini Hall, Virginia, a James River manor house, portrayed by Sir Joshua Reynolds as an English gentleman. (Courtesy Louise A. Patten; photo Colonial Williamsburg, Virginia.)*

102

the Reverend James Murray in 1762, "will expend on their Son's Education the Sums requisite to carry them thro' a regular Course of Studies." William and Mary College, well endowed by the established Anglican church, opened in Williamsburg, Virginia, soon to become the provincial capital, in 1693; but few students spent more than a year there, that year usually given to indolence and sport. Some planters sent their sons to England for sound classical instruction; but those who profited from such excursions often remained permanently abroad. What reading the planters did themselves usually dealt with practical subjects like law, medicine, commerce, and surveying. Observers noted that they were an outdoor people, fonder of fox-hunting and horse-racing and long week-end house parties than of polite learning. More than ignorance they feared rusticity and inelegance. The dancing master was as much in demand as the tutor.

Although highly conscious of their rank as gentlemen, the Chesapeake planters took the management of their tobacco plantations seriously. At the same time they continued to splurge on fine imports supplied by their British agents, usually on long-term credits which further encouraged them to live above their means. Land, which represented their greatest wealth, was also their downfall. "Such amazing property," observed Philip Fithian, tutor to the Carters in their heyday, "no matter how deeply it is involved [in debt], blows up the owners to an imagination, which is visible to all." They "live up their suppositions," a Londoner remarked, "without providing against Calamities and accidents." The slave system reinforced the sense of mastery arising from majestic land holdings.

From the 1730s to the 1750s, when the price of Virginia tobacco soared, the rising profits from their staple also put a premium on the planters' land. In this period, the Chesapeake gentry enjoyed their "golden age," the age of "the gauntlet and the glove," in which the myth of southern chivalry and romance took root. Yet few could afford for

long the high life of cavaliers, the expenditures for clothes, carriages, and body slaves, mansions, parks, and wine. Eventually, the Virginians' debts for imported indulgences grew so calamitously high that Governor Francis Farquier remarked in 1766 that their "Blood . . . is soured by their private distresses." To those who crashed, the West loomed more beguilingly than ever as a refuge or new springboard to success. It also fed grand ideas of empire among such Virginians as young George Washington and Thomas Jefferson, whose vision encompassed the entire continent, even the entire hemisphere.

Of all the mainland settlements, tidewater South Carolina was closest to the West Indian sugar islands, most distant from England, in character. As we have seen (p. 69), many of the early settlers had come to South Carolina from Barbados and from among the Huguenots of the French West Indian islands and France herself. In the middle of the eighteenth century, South Carolina was the only mainland colony in which Negroes outnumbered whites, as in the islands. The whites below the 2000 leading families, moreover, were the most depressed on the continent, showing the lowest literacy rate and the strongest antagonism to the ruling group.

Under the English navigation acts (see p. 78), Carolina rice had been made an enumerated commodity in 1704, thus requiring that it be sent to the mother country for reshipment by English merchants to the European continent which offered the major market. Spoilage from excessive handling and delays in reaching users soon forced the English to reconsider, and in 1729 they allowed rice once more to go directly to European ports. This decision helped greatly to enlarge South Carolina's trade and profits. By the 1750s, their land hunger as great as that of the Virginians, South Carolina's planters had extended their fields and their forest holdings well into neighboring Georgia, soon virtually their captive colony. By then, too, encouraged by a parliamentary bounty, many of the rice planters had turned to growing indigo, heavily in de-

The Start of the Hunt, *artist unknown, is a mid-eighteenth-century scene of country gentlemen at leisure. (National Gallery of Art, Washington, D.C., gift of Edgar William and Bernice Chrysler Garbisch.)*

mand as the source of a dye much wanted in the booming English textile industry. Indigo, together with rice, provided Carolinians with income less subject to price fluctuations and other market hazards than tobacco. The Carolina grandees, unlike the Chesapeake gentry, thus were less victimized by debt. "The planters are full of money," noted Henry Laurens, himself one of the richest of the rich, in 1750.

Since the Carolina rivers, unlike those of the Chesapeake region, did not afford seagoing vessels sufficient depth for sailing inland direct to the plantations, the colony's produce usually was brought down to Charleston for shipment abroad. Where the Chesapeake region remained virtually devoid of towns for generations, and its culture rural, Charleston, South Carolina, by the 1750s had become the fourth largest colonial city. Its mid-century population of 10,000 was almost equally divided by color, with a sizable proportion of the blacks serving as household and body slaves to planters who maintained homes there.

The heavy preponderance of blacks on South Carolina plantations gave rise to the gravest fears of servile restiveness and revolt and hence to the severest restraints and repression.

Relations between blacks and whites were aggravated by the masters living most of the year distant from the hot and enervating fields where overseers alone were charged with getting out the crops, come what may. A petition of the South Carolina assembly to the Board of Trade in London in 1728 spoke of "such vast numbers of enemies, as are the Spaniards on one side, the Indians on the other and a more dreadful one amongst ourselves, viz., such vast quantities of negroes to grapple with." Forty years later, Lieutenant-Governor William Bull wrote similarly to Lord Hillsborough in England that the colony's Negroes constituted a "numerous domestic Enemy . . . thick sown in our plantations, and require our utmost attention to keep them in order."

In mid-century, rich Carolina planter families like the Draytons, Izards and Manigaults, Hugers, Rutledges and Pinckneys, lived on a handsome scale. Their summers they were

103

104

likely to spend at Newport, Rhode Island, or abroad. For much of the rest of the year they occupied their Charleston town houses, enjoying the city's genteel entertainments: music, the theater, dancing parties, and horseracing. Architectural styles borrowed from the West Indies—the pastel-shaded brick and stucco houses embellished with wrought-iron balconies and gates, and the lush private gardens —helped give eighteenth-century Charleston its distinctive and exotic charm. Handsome churches and public buildings lent an added dignity, while the wholesale and retail establishments, warehouses, and business offices clustered around the wharves gave evidence of the city's commercial vigor.

Charleston's economic growth permitted ambitious businessmen as well as traditional planters to amass fortunes. While the old names persisted in the ranks of the rich and powerful, new men also could buy land, marry into older families, and set themselves up as grandees. There were probably more rich men in South Carolina in the 1760s than in any other colony. At the same time, the concentration of wealth in Charleston seems to have supplied an unusually strong impulse for further accumulation and display. "Their whole lives," said the *South Carolina Gazette,* of the colony's leaders on the eve of the Revolution,

are one continued Race in which everyone is endeavoring to distance all behind him; and to overtake or pass by, all before him; everyone is flying from his inferiors in Pursuit of his Superiors. . . . Every Tradesman is a Merchant, every Merchant is a Gentleman, and every Gentleman one of the Noblesse. We are a Country of Gentry. . . . We have no such Thing as a common People among us: Between Vanity and Fashion, the Species is utterly destroyd.

### THE "BACK PARTS"

On the eve of the American Revolution, about 250,000 persons—runaway Negroes and servants who had established their freedom and black slaves, together with a mixed white population of recent foreign immigrants and migrants from the tidewater—had displaced most of the aborigines of the Chesapeake back country and the "back parts," as they were called, of South Carolina and Georgia and developed a society of their own.

During the first years of life in the back country, the poorer settlers lived in crude shanties of unsplit logs enclosed only on three sides; later on, they constructed more substantial log houses. Although the entire back country at first offered a paradise for hunter and trapper, a mixed subsistence agriculture producing cereals, potatoes, fruits, and meat, as well as flax and hemp, gradually developed in the Chesapeake hinterlands. Soon small market centers emerged along the main routes and at the ferry crossings, and even before mid-century such thriving crossroads communities as Fredericksburg and Hagerstown in Maryland (dominated by the German newcomers), and Martinsburg and Winchester in Virginia, and Charlotte in North Carolina (where the Scotch-Irish prevailed) had been built, each with its grist mills, country stores, bakers, masons, carpenters, coopers, brickmakers, and weavers. Yet rough conditions continued to breed rough manners, and travelers often remarked on the primitive life of the early pioneers in the upland South and on the shiftlessness and intemperance of the "poor whites" who made up an illiterate yeomanry. Most travelers agreed, moreover, that the well-to-do frontiersmen and the poorer yeomanry alike lacked the initiative so characteristic of their counterparts in the Middle colonies and New England.

The "back parts" of the Carolina country were more isolated and much rougher even than those of the Chesapeake region. It must have been particularly hard on settlers fresh from Ulster or German villages to spend lonely years in a country still ringing with the cries of wolves and panthers. Malaria was endemic here and only added to the difficulty of facing the prospect of unending labor to clear the land. Many settlers soon fell back into the nomadic life from which civilization had worked for centuries to raise mankind. They became herdsmen of wild swine and cattle, often stolen from the red men. Itinerant clergymen reported with dismay how the people in this region dwelt together in "Concubinage, swapping their wives as Cattel, and living in a State of Nature, more irregularly and unchastely than the Indians." A few, nevertheless, found this life so satisfactory that they made fortunes out of meat and skins and tallow. Such men became a regular back-country gentry living on the most extensive cattle ranges on the entire mainland. Most others, however, continued their slide on the social scale into the life of primitive huntsmen constantly on the prowl for elusive game, including Indians.

Gradually, tidewater institutions, both legal and political, were imposed on the Maryland and Virginia back country, although the incompleteness of tidewater control was shown even as late as 1863, when the West Virginians seceded from the slave-holding and slave-breeding East. Resistance to Charleston domination in hinterland South Carolina and Georgia was even stronger. Throughout the eighteenth century, the back parts of these colonies complained frequently of the "mixt Multitude" of "white-collar parasites" from Charleston, the "mercenary tricking Attornies, Clerks, and other little Officials," who came to prey upon them, taking full advantage of their poor knowledge of English, their ignorance, their friendlessness. "Finding . . . they were only amus'd and trifled with," they said at last, "all Confidence of the Poor in the Great is destroy'd and . . . will never exist again." In the Revolution, when the Carolina planters themselves fought the British, the non-English in the "back parts," Anglophobe though they were to the marrow, chose to fight the planters. And yet, their very Indian wars, their pursuit of Indian slaves, by bringing them into confrontation with the French in Louisiana and the Spanish in Florida, worked to develop the idea of empire and the hunger for the whole continent, unaware though they remained of its true extent.

## III  *The Middle Colonies*

### PENNSYLVANIA

During the eighteenth century the Middle colonies formed the most heterogeneous part of British North America, Pennsylvania, the newest, quickly becoming the largest and most diversified among them. By 1755, Philadelphia, with 28,000 inhabitants, had passed Boston for first place among colonial cities. Though Quakers no longer were a majority in Philadelphia, the Quaker merchants comprised the city's wealthiest group and dominated the whole settlement. Their wealth stemmed largely from their extensive trade, including the slave trade, the profits from which they invested in mining and manufacturing enterprises and in urban and forest land.

The Quakers' religious beliefs, like the Puritans', inspired the thrift, industry, and reliability essential to business success. The persecution of the Friends for their beliefs both in Europe and America had scattered them over the western world, a circumstance they also turned to commercial advantage. Frederick B. Tolles, the historian of colonial Quaker life, writes:

There were Quakers in most of the ports with which Philadelphia had commercial relations. A number of them, like the Hills in Madeira, the Lloyds in London, the Callenders in Barbados, the Wantons in Newport, and the Franklins in New York, were related by marriage to the leading Quaker families of Philadelphia. . . . The intelligence which they received through their correspondence and from itinerant "public Friends" . . . from Nova Scotia to Curaçao and from Hamburg to Lisbon . . . was chiefly concerned with prices current and the prosperity of Truth.

The industrious farmers Penn brought to the back country of his colony supplied Philadelphia's merchants with excellent grain and other staples for export and a thriving market for imported goods. Philadelphia shipyards turned out vessels the equal of any in the world, and their captains were second to none, especially in evading the British navigation acts.

Prosperity and the intricacies of business led to a loosening of the Friends' restrictions against worldly pleasures. A great Quaker merchant in 1719 might declare: "I always suspect the furniture of the Inside Where too much application is Shewn for a Gay or fantasticall outside." But the next generation was not so suspicious. They cultivated an expensive simplicity. Their clothes, though unadorned, were cut from the most expensive materials. Their Georgian houses lacked the external decoration and the more elaborate doorways of non-Quaker mansions, but the interiors were just as sumptuous. Objections to the fine arts still lingered on in the mid-eighteenth century, but rich Quakers, like other rich colonials, had their portraits painted in England, and even orthodox Friends tolerated profile silhouettes. Like the Chesapeake and Carolina aristocracy, the Philadelphia merchants kept elaborate carriages to travel between the city and their country estates. They entertained lavishly, cultivated magnificent gardens, and enjoyed "free sociable Conversation." Orthodox Quakers did not condone gambling, dancing, theatergoing, and tippling—the "world's" pleasures; yet some so-called "Wet Quakers" yielded to the temptations of the *beau monde,* to horse racing, punch-drinking, and card-playing. Some even left the Friends for the more engaging Anglican church where they were not required to report their private affairs publicly, as at the Friends meetings. Still others, drawn perhaps by their traditional attachment to "Laborious Handicrafts," became involved with Newtonian science and experimentation. Among the more interesting imports of the Philadelphia merchants were the books, instruments, and mixtures of the science of the day. Such men frequently became Deists, for whom God was but the "Heavenly Engineer."

Far from unknown among the educated planters of Virginia and the intellectuals of New England, Deism flourished in Philadelphia. Its greatest New World apostle was Philadelphia's leading citizen, Ben Franklin (see p. 132).

The liberal government that William Penn had created for his settlement was, by the early years of the eighteenth century, already on the way to being corrupted by his absentee successors. The rising Quaker merchants grew most vocal in attacking the regime and in proposing the strengthening of the local assembly at the expense of the proprietors. After 1740 the struggle quickened between the proprietary party (which stood for centralized authority in the hands of the governor and council) and the popular party (composed of city merchants and property-holding farmers). Liberal suffrage laws and the support of the German element enabled the anti-proprietary Quaker party to outmaneuver the deputies of the Penns.

For a time, the assembly enjoyed the confidence of all sections of the colony. But in 1754 its failure to protect the frontier from Indian raids the frontiersmen themselves had inspired by land-grabbing and violence

brought the assembly under attack. Actually, the assembly did not object to appropriating funds for frontier defense, but it insisted that the proprietors share the expense by accepting a tax on their lands. A deadlock resulted until the proprietors agreed to put up £5000 for the defense of the colony and the assembly voted the necessary funds. The Pennsylvania frontier, nevertheless, continued right up to the Revolution to be the scene of bloodshed as the "thirst for large tracts of land . . . prevailed with a singular rage" among the grandees, and the hunger for space at the red man's expense remained unappeased among the frontier settlers.

## NEW JERSEY AND NEW YORK

Travelers passing through New Jersey in the eighteenth century sometimes stopped long enough to comment on its natural beauty, its prosperity, or the succulence of its oysters. But there was little more to detain the curious, who usually hastened on to New York. Jerseyites, to a degree, felt the same way about their settlement. In the 1750s about 70,000 people lived in New Jersey, and many of them looked upon it as a "keg tapped at both ends,"

107

the colony transporting its surplus hemp, grain, flax, hay, and Indian corn either to New York or Philadelphia for shipment overseas.

The movement of Yankee Puritans from Long Island to East New Jersey, which had begun while the Dutch still held New Netherland, was perhaps the most significant of early intercolonial migrations (see p. 72). The cultural influence of New England continued strong in East New Jersey, particularly in the towns of Newark, Elizabeth, and Woodbridge. But elsewhere in the colony by the eighteenth century the old New England ways were modified and the transplanted village community, with its town meetings and its close social and religious supervision, had broken down. The influence of neighboring Pennsylvania thereafter grew stronger, and the farm rather than the village became the basic social unit. The New England influence persisted, however, in the Georgian farmhouses, inns, and churches.

*East prospect of Philadelphia, 1754, engraved by George Heap. This view, from the Jersey side of the Delaware River, shows the tall spire of the Episcopalian Christ Church in the center. (Stokes Collection, New York Public Library.)*

108

Nature endowed New York City with the finest harbor in the Atlantic world, yet its growth was far slower than that of Philadelphia, Boston, or Charleston. Patroon control of the Hudson Valley (see p. 30) and Indian control of the interior were partly responsible for New York's low state. Until 1720, the pirate taint also held back the development of legitimate trade. New York merchants liked pirate goods, which they could buy cheap and sell dear. Pirate crews also were good customers when they came ashore. A pirate rendezvous, however, offered no attraction to legitimate captains and shippers who could easily ply an active trade elsewhere. Early in the 1700s, New York's governor pressed London for vessels swift enough to "destroye these vermin who have hitherto made New York their nest of safety." But a quarter of a century passed before effective action was taken. Thereafter, Yorkers entered more vigorously into competition with the Yankees to the north and the Quakers to the south and earned a growing share of American, West Indian, and world trade.

At mid-century, New York City boasted 13,000 inhabitants. Shade trees grew along the paved streets, which were clean by colonial standards, and the public and private build-ings usually drew favorable comments, though some visitors ranked New York below Philadelphia in beauty. Dr. Alexander Hamilton, an amusing and perceptive Marylander who toured the northern colonies in 1744, accompanied by his slave, Dromo, found the New York atmosphere more electric than that of Philadelphia. "The houses," he wrote, "are more compact and regular, and in general higher built, most of them after the Dutch model, with their gravell ends fronting the street." Otherwise, the city had begun to lose many of its Dutch features, and the Dutch language itself was less commonly heard. The absence of a Dutch press or a Dutch colonial literature left the dying culture with few supports, and the opening of King's College, future Columbia University, in 1754 made it certain that English speech and culture would predominate.

As cosmopolitan as Philadelphia, New York's rich inhabitants enjoyed the same pleasures as their Pennsylvania neighbors, but with an easier conscience. They listened to choral and instrumental music and, despite the opposition of local Calvinists, patronized the theaters where traveling English companies produced the standard English dramas.

Having noticed the decline of Dutch influ-

This view of the Hand-in-Hand Fire Company of New York at work embellished a notice of a meeting sent out by Isaac Roosevelt on March 3, 1762. (Stokes Collection, New York Public Library.)

ence in New York City, travelers sailing north by sloop were the more sharply struck by its persistence in the Hudson Valley. The voyage up the Hudson was punctuated by stops at small settlements like Poughkeepsie. Long before Washington Irving exploited the romance and mystery of this region, visitors experienced delicious shudders as they surveyed the solitary river scenery "where nothing presents but huge precipices and inaccessible steeps, where foot of man never was." At the end of this scenic route lay Albany, where the Dutch language remained the predominant one as late as the 1740s.

Exposed to Indian raiders from French Canada until the British dislodged the French in 1763 (see p. 164), colonial Albany kept the look of a frontier outpost. Wooded palisades enclosed the town. At its center stood a square stone fortress manned by 300 of the king's troops. But the domestic architecture was comfortable enough. Observers spoke of the "superstitiously clean" look of the wood and brick houses, their ends characteristically facing the streets.

> Their chambers and rooms are large and handsome [wrote a contemporary]. They have their beds generally in alcoves, so that you may go thro' all the rooms of a great house and never see a bed. They affect pictures much, particularly scripture history, with which they adorn their rooms. They set out their cabinets and *buffets* much with china. Their kitchens are likewise very clean, and they hang earthen or delft plates and dishes around the walls, in manner of pictures.

Eighteenth-century travel accounts often mention "the avarice, selfishness, and immeasurable love of money" of the Albany Dutch. They were even charged with trading with the enemy when Indian war-parties led by the French were burning New England settlements (1702–1706). But this materialism and particularism was not unusual in the colonies.

The Hudson Valley between New York City and Albany was the only part of the entire province that was well settled as late as 1750. Yet even here the landscape was characterized by huge primeval tracts owned by a few rich men. From the start of the eighteenth century, British governors of New York, emulating the Dutch patroon system, rewarded their favorites with land grants ranging from 50,000 to a million acres. As a result, the richest land was monopolized by owners who sometimes paid nothing but a token tax on their property and thus had small incentive to sell. They leased occasional tracts to tenant farmers. Otherwise, bona-fide settlers were discouraged. German, Scotch-Irish, and other "squatters," however, took advantage of the unpatrolled country. Between 1720 and 1756 New York's population grew from 30,000 to 85,000, much of the increase occurring in the Hudson Valley. When, in later years, the patroons tried to collect rents from families that had squatted here for generations, they were resisted with spirit.

## IV  *Eighteenth-Century New England*

### RHODE ISLAND

Eighteenth-century Boston was regarded by many as the most impressive and the most English city in the colonies. Many roads led to Boston, but the most common way from the Middle colonies, or at least from New York, was to sail out Long Island Sound to New London, Connecticut, or to cross over from Long Island itself by ferry. From New London, most travelers would stop first at Newport, Rhode Island, the fifth largest city in the colonies, and one already renowned among vacationists for its pleasing and healthful climate. Planters from the Carolinas and the West Indies were coming to Newport as early as the 1730s to escape the tropical heat. Bishop Berkeley, the famous English philosopher, lived here between 1720 and 1731, and Newport was the home of one of America's first artists, Robert Feke, whose portraits

109

tell us so much about the values and aspirations of the New England and Pennsylvania aristocracy. The magnificence of Newport's private and public buildings rivaled those of Boston, Philadelphia, and Charleston. In Peter Harrison, the town could claim the most distinguished American architect, who in the 1750s introduced the classical temple form that was eventually adopted everywhere in the colonies. King's Chapel in Boston, completed in 1754, is perhaps Harrison's most famous structure, but other fine examples of his work are Christ Church in Cambridge, Massachusetts, and the Touro Synogogue in Newport itself.

Approximately 7000 people lived in Newport in the 1750s and many of them lived off what we, today, would call the tourist trade. But the city was also a flourishing port dominated by the slave-traders. Its shippers, like those of the rest of seaboard New England, also engaged in supplying the West Indies with foodstuffs, timber, and other commodities assembled at ports all over the world and carrying away sugar and molasses for the manufacture of the rum used in slave-buying. As a British customs man said of Yankees generally, Newporters were careful "to keep their ships in constant employ, which makes them trye all ports to force a trade."

Yet Rhode Island had still to live down its reputation for radicalism that it had earned in Roger Williams's day. "The private people," declared one English visitor, "are cunning, deceitful, and selfish; they live almost entirely by unfair and illicit trading." Dr. Hamilton, on his visit to the colony in 1744, decided that Rhode Island with its "rural scenes and pretty frank girls," was the most agreeable place he had struck in his travels, but he had to admit that the people had "as bad a character for chicane and disingenuity as any of our American Colonies."

### MASSACHUSETTS

The city of Boston, if not yet the "hub of the universe," was the heart of Massachusetts,

as Massachusetts was the heart of New England. Even prejudiced observers from other sections, who came with preconceived notions about the "enthusiastical" or "canting" Yankees, were amazed by the richness and graciousness of Boston's upper-class life and the general comfort of the rest of the people. North of Boston such ports as Salem, Marblehead, and Gloucester, which much later were to supply many of the "proper Bostonians" of the Victorian era, were already enjoying a thriving trade. But the capital of the commonwealth, with over 15,000 people in 1750, the best harbor, and the biggest hinterland markets, was still far ahead of the other towns and growing faster.

Boston's commercial prosperity had begun, as we have seen (p. 67), virtually from the beginning of settlement there. Her merchants were quick to take all the advantage they could of England's wars with the Dutch which, in the seventeenth century, diverted the vessels of the two greatest commercial nations of the time from the world's trading routes. Early in the eighteenth century, it was peace rather than war that gave the strongest impetus to Boston's prosperity, especially the Peace of Utrecht of 1713 (see p. 159). In the West Indies, the growing demand for all necessities sent prices and profits soaring. By the terms of the Peace of Utrecht, Britain obtained Newfoundland and Nova Scotia from France, and the vast fisheries of their waters were opened to Yankee enterprise. At the same time, Nantucket whalers began to sail far from their home waters on long voyages to the Arctic Ocean and Brazilian shores. "Farming the sea," as the Yankee said, was itself procreative. The demand for more and better ships promoted such land-based businesses as rope- and sail-making. These drew artisans from nearby and foreign towns, and their growing number fostered new home and business construction. Agriculture in the surrounding countryside also felt the surge of prosperity as town populations had to be fed. New road-building gave its own impetus to growth and speeded the exchange of goods.

As in Pennsylvania and the South, so in Massachusetts wealth enlarged the demands of nature. Calvin, it is true, warned the Saints "perpetually and resolutely [to] exert themselves to retrench all superfluities and to restrain luxury." He particularly commanded the "elect" to "give an account of thy stewardship." But by the eighteenth century, the richest Puritans, like the richest Quakers, had

*General Samuel Waldo, a life-sized portrait by Robert Feke, c. 1748. The general, assuming a courtly pose, rests his spyglass on a rock. In the distance, the citadel of Louisbourg is under bombardment. (Bowdoin College Museum of Art.)*

*Interior view of King's Chapel, Boston, showing Peter Harrison's use of double Corinthian columns to support a vaulted ceiling. (Wayne Andrews.)*

moved away from the old religion to the more congenial Anglican communion, where there was no requirement to make "a public relation of their experiences." King's Chapel, the first Anglican Church in Boston, was opened in 1688, and there, as in their new brick mansions on Beacon Hill, even before Peter Harrison built its fine new house of worship in mid-century (p. 110), the "visible elect" might display God's bounty without having to disclose how it fell to their lot.

Boston's "codfish aristocracy" and its emulators in other Yankee ports now affected swords, satins, and sturdy English broadcloths. 111

112

In the country, comfortable "colonial" homes replaced the rude structures of pioneer days, and the gentry drank and dressed as befitted their new substance and standing. The requirement that all Puritan residences be within half a mile of the town church remained but a faint reminder of narrower times, and with its passing went the stringency of religious observance, the strength of the public school plan. Boston and other towns merely breathed easier for the change.

John Singleton Copley's realistic portraits of eighteenth-century brocaded Boston merchants and their wives not only reveal their down-to-earth materialistic outlook, but also their frills and finery. The new preference for easy manners and politeness could be detected, too, in the abandonment of thorny seventeenth-century prose for a smooth and easy diction that would be less jarring to refined ears. Even Cotton Mather, Boston's leading minister and savant and a stanch defender of old doctrines and old ways, admitted in 1720: "I am too liable to an Infirmity of Salting my Sentences . . . with Intermixtures of something or other that I have Read of." Mather realized that, among a people whose trade had become world-wide and whose taste had be-

come enriched, pedantry was old-fashioned and provincial.

The growing secularization so characteristic of colonial society everywhere in the eighteenth century showed itself clearly in the turbulence and irreverence of life in the cities. Samuel Sewall, judge, spirited diarist, and epitome of the new bourgeoisie, was reporting the tumults and riots of the Boston streets as early as the 1680s. Fifty years later, Boston mobs attacked bawdy houses and public market houses indiscriminately, according to one contemporary. When Cotton Mather warned a local reprobate that every time he drank rum he was selling the blood of Christ, this was the response: "Truly, Sir, when we are going to make ourselves drunk, we never think of that."

Self-indulgence gave still another impetus to trade; but Massachusetts had no staple that was wanted where the luxuries she craved originated. Problems involving the imperial navigation system only enlarged the challenge to Yankee ingenuity on the sea. In resolving their problems, Yankee merchants were not constrained by conscience or by consciousness of crime. Like others, they engaged in much illicit traffic, and some did not scruple about practicing sheer piracy. New England's most

*Mr. and Mrs. Isaac Winslow by John Singleton Copley, 1774. (Museum of Fine Arts, Boston, M. and M. Karolik Collection.)*

lucrative legitimate voyages involved the so-called slave-trade triangle, in which Bostonians gained their full share. The American South was usually supplied with slaves by British or southern ships, although Rhode Islanders also participated in this part of the slave traffic. On the typical Boston slaving voyage, Boston rum was carried to Africa to pay for or otherwise obtain the human cargo. The Africans then were carried to the British West Indies, the notorious "Middle Passage." In the West Indies, precious coin was taken on along with the molasses for the production of more rum, and so around once more. When British West Indian sugar production began to fall off, Boston captains took to visiting "closed" French and Spanish islands to pick up their molasses. In 1733 Parliament yielded to the protests of France and Spain as well as British West Indian planters and adopted the Molasses Act, prohibiting mainland merchants from trading with the foreigners. This was a blow Yankee merchants knew well how to parry. Smuggling became at once a common and a fine art. When Britain, in 1764, decided to strengthen the enforcement of the Molasses Act, Yankee resistance quickly took on a revolutionary tinge (see p. 179).

Distant commerce has always involved a strong element of risk. To reduce the risk, Yankee merchants often installed their brothers, sons, and in-laws as their agents in foreign lands. In Britain itself they turned, when they could find them, to relatives who had resisted the lures of the New World. Family connections failing, they, like the Quakers, sought out their co-religionist. As a last recourse, in Dutch or Spanish, French or Portuguese ports, they employed their own countrymen to look after their interests. Characteristically, family businesses were enlarged and family ties multiplied by intermarriage among mercantile families. In this way, wealth was consolidated; yet a strong start could be made with little capital and the established elite itself was pleased to make room for proven competitors, especially when it had daughters to provide for.

To the west, north, and south of Boston, simpler ways persisted, even though the conservatives thought that the new settlements springing up everywhere in the first third of the eighteenth century displayed a shocking disregard for authority. These "ungospelized" plantations, according to Cotton Mather, were "the very Brothel houses of Satan," and the inhabitants in the hinterlands were said to be "Indianizing" themselves. But to the outsider, the New England villages still seemed remarkable for their tidiness and decency.

Living frugally in simple frame houses, tilling an indifferent soil, the New England farmers developed into the tough, uncommunicative (though sometimes garrulous) American stereotype. Travelers thought them too democratic and careless of social distinctions. "They seem to be a good substantial Kind of Farmers," remarked one visitor, "but there is no break in their Society; their Government, Religion, and Manners all tend to support an equality. Whoever brings in your Victuals sits down and chats to you." When they did "chat," moreover, their superior education, compared to that of rustics farther south, soon became evident. One observer from the South seemed surprised that these people, who looked "rather more like clowns, than the riff-raff of our Maryland planters," should discuss matters "that in our parts would be like Greek, Hebrew, or Arabick."

Actually, however, the plain people of New England, especially in Massachusetts, did not condone unlimited democracy, and they observed their own social distinctions. The large landowners in southern and western New England were the acknowledged leaders, along with the ministers, physicians, and innkeepers. The church meeting enforced a practical social discipline, and what often seemed like loose behavior (for example, the courtship custom known as "bundling" or "tarrying") simply illustrated rural innocence.

The Yankee, tight with his money yet

114

philanthropic for the public good, loyal to his neighbors but regarding the world beyond his village as fair game, gradually became a kind of colonial paradox. He was admired for his industry and his institutions, but disdained for his shrewdness. Though deeply conservative and wary of sudden change, he was susceptible to emotional appeals in religion and to heresies in politics and economics.

## v  *The Spirit of Provincial Politics*

### THE BONDS OF SOCIAL INTERCOURSE

When John Adams of Massachusetts, while attending the Continental Congress in Philadelphia in 1774, first saw in the flesh well-horsed, saber-rattling southerners with their flashy body slaves, he suffered the greatest anxiety of his life. He hastened to write home to his wife how he dreaded "the consequences of this dissimilitude of character" between Yankees and planters, and added that, "without the utmost caution on both sides, and the most considerate forbearance with one another, . . . they will certainly be fatal."

Long before Adams's unsettling experience it had become apparent to many in America and abroad that a country so diverse, geographically and culturally, as the American mainland colonies had become, was not likely to unify itself. Idiom, custom, and economic interest divided the provinces. The vague definition of colonial boundaries in the colonial charters was the source of many conflicts. Maryland, Pennsylvania, and Virginia, and Massachusetts and New York, engaged in drawn-out boundary disputes which grew especially acrimonious in the middle of the eighteenth century when great land speculators from the different colonies staked out overlapping claims. These disputes eventually turned colony against colony in feuds that later helped drag out the Revolutionary War and postponed the establishment of a perma-

nent federal government once independence had been declared. The movement of speculators and settlers westward also stirred the Indians to stronger resistance, and the colonies again fell out among themselves in trying to meet the recurrent challenges. Other issues involving the exchange of currency, piracy and smuggling, religion and politics, further complicated colonial relationships—to such a degree, indeed, that to many at home and abroad it seemed that only the stabilizing control of the mother country prevented colonial anarchy.

And yet, unifying influences also were at work. The insularity and provincialism that undoubtedly existed throughout colonial America was frequently noted by American and foreign travelers. But long before the Revolution, many intellectual barriers were being broken down, especially among the leaders in the different settlements who, despite their differences, shared many interests, beliefs, experiences, and aspirations. Waterways and roads brought the businessmen of New York, Philadelphia, Boston, and Charleston into a vital economic network. Itinerant peddlers, printers, and artists passed from colony to colony. Invalids took long journeys to improve their health, and vacationers to broaden their horizons. Well-to-do families paid visits to distant kin; Quakers and Jews sought out their scattered co-religionists. The colleges at Princeton, New Haven, and Cambridge attracted students from the South and the West Indies as well as from neighboring colonies. John Bartram of Philadelphia, one of many naturalists, botanized across the countryside and entertained fellow enthusiasts who came from afar to see his celebrated gardens. Fraternal societies, which were organized in the principal cities as early as the 1730s, welcomed members from other colonies; Washington, Franklin, and other colonial leaders were Masons even before their revolutionary activities brought them closer together. Finally, colonists read one another's newspapers, circular letters, sermons, pamphlets, and almanacs.

The literate colonial had at his disposal a

variety of information on matters outside his immediate sphere of interest—political, cultural, and economic—that linked him with the destiny of his continent. When the time came, colonial spokesmen were able to appeal to a set of widely shared beliefs and ex-

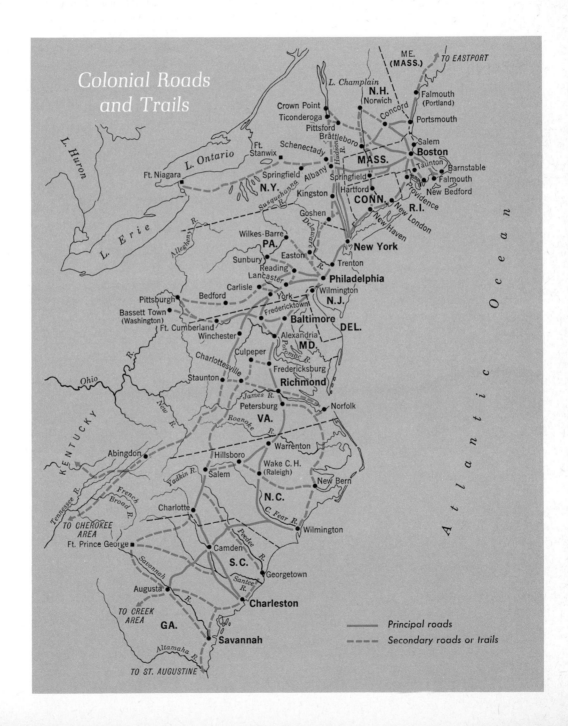

Colonial Roads and Trails

periences, especially among a few thousand leading families, a few hundred in each colony, whose remarkable gains in wealth and power underlay their more subtle claims to primacy.

### THE SEAT OF POLITICAL POWER

Nowhere was the emergence of the colonial elite more evident than in the structure and tendency of colonial politics. In each of the colonies in the mid-eighteenth century, the governor nominally was at the head of the government. Only in Connecticut and Rhode Island was he elected by the legislature. In Maryland and Pennsylvania he continued to be appointed by the absentee proprietor in England. In all the other colonies, including Georgia after 1752, he was appointed by the king. The governor himself appointed his council, which formed the upper house of the legislature. The lower house, usually called the assembly, represented those qualified electors who bothered to exercise their franchise. Local government differed from colony to colony; but even in Virginia, where the governor, like the king at home, appointed the justices of the peace, the most important local officers, the justices themselves firmly resisted interference once they had gained their commissions.

The governor's main strength lay in his right to veto provincial legislation. If he was a man of acumen and ability, he could of course influence the legislators to act in conformity with the king's policy; he could temper or constrain assembly actions before abrasive vetoes became necessary. But success in managing the elected representatives depended on mutual confidence between them and the governor, and confidence dwindled in the eighteenth century.

The assembly's main strength lay in its control of appropriations, including those for the governor's salary and for carrying out relevant parliamentary measures. In the eighteenth century, most of the colonial assemblies, like Parliament in England, used their control of the purse to control the entire government.

The leading families, in turn, used their wealth and standing to control the assemblies for generations.

Two conditions helped perpetuate oligarchic power. One was the limitation of the franchise in practically all the colonies to those with considerable property, preferably in land. In some colonies, to be sure, such as Massachusetts and Pennsylvania, property qualifications were low enough and land ownership common enough to insure a substantial electorate, more or less representative of the whole adult population. But even in the North, as in New York and Connecticut, for example, many could not meet the property qualifications; in the South, the requirements usually were higher than in the North, and eligible voters relatively fewer. Certain colonies also had religious qualifications for voting, but with the exception of the almost universal disfranchisement of Catholics and Jews, these qualifications tended to be questioned less and less frequently where property qualifications could be met. So-called plural voting also was common. In Virginia and elsewhere, those who met the specific property qualification in each of two or more counties could vote two or more times; to make it easier for the gentry to exercise this privilege where they held land, election dates often were staggered. Property qualifications for office-holding, in turn, were usually much higher than for the franchise itself. A member of the South Carolina assembly, for example, had to own at least 500 acres of land, 10 slaves, or other property worth at least £1000.

The second objective condition tending to perpetuate oligarchic control was the underrepresentation of new inland settlements in the asemblies. The assemblies themselves often refused to establish new counties and towns in distant regions and to reapportion seats in the legislature in accord with changing population density. Inland regions sometimes were happy to be left without responsibility for paying for county or town government or for representation in the assembly and often did not complain of neglect until crises involving Indians or taxation aroused them. In South Carolina throughout the colonial period the inland settlements had no representatives whatever, and no local courts; and the planters in Charleston heard about this often enough.

These objective characteristics of colonial politics may have made it more difficult to overthrow the oligarchs in times of stress; but their rule tended to be sustained by the even stronger sanctions arising from the popular recognition of merit based on family and fortune. Locke's conception of property, on which the defense of oligarchic pretensions rested, went beyond the crassness of mere ownership, exploitation, and accumulation. Property was the foundation of moral independence, morality the foundation of welfare. Property carried obligation as well as power; great property incurred the obligation of great power employed for the common good.

Colonial history is well marked with local rebellions against the ruling oligarchs. One of the most persistent issues between them on the one hand, and businessmen on the make and the general population on the other, was the supply of money. The primary need for currency among the small farmers who made up by far the majority of the white population everywhere was for taxes, which in their judgement, and usually they were right, were both too high and unfairly apportioned. At the same time, many such farmers along with enterprising business and professional men, noting the expansive tendency of the entire colonial economy, became increasingly engaged in trade, and also in land speculation to a degree commensurate with their aspirations if not their means. Since money, or at any rate credit in the form of liberal issues of negotiable currency, was the food of trade and the drink of speculation, such men naturally sought a plentiful supply of it, far above the quantity needed to meet mere tax obligations and other current debts. The normal scarcity of specie in the colonies was aggravated by the mercantilist system which drained gold and silver to the mother country. Thus it became the common practice for those seeking financial assistance to demand more and more paper money. Often enough their demands were heeded. But since paper money had a tendency to be overissued and thus to decline in value, easy-money policies usually were reversed at what appeared to be the most inconvenient times. At such times, taxes, interest, rent, and loans would go unpaid, and creditors trying to collect what was due them might be tarred and feathered and chased from the debtors' vicinity at gun point.

A classic battle over the currency supply occurred in Massachusetts in 1740 and 1741, when many enterprising colonists sought to establish a land bank to lend money in the form of "bills of credit," or paper notes, on the security of land mortgages. Two far-reaching changes in the colony's affairs had greatly improved the chances for such a bank after an agitation of nearly 20 years. One was the realization that the Indian menace on the frontiers had receded to such an extent that western lands could now be sold freely to speculators in large tracts without the requirement that they be settled immediately as a protective measure. The second was the decision of the government in London in 1739 to require that the £30,000 in paper money that the colony had long been permitted to issue each year for government expenses, without strict time periods for the redemption of such money, must now be called in promptly every two years. Heretofore, the colony had allowed its issues to accumulate, so that more than £250,000 in such currency actively circulated.

A calling in of most of this money and the strict limitations imposed on future issues foreshadowed a financial calamity. At the same time, the London order did not forbid *private* issues of paper money, so that the veteran proponents of the land-bank idea saw the loophole through which to jump. The growth in land speculation allowed them to anticipate both an active demand for their issues and a broad base in land mortgages to insure the acceptance of their currency by creditors of all kinds. Their own opportunity, unfortunately for them, also alerted their opponents among the richest Boston merchants and creditors in the Governor's circle. These men had a constitutional loathing for paper money, especially if unsecured by specie or by their own high character. To meet the financial emergency and undermine the land bank at the same time, they immediately set up a silver bank. Its notes were to be redeemable only in specie, but specie being in such short supply, it was not to be paid out before 15 years had passed, during which the business probity of the oligarchs was to be considered sufficient security.

The advocates of each plan sought government approval; and while the land bank gained much support in the assembly elected in May 1740, Governor Jonathan Belcher and his council backed the silver scheme. While the deadlock held, both banks began to issue notes without official sanction, a step which led the Governor and council to threaten the land-bank directors with the direct penalties. Within six months their campaign of abuse had wholly discredited land-bank paper. Early the next year, on their application, Parliament voted to prohibit land banks in Massachusetts. Even-handedly, the London authorities extended the prohibition to the silver bank as well, a move Boston's leaders could bear with resignation since their principal goal in establishing the silver bank had been the destruction of the land bank, a goal now fully gained. Their success, however, led to such widespread discontent that their friend Belcher was recalled before the year 1741 ended. The destruction of the Massachusetts land bank, John Adams observed a generation later, "raised a greater ferment in the province than the stamp-act did" in 1765.

In 1751, owing largely to the depreciation of paper currency in Rhode Island, Parliament passed the first Currency Act. New land banks were prohibited in New England, old issues of currency were to be called in at the date of their retirement, and new issues had to be guaranteed by taxes and retired after a limited period. These regulations widened the split between Parliament and rural New Eng-

landers, whose violent response a few years later bore out Franklin's warning to London in 1764: "I wish some good Angel would forever whisper in the Ears of your great Men that Dominion is founded in Opinion."

Conflicts over the money supply, taxation, and debt were not necessarily sectional ones, although they became most acute where the "back parts" felt the weight of tidewater and town leaders. Other political conflicts were specifically sectional in origin. One of the most persistent of them arose over the complaints of new settlers on the moving frontier against the failure of the provincial governments to protect them from the Indians, the French, and the Spanish. The failure of the provincial governments to provide passable roads to markets was a second source of sectional conflict. A third was the failure of such governments to set up courts in the back country and thus save the farmers the heavy cost of several days' travel and neglect of crops to have even minor controversies settled. A fourth was the collection of tithes for the established churches, which had few ministers and few communicants in the wilderness. The failure to extend representation and the suffrage to back-country residents grew into a major issue largely because of the gentry's reluctance to correct the back country's other grievances.

Yet the colonial rank and file rarely challenged patrician claims to political place and power. Probably a fourth of the white population of the colonies was illiterate; probably a fifth of those who could read and write knew little or no English. Many others used it awkwardly. Most rustics, moreover, illiterate or not, could think of no more unnerving experience than having to address constituents in public meetings or to take effective places in legislative bodies. City artisans, shopkeepers, and laborers no doubt shared the misgivings of their country cousins. By and large, the common run of voters were still proud to be represented by the great men of their neighborhood or of the colony as a whole. Thus they returned to office generation after generation of Byrds, Carters, Harrisons, and Washingtons in Virginia; of Van Rensselaers, Schuylers, and Livingstons in New York; of Logans, Norrises, Pembertons, and Dickinsons in Pennsylvania. Even in Masschusetts, where the suffrage qualifications were light and educational levels and literacy higher than elsewhere in America, Hutchinsons, Hancocks, Olivers, Bowdoins, and Brattles all were repeatedly returned to rule. A popular political genius like Sam Adams in Massachusetts, the first great rabble-rouser in the colonies, developed a "machine" of his own, known at the outset of the Revolution as the "Caucus Club." But even an Adams made little progress against the oligarchs until they wanted his support to meet the British challenge.

# READINGS

M.L. Hansen, *The Atlantic Migration 1607–1860* (1940), is the standard account of the movement of Europeans to America before the Civil War. Carl Wittke, *We Who Built America: The Saga of the Immigrant* (1967), is fuller on the major colonial immigrant groups. A.E. Smith, *Colonists in Bondage* (1947), is authoritative on white-servant immigration. Much useful material on this subject will also be found in M.W. Jernegan, *Laboring and Dependent Classes in Colonial America 1607–1783* (1931). Dietmar Rothermund, *The Layman's Progress, Religious and Political Experience in Colonial Pennsylvania 1740–1770* (1961), offers a penetrating analysis of the religious sects and their role in society. E.T. Clark, *The Small Sects in America* (1949), is informative on their background and history, Rufus Jones, *The Quakers in the American Colonies* (1911), a standard study, may be supplemented by S.V. James, *A People Among Peoples, Quaker Benevolence in Eighteenth-Century America* (1963).

On the major national groups the following older works, although sometimes apologetic in tone, remain invaluable: A.B. Faust, *The German Element in the United States* (2 vols., 1909); F.R. Diffenderffer, *The German Immigration into Pennsylvania through the Port of Philadelphia 1700–1775,* bound with his *The Redemptioners* (1900); and H.J. Ford, *The Scotch-Irish in America* (1915). R.J. Dickson, *Ulster Emigration to Colonial America 1718–1775* (1966), is especially valuable for conditions in North Ireland. I.C.C. Graham, *Colonists from Scotland, Emigration to North America 1707–1783* (1956), is good on that group. F.J. Turner, "The Old West," in *The Frontier in American History* (1920), is the classic short account of the penetration of the interior.

J. H. Franklin, *From Slavery to Freedom, a History of Negro Americans* (1967), the standard work with an up-to-date bibliography, covers the colonial period in detail. August Meier and E.M. Rudwick, *From Plantation to Ghetto* (1966), is an authoritative short history. Elizabeth Donnan, ed., *Documents Illustrative of the History of the Slave Trade to America* (4 vols., 1930–1935), is the prime source. W.E.B. DuBois, *The Suppression of the African Slave-Trade to the United States of America* (1896), is valuable for many aspects of the "institution" in colonial times as well as for the slave traffic. Basil Davidson, *Black Mother, the Years of the African Slave Trade* (1961), is an able modern account. Herbert Aptheker, *American Negro Slave Revolts* (1943), tells much about Negro life in general. D.B. Davis, *The Problem of Slavery in Western Culture* (1966), and W.D. Jordan,

*White Over Black, American Attitudes toward the Negro 1550–1812* (1968), together have significantly raised the level of the study of Negro history.

J.T. Adams, *Provincial Society 1690–1763* (1927), is a substantial general account. See also the books by T.J. Wertenbaker cited for Chapter Two under the general title, *The Founding of American Civilization*. Carl Bridenbaugh, *Myths and Realities: Societies of the Colonial South* (1952), is short, iconoclastic, and stimulating. Chesapeake society is well described in D.S. Freeman, *The Young Washington* (2 vols., 1948), the opening volumes of his multivolume biography. On Charleston and its leadership, see M.E. Sirmans, *Colonial South Carolina, a Political History 1663–1763* (1966). Volume I of L.C. Gray, *History of Agriculture in the Southern United States to 1860* (2 vols., 1933), offers a wide-ranging analysis. V.W. Crane, *The Southern Frontier 1670–1732* (1929), is excellent on life in the interior. F.H. Hart, *The Valley of Virginia in the American Revolution 1763–1789* (1942), tells much about the backcountry of the Old Dominion. *The Carolina Backcountry on the Eve of the Revolution, by Charles Woodmason,* edited by R.J. Hooker (1933), is a revealing contemporary account. A.W. Lauber, *Indian Slavery in Colonial Times* (1913), is a good study of a neglected subject.

In addition to the works on the immigrants cited above, the following are particularly valuable on eighteenth-century Pennsylvania: Carl and Jessica Bridenbaugh, *Rebels and Gentlemen: Philadelphia in the Age of Franklin* (1942); F.B. Tolles, *Meeting House and Counting House, The Quaker Merchants of Colonial Philadelphia* (1948); and the opening chapters of S.B. Warner, Jr., *The Private City, Philadelphia in Three Periods of its Growth* (1968). Urban life here and elsewhere in the colonial period is authoritatively dealt with by Carl Bridenbaugh in *Cities in the Wilderness . . . 1625–1742* (1938) and *Cities in Revolt . . . 1743–1776* (1955). Bridenbaugh, ed., *Gentleman's Progress* (1948), is the account, by Dr. Alexander Hamilton, of his trip from Maryland to New England in 1744.

New England society is adequately if not impartially covered in J.T. Adams, *Revolutionary New England 1691–1776* (1923). Correctives for Adam's anti-Puritan bias will be found in S.E. Morison, *Intellectual Life of Colonial New England* (1956); K.B. Murdock, *Increase Mather, the Foremost American Puritan* (1925); and Perry Miller, *The New England Mind: From Colony to Province* (1953). C.K. Shipton, *New England Life in the 18th Century* (1963), affords a vivid panorama of elite activities. W.B. Weeden, *Economic and Social History of New England 1620–1789* (2 vols., 1890), remains the best survey. It may be supplemented for the later colonial period by J.B. Hedges, *The Browns of Providence Plantations, Colonial Years* (1952), and W.T. Baxter, *The House of Hancock, Business in Boston 1724–1775* (1945). More specialized studies include Bernard and Lotte Bailyn, *Massachusetts Shipping 1697–1714* (1959), and G.A. Billias, *The Massachusetts Land Bankers of 1740* (1959). Information on the New England backcountry can be found in L.K. Mathews, *The Expansion of New England* (1909), and the early chapters of L.N. Newcomer, *The Embattled Farmers: A Massachusetts Countryside in the American Revolution* (1953).

Leonard Labaree, *Royal Government in America, a Study of the British Colonial System before 1783* (1930), is a comprehensive survey of administration and legislation. T.C. Barrow, *Trade and Empire: The British Customs Service in Colonial America 1660–1775* (1967), emphasizes the central role of commerce in colonial–mother-country relations. Sectional works of importance for imperial politics include J.P. Greene, *The Quest for Power, the Lower Houses of the Assembly in the Southern Royal Colonies 1689–1776*

(1963), and J.A. Schutz, *William Shirley, King's Governor of Massachusetts* (1961). The colonial franchise and representation have been thoroughly restudied in such works as R.E. Brown, *Middle-Class Democracy and the Revolution in Massachusetts 1691–1780* (1955); Theodore Thayer, *Pennsylvania Politics and the Growth of Democracy 1740–1776* (1953); and R.P. McCormick, *The History of Voting in New Jersey* (1953). Their general conclusions about the liberality of the franchise are challenged in such works as C.S. Grant, *Democracy in the Connecticut Frontier Town of Kent* (1961), and C.S. Sydnor, *Gentlemen Freeholders, Political Practices in Washington's Virginia* (1952). The early chapters of Chilton Williamson, *American Suffrage, from Property to Democracy 1760–1860* (1960), afford a scholarly survey of colonial practice.

*The William and Mary Quarterly, a Magazine of Early American History,* is invaluable for current scholarship on, and contemporary documents of, the colonial period.

# FOUR

The epithets "colonial" and "provincial" carry a connotation of narrowness, rusticity, isolation from the main stream of thought and action in the world. And it is true that in many parts of eighteenth-century America whatever intellectual baggage the early settlers had brought over had become obsolete and threadbare—if, indeed, it had not been altogether cast off in the wilderness. Few people could find time for philosophy or even for contemplation; when work was set aside for the day, the old forms of religion continued to serve most of those who had not entirely abandoned activites of the mind and nourishment of the spirit.

Yet the "New World" was in fact new; and even in the realm of traditional religious observance important changes were apparent. By the beginning of the eighteenth century the traditional churches, the Anglicans, Presbyterians, and New England Congregationalists, were losing ground in a number of ways. In one quarter, the once-hot fires of sectarian commitment seemed to have been banked. With the passing of the generations, the comfortable, often wealthy members of seaboard congregations, as we have seen (p. 111), relaxed the severity of their religious views and chose preachers who made smaller emotional demands upon them, preachers who themselves often were broadened intellectually by new currents of thought. Some of the more advanced divines, like their advanced parishioners, even flirted with the "religion of reason," and this tendency grew stronger as the century wore on.

In another quarter, traditional churches were afflicted by a quite different kind of loss. Preachers who had surrendered the old orthodoxies and yet had no stomach for the new

# THE MATURE
# COLONIAL MIND

modes of thought became simply cold and ineffectual and left their congregations dissatisfied. Members of such congregations gradually turned to the revivalist preachers of the Great Awakening of the 1730s and 1740s who aroused waves of religious "enthusiasm," as it was called (see p. 125). Their passion often split established congregations and denominations into irreconcilable camps, so much so that by the end of the colonial period America embraced an extraordinarily wide range of religious views, running from austere rationalism to obscure pietism.

Although Europeans, and Englishmen in particular, continued to scorn the "colonials" as bumpkins and barbarians, certain leaders of thought had begun to give a distinctive American cast to secular as well as religious ideas. Benjamin Franklin, for example, honored and respected in the great world of learning, could have sprouted nowhere but in the mainland colonies. By the eighteenth century American prosperity permitted a cultivated minority, at least, to engage in nonutilitarian pursuits and to keep up with the latest intellectual developments on the Continent. This minority created a staunch little world of its own where American savants could talk and speculate and experiment. The Enlightenment became the intellectual hallmark of the eighteenth cen-

tury; and Americans not only shared in the new universe it opened to the mind, but actually broadened its perspectives and its scope. The idea of political independence itself most probably would have gone unthought of had not intellectual independence and maturity preceded it.

## 1   The Religious Mind

### PURITANS UNDER STRESS

The sapping of orthodoxy in religion was particularly striking in New England, where the demands of the old divines had been most rigorous and had contrasted most markedly with the growing wealth and cosmopolitanism of the townspeople. The social changes also affected many of the clergy, costing the church its former internal solidarity and outward high prestige.

Puritan orthodoxy suffered its first serious blow in the "Half-Way Covenant" of 1662 (see p. 63), which permitted church members who had no religious experiences to confess in public to remain in the church and to have their children baptized. A series of dramatic setbacks followed this first one. Under the

124

short administration of Governor Andros (1686–89), the legal foundations of Puritanism were undermined in the Bay Colony and Anglicanism was introduced. The revised Massachusetts charter of 1691 then substituted property for religious tests as a qualification for voting. The excesses of the Salem witchcraft hysteria that followed in 1692 further weakened ministerial authority.

This episode began when two Salem girls accused certain townspeople of bewitching them. Soon a perfect epidemic of witch-hunting infected the community, claiming 20 lives by execution after trials under leading ministers and magistrates. A hundred others were jailed and stood awaiting their fate until the judges, finding some of the most eminent and respected citizens among those charged with being the Devil's emissaries, at last came to their senses. Both Increase and Cotton Mather had inadvertently encouraged the outbreak by publishing books proving the existence of witches—this at a time when William Penn dismissed a case against a woman charged with riding on a broomstick by saying "that there was no law in Pennsylvania against riding on broomsticks." During the trials, the Mathers had cautioned the court not to accept as evidence the reports of persons allegedly afflicted by witchcraft. Since neither the Mathers nor the other ministers actively opposed the trials, however, they were subsequently blamed for the abuses, and their reputations suffered.

### JONATHAN EDWARDS: YANKEE REVIVALIST

The theological luminary of the next generation in New England was the great revivalist, Jonathan Edwards (1703–1758). A devoted Congregationalist, Edwards was nevertheless strongly attracted to new modes of religious contemplation. In his concern for truths that lay beyond concrete experience, in his rapturous and at the same time astute analysis of religious feeling, evil, and grace, Edwards demonstrated a characteristically American spirit as diverse and contradictory

as the country itself: visionary and down-to-earth, deeply radical and solidly conservative, coldly prudent and unexpectedly wild.

Edwards, in 1729, succeeded his grandfather, the eminent Solomon Stoddard, in the Northampton, Massachusetts, pastorate where he served for 21 year before his congregation dismissed him. The significance—and the tragedy—of Edwards' career was his unsuccessful attempt to restore the sense of God's omnipotence to a people for whom religion had become a conventional routine. Because his own religious experience was so intense, he sought to awaken in his congregation a similar emotion. Ever since his student days at Yale, Edwards had been a reader of Newton and John Locke; the science and philosophy of the Enlightenment interested him enormously. But his mystical and poetic disposition prevented him from becoming a rationalist like Charles Chauncy of Boston, Edwards's chief theological opponent. Locke taught Edwards that men's hearts could be touched only by making the abstract come alive. A later generation was to abuse him for his apparent pleasure in threatening his listeners with hellfire. Actually, most of his sermons dealt with God's mercy, but by occasionally playing on the nerves of his auditors, by reducing hell to something vividly physical, he awakened slumbering hearts. His horrendous picture of evil sprang from a dazzling vision of its opposite; evil was the antithesis of that perfect harmony and virtue and Being, which is God.

Between 1733 and 1735, under the influence of Edwards's teachings, Northampton underwent an intense religious revival. Edwards attacked the widely held doctrine that salvation depended on "moral sincerity" and good works, that every man possessed the power to save himself. In place of the humanized Deity, genial and benevolent, who made salvation easy for reputable citizens (the God of his grandfather, Stoddard), he resurrected the omnipotent and splendid God of Calvin. His revival efforts in the mid-1730s won him as many as 30 conversions a week; but they also further divided his congregation and forced some of the members to abandon it in favor of the more lenient Anglican system. Edwards's unswerving devotion to the revived Calvinism eventually led to his dismissal in 1750. By then, in New England and elsewhere in America, revivalism had gained many more converts, thanks to the frequent visits of the electrifying English evangelist George Whitefield, one of the precursors of American Methodism. But revivalism, as preached by Whitefield's cruder imitators, had also gained numerous enemies and sharpened sectarian divisions in Protestantism.

### THE GREAT AWAKENING

In the early decades of the eighteenth century, religion had fallen even further in esteem outside of New England than in it. Many back-country settlers, particularly in the South, rarely saw a minister. In some frontier areas, no provision at all had been made for religious instruction and guidance. Whitefield's tours soon brought widespread changes in religious practices and indeed in other areas of American life.

The Great Awakening was actually part of a world-wide evangelical movement that had put down its roots in Germany and England. Its leading native spirits in the colonies, in addition to Jonathan Edwards, were Theodore Frelinghuysen, a Dutch-Reformed minister living in New Jersey, and William Tennent and his sons, Pennsylvania Presbyterians. The full force of the Great Awakening in America began to be felt during Whitefield's first tour, 1739–41, when he and some 17 assistants who came with him harangued enormous crowds everywhere from Georgia to Massachusetts. Many of his listeners traveled miles to hear him, his theatrical performances appealing to the emotions of his audience. Although Whitefield did not mix politics with religion, some of his enthusiastic co-workers offended the conservatives by their extravagant behavior and upset the social order by rejecting all forms and creeds. Too often they took weeping and screaming and bodily gyrations as

evidence of the entrance of the spirit of God.

Enemies of the revival were shocked by ministers grotesquely enacting the sufferings of Christ on the pulpit. Revivalist preachers who passed from place to place censuring the local clergy for their lack of piety were themselves most severely censured. In his *Seasonable Thoughts on the State of Religion in New England* (1743), Charles Chauncy referred to these itinerant preachers as "Men who, though they have *no Learning,* and but *small Capacities,* yet imagine they are able, and without Study too, to speak to the *spiritual Profit* of such as are willing to hear them." Chauncy especially deplored the contention that the sudden awareness of sin with all the motions that accompanied it—"bitter *Shriekings* and *Screaming; Convulsion-like*

125

*Jonathan Edwards, the outstanding preacher of the Great Awakening in New England. Detail of an engraving after a painting by Charles Willson Peale. (Courtesy of the New-York Historical Society, New York City.)*

126

*Tremblings* and *Agitations, Struggling* and *Tumblings*"—signified conversion.

Between arch-conservatives like Chauncy and uncompromising revival enthusiasts like Tennent, stood a third group—moderates typified by Edwards and Benjamin Colman in Boston. Unwilling to condone the excesses of the Great Awakening, they nevertheless welcomed it, at least in the beginning, as a mighty manifestation of God's spirit moving over the land. Many others, recognizing the isolation and spiritual starvation of frontier life in particular, shared their view. It is easy to harp on the extravagances of the Great Awakening, the foamings and frothings and trances, but it cannot be dismissed as a mere emotional orgy. Its consequences, moreover, appear to have been far-reaching.

*Religious consequences.* The Great Awakening split the old denominations into two main groups, one espousing the traditional conservative doctrines or forms, the other adopting the "New Divinity." The latter was a religion of personal experience as against a religion of custom or habit. The "New Light" or "New Side" wing, as the revivalists were called, demanded a universal priesthood of believers, a kind of spiritual democracy. The great revival increased the membership of the small dissenting sects at the expense of the established denominations. Presbyterians and Baptists, for example, made impressive gains, and in the back country a new group, later to be known as the Methodists, gathered strength. Large numbers of the unchurched were converted. In New England alone, some 40,000 to 50,000 joined churches. Although a distaste for "enthusiasm" drove many of the antirevivalists into the Anglican fold, the establishment was shaken.

*Political consequences.* Some historians believe that the weakening of the established Anglican Church helped to loosen British authority in the colonies, particularly in Virginia where the Baptists and Methodists led the fight against the Anglicans. Elsewhere, too, it has been argued, the Great Awakening served as a leveling movement, preparing the

way for the separation of church and state. It required no great stretch of the imagination to extend the liberties of conscience to economic and political liberties.

*Social consequences.* The huge crowds that came to hear Whitefield and the other preachers yearned for social contact. In the vast outdoor meetings that were to become a common feature of subsequent revivals, they found release for social and spiritual emotions long repressed. Despite the excesses accompanying the Great Awakening and the backsliding that followed, morals and manners improved as a result of it. Despite its initial emphasis on miraculous conversions, among the Baptists, the Methodists, and the Presbyterians, as

*The English evangelist George Whitefield with a spellbound congregation. (National Portrait Gallery, London.)*

among the Anglicans themselves, righteous conduct became the test of grace.

Although many of the revivalists were suspicious of an educated clergy who (in James Davenport's words) were "leading their People blindfold to Hell," the Great Awakening spawned a number of educational institutions. William Tennent's famous "Log College" at Neshaminy, Pennsylvania, founded in 1736, fathered similar schools for the preparation of Presbyterian ministers. The Baptists lagged behind the Presbyterians, but they established their own schools—Hopewell Academy, and later the College of Rhode Island (Brown) in 1764. Princeton (Presbyterian), Rutgers (Dutch-Reformed), and Dartmouth (Congregational) were all founded under the impetus of the revival movement. The new colleges hardly represented the spirit of the Enlightenment, for their main purpose was to prepare ministers in an atmosphere uncontaminated by the doctrines of rival denominations or by secular infidelities. In time, however, the narrow sectarian objectives of these new colleges were less emphasized and some grew into great universities.

The Great Awakening, furthermore, quickened the humanitarian spirit of the eighteenth century by forcing men to pay attention to their social as well as their spiritual condition. When Jonathan Edwards defined virtue as "love of Being in general," he was suggesting that there was a divine element in everyone that ought to be recognized out of love for God. Orphans, paupers, Indians, and Negroes shared in this being and became the objects of Christian concern.

For the Negro, in particular, the Great Awakening was to have momentous consequences. In the heat of religious emotions, racial exclusiveness softened. Blacks as well as whites offered testimony of religious conversion, both in segregated and unsegregated gatherings, and some Negroes became well known for their powers of exhortation. The revivalists did not try to invalidate slavery as an institution, but in preaching that every man, no matter what his color, was (as White-field reminded the planters) "conceived and born in sin," the spiritual equality of the Negro could no longer be denied. That point assured, the antislavery men could now move on to the radical correlative: the sinfulness of enslaving a fellow-being endowed with an immortal soul.

It was no accident that leading antislavery advocates among the revivalists were Quakers, for holding men in bondage seemed grievously at odds with their equalitarian and humane convictions. Well-known Quakers like John Woolman and, later, Anthony Benezet, exposed the horrors of the Middle Passage, the slave-ship voyage, and sought to correct the popular notion that Negroes were unteachable barbarians. Each spoke out eloquently on behalf of the despised blacks and eventually persuaded other Quakers to join their quiet crusade.

Woolman, a mild but determined humanitarian, began his opposition to slavery in 1743 and from then until his death never ceased to admonish his coreligionists in New Jersey, Maryland, and Virginia on the sin of human exploitation. Not only did he tabulate the crippling effects of slavery on men who were reckoned as animals and deprived of physical and mental nurture; he also warned against the spiritual debasement of the white overlords:

Placing on men the ignominious Title, SLAVE, dressing them in uncomely Garments, keeping them to servile Labour, in which they are often dirty, tends gradually to fix a notion in the Mind, that they are a sort of people below us in Nature, and leads us to consider them as such in all our Conclusions about them.

"To labor hard," he wrote again in his homely way, "or cause others to do so, that we may live conformably to customs which our redeemer discountenanced by his example, and which are contrary to divine order, is to manure a soil for propagating an evil seed on earth." Woolman never resorted to harsh abuse, but his journal, as the Quaker poet and abolitionist John Greenleaf Whittier said later, was a life-long testimony against wrong, and one of the finest expressions of eighteenth-century benevolence.

## THE CHURCHES

At the end of the colonial period, there was approximately one church for every 900 people. Despite the Great Awakening, the majority of the colonial population had no church affiliation. Established churches (those that were officially supported by the state) existed in some colonies—Anglican in the South and Congregational in New England. But almost from the beginning many colonies had been battlegrounds for competing sects. When Quakers, Anglicans, Presbyterians, Dutch-Reformed, Catholics, and Jews lived in the same province, as they did in Pennsylvania, an established church became inadvisable if not impossible. The dissenting spirit of Protestantism did not fade away in America. Rather, it took on a new energy as denominations splintered and new sects sprang up. The very multiplicity of religions insured a practical tolerance and the acceptance of what finally came to be the American principle of the separation of church and state.

Despite the variety of sects and the ethnic and geographical divisions among the denominations, the following generalizations about colonial religion in the 1750s seem valid:

*First,* colonial religion was overwhelmingly Protestant. Although the colonies provided a refuge for the persecuted of all the Old-World religions, only about 25,000 Catholics and 2000 Jews were living in America on the eve of the Revolution. The colonists were in a real sense the children of the Reformation, differing markedly among themselves in creed and doctrine yet joined in common opposition to Rome. Catholics were not physically molested in eighteenth-century America, but they were the victims of anti-Catholic propaganda spread by Protestant ministers, educators, editors, and publishers of the popular almanacs. England's wars with Catholic France partly

explain this anti-Catholic feeling, but the hostility went far deeper. Particularly in New England, but elsewhere as well, the inhabitants passed on their inherited prejudices against Catholic practices.

*Second,* the doctrine and organization of American churches reflected the social background of the members. The most powerful and influential denominations in the New World were the New England Congregationalists, the Presbyterians, and the Anglicans. These Churches numbered among their adherents many plain folk, in addition to most of the established mercantile and landed middle-class families; but a higher proportion of persons of modest means was found in the Baptist churches, among the Methodists who emerged in the late 1760s, and in various small sects. By making frankly evangelical appeals, they reached elements in the colonial population that had hitherto been neglected by the older churches. Poor and despised at the beginning, their frugality, perserverance, and industry—the practical morality characteristic of the sects—brought them prosperity in turn, and with prosperity came acceptance and respectability. This cycle was repeated again and again throughout American religious history.

*Third,* the churches of the non-English-speaking settlers in eighteenth-century America, where such churches survived the strains of frontier life, had little influence on the main currents of colonial religion, but they served as vital social organizations. It took some time for European immigrants to accommodate themselves to American ways. Speaking a variety of tongues and forming ethnic centers of their own, these settlers often looked to their respective churches for guidance. The ministers delivered their sermons in the language of their congregations and sought to keep alive the Old-World traditions as a kind of social cement, an endeavor in which they often failed. The German immigrant churches survived best, and thus by the middle of the eighteenth century were most strongly confronted with the question that ultimately faced all foreign-language groups: Should English be substituted for their native tongue? Only by insisting on racial and cultural distinctiveness could the religious leaders prevent their compatriots from being absorbed by the aggressive American sects. Having lost the official sanction that some of these churches had enjoyed in their European homeland they had to become more sectarian in order to survive, unfortunately a self-defeating recourse.

*Fourth,* the tendency throughout the eighteenth century was toward greater religious freedom. To the sectarian-minded worshipper of the seventeenth century, tolerance, or "polypiety," was the greatest impiety, but no state-enforced religion could survive where dissenters continued to dissent and where men of diverse backgrounds and religions soon lived side by side. Even in orthodox New England the persecution of Quakers and Baptists had ceased by 1700, and a robust minister like John Wise of Ipswich could almost single-handedly foil the attempt of an organized clique of ministers to centralize church government and destroy the autonomy of the independent congregation. In defending the congregational principle and church democracy (in *The Churches' Quarrel Espoused,* 1710, and *The Vindication of the Government of the New England Churches,* 1717), Wise introduced arguments that were later adopted by the Revolutionary patriots in defense of political democracy. All men are born free, he said, and "Democracy is Christ's government in Church and State."

With the breakdown of Puritan control in New England after 1691, all the dissenting Protestant sects could ally themselves against the Anglican Church, which was regarded by many colonists as the tool of the British absolutism. In 1763, the possibility that an Anglican bishop might be appointed for New England aroused as much heat as the Stamp Act was to generate two years later. Dissenters everywhere saw in the proposition to establish a resident bishop in America a horrible threat to liberty: "We should soon be obliged," read

one manifesto, "to bid farewell to that religious Liberty, in which CHRIST hath set us free." Even southern Anglicans agreed with northern dissenters in opposing the appointment of an American bishop.

By 1776, the atmosphere in the colonies made wide religious toleration inevitable. Colonial proprietors found that toleration was good for business, for it attracted foreign settlers. The experience of colonies like Rhode Island and Pennsylvania, which had prospered without an established church, and the opposition of the unchurched and dissenters also contributed to religious liberty.

### BETWEEN FAITH AND REASON

As eighteenth-century Americans tended to become humanitarian, secular, and liberal, turning their attention away from God in Heaven toward man on earth, their God also grew more tractable, less demanding, more involved with the happiness of His Children. The domestication of Calvin's God did not occur suddenly, but by 1755 John Adams could speak of "the frigid John Calvin," and turn elsewhere for peace of mind.

The drift toward liberalism was expressed in many ways, even in graveyards. The early Puritans marked their headstones with the skull and crossbones, grim symbols of an austere faith. By the eighteenth century, the headstone skulls had begun to sprout wings, (emblems of resurrection), and before the century was over cherubs and finally the urn and the cypress (secular symbols of pagan origin) had displaced skulls altogether.

The new way of looking at the world comes through strongly in the lives of three men on the eve of the Enlightenment.

Samuel Sewall (1652–1730), Boston-born and bred, bore the stamp of his Puritan forebears, yet shared fully in the new secular attitude. As one of the "Stewards" of his province, a conservative man of affairs and a bulwark of the church, he necessarily spoke in the accents of piety. His wonderful *Diary,* a record of his activities between 1674 and 1677 and from 1685 to 1729, is full of reports of sermons, funerals, weddings, of visits to graveyards ("an awful yet pleasing treat"), and humorlessly amusing accounts of his courtships. But hard as Sewall tried to present himself as a pious and other-worldly man ("The Lord add or take away from this our corporeal weight," he heavily comments on his durable 193 pounds, "so as shall be most advantageous for our spiritual growth"), we are always aware of him as the curious busybody, the humanitarian who opposed the selling of blacks, the chronicler of succulent dinners. His religious sense and training told him that life on earth was transient; every accident, from losing a tooth to breaking a glass, became for him a lesson of mortality. Yet Sewall, involved in a world of tangible

*Samuel Sewall, c. 1730 by Nathaniel Emmons. (Massachusetts Historical Society.)*

delights, made much the best of his earthly passage. This side of him emerges in the diary entry: "Six swallows together flying and chippering very rapturously."

Sewall typified Boston's merchant class in the age of transition. William Byrd II (1674–1744) represented the Virginia planter aristocracy of the same period. Byrd grew up in a society preoccupied with hunting and horse-racing, politics, military pursuits, and social affairs. Yet such gentry were by no means irreligious or free-thinking. One of the great Virginia planters, Robert Carter, constantly turned to religious themes in his letters and strove for what he called "Practical godliness." Byrd himself, educated in London and displaying the manners and sometimes the looseness of Restoration courtiers, had his serious side. His graphic and candid diary shows him to have been a scholar who, besides reading Hebrew every morning, read several pages of the Greek version of Josephus, and perhaps a bit of Bishop Tillotson, the liberal English Anglican churchman. His library of 3600 volumes was equaled in North America only by Cotton Mather's. Like Sewall, Byrd despised the slave trade, and his religious credo, rational and benevolent, evokes the spirit of the new secularism:

I believe that God made man . . . and inspired him with a reasonable soul to distinguish between good and evil; that the law of nature taught him to follow the good and avoid the evil because the good tends manifestly to his happiness and preservation, but the evil to his misery and destruction.

Cotton Mather (1663–1728), grandson of Richard Mather, one of the original Massachusetts "Saints," a "very hard student" and inflexible Puritan, reflected the transition from faith to reason in a more interesting way than his contemporaries, Sewall or Byrd. His father, Increase Mather, "swam quietly in a stream of impiety and carnal security for many years together," as he phrased it, until he was converted in 1654. Cotton Mather

*Cotton Mather by Peter Pelham. Done in 1728, this is the first mezzotint engraving known to have been made in this country. (Prints Division, New York Public Library.)*

reflected his father's improvement. "I began to pray, even when I began to speak," he wrote of himself. At the same time he began to study. An understanding of Nature, he found, was the best antidote to atheism, and his religious zeal in no way interfered with his lively interest in medicine, agriculture, and other rational means of human betterment. In fact, his curiosity about every aspect of the natural world, his loving attention to the humblest practical problem—which drew from him the characteristic observation, "The very wheelbarrow is to be with respect looked upon"—sprang directly from his Christian piety. Implicit in Puritanism was the conviction that scriptural truths might be discerned by "right reason," and although God might set aside natural laws when He chose to do so, He created a rational universe whose order any

rational man might detect. Peter Ramus, a French Protestant scientist much in vogue among New England thinkers, sanctioned this view, and Cotton Mather (without abandoning his faith in God's miraculous ways nor his belief in the threat of the Devil's) saw God's hand in the visible order of the universe.

It may seem a far cry from the kind of rationalism espoused by Puritan thinkers like the Mathers to the rationalism of the later Deists. And yet both believed that the Almighty had given them a thoroughly rational physical universe and the rational faculties with which to understand it. Puritans might use these faculties more for the glory of God, Deists more for their own pleasure.

Deism offered a mechanical universe run by a Heavenly Engineer who had no need to resort to miracles to demonstrate His glory. Deists dismissed the Trinity, the divinity of Christ, and the Biblical account of the creation of man as superstitions. The moral truths of Christianity, they said, were the heart of it, and were better defended by science than by revelation. They emphasized the ethics of Jesus and his way of life on earth, not his ascension. The Deists were not atheists (although they were so labeled by their enemies); but neither were they mystics. As rational men, the truest was for them the clearest, and the most logical. A philosophy of life rather than a religion, Deism reflected the emerging secular view of the world and also promoted it.

## II  *The Secular Mind*

### THE ENLIGHTENMENT

When Nicholas Copernicus, a Polish-born mathematician and astronomer, published his *Concerning the Revolution of Heavenly Bodies* in 1543, he dismissed the traditional conception of the universe, which pictured the earth at the center with the planets revolving around it, and replaced it with the

132

conception of a solar system, or sun-centered universe. In so doing, he cast suspicion on man's kinship with the angels and suggested that the whole of creation was governed by unchanging natural laws. Subsequently, a growing number of scholars, philosophers, and scientists began to study man and his environment more objectively, to make orderly observations and experiments. Their discoveries in astronomy, physics, anatomy, geology, and chemistry further weakened the old Biblical dogmas. By the eighteenth century the learned world accepted the idea of the universe as it appeared in the treatises of the great English mathematician Sir Isaac Newton (1642–1727). On his conception rested the Enlightenment in philosophy.

According to Newton, neither chance nor miracle governed the physical world. Instead, it appeared to be a perfect mechanical structure functioning under fixed mathematical laws. If that was the character of the universe, it must also be the character of mankind, who was part of it. Thus the Enlightenment philosophers proceeded to extend Newton's idea of the physical world to the moral world as well. By means of objective investigation and reason, they said, men would discover the mechanism of society itself and the fixed laws of its orderly life. Once these were found, all archaic growths and evil obstructions (how these appeared in the first place, they did not say) could be removed. They held bad environment rather than original sin responsible for social evils. By means of science and reason, philosophers could create an ideal environment in which the natural man would flower. The philosophers of the Enlightenment carried their optimism even further. The qualities they valued most highly in the study of physics and political economy—reasonableness, clarity, balance—they made the criteria of art and literary expression as well. What their aesthetics lacked in spirit it made up for in form, or so it seemed. For political and social perfection they looked most hopefully to America itself, where the encrustations of the evil past were fewest and natural man might find a virgin environment at his disposal.

## BENJAMIN FRANKLIN

The exemplar of the American Enlightenment and one of the greatest men of his age was the renegade Bostonian and adopted Philadelphian, Benjamin Franklin (1706–1790), a living example of what might be accomplished by reason, measure, and clarity:

Printer, postmaster, almanac maker, essayist, chemist, orator, tinker, professor of housewifery, ambassador, projector, maxim-monger, herb-doctor, wit:—Jack of all trades, master of each and mastered by none—the type and genius of the land.

So Herman Melville, the great nineteenth-century American novelist, later described Franklin, observing at the same time that he was "everything but a poet." Melville was right. Franklin, like the other *philosophes,* abhorred mysteries and metaphysics. Incapable of deep religious emotion, he worked out a complacent practical faith for himself and a cool tolerance for the beliefs of others. In his own eyes, he never "sinned"; rather, he "erred." In that distinction we may measure the gulf between the piety of his seventeenth-century forebears and the naturalism of the eighteenth century.

Franklin's admirable worldliness was neither greedy nor materialistic. He respected tools and the people who used them artfully. His close attention to the humblest as well as to the loftier occupations arose from his desire to produce "something for the common benefit of mankind." When he had acquired enough money to support himself (by the conscientious application of the principles he outlined in his celebrated *Autobiography*), he gave up business and devoted his energies to science, public affairs, and writing. He wanted people, he once confessed, to say after his death that "He lived usefully" rather than that "He died rich."

And so Franklin improved the printing press, tinkered successfully with smokey chimneys, suggested changes in the shape and rigging of ships, plotted cyclonic storms, introduced various new plants into the New World, drained swampy land, improved carriage wheels, founded the first American club for mutual improvement, invented the bifocal lens, designed an effective iron stove, recommended a more practical watering trough for horses, showed navigators how to shorten the crossing to Europe by following the Gulf Stream, demonstrated a way of heating public buildings, and constructed a fan for his chair to keep off the flies. This is only a partial list of his accomplishments, which included pioneer work in the science of electricity, studies in American population growth, and an extraordinarily long and successful public career. Franklin asked for no rewards beyond the doing itself. He took out no patents on his inventions, because "as we enjoy great advantages from the inventions of others, we should be glad of an opportunity to serve others by any invention of ours." His entire life was a fulfillment of one of his deepest beliefs: "Serving God is doing good to men."

Franklin's many-sidedness and his zeal for the practical make it hard to think of him as a philosopher and a man of letters at all. Yet he took to writing as he took to politics, religion, ethics, science, agriculture, and mechanics—easily and engagingly. Through his writings he expressed the values of thousands of his fellow Americans, the common citizens whose virtues he so uncommonly represented. Their materialistic aspirations he caught in his capitalistic homily, "The Way to Wealth." But his shrewd practicality went beyond concern for the dollar. In his humorous maxims he embodied the folk-wisdom of the American people:

Fish and visitors stink in three days. Write with the learned, pronounce with the vulgar. Eat to please thyself but dress to please others. Neither a fortress nor a maid will hold out long after they begin to parley. Let thy maidservant be faithful, strong, and homely. Keep your eyes wide open before marriage, half shut afterwards. Where there's marriage without love there will be love without marriage. The most exquisite folly is made of wisdom spun too fine.

Even Franklin's scientific papers, which won him world-wide acclaim during and after his lifetime, were couched in terms that could be readily understood. As Franklin's younger contemporary, the chemist Sir Humphry Davy, expressed it in his fine tribute to the American:

A singular felicity of induction guided all Franklin's researchers, and by very small means he established very grand truths. The style and manner of his publications on electricity are almost as worthy of admiration as the doctrine it contains. He has endeavored to remove all mystery and obscurity from the subject. He has written equally for the uninitiated and for the philosopher; and he has rendered his details amusing as well as perspicuous, elegant as well as simple. Science appears in his language in a dress wonderfully decorous, the best adapted

*Benjamin Franklin at 50 by Matthew Pratt. (Culver Pictures.)*

133

134

to display her native loveliness. He has in no instance exhibited that false dignity, by which philosophy is kept aloof from common applications; and he has sought to make her a useful inmate and servant in the common habitations of man, than to preserve her merely as an object of admiration in temples and palaces.

### SCIENCE IN THE COLONIES

The brilliance of Franklin's career and his exhalted reputation abroad have obscured the attainment of his lesser contemporaries whose investigations he encouraged and assisted. They shared his reliance on Enlightenment thought and like him believed not only that natural philosophy demonstrated the immutable ways of God, but also that it could be put to practical use. "Science," Francis Bacon had written, "must be known by its works. It is by the witness of works rather than by logic or even observation that truth is revealed and established. It follows from this that the improvement of man's lot and the improvement of man's mind are one and the same thing." The American scientists who shared the Baconian attitude were not mere utilitarians, but like scientists in Europe they were motivated by disinterested curiosity and a desire for scholarly recognition. Living in a society without wealth, without patronage, and without a learned class, they naturally looked to Europe for sustenance.

Fortunately for the physicians, the teachers, the self-taught botanists, and the amateur mathematicians and astronomers who made up the scientific community in North America, the European savants were keenly interested in the New World. They encouraged the Americans to report their findings on flora and fauna, Indian ethnology, medical lore, earthquakes. By collecting unknown plants, for example, the Americans could help the Swedish scholar Carl Linnaeus to complete his biological classifications. By the middle of the eighteenth century, European scientists had developed a system of communication which kept them informed about one another's findings, and they made the Americans a link in this intellectual chain. Thanks to the efforts of Peter Collinson, a Quaker merchant of London and an influential member of the Royal Society, the reports of the Americans were transmitted to interested Europeans. Through Collinson, isolated Americans also were kept informed of the activities of colleagues in other colonies.

New England from the outset had assumed the leadership in scientific investigation. Many of her leaders and professional men had been trained in English universities, and Harvard teachers and graduates had been elected to the Royal Society before 1700. John Winthrop, Jr., of Connecticut, a charter member of the Society, donated a telescope to Harvard in 1672, the one that enabled Thomas Brattle to observe the comet of 1676. Newton used Brattle's observations in his *Principia Mathematicia* to illustrate how the orbits of comets are fixed by gravitational force. No less important were the 82 letters the formidable Cotton Mather sent to the Royal Society's *Transactions* between 1712 and 1724. Among them were reports on the hybridization of plants and inoculation against smallpox.

But New England soon lost its pre-eminence to Philadelphia, which by 1750 had become the center of colonial science. Commercial prosperity was partly responsible for the willingness of Philadelphians to support scientific enterprises (see p. 106). Equally important was the Quaker connection of certain Philadelphians with intellectuals abroad. It was the English merchant, Collinson, again, who put the self-taught naturalist John Bartram in touch with Linnaeus. When Peter Kalm, a pupil of Linnaeus, visited America in 1748, he came straight to Philadelphia to see Bartram. Their discussions, according to Kalm, ranged from silk culture, vineyards, stalactites, and truffles to Indian pottery, hummingbirds, and cures for snake bite. Bartram had a genius for collecting specimens and a knack of communicating his enthusiasm to others. Half-mystic, half-rationalist, this independent Quaker saw "God in his glory" through the telescope, the first instrument of space exploration.

Bartram received aid and encouragement from another notable Philadelphia Quaker, James Logan, a rich and highly intelligent merchant who conducted important experiments on the role of pollen in the fertilization of plants. Logan also befriended Thomas Godfrey, who invented an improved quadrant, and Cadwallader Colden, a plant collector highly honored in Europe and author of one of the earliest scholarly treatises on the Indians.

In 1743 Franklin and Bartram tried to set up a scientific society that would correlate the work of experimenters throughout the colonies. The attempt seemed promising at first but had to be abandoned. Twenty-five years later (1768), it was revived as the American Philosophical Society. The 1771 *Transactions* of the Society carried reports by a number of colonial scientists on a transit of Venus across the sun that had taken place in 1769. In Philadelphia, where the observation took on the proportions of a community enterprise, David Rittenhouse, an ingenious clockmaker and builder of the celebrated orrery (a mechanical planetarium), was the principal contributor. European scientists hailed the Society's *Transactions* as evidence that American science had attained a surprising maturity.

## III  Cultural Progress

### EDUCATION

The educational system of the colonies was largely English in origin. The idea of the public grammer school was already a century old before its introduction to North America in 1642, and English universities served as the models for the first colleges in the New

*John Bartram, the Pennsylvania naturalist. (National Portrait Gallery, Smithsonian Institution, Washington, D.C.)*

World. English pedagogy and textbooks, and English schoolmasters and scholars, enjoyed great prestige.

In the seventeenth century education had been closely tied to religion and the church. But in the eighteenth century the introduction of secular subjects modified the religious emphasis. Social usefulness became an educational goal essential to the eighteenth-century ideal—the public-spirited man. The social importance of education was suggested by a well-known Massachusetts clergyman in 1716:

That *Good Order in Families and schools* for the well Educating of Children, are unspeakably useful and needful for a Peoples

135

welfare. Every Child that grows up, will be a useful or hurtful Member of the body Politick and persons thus growing up, are most like to prove *useful* or *hurtful,* according to the good or bad Methods taken in their Education. Those well *instructed, Governed,* Imployed in their Youth; are most likely to be harmless and serviceable in their Generation. Those brought up in *Ignorance* & *Idleness, Pride,* and *Luxory;* are likely to prove Vicious themselves, and be *Poysonous Infexious Plagues* to the Publick. A little Leaven, Leavens the whole lump; what will one *scabby sheep* do?

Education reflected the social cleavages that existed not only in the South, where class lines were especially sharply drawn, but also in the Middle and New England colonies. Rich children received a different kind of education from that received by poor children, who, if they were educated at all, were prepared solely for their limited stations in life. Even liberal-minded men in the mid-eighteenth century—revolutionists in the making—accepted these social distinctions as natural and proper. Jonathan Mayhew, a liberal minister of Boston, the epitome of the Revolutionary preacher and the counselor of rebels, bluntly distinguished between the abilities of the base-born and the well-born. "That which principally distinguishes some men from the beasts of the field," he said, "is the different formation of their bodies. Their bodies are *human,* but they are in a manner *brute* all beside. . . . Those of the lower class can go but a little ways in their inquiries into the natural and moral constitution of the world." The Revolutionary decades saw a weakening of this two-class system, but traditional attitudes lingered on into the national period that followed.

The kind and quality of education in eighteenth-century America depended also on the section, the national origin of the settlers, their religion, and their closeness to settled areas. Education in the South, for example, where it was difficult to establish any kind of organized educational system for the scat-

tered plantations, lagged behind that in the North. Pauper schools gave rudimentary instruction to orphans and the children of the poor, but in general only the children of the rich were educated. Higher standards prevailed in the Middle colonies, where the dissenting Protestant denominations emphasized Bible-reading, but the amount and quality of education that most children received was limited to what their parents could afford.

Only in Massachusetts and Connecticut did education become a public responsibility. The Massachusetts school laws of 1642 and 1647 (see p. 63) meant, in effect, that all children must be taught to read. These standards—unique in the English-speaking world at the time—deteriorated as New England society became more decentralized and as educational control passed to the local authorities. By 1700, education was at a low ebb in New England, and illiteracy was prevalent on the frontier. But conditions rapidly improved. During the 40-year period from 1720 to 1760, a number of excellent semi-private academies were established, and New Englanders once again could proudly claim to be the best-educated people in all North America.

In the cities, several interesting educational experiments were carried on in the eighteenth century. Philadelphia, Boston, and New York, besides having the best private academies, also had a number of private evening schools that featured practical courses ignored by classical academies. Such subjects as geography, navigation, bookkeeping, mathematics, and surveying had a high practical value in a commercial society. All classes attended evening schools, but the majority of students, of both sexes, came from middle-class homes.

A relatively small number of well-to-do students attended the seven colonial colleges that had been established by 1764. These and the private academies retained the European curriculum (Latin, Greek, Hebrew, and Science) and fostered aristocratic, conservative ideals. Religious training remained ostensibly the chief function of the colleges, but the

*Harvard College in 1767, from an engraving by Paul Revere. Buildings shown from right to left: Massachusetts Hall; Stoughton Hall; Harvard Hall; Hollis Hall; Holden Chapel. (Essex Institute.)*

liberal and rational influences of the age began to be felt as the century waned. The students of the second-oldest college in British America, William and Mary, began to debate the philosophy of politics and natural rights. Such eminently practical leaders as Thomas Jefferson and James Monroe were trained here. Harvard became a center of science; the College of Philadelphia became an advocate of "*every thing* that is useful, and *every thing* that is ornamental." King's College (later Columbia) advertised that while the teaching of religion was its principal objective, "it is further the Design of this College, to instruct and perfect the Youth in . . . The Arts of *Numbering* and *Measuring,* of *Surveying* and *Navigation,* of *Geography* and *History,* of Husbandry, Commerce and Government." The colonial colleges did not ignore classical learning, but their graduates began to embody more and more the American ideal of the useful citizen equipped to meet practical realities.

Naturally enough, the colleges had become the centers of the new science by the first quarter of the eighteenth century. True, no college professor ever matched the self-taught Benjamin Franklin or John Bartram in originality. But America's ablest astronomer, John Winthrop, taught at Harvard College, and David Rittenhouse, astronomer and mathematician, lectured at the College of Philadelphia,

as did Dr. Benjamin Rush, the first professor of chemistry in America.

### JOURNALISM AND LETTERS

Literacy, by European standards, was high in the colonies but only a few Americans kept up with the new learning. A somewhat larger number read colonial newspapers. During Franklin's term as Deputy Postmaster for the colonies (1753–55), he succeeded in reducing postal rates for newspapers and in speeding up their distribution. But throughout the pre-Revolutionary period they remained too expensive for the poor. By 1765, nevertheless, 25 weekly papers were being published in 11 colonies. Most of the columns were filled with excerpts from English papers, but after the famous trial of John Peter Zenger in New York in 1735, greater opportunities opened up for independent reporting.

Zenger was charged with criminal libel for printing an unfavorable report about a crown official. He was defended by the eminent Philadelphia lawyer, Andrew Hamilton, who appealed to the jury to define libel in a way contrary to the current English rule. For the judges, the question was merely whether

137

colonial almanac appeared in New England in 1639; by 1731, almanacs were being read in all the colonies. Pocket-sized and paper-bound, they served as calendars, astrological guides, recipe books, and children's primers. Sandwiched in between bits of practical information were jokes, poems, and maxims. The better almanacs (published by Nathaniel Ames and Benjamin Franklin) punctured superstition, provided simplified summaries of the new science, and presented tasteful selections from the best British authors. Franklin's *Poor Richard's Almanack,* first published in 1732, soon sold 10,000 copies a year.

Literature received more attention in the eighteenth century than it had in the seventeenth, though the Puritan suspicion of the secular imagination had not entirely relaxed. A commercially and politically minded population, however, had little interest in *belles lettres.*

By the 1740s, Philadelphia had become the literary center of the colonies and the first city to manifest a literary self-consciousness. But even here, the coterie of young men who gathered around the educator and magazine editor William Smith became even more fettered by English literary conventions than their predecessors had been. Not one of them measured up to the gifted Puritan poet Edward Taylor, whose verse blended homely details of New England life with magnificent visions of God. None wrote with the urbanity, robustness, and wit of William Byrd II, or with the charm and lucidity of Franklin.

The neo-classic eighteenth-century writers took their cue from the English critic Lord Kames, whose influential book, *Elements of Criticism* (1762), dictated the aesthetic standards accepted by the literate. "We have," Kames wrote, "the same standard for ascertaining in all the fine arts, what is beautiful or ugly, high or low, proper or improper, proportioned and unproportioned. And here, as in morals, we justly condemn every taste that swerves from what is thus ascertained by the common standard." Ardent young poets were becoming aware of their American-ness, but

Zenger had published the offending articles; for Hamilton, the question was whether the contents of the articles were true. The jury accepted Hamilton's advanced version of libel and held that since the articles were true, Zenger was not guilty as charged. Fifty years passed before the finding in this case became formal law, but the decision did encourage other journalists to become more outspoken.

A more popular medium than newspapers for spreading scientific and political information, especially to rural Americans, was the almanac, an old English institution. The first

they expressed their emotions in conventional and "proper" poetic diction and sang about "swains" and "snowy lambkins" haunting the banks of the Schuylkill River. After 1750, they became absorbed in political issues and expended their talents on satire and polemics.

Literally as well as metaphorically, everyday Americans in this period had begun to speak

*Poor Richard's Almanack, by Benjamin Franklin, was one of the most popular publications in the colonies.*

Poor Richard, 1747.
AN
Almanack
For the Year of Chrift
1747,
It being the Third after
LEAP-YEAR,

| And makes fince the Creation | Years |
|---|---|
| By the Account of the Eaftern *Greeks* | 7255 |
| By the Latin Church, when ☉ ent. ♈ | 6946 |
| By the Computation of *W. W.* | 5756 |
| By the *Roman* Chronology | 5696 |
| By the *Jewifh* Rabbies | 5508 |

*Wherein is contained,*
The Lunations, Eclipfes, Judgment of the Weather, Spring Tides, Planets Motions & mutual Afpects, Sun and Moon's Rifing and Setting, Length of Days, Time of High Water, Fairs, Courts, and obfervable Days.
Fitted to the Latitude of Forty Degrees, and a Meridian of Five Hours Weft from *London*, but may without fenfible Error, ferve all the adjacent Places, even from *Newfoundland* to *South Carolina.*

By RICHARD SAUNDERS, Philom.

PHILADELPHIA:
Printed and fold by *B. FRANKLIN.*

a different language from the English. In the seventeenth and eighteenth centuries, English lexicographers and scholars like Dr. Samuel Johnson had pruned and refined Elizabethan English, but many of the barbarisms they eliminated continued to be good usage in the colonies. Surviving archaisms like *I guess, chump, flap-jack, home-spun, to hustle,* and many others came to be regarded as Americanisms. American speech also absorbed words from the Dutch, French, German, and Spanish. New plants, animals, and birds tested the wit of the colonists, as did the peculiar American geography. *Poke-weed, bottom-land, rolling-country, back-woods, land office,* and *crazy-quilt* were all colonial words that described new scenery, new objects, and new situations. Until the appearance of Philip Freneau's earliest poems in the 1770s, however, formal American writing remained derivative and provincial.

### POLITICAL IDEAS

The most important colonial writing in the eighteenth century and the most widely read was not the work of literary men but of theologians, scientists, and political theorists. Among the political writers were some of the ablest and most highly cultivated minds in the New World.

The political philosophy of most thinking Americans before the Revolution derived partly from colonial experience and partly from English and continental sources. Even during the seventeenth century, when faith, revelation, and authority carried more weight than reason, the foreshadowings of democracy were dimly visible. Puritanism, as well as the Enlightenment, nourished ideas of liberty, success, and self-fulfillment. As rationalism gradually undermined old dogmas and as democratic tendencies grew more noticeable, Americans became receptive to ideas from abroad congenial to their own experiences. The leading imported idea was the doctrine of natural rights as formulated by John Locke in his *Two Treatises of Civil Government.*

Published in 1690, Locke's essays helped explode the divine-right theory of kingship which had brought the prestige of religion to the support of absolute political authority.

Philosophers long before Locke, as we have see (p. 45), had attacked the divine-right theory. Locke's distinction lay in his restatement of English constitutional ideas in their most persuasive and popular form. Government, he said (by which he meant king, parliament, or any other political agency), was responsible to the people, to the community it ruled. Its power was limited both by constitutional traditions, popular conventions, and the moral law deducible from the laws of nature.

But what, precisely, were the natural laws that governed the political activities of man? It was one thing for Newton to demonstrate the laws governing the heavenly spheres but quite another thing to demonstrate the existence of a natural order in society. The early theorists of natural law tackled the problem by trying to identify man's elemental needs and faculties. How would man behave, they asked, if he acted solely in accordance with his nature, without social restraints of any sort? Of one thing they were sure: in a natural state men would never consent to live under any form of government that did not protect their life, liberty, and property. Hence, when men accepted government, they entered into a "social contract" with their rulers; in return for security and protection, they accepted the ruler's authority. But if the rulers violated their part of the bargain, the people were no longer bound by the contract. Then they had the right to overthrow the government and establish a new one. These Lockeian ideas were easily digested by practical people. In business, contractual relationships were becoming more and more common, and society was familiar with the Puritan idea of a "covenant" between God and man.

Locke's treatises were widely regarded as the best justification of the Glorious Revolution of 1688 (see p. 77). Originally, his sallies were directed against kingly government and

were meant to justify the supremacy of Parliament. But Locke phrased his criticisms in such general terms that the colonists found it easy to convert them into a challenge to Parliament itself. Other beliefs, widely held in the colonies, strengthened his natural-rights philosophy. The common-law rights of freeborn Englishmen, for example, were closely identified with the natural rights of men. And these legal rights were sustained by two English authorities who were immensely influential in America: Sir William Blackstone, known through his *Commentaries on the Laws of England* (1765–69), and Sir Edward Coke, the seventeenth-century English lawyer (see p. 46). From Blackstone the colonists quoted that man's first allegiance was to a God whose will was the universal law of nature, and that human laws were clearly invalid when they conflicted with natural law. The colonial pamphleteers cherished particularly this pronouncement by Coke:

The law of nature is that which God at the time of creation of the nature of man infused into his heart, for his preservation and direction; and this is *Lex aeterna,* the moral law, called also the law of Nature. And by this law, written with the finger of God in the heart of man, were the people of God a long time governed before the law was written by Moses who was the first reporter or writer of law in the world.

Ideas about natural rights were in the air, then, long before the Declaration of Independence was written. They seemed especially appropriate to a people who had in fact created government while still living in a state of nature. When these ideas were challenged in the developing conflict with Britain, colonial pamphleteers increasingly used American experiences to defend them. John Wise based his support of the incipient rebels on the congregational principle. When Jonathan Mayhew composed his famous "Discourse Concerning Unlimited Submission and Non-Resistance to the Higher Powers" (1750), he provided political ammunition for the later

Revolutionary pamphleteers. Mayhew admitted that civil authority required obedience, that disobedience was morally as well as politically sinful. But, he added, when rulers pillage the public instead of protecting it, they stop being emissaries of God and become "common pirates and highwaymen." To support a tyrant was to abet him in promoting misery. For Mayhew, the doctrine of the divine right of kings (with its corollary of nonresistance) was "altogether as fabulous and chimerical as transubstantiation; or any reveries of ancient or modern visionaries." The form that a government took was less important than the need for it to have popular support. If government derived from God, as the absolutists said, it was because God moved the people to organize it.

Here was a reasonable and religious basis for popular assemblies that made sense to the learned and the unlearned alike. A century and a half of colonial history, as a conservative Swedish observer noted in 1775, had created a new kind of political animal peculiar to North America:

The chief trait in the character of an American is an immoderate love of liberty, or rather license. . . . And this enthusiasm rules in the breasts of all from the highest to the lowest. Education, manner of life, religion, and government—all contribute to it. Parents exercise no authority over children, beyond letting them for the most part do what pleases them. Everyone can maintain himself without trouble, for here there is room enough, and wages are high. No one, therefore, knows oppression or dependence. All are equally good; birth, office and merits do not make much distinction. Freedom of conscience is unlimited, without the least control by secular law, and church discipline means nothing. The English method of government is in itself quite mild, and is all the less able, in this remote part of the empire, to exercise a reasonable strictness. The reins of government lie so slack that they seldom are noticed, and the hand that guides is never seen. The result of all this is that the people neither know nor will know of any control, and everyone regards himself as an independent Prince. One can grow weary of continually hearing and reading about noble liberty. Many, as stupid and shameless, regard all other nations as slaves. Their imagination constantly sees apparitions coming to steal away that goddess of theirs. All the enterprises of the government arouse suspicion. The most reasonable regulations are invasions of their rights and liberties; light and necessary taxes, robbery and plunder; well-merited punishment, unheard-of tyranny.

# READINGS

Merle Curti, *The Growth of American Thought* (1943), a comprehensive work, and vol. 1 of V.L. Parrington, *Main Currents in American Thought* (3 vols., 1927), afford useful introductions to the mature colonial mind. Michael Kraus, *The Atlantic Civilization* (1949), is especially good on overseas intellectual connections. Max Savelle, *Seeds of Liberty* (1948), and Clinton Rossiter, *Seedtime of the Republic* (1953), are outstanding intellectual histories with emphasis on political ideas. Rossiter, *The First American Revolution* (1953), is a useful reprint of Part I of his larger work.

Modern introductions to the religious history of the period will be found in S.E. Mead, *The Lively Experiment: The Shaping of Christianity in America* (1963), and W.S. Hudson, *Religion in America* (1965). T.C. Hall, *The Religious Background of American Culture* (1930), covers the origins of the dissenting tradition in England and its spread in

America. L.J. Trinterud, *The Forming of an American Tradition* (1949), is outstanding on Presbyterianism. The liberal reaction and its opponents is well presented in Conrad Wright, *The Beginnings of Unitarianism in America* (1955). W.W. Sweet, *Religion in Colonial America* (1942), is a useful survey of church history. Perry Miller, *The New England Mind: From Colony to Province* (1953), has an excellent discussion of the Salem witchcraft hysteria. M.L. Starkey, *The Devil in Massachusetts* (1949), offers a more extended account which should be read with the caution suggested in Chadwick Hansen, *Witchcraft in Salem* (1969).

Perry Miller, *Jonathan Edwards* (1949), and O.E. Winslow, *Jonathan Edwards 1703–1758* (1940), are the leading biographies of the New England divine. S.C. Henry, *George Whitefield, Wayfaring Witness* (1957), is excellent on the revivalist. Alan Heimert and Perry Miller, eds., *The Great Awakening, Documents Illustrating the Crisis and Its Consequences* (1967), provides the best general survey. On the Great Awakening regionally, see E.S. Gaustad, *The Great Awakening in New England* (1957); C.H. Maxson, *The Great Awakening in the Middle Colonies* (1920); and W. M. Gewehr, *The Great Awakening in Virginia 1740–1790* (1930). On the relation of the religious revival to slavery and the blacks, see especially Chapter 7 in D.B. Davis, *The Problem of Slavery in Western Culture* (1965); and Chapters 5 and 7 in W.D. Jordan, *White Over Black, American Attitudes toward the Negro 1550–1812* (1968). D.G. Mathews, *Slavery and Methodism: A Chapter in American Morality 1780–1845* (1965), is a valuable special study. E.B. Greene, *Religion and the State, The Making and Testing of an American Tradition* (1941), is a good, short study of the separation of church and state. R.B. Perry, *Puritanism and Democracy* (1944), is a penetrating investigation of the relations of religion and politics. On deism, see G.A. Koch, *Republican Religion: The American Revolution and the Cult of Reason* (1933) and Herbert Morais, *Deism in Eighteenth Century America* (1934).

The impact of the Enlightenment is well presented in the general works cited at the head of these Readings. Its relevance to the life of the Negro is examined in detail in Chapters 13 and 14 in Davis, *The Problem of Slavery in Western Culture*, cited above. Numerous works by and on Benjamin Franklin help give substance to Enlightenment thought: A.O. Aldridge, *Benjamin Franklin: Philosopher and Man* (1965); Carl Van Doren, *Benjamin Franklin* (1938); I.B. Cohen, *Franklin and Newton* (1956); Franklin's *Autobiography* (first published 1868); and two well-edited anthologies: I.B. Cohen, *Benjamin Franklin* (1953); and F.L. Mott and C.E. Jorgenson, *Benjamin Franklin* (1936). For a very critical estimate see the essay on Franklin in D.H. Lawrence, *Studies in Classic American Literature* (1953). The Enlightenment in Philadelphia may be pursued further in F.B. Tolles, *James Logan and Culture of Provincial America* (1957). Brooke Hindle, *The Pursuit of Science in Revolutionary America, 1735–1789* (1956), is a scholarly monograph. Maurice Cranston, *John Locke* (1957), is a readable modern biography. John Locke, *Two Treatises of Civil Government* (1690), lays the foundation for political thought in the Enlightenment. Caroline Robbins, *The Eighteenth-Century Commonwealthman* (1959), is an indispensable study, as its subtitle says, "in the Transmission, Development and Circumstance of English Liberal Thought from the Restoration of Charles II until the War with the Thirteen Colonies." The Readings for Chapter Five supply further references on this subject and its relation to the American Revolution. Adrienne Koch, ed., *The American Enlightenment: The Shaping of the American Experiment and a Free Society* (1965), is an outstanding anthology, relevant to this and later chapters.

Paul Monroe, *The Founding of the American Public School System: A History of*

*Education in the United States from the Early Settlements to the Close of the Civil War Period* (2 vols., 1940), is a standard source. Robert Middlekauff, *Ancients and Axioms, Secondary Education in Eighteenth-Century New England* (1963), is excellent on an important region. On higher education, see Frederick Rudolph, *The American College and University* (1962); Richard Hofstadter, *Academic Freedom in the Age of the College* (1955); and the masterly work by S.E. Morison, *Harvard College in the Seventeenth Century* (1936).

On popular culture, see Sidney Kobre, *The Development of the Colonial Newspaper* (1944), and vol. 1 of F.L. Mott, *A History of American Magazines* (5 vols., 1930–1968). Richard McLanathan, *The American Tradition in the Arts* (1968), provides a fresh view of all the fine and decorative arts. See also Oliver Larkin, *Art and Life in America* (1949). On colonial literature see the work of V.L. Parrington, above, and M.C. Tyler, *A History of American Literature 1607–1765* (1949). Worth reading for quick surveys are the first chapter of Marcus Cunliffe, *The Literature of the United States* (1954), and an excellent essay on colonial writing in H.M. Jones, *Ideas in America* (1944). Chapters I and II of Robert Spiller, et al., *Literary History of the United States* (3 vols., 1948), contain up-to-date and scholarly treatments by specialists in colonial literature.

143

# FIVE

In the broad panorama of North American history as a whole [writes John Bartlet Brebner in his fine study of *The Explorers of North America*], perhaps the greatest persistent theme is the westward flow of population from the Atlantic to the Pacific, and it has become such a commonplace that there is some danger of its being taken for granted as a feature of the colonial history of the seventeenth century. As a matter of fact, it was not until 1768 that the expanding population of the coastal colonies burst through the Appalachians to *occupy* the heart of the continent. When they did so, they found weather-beaten trails, skilful, knowledgeable guides, and Indians who had dealt with the white man for a century, [all] almost anonymously risk[ing] their lives to provide Europe with its furs and buckskins.

Until the end of the eighteenth century, the "wilderness" between the Appalachians and the Mississippi was as much a battlefield as a wilderness. True, nature had thrown up formidable obstacles to permanent white settlement. The high, broad mountains, ranging north and south for nearly a thousand miles, offered few passes for man and his goods. Beyond the mountains lay the impenetrable woods and marshes of the Ohio and Mississippi valleys, where, for all one knew, monstrous griffin-vultures (with eagle head and wings and hindquarters of the lion) prowled and preyed. Had these been the only deterrents, however, white settlement surely would have started earlier than it did and proceeded more gradually than the explosive pace at which the region was overrun once *man-made* barriers and *human* enemies had been leveled or dislodged.

Within the depths of this western country, Indian tribes and groups of tribes had long

# THE WORLD
# AND THE WILDERNESS

since marked out "states" with vague but well-defended borders that trespassers, native and European alike, had learned to respect, to be wary of, or at least not to assault without due cause and preparation. By the beginning of the eighteenth century the great lakes and rivers that dominated the region, as well as many of their tributary streams, had been discovered and explored by the white man. Strategic points had been located and many of them fortified. Diplomacy, especially between aborigines and white aggressors, had become a continuous complement to trade. When diplomacy broke down, arms were plentiful on both sides—and promptly used.

The Indians of this overwhelming forest warred among themselves for lands to insure their supply of game and fish and grain, or for territory rich in the furs that the white man was so eager to buy, or for control of the watercourses and woodland paths over which pelts and skins were hauled to the white man's posts. The invaders, in turn, clashed among themselves, first over control of the hunting and trading tribes, then over the lands in the great drainage basins, and ultimately over the whole of North America. In a sense, the American Revolution was a late phase of this struggle which did not finally flicker out until the end of the Indian wars on the plains following the American Civil War.

## 1 *The "Wilderness" Prize*

### CIVILIZED RED MEN AND WHITE

Few understood the terms of the enduring warfare for the "wilderness" better than the civilized Indian tribes—above all, the five Iroquois Nations (Mohawk, Oneida, Onondaga, Cayuga, and Seneca) whose empire it was that all contended for.

"Among all the barbarous nations of the continent," writes the brilliant Francis Parkman, "the Iroquois of New York stand paramount. . . . The Iroquois was the Indian of the Indians. . . . Their organization and their history evince their intrinsic superiority." Parkman writes of the Iroquois' "ferocious vitality, which, but for the presence of the Europeans, would probably have subjected, absorbed, or exterminated every other Indian community east of the Mississippi and north of the Ohio." The Europeans' own ferocious vitality brought out other traits in these worthy antagonists. "It is by the most subtle policy," said the Jesuit Lafitau, who knew the Iroquois at the peak of their prosperity toward the end of the seventeenth century, "that they have taken the ascendant over the other na-

145

146

tions, divided and overcome the most warlike, made themselves a terror to the most remote, and now hold a peaceful neutrality between the French and the English, courted and feared by both."

The heart of the Iroquois empire extended across the rich central valley of present-day New York State, from the Hudson River to the Genesee. Here lay the first sea-level route to the West, north of Georgia. To the east of the Iroquois heartland glistened the waters of Lake Champlain, to the north the upper St. Lawrence, to the north and west lakes Ontario and Erie, to the south the sources of the rivers bound for the Atlantic and the northern tributaries of the Ohio, and the eastern tributaries of the Mississippi. No more strategic terrain could be found in all North America. In Parkman's judgment, it "gave the ambitious and aggressive [Iroquois] confederates advantages they perfectly understood, and by which they profited to the utmost."

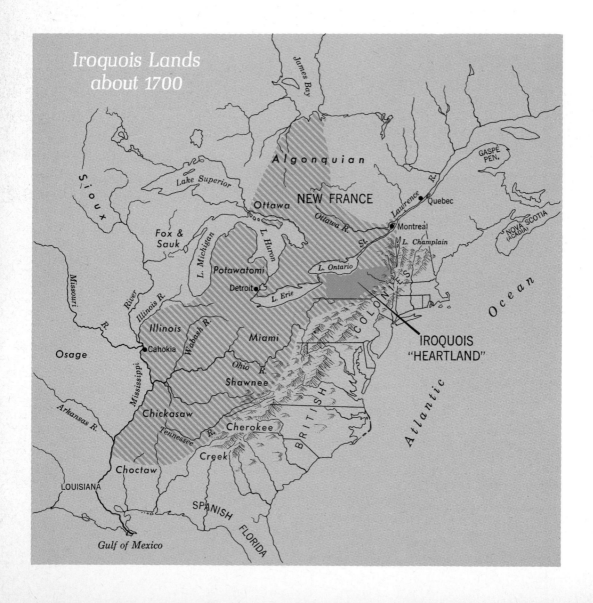

*Iroquois Lands about 1700*

The Iroquois had not always been so ambitious and aggressive. In fact, their great League or Confederation had been known as "The Great Peace" when it was first brought together in the middle of the sixteenth century by the imaginative chieftain Hiawatha, a leader thoroughly libeled in Longfellow's sentimental poem derived from threadbare legends of hostile Chippewas. The purpose of the League had been to end warfare among the Five Nations of the New York Valley, and, by presenting a united front, to discourage the surrounding tribes from aggression.* The Iroquois League lasted 300 years, and vestiges of its traditions are still sustained by the few thousand tribesmen who continue to occupy the grounds of their vanished glory. "The Great Peace" had a much shorter life.

At the time "The Great Peace" was organized, the Iroquois heartland formed an enclave within the vast territory reaching from the Atlantic to the Great Lakes claimed by the Algonquians. About half a century after "The Great Peace," Champlain established the French in the New World and his followers organized systematic fur-trading with the aborigines. The Algonquians became their chief suppliers, hunting the fur-bearing animals, mainly beavers, stripping them of their pelts, and carrying them to primitive Quebec and Montreal for shipment overseas. The vogue of beaver arose not only from its intrinsic beauty but from the fact that the hairs of the fur had fine barbs which clung readily to felt and facilitated the manufacture of beaver hats. So eager did Europe become for American furs that Algonquian territory for hundreds of miles around was quickly shorn of its animal life. During the same period the Dutch at New Amsterdam and Albany established fur-trading relations with the touchy Iroquois, and their lands too were soon depleted of beaver.

* The "Five Nations" became the "Six Nations" about 1715, when the Tuscaroras of South Carolina, a tribe related to the northern Iroquois, were routed by provincial forces, chased from their lands, and accepted into the northern League.

*The fabrication of beaver hats, 1750. (William L. Clements Library.)*

Trade with the Europeans drew even the most stalwart Indians into dependence on the white man's goods. Metal axes, knives, hoes, and kettles, as well as woolen blankets and colored calico, were so superior to Stone Age tools and pottery, and to raiment of deer and buffalo skins, that the Indians' crafts deteriorated and among some tribes disappeared entirely. More demoralizing was French and Spanish brandy, which the Jesuits and other missionaries tried with little success to keep their countrymen from selling to the susceptible red men, and Dutch (and later English and American) rum, against which there were few or no prohibitions. But worst of all were European firearms, to which the Dutch first introduced the red men. French traders, ignor-

148

### THE IROQUOIS IMPERIUM

Almost from the start of the fur trade early in the seventeenth century, the Iroquois had terrorized the surrounding Algonquians and eventually had driven them from the trapping grounds eastward to the sea. Along the coast, the displaced Algonquians became the scourge of New England's struggling fishing villages and inland settlements. Confronted with the denuded trapping grounds and the rout of the Algonquians, the French traders turned westward. As early as the 1620s they had established relations with the highly civilized Hurons who occupied the strategic territory between Lake Huron on the north and Lakes Erie and Ontario on the south. This territory was bounded on the east by the Ottawa River, which flowed southeastward to the St. Lawrence, just above Montreal. It was far more difficult for the French to ship their furs to Montreal over the Ottawa River route than by way of the Great Lakes; but the hostile Iroquois dominated the Lakes, and the French had little choice.

Soon even the Ottawa River route became untenable. The Hurons served exclusively as middlemen between the hunting Indians north and west of them and the French traders to the east. But the Dutch, who wanted the western pelts as desperately as the French, urged their Iroquois allies to break up the Huron monopoly. Iroquois efforts to gain an advantage by diplomatic means were persistently rebuffed, and by 1640 the Five Nations were sending marauding parties to the Ottawa River to rob and kill the Huron carriers. The Hurons responded by mobilizing the tribes of the river region to form a buffer against the Iroquois menace. The Iroquois assaults on the French fur trade spread to Montreal itself, which the Five Nations permitted the French to retain only to provide themselves with a docile market to play off

against the Dutch when they bargained too hard. Finally, in 1649, the Iroquois launched a brutal invasion of the Huron peninsula, demolished the Hurons' settlements, destroyed their civilization, and sent most of the hunting tribes even of the upper Mississippi Valley flying across the prairie to pile up against the borders of the inhospitable Sioux, the fiercest horse Indians of the plains.

The extinction of the Hurons brought the French fur trade to a standstill. But so ferocious had been the Iroquois' assault, so bloodthirsty their subsequent mopping up and marauding, that neither they nor the Dutch profited from the triumph. Commenting on

*This tattooed Iroquois (probably a Mohawk), drawn by Charles Bécard de Granville, a French official in Canada about 1700, is one of the earliest drawings of Indians of the St. Lawrence Valley. (Public Archives of Canada.)*

the bands of Iroquois that were roving as far west as Lake Michigan in 1652, a French observer said, "They came like foxes, attacked like lions, and fled like birds." Only after the Iroquois and the French had made peace in 1654 would the western hunting Indians return to the beaver grounds. Gradually other tribes, famished for European commodities, dared to assume the role of middlemen that the vanquished Hurons had performed.

Everyone knew that the peace of 1654 was only a temporary truce. By the 1660s, Iroquois harassment of the new middlemen had again grown so vicious that Louis XIV was prevailed upon to send a crack military force to Canada to quell the Five Nations. In 1666 this force struck at the Iroquois with such stunning impact that henceforth they were to retain a healthy respect for French arms. The setback also caused them to place a higher value on their connections with the English, who had supplanted the Dutch at Albany and New Amsterdam two years before. So it was that after 1666 the Iroquois looked southward to satisfy their own imperial ambitions—to the country that was to become the heartland of the United States. The fear they had instilled in all the northern tribes persisted, however, and their intermittent raids in later years, often under English prompting, helped keep it fresh. The mere rumor that the Iroquois were on the warpath struck terror into the hearts of the Canadian tribes—a circumstance the French regime made use of to keep the exploited northern natives under the protection of French arms. Otherwise they might have been lured to the English trade by the cheapness and superiority of English soft goods and implements.

At its peak in the eighteenth century, the Iroquois empire spread some 800 miles between the Appalachians and the Mississippi, southwesterly from the Five Nations' home valley in New York. The northern limit formed a broad arc from Lake Champlain across the headwaters of the St. Lawrence to the eastern shores of Lake Michigan. Iroquois warriors probably never numbered more than 2500, and the task of subduing and holding tributary the hunting and trapping tribes in this vast domain strained the Five Nations to the utmost. Yet until past the middle of the century the Iroquois League managed to dissuade even their English allies from settling permanently in its immensely rich fur empire. And the French, compelled to range exhausting distances for furs north and west of their capital at Quebec, were never permitted to forget the menace of the League at their rear.

## II  *The French Barrier*

### THE ANCIEN RÉGIME IN CANADA

For a hundred years after the extinction of the Hurons the fur trade north of the Ohio could as accurately be described as "the fur war." Senseless raids and bloody reprisals kept the wilderness and the settlements that bordered on it in constant turmoil and their denizens, red and white alike, watchful, suspicious, on edge. Armed conflict was supplemented by rival missionary activity, espionage, secret pacts, and frequent treachery.

But the war had its constructive side: the brutal competition for fur provided an overpowering impulse to discovery and exploration. One of the heaviest costs of the fur trade was transportation; and one of the traders' most urgent quests, aside from new beaver lands themselves, was for new waterways to carry the pelts to Atlantic ports. More than geography was involved. As the Jesuit, Albanel, observed in the 1670s, "It is no new thing for the Savages to be extremely cautious in granting strangers a passage, by way of their rivers, to distant Nations. The rivers are to them . . . their sole source of subsistence—whether in the form of fish or game, or in that of traffic." The dynamics of the fur trade drew rival European explorers on an endless search for territory until they spanned the continent; diplomacy, intimidation, and conquest opened up the strategic waterways by which the continent's wealth was realized.

150

France, it is often said, had many advantages over England in the contest for North America, while Spain is supposed to have lain dormant. In fact, the Spanish North American empire grew at France's expense during the half-century and more preceding the expulsion of the French in 1763, and survived another half-century after the French had gone. France's alleged advantages over England include: (1) the absolute power of the governor-general of Canada, especially in emergencies, in contrast to the multiplicity of authorities in the English colonies; (2) the professionalism of the permanent military forces in Canada, in contrast to the improvised citizen militias of the English provinces; and (3) the success of French missionaries in converting the natives, and of French lay administrators and traders in holding their affections and allegiance, in contrast to the hatred with which the red man viewed the permanent English settlers who were depriving them of their ancient lands by violence and chicanery.

But on analysis these alleged French advantages appear dubious; in any case, they were more than offset by the advantages enjoyed by England and her American plantations. The governor-general of Canada was appointed by an absolute king at home and served nominally as the king's surrogate in the New World. Since power theoretically was centralized in his office, prompt and decisive action on his part was always possible. But in 1665 the king also endowed New France with an "intendant," whose duty it was to report directly to the monarch on judicial and financial matters and on anything else that might engage his notice, malicious or otherwise. "The intendant," Parkman writes, "was virtually a spy on the governor-general." In addition, New France was blessed with a bishop—the spiritual head of the empire, and the temporal head of the empire's largest property-owner, the Roman Catholic Church.

These three—governor, intendant, and bishop, each with a sycophantic corps of functionaries and talebearers—ruled Canada. But they were always on short tether from Ver-

sailles. Far from centralizing power, the system left New France at the mercy of petty jealousies, selfish cliques, and profound clashes of authority. "Canada," cried the frustrated Antoine de La Mothe-Cadillac in 1699, when he was pleading for permission to build a fort at Detroit, "is a country of cabals and intrigues, and it is impossible to reconcile so many different interests."

Undeniably, the French proved capable of magnificent efforts in enlarging and protecting their realm. But these efforts often were made in eleventh-hour attempts to compensate for the failures of the central government, and sometimes were carried forward in defiance of it and despite its obstructionism. One of the fundamental failures of the regime was the seigniorial system of landholding. Early in the history of New France, the best river-front lands had been granted under feudal tenure to army officers and other *gentilshommes* who made little effort to bring them under cultivation. Eventually some of the fiefs fell into the possession of thrifty merchants and unusually gifted *habitants,* or peasants, who by scrimping and scraping over the years somehow managed to accumulate enough capital to buy out cash-hungry noblemen at bargain prices. Such self-made *seigneurs* often made farming pay. Yet for generations the domestic food supply of New France remained poorer even than that of the savages before the white man came. As a consequence, the vaunted professional soldiers of New France were always dependent on the home country and on neighboring New England for sustenance.

Canadian industry was even more backward than its agriculture, which meant that the colonials had to rely on ocean-going vessels to bring in munitions, trading goods, and other hardware. But the only navigable entry to French warehouses in Montreal and Quebec was by way of the St. Lawrence, which was either frozen or clogged with ice floes half the year. This inadequate supply line from the sea made it easy in times of crisis for the English navy and English and Yankee privateers to offset the nominal military superiority of the enemy. In the interior, moreover, the French could never count with absolute confidence on the loyalty of the Christianized Indians. "Thus far," Cadillac observed in 1699, "all the fruits of the missions consist in the baptism of infants who die before reaching the age of reason."

Besides its internal problems, the French regime in Quebec faced other difficulties. Compared, for example, with the lush sugar islands of the West Indies, Canada ranked low in the French scheme of overseas empire. This empire itself, moreover, ranked far below the commitments and ambitions of the Bourbon dynasty in Europe. Louis XIV and his successors considered Canada an arctic waste, little better than a place of exile for aristocratic busy-bodies and other nuisances. All the more astonishing, then, are the successes these outcasts and a handful of devoted empire-builders achieved in the distant reaches of North America.

### THE JESUIT MONOPOLY

From the extraordinary explorations of Champlain and his young men early in the century (see p. 28) until the quieting of the Iroquois menace in 1666, Quebec had permitted almost no one but Jesuits to venture into the western country. There were good reasons for granting a monopoly of western exploration to the churchmen. For one thing, no other men could be spared from the defense of the three administrative towns on the St. Lawrence—Quebec, Three Rivers, and Montreal—whose loss to the Dutch or the English would have meant the extinction of the whole French imperial venture in North America. Second, the Jesuits required no western forts, and hence no garrisons to house soldiers, no agriculture to feed them, no women and wine for amusement, above all no colonies of merchants with their families, wagons, roads, and other domesticating influences. All elements in the fur trade—natives and whites, Dutch, English, Spanish, and French—abhorred the spread of permanent white settlement, which inevitably disrupted or dislodged Indian society and destroyed the forests and the game. The Jesuits could best be trusted to preserve the West for their Indian converts—and for themselves.

A third condition helped to solidify the Jesuits' monopoly. As the administration of New France learned early, among lay adventurers the distant West could be an underminer of discipline and a breeder of disloyalty. In 1629, one of Champlain's most trusted young lieutenants, Etienne Brulé, went west with a group of comrades. In the stillness of the forest they quickly felt the slackening of French fetters, struck out as independent traders, and shipped their furs not to Quebec but to the hated English on the Connecticut and Delaware rivers, who offered them a better price. Later Frenchmen, preferring negotiable income to the nebulous benefits of empire, traded *sub rosa* with the Dutch and the Iroquois. Such horrible examples were not lost on the crown councillors in Quebec nor on their superiors at Versailles. Jesuit confessors, moreover, were always on hand to ferret out the "interlopers," and to retail the news of their treachery to the authorities.

Still another circumstance strengthened the Jesuits' position. French laymen were subservient only to the civil government on the St. Lawrence; the Jesuits, in addition, were indissolubly tied to the church hierarchy there. Even loyal laymen might discover shorter, safer paths to the sea and bypass the St. Lawrence route. Such discoveries, by diverting revenues from Quebec (though not from the French themselves), would only undermine the regime at the capital and destroy the most strategic bastion of the empire. To forestall such as disaster, the civil authorities preferred to leave control of the West to the Jesuits, and to the bishops in Quebec who could insure their political soundness and good faith.

The Jesuits made much of their opportunity. During the Iroquois wars of the 1640s and 1650s they skirted the battlefield to the north and established French missions and French claims as far west as La Pointe in

152

present-day Wisconsin, at the farthermost reach of Lake Superior. Once the Iroquois were quelled in 1666 and the tribes that fled before them had returned to their hastily abandoned territory in eastern Wisconsin, Illinois, and Michigan, the Jesuits themselves turned back toward the east. From missions at Michilimackinac and Green Bay on Lake Michigan, and Sault Ste. Marie on the portage between lakes Huron and Superior, ambitious church fathers conducted the first thorough explorations of the waters of the Great Lakes region—notably the Illinois, Fox, and Wisconsin rivers. At last, in June 1671, on the basis of their work, the "Great Intendant," Jean Talon, ordered a regal ceremony at the Sault to be attended by the chiefs of 14 tribes and their retinues, as well as by missionary leaders and their own henchmen. Here Talon's emissary, François Daumont, Sieur de St. Lusson, fresh from the home country, raised the standard of France and claimed for the French crown all the known lands of Canada and "all other countries, rivers, lakes and territories, contiguous and adjacent thereunto, as well discovered as to be discovered, which are bounded on the one side by the Northern and Western Seas and on the other side by the South Sea, including all its length and breadth."

One of the rivers "to be discovered" was the Mississippi. Explorers had heard of the "great water" for more than a century, but as late as the 1670s the whereabouts of both its source and its mouth remained in doubt. To explore the Mississippi's course and to discover where it emptied, Talon chose Louis Jolliet, who had "already been quite near this great river" while prospecting for copper on the shores of Lake Superior. Jolliet, among other qualifications, had a reputation for getting along with the Jesuits. Father Claude Dablon, one of the most energetic organizers of Jesuit explorations and one of the most jealous guardians of their monopoly of the West, talked Talon into letting Father Marquette accompany Jolliet "as chaplain and Christian spokesman."

In December 1672 Jolliet arrived at Marquette's mission of St. Ignace on the Michigan peninsula, and the following spring they set out together for the Wisconsin River. In mid-June, according to Jolliet's account, "we safely entered Mississippi . . . with a joy I cannot express," and in one of the epic voyages of American exploration he and Marquette followed the river south almost to its juncture with the Arkansas. Here they learned from the local Indians that, "Beyond a doubt, the Mississippi River discharged into the Florida or Mexican Gulf, and not to the east in Virginia . . . or to the west in California." They decided to take the Indians' word instead of pushing on, for, as they explained. "We could give no information if we proceeded to fling ourselves into the hands of the Spanish, who, without doubt, would at least have detained us as captives.

The voyage over, Marquette returned directly to his mission. Disappointed in not finding the South Sea, Jolliet was at least able to report to Quebec in 1674 the gratifying news of a route from the St. Lawrence to the Spanish Gulf that could be traversed almost entirely by water. By controlling this route, the French, in Talon's words, might "confine [the English and the Iroquois] within very narrow limits." The prospect, at the same time, of splitting the Spanish empire in two and taking the "kingdom of Theguaio and Quivira, which border on Canada, and in which numerous gold mines are reported to exist," did not pass unnoticed.

## THE THRUST OF EMPIRE

Jesuit explorers did well for the Quebec regime; but not well enough to justify their obstructionist tactics in times of crisis against less pious Frenchmen who, in fact, could not be kept out of the woods and the West. During the Iroquois wars of the 1640s and 1650s, Quebec's income from the fur trade fell disastrously, and the urgent need for more revenue than the Jesuits were providing prompted the administration to risk its first guarded ex-

*Indians performing a tribal dance for Marquette and Jolliet (seated at upper left). (New York Public Library.)*

ceptions to the churchmen's monopoly. As the defenders of the monopoly warned, these exceptions eventually undermined the whole French North American empire, but not before this empire itself had been magnificently extended. The agents of imperial expansion and (not altogether unwittingly) of the ultimate collapse were the fabulous *coureurs de bois*—rangers of the woods—and the militant young captains who followed in their paths.

Much romantic nonsense has been written about the *coureurs de bois,* inspired no doubt by stories of the readiness with which they threw off the restraints of civilization, took on Indian women and Indian ways, and in other respects returned to the nomadic life of the "Noble Savage." In reality, most of the *coureurs* had shed the restraints of civilization before they ever entered the woods. It is true that many of their leaders were upper-class young Frenchmen come to America to seek their fortunes. But typically, the *coureurs* were the sons of impoverished Canadian *gentilshommes,* brought up amidst the pride, sloth,

and squalor of the *seigneuries*—uneducated, illiterate, wild. As likely as not it was their fathers who first drove them into the woods to find Indians with furs and to kill and steal. Later they might join up with a natural leader like Daniel Greysolon, Sieur Du Lhut, who gave his name, "irretrievably Anglicized," to modern Duluth, whose site he first visited in 1679. "The famous Du Lhut," writes Parkman, "is said to have made a general combination of the young men of Canada to follow him into the woods. Their plan was to be absent four years, in order that the edicts against them might have time to relent."

Once in the woods, moreover, the *coureur* led a life far removed from the simple pleasures of the wigwam, the fire, and the feast of venison. One of the greatest of the rangers, Pierre Esprit Radisson, set down the realities of the woodsman's existence:

What fairer bastion [of self-confidence] than a good tongue, especially when one sees his owne chimney smoak, or when we can kiss our owne wives or kiss our neighbour's wife with ease and

153

154

delight? It is a different thing when victualls are wanting, worke whole nights & dayes, lye down on the bare ground, & not always that hap, the breech in the water, the feare in the buttocks, to have the belly empty, the weariness in the bones, and drowsinesse of the body by the bad weather that you are to suffer, having nothing to keep you from such calamity.

The *coureurs de bois*—or outlaws of the bush, as Parkman brands them—received their first official encouragement to infringe on the Jesuit monopoly in 1654. In the spring of that year, the first spring of peace following the extinction of the Huron middlemen, an argosy of canoes with a cargo of fine furs unexpectedly arrived at Three Rivers after a hazardous passage from the Wisconsin country. At their helm were Indians hungry for European goods, and full of tales of western braves pining for trade. "To bring backe, if possible, those wildmen the next year, or others, being that fur is the best manna of the countrey," Governor Jean de Lauzon of New France licensed the hardheaded adventurer Médard Chouart, Sieur des Groseilliers, and a companion to return west with the natives. In 1656, Groseilliers (or "Gooseberry," as the English fondly called him later on) and his associate arrived back in Three Rivers with 50 canoes, "laden with goods which the French come to this end of the world to procure." Their smashing success inflamed the starving sons of the seigniories, and in a short time 30 or more of them had plunged, unauthorized, into the woods.

One profitable venture led to another until, by the 1670s, some 800 *coureurs,* out of a total French population of less than 10,000, "had vanished from sight in the immensity of a boundless wilderness." By the 1680s the adult population of the St. Lawrence had become so thinned out that the king ordered the execution of anyone going into the woods unlicensed. But the profits of disobedience seem to have averted the penalties. "All has been in vain," the intendant, Duchesneau, wrote home about 1679, "inasmuch as some of the most considerable families are interested with . . .

the *coureurs de bois* . . . and the governor lets them go and even shares in their gains."

Besides depleting the population along the St. Lawrence, the far-ranging *coureurs* brought other griefs to the administration at Quebec. Groseilliers, the sharp trader, and Radisson, his brother-in-law and a brilliant explorer, were the first important offenders. In order to shake off two observers whom the governor insisted they take along to insure him half the profits of the venture, they stole silently from the capital in August 1659 and made a marvelously rapid journey around the Iroquois empire to the southern shores of Lake Superior. There, before the winter had settled in, they threw up a sturdy trading station on Chequamegon Bay. The primitive hunting tribes of the interior were lured to their metal trading goods like bears to honey. Direct dealings with the Indians meant that no troublesome middlemen were needed; more important, Radisson quickly grasped the idea that the hazardous journey through hostile country back to the St. Lawrence with heavy loads of fur could be avoided by using Hudson Bay, much talked of among the red men, as an outlet to the sea.

Impatient to explore the exciting new prospect, the two *coureurs* hurried back to Quebec in the summer of 1660, proud leaders of a majectic flotilla of 60 canoes groaning under their cargo of fine pelts. The scene on arrival was impressive; but not sufficiently so to thaw the governor. For their effrontery in going off as they did, the *coureurs'* cargo was almost wholly confiscated. Worse, the administration would not hear a word of a route that bypassed the St. Lawrence citadel, however advantageous it might prove commercially. Groseilliers and Radisson hastened to France to persuade the home government to overrule the provincials. When Versailles rebuffed them, they turned for backing to some private French merchants at Cadiz, with no greater luck. Fed up with their countrymen, they daringly approached the English and, after the failure of an expedition from Boston to reach Hudson Bay in 1662, they won the support of Charles II and a group of merchants in London who basked in the patronage of the King's cousin, Prince Rupert. In August 1668, for the first time since Henry Hudson's voyage in 1610 or 1611, a white man's vessel entered Hudson Bay, to return to London the next year laden with furs. In 1670, Prince Rupert helped float the renowned Hudson's Bay Company—"The Governor and Company of Adventurers of England trading into Hudson's Bay," to give

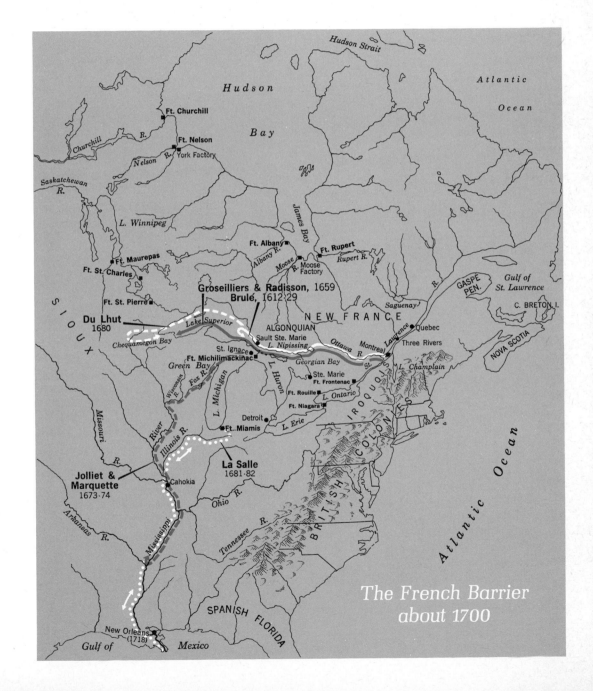

The French Barrier
about 1700

156

it its resounding official title—to exploit England's unexpected gift from the French.

Hudson Bay was a phenomenally strategic body of water, and news of English vessels "interloping" there had a phenomenal effect on the French. The Bay's value lay only partly in its own vast protected extent and its connection with the Atlantic—for a few ice-free months each year—by way of Hudson Strait. Equally important were the strategic rivers, like the ribs of a gigantic fan, that emptied into it. The two westernmost of these rivers (see map, p. 155), the Churchill and the Nelson, commanded the Canadian great plains and the Rockies beyond. The easternmost, the Rupert, threatened the St. Lawrence country itself. But most menacing to the French were the Moose and the Albany, whose drainage systems converged on the cross-roads of the entire continent: the north-south Mississippi Basin, and the east-west Great Lakes.

Groseilliers and Radisson had tilted the whole French-Canadian world and urgent measures were needed to set it right once more. The Jesuits, characteristically, concentrated on preserving the St. Lawrence entrepôts; in the 1670s and 1680s, they planted vigorous new missions in the Minnesota country to dissuade converted red men (and to convert others) from commerce with the white men of the Hudson Bay "factories," or warehouses, who were little better than infidels. The imaginative *coureurs de bois* and the importunate military adventurers had far more aggressive ideas—ideas that a new political administration sometimes supported with vigor against persistent Jesuit caviling. Their strategy naturally focused on the Mississippi River, but their plans for the envelopment of the distant West and the subjugation of the populous English East were no less grandiose.

The Mississippi had many attractions besides its grandeur. Control of its whole length would confine the incorrigible Iroquois to the eastern valley and in addition would frustrate plans to link up the Iroquois empire with the new British satrapy at the northern bay. At the same time it would split the Spanish empire to the south and open the vast American plains to French exploitation. Above all, perhaps, the Mississippi offered an all-weather outlet to the sea for the furs of the virgin lands it dominated. All these considerations, no doubt, burned in the mind of the intendant, Talon, when he sponsored the epochal journey of Jolliet and Marquette in 1672.

### THE CONVERGENCE OF ENEMIES

When Jolliet returned to Quebec in 1674 with his news of a virtually all-water route from the St. Lawrence to the Spanish Gulf, the redoubtable Talon had been replaced by the "Iron Governor," Louis Comte de Frontenac. Among the governor's protégés was the *coureur* extraordinary, Robert Cavelier, Sieur de La Salle, who after a hasty voyage to Paris following Jolliet's report, returned to Quebec in 1675 armed with the royal blessing and a five-year monopoly of the Mississippi fur trade. There were no limits to La Salle's imagination nor to Frontenac's endorsement of his plans. On April 9, 1682, as a mere preliminary to his breathtaking scheme for a comprehensive commercial system on the waters of the West, La Salle and a score of fellow *coureurs* completed the exploration of the Mississippi all the way to the Gulf. There the great leader claimed for France "possession of that river, of all the rivers that enter into it, and all the country watered by them." To this claim he gave the name Louisiana, in honor of his sovereign.

December 1682 found La Salle and his company, on their journey upstream, at the confluence of the Mississippi and the Illinois rivers. There, on a towering precipice, La Salle ordered the construction of an armed post, Fort St. Louis, to serve at once as a beacon to friendly braves eager for trade and a bastion against the aroused Iroquois who had sworn his death. Trade flourished during the first spring; but the fickle government of Louis XIV had just replaced Frontenac with a new governor, Le Febvre de la Barre, who grew jealous of La Salle's monopoly and was unwilling to assist in its defense. Desperate to conclude this phase of his work, La Salle left subordinates in charge at St. Louis to defend it as best they could and took ship for France to get additional backing for the construction of a post at the very mouth of the Mississippi. His aim was to protect Louisiana from the Spanish and provide a port from which the furs of the whole vast valley could be exported to the world. During his absence St. Louis became untenable, and La Salle's own excursion cost him his life. Having found backing in Paris, in 1684 La Salle was on his triumphant way back to the future site of New Orleans with four strong ships. However, the weather turned stormy, the crew rebellious, and navigation blind. Failing to find the Mississippi, the company piled up hundreds of miles away at Spanish Matagorda Bay. Here the imperious commander was unceremoniously murdered by his men, who in turn were massacred by wild Comanche warriors.

La Salle's original delay in getting started between 1675 and 1682, was itself the result of the Iroquois' raids on all interlopers, red or white, who violated the borders of their preserve. Daniel Greysolon, Sieur Du Lhut, determined to profit from La Salle's experience. In 1678, while Frontenac still was governor and still giving the *coureurs* enthusiastic support—for a fat share in the proceeds of their trade—Du Lhut proposed to divert the pelts of the virgin West from the British at Hudson Bay by resuming the quest for a northwest passage to the pacific. The best fur-bearing lands themselves now lay north and west of Lake Superior in the direction of the elusive "western sea"; best of all, there would be no Iroquois to contend with.

In the next three years Du Lhut and his rangers explored the northern reaches of the Mississippi River and claimed much of the country beyond it for France. But in place of the Iroquois they soon encountered the ferocious Sioux. "The hand of the Sioux," Brebner writes, "was raised against every man and the Canadians found it easiest in the long run to go around their territory." But the only way around the Sioux open to the French was through the frigid Saskatchewan Valley and the forbidding country still farther north (see map, p. 155)—country that other Frenchmen were to penetrate and explore before the end of the eighteenth century. Du Lhut returned to Quebec in 1681 to answer Jesuit charges that, through dealings with wild, unlicensed traders, he was setting up a private fur empire and undermining the central administration. The charges were never made to stick, but Du Lhut never strayed so far again. In 1684 he built Fort Tourette north of Lake Nipigon, which itself was due north of Lake Superior on the eastern edge of the Sioux domains. The same year, however, the Iroquois, prompted by the British, took to the warpath and forced Du Lhut to seek the protection of the St. Lawrence once more.

Failures like La Salle's and Du Lhut's convinced Canadian officials that they would have to resort to military terror if the Iroquois and other enemy tribes were to be controlled and if the English and the Spanish were to be ousted from the French empire. The Jesuits fought the military policy even more pertinaciously than they opposed the *coureurs;* and the aging Louis XIV, increasingly concerned over his eternal soul, supported the churchmen. Frontenac, however, who had returned as governor in 1689, took his own militant course. And before his death in 1698 the French had begun to construct forts along the length of the Mississippi and across the Great Lakes country. The northern anchor of this system was Fort Detroit, which Cadillac, after bitter controversies with the Jesuits, managed to finish in 1699. Among the last of the forts was the one erected at New Orleans, where in 1718 the southernmost citadel of the French North American empire was established.

Nor where the French content just to build defensive military outposts. Their larger pol-

158

icy was to oust the British entirely. King Philip's War of 1675 (see p. 66) marked one of the earliest French-inspired Indian attacks on the New England colonies. Others followed so regularly and threatened so overwhelmingly that in 1690, on the eve of the grim Salem witch trials (see p. 124), Cotton Mather cried, "It was Canada that was the chief source of New England's miseries. There was the main strength of the French. . . . *Canada must be reduced.*" During the witch trials themselves two years later, it was charged against John Alden, one of the most prominent of the accused, that "He sells powder and shot to the Indians and the French and lies with Indian squaws and has Indian papooses."

III   *The World Wars of the Eighteenth Century*

**PARTIES TO THE CONFLICT**

Virtually from the beginning of settlement in America the Protestant English and the Catholic French, each with their tentative Indian allies, had been warring on one another. Besides the fur trade, the Canadian fisheries created tensions between the two camps that were not to be satisfactorily settled until the end of the nineteenth century. As early as 1613, an expedition under Captain Samuel Argall set forth from primitive Virginia and exterminated the French pioneers in Acadia (modern Nova Scotia). Sixteen years later intolerant Puritans sallied forth against Quebec, which they seized and held for a time. Algonquian Indian raids on New England's fishing villages somewhat compensated the French, the Algonquians' friends; but the brutal exchange of raids and massacres continued. After the Catholic Stuarts came to the English throne in 1660, the kingdom's policy was largely dictated by their Catholic cousin across the Channel, Louis

XIV. But this royal liaison did not deter individual English aristocrats and merchants from bedeviling the French empire in pursuit of private profit. The incredible coup by which the English turned the work of Groseilliers and Radisson at Hudson Bay in 1670 to their own benefit marked a turning point in American if not in world history. And the work of Jolliet and Marquette, La Salle, Du Lhut, and Cadillac—not to mention their great superiors, Talon and Frontenac—in counteracting the English coup gave momentum to the larger struggle that was brewing in Europe.

In 1689 Protestant King William of Orange, as we have seen (p. 77), came to the throne of England as William III, anxious to settle accounts with Louis XIV for his aggressions against Holland. The resulting conflict foreshadowed the great wars that were to mar the eighteenth century. Known in Europe as the War of the League of Augsburg (after the coalition William had organized to suppress Louis XIV's claims to hegemony over the Continent) and known in America as King William's War, this struggle dragged on in the Old World and the New until 1697. While William's League may have had the best of the fighting on the Continent, the French surely had all the best of it in America. Their forces captured York Factory on Hudson Bay and disrupted the trade of the other English establishments there. They also collaborated with the Indians in ferocious raids against English settlements at Schenectady, New York, and on the Maine and New Hampshire frontiers, and harassed the Massachusetts fishing fleet. At the same time, Frontenac turned back a vigorous assault on Quebec led by a worthy antagonist, William Phips, Governor of Massachusetts.

The Peace of Ryswick brought King William's war to an end in 1697 without settling any of the issues between the combatants. By then, moreover, other parties to the looming universal conflict had strengthened their New World positions. The Iroquois, alarmed by the new show of French strength under Frontenac, reaffirmed their allegiance to the English; it was on this pledge that English claims to the Ohio and Mississippi valleys were henceforth to rest. As part of the agreement, the Five Nations promised to end their bedevilment of the American settlements verging on their domains. Americans in the Carolinas, meanwhile, had found their way around the southern end of the Appalachians and were pushing their own hunting and trading activities to the very shores of the Mississippi below St. Louis. Farther south and west, the Spanish, first aroused by La Salle's activities at the Mississippi's mouth, began pushing into West Florida, Texas, and New Mexico. Spanish moves into the western plains, like the earlier advances of the French beyond Lake Superior and the English beyond the Mohawk, were promptly thrown back by the Indian barrier. This time the Comanches and Apaches played the roles that earlier had fallen to the more northerly Iroquois and Sioux. But a Spanish base established at Pensacola, Florida, in 1696 effectively retarded the French development of Louisiana and the progress of the Carolinians as well.

The Peace of Ryswick came to a violent end in 1702. Two years before, the Spanish king had died without an heir, and Louis XIV had grasped the opportunity to extend Bourbon influence to the Iberian Peninsula by installing his grandson on the throne. William III, backing a candidate of his own, allied himself with other continental powers to expel Louis' young protégé. But they had more than that in mind, showing the growing importance of the New World in the world-wide scheme of things; for as one of the coalition's own treaties said, its members had come together, "especially in order that the French shall never come into possession of the Spanish Indies nor be permitted . . . to navigate there for the purpose of carrying on trade."

William died in 1702. His successor, Queen Anne, persisting in his policies, fought France

and Spain for 11 bitter years in the conflict known in America as Queen Anne's war, in Europe as the War of the Spanish Succession. In the New World the struggle ranged from the Atlantic to the Mississippi, from the Gulf of Mexico to Hudson Bay. From it, Carolina in the south and Massachusetts in the north emerged as the bulwarks of the English mainland empire. The first remained exposed to Spanish attack, the second to French attack, for many decades; the "plantations" in between enjoyed the protection of Iroquois warriors while England herself concentrated on her European affairs.

Although Carolina and Massachusetts suffered severely from the long struggle, the French and their Spanish allies eventually were defeated everywhere. The Peace of Utrecht of 1713, which ended Queen Anne's War after years of negotiation, hastened the decline of Spain as a world power and the expulsion of the French from the New World. The Peace of Utrecht confirmed the Bourbon's occupation of the Spanish throne, which remained in their family until 1931. But in the New World, France surrendered to her Protestant enemy her part of rich St. Christopher in the West Indies (renamed St. Kitts, after the British settlement on the island), confirmed British supremacy over Hudson Bay, and yielded Acadia as well. Above all, the French recognized the Iroquois as British subjects and the Iroquois empire as a British domain. Britain also won from both France and Spain commercial concessions that boosted American as well as English trade with the Spanish Main and Spanish islands in the Caribbean. The most momentous of these was the *asiento,* under which they, rather than the French, gained the exclusive privilege of selling African slaves to the Spanish Indies and the Spanish Main (see p. 97).

The British took such gluttonous advantage of Spain's commercial concessions that the Spanish organized a special Caribbean coast guard, manned by the roughest pirates they could enlist, to keep from being swallowed

*Capture of Louisbourg by colonial forces, 1745. (Courtesy Kenneth M. Newman, The Old Print Shop, N.Y.C.)*

whole. In 1739 a British seaman named Robert Jenkins was haled before Parliament by the "war party" that was growing in opposition to Spanish manhandling of British seamen. In a little box he carried a carefully preserved human ear, which he claimed a Spanish officer had cut from his head as a bloody warning against British interference. This dramatic tableau created a sensation, and Britain promptly embarked on "The War of Jenkins' Ear." Disaster followed disaster as the British staged a series of unsuccessful attacks on the Atlantic and Pacific coasts of Spanish America. No final decision was reached until a new general European war broke out in 1745, this one a struggle over the Austrian succession.

One of the places Britain had failed to take from the French in 1713 was Cape Breton Island, just to the north of Acadia, which commanded the entrance to the Gulf of St. Lawrence. Here the French built the mighty fortress of Louisbourg, the "Gibraltar of the New World." In the third of the great international conflicts, the War of the Austrian Succession, or King George's War (1745–1748), Massachusetts forces assaulted Louisbourg and, to everyone's surprise, including their own, they managed to capture it. Colonial love for the mother country was hardly warmed by Britain's restoration of Louisbourg to the French in the Peace of Aix-la-Chapelle, which ended this latest struggle. In return, Britain received Madras in India.

## THE FRENCH AND INDIAN WAR

Like the Peace of Ryswick in 1697, the Treaty of Aix-la-Chapelle was more a truce than a permanent settlement. Even before it was signed, both the French and the British had begun preparations for a final showdown. In 1747, with the formation of the Ohio Company of Virginia, Britain had embarked on a shrewd program of encouraging colonial land speculators to stake out huge tracts in the Ohio Valley, "inasmuch as nothing can more effectively tend to defeat the dangerous designs of the French." In 1749, the governor of Canada sent his own representative, Jean Baptiste le Moyne de Bienville, to occupy the valley. During the next few years other Frenchmen followed to work out a system of military defenses. Governor Dinwiddie of Virginia, an investor in the Ohio Company, caught wind of French activity in 1753 and ordered young George Washington to travel west with a protest. When this mission failed, Washington was sent out the next year with a small force and orders to halt the French. This mission ran up against the newly erected French Fort Duquesne at the forks of the Ohio, the site of modern Pittsburgh. Washington proceeded to build his own Fort Necessity at nearby Great Meadows, but in July was forced to capitulate to a French attack upon it. Although the formal declaration of war between the French and the English did not come until 1756, actual fighting had already begun, appropriately enough, in the New World.

The extension of French fort-building in the West caused the Privy Council in England to look to its own strength in America. This rested heavily on the Iroquois; but the British now sensed the growing discontent of their native allies in the face of policies that had prompted the creation of the Ohio Company. American land hunger and frequent confrontations between red men and white on the moving frontier further deepened

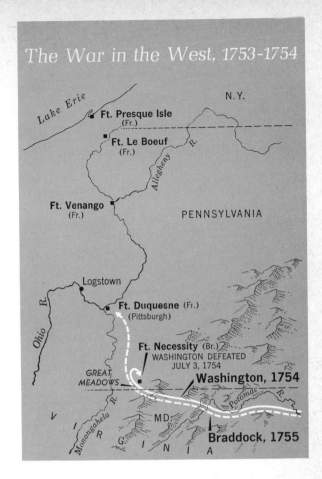

## The War in the West, 1753-1754

Indian suspicions of the sanctity of their preserves. In an attempt to restore, Iroquois confidence on the eve of certain war with the French, the Privy Council called for a meeting at Albany, New York, in June 1754, at which delegates from all the northern colonies were to meet with Iroquois and other Indian leaders. At the Albany Congress the Iroquois accepted the lavish British gifts but made no promises of their own. To their suspicions of the British were added their traditional respect for the military prowess of the French, now much enhanced.

One objective of the Albany Congress was the formation of an intercolonial union to bring some consistency into colonial Indian policies. Under Benjamin Franklin's leader-

161

162

ship a Plan of Union was presented and accepted by the delegates. It called for a "General Government . . . under which Government each Colony may retain its present constitution" except for certain particulars. The supergovernment could consist of a grand council made up of representatives drawn from each colony on the basis of population and wealth. A president-general (to be appointed by the king) and a treasurer would comprise the executive branch, advised by the grand council but with final authority in matters of peace and war. The grand council would handle Indian affairs, administer the disposal of western lands, govern the frontier territories beyond the precincts of the colonies until the Crown took over, and levy taxes to maintain a colonial army.

Neither the British government nor the in-

dividual colonial governments would even consider this enlightened proposal. Not a single colony supported its spokesmen, and Britain herself rejected their work. "The Assemblies," Franklin wrote, ". . . thought there was too much *prerogative* in it, and in England it was judged to have too much of the *democratic*." Land speculators, particularly strong in the Virginia government, which had not even bothered to send delegates to Albany, had no intention of entrusting the distribution of the Ohio lands to an intercolonial congress, and every colonial assembly was jealous of its own control of taxation. The colonies were not ready for union in 1754, and the war against the French was conducted inefficiently and with constant bickering among the Americans and between them and the mother country.

Neither the French nor the British welcomed a resumption of the world conflict; in fact, the Duke of Newcastle, the First Secretary of State, hoped at first that the war

*General Braddock and his troops on their ill-fated march toward Fort Duquesne. (Culver Pictures.)*

might be localized. Seeking to gain his objective with a great show of strength, in April 1775, he sent General Edward Braddock and 1400 regulars to America to level Fort Duquesne. Braddock was to be assisted by 450 colonials under Lieutenant Colonel Washington. Unfortunately for British hopes, Braddock's entire force was ambushed and savagely mauled in July by a force of French and Indians on the Monongahela River about eight miles below the fort, and Braddock himself was mortally wounded.

Braddock's defeat opened the eyes of the colonials, whose regard for British redcoats declined swiftly thereafter. The survivors of the expedition were saved only by the timely work of Washington and his militia, a circumstance, in turn, that caused the Colonel's estimation of the Americans' own prowess to soar. Braddock's defeat also weakened the waning prestige of the British among the Indians. The French and Indian victory soon exposed the western settlements of Pennsylvania, Maryland, and Virginia to a series of French and Indian raids. Other British operations that year were also largely unsuccessful. General William Johnson, with 2000 British troops and 250 Mohawks, rebuffed a strong French assault on Lake George. Elsewhere, however, the British failed to take Fort Niagara, the key to French control of the West, or Crown Point on Lake Champlain.

In the meantime, the struggle for America once more became part of a world war raging on the Continent, in the Mediterranean, the Indian Ocean, the West Indies, and finally even the Philippines. In a new shift of alliances, France, Austria, Russia, Sweden, many of the German states, and later Spain, were arrayed against Britain, Portugal, and Prussia. Until 1758 the contest went so dismally for Britain and her allies almost everywhere that the Earl of Chesterfield was driven to write: "The French are masters to do what they please in America. We are no longer a nation. I never yet saw so dreadful a prospect." In that year, however, the brilliant organizer and strategist William Pitt became Secretary

of State and British fortunes picked up. At a moment of grave discouragment, Pitt showed amazing confidence. "I am sure," he said, "that I can save the country, and that no one else can." Perceiving the central importance of seapower and of the American theater of action, Pitt subsidized Frederick the Great of Prussia to carry the burden of war in Europe, used the British fleet to bottle up French ships in French ports, and brought greater energy to bear in the New World. For Pitt the central strategic objective was the conquest of Canada and the capture of the American interior. To this end he used British superiority at sea to strike hardest at the two focal points of French power—Louisbourg and Quebec.

In 1758 the British recaptured Louisbourg, "the strongest fortress in the New World," the key to the St. Lawrence River and the Atlantic fisheries, and a standing threat to New England. The event was celebrated with great bonfires in London, Philadelphia, Boston, and New York. "A hundred thousand million of congratulations report this great and glorious event, the salvation of Europe," wrote one of Pitt's enthusiastic English correspondents. In the same year George Washington, now on the staff of Brigadier John

163

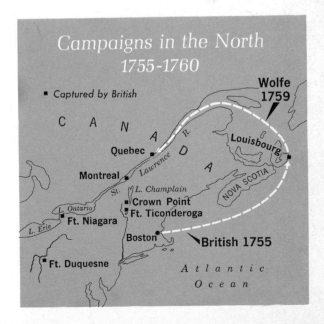

164

Forbes, had the satisfaction at last of taking part in the capture of Fort Duquesne, now renamed "Pitts-bourgh" in honor of the British leader. Frederick the Great, meanwhile, turned the tide on the Continent, and Clive began to tame the French in India.

The climax among the victories of the following year came when a brilliant young brigadier general, James Wolfe, after bringing a large army up the St. Lawrence from Louisbourg, stormed the Heights of Abraham outside Quebec and took the city from a smaller force under General Montcalm, thus gaining strategic control of the St. Lawrence. Both generals were killed in the battle, but Wolfe lived long enough to know that he had won Canada for the empire. Since the British were also winning on the sea, in the West Indies, in India, and in the American West, the crisis in the war had passed. "Some time ago," said Pitt in the midst of all these triumphs, "I would have been content to bring France to her knees, now I will not rest till I have laid her on her back." Thus the war dragged on until 1763, when the opposing coalition at last agreed to make peace.

By the Treaty of Paris, concluded in February 1763, Britain won from France all of Canada and all the great interior east of the Mississippi except for the port of New Orleans. France (to the dismay of Pitt, who had been dismissed by George III) retained fishing rights on the Newfoundland banks and two small islands as fishing bases there. Britain also returned to her the captured West Indies islands of Martinique and Guadeloupe. Spain surrendered East and West Florida to the British in return for the restoration of Cuba, which had been overrun the preceding year. By a treaty contracted between France and Spain in 1762, which had induced Spain to enter the war, France compensated her ally by yielding to her all the French territories west of the Mississippi, together with the Isle of Orleans east of it.

Even before the negotiations leading to the Treaty of Paris, British statesmen realized that they could not have both Guadeloupe and Canada—that if they demanded both, the French would continue the fight. Perhaps most influential in the decision to keep Canada and renounce Guadeloupe was the pressure exerted by plantation owners in the British West Indies, who feared competition from Guadeloupe sugar if that island were brought into the empire. The attractions of Canada's fur trade likewise were not lost on the British negotiators. But more general con-

"Quebec, The Capital of New France, a Bishoprick, and Seat of the Soverain Court." This line engraving, done in 1759 by Thomas Johnson, is the earliest American engraved view of Quebec. The small structure (upper left) to the immediate right of the tree is the fortification called the Citadel. The Plains of Abraham are to the left of this, off the picture. (Stokes Collection, New York Public Library.)

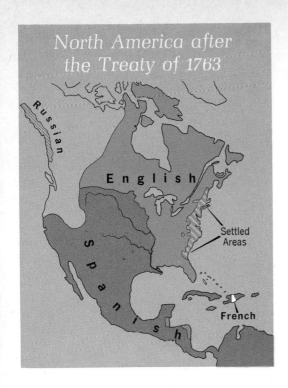

North America after the Treaty of 1763

Russian

English

Settled Areas

Spanish

French

this area, even at the cost of another sugar island, seemed sound policy.

During the argument over the treaty, it was asked whether Canada would not some day revolt and announce its independence of Britain. It was also said that if the French were expelled from Canada, the American colonists themselves would no longer feel so dependent on the mother country for protection. Benjamin Franklin, then in London as a colonial agent, wrote a pamphlet on the subject in which he argued for retaining Canada as part of an American agricultural empire that would offer a vast and rapidly expanding market for British manufactures. The idea of independence Franklin brushed lightly aside. If the North American colonists had been incapable of uniting against the French and Indians, he asked, was there any likelihood that they would unite against "their own nation" which "they love much more than they love one another?" A union among the colonies, he went on, "is not merely improbable it is impossible."

But here Franklin added an explanation which, though he did not mean it as a warning, might well have been taken as such: "When I say such a union is impossible, I mean without the most grievous tyranny and oppression." There was no assurance, of course, that Englishmen and Americans would agree on precisely what constituted grievous tyranny. When Franklin published his essay in 1760, he could hardly have imagined that 16 years later he would put his signature to a Declaration of Independence and negotiate for loans with Britain's enemies.

siderations also had their effect. Most important among these was the growing realization of the importance of Britain's mainland colonies, especially the rapidly growing Middle colonies and New England, as markets for British goods. Heretofore, the American empire had been valued mainly as a source of raw materials—tobacco and rice in the mainland South, sugar in the West Indies; in 1698, seven-eighths of Britain's American trade had been with these staple-producing regions. By the 1760s, however, two-thirds of Britain's American exports were going to areas north of Maryland. Removing France in Canada from

# READINGS

Between 1851 and 1892, Francis Parkman published the eight volumes that make up his study of *France and England in North America*, which is devoted almost entirely to the period discussed in the present chapter. Parkman's analysis of Indian civilization was written before modern anthropology took over the field; but it retains historical values of its own, often neglected in modern social science, that justify its close examination even now. Later historical scholarship has also altered some of Parkman's findings in other areas. Yet his books remain a monument to one of the greatest of American historians and an unfailing pleasure to read. Short passages may be found in the far from fragmentary one-volume *The Parkman Reader* (1955), edited by S.E. Morison. J.B. Brebner, *The Explorers of North America 1492–1806* (1933), is a superb study based largely on the explorers' own accounts but illuminated by the author's grasp of the implications of exploration for American, Canadian, and world history.

The general books on the American Indians mentioned in the Readings for Chapter One may be supplemented by A.M. Josephy, *The Patriot Chiefs, a Chronicle of Indian Leadership* (1961), and Oliver La Farge, *A Pictorial History of the American Indian* (1957). Of value on more specific topics are G.T. Hunt, *The Wars of the Iroquois* (1940), and W.R. Jacobs, *Diplomacy and Indian Gifts, Anglo-French Rivalry along the Ohio and Northwest Frontiers 1748–1763* (1950). Authoritative on early Canadian history are G.M. Wrong, *The Rise and Fall of New France* (2 vols., 1928), and his shorter work, *The Conquest of New France* (1918). W.B. Munro, *Crusaders of New France* (1918), also merits examination. Two admirable histories of Canada cover the period of this chapter at length: W.T. Easterbrook and H.G.J. Aitken, *Canadian Economic History* (1956), and D.G. Creighton, *A History of Canada* (1958). A useful work on more southerly country is W.E. Dunn, *Spanish and French Rivalry in the Gulf Region of the United States 1678–1702* (1917).

Three general works on exploration and settlement give much attention to the international struggle for control of North America: V.B. Holmes, *A History of the Americas From Discovery to Nationhood* (1950); Bernard DeVoto, *The Course of Empire* (1952); and L.D. Baldwin, *The Story of the Americas* (1943). The background of the international wars of the first half of the eighteenth century is brilliantly set forth in W.L. Dorn, *Competition for Empire 1740–1763* (1940), an indispensable book. Max Savelle, *The Origins of American Diplomacy, the International History of Anglo-America 1492–1763* (1967), also is outstanding. As illuminating as it was influential is A.T. Mahan, *The Influence of Sea Power upon History 1660–1783* (1894). Excellent accounts of the period and topics covered in this chapter may be found in vol. II of Edward Channing, *A History of the United States,* and R.A. Billington, *Westward Expansion,* both listed in our General Bibliography.

First-rate special studies of the fur trade include: Volume I of E.E. Rich, *Hudson's Bay Company* (3 vols., 1960), on the period 1670–1763; C.A. Vandiveer, *The Fur Trade and Early Western Exploration* (1929); H.A. Innis, *The Fur Trade in Canada* (1930); and V.W. Crane, *The Southern Frontier 1670–1732* (1929). G.L. Nute, *Caesars of the Wilderness: Médard Chouart, Sieur des Groseilliers, and Pierre Esprit Radisson* (1943), is a fine study of the leading *coureurs de bois*. See also L.P. Kellogg, *The French Regime in Wisconsin and the Northwest* (1925). C.H. Ambler, *Washington and the West* (1936), is a useful introduction to the role of land-speculation in the international contest. A.P. James, *The Ohio Company, its Inner History* (1959), is authoritative. Biographies of Washington, Jefferson, Marshall, and Franklin, suggested for other chapters, have illuminating material on early western land problems.

    H.H. Peckham, *The Colonial Wars 1689–1762* (1964), offers a short, scholarly account of the military side of the conflict for empire in America. The most elaborate account of the French and Indian War is to be found in L.H. Gipson, *The British Empire before the American Revolution* (13 vols., 1936–1967). E.P. Hamilton, *The French and Indian Wars* (1962), is especially good on the terrain, boats, and weapons of the conflict. O.A. Sherrard, *Lord Chatham* (3 vols., 1952–1958), is outstanding on William Pitt the Elder. Interesting shorter works include J. H. Plumb, *Chatham* (1953), and C.G. Robertson, *Chatham and the British Empire* (1946).

167

# SIX

In 1763, when the French and Indian War ended, France seemed ruined. Although she was not beyond recovery, as William Pitt warned with characteristic insight, even few Frenchmen expected that she would soon be able to resume the imperial contest. Britain, by contrast, appeared to be at the peak of her imperial glory; yet her North American mainland colonies were to rebel against her "tyranny" much earlier than the French would turn on the absolutist Bourbons, and indeed they would win their independence with French aid.

Few changes in national fortunes have come about so swiftly and with so little apparent incitement. Indeed, on both sides of the ocean reasonable men found the revolutionary movement in America incomprehensible—and who could blame them when rebel spokesmen talked of little but preserving *English* liberties? For all their chafing under the imperial system, the colonials, said the rebel leader John Adams of Massachusetts, "had been educated in an habitual affection for England." Many colonials, even in Boston in fact had no more affection for England than for New England (see Chapter Three). The "affectionate" colonials Adams had in mind were the articulate leaders of his own commonwealth, the most English of all the American "plantations," and the heirs of early English settlers in other colonies suddenly beset by swarms of alien and abrasive poor assaulting their landed as well as their cultural heritage. And yet it was these English who stood in the forefront of the rebellion against the mother country.

Ambrose Serle, civilian secretary to Lord Richard Howe, the British naval commander in America during the early years of the

# THE AMERICAN REVOLUTION

fighting, declared that, "The Annals of no Country can produce an Instance of so virulent a Rebellion, of such implacable madness and Fury, originating from such trivial Causes as those alleged by these unhappy People." Serle's description hardly characterizes the eight dreary years of spasmodic revolutionary warfare; but even if it did, the Revolution was effected less by popular "virulence" than by learned argument, "the energies of well-weighed choice"; less by "those mad tumultuous actions which disgraced many of the great revolutions of antiquity," than by the force of continental aspirations.

By the 1770s, nearly 700,000 of the white inhabitants of the 13 rebellious colonies—almost two-fifths of their entire white population—were of non-English extraction. Of the Scotch-Irish and Germans who predominated among them, the former, as we have seen (Chapter Three), had few reasons to love the mother country, the latter strong leanings toward their own traditions. Even among English-born colonials or those with English forebears, there were many religious dissenters or descendants of religious dissenters who had neither forgiven nor forgotten persecution at home. These, together with convicts or the offspring of convicts forcibly banished to New World servitude, made poor material from which to fashion dutiful subjects.

Still another 450,000 Americans at this time were Negroes from Africa or of African descent, most of them submerged in slavery. Had more of them been aware of England's predominant role in the eighteenth-century slave trade and of Parliament's role in forcing captive blacks on ambivalent colonies for the benefit of commercial carriers (see pp. 96–97), they may have loved the English even less than they loved their masters. As it was, tens of thousands of them responded to British promises of freedom for abandoning the fields and joining the fighting on the loyal side, and even greater numbers left with the British at the end of the war or were taken beyond the boundaries of the victors by their loyalist owners. At the same time, about 5000 Negroes, free and slave, largely from northern colonies, joined the rebels when reluctantly permitted to do so by American leaders, no doubt in the hope of securing that liberty and equality which, it was said, the fighting was all about.

Many Scotch-Irish, Germans, and members of other minority groups, of course, although they often had as little sympathy for the Revolution as for the British, also were won over to the conflict by rebel leaders. When, in

170

1775, a North Carolina convention elected delegates to the Continental Congress (see p. 190), Andrew Miller, a loyalist merchant, asked the westerners in the colony to pay no part of their expenses,

> as they had no share in the Nomination, having only one or two members for a County, and the Southern and lower Countys had some of them 6 Votes. It is not in Character, to dispute the power of Parliament when we say we are not represented, and yet quickly Submit to so unequal a Representation in a body formed by ourselves. But I am afraid I am only repeating what you must have before heard from others.

Sometimes, ethnic-group participation was gained by promises of attention to such frontier complaints, more often by the westerners' own generalized expectations of equality of opportunity with the English in the future.

Support of the fighting, nevertheless, proved no stronger in the colonies than in the distant mother country. By December 1776 the 16,000 men Washington had taken under his command 18 months earlier (see p. 194) had dwindled to 2400 bitter-enders; and frequently in succeeding years it seemed that the British might be near victory for want of opposition and the rebels near disintegration for want of pay.

Popular apathy toward the war may have given the large number of loyalists in the colonies encouragement to persist in their opposition to the rebellion despite widespread personal harrassment; and the more so, since many of them believed that only the authority of the mother country could maintain political stability in an America of antagonistic commonwealths, each swelling with violent foreigners on the Indian frontiers and unruly mobs in the cities, neither class to be trusted with English liberties. Yet the challenge of British authority and loyalist sentiment from the top, and of rural squatters and urban workers from the bottom, only deepened the commitment of such conservative rebel leaders as Adams of Massachusetts,

Franklin of Pennsylvania, and Washington of Virginia to the necessity of ridding English liberties themselves of the "systems of civil and priestly hierarchy" under which they had become corrupted in the mother country and of defending their purity here.

Americans were "born heirs of freedom," declared one of their leaders, forgetting the servants and the slaves; whereas in England, as early as the 1750s, Franklin had found "an extream corruption prevalent among all orders of men in this rotton state." Somewhat later, Adams observed of the mother country that, "Corruption, like a cancer . . . eats faster and faster every hour. The revenue creates pensioners, and the pensioners urge for more revenue, . . . until virtue, integrity, public spirit, simplicity, and frugality, become the objects of ridicule, and . . . foppery, selfishness, meanness, and downright venality swallow up the whole society." "Every American of fortune and common sense," he said, "must look upon his property to be sunk downright half of its value" the moment "an absolute subjection" to the Parliament of such a society "is established."

The heart of the rebellion lay in the threatened infection of America with the pox that in colonial opinion had killed English liberties at home. As John Dickinson of Pennsylvania put it in 1768, the critical question was "not, what evil *has actually attended* particular measures,—but what evil in the nature of things, is *likely to attend* them." The colonials, their friend Edmund Burke told the Commons seven years later, "auger misgovernment at a distance and snuff the approach of tyranny in every tainted breeze."

Reminiscing long after American independence had been won, John Adams asked, "What do we mean by the Revolution? The War? That was no part of the Revolution. It was only an Effect and Consequence of it. The Revolution was in the minds of the people, and this was effected, from 1760 to 1775, in the course of fifteen years before a drop of blood was drawn at Lexington." He meant, of course, the people of "principle and property," not the "turbulent and changing" rabble "of no importance"; the "friends of order," not its foes.

And yet, despite the leaders' detestation of "Christian White Savages" on the frontiers, Franklin's epithet, the political Revolution became a social revolution of a new and lasting kind. It created not a purified England but an open America, one characterized not by virgin leaders but (forgetting the *red* "savages") by virgin lands. Thomas Jefferson identified the emerging American vision when he talked of our "Empire for Liberty." He would preserve it for English "yeomen"; but it had already engaged the imagination of other Old World subjects and for a century would continue to offer them unprecedented opportunities for a fresh start.

## 1 *The Onset of British Mismanagement*

### THE NEGLECTED ISSUES OF EMPIRE

The most divisive imperial problem raised by the French and Indian War was that of taxation. "It is unreasonable, and inconsistent with the Principles and Spirit of the *British* Constitution," said the "Declaration of Rights and Grievances" of the Stamp Act Congress in 1765 (see p. 181), for the People of *Great Britain* to grant his Majesty the Property of the Colonists." And yet Britain's long and costly struggles for empire had boosted tax rates at home to such staggering heights that landowners were yielding about a third of their income to the government. The French and Indian War alone had added £58 million to the public debt which stood in 1763 at about £130 million. Now the British had to face the cost of garrisoning their expanded possessions around the world. Lord Amherst, the military commander in North America, wanted to keep 5000 men there. Policy-makers in London, perhaps more fearful than Amhert of the quick resurgence of their French

rivals and perhaps more sordid in their quest for jobs, preferred 10,000 men. In any case, Parliament believed that the colonies should share the cost, which after all would go largely to pay for their protection. The British felt especially justified in their stand by the manifest good thing the northern colonials in particular had made of the war. "You cannot well imagine," a visitor wrote from Boston in 1760, "what a land of health, plenty and contentment this is among all the ranks, vastly improved within these ten years. The war on this continent has been equally a blessing to the English subjects and a Calamity to the French."

Colonial leaders, however, for all their English customs and manners and their avowed loyalty to the Crown, had long since learned to arrange their home finances without British interference and now demanded that the British solve the empire's financial crisis without troubling them. For one thing, the colonies had worked up a war debt of their own of £2.5 million which they would have to pay and service. In addition, by Pitt's estimate, British merchants, under the mercantilist tendency of trade, made profits of no less than £2 million a year on colonial commerce, and such profits seemed to Americans to be "tax" enough. The very prosperity that made the colonials seem fair game to the British, morevover, had given them, in the words of Lieutenant-Governor Hutchinson of Massachusetts, "a higher sense" of their "grandeur and importance," and stiffened their stand against Parliament's financial innovations and in support of their own scholarly ideas.

As the constitutional debate developed, British spokesmen realized that they had fallen into the comfortable habit of evading serious conflict with the colonials. Even in the 1760s, they looked upon the new "American problem" only as a minor disturbance. By the 1770s, their gaze was rudely jerked around, but too late to save them.

After the French and Indian War, the task of coping with the vast new problems of

172

worldwide empire fell first upon the ministry of George Grenville, which lasted from 1763 to 1765. Although men continued to be known at this time by the seventeenth-century designations of Whig and Tory, representing Low Church and High Church factions respectively within the Church of England, actually the two-party system with its foundation in the idea of a "loyal opposition" had long since disappeared from English politics. Many High Church people had continued to support the legitimacy of the Stuart line, despite its Catholic leanings, even after the succession settlement at the time of the Glorious Revolution of 1688 had barred Cath-

*The young monarch, King George III. (New York Public Library.)*

olics from the throne forever (see p. 77). In 1715, indeed, a Tory faction tried to overthrow George I, successor to Queen Anne on her death the year before, in favor of the Stuart "Pretender," James III, and for their pains their party became tainted with treason. The Whigs' success in protecting the King, at the same time, enhanced their own position. This was further strengthened by the fact that George I and his son George II, who succeeded him in 1727, were German relatives of Anne, neither of whom learned English and both of whom gave most of their attention to the family estates in Hanover. Their preoccupation with German affairs made it easier for the Whigs virtually to run Britain for 50 years.

The heyday of Whig control came during the regime of Robert Walpole, the first genuine Prime Minister, 1721–1742, when his determination to perfect the machinery of parliamentary supremacy at home led both to the long peace with Britain's imperial rivals on the Continent and the long period of "salutary neglect" in America. Suppression of the revolt of "Bonnie Prince Charlie," the new Stuart "Pretender," in 1745, again strengthened the Whigs, who were protected from more popular discontent by the severe limitations of the English franchise at this time (it was among the leading proponents of greater democracy in England that the rebellious Americans would find their staunchest supporters in the mother country). The expansion of the British empire after 1713 as after 1763 had created vast new administrative problems, leading to vast new government patronage; and Whig leaders gradually adopted the practice of using government favors to hold the support of the disgruntled within their ranks and to reward their friends. It was while their genuine hold on the people declined that they resorted to the ever more widespread corruption that so repelled the American revolutionary purists.

On taking the throne in 1760, when Whig domination had become especially shaky because of early British failures in the French and Indian War, George III, English born and raised, proved far less docile than his Hanoverian predecessors. Only 22 years of age at this time, and lacking both experience and imagination, George after 1765 was troubled in addition by intermittent attacks of the apparent insanity that clouded his last years. Yet he was conscientious and energetic. Thoroughly schooled in the rightful role of a "patriotic king," he at the same time gained independent ideas of the rightful role of Parliament. His unswerving support of Parliament, indeed, is what got him into so much trouble with his subjects in America who, as they insisted, had no representation in England and no parliaments of their own at home.

The Parliament George cherished, however, was not that of the Whig families. To break their hold on the "popular" Commons in particular, George was early advised to subsidize certain members who became known as the "King's Friends." But Walpole's heir in command of the Whigs, the veteran Duke of Newcastle, could play this game with far greater dexterity than the young monarch. The competition between Crown and "Government" for Commons votes, given the long tradition of purchase, soon made it impossible for anyone to remain untarnished. As a contemporary slogan went, the mood in Parliament was, "Everyone for himself and the Exchequer for us all." The speed with which ministries came and went between Grenville's fall in 1765 and Lord North's rise in 1770, to serve for 12 years, underscored the instability of parliamentary factions just when the empire hung in the balance.

In a sense, the American Revolution was fostered less by British tyranny than by British weakness and overconfidence. Yet it would be a mistake to assume that any rebel leaders, on principle, wanted to break out of the empire. What they insisted upon was the preservation of their traditional right (see p. 186) to manage their own affairs within it. A month after fighting had begun at Lexington and Concord, the Continental Congress actually voted to make a careful list of supplies captured at Fort Ticonderoga so that they could be returned when "restoration of the former harmony" made it possible. Not until the colonials realized that there was no way to win self-government within the empire did rebellion become revolution, with independence its goal.

### GIVING OFFENSE TO THE MERCHANTS

Rumblings of serious trouble in America were heard even before the French and Indian War ended. From the start of the war, colonial merchants, with characteristic disregard for British policy, had sold supplies to the enemy on the North American mainland and had carried on (illicit) business as usual with enemy islands in the West Indies. In 1760 Pitt's ministry had ordered colonial governors to make a more vigorous effort to enforce the standing customs regulations. To carry out the governor's orders in Massachusetts, the principal center of illicit trade, royal customs collectors applied to the Superior Court of the colony for writs of assistance allowing them to call upon constabulary aid in searching the premises of merchants suspected of smuggling. Such writs, by giving customs officers the backing of a police force, made it difficult if not impossible for the proud and overbearing merchants to debar customs officers from their premises.

Writs of assistance had been in common use for a long time, both in Britain and America (see p. 79). Authorized by acts of Parliament, they had to be renewed each time a new sovereign came to the throne. Thus when George II died in 1760, new writs had to be authorized in the name of George III, and the Massachusetts merchants seized on this opportunity to denounce the whole practice. They engaged as counsel the eccentric young Boston lawyer James Otis, described by a contemporary as "a plump, round-faced, smooth-skinned, short-necked, eagle-eyed politician."

Otis was a member of an old Massachusetts

family long in the King's service. When, in 1760, however, Governor William Shirley, after promising to appoint young Otis's father to the Supreme Judicial Court, gave the place instead to the wealthy merchant Thomas Hutchinson, father and son turned against the Governor's faction. When offered the opportunity the next year to square accounts with Hutchinson in particular, who was now charged with the responsibility for issuing the new writs in the colony, Otis promptly resigned his lucrative job as King's advocate-general of the admiralty court in order to speak for the merchants. Soon he had become one of their most active supporters.

Early in 1761, when Otis appeared in court to protest against some writs that Hutchinson had drafted, he delivered one of the most momentous speeches ever heard in North America. As John Adams, who was on hand, remembered many years later: "Otis was a flame of fire! . . . he hurried away everything before him. American independence was then and there born." Although the speech itself has been lost to history, we know that Otis rested his case not on legal technicalities but on broad philosophical grounds. An act of Parliament contrary to the principles of "natural equity"—that is, natural law—or to the principles of the unwritten British constitution, he declared, should be regarded by the courts as void and unenforceable. In this argument he was harking back to the doctrines elaborated by Edward Coke, the great English jurist of the seventeenth century. More important, Otis laid down principles of opposition to Parliament to which the colonials would return again and again. Parliament had no legal right, he said, to break natural law either in Britain or in America. Fundamental human rights could not be infringed by legislation.

Although the legality of the writs was upheld in this instance and the writs themselves were issued, other colonies soon joined in the protest against them and judges frequently refused to issue them in spite of heavy pressure from imperial customs commissioners.

## MISHANDLING THE WEST

British interference with colonial commerce during the French and Indian War angered Americans especially in New England, New York, and Pennsylvania. Britain's taking Canada from France at the end of the war gave colonials in all the 13 commonwealths greater freedom and more frequent occasions to vent their anger. So long as France owned Canada, the Americans had been drawn toward the mother country by the menace of an alien neighbor. The expulsion of France removed this menace, but subsequent British administration of Indian affairs in particular quickly presented new dangers all along the frontiers. Most of the tribes, grown fearful of British expansionism, had become allies of the French during the war and were now extremely restive over impending British domination. Indian and related frontier issues were among the first to confront the new Grenville ministry in 1763, and its management of them hastened the American rebellion along.

Probably no one could have satisfied all the clashing interests on the frontier. The established fur traders in the colonies as well as in Canada wanted the West permanently reserved for the Indian hunters and for the animals that bore the precious pelts. The newly influential land speculators, on the other hand, were urging settlers to go west, and wanted the frontier made safe for them. Both sides had powerful friends in British politics. Colonial land speculators were particularly active in Pennsylvania and Virginia, and their claims often conflicted with one another's as well as with those of rivals in Britain. Benjamin Franklin represented a group of wealthy Pennsylvanians interested in lands along the Ohio. One of the Virginia enterprises was promoted by George Washington, whose Mississippi Company, formed as recently as 1763 as a successor to the old Ohio Company (see p. 161), had its eye on thousands of acres at the junction of the Ohio and Mississippi rivers.

While the British government struggled to piece together a western policy, the Indians decided to look after themselves. Especially with the French power gone they felt they had to assert their rights more fiercely against the British traders, who were cheating them without remorse. Still more menacing was the flood of settlement that would sweep over their lands if the speculators had their way.

Goaded by friendly Gallic traders who talked persuasively of the return of French power to North America, the red men, under the able Ottawa chief, Pontiac (hence the name, "Pontiac's Conspiracy") went into action in May 1763. Pontiac had planned a concerted attack on British forts with the objective of sweeping the entire white population into the sea. By the end of June the Indians had destroyed seven of the nine British garrisons west of Niagara. So desperate had the British become by July 1763 that they employed infected blankets to "send the *Small Pox*" among the "disaffected tribes." Thousands of braves soon died of the disease and by September 1764 most of the West had been pacified by such germ warfare and more conventional means.

One notorious instance of conventional "pacification" occurred in December 1763, when the "Paxton Boys" of Paxton and Donegal townships in Lancaster County, Pennsylvania, in retaliation for Indian raids on their frontier homes, fell upon the peaceful and innocent Conestoga braves near the town of Lancaster, murdered six of them and then stormed the workhouse where 14 others had found refuge and "put old and young to the hatchet." Encouraged by the townspeople, the "Paxton Boys" soon grew into a mob of hundreds and moved toward Philadelphia. Ten miles from the city, Franklin and four others met them. "The fighting face we put on," wrote Franklin, "and the reasonings we used with the insurgents . . . turned them back." But the "White Savages" nursed an even fiercer hate of the eastern grandees than before.

News of Pontiac's Conspiracy reached London in August 1763, and in October the government there issued the Proclamation of 1763, intended as a temporary measure to give Britain time to work out a permanent western policy. The Proclamation set boundaries for three new crown colonies: Quebec, East Florida, and West Florida. Virtually all other western territory stretching from the Alleghenies to the Mississippi, and from Florida to 50° north latitude, was reserved for the time being for the red men (see map, p. 176). Fur traders, land speculators, settlers, all were excluded.

But no proclamation issued thousands of miles away could keep speculators and frontiersmen out. Many of the colonials must have agreed with George Washington when he urged in effect that the Proclamation of 1763 be disobeyed: "I can never look upon that proclamation in any other light . . . than as a temporary expedient to quiet the minds of Indians. . . . Any person, therefore, who neglects the present opportunity of hunting out good lands, and in some measure marking and distinguishing them for his own (in order to keep others from settling them), will never regain it." Washington practiced what he preached, and maintained an agent in the Ohio Valley to stake out his claims. Others, like the Pennsylvanian George Croghan and the North Carolinian Richard Henderson followed suit by searching out good lands from Fort Pitt to the Kentucky country.

In fact, opposition to the Proclamation of 1763 grew so strong that within a few years the British government began to revise its western policy, making a series of treaties with the Indians to give the speculators more room. One such treaty was made with the Choctaws and Chickasaws in 1765 to set the boundary of the Floridas. Three more followed in 1768: one with the Creeks at Pensacola, which affected the borders of South Carolina and Georgia; one with the Cherokees at their village of Hard Labor, which affected the boundary of western Virginia; and one with the Iroquois at Fort Stanwix in New York, which defined and in some places extended that colony's northern boundary. By the treaty of

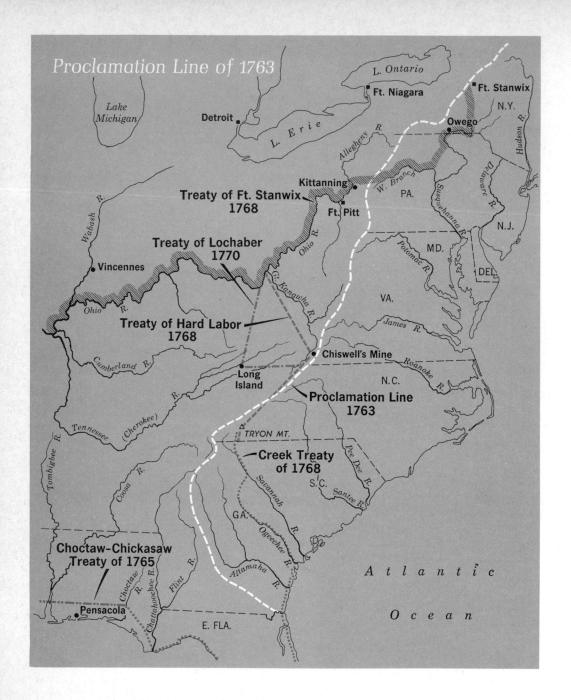

Lake Michigan

L. Ontario

Ft. Niagara

Ft. Stanwix

N.Y.

Detroit

L. Erie

Owego

Hudson R.

Allegheny R.

Kittanning

W. Branch

**Treaty of Ft. Stanwix 1768**

PA.

Ft. Pitt

Susquehanna R.

Delaware R.

N.J.

**Treaty of Lochaber 1770**

Wabash R.

Ohio R.

MD.

DEL.

Potomac R.

Vincennes

Gt. Kanawha R.

VA.

Ohio R.

**Treaty of Hard Labor 1768**

James R.

Cumberland R.

Chiswell's Mine

Roanoke R.

Long Island

**Proclamation Line 1763**

N.C.

Tennessee R. (Cherokee)

TRYON MT.

Pee Dee R.

**Creek Treaty of 1768**

Tombigbee R.

Coosa R.

S.C.

Santee R.

Savannah R.

GA.

Ogeechee R.

**Choctaw-Chickasaw Treaty of 1765**

Choctaw R.

Flint R.

Chattahoochee R.

Altamaha R.

*Atlantic*

Pensacola

*Ocean*

E. FLA.

Lochaber in 1770, the Cherokees, for a price, accepted a line even farther west than that set at Hard Labor.

Every extension of the boundary line deeper into the continent touched off new bursts of speculation. In 1768 the first actual settlers be-

yond the Blue Ridge barrier occupied the Watauga Valley of North Carolina. In 1769, having made his first trip west two years before, Daniel Boone traversed the future "Wilderness Road" from the Holston River, through the Cumberland Gap, into Kentucky (see map below). Here he spent two years exploring the river valleys north to the Ohio, and in 1775, spurred on by Richard Henderson's land enterprises (see p. 233), he guided the first group of permanent settlers to the blue grass region. Unfortunately for the British, the deeper the Americans moved into the West and away from the old centers of power the more determined on self-government did they become.

#### THE PLANTERS' DISENCHANTMENT

Historians disagree about how important colonial discontent over Britain's western policy was in nourishing the impulse to revolution. But some influential Americans seem to have become convinced that their lives would be simpler and their business operations more secure and profitable if they did not have to reckon with British authority beyond the mountains. A few years after the Indian treaties were signed, the newly appointed governor of Virginia, Lord Dunmore, who was himself involved with speculators, warned the home government that it would be difficult to deny the western territory to "a people who are constantly in search of new lands."

In Virginia the drive toward the frontier was intensified by the plight of the planters. By concentrating on their one money-making crop, tobacco, they had badly depleted the soil of both tidewater and piedmont, and there was little fresh land to be had except across the

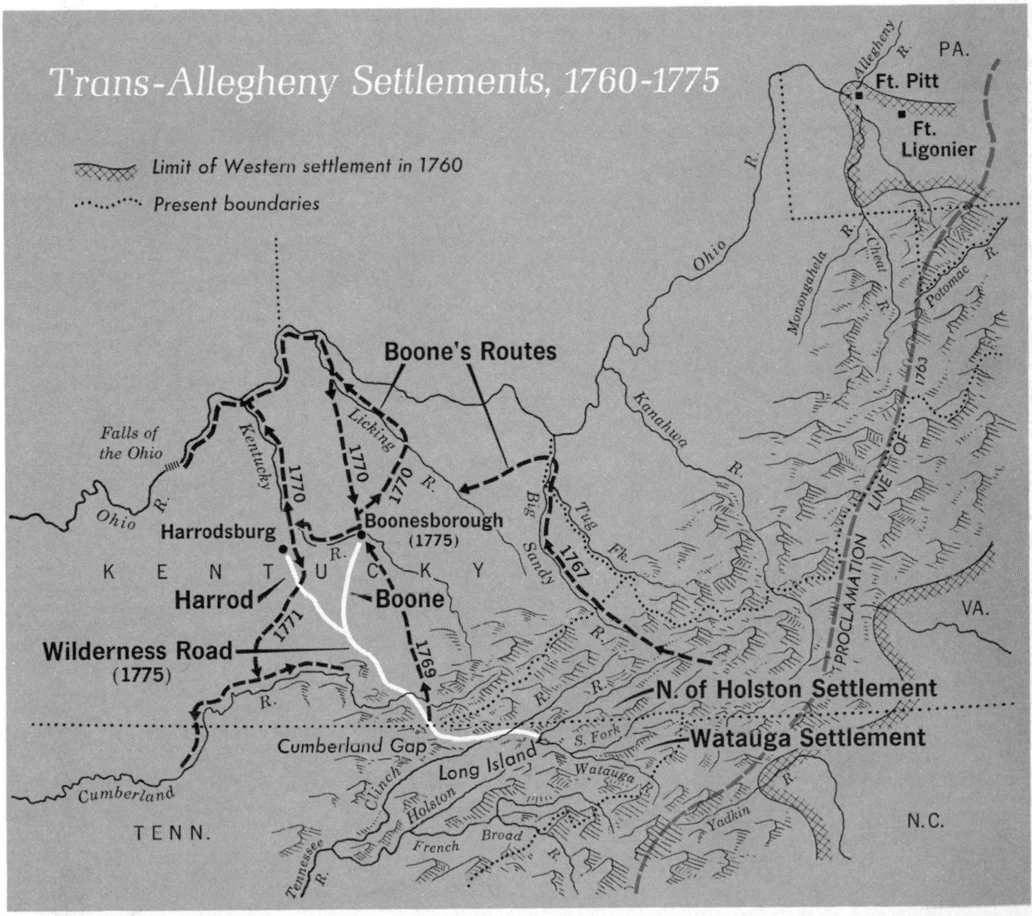

Trans-Allegheny Settlements, 1760-1775
Limit of Western settlement in 1760
Present boundaries
Boone's Routes
Falls of the Ohio
Ohio R.
Kentucky
Licking R.
1770
1770
1770
Harrodsburg
Boonesborough (1775)
K E N T U C K Y
R.
Harrod
Boone
1771
1769
Wilderness Road (1775)
Cumberland Gap
Long Island
Cumberland
TENN.
Clinch
Holston
Tennessee R.
French Broad R.
Watauga R.
S. Fork
Yadkin R.
N. of Holston Settlement
Watauga Settlement
Big Sandy
Tug Fk.
1767
Kanahwa R.
Ohio R.
Monongahela R.
Cheat R.
Potomac R.
Allegheny R.
Ft. Pitt
Ft. Ligonier
PA.
VA.
N.C.
PROCLAMATION LINE OF 1763

mountains. "The greatest estates we have in the colony," Washington pointed out in 1767, had been established "by taking up . . . at very low rates the rich back lands which we thought nothing of in those days but are now the most valuable lands we possess." Cheap lands still farther west seemed the only solution to the problem of growth, and some, like Washington, were already shifting from tobacco to wheat-growing in anticipation of moving inland.

Land policy was only one source of planter discontent with British rule. British merchants served as middlemen, at exorbitant commission fees, for everything the southerners bought abroad as well as for everything they sold. In addition, British shipowners charged high rates for carrying the planters' produce and purchases across the ocean. As their returns from the depleted lands dwindled, the southerners' debts mounted. Jefferson once estimated that Virginia planters owed at least £2 million to British merchants, and observed that these debts "had become hereditary from father to son, for many generations, so that the planters were a species of property annexed to certain mercantile houses in London." When the planters tried to pay their debts in American paper currency, such a howl of protest arose from the British merchants that Parliament passed the Currency Act of 1764 forbidding this practice and warning that a burdensome penalty would be laid on any colonial governor who signed a paper-money bill.

The Virginians' discontent became a broad colonial issue as a result of the "Parson's Cause" of 1763. This dispute over how the clergy of the established church were to be paid first brought Patrick Henry to notice. Traditionally, the Virginia clergy's salary was stated in pounds of tobacco; but when a tobacco shortage in 1755 drove prices far above their usual level, the assembly passed the Twopenny Act (reenacted in 1758) which allowed taxpayers to meet their obligation to the clergy at the rate of two cents for each pound of tobacco due, even though tobacco had soared

to five and a half cents a pound. The Virginia clergy—who were often embroiled with the laymen over one issue or another—appealed to the Bishop of London, arguing that since their salaries had been kept low when tobacco prices were low they should go up when prices were high. Their appeal was successful and, as a result, the Twopenny Act was disallowed by the Crown in 1759.

But several members of the Virginia clergy, not content to let the matter rest, sued for a year's back pay. In one of these suits, which reached the courts in 1763, Henry represented the tax-collectors of the province. In an inflammatory speech to the jury, the young lawyer not only attacked the clergy but argued that the King by disallowing the Virginia law of 1758, had "degenerated into a tyrant, and forfeits all rights to his subjects' obedience." The opposing attorney called this "treason," but Henry knew his strong language was safe in a country made up largely of dissenters. The jury awarded only one penny in damages to the churchmen who had brought the case, and Henry's victory made him famous.

In 1764 the frontier region in which Patrick Henry lived voted him into the House of Burgesses. From then on he was an effective spokesman for Virginia religious dissenters and the common people generally. Since Virginia herself was so predominant a power in the South, her hurts and her heroes furthered her neighbors' as well as her own preparation for cooperating with rebellious colonists to the north.

## II  *The Passion for Self-Government*

### THE CHALLENGE OF THE SUGAR ACT

Rebelliousness in the ports and violence on the frontier only deepened the Grenville ministry's sense of urgency about money for troops and administrative personnel to restore law and order in America.

In April 1764 the ministry took its first financial plunge by imposing on the American colonies what became known as the Sugar Act. By this measure Grenville hoped to raise £45,-000 a year. Instead he raised the spirit of revolt.

A duty of six cents a gallon on the importation of foreign molasses essential to the distilling of Yankee rum had been imposed on the colonies in 1733 but was weakly enforced. The new act halved the duty but made it clear that it would be collected to the penny. Duties on many other essential imports were raised at the same time. To insure collection, suits over the payment of the new duties and charges of smuggling on other grounds as well were removed from the regular colonial courts, where Americans usually were let off by friendly juries, to the hated admiralty courts, where there were no juries. This provision excited American merchants even more than the ruin they saw in store for them because of the Sugar Act's direct interference with the whole range of colonial commerce.

But what aroused Americans most of all were the ominous implications of the official title of the act—the Revenue Act—and the preamble which elaborated its purpose to tax the colonists directly. Heretofore the charges placed upon the colonials had been explained and excused as a legitimate part of imperial administration. The Sugar Act was the first law ever passed by Parliament with the avowed objective of raising money in the colonies.

The Currency Act, passed in the same month as the Sugar Act (see p. 178), worsened the situation. Faced with one measure designed to draw money from America and another to forbid expansion of American currency, many groaned under the heavy hand of empire. The town of Boston, preparing instructions for its representatives in the general assembly at this time, asked an ominous question: "If taxes are laid upon us in any shape without ever having a legal representation where they are laid, are we not reduced from the character of free subjects to the miserable state of tributary slaves?" James Otis wrote a thundering pamphlet in which he declared: "No parts of his Majesty's dominions can be taxed without their consent." The Massachusetts House of Representatives authorized a committee of correspondence to write to other provinces about the issue. In Boston, New York, and elsewhere, merchants and mechanics pledged themselves not to buy or use certain British goods. The Sugar Act spawned the idea of nonimportation, which soon became so effective a revolutionary weapon.

### THE STAMP ACT

When Grenville announced the Sugar Act, he served notice that another revenue measure was being prepared. This was the Stamp Act, passed by Parliament in March 1765, to go into effect in November. Grenville had even higher hopes for this act than for the Sugar Act, for he expected it to bring in £60,000 a year. Every time a colonial wanted a legal document, or a license, newspaper, pamphlet, almanac, playing cards, or dice, this act required that he purchase a stamp for it ranging in value from a half-penny to £10.

One section of the Stamp Act especially alarmed the dissenting clergy, who were to become among the most influential of the rebels. This was the section that required stamps on "every skin or piece of vellum or parchment, or sheet or piece of paper," as the act said, issuing from any court, including courts "exercising ecclesiastical jurisdiction within the said colonies." There were, as yet, no courts in the colonies "exercising ecclesiastical jurisdiction"; but there was a justifiable fear, growing since 1763, that the Church of England might gain the authority to set them up under the bishop it was urging for America. When the Stamp Act seemed to assume that these courts, and this centralized religious authority, would be imposed, it galvanized the resistance of the many colonials whose whole tradition was based on congregational self-determination (see p. 129). The Stamp Act provided further that all violators were to be tried

180

in the same hated juryless admiralty courts in which smugglers were brought to account, and heavily fined if found guilty. The Sugar Act had struck mainly at merchants. The Stamp Act hit every articulate and influential person in the colonies—lawyers, printers, editors, tavern-owners, and dissenting preachers. Great men like Walpole and Pitt had steered clear of stamp acts in England; but in the even more touchy colonies Grenville, who fancied himself a financial expert, risked one to his misfortune.

"One single act of Parliament," said James Otis of the Sugar Act, "set the people a-thinking in six months, more than they had done in their whole lives before." That was in New England. The fatal flaw of the Stamp Act was that it set people *talking* everywhere. It was during a stormy session on this issue in the Virginia House of Burgesses that the frontier leader, Patrick Henry, in defiance of the old tidewater families, issued his famous warning to George III: "Caesar had his Brutus— Charles the first, his Cromwell—and George the third—may profit by their example." The Stamp Act, in fact, set people to acting as well as talking. In response to this Act colonial leaders began to develop the revolutionary machinery by which they ultimately separated from Great Britain and set up their own independent governments.

No sooner had news of the Stamp Act reached America than the Massachusetts House of Representatives, on Otis's motion in June 1765, resolved to call for a full-scale intercolonial congress, the first ever to be convened on American initiative, to meet in New York City in October, to combat it. In the intervening months the Sons of Liberty, secret organizations often lead by men of wealth and standing, were formed to intimidate stamp agents and others insufficiently rebellious. In Boston, Philadelphia, Newport, New York, and Charleston, mobs led by merchants themselves pillaged the houses of Stamp Act defenders and the King's officials. In August 1765 a Boston mob burned the records of the admiralty court, ransacked the home of the

This cartoon of 1769, an expression of colonists' antagonism against ecclesiastic domination, shows an irate mob composed primarily of anticlerics taunting a frightened bishop as the boat on which he is riding is shoved away from a Boston dock. (The John Carter Brown Library.)

comptroller of the customs, and then entered, looted, and wrecked the elegant Hutchinson mansion, stealing or destroying everything down to the last shirt. Even before November 1, when the Stamp Act was to go into effect, every stamp agent in the colonies had been badgered into resigning or promising not to execute his commission.

When the Stamp Act Congress met in New York in October 1765, nine colonies were represented. Of the four absentees, Virginia, Georgia, and North Carolina had failed to send delegates only because their royal governors would permit none to be selected. The fourth missing colony was New Hampshire.

It was at the Stamp Act Congress that Christopher Gadsden of South Carolina proposed that "there ought to be no New England man, no New Yorker, known on this continent, but all of us Americans." This Congress neither threatened rebellion nor urged independence, but it greatly advanced the constitutional argument by clarifying the American position. Its moderate "Declaration of Rights and Grievances" began by acknowledging "all due Subordination" not only to the Crown, but also "to that August Body the Parliament of Great Britain." At the same time, the Declaration stated, "That the people of these Colonies are not, and from their local Circumstances cannot be, Represented in the House of Commons in *Great Britain;* That the only Representatives of the People of these Colonies, are Persons chosen therein by themselves, and that no Taxes ever have been, or can be Constitutionally imposed on them, but by their respective Legislatures."

The Declaration went on to assert that the colonists were "entitled to all the inherent Rights and Liberties" of Englishmen born in Great Britain; that the extension of the jurisdiction of the admiralty courts in particular had "a manifest Tendency to subvert" these "Rights and Liberties"; that among such "Rights and Liberties," was "the Right . . . to Petition the King, or either House of Parliament"; and lastly, that the colonists were hereby exercising the right of petition "to procure the Repeal" of the Stamp Act and "any other Acts of Parliament, whereby the Jurisdiction of the Admiralty is extended," or "*American* Commerce" is restricted.

The Stamp Act Congress was followed by signed agreements among hundreds of merchants in each of the major ports not to buy British goods until the hated law and the other objectionable trade regulations had been repealed. When the Stamp Act went into force in November, merchants almost everywhere suspended business in protest. When they resumed business by the end of the year, they did so without using stamps, and not a single one ever was sold in America.

By November 1765 Grenville had been relieved of his ministry, more for boring the young King who had developed "a kind of horror of the interminable persistency of his conversation," than for overburdening the Americans. His successor, the Marquis of Rockingham, had never supported the Stamp Act, and when pressure from British merchants who were feeling the pinch of the American boycott was added to that of the Americans themselves, he took steps to repeal it. In January 1766 Pitt speeded repeal along with a devastating speech in Parliament, declaring, "I rejoice that America has resisted." The Government had but one course, he warned: "It is that the Stamp Act be repealed, absolutely, totally, and immediately." The Commons soon voted for repeal by a wide margin, and on March 17, 1766, the Lords, urged on by the King, also gave their consent.

Few British leaders, however, were ready to admit that the Stamp Act had been repealed because, as Pitt put it, "it was founded on an erroneous principle." To make it clear that repeal was not a renunciation of revenue-raising powers, Parliament, along with the repeal measure, passed the Declaratory Act, which asserted that *it* had the unquestionable right to make laws "to bind the colonies and people of America . . . in all cases whatsoever."

Parliament, unfortunately, did more. On Lord Amherst's departure from Canada in 1763, General Thomas Gage had risen to Commander-in-Chief of the few thousand British troops still holding western posts. On his elevation, Gage, something of a social lion, moved from Montreal to more cosmopolitan New York City, and in March 1765 within a few days of the Stamp Act, Parliament had passed a "Quartering Act" requiring the colonies to supply barracks for Gage's men and

182

other materials heretofore furnished by the British army. Compliance lagged. When the Stamp Act Congress made New York appear to have become the center of rebellious activity, Gage called in more of his men to join him in the city. Chiefly to house them, Parliament, in 1766, passed a second Quartering Act requiring the colonies to supplement barracks where necessary with accommodations for the troops in public inns, alehouses, unoccupied buildings, and even private barns.

New York's legislature and the city's residents both resisted the new law and defied the redcoats in their midst. In August 1766, almost two years before the Boston Massacre (see p. 183), redcoats and rebels clashed, and Isaac Sears, the leader of the City's Sons of Liberty, was wounded. A larger clash on the same issue, known as the Battle of Golden Hill, took place in New York in January 1770, with no fatalities but with numerous casualties among the Sons of Liberty and the sons of Britain.

The Declaratory Act's assertion of power in London and the mobilization of "standing armies" in the colonies to back it augured ill for the future despite the rejoicing with which repeal of the Stamp Act had been hailed.

### THE TOWNSHEND ACTS

About four months after repeal, the Rockingham ministry fell and Pitt was asked to form a government. But Pitt soon became so ill that he was forced to retire temporarily in favor of the overly clever Chancellor of the Exchequer, Charles Townshend. If Grenville's fiscal measures had awakened Americans to resistance, Townshend's turned them to revolution, a turn Pitt might have averted.

American arguments in 1765 and 1766 had led Townshend to believe that the colonials would accept revenue-raising acts presented not as "internal taxes" but as traditional "external" trade regulations. Accordingly, in June 1767, on his recommendation, Parliament passed the Townshend Acts imposing new *import* duties—on glass, lead, paints, paper, and tea. Such thinking did not impress Ameri-

can spokesmen, but the extraordinary thoughtlessness of other provisions of the Townshend Acts did. To insure collection of the new duties, the Acts reasserted the power of imperial courts in the colonies to issue writs of assistance. Provocative as this assertion was, worse lay ahead, for the acts also provided that violators of the new regulations be tried in the hated admiralty courts. Resentment was heightened further by the Acts' creation of a new Board of Customs Commissioners whose job it was to spy out every petty violation, and even to invent violations under technicalities the more surely to harass the colonials. The crowning insult was the provision that the salaries of the King's new appointees be paid out of the fines and judgments levied against violaters convicted in the admiralty courts, a scheme devised to make the customs commissioners independent of both Parliament and the colonial assemblies. The final section of the Townshend Acts hit specifically at New York for noncompliance with the Quartering Act of 1766. After October 1, 1767, all legislative functions of the New York Assembly were to be suspended.

Alert now to the traps in parliamentary language, emerging colonial leaders had also become adept at resistance to parliamentary objectives. Even before the customs commissioners reached Boston in November, the nonimportations agreements that British merchants found so costly the year before had been revived. Beginning early in December 1767 and continuing through February 1768, the moderate, and hence more effective, John Dickinson published in the *Pennsylvania Chronicle and Universal Advertiser* his series of *Letters from a Farmer in Pennsylvania to the Inhabitants of the British Colonies*. These were copied in many other colonial newspapers and also widely distributed in pamphlet form. In his *Letters*, Dickinson assailed the Townshend Acts as unconstitutional, and denounced Parliament's treatment of the New York Assembly in particular as a threat to the liberties of all the colonies. We must not sacrifice "a single iota" of our privileges, he

*Sam Adams in 1774 by Paul Revere. (Spencer Collection, New York Public Library.)*

asserted; yet they must be defended not violently, but *"peaceably—prudently—firmly—jointly."* In February 1768, on behalf of the Massachusetts legislature, Samuel Adams already the acknowledged leader of the "popular party" in the House of Representatives to which he had been elected in 1766, wrote a "circular letter" to be sent to the other colonies restating Dickinson's points.

Sam Adams's work drew from the newly created office of Secretary of State for America an arrogant reply instructing all colonial governors to see to it that their assemblies treated it with "the contempt it deserves," even if they had to dissolve the assemblies to enforce this policy. The Secretary's order came too late to stop the assemblies of New Hampshire, New Jersey, and Connecticut from openly endorsing Massachusetts's stand and to prevent Virginia from issuing her own circular letter in support of it. Massachusetts, nevertheless, was made to suffer. Governor Francis Bernard, Shirley's successor in 1760, had been specifically admonished to dissolve the legislature should it fail to rescind Adams's letter. On June 30, 1768, the Massachusetts House of Representatives voted 92 to 17 not to rescind. On July 1 Bernard carried out his instructions.

Certain to be provocative at any time, Bernard's act at this juncture proved peculiarly ill-timed. Earlier in June, the customs commissioners had ordered the seizure of John Hancock's sloop *Liberty,* for attempting to land a cargo of wine on Boston's wharf without paying the duty, her officers having locked a wharf official in the sloop's cabin to improve their chances of success. *Liberty's* seizure led crowds to attack other customs officials in the port and to menace their homes. In response, they demanded the protection of British troops. Rumors of the redcoats' coming spread through Boston daily until, in fact, at the end of September 1768, two well-equipped infantry regiments dispatched by Gage arrived, the General himself following in two weeks.

Redcoats in Boston now, as in New York earlier, was ample incitement to riot, and it is remarkable that serious violence was averted for 18 months. One cause of friction was competition for jobs between Yankee laborers in the port and redcoats seeking work in off-duty hours. A fist fight over this issue on the afternoon of March 5, 1770, raised tension to a peak and that night, the "victualling houses" having done good business, the "Boston Massacre" took place. Ten British soldiers, goaded by an unruly crowd, fired at their tormentors despite their officer's efforts to restrain them, and killed five while wounding others.

John Adams defended the soldiers in court against a murder indictment. The civilian dead, he said later, were among "the most obscure and inconsiderable [men] that could have been found upon this continent." They were not even genuine Bostonians, but out-

*This view, by Paul Revere, of "The Bloody Massacre" and its numerous variants (including the original by Henry Pelham from which this was copied) are regarded as major pre-Revolutionary propaganda helping to focus the rancor of many Colonials on the British. The pen and ink diagram (facing page) is Revere's representation of the skirmish as it actually took place. It was used at the trial of the British soldiers. (Print: Metropolitan Museum of Art; Sketch: Boston Public Library.)*

siders looking for trouble. "And it is in this manner," he told the trial jury, that "this town has often been treated; a Carr from Ireland, and an Attucks from Framingham, happening to be here, . . . sally out upon their thoughtless enterprises, at the head of such a rabble of negroes, &c, as they can collect together."

Adams's plea won acquittal from the Boston jury on the murder charge. Two soldiers, found guilty of manslaughter, were released after minor punishment. But the "massacre" itself was picked up as a favorite theme for oratory. Here is how one Bostonian used it:

Has the grim savage rushed again from the wilderness? Or does some fiend, fierce from the depths of Hell, with all the rancorous malice which the apostate damned can feel, twang her deadly arrows at our breast? No: none of these . . . it is the hand of Britain that inflicts the wound.

In the meantime, nonimportation progressed in the South as well as in the North, Vir-

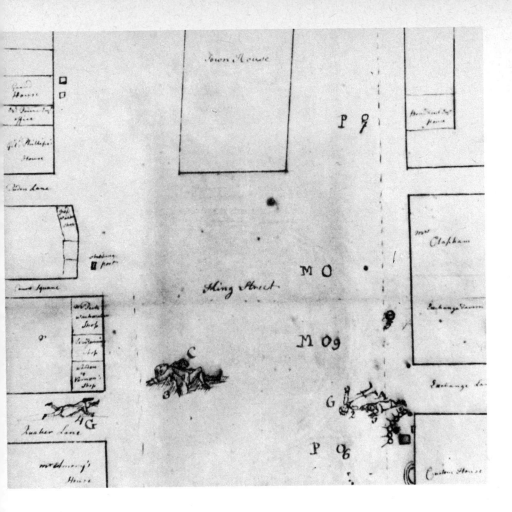

ginia's "Resolves" for this purpose being adopted in May 1769 at a meeting led by George Washington in a private home after the Governor had dissolved the legislature for denying Parliament's right to tax the colonies. By 1770, every colony but New Hampshire had agreed to participate in enforcement, thereby leaving few loopholes for evasion by Americans as yet unaccustomed to working together. That year, colonial trade with the mother country fell off by a third.

Sir Frederick, Lord North, who became Prime Minister in March 1770, could not help but realize that the Townshend Acts were costing more than they would ever bring in,

and he promptly called on Parliament to repeal all the duties except that on tea. This *one* must continue simply to maintain the principle of parliamentary power. Parliament complied in April, without yet having heard of the "Boston Massacre." Against the urging of the Sons of Liberty, most Americans, on learning of Lord North's apparently conciliatory step, let nonimportation drop. It had to be acknowledged, however, that the British had so far failed to force the colonials to yield a regular revenue, even for their own protection, while the Americans had failed to win their point on the unconstitutionality of Parliament's efforts.

185

186  THE PROGRESS OF IDEAS

The abatement of tension in the period between the repeal of the Townshend Acts in April 1770 and the "Boston Tea Party" of December 16, 1773, (see p. 189) was such that English and Scotch-Irish immigration to the mainland colonies reached their peak of the entire colonial period in these years, while German immigration continued strong. Yet the Americans soon were driven to resume their increasingly rebellious stand against the mother country not merely by the course of events but also by the logic of their arguments. Each time they came close to accepting some parliamentary authority, short of agreeing to direct taxation, they were put off by the British leaders' intellectual inertia. Instead of retreating as the British hoped they would, they moved determinedly along their own ever-clearer intellectual course and eventually carried many British spokesmen with them.

The "Declaration" of the Stamp Act Congress, the resolves of provincial assemblies, the testimony of Americans abroad, the pamphlets published by colonial lawyers like Otis, Dickinson, and Daniel Dulany of Maryland, all help clarify the positions of articulate Americans. In his *Considerations* of 1765, Dulany accepted without question, "the authority of the mother country to regulate the trade of the colonies." He even admitted that they might allow Britain an "incidental revenue" arising from such regulation. But Parliament's right "to impose an internal tax . . . without their consent *for the single purpose of revenue,*" they would never grant. In his *Letters from a Farmer,* in 1768, Dickinson said of the Townshend measures:

I regard the late act as an *experiment made of our disposition.* It is a bird sent over the waters, to discover, whether the waves, that lately agitated this part of the world with such violence [meaning the Stamp Act], have yet *subsided.* If *this adventurer* gets footing here, we shall quickly find that it be of the kind described by the poet.—

*"Infelix vates."*
A direful foreteller of future calamities.

"Tho' your devotion to *Great Britain* is the most affectionate," Dickinson concluded, "yet you can make PROPER DISTINCTIONS, and know what you owe to *yourselves,* as well as *to her.*"

Later that year, Franklin's "distinctions" had been made. Testifying before Parliament in 1766 on American views, Franklin observed: "I never heard any objection [in America] to the right of laying duties to regulate commerce; but a right of laying internal taxes was never supposed to be in Parliament." In 1768 Franklin was prepared to go further. After mulling over the question, he said, he found it

difficult to draw lines between duties for regulation and those for revenue; and if the Parliament is to be the judge, it seems to me that establishing such a principle of distinction will amount to little. The more I have thought and read on the subject, the more I find myself confirmed in opinion, that no middle ground can be well maintained. . . . Something might be made of either of the extremes: that Parliament has a power to make *all laws* for us, or that it has a power to make *no laws* for us; and I think the arguments for the latter more numerous and weighty, than those for the former. Supposing that doctrine established, the colonies would then be so many separate states, only subject to the same king, as England and Scotland were before the union.

These last bold words laid bare the direction the colonial argument was taking—that the colonists should become completely independent of Parliament and united to Britain only by their loyalty to the Crown. Such distinguished American lawyers as James Wilson of Pennsylvania, John Adams, and Thomas Jefferson shared this view.

Algernon Sidney, the seventeenth-century republican who opposed both the absolutism of Charles I and the dictatorship of Cromwell —and with James Harrington and John Locke was most quoted by the American rebel philosophers—once wrote: "Peace is seldom made, and never kept, unless the subject retain such power in his hands as may oblige the prince to stand on what is agreed." Sidney had followers in eighteenth-century England as well as in America who willingly conceded that history, the British constitution, and the rights of man all supported the colonial argument against having their money taken from them, as they put it, by a legislature in which they had no voice. Parliament itself, however, until too late, offered in rebuttal only the sophistry of "virtual representation." True, said the government defenders, Americans were not directly represented in Parliament. But neither were the people of Manchester, Birmingham, and other growing industrial cities in England represented by men of their own choosing. Yet they willingly paid taxes levied by members elected elsewhere in the kingdom who "virtually represented" them—and the colonials should profit from *that* example.

Americans failed to be impressed with this argument. To them, 3000 miles from London, "virtual representation" by men who never saw them from one year to the next and knew little and cared less about their happiness was no representation at all. To their friend Pitt, "virtual representation" was "the most contemptible idea that ever entered into the head of man." His friend Camden told Parliament, "virtual representation . . . is so absurd as not to deserve an answer."

If, as the Stamp Act Congress said in 1765, Americans, "from their local circumstances cannot be represented in the House of Commons in Great Britain," and if "virtual representation" was a fraud, where, then, were they to turn for relief from mounting impositions? To their "enlightened despot," the half-mad King? In 1771, in his oration commemorating the first anniversary of the "Boston Massacre," the rebel James Lovell stated that by now the colonials wanted more than to be spared oppression; free people are "those who have a *constitutional check* upon the power to oppress." Some years later, other patriots would be quoting Franklin's English friend Dr. Richard Price to the effect that, "Liberty in a State is self-government."

"Happy are the men, and *happy the people who grow wise by the* misfortunes of others," said one of the rebel philosophers. To attain such wisdom, John Adams admonished his friends, "Let us . . . read the histories of ancient ages; contemplate the great examples of Greece and Rome; set before us the conduct of our British ancestors, who have defended for us the inherent rights of mankind against foreign and domestic tyrants and usurpers." Others, led by John's cousin Sam, were more impatient. "UNLESS THE MOST WATCHFUL ATTENTION BE EXERTED," John Dickinson had warned, "A NEW SERVITUDE MAY BE SLIPPED UPON US UNDER THE SANCTION OF USUAL AND RESPECTABLE TERMS." While some rebels studied, Sam Adams watched. While some argued, Sam exhorted. "I doubt whether there is a greater incendiary in the King's dominion," Governor Hutchinson said of him in 1771. Yet he had barely begun to act.

While tension abated following repeal of the Townshend measures and merchants and others went about their accustomed business, British administration of the ports and the courts also continued its abrasive course. Ships were stopped and searched, their officers abused, their owners hailed before admiralty judges, warehouses entered with constabulary aid. Many, like John Hancock, disenchanted by the rumor that Adams "led him by the nose," learned to endure the painful British presence patiently, hoping only that nothing worse would befall them. Sam Adams, writing tirelessly for his favorite *Boston Gazette* and other Boston newspapers, made the most of every petty incident, regretting only that none was sufficiently combustible to feed the flame of rebellion. He also wrote letters to correspondents in other colonies, looking ahead to the time when he would be able to form them into permanent committees to keep the patriot spirit high.

"If it were not for two or three Adamses," Hutchinson reported to London in 1771, "we

188

should do well enough. We have not been so quiet these five years." Later letters announcing the decline of Adams's "popular party," a fact confirmed by Sam's much narrowed margin of victory on being reelected to the provincial House of Representatives in 1772, came like the music of sirens to Lord North's ministers. But Adams was sufficiently contemptuous of the British to believe that sooner or later they would be lulled into playing his game, and in fact he found his opening sooner than he expected.

Late in 1771, Boston learned that henceforth the royal governor was to be paid by the Crown, not the colony. In September 1772 the rumor of a similar change in the method of paying judges was confirmed. This was the "FINISHING STROKE," cried the Boston Sons of Liberty in October; Americans will become "as complete slaves as the inhabitants of Turkey or Japan." In November, on Adams's motion, a very divided Boston Town Meeting appointed an official "committee of correspondence . . . to state the rights of the Colonists and of this Province in particular, as men, as Christians, and as Subjects; and to communicate the same to the several towns and the world." Having carried this day against the opposition of Hancock and others, Sam Adams now embarked on his successful campaign to arouse the people everywhere to assert their natural rights, "exclusive of all charters from the Crown." "All Men," he asserted, "have a Right to remain in a State of Nature as long as they please; And in case of intollerable Oppression, Civil or Religious, to leave the Society they belong to, and enter into another."

The *Gaspee* incident in 1772 advanced Adams's intercolonial campaign. On June 9, that year, the British customs schooner, *Gaspee,* a thorn in the flesh to Rhode Island merchants in Narragansett Bay, ran aground seven miles below Providence while pursuing a local vessel. That evening, eight boatloads of men led by prominent Providence merchants attacked the stranded revenuer, removed her crew, and burned her to the ground. Aware that Rhode Island courts would never punish the offenders even if they could be caught, the King, on learning of the affair, named a special commission of inquiry to find the perpetrators and ship them to England for trial. Although Rhode Island recalcitrance utterly frustrated the commission, the plan to send colonials to England for trial jarred Americans all the way to Virginia and Charleston. By February 1774 every colony but North Carolina and Pennsylvania had formed committees of correspondence by which Sons of Liberty might keep one another informed on further breaches of their natural rights. Thus, Hutchinson lamented, "was the Contagion which began in Boston" diffused. "From a state of peace, order, and general contentment," the entire continent "was brought into a state of contention, disorder, and general dissatisfaction." The committees, Sam Adams boasted, turned people from "picking up pins, and directed their View to great objects."

### TO THE BREAKING POINT

By 1774, of course, Britain had again been as effective as the committees. Perhaps the revolutionary tendency became irreversible when Parliament passed the incredibly provocative East India, or Tea, Act, May 10, 1773.

No ordinary commercial organization, the East India Company was a gigantic monopoly to which Parliament had entrusted even the government of India. Like the British government itself, the company now was shot through with corruption and mismanagement. Trembling on the brink of bankruptcy, it demanded that Parliament bail it out. The warehouses of the East India Company in England were bulging with 17 million pounds of tea. The Tea Act granted the company the right to ship this tea to America and to sell it there through its own agents. Cheap tea for colonial consumers was one thing. Cheap tea at the expense of colonial importers was another. Moreover, these importers asked their sympathetic fellow Americans: If Parliament could now bestow a tea monopoly on the East India Company, what was to stop it from granting similar monopolies over other commodities?

By December 1773 East India Company tea had reached Boston, where it sat under the protection of British troops. To rid themselves of it, patriots under Sam Adams's direction hit on the device of disguising themselves as Indians, boarding the tea ships, and throwing the tea into the harbor. This feat, famous as the "Boston Tea Party," was performed on December 16, 1773.

The North ministry could not ignore so defiant an act, nor could friends of the colonies in Parliament condone it. To punish the Americans, Parliament passed a series of acts early in 1774, called in the colonies Coercive, or "Intolerable," Acts, which killed whatever hope of reconciliation remained: (1) The Port of Boston was to be closed until the East India Company and the British customs had been reimbursed for their losses. (2) Any British official indicted by Massachusetts courts for capital offenses committed while enforcing British laws could be tried at home, away from hostile colonials. (3) In Massachusetts, the King or his governor was given power to fill by appointment many offices heretofore elective; and no town meeting could be held without the governor's permission, and then only on business he approved. (4) A new quartering act was imposed on all the colonies.

With characteristically poor timing, Parliament also picked May 1774 to pass the Quebec Act, which, by recognizing certain features of French law, gratified the former Canadian subjects of France. But these features included trials without juries, and political equality for Catholics—two items which especially alarmed the wary Protestants of neighboring Massachusetts. More objectionable still, to the rest of the colonists, the act enlarged the Province of Quebec to include the territory north of the Ohio and east of the Mississippi where Massachusetts, Connecticut, and Virginia all had claims which the Quebec Act ignored. No longer did the radicals in America have to exaggerate the danger to traditional

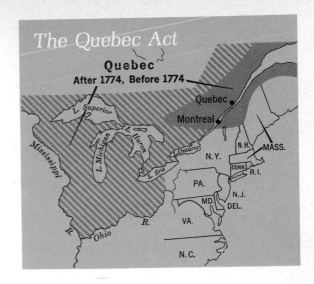

The Quebec Act

Quebec
After 1774, Before 1774

liberties; the danger had been plainly revealed for all to see. And they had good reason to believe, as Edmund Burke advised the New York Assembly from London, that the purpose of the Quebec Act had been to hem in the old English colonies and to cut off their growth.

The Massachusetts House of Representatives replied to these measures by asking all the colonies to send delegates to Philadelphia in September 1774 to voice their opposition. The result was the First Continental Congress, in which only Georgia, of the thirteen colonies, was unrepresented. The delegates to this Congress had been named by extralegal conventions called to elect them and to perform other revolutionary acts unthinkable for regular legislatures and governors.

Work began in Philadelphia with the proposal of the conservative Joseph Galloway of Pennsylvania that a grand colonial council be set up to share power with Parliament on colonial matters. But, spurred on perhaps by false rumors that General Thomas Gage (recently appointed governor of Massachusetts) had bombarded Boston and that New England had taken up arms, the Congress rejected Galloway's scheme by a single vote and resolved on more drastic action.

A meeting of delegates from Massachusetts towns had just adopted the "Suffolk Resolves," which advocated two bold measures: (1) that

189

190

the colonies raise their own troops; and (2) that they suspend all trade with Britain, Ireland, and the British West Indies. The Congress endorsed these proposals. Companies of "minutemen" soon began to drill on the village greens. To insure that the boycott of British trade be complete, Congress organized a "Continental Association" and authorized the selection of committees "in every County, City, and Town" to enforce the "Non-Importation, Non-Consumption, and Non-Exportation" policy. These committees were also to "encourage Frugality, Economy, and Industry, and . . . discountenance and discourage every species of extravagance and dissipation, especially horseracing, and all kinds of gaming, cock fighting, exhibitions of plays, shews and other expensive diversions and entertainments." They were empowered, moreover, to publish the names of all violators as "enemies of *American* liberty," the better to expose them to public attack. These committees became virtual local governments. Few dared attract their enmity and the Association proved a great success.

The First Continental Congress may rightly be described as the first national government in America. "By assuming the powers of legislation," wrote a Tory critic of the Association and other congressional acts, "the Congress have not only superseded our provincial legislatures, but have excluded every idea of monarchy; and not content with the havoc already made in our constitution, in the plentitude of their power have appointed another Congress to be held in May."

Before adjourning on October 26, 1774, the First Continental Congress did in fact agree, unless their grievances had been fully met, to reconvene on May 10, 1775. The date proved to be none too early. Unnerved by the gathering of minutemen around Boston, General Gage, on April 19, 1775, sent 700 troops to destroy the large amount of munitions and supplies that the colonists appeared to be collecting in Concord, about 20 miles north. Boston patriots, in turn, sent Paul Revere, William Dawes, and Dr. Samuel Prescott to arouse the minutemen along the way, and at Lexington green, five miles short of Concord, the redcoats encountered a line of armed farmers and townsmen. Eight minutemen fell here, and the British moved on. Revere and Dawes were halted by the British before reaching Concord, but Dr. Prescott got through in time to warn the minutemen there to get their supplies away, which they did. Frustrated at Concord, Gage's men turned back toward Boston; but by then, thousands of minutemen lined the road and shot down the redcoats as they passed. By the time they reached Boston the British counted 273 casualties. Nintey-three Americans had been killed or wounded.

There remained many men on both sides who tried, still, to avert war. But the battle of pamphlets and protest clearly had yielded to a battle of rifles and cannon, and as the news of the start of actual fighting spread, Americans looked anxiously to the Philadelphia meeting for leadership.

III  *Patriots and Loyalists*

### FAILURE OF CONCILIATION

When the Second Continental Congress convened hastily in Philadelphia in May 1775 (all thirteen colonies were now to be represented, but distant Georgians did not arrive until September), few of the delegates could have imagined that they were to remain in session almost continuously for 14 years. They were a distinguished, if divided, group; sitting among them were the men who were to be the first three presidents of the United States. The appearance of the delegates in the Philadelphia streets drew shouts of admiration from the crowds who, excited by the news of Lexington and Concord, now gathered every day to watch the militia going through its drill. Even the dignified John Adams was moved to write to his wife, Abigail, "Oh, that I were a soldier!"

Most of the delegates found in the mood of the crowds an echo of their own. It was clear that the Congress would support the action Massachusetts had taken, and yet there was no formal resolve that the Continental Congress create a Continental army, whose existence was recognized only in an off-hand announcement of the Congress that it would "adopt" the army then congregating around Boston, for "the general defense of the right of America." The delegates were sharply divided on what additional course of action to follow. There were three fairly distinct factions: A few still hoped for conciliation; these delegates represented well-established and wealthy families in the strategic provinces of New York and Pennsylvania. But even these men were committed to the defense of American rights. At the opposite extreme were the militants, who were firmly convinced that Britain would not yield to purely defensive armed resistance. They were either flatly in favor of independence or else regarded it as inevitable. This was the party of Washington, Franklin, John and Sam Adams, and Jefferson. The largest group was made up of the moderates, who believed that a vigorous show of armed strength would force Britain to back down and give in to the demands of Congress. This group felt that independence was neither desirable nor necessary.

These differences of opinion were compounded by clashes of interest between the delegates from various sections of the colonies. Even so, the Congress was almost unanimous in choosing Washington as commander-in-chief of the American forces. Washington inspired confidence. His courage, honesty, and dignity, his willingness to sacrifice his personal fortune to the cause, all proved in the long run more vital than military genius to rebel success. It was quite in character for Washington even to refuse the pay that Congress voted him and to serve through the war without compensation.

Many in the Second Continental Congress still hoped that Washington, as general, would find little to do. On July 6, 1775,

Congress adopted a "Declaration of the Causes and Necessity of Taking up Arms": "Our cause is just," they confidently declared. "Our union is perfect." Then came an open threat: "Our internal resources are great, and, if necessary, foreign assistance is undoubtedly attainable. . . . The arms we have been compelled by our enemies to assume, we will . . . employ for the preservation of our liberties, being with one mind resolved to die free men rather than live slaves." But there was also a note of hope: "We have not raised armies with ambitious designs of separating from Great Britain, and establishing independent States."

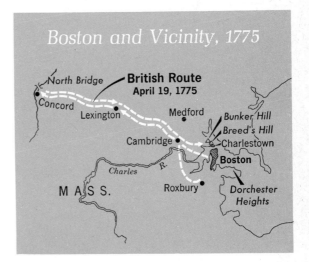

At this time Congress also adopted the "Olive Branch Petition," the work of its most cautious members, which begged the King to keep Parliament from further tyrannical measures so that a plan of reconciliation could be worked out. On receiving this petition in August, however, the incautious King himself brushed it aside and issued a proclamation of his own. Americans were rebels, he said, and he warned all loyal persons to refrain from assisting them.

These plates depicting the engagements of Lexington and Concord were drawn by Ralph Earle and engraved by Amos Doolittle (both soldiers) and published late in 1775. The engravings show not only the surprisingly effective stand of the colonial militia against the experienced British army, but also the sensitivity to design of our early artists. Plate I (Above). In the center are shown the British Grenadiers under the command of Major Pitcairn, on horseback, firing on the provincials (minutemen) at the far left. The British regulars, in the background, are marching to Concord. Plate II (Below). Major Pitcairn and his aide (with spyglass), watch the patriots regroup while the British troops march into Concord.

Plate III (Above). The skirmish at Concord bridge. The British (right) are already starting to withdraw. Plate IV (Below). The provincials snipe away at the columns of retreating British troops from behind their protective stone fence. The flames are from burning houses in Lexington. (Stokes Collection, New York Public Library.)

194

Still, there were conciliators in Britain too. In March 1775 Edmund Burke, in one of his great speeches, urged Parliament to meet American demands and surrender the right to tax. "An Englishman," he cried, "is the unfittest person on earth to argue another Englishman into slavery." Burke went largely unheeded, but Lord North himself persuaded Parliament to offer last-ditch concessions that might have helped in 1765 but in 1775 were too late.

By the time the North plan of conciliation reached Philadelphia, the Battle of Bunker Hill, the bloodiest engagement of the entire war, had been fought. The battle actually took place on Breed's Hill, overlooking Boston, where hundreds of American militiamen had gathered soon after the surviving redcoats had returned from Concord (see map, p. 191). On June 17, 1775, General Gage, strengthened by fresh troops, decided that he would drive the patriots off. He did manage to dislodge them, but at a frightful cost. The Americans lost almost 400 men, but Gage lost more than 1000—over 40 per cent of those he had moved into battle. Two weeks later, General Washington arrived at Cambridge, outside Boston, to take command.

By this time, too, fighting had begun farther north. Early in May 1775, in an effort to gain control of Canada, Ethan Allen, from future Vermont, captured the British posts at Crown Point and Ticonderoga in New York. On May 29, the Congress approved an address to their "fellow-sufferers" in Canada, inviting them to join the rebellion; but Canadian "sufferings" had been assuaged by the Quebec Act of 1774 (see p. 189), and their loyalty was not to be shaken. When the British organized a force in Canada to invade New York themselves, Washington decided to try to forestall them. In September 1775 Benedict Arnold set out for Quebec from Cambridge with about 1000 men, and early in December was joined below the town by a smaller contingent under Richard Montgomery, which had already taken Montreal. On New Year's Eve, 1775, Arnold and Montgomery made their assault, and it ended in Montgomery's death and Arnold's defeat. Arnold's force kept Quebec isolated through the bitter winter; but with the arrival of British reinforcements in the spring, he was forced to retire to Ticonderoga. The venture only sharpened British concern for Canada's safety, and coming as it did just after Congress had rejected Lord North's last effort at conciliation, it also prompted George III to build up his forces there for the fight to the finish against the rebels to the south.

### THE DECLARATION OF INDEPENDENCE

The average Englishman had no heart for the fight against the colonials, and the mother country was obliged to hire foreign mercenaries. Almost 30,000 "Hessians," as they came

*Thomas Paine at 70 by John Wesley Jarvis. (National Gallery of Art, Washington, D.C.)*

to be called since so many of them came from the German principalities of Hesse-Kassel and Hesse-Hanau, ultimately served with the British army in America.

Colonial propagandists and America's sympathizers in Parliament were quick to exploit this move, which stiffened the will of those Americans who had already declared for separation. The number of such Americans was raised early in 1776 by a pamphlet called *Common Sense* that appeared in Philadelphia from the hand of Thomas Paine. More than 120,000 copies were quickly sold. "There is something very absurd," Paine said, "in supposing a Continent to be perpetually governed by an island." And he added: "Freedom hath been hunted round the globe. . . . England hath given her warning to depart. O receive the fugitive, and prepare in time an asylum for mankind."

Such preparation was indeed under way. On April 6, 1776, the Congress had opened American ports to the commerce of all nations except Britain. This, in itself, placed America independent of Britain, as many in Congress realized when they debated the step. A month later Congress advised such colonies as had not already done so to form new state governments (see p. 214). Then on July 2, 1776, after nine hours of debate the day before had helped bring certain reluctant delegates around, Congress adopted Richard Henry Lee's "Resolution of Independence":

RESOLVED, That these United Colonies are, and of right ought to be, free and independent States, that they are absolved from all allegiance to the British Crown, and that all political connection between them and the State of Great Britain is, and ought to be, totally dissolved.

The adoption of this resolution was the great step, but in order to help enlist the support of foreign powers one more step seemed desirable. As Jefferson put it, "a decent respect to the opinions of mankind requires that they should declare the causes which impel them to the separation." On July 4, having made numerous changes in Jeffer-

First page of Jefferson's rough draft of the Declaration of Independence, showing corrections made by Jefferson, John Adams, and Franklin. (Library of Congress.)

son's draft of this declaration of causes, Congress finally ordered it "authenticated and printed," and "proclaimed in each of the united states & at the head of the army."

One of Congress's great goals was unanimity before the world; but not until July 19 was it possible to give the declaration its lasting title: "The Unanimous Declaration of the

195

*Detail from John Trumbull's* Declaration of Independence *showing the committee assigned to draft the Declaration submitting it to Congress. At the table before John Hancock stand John Adams, Roger Sherman, Robert Livingston, Thomas Jefferson, and Benjamin Franklin. (Yale University Art Gallery.)*

Thirteen United States of America." In order that unanimity be attained, what John Adams called Jefferson's "vehement philippic against negro slavery" had to be struck out, "in complaisance," as Jefferson noted at the time, "to South Carolina and Georgia. . . . Our northern brethren," he added, "also I believe felt a little tender under these censures; for tho' their people have very few slaves themselves, yet they have been pretty considerable carriers of them to others." There was no difficulty, however, about the ringing opening phrases of the Declaration, "these truths" we hold "to be self-evident." Many years later, John Adams was to belittle Jefferson's achievement, holding that the Declara-

tion merely repeated what men had been saying all along. But Jefferson replied that this was exactly what he had intended to do. The Declaration, Jefferson said, was "to be an expression of the American mind. . . . All its authority rests on the harmonizing sentiments of the day."

Although most of their quarrels had been with acts of Parliament, the list of grievances the Congress subscribed to in the Declaration was directed at "the present King of Great Britain." This was done deliberately. If the delegates had made their case against Parliament, they would have implied that they might still be persuaded to remain loyal subjects of the King. By attacking George himself, they served notice that they accepted no British authority whatever, and that they were cutting every tie connecting them with the mother country.

The "self-evident" truths in the preamble to the list of grievances were meant to justify this revolutionary step in terms of the doctrine of natural rights, including the right of revolution. John Locke had given the doctrine of natural rights its classic formulation in defending the Glorious Revolution of 1688 in England (see p. 140). By 1776 his ideas had become virtually axiomatic in America. What they meant was that all men share equally in certain basic *political* rights, which government must not invade. "Governments long established," the Declaration acknowledged, "should not be changed for light and transient causes." But in America, Britain's "invasion" involved "a long train of abuses and usurpations" which showed an intention to place the colonists "under absolute Despotism." This a free people had more than a right to oppose; they had a duty to rebel against such tyranny.

The Declaration of Independence, when it stated that "all men are created equal," may not have seemed to Congress to venture beyond the conventional political equality of free citizens. But even before the Declaration was made there were those deeply troubled by the discrepancy between the institution of slavery and the rebels' bold avowals about liberty as their goal. The Association of 1774 (see p. 190), and other nonintercourse proposals of the time, explicitly named the slave trade as one to be boycotted to make unmistakable the aversion to it. When in May of the following year, the question of using slaves as soldiers came up in Massachusetts, it was decided that their enlistment would be "inconsistent with the principles that are to be supported," and they were rejected. When the British, that November, began to make overtures to the slaves to enlist against their masters, however, Americans recognized the danger and altered their stand. Most of the slaves among the 5000 Negroes who served with the American revolutionary army were freed on enlistment. In his attack upon slavery in the early drafts of the Declaration, moreover, Jefferson included bondmen among those whose "sacred rights of life and liberty" had been violated by His Royal Majesty, George III.

Like all great political documents, the Declaration of Independence instantly took on a life of its own, consistent with the hopes and aspirations of all men under fetters, not merely white men in the America of 1776. Manumission in the South, abolition in the North, during and after the Revolutionary War itself, gained momentum from the Declaration's self-evident truths (see p. 196). In 1789, when the French rebelled against Bourbon absolutism, the Declaration helped light the way for their leaders. In our own time, among colonial peoples abroad and the repressed at home, the Declaration continues to serve the cause of revolution and of social as well as political equality.

## THE LOYALISTS

While Congress, as a revolutionary body, might easily be won around to the ringing phrases of the Declaration, and while other Americans might even extend the meaning of these phrases to suit their own more advanced thought, a good many colonials, often after agonizing indecision, concluded that they must remain loyal to the Crown.

These Loyalists—scornfully called Tories by the patriots—came from several social classes and allied themselves with king and Parliament from a variety of motives. Among those content with the old order or tied to it by personal interests were many rich merchants and landholders fearful of what might happen to their property in a mass uprising; they were convinced that, even though British measures sometimes caused them heavy losses, they had far more to lose than to gain by a social upheaval. With them stood many influential lawyers and professional men who had pushed their way up the social ladder, as well as officeholders in the service of the Crown, recent arrivals in the colonies, and Anglican clergymen. Almost every major seaport town—Boston, Newport, New York, Philadelphia, Charleston, Savannah—had a social nucleus of the well-to-do, the official, and the prominent, a glittering high society dominated by aristocratic prejudices and Loyalist sentiments. But there were in addition many ordinary citizens who were slow to shift their loyalty and who resented being hurried into the risks of war and rebellion. "Damn the Rebels," shouted one vehement farmer in western Massachusetts. "I would cut their thumbs, boil them on the coals, and eat them. . . . I wish I had the Keys of Hell, I would turn on all the damned Rebels and kick them along. . . . I wish they were all Scalped: damn the Congress to hell."

Some ordinary Americans, indeed, embraced the Crown with new fervor rather than support the hated *colonial* aristocrats often found among the rebels. In North Carolina, the Regulators, as such back-country Tories were called, even took up arms against the seaboard patriots. Others remained Tories simply because they felt the colonials could not win the war. In some provinces, the aristocracy itself was split, and old factional animosities were now reflected in the division between Whig and Tory. In New York, for instance, the supporters of a Presbyterian faction led by the Livingston family had been feuding for years with an Anglican faction led by the De Lanceys; with the Revolution, the former took their stand as Whigs, the latter as Loyalists.

In the war of words that preceded the Declaration of Independence, Tory spokesmen held their own against the arguments of the patriots. True, they sometimes indulged in violent statements of aristocratic prejudices, like the outburst of the New York Tory Samuel Seabury: "If I must be enslaved, let it be by a *King* at least, and not by a parcel of upstart lawless Committeemen. If I must be devoured, let me be devoured by the jaws of a lion, and not gnawed to death by rats and vermin." Some Tories, among them the Maryland Anglican Jonathan Boucher, even harked back to ancient and outmoded arguments like the divine right of kings: "Unless we are good subjects," wrote Boucher, "we cannot be good Christians." But there were also those who invoked legal and philosophical notions that command widespread respect. Daniel Leonard, a talented and forceful lawyer from Taunton, Massachusetts, drew upon the philosophy of Thomas Hobbes to defend royal authority. Grimly he described the fate of society when brute force prevails and rebels defy their God-appointed rulers:

> Rebellion is the most atrocious offense that can be perpetrated by man. . . . It dissolves the social bond, annihilates the security resulting from law and government, introduces fraud, violence, rapine, murder, sacrilege, and the long train of evils that riot, uncontrolled, in a state of nature.

With Tory bluntness, Leonard reminded his readers that the common people, "confined to the humbler walks of business or retirement," had little knowledge of state affairs, and he warned of the swift retribution certain to overtake the colonists if they defied the King's armies.

Leonard's case shows that Loyalist spokesmen were by no means simple-minded reactionaries. Most of them subscribed as readily as the patriots themselves to the general ideas of popular representation that had gained currency in England through long years of struggle. That taxation without representation was tyranny they admitted; but they felt that the House of Commons offered safeguards against abuse, and that the absence of American representatives there did not make Parliament's taxation of the colonies a form of tyranny. One group of New York Loyalists drew up an imitation "Declaration of Independence" in which the preamble repeated almost the exact words of Jefferson, including his statement of the natural right of revolution. But when they came to their bill of grievances, they substituted the actions of the Continental Congress for those of the King, enumerating them as evidence of "a long train of the most licentious and despotic abuses."

There is no question that the Tories were on the whole more conservative, less libertarian, and less friendly to democratic ideas and practices than the patriots. But the lines in this fraternal struggle were also drawn on practical issues, conflicts of temperament, and accidents of personal situation.

In this struggle the Whigs usually held the advantage, for they had taken the initiative. While the Loyalists were still expressing their disdain for patriotic agitations and waiting for the hand of British authority to fall upon their foes, the Whigs organized "Tory committees" which imprisoned many of them and drove others out of their homes and communities. Patriots refused to trade with Loyalists or work for them. Loyalist estates and personal property often were confiscated. Few Loyalists, however, lost their lives. American Whigs who lived long enough to learn of the horrors of the French Revolutionary terror sometimes remarked on the relative mildness of their own earlier behavior toward the counterrevolutionaries. Clearly, some kind of repression was in order. As Washington asked in 1775, "Why should persons, who are preying on the vitals of the country, be suffered to stalk at large, whilst we know that they will do us every mischief in their power?"

The British forces never used the full potential of Loyalist support, but Loyalists did render important services as spies, informants, workmen, providers of supplies, and soldiers. Their greatest value was as propagandists; they went among their wavering neighbors, warned them of the danger of taking part in the rebellion, appealed to old loyalties, and put sympathetic merchants in touch with British quartermasters eager for supplies. Many Loyalists fled behind the British lines and enjoyed the comfort of British protection, especially in New York City and Philadelphia. Thousands moved for good to England or Canada, where they were warmly welcomed and helped to start a new life. It has been estimated that the British government later spent about £3 million in compensating the Loyalists for their losses.

## IV  *The War of Independence*

### THE OPPOSING CAMPS

Loyalist warnings that Britain possessed enormous military advantages in the looming war were well founded. A disorganized population of about 2.5 million, with no army or navy and no true central government, was ranged against an imperial power of 10 million persons, the mistress of the seas, with thousands of experienced troops at her command.

Yet Britain suffered many strategic disadvantages to which the United States was to grow accustomed in the twentieth century. She had to wage the war across 3000 miles of ocean, on unfamiliar terrain, much of it trackless forest. As one of her officers put it, the difficulty of moving supplies into the interior "absolutely prevented us this whole war from going fifteen miles from a navigable river." In contrast, the Americans were swift and mobile, adept at swooping down for short skirmishes, pecking away at the enemy's supply lines, and taking cover in the woods.

This sort of "guerrilla warfare," a term to be applied to other colonial conflicts later on, left British officers bewildered. In Lord George

Germain, the Colonial Secretary, they had an intelligent and meticulous organizer who fully appreciated the difficulties "of opposing an enemy that avoids facing you in the open field." Germain gave his American commanders wide latitude in planning their maneuvers under the new conditions. As time proved, however, he was too optimistic about Loyalist assistance and trusted too much in officers who lacked energy and imagination. One of their failings was contempt for the American "yokels" (less widespread at the war's end than at the beginning), an attitude that led to careless and extravagant behavior. Even at Yorktown many of them were to surrender gracelessly, preferring to bow before the trim French forces instead of the ragged Yanks. The morale of the British troops was further weakened by faltering support on the home front. British civilians as a rule were almost as confused as their troops. Many were not even sure of what they were trying to accomplish. Hence their support of the war was lukewarm at best.

On their part, most Americans tended to underestimate their own difficulties. The same stubborn individualism, the same jealous attachment to their liberties that had made the Americans quick to resist the assaults of Parliament, now made them slow to accept the tight organization and the onerous discipline that were needed to carry on a war. Raising an army was hard enough; whipping it into a disciplined force was harder; and keeping it active in the field was all but impossible. Although some 300,000 persons may have taken up arms in the rebel cause, the largest army Washington ever pieced together at one time amounted to a little over 20,000 men. Usually he had hardly as many as 5000, most of them state militia accustomed to marching under friendly officers elected by themselves and resentful of outside commanders. Most soldiers, concerned with families and farms back home, were reluctant to sign up for more than a few winter months, and few were ready to re-enlist. Southerners resented being sent to New England to fight, and New Englanders returned the compliment. With the Continental army sadly in need of professionals, the Americans were glad to welcome such foreign volunteers and sympathizers as Baron Friedrich W. A. von Steuben of Prussia, Count Casimir Pulaski of Poland, and the Marquis de Lafayette, a 20-year-old volunteer from France. Von Steuben in particular was the kind of drillmaster raw troops most needed.

As long as the war lasted, Washington plagued Congress with requests for fighting men. The delegates were powerless to do anything more than pass his demands on to

General Washington at Princeton *by Charles Peale Polk (1767–1822). (National Gallery of Art, Washington, D.C.)*

the states. No one was satisfied with the results. Yet Congress's record was not as poor as it is often painted. The new nation, which had previously looked to the mother country for its manufactures, was always hard put to feed, clothe, arm, and pay the relatively few soldiers it could put in the field at any time. Washington's army was desperately small. And yet the country could not have supported a much larger one than Congress supplied.

The story of the wartime economy is similar. Congress lacked not only the power to tax, but also—given the origins of the Revolution—the inclination to do so. Moreover, much of the taxable specie in the country—English guineas, Spanish pieces of eight, Dutch florins, and, for that matter, household silver—had gone with the Loyalists. Specie loans, foreign and domestic, were slow in coming, and they were used up with disheartening swiftness. Thus the war was financed mainly with paper money (especially the Continental currency, which had no observable resources behind it) and a whole Pandora's box of I.O.U.'s, the variety of which reflects credit only on Congress's ingenuity. The paper money eventually became valueless and the I.O.U.'s depreciated greatly.

The riot of speculation that accompanied the rise of commodity prices, expressed in terms of the depreciated currency, angered Washington more deeply than almost any other problem of the Revolution. At the same time, rising prices served to induce legitimate producers among farmers, miners, and manufacturers to increase their output greatly. Profits soared; but so did the quantity of goods available to the Continental army. Robert Morris expressed the philosophy of the wartime entrepreneurs, a philosophy that did not cost them the good opinion of their friends: "It seems to me that the present oppert'y of improving our fortunes ought not to be lost, especially as the very means of doing it will contribute to the service of our country." It is doubtful if any greater economic effort could have been elicited had the Congress's money been as sound as that of the Bank of

*A German impression, from 1784, of a uniformed American rifleman and a regular infantryman. (New York Public Library.)*

England and its credit buttressed (as it later was) by a bank of its own.

### FROM LONG ISLAND TO SARATOGA

On being dislodged from Breed's Hill in June 1775, patriot forces successfully occupied Dorchester Heights overlooking Boston. There, Washington armed his men with cannon laboriously hauled down from Fort Ticonderoga early in 1776. Confronted by this force, the British General, Sir William Howe,

who had supplanted General Gage, decided in March 1776 to evacuate Boston for Halifax, Nova Scotia. From there he would assault New York City, which, with its heavy Loyalist population and fine harbor, he hoped to make his headquarters. Washington expected this move, and in April he rallied as many soldiers as he could and marched them off to protect the city. But here he soon found himself confronted with Howe's army of 32,000 men on Staten Island. Sensing that it would be risky to concentrate his troops in the city itself, Washington fortified Brooklyn Heights on Long Island, hoping thereby to gain control of Manhattan as Dorchester Heights had given him control of Boston. On August 27, however, Howe defeated the rebels on Long Island. Two days later Washington entered Manhattan itself, where he was chased up the island to White Plains. Here he was beaten again, and fled to Hackensack, New Jersey, where he reformed his ranks.

By now Washington had his strategy firmly in mind. "We should on all occasions avoid a general action," he told Congress, "or put anything to the risque, unless compelled by a necessity, into which we ought never to be drawn." These tactics were made all the easier by Howe's own lethargy on the attack.

In December 1776, nevertheless, Howe did chase Washington from Hackensack to Trenton, New Jersey, and then across the Delaware River into Pennsylvania. Washington wrote to Congress that he must have more troops, or "I think the game will be pretty much up." But he did not wait for Congress's help before acting. Realizing that Howe's troops must be spread thin, Washington counterattacked brilliantly. On the stormy Christmas night of 1776 he recrossed the Delaware, surprised the sleepy Hessians at Trenton, killed their commander, and took almost 2000 prisoners. Washington followed up this victory with another near Princeton, January 3, 1777. Before retiring for the winter near Morristown, he had cleared the British out of the state and once again dared hope for ultimate success.

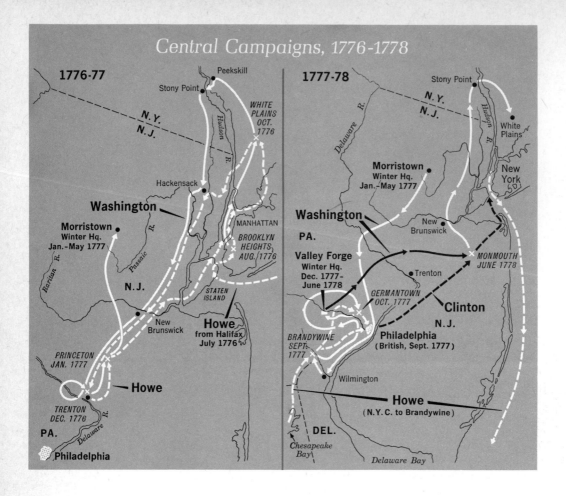

## Central Campaigns, 1776-1778

**1776-77**

Peekskill
Stony Point
WHITE PLAINS OCT. 1776
N.Y.
N.J.
Hudson R.
Hackensack
**Washington**
Morristown Winter Hq. Jan.-May 1777
MANHATTAN
BROOKLYN HEIGHTS AUG. 1776
Passaic R.
N.J.
STATEN ISLAND
New Brunswick
**Howe** from Halifax July 1776
Raritan R.
PRINCETON JAN. 1777
**Howe**
TRENTON DEC. 1776
Delaware R.
PA.
**Philadelphia**

**1777-78**

Stony Point
N.Y.
N.J.
Delaware R.
Hudson R.
White Plains
Morristown Winter Hq. Jan.-May 1777
New York
**Washington**
PA.
New Brunswick
**Valley Forge** Winter Hq. Dec. 1777-June 1778
Trenton
MONMOUTH JUNE 1778
GERMANTOWN OCT. 1777
**Clinton**
N.J.
BRANDYWINE SEPT. 1777
**Philadelphia** (British, Sept. 1777)
Wilmington
**Howe** (N.Y.C. to Brandywine)
DEL.
Chesapeake Bay
Delaware Bay

These hopes soared with the defeat of "Gentleman Johnny" Burgoyne at Saratoga, New York, in October 1777. General Burgoyne had worked out an elaborate plan to divide and conquer the rebels. With a large force from Canada he himself would push southward along Lake Champlain. At the same time, a smaller force under Colonel Barry St. Leger would march eastward through the Mohawk Valley from Fort Oswego on Lake Ontario. Still a third force, under General Howe, was to move northward up the Hudson Valley from New York City. Converging on Albany, the three armies would crush any American opposition, proceed to control New York and cut New England off from the south. Then the independent rebel states could be picked off, one by one.

Burgoyne's strategy was sounder than his communications. With Germain's permission, Howe undertook to nail down Philadelphia, the rebel capital, before moving north. On September 11 he overcame the defenders at Brandywine Creek, but not until September 26 could he enter the city itself. On October 3, at nearby Germantown, Howe repelled Washington's attempt to dislodge him. When Franklin, in Paris (see p. 204), heard that Howe had captured Philadelphia, he dissented. "No," he said, "Philadelphia has captured Howe." And so it was. Deserting Burgoyne, the pleasure-loving Howe lolled in the lap of Philadelphia's grateful Loyalist society.

Although tempted by fewer attractions than Howe, St. Leger was also lost to Burgoyne. On August 22, after Benedict Arnold's clever ruse at Fort Stanwix deprived him of his Indian contingents, St. Leger, battered in earlier engagements on the way, decided to return to Fort Oswego.

Of the three British armies essential to Burgoyne's compaign, only one remained to him—his own. Blissfully unaware of his predicament, "Gentleman Johnny" started southward from Canada on June 17, with his wine, his fine clothes, his camp-following women, and almost 8000 redcoats.

Misfortune dogged Burgoyne at almost every step, and of a kind that he and his men most detested. Impromptu bands of "country yokels," materializing suddenly, riddled his proper formations and as suddenly dissolved. On August 11, at Bennington, a group of Green Mountain Boys led by John Stark fell fiercely upon a force of 700 men whom Burgoyne had sent out to forage, and destroyed them entirely. A few days before, Burgoyne had received the dismal news of Howe's Philadelphia enterprise. "I little foresaw," Burgoyne wrote to Germain, "that I was to be left to pursue my way through such a tract of country, and hosts of foes, without any co-operation from New York." But he pushed on to the vicinity of Saratoga, where on September 19 he was checked at the battle of Freeman's Farm. At last, his defeated force overwhelmingly outnumbered, he was met by Gates and Arnold at Bemis Heights. While Gates was arguing in his quarters with a captured British officer about the merits of the Revolutionary cause, Arnold led a magnificent assault. On October 17, 1777, Burgoyne surrendered his battered army.

Arnold's victory was an eye-opener to the redcoats. As one British officer captured at Saratoga wrote:

The courage and obstinacy with which the Americans fought were the astonishment of every one, and we now become fully convinced, they are not that contemptible enemy we had hitherto imagined them, incapable of standing a regular engagement, and that they would only fight behind strong and powerful works.

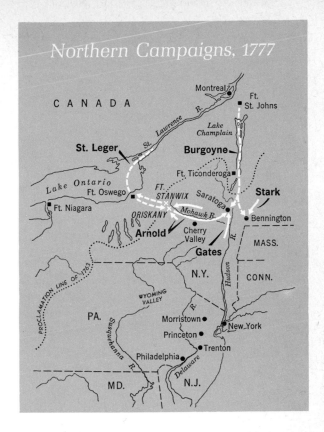

## Northern Campaigns, 1777

Burgoyne's dramatic defeat in turn electrified all Europe.

### THE FORCE OF THE FRENCH ALLIANCE

From the start of the Revolution, European governments had looked with mixed pleasure and concern at Britain's plight. On the one hand they yearned to see the island kingdom humbled and the balance of power restored; on the other, they feared the example of American success among their own people, at home as well as in their overseas possessions.

As early as November 1775, Congress began to play upon Europe's hopes and fears by sending Silas Deane to France. Deane was successful in gaining secret assistance in the war both from France and from her ally, Spain. After the Declaration of Independence, Congress lifted its sights and dispatched Arthur Lee, then serving secretly in London, and the renowned and engaging Franklin, to as-

203

sist Deane in Paris in negotiating a formal alliance. Franklin charmed the French, but they did not capitulate until they had learned of Burgoyne's surrender at Saratoga. In order to short-circuit Franco-American negotiations, Lord North's government, following Burgoyne's defeat, offered to suspend all laws passed in relation to America since 1763, and also appointed a peace commissioner to seek to end the war on these terms. In order to short-circuit Anglo-American negotiations which might restore British strength in America, France was ready to jump into the war on the rebel's side.

Congress rebuffed Lord North's offer. Nothing short of recognition of independence would do, and this the British could not grant. Congress also, on March 4, 1778, ratified the treaty with France which Franklin and Deane had concluded on February 6: "The essential and direct end" of the alliance cemented by the treaty was "to maintain . . . the liberty, sovereignty, and independence absolute and unlimited, of the United States." In case war broke out between Britain and France (Britain did declare war in June 1778), the United States and France agreed "to make it a common cause," and neither party was to make peace without consulting the other. The French generously consented not to interfere if the Americans could conquer Canada and Bermuda; and, not to be outdone in generosity at Britain's expense, the Americans gave the French *carte blanche* in the British West Indies. In a separate commercial treaty negotiated at the same time, the two nations also granted one another favorable trade terms.

Before the French alliance American privateers did plenty of damage to British commerce, but American efforts to build a navy had come to little, partly because the privateersmen themselves outbid Congress for good men and ships. John Paul Jones and other commissioned sea captains, sometimes using French bases, harassed British coastal towns, but there and elsewhere, simply "to Surprise and spread Alarm," as Jones said, they operated individually or in small, uncooperative

squadrons, not as an effective fleet. With the French alliance, the rebels acquired naval support ready made, even though for some years it took the form of independent French actions against the common enemy.

One exception to this policy was French cooperation with John Paul Jones in September 1779 in the battle of which the famous engagement between *Bonhomme Richard* and the British warship *Serapis* was a part. Although *Bonhomme Richard* was sunk in the meeting, Jones and his men successfully boarded *Serapis* and took her to port in France. It was during this engagement, when invited to surrender by the heavier British vessel, that Jones is said to have replied, "I have not yet begun to fight." Fight he did, as he never had before even during his own extraordinarily violent career, but the outcome had no military effect on the progress of the cause.

The French alliance transformed the American war for independence into a renewal of the European struggle for power. Spain, Holland, and Russia soon joined the fray to nibble at British trade and feast on British shipping. The British held their own against these rivals, and their own privateers continued to improve their showing against rebel shipping itself. At the same time, foreign pressure on her control of the seas forced the British henceforth to wage a defensive war in America and eventually to capitulate. The Americans' success was delayed in part because, so divided were the states, so poor the people, they could not long sustain the buoyant spirit of Saratoga and the French alliance; and in part because the French, belatedly concerned for the safety of their West Indian possessions, were slow in making their critical naval contributions to America's final victory.

### THE NADIR OF THE CAUSE

After his defeat at Germantown (p. 202), Washington had taken his battered bitter-enders to nearby Valley Forge where they endured their well-known winter ordeal. Howe's pleasures in Philadelphia at the same time were wearing thin and he asked to be relieved of "this very painful service." His failure to disperse Washington's ragged, starving army prompted Germain to accede to his request, and in May 1778 Howe was supplanted at the head of the British forces by General Henry Clinton. Clinton's orders were to evacuate Philadelphia and to prosecute a vigorous new campaign in New York.

When Clinton began his move from Philadelphia on June 18, Washington emerged from Valley Forge to intercept him. On June 28, the two armies met at Monmouth Courthouse in New Jersey, in an action that was a credit to neither side. General Charles Lee, at the head of Washington's advance force, behaved in a way that soon led to his court-martial. When Clinton, however, tried to take advantage of Lee's mistakes, other Americans checked him. Clinton was allowed to steal away under cover of night to Sandy Hook, where his troops embarked on waiting transports for Manhattan.

Except for an expedition to South Carolina in December 1779 (see p. 206), Clinton remained in New York until the end of the war. Washington himself followed Clinton to New York and again encamped at White Plains to keep an eye on the enemy. In the meantime, Loyalist and Indian bands terrorized frontier settlements in the Wyoming Valley in Pennsylvania's eastern interior and in Cherry Valley in central New York.

While the principal armies thus were playing their waiting game in the East, Virginia's own forces under George Rogers Clark undertook to destroy the Indians assisting the British in the West (see map. p. 207). In May 1778, with 175 riflemen, Clark floated down the Ohio almost to the Mississippi and proceeded to take the undefended old French towns of Kaskaskia, Cahokia, and Vincennes. Colonel Henry Hamilton, the hated English commandant at Detroit, known as the "Hair Buyer" for paying his Indian auxiliaries for American scalps, counterattacked and recaptured Vincennes. Clark then performed one of the most remarkable feats of the war. With

an "army" of 127 men, half of them French, he marched 180 miles from Kaskaskia to Vincennes—triumphing over cold, floods, and hunger—and forced Hamilton to surrender on February 24, 1779. Clark never reached Detroit, as he hoped, nor did his victories clinch the lower Ohio and Illinois country for the Americans. But he lifted the Indian pressure from the settlements in Kentucky and West Virginia.

In accordance with his orders as he understood them, Clinton, beginning in May 1779, began making sporadic forays against rebel forts in upstate New York, which Washington's contingents, especially the one under General Anthony Wayne, repulsed. Other rebel forces, in turn, took the offensive against the marauding Loyalist and Indian bands in New York and by August 1779 had destroyed 40 Seneca and Cayuga villages. These actions neutralized the Iroquois menace in the East as Clark's had quieted the other tribes in the West.

Success against Britain's Indian allies in the interior, however, could not offset the deterioration in numbers and morale of Washington's main army in New York. Unpaid, ill-clothed, miserably fed, this army grew ever more restive as it saw, on the one hand, Congress's inability to stem the inflation that forced up the cost of war supplies, and on the other the high life of civilian profiteers. Late in 1779, Washington took this army to winter quarters in Morristown, New Jersey, where its sufferings outdid those at Valley Forge, and where hope for improvement vanished. Desertions soared, and before camp was broken in the spring of 1780, Washington had to quell an armed mutiny of Connecticut regiments.

The British tried to make capital of the rebels' plight by offering handsome bribes to alienated officers. Their best catch was the brilliant Benedict Arnold, already conscious of real and imagined snubs, who began sending Clinton information on American troop movements as early as May 1779. Arnold was soon found out, but escaped with reprimands.

206

The next year, his plot to gain command at West Point and to turn the fortress over to the British collapsed when the enemy agent, Major John André, was caught behind the American lines with incriminating evidence and hanged as a spy. On learning of André's fate, Arnold, on September 25, 1780, fled to a British warship on the Hudson. The British soon made him a general and enriched him besides, and he fought the rest of the war on their side.

Back in 1778, in the so-called "Conway Cabal," a group in Congress had given serious consideration to supplanting Washington with a more manageable commander. Under the changed circumstances of 1780, a new congressional delegation set out for Morristown in April empowered, as they said, to offer him "a kind of dictatorial power, in order to afford satisfaction to the army." As Washington ignored the Conways, so he rejected the desperate alternative. The delegation was warmly received by General Nathanael Greene and other officers who had similar plans of their own, but Greene sensibly steered them away from his chief. "He has strange notions about the cause," Greene said, "and the obligation there is for people to sacrifice fortune and reputation in support thereof." Washington never forgot that he was engaged in a war on tyranny as well as on tyrants, and his patience with the people soon had its reward.

### TO YORKTOWN

The final battles of the war were fought in the South. Although Henry Clinton, along with Lord Cornwallis and Admiral Sir Peter Parker, had failed to take Charleston, South Carolina, in a combined sea and land attack back in June 1776, Clinton believed that Loyalist support was heavy in the South and could be more fully exploited. Soon after he had taken over from Howe in 1778, Clinton planned an attack on Savannah, Georgia, which was successfully carried out in December that year. From Savannah, Georgia was overrun. One year later, Clinton personally led the new expedition against Charleston from New York, and on May 12, 1780, the town fell and with it over 5000 men, 300 cannon, and four ships. Clinton then returned to New York, leaving Cornwallis in charge. Cornwallis followed up with a smashing victory over General Gates at Camden, South Carolina, on August 16, 1780.

With Georgia and South Carolina firmly held (despite the partisan warfare of South Carolina guerrillas like the daring "Swamp Fox," Francis Marion), the British commanders now turned to North Carolina, but here the tables were rudely turned. At King's Mountain, on October 7, 1780, an army of 1100 Tories was shot up by back-country patriots. Then, General Daniel Morgan's victory at Cowpens on January 16, 1781, and a severe engagement at Guilford Courthouse in March, at last persuaded Cornwallis to abandon the state and move on to Virginia. General Nathanael Greene, who after Gates's disheartening defeat at Camden had taken over the command of the Continental army in the South, then cleared the British out of most of South Carolina in 1781. Not until December 1782, however, did the British defense of Charleston itself collapse.

When Cornwallis, after raiding villages and farms, took up his position at Yorktown, Virginia, on August 1, 1781, he believed that British naval superiority would assure the evacuation of his troops, if such a move became necessary. In two months it did, but the evacuation was foiled by France's greatest contribution to rebel success.

In 1778, and again in 1780, French fleets had arrived in America, the first soon to leave again for the West Indies, the second to find itself bottled up by the British in Newport, Rhode Island, after landing the Comte de Rochambeau and 5000 men. In May 1781 Washington, still eyeing Clinton in New York, learned of the approach of a third French fleet of 20 warships under Admiral de Grasse. He tried to get Rochambeau to use this fleet to help get Clinton out of New York; but de Grasse himself was headed south and

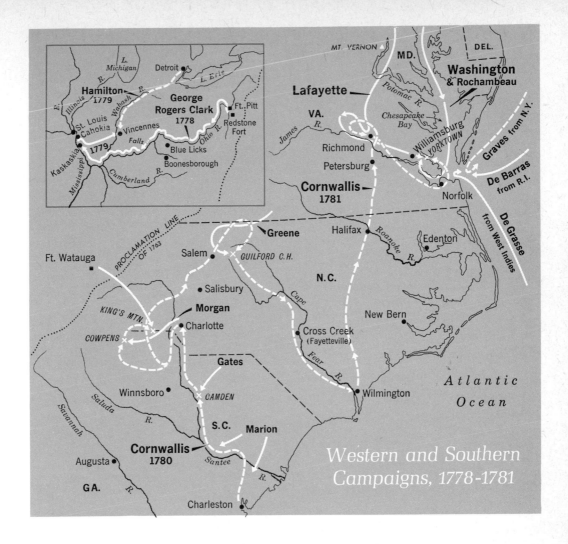

**Western and Southern Campaigns, 1778-1781**

Washington promptly decamped and marched his men to meet him. British naval units around New York also sailed south; but on discovering the French strength, they sailed right back again and Cornwallis was finished. Pinned down between the French fleet and a combined Franco-American force of 16,000 men, Cornwallis had to yield. As his defeated troops, numbering about 7000, stacked their arms, American bands played a march called "The World Turned Upside Down."

The British surrender at Yorktown on October 19, 1781, virtually ended hostilities. Lord North, on learning the news, cried out again and again, "Oh God! it is all over!" In March 1782 he resigned in favor of the Marquis of Rockingham, and his long and disastrous ministry came to an end.

The British, however, showed signs of fight even after Yorktown. The final peace was not worked out until almost two years later, and during that time Admiral Rodney defeated a French fleet at the Battle of the Saints in the West Indies in April 1782. This belated victory went far toward redressing the balance of power at sea. The following autumn, the British turned back with heavy enemy losses a well-prepared French and Spanish attack on the fortress of Gibraltar. These successes did not alter the fact that Britain had lost the

208

war, but they did enable her to hold out for less costly peace terms.

### THE TREATY OF PARIS

The American peace commissioners, Benjamin Franklin, John Jay, and John Adams, who were sent by Congress to Paris in 1782, had to proceed very delicately in their negotiations. Congress had instructed them to consult with France on matters of diplomacy, but the commissioners knew that Spain had never approved of American independence and that she opposed the Mississippi River boundary the envoys were seeking. Since it seemed

likely that France would support Spain, the three Americans ignored their instructions and reached a preliminary independent agreement with the British delegation that gave America the territory she coveted up to the Mississippi shore. In return, America renounced all claims to Canada. Vergennes, the French minister, was chagrined by these behind-the-scenes deals, but the adroit Franklin managed to soothe him and even to extract another fat loan for the United States.

The treaty between the United States of America and Great Britain was signed in Paris on September 3, 1783, and ratified in Philadelphia on January 14, 1784. Known as

United States in 1783

the Treaty of Paris, it included the following provisions: (1) Britain recognized American independence. (2) America obtained all the territory bounded by the Mississippi River on the west, the 31st parallel on the south (the line agreed upon if Britain ceded Florida to Spain, which she did), and the Great Lakes on the north. (3) Britain acknowledged America's right to the Newfoundland fisheries, but (4) retained the privilege with America of navigating the Mississippi. The United States agreed (5) to impose "no lawful impediment" to the recovery by British creditors of private debts due them but (6) consented only to "recommend" that the states restore Loyalist property.

The American negotiators had done well. Although the treaty left many important issues unresolved, many commercial agreements uncertain, and some boundaries dangerously inexact, American independence was a recognized fact, and a vast area from the Alleghenies to the Mississippi lay open to settlement. An epoch had begun, a New Jersey congressman observed. "It opens a new scene to Mankind, and is big with inconceivable Effects

in the political and I hope in the moral world." Washington, for all his disappointments and disgusts, agreed. Back in 1778, he cried out in anguish: "The States separately, have very inadequate ideas of the present danger. . . . Party disputes and personal quarrels are the great business of the day, whilst the momentous concerns of empire . . . are but secondary considerations." But in 1783, the opportunity for empire, and for the "self-evident truths" that would make empire in America different from empire abroad, seemed much brighter. In that year, the war at an end, victory attained, Washington said:

The citizens of America, placed in the most enviable condition, as the sole lords and proprietors of a vast tract of continent, comprehending all the various soils and climates of the world, and abounding with all the necessaries and conveniences of life, are now, by the late satisfactory pacification, acknowledged to be possessed of absolute freedom and independency. They are, from this period, to be considered as the actors on a most conspicuous theatre, which seems to be peculiarly designated by Providence for the display of human greatness and felicity.

# READINGS

E.S. Morgan, *The American Revolution: Two Centuries of Interpretation* (1965), is a good introduction to the contesting views on the origins and character of the break with England. Morgan's *The Birth of the Republic 1763–1789* (1956) is a statement of his own view. L.H. Gipson, *The Coming of the Revolution 1763–1775* (1954), is an authoritative short version of the later volumes of his 13-volume *The British Empire Before the American Revolution* (1936–1967). Merrill Jensen, *The Founding of a Nation* (1968), reflects modern scholarship on the period 1763–1776. See also Bernhard Knollenberg, *Origin of the American Revolution* (1960). Valuable older works include C.L. Becker, *The Eve of the Revolution* (1918); C.M. Andrews, *The Colonial Background of the American Revolution* (1924); and J.C. Miller, *Origins of the American Revolution* (1943). E.B. Greene, *The Revolutionary Generation 1763–1790* (1943), is a social history of the period. Eric Robson, *The American Revolution 1763–1783* (1955), is a succinct discussion of imperial problems by an English scholar. John Shy, *Toward Lexington, The Role of the British Army in the Coming of the American Revolution* (1965), is an illuminating work.

Three books by Sir Lewis Namier remain important on British politics in the revolutionary period despite certain recent criticisms of them: *England in the Age of the American Revolution* (1930); *The Structure of Politics on the Accession of George III* (1957 ed.); and *Personalities and Powers* (1955). Namier and John Brooke, *Charles Townshend* (1964), goes beyond biography to study the policies of the controversial minister. Richard Pares, *King George III and the Politicians* (1953), is in the Namier tradition. Herbert Butterfield, *George III and the Historians* (1957), is a good statement of the dissenting view. The older view of party conflict which Namier attacked but which has regained interest is presented in G.O. Trevelyan, *The Early History of Charles James Fox* (1901), and *The American Revolution* (4 vols., 1898–1907; reduced to one useful volume by Richard Morris, 1964). O.A. Sherrard, *Lord Chatham and America* (1958), volume 3 of Sherrard's life of William Pitt, is excellent on America's great champion. George Rudé, *Wilkes and Liberty, A Social Study of 1763 to 1774* (1962), is good on social ferment in England on the eve of the Revolution in America.

Bernard Bailyn, ed., *Pamphlets of the American Revolution,* vol. 1, 1750–1765 (1965), is a fruitful anthology with a penetrating introduction on the colonial response to British measures. Bailyn's *The Ideological Origins of the American Revolution* (1967), is an elaboration of this introduction. Some of the fruits of this work appear in H.T. Colbourn, *The Lamp of Experience: Whig History and the Intellectual Origins of the American Revolution* (1965), and G.S. Wood, *The Creation of the American Republic 1776–1787* (1969). The background in English thinking is well supplied in Caroline Robbins, *The Eighteenth-Century Commonwealthman, . . . from the Restoration of Charles II until the War with the Thirteen Colonies* (1959). Max Beloff, ed., *The Debate on the American Revolution 1761–1783* (1949), combines British and American documents. The thrust of American ideas of liberty and empire is illuminated in Clinton Rossiter, *Seedtime of the Republic* (1953); Max Savelle, *Seeds of Liberty* (1948); and Gerald Stourzh, *Benjamin Franklin and American Foreign Policy* (1954). Carl Bridenbaugh, *Mitre and Sceptre: Transatlantic Faiths, Ideas, Personalities and Politics 1689–1775* (1962), is authoritative on the Anglican threat to religious liberty in America and its role in the revolutionary movement. A.M. Schlesinger, *Prelude to Independence: The Newspaper War on Britain 1764–1776* (1958); Philip Davidson, *Propaganda and the American Revolution* (1941); and B.I. Granger, *Political Satire in the American Revolution 1760–1783* (1960)—all supply evidence of the attempts to engage the popular mind. Thomas Paine, *Common Sense,* is available in M.D. Conway, *The Writings of Thomas Paine* (4 vols., 1894–1896), and in numerous other editions. C.L. Becker, *The Declaration of Independence* (1922), is the outstanding study of that document. The background for it and many other related subjects is fully revealed in J.P. Boyd, ed., *The Papers of Thomas Jefferson,* vol. I, 1760–1776 (1950).

Special studies of British action and colonial reaction include T.C. Barrow, *Trade and Empire: The British Customs Service in Colonial America 1660–1775* (1967); A.M. Schlesinger, *Colonial Merchants and the American Revolution 1763–1776* (1918); Carl Bridenbaugh, *Cities in Revolt, Urban Life in America 1743–1776* (1955); E.S. and H.M. Morgan, *The Stamp Act Crisis: Prologue to Revolution* (1953); B.W. Labaree, *The Boston Tea Party* (1964); and three excellent books on the West: Clarence Alvord, *The Mississippi Valley in British Politics* (2 vols., 1916); J.M. Sosin, *Whitehall and Wilderness: The Middle West in British Colonial Policy 1760–1775* (1961); and T.P. Abernethy, *Western Lands and the American Revolution* (1937). J.R. Alden, *The South in the Revolution 1763–*

*1789* (1957), ably covers that section's participation. G.M. Wrong, *Canada and the American Revolution* (1935), is an authoritative study. An exceptionally valuable collection of essays will be found in R.B. Morris, ed., *The Era of the American Revolution* (1935).

In addition to certain biographically oriented works cited above, the following lives of leading figures are of value: D.S. Freeman, *George Washington: A Biography* (6 vols., 1948–1954), completed by J.A. Carroll and M.W. Ashworth (vol. 7, 1957); Marcus Cunliffe, *George Washington, Man and Monument* (1959); Carl Van Doren, *Benjamin Franklin* (1938); V.W. Crane, *Benjamin Franklin and a Rising People* (1954); Page Smith, *John Adams* (2 vols., 1962); Gilbert Chinard, *Honest John Adams* (1933) and *Thomas Jefferson, The Apostle of Americanism* (1929); Dumas Malone, *Jefferson and His Time* (3 vols., 1948–1962); J.C. Miller, *Sam Adams: Pioneer in Propaganda* (1936); R.D. Meade, *Patrick Henry* (2 vols., 1957, 1969); Esther Forbes, *Paul Revere and the World He Lived In* (1942). W.H. Nelson, *The American Tory* (1961); Wallace Brown, *The King's Friends* (1965); and P.H. Smith, *Loyalists and Redcoats* (1964) are good modern studies.

H.S. Commager and R.B. Morris, eds., *The Spirit of "Seventy-Six"* (2 vols., 1958), is a superb anthology of participant accounts covering the war on the battlefronts and in civilian life. S.E. Morrison, *John Paul Jones, A Sailor's Biography* (1959), offers an admirable introduction to the war at sea. Especially useful on the military phases of the war are W.M. Wallace, *Appeal to Arms* (1951); Howard Peckham, *The War for Independence* (1958); and J.R. Alden, *A History of the American Revolution* (1969). And from the British side: Piers Mackesy, *The War for America 1775–1783* (1965); G.A. Billias, ed., *George Washington's Opponents* (1969); and G.S. Brown, *The American Secretary: The Colonial Policy of Lord George Germain 1775–1778* (1963).

S.F. Bemis, *The Diplomacy of the American Revolution* (1935), is a scholarly account. American relations with France are well presented in E.S. Corwin, *French Policy and the American Alliance* (1916). R.B. Morris, *The Peacemakers: The Great Powers and American Independence* (1965), is the indispensable study of the Peace of Paris. On the effects of the Revolution in Great Britain, see R. Coupland, *The American Revolution and the British Empire* (1930).

The financing of the Revolution is ably dealt with in Clarence Ver Steeg, *Robert Morris* (1954), and E.J. Ferguson, *The Power of the Purse: A History of American Public Finance 1776–1790* (1961). On the Continental Congress, see Lynn Montross, *The Reluctant Rebels* (1950), and E.C. Burnett, *The Continental Congress* (1941). For the impact of the Revolution on American society, see Readings for Chapter Seven.

# SEVEN

In December 1776, when Washington's "rabble in arms" were running before the redcoats southward across New Jersey and the Continental Congress itself had flown from menaced Philadelphia to Baltimore, Tom Paine published the first number of *The American Crisis,* which opened with the famous words:

These are the times that try men's souls. The summer soldier and the sunshine patriot will, in this crisis, shrink from the service of their country; but he that stands it *now,* deserves the love and thanks of man and woman.

Intermittently during the war Paine published about a dozen more *Crisis* essays on current issues—how to treat Tories, what to do with Loyalist and western lands, the need for *federal* taxation—issues that were seriously dividing the "united colonies." The last *Crisis* appeared on April 19, 1783, the eighth anniversary of Lexington and Concord, when America's triumph had been all but formally signed and sealed. " 'The times that tried men's souls,' are over—," Paine began his valedictory, "and the greatest and completest revolution the world ever knew, gloriously and happily accomplished."

"So far as my endeavours could go," the pamphleteer reminded his public, "they have all been directed to conciliate the affections, unite the interests, and draw and keep the mind of the country together." Then he underscored his transcendent theme:

We have no other national sovereignty than as United States. . . . Individuals, or individual states, may call themselves what they please; but the world, and especially the world of ene-

# THE CRITICAL
# PERIOD

mies, is not to be held in awe by the whistling of a name. Sovereignty must have power to protect all the parts that compose and constitute it; and as UNITED STATES we are equal to the importance of the title, but otherwise we are not. Our Union, well and wisely regulated and cemented, is the cheapest way of being great—the easiest way of being powerful, and the happiest invention in government which the circumstances of America can admit of.—Because it collects from each state, that which, by being inadequate, can be of no use to it, and forms an aggregate that serves for all.

Paine's resounding periods fell sweetly on the ears of many Americans; yet by 1783 the very patriots who were most sympathetic to his views had grown sadly aware that "the times that tried men's souls" were far from over. They saw in the recent war the only guarantee of national unity (such as it was), and in the Revolution's end a perilous threat to the United States. Indeed, to some of them, Paine's "aggregate that serves for all" had already become little more than a floating fiction, a derelict castle in the air, leaderless, unguarded, barren of treasure and of hope. Worst of all, perhaps the majority of Americans preferred it that way, now that independence had been won. Their experience with the mother country made them only the more

suspicious of any new centralizing agency that might interefere in their local affairs, and indeed suspicious of local government itself and its nosing into their private lives. So far as these Americans were concerned, government meant snooping tax-collectors, mortgage-foreclosing courts, hamstringing regulations, and little else—and the less of it the better.

Some of the men who drew up the new state constitutions that followed the Declaration of Independence understood this attitude, and the weak Articles of Confederation of 1777 are a monument to it. By 1787, however, even many of the localists had grown disillusioned with their disintegrating central administration and had come around to Paine's high view of a sovereign nation.

## I The First State Constitutions

### TOWARD STATE SOVEREIGNTY

As early as the fall of 1774, as we have seen (p. 189), all the colonies but Georgia had set up provincial congresses (or conventions, as they were called in some places) to elect representatives to the First Continental

213

214

Congress and to perform other revolutionary acts. Georgia joined the procession almost a year later. These congresses were not only provincial; they were provisional. Even after Lexington and Concord in April 1775, most colonies continued to hope for reconciliation with the mother country; and in November of that year, to forestall a movement that promised to become widespread, the Second Continental Congress had to squelch as "very dangerous to the liberties and welfare of America," a New Jersey petition to the King, "humbly beseeching . . . a restoration of peace and harmony with the Parent State, on constitutional principles."

The Continental Congress at this juncture faced a critical dilemma. If it acted on its pretensions to speak for "America" (a term that was appearing more and more frequently in political parlance), it could not condone random approaches to the "enemy" by each of the rebel commonwealths. On the other hand, if it stiffened the will of these commonwealths to break finally with Britain, it might find itself confronted with 13 independent states, each standing all the more proudly on its dignity as a sovereign power. The Congress faced up to its predicament with spirit, and indeed, on the part of nationalist enthusiasts like Sam and John Adams, with relish. At about the same time as New Jersey's projected free-lance petition to George III, Congress received a communication from New Hampshire describing the "convuls'd state" of that province under its makeshift provisional government and asking direction from Congress "with respect to a method for our administering justice, and regulating our civil police." And just as New Jersey had been warned not to test Congress's determination to control America's foreign affairs, so New Hampshire was advised no longer to consider Britain's role in the state's domestic affairs. Call "a full and free representation of the people," Congress told the New Hampshire delegates, and let this body "establish such a form of government, as, in their judgement, will best produce the happiness of the

*The first number of* The American Crisis, *published in December 1776. (New York Public Library.)*

people, and most effectually secure peace and good order in the province."

Soon after, Congress gave similar advice on similar inquiries from South Carolina, Massachusetts, Virginia, and North Carolina, all of them former royal colonies now suffering from the vacuum in royal power. Each decision was embraced by those in favor—and denounced by those opposed—as one step nearer a united declaration of independence. "Gentlemen seem more and more to enlarge their views," Sam Adams happily observed of Congress in December 1775. By May 1776, "enlargement" had grown so general that on the tenth of that month Congress took the initiative to recommend to those provinces "where no government sufficient to the exigencies of their affairs have been hitherto established," that they "adopt such government as shall best conduce to the happiness and safety of their constituents in particular, and America in general." "It is necessary," said the preamble to this recommendation, "that the exercise of every kind of authority under the . . . crown of Great Britain . . . should be totally suppressed."

"This day the Congress has passed the most important Resolution that ever was taken in America," exulted its author, John Adams. Writing of this resolution in later years, Adams said, "I thought it was independence itself, but we must have it with more formality yet." Some states did delay until after July 4, 1776, to act on Congress's recommendation, but within a year of Adams's resolution all but Rhode Island, Connecticut, and Massachusetts had framed new forms of government. Rhode Island and Connecticut both had long enjoyed liberal charters under which even the provincial governors were elected by the voters (see p. 65); simply by deleting all references to the king, both commonwealths were left with "constitutions" that served them for many decades to come. Massachusetts, waiting for what Edmund Randolph of Virginia called "the then infancy of the science of constitutions, & of confederacies" to pass, also struggled along under its old charter—with a cumbersome 28-member council as executive—until 1780.

## THE FUNDAMENTAL LAW

In most of the states, the revolutionary provincial congresses, self-conscious tribunes of the people, drew up and adopted the new constitutions without troubling to consult voters. The delay in constitution-making in Massachusetts was not due entirely to the scientific caution of her leaders; in September 1776, tardily following the advice of the Continental Congress, the provisional government there asked the people of the state for permission to write a new constitution that would regularize the revolutionary administration. The people, acting through their town meetings, gave their consent and the provincial congress set about its task. The town meeting of Concord, however, objected strenuously to the proceedings. In resolutions published in October 1776, it said:

We Conceive that a Constitution . . . intends a System of Principles Established to Secure the Subject in the Possession & enjoyment of their Rights and Privileges, *against any Encroachments of the Governing Part.* . . . A Constitution alterable by the Supreme Legislative is no Security at all to the Subject against any Encroachment of the Governing part on any, or on all of their Rights and privileges.

If the provincial congress makes the constitution, argued the Concord meeting, what is to prevent it from unmaking it? If the fundamental law has no sanction superior to that of ordinary legislation, what will protect our liberties? Concord demanded that a special "Convention . . . be immediately Chosen, to form & establish a Constitution," and for no other purpose.

The Massachusetts provincial government, paying no particular notice to Concord's novel proposal, proceeded to draft the new constitution itself. But the Concord notion spread, and when the provincial congress presented its constitution to the people in 1778 they rejected it by a rousing 5-to-1 majority. This constitution had many defects, but no more than some that were adopted elsewhere. Recognizing that the principal objection to it was indeed its authorship, the provincial congress voted in June 1779 to embrace the Concord idea. By March 1780, under the leadership of John Adams, a specially elected convention completed a new framework of government that has lasted—with amendments, of course—for almost two centuries. By June, the voters had approved.

In calling a special constitutional conven-

216

tion and in submitting its work to the people, Massachusetts established precedents later adopted by the other states when they came to rewrite their fundamental laws, and, of course, by the Republic itself when the Great Convention of 1787 wrote the fundamental law of the land. Moreover, even the state constitutions written and adopted by the provincial congresses, after declaring their independence of all authority except that of the people, set forth at the outset the "bill" or "declaration" of "unalienable" or "natural" or "inherent" rights, of which the "Governing Part," as the Virginia Constitution said, "cannot by any compact deprive or divest their posterity."

Although from the start of settlement in America the colonists had lived under explicit charters and had been governed, in addition, by written instructions from kings and proprietors, both charters and instructions were expected to conform to the nebulous English Constitution—the uncodified common law and the unwritten "customs and usages of the realm." These, in turn, were expected to conform to the even more fundamental "natural laws" of all rational societies as expressed most comprehensively in the philosophical writings of John Locke (see p. 139). The "decisive event," as John Adams called it, of the Continental Congress's instructions to the states to renounce British rule and to form their own governments meant inevitably that Americans were now cut off from the English Constitution and from the Lockeian "Bill of Rights" of 1689 that had become so basic a part of the "privileges and immunities" of British subjects. It was essentially to reassert these privileges and immunities on the foundation of natural law alone that the new state constitutions were written. Although these constitutions were derived directly from the old written colonial charters, they went radically beyond the charters in this one respect: They set forth for the first time not only the supreme law for each state, but also the "higher law" of nature from which the supreme law itself derived its validity. It is in

this extension of the old written charters (and not merely in the fact that the new frameworks of government were themselves written down) that the originality of the new state constitutions lies.

Soon after the new state constitutions were written, Congress had them collected and printed for general distribution, and numerous editions were required to meet the demand from savants and statesmen at home and abroad. The bills of rights, setting forth the "higher law" of nature from which the supreme law itself derived its validity, aroused the greatest interest. This interest has survived the test of time. The bills of rights have been the most enduring parts of the state constitutions, and along with the Bill of Rights in the first ten amendments to the federal Constitution have figured most prominently in constitutional issues since raised and resolved by the courts and the people.

The fundamental rights in these "bills" or "declarations" included: "acquiring, possessing, and protecting property"; freedom of worship, speech, and assembly; moderate bail, prompt hearings, trial by jury, and punishments to fit the crime; protection from general search warrants and from liability to serve in or support standing armies; exemption from maintaining any special class of men by "exclusive or separate emoluments or privileges from the community, but in consideration of publick services." Above all, "when any government shall be found inadequate or contrary to [the people's wishes] . . . a majority of the community hath an indubitable, unalienable and indefeasible right to reform, alter or abolish it." To reduce the likelihood of revolutions, elections must be "free, . . . frequent, certain, and regular." And in such elections, all "men having sufficient evidence to permanent common interest with, and attachment to the community, have the right of suffrage."

Conservatives found it easy enough to live with these gaudy generalizations. An equal right to acquire property was scarcely an open sesame for social climbers. Freedom to worship as one pleased seemed not necessarily inconsistent with the continuation of compulsory tithes for established churches. Moderate bail and humane penalties were after all, elastic injunctions. "Free, frequent, certain, and regular" elections could, with good conscience, be limited to the popular lower house of the legislature. "Sufficient evidence to permanent common interest with, and attachment to the community," gave oligarchs wrapped in deep esteem for their own social values ample latitude for sharp restrictions on the privilege to vote. Nor did the constitutional requirements undo in the least such old dodges as underrepresenting western counties, setting election days at inconvenient seasons, naming polling places at inaccessible sites.

And yet the "bills of rights" gave the populace, in the language of the times, "a standing law to live by." Without the promise of such a Bill of Rights they almost certainly would have rejected the new federal Constitution of 1787 (see p. 263). Reformers, moreover, eventually used the leverage afforded by the liberal language of these bills to open the land on easy terms, abolish imprisonment for debt, provide free schools, prohibit the use of public funds for favored religious sects, promote free expression in the press, reform the courts, improve the jails, liberalize the qualifications for office-holding, and broaden the franchise. They turned the principle of liberty against the "governing part" into the pursuit of equality with the governing parties, employing government itself to remove the barriers to liberty defined as opportunity (see Chapter Thirteen).

Such reforms were often slow in coming, and sometimes disappointing in their practical consequences. Among the earliest reforms based explicitly on the bills of rights in the constitution-making period itself were the gradual abolition of slavery north of Delaware and (at least for the time being) the removal of many restrictions on manumission, especially in Virginia.

The bill of rights of the first Vermont constitution of 1777 (see p. 231), straightforwardly abolished slavery, and when Vermont after entering the Union in 1791 drew up a new constitution two years later, the abolition provision was carried over. In Massachusetts, a court decision in 1783 used the bill of rights to justify fining a slaveholder on the charge of assaulting and shackling a runaway. Thereafter, slaves began to leave their masters, and in the first national census of 1790 Massachusetts was the only state to report no slaves. New Hampshire soon was in the same position. Between 1780 and 1804, all the states from Rhode Island to New Jersey put abolition in process by legislation freeing children of slave mothers once they had reached a certain age, ranging from 18 to 28.

In the northern states the slave population was relatively small and the number of free Negroes grew only slowly. In Virginia, after private manumission was eased in 1782, the number of free Negroes jumped from 2000 to almost 13,000 in 1790, and to 30,500 in 1810. In Maryland, the legislature rejected easing bills, but the restrictions there had been comparatively mild. In 1790 more than 8000 free Negroes lived in Maryland, and thereafter their number multiplied as rapidly as in Virginia. Farther south, although abolition and manumission were often mentioned in connection with the struggle for liberty, progress was slight.

The leaders of the revolutionary generation had profound faith in the concrete definition of rights and duties. "The blessings of society," John Adams in 1776 advised the states then framing their new basic laws, "depend entirely on the constitutions of government." Yet the Negro freed by abolition or manumission, by legislation or by courts, north or south, hardly entered the free world the law prescribed. Adams himself, in 1795, told how slavery really ended in his state:

Argument might have [had] some weight in the abolition of slavery in Massachusetts, but the real cause was the multiplication of labouring white people, who would no longer suffer the rich to employ these sable rivals so much to

218

their injury. . . . If the gentlemen had been permitted by law to hold slaves, the common white people would have put the negroes to death, and their masters, too, perhaps. . . . The common white people, or rather the labouring people, were the cause of rendering negroes unprofitable servants. Their scoffs and insults, their continual insinuations, filled the negroes with discontent, made them lazy, idle, proud, vicious, and at length wholly useless to their masters, to such a degree that the abolition of slavery became a measure of economy.

In the North as well as in the South, as the numbers of free Negroes grew, their social fetters multiplied. As a result, they seemed to become incorrigible public problems and costly public charges. Sometimes the very laws designed to open up the world of opportunity for the whites explicitly closed that world to the blacks and hardened their pariah status (see p. 399).

### THE FRAMEWORK OF GOVERNMENT

The new state constitutions were all fairly brief documents, ranging from a mere 1000 to no more than 12,000 words. The bills of rights were themselves the briefest, if the most far-reaching, parts of the constitutions. Provisions for the actual "framework of government," the least original parts of the documents, took up by far the most space.

The new state constitutions undertook carefully to define the emergent political societies of the new states, to make explicit who could vote and who could rule and what the powers of each group were. Generally speaking, where the old colonial charters had been conservative in nature—as in Maryland and New York—the early state constitutions also were conservative. Where the colonial charters had been more democratic—as in Pennsylvania and Georgia—the constitutions tended in the same direction. Where the colonial charters had been moderately liberal—as in Virginia and Massachusetts—the new constitutions also reflected the past.

These terms—conservative, democratic, and moderate—refer basically to two subjects: qualifications for the franchise, and qualifications for office-holding. In conservative New York, for example, no one could vote for members of the upper house of the legislature who did not own land worth £100; in conservative Maryland, no one could *sit* in the upper house who did not own property worth £1000. In democratic Georgia, all white male inhabitants who paid taxes (whether they owned property or not) could vote for all state legislators; in democratic Pennsylvania, *membership* in the legislature was open to all taxpaying freemen. In moderate Virginia, all landowners could vote for members of both houses; in moderate Massachusetts, a freehold of £300 or personal property worth £600 was required for *membership* in the upper house.

But there were other phases of government to which these characterizations also apply. In conservative Maryland, for example, while the membership of the lower house of the legislature was renewed each year, the upper house was elected for a solid five years. Democratic Pennsylvania, on the other hand, having resisted for decades efforts of the colonial governor's council to share in legislation, now dispensed with an upper house altogether and concentrated power in a unicameral legislature elected afresh by the people each year. Moderate Virginia, while providing a four-year term for members of its upper chamber (as against a one-year term for the lower house), also stipulated that one-fourth of this chamber must retire annually.

"The oftener power Returns into the hands of the people the Better," the manifesto of a Massachusetts town meeting declared in 1778. As the terms of legislators in many of the new states indicate, a frequent popular mandate had already become one of the political shibboleths of the age: in ten states the lower house was elected for twelve months; in Connecticut and Rhode Island for but six; only in South Carolina did representatives serve as long as two years. A second shibboleth, deriving from Montesquieu's attack on "despotism" in his *The Spirit of Laws* (first published in France in 1748 and widely read in the colonies), was the "separation" and "balance" of powers (see p. 250). Article XXX of "Part the First" of the Massachusetts constitution of 1780 was most explicit on this point:

In the government of this commonwealth, the legislative department shall never exercise the executive and judicial powers, or either of them: the executives shall never exercise the legislative and judicial powers, or either of them: the judicial shall never exercise the legislative and executive powers, or either of them: to the end it may be a government of laws and not of men.

Almost 200 years of independent political practice in America (not to speak of an even longer history in England, and in America under English rule) have failed to clarify in any absolute way where legislative, executive, or judicial power begins and ends. Separated in theory, these departments of government have always been dependent on and usually at war with one another. We have already seen (p. 77) how in England after 1688, for example, Parliament made the crown and the crown courts virtual captives of the legislature; and how, in the colonies themselves, parallel developments had divested royal governors of many of their nominal prerogatives and had made the assemblies nearly supreme (p. 116). Colonial governors could veto legislation, control the speakership of the house, summon or adjourn the assembly, make key political appointments with the advice of their handpicked councils, and otherwise enjoy the privileges of patronage. But the assemblies, by their control over money and by other means, had gradually sucked the strength from the governor's position and had made him, for all the verbal force of his functions, often little more than functionary. At the same time, the assemblies had asserted control over local judiciaries and had shown contempt for royal tribunals like the admiralty courts.

When the time came to write the new state constitutions, the power of the purse was universally retained in the legislature. And in three states—Virginia, South Carolina, and New Jersey—it was assigned exclusively to the lower house. But the constitution-making congresses and conventions were hardly satisfied to insure legislative control over the executive simply by keeping the money power in legislative hands. Conservatives, democrats, and moderates alike, all explicitly stripped the executive of the absolute veto power, and in all but two states—Massachusetts and New York—of any veto power whatever. Only in New York, moreover, did the governor retain a certain limited control over the date and duration of legislative sessions; elsewhere the constitutions specifically set forth when the legislature should convene, and left the houses themselves to make their own rules and elect their own officers. Almost everywhere the governor retained the right of appointment, with the advice of the upper house; but now the upper house, like the lower, was an elected body far more jealous of legislative prerogatives than the old colonial councils had been.

The degradation of the executive was capped by the mode of his election and the nature of his tenure. In New England and New York the governor was elected by the voters; but from New Jersey southward—in eight states—he was elected by the legislature. In New York, Pennsylvania (where he was simply the "president" of an executive council), and Delaware, his term ran three years; in South Carolina, two. But in the remaining nine states, the governor was elected for only 12 months. Most states, moreover, now applied the policy of rotation in office with peculiar severity to the governorship. In New England, New York, and New Jersey the same man was eligible to run for two or more consecutive terms. Elsewhere—in seven states—his eligibility was circumscribed by provisions like that of conservative Maryland, where he could serve his one-year term only three years in any seven; or like that of moderate South Carolina, where he was ineligible for a second two-year term until four years had elapsed since his first.

220

In most states the qualifications for governor were higher than for any other office. He had to own more land and pay more taxes than members of the legislative upper house. And he usually had to meet religious qualifications—either as a member of an established church or at least a Protestant in good standing. But these requirements only made the office prey to gilded figureheads aglow with piety, although some governors, of course, surpassed the limitations of the office. The fact that they had to be men of exceptional wealth often gave them a certain leverage in the community, and, as in colonial times, if they knew how to bend the legislative will to their own, they could make the governorship a position of strength as well as honor. In politics, personality weighed as much as formal powers, and strong governors could operate successfully where senators and representatives were at one another's throats. On the whole, however, the governors—and the state governments—suffered severely from what Jefferson once denounced as "legislative tyranny."

Even the courts did not escape the pervasive power of the legislatures. Every state constitution provided that the legislature "have full power and authority to erect and constitute judicatures," to use the words of the Massachusetts document. In Connecticut, Rhode Island, and South Carolina, moreover, the legislature alone named the judges; and in no state was the legislature without some voice in their appointment or their removal.

In 1787, while addressing the Great Convention in Philadelphia, James Madison said: "Experience in all the States has evinced a powerful tendency in the legislature to absorb all power into its vortex. This was the real source of danger to the American Constitutions; and suggested the necessity of giving every defensive authority to the other departments that was consistent with republican principles." In later years, constitutional conventions in all the states—either by proposing

amendments or by rewriting the entire fundamental law—undertook to rectify this gross imbalance among the "separated" departments. The principal changes enlarged the governor's freedom of action; but not until long-lived political parties developed and the governor became the head of his party in the state (see Chapter Thirteen) was he able to assert executive leadership and overcome the fruitless factionalism of legislative supremacy. "The States separately," Washington complained in 1778, after three years of struggle to maintain a continental army in the field, "have very inadequate ideas of the present danger. . . . Party disputes and personal quarrels are the great business of the day, whilst the momentous concerns of empire . . . are but secondary considerations." To this observation, many a helpless governor would have cried, "Amen!"

## II  *The "Firm League of Friendship"*

### THE FIRST FEDERAL CONSTITUTION

In July 1775, ten months before the revolutionary instructions to form permanent governments went out to the states, Benjamin Franklin disclosed to certain members of the Second Continental Congress a draft of "Articles of Confederation and Perpetual Union" under which a permanent national government might also be set up. Franklin's friends found that too many delegates "were revolted" by the idea of creating a permanent government while some lingering hope of conciliation with Britain remained, and the trial balloon was laid aside until the next year. In June 1776, Congress named a committee to work over Franklin's plan; but no less than a year and a half passed before its own draft was sufficiently advanced to be submitted to the states. John Dickinson of Pennsylvania was the principal author of the new document, which undertook to establish a firm national government without weakening the self-determination of the individual commonwealths. This, of course, was difficult to accomplish. Dickinson's own name for his government, "A firm league of friendship," strongly suggests that where there might be conflict of authority, the states, not the new government, would triumph.

Congress was only too aware of the defects of its offspring. In its letter to the states in November 1777 asking formal approval, it apologized for the "uncommon embarrassment and delay" in framing the Articles and solicited the most generous considerations of their form, "as that alone which affords any tolerable prospect of general ratification." Franklin's draft offered membership in "our Association" to "any and every Colony from Great Britain upon the Continent of North America," including the islands of the West Indies. He even opened the door to Ireland. Congress's aspirations were more sober. It ordered the Articles translated into French so that "the inhabitants of Canada, &c." might subscribe.

Under the Articles of Confederation, each state elected and paid the salaries of its delegates and reserved the right to recall them. Voting in the single-chamber legislature was by state, and each state had only one vote, no matter how many delegates it sent. Important legislation required a two-thirds majority of the states, a margin made more difficult to attain by the provision nullifying a state's vote if its delegation were evenly split. The administration of such laws as could be passed was hamstrung by the provision making the only executive a "committee of the states" consisting of one delegate from each state. Nor could the Articles be amended except by the unanimous consent of the states.

The Articles gave the new government considerable powers: Congress might (1) make war or peace and fix state quotas of men and money for the national army; (2) make treaties and alliances; (3) decide inter-

state disputes, limit state boundaries, and admit new states; (4) borrow money and regulate standards of coinage and weights and measures; and (5) establish post offices. But such basic perquisites of sovereignty as levying taxes, raising its own troops, and regulating commerce were denied it.

The framers of the Articles, having made every concession they could to the states' own freedom of action, expected quick approval by the state governments. One last concession to Virginia, however, aroused the suspicion of Maryland and other "landless" states and delayed ratification for almost four more years. This concession stated that, "no state should be deprived of territory for the benefit of the United States."

Seven "landed" states—Virginia, New York, the two Carolinas, Georgia, Massachusetts and Connecticut—on the basis of their original charters or on other grounds, laid claim to territory extending either to the Mississippi or all the way to the Pacific. By the Quebec Act of 1774 (see p. 189), the British had overridden these claims; and Maryland now argued that since the war against Britain was a common effort, the western territories claimed by the "landed" states should be "considered as common property, subject to be parceled by Congress into free, convenient, and independent governments." New Jersey and Delaware soon aligned themselves with Maryland. As the costs of the war mounted, these "landless" states became increasingly alarmed at the high taxes they would be forced to levy, whereas the "landed" states would be able to pay their shares out of land sales. The "landless" states were also troubled by the likely growth in population and power of the others; they feared that their own people would be lured by low taxes to the western territories of the "landed" states, which would make these states predominant in any central government. Speculators in certain "landless" states added their influential voices to those of their representatives. Before the Revolution, such speculators had purchased millions

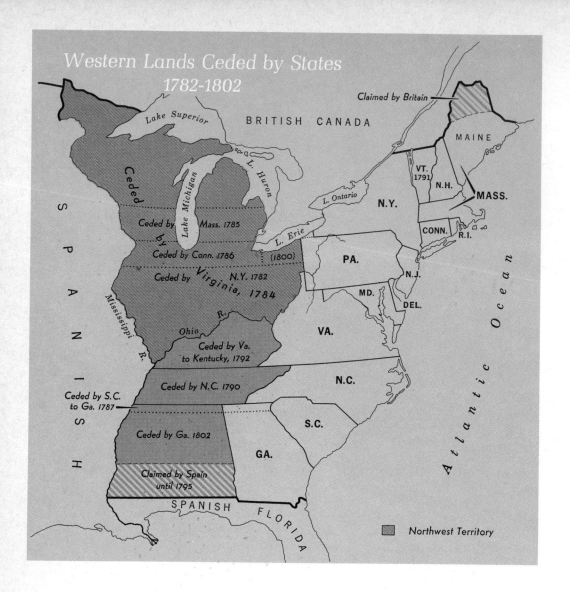

**Western Lands Ceded by States 1782-1802**

Claimed by Britain

BRITISH CANADA

Lake Superior

L. Huron

Lake Michigan

Ceded by Mass. 1785

Ceded by Conn. 1786   (1800)

Ceded by Virginia, 1784   N.Y. 1782

L. Ontario

L. Erie

MAINE

VT. 1791

N.H.

MASS.

N.Y.

CONN.

R.I.

PA.

N.J.

MD.

DEL.

VA.

Ceded

by

Ceded by

S    P    A    N    I    S    H

Mississippi R.

Ohio R.

Ceded by Va. to Kentucky, 1792

Ceded by N.C. 1790

Ceded by S.C. to Ga. 1787

Ceded by Ga. 1802

Claimed by Spain until 1795

N.C.

S.C.

GA.

SPANISH   FLORIDA

Atlantic Ocean

Northwest Territory

---

of acres from the Indians in areas claimed especially by Virginia. If Virginia's claims were now allowed to stand, their own claims surely would be invalidated in favor of Virginia speculators.

The deadlock over ratification of the Articles held until early in 1780. In February, that year, finding, because of the weight of taxes, "a violent inclination in most of the States to appropriate all the western Lands to the use of the United States," New York proposed, "especially to accelerate the federal alliance," to tender its lands to Congress. Con-

necticut soon followed suit. When Virginia at last yielded in January 1781, Maryland withdrew its objections to the Articles. In February, Congress named March 1 as the day to proclaim the start of the new government. The Second Continental Congress then became the formal ruling body of "The United States of America," the "Stile," as the Articles said, "of this confederacy."

Shortly after ratification of the Articles, Congress succeeded in settling a long-standing dispute between Pennsylvania and Connecticut over some western land remaining in state hands. "There are few instances," observed Robert R. Livingston of New York, "of independent states submitting their cause to a court of justice." Livingston went on to predict: "The day will come when all disputes in the great republic of Europe will be tried in the same way, and America will be quoted to exemplify the wisdom of the measure." But Livingston's optimism was misplaced and premature. The succeeding years were to make abundantly clear that a mere federation of states could not function properly as a nation, that a national government sovereign in its own right could alone substantiate its claims to power and the world's respect.

### NO VISIBLE HEAD

When Franklin, in July 1775, first proposed a "firm" (but not yet "perpetual") union of the colonies, he had also suggested as "a Rule" (so jealous were the fledgling free commonwealths of one another) "that each succeeding Congress be held in a different Colony till the whole Number be gone through, and so in . . . Rotation." In Dickinson's plan for a "perpetual Confederation," Congress was given the dignity of a permanent abode in Philadelphia; but the delegates might have spared themselves the sacrifice, for within 15 months Congress had been chased twice from its capital (and subsequently from other towns where it alighted) by British troops.

In June 1783, just two months after Paine's optimistic farewell to his reading public, Congress was once more in exile. Apprised that the Philadelphia militia would not raise a single musket against mutinous Pennsylvania regiments, and having no force of their own with which to "hazard the authority of government," the few delegates in attendance hied themselves to the hamlet of Princeton, New Jersey. "The great Sanhedrin of the Nation," jeered the unpaid Pennsylvania officer, Major John Armstrong, "with all their solemnity and emptiness, have . . . left a state, where there wisdom has long been question'd, their virtue suspected, and their dignity a

jest." Congress, delegate Benjamin Hawkins of North Carolina dolefully observed, was "responsible for every thing, and unable to do any thing, hated by the public creditors, insulted by the Soldiery and unsupported by the citizens."

Thereafter humiliations followed in threes. In January 1783, John Adams, having been handsomely greeted and entertained, had concluded a favorable treaty of amity and commerce with Holland, and early in October the first Dutch minister to the United States, Peter John van Berkel, arrived in Philadelphia. Finding no officials to greet him, he innocently looked about for a government to which he could present his credentials. Ten days of mortified waiting passed before he took it upon himself to inform Princeton of his presence, and another ten days before the delegates there were able to round up an absent member who alone could decipher the Low Dutch in which the minister's papers were inscribed. "Congress are in a charming situation to receive him," Madison expostulated in dismay; "in an obscure village undetermined where they will spend the Winter and without a Minister of F[oreign] A[ffairs]." The government had provision for such a minister, but the last one, Robert R. Livingston, relinquished the office in June 1783, after having formally resigned the previous December. A faction in Congress that preferred no foreign minister to one it disapproved of, succeeded in blocking the appointment of a successor.

This embarrassment with the friendly Dutch had been somehow smoothed over, and the momentous decision to spend the winter in Annapolis had been made, when, in November 1783, Congress at last was confronted with the definitive treaty of peace with Britain. This treaty, as we have seen (p. 208), had been signed in Paris on September 3. One provision required that for the peace terms to become operative, ratified copies had to be exchanged by the two countries within six months of that date. Even with slow eighteenth-century communications this was a fair

*The "provincials" of the Continental Congress in a contemporary European view. (Courtesy Kenneth M. Newman, The Old Print Shop, N.Y.C.)*

time allowance. Those who made it, however, reckoned without Congress. The delegates could not act until nine states were fully represented; but at least two states, New York and Georgia, had not even troubled to elect delegates, and those of Maryland consistently boycotted the meetings even though Congress, as a member complained, was "actually seated in the Capital of the State." By the end of the year, one South Carolinian, Richard Beresford, sick in bed in Philadelphia, would at last have filled out a quorum, and so nervous had the leaders grown that on January 1 Jefferson proposed that "if Beresford will not come to Congress, Congress must go to him for this one act."

Fortunately, an unseemly procession back to Philadelphia was averted. By January 14 Beresford felt well enough to visit Annapolis, and on that day, with 23 members present, the treaty acknowledging the independence of the United States was ratified without dissent. Scarcely seven weeks remained to the deadline and these, alas, were lost when a mishap at sea delayed delivery of the American papers until May 12. The British, however, contented themselves with jibes at the fumbling new nation, and the treaty went into effect more than two months late.

The formal establishment of American independence seemed almost a signal for the formal abdication of the American government. January 14–16, 1784, were the only three days in a period of four months on which as many as nine states were represented in Congress. Sometimes the number fell to as low as three. On February 20, Madison noted. "We have not sat above 3 days I believe in as many weeks. Admonition after admonition has been sent to the states, to no effect. We have sent one today. If it fails, it seems as well we should all retire."

Only because a fanatical little group "were unwilling to familiarize the idea of a dissolution of the federal government," did efforts to build a "peace establishment" continue. This group had its reward on March 1, when the arrival of a New Hampshire member once again brought the number of states represented up to the desired nine. For the next three months Congress met regularly and legislated wisely (see p. 234), but following the day set for summer adjournment, June 3, the nation once more was without a "visible head." Jefferson in particular had urged the appointment of members to the "Committee of the States" as a symbol of continuity while Congress recessed, and reluctantly a majority approved. Some of the men named to the Committee, however, had opposed its creation and sat with it only to hasten its demise. In September, asked by Committee Chairman Samuel Hardy to relieve him for a time, John Francis Mercer journeyed from Virginia to Annapolis, but found no trace of the members. Pushing hopefully on to Philadelphia, he was again disappointed. "A desire," he wrote to a friend, "that the State of Virginia might shew her respect for the Confoederal Government (if it is not a prostitution of the name of Government to apply it to such a vagabond, strolling contemptible Crew as Congress) will induce me to spin out a Couple of weeks here." But not even the ghost of a government materialized to receive Virginia's respects.

Jefferson had gone to France the previous July as American envoy. In October, his secretary wrote him from Monticello: "This invisibility of a federal head will have little effect on our affairs here, or on the minds of the citizens of the United States who can easily reconcile themselves to it and who will view it in no other light than the rising or dissolution of their several legislatures to which they have been accustomed." American spokesmen were more concerned over the figure a headless government cut in a "world of enemies" than they were over the vacuum in the central administration at home. "Whatever little politicians may think," wrote Charles Thomson, the "perpetual secretary" of Congress, late in September, "a government without a visible head must appear a strange phenomenon to European politicians and will I fear lead them to form no very favourable opinion of our stability, wisdom or Union."

Just before adjourning in Annapolis on June 3, 1784, Congress had set October 30 for its next meeting, this one to take place in Trenton, New Jersey. Many delegates showed their disgust with the government's wanderings by staying away, and, typically, a month passed before a quorum assembled. Most of the following month was spent debating the question of still another move, this one to a "permanent home," and on Christmas Eve the delegates were on their way to New York, where they did in fact fill out their last four years.

There had already been considerable discussion among nationalist leaders (see p. 244) about calling a convention for a drastic revision of the general government, "to enable Congress," in the words of Richard Henry Lee of Virginia, "to execute with more energy, effect, and vigor, the powers assigned to it." Yet, as delegate William S. Johnson of Connecticut observed soon after the members had savored the exhilarating atmosphere of New York, "there appear on all sides, and in every Body here, good Dispositions to enter into the Consideration and Discussion of public Affairs with Diligence, Zeal, and Integrity." Others were so encouraged by the early arrival of delegates from nearly all the states that, as Madison said, "the conversation concerning a Continental Convention has ceased for some time, so that perhaps it may not be revived again." He was wrong, of course. The new nation remained abused abroad, divided at home, its government weak and inadequate, its future critical.

Historians have debated few questions more hotly than that of the need for the stern centralization of national power imposed by the new Constitution of 1787 (see p. 265). Only less interesting have been these questions: Did the new Constitution, the change in political organization alone, actually unify the country, or did unification follow more directly the opening of the West, improvements in communication, and the spread of trade and industry, to all of which the Revolution had given some impetus and the old Congress even more? It was in the political

226

crisis that ended with the writing of the Constitution, wrote John Fiske in his exceedingly influential *The Critical Period of American History, 1783–1789*, "that the pliant twig was bent; and as it was bent, so has it grown; until it has become indeed a goodly and a sturdy tree." To suggest that the pliant twig was bent as far and fed as well by the economic and social changes of the Revolutionary and early national periods as by the Constitution itself is to deny neither the reality of the political crisis that persisted after the Revolution nor the value of the Constitution in helping to end that crisis.

## III  *The Confederation's Crisis*

### THE EMERGENCY IN FOREIGN AFFAIRS

"As to the future grandeur of America," wrote the influential Englishman Josiah Tucker, Dean of Gloucester, after the close of the Revolution, "and its being a rising empire under one head, whether republican or monarchical, it is one of the idlest and most visionary notions that ever was conceived even by writers of romance. . . . A disunited people till the end of time, suspicious and distrustful of each other, [the Americans] will be divided and subdivided into little commonwealths or principalities . . . [with] no centre of union and no common interest."

One of the traditional panaceas for domestic disunion is to venture dangerously abroad. Where domestic affairs divide, foreign affairs unite. The Revolution itself had shown the coalescing tendency of foreign conflicts, and as early as 1781 nationalists like Gouverneur Morris of New York were suggesting that peace be indefinitely postponed until "that great friend to sovereign authority, a foreign war," might speed the day when the American "government would acquire force." After 1783, Congress itself may have looked forward to the foreign problems arising from the peace

treaty and from independence to strengthen its hand at home. If it did, it was once more proved wrong, the scornful Dean Tucker right.

The persistence of the British government in retaining armed posts in the American West, the persistence of British merchants in seeking to collect pre-Revolutionary debts, the persistence of Loyalists in seeking to recover pre-Revolutionary property, the persistence of the Spanish in obstructing American commerce on the Mississippi—all these, along with Indian problems once the burden of the British but now America's own, presented Congress with difficult, frustrating, and embarrassing issues.

According to the treaty of peace, the British were to surrender "with all convenient speed" their military and fur-trading posts in the Northwest—Dutchman's Point, Pointe-au-Fer, Oswegatchie, Oswego, Niagara, Detroit, and Michilimackinac, names redolent of the Colonial fur traffic and bloody Indian engagements. This the British firmly refused to do. The treaty of peace gave the United States control of the northwest country, but made no provision for the local Indian tribes. The British, who had painful memories of Pontiac's conspiracy 20 years before, feared that American settlement of the West would provoke new native uprisings in defense of their lands, and were determined to retain their posts in order to protect the rich Canadian fur trade in the region, which had expanded tremendously at American expense following the Quebec Act of 1774 (see p. 189). In 1784–86 and in 1789, Congress negotiated four separate treaties with the Indians who ranged over this territory, and forbade Americans to settle on any land that had not been ceded by these treaties. But Congress had neither the money nor the military power to remove the Indians from the purchased land or to keep the Americans off forbidden ground.

Under British prodding, the Indians soon renounced the American treaties and attacked the American settlers. While Congress pressed the British to conform to the peace treaty terms, the old enemy responded defiantly by renegotiating their own trading agreements with the Indians. Besides retaining their posts, the British went so far as to use force to deny Americans use of the Great Lakes.

Indian problems also arose in the Southwest, where Spain, in turn, was determined to keep out American settlers. During the Revolution, Spain had offered to mediate between the colonists and Britain if Congress would cede to her the territory between the Ohio River and the Gulf of Mexico and between the Appalachians and the Mississippi. Congress had refused this offer, but Spain had entered the war anyway in support of France. In a separate treaty in 1783, she received East and West Florida from Britain. Here she established forts and in 1784 made treaties with the local Indians obliging them to join in the harassment of American frontiersmen.

British (and for that matter, Spanish) recalcitrance over the West hardened as American weakness in other areas was disclosed. Although the treaty of peace had declared that no legal impediments should hinder creditors on either side from collecting old debts, actually the great bulk of the debts were owed by the ex-colonials. And although Congress urged the new states themselves to honor the treaty provision, it had no power to prevent their passing legislation to frustrate the British instead. Not until 1802 did the United States settle private debts incurred by Americans before the war by agreeing to pay the sum of £600,000 to British creditors.

In accordance with the terms of the peace treaty, Congress had also made "earnest recommendation" to the states to restore confiscated Loyalist property to its former owners. But most states chose to ignore this recommendation, and even after the war, patriots continued to confiscate Loyalist lands without punishment by the courts. The treaty also permitted Loyalists to return for 12 months to try to recoup their losses, but many who came back received only tar and feathers for

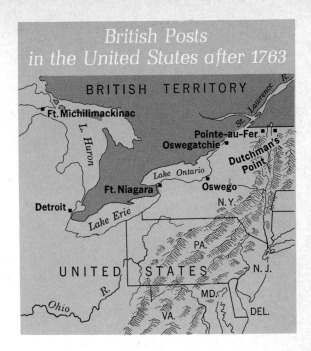

British Posts in the United States after 1763

their pains. Years later, Britain awarded £3.3 million to about 5000 Loyalists for property lost in America during the Revolution.

In the peace treaty, Britain had agreed that Americans were to have the right to navigate the Mississippi and use the port of New Orleans as a place to deposit their export goods. But now Spain insisted that these rights had not been Britain's to grant. Spain had acquired control of New Orleans from France in 1763 and had captured the port of Natchez, north of New Orleans, from the British in 1779. At the end of the war Spain refused to open New Orleans to American shipping and to yield Natchez to the United States, in whose territory it lay, and Congress had no means of forcing her to alter her policy.

Westerners were especially outraged with Congress over this failure, and Spain lost little time in trying to capitalize on their unhappiness by suggesting that they secede from the United States and join the Spanish empire. Congress's negotiations for a commercial treaty with Spain in 1785, conducted by John Jay, now Secretary for Foreign Affairs, only deepened western discontent. An urbane New Yorker, Jay feared that the development of the West would only "fill the wilderness with

227

228

white savages . . . more formidable to us than the tawny ones which now inhabit it." Perhaps because of his apprehensions, he concluded his drawn out talks with Don Diego de Gardoqui, the first Spanish minister to the United States, by agreeing to surrender American claims to the use of the Mississippi for 25 years, in exchange for favorable treatment of American ships in Spanish ports elsewhere. Seven states, most of them in the commercial North, supported Jay's agreement in Congress against the opposition of the southern states, which had ambitions of their own in the Southwest. Seven states were not enough to approve the agreement and it fell through. The mere act of negotiating and supporting such a treaty, however, made Jay and the commercial interests suspect in the West and in the South for decades. The failure of the treaty, in turn, cost Congress the support of the commercial interests of the East. Congress's growing weakness at home, in turn, only worsened its standing abroad.

### FINANCIAL DEBILITY AT HOME

Besides international problems arising from the peace treaty, Congress was confronted after 1783 by domestic problems growing out of independence. Bereft of the power to lay and collect taxes, it had to face its predicament without the sinews of sound finance. Worse, with no money to pay the Continental troops, Congress was physically menaced by its own army, which, sharing the almost universal lack of confidence in the government, refused to disband without first receiving its due compensation.

Many other claims arising from the war poured in upon Congress. Above all there was the back interest to be paid on the public debt, not to speak of the principal itself. Robert Morris, named Secretary of Finance in 1781, urged Congress to establish a national tariff so that it would no longer have to beg the states for funds; he also proposed a land tax, a poll tax, an excise on distilled liquors. But none of these measures would the state

delegates in Congress enact. When Congress in 1782 then requested $10 million from the states for the next year, it received less than $1.5 million.

In January 1783, his patience exhausted, Morris wrote to Congress: "To increase our debts, while the prospect of paying them diminishes does not consist with my ideas of integrity. I must therefore quit a situation which becomes utterly insupportable." No successor could be found to take over the thankless job, however, and Morris was prevailed upon to remain until the army had been paid. In June, Washington managed to get the troops to go home, even though they were not to be paid for some months to come, and even then not in cash but in warrants to western lands from which the Indians were determined to bar white settlers. A loan from Holland enabled the government to limp along for a time; but when Morris finally left in September 1784, having made no dent on the localism of the states, the treasury was empty as usual.

Morris' efforts were not totally in vain, however. In 1781 he proposed to Congress the creation of a commercial bank, the first of its kind in America, and that same year Congress chartered the Bank of North America with a paid-in capital of $400,000, to be located in Philadelphia. This bank eventually lent millions to the government and saw it through some of its most critical situations, but most of the bank's business was with private entrepreneurs. Like other American institutions under the Confederation, this bank—and others modeled after it in New York and Massachusetts in 1784—performed strongly even though the government itself continued to languish.

### CONGRESS AND THE PRIVATE ECONOMY

Historians still disagree about how dark or how bright general economic conditions actually were during the Confederation years from 1783 to 1787. But it is certain that specific areas were hurt by a postwar depression.

American shipowners were especially hard hit by the loss of their favored position in the trade with Britain and the British West Indies. When Congressional envoys tried to get Britain to reopen the West Indian trade in particular to American goods and American ships, they were laughed out of court. The loss of British trade was only in part offset by West Indian smuggling, by the new trade opened up with China in 1784, and by increased trade following upon commercial treaties with Baltic nations, France, and other continental countries.

When Congress tried to retaliate against the British commercial affronts, it succeeded only in displaying once more its own impotence and that of the new nation. Lord Sheffield, who promoted the British anti-American policy, wrote in his *Observations on the Commerce of the American States* (1783): "America cannot retaliate. It will not be an easy matter to bring the American States to act as a nation. They are not to be feared as such to us."

Immediately after the war, the pent-up American hunger for British finery and other goods had given American importers a taste of prosperity. But once the splurge was over, importers joined the chorus of protest against Congress. Blaming their plight on the shortage of domestic currency and the insecurity of domestic credit, they demanded financial reforms. American manufacturers, in turn, who had practically monopolized the American market during the conflict, demanded protection against the influx of British goods and sought subsidies to support their own programs of industrial expansion—neither of which Congress was in a position to provide.

For all its potential wealth, the United States was still a poor and wild country. Settlement had to precede intensive development; subsistence had to be gained before capital for long-term investment could be spared. The United States, and indeed the world, though on the threshold of the industrial revolution, were still far from becoming industrial-minded. In Pennsylvania, for example, in the 1780s, Oliver Evans perfected a

*View of the bridge over the Charles River engraved in 1789. (Library of Congress.)*

SEVEN *The Critical Period*

230

much-needed machine to make wool "cards"—the toothed instruments used for combing out strands of wool—but he found few takers. Evans anticipated modern assembly-line techniques by developing a "straight-line" method which, without the intervention of manual labor, allowed raw grain to be put through all the steps needed to transform it into flour ready for shipment. But conservative farmers resisted his innovations. Evans's greatest achievement, though he never found backing for it, was the development of plans for a "steam carriage," the forerunner of the railroad locomotive. Evans's well-known contemporaries, James Rumsey in Virginia and John Fitch in Pennsylvania, also worked on steam boilers, especially for steam boats, with sympathetic encouragement from intellectual leaders. Neither capitalists nor potential users, however, supplied them with financial backing or with markets, and both died in the 1790s broken in spirit.

Fortunately, most Americans, especially the inarticulate farmers who made up 90 per cent of the population, did not depend on Congress for their well-being. Even of those who did, many often seemed to get along better than their petitions to Congress suggested. Public creditors, in particular, although angry over the government's continuing failure even to keep up interest payments, apparently had enough reserve capital to sponsor new business ventures, especially in domestic trade and the expansion of the domestic economy, and the years immediately following the war saw unprecedented activity in road and canal construction, bridge building, house building, insurance, land sales, and banking. In Pennsylvania in 1784 Washington found a "spirit of enterprise [which] may achieve almost anything." In New York he noted a "temper, genius, and policy" directed single-mindedly toward commercial expansion. Washington advised Virginia to display a comparable commercial spirit and show "to our countrymen the superior advantages we possess beyond others." Otherwise, Virginia "must submit to the evils arising [from commercial competition] without receiving its benefits."

Perhaps the most significant signs of economic progress during the period of political crisis were the resumption of immigration to America, the rapid growth in the number and size of families, and the settlement of new lands on the frontiers in the North and West. What order there was in these developments can be attributed mainly to individual land-speculators—evidence again of the weakness of Congress. But the developments themselves proceeded apace, thanks to the vigor of the native-born, the immigrants, and the country at large.

## IV  Congress and the West

### THE SPECULATOR'S FRONTIER

In writings about American history, the term "frontier" is usually used to describe the West in an early phase of its development, and the "moving frontier" is taken to be the line marking the latest advance of permanent western settlement. This is as it should be; the history of the frontier is essentially the history of the westward movement of population. But this limitation of the term tends to obscure the opening of and the advance of population into the "northern frontier" of Vermont, New Hampshire, and Maine. In the early decades of the nineteenth century, great areas in each of these New England states remained wilder than much of Kentucky or Tennessee, Ohio or Michigan. During most of the eighteenth century, they remained as virgin and primitive as in Champlain's time.

Vermont, unlike Maine and New Hampshire, was a wholly landlocked territory, and the last part of the northern frontier to be penetrated by white settlers. Besides difficulty of access, political conflicts and the consequent uncertainties of land titles kept adventurers away. Both New York and New Hampshire claimed Vermont, but not until 1769 did migrants from either state venture into it to build permanent homes. In 1770, fishing in troubled waters, Ethan Allen and

*John Fitch's early paddle steamboat on the Delaware River at Philadelphia. (New York Public Library.)*

his brother Levi organized and armed the "Green Mountain Boys" in an attempt to establish their own independent hegemony in the region. Gradually they staked out large land holdings and in 1775, following Ethan's victory for the rebel states at Fort Ticonderoga, New York, on the Vermont border (see p. 194), he and brother Levi tried to get the Governor of Canada to guarantee Vermont's independence in exchange for their future neutrality in the war. Failing here, the Allens, in 1777, when about 30,000 persons had settled in Vermont, set up a government of their own. When the Revolution ended, they offered to "raise a regiment of Green Mountain Boys for His Majesty's Service." By then the population of Vermont had reached about 80,000, and many wanted to join the Union. Ethan and Levi, however, were determined "at all risks . . . that Congress shall not have the parcelling of [Vermont] lands to their avaricious Minions." Congress did nothing for the unionists and not until 1791 did Vermont become the fourteenth state.

Far to the southwest, meanwhile, other individualists were also staking out territory for independent states. In 1770 James Robertson and in 1773 John Sevier—both Virginians and both speculators—led settlers into the region of the Watauga and Holston rivers that now lies in eastern Tennessee but was then claimed by North Carolina. Isolated from organized society, they took practical steps for their self-protection by drawing up a compact of government called the Watauga Association. In 1780 Robertson pushed still farther west to establish a new settlement near present-day Nashville, leaving Sevier more or less unchallenged in the Watauga country. A brilliant victory over the British at King's Mountain in 1780 cemented Sevier's position among the pioneers, and subsequent raids on and deals with the Indians furthered his private speculative interests.

In 1784, following the lead of Maryland, Virginia, and other states, North Carolina ceded the Watauga region to Congress. At her own expense, and to the disgust of her tidewater taxpayers, North Carolina had succeeded in keeping the Indians in the western country under control. Now the Wataugans, about 10,000 strong, realizing the futility of counting on the helpless Congress for protection, decided to set up a separate state of their own. Sevier opposed this scheme, but when he sensed the determination of the Wataugans he decided to put himself at the head of the movement. The new state, called Franklin, was proclaimed in 1784. The next year, with enthusiasm for independence running strong, a highly democratic constitution was promulgated; but once the woodsmen had exhausted

231

their political energy and returned to their struggle with the forest and the soil, Sevier managed to have the constitution altered in a way that restored his own nearly absolute control.

His administration apparently safe, Sevier set off on an unpopular adventure to clear the Indians out of territory he was developing near Muscle Shoals in present Alabama. Failure here and in other undertakings gradually

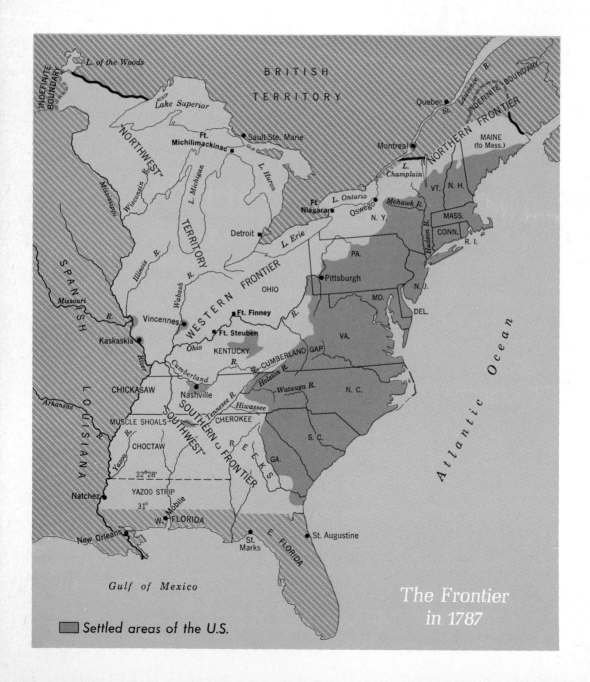

The Frontier in 1787

Settled areas of the U.S.

*John Sevier, from a portrait by George Washington Cooper. (Tennessee Historical Society, Nashville.)*

acquired from the Indians by private treaty in 1775, Henderson organized the Transylvania Company, with a government no more democratic than that of Watauga under Sevier, and as the years passed thousands of land-hungry settlers flooded into Henderson's domain. Virginia, claiming the land all the way to the "South Sea," including future Kentucky, had not renounced her claim to this adjacent territory when she ceded the rest of her western lands to Congress in 1783. Throughout the Confederation period, Henderson's satrapy was torn by strife between settlers who wanted to join forces with Spain in order to win commercial privileges on the Mississippi, and those who wanted to retain their standing in the United States. During these years, ten conventions were held in Kentucky by settlers seeking statehood, and on three occasions Virginia herself supported their demands. Once again, Congress did no more than it had about Vermont; but once again future Kentucky continued to burgeon despite official neglect.

undermined his standing in the area, and by 1788 the lack of local leadership and other problems of independence moved the Franklinites to try to return to the fold. North Carolina, having by this time rescinded her cession of the Watauga region, encouraged the Franklinites by offering renewed protection and support. Then in 1789 North Carolina surrendered the territory to Congress once again. By then most of the land had been carefully staked out by private speculators, and when Congress finally gained jurisdiction over the region, it gained little new federal territory.

Richard Henderson, a North Carolina judge who had supported James Robertson in Nashville and who had earlier backed Daniel Boone, also became engaged during this fluid wartime and postwar era in establishing an empire of his own in territory that was to become Kentucky. To develop land

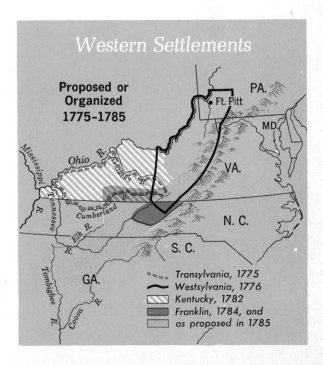

Western Settlements

Proposed or Organized 1775-1785

Mississippi R.
Ohio R.
Kentucky R.
Tennessee R.
Cumberland
Elk R.
R.
Tombigbee R.
Coosa R.

Ft. Pitt
PA.
MD.
VA.
N. C.
S. C.
GA.

- - - Transylvania, 1775
—— Westsylvania, 1776
▨ Kentucky, 1782
▨ Franklin, 1784, and
▤ as proposed in 1785

### ORGANIZING THE NORTHWEST TERRITORY

Organization of the southwestern frontier had been so haphazard and disorderly that Washington, after a visit to the region in 1784, warned Congress "that scarce a valuable spot within a tolerable distance of [the Ohio River] is left without a claimant." He urged Congress, in developing the land north of the Ohio, to follow the Yankee tradition of orderly survey and purchase. Discounting Britain's continuing hold on her armed posts in this area and her continuing hope that the "Old Northwest" might yet revert to the Empire, Congress itself had become the only formal authority in this region, and once the cessions of the landed states (see p. 222) were completed and the Indian title "quieted," the delegates undertook to follow Washington's advice. Yet here, as in the Southwest, although Congress made the rules, the actual development and settlement of the land remained largely in private hands.

In making the rules, Congress followed the lead of New York State, whose cession of its western lands to the Confederation in 1780 contained certain stipulations. New York required that her ceded territory "shall be formed into distinct republican States, which shall become members of the Federal Union, and have the same rights of sovereignty, freedom, and independence as the other States." In 1784, Congress named a committee, with Jefferson as chairman, to settle the question of how this stipulation might be observed in all ceded land. The result of the committee's work was the Northwest Ordinance of 1784, the first official attempt to outline the procedure for establishing territorial government and effecting the transition to statehood. Congress never put this ordinance to use, but it served as the basis for the more famous Northwest Ordinance of 1787 (see p. 236).

No government, of course, was needed in the Northwest Territory, as the "Old Northwest" came officially to be called, until the land had been organized and peopled. By 1785, though the Indians and the British still menaced settlement, Congress had succeeded in opening up some of the territory, and it now named a second committee, again with Jefferson as chairman, to recommend orderly methods for selling homesteads. Acting on the committee's report, Congress adopted the Land Ordinance of 1785.

The Land Ordinance reserved no less than one-seventh of the Northwest Territory "for the use of the continental army." It also reserved four lots in each township for the United States, and one lot "for the maintenance of public schools." Except for a small sector in future Ohio retained by Connecticut as its "Western Reserve," the rest of the Northwest Territory was to be surveyed into townships of 36 sections, each section 640 acres, or 1 square mile, in area. The minimum purchase, at auctions to be held at convenient locations, was to be one section; the minimum price, $1 per acre in cash. Congress hoped that good land would command a better price.

In colonial times, unclaimed public land had gone free, or nearly free, to all comers; clearing, cultivation, and help in keeping down the Indians had been considered sufficient payment to the government for a good farm. But Congress, now desperate for funds to carry on the government, hoped to raise revenue from land sales. The results were disappointing, for the minimum requirement of $640, in cash, effectively shut out most of the settlers who were eager to push westward, while the price of $1 per acre discouraged speculators. In later years, the minimum acreage and the minimum price were both reduced, and long-term credit made it easier for small farmers to pay for their land. Not until the Homestead Act of 1862, however, did the United States revert to the colonial tradition of offering free land to bona-fide settlers.

After the first seven ranges of townships surveyed in the Northwest Territory had failed to produce the revenue for which Congress longed, the delegates reluctantly yielded to the blandishments of speculators who now proffered pennies rather than dollars per acre for tremendous tracts. The principal proposal came from a group of army officers who in 1786 organized the Ohio Company to purchase a million dollars' worth of land. They planned to pay for this by distributing company stock to fellow officers in exchange for land warrants the officers had received from Congress in lieu of back pay. Congress was asked to accept these warrants at face value, even though the company had acquired them at their depreciated price of about nine cents on the dollar.

The delegates refused to be pressured into such a deal until two men, the Reverend Manassah Cutler, an exceedingly persuasive lobbyist for the Ohio Company, and William Duer, a rich wartime profiteer recently appointed secretary to the Board of the Treasury,

took a hand in the proceedings early in 1787. Armed with more forceful techniques than mere persuasion, Duer forced the deal through Congress by devising a scheme permitting himself and others in the government to share in the profits without seeming to be connected with the business in any way. Duer's idea was for Cutler's Ohio Company to purchase a million acres of land for itself, and to take an option on another 5 million which would be turned over to a second enterprise, the Scioto Company, in which Duer and his cronies would have controlling interest. Duer's scheme worked for the moment and the Ohio Company actually picked up 1 million acres at about nine cents an acre; but the contrived Scioto Company quickly became entangled in various frauds and suits and never earned anything for the shady schemers.

Having swung the deal, the Ohio Com-

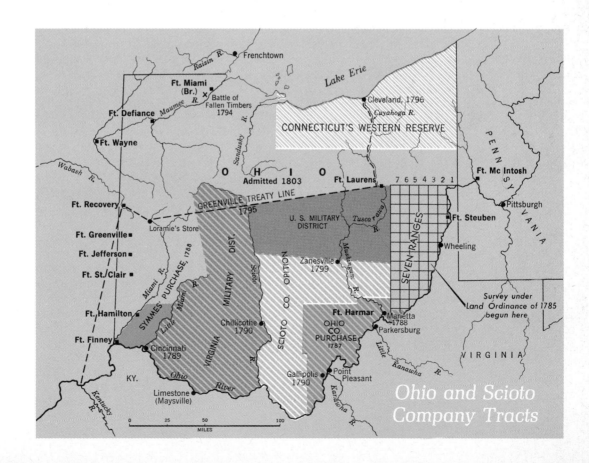

*Ohio and Scioto Company Tracts*

236

pany's first order of business was to prod Congress into getting the government of the new territory established so that the speculators could move ahead with the sale and settlement of their vast holdings. The result of their efforts was the Northwest Ordinance of 1787, Congress's most important piece of legislation.

By the terms of this Ordinance, the Northwest Territory was to be set up as a single unit with a governor to be appointed by Congress. When 5000 free male inhabitants had settled in the Territory, those who owned at least 50 acres apiece were to elect a territorial legislature whose acts would be subject only to the governor's veto. The voters would also send a nonvoting delegate to Congress. No less than three and no more than five states were to be carved out of the Territory, and the boundaries of three future states were tentatively laid out. When a potential state had 60,000 free inhabitants, it was to be admitted to the Union "on an equal footing with the original States in all respects whatever." The Northwest Ordinance required, in addition that "the people and states" in the Territory, adopt "articles of compact" with the "original states" which shall "forever remain unalterable, unless by common consent." These articles in effect set forth the first *federal* bill of rights, similar to those in the first state constitutions (see p. 216), and with the momentous provision prohibiting slavery in the Territory and in the states to be carved from it.

It has been persuasively argued (the actual negotiations presumably were secret) that the southern delegates in Congress accepted this provision in return for the three-fifths rule in the Constitution permitting five slaves to be counted as three persons in apportioning representation in the new national legislature. Congress, in New York, enacted the Northwest Ordinance in July 1787, just when the "Great Convention" was sweltering in Philadelphia over the issue of representation (see p. 252), and a compromise could easily have been worked out.

Following enactment of the Ordinance, the Ohio Company, in December 1787, sent out its first group of 47 settlers. In the spring of 1788, they floated down the Ohio in a flat boat and launched the settlement of Marietta at the junction of the Ohio and Muskingum rivers. The Scioto Company, meanwhile, still with only an option on the land it was trying to sell, and afraid that local purchasers might be tempted to scrutinize its title, dispatched the poet and diplomat Joel Barlow to Europe to find more gullible buyers far from the scene. By 1790 Barlow had rounded up some 600 Frenchmen who, on arriving in America, settled by mistake not on Scioto land but on land belonging to the Ohio Company itself. At their village of Gallipolis, these inexperienced pioneers endured all the hardships of the frontier aggravated by doubtful land titles, and were barely saved from extinction by a new grant of land from Congress and other timely assistance.

A third group of settlers, sent out by the New Jersey speculator, John Cleves Symmes, to develop a tract he also had purchased from Congress, laid the foundations of Cincinnati in 1788. Eight years later Moses Cleaveland led a band of pioneers to Connecticut's Western Reserve, where they built the town of Cleveland on Lake Erie.

## v  *The Final Shocks*

Besides the Northwest Ordinance and the beginning of settlement in the Northwest Territory, Congress could boast of few achievements during the postwar years. American ships were harassed on the high seas, their cargoes barred from foreign ports. Attempts by congressional envoys abroad to improve commercial relations with foreign countries met only with insults. At home, American manufacturers suffered from foreign competition that Congress was at a loss to regulate by tariffs or other means. Even on the frontiers, new settlers were left almost entirely to their own resources in combating the Indians, the British, and the Spanish. Frontier violence and threats of violence stifled the

Fort Harmer, Ohio, 1790. This nineteenth-century impression shows the recently founded town of Marietta on the opposite bank of the Ohio River. (Courtesy of the New-York Historical Society, New York City.)

demand for land and caused speculators to grumble as their holdings failed to appreciate in value.

Only the established small farmer in the older sections of the country had remained secure—he was exposed neither abroad nor at home, neither on the sea nor on the land. So long as British, French, and Continental forces remained mobilized in America and needed his stores and supplies, his market for cash crops remained lively. Subsistence farmers fared even better when cheap British imports started to come in after the war. By 1785, however, the foreign troops had been withdrawn, the American army had been disbanded, and the farmer's market had shrunk. Wartime creditors began to press the farmers for back interest. To make matters worse, the state legislatures began to raise taxes and to demand that they be paid in specie, so that the states themselves could pay the back interest on their Revolutionary debts. Stunned by this bitter reversal of fortune, the farmers, and the small retailers who depended on them, cried out for relief. As in colonial times, they and other debtors agitated for the states to issue paper money that would serve

as legal tender in the payment of all debts, public and private; and they demanded that the states enact stay laws that would postpone the foreclosure of farms and other property on which mortgage payments were in arrears.

In most of the states, the farmers did win certain concessions. Seven states issued some form of paper money, often to good effect. But in states like Massachusetts, the creditors and the conservatives in the legislature successfully resisted the debtors' demands, and the seaboard commercial towns managed to shift a disproportionate part of the tax burden onto the inland landholders. It has been estimated that after 1780 the average Massachusetts farmer had to surrender a third of his income in taxes.

Even in Rhode Island, where debtors were particularly influential, farmers suffered sharply from the market slump. Together with other debtors, they persuaded the legis-

237

lature to issue paper money in 1786, but its value depreciated so rapidly that merchants soon refused to accept it, and even began to avoid their debtors for fear that they might be paid. The legislature responded by passing a law that made refusal to accept the paper money a crime punishable by fines, without even the ceremony of a jury trial. One Rhode Island butcher, John Weeden, appealed his conviction under this law to the state supreme court. In the famous case of *Trevett v. Weeden* (1786), the court dismissed Weeden's complaint on the ground that it had no jurisdiction over the case, volunteering the opinion that the law was repugnant to the provisions of the Rhode Island charter and was therefore unconstitutional.

In New Hampshire, the militia had to be called out in 1786 to disperse a mob that had surrounded the legislative meeting house in an effort to coerce the members to issue paper money. It was in Massachusetts, however, that conservatives experienced the greatest shock. Here the legislature, its upper house dominated by merchants, failed to heed the debtors' demands for relief, and actually levied higher taxes that had to be paid in specie. On July 31, 1786, to evade the debtors' protests, the legislature adjourned until the following January 31. This cowardly act precipitated the violent uprisings subsequently known as Shays' Rebellion.

Thirty-nine at the outbreak of the Rebellion, Daniel Shays was typical of the thousand men who eventually participated in it. He had been born into poverty in Middlesex County in eastern Massachusetts, but before the Revolution had moved to the western part of the state where he found work as a farm laborer. Following Lexington and Concord he enlisted in time to see action at Bunker Hill in June 1775. "A brave and good soldier," as a subordinate described him after the war, he had won early promotion to sergeant; but the four years he had to wait for a promised commission to captain embittered him. After a year in this exalted position, he was mustered out in 1780 and re-

turned to his home in Pelham in Hampshire County to await payment, like thousands of other disappointed officers, for his long service to his country. His farming went badly, his army compensation was long delayed, his obligations accumulated, and "the specter of debtors' jail always hovered close by."

An articulate rebel, Captain Shays became a spokesman for his neighbors when the western counties became increasingly agitated over their worsening economic straits. Some of these counties were too poor to afford to send delegates to the legislature in far-off Boston; and in some of the towns no men were to be found who could meet the property qualifications to sit in the general court. In effect, the debtors, most of them veterans of the Revolution, were deprived of any voice in the state government, and the nabobs of Boston and other port towns were quick to take advantage of this agrarian weakness. To make their protests heard, the debtor leaders resorted to the time-honored device of county conventions. Here men from neighboring towns would gather at the county seats on a basis of personal equality and give voice to their political feelings by means of published resolutions and petitions to the legislature. After the legislature adjourned in July 1786, having ignored the petitions of the disfranchised and having done nothing to relieve their mounting distress, more and more county conventions were called in all parts of the state.

Under the leadership of ex-officers like Shays—plain depressed citizens, none of them brilliant agitators or commanders—the members were warned to "abstain from all mobs and unlawful assemblies until a constitutional method of redress can be obtained." But popular discontent soon overrode these cautionings, and hotheads, exploiting the popular convulsion, began to assemble riotous mobs. Their targets were the civil courts where foreclosure proceedings by the hundreds were scheduled. After forcing the suspension of many civil court sessions, the mobs attacked the criminal courts to prevent the trial of rioters. When they next menaced the federal arsenals, the government no longer could postpone action.

By October 1786, the fires of rebellion had been fanned by numerous Massachusetts merchants and other businessmen eager to prove the impossibility of democratic government. At the same time, moderate leaders were forced to put themselves at the head of the mobs if only to restrain them from greater violence. Somehow Shays had risen to the leadership of the whole movement and the troops who rallied to him became the targets of state forces hastily gathered by General Benjamin Lincoln at the behest of Governor James Bowdoin. Fighting between Shays' forces and Lincoln's continued from mid-January to the end of February 1787, when the Rebellion finally was crushed and Shays fled to Vermont. A number of his straggling followers, captured during the fighting, were freed by the legislature in June. The bitterness that followed in the wake of this uprising emerged in the subsequent elections, when the aging John Hancock defeated Governor Bowdoin. No reprisals of an enduring kind, however, were imposed on Shays or his followers, and the Massachusetts legislature itself held off harsher taxes that were on its agenda and passed laws exempting household goods and workmen's tools from confiscation for debt.

Shays' Rebellion shocked conservatives throughout the nation. They now felt more acutely than before the necessity of preventing attacks on courts of law and physical intimidation of legislatures. To protect their interests, they sought to prevent legislatures from impairing the obligations of private contracts and from establishing depreciated currencies as legal tender for the payment of debts. Many of them also joined the movement, by then well underway, for a stronger central government which would itself be sovereign in critical areas, thereby reducing the power and pretensions of the states while protecting them from mob pressures.

The "critical period," beginning almost simultaneously with the enthusiasm for independence, had driven many Americans into renewed violence once the War of Independence had ended. Their abhorrence of domestic if not international violence and the urgency to protect themselves in the future, led many of the new leaders to subscribe to the sentiments of the respected Dr. Benjamin Rush, who in his *Address to the People of the United States,* in January 1787, said:

There is nothing more common than to confound the terms of the American revolution with those of the late American war. The American war is over; but this is far from being the case with the American revolution. On the contrary, nothing but the first act of the great drama is disclosed. It remains yet to establish and perfect our new forms of government; and to prepare the principles, morals, and manners of our citizens, for these forms of government, after they are established and brought to perfection.

Washington, embittered by the spectacle of the faltering Congress, referred to it as "a half-starved, limping government, always moving upon crutches and tottering at every step." But the immediate "crisis" was soon to be over and the nation more soundly launched.

# READINGS

Allan Nevins, *The American States During and After the Revolution 1775–1789* (1924), although superseded on many points by more recent scholarship, remains the most substantial account of state politics during the "critical period." A useful survey of the recent scholarship is available in the chapters on Charles Beard and the accompanying bibliographical essays in Richard Hofstadter, *The Progressive Historians: Turner, Beard, Parrington* (1968). Two outstanding books by scholars involved with other countries but whose work is directly relevant to the United States may be noted here: J.R. Pole, *Political Representation in England and the Origins of the American Republic* (1967), and R.R. Palmer, *The Age of Democratic Revolution, A Political History of Europe and America 1760–1800* (vol. I, "The Challenge," 1959). On constitution-making in the states in particular, see R.J. Taylor, ed., *Massachusetts, Colony to Commonwealth, Documents on the Formation of Its Constitution* (1961); Oscar and M.F. Handlin, *The Popular Sources of Political Authority* (1966), a collection of sources on the Massachusetts convention of 1780; Richard McCormick, *Experiment in Independence: New Jersey in the Critical Period 1781–1789* (1950); E.W. Spaulding, *New York in the Critical Period* (1932); R.L. Brunhouse, *The Counter-Revolution in Pennsylvania 1776–1790* (1942); and Dumas Malone, *Jefferson the Virginian* (1948). Other biographies of the Founding Fathers that deal extensively with the "Critical Period" are Irving Brant, *James Madison* (6 vols., 1941–1961), and Broadus Mitchell, *Alexander Hamilton* (2 vols., 1957–1962). Louis Gottschalk, *Lafayette: Between the American and the French Revolution 1783–1789* (1950), is especially rewarding. E.P. Douglass, *Rebels and Democrats* (1955), is best described by its subtitle, "The Struggle for Equal Political Rights and Majority Rule during the American Revolution." R.A. Rutland, *The Birth of the Bill of Rights 1776–1791* (1955), covers the subject in the states, the Constitutional Convention, and the ratifying process. Here, as elsewhere, W.D. Jordan, *White over Black* (1968), is illuminating; see especially Parts Three and Four.

E.C. Burnett, *The Continental Congress* (1941), is the standard and indispensable study of the national government in the "critical period." Lynn Montross, *The Reluctant Rebels, The Story of the Continental Congress 1774–1789* (1950), is more highly colored, but judicious in its emphases. On the central issue of public finance, see E.J. Ferguson, *The Power of the Purse, A History of American Public Finance 1776–1790* (1961).

The old but exceedingly influential work by John Fiske, *The Critical Period of American History 1783–1789* (1888), still merits serious consideration. Merrill Jensen, *The New Nation: A History of the United States During the Confederation 1781–1789* (1950), is a comprehensive study of American politics and society. Jensen develops the idea that conditions in this period were not as bad as proponents of a new constitution claimed. His work derives from C.A. Beard's outstanding scholarly monograph *An Economic Interpretation of the Constitution of the United States* (1913). Beard's principal critics include R.E. Brown in *Charles Beard and the Constitution* (1956), and Forrest McDonald, *We the People: The Economic Origins of the Constitution* (1958). Criticisms of the critics, with illuminating observations of their own, include Lee Benson, *Turner and Beard: American Historical Writing Reconsidered* (1960), and J.T. Main, *The Anti-Federalists, Critics of the Constitution 1781–1788* (1961). Informative but perhaps exaggerated accounts of the social impact of the Revolution include J.F. Jameson, *The American Revolution Considered as a Social Movement* (1926), and E.B. Greene, *The Revolutionary Generation 1763–1790* (1943). J.T. Main, *The Social Structure of Revolutionary America* (1965), does as much as appears possible with the statistical evidence that remains on the distribution of property and related matters.

The state of American business under the Articles is well described in R.A. East, *Business Enterprise in the American Revolutionary Era* (1938). Edward Channing, *A History of the United States* (vol. III, 1912), is good on all phases of the era of the Confederation but especially useful on the efforts to rebuild commercial relations with Britain and the world. On the land problems see the early chapters in P.J. Treat, *The National Land System 1785–1820* (1910), and B.H. Hibbard, *A History of the Public Land Policies* (1924). Excellent on the early land companies is T.P. Abernethy, *Western Lands and the American Revolution* (1937). On early western settlement, see F.S. Philbrick, *The Rise of the West 1754–1830* (1965); B.W. Bond, Jr., *The Civilization of the Old Northwest* (1934); and A.P. Whitaker, *The Spanish-American Frontier 1783–1795* (1927). For background on the Northwest Ordinance and slavery, see Staughton Lynd, "Slavery and the Founding Fathers," in Melvin Drimmer, ed., *Black History, A Reappraisal* (1968). Useful biographies of early western speculators include C.S. Driver, *John Sevier: Pioneer of the Old Southwest* (1932), and W.H. Masterson, *William Blount* (1954). On the same subject, T.P. Abernethy, *From Frontier to Plantation in Tennessee* (1932), is an illuminating work.

M.L. Starkey, *A Little Rebellion* (1955), is excellent on Shays' revolt. A good shorter account is R.B. Morris, "Insurrection in Massachusetts," an essay in Daniel Aaron, ed., *America in Crisis* (1952).

# EIGHT

Under the Articles of Confederation, the government of the new Republic had shown itself to be weak and contemptible. The high hopes of the victorious patriots, dashed by the economic distress and domestic violence of the postwar years, were almost entirely dissipated by the political separatism of the states and sections. Some, like General Benjamin Lincoln of Massachusetts, had grown so dispirited they felt geography itself to be against them. In 1786 Lincoln wrote to the more sanguine Rufus King:

Did the United States extend from east to west, . . . instead of their extending, as they do now, from north to south, their union would, probably, be much more permanent, and they would be easier governed by the same legislative body than in their present situation. . . . [Given] the evils, which are consequent on the extent of the United States, their different climates, their different productions, and the different views of the people in consequence thereof, . . . I cannot believe that these states ever will, or ever can, be governed . . . by laws which have a general operation.

General Lincoln thought it inevitable that the people must accept "a division" into many parts and seek "safety by a firm alliance" among them.

At this very time, Dr. Rush was writing to a friend abroad: "Some of our enlightened men who begin to despair of a more complete union of the States in Congress have secretly proposed an Eastern, Middle, and Southern Confederacy, to be united by an alliance, offensive and defensive." Their secret was soon out, for in the spring of 1787 several newspapers published a circular letter urging a similar three-part plan.

# THE CONSTITUTION

Such proposals shocked moderates like Washington, Madison, and Jay. "The honor, power, and true interest of this country," Washington wrote, "must be measured by a Continental scale." He and his friends feared that the fragments of the Union, like the states of Europe, would be eternally at war with one another, and all weaker prey to European enemies unwilling to acknowledge their independence. In the Northwest, as they knew only too well, Britain still clung to her aspirations for American territory. In the Southwest, Spain clearly nursed her ancient colonial claims. Nor had France surrendered her ambitions to regain her lost New World empire.

Quite as alarming to these moderates, who had hoped that America might stand before the world as a model of unity and liberty, were the advocates of a military dictatorship to hold the states and sections together by force, one made more palatable by Washington's consenting to head it. As early as 1782, Colonel Lewis Nicola wrote to the General in this vein, stressing how "military men in particular" understood "the weakness of republics." General James M. Varnum undertook to strengthen Nicola's appeal: Since the citizenry at large, he told Washington, did not have "that love of equality which is ab-

solutely requisite to support a democratic Republic, . . . absolute monarchy or a military State can alone rescue them from the horrors of subjugation."

"What a triumph for our enemies," the General exclaimed, "to verify their predictions! What a triumph for the advocates of despotism to find we are incapable of governing ourselves, and that systems founded on the basis of equal liberty are merely fallacious."

None of these plans gained much support outside the military, yet as time passed, Washington himself observed that "even respectable characters speak of a monarchical form of government without horror." Such talk spurred the moderates to action. As Jay wrote to Washington in June 1786, shortly before Shays' Rebellion:

What I most fear is that the better kind of people (by which I mean the people who are orderly and industrious, who are content with their situations, and not uneasy in their circumstances) will be led, by the insecurity of property, the loss of confidence in their rulers, and the want of public faith and rectitude, to consider the charms of liberty as imaginary and delusive. A state of fluctuation and uncertainty must disgust and alarm such men, and prepare their minds for almost any change that may promise them quiet and security.

243

244

Once Shays' Rebellion occurred, the moderates' alarm deepened. John Marshall, far from the scene in Virginia, expressed the growing perturbation of substantial citizens everywhere when he wrote that "these violent . . . dissensions" in a state thought so rational and orderly would be a blow to free government "throughout the globe." Perhaps it was true that man really was incapable of governing himself. "I fear we may live to see another revolution." Washington himself warned early in 1787, "Something must be done or the fabric will fall." Again he declared: "We cannot exist long as a nation without having lodged somewhere a power which will pervade the whole Union in as energetic a manner, as the authority of the State Governments extends over the several States."

Something, as we know, was done.

## I  *The Great Convention*

### PRELIMINARY MANEUVERS

As early as 1780, Alexander Hamilton had asked for the formation of a new and more energetic government to press the Revolutionary War forward. In 1782 the New York legislature and in 1785 the Massachusetts legislature passed resolutions calling for conventions to supplant the Articles. Nothing came of these proposals, but a dispute between Maryland and Virginia early in 1785 started a chain of events that led at last to the Great Convention of 1787.

Maryland and Virginia had fallen out over the navigation of the Potomac River and Chesapeake Bay. Early in 1785 representatives of the two states met at Alexandria, Virginia, in an attempt to settle their differences. From there they moved to Washington's home at Mount Vernon, where representatives from neighboring Delaware and Pennsylvania were invited to join the discussion. Their talks at this time were broadened to explore the possibility of establishing water communication between Chesapeake Bay and the Ohio River, a subject of keen interest to those who would give cohesion to the Union as well as to speculators and western settlers. Encouraged by the progress of the talks, Madison suggested to the Virginia legislature that it invite all the states to a commercial convention at Annapolis. The legislature accepted the idea and the invitations went out.

Only five of the 13 states sent delegates to Annapolis, but one of them was New York, and among her delegates was the indefatigable Hamilton. His ideas had long since soared beyond mere commercial arrangements, but to attempt more with only five states represented appeared impracticable, and at his suggestion, after agreeing that the New Yorker write the report of the meeting, the Annapolis Convention adjourned. In his report, Hamilton stressed not commercial difficulties but the numerous hamstringing defects of the Confederation, and he closed with a call for a great new convention of all the states to meet in Philadelphia the following May to amend the Articles. This call was made official, if not strengthened, by the resolution of the Confederation Congress, February 21, 1787, setting the "second Monday in May next" as the date of the Philadelphia meeting "for the sole and express purpose of revising the Articles of Confederation."

The second Monday in May was the 14th, but following the leisurely fashion of the age, it was not until May 25 that delegates from the required majority of states reached Philadelphia to begin the Convention's business. The call to Philadelphia was better heeded than the one to Annapolis, and eventually every state but Rhode Island was at some time represented there.

### THE DELEGATE LEADERS

Arguing for the Constitution in the *Federalist* papers in 1788 (see p. 263), John Jay wrote: "When once an efficient national government is established, the best men in the country will not only consent to serve, but also will be generally appointed to manage it." Questionable as this prediction became in later years, the new government not only elicited the services of the country's best men but was set up by them.

Not all the eminent leaders attended the Philadelphia meeting. Jay himself, Jefferson, and John Adams were abroad on other duties. Sam Adams failed of election as a delegate, while Patrick Henry, appointed by the Virginia legislature, refused to serve. Yet it was a brilliant gathering. James Madison, one of the most brilliant of all, once observed that "there never was an assembly of men, charged with a great and arduous trust, who were more pure in their motives or more exclusively or anxiously devoted to the object committed to them to . . . best secure the permanent liberty and happiness of their country."

From Pennsylvania came Benjamin Franklin, at 81 the oldest member and the sage of the Convention, more influential among his fellows for his kindliness and humor than for his political views; Gouverneur Morris, a witty and cynical Philadelphia lawyer with a gift for rhetoric; Robert Morris, the financier of the Revolution, now heavily involved in the land-speculations that were eventually to ruin him; and the immigrant Scot, James Wilson, a learned lawyer and man of affairs who became an active and ardent advocate of popular sovereignty. From Massachusetts came Rufus King, a veteran of the Continental Congress whom Hamilton had converted into a supporter of strong, centralized government; and the mercurial and opinionated Elbridge Gerry, who sat through the Convention but then refused to sign the Constitution. Roger Sherman, an eccentric self-made businessman who had built a respectable political career, led the Connecticut delegation. Delaware sent John Dickinson, an advocate of the interests of the small states, but one seasoned in intercolonial politics and with strong national sympathies.

Hamilton, perhaps the most ardent backer of centralized government, was accompanied in the New York delegation by two colleagues devoted to state sovereignty, Robert Yates and John Lansing. Until Yates and Lansing defected from the Convention on July 5, they consistently outvoted Hamilton; after their departure deprived New York of its vote because it no longer could muster a quorum, Hamilton's own attendance became spotty. His extreme views on centralization further weakened his position.

From New Jersey came the astute William Paterson, a resolute spokesman for the small states; from Maryland, her Attorney-General, Luther Martin, who wearied the delegates with lengthy speeches and in the end refused to endorse their work.

Virginia, the most populous state, sent perhaps the most scintillating delegation, headed by the silent but impressive Washington, suffering from rheumatism. With him came young Madison, the most gifted apologist for the Constitution, on whose detailed notes (not made public until 1840) we depend for much of our firsthand knowledge of the proceedings; George Wythe, Jefferson's law professor, who helped codify the laws of the state; George Mason, planter and patriot, who had drafted the Virginia Declaration of Rights, but who could not bring himself to support the Constitution; and the youthful Virginia Governor, Edmund Randolph, who finally urged adoption of the Constitution upon his state's ratifying convention after having refused to sign it.

North Carolina sent a quiet five-man group. South Carolina's delegation was led by Charles Pinckney, the eminent Charleston lawyer and slave-owner, and his cousin, General Charles Cotesworth Pinckney, lawyer, planter, and heavy investor in public securities. William Few, former North Carolina "Regulator," yet an active revolutionary fighter, headed the Georgia contingent. New Hampshire felt it could not afford to send delegates, but at last the wealthy Portsmouth merchant, John Langdon, offered to pay his own expenses and those of a fellow delegate, Nicholas Gilman, both reaching Philadelphia two months after the Convention had begun.

In all, 74 delegates had been named but

only 55 attended. Their average age of 42 attests to the youthfulness of most of them. Many had been officers in the Revolution, and 27 belonged to the Society of Cincinnati, an organization formed to look after officer interests. A mere eight were signers of the Declaration of Independence. In an age when few Americans went to college, a majority of the delegates were college graduates. While lawyers predominated, many of them were also businessmen or planters. Only Few of Georgia could be said to represent the plain farmer class; but he was no novice in politics, having had years of experience in his state legislature and the Continental Congress.

### THEIR SOVEREIGN BENT

The Convention's first business on May 25 was the election of a presiding officer, and the 29 delegates then present voted unanimously for George Washington.

The Convention's second decision, also unanimous, elicited controversy then and since: the ruling that the proceedings be secret. The official journal, kept by the secretary, was to be available only to members; press and public were to be barred from the sessions, and nothing said on the floor of the Convention was to be written or spoken of outside without permission. Jefferson, when he learned of the ruling in Paris, thought it a sad commentary on the delegates' democratic faith. Yet, as Madison later pointed out, it probably helped keep the members open-minded and flexible in debate. Many of the opinions expressed, he said, were "so various and at first so crude" that hours, sometimes days, of discussion were required before the delegates could come to any agreement on them. Had the members been obliged to commit themselves publicly to one opinion or another at the outset, they might have been reluctant to take any stand on divisive issues, or to change their minds once their positions had become known.

One of the first divisive issues, in fact, was the delegates' avowed purpose in coming together. The call, as we have said, was clear: They were there to "revise" the Articles. Some held to the very letter of their instructions and even insisted that revisions be unanimous, one of the requirements of the Articles most in need of revision. Others, however, lest they

Delegates to the Second Continental Congress, reading from top left, included: James Madison of Virginia (Colonial Williamsburg Collection); Gouverneur Morris of Pennsylvania (Courtesy of the New-York Historical Society, New York City); Roger Sherman of Connecticut (detail, Yale University Art Gallery, gift of Roger Sherman White); James Wilson of Pennsylvania (Smithsonian Institution, National Collection of Fine Arts); and Charles Cotesworth Pinckney of South Carolina (Courtesy Carolina Art Association, Gibbes Gallery, Charleston).

"let slip the golden opportunity," as Hamilton put it, took a freer view. When Edmund Randolph of Virginia declared that he was not "scrupulous on the point of power," Hamilton seconded his stand, and the Convention, over the misgivings of some, proceeded to supplant, not revise, the Articles.

On May 30, only five days after the opening session, Edmund Randolph disclosed something of the revolutionary temper of the leaders by offering these resolutions:

1. That a union of the states merely federal will not accomplish the objects proposed by the Articles of Confederation—namely common defense, security of liberty, and general welfare.

2. That no treaty or treaties among the whole or part of the states, as individual sovereignties, would be sufficient.

3. That a *national* government ought to be established, consisting of a *supreme* legislative, executive, and judiciary.

Congress promptly agreed to put off debate on propositions 1 and 2; but sitting as the *"Committee of the Whole* on the state of the Union" —not on the state of the Articles—it directly applied itself to the summer-long task of shaping an instrument of government conforming to proposition 3.

## II   *The Convention at Work*

### THE OVERARCHING ISSUES

Having secretly decided to jettison the "Firm League of Friendship" for a sovereign national state, the Convention delegates now faced two overarching issues: the problem of *power* and the problem of *federalism*. From their wartime experiences and the failures of the Confederation they knew at first hand the frightening costs of vague, divided, and often absent authority. At the same time, they required no reminders of their prewar experiences with what they regarded as overbearing and repressive power. While they, in many

instances, continued to hold others in the most oppressive bondage, they retained an almost anarchic suspicion of controls over their own jealously guarded liberties, so recently retrieved, as they saw it, from King and Parliament. Their first challenge, then, was to design a government sufficiently constrained to protect the individual citizen yet authoritative enough really to rule the nation. Abraham Lincoln, faced with an even graver challenge 75 years later, defined the same issue: "Must a government, of necessity, be too strong for the liberties of its own people or too weak to maintain its own existence?" The Founding Fathers thought not.

The problem of federalism was almost as old as the problem of power. Even in ancient times separate states had joined forces in federations for mutual safety and advantage. In the history of Western society we find, as the Founding Fathers found, many confederated unions in which member states shared power with a central government: ancient Greece, the Swiss Confederation, the United Provinces of the Netherlands. Even the American provinces had experimented with this sort of arrangement in the New England Confederation of 1643. As early as 1701, Robert Livingston of New York had spoken of establishing three colonial confederacies, while 20 years later the Earl of Stair devised a federal plan embracing both the mainland colonies and the British West Indies. In the Albany Plan of Union, 1754, Franklin proposed granting a central government authority to levy duties and taxes on the provinces. Subsequently, several thinkers on both sides of the Atlantic had suggested that the colonies be joined into a loose federal structure where, while linked to Britain by common interests and loyalty to the Crown, they would be substantially self-governing. On the very eve of the Revolution, the Loyalist Joseph Galloway had proposed a plan of union that might earlier have saved the empire (see p. 189).

Finally, there were the Articles of Confederation, a questionable model, to be sure, for the leading Convention delegates, yet one to which many enamored of state power still clung. Among the latter, those in the larger states were determined that their influence in any new central government be proportionate to their population and wealth. At the same time, those in the smaller states sought guarantees that their interests would not be sacrificed. The question of slavery, essentially sectional in character, aggravated, indeed poisoned, each issue, not least such critical ones as property to be taxed by, and persons to be represented in, any new national establishment.

The claims of federalism could not be, and as we know were not, put aside. Yet to the Convention leaders the claims of power stood paramount, and their major concessions to federalism were made only to facilitate the attainment of strength.

## THE PHILOSOPHIC GUIDELINES

Before recounting how the Founding Fathers solved the problems of power and federalism, it appears worthwhile to examine how they formulated these problems for themselves. Almost without exception they were practical men of affairs who, if pressed, probably would have agreed with the comment John Rutledge of South Carolina made during a warm discussion of the slave trade: "Religion & humanity had nothing to do with this question—Interest alone is the governing principle with Nations." At the same time, as thoughtful and exceptionally well-educated men, they realized, when not too closely involved, that considerations of "interest alone" usually led nowhere but to warfare. Thus their overriding aim was to temper interest with reason, to bring human nature under the discipline of the optimistic philosophy of the Enlightenment, so that "civilization," a term then just coming into general use, might be improved and conflict avoided.

Not all the members of the Convention, once more, nor even all those who rallied to the Constitution later on, agreed on the best political means by which civilization might be improved. Most of the Philadelphia assemblage, nevertheless, managed to negotiate successfully between the extreme state-rights and centralization positions that so conspicuously frustrated the New York delegation. We may reconstruct the broad outlines of their thinking from their observations in the Convention and in the ratification debates, from works of political philosophy like the *Federalist* papers (see p. 263) and John Adams's *Defence of the Constitutions of Government of the United States of America* (which was read and cited with approval by a number of delegates), and from their private letters.

The Founding Fathers permitted themselves to be optimistic about constructing a suitable government—one, in Washington's words, with a "liberal and energetic Constitution," yet "well guarded and closely watched to prevent encroachments"—because they expected their profound pessimism about human nature to impel them to leave nothing undone to control it.

Human nature, they believed, was universally fallible. "Men," said Hamilton in a characteristic generalization, "are ambitious, vindictive, and rapacious." Madison agreed. Vice, he argued, could not be checked with virtue; vice must be checked with vice:

Ambition must be made to counteract ambition. The interest of the man must be connected with the constitutional rights of the place. It may be a reflection on human nature that such devices should be necessary to control the abuses of government. But what is government itself, but the greatest of all reflections on human nature? If men were angels, no government would be necessary.

Madison said the time might come when the majority of Americans, possessing no property of any kind, would destroy "the rights of property and the public liberty." For this reason the envy of the poor must be controlled. Yet even a wealthy aristocrat like Gouverneur Morris acknowledged that "wealth tends to corrupt the mind," and that rich men as well as poor would use power to their own advan-

250

tage if given the opportunity. Thus the greed and pride of the rich must also be held in check.

To control the poor and check the rich while allowing each their liberties, the Framers looked to a republican rather than a democratic form of government. In a republic, as Madison defined it, the "public views" of each class will be "refined and enlarged" by "passing them through the medium of a chosen body of citizens, whose wisdom may best discern the true interest of their country, and whose patriotism and love of justice, will be least likely to sacrifice it to temporary or partial considerations."

The Founding Fathers were as reluctant to entrust power to interests as to individuals or social classes. They believed that a landed interest, a moneyed interest, a commercial interest, a manufacturing interest, if it could seize full control of government, would tyrannize over the rest of society. And the danger would be even greater if several interests were to join forces and form a majority that could control the nation.

In meeting this problem, the advocates of a stronger constitution turned to a *federal* republic rather than a consolidated one, looking to the political identity of the parts to offset the power grabs of boundless material interests working in concert.

Heretofore it had been commonly believed that, at best, republics were suitable only for small territories, such as the individual American states, and that large areas had to be governed by monarchs. Madison boldly argued the contrary: the larger the society, the stronger the safeguards of liberty on the one hand and of the general welfare on the other. His most comprehensive statement appeared in *Federalist* Number 10:

The influence of factious leaders may kindle a flame within their particular States, but will be unable to spread a general conflagration through the other States. A religious sect may degenerate into a political faction in a part of the Confederacy; but the variety of sects dispersed over the entire face of it must secure the national councils against any danger from that source. A rage for paper money, for an abolition of debts, for an equal division of property, or for any other improper or wicked project, will be less apt to pervade the whole body of the Union than a particular member of it.

Small republics in the past had suffered from political instability not because they were republics, but because their comparatively small number of people made it difficult to keep them from tending toward "pure democracies" where insufficient checks upon popular vagaries soon led to the single alternative of tyranny. Even the republican constitutions of the new American states, whose "valuable improvements . . . on the popular models, both ancient and modern," Madison conceded, "cannot certainly be too much admired," had not "effectually obviated the danger on this side as was wished and expected." At the same time, the comparatively small number of interests in small states made it easier for them to combine against the public interest. But a sovereign republican government resting upon an extensive territory, a large population, and a great variety of interests, could risk popular liberties because it contained within itself all the necessary "checks and balances." Persons, classes, and interests all would be free to contend; none would become powerful enough to domineer.

The concept of offsetting interests in *politics* was as old as Aristotle. In the eighteenth century, it gained great force as an instrument of *government* through the works of the French philosopher of the Enlightenment, Montesquieu. True to the mechanistic spirit of the age, Montesquieu offered along with classical political propositions modern means of applying them. His most powerful instrument, of which we have spoken in connection with the constitutions of the new American states (see p. 219), was the system of checks and balances both among the segments of society and also the functions of government.

In America, as in England, Montesquieu's favorite model, three separate functions of government commonly were distinguished in political treatises: the executive, the legislative, and the judicial. If the three agencies performing these functions could be made equal in power and sufficiently independent of one another, they would, it was believed, offset the ambitions of each in such a way as to prevent any one from tyrannizing over all. John Adams stated the argument succinctly:

A legislative, an executive, and a judicial power comprehend the whole of what is meant and understood by government. It is by balancing each of these powers against the other two, that the efforts of human nature toward tyranny can alone be checked and restrained, and any degree of freedom preserved in the constitution.

American practice and American conditions offered the delegates still another opportunity to introduce balance into the new national government, which they grasped. In the provincial and state legislatures, the lower house usually served as the "democratical branch" elected by a broad suffrage. In the new national legislature, most delegates agreed, there must also be two houses, the "democratical" one to check and in turn be checked by a second, representing the wealthier and more aristocratic elements. John Adams declared that there could be "no free government without a democratical branch in the constitution"; and most fearful though the delegates almost uniformly were of "pure democracy," no one, not even Hamilton, would contradict him. A few delegates feared that a two-house legislature, by pulling in opposite directions, would be incapable of effective action. But advocates of bicameralism pointed out that a strong and independent executive could prevent this. Some delegates, in turn, worried about creating a single strong executive—Edmund Randolph declared that such a position would be a "foetus of monarchy." But others, among them Gouverneur Morris, envisaged the President as "the guardian of the people, even of the lower classes, against legislative tyranny; against the great and wealthy who in the course of things will necessarily compose the legislative body."

John Adams felicitously expressed the spirit of the age of the Framers when he observed that, "the blessings of society depend entirely on the constitutions of government." Buoyed up by that faith, the delegates in the Great Convention, often sorely tried by controversy, managed to balance out all contending claims and complete their great instrument.

### COMPROMISE IN THE CONVENTION

Although the delegates were largely in agreement on their basic aims and general philosophy, they nevertheless were quickly confronted by certain issues that almost wrecked the Convention. One of these had to do with the relative power of large and small states.

Once the delegates had agreed to go beyond the idea of amending the Articles they took up Edmund Randolph's so-called "Virginia Plan" for a new government structure especially attractive to the large states. Randolph proposed a two-house "National Legislature" with membership in both houses allotted among the states in proportion to their free population. Members of the upper house were to be elected by the members of the lower, who were themselves to be elected by the people. The whole "National Legislature" was then to elect the "National Executive" and the "National Judiciary." A council of revision, made up of the executive and some members of the judiciary, would have the power to veto acts that had been passed by the legislature.

This proposal, by violating the principle of the separation of powers, for the government would derive all its authority from a single base, a popularly elected lower house, aroused general disapproval. It particularly alarmed delegates from the small states, who feared that their commonwealths would be overwhelmed in the popularly elected house, and that some of them might get no representatives at all in the second house. Thus they insisted that all the states have *equal* representation in the legislature rather than

252

*proportional* representation. To gain their objective, the small states promptly offered a plan of their own, presented to the Convention by Paterson of New Jersey and known since as the "New Jersey Plan." According to this proposal Congress would remain a single house, as under the Articles, where all states, large and small alike, would continue to have but one vote apiece. The delegates rejected this futile proposal and took the Virginia Plan as their preliminary model from which to construct the final document.

The debate on the issue of state representation and hence state strength in the new Congress grew long and sharp in the hot Philadelphia summer. A climax was reached on June 30, when Gunning Bedford of Delaware made a violent and accusatory speech against the large states. Near the end of his attack he made this "warm & rash" declaration: "The large states dare not dissolve the Confederation. If they do, the small ones will find some foreign ally, of more honor and good faith, who will take them by the hand, and do them justice." The small-state delegates, in fact, were on the verge of going home and disrupting the entire Convention; and the large states, if the influential James Wilson of the large state of Pennsylvania is to be credited, were not unwilling for them to do so. In reply to Bedford, Wilson said: "A separation to the north of Pennsylvania . . . neither staggers me in my sentiments or my duty. If a minority should refuse their assent to the new plan of a general government, and if they will have their own will, and without it, separate the union, let it be done."

On July 2, cooler heads succeeded in getting a "grand committee" appointed to review the issue, Elbridge Gerry of Massachusetts being named chairman; and on July 5 this committee offered the Convention a compromise scheme devised largely by Franklin: There would be a two-house legislature, with membership in the lower house apportioned according to population, thus satisfying the large states, and with membership in the upper house equal for all states, thus satisfying the

small ones. This arrangement, adopted only after much further argument, provided the basis for the "Great Compromise" of the Constitution and determined the general character of the two bodies that soon came to be called the House of Representatives and the Senate.

The two-house plan enabled the delegates to establish the lower house as the people's branch. The members of this house were to be elected by all voters in each state who were eligible to vote for "the most numerous branch of the State Legislature." The upper house, whose members were to be chosen, more restrictively, by the state legislatures, was expected to be more friendly to property and more conservative in other ways.

With the Great Compromise, one issue that might have broken up the Convention had been settled, but the settlement quickly spawned two new issues which divided the free and slave states. Conflict over these issues, as over the earlier one between the large and small states, soon found sectional rivals among the delegates threatening to go home.

After Gerry's special committee offered the Great Compromise, the main body of the Convention agreed that the "direct taxes" the new government would be given the power to levy were to be apportioned among the states according to their population, just as representation was to be apportioned in the lower house. This decision led the slave South to demand that Negro slaves in the population, if they were counted at all in apportioning taxes, be given less weight than free men. The North wanted Negroes to be given less weight only in apportioning representation in the House of Representatives. Some leaders wanted them to be given no weight. Rufus King of Massachusetts, for example, told the delegates that, "in fixing numbers as the rule of representation . . . he thought the admission of [blacks] . . . along with Whites at all, would excite great discontents among the States having no slaves." In the debate, the proportion "three-fifths" was proposed many times. But Wilson of Pennsylvania "did not well see on what principle the admission of blacks in the proportion of three-fifths could be explained. Are they admitted as Citizens? Then why are they not admitted on an equality with White Citizens? Are they admitted as property? Then why is not other property admitted into the computation?" At the same time, strong southern spokesmen demanded that blacks and whites be given equal consideration, but on terms that few blacks would have admired. Pierce Butler of South Carolina, for example, "insisted that the labour of a slave in S. Carola was as productive & valuable as that of a freeman in Massts. . . . and that consequently an equal representation ought to be allowed for them in a Government which was instituted principally for the protection of property, and was itself to be supported by property."

Rufus King acknowledged that "he had never said . . . that he would in no event acquiesce in & support" the three-fifth rule for representation as well as taxes; and Wilson also talked of "the necessity of compromise." Some southerners, like Mason of Virginia, also thought Butler's demands "unjust," but that slaves "ought not to be excluded from the estimate of Representation" altogether. The upshot was a second compromise, the so-called "three-fifths compromise," which specified that both for direct taxes and for representation five Negroes were to be counted as equivalent to three whites.

In arguing for ratification of the Constitution in *Federalist* Number 54, Madison urged that "the compromising expedient of the Constitution be . . . adopted, which regards [the slaves] as inhabitants, but as debased by servitude below the equal level of free inhabitants; which regards the *slave* as divested of two-fifths of the *man*." This, Madison privately believed, was precisely what was so evil in slavery; but the Constitutional Convention could not have survived an attack on the "peculiar case" of the blacks, nor even one on the slave trade. Gouverneur Morris of Pennsylvania said "he did not believe that those [Southern] States would ever confederate on terms that would deprive them of that trade." Rutledge of South Carolina agreed: "The true question," he told the delegates, "is whether the Southn. States shall or shall not be parties to the Union. If the Northern States consult their interest, they will not oppose the increase of Slaves which will increase the commodities of which they will become the carriers."

Yet the slave trade, even though many slaveholders detested it, did arise as an issue and again stretched the compromising ingenuity of the Convention.

Delegates from the commercial North had urged that the new government be granted full power to regulate interstate and foreign commerce and to make treaties which the states must obey. The Convention readily agreed on these points. But the South, fearful of being outvoted in the new Congress, demanded that commercial regulations and all treaties require the consent of a two-thirds majority of the Senate rather than a simple majority. The southerners were particularly concerned about taxes on exports, for they were heavily dependent on selling tobacco and other staples in competitive world markets. They were also worried lest Congress, after the Convention, tamper with the importation of slaves.

To allay these fears, the Convention negotiated its third major compromise. To conciliate the South, the Constitution prohibited all taxes on exports; it also guaranteed that for at least 20 years there would be no ban on "the migration" or importation of such persons as any of the states now existing shall think proper to admit;" and that any "person held to service or labor in one State . . . escaping into another, . . . shall be delivered up on the claim of the party to whom such service or labor may be due." By these provisions, prohibition of the slave trade was delayed and slaves seeking freedom were frustrated, even though many delegates hated slavery sufficiently, in the words of Paterson of New Jersey, to have "been ashamed to use the term 'Slaves' & had substituted a description." "The

254

thing," as Lincoln said later, "is hid away in the Constitution, just as an afflicted man hides away a wen or cancer which he dares not cut out at once, lest he bleed to death." Finally, the South won the provision requiring a two-thirds vote in the Senate for the ratification of all treaties. In exchange for these concessions, northerners won their point on a simple congressional majority for acts regulating commerce.

A final issue, the Presidency, although less controversial than the representation issue, was compromised only after extended debate. How was the President to be elected—by direct popular vote, by the state legislatures, by the federal legislature, or by the state executives? How long should his term be? Some said as few as three years, others as many as 15. A few agreed with Hamilton on life tenure during good behavior.

James Wilson favored the election of the President by popular vote, but the Convention's suspicion of democracy killed this suggestion. Still the delegates found it easier to arrive at a negative decision—that the President was *not* to be elected by a direct popular vote—than to determine just what sort of indirect election procedure should be followed. Here the jealousies of large and small states once again came into play, for if the number of a state's presidential electors were determined by population, the large states would hold the advantage. Finally, the delegates turned this question over to another special committee, whose recommendations they accepted with only minor changes. In a manner to be decided by its own legislature, each state was to choose a number of presidential electors equal to the number of its senators and representatives. These electors (who would make up the "electoral college") might be chosen by popular vote or by the state legislature alone—the procedure followed by most of the states. The electors, meeting in their own states, would vote for two persons, at least one of them from another state. The person having the largest number of votes

would become President, if these votes constituted a majority; and the person having the next-largest number would become Vice-president.

Thus far, the method of election favored the large states. But the delegates, believing that the electors in each state would normally vote first for citizens of their state, expected that no candidate would receive the required majority of the ballots. In that case, or in case two candidates, each with a majority, were tied, they stipulated that the election be decided in the House of Representatives where each state, regardless of population, would cast but one vote. This gave the small states equal standing with the large in ultimately choosing the President from among candidates whom the large states, because of their preponderance of votes in the electoral college, would in effect nominate.

This complex scheme was based on the assumption that each state would constitute its own party. But the emergence of national parties early in American history nullified the Framers' elaborate machinery. The two-party system eventually made it possible for voters throughout the country to choose electors pledged to one of a few leading candidates. While such electors retained the privilege of exercising personal choice in the electoral college, their party affiliation usually obliged them to, vote for the party nominees. Only in two elections has the original electoral plan ever been brought into full play—in 1800, when Jefferson and Burr were tied in the electoral college; and in 1824, when no candidate won a majority in the electoral college.

### AGREEMENT IN THE CONVENTION

Although the delegates in Philadelphia spent much time resolving very sharp differences among themselves, their states, and their sections, they remained in substantial accord on many issues and objectives, as their common political faith would lead one to suppose.

But more than this faith alone, they shared other attributes that made agreement easier. Nearly all were well-to-do and some were very rich; the ordinary town laborer, farmer, frontiersman, or angry debtor found few spokesmen among these worthies. Most of them are known to have held public securities a few years after the Convention, testimony, no doubt, to their confidence in the lasting strength of their work there. Many of them undoubtedly held such securities while the Convention was in progress, testimony also to their interest in doing their work well. By and large, they were private as well as public creditors, with money out on loan to individual and business borrowers; and holders of private as well as public securities, typically in land companies or commercial enterprises. At least 15 were slave-owners, usually large ones. It is not surprising, therefore, to find them showing a greater degree of harmony on the economic clauses of the Constitution even than on most political clauses.

Every delegate but Gerry of Massachusetts, for example, voted to give the new national government the power to collect taxes and tariffs. The clause granting Congress the power to pay the debts of the United States passed unanimously. Ten states of the 11 voting supported the provision that all debts incurred "before the adoption of this Constitution shall be as valid against the United States under this Constitution as under the Confederation." No one opposed giving Congress the power to coin money and "regulate the value thereof," nor the power to borrow money on the credit of the United States, nor the power to regulate commerce among the states or with foreign nations and Indian tribes.

James Madison once said that even more than the weaknesses of the Confederation Congress, the "mutability of the laws of the states" deepened the discontents that led eventually to the Great Convention. Madison had most particularly in mind state laws that made credit more risky, investment more hazardous, long-term business planning more dubious—the principal culprit in all instances being state issues of paper money. One could hardly overstate, he said, "the loss which America has sustained since the peace from the pestilent effects of paper money on the necessary confidence between man and man, on the necessary confidence in the public councils, on the industry and morals of the people, and on the character of republican government." The delegates so strongly subscribed to Madison's analysis that almost without demur they forbade the states to issue "bills of credit," that is, paper money; to make anything but gold and silver legal tender for the payment of private or public debts; to interfere with the obligations of contracts; to tax imports or exports in commercial wars with one another.

The delegates went further still, to reassure the business community. Beyond the sovereign power of the purse, they gave the new government the sovereign power of the sword: to "provide for the common defence"; "to declare war"; "to raise and support armies"; "to provide and maintain a navy"; "to provide for calling forth the militia to execute the laws of the Union, suppress insurrections and repel invasions."

For the special benefit of those who had been so alarmed by Shays' Rebellion, Hamilton devoted a large part of *Federalist* Number 9 to arguing the "utility" of a strong federal republic, "as well to suppress faction and to guard the internal tranquility of the States, as to increase their external force and security." For protecting domestic property and maintaining internal peace, the militia and the army would serve. As for the economic and other national advantages of "external force," he devoted most of *Federalist* Number 11 to arguing the tremendous value of a navy.

"If we mean to be a commercial people," Hamilton wrote, "or ever to be secure on our Atlantic side, we must endeavor, as soon as possible, to have a navy." No individual state could afford a navy of its own. But a federal union could weld into a respectable fleet the tar, wood, pitch, and turpentine of the southern states, the iron of the Middle states, and the seamen and craftsmen of New England. Such a fleet may not at first "vie with those of the great maritime powers [but] would at least be of respectable weight, if thrown into the scale of either of two contending parties." Hamilton continued:

This would be more particularly the case in relation to operations in the West-Indies. A few ships of the line sent opportunely to the reinforcement of either side, would often be sufficient to decide the fate of a campaign, on the event of which interests of the greatest magnitude were suspended. Our position is in this respect a very commanding one. And if to this consideration we add that of the usefulness of supplies from this country, in the prosecution of military operations in the West-Indies, it will readily be perceived that a situation so favorable would enable us to bargain with great advantage for commercial privileges. A price would be set not only upon our friendship, but upon our neutrality. By a steady adherence to the Union, we may hope ere long to become the Arbiter of Europe in America, and to be able to incline the balance of European competitions in this part of the world as our interest may dictate.

A disunited people, Hamilton warned, could not hope to grasp such advantages; and the longer unity was postponed, the weaker hope would grow.

## III  *A Federal Form of Government*

### THE STATES IN THE SOVEREIGN REPUBLIC

The solution to the problem of power embodied in the Constitution endowed the new central government with supreme power in the areas delegated to it:

This Constitution, and the laws of the United States, which shall be made in pursuance thereof; and all treaties made, or which shall be made, under the authority of the United States, shall be the supreme law of the land; and the Judges in every State shall be bound thereby, anything in the Constitution or laws of any State to the contrary notwithstanding. [Article VI, section 2]

The solution of the problem of federalism, at the same time, reserved many fundamental public functions for the states. They, not the central government, for example, retained almost unlimited "police power" to protect and foster the health and safety of their citizens. Municipal and local governments continued to operate only under state charters or other state grants of power. The control of education and the chartering of corporations remained almost exclusively state domains, as did the regulation of labor organizations and working conditions. The formation and administration of civil and criminal law codes also remained state prerogatives.

As if the specifications in the original draft of the Constitution were not clear enough, the Tenth Amendment, which went into effect at the end of 1791, declared: "The powers not delegated to the United States by the Constitution, nor prohibited by it to the States, are reserved to the States respectively, or to the people."

In spite of the Constitution and the Tenth Amendment, the states and the central government have battled for nearly 200 years over alleged encroachments on one another's spheres. Indeed, the history of the Supreme Court has been largely the history of repeated attempts to define their respective areas of authority. The Constitution, nevertheless, by granting the new central government sovereign powers over the purse and the sword and related subjects in domestic and international life, helped limit the range of state and national conflicts and interposed a counterweight to destructive rivalries among the states and to the authority of each over its own citizens.

## SAFEGUARDS
## AGAINST FEDERAL TYRANNY

While granting the central government sovereign powers in specific areas, the Framers carefully provided safeguards against the misuse of those powers by any person, interest, or single branch of government. Before a law could be passed, for example, the Constitution required that it be approved by both houses of Congress and signed by the President. All revenue bills, moreover, must originate in the House of Representatives exclusively, where members representing the broadest electorate would thus have the strongest check on the vital power to spend money. The power of the judiciary, in turn, to validate or void as unconstitutional acts passed by the legislature and signed by the executive was soon to be clarified and strengthened (see p. 317).

The strong single executive prescribed by the Constitution in place of the Confederation's executive committee, while endowed with formidable powers, was also checked by Congress as well as by the courts. The executive, or President, could veto as well as approve congressional measures, for example, but a two-thirds vote in both houses of Congress could override his vetoes. While empowered to negotiate treaties, the President could not put them into effect until confirmed by two-thirds of the Senate; and if money were needed to enforce them, he had, in addition, to seek appropriations from the House of Representatives. Under the Constitution, the President may call Congress into special session, but he may not adjourn it except in the case of a disagreement on adjournment between the Senate and the House (this has never happened). The Constitution empowered him to appoint his own advisors and administrators and other major officers such as ambassadors, ministers, and Supreme Court justices, but only "with the advice and consent of the Senate." (The power of removing such appointees, although not mentioned in the Constitution, was later adjudged to be included, and without approval of the Senate. As federal activities grew more numerous—and more costly, the need for administrative funds in addition to those for treaties grew greater, thereby making the executive increasingly dependent upon House willingness to supply money.

All these manifestations of the principle of the separation of powers must have reassured many of the skeptics that the new Constitution would not be used as an instrument of tyranny. And yet we may wonder how effectively the new government would have worked had there not developed a two-party system to give force and direction to its powers. One of the most persistent criticisms of the Constitution held that it separated the powers of the President and Congress all too much, and that by emphasizing mutual checks rather than mutual cooperation it made effective presidential leadership too difficult to attain. But the national party system soon quieted such fears.

The Framers usually thought of political parties not as useful agencies of constitutional government but as the source of mischief and danger. Madison spent a large part of the *Federalist* Number 10 discussing what he called "the violence of faction"—by which he meant the random, shifting alliances for temporary purposes, which in the states reflected the turbulence of pure democracy he and his colleagues detested, or the machinations of sordid interests they deplored. It was natural, then, for them to think of political parties as a nuisance if not, in fact, as a menace. Yet the emergence of the American two-party system eventually made possible the development of responsible majority coalitions capable of governing effectively by reducing the likelihood of the President and Congress paralyzing each other. The rise of the national party system also helped stimulate interest in national as against merely factional issues, thereby affording national leaders a groundswell of national support and a sense of general consent.

### JUDICIAL REVIEW

The power of "judicial review"—that is, the right of the courts to declare legislative acts unconstitutional—is not even mentioned in the Constitution, and scholars disagree about whether the delegates at Philadelphia meant the courts to exercise it, and if so to what extent. Article VI, paragraph 2, as we have seen (p. 256), declares only that the federal Constitution and the laws and treaties made under its authority are "the supreme law of the land," and that state judges must hold the Constitution superior to their state constitutions and laws. Had state judges not been required to do this, or if the national Supreme Court had refused to reject state laws, and even provisions of state constitutions, found to be at odds with the federal Constitution, the Union would surely have fallen to pieces.

A more spirited argument has grown up over whether the delegates intended to empower the Supreme Court to declare acts of the *national Congress* unconstitutional. If they meant to do so, it has been asked, why did they not spell out that power in clear terms? American political theorists at the time were quite familiar with the idea that legislative acts contrary to a constitution or to fundamental law should be regarded as void. Before the Revolution, when James Otis denounced writs of assistance, he asserted that an act of Parliament authorizing such writs was void because it violated "natural equity" and the unwritten British constitution. Moreover, the Privy Council in London frequently had "disallowed" particular acts of colonial legislatures—a procedure similar to judicial review. A few colonial cases, notably that of *Trevett* v. *Weeden* (see p. 238), may also have served as precedents in the thinking of some of the delegates.

Even though the Constitution is silent on the subject, the issue was discussed in the Convention where it seems to have provoked little debate. The Virginia Plan had proposed a "council of revision," composed of members from the executive and judicial departments and empowered to veto acts of Congress. But in the end the veto power was granted to the President alone. During the discussion, some delegates who opposed a presidential veto made it plain that they expected the Supreme Court to exercise the power of judicial review, and saw no reason for still another check.

In the debates over ratification as well, the leading advocates of the Constitution declared that they expected judicial review to be exercised by the Court over acts of Congress. Hamilton bluntly stated in *Federalist* Number 78 that he expected the judiciary to throw out acts of "the legislative body" when those acts were at variance with the Constitution. Otherwise, he argued, the whole idea of a fundamental law would be meaningless:

No legislative act, therefore, contrary to the Constitution, can be valid. To deny this would be to affirm, that the deputy is greater than his principal; that the servant is above his master; that the representatives of the people are superior to the people themselves.

Still more emphatic was young John Marshall's statement to the Virginia ratifying Convention:

If they [the legislature] were to make a law not warranted by any of the powers enumerated, it would be considered by the judges as an infringement of the Constitution which they are to guard. They would not consider such a law as coming under their jurisdiction. They would declare it void.

When Marshall became Chief Justice in 1801, he firmly established this power in the Supreme Court (see p. 318).

Over the years most American have shown an attitude of veneration toward the Supreme Court, which made the severe criticisms of the Court from time to time all the more telling. Of all the criticisms of the American constitutional system itself, one of the most cogent has been that the extraordinary powers enjoyed by the Court are undemocratic. The

Court is simply a body of nine men (the number has varied from time to time), usually elderly and out of sympathy with the current generation, holding virtual life tenure, with the power to strike down laws, no matter how overwhelmingly endorsed by Congress, no matter how willingly signed by the President, no matter how enthusiastically supported by the people. The Court decides on the meaning of the Constitution itself, and determines whether the laws passed by Congress fit its language. Charles Evans Hughes, a former Chief Justice, once said: "We are under a Constitution, but the Constitution is what the judges says it is." In the administrations of Jefferson, Jackson, Buchanan, and Lincoln in the nineteenth century and in most administrations of the twentieth century, many people denounced the Court's sweeping use of the power of judicial review. Yet in 1937 when Franklin D. Roosevelt tried to transform the character of the Court in response to changing times, he suffered one of his worst political defeats which since then has served to remind later Presidents of the great risk in laying hands on this sanctified body.

**A FLEXIBLE INSTRUMENT**

"The government we mean to erect," said Madison, "is intended to last for ages." One of the sources of the government's longevity under the Constitution is that document's remarkable flexibility. One of the sources of this flexibility, in turn, is the process by which the Constitution may be amended. The futility of trying to amend the Articles by the required unanimous consent of the states had hastened their demise. The easier amending process in the Constitution (Article V*) was at first

* The only place where the Constitution retained the requirement of unanimity for amending it was in the provision at the end of Article V, that "no State, without its consent, shall be deprived of its equal suffrage in the Senate," a stipulation that clearly gave any single state a veto on altering the Constitution in this respect. This limitation gained greater significance after the Supreme Court's epochal enunciation in 1964 of the "one man,

sparingly used—but only after the promised first ten amendments constituting the much-desired federal Bill of Rights had been adopted (see p. 271). Patrick Henry had opposed the movement for the Constitution and fought its ratification in Virginia. Once he had lost this fight, the amending process alone reconciled him to the new system. "I will be a peaceable citizen," he said. "My head, my hand, and my heart shall be at liberty to retrieve the loss of liberty, and remove the defects of that system in a constitutional way."

A second, somewhat less tangible source of the Constitution's long life lies in the general terms in which the document is written—no accident, but a result of the Framers' classical training and universal way of thinking. Statesmanship required that they leave important powers to the jealous states. Having done this, they wrote down the prerogatives of the sovereign national government so broadly that essential powers could be retrieved when changes in national life made it imperative that they be exercised on the national level. The Constitution is an extremely brief document to have been successfully applied to the government of a vast continent during almost two centuries of unprecedentedly rapid social change. It would have been neither so brief nor so successful had its framers tried to spell out the meaning of all its difficult phrases, instead of leaving them to be reinterpreted by future generations in response to future needs.

One of the flexible clauses of the Constitution gives Congress power "to regulate commerce with foreign nations, and among the several States, and with the Indian tribes." How widely should the word "commerce" be construed? Does it mean merely buying and selling, or does it encompass a wide range of activities? Precisely what did Congress have

one vote" rule to validate the constitutional guarantee to all citizens, under the Fourteenth Amendment, of "equal protection of the laws." This Amendment, like the Court's decision, referred only to the state legislatures, but its philosophy clearly was suggestive in relation to the United States Senate as well.

the power to do when it undertook to "regulate"? How much latitude did the phrase "among the several States" give Congress in regulating the interior traffic of a state? Over the years, these questions have given the Supreme Court a great deal of business, and have presented it with some knotty questions differently answered at different times.

Other flexible provisions include the famous "elastic clause," giving Congress the power to make "all laws which shall be necessary and proper" to carry out its enumerated powers—an extremely broad grant of authority; and the "general welfare" clause, giving Congress the power to "provide . . . for the the general welfare," but which does not say how broadly "the general welfare" may be interpreted.

Further flexibility has sprung from the delegates' decision to say nothing at all in the Constitution about several important problems, even though they were discussed in the Convention. Robert L. Schuyler writes of what he calls "the silences of the Constitution":

Had it [the Constitution] been more explicit in all cases, had the intent of the framers been always clearly expressed, had it borne on its face clearer evidence of the economic struggle through which it was established, it could not have been so readily appealed to and cherished by both parties. The Constitution makes no mention of a number of matters that were considered in the Philadelphia Convention and that later became subjects of acute party conflict—the assumption of state debts, for example, and the establishment of a national bank. When, therefore, assumption and the bank came up as party measures under the Constitution it was possible alike for those who advocated and those who opposed them, while bitterly contending with one another, to appeal to the same document in defence of their respective positions. Again, the large majority of the framers were certainly opposed to universal manhood suffrage, but their attitude toward it was not betrayed in the document which they drafted. Aristocrats and democrats could both stand on the broad bottom of the Constitution.

Institutional as well as verbal innovations not contemplated by the Constitution also helped preserve it for the ages by strengthening the government it designed. One of the most important of these, as we have said (p. 254), is the two-party political system that tends to sponge up a host of divisive issues. Others included the enlargement of the role of the Cabinet and the strength it added to the administrative powers of the executive; the committee system in the House and Senate, which, though often obstructive, nevertheless gave order and insight to legislation; and the bureaucratic civil service, which preserved professional continuity (sometimes, indeed, against the public wish, if not the public interest) in spite of the frequency of elections and changes of political chiefs.

### THE CONVENTION'S ACHIEVEMENT

The Constitutional Convention, for all its conservatism, set up what was surely by world-wide standards a radical government—a republic among oppressive monarchies, a democratic nation among aristocracies. "It is *essential* to such a government," Madison had written, "that it be derived from the great body of the society, not from an inconsiderable proportion, or a favored class of it." Under the Constitution, said John Marshall, who rose as a new leader during the ratification controversy in Virginia, "it is the people that give power, and can take it back. What shall restrain them? They are the masters who give it, and of whom their servants hold it."

Moreover, for all its stress on private property, which, in the eighteenth century was thought to be the best foundation for public responsibility, the Constitution stipulated no property qualification for office, not even that of President. It also required "a compensation —to be ascertained by law, and paid out of the Treasury of the United States" for all elective posts, so that men need not be rich to hold them. In the instrument itself, even before the Bill of Rights was appended, the Constitution forbade religious tests for any federal position. It provided that "for any speech or debate in either House," senators and representatives "shall not be questioned in any other place," thereby assuring their fullest freedom of expression. It also guaranteed trial by jury for all crimes, "except in cases of impeachment"; and forbade suspension of "the privilege of the writ of habeas corpus" except in times of invasion or rebellion.

The Founding Fathers were too wise to regard their handiwork as perfect, but they were also too wise to expect perfection. Near the close of the Convention, Franklin expressed his views in a little address that was read for him by James Wilson. "I confess," he declared, "that there are several parts of this constitution which I do not at present approve." But he added that he was not sure that he would *never* approve them. He had lived a long time and had already changed his mind on many things. "The older I grow, the more apt I am to doubt my own judgment, and to pay more respect to the judgment of others." When men sat down to make laws or constitutions, he said, they brought with them all their prejudices, passions, errors, local interests, and selfish views. "It therefore astonishes me, Sir," he concluded, in words addressed to Washington in the chair, "to find this system approaching so near to perfection as it does. . . . Thus I consent, Sir, to this Constitution, because I expect no better, and because I am not sure that it is not the best. The opinions I have had of its errors, I sacrifice to the public good."

## IV  *Persuading the People*

### RATIFICATION

The Constitutional Convention sat from May 25 to September 16, 1787. Of the 55 delegates who took some part in the deliberations, 42 stayed to the end, and 39 signed the document. The other three, Gerry of Massachusetts and Randolph and Mason of Virginia,

refused to go along, their reasons accumulating as the sessions drew out. These refusals gave warning of the battle ahead when the Constitution would be offered to "we the people" for approval. But the signers were not to be diverted from their course by fear. The day after the Convention adopted the Constitution, a copy was sent to Congress, largely out of courtesy, and with a letter that did not mince words. "In all our deliberations on this subject," said the signers, "we kept steadily in our view that which appeared to us the greatest interest of every true American—the consolidation of the Union—in which is involved our prosperity, felicity, safety, perhaps our national existence." They petitioned Congress for no vote. Nor would they apply to the state legislatures for confirmation. In keeping with their revulsion from existing governments, in the Constitution itself they asked only the assent of nine special conventions like their own.

While the election of delegates to these conventions was in progress, people throughout the country discussed and debated the Constitution. Its opponents revived the old suspicion of centralization, and with it the fear of governmental power overriding personal freedom. A rural delegate to the Massachusetts ratifying convention put this in plain words:

These lawyers, and men of learning, and moneyed men, that talk so finely, and gloss over matters so smoothly, to make us poor, illiterate people swallow down the pill, expect to get into Congress themselves; they expect to be managers of this Constitution, and get all the power and all the money into their own hands, and then they will swallow up all us little folks, like the great leviathan, Mr. President; yes, just as the whale swallowed up Jonah. This is what I am afraid of.

Rufus King, a member of the same convention, summed up the feelings of the opposition, though he did not share them, in a letter to James Madison in January 1788: "An apprehension that the liberties of the people are in danger, and a distrust of men of property

and education have a more powerful effect upon the minds of our opponents than any specific objections against the Constitution."

But the Constitution's critics, named "Antifederalists" by the Constitution's friends, did offer plenty of specific objections: There was no bill of rights; state sovereignty would be destroyed; the President might become king; the standing army would be everywhere; only the rich and well-born could afford to hold office; tax collectors would swarm over the countryside; the people could not bear to be taxed by both state and national governments; commercial treaties would sell out the West and the South; debtors would no longer be able to defend themselves through recourse to state paper money and state stay laws. In

March 1787 George Washington had remarked that "A thirst for power [has] taken fast hold of the states individually; . . . the many whose personal consequence in the control of state politics will be annihilated [by a national government] will form a strong phalanx against it." But it was not merely local lions who felt themselves menaced by the proposal. Many honest citizens shrank from so drastic an innovation.

Ratification, nevertheless, started out smoothly enough. Between December 7, 1787, and January 9, 1788, five states approved the Constitution, three of them (Delaware, New Jersey, and Georgia) without a single opposing vote. A fourth state, Connecticut, ratified by 128 to 40. In Pennsylvania alone among the first five, controversy flared up. By staying away, opponents of the Constitution tried to prevent the legislature from obtaining the quorum needed to vote on the call for the ratifying convention. The Federalists responded with strong-arm tactics, forcibly dragging enough of the laggards into the chamber to make up the quorum. In the Pennsylvania ratifying convention itself the Federalists won handily, 46 to 23.

In Massachusetts, the sixth state to ratify, the convention debated the Constitution from early January to early February without result, until Federalist leaders, playing upon their vanity, ingeniously won over such popular opponents as John Hancock and Sam Adams, and placated others by promising to support amendments in the new Congress guaranteeing popular liberties. Yet the Constitution barely squeaked through, 187 to 168.

Maryland and South Carolina ratified with little conflict. In New Hampshire, the Antifederalists proved strong enough to prevent a vote in the first convention, and in the second, on June 21, 1788, to hold the margin of approval to 57 to 46. By this margin New Hampshire became the ninth state to ratify, and technically the new government could now be organized. No one believed, however, that it could function without Virginia and New York, where the outcome remained very doubtful.

In the Virginia convention, in an extraordinarily brilliant examination of the Constitution during which every implication of the new document was sifted "clause by clause," the scholarly George Mason and the inflammatory Patrick Henry led the opposition. Washington's influence and the knowledge that he would consent to serve as first President was responsible for the unexpected conversion of Edmund Randolph, who had refused to sign the Constitution in Philadelphia. These gains and the promised addition of a bill of rights eventually softened the opposition, permitting Virginia to fall in line, 89 to 79, four days after New Hampshire.

By arrangement between Madison and Hamilton, couriers promptly carried the good news from Virginia to New York, where Hamilton and fellow Federalists were engaged with an embattled opposition led by Governor George Clinton, along with the disenchanted Great Convention delegates, Lansing and Yates. Well aware of Clinton's strength, Hamilton, assisted on a few occasions by John

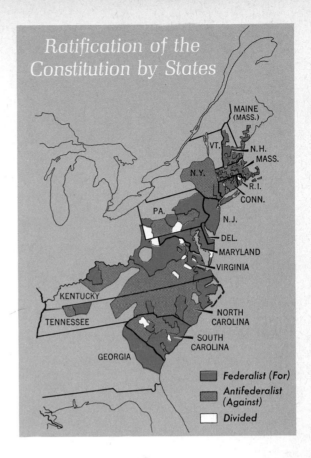

Ratification of the Constitution by States

MAINE (MASS.)
VT.
N.H.
MASS.
N.Y.
R.I.
CONN.
PA.
N.J.
DEL.
MARYLAND
VIRGINIA
KENTUCKY
TENNESSEE
NORTH CAROLINA
SOUTH CAROLINA
GEORGIA

■ Federalist (For)
■ Antifederalist (Against)
□ Divided

Jay and more elaborately by Madison, had begun as early as October 1787 to write those articles in the press in support of the Constitution, later published as *The Federalist,* by far the best commentary on the Constitution by its contemporary advocates. Persuasive as they were and indeed still remain, the *Federalist* papers proved less important in shaping the vote in the hard-nosed New York convention than the news from New Hampshire and Virginia. The success of the Constitution in the first of these states changed the issue from helping to form a new union to joining one that seemed almost certain to be established. The success in the second left New York as the single great state still outside the fold. Once again, the promise of amendments constituting a bill of rights also overcame some opposition. Having agreed to support such amendments, the Federalists barely won at last on July 26, 1788, by 30 to 27.

263

264

So hostile were Rhode Island and North Carolina to the Constitution, they did not join the Union until the new government was in operation. North Carolina, by a wide margin, ratified the Constitution in November 1789, Rhode Island waited until May 1790, when Congress considered placing her on the footing of a foreign nation. Even then she decided to enter only by the narrowest vote.

The bills of rights in the first state constitutions, as we have seen (p. 216), gave the

*(Right) Title page of* The Federalist *in its first collected version published in 1788. (New York Public Library.)*

*(Below) Narrow though their victory was, New York City's Federalists were so certain of victory in the ratifying convention that they celebrated it three days before the event with a banquet at this grand pavilion seating 6000 persons. (Courtesy of the New-York Historical Society, New York City.)*

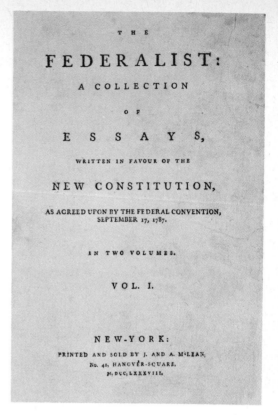

THE

# FEDERALIST:

A COLLECTION

OF

# ESSAYS,

WRITTEN IN FAVOUR OF THE

## NEW CONSTITUTION,

AS AGREED UPON BY THE FEDERAL CONVENTION,
SEPTEMBER 17, 1787.

IN TWO VOLUMES.

### VOL. I.

### NEW-YORK:

PRINTED AND SOLD BY J. AND A. McLEAN,
No. 41, HANOVER-SQUARE,
M,DCC,LXXXVIII.

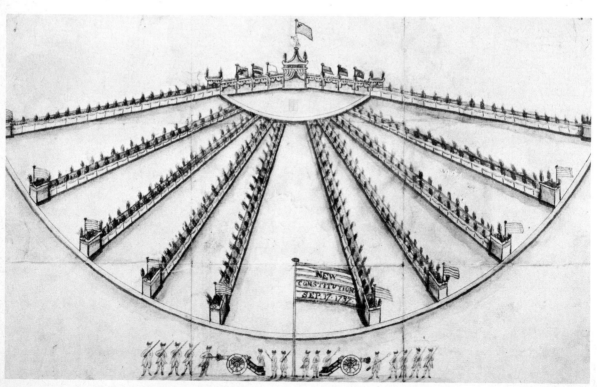

people the strongest and most enduring guarantees of their liberties against encroachment even by their own chosen governments. Why, then, was there no bill of rights in the new federal Constitution to assure freedom of religion, speech, and the press, security against unreasonable searches and seizures and excessive bail, and to guarantee life, liberty, and property through due process of law? This became the hardest question for the Federalists to answer. In the Convention a bill of rights had been suggested by George Mason, but only near the very end. By then most delegates seem to have agreed with Roger Sherman, who felt that no federal bill of rights was needed because those in the state constitutions adequately protected the people, all of whom remained citizens of their respective states, not of the Union. After all, there had been no bill of rights in the Articles of Confederation. These delegates appear to have underestimated the strong new centralizing tendency of their own document, and the strong new fears it aroused.

It may fairly be said that without the promise of such guarantees once the new national government was elected, the federal Constitution may never have been approved. The more flexible Federalist leaders in Massachusetts, Virginia, New York, and elsewhere obviously realized this as Antifederalist opposition mounted. It was to redeem the promise made in so many ratifying conventions that James Madison arose in the first Congress to introduce the proposals for the first ten amendments, which finally became the Constitution's Bill of Rights. This charter of liberties was the great achievement of the Antifederalists; it demonstrated the value of a strong opposition party and of sustained public discussion.

## THE MEANING OF RATIFICATION

About 60 years ago, the distinguished historian Charles A. Beard tried to show that the vote for and against ratification of the Constitution followed class and sectional lines. Speculators, capitalists with large holdings in public securities, and other investors favored ratification, Beard wrote, while frontiersmen, small farmers, and debtors opposed it. The bitter contest over ratification, he argued, was won by the Federalists against the wishes of the majority, largely because so many of their opponents did not have the right to vote and lacked leadership, whereas the Federalists enjoyed all the advantages of wealth and were accustomed to run the show. Not the idealism of bills of rights, but the interests of property had carried the day.

This materialistic view shocked many in Beard's day, and ever since it has arrayed historians in contesting camps. Few subjects have so aroused students of American politics; and the subject refuses to die because of its great interest on the one hand, and the inconclusiveness of the data on the other. More than a generation of further research, however, has made it clear that the simple lines of division in Beard's pioneer work cannot be sustained.

In the Virginia ratifying convention, to give but one instance, the Antifederalists were much the same sort of people as the Federalists —so far as landholding, slaveholding, military rank, and other measurable qualities go. Again, in Massachusetts, we might expect the former Shaysites to have been vigorous opponents of ratification, and it is true that the delegates from several counties in the center of the state did oppose it. But the delegates from almost all the Shaysite territory north and west of Springfield voted in favor of ratification. Finally, although the great financial center of New York City supported the Constitution, as we would expect if Beard's thesis was sound, the predominantly agricultural state of New Jersey supported it just as strongly, which we would *not* expect from Beard's thesis.

Nor was the struggle waged over democratic principles. In the public debates over ratification, many Antifederalists attacked the Constitution as an effort to limit democracy, to thwart the popular will, to subvert popular liberties. But recent research has shown that leading Antifederalists—among them George Mason and Elbridge Gerry—were as skeptical about the merits of democracy as the Federalists were. Although the political role of the common man was as advanced in the American states as it was anywhere, we must remember that the Constitution was not framed in a democratic age. Even so, it is possible, though not certain, that the Constitution was accepted by a majority of those Americans who cared anything at all about political matters. The vote for delegates to the ratifying conventions was thrown open to a very extensive electorate. Except in New York and Connecticut, everyone was allowed to vote who satisfied the minimum qualifications for the election of his own state officers, and in these two exceptions, the qualifications were broadened, not narrowed, so that they might be brought into line with other commonwealths.

Although we have no popular vote on the Constitution, we do know the votes of the delegates the people chose. In the 11 states that ratified the Constitution before it went into effect, the elected delegates voted 844 to 467 to adopt it. Many of them had no instructions from the voters and ran for election without committing themselves on the issue of ratification. It is thus impossible to know whether they reflected the wishes of their constituents. Some of them were simply endorsed by the electorate as trusted representatives and were sent off to the convention to make up their own minds. Some—we have the distinguished examples of Edmund Randolph in Virginia and Melancton Smith in New York—actually changed their minds in the course of the debates.

Had all the adult males in the country been able to vote, would the opposition to the Constitution have been more powerful? It is impossible to be certain, for a wider electorate may have meant simply that the proportion of nonvoters would have been greater. Despite all the emphasis that historians have put upon the bitterness and the closeness of the contest in some of the ratifying conventions, it seems true that for many Americans, as Robert E. Brown has said "the Constitution was adopted with a great show of indifference." Although some men felt the issue keenly and discussed it hotly with their neighbors, many who had the right to go to the polls simply failed to make the effort. They had not yet developed a lively interest in political matters outside their own states. In Philadelphia, for example, the voting turnout over the Constitution was only a fraction of what it had been years before in a closely contested local election. In Massachusetts, the vote was smaller than it had been in the relatively exciting Bowdoin-Hancock election that followed Shays' Rebellion. Perhaps part of the explanation is that the ordinary citizen in the American states was not a very active political man, and that he put extraordinary trust in the judgment of established political leaders. Yet even so political a young man as John Quincy Adams, when he heard that his state had ratified the Constitution, wrote in his diary:

In this town [Newburyport, Massachusetts] the satisfaction is almost universal; for my own part, I have not been pleased with this system. . . . But I am now converted, though not convinced. My feelings upon the occasion have not been passionate nor violent; and, as upon the decision of this question I find myself on the weaker side, I think it my duty to submit without murmuring against what is not to be helped.

The Constitution was conceived, drawn up, and promoted by an extraordinary generation of political leaders who had no false modesty about their own abilities, as few leaders did in their day. For all the controversy their work stirred up, these leaders had persuaded the politically active public to accept a drastic change in the structure of their government without violence, without bloodshed, without coercion. Most of them were promptly given the opportunity to show that the Constitution which had been won on paper could be made to work in actuality.

# READINGS

The best text of the Constitution, with an analysis of each clause and summaries of Supreme Court interpretations, is E.S. Corwin, *The Constitution of the United States of America* (1953). The classic commentary on the Constitution is *The Federalist,* written in 1787–1788 by Hamilton, Madison, and Jay. The definitive modern edition is that by J.E. Cooke (1961). The spirit of the Constitution and its makers is best indicated in Max Farrand, ed., *Records of the Federal Convention* (4 vols., 1911–1937). For its reception by the ratifying conventions see Jonathan Elliot, ed., *The Debates in the Several State Conventions on the Adoption of the Federal Constitution* (5 vols., 1836–1845). A.T. Prescott, ed., *Drafting the Federal Constitution* (1941), rearranges the Convention debates by subject matter. Perhaps the best brief book on making the Constitution is R.L. Schuyler, *The Constitution of the United States* (1923). See also Max Farrand, *The Framing of the Constitution of the United States* (1913); Carl Van Doren, *The Great Rehearsal* (1948) and Clinton Rossiter, *1787—The Grand Convention* (1966).

J.A. Smith, *The Spirit of American Government, A Study of the Constitution: Its Origin, Influence and Relation to Democracy* (1907), foreshadowed C.A. Beard's monograph, *An Economic Interpretation of the Constitution of the United States* (1913). For criticisms of Beard and more recent revisionist works see the Readings for Chapter Seven and the relevant chapters in Richard Hofstadter, *The Progressive Historians* (1968). Staughton Lynd, "Slavery and the Founding Fathers" in Melvin Drimmer, ed., *Black History* (1968), is suggestive.

Leading biographies of proponents of the Constitution include Irving Brant, *James Madison: The Nationalist 1780–1787* (1948), and *James Madison: Father of the Constitution 1787–1800* (1950); Broadus Mitchell, *Alexander Hamilton: Youth to Maturity 1755–1788* (1957), with an extended account of the New York ratifying convention; Frank Monaghan, *John Jay* (1935); and A.J. Beveridge, *The Life of John Marshall* Vol. I (1916), especially good on the Virginia ratifying convention. For opponents of the Constitution see E.W. Spaulding, *His Excellency, George Clinton* (1938), and Helen Hill, *George Mason* (1938). Richard Henry Lee, *Letters from the Federal Farmer* (originally published in 1787 and 1788 and available in Forrest McDonald, ed., *Empire and Nation* (1962), became the Antifederalist equivalent of the Federalist papers. Cecelia Kenyon, ed., *The Antifederalist* (1967), is an outstanding anthology.

On judicial review, R.K. Carr, *The Supreme Court and Judicial Review* (1942), is brief and clear. Other leading studies include C.G. Haines, *The American Doctrine of Judicial Supremacy* (1932); E.S. Corwin, *The Doctrine of Judicial Review* (1914); and C.A. Beard, *The Supreme Court and the Constitution* (1912).

On ratification in the states, in addition to Mitchell and Beveridge above, see F.G. Bates, *Rhode Island and the Formation of the Union* (1898); R.L. Brunhouse, *The Counter-Revolution in Pennsylvania 1776–1790* (1942); L.I. Trenholme, *The Ratification of the Federal Constitution in North Carolina* (1932); S.B. Harding, *The Contest over Ratification of the Federal Constitution in the State of Massachusetts* (1896); C.H. Ambler, *Sectionalism in Virginia from 1776 to 1851* (1910); L.G. DePauw, *The Eleventh Pillar* (1967), on New York; and O.G. Libby, *The Geographical Distribution of the Vote of the Thirteen States on the Federal Constitution 1787–1788* (1894).

# NINE

March 4, 1789, was the date set for the new Congress to assemble in New York, and at dawn the guns at the Battery on the southern tip of Manhattan Island saluted the great day and the city's church bells rang out. But these were empty gestures. The month of March came to an end, and still no quorum of representatives or of senators had completed the rough journey to the capital. New York's City Hall, at Broad and Wall streets, had been carefully remodeled under the supervision of the French architect Pierre Charles L'Enfant, and now, as Federal Hall, it stood ready for the national lawmakers. Its elegance, one historian has said, "was enough to disturb the republican souls of members from the rural districts and the small towns." But it was the emptiness of Federal Hall that most disturbed Federalist leaders already in New York. "The people will forget the new government before it is born," moaned Fisher Ames of Boston, the gloomy conservative who had shepherded the federal Constitution through the Massachusetts ratifying convention against the forces of redoubtable Sam Adams, and who had gone on to defeat Adams for Congress.

By April 1 the House of Representatives was at last ready to convene, and by April 6 the Senate had its quorum and could join the House in examining the ballots of the presidential electors. Washington, with 69 votes, was found to have been chosen President unanimously. John Adams, second in the balloting with 34 votes, was named Vice-president. After a triumphal journey from Mount Vernon, Washington arrived in New York on April 23, 1789. On April 30, with the sun shining on the gaily decorated streets, he was inaugurated.

# THE FEDERALIST

# DECADE

The choice of New York as the national capital gave a fillip to the already dashing social life of the country's second largest city. Madison's unhappiness over the "scanty proportion" of representatives "who will share in the drudgery of the business" was scarcely dispelled by the round of dinners, dances, and balls that quickly caught up his colleagues. The sun had begun to shine once more on the American economy as brightly as it did on the inauguration, and the prospect of prosperity was reflected in the boisterousness and ostentation of the capital's entertainments. These enticed even the more temperate members of what was soon to be called the "Federalist Court."

Congress, nevertheless, got on with its business. The leaders of the First Congress were determined to make good—and to make a good impression. John Adams, as President of the Senate, a body that Gouverneur Morris hoped would "show us the might of aristocracy," so loved dignified titles and formal procedures that the Antifederalists, pointing gleefully to his stoutness, promptly dubbed him "His Rotundity." The Constitution named Washington simply "President of the United States," but that was not good enough for Adams. With that title, said the Vice-president, "the common people of foreign countries, the soldiers and sailors . . . will despise [the President] to all eternity." He preferred "Majesty" or "Excellency." Others suggested "Highness," and "Elective Highness." Moreover, when the President came to address Congress, should he, Adams asked, be received sitting down (as in the House of Lords), or standing (as in the Commons); by a committee, or by the "Usher of the Black Rod," Adams's title for the Sergeant-at-Arms?

Such preoccupation with decorum made Congress seem rather ridiculous at first, especially to "back parts" members who knew little of the value of trappings in royal courts. But the need for getting down to more serious business soon sobered it up. The Constitution offered few suggestions on punctilio or procedure, but it was clear enough on objectives, and the times were making their own urgent demands.

New York was the capital of what was still a weak nation—one beset by foreign and domestic debts, surrounded by enemies, harassed on its borders by hostile Indians, on the sea by bold pirates, and in foreign ports and foreign waters by unfriendly navies. Nor was there to be unity at home.

270

## 1  *The New Government at Work*

### FIRST FEDERALIST MEASURES

"Few who are not philosophical spectators," President Washington wrote at the outset of his administration,

can realize the difficult and delicate part, which a man in my situation has to act. . . . my station is new, and, if I may use the expression, I walk on untrodden ground. There is scarcely an action, the motive of which may not be subject to a double interpretation. There is scarcely any part of my conduct which may not hereafter be drawn into precedent.

Much has been made of the "furious pace" with which Alexander Hamilton in particular worked to get the new government off the

*"View of the Triumphal Arch, and the manner of receiving General Washington at Trenton" on his way to the inauguration ceremonies in New York. In 1789 Trenton was just a hamlet—no more than 50 people are shown—gathered to cheer the new President on his white horse.* (Columbian Magazine, 1789.)

ground. One reason for Hamilton's administrative zeal may have been that Washington had allowed a precious five months to elapse before commissioning the new Secretary of the Treasury on September 11, 1789. In taking other steps the first President acted with similar deliberation, and the first Congress followed his example.

The Constitution placed on Congress the responsibility of raising money for government expenses; now the delicate business of designing and collecting taxes had to be faced. The Constitution gave Congress the power "to raise armies" and "maintain a navy"; now the size and scope of each in peacetime as well as wartime had to be determined. The Constitution created a national judiciary made up of a Supreme Court and "such inferior courts as Congress may from time to time ordain and establish"; now the machinery for federal law enforcement had to be built. The Constitution created a potentially strong executive; now the executive departments had to be organized and manned. While Congress, for all its dilatoriness in getting under way, dealt successfully with most of these constitutional tasks in its first session, one of its earliest substantive steps was to enact and submit to the states the promised amendments to the

*Inauguration of George Washington on the balcony of Federal Hall, New York City, April 30, 1789. From an engraving made in 1790 by Amos Doolittle after a drawing by Peter Lacour. (Stokes Collection, New York Public Library.)*

Constitution creating a federal "Bill of Rights."

The promise of such amendments as we have seen (p. 263), induced many in the state ratifying conventions to endorse the Constitution as it stood. To allay any possible alarm over whether this promise would be fulfilled, Washington, in his first inaugural address, April 30, 1789, urged Congress to act on the amendments at once. Each of the ten amendments ultimately adopted circumscribed the powers of the federal government in relation to the individual, and the last two reasserted certain fundamental rights of the states.

Yet these amendments met with scant opposition in the House and Senate, strongly nationalist though the members were, and by December 1791 the required three-fourths of the states had ratified them.

Washington grew disappointed when few other measures passed through Congress with the unanimity of these amendments. When

272

some legislation even in this first session re-opened sectional rifts he viewed the future with dismay.

The new government's most urgent need was for money to meet its day-to-day expenses, and more important, as Madison put it, "to revive those principles of honor and honesty that have too long lain dormant" by paying the national debt. Madison, the acknowledged leader in the first House of Representatives and the President's closest advisor, hoped to raise the necessary funds principally by a modest tariff bill which he submitted to the House even before Washington was inaugurated. By touching "such articles . . . only as are likely to occasion the least difficulty," Madison expected prompt enactment of his measure. The very proposal, however, found merchants adding the anticipated tax to their prices. They gave no encouragement to its early passage which would yield their extra profits to the government. With lobbying and log-rolling tactics that became notorious later on, manufacturers also combined to hold up the bill until each obtained special protection for his products.

The claims of competing economic interests would have been settled sooner had not Madison conceived of his tariff as a weapon in the new nation's commercial war with Britain as well as a money-raising bill. Once the Revolution ended, Britain, as we have seen (p. 229), had deprived Americans of their extensive prewar commerce with the British West Indies, while in her home ports she treated American goods and ships as she treated those of other nations with whom she had no commercial treaties. Nor, rightfully skeptical of enforcement here, would she make commercial treaties with the Confederation Congress. In an effort to compel her now to restore the old privileges and grant new ones, Madison, in his tariff bill, asked for higher duties on goods entering American ports from countries without treaties with the United States, such as Britain, and lower duties on similar goods from countries with treaties, such as France, her ally in the Revolution. He also asked for higher duties on goods entering in foreign ships, and higher port charges on such ships.

These discriminatory proposals presented welcome opportunities for oratory by restored loyalists, renascent monarchists, and others whose "habitual affection for England" had revived or regained respectability during the Critical Period in America. Even though Madison, the author of these proposals, was a Virginian, they also galvanized the never really dormant suspicion of the commercial North in the agrarian South, where planters simply wanted cheap and plentiful shipping under any flag to carry their staples overseas, and feared a Yankee shipping monopoly at Britain's and their own expense. Commercial-minded Yankees, Yorkers, and Quakers, at the same time, also opposed Madison's commercial warfare, preferring friendliness to hostility as the policy most likely to move Britain to restore normal trade relations between the new nation and the old.

As finally enacted in July 1789, Madison's tariff made no reference to countries with or without commercial treaties with the United States. It placed duties averaging about 8½ per cent on the value of certain listed imports, but provided, for the benefit of American carriers, that goods imported in American ships be taxed at a rate 10 per cent lower than goods arriving in foreign ships. A second act passed later in the month set tonnage duties of 6 per cent per ton on American ships entering American ports and 50 cents per ton on foreign ships.

Explicit discrimination against Britain had been rejected; yet so sensitive was London to America's every independent step that as soon as the government there learned of the differentials in favor of American carriers, it dispatched Major George Beckwith, an officer familiar with America and American leaders through his experiences in the Revolution, to serve as a secret agent in New York. Besides working to remove these tariff differentials, Beckwith was to uncover and report on American attitudes toward all other outstanding problems with Britain and to bend these attitudes toward London's own policy. Beckwith soon penetrated the highest ranks of the new national government, his path smoothed by the active Anglophiles now in it. He became especially close to Hamilton, whose love for everything English matched his love for power and soon led him deliberately to mislead Washington himself in order to further his own favorite policy of a permanent alliance with Britain involving far more than commercial reciprocity. Hamilton, indeed, using the code number "7," secretly became Beckwith's principal source of information and misinformation, asserting as fixed American policy at critical junctures positions he then undertook to impose upon the President by falsifying the nature of Beckwith's mission as well as his communications.

No Anglo-American alliance was made in this period, and no commercial treaty was negotiated with Britain until Jay's Treaty of 1794, which Hamilton characteristically helped bend toward London's desires (see p. 287). His secret activities did not go unsuspected; had they actually been uncovered, his own national career would have been checked at the outset, an event that would have had more far-reaching consequences than the tariff act itself.

Under this act, no revenue could be collected until inspectors, weighers, and other port personnel were appointed. Thereafter, for more than a hundred years (except for the single year 1836, when federal land sales surpassed them), the customs annually yielded far more federal revenue than any other single source, and customhouse jobs remained the staple of federal patronage.

While the House was occupied with debate on the tariff, the Senate started work on what was to become the Judiciary Act of September 1789. This act helped cement the federal system by spelling out the procedure by which new federal courts could review state laws and state court decisions involving powers and duties delegated by the Constitution to the federal government. It also specified that the Supreme Court be manned by a chief justice and five associate justices. The system of federal courts was to be completed by three circuit courts and thirteen district courts. The circuit courts, when sitting, were to have a three-man bench consisting of two federal Supreme Court justices and one district court judge, the Supreme Court justices being obliged to make arduous journeys on their circuits to sit with the local judge of the different district courts. The district courts, the lowest in the federal system, were to have but one judge. Attached to each district court were United States attorneys and their deputies to serve as federal prosecutors, and United States marshals and their deputies to serve as federal police.

One of the duties of these marshals and deputies, and of numerous special assistants, was to take the first census in 1790, as provided in Article I, Section 2 of the Constitution, for the primary purpose of apportioning seats, by states, thereafter, in the House of Representatives. Madison had a typically scholarly concept of the value of a census. The first bill for its establishment, he wrote Jefferson early in 1790, "contained a schedule for ascertaining [not merely the number of persons in the country, which was all the Constitution prescribed, but] the component classes of the Society, a kind of information extremely requisite to the Legislator, and much wanted for the science of Political Economy." This bill passed the House, but, said Madison, "It was thrown out by the Senate as a waste of trouble and supplying materials for idle people to make a book." Fortunately, the Senate soon relented and permitted the making of a useful "enumeration." The information gathered by the census-takers was enlarged in each subsequent decade; but not until 1870 did it offer thoroughly reliable statistics on the state of the nation and the rate and character of its growth.

The executive had been one of the weakest links in the old Confederation. Yet the three executive departments created under the Articles of 1781—Foreign Affairs, Treasury, and

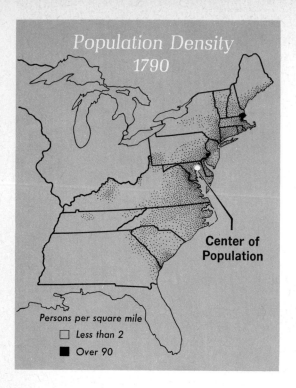

**Population Density 1790**

Center of Population

Persons per square mile
☐ Less than 2
■ Over 90

ing even minor posts. "A single disgust excited in a particular state, on this account," he wrote, "might perhaps raise the flame of opposition that could not easily, if ever, be extinguished. . . . Perfectly convinced I am, that if injudicious or unpopular measures should be taken by the executive under the new government, with regard to appointments, the government itself would be in the utmost danger of being utterly subverted by those measures."

Washington also was reluctant to appoint an opponent of the Constitution to any office, however insignificant, when a sympathizer could be found. Finally, he gave preference, when he could, to men whose measure he personally had taken during the heat of the Revolution. General Henry Knox of Massachusetts, Washington's chief of artillery and one of the army's most outspoken opponents of the old Congress, became the first Secretary of War. To Edmund Randolph of Virginia, one of Washington's wartime aides-de-camp, went the Attorney-Generalship. The Treasury seems to have been reserved for the Middle states, for when Robert Morris of Pennsylvania declined the appointment as Secretary of that department the President turned to another of his military aides, Hamilton of New York. John Jay of New York, in charge of foreign affairs for the old Congress, continued to direct them until April 1790, when Thomas Jefferson of Virginia took over and Jay became the first Chief Justice of the Supreme Court.

The Constitution made no provision for a presidential Cabinet, but early in his administration Washington established the practice of taking action only on matters that had been referred to him by the secretaries of the three departments or the Attorney-General. Gradually, he began to consult these secretaries on questions that arose outside their departments. In the spring of 1791, in anticipation of a journey to the South that would keep him from the capital for an extended period, Washington wrote to each of the three secre-

War—continued unchanged for months under the new government. Not until July 1789 did Congress create the new Department of State to manage foreign relations. The new War Department was set up soon after; the Treasury, not until September. An act of February 1792 stipulated that there should be "one Postmaster General," but this official remained in the Treasury Department until 1829. The Judiciary Act of September 24, 1789, created the office of Attorney-General, but the Department of Justice was not established until 1870.

While Congress busied itself with these basic measures, the President gave his most serious attention to the appointments he knew he must make to fill the positions Congress was creating. Washington wanted to surround himself with the best men available, but other considerations carried great weight in his thinking. It is impossible to exaggerate Washington's awareness of the tenuousness of the thread that held the states together, or his care not to give offense to local sensibilities in fill-

taries, "to express my wish, if any serious and important cases should arise during my absence, . . . that the Secretaries for the Departments of State, Treasury, and War may hold consultations thereon." Washington went further. While holding himself in readiness to return to the capital in an emergency, he told the secretaries that, "should they determine that measures, relevant to the case, may be legally and properly pursued without the immediate agency of the President, I will approve and ratify the measures, which may be conformed to such determination." Thereafter, the three secretaries began to meet from time to time for *collective* action; and after the crisis in foreign affairs in 1793, arising from the wars of the French Revolution (see p. 284), these meetings, which Washington himself had begun to call, became regular events. In this way the Cabinet became a permanent cog in the machinery of the federal government.

The Constitution required the "advice and consent of the Senate" for high presidential appointments like those of Cabinet officers. Had it required Congressional consent for removal as well, the American government may have gone the way of the British government at this time toward a Cabinet wholly responsible to the legislature, not the executive. Madison's bill proposing creation of the Department of State in May 1789 explicitly gave the President the right to remove the Department Secretary without consulting Congress. Many members of the First Congress fought this provision, but Madison backed Washington's policy of an executive relatively free from legislative control and carried the point. Hamilton, as we shall see in a moment, went even further, seeking to impose executive policy on the legislature.

THE FUNDING PROGRAM

The Constitution stipulated that the President "shall from time to time give to the Congress information of the state of the

*General Henry Knox. On becoming Secretary of War, Knox inherited an army of 672 officers and men. In 1790 Congress raised this force to 1216, half the number Knox requested, and at the same time cut private's pay from $4 to $3 a month. At this rate it was said, none would come in but men "purchased from prisons, wheel barrows, and brothels." (Courtesy, Museum of Fine Arts, Boston.)*

Union, and recommend to their consideration such measures as he shall judge necessary and expedient." But the act creating the Treasury Department (on Hamilton's insistence, which coincided nicely with Congress's jealousy of its prerogatives in money matters) gave the Secretary of the Treasury the right to advise Congress directly on finance. Hamilton would have preferred to give his advice in person to the assembled legislators; but Congress decided that he submit reports in writing, and near the end of the first session asked him to prepare fiscal reports for the new session to begin in December 1789. Hamilton had his first report, "for the Support of Public Credit," ready in January 1790. In December he submitted his report on a national bank,

275

*Alexander Hamilton in military uniform, painted in 1791 by Charles Willson Peale. (Courtesy of the New-York Historical Society, New York City.)*

and in 1791 he reported to the Second Congress on the mint and manufactures.

While many of his colleagues floundered amidst the perplexities of an infant republic in an age of almost universal monarchy, Hamilton's step never veered from the high road of national authority. The new Congress rang with a multiplicity of counsels, most of them in the voice of inexperience, and Hamilton grasped the strategic opportunity for what he called the "Executive Impulse." Thirty-four years old at this time, he had been close to great men and great events for more than 12 years and was now at the height of his faculties. Even his enemies in Congress acknowledged "the force of his genius." While he complied with the decision that he report to Congress in writing, he refused to leave the implementation of his work to ignorant, careless, or antagonistic hands. During his first years as Secretary of the Treasury, Hamilton frequently sat with House committees to help them frame the legislation required by

his "advice." He also became conspicuous on the floor of Congress, whipping Federalist forces into line behind his measures. The saturnine Senator from Pennsylvania, William Maclay, observed that,

Nothing is done [in the House] without him. . . . Mr. Hamilton . . . was here early to wait on the Speaker, and I believe spent most of his time running from place to place among the members.

At the Constitutional Convention, Hamilton had observed that "the views of the governed are often materially different from those who govern." He was determined to array "those who govern" behind the new administration, whatever the "governed" might think. But even among those who govern, he made an additional differentiation. Early in his report on the public credit, he noted a rise of over 80 per cent in the market value of public securities during the previous year, most of it in the previous two months, simply in anticipation of his recommendations. "It cannot but merit particular attention," he added directly, "that among ourselves the most enlightened friends of good government are those, whose expectations are highest." None nursed higher expectations of the new government than the speculators in public securities.

Besides Hamilton himself, the speculators had a great friend at court in the person of William Duer, the New York profiteer who was Hamilton's client in his private law practice. Within but three days of his own appointment as Secretary, Hamilton had named Duer Assistant Secretary of the Treasury. Even then Duer had in hand an elaborate scheme for speculating in heavily depreciated public securities, the initial success of which —depending on advance knowledge of Hamilton's program among insiders and ignorance of it among other security holders—probably was reflected in the dramatic rise in security prices of which Hamilton had boasted.

Most of the speculators were northern capitalists schooled in security dealings and in command of cash and credit when opportunity offered. Many of them were members of Congress, primed to vote for Hamilton's program as presented by the Secretary. The cash and credit of southern planters were more likely to be tied up in land and slaves and in obligations to British merchants. Even among planters "who governed" in their states and ranked high in the counsels of the new nation, few were able to compete with Yankees and Yorkers in security manipulation.

No one could deny Hamilton's assertion in his report on the public credit, that "the debt of the United States . . . was the price of liberty. The faith of America has been repeatedly pledged for it," he added, "and with solemnities, that give particular force to the obligation." His assertion that funding the debt by "a punctual performance of contracts" with the holders of public securities would "cement more closely the union of the states," was another proposition. The scandals attached to the funding divided many from Washington's administration even among "enlightened & discriminating" men in the North, while the sectionalism of the Secretary's program alienated some southerners from the Union itself, many of them hardly the "ignorant and designing men" Hamilton's friends called his enemies. Most such men acknowledged the new nation's obligations as openly as the Secretary and conceded the benefits to flow from meeting them promptly and in full, as Hamilton proposed. But they resented the imputation that their quarrels with the Secretary's methods, and especially the methods of his closest friends, reflected a lack of patriotism and a cavalier disregard for obligations solemnly undertaken. When, in April 1790, in the midst of the session-long Congressional debate on Hamilton's report, Ducr decided that it probably was politically advisable to resign his Treasury post, Hamilton wrote him that, "*upon reflection* I cannot help thinking you have decided rightly."

In his report on the public credit, Hamilton made three major recommendations: (1) that the foreign debt, of almost $12 million, including arrears of interest, be repaid by means of a new bond issue; (2) that the domestic debt, made up of many kinds of Revolutionary securities valued in 1789 at about 25 cents on the dollar, be exchanged at its face value, plus back interest, for additional new bonds amounting to some $40 million; (3) that the remaining state debts, totaling about $21 million, be assumed by the federal government and refunded on a similar basis.

Congress enacted Hamilton's proposal for refunding the foreign debt with very little debate. Despite his pertinacity on its behalf, his program for the domestic debt had much tougher going. The plan had become known to certain of his friends before he made his report, and by the time the House took up the bill speculators in and out of Congress had surreptitiously begun to buy up old securities. Included in the issues to be refunded were the certificates with which the Revolutionary veterans had been paid. Large amounts of these certificates along with other issues, were scattered through the hinterland, and many eastern speculators dispatched fast boats and coaches loaded with cash to beat the news to the back country, where their agents bought up for a song securities that were soon to soar in value. The Antifederalists, led in the House by Madison, cried corruption; but they could offer only a cumbersome, hastily prepared bill as an alternative to Hamilton's plan. Madison and his followers proposed to discriminate between the original holders of the securities representing the domestic debt and those who purchased them later on speculation. The latter, the Antifederalists held, should not be permitted to profit at the general public's expense. Madison's efforts were wasted, however, and Hamilton's proposal won.

Although funding of the foreign and the federal war debt had now been approved, there remained the further question of the war debts the states had accumulated in the revolutionary cause. Certain states, especially in the South, had paid off substantial portions of their revolutionary obligations; others, led by Massachusetts, the principal storm center of the Revolution, had paid none. With federal securities at their peak in value now, Hamilton's friends among the speculators buzzing around Federal Hall in New York had turned to the deeply depreciated state securities to make their latest killing. Hamilton, as they knew, viewed the debts incurred by the states during the war as a responsibility of the entire new nation which victory in the war had preserved. They wondered, nevertheless, how far he would go in endangering national unity by pressing this position upon reluctant southern legislators. Their wonder was deepened by the crucial consideration that no money had as yet been appropriated for funding even the approved foreign and federal debt. They realized that the entire funding program might collapse if the assumption of state debts was urged too obdurately upon rebellious congressmen who could kill appropriations for any funding at all.

Southern intransigence on the subject of assumption, aroused by the fact that mainly northern debts would be assumed, was fed by the additional fear that in paying for assumption Congress would preempt the remaining tax sources of the nation, thereby endangering the fiscal standing of the states and state rights themselves. Thus, when assumption came up for a House vote in April 1790, southerners ganged up to defeat it by two votes. By taking the lead in mobilizing the opposition, Madison deepened his breach with Washington and the administration, but at the same time strengthened his political position in his own state.

Like Hamilton and the speculators, nevertheless, Madison was unwilling to see the whole funding program, and hence the credit of the new nation, founder on the question of assumption. Jefferson, recently returned from France to take up his duties as Secretary of State, agreed with him. On recognizing that Hamilton was irretrievably committed to assumption, they finally yielded in June in exchange for objectives of their own. The subject of the permanent "residence" of the new government deeply agitated Congress at the same time as the funding program. New York and Philadelphia both wanted it. When, after numerous failures to reverse the House vote on assumption, Hamilton at last proposed to Madison and Jefferson that in exchange for their support of the whole funding program he would undertake to swing enough northern votes behind the proposition to locate the permanent capital in the South, the deal was made.

By the time assumption passed late in July, Hamilton and his followers had already carried out their part of the bargain by sponsoring the measure which made Philadelphia the capital for ten years, starting late in 1790, and designated a site on the Potomac to be ready in 1800 as the permanent seat of the government. In 1791, the commissioners for the development of the new "Federal City" let it be known that the capital would be named for the first President.

### THE FIRST BANK OF THE UNITED STATES

It is "a fundamental maxim, in the system of public credit of the United States," Hamilton said, "that the creation of debt should always be accompanied with the means of its extinguishment." But in practice Hamilton undertook to supply only the means for paying the interest, not the principal of the debt. He had no intention of eliminating the bonds that served the moneyed classes as a source of income and as collateral for further speculation. The annual interest on all the new bonds averaged about $2 million for the period 1791–95, and came to nearly half the government's total expenditures for these years. Although the American carrying trade benefited from the tariff differentials of 1789 and from opportunities for neutral shipping once the wars of the French Revolution began in 1793 (see p. 284), the customs duties failed to provide even this small amount. Thus, besides successfully urging an increase in the tariff, Hamilton made two more proposals. Both were adopted, but not without further factional and sectional strife.

The first of these proposals called for a

Bank of the United States, modeled explicitly on the Bank of England, with a capital of $10 million, one-fifth to be subscribed by the government, the rest by private capitalists. The Federalists, opposed on principle to government paper money, planned to have the Treasury issue only minted gold and silver. Consequently, Hamilton argued, a commercial bank was needed to supply notes that would serve as currency in business transactions. This bank would also assist the government by lending it money to meet its short-term obligations and by serving as a depository for government funds. Finally, by providing personal loans, the bank would make it easier for individuals to pay their taxes.

"This plan for a national bank," objected Representative James Jackson of Georgia, "is calculated to benefit a small part of the United States, the mercantilist interests only; the farmers, the yeomanry, will derive no advantage from it." But Hamilton's bill passed the House, 39 to 20. Thirty-six of the favoring votes came from the commercial North, 19 of the opposing votes from the agrarian South. In February 1791 the Bank of the United States was chartered for 20 years with headquarters in Philadelphia, and in December it opened. Ultimately, eight branches were established in port cities from Boston to New Orleans.

In the House debate on the bank bill, Madison had argued that a national bank would be unconstitutional. The Constitutional Convention, he insisted, had expressly rejected the proposition that the federal government be empowered to charter companies. When the bill was sent to Washington for his signature, he asked Jefferson and Hamilton as well as Attorney-General Randolph for their opinions on its constitutionality. Jefferson supported Madison. But Hamilton argued that since the government had been delegated the power to regulate currency, it had the "implied power" to establish a bank to issue that currency. Randolph equivocated on the constitutional problem, and it seems that Washington himself never resolved it. He rejected Jefferson's and Madison's "strict interpretation" of

the Constitution in favor of Hamilton's "broad interpretation"; but his decision on the bank was not based on the constitutional reasoning of any of these spokesmen. Washington's administrative credo required him to give his support, when in doubt on an issue, to the Cabinet member whose office was most closely involved. On these grounds Hamilton won his bank.

### THE MILITARY ON THE FRONTIER

Hamilton's second proposal for raising money called for an excise tax on various commodities, including distilled liquors, from which he hoped to realize as much as $800,000 annually to apply against the interest costs of the funding system. Hamilton's excise was enacted in March 1791, and soon after, federal taxgatherers were in the field. The excise, said Jackson of Georgia, "was odious, unequal, unpopular, and oppressive, more particularly in the Southern states" where whiskey was held to be essential to men working in the hot climate. Opposition to the new tax, however, grew most violent in western Pennsylvania, where, to save transportation costs on bulky grain, backcountry farmers often converted it into hard liquor. To the people in this and other regions where coin was scarce, whiskey had actually become a medium of exchange, and the tax on it seemed to be a tax on money itself.

There were also deeper reasons for resentment. In Number 12 of *The Federalist,* Hamilton himself had observed that "the genius of the people will ill brook the inquisitive and peremptory spirit of excise laws." Hamilton's insight into the American "genius" was confirmed in September 1791, when an early meeting at Pittsburgh of opponents of the excise resolved that, "It is insulting to the feelings of the people to have their vessels marked, houses . . . ransacked, to be subject to informers," and so forth. One of the most objectionable features of the measure was the provision requiring those prosecuted for infractions to stand trial in federal courts, the nearest one to the Pittsburgh district, for ex-

280

ample, being 350 miles away in Philadelphia. Besides obliging farmers to halt all work to attend court, the trip itself was equivalent to a serious pecuniary fine, owing to the distance and difficulty of communication.

Resistance to collection of the excise grew so strong that it never yielded much more than half of what Hamilton had expected, and of this amount the cost of gathering the tax annually took more than 15 per cent, far too big a bite. In May 1792 Congress responded to pressure from the whiskey country by reducing the excise materially, especially on small stills. But the very idea of the tax still rankled, and in September that year Washington was forced to issue a proclamation warning "malcontents" to "desist from all unlawful combinations . . . tending to obstruct the operations of the laws." Nothing was done, moreover, about "the great popular grievance" of the trial site until June 1794, when Congress permitted state courts to exercise jurisdiction in excise cases which arose more than 50 miles from the nearest federal court. Far from being received as a concession, however,

this act was looked upon as inflammatory, for its application was specifically withheld from "distillers who had previously to its enactment incurred a penalty." To make matters worse, in May 1794 the federal court in Philadelphia had issued writs against 75 western Pennsylvania distillers returnable in that court, but had delayed until July to serve them. When federal marshals came west with the writs, they were attacked by a mob shouting, "The Federal Sheriff is taking away men to Philadelphia!"

Hamilton interpreted the uprising that followed against all federal collectors in the disaffected area as a rebellion against the United States and prevailed upon Washington early in August 1794 to order the mobilization of 13,000 militiamen to crush the farmers. Hamilton, naturally, rode west with the troops, whom Washington himself journeyed out to inspect at Carlisle. Although they found no organized opposition, the militia rounded up about a hundred men. Two of them were later convicted of treason and sentenced to death, but Washington eventually pardoned them.

In the year of the so-called "Whiskey Insurrection," receipts from the excise on distilled liquors fell lower than ever and the cost

*A tarred and feathered tax collector, victim of the "rebels" during the Whiskey Insurrection. (New York Public Library.)*

of collection, including the cost of the military display, naturally skyrocketed. But Hamilton, having already devised excises on additional essentials like salt and coal, and boots and shoes, to eke out the interest on the government debt, persisted in the "experiment" of collection to prove to the skeptical capitalists of the world that a republic could coerce its citizens where financial responsibility was at issue.

If the excise venture advanced the standing of the administration abroad, it only aggravated opposition on the frontier already aroused by other grievances.

On the southwestern frontier Spain put pressure on Washington's administration by continuing to contest the Florida border as defined in the Treaty of Paris (see p. 209), and by keeping the Mississippi at New Orleans closed to American shipping. In the Northwest, Britain persisted in using military power based at posts on American territory to help Canadian fur trappers against American entrepreneurs. Neither Spain nor Britain tried to restrain the Indians in their territories from systematically molesting American frontiersmen. Coupled with the failure of Washington's own efforts to deal with the Indians on American territory, this situation was doubly depressing to settlers on the borders who had looked to a strong central government for protection against repeated Indian raids.

In 1790 Washington had invited Alexander McGillivray, a half-breed Creek who led the tribes of the Southwest, to come to New York. Here a treaty was drawn up by which McGillivray agreed, in exchange for a substantial yearly pension, to keep peace on the frontier. He abided by this treaty only as long as it took him to get back to Tennessee, where bloodshed was promptly resumed. In the Northwest, Washington tried to use force against the Indians, but with no more success than he had won with diplomacy. In 1790 in the Ohio country, the Indians ambushed General Josiah Harmar and 1500 militiamen. In 1791 Governor Arthur St. Clair of the North-

Indian Wars in the Northwest

Lands ceded by Indians in Greenville Treaty, 1795

west Territory suffered a worse fate. Most of his 2000 ill-equipped and untrained men deserted even before they had met any Indians, and the rest were trapped and forced to flee for their lives.

"Here in this very room," Washington stormed on learning of this latest failure, "I warned General St. Clair against being surprised." The explanation of the President's fury by John C. Fitzpatrick, one of Washington's better biographers, helps us understand the plight of the poor, struggling country: "The Commander-in-chief of the Continental Army . . . knew by bitter experience what it meant to collect, arm and equip a force, only to have it annihilated, the man-power wasted, and all the time and expense for naught. . . . It took two years to gather another army."

When the new force was ready in 1794, Washington was more careful in selecting his commander. That year, under General "Mad Anthony" Wayne, the federal troops routed the northwestern tribes in the Battle of Fallen Timbers, and in 1795, by the Treaty of Fort Greenville, these tribes yielded most of their Ohio land. At about the same time, local action by John Sevier and James Robert-

282

son quieted the southwestern tribes. But the Treaty of Fort Greenville won the Federalists less favor on the frontier than their earlier failures had cost them. And for the accomplishments of Sevier and Robertson, the Federalists received no credit at all.

## II *Political Issues and Party Strife*

### CONSOLIDATING THE REPUBLICAN OPPOSITION

Hamilton's ambition for America was greater than that of most of his followers, and his vision far exceeded theirs. His blueprint for converting the United States into a powerful industrial nation was his celebrated Report on Manufactures, sent to Congress in December 1791. In it he urged the value of industry to the community, and the need for protective tariffs, subsidies, and other aids while industry was in its infancy. Congress gave this report a cold reception. The merchants, moreover, in whose hands the money of the country was concentrated were to remain cool to industrial enterprise, and hence to tariffs and subsidies, for another quarter of a century.

Hamilton's agrarian opponents outstripped him in vision. Hamilton had no respect for the men who were opening up the vast reaches of the new country. He despised farmers, and he hated westerners as troublemakers. In his plan to unify the nation, he assigned to both groups inferior roles. In less than a decade after the start of the new government, however, the majority who lived on the land were to show that they counted for more than the minority in the cities, and that votes counted for more than wealth. The rise of the agrarian Republican party insured that Hamilton's program and that of the Federalists would not enjoy a long life. Without Washington's support, the party would not have ruled as long as it did.

We cannot assign specific dates to the beginnings of political parties in America. During the colonial period so-called "factions" came and went, with as little continuity as Washington hoped the "factions" of his own time would have. The issue of the Constitution again divided the country into what became known as "Antifederalists" and "Federalists." The latter, as the victors in this confrontation, while trying to strengthen the opinions and mobilize the votes of their followers, succeeded rather in consolidating the opposition.

In the looming contest between these two camps, the Federalists at first enjoyed great advantages. Above all, they had a strong, clear program and, in Hamilton, a resourceful, energetic, and uncompromising leader. Most of the well-educated, wealthy men in the country were Federalists; so were most of the newspaper editors, clergymen, and other makers of opinion. Hamilton showed, too, that the Federalists controlled the army, and were quite willing to use it. A readymade network of chambers of commerce, units of the Society of Cincinnati, and other going organizations worked for Federalism on the local level, and the party quickly developed a grassroots patronage system to give sinecures to local party workers. Even during the First Congress, Federalist leaders caucused and corresponded on platforms, candidates, and campaigns as though they were members of an organized machine.

The men who opposed the Federalists showed a preference for the prerogatives of the states and the privacy of the people as against the national government as conducted under the Constitution by Hamilton and his friends. In the contest for national power this preference seemed to be a weakness that the Federalists quickly exploited—to their own undoing.

Far from uniting the states and the people, Hamilton's program only magnified existing antagonisms. Every Hamiltonian measure was essentially a northeastern measure: funding, assumption, the national bank, the excise, pro-

283

tective tariffs—all served to divide the South from the North, the West from the East. Every Hamiltonian measure was a capitalist's measure that alienated debtors from creditors, even in the Northeast. Every Hamiltonian attitude was an aristocratic attitude that pleased the "gentlemen of principle and property" and offended the "people of no particular importance."

Jefferson, as much as Hamilton, sought stability and dignity for the new government, but he believed that men "habituated to think for themselves"—American yeomen, in short—were much easier to govern than men (usually city-dwellers, he thought) who were "debased by ignorance, indigence, and oppression." By 1791 Jefferson was convinced that Hamilton and his "corrupt squadron" menaced the country, and he wrote Washington to say so. More than that, he began to exert systematic pressure on Hamilton's Treasury Department which, he told the President, under the present Secretary "possessed already such an influence as to swallow up the whole Executive powers." Jefferson first tried to place his own sympathizers in Hamilton's department. Next he tried to divest the Treasury of the Post Office. Then he tried to have Hamilton's department cut in two, transferring to an independent administrator the collection of the tariff, and leaving other collections where they then were. In none of these stratagems did Jefferson succeed; but as tactics in his distressing feud with Hamilton they at least kept the Treasury on the defensive and impeded it from extending its power. Having accomplished this much, Jefferson, with Madison's support, worked out a plan to save the United States in his own way. Essential to his program was getting the people to use their great privilege of the franchise.

To no other people, said a traveler about Americans at this time, were the "smiles and frowns of political government" of so little consequence. How right he was is shown by the vote: Hardly one-fourth of those eligible had voted for delegates to the state conventions to ratify the Constitution; the percentage voting for representatives to the First Congress was still smaller. Jefferson's approach to getting out the vote was to explain what, indeed, individuals could do for themselves if each flexed his political muscle.

"If left to me to decide whether we should have a government without newspapers, or newspapers without a government," Jefferson once wrote, "I should not hesitate for a moment to prefer the latter." He had disapproved of the secrecy of the Constitutional Convention, and his first step in the looming party battle was to enlist the best man available to keep the public informed of what he believed to be the plot of the Convention victors. This man proved to be the poet Philip Freneau, Madison's classmate at Princeton. In October 1791 Freneau issued the first number of the *National Gazette,* a new Antifederalist paper published in Philadelphia, for the time being the national capital. Freneau so quickly took the play away from John Fenno, the editor of the Hamiltonian *United States Gazette,* that Hamilton felt obliged to enter the newspaper battle himself.

If Jefferson was the philosopher of agrarian politics, Madison, strategically situated in Congress where issues were argued and supporters mobilized, soon emerged as "the great man of the *party.*" Serious party work began as early as the winter of 1791–92, when Madison wrote a number of articles for the *National Gazette* in which he gradually developed the position of "the Republican party, as it may be termed." Thereafter, influential allies, local lieutenants, grass-roots clubs, and candidates who could afford the time and money to campaign and hold office were all arranged for. Besides Jefferson and Madison, those enlisted under the new banner included Governor George Clinton of New York, who, in opposition to General Schuyler, Hamilton's rich father-in-law, controlled the upstate vote; and Aaron Burr of New York City (Clinton had recently helped Burr defeat Schuyler for the Senate), whose followers in the Society of Tammany, a drinking club and benevolent association, already were hungering for pat-

284

ronage. The leaders in Virginia and New York were soon joined by the brilliant young Swiss Albert Gallatin, who had settled on the frontier in western Pennsylvania. In all the other states, intellectual, professional, and literary luminaries helped fill out the Republican officers' corps.

The Republican party was too young to run a presidential candidate in 1792, and in any event its leaders preferred Washington to any other man. The Federalists, in turn, were far from ready to risk going on without him. Once more the reluctant General was elected unanimously; the Republicans, however, had the satisfaction of throwing a scare into the Vice-president, John Adams. Their candidate, Governor Clinton, carried the great states of Virginia and New York, together with North Carolina and Georgia. All told, Clinton polled 50 electoral votes to Adams's 77.

## REPUBLICANISM ABROAD AND AT HOME

During Washington's first administration, party lines had been drawn over financial issues and difficulties on the frontier. In his second administration, problems of foreign policy, as Colonel Higginson of Massachusetts said, "not merely divided parties, but moulded them; gave them their demarcations, their watchwords, and their bitterness." Some of these problems were carry-overs from the war with England. But the French Revolution, which began just a few weeks after Washington first took office in 1789, was the source of most of the trouble.

At first, all but the most conservative Americans welcomed the French Revolution. In 1790, when Lafayette sent Washington the key to the Bastille, the President acknowledged it as a "token of victory gained by liberty over despotism." After Edmund Burke's condemnatory *Reflections on the Revolution in France*, first published in England late in 1790, had reached the United States, Hamiltonians tended to align themselves with it, and all the more so, when the Jeffersonians cham-

pioned Tom Paine's libertarian response, *The Rights of Man*.

The unicameral legislature and other leveling features of the French Constitution of 1791 (borrowed unfortunately from the discredited American Articles of Confederation) prompted John Adams, that year, to publish his *Discourses on Davila,* in which he reiterated the theory of checks and balances built into the very *structure* of government as the only possible way to offset the vanity and selfishness innate in mankind.

It is not to flatter the passions of the people [Adams wrote] . . . to tell them that in a single assembly they will act as arbitrarily as any despot, but it is a sacred truth . . . that a sovereignty in a single assembly must necessarily and will certainly be exercised by a majority, as tyrannically as any sovereignty was ever exercised by kings or nobles. And if a balance of passions and interests is not scientifically concerted, the present struggle in Europe will be little beneficial to mankind, and produce nothing but another thousand years of feudal fanaticism, under new and strange names.

His *Discourses*, Adams noted, were not "the way to obtain a present enthusiastic popularity." Yet they helped rally conservative— that is, Federalist—opinion against France, even before events in that unhappy country had dissipated the initial American sympathy for the Revolution. The execution of Louis XVI in January 1793 disgusted most American conservatives, and the Jacobin "reign of terror" that followed confirmed their deepest misgivings about excessive democracy. In the meantime, the French wars against the continental monarchs, who had combined to end the threat of republicanism, had begun in 1792, and early in 1793 they spread to Britain and Spain.

For weeks, westerly gales kept news of the execution and the wars from reaching America. When all the news flooded in at once, in April 1793, it strengthened the Hamiltonians in their stand against France. The Jeffersonians, on the other hand, held to their hatred of monarchs and monarchy and voiced their confidence in the people of France against the autocrats of Britain.

News of the French war with Britain heightened the conflict in American opinion. More important, it created a dispute over foreign policy. The French treaty of 1778 (see p. 204) provided that the United States must defend the French West Indies in case of an attack on France herself, and also that American ports must receive prizes captured at sea by French privateers and men-of-war. The Girondists, who ruled revolutionary France in 1792, assumed that this treaty remained in force, as indeed it did, and they sent "Citizen" Edmond Genêt as envoy to America to see that it was carried out. Genêt had other instructions as well. He was to organize expeditions from America to detach Louisiana and Florida from Spain, and to outfit American privateers to prey on British shipping. These enterprises were to be financed with American funds made available to him by a speed-up in American payments on outstanding French loans. Genêt had one more project: to organize Jacobin clubs in America to advance the cause of Liberty, Equality, and Fraternity—just at the time when Jefferson himself began to sponsor Republican political clubs of his own.

Genêt, an attractive and enterprising young man, landed in Charleston, South Carolina, a pro-French stronghold, on April 8, 1793, and, after a warm welcome, went right to work without even bothering to present his credentials to the government in Philadelphia. By the time he finally arrived at the capital, the President, after consulting Jefferson and Hamilton, had issued his Neutrality Proclamation of April 22, making it clear that the United States would not participate in the French wars. Jefferson argued that the treaty of 1778 had been entered into with the French nation, no matter what its government might be, and this interpretation was strictly true under international law. He also argued that since only Congress could declare war, only Congress could proclaim neutrality. Thus

a presidential proclamation of neutrality was unconstitutional. Jefferson felt, too, that if such a proclamation were actually issued, Britain should be forced to make certain commercial concessions in return. Hamilton, on the contrary, held that the French treaty had died with the French king, and that neutrality in any case was the only feasible American policy. Jefferson did not persist in his argument, and Washington's so-called Neutrality Proclamation was announced.

By this time, Genêt had already commissioned enthusiastic Charleston ship captains as French privateers to prey on British shipping; he had also organized a South Carolina military adventure against Spain in Florida, and had induced George Rogers Clark and other Kentuckians to float down the Mississippi and dislodge the Spanish from New Orleans, a mission dear to Kentuckian hearts. The warmth of Genêt's reception had convinced him that the people were with him, whatever the government might do. Thus when Washington received Genêt with forbidding coldness and gave him to understand that the government would no longer tolerate his operations, let alone abet them under the old treaty, Genêt decided to ignore the President and proceed with his revolutionary work on his own.

Even Jefferson was put out by this persistence, and when Genêt, contrary to Washington's express warnings, permitted *Little Democrat,* a prize ship converted into an armed vessel, to sail as a privateer, Jefferson voted with the President and the rest of the Cabinet to ask for Genêt's recall. By then, Genêt's group had fallen out of favor at home and, fearing for his life, the young envoy decided to remain in America. He married Governor Clinton's daughter and retired to a country estate on the Hudson.

The repercussions of this affair in the American government were less romantic. Washington's Neutrality Proclamation had reflected the President's determination, at almost any price, to keep the infant nation at peace. Jefferson shared this determination,

286

but his apparent sympathy for Genêt's early machinations prompted the President to read the most sinister meaning into the conduct of his Secretary of State. The American "party battle" was growing more and more feverish at this point—a development that only heightened Washington's concern. In a letter to his friend Richard Henry Lee, on October 24, 1793, he spelled out his feelings:

> The conduct of those, who are arraigning and constantly (so far as they are able) embarrassing the measure of government [that is, the Neutrality Proclamation] with respect to its pacific disposition towards belligerent powers are too obvious. . . . It is not the cause of France, nor I believe of liberty, which they regard; for, could they involve this country in war (no matter with whom) and disgrace, they would be among the first and loudest of the clamorers against the expense and impolicy of the measure.

### THE PROFITS AND PROBLEMS OF NEUTRALITY

The war in Europe greatly increased the belligerents' need for food and other materials, and at the same time tied up the commercial ships that might have brought in the needed supplies. This situation opened the way for a boom in the carrying trade of neutrals; as a leading maritime nation, the United States was among the greatest gainers. Since the French, particularly, had only a small fleet, painfully vulnerable to British attack, they desperately needed neutral assistance. Early in the war, France at last surrendered her monopoly of the French West Indian trade and opened the islands' ports to American ships and American produce—a turn of events that gave great impetus to American commerce.

The British, determined to monopolize world shipping and especially to keep the late rebels down, retaliated quickly. Trade, according to them, was simply an arm of war. They resurrected the "rule of the War of 1756," which held that trade barred to a nation in peacetime could not with im-

punity be opened to it during hostilities. This applied with special force to the French West Indian trade. In November 1793 they decreed that all shipping to or from the French colonies would be subject to British seizure. Americans by then had swarmed into the Caribbean to serve the French islands, and the British seized about 300 United States vessels, abused their passengers, and forced many of their sailors into the British navy.

Even so, American trade continued to grow. Many ships were captured, but many more slipped through with profits that more than compensated for the great risks involved. Ship losses served as an additional stimulus to the shipbuilding industry. By 1794, however, the British had become so brazen that even the Federalists expected war. The United States insisted that neutral ships made neutral goods, but the British enforced the right to search for enemy supplies anywhere in any ship. The United States insisted that a blockade, to be effective, must be enforced by actual patrols of the closed ports. But the British simply announced "paper blockades" and undertook to enforce them on the oceans wherever they found a vessel presumably bound for a forbidden harbor. Food, the United States insisted most firmly, could not be classified as contraband. But the British were more realistic and did not hesitate to capture ships sailing with food for France and her allies.

Painful as Federalist shippers found these British measures, it was the Republicans who made the most of them by labeling them monarchist affronts to the American flag. Recalling how effective commercial retaliation had been against the British in the great days of the Revolution, the Republicans now demanded an embargo to keep British ships out of American ports and American ships off the seas, where they were subject to British seizure.

As if to keep American memories fresh, the British in Canada chose this time to incite the Indians to raid the Ohio country, where thousands of farmers were settling. The British also made it clear that they had no intention of relinquishing their armed posts on American territory, which were giving assistance and encouragement to the Indians. Public opinion, aroused over the hot issues of trade and territory, forced the Republicans' embargo through Congress early in 1794. It was to remain in effect for one month, but at the expiration of that period it was extended for two months more.

## JAY'S TREATY

When the British, in March 1794, sought to end the embargo by revoking the harshest of their rules for neutrals, the Federalists decided to try to gain additional concessions through diplomacy. On April 16, 1794, Washington named John Jay, now Chief Justice, to go to England and settle the main differences between the two countries. Jay was instructed (1) to get the British to surrender their military posts in the Northwest, (2) to pay for American ships that had been captured illegally, and, (3) to accept and respect the American position on the rights and privileges of neutrals. Jay was also to negotiate the best commercial treaty he could. Failing to get the British to agree on all these points, Jay was to try to get the northern countries of Europe to agree jointly with the United States to enforce the rights of neutrals.

Jay had a good case, and the British needed American friendship. But Hamilton nullified these advantages. Once the French Revolution began and democracy seemed to be making headway in the world, his own commitment to monarchical Britain became ever stronger. As early as October 1789, Hamilton told Major George Beckwith, his secret contact reporting on American affairs (see p. 273): "I have always preferred a connexion with you, to that of any other country, *we think in English,* and have a similarity of prejudices and predilections." Thereafter, Hamilton had let nothing pass to Britain's disadvantage. In 1794, while Jay was still at sea on his voyage to England, Washington received a proposal from Sweden and Denmark, two of the north-

ern neutrals Jay was to consult if he failed to gain British concessions. They suggested to the United States just what Jay was instructed to suggest to them—that all three nations unite in combating British assaults on neutral shipping. Washington naturally inclined toward adopting a proposal so similar to his own. In this he had the support of Edmund Randolph, Jefferson's successor as Secretary of State. Nevertheless Hamilton managed to dissuade him, arguing that far from strengthening Jay's hand in his negotiations, such action would only make the British all the more difficult to deal with. Hamilton, moreover, promptly told George Hammond, the British minister in New York, of Washington's decision; and Hammond lost no time in conveying this information to the British negotiators. Jay's bargaining power thus was short-circuited. The result was an uphill fight for the American envoy and a very unsatisfactory agreement.

By the Treaty of London (completed on November 19, 1794, and henceforth known in America as Jay's Treaty), the British agreed once more to evacuate their posts in the Northwest, and by 1796 had done so. But Jay had to barter away a great deal in return. The British could still carry on the fur trade on the American side of the Canadian border and they could still trade with the Indians, who were hostile to advancing American settlement. These concessions almost nullified the surrender of the posts and hardly pleased the westerners, who had remained suspicious of Jay ever since his negotiations with Gardoqui (see p. 228). As for the British paying for captured ships, settlement of this issue was left to a future joint commission which would determine what, if anything, was owed. On the rights of neutrals, Jay failed altogether. The Treaty of London said nothing that would keep the British from continuing to stop and search all ships on the seas and to impress their crews at will. The treaty also left the British the privilege of defining contraband goods as best suited their purposes. Jay's efforts to get commercial concessions

288

were equally abortive. The treaty did assert the so-called "most-favored-nation" principle, by which American goods entering British home ports and British goods entering American ports were to be treated on the same terms as the goods of the nation having the most favorable commercial agreement with each. But the jewel of the British empire, so far as American merchants were concerned, was the British West Indies, and here Jay made his most objectionable arrangement. For the privilege of visiting Indies ports (a privilege limited to small American ships of no more than 70 tons), American cargoes of molasses, coffee, cocoa, sugar, and cotton—the only worthwhile British West Indian commodities —had to be carried directly to American ports. World trade in these commodities was denied to American merchants, but the British could continue to carry them anywhere, including American ports. The Senate forced the removal of this provision before it would ratify the treaty.

Jay's whole agreement was so unsatisfactory that Washington hesitated a long time before he even sent it to the Senate. The Senate, in turn, made every effort to keep the terms from the people lest the call for war against Britain become too strong to withstand. The terms did leak out before the treaty was ratified in the Senate on June 25, 1795, by the slenderest possible two-thirds majority. The public response was as violent as expected. In the months following, "Sir John Jay" was hanged in effigy throughout the country. One zealot caught the spirit of the whole people when he chalked up in large letters on a Boston street wall: "DAMN JOHN JAY! DAMN EVERY ONE WHO WON'T DAMN JOHN JAY!! DAMN EVERY ONE WHO WON'T SIT UP ALL NIGHT DAMNING JOHN JAY!!!"

In the Congress that met in December 1795, the question was asked whether the House of Representatives, by failing to vote appropriations required under the agreement, could in effect reject the treaty even though the Senate had accepted it. The House voted 57 to 35 that it had the constitutional right to reject treaties by withholding funds, but it went on to approve the appropriations in April 1796 by a vote of 51 to 48.

### PINCKNEY'S TREATY

In June 1795, while the Senate was considering Jay's Treaty with Britain, Spain withdrew from the British coalition against France

*"Stop the Wheels of Government".*

*A Federalist view of Congressman Albert Gallatin in 1796 when he was arguing that the House could, by withholding appropriations, effectively veto a treaty made by the President and the Senate, and thereby "stop the wheels of government." The guillotine signifies the Federalists' resentment of Gallatin's French-speaking noble ancestry. (New York Public Library.)*

and made peace with the revolutionary government there. This step made her fearful of British reprisals which might take the form of attacks on her empire in America. She also feared attacks from American frontiersmen. When Britain and America concluded Jay's Treaty, however unsatisfactory its terms for the United States, Spain's fears for her empire grew, and she decided to try to win American friendship to offset Britain's enmity. After several proposals failed to lure Thomas Pinckney, the American minister who had gone to Madrid on Spain's invitation in 1794, Pinckney was able to write home in August 1795 that the King of Spain was now prepared "to sacrifice something of what he considered as his right, to testify to his good will to us."

Pinckney proceeded to negotiate the Treaty of San Lorenzo, usually called Pinckney's Treaty, which the Spanish signed in October 1785 and the United States Senate unanimously approved in March 1796. This agreement settled the northern boundary of Florida at the latitude of 31 degrees. Much more important, Spain consented to open the Mississippi "in its whole length from its source to the ocean" to American traffic and to allow Americans the free use of the port of New Orleans for three years, after which time the arrangement could be renewed.

III *John Adams's Adminstration*

### THE ELECTION OF 1796

Washington had been so serious about not running again in 1792 that he had asked Madison and others to draw up ideas for a "valedictory address" to the nation. Early in 1796 he resurrected these papers and turned them over to Hamilton (who had resigned from the Cabinet in 1795) with a request for a new draft. Nothing could deter Washington now from leaving his high office. He looked with deepest dismay, he said, on the "baneful effects of the spirit of party," but at the same time he took keen satisfaction in many of his accomplishments.

Washington did not deliver his Farewell Address in person; he simply published it in the newspapers on September 17, 1796, a date so close to the presidential elections that it stirred the keenest resentment among the opposition leaders, who felt that his de-

lay in announcing his decision handicapped them in mounting an effective campaign. They felt, also, that his strictures on party spirit were attacks on them and not equally on the governing party.

Washington noted as a "matter of serious concern that any ground should have been furnished for characterizing parties by *geographical* discriminations—*Northern* and *Southern*, *Atlantic* and *Western*." In much of his address he urged upon the country the need for preserving "the unity of government which constitutes you one people." Only toward the end did he discuss foreign affairs; nowhere was there an admonition against all "entangling alliances." Washington actually said:

> The great rule of conduct for us in regard to foreign nations is, in extending our commercial relations to have with them as little *political* connection as possible. . . . It is our true policy to steer clear of permanent alliances with any portion of the foreign world. . . . Taking care always to keep ourselves . . . on a respectable defensive posture, we may safely trust to temporary alliances for extraordinary emergencies.

The party strife that Washington deplored was nearing its peak when he retired. Debate in the House over Jay's Treaty had continued well into 1796, and Washington's own decision intensified the conflict by opening up the highest office to the rising political machines. The Federalists had considered Jay as a candidate, but the furor over the treaty killed his chances. Widespread satisfaction with the Treaty of San Lorenzo, on the other hand, made Thomas Pinckney a plausible choice. In the end, the Federalists brought out a ticket of John Adams of New England and Pinckney of South Carolina. The Republicans named Jefferson as their standard-bearer, and Aaron Burr of New York for Vice-president.

Hamilton and Adams had long since grown cool toward each other, and Hamilton went to great pains to maneuver Pinckney into the Presidency. But his elaborate scheme backfired. Not only did Adams, with 71 votes, win the Presidency, but Jefferson, with 68 votes, was second in the balloting and defeated Pinckney even for the Vice-presidency.

### JOHN ADAMS AS PRESIDENT

Americans now take the transition from one presidential administration to another as a matter of course; but in 1796 the public was experiencing its first transfer of power from one man to another. The excitement of the nation was enhanced by the fact that a leader of Washington's stature was about to retire. The President, writes Leonard D. White, in his history of Federalist administration, "had already determined to demonstrate to the world the supreme achievement of democratic government—the peaceful and orderly change of the head of the state in accordance with the voice of the people." John Adams himself was moved by the historic event; reporting his inauguration to his wife, he wrote: "A solemn scene it was, indeed. . . . In the chamber of the House of Representatives was a multitude as great as the space could contain, and I believe scarcely a dry eye but Washington's. . . . All agree that, taken together, it was the sublimest thing ever exhibited in America."

No one in the United States had written more than John Adams about the nature of man. But, as Jefferson shrewdly observed, in practice Adams was "a bad calculator" of the "motives of men." He made the mistake of retaining in his Cabinet such second-rate Hamiltonians as Secretary of State Timothy Pickering and Secretary of the Treasury Oliver Wolcott, who had surrounded Washington toward the end when even the great General himself could not induce able administrators any longer to forego private business for the public service. Worse, by being absent from his post more often, perhaps, than any President in history, Adams inadvertently gave these Hamiltonians free rein. "The worst evil that can happen to any government," Adams wrote to Pickering in 1797, "is a divided executive. . . . A plural executive must, from the nature of men, be forever divided; this is a

demonstration that a plural executive is a great evil, and incompatible with liberty." Yet the nation was ruled by a "plural executive" during much of Adams's administration. Where Washington in eight years had been absent from his post in Philadelphia only 181 days, Adams in four years was absent 385 days, and often for months at a time. Usually he was communing with his books at home in Quincy, Massachusetts; often he left Philadelphia "precipitately," and could not easily be reached. At one point Secretary of the Treasury Wolcott asserted that "Mr. Stoddert, Mr. Dexter, and myself govern this great nation." Stoddert was Secretary of the Navy Department, newly created in 1798 (see below); and Dexter was Secretary of War.

### JOHN ADAMS'S FOREIGN POLICY

In later years, after his retirement, John Adams counted as one of his major achievements that he, like Washington, had kept the United States at peace with France. Hamilton's anti-French friends in Adams's virtually autonomous Cabinet, however, carried the administration to the brink of all-out hostilities despite the President.

The French had taken less kindly than the Spanish to Jay's Treaty; interpreting it as a British diplomatic victory, they intensified their attacks on American ships bound for British ports. By the time of Adams's inauguration in March 1797, the French had captured about 300 American vessels and had manhandled their crews. In the meantime, Washington had recalled the francophile minister, James Monroe, for having told the French first that Jay's Treaty would never be ratified, and then that it would never become operative because Washington would be defeated in the forthcoming election. Washington sent Charles C. Pinckney to replace Monroe, but after he had been in France the two months permitted foreigners, the French police notified him that unless he obtained a permit to remain they would arrest him. Pinckney fled to Amsterdam in a rage. By the time news of Pinckney's treatment reached Philadelphia, Adams had become President and high Federalists were clamoring for war with the brutal French.

Adams withstood their demands, but without querying the French government, he decided as one of his first presidential measures to send a three-man mission to Paris to persuade the French to stop their raids on American shipping. Pinckney, ordered back to France, was joined in Paris by the Federalist John Marshall and the Republican Elbridge Gerry. When Talleyrand, then foreign minister of France, refused to negotiate until the Americans had given a bribe of $250,000 to three subordinates, Gerry's Federalist colleagues left Paris in a huff. Gerry stayed on to parley with Talleyrand, and came home only when Adams demanded that he cease dallying with the revolutionists.

In their reports home the American envoys had referred to Talleyrand's three subordinates as X, Y, and Z. When the reports became public, an uproar broke out among the partisans of both parties over the so-called "X.Y.Z. Dispatches," during which someone is said to have cried, "Millions for defense, but not one cent for tribute." Congress did vote millions for the expansion of the army and navy in 1798 and 1799; it also created a separate Navy Department and repealed all treaties with France.

To the chagrin of Hamilton, who was aching to lead it into battle, the new army materialized very slowly. Adams himself saw little use for it in fighting for the freedom of the seas and was most reluctant to burden the country with mounting military costs. The new Navy Department, on the other hand, promptly pushed to completion three well-armed frigates that had been under construction, produced 20 other ships of war, and unleashed hundreds of American privateers to prey upon the French. In 1798 and 1799, an "undeclared naval war" raged with France in which American ships, operating mainly in the Caribbean, took almost a hundred French vessels, and suffered losses themselves.

Hamilton's friends in the Cabinet and Congress, meanwhile, were pushing the expansion of the army with such zeal that many suspected a plan to use it against domestic as well as foreign enemies. Their suspicions were confirmed in February 1799, when troops were sent once more to western Pennsylvania to put down a rebellion led by John Fries against the collection of new taxes just levied to pay for the army itself. The Hamiltonians even induced Washington, only a few months before his death, to take nominal command of the army once more, a step that helped

*John Adams (1801) by Charles Balthazar Julien Fevret de Saint-Memin. This "physiognotrace" portrait was done in crayon with an instrument that traced off the subject's profile. (The Metropolitan Museum of Art, gift of William H. Huntington, 1883.)*

persuade Adams, much against his inclination, to name Hamilton as next in command and effectively in charge. But Adams would go no further. To the consternation of Hamilton and his friends, the President refused to make any use of the army against foreign enemies or to ask Congress to make the war with France official.

News that France was relenting in her attitude in the face of Adams's naval policy confirmed the President in his hopes for peace. The same news only drove the Hamiltonians to desperation and the Federalist party to defeat and to the verge of destruction. When, early in 1799, Adams named a new three-man commission to reopen negotiations with Talleyrand, the Hamiltonians berated him fiercely, and Hamilton's friend, Timothy Pickering, still Secretary of State, went so far as to delay the sailing of two of the three com-

missioners not already in Europe. When the three Americans finally assembled in France early in 1800, they found that the best they could get from her negotiators was confirmation of the principle that "neutral ships make neutral goods." An indemnity for losses already suffered on the high seas in violation of this principle proved to be out of the question.

When the Hamiltonians learned in September that the American envoys had agreed to peace on these meager terms, they launched their fiercest attack yet on John Adams. Hamilton himself gave the signal in a "fatal tirade" against the President early in October, in which he referred to Adams's "extreme egotism," "terrible jealousy," and "violent rage," and proceeded to question even "the solidity of his understanding." This attack so shattered the Federalist party that, as one former leader said to another, "We have no rallying-point;

*"Preparation for War to defend Commerce," contemporary engraving by William Russell Birch of Southwark shipyard, Philadelphia, showing the 36-gun frigate Philadelphia under construction, 1799. Swedish Church shown in background. Philadelphia was captured during the war with Barbary pirates in 1804 and destroyed by Stephen Decatur (see p. 312). (Stokes Collection, New York Public Library.)*

*The Boston troops, as reviewed on President Adams's birthday, on the Common, 1799. The State House, completed in that year from plans by Charles Bulfinch, can be seen at the upper right. (Stokes Collection, New York Public Library.)*

and no mortal can divine where and when we shall again collect our strength. . . . Shadows, clouds, and darkness rest on our future prospects."

### THE ALIEN AND SEDITION ACTS

At the time of Adams's election, Madison had written to Jefferson: "You know the temper of Mr. A. better than I do, but I have always conceived it to be rather a ticklish one." One thing Adams soon became most "ticklish" about was the Republican taunt that he was "President by three votes." Other partisan attacks on him and his administration aroused him, early in the summer of 1798, to strike out at his detractors. Adams felt especially imposed upon by Albert Gallatin, who on Madison's retirement from Congress in 1797 had become Republican leader of the House; by the English radical Thomas Cooper who had come to America in 1794 and soon proved himself a vigorous Republican pam-

293

phleteer; and by a number of recently arrived French intellectuals, including the chemist Pierre A. Adet, the botanist André Michaux, and Victor Du Pont, all of whom Adams suspected of engaging in espionage. Many undistinguished but noisy French Jacobins who had fled the repression of the Directory after 1795 also set up a clamor against Adams. Most offensive of all, perhaps, to anglophile Federalists, were the defeated fighters for Irish freedom, who chose this time to carry their insatiable hatred of Britain to the United States.

Nor did Adams forget American-born Republican journalists. Outstanding among them was Franklin's grandson, Benjamin Bache, known as "Lightning-rod Junior," whose Philadelphia *Aurora* had supplanted Freneau's *National Gazette* after 1793 as the leading Republican paper.

Adams might easily have overcome his pique had not the most violent men of his party in June and July 1798 pushed through Congress a series of measures known as the Alien and Sedition Acts. Angered as he was, the President grasped the weapons so gratuitously presented. The first of these measures was a Naturalization Act which raised the residence requirement for American citizenship from five to fourteen years and would have meant permanent disfranchisement for many. The second, the Alien Act, empowered the President in peacetime to order any alien from the country, and to jail for not more than three years those who refused to go. The third, the Alien Enemies Act, permitted the President in wartime to jail enemy aliens at his pleasure. No arrests were made under either alien act, but they did scare hundreds of foreigners from the country.

The fourth measure was the Sedition Act. Its principal clause prescribed fines and jail penalties for anyone speaking, writing, or publishing "with intent to defame . . . or bring into contempt or disrepute" the President or other members of the government. Its intent to gag the Republican opposition until after the next presidential election is evident in the provision continuing the act, "in force until March 3, 1801, and no longer."

Matthew Lyon, an outspoken Irish-born Republican congressman from Vermont, while campaigning for re-election against a "government" man, was the first to be jailed under the Sedition Act. No respect was paid to his person. Jefferson protested that Lyon was treated the same as the vilest criminals of the day; Lyon himself wrote of his filthy cell with nothing "but iron bars to keep the cold out." It was "the common receptacle," he said, "for horse-thieves, . . . or any kind of felons," "I know not which mortifies me most," Jefferson remarked on learning of Lyon's fate, "that I should fear to write what I think, or my country should bear such a state of things." Lyon's constituents backed him to the hilt. During his four-month jail term they re-elected him to Congress.

Many others, most of them Republican editors, followed Lyon to jail and Republican papers had to shut down. With few exceptions the trials were travesties of justice dominated by judges who saw treason behind every expression of Republican sentiments. Grand juries for bringing in the indictments and trial juries for rendering the monotonous verdict of guilty were hand-picked by Federalist United States marshals in defiance of statutes prescribing orderly procedure. The presiding judges often ridiculed the defendants' lawyers and interrupted their presentations so outrageously that many threw up their hands and their cases, leaving the accused to the mercy of the courts.

By far the worst offender was Justice Samuel Chase of the United States Supreme Court before whom, while he was on circuit court duty, both the Republican scholar Thomas Cooper and the unbalanced Republican pamphleteer James Thomas Callender had the misfortune to be haled. "I cannot suppress my feelings at this gross attack upon the President," the Justice declared during Cooper's trial; and then he embarked on a

*"Congressional Pugilists,"* Republican Representative Matthew Lyon, with tongs, attacking Federalist, Roger Griswold, for alleged slurs on Lyon's Revolutionary War record. This cartoon, done by an unknown artist, reveals the bitter feeling prevailing between the parties at the time. (Maryland Historical Society.)

gross attack of his own on Republican principles, as if real republicanism could "only be found in the happy soil of France," where "Liberty, like the religion of Mahomet, is propagated by the sword." When, on his journey to the scene of Callender's trial, Chase was informed that the pamphleteer had once been taken into custody as a vagrant, he replied, "It is a pity that they had not hanged the rascal." Chase harangued juries by the hour spouting Federalist doctrine of such a partisan nature that sensible party colleagues like John Marshall were mortified. The carefully chosen juries loved it and delivered the desired verdicts. Cooper got six months and Callender nine.

The courts, at the same time, fell sharply in the estimation of the people. In January 1798 the states had ratified the eleventh amendment to the Constitution excluding "the judicial power of the United States" from countenancing any suit "against one of the United States by citizens of another State, or by citizens of any foreign state." This amendment had grown out of a Supreme Court verdict against the state of Georgia in *Chisholm* v. *Georgia* in 1794, in a case in which the state had been sued by a British creditor. The amendment was a blow to the federal court system which stirred John Marshall a few years later to heroic efforts to restore the standing of the judiciary (see p. 317). His task was made all the harder by the conduct of the courts in Sedition Act cases.

Madison called the Sedition Act "a monster that must forever disgrace its parents." He and Jefferson both recognized it as the start of the Federalist campaign for the elections of 1800, and they quickly set in motion a broad-gauged attack on the whole Federalist philosophy. Their offensive took the form of a series of resolutions for which their allies won the approval of the legislatures of Kentucky and Virginia in November and December 1798. The resolutions were then circulated among the rest of the states.

Jefferson wrote the Kentucky Resolutions, Madison those adopted in Virginia. Both sets attacked the Hamiltonian "broad interpretation" of the Constitution and developed the state-rights position later used to justify nullification and secession. In Jefferson's words, "the several states composing the United

States of America, are not united on the principle of unlimited submission to their general government"; that government, in Madison's terms, is but a "compact to which the states are parties." The Kentucky Resolutions held that, as parties to the "compact," the states had the right to declare what measures went beyond their agreement and were "unauthoritative, void, and of no force," and to decide what remedies were appropriate. Madison, in the Virginia Resolutions, said that the states together might "interpose" to check the exercise of unauthorized powers. Jefferson, in his Kentucky Resolutions, went further: he held that the legislature *of each individual state* had this right.

No interpretation of the intent, purpose, or action of the Great Convention of 1787 could have been more far-fetched than that expressed in these partisan Resolutions. But Madison and Jefferson at least had a liberalizing goal absent from later state-rights movements in pressing their argument this far. As Jefferson put it in the Kentucky Resolutions, the Alien and Sedition Acts, by employing the loosest construction of the Constitution to impose the tightest tyranny, soured "the mild spirit of our country and its laws."

### THE ELECTION OF 1800

While the "X.Y.Z." affair (p. 291) and other affronts by France had cost the francophile Republicans some strength in the country, their prospects for the presidential campaign of 1800 were brightened by the sharp split in Federalist ranks between the Adams men and the Hamiltonians.

For the campaign of 1800 the Republican caucus named Jefferson and Burr. The Federalists were so divided that no caucus of their leaders was possible. By devices difficult to disentangle, the ticket of Adams and C. C. Pinckney finally was made public; but once again, as in 1796, the central drama revolved around Hamilton's determination to defeat Adams by means of his own running mate. No one was willing to go along with Hamil-

ton's strategy, however, and what was worse, the Republicans, as many Federalists expected, polled enough votes to make the maneuver meaningless. The electoral college voted 65 for Adams and 64 for Pinckney; Jefferson and Burr each received 73 votes.

The Republicans triumphed in a campaign that one writer describes as "a havoc of virulence." But worse was to come. Burr had no pretensions to the Presidency at this time; but many Federalists, especially those from commercial New England and New York, saw in his tie vote with Jefferson an opportunity to raise to the Presidency, "a friend of the Constitution . . . a friend of the commercial interests . . . the firm and decided friend of the *navy*." The *Washington Federalist,* which carried these words in January 1801, went on to say: "The *Eastern* States have had a President and Vice President; So have the *Southern*. It is proper that the *middle* states should also be respected. . . . Mr. Burr can be raised to the Presidency without any *insult* to the feelings of the Federalists, the friends of Government."

According to the Constitution, the House would have to decide between the two Republicans. There the voting was to be by states, not individuals, and nine states (out of 16) were needed to win. On January 9, 1801, Jefferson wrote to a fellow Virginian:

We have eight votes in the House of Representatives certain and there are three other states, Maryland, Delaware, and Vermont, from either of which if a single individual comes over it settles the matter. But I am far from confiding that a single one will come over; . . . nothing seems to bend the spirit of our opponents.

The first ballot in the House was taken on February 11, with the results that Jefferson had foreseen: he carried eight states, Burr six, and two were undecided. And so it went for a feverish week during which 35 tense ballots were taken.

While the deadlock persisted, Federalist strategists, whose party still retained a majority in Congress, began to think in terms of having the Senate "appoint a Presidt. till another election is made," as Monroe reported to Jefferson. The Republicans retorted to rumors of such a "violation of the Constitution," by openly declaring in the press (in the words of "Hortensius"—Monroe's son-in-law, George Hay) that "The usurpation . . . will be instantly and firmly repelled." Jefferson himself warned on February 15: "We thought best to declare openly and firmly, one & all, that the day such an act passed, the Middle States would arm, & that no such usurpation, even for a single day, should be submitted to." Resistance would not only be by arms but by abrogating the Constitution entirely and calling "a convention to reorganize and amend the government." The *Washington Federalist* promptly boasted of what "the militia of Massachusetts consisting of 70,000 in arms— with those of New Hampshire and Connecticut united almost to a man," would do to the "factious foreigners in Pennsylvania or a few *fighting* bacchanals of Virginia . . . farcically performing the manual exercise with *cornstalks* instead of muskets."

"By deceiving one man (a great blockhead) and tempting two (not incorruptible)," Congressman Bayard of Delaware wrote to Hamilton, Burr "might have secured a majority of the states." But Burr resisted Federalist blandishments in such an "honourable and decisive way," as Jefferson himself acknowledged, that worried Federalist leaders began to sound out Jefferson on what they might really expect from him concerning the preservation of Hamilton's fiscal system, the development of the navy, and the future of Federalist office-holders. Some Federalists thought they had actually made a deal with the candidate on these matters; but Jefferson wrote to Monroe on the same day he was approached: "Many attempts have been made to obtain terms and promises from me. I have declared to them unequivocally, that I would not receive the government on capitulation, that I would not go into it with my hands tied."

The deadlock finally was broken on February 17 on the 36th ballot. Hamilton is often given credit for terminating the disastrous struggle; and it is true, as Jefferson wrote to his daughter as early as January 26, "Hamilton is using his uttermost influence to procure my election rather than Colonel Burr's." Hamilton, nevertheless, was deeply out of favor with the Federalist diehards, and his "uttermost influence" fell mainly on deaf ears. Jefferson himself suggested that the Republicans' militant stand against "stretching the Constitution" had brought enough Federalists

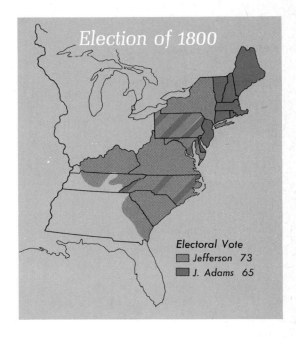

Election of 1800

Electoral Vote
Jefferson 73
J. Adams 65

to their senses. On the other hand, the day after his victory, he wrote to Thomas Mann Randolph: "After exactly a week's balloting there at length appeared ten states for me, four for Burr, and two voted blanks. *This was done without a single vote coming over.*" Jefferson went on to explain the intricacies of Federalist strategy, and continued: "They had before deliberated whether they would come over in a body, when they saw they could not force Burr on the republicans, or keep their body entire and unbroken to act in phalanx

298

on such grounds of opposition as they shall hereafter be able to conjure up. Their vote [none whatever having been cast directly for Jefferson] showed what they had decided on, and is considered a declaration of perpetual war."

The next Congress put an end to this kind of problem by sending the Twelfth Amendment to the states, which ratified it by September 1804. This amendment provided that, henceforth, "The electors . . . shall name in their ballots the person voted for as President, and in distinct ballots the person voted for as Vice-President."

The transfer of power from the Federalists to the Republicans had been much more foreboding than the transfer of the Presidency from Washington to Adams in 1796. Yet it had been accomplished peacefully after all, and henceforth an organized opposition was to be allowed its own free voice and aspirations to power without any taint of treason or disloyalty.

Although the Republicans in 1800 captured the Presidency and control of both the House and the Senate, nevertheless the country's first great shift in political power was not quite complete. Just before adjourning, in March 1801, the retiring Federalist Congress gave Adams a new judiciary act which relieved Supreme Court and district court justices from riding to the circuit courts, created a whole new group of circuit court judges, and increased the number of district court judges. Adams filled these life-time jobs and other new judicial posts with Federalist sympathizers. Most important, he named his interim Secretary of State, John Marshall, as Chief Justice of the Supreme Court. Adams was the last Federalist President, but during more than 30 years of Republican political control Justice Marshall continued to hand down Federalist interpretations of the law.

### THE FEDERALIST DECADE

The Federalist decade was a great one in the history of the country and of the world.

Practical men, their minds and hearts more at home with problems of commerce, currency, and speculation than with politics and diplomacy, had nevertheless transformed an infant and shaky nation devoted to individualism and fractious under restraint, into a respected commonwealth. Very early in the Federalist regime, many of the leaders of the government had returned with relief to their private occupations. Their successors clung to political office largely for the emoluments of power until they too, now against their will, were turned out to private pastures. Businessmen were never to make satisfactory political leaders in America. This circumstance makes only the more remarkable the achievement of the businessmen among the first great Federalists.

Cautious, conservative, preferring the order of things under which they had achieved success, the established seaboard businessmen remained skeptical of the incredible opportunities of the American continent, scornful of the aspirations of those of low breeding and poor education to participate in American development. John Jay in 1809 expressed the old Federalist position well when he wrote, "that those who own the country are most fit persons to participate in the government of it." Much later, in 1821, when New York State's Federalist constitution was on the verge of replacement, Chancellor Kent recalled the aristocratic view, "that to the beneficence and liberality of those who have property, we owe all the embellishments and comforts and blessings of life." These, after all, were sound Lockeian principles; and while no longer in the nineteenth century revolutionary principles, they still suggest the grounds on which the Federalist oligarchy had preserved the independence of the United States.

The "people" for a long time had looked to the "beneficence and liberality of those who have property" for the preservation of their political well-being. In the Jeffersonian era and for much of the rest of the nineteenth century in resource-rich America, Federalist leadership was no longer wanted; nor did the Federalist worthies any longer wish to lead.

When the country became Republican and nationalistic, they became sectional and narrow. On the morning of Jefferson's inauguration, John Marshall wrote of his fears to C. C. Pinckney: "The Democrats are divided into speculative theorists & absolute terrorists. With the latter I am disposed to class Mr. Jefferson." A few months later, the Boston merchant, George Cabot, described by Marshall's biographer Albert J. Beveridge as "the ablest, most moderate and far-seeing of the New England Federalists," wrote: "We are doomed to suffer all the evils of *excessive* democracy through the United States. . . . Maratists and Robespierrians everywhere raise their heads. . . . There will be neither justice nor stability in any system, if some material parts of it are not independent of popular control."

Jefferson himself was more sanguine. Two days after his inauguration he wrote to John Dickinson:

What a satisfaction have we in the contemplation of the benevolent effects of our efforts, compared with those of the leaders on the other side, who have discountenanced all advances in science as dangerous innovations, have endeavoured to render all philosophy and republicanism terms of reproach, to persuade us that man cannot be governed but by the rod, etc. I shall have the happiness of living and dying in the contrary hope.

# READINGS

J.C. Miller, *The Federalist Era 1789–1801* (1960), is the best modern introduction to the period of this chapter, and rich in bibliography. H.J. Ford, *Washington and His Colleagues* (1921), and J.S. Bassett, *The Federalist System* (1906), are worthwhile older surveys. C.G. Bowers, *Jefferson and Hamilton* (1925), is a colorful account with a strong Antifederalist bias. Equally good reading on the Federalist side are vols. II and III of A.J. Beveridge, *The Life of John Marshall* (4 vols., 1916–1919). E.S. Maclay, ed., *The Journal of William Maclay* (1928), provides lively comment on the First Congress by an Anti-federalist senator. His views may be compared with those of an arch-Federalist from Massachusetts in Seth Ames, ed., *Works of Fisher Ames* (2 vols., Boston, 1854).

The first two volumes of the distinguished series on administrative history by L.D. White: *The Federalists* (1948) and *The Jeffersonians* (1951) are comprehensive. The following works, whose coverage is clear from thir titles, are useful on special phases of Federalist precedent-making: R.V. Harlow, *The History of Legislative Methods in the Period before 1825* (1927); E.S. Corwin, *The President: Office and Powers 1787–1948* (1948); H.B. Learned, *The President's Cabinet: Studies in the Origin, Formation and Structure of an American Institution* (1912); D.S. Alexander, *History and Procedure of the House of Representatives* (1916); and G.H. Haynes, *The Senate of the United States: Its History and Practice* (2 vols., 1938).

The best approach to Hamilton's thinking is through his *Papers,* now being edited by H.C. Syrett and J.E. Cooke. By 1969, 15 volumes had been issued, reaching to January 1794. J.C. Miller, *Alexander Hamilton: Portrait in Paradox* (1959), is probably the fairest biography of this controversial figure. It should be supplemented by J.P. Boyd, *Number 7, Alexander Hamilton's Secret Attempts To Control American Foreign Policy* (1964). Other useful studies, though partial and defensive in tone, include Broadus Mitchell, *Alexander Hamilton* (2 vols., 1957, 1962), and Clinton Rossiter, *Alexander Hamilton and the Constitution* (1964). Bray Hammond, *Banks and Politics in America: From the Revolution to the Civil War* (1957), and the later chapters of E.J. Ferguson, *The Power of the Purse, A History of American Public Finance 1776–1790* (1961), put Hamilton's economic program in context. The biographies of Washington, Madison, and Jay, cited in earlier chapters, and of Jefferson, cited in Readings for Chapter Ten, all are essential for the Federalist period and party rivalry.

Richard Hofstadter, *The Idea of a Party System: The Rise of Legitimate Opposition in the United States 1780–1840* (1969), traces the gradual acceptance of party competition, with some background on the English experience. Joseph Charles, *The Origins of the American Party System* (1961), is a penetrating short account. Valuable also are W.N. Chambers, *Political Parties in a New Nation, The American Experience 1776–1809* (1963), and Chambers and W.D. Burnham, eds., *The American Party Systems: Stages of Development* (1967). C.A. Beard, *The Economic Origins of Jeffersonian Democracy* (1915), may be supplemented by two books by N.E. Cunningham, Jr., *The Jeffersonian Republicans: The Formation of Party Organization 1789–1801* (1957), and *The Jeffer-*

*sonian Republicans in Power: Party Operations 1801–1809* (1963). E.P. Link, *Democratic-Republican Societies 1790–1800* (1942), covers these sources of early Republican strength.

Foreign affairs in the Federalist period, and their inescapable impact on party development, are dealt with illuminatingly in the following works: Felix Gilbert, *To the Farewell Address, Ideas of Early American Foreign Policy* (1961); Alexander De Conde, *Entangling Alliance: Politics and Diplomacy under George Washington* (1958), and *The Quasi-War: The Politics and Diplomacy of the Undeclared War with France 1797–1801* (1966); P.A. Varg, *Foreign Policies of the Founding Fathers* (1963); C.D. Hazen, *Contemporary American Opinion of the French Revolution* (1897); L.S. Kaplan, *Jefferson and France* (1967); and S.F. Bemis, *Jay's Treaty* (1923), and *Pinckney's Treaty* (1926). L.B. Dunbar, *A Study of the "Monarchical" Tendencies in the United States from 1776 to 1801* (1923), is suggestive on the lasting attraction of the English system.

The frontier and foreign policy are covered thoroughly in A.P. Whitaker, *The Spanish-American Frontier 1783–1795* (1927), and *The Mississippi Question 1795–1803* (1934), and in F.S. Philbrick, *The Rise of the West 1754–1830* (1965). L.D. Baldwin, *Whiskey Rebels: The Story of a Frontier Uprising* (1939), is a readable account.

Gilbert Chinard, *Honest John Adams* (1933), and Page Smith, *John Adams* (2 vols., 1962), are good biographies of the second President. Authoritative works on his administration include M.J. Dauer, *The Adams Federalists* (1953), and S.G. Kurtz, *The Presidency of John Adams: The Collapse of Federalism 1795–1800* (1958). Adams was one of the most cogent thinkers of his day. A fascinating work made up of his marginal comments on books by his contemporary philosophers is Zoltán Haraszti, *John Adams and the Prophets of Progress* (1952). A more conventional anthology is Adrienne Koch and William Peden, eds., *The Selected Writings of John and John Quincy Adams* (1946). J.C. Miller, *Crises in Freedom: The Alien and Sedition Acts* (1951), and J.M. Smith, *Freedom's Fetters* (1956), are good on the origins and impact of these early attempts at repression of opinion. L.W. Levy, *Legacy of Suppression: Freedom of Speech and Press in Early American History* (1960), is useful for background on issues raised by the Sedition Act. Morton Borden, *The Federalism of James A. Bayard* (1955), is especially good on the election of 1800.

# TEN

Of all the great figures among the Founding Fathers, Thomas Jefferson was at once the most approachable and the most aloof. The rustic dress he affected, and his casual pose even on solemn public occasions, furthered the illusion of informality in his manner. Senator Maclay of Pennsylvania left us a characteristic picture of Jefferson in 1790, when, on the latter's return from five years in Paris to take up his duties as Secretary of State, he appeared before a committee of the Upper House to answer questions on foreign affairs:

His clothes seem too small for him. He sits in a lounging manner, on one hip commonly, and with one of his shoulders elevated much above the other. . . . His whole figure has a loose, shackling air. He had a rambling, vacant look, and nothing of that firm collected deportment which I expected would dignify the presence of a secretary or minister. I looked for gravity, but a laxity of manner seemed shed about him.

Jefferson tended to underscore this impression as he grew older. In 1804, for example, Augustus Foster, secretary of the British Legation in Washington, described the President's dress in detail, not omitting his "yarn stockings, and slippers down at the heels," and concluded that he looked, to the life, "very much like . . . a tall, large-boned farmer." Yet Maclay, while commenting that Jefferson's face had "a sunny aspect," felt constrained to add that he "has rather the air of stiffness in his manner." And Foster, noting that Jefferson appeared "good natured, frank, and rather friendly," remarked also that "he had somewhat of a cynical expression of countenance." "The people," writes Albert Jay Nock, one of Jefferson's most perceptive biographers, "could

# JEFFERSON
# IN POWER

have quite taken him to their hearts if they had not felt, as every one felt in his presence, that he was always graciously but firmly holding them off."

Jefferson had three great loves: music, "the favorite passion of my soul"; science, "my supreme delight"; and Martha Wayles Skelton, "the cherished companion of my life, in whose affections, unabated on both sides, I . . . lived ten years in unchequered happiness." Jefferson had married the widow Skelton in his 29th year, on New Year's Day, 1772. Her father, John Wayles, died only months after the wedding, leaving her an inheritance, as Jefferson observed, "about equal to my own patrimony [which was large], and consequently doubled the ease of our circumstances." Before her death in 1782, Mrs. Jefferson bore her husband six children, four of whom failed to reach the age of two; only Martha Jefferson, their first-born, outlived her father. Although Jefferson was a prolific writer on many subjects, virtually everything we know of his wife is confined to the short record of births and deaths, including her own, which he kept on the leaf of his prayer book.

By 1782, Jefferson felt that he had given the nation and Virginia all the service a republic or a republican state could demand.

To be dragooned longer away from "my family, my friends, my farm and my books," he wrote to James Monroe early that year, "would be slavery, and not that liberty which the Bill of Rights has made inviolable." But his bereavement in September left him in "the stupor of mind which rendered me as dead to the world as was she whose loss occasioned it." "A single event," he wrote to his French friend, the Marquis de Chastellux, "wiped away all my plans [of retirement], and left me a blank which I had not the spirits to fill up." Music and science, upon which had "rested all prospects of future happiness," had lost their charm, along with all other "domestic and literary objects." Public life, once his reluctant response to duty as a landed Virginia gentleman, now became his chief diversion. Politics, once his avocation, became his shield.

Inured by personal tragedy to "hiding the inner springs of sentiment," Jefferson henceforth faced politicians and political issues with far more equanimity than Washington, Hamilton, and most of his other colleagues. His stoicism, nevertheless, was sometimes strained beyond endurance, especially by antagonists who lacked his restraint. During the acrimonious 1796 presidential campaign, Jefferson wrote to a friend with characteristic

303

304

discontent: "It has been a source of great pain to me to have met with so many among our opponents who had not the liberality to distinguish between political and social opposition; who transferred at once to the person the hatred they bore to his political opinions." After 1796, he was to meet many more of this type and in relation to them to succumb himself to their defects of character.

## 1   *The Republicans Take Office*

### THE INAUGURAL PROMISE

Jefferson took the Republican victory in 1800 much more seriously than some historians have taken it since. "The Federalists," he wrote later in life from a perspective of many years, "wished for everything which would approach our new government to a monarchy; the Republicans, to preserve it essentially republican." This preservation, he held, had been assured by his triumph. "The revolution of 1800 was as real a revolution in the principles of government as that of 1776 was in its form."

At the time of the Republican success at the polls, Jefferson could hardly deny that the Federalist leaders had put up a hard fight and that their followers had been numerous. But the desperate maneuvers during the struggle with Burr in the House, he held, foreshadowed the Federalist party's early extinction. "Our information from all quarters," he wrote to a fellow Virginian soon after his victory, "is that the whole body of federalists" in the country had been alienated from the Federalist leadership, "and I verily believe they will remain embodied with us, so that this conduct of the minority [in Congress] has done in one week what very probably could hardly have been effected by years of mild and impartial administration."

When the day came for his inaugural address, March 4, 1801, Jefferson was prepared to embrace the opportunity presented by the Federalist leaders' perversity. He had taken great pains over the tone and content of this address, which has properly been described since as "a classic exposition of democratic philosophy." Very early in it, he said:

Let us, then, fellow-citizens, unite with one heart and one mind. Let us restore to social intercourse that harmony and affection without which liberty and even life itself are but dreary things. And let us reflect that, having banished from our land that religious intolerance under which mankind so long bled and suffered, we have yet gained little if we countenance a political intolerance as despotic, as wicked, and capable of as bitter and bloody persecutions.

*Unusual pencil sketch of Thomas Jefferson, 1799, by one of the architects of the Capitol, Benjamin H. Latrobe. (Maryland Historical Society.)*

Having thus characterized the Federalist "reign of terror" under the Alien and Sedition Acts, Jefferson continued his conciliatory discourse:

But every difference of opinion is not a difference of principle. We have called by different names brethren of the same principle. We are all Republicans, we are all Federalists. If there be any among us who would wish to dissolve this Union or to change its republican form, let them stand undisturbed as monuments of the safety with which error of opinion may be tolerated where reason is left free to combat it.

The President then disclosed the natural and social foundations of his vision for his country:

Kindly separated by nature and a wide ocean from the exterminating havoc of one quarter of the globe; . . . possessing a chosen country, with room enough for our descendants to the hundredth and thousandth generation; entertaining a due sense of our equal right to the use of our own faculties, to the acquisitions of our own industry, to honor and confidence from our fellow-citizens, resulting not from birth, but from our actions and their sense of them; enlightened by a benign religion, professed, indeed, and practiced in various forms, yet all of them inculcating honesty, truth, temperance, gratitude, and the love of man . . .—with all these blessings, what more is necessary to make us a happy and a prosperous people?

Jefferson answered his question:

Still one thing more, fellow-citizens—a wise and frugal government, which shall restrain men from injuring one another, shall leave them otherwise free to regulate their own pursuits of industry and improvement, and shall not take from the mouth of labor the bread it has earned. This is the sum of good government, and this is necessary to close the circle of our felicities.

Even John Marshall grudgingly praised the President's remarks. Although the new Chief Justice had been excoriating Jefferson ever since 1776, when he thought his cousin a coward for not joining in the Revolutionary fighting, Jefferson generously invited him to officiate at the inaugural ceremony. "I have administered the oath to the Presdt.," Marshall reported to Charles Pinckney, the same day. "His inauguration speech . . . is in general well judged and conciliatory. It is in direct terms giving the lie to the violent party declamation which has elected him, but it is strongly characteristic of the general cast of this political theory."

Jefferson little expected to hold the sympathy of men like the Chief Justice, but his "hopes [that] we shall be able to restore union to our country" were well nurtured by his realization of what failure to do so might mean. "The clergy, who have missed their union with the State," he wrote in May 1801, "the Anglo men, who have missed their union with England, and the political adventurers who have lost the chance of swindling & plunder in the waste of public money, will never cease to bawl, on the breaking up of their sanctuary." Such men, whose tactics during the contest with Burr had opened "upon us an abyss, at which every sincere patriot must shudder," remained beyond the pale of his approaches. "They are invincibles," he wrote, "but I really hope their followers may . . . be brought over. . . . The bulk of these last were real republicans, carried away from us by French excesses. . . . A moderate conduct throughout, which may not revolt our new friends and may give them tenets with us, must be observed."

Federalist die-hards clung to the belief that Jefferson's "moderate conduct" reflected nothing more worthy than the new President's "immoderate thirst for popularity." "In dress, conversation and demeanor," observed one of them, "he studiously sought and displayed the arts of a low demagogue seeking gratification of the democracy on whose voices and votes he laid the foundation of his power."

Yet it was Jefferson who refused to let the date of his birth become known when well-wishers proposed that it be made a public holiday, explaining that he did not approve of "transferring the honour and veneration for

306

the great birthday of our Republic to any individual, or of dividing them with individuals." Unlike Washington, he also rejected proposals for political grand tours. "I am not reconciled," he once remarked, "to the idea of a chief magistrate parading himself through the several States as an object of public gaze and in quest of applause which, to be valuable, should be purely voluntary. I had rather acquire silent good will by a faithful discharge of my duties than owe expressions of it to my putting myself in the way of receiving them."

### THE INNER CIRCLE

Jefferson was much too wise a politician to permit the urgency he felt for conciliation to warp the unity of his own regime. "I have firmly refused," he warned Monroe during his first week in the "President's Palace" (as the White House was then called), "to follow the counsels of those who desired giving offices to some [Federalist] leaders in order to reconcile. I have given and will give only to Republicans."

Of the five Cabinet positions at his disposal, nevertheless, Jefferson calculatingly granted two to New England, where Federalism was most intransigent. Levi Lincoln of Worcester, Massachusetts, was appointed Attorney-General; and Henry Dearborn, of the Maine district, became Secretary of War. Jefferson also named a New Englander, Gideon Granger, Postmaster-General, an office not yet of Cabinet rank. "Union is already effected from New York southward almost completely," Jefferson wrote to General Henry Knox, the Massachusetts Federalist who had been Washington's Secretary of War and who took the trouble to commend Jefferson on his fair-mindedness. "In the New England States it will be slower than elsewhere, from peculiar circumstances better known to yourself than to me. But we will go on attending with the utmost solicitude to their interests and doing them impartial justice, and I have no doubt they will in time do justice to us."

Robert Smith of Baltimore, a wealthy ad-

miralty lawyer avid for political preferment, became Jefferson's Secretary of the Navy. The two most important Cabinet posts went to the two most important Republicans after the President: James Madison became Secretary of State; and Albert Gallatin, Secretary of the Treasury.

In filling the hundreds of other federal jobs, Jefferson moved with feline caution. Virginia Congressman William Branch Giles, in recommending a neighbor of his to the President, wrote, "A pretty general purgation of office has been one of the benefits expected by the friends of the new order of things." Yet the friends of the new order were made to wait for vacancies to occur. "Deprivations of office, if made on the ground of political principles alone," Jefferson wrote, "would revolt our new converts, and give a body to leaders who now stand alone. Some [removals], I know, must be made," he conceded. But "they must be as few as possible, done gradually, and bottomed on some malversation or inherent disqualification."

To this general principle Jefferson maintained one overweening reservation, which he put in some of his harshest language. The "midnight appointments" which John Adams had "crowded in with whip and spur" when he was aware "that he was making appointments not for himself but his successor . . . I consider . . . as nullities, and will not view the persons appointed as even candidates for their office, much less as possessing it by any title meriting respect." Adams's "filling all offices . . . with the bitterest Federalists, and providing for me the alternative either to execute the government by my enemies, . . . or to incur the odium of such numerous removals . . . as might bear me down," was an "outrage on decency" that "should not have its effect."

The problem of patronage has always been considered a sordid one in American politics compared with other issues of domestic policy and foreign relations. Jefferson put the case succinctly when he said, "whenever a man has cast a longing eye on offices, a rottenness begins in his conduct." Yet patronage is the blood stream of the two-party system, which itself has lent stability and continuity to American political affairs. Neither Federalists nor Republicans succeeded in grasping the idea of a permanent two-party system. They could not, of course, blind themselves to the harsh political divisions in the young country; but such divisions only deepened the feeling in the respective camps that their opponents were at best factionalists and feudists, at worst subversives and traitors, who willfully menaced the still fragile Union. The problem of partisanship was not so severe for the Federalists, who felt that God and Nature had formed them expressly for leadership. For the Republicans, however, it posed a shattering dilemma.

"The elective principle becomes nothing," Jefferson said, "if it may be smothered by the enormous patronage of the General Government." He was, of course, complaining of the Federalists who had stacked the government with his political opponents. But what of himself, now? "Those who have once got the ascendency," he complained during Adams's administration, "and possessed themselves of all the resources of the nation, their revenues and offices, have immense means for retaining their advantage." Was he not, then, politically if not morally obligated to use these means for perpetuating Republicanism? There were many in his party who believed he was —Vice-president Burr, of New York, for example; and Congressman Giles of Virginia, and Robert and Samuel Smith of Maryland, and editor William Duane, and demagogue Michael Leib of Pennsylvania. All of them had done the unpleasant work, the local politicking, that had carried Jefferson to his exalted office. For them, the very nub of the "elective principle" was the availability of the "enormous patronage of the General Government." When Jefferson insisted that they wait for vacancies in order to fulfill the promises of jobs they had made during the campaign, they quickly became incensed and schismatic.

Problems of patronage were to contribute heavily to the fragmentation of the Republican party, as the President sagely predicted they would when the leaders "shall be so strong as to fear no other enemy." But Jefferson, Madison, and Gallatin, the innermost triumvirate, by insisting on the priority of national over party unity, managed to postpone the crack-up for a generation.

## REPUBLICANISM
## IN SPIRIT AND SUBSTANCE

It is fitting that Jefferson should have been the first President to begin his term in the rude capital on the Potomac. He himself had suggested the layout of Pennsylvania Avenue, and on many other details had advised Major L'Enfant, the French engineer who designed the city of Washington. "I have examined my papers and found the plans of Frankfort-on-the-Mayne, Carlsruhe, Amsterdam, Strasburg, Paris, Orleans, Bordeaux, Lyons, Montpelier, Marseilles, Turin, and Milan, which I send in a roll by the post." So Jefferson wrote to Major L'Enfant in April 1791, urging him to study these ancient models. On the same day, he wrote to Washington:

Whenever it is proposed to prepare plans for the Capitol I should prefer the adoption of some one of the models of antiquity which have had the approbation of thousands of years; and for the President's house I should prefer the celebrated fronts of modern buildings which have already received the approbation of all good judges. . . . While in Europe I selected about a dozen or two of the handsomest fronts of private buildings, of which I have the plates.

Such architectural conservatism may seem out of character in the philosopher of revolution; yet it must be acknowledged that his views reflected a sort of centuries' long popular ballot. Actually, Jefferson's final plans for "Federal City," though similar in outline to L'Enfant's, were much more modest and cramped, and irked the Frenchman. L'Enfant's grander proposals ultimately won approval; but for decades little progress was made in alleviating the Republican simplicity of the

308

swamp site. Early in 1804, members of the government grew so distressed with the state of the "little village in the midst of the woods," that a spirited debate took place in Congress on a measure to move the capital permanently to Baltimore. After a visit to Washington later the same year, the British poet Thomas Moore lampooned the city and its pretensions:

This embryo capital, where Fancy sees
Squares in morasses, obelisks in trees;
Where second-sighted seers, even now adorn
With shrines unbuilt and heroes yet unborn,
Though nought but woods and Jefferson they see,
Where streets should run and sages *ought* to be.

Besides employing the Frenchman L'Enfant to plan "Federal City," the young country looked to an Irishman, James Hoban, to design the White House, and to an Englishman, Benjamin H. Latrobe (working with the American, William Thornton), to design the Capitol. Adams's Alien Act offered poor hospitality to such men, and Jefferson, once he had named his advisers and manned his administration, saw to it that Congress allowed this "libel on legislation" to lapse. Once more, distinguished foreigners were welcomed to the United States. Next, Jefferson freed all who had been jailed for infractions of the Sedition Act, and asked Congress to return all fines collected under it. He also recommended the restoration of the five-year residence requirement (instead of the Naturalization Act's fourteen-year requirement) for foreigners who wanted to become American citizens. Congress acted favorably on both suggestions.

Having thus righted matters of the spirit, Jefferson turned to matters of the purse. During his occupancy of the "President's Palace," he did away with Washington's regular lavish "levees" and "the mimicry I found established of royal forms and ceremonies." On the other hand, his personal hospitality became legendary, and murmurings were heard that whereas Washington entertained once a week, Jefferson held a levee every night: "Mr. Madison," a White House guest reported on one occa-

sion, observed that the wine the President was serving "was the most delightful wine when drank in moderation, but that more than a few glasses always produced a headache the next day. . . . Mr. Granger [the Postmaster-General] remarked with point that this was the very time to try the experiment, as the next day being Sunday would allow time for a recovery from its effects. The point was not lost upon the host and bottle after bottle came in."

Tales of such indulgence were circulated at the time (and have been used since) to suggest that tippling might be included among Jefferson's taints of character. But more sanguine souls were grateful that his wine cellar, well stocked at his own expense during his tenure in France, became an oasis in "this desert city."

Retrenchment in the "President's Palace" was a relatively simple matter in the wilds of Washington, where social climbers determined to shake the President's hand were far fewer than in Philadelphia or New York. In economizing in other areas of government, Jefferson moved with the same caution as in distributing patronage, and for the same reason: to avoid presenting "a handle to the malcontents among us" who might weaken national unity. Federalist leaders had a less flattering interpretation of the President's "temporizing," which nevertheless served his purpose of prolonging their patience with him. Hamilton stated this version well in a letter to Congressman Bayard during the Burr controversy in the House:

[Jefferson] is as likely as any man I know to temporize, to calculate what will be likely to promote his own reputation and advantage; and the probable result of such a temper is the preservation of systems, though originally opposed, which, being once established, could not be overturned without danger to the person who did it. To my mind, a true estimate of Mr. Jefferson's character warrants the expectation of a temporizing rather than a violent system.

Jefferson's own remarks after taking office seemed to confirm this view of his policy, and have led later historians to conclude that once

in office he merely "domesticated" Hamiltonian practices. Jefferson dared not, for example, attempt to overthrow the Federalists' assumption of state debts nor repudiate the securities by which this and other Hamiltonian fiscal operations had been funded and the public credit maintained. "It mortifies me," he complained, "to be strengthening principles which I deem radically vicious, but this vice is entailed on us by the first error. . . . What is practicable must often control what is pure theory."

The banking system also was safe, at least from extinction. "It is certainly for the public good," Jefferson advised Gallatin in 1802, "to keep all the banks competitors for our favours by a judicious distribution of [public deposits] and thus to engage the individuals who belong to them in support of the reformed order of things, or at least in an acquiescence under it." When, late in 1803, soon after the Louisiana Purchase (see p. 326), there was a movement for the establishment of a branch of the Bank of the United States in recently acquired New Orleans, Jefferson wrote to Gallatin:

This institution is one of the most deadly hostility existing against the principles and form of our Constitution. . . . Penetrating by its branches every part of the Union, acting by command and in phalanx [it] may, in a critical moment, upset the government. I deem no government safe which is under the vassalage of any self-constituted authorities, or any other authority than that of the nation or its regular functionaries.

He acknowledged, nevertheless, that "the nation is at this time so strong and united in [the Bank's] sentiments that it cannot be shaken at this moment," and signed the authorization for the new branch that Gallatin wanted. Republican proposals for the abolition of the costly mint and still more costly navy,

309

310

in turn, were withdrawn on the first show of serious Federalist opposition.

Yet Hamilton knew as well as anyone that Jefferson would make a strong President. "It is not true," he wrote, "that [Jefferson] is an enemy to the power of the Executive. . . . It is a fact which I have frequently mentioned, that, while we were in the administration together, he was generally for a large construction of the Executive authority and not backward to act upon it in cases which coincided with his views." This opinion, of course, is but another brush stroke in the portrait of Jefferson as nothing but a Federal centralist in Republican clothing. And it is true that his show of nationalism, especially in the conduct of foreign affairs, did complete the alienation from him of the zealous state-rights Republicans who had already become disillusioned by the President's strong stand on federal patronage (see p. 306).

But the "cases that coincided with his views" were far from Federalist ones. "Among the first and most important" of these was ridding the country of "a debt of a hundred millions, growing by usurious interest, and an artificial paper phalanx overruling the agricultural mass of our country." In this "case," according to Jefferson, Madison, and Gallatin, lay the crux of Republicanism, and the crux of the country's future. Was it true, as Hamilton insisted, that in order to survive, the Union had to hold the favor of the rich by means of public securities that carried high interest rates and would not soon be "extinguished"? Or was it true that rich rentiers were, in Gallatin's words, "idle and dissipated members of the community," whose claims on the Treasury needlessly sucked up through taxation the small amounts of capital accumulated by the men on the frontier who were undertaking the real development of the resources of the land? Jefferson and his friends knew what their answer was. They could not repudiate the national debt. But they could "reform the waste of public money and thus drive away the vultures who prey upon it."

"Hamilton," Jefferson wrote in an early memorandum to Gallatin on this subject,

in order that he might have the entire government of his [political] machine, determined so to complicate it that neither the President nor Congress should be able to understand it or to control him. He succeeded in doing this, not only beyond their reach, but so that at length he could not unravel it himself. He gave to the debt in the first instance, in funding it, the most artificial and mysterious form he could devise. He then moulded up his appropriations of a number of scraps and remnants, . . . until the whole system was involved in impenetrable fog; and while he was giving himself the airs of providing for the payment of the debt, he left himself free to add to it continually, as he did in fact, instead of paying it.

Jefferson then admonished Gallatin to keep the country's finances so simple "that every member of the Congress and every man of any mind in the Union should be able to comprehend them." He himself, meanwhile, halted the expansion of the navy, began a "chaste reformation" of the army, dismembered the diplomatic corps, ordered the Postmaster-General to employ no printers, and eliminated many tax-collectors. He reported these economies in his first "State of the Union" message, which he sent to Congress in December 1801, instead of delivering it "from the throne" as Washington and Adams had done. Jefferson went on to urge that Congress profit by his example.

To keep waste to a minimum, Jefferson recommended that Congress henceforth appropriate funds only for specific purposes, rather than in lump sums for the different departments, as had previously been the practice. He also advised Congress to require annual accountings from the Secretary of the Treasury showing how each of the departments had actually spent its money. Such frugality and good management, Jefferson thought, would make it possible for Congress to repeal the hated excise taxes immediately, and cancel all postage on newspapers "to facilitate the progress of information." Commercial prospects, and hence the prospects of revenue from import duties, were so good, Jefferson believed, that even without internal taxes, payment of the public debt could be speeded up and millions of dollars in interest saved.

By the end of 1802, Jefferson's calculations had been fully justified. In one year, he told Congress in his second annual message in December, "without a direct tax, without internal taxes, and without borrowing, . . . upward of eight millions of dollars, principal and interest, of the public debt," had been paid, and the Treasury had, besides, a surplus of $4.5 million. "When merely by avoiding false objects of expense," he concluded, "we are able . . . to make large and effectual payments toward the . . . emancipation of our posterity from that moral canker [the public debt], it is an encouragement . . . of the highest order to proceed, as we have begun, in substituting economy for taxation." Two years later, near the end of his first term, Jefferson was able proudly to proclaim that "it may be the pleasure and pride of an American to ask what farmer, what mechanic, what labourer, ever sees a taxgatherer of the United States."

## THE BARBARY CORSAIRS

Jefferson's economies in the naval and military establishments were prompted in part by the theory, a favorite of his, that American commerce and commercial friendship alone were formidable weapons in foreign relations. Every foreign nation, he argued, felt such a vital interest in American trade and the use of American ships and harbors, that none would dare risk war. But this blanket proposition failed to cover such outlaw nations as Morocco, Algiers, Tunis, and Tripoli, whose rulers were in league with the Barbary pirates operating off their shores. For centuries such pirates had preyed on vessels sailing Atlantic and Mediterranean routes, stealing their cargoes and selling their crews and passengers into slavery. In exchange for promises of protection, the rulers of the Barbary states demanded tribute from the commercial nations; and even though the "protection" proved to

be little more than nominal, these nations found it the better part of valor to pay. Britain, mistress of the seas, paid tribute herself and often connived with the pirates to keep other nations from encroaching on her trade.

When the United States became an independent nation, American shipping, the favorite target of the British, proved especially vulnerable to pirate attack. As Franklin's assistant in Paris in 1784, Jefferson asked, "Why not go to war with them?" He continued in a letter to Monroe: "We ought to begin a naval power if we mean to carry on our own commerce. Can we begin it on a more honorable occasion, or with a weaker foe? I am of the opinion Paul Jones with half a dozen frigates would totally destroy their commerce." Nothing came of this uncharacteristic bellicosity or of Jefferson's later efforts as envoy in Paris and as Washington's Secretary of State to organize a coalition of maritime powers to blockade the Barbary coast and keep the pirates off the sea. "When this idea [of paying them tribute] comes across my mind," Jefferson cried in 1786, "my faculties are absolutely suspended between indignation and impatience." Yet over a period of ten years he sadly watched the administrations of Washington and Adams sweeten pirate treasuries with $2 million, while losses of ships, cargoes, and men mounted. Early in May 1801 Jusuf Caramelli, the Bashaw of Tripoli, suddenly demanded an increase in American payments. When Jefferson bridled at this news, the Bashaw ordered the flag-staff in front of the American consul's residence in Tripoli cut down, in effect, a declaration of outright war. Jefferson, eager to put an end to Barbary extortions once and for all, accepted the challenge.

Like most wars, the conflict with the Barbary buccaneers was more easily begun than ended. Jefferson promptly ordered a naval squadron to sew up the pirates in their home ports, but this proved difficult for a navy "supported" by an economy-minded administration. Confusion in Republican councils at home and indecisiveness of command at the scenes

of battle prolonged the war. The only bright spot for the Americans occurred early in 1804 when Lieutenant Stephen Decatur stole into the harbor at Tripoli with a small force of men and burned the frigate *Philadelphia*, which had run aground and been captured by the Tripolitans. Fortunately for the Americans, the Bashaw himself was having domestic troubles, and at last, in 1805, threatened with the loss of his throne from other quarters, he sued for peace with the United States. The peace treaty, in the words of Commodore Preble, the American naval commander during most of the fighting, put American relations with Tripoli "on more honorable terms than any other nation has ever been able to command."

The United States continued to pay tribute to the pirate states until 1816, but at a much lower rate than before. The New England merchant community and other maritime centers were as pleased as the administration by this particular economy. The costs of the war, however, sucked much of the satisfaction from it. Determined that these costs should not delay eradication of the public debt inherited from the Federalists, Gallatin devised new tariffs in 1804 to make up a special "Mediterranean Fund." Henceforth, the cost of protecting the commerce and seamen of the United States from pirate attacks was kept out of the general budget and defrayed by the special duties. This was a financial dodge, but one in keeping with the salutary Republican

principle of letting the public know what it was paying for.

## II  *The War with the Judiciary*

### THE LAW AND THE PEOPLE

In the same State of the Union message of December 8, 1801, in which he urged his "case" for economy on Congress, Jefferson recurred to his second great issue with the Federalists: the question of the national Judiciary, which, unlike the Legislature and the Executive, remained in Federalist hands.

No department of government touched the everyday life and interests of the people more directly than the courts. With the rush of settlers to the frontier following the quieting of the Indian menace in the West (see p. 281), land titles in particular had fallen into a terrible tangle, and fear of litigation was widespread. Cases also arose regularly over the collection of debts and taxes, the settlement of bankruptcies, the liquidation of foreclosed property, the assessment of damages arising from trespass or accident, and the probation of wills and the settlement of estates. When out-of-state claimants and creditors were involved in such cases, they were tried initially not in local courts, which were often manned by the defendant's friends and neighbors, but in the lower federal courts inevitably manned by strangers. Federal courts could also take "original cognizance" in suits that might arise from dereliction in payment of federal excises and other federal taxes, and from alleged violations of federal statutes like the Sedition Act of 1798, of agreements like Jay's Treaty of 1794, and of the Constitution itself.

Still other cases, much more dubious in their origins, were avidly accepted by the federal courts under anglophile Federalist judges. These cases arose over alleged infractions of executive edicts like the Neutrality Proclamation of 1793, to which the courts gave the force of legislation, and over numerous other international disputes occasioned by the "disturbances which agitate Europe." No federal laws imposed penalties in these cases; but the judges justified taking jurisdiction under the English common law, which they held to be in force against "crimes" upon which Congress had not yet acted.

One ironic doctrine of the common law was expressed in the edict, "born a subject, always a subject," which Americans had forcibly rejected by the Revolution. Federalist judges, at Britain's behest, employed this doctrine against Americans—Republicans, by and large—who had turned naturalized Frenchmen to prey on British shipping during the wars of the French Revolution. The English common law, in addition, was harsher even than the Sedition Act in matters of freedom of thought, assembly, and expression, and Federalist judges had not hesitated to try Republican spokesmen by English precedents when the American legislation did not cover the grounds. The English common law, finally, was especially hard on debtors, defaulters, and bankrupts, toward whom state courts and state legislatures, recognizing the unusual instability of the American economy, had begun to take a more lenient stance.

Jefferson put the Republican case against Federalist adoption of the common law most strongly to Edmund Randolph in August 1799:

Of all the doctrines which have ever been broached by the federal government, the novel one, of the common law being in force . . . in their courts, is to me the most formidable. . . . The bank law, the treaty doctrine, the sedition act, alien act, . . . etc., etc., have been solitary, unconsequential, timid things, in comparison with the audacious, barefaced, and sweeping pretension to a system of law for the United States, without the adoption of their Legislature, and so infinitively beyond their power to adopt. If this assumption be yielded to, the State courts may be shut up, as there will then be nothing to hinder citizens of the same State suing each other in the federal courts in every case, as on a bond for instance, because the common law obliges payment of it, and the common law they say is their law.

Court procedure—the delays imposed by infrequency of court sittings, the bullying of litigants and jurors by court attendants, the knavery of lawyers, and the vulgar and prejudiced conduct of most judges—contributed as much as the content of the law itself to the

Latrobe's "Richmond: Sketch in the Court of Appeals," 1798—an ironic view of the judiciary. The quotation, "Brekekexkoax-koax-koax . . .," is from Aristophanes' satire, "The Frogs." (Maryland Historical Society.)

almost universal hatred of the whole business of the "administration of justice" under the Federalist regime. Since almost every defect

314

of court procedure was magnified in the federal courts, the hatred of federal justice had grown most intense. The establishment of the federal court system by the Judiciary Act of 1789 (see p. 273) had been received at the time with considerable popular misgiving. "It swallows up every shadow of a State judiciary," cried James Jackson of Georgia in the House. "This department I dread as an awful tribunal," added a congressman from New York. "By its institution, the Judges are completely independent, being secure of their salaries, and removable only by impeachment." The enlargement of the federal court system by the Judiciary Act of February 1801, under which Adams made his notorious "midnight appointments" (see p. 298), only deepened the suspicions of those fearful of the spread of Federalist usurpation and "tyranny." The Federalists, Jefferson wrote to John Dickinson soon after this Act was passed,

have retired into the judiciary as a stronghold. There the remains of Federalism are to be preserved and fed from the Treasury, and from that battery all the works of Republicanism are to be beaten down and erased. By a fraudulent use of the Constitution, which has made judges irremovable, they have multiplied useless judges merely to strengthen their phalanx.

Representative Giles of Virginia was even more forthright: "The revolution [of 1800] is incomplete so long as that strong fortress [the judiciary] is in possession of the enemy." To complete the revolution, he demanded "the absolute repeal of the whole judiciary system."

### THE REPEAL PROJECT

Repeal of the Judiciary Act of February 1801 (not to speak of "the whole judiciary system") had to wait until the new Republican-controlled Congress convened in December. But the President did not delay that long in opening his war on the "enemy." "The only shield for our Republican citizens against the federalism of the courts," Jefferson wrote in April 1801, "is to have attorneys & Marshals republicans." Despite his strategy of caution in dispensing patronage, he unceremoniously kicked out Adams's appointees to these jobs and filled them with his own.

Not all Republicans were as sanguine as Giles and Jefferson about the constitutionality of repeal of the Federalists' Judiciary Act. The Constitution explicitly states that federal judges, "both of the Supreme and inferior courts, shall hold their offices during good behavior." Would it be legal, then, for the two other departments, for the President and Congress, in effect, to remove the new Federalist members of the judiciary simply by eliminating their jobs? Would not Marshall's Federalist Supreme Court nullify repeal on these grounds at the first opportunity—as rumor said it was preparing to?

When writing his State of the Union address to the new Congress, Jefferson at first took explicit cognizance of these questions. In a long paragraph on the great constitutional issue of judicial review he reasserted his old belief that, under the principle of the separation of executive, legislative, and judicial departments, each, "according to its own judgment and uncontrolled by the opinions of any other departments, . . . must have a right . . . to decide on the validity of an act." To reinforce his stand on the equality of the three departments, he then reviewed his conduct as President in relation to the Sedition Act:

Called on by the position in which the nation had placed me to exercise in their behalf my free and independent judgment, I took that act into consideration, compared it with the Constitution, viewed it under every aspect of which I thought it susceptible, and gave it all the attention which the magnitude of the case demanded. On mature deliberation . . . I do declare that I hold that act to be in palpable and unqualified contradiction to the Constitution. Considering it then as a nullity, I have relieved from oppression under it those of my fellow citizens who were within reach of the functions confided in me.

Although he had referred in his letter to Dickinson to the Federalists' "fraudulent use of the Constitution" in loading his administration with "irremovable judges," Jefferson does not appear to have intended to employ the power he claimed by "Executive Review" to declare the Federalists' Judiciary Act unconstitutional. His primary aim was rather to assure Republican legislators that they could meddle with the "permanent" judiciary as long as their constituencies—the last repository of power—did not vote them out, and that the Executive would back them up. He also meant to warn Marshall in advance that nullification by the Supreme Court of congressional repeal of the Federalists' Judiciary Act would create a deadlock perilous to the Union.

Jefferson had already signed the address with this long philosophical treatise included, when he recalled his larger strategy of wooing as many moderate Federalists as he could. At the last moment before sending it to the Capitol to be read, he struck out the entire incendiary theme. "This whole paragraph," he noted on the margin of the final draft itself, "was omitted as capable of being chicaned, and furnishing something to the opposition to make a handle of. It was thought better that the message should be clear of everything which the public might be made to misunderstand."

In the "cleared up" address, Jefferson's reference to the judiciary was the soul of mildness, short and sweet: "The judiciary system of the United States, and especially that portion of it recently erected, will of course present itself to the contemplation of Congress." To assist the legislators, Jefferson presented at the same time "an exact statement of all the causes decided since the first establishment of the courts, and of those which were depending when additional courts and judges were brought in to their aid." This summary showed that the business of the federal courts had in fact been declining, and that on the relatively innocuous grounds of frugality alone the Federalists' expansion of the judiciary had been wholly uncalled for.

Jefferson's last-minute "temporizing" failed to conceal the poison pen behind the innocuous language. The arch-Federalist, Fisher Ames, promptly reported that the State of the Union message "announces the downfall of the late revision of the Judiciary. . . . The U.S. Gov't . . . is to be dismantled like an old ship. . . . The state gov'ts are to be exhibited as alone safe and salutary." Marshall's Supreme Court, moreover, immediately accepted the challenge. The now famous case of *Marbury* v. *Madison,* trivial though it was on its merits, offered Marshall an opportunity too good to miss for striking right back at the executive department, and at Jefferson himself.

William Marbury, among the very last of Adams's "midnight appointees," had been named for a five-year term as one of the new justices of the peace in the District of Columbia on March 2, 1801, and confirmed by the Senate the next day. But the papers had been handled "with his customary negligence of details" by Marshall himself as Adams's Secretary of State (that office was charged in those days with certain domestic duties as well as with the conduct of foreign affairs) and were not delivered to Marbury before Jefferson took office on March 4. Jefferson promptly ordered his Secretary of State, Madison, not to deliver Marbury's commission. Marbury then asked the Supreme Court to issue an order—a so-called "writ of mandamus"—requiring Madison to install him. The case came before the Court on December 21, 1801, just two weeks after Jefferson's State of the Union message. Finding his colleagues unprepared to make a final decision on such short notice, Marshall and the Court on December 22 issued a "preliminary rule" requiring Madison and the administration to "show cause" at the next term of the Court why a writ of mandamus confirming Marbury's possession of his job should not be obeyed.

Technically, a writ of mandamus is an order by a superior authority (in the common law, an order by the king) instructing an inferior one to redress a wrong; and Republican spokesmen lost no time in denouncing Mar-

316

shall's "preliminary rule" as a barefaced bid by the Federalist judiciary to denigrate the executive and intimidate the legislature at one blow. "I think it proper to tell you," wrote a Washington correspondent to the *Salem Register,* "that the late mandamus business in the Supreme Court was calculated expressly with a view to deter from any attempt to repeal [the Federalists' judiciary] law." Congress, concluded this writer, must "rescue the country" from "judges who have so much controul over life and property." There is "reason to believe," he added optimistically, "that Congress will not be deterred from its duty and that the law will be repealed."

Repealed it was. Far from intimidating Congress, Marshall's action in the "mandamus business," as Senator Stevens Thomas Mason of Virginia remarked, "excited a very general indignation and will secure the repeal of the Judiciary Law of the last session, about the propriety of which some of our Republican friends were hesitating."

Congress began its "contemplation" of the "judiciary system of the United States, and especially that portion of it recently erected," on January 6, 1802, when Senator John Breckenridge of Kentucky introduced a modest bill seeking by repeal only to return the country to the court structure that had served it satisfactorily since 1789. An ardent state-rights man, Breckenridge had been entrusted by Jefferson in 1798 with the task of shepherding the Kentucky Resolutions through the legislature of his state, of which he was a leading member. In the succeeding four years, despite his elevation to the Upper House of the national Congress, his zeal for the localist philosophy of these Resolutions had, if anything, grown warmer. One reason for this was that land titles in Kentucky probably were the muddiest in the country and the most susceptible to attack in federal courts by out-of-state speculators.

In his initial presentation of the repeal bill, nevertheless, Breckenridge eschewed philosophy and, following Jefferson's strategy, stressed economy and frugality. The existing law, he cried, was "a wanton waste of the public treasure. . . . The time will never arrive when America will stand in need of thirty-eight Federal judges." But it was not long before Federalist senators, overriding all Jefferson's and Breckenridge's caution, brought the debate around to the great constitutional questions.

Most deeply at issue was the Republican emphasis on the "Elective Principle" as against Federalist insistence on an "independent judiciary" to preserve the country from "the ruin of every Republic, the vile love of popularity." "Why are we here?" cried that most authentic of Federalists, Gouverneur Morris, during the debate. "To save the people from their most dangerous enemy; to save them from themselves." Should all else fail, "the Constitution has given us an independent judiciary," which, if "you trench upon the rights of your fellow citizens, by passing an unconstitutional law, . . . will stop you short."

Breckenridge, after some intervening debate, replied: "I did not expect, sir, to find the doctrine of the power of the courts to annul the laws of Congress as unconstitutional, so seriously insisted on. . . . I would ask where they got that power, and who checks the courts when they violate the Constitution?" The doctrine that the courts may nullify legislation, Breckenridge said, would give them "the absolute direction of the Government, . . . [for] to whom are they responsible?" To which Morris rose again to answer: "The moment the legislature . . . declare themselves supreme, they become so . . . and the Constitution is whatever they choose to make it."

Thus was the debate in the Senate deadlocked. But not the vote. Republican caution was well justified by the party's slender margin in that chamber. But the margin held up, and by a strictly partisan tally of 16 to 15 the Senate on February 3, 1802, adopted the repeal bill.

In deep dejection, Gouverneur Morris wrote in his *Diary* that in the House, "A band of ministerial mutes stand ready to pass [the repeal measure] without debate." In fact, the argument in the "democratical branch" of Congress was on as high a level as in the Senate and almost as prolonged. No earlier debate had been so widely reported in the newspapers or had so strongly whipped up the people. Giles, in Jefferson's opinion "the ablest debater of the age," epitomized the whole Jeffersonian position when he observed that the central issue was "the doctrine of irresponsibility against the doctrine of responsibility [to the public]. . . . The doctrine of despotism in opposition to the representative system." For the Federalists, in a speech praised by John Adams as "the most comprehensive masterly and compleat argument that has been published in either House," Bayard of Delaware threatened:

There are many now willing to spill their blood to defend that Constitution. Are gentlemen disposed to risk the consequences? [Destroy the independence of the national judiciary and] the moment is not far off when this fair country is to be desolated by civil war.

But the House was to be swayed no more than the Senate. On March 3, 1802, feeling that they had "wandered long enough in those regions of fancy and terror to which [Federalist spokesmen have] led us," the Republican leadership brought the issue to a vote and carried repeal by 59 to 32.

"Should Mr. Breckenridge now bring forward a resolution to repeal the law establishing the Supreme Court of the United States," wrote the influential *Washington Federalist* on the day the vote was announced, "we should only consider it a part of the system to be pursued. . . . We sincerely expect it will be done next session. . . . Such is democracy." That this opinion was not merely inflammatory propaganda was proved soon enough. On April 8, 1802, without debate, the Senate enacted a supplementary judiciary bill abolishing the imminent June term of the Supreme Court and the following December

term as well, and establishing it as law that the Court should hold but one term annually, beginning the second Monday of each February. On April 23 the House adopted the same bill and the President promptly signed it.

"This act," cried Bayard, "is to prevent the court from expressing their opinion upon the validity of the act lately passed . . . until the act has gone into full execution, and the excitement of the public mind is abated."

### MARBURY V. MADISON DECIDED

When the repeal and Court-postponement measures had become law, and the Supreme Court justices had been forced, under the restored provisions of the Judiciary Act of 1789, to resume onerous circuit court duty, Chief Justice Marshall moved instantly to rally his fellow members of the highest bench to refuse to serve in the lower courts and "risk the consequences." But this medicine was too strong for the jurists, and in the fall of 1802, filled with disgust, Marshall himself sat on circuit court cases in Richmond. By then, too, a second piece of strategy had sputtered out. To create an opportunity for the Supreme Court to review the repeal act when it finally convened in February 1803, Marshall and other Federalist leaders tried to induce some of Adams's dispossessed circuit court appointees to sue for their jobs. "But their energies flagged," writes Albert J. Beveridge, Marshall's spirited biographer, "their hearts failed, and their only action was a futile and foolish protest to the very Congress that had wrested their judicial seats from under them." Republican strategy, as Bayard had accurately defined it, was obviously working so well that in November 1802 Jefferson was able to write almost smugly:

The path we have to pursue is so quiet that we have nothing scarcely to propose to our Legislature. A noiseless course, not meddling with the affairs of others, unattractive to notice, is a mark that society is going on in happiness. If we can prevent the government from wasting the labors of the people, under the pretense of taking care of them, they must become happy.

Yet Jefferson, as he put it only a month earlier, had not lost sight of his objective, "to sink Federalism into an abyss from which there shall be no resurrection for it." And Marshall, frustrated by Republican tactics and Federalist timidity, only hardened his resolve to plant an "independent judiciary" in the path of "turbulent democracy" at the earliest possible moment. If no better occasion presented itself than the trivial case of *Marbury v. Madison,* it would have to serve. During the Supreme Court's enforced 14-month interregnum, the mandamus controversy had practically disappeared from official as well as popular notice. Marshall would revive it with a bang. On this the Chief Justice had decided months before the 1803 term of the Supreme Court opened on February 9.

Of all the parties to the mandamus case, Marbury himself, his proposed five-year term in an office of "such slight dignity and such insignificant emoluments" already almost half over, had perhaps least interest in the outcome. But the administration was scarcely more concerned. In effect, it could not lose. If Marshall's Court dismissed Marbury's suit and withheld the mandamus, it would only be conceding the Republicans' contention that the national judiciary had no legal grounds on which to enjoin the executive to obey even the constitutional laws of Congress. The executive would be a law unto itself, not subject to judicial restraint. If, on the other hand, the justices ruled, as the Republicans universally expected they would, that Madison must obey a mandamus to deliver Marbury's commission, what means could it employ to carry out its order? Jefferson almost certainly would have said in this situation what Andrew Jackson is reputed to have said somewhat later: "John Marshall has made his decision. Now let him enforce it." The contempt in which the Court was still widely held would only have deepened. So confident was the administration in its invulnerability, that Secretary of State Madison neglected even to dignify the proceedings by his presence when the case was called.

The Republicans, alas, had failed to gauge Marshall's determination and audacity, and got a shock. Ironically, they won the case. Sympathetic as he may have been toward Marbury's predicament, Marshall could only extricate himself from his own dilemma by denying the mandamus. It was the argument on which he grounded his denial that rocked the administration and made history.

The decision in *Marbury* v. *Madison* was handed down on February 24, 1803. Even the external circumstances surrounding the decision were historic. Heretofore, in every case decided by the Supreme Court, each justice had written a separate opinion and the ruling was made by majority vote. It did not matter whether the reasoning of the justices differed, or whether they contradicted one another in interpreting the law. The vote stood, even though the opinions behind it left the legal profession at sea. Marshall found this procedure intolerable. Beginning with *Marbury* v. *Madison,* he alone, during his 34 years as Chief Justice, wrote most of the important decisions. The other justices were consulted, and they might concur or dissent as they chose. A majority vote still was needed. But the majority now spoke with one clear voice, the voice of Marshall.

The Chief Justice saw to it that no one dissented in *Marbury* v. *Madison.* "Has the applicant a right to the commission he demands?" Marshall asked. "If he has a right, and that right has been violated, do the laws of his country afford him a remedy? If they do afford him a remedy, is it a *mandamus* issuing from this court?"

Yes, the applicant has a right to his commission. Yes, refusal to deliver it "is a plain violation of that right, for which the laws of his country afford him a remedy." Yes, the remedy is a mandamus; "this is a plain case for a mandamus." *But this court may not issue it!*—"because the law [granting the Court the power] is unconstitutional, and therefore absolutely incapable of conferring the authority and assigning the duties which its words purport to confer and assign."

What is this law? It is Section 13 of the Judiciary Act of 1789. This act had been drafted by no less a person than Oliver Ellsworth, Marshall's predecessor as Chief Justice; and William Paterson, now a member of Marshall's Court, had been a member of the committee that reported it to the Senate. The act, indeed, had passed utterly unquestioned when Marshall himself first took "original cognizance" of Marbury's suit in 1801. The Constitution (Art. III, Sec. 2), Marshall argued, gave the Supreme Court original jurisdiction in a few specified instances only. The power to issue mandamuses was not among them. The Judiciary Act conferred this power on the Court. In doing so, it went beyond the supreme law of the land. The section of the Constitution in question goes on to define areas of the Supreme Court's appellate jurisdiction, and then closes with the words, "with such exceptions, and under such regulations as Congress shall make." Most lawyers then and since have held that these closing words gave Congress the authority to enlarge (but not diminish) the Court's original as well as appellate jurisdiction. But not Marshall. Over original jurisdiction, these words "have no operation at all."

This was novel as well as questionable law. But political power, not law, was at issue, and the partisan bench swallowed it. There remained, then, the great question: "The question whether an act repugnant to the constitution can become the law of the land."

Granting that the Court may declare unconstitutional an act passed by Congress and signed by the President, can it—and it alone —invalidate that law? Jefferson's cherished "Elective Principle" answers, "No." The judiciary may declare an act of the legislature unconstitutional; but the legislature may then impeach the judges and at the next election take its chances with the people with whom the final decision lay. The executive, at his own discretion, meanwhile, may continue to execute the law as though the Court had not spoken, and until the people in the next election voted to sustain or discredit his action.

Slow? Cumbersome? Yes. But to Jefferson and his colleagues here lay the essence of representative republican government. To Marshall, here lay the very definition of anarchy: "If an act of the legislature repugnant to the constitution is void, does it, . . . though it be not law, . . . constitute a rule

*Chief Justice John Marshall by Rembrandt Peale, 1834. (The Virginia Museum of Fine Arts, Glasgow Fund, 1956.)*

320

as operative as if it was a law? This would be
. . . an absurdity too gross to be insisted on."
In defense of his dictum that "It is emphati-
cally the province and duty of the judicial
department to say what the law is," Marshall
put heaviest emphasis on that "greatest improvement on political institutions, a written
constitution." The government of the United
States, he argued, is one in which the powers
of the different departments are

defined and limited; and that those limits may
not be mistaken or forgotten, the constitution is
written. . . .

Those, then, who controvert the principle
that the constitution is to be considered in court
as a paramount law, are reduced to the necessity
of maintaining that courts must close their eyes
on the constitution and see only the law. This
doctrine . . . would declare that an act which,
according to the principles and theory of our
government is entirely void, is yet, in practice,
completely obligatory. It would declare that if
the legislature shall do what is expressly forbidden, such act, notwithstanding the express
prohibition, is in reality effectual.

It is "the very essence of judicial duty,"
Marshall concluded, to check this "extravagant" doctrine. "The particular phraseology
of the constitution of the United States confirms and strengthens the principle, supposed
to be essential to all written constitutions, that
a law repugnant to the constitution is void,
and that courts, as well as other departments,
are bound by this instrument."

"Thus by a coup as bold in design and as
daring in execution as that by which the
Constitution had been framed," writes Beveridge, "John Marshall set up a landmark in
American history so high that all the future
could take bearings from it." Not for more
than 50 years, in fact, was the Supreme Court
again to declare an act of Congress unconstitutional. That declaration was made in the
momentous case of the slave Dred Scott in
1857 (see p. 570). But the independence of
the judiciary was henceforth to be seldom
challenged and "judiciary review" was to become as firm a constitutional principle as
though it had been written explicitly into the
supreme law of the land.

## THE IMPEACHMENT GAMBIT

The *Marbury* decision did not end the war
between the Republican administration and
the judiciary by any means. But nothing revealed the soundness of Marshall's political
*coup* more convincingly than its farcical
sequel.

The Republican conception of the impeachment power was adequately based in logic if
not in law; and even before the *Marbury* decision (and no doubt with an eye toward
intimidating the Supreme Court) the impeachment machinery of the federal government had been set in motion. A precedent
had been established in Pennsylvania, where,
after the Republican party captured control
of the state legislature in the elections of 1799,
the state House of Representatives proceeded
to impeach an outstanding local Federalist
judge and the state Senate to convict and remove him. The Senate's action was taken in
January 1803. Its victim was Alexander Addi-
son. The grounds were not "high crimes and
misdemeanors," as the law required, but
"manners and morals" offensive to the popular party. In the middle of February 1803, a
week before the *Marbury* climax, the United
States House of Representatives began to take
steps to impeach federal district court Judge
John Pickering of New Hampshire on similar
grounds, and on March 2 voted his impeachment overwhelmingly.

The unfortunate Pickering had been hopelessly insane for three years, had become an
alcoholic as a result, and his conduct on the
bench reflected his condition. His attacks on
the Republicans were not merely partisan;
they were spoken in the vilest language. An
insane man could not legally be tried for high
crimes and misdemeanors; but the Republicans held that the Senate, in impeachment
trials, did not really sit as a court. "Impeach-

ment," the consistent Giles explained, "was not a criminal prosecution, it was no prosecution at all. . . . Removal by impeachment was nothing more than a declaration by Congress to this effect: You hold dangerous opinions, and if you are suffered to carry them into effect you will work the destruction of the Union." Pickering was held liable, and on March 12, 1804, by a strictly party vote of 19 to 7 the Senate convicted him. Three Republican senators broke ranks; they dared not defy party discipline and vote against conviction; they merely showed they had no stomach for the proceedings by absenting themselves when the ballot was taken. Vice-president Burr, in turn, finding suddenly that he had to leave Washington to mend his political fences in New York in preparation for the elections of 1804, let Senator Franklin of North Carolina preside.

The worst was yet to come. Within an hour of Pickering's conviction in the Senate, the House impeached Supreme Court Justice Samuel Chase, notorious for his conduct during the heyday of the Sedition Act (see p. 294). Chase's career had been a triumph over his imperfections of character. A man of brilliant mind, as all parties conceded, he had survived numerous business and political disasters before ascending to the highest bench in 1796. Along the way his vitriolic tongue had offended many. His latest transgression occurred in May 1803, when he harangued a Baltimore grand jury for hours on Republican failings, including "the late alteration of the federal judiciary," by which "our republican constitution will sink into a mobocracy, the worst of all possible governments."

Chase had been impeached on eight counts, all but the last covering incidents four or five years old. The last was the recent Baltimore affair, characterized by the House as "an intemperate and inflammatory political harangue," delivered "with intent to excite the fears and resentment of the good people of Maryland . . . against the Government of the United States." "These articles," John

Quincy Adams wrote to his father, "contained in themselves a virtual impeachment not only of Mr. Chase, but of all the Judges of the Supreme Court from the first establishment of the national judiciary." No crime or misdemeanor was attested; on Giles' theory none was needed.

Chase's trial began on February 4, 1805, in the Senate chamber, garishly redecorated for the occasion and presided over once again by the Vice-president, himself with the blood of Hamilton on his hands (see p. 329). Chase's chief counsel was Luther Martin, slack-jawed, slovenly, his speech "shackled by a preternatural secretion of saliva," yet the acknowledged leader of the American bar. John Randolph of Roanoke, the intemperate Republican leader in the House whose vitriolic oratory had already made him many enemies, headed the impeachment advocates. No lawyer, Randolph failed to hold in line the Republican legal luminaries in his group who rebelled against Giles's political theory of impeachment. Republican evidence was discredited on every charge; Randolph's summations became models of contradiction and confusion. As the tendency of the trial grew clear, Burr, the Judas of the party since the election of 1800, suddenly found himself regaled with presents and patronage in a disgraceful maneuver by the administration to swing the power of the President of the Senate against Marshall's man. Nothing worked. Chase was acquitted on each count, and returned to the bench triumphant.

Few doubted, least of all Marshall himself, that if Chase had been convicted on this transparent political indictment, the Chief Justice would have been attacked next. When John Adams, at the end of his administration, named Marshall to the Court, he had short-circuited the incoming President's clear intention to give the chief justiceship to his friend and fellow-Virginian, the fervid state-rights enthusiast, Spencer Roane, of the Old Dominion's highest court. Jefferson found it especially hard to forgive and forget having been

322

forestalled in this manner. But after the Chase debacle he hastily acknowledged that impeachment was not the means to even the score. Jefferson himself branded the trial of Chase a "farce," and soon put impeachment aside as a political weapon, trusting to the growing popularity of the Republican program to bring the courts into closer harmony with the election returns.

## III  *Jefferson and the West*

### SPURS TO SETTLEMENT

Late in 1801 Jefferson wrote: "The increase of [our] numbers during the last ten years . . . we contemplate . . . not with a view to the injuries it may enable us to do to others in some future day, but to the settlement of the extensive country still remaining vacant within our limits." On another occasion that year, he grew even more expansive: "However our present interests may restrain us within our own limits, it is impossible not to look forward to distant times, when our rapid multiplication will expand beyond those limits and cover the whole northern, if not the southern, continent with a people speaking the same language, governed in similar forms and by similar laws." This, as others were to insist in the great years ahead, was America's "manifest destiny."

Jefferson, as we shall see, had every intention of hastening spectacularly the coming of these "distant times." But he did not neglect on that account to speed as well the settlement of the vast territory already in American possession by his favorite yeoman white farmers. To encourage settlement of the public lands and the creation of new states, Congress, in 1796 and 1800, had lowered both the minimum acreage a pioneer had to buy and the actual cash he had to put down. In 1804 Jefferson got Congress to reduce requirements to the point where, for a down payment of about $65 a man could gain title to a quarter section of 160 acres.

These measures promoted the settlement of the Northwest Territory, from which Ohio (admitted to the Union in 1803) was the first state to be formed. Under the Land Ordinance of 1785 (see p. 234), each state created in the Northwest Territory was to receive from Congress one section of land (640 acres) in every township, the proceeds from the sale of this section to be used to support education in the state. In the act by which Ohio was admitted to the Union, Congress specifically made this grant for the first time. The act also provided that 3 per cent of federal income from the sale of public land in Ohio was to be used to help the state develop new roads— a provision that established a precedent for national aid to transportation.

Jefferson also tried to promote settlement in the Southwest, where conflicting claims to huge tracts of land near the Yazoo River in present-day Mississippi presented a major obstacle. In 1789 the state of Georgia, which then owned this territory, sold about 25 million acres of it to speculators. When the buyers failed in their operation, Georgia, in 1795, resold much of the same land to other companies at the extraordinarily favorable price of 1½ cents an acre. All but one of the members of the Georgia legislature participated in the second deal. Responding to a charge of fraud, a new legislature the next year rescinded the sale. But in the meantime the companies had sold stock widely, and the owners of the stock demanded delivery of the land.

When Georgia finally ceded her western lands to the federal government in 1802, the Yazoo stockholders carried their demands along to President Jefferson. He set up a commission which in 1803 recommended that the Yazoo claimants be reimbursed through the sale of 5 million acres of Yazoo land. The commission also recommended that the United States quiet the Indian claim to territory within the boundaries of Georgia, and that the rest of the land ceded by Georgia should itself become a state when its population reached 60,000.

Georgia and the federal government accepted these recommendations. In the House of Representatives, however, John Randolph led the fight against compensating the Yazoo claimants, insisting that the precious rights of the soverign state of Georgia had been forfeited, with Jefferson's connivance, for the benefit of corrupt speculators. On these grounds he successfully opposed payment for more than ten years, and split the Republican party in the process. Randolph was supported by the die-hard state-rights Republicans whose philosophy Jefferson himself had buttressed with the Kentucky Resolutions of 1798. Jefferson, however, was to prove no stickler for state rights or for a narrow interpretation of the Constitution where America's expansion was concerned, and the majority of the Republican party clung to his leadership.

In 1810 John Marshall added his resounding voice to the Yazoo argument. In the case of *Fletcher* v. *Peck,* the Chief Justice declared the Georgia sale of 1795 a legitimate contract which the next legislature had no power to break without the consent of the other party to it. This decision strengthened the position of the Yazoo stockholders and finally, in 1814, with Randolph out of Congress for the time being, Congress awarded them $5 million. Within five years, Alabama and Mississippi, both made up of territory ceded by Georgia, were admitted as states.

## TRANSCONTINENTAL VENTURES

Gratifying as Jefferson found the filling up of the country, he remained much more intrigued by his vision of encompassing the entire continent and indeed the hemisphere in his "empire for liberty." Back in 1786 he had already tried to bring the "distant times" for this achievement a little closer by supporting a fantastic expedition led by "the mad, romantic, dreaming Ledyard." John Ledyard of Connecticut, a natural-born roamer of the world, once sailed with Captain Cook. With Jefferson's encouragement, he hoped to tramp across Siberia, traverse the Bering Straits, and, from Alaska, explore the wild North American interior. Russian police picked Ledyard up before he got properly started and packed him off home. Six years later, in 1792, Jefferson persuaded the American Philosophical Society to finance a far-western journey under the leadership of the French botanist André Michaux. But this venture also failed when the Frenchman showed more interest in his countryman Genêt's political expeditions than in Jefferson's natural-history ones.

Finally, early in 1803, Jefferson induced Congress to appropriate money for an expedition across the continent, ostensibly for scientific purposes, but also to search out new supplies and new outlets for American fur-trappers and traders. The appropriation was to be kept secret, for the proposed expedition would traverse foreign territory.

For this venture, Jefferson chose the experienced wilderness explorer, Meriwether Lewis, who took as his colleague William Clark, the younger brother of George Rogers Clark and a well-known Indian-fighter and frontiersman in his own right. By the time their party of about 45 men set out for the Missouri River on July 5, 1803, much of the territory they planned to explore had become American property through the Louisiana Purchase. Lewis and Clark, however, had been commissioned to go well beyond Louisiana in order to discover a route from the Missouri River to the Pacific. They crossed the Rockies at the Continental Divide and traced the Columbia River to its mouth, thereby establishing an American claim to the Oregon country. After their return in 1806, they published a journal of their expedition which has since become a classic, and which in its own time supplied much useful information for map-makers and settlers.

In 1806, the year of Lewis and Clark's return from the Northwest, Zebulon N. Pike was sent to explore the Southwest. His party discovered the gigantic Colorado peak that now bears his name, and then pushed deeper into Spanish territory in New Mexico. Pike was arrested by the Spanish but soon freed. In 1810 he published *An Account of Expedi-*

*Two sketches from the* Journal *of Sergeant Patrick Gass (1812) kept during the Lewis and Clark expedition to the Pacific and back. Gass accompanied the explorers on the entire journey. (Upper) Captains Lewis and Clark holding a council with the Indians. (Lower) The captains fighting off an attack by Indians. (New York Public Library.)*

tions to the Sources of the Mississippi—sources which in fact he had failed to discover. His report, like that of Lewis and Clark, nevertheless added appreciably to information about the continent that many in Europe as well as in America coveted.

### THE LOUISIANA PURCHASE

Exploration, fascinating to Jefferson's scientific mind, and trade, the material justification for exploration, were but preliminary steps toward his ultimate political goal: the peaceful acquisition of territory for the United States. Spain, with Jefferson's blessing, held Louisiana—or New Orleans, as the whole

western country was sometimes called—from 1762 to 1800. "Till our population can be sufficiently advanced [in numbers] to gain it from them piece by piece," Jefferson thought, it could not "be in better hands." It is not difficult, therefore, to imagine the President's anxiety on learning early in 1802 from Rufus King, the American minister in London, that by a secret treaty of October 1800 the insatiable Napoleon, compensating Spain with territory elsewhere, had retrieved Louisiana for France.

In April 1802 Jefferson let the French know by means of a long dispatch to the American minister in Paris, Robert R. Livingston, that their retaking Louisiana must force us to "marry ourselves to the British fleet and nation." The action of France, Jefferson wrote, "completely reverses all the political relations of the United States, and will form a new epoch in our political course. . . . There is on the globe one single spot," the President continued, "the possessor of which is our natural and habitual enemy. It is New Orleans, through which the produce of three-eighths of our territory must pass to market, and from its fertility it will ere long yield more than half of our whole produce and contain more than half of our inhabitants." Spain, feeble, pacific, and cooperative, he added, "might have retained it quietly for years." But "France placing herself in that door assumes to us the attitude of defiance."

Although Napoleon formally re-acquired Louisiana in 1800, he had reasons enough to postpone taking actual possession of it. For one thing, he had not a sou to spare for the costs of occupation. He intended to develop Louisiana into a source of food for the French West Indies, thus ending their dependence on the United States; but he could not proceed with this plan until he had secured his position in Europe, something he was unable to do until late in 1801. To protect Louisiana from the British, moreover, the French colony of Santo Domingo, in the Caribbean, was essential as a naval base. Unfortunately for Napoleon, a stubborn slave insurrection in

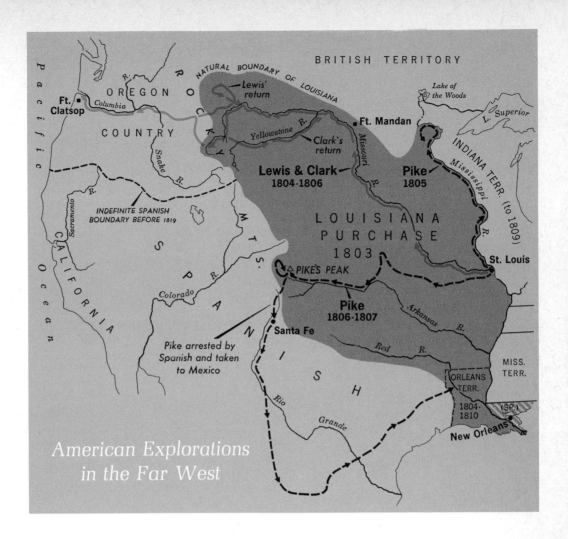

American Explorations
in the Far West

Santo Domingo, led by the Negro General Toussaint L'Ouverture, who claimed to have liberated the island from France, was still going on. Worse, the uprising threatened to spread to the rest of the French West Indies and thus ruin Napoleon's whole vision of a new American empire.

Once Napoleon had settled his European affairs at the preliminary Peace of Amiens in 1801, he felt secure enough to send his brother-in-law, General Charles Leclerc, and 17,000 men to crush Toussaint, and to plan a second expedition to occupy New Orleans. Combat in Santo Domingo quickly became bestial and disorganized. By the fall of 1802, Leclerc's first army had been butchered by

the defenders, and its reinforcements scourged by an epidemic of yellow fever. In November, France learned that Leclerc himself had followed his soldiers to the grave. The disaster was so complete that Napoleon never sent the expedition to occupy New Orleans, gave up his entire Louisiana policy, and decided, instead, to sell out—something he was expressly forbidden to do by the terms of his secret treaty of 1800 with Spain.

As early as May 1802, Jefferson had instructed Robert Livingston in Paris to try to get the French to put a price on New Orleans (and the Floridas, which Jefferson mistakenly assumed had also passed into French possession). Before the end of the year, two items

325

326

of news reached Washington which made the acquisition of New Orleans urgent, even by warlike means, and at the same time brightened the prospects of its falling to the United States. The first news told of the suspension in October 1802 of the American right of deposit at New Orleans by the Spanish intendant still in charge of the port. This right had been won for three years in Pinckney's Treaty of 1795 (see p. 288), and until now Spain and France both had continued to recognize it. The second piece of news reported Leclerc's disaster in the Caribbean.

"The agitation of the public mind on occasion of the late suspension of our right of deposit at New Orleans," Jefferson wrote in January 1803, "is extreme." And he continued with an analysis of American opinion:

In the western country [the agitation] is natural, and grounded on honest motives; in the seaports it proceeds from a desire for war, which increases the mercantile lottery; in the Federalists generally, and especially those of Congress, the object is to force us into war if possible, in order to derange our finances; or if this cannot be done, to attach the western country to them as their best friends, and thus get again into power.

Jefferson was determined that "nothing but the failure of every peaceable mode of redress, nothing but dire necessity, should force us from the path of peace." To quiet the agitation for war, he sent to the Senate, in January 1803, his nomination of James Monroe as minister extraordinary to France and Spain to assist Livingston in Paris. The nomination was quickly confirmed, and $2 million was appropriated for Monroe's use in negotiations. The new minister sailed early in March with instructions to offer up to $10 million for New Orleans and the Floridas. If France refused to sell and persisted in addition in keeping New Orleans closed to American commerce by force, Monroe and Livingston were authorized to approach Britain with the suggestion that she join with the United States in the event of a new war with Napoleon. By the time Monroe arrived in Paris, he found

his elaborate instructions obsolete. A staggering offer of the whole Louisiana Territory had been made to Livingston, and on April 30, 1803, the two Americans closed the deal.

Monroe and Livingston could not state with certainty just what they had purchased; the terms said simply that the United States was to receive Louisiana with the boundaries "that it now has in the hands of Spain." If this seemed vague, said Talleyrand, Napoleon's negotiator, "I suppose you will make the most of it." The final price was $15 million, a fourth of which was to be used to settle the claims of American shippers and shipowners against the French government. The purchase treaty also specified that the inhabitants of Louisiana, most of whom were Catholic, were to become American citizens and were to be protected in the practice of their religion.

Jefferson was ecstatic over the *"denouement"*: "The territory acquired, as it includes all the waters of the Missouri and Mississippi, has more than doubled the area of the United States, and the new part is not inferior to the old in soil, climate, productions, and important communications." In addition, "giving us the sole dominion of the Mississippi, it excludes those bickerings with foreign powers which we know of a certainty would have put as at war with France immediately."

Nevertheless there remained certain difficulties about the "noble bargain," as Talleyrand called it. The French Constitution prohibited the disposal of territory without a legislative vote, a step Napoleon had dispensed with. The American Constitution, in turn, did not explicitly delegate power to the Executive or any other department to purchase foreign territory. Jefferson was so troubled on this score that he suggested an amendment to make the treaty legitimate. When warned that delay in adopting an amendment might cause Napoleon to renege, the President swallowed his scruples and pushed the treaty through. In October 1803 the Senate approved it 24 to 7; and the House, overwhelming the opponents of the enlargement of executive powers in foreign affairs, appropriated the purchase

*Aquatint of New Orleans, 1804, issued to commemorate Louisiana Purchase. The American artist, J.L. Boqueta de Woiseri, was one of the first to employ the aquatint technique; he also did views of Philadelphia, New York, and other cities. (Mariners Museum, Newport News, Virginia.)*

money 90 to 25. Gallatin typically saw to it that the Treasury could service the bonds required without raising taxes a penny.

On December 20, 1803, the United States formally took possession of Louisiana. The next year the Purchase was divided into two territories, each to be administered according to the procedure outlined in the Northwest Ordinance of 1787 (see p. 236). By this procedure one of the two territories, with its present-day boundaries, became the state of Louisiana in 1812.

Territorial expansion, like governmental economy and the "elective principle," held a very high priority among those "cases" Hamilton had referred to in which Jefferson "was generally for a large construction of the Executive authority and not backward to act upon it." In later years the President rationalized his "unconstitutional" behavior in this way:

A strict observance to the written laws is doubtless *one* of the high duties of a good citizen, but it is not the *highest*. The laws of necessity, of self-preservation, of saving our country when in danger, are of a higher obligation.

Inconsistent though Jefferson may sound, he was only once again seeking cover under the "higher-law" doctrine of the Revolution and the Declaration of Independence.

Florida had not been included in the deal with Napoleon, since Spain had not yielded it to France. But Jefferson was far from discouraged. "If we push them strongly with one hand, holding out a price in the other," he said, "we shall certainly obtain the Floridas, and all in good time." This, of course, was a sound prediction—one, once again, that the higher-law doctrine hastened to fulfillment (see p. 360).

IV *The Whiplash of Politics and War*

### CRISIS IN NEW ENGLAND

John Randolph of Roanoke, reflecting in his old age on the first three years of Jefferson's reign, when he himself, booted and spurred and flashing a horsewhip, rode herd on the Republicans in the House, said: "Never was there an administration more

328

brilliant than that of Mr. Jefferson up to this period. We were indeed in the 'full tide of successful experiment.' Taxes repealed; the public debt amply provided for . . . ; sinecures abolished; Louisiana acquired; public confidence unbounded." Even in New England the congressional elections of 1802–03 showed the surge of Republican strength, and by 1804 the legislatures of but three Yankee states—Massachusetts, Connecticut, and New Hampshire—remained (rather shakily) in Federalist hands. Yet there were those still in New England upon whom every new wave of Republican sentiment cast a blistering spray. Their leader was John Adams's treacherous old Secretary of State, Senator Timothy Pickering of Massachusetts.

Early in 1804, when the acquisition of Louisiana seemed to destroy all hope of future Federalist influence in the nation, and when the progress of the impeachment proceedings against Federalist judges menaced even the party's present strength, Pickering wrote: "The people of the East cannot reconcile their habits, views, and interests with those of the South and West. The latter are beginning to rule with a rod of iron." His prescription was "separation," and the formation of a "Northern Confederacy." "The magnitude and jealousy of Massachusetts," wrote Pickering's fellow conspirator, Congressman Roger Griswold of Connecticut, "would render it necessary that the operation should be commenced there." "But," Pickering added, "New York must be associated; and how is her concurrence to be obtained? She must be made the centre of the confederacy. Vermont and New Jersey would follow of course, and Rhode Island of necessity. Who can be consulted, and who will take the lead?"

Pickering had every hope of enlisting Hamilton himself; but the ambitious ex-Secretary recoiled from attempting to destroy the Union he had helped to create. Other Federalist invincibles—Fisher Ames, Theophilus Parsons, John Quincy Adams, George Cabot—all took Hamilton's position. Jefferson, they agreed, was the incarnation of evil—atheist, Francophile, terrorist. All the better, then, to give him his head. "We shall go the way of all governments wholly popular," Cabot advised Pickering, "—from bad to worse,—until the evils, no longer tolerable, shall generate their own remedies." Democracy must end in crisis; when the time came, a stern Yankee oligarch would find his opportunity to regain supremacy for "right principles" throughout the land. Patience, not disunion, was the remedy.

Pickering, Griswold, and company had no time for patience. "If Federalism is crumbling away in New England," Pickering wrote, "there is no time to be lost, lest it should be overwhelmed and become unable to attempt its own relief." Hamilton unwilling, they would turn desperately to one as desperate as themselves, Hamilton's mortal enemy, Aaron Burr.

By 1804 Burr's relations with Jefferson and the Virginia Republicans were at their worst, and the Vice-president had decided to seek vindication from the people of New York by running for governor in the April elections. Burr's decision was the New Englanders' opportunity. Would he, a Yankee delegation asked, if victorious in the Empire State, bring New York into a new northern confederation under England's wing? Presumably Burr agreed; but even Griswold acknowledged that his consent was "of a doubtful nature." The question, in any case, was soon to become academic. To win against the regular Republican machine in New York under the able control of Governor George Clinton, Burr needed heavy Federalist support. Hamilton, who saw his own preeminence in the party passing to the Vice-president, did everything he could to defeat him. Burr lost, and the projected northern confederacy collapsed.

The sequel ended with the tragedy of Hamilton's death. Embittered by Hamilton's opposition and by other offenses, real and imaginery, that had festered in his mind for two months, Burr in mid-June challenged Hamilton to a duel. Hamilton, as he made abundantly clear, accepted the challenge more as a political than a personal gesture. The

*Aaron Burr, a profile by the French engraver Charles Balthazar Julien Fevret de Saint-Memin. (New York Public Library.)*

vision of a democratic crisis had not left his mind; his ambition from boyhood to become the man on a white horse made this vision all the more alluring. When the opportunity came to elevate himself and save the country, he could not act were there a shadow of cowardice on his record. Duel he must, not to kill, but to keep the story of his courage alive. Hamilton intended to miss his opponent; Burr did not. When they met on July 11, 1804, Hamilton was struck below the chest. Thirty hours later he was dead.

### BURR'S CONSPIRACY

The schemes of the "Essex Junto," as Burr's Yankee co-conspirators were called (after the Massachusetts county in which they predominated), almost ruined the Federalist party, even in New England. In the presidential elections of 1804, Jefferson, unanimously renominated by the Republican congressional caucus, carried every state in New England except Connecticut, and every other state in the Union but Delaware. As against Jefferson's 162 electoral votes, his Federalist opponent, Charles C. Pinckney of South Carolina, received a meager 14. Clinton, to whom, instead of Burr, Jefferson had entrusted the distribution of federal patronage in New York, became the new Vice-president. He and his Federalist opponent, Rufus King of New York, were the first to run for that office under the terms of the Twelfth Amendment (see p. 298), and Clinton won 162 to 14.

Jefferson's second inauguration took place on March 4, 1805, three days after Chase's resounding vindication in the Senate. Burr's conduct of the trial had won outspoken Federalist approval, but the former Vice-president personally still bore the brand of Hamilton's murderer. An untouchable to both parties, his political future was nonexistent, while his private future was boxed in by debt. He dared not return to his law practice in New York, where he was under indictment for precipitating the fatal duel. He had little choice, indeed, but to take refuge, like many other discredited Americans, in the depths of the West. Before leaving Washington, Burr cynically approached the British minister with an offer to detach the western states from the Union in return for half a million dollars. This was the same minister, Anthony Merry, who had conspired in the projected secession of New England, and he was interested enough in this new adventure to convey Burr's proposition to London.

While Merry awaited a response, Burr took himself off. No response came from London; and once in the West Burr began to talk openly of many different plans, some pro-British, some pro-Spanish, some possibly treasonable. Eventually he fell in with General James Wilkinson, a scoundrel "from the bark to the very core," whom Jefferson unaccountably had made military commandant of Louisiana, and one Harman Blennerhassett, an Irish exile who lived in style on an island he owned in the Ohio River. Burr's ultimate plan for the winter of 1806 was to use Blenner-

329

330

hasset's island as a taking-off place from which to join up with Wilkinson's troops for purposes that were not very clearly specified.

The unscrupulous Wilkinson, acting in character, soon double-crossed his wayward accomplice, and to save his own skin disclosed to Jefferson something of Burr's intentions. The President lost little time in issuing a proclamation for Burr's arrest. Burr barely missed making good his escape to Spanish territory when he was picked up at Wakefield, Alabama, on February 19, 1807. On March 30 he was brought before the United States Circuit Court at Richmond, presided over, of all people, by John Marshall. Arraigned at first on lesser charges, Burr was indicted for treason on June 24. On August 3 his trial, one of the most memorable criminal prosecutions in American history, began.

During the arraignment proceedings, Marshall, on behalf of the accused, issued to the President himself a "compulsory process for obtaining witnesses," requiring Jefferson's attendance and testimony. Jefferson scorned the order; and, by refusing to appear, set a precedent for future Presidents. But much more important were the grounds of Burr's eventual acquittal. Treason is defined in the Constitution (Art. III, Sec. 3) as follows:

Treason against the United States shall consist only in levying war against them, or in adhering to their enemies, giving them aid and comfort.

This section continues:

No person shall be convicted of treason unless on the testimony of two witnesses to the same overt act, or on confession in open court.

What the Constitution does not answer is the question, does each individual involved in a conspiracy to levy war on the country or to adhere to its enemies have, in fact, to participate in the actual war itself? Or is it enough for the "testimony of two witnesses to the same overt act" simply to connect him with the overt conspiracy? The English common law does answer this question. "In trea-

son all are principals," is the common-law doctrine. "What one does through another, he does himself." In an earlier trial growing out of Burr's activities, moreover, Marshall explicitly accepted this tenet:

It is not the intention of the Court to say that no individual can be guilty of this crime who has not appeared in arms against his country; on the contrary, . . . all those who perform any part however minute, or however remote from the scene of action, and who are actually leagued in the general conspiracy, are to be considered traitors.

But not Burr. In prosecuting the prisoner, the lawyers for the administration seemed not in the least embarassed on going right down the line with the common law. In instructing the jury, on the other hand, the Chief Justice, "as unconvincing as he was labored," turned tail. Jefferson not Burr was on trial in Marshall's mind, and Jefferson could not be permitted to win. In the opinion of Edward S. Corwin, one of the most eminent of constitutional historians, "Marshall's conduct of Burr's trial for treason is the one serious blemish on his judicial record." In extenuation, it may be said that the President's own conduct in hounding his party enemy was ferocious.

Ironically, Marshall's dictum in his charge to the jury that "the testimony of two witnesses" was needed on actual warlike activity by Burr personally, became the touchstone of the American doctrine of "constructive treason"—the doctrine which, in Marshall's words, stated that "the crime of treason should not be extended by construction to doubtful cases." But the law has managed at the same time to evade that monument to the great Chief Justice by leaving "treason" as he defined it, but giving to "espionage" the construction that "treason" had under the common law.

## TRIALS OF A NEUTRAL

Jefferson's first term had coincided more or less with the first years of peace Europe had

331

known since the French Revolution of 1789. But the European wars were resumed in 1803, and by 1805 Napoleon's victory at Austerlitz had given France control of much of the European continent, while Nelson's victory at Trafalgar had confirmed British control of the seas. This apparent stalemate led to a brutal war of attrition, with disastrous results for neutrals, including the United States. While both belligerents tried to involve the Republic on their behalf, they also made it hazardous for Americans to continue to trade with either party. Jefferson was aware of America's explosive international predicament. Yet he wrote to Monroe on the resumption of hostilities in Europe:

If we go to war now, I fear we may renounce forever the hope of seeing an end of our national debt. If we can keep at peace eight years longer, our income, liberated from debt, will be adequate to any war, without new taxes or loans, and our position and increasing strength put us *hors d'insulte* from any nation.

Jefferson, in dealing with the Barbary pirates, had shown that he was not a dogmatic pacifist. As Secretary of State in 1793, when it seemed that Britain might wrest Louisiana from Spain, he had advised Washington, "I am so impressed with the magnitude of the dangers [attendant upon a change of ownership of Louisiana] that in my opinion we ought to make ourselves parties in the general war expected to take place, should this be the only means of preventing the calamity." But Louisiana was one thing—a colossal opportunity for agrarian expansion. Commerce was another; and Jefferson proved exceedingly reluctant to sink the Treasury if not the nation itself in martial adventures from which the gains were obscure.

The first new blow against neutral American shipping fell in 1805, when a British court handed down a ruling in the case of the vessel *Essex*. In 1800 a British court had ruled that American ships could carry goods from the French West Indies to France provided the goods were first landed on American shores, duty-free. This decision had given a strong impetus to the so-called "re-export" trade which, by 1805, accounted for more than half of America's booming neutral commerce. In the Essex case, however, the earlier decision was revoked. The British court now held that French colonial goods could be sent to France in American ships only if a duty had been paid on them in America and only if there were other evidence to prove that the goods had not been intended for France in the first place. Any ship that could not produce this evidence to Britain's satisfaction was vulnerable to British capture.

Britain also stepped up her attacks on other American commerce, and the impending termination of the 12-year commercial agreement made at the time of Jay's Treaty in 1794 threatened to leave American shipping still more vulnerable. Jefferson took steps to remedy the situation. In 1806, he induced Congress to pass a nonimportation act prohibiting the landing of any British goods that could either be purchased elsewhere or manufactured in the United States. With this as a club (the act was not actually enforced until later), he sent William Pinkney to join Monroe, who was now the regular minister in London, in an effort to make a new commercial treaty and otherwise put an end to British depredations.

Napoleon in the meantime, as a result of new victories on land, was preparing to close the entire Continent to Britain, her goods, and her friends, and to blockade the British Isles. For this purpose, he issued the Berlin Decrees of November 1806. Pinkney and Monroe succeeded in negotiating a treaty in London, but the British stipulated as a condition of enforcement that the United States must resist these Berlin Decrees. Jefferson rejected such dictation, however, and refused even to submit the treaty to the Senate. In 1807 Napoleon added the Milan Decrees to the Berlin Decrees, ordering the confiscation of all ships, especially neutral ships, that had visited a British port or might be bound for one. Britain responded

332

with a series of "orders-in-council." The major orders, in January and November 1807, stated that "all ports and places of France and her allies or of any country at war with His Majesty" were blockaded, and that neutral ships that frequented such ports or sailed toward them did so at their peril.

## IMPRESSMENT AND EMBARGO

Between 1804 and 1807, the United States lost hundreds of ships to the British, who had bottled up the French navy even more successfully than they had blockaded the French ports. Still more obnoxious was the British practice of stopping ships on the high seas to search for and take off alleged deserters from the British navy, a practice known as impressment.

The British navy, a harsh institution that had been enormously expanded for the fight against Napoleon, was characteristically short of men. The American merchant marine, in turn, growing rapidly as a result of the neutral trade, also needed new hands. American commerce, despite all the losses to the British navy, had become so profitable that American shipowners could offer consistently higher wages and better working conditions than the British. Consequently, thousands of British sailors who happened to be in American ports signed on American ships. The United States government also attracted foreign sailors to man American warships. In 1807 the crew of 419 on the frigate *U.S.S. Constitution* had only 241 who claimed American citizenship, and 149 who admitted to being English. To the beleaguered British, who believed that "Once an Englishman, always an Englishman," this was an intolerable situation.

Britain had practiced impressment, and Americans had complained of it, ever since 1776; after 1804, however, the British redoubled their efforts to fill out their crews. In June 1807 one affront led to violence and to talk of war. The new American frigate *Chesapeake,* suspected by the British of having a certain deserter on board, was sailing off Norfolk, Virginia, outside the three-mile limit, when the British warship *Leopard* intercepted her and demanded the right of search. *Chesapeake's* captain refused, and a few minutes later *Leopard* opened fire. *Chesapeake,* her new guns ill-mounted, and her decks cluttered with as yet undistributed gear, suffered 21 casualties before being boarded by *Leopard's* officers, who found the deserter they were after and took him off, along with three Americans who had served in the British navy.

The country demanded that Jefferson retaliate against force with force, and in response the President called a special session of Congress for October 1807, when the members promptly voted an appropriation of $850,000 to strengthen the navy. But Jefferson had his own favorite policy of "peaceful coercion," which he was determined to try before the navy went into action. The best way to protect American ships from capture and the country from incendiary insults, the President's argument ran, was to keep American commercial vessels off the seas. Deprived in this manner of American goods and American carriers, without which the warring powers could not get along, these powers would soon be forced to recognize neutral, and hence American, rights. When the regular session of Congress convened in December 1807, the overwhelming Republican majority promptly (December 22) passed the First Embargo Act embodying Jefferson's program, By this measure no ships (with certain essential exceptions) were permitted to leave United States ports, and no goods could be shipped out, even overland. Three subsequent embargo measures, the last in January 1809, tightened the regulations, increased the severity of penalties for infractions, and strengthened enforcement procedures.

The embargo proved as great a disaster as Jefferson had hoped; the trouble was that it hurt not the warring powers of Europe, but American commerce and American ports. Jefferson's use of the army and navy, both

enlarged for the purpose, in forcibly imposing his policy on the mercantile community
seemed to many to have reached the point of
his making war on his own citizens while
the obvious foreign enemy went scot free. But
his determination to avoid a large new war
debt to eat out the substance of small farmers by taxation was as strong as his determination to gain the continental expanse for future
generations of such farmers; and here, as in
the Louisiana Purchase (see p. 326), he
allowed himself to override his constitutional
scruples.

In spite of the losses caused by the European wars, between 1803 and 1807 American
exports had grown from $55 million to $108
million. By 1808, with the embargo in force,
they had dwindled to the little that could be
smuggled out of the country by one ruse or
another. New England's Federalist merchants
felt that they were the only ones being "peacefully coerced" by Jefferson's Republican policy. Actually, all ports suffered alike. In New
York, as one traveler reported, "Not a box,
bale, cask, barrel or package was to be seen.
. . . The streets near the waterside were almost deserted; the grass had begun to grow
upon the wharves." The industries associated
with commerce, such as shipbuilding and sail-
making, were also at a standstill, and their
artisans unemployed.

Fourteen months of embargo were enough
even for many Republicans, and on March 1,
1809, three days before Jefferson's retirement,
he was obliged to sign an act repealing the
measures. He also approved a strong substitute
—a Nonintercourse Act proscribing trade
with Britain and France, but opening trade
with all other countries. If either Britain or
France would cancel its orders or decrees
against American shipping, then the nonintercourse ban would apply only to the other.

## v  *Jefferson's Retirement*

Jefferson was even more passionate than
Washington in wanting to keep America free

from European entanglements; his embargo
illustrates the extremes to which he would go
to accomplish this end. More passionate still
was his compulsion to get Europe out of America, as evidenced by the Louisiana Purchase
and his thirst for Florida, to say nothing of

Cartoonist Alexander Anderson's version of how
to check a tobacco exporter trying to smuggle out
a barrel of his "superfine" product in defiance of
the "Ograbme" (embargo spelled backwards).
(Courtesy of the New-York Historical Society,
New York City.)

South America and Canada. In spite of all his
efforts, however, the United States became increasingly involved in Europe's affairs, and
after 1806 Jefferson found himself "panting
for retirement."

Jefferson was especially anxious to safe-
guard the surplus that Gallatin had so painstakingly built up in the Treasury by 1807
(the President hated to admit, of course, that
it had come mainly from European trade),
and the last thing he wanted was to squander
this reserve on defense measures. If American

334

commerce could be protected from foreign on-slaughts and affronts only by a strong, expensive navy, it would be better to have no commerce. Rather, argued Jefferson, was not America's best defense her own internal development? America's continental destiny would supply all the land needed for a vast and varied civilization safe in the Western Hemisphere. And an "American system" of tariffs and other aids to home manufactures would supply the needed industrial capacity. This was the vision that Jefferson disclosed in his message to Congress in December 1806:

The question now comes forward—to what . . . objects shall these surpluses be appropriated . . . when the purposes of war shall not call for them? Shall we suppress the impost and give that advantage to foreign over domestic manufactures? . . . Patriotism would certainly prefer its continuance and application to the great purposes of the public education, roads, rivers, canals, and such other objects of public improvement as it may be thought proper to add to the constitutional enumeration of federal powers. By these operations new channels of communications will be opened between the states, the lines of separation will disappear, their interests will be identified, and their union cemented by new and indissoluble ties.

In 1805 Jefferson had written: "General Washington set the example of voluntary retirement after eight years. I shall follow it. And a few more precedents will oppose the obstacle of habit to anyone after a while who shall endeavor to extend his term. Perhaps," he added, foreseeing the possibility of what actually occurred in 1951, "it may beget a disposition to establish it by an amendment to the Constitution" (see Amendment XXII).

By the time of the presidential election of 1808, the Republican party had already split into various factions, and Jefferson's withdrawal as a candidate heightened the ambitions of the different leaders. To make matters worse, the embargo seemed to have resurrected the Federalist opposition. In 1807 every New England state but Connecticut had a Republican governor. By the summer of 1808, after six months of embargo, every Republican governor in New England had been turned out in favor of a Federalist. Federalist representation in the House, moreover, while it reached only a third of that of the Republicans, was to double between 1807 and 1809.

Obviously a real contest loomed for Jefferson's successor, a contest that was made more difficult for his party by the deep dissension in the ranks. The call for a meeting of the Republican congressional caucus for January 23, 1808, to name the party's candidates for President and Vice-president, was so unfortunately worded by the caucus president, Senator Stephen R. Bradley of Vermont, that it prompted Congressman Edwin Gray of Virginia, a supporter of James Monroe, to write to Bradley to "take the earliest moment to declare my abhorrence of the usurpation of power declared to be vested in you—of your mandatory style, and the object contemplated." Gray wanted the nomination to be made by "the people"; and indeed two local caucuses had already been held in Virginia, the first of which had named Monroe for the presidency, and the second, a much larger group, James Madison. Other meetings in New York, called by seaboard Republicans as mortified as the Federalists by the embargo and determined to punish Jefferson and Madison for it, were soon to name Vice-president George Clinton for the highest office. Despite the rumbling against it and the renegades from it, the Republican congressional caucus met. And when the chips were down, the loyal Jeffersonians rallied to the President's strong favorite, James Madison, and nominated him overwhelmingly. Of 89 votes cast, Madison received all but 6, which were divided equally between Monroe, the choice of the Randolph state-rights camp, and Clinton, the maritime candidate. Monroe at first refused to accept the verdict, but pressure from Jefferson himself ultimately nipped an outright rebellion at election time. Clinton was somewhat mollified by his easy renomination for Vice-president.

The Federalists seem to have agreed on their old 1804 ticket without the formality of a caucus. Now, as in the earlier election, they made a demonstration of their status as a national rather than a New England party by renaming Charles C. Pinckney of South Carolina for the Presidency, and Rufus King of New York as his running mate. In 1808, moreover, the Federalist ticket did manage to carry Maryland, North Carolina, and Delaware as well as all New England but Vermont. All told, Pinckney and King each garnered 47 electoral votes. Madison won with 122, while Clinton carried New York's 6. Clinton won the vice-presidency with 113 electoral ballots.

Jefferson's successor had been established. Far from retiring from political affairs, however, the aging political philosopher made his home, Monticello, the shrine to which younger Republicans beat a much used path, and made himself the "sage of Monticello" who consulted regularly with them for the next 17 years.

336

# READINGS

Many of the books recommended in the Readings for Chapter Nine are useful for this chapter. Much the best approach to Jefferson is to read his own writing. Jefferson, perhaps more than any other American President, merits the 60 or more volumes into which his writings are being collected under the editorship of J.P. Boyd. By 1969, 17 volumes of this edition had been issued, covering the period up to December 1790. The most satisfactory earlier large edition is that edited by P.L. Ford (10 vols., 1892–1899). Good one-volume editions include Bernard Mayo, ed., *Jefferson Himself* (1942), and Adrienne Koch and William Peden, *The Life and Selected Writings of Thomas Jefferson* (1944). L.J. Cappon, ed., *The Adams-Jefferson Letters* (2 vols., 1959), is invaluable.

The standard modern biography of Jefferson is Dumas Malone, *Jefferson and His Times* (3 vols., 1948–1962), which so far only carries through the election of 1800. The standard older biography, with many original writings quoted at length is H.S. Randall, *The Life of Thomas Jefferson* (3 vols., 1865). Two one-volume biographies merit special mention: A.J. Nock, *Thomas Jefferson* (1926), and Gilbert Chinard, *Thomas Jefferson, The Apostle of Americanism* (1939). Adrienne Koch, *Jefferson and Madison, The Great Collaboration* (1950), might be read most profitably with L.W. Levy, *Jefferson and Civil Liberties, The Darker Side* (1963). Irving Brant, *James Madison: Secretary of State 1801–1809* (1953), is the relevant volume here in Brant's six-volume life of Madison. Raymond Walters, Jr., *Albert Gallatin* (1957), and James Parton, *The Life and Times of Aaron Burr* (1858), may be recommended. H.S. Syrett and J.G. Cooke, eds., *Interview in Weehawken, The Burr-Hamilton Duel as Told in the Original Documents* (1960), covers that tragic event. D.J. Boorstin, *The Lost World of Thomas Jefferson* (1948), and R.B. Davis, *Intellectual Life in Jefferson's Virginia 1790–1830* (1964), help recreate the intellectual environment of the period. The Jeffersonian heritage is emphasized in C.M. Wiltse, *The Jeffersonian Tradition in American Democracy* (1935), and M.D. Peterson, *The Jefferson Image in The American Mind* (1960). N.K. Risjord, *The Old Republicans, Southern Conservatism in the Age of Jefferson* (1965), is a valuable special study.

Henry Adams, *History of the United States during the Administrations of Jefferson and Madison* (9 vols., 1889–1891), is the classic account, of which abridged versions are available in paperback. Edward Channing, *The Jeffersonian System* (1906), and vol. IV of Channing's *A History of the United States* (6 vols., 1905–1925) also are important older works. Good introductions to modern scholarship on this subject are N.E. Cunningham, Jr., *The Jeffersonian Republicans: The Formation of Party Organization 1789–1801* (1957), and *The Jeffersonian Republicans in Power: Party Operations 1801–1809* (1963), W.N. Chambers, *Political Parties in a New Nation, The American Experience 1776–1809* (1963), and J.S. Young, *The Washington Community 1800–1829* (1966), are also illuminating. L.D. White, *The Jeffersonians* (1951), maintains the high level of his related works on government administration. Malcolm Rohrbough, *The Land Office Business: The Settlement and Administration of American Public Lands 1789–1837* (1968), is excellent. C.P. Magrath, *Yazoo, The Case of Fletcher v. Peck* (1966), is a special study with wide ramifications. On "The Federalist Party in the Era of Jeffersonian Democracy," to quote the subtitle, see D.H. Fischer, *The Revolution of American Conservatism* (1965).

Four outstanding works cover the war with the judiciary: vol. III of A.J. Beveridge, *The Life of John Marshall* (4 vols., 1916–1919); vol. I of Charles Warren, *The Supreme Court in United States History* (2 vols., 1937); C.G. Haines, *The Role of the Supreme Court in American Government and Politics 1789–1835* (1944); and the incisive short book by E.S. Corwin, *John Marshall and the Constitution* (1919). Roscoe Pound, *The Formative Era of American Law* (1938), is an unusually penetrating book.

Foreign relations in Jefferson's administration are dealt with generally in Bradford Perkins, *First Rapprochement: England and the United States 1795–1805* (1955), and *Prologue to War: England and the United States 1805–1812* (1961). J.A. Field, Jr., *America and the Mediterranean World 1776–1882* (1969), is authoritative on the Barbary War and related subjects. See also G.W. Allen, *Our Navy and the Barbary Corsairs* (1905), and R.W. Irwin, *Diplomatic Relations of the United States with the Barbary Powers 1776–1816* (1931). Outstanding on the background of the Louisiana Purchase is E.W. Lyon, *Louisiana in French Diplomacy 1759–1804* (1934). Other worthwhile studies of this subject include J.K. Hosmer, *History of the Louisiana Purchase* (1902), and F.A. Ogg, *The Opening of the Mississippi* (1904). J.E. Bakeless, *Lewis and Clark, Partners in Discovery* (1947), is good on the two explorers. The most scholarly account of Burr's western maneuvers is T.P. Abernethy, *The Burr Conspiracy* (1954). J.F. Zimmerman, *Impressment of American Seamen* (1925), is a useful work. The books by L.W. Levy on civil liberties, and by L.D. White on government administration, cited above, are illuminating on the embargo issue. Useful older studies of the embargo policy are L.M. Sears, *Jefferson and the Embargo* (1927), and W.W. Jennings, *The American Embargo 1807–1809* (1921).

# ELEVEN

"Our lawyers and priests," Jefferson once wrote, "suppose that the preceding generations held the earth more freely than we do; had a right to impose laws on us, unalterable by ourselves." Jefferson supposed quite the contrary. He believed that "the earth belongs to the living not to the dead," that each generation must make its own laws. When, in 1809, he turned over to his friend and protégé, James Madison, all the problems his embargo had failed to solve, he saw an exciting new generation on the threshold of power in the United States and optimistically awaited the future that lay in its hands.

Benjamin Franklin, John Hancock, Washington, and Patrick Henry had died in the 1790s. Between 1803 and 1806, Sam Adams, Hamilton, and Robert Morris had followed them to the grave. Ready to take their places were men like Henry Clay, the idol of the West; John C. Calhoun, the idol of the South; and Daniel Webster, the idol of New England, all youthful enough never to have been British subjects, all eager to build a great American empire of their own. The oldest of the new group, at 42, was Andrew Jackson, North Carolina-born, who, one fine day in his early twenties, it is said, loomed on the Tennessee frontier astride a grand horse and equipped with dueling pistols and fox hounds, all picked up during a spree in Charleston financed by a legacy from an Irish relative. "Knowing little about jurisprudence but a great deal about making his own way," Jackson promptly set up as a lawyer to seek his fortune among the influential and well-to-do.

The earlier generation of statesmen had won independence and established a nation. It was the role of the new generation to overcome, if they could, the persistent problems

# THE

# NATIONAL FOCUS

of sectionalism at home and contempt abroad, to infuse the people with a national spirit, and foreign nations with respect.

## 1 Opportunities for Smart Young Men

In the first decade of the ninteenth century, while Europe was bled and impoverished by war, the United States blossomed with opportunities for smart young men. The Louisiana Purchase, by doubling American territory, seemed to have insured the future indefinitely. To the east of the Purchase, tens of thousands of new settlers each year were clearing the forests and bringing new land under cultivation. By 1810, more than a million persons lived between the Appalachians and the Mississippi, most of them in a great triangle with its apex at St. Louis, a thousand miles from the Atlantic coast. Outside this triangle to the north, Indiana had already become a territory and Illinois was soon to seek admission to the Union. In the South, Alabama, Mississippi, and Louisiana were on the verge of statehood.

In all of these new areas, speculators were doing a land-office business, and the litigation that grew out of conflicting claims enriched lawyers as well. Some frontier families did settle down to produce goods for market, and by 1810 thousands of flat boats were floating down the western rivers each year, themselves to be broken up into saleable lumber at the end of the voyage and added to the cargo supplied by farmers, woodsmen, and trappers. Hardy sailors sometimes poled small shipments of provisions, clothing, and tools upriver in keel boats. Where there were no navigable streams or where the current was too strong to oppose, road construction had begun. Men talked again of canals and, wonder of wonders, the steamboat, which Robert Fulton in 1807 proved could be propelled even against the current of the mighty Hudson.

In 1808, John Jacob Astor in New York organized the American Fur Company (see p. 376) to extend the fur-trading frontier overland to the Pacific, thereby showing the continental sweep of American enterprise. Yankee, Yorker, and Quaker ship captains, meanwhile, were capturing much of the world's carrying trade from the beleaguered British. Driven by the embargo to give their home ports a wide berth, many of them sailed all the seas, serving Russian, Chinese, Japanese, Turkish, and South American traders. In South America they often turned a pretty

Spanish dollar buying and selling cargo on their own account. Some of them married Spanish girls, raised families, and took active parts in the revolts against Spain that early in the nineteenth century established the independence of the Latin-American nations, hopefully on the model of the United States (see p. 360).

Enterprising southerners, in the meantime, finding their tobacco shut out of European markets by the French wars, were taking up new lands easily adaptable to cotton-growing (see p. 380). By 1810, South Carolina and Georgia were producing enough cotton to account for almost one-fourth of all American exports and also to supply the new cotton-spinning industry that had arisen in New England. Innovations in wool production kept up with improvements in cotton. Spanish sheep of the extraordinarily fine merino strain were introduced into the United States in 1802. By 1810, some 20,000 merinos, along with millions of ordinary sheep raised in Pennsylvania, New York, and New England, were supplying raw wool to a number of new factories and to thousands of spinners and weavers working at home.

Cut off from vital supplies by the European wars and Jefferson's embargo, the United States became nearly self-sufficient in many manufactures besides cottons and woolens. By 1810, the value of such manufactures (most of them produced as yet in homes, not factories) was placed at almost $200 million annually. To help move such products, as well as the raw materials, of farm, forest, and sea, almost 200 turnpike companies had been chartered in New England by 1810, almost 100 in New York, and about 40 in Pennsylvania, while hundreds of miles of good free roads had been built across the face of the land.

Some critics had predicted that capital would flee the country under a "dangerous" president like Jefferson. Actually it multiplied as never before—sometimes hindered, but more often prodded, by war abroad. Rapidly rising business activity called for expanding credit. To meet the need, 58 new state banks were opened between 1800 and 1811, more than doubling the country's total. Private banks added to the sources of domestic credit, and foreign bankers, notably the English Barings, extended liberal credit to American merchants.

## II  *The War of 1812*

### PRESIDENT MADISON

James Madison was 58 when he was sworn in as fourth president of the United States by Chief Justice Marshall on March 4, 1809. Although he was many years older than the enterprising new generation, he showed his sympathy with their ideas by appearing for his inauguration ceremonies dressed in "a full suit of cloth of American manufacture." In his inaugural address he spoke warmly of the need to promote American industry and "external as well as internal commerce." Albert Gallatin, Madison's Secretary of the Treasury and strong right arm throughout his first administration, shared the views of his chief. "I cannot be content," Gallatin wrote in 1809, "to act the part of a mere financier, to become a contriver of taxes, a dealer of loans." In his Report on Roads and Canals in 1808, and in his more famous Report on American Manufactures in 1810, Gallatin laid out an ambitious program of federal aid to American industry, independedent of European raw materials, markets, or wars. This program foreshadowed Henry Clay's "American System" of later years (see p. 401). Before it could be realized, however, the nation itself had first to be preserved.

Unfortunately, James Madison was not quite the man for the crises he inherited from President Jefferson. "Madison," John Quincy Adams confided in his diary in the 1830s, "was in truth a greater and far more estimable man" than Jefferson. But this view was shared only by those whose aversion for the "Sage of Monticello" grew with Jefferson's own rise in repute. "Our President," John C. Calhoun observed more accurately during Madison's first term, "tho a man of amiable manners and great talents, has not I fear those commanding talents which are necessary to control those about him." One of Madison's disabilities was his small size and frail constitution. "As to Jemmy Madison—oh, poor Jemmy!" Washington Irving lampooned him in 1812, "he is but a withered little apple-john." After a period of melancholia at the age of 20, from which he was roused only by the struggle of the colonies with Great Britain, Madison himself had decided that he could not "expect a long or healthy life," and he determined to withhold his energies from those things that were "useless in possessing after one has exchanged time for eternity."

Appparently, Madison did not include

*James Madison, age 82, from a drawing by J.B. Longacre taken from life at Montpelier, Virginia, July 1833. (The Bettmann Archive.)*

knowledge among the "useless" things. Throughout his long career, more robust men pinned the tag "scholar in politics" on their rather didactic colleague, whose mode of dress heightened his bookish aspect. "He . . . always appeared neat and genteel," recorded one long-term observer, "and in the costume of a well-bred and testy old-school gentleman. I have heard in early life he sometimes wore light-colored clothes; but from the time I first knew him . . . never any other color than black."

Yet, when he chose, Madison could carry his learning lightly. Augustus Foster found him "better informed" than Jefferson, but also more of "a social, jovial, and good-natured companion, full of anecdote, sometimes rather of a loose description." A visitor to Madison's Virginia home, "Montpelier," described his conversation as "a stream of history . . . so rich in sentiment and fact, so enlivened by anecdotes and epigrammatic remarks, so frank and confidential, . . . that it had an interest and charm, which the conversation of few men now living, could have. . . . His little blue eyes sparkled like stars from under his bushy grey eye-brows and amidst the deep wrinkles of his poor thin face." But one visitor late in Madison's life also observed that, "this entertaining, interesting and communicative personage, had a single stranger or indifferent person been present, would have been mute, cold and repulsive." Unfortunately, Madison was surrounded during his Presidency by strangers and indifferent persons, not to speak of self-seekers and betrayers.

Madison was perhaps most poorly equipped for executive positions. In congresses, conferences, and conventions the weight of his intellectual equipment was most telling. In political in-fighting and cloakroom bargaining he was no match for Hamilton among the older generation nor for Clay among the younger. At the very outset of his presidential term, he lost control of his Cabinet and even the privilege of making his own selections. By training, experience, aspiration, and right, Albert Gallatin had first claim on the position of Secretary of State, a claim Madison had intended to honor. Yet powerful shipping interests in the Senate, led by Samuel Smith of Maryland, let it be known that Gallatin's nomination would not be confirmed. Smith, like almost everyone else in politics at this time, was nominally a Republican; yet he detested Jefferson's policy of dismantling the navy, and the embargo made him and the "Invisibles," as the Smith faction was called, blind with rage. Gallatin's connection with these policies earned him Smith's eternal enmity.

Other Republicans, like William Duane, Bache's successor as editor of the Republican *Aurora,* and Dr. Michael Leib, a physician whose craving for political power was fed by his ability to deliver the German vote in Pennsylvania, took out on Madison and Gallatin their disgust with Jefferson's parsimonious and insufficiently partisan approach to patronage. Smith, Duane, and Leib found a ready welcome in the Randolph Republican faction (though not always from Randolph personally), whose strongest bond was hatred of the retired President and his friends. Jefferson had been able to smother such local malcontents. But in 1809 they forced Madison to appoint Samuel Smith's brother Robert as Secretary of State, and to yield all other Cabinet posts but one to party hacks. Gallatin, powerless to avert this undermining of the executive in the midst of the most critical international situation the young nation had yet faced, selflessly agreed to continue as Secretary of the Treasury.

Duane, at one stage, attacked Gallatin in the *Aurora* with the sinister observation that he was "to all intents and purposes the president, and even more than, the president of the United States." But if Gallatin did in fact share Madison's responsibilities, he did not share his power. When in 1813 Madison was obliged by Governor Tomkins of New York and his political friends to appoint General John Armstrong, a profiteering New York politician, Secretary of War, and to give Duane a lucrative military post, Gallatin felt

obliged to resign. Duane's conduct in particular, Gallatin wrote to a friend in May 1813, "has disgusted me so far as to make me desirous of not being any longer associated with those who appointed him." Gallatin's departure was almost the last straw for Madison, who, when visited by William Wirt in October 1814, was described as looking "miserably shattered and woe-begone. In short, he looked heart-broken."

Yet Madison, like Jefferson before him, somehow survived his eight years of "splendid misery." He also survived the alleged miseries of his constitution. Jefferson, who insisted that health was worth more than learning and who took two hours of intensive exercise—"the sovereign invigorator of the body," as he put it—every day, lived to the ripe old age of 83. Madison, frail, gray, and bookish, whose body would have collapsed under Jefferson's regimen, lived to a gratifying 87.

## THE FAILURE OF DIPLOMACY

Madison, along with other presidents in American history, believed he had only to issue orders or confer responsibility to fulfill his obligations as chief executive or commander-in-chief. But subordinates, whose divided political loyalties inside the Republican party made them uncertain whether their main allegiance was to their country, their superior, or themselves, often ignored or countermanded his orders. This lack of unity in the administration was aggravated by the persistent sectional controversies carried over from Jefferson's time, most recently those involving Jefferson's embargo of 1807 and the Non-intercourse Act of 1809 (see p. 333). The first of these measures had made influential New Englanders more determined than ever to escape the scourge of the Virginia dynasty and return to the British Empire. Many southerners, in turn, viewed the closing of American ports to British ships by the Non-Intercourse Act as a surrender of the southern export economy to New England shipping interests. These southerners might have been glad to see the Yankees withdraw from the Union. Under Madison the sectional controversies grew so acrimonious that even a foreign war failed to unite the country. This war probably was postponed until 1812 only because Britain was too occupied with her own internal and international problems to exploit American sectionalism.

When Madison took office in 1809, many nostalgic Englishmen still had not forgiven their American cousins for the Revolution and lived for the day when the American flag would be wiped off the seas. Their policy was to keep at a high level the pressure of impressments and captures that had forced Jefferson so to offend New England. Wiser English heads, looking ahead to Britain's progress in the Industrial Revolution, realized that her future lay in manufacturing more than in carrying trade. They were willing to tolerate commercial rivalry if it helped preserve American markets for British industrial goods and if it kept the United States and Britain at peace. Foreign Minister George Canning, though himself a leader of the anti-American die-hards, recognized the merit in the tolerant position of the other camp. Rule of the seas was his preferred policy, but the fact that Napoleon's Continental System (see p. 331) had left the United States as Britain's only sizable customer for manufactures led Canning to accept the policy of conciliation that the British industrialists demanded. At least he seemed to accept it.

Canning had come into office in 1807. In one of his first steps, taken probably for home consumption, he sent George Rose to America in 1808 to try to settle the differences with the United States. Since Rose was empowered to make no concessions and actually made some new demands, he got nowhere, as Canning probably intended. Just after Madison's inauguration in 1809, the British minister in Washington, David Erskine, who had married an American woman and who showed a fondness for American society, was instructed by Canning to try where Rose had failed. Erskine offered to withdraw the British orders-in-council (see p. 331) if, among other things, the United States would end nonintercourse with Britain while retaining it with France. The offer was sweetened in other ways, and Madison grasped it. Scores of American ships, loaded with goods, now hovered around British ports awaiting the resumption of trade, while hundreds of other American vessels set sail. Commerce boomed; but the situation proved too good to last.

Actually, Erskine had never been granted the power to rescind the orders-in-council. And in his eagerness to befriend America he had failed to insist on explicit acceptance of certain more onerous terms of his instructions. When Canning learned of the settlement, he immediately disavowed it and then recalled Erskine. In Erskine's place, he sent Francis J. Jackson, an implacable anti-American who spent a year exasperating everyone he met. On Jackson's recall, no replacement was named. Madison, in the meantime, had been obliged to restore nonintercourse with Britain and to continue it with France.

Talk of war grew louder when Congress reconvened in December 1809 and added inflammatory debate to ill-conceived legislation. One unfortunate measure, effective May 1, 1810, was the so-called "Macon's Bill Number 2," named for the chairman of the House Committee on Foreign Affairs. This act put an end to nonintercourse, but provided for its revival against France if Britain rescinded her orders-in-council, and its revival against Britain if France agreed to rescind her Berlin and Milan decrees (see p. 331). With little to lose, Napoleon instructed his foreign minister to let the Americans know that the French decrees were revoked as of November 1, 1810. To the consternation of New England, Madison took the bait and restored nonintercourse against the British, a step Congress confirmed with a new Non-Intercourse Act in March 1811. Napoleon, as many had foreseen, failed to abide by his announced revocation, and French attacks on American commerce continued. At the same time, William Pinkney, the American minister in London, discovered

344

that the revocation of nonintercourse with France had failed to coerce Canning to withdraw the British orders. Soon after, Pinkney returned home. With no British minister in Washington and no American representative in London, there was little chance for improvement in Anglo-American relations.

### THE URGE TO WAR

Popular disgust with the stalemate in foreign affairs was registered in the elections of 1810 and 1811, in which the voters unseated many members of the Eleventh Congress. Conspicuous among the replacements who arrived in Washington in November 1811 were bristling young men from the southern, western, and northern frontiers. Unconcerned with foreign attacks on American ships, except as affronts to the American flag, these newcomers were determined to extend American territory at the expense of embattled European nations continuing to hold land in North America.

On the southern frontier, Spain still held the Floridas, now a haven for runaway slaves and marauding pirates and a home for hostile Indians. By 1810, however, most of the settlers on the rich lands of West Florida were Americans, who, bemoaning Spain's inability to protect them, revolted and asked to be annexed by the United States. Madison, as eager as Jefferson to acquire new territory, had connived in this uprising. He proclaimed the annexation of West Florida in October 1810, and early in 1812 an armed American expedition set out to take weakly defended East Florida as well. Spain's threat to declare war, and New England's threat to revolt if war came, obliged Madison to recall the troops. This action appeased Spain and New England, but it was deemed treachery by the expansionists of the Southwest.

North of the Floridas, on American territory, an Indian war was imminent. All along the frontier, the Indian tribes had been tricked into making grant after grant of land by treaties they ill understood. Between 1801

and 1810, about 110,000,000 acres in the Ohio Valley had been taken from them by such means; but having formally ceded this territory, the Indians were slow in moving out, and the sporadic violence between red men and whites increased. By force of arms white settlers gradually made American title to the land effective while the dislodged aborigines of the Valley—Creeks, Cherokees, Kaskaskias, Shawnees, and others—were forced ever closer to the Mississippi and on to lands of the aggressive Sioux and Chippewas, who gave them only the fiercest kind of welcome. In 1811 the great Shawnee chief, Tecumseh, decided to make a stand against the frontiersmen. The land belonged to all Indians, he insisted, and no individual tribe had the right to trade away a single acre; further attempts at settlement, he said, would be resisted by a united force.

In July 1811 Tecumseh warned Governor William Henry Harrison of Indiana Territory that he intended to enlist southern tribes for a general defense. This announcement, meant to intimidate Harrison, only aroused him. Once Tecumseh had left for the South to mobilize his allies, Harrison moved on Prophetstown, the main Shawnee village on the Wabash, with a thousand men. On discovering this force at Tippecanoe Creek adjacent to Prophetstown, the leaderless Shawnee braves attacked it at dawn, November 7, 1811. Harrison's men repulsed them, though suffering heavy losses, and proceeded to burn Prophetstown to the ground. Finding the charred ruins of the village on his return, Tecumseh mobilized the survivors and swore them to eternal war against the white man. By the spring of 1812, many families of would-be settlers were fleeing for their lives to more protected areas.

Frontiersmen had long blamed the British in Canada for supplying Tecumseh with arms and egging him on against the settlers. Hence they acclaimed the victory at Tippecanoe as a triumph over the British as well as over the Indians and interpreted Tecumseh's retaliatory assaults after the battle as part of a British plot. The cry thus grew louder on the frontier for the conquest of all Canada as the first step in the ultimate elimination of Britain from "Our Continent," and for the conquest of all Florida, lest Spain be used as a cat's-paw for Britain's re-entry.

The handful of frontiersmen who carried this cry to the halls of Congress in November 1811 were promptly branded by easterners as "War Hawks." Among them were Calhoun, from upland South Carolina, whose grandmother had been scalped by Cherokees, and

Felix Grundy, of Tennessee, who had lost three brothers in Indian raids. Their leader was "Harry of the West," Henry Clay of Kentucky.

Taking advantage of the political rivalry among the older members of the decaying Republican party, Clay's friends quickly elected him Speaker of the House; he then used the Speaker's prerogative to name them chairmen of the major committees. Soon Clay and his backers placed before the House bills for en-

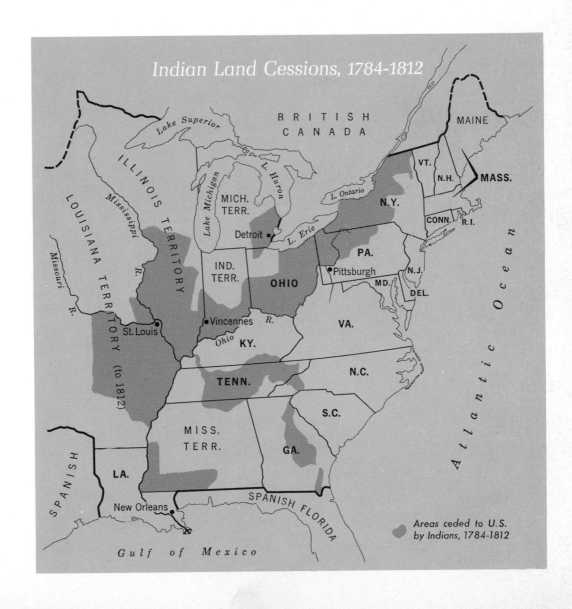

Indian Land Cessions, 1784-1812

Areas ceded to U.S. by Indians, 1784-1812

listing a large army, recruiting a modest navy, and letting the world know, as Clay said, that "we could fight France too, if necessary, in a good cause—the cause of honor and independence."

Congressional opinion on these bills was sharply divided, but events played into the hands of the war party. Early in May 1811, for example, the British became unusually active in impressment raids off New York harbor, and the American frigate *President,* a formidable 44-gun man-of-war, was ordered to patrol these waters to protect American ships. The British *Guerrière* (38 guns) had been an especially successful raider, and when the captain of *President* thought he had spotted her off Sandy Hook, he immediately gave chase. When his prey refused to identify herself, the captain ordered her bombarded. Nine British were killed and 23 wounded. *President* suffered no casualties, for the good reason that the British ship was not *Guerrière* at all, but a little 20-gun corvette, *Little Belt,* which could offer small resistance. The American government tried to settle British claims amicably in exchange for revocation of the orders-in-council. The British refused to be pressured in this manner, and the American public was just as happy. The pounding of *Little Belt* was hailed as a great triumph in the United States and helped dissolve any lingering fears of "the mistress of the seas."

A few months after the *Little Belt* affair, disclosure of the notorious "Henry Letters" further inflamed America's warlike ardor. These letters included reports of a Canadian secret agent, John Henry, on the extent of disunion sentiment in New England at this time. British interest in this subject enraged many Americans and brought the pressure on Madison to declare war to a level beyond his power to withstand.

On June 1, 1812, the President reluctantly sent a war message to the House. On the 18th he announced that both the Senate and the House had declared for war on Britain. "I verily believe that the militia of Kentucky are alone competent to place Montreal and

Upper Canada at your feet," boasted Henry Clay during the congressional debates. Congress must have believed him, for when it adjourned on July 6 it had voted no new taxes and only a few new men to carry on the war it had declared.

In his war message, Madison had said nothing about Canada and Florida, territories dear to the War Hawks' hearts, and little about the allegedly British-inspired Indian troubles on the frontier. Instead, he stressed the accumulation of intolerable offenses against American citizens, American ports, American ships, and American commerce. Impressment topped his list of war issues, and he attacked most bitterly the hovering of British men-of-war around American harbors, the "pretended blockades," and the "sweeping system" of orders-in-council.

The maritime areas in the Middle States as well as in New England had voted against the war mainly because they knew that their ships would bear the brunt of the fighting and their commerce the brunt of the cost. The South, which had lost its European tobacco market because of Napoleon's Continental System, and which was losing cotton sales because the British could no longer sell their manufactured cotton textiles across the Channel, supported the war. Except in upper New York State and part of upper Vermont, where relations with Canada were close and where trade across the border was profitable, the war had the vociferous support of the exposed frontier. Some doubted, however, that western deeds would prove as brave as western words. "When a man rises in this House," said Representative Stow of New York in January 1812, "you may almost tell how ardent he will be, by knowing how far distant he lives from the sea."

Two days before Congress declared war, Castlereagh, Canning's successor as British foreign minister, had announced the repeal of the orders-in-council. A few days later, James Monroe, now Secretary of State, instructed Jonathan Russell, the American *chargé* in Paris who was filling in at London, to arrange an armistice "if the orders-in-council are repealed, and no illegal blockades are substituted for them, and orders are given to discontinue the impressment of seamen from our vessels, and to restore those already impressed." Castlereagh's repeal and Monroe's letter crossed at sea, but neither could have prevented war. Monroe demanded too much;

*Battle of* President *and* Little Belt, *aquatint by William Elmes, 1811. Unlike most sloops-of-war,* Little Belt *had a high poop deck (not depicted in this print) which caused it to be mistaken for the frigate* Guerriére. *(Courtesy of the New-York Historical Society, New York City.)*

348

on learning of his armistice offer from Russell, Castlereagh exclaimed, "No administration could expect to remain in power that should consent to renounce the right of impressment, or to suspend the practice." Castlereagh, in turn, offered too little. That strictly maritime concessions would scarcely have been enough to swing the frontier to peace is indicated in a letter that Andrew Jackson had written the previous March:

We are going to fight for the reestablishment of our national character, . . . for the protection of our maritime citizens impressed on board British ships of war, . . . to vindicate our right to a free trade, and open market for the productions of our soil now perishing on our hands because the *mistress of the ocean* has forbid us to carry them to any foreign nation; in fine, to seek some indemnity for past injuries, some security against future aggression, by the conquest of all the British dominions upon the continent of North America.

### PREPARING FOR HOSTILITIES

Jackson's spirit had not carried over into measures required to make the grand war a success. Early in 1811, the war party in Congress had allowed the Bank of the United States to die at the expiration of its 20-year charter—an action that deprived the government of one of its main fiscal agencies just when it was needed most. Despite the urging of Secretary Gallatin, Congress put off consideration of war taxes until 1813. In the meantime, with no bank to lend assistance, only half of an authorized bond issue of $11 million could be sold. Throughout the war, new taxes were reluctantly voted and expertly evaded; new loans were optimistically authorized and niggardly subscribed.

Madison said the war was to be fought for freedom of the seas. Jackson said it was to be fought against the "mistress of the ocean." Yet not until six months after war had been declared did Congress appropriate money to enlarge the meager American navy. The army

faced a similar plight. "Such is the structure of our society," wrote Henry Clay in 1812, "that I doubt whether many men can be engaged for a longer term than six months." Yet Clay and other War Hawks had voted for an addition of 25,000 men to the regular army (making a total of 35,000), all to be enlisted for five years. Kentucky, Clay's state, had panted for war more hotly than any other; yet in the first two months of the war only 400 Kentuckians enlisted. In Vermont, which, according to a local correspondent of Madison's, "appeared to wish for war more than . . . other northern states . . . perhaps not one thousand" were ready to fight. To augment the regular army, early in 1812 the President was authorized to accept 50,000 volunteers for a year's service. But scarcely 5000 signed up in the following six months. A little later, the President was authorized to call out 100,-000 state militia, but few of those who took up arms would follow their officers across the borders of their own states. At the outset of the war, the free population of the United States was about 12 times the population of Canada; yet, according to Henry Adams, two months after the declaration of war "the Canadian outnumbered the American forces at every point of danger on the frontier."

The American army was no worse than its generals deserved. "The old officers," observed the rising Winfield Scott at the outset of hostilities, "had very generally slunk into either sloth, ignorance, or habits of intemperate drinking." The newer ones, mainly political appointees, included a few good men, Scott acknowledged. But most were "coarse and ignorant"; or, if educated, were "swaggerers, dependents, decayed gentlemen, and others unfit for anything else." Admittedly it would have been difficult for anyone to uncover talent in the army as it was then constituted. But Madison magnified the difficulty by permitting "the advisory Branch of the appointing Department," as he called the Senate, to dictate to, overrule, and intimidate the executive department.

## STRATEGY ON LAND AND SEA

Confusion in American minds over the objectives of the war muddied strategy from the outset. Canada, it was agreed, was the only "tangible" place to engage Great Britain, but New England, the logical base for an invasion of Canada, opposed the whole war (see p. 354). The South proved to be no more enthusiastic, fearing that the acquisition of Canada "as an object of the war," would, if successful, put slaveholders at a great disadvantage in the government in the future. The West agreed with Jefferson that "the cession of Canada . . . must be a *sine qua non* at a treaty of peace." But for all its hunger for Canada, the West in turn would not tolerate the withdrawal of troops to the north from the garrisons guarding the western frontier against the Indians.

To conquer Canada, Montreal, the main port of entry for British assistance, had first to be taken and held. But checked by such antipathy at home from making a quick and concerted push on Montreal, the United States, at the opening of the war, tried three timid and uncoordinated forays against Canada, scattered over almost a thousand miles of border. The principal results of these were to cause Canadians to accuse their southern neighbors of naked aggression and to sour future relations between the countries. The first of these forays, in July 1812, found General William Hull not only failing to penetrate Canada from Detroit but being forced to yield Detroit to the brilliant Canadian, General Isaac Brock, who had infiltrated his rear from Niagara. In 1814, Hull was sentenced to death by a court-martial for cowardice and neglect of duty, but he was allowed to escape the penalty because of his record in the Revolution.

The second American foray took place early in October and cost the Canadian General Brock's life. Captain John Wool led an American detachment across the Niagara River and took Queenston Heights, where New York militia were to join him and push on. But New York's militiamen refused to cross their state line and stood by while Canadian reinforcements mowed down Wool's men. The third foray in November, this one directed at last against Montreal itself from Plattsburg on Lake Champlain in New York, was no less disgraceful. Here militia under General Henry Dearborn marched north 20 miles, decided that was far enough from home, and marched back again.

Before 1812 was over, a new American force under the vigorous direction of General William Henry Harrison stood poised to recapture Detroit. When the Canadians routed a large detachment of Harrison's troops under General James Winchester at Frenchtown on the Raisin River, January 22, 1813, Harrison postponed further action, but he was to be heard from later on.

Canada clearly was not as "tangible" as had been supposed. Far from occupying it (it "will be a mere matter of marching," Jefferson had said), after six months of fighting the Americans found their own frontier pushed back to Ohio.

At sea, a more satisfactory story was unfolding. Statistically the American navy was no match for the enemy. In American waters alone, the British had 11 huge ships-of-the-line, 34 frigates, and 52 smaller warships. The United States had 16 ocean-going warships in all, including only three frigates, *Constitution, United States,* and *President,* to which, before long, a fourth, the reconstructed *Chesapeake,* was added. In the opening months of the conflict, these men-of-war scored startling victories over the British in single-ship engagements. The winter of 1812–13 found most of the American navy back in harbor, where the British, intensifying their blockade of American ports south of New London, Connecticut (they left friendly Rhode Island and Massachusetts ports alone), succeeded in bottling it up for the rest of the war. But they could not discourage American privateers, who, all told, captured more than 800 British merchantmen, most of them after 1813.

### WITHSTANDING THE BRITISH REGULARS

A week after the American declaration of war, the Czar of Russia joined Britain in the struggle against Napoleon. One of his first moves was to sound out the American minister in St. Petersburg, John Quincy Adams, on the chances of peace between his new ally and her old colonies in order to free Britain for the greater struggle on the Continent. No one wanted peace more than Madison, especially with the presidential elections of 1812 coming up. As soon as he learned of the Czar's thinking, he sent Gallatin and the former Federalist Senator, James A. Bayard, to join Adams in Russia. The British, however, spurned both the Czar's approaches and the American envoys, and the war sputtered on.

It is one of the ironies of the presidential election of 1812 that Madison should have found himself the champion of the "war party." The "peace party" had the solid allegiance of the maritime interests in every state north of Maryland. Supporting the maritime interests were thousands who had become discouraged with the country's military prospects after the failures of the most recent few months. Thousands more who detested fighting on the same side as the despot, Napoleon, turned against Madison.

De Witt Clinton of New York, an antiadministration Republican, won the "peace party" nomination with the aid of surviving New England Federalists. His own position remained ambiguous. His Republican supporters claimed that he would bring peace by fighting the war more vigorously than the administration; his Federalist backers said he would accomplish this by promptly ending the fighting. Apparently carrying water on both shoulders, Clinton also carried every northern state except Pennsylvania and Vermont. The solid backing of the South and West, however, put Madison across, and in the electoral college he won by 128 to 89.

The success of the "war party" at the polls gave the administration men in Congress new confidence, and on convening in December 1812, they promptly authorized the construc-

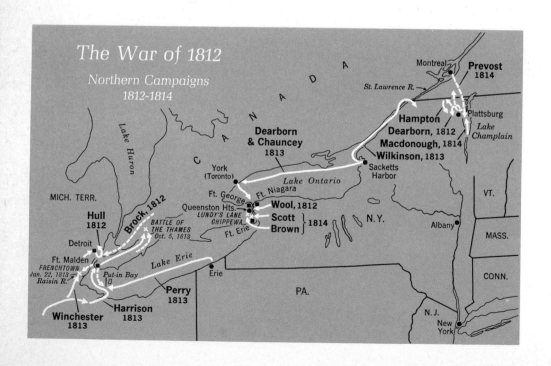

## The War of 1812
### Northern Campaigns 1812-1814

*This cartoon appeared soon after Perry's victory on Lake Erie. "Brother Jonathan" is shown forcing "John Bull" to down a draught of Perry. (The Bettmann Archive.)*

tion of four new ships-of-the-line and six new frigates. The armed forces, in the meantime, reviewed their strategy and replanned their campaigns. Even before his loss of Detroit to Brock, General Hull had been skeptical of holding the city without control of Lake Erie. General Harrison shared Hull's views. After Winchester's defeat at Frenchtown, Harrison decided to wait until the Canadians had been cleared off the water before making another overland assault on Detroit. The task of clearing Lake Erie was given to young Captain Oliver Hazard Perry, who early in 1813 began to construct a small fleet at Presqu'ile, off the Pennsylvania shore of the Lake. Sails, cordage, ordnance, and most of the other supplies Perry needed had to be hauled across the Alleghenies from eastern cities and then poled laboriously up river from Pittsburgh. By August 1813, nevertheless, Perry's fleet was ready, and on September 10 he won a bloody but decisive victory over the British lake squadron, which he caught in Put-in Bay at the western end of the water. Since Perry's ships penned the British in, the fight was more like a land action, with both sides firing away at each other. At the end of the engagement Perry reported to Harrison, "We have met the enemy and they are ours."

Harrison followed up Perry's victory by setting out after the Canadian General Henry Proctor, who had abandoned Detroit when he lost his naval support. Proctor marched east toward Lake Ontario, where another British naval squadron was in control, but Harrison's forces caught and defeated him on the way, at the battle of Thames River, October 5. Tecumseh, who had earlier gone over to the British, was killed in this engagement and his Indian forces ceased to be a factor in the war.

Encouraged by Perry's success on Lake Erie, Captain Isaac Chauncey of the United States navy collected a few vessels on Lake Ontario and, in collaboration with General Dearborn, attacked York (present-day Toronto), the capital of Upper Canada. Dearborn's men took the town, but not before a powder magazine near the town exploded, killing 300 American soldiers and giving the survivors an excuse to burn the capital's parliament houses. Since Chauncey could not establish American naval supremacy on Lake Ontario, Dearborn's hold on York remained tenuous and the United States forces soon abandoned it. Still farther east, Generals James Wilkinson and Wade Hampton planned a new march on Montreal, but, characteristically, turned back after brief skirmishes near the Canadian border.

In April 1814 Napoleon abdicated and Britain was eager for peace. But peace could wait until she had put the upstart Americans in their place. First, in May 1814, the British

351

*Contemporary British version of the attack on Washington under Major General Ross, 1814. ". . . we burnt and destroyed their Dock Yard with a Frigate and a Sloop of War, Rope-walk Arsenal, Senate House, President's Palace, War Office, Treasury and the Great Bridge. With the Flotilla the public property destroyed amounted to thirty Million of Dollars." (Library of Congress.)*

extended their blockade to northern New England ports and strengthened it elsewhere, steps that permitted the harassment of American seaboard cities all the way to Maine and the incitement of slave insurrections in and around southern ports. On one such adventure, emanating from Chesapeake Bay, a force of British regulars supported by a British fleet began a march on Washington. The hastily mobilized defenders, led by the incompetent General William H. Winder, were routed at Bladensburg, leaving Washington open to the invaders. On August 24, in retaliation for the exploit at York, the British set fire to the Capitol and the White House. The failure of an assault the next month against Baltimore and Fort McHenry prompted the British to withdraw from the area on October 14.

The burning of the government buildings was of little military importance, but, as Leonard D. White writes, it marked "probably the lowest point ever attained in the prestige of the presidency." Before the burning, Secretary of War Armstrong had rejected

Madison's warnings that a British attack was imminent and had taken no measures to prepare for it. When Madison took the city's defense on his own shoulders, Armstrong washed his hands of the capital and rode off to Maryland. Unfortunately for Madison, his tactics were disastrous. After the debacle, the President wrote to Armstrong that "threats of personal violence had . . . been thrown out against us both." He warned the absent Secretary to stay away from the troops, and explained by saying that "I had within a few hours received a message from the commanding general of the Militia informing me that every officer would tear off his epaulets if Gen'l Armstrong was to have anything to do with them."

Only after further delay did Madison demand Armstrong's resignation; and only after still more procrastination did he appoint Monroe, virtually on the latter's demand, as Secretary of War.

Of greater military significance than the burning of Washington was a three-pronged attack that the British directed against Niagara, Lake Champlain, and New Orleans. By mid-1814 the United States had managed to uncover a few vigorous new commanders, including General Jacob Brown and his subordinate, Winfield Scott. Having learned of the British push on Niagara before it had got under way, General Brown took the initiative himself. On the fourth of July he captured Fort Erie, on the Canadian side of the Niagara River; the next day, Scott defeated the British at Chippewa. On July 25, Brown outfought the enemy at Lundy's Lane, near Niagara Falls, but fell back upon learning that strong British reinforcements were on the way.

In August these reinforcements, 10,000 veterans of Wellington's Napoleonic campaigns, arrived at Montreal ready for the second phase of the British offensive—a march toward Lake Champlain under Sir George Prevost. Their objective might have been to detach northern New York and New England from the United States and restore them to the British empire. Whatever their purpose, they were foiled in the battle of Plattsburg Bay (see map, p. 350).

Although heavily outnumbered by the British at Plattsburg, the Americans had two advantages: First, they were installed in fortifications erected by the new army engineers, the first experienced graduates of West Point, which had been established in 1802. Second, they were protected by Captain Thomas Macdonough's flotilla on Lake Champlain. Early in September, Prevost moved his fine army toward Plattsburg in coordination with a British flotilla on the lake. Macdonough's men and ships took a battering in the ensuing battle of Plattsburg Bay; yet they won so complete a victory that Prevost, rather than try a match of arms on land, turned back.

Plattsburg Bay, the last battle before the Treaty of Ghent officially ended hostilities (see p. 356), was not the last battle of the war. In the Southwest, Andrew Jackson had been campaigning more or less on his own against the Indians, and after routing the Creeks at the battle of Horseshoe Bend in Alabama in March 1814 (see map, p. 354), he forced them to yield by treaty many thousands of acres of excellent land. The vigor of Jackson's actions brought him full command in the southwestern theater and the responsibility for checking the British attack in that sector—the third prong of their comprehensive assault. Aware that the British might use Pensacola in Spanish Florida as a base, Jackson invaded the area and burned the town. Marching on to New Orleans, he was ready for the British when they arrived there from Jamaica. In the battle between 8000 British veterans of the Napoleonic campaigns and a rag-tail collection of American militiamen, sailors, and pirates, Jackson's rifles and artillery mowed down the redcoats. British casualties in this unnecessary battle amounted to more than 2000 men, including the commanding general, Sir Edward Pakenham, whereas the well-entrenched Americans suffered only 8 killed and 13 wounded. The battle of New Orleans took place on January 8, 1815, two weeks after the Treaty of Ghent had been signed but over a

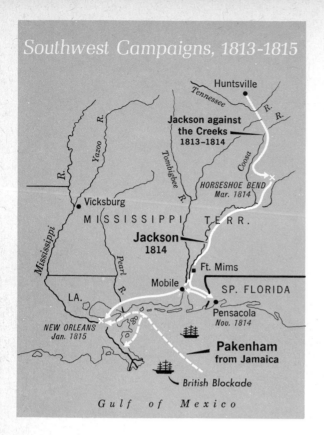

Huntsville

Tennessee R.

**Jackson against the Creeks 1813–1814**

Yazoo R.

Coosa R.

Tombigbee R.

*HORSESHOE BEND Mar. 1814*

• Vicksburg

M I S S I S S I P P I    T E R R.

**Jackson 1814**

Mississippi R.

Pearl R.

■ Ft. Mims

Mobile ●

SP. FLORIDA

LA.

Pensacola
*Nov. 1814*

*NEW ORLEANS Jan. 1815*

**Pakenham from Jamaica**

↘ British Blockade

*Gulf    of    Mexico*

---

aration—amicably if they can, violently if they must." Once "Mr. Madison's War" began, New England decided to have as little to do with it as possible, except insofar as it feathered her nest.

The British blockade of the American coast below New London, Connecticut, at the outset of the war (see p. 349) had left the rest of the nation at the mercy of Massachusetts and Rhode Island for imports, and Yankee merchants in these states made the hated administration pay dearly for wartime goods. New England's commercial prosperity was matched by that of her manufacturers. New England produced many critical commodities, but the boom was especially marked in cotton textiles. Between 1810 and 1814 the number

*Broadside giving Bostonians the news of the signing of the Treaty of Ghent. (Courtesy of the New-York Historical Society, New York City.)*

## PEACE!

### Treaty of PEACE signed & arrived!

CENTINEL-OFFICE, *Feb.* 13, 8 o'clock in the morning.

WE have this instant received in Thirty-two hours from N. York, the following

#### Great and Happy News!

To BENJAMIN RUSSELL, Esq. Centinel-Office, Boston,
New-York, Feb. 11, 1815.—Saturday Evening, 10 o'clock.

SIR—

I HASTEN to acquaint you, for the information of the Public, of the arrival here this afternoon of H. Br. Majesty's Sloop of War FAVORITE, in which has come passenger Mr. CARROL, American Messenger, having in his possession a

## TREATY OF PEACE

Between this Country and Great-Britain, signed on the 26th December last.

Mr. BAKER also is on board, as Agent for the British Government, the same who was formerly Charge de Affairs here.

Mr. Carroll reached town at eight o'clock this evening. He shewed to a friend of mine who is acquainted with him, the pacquet containing the Treaty, and a London Newspaper of the last date of December, announcing the signing of the Treaty.

It depends, however, as my friend observed, upon the act of the President to suspend hostilities on this side.

The gentlemen left London the 2d Jan. The Transit had sailed previously from a port on the Continent.

This city is in a perfect uproar of joy, shouts, illuminations, &c. &c.

I have undertaken to send you this by Express—the rider engaging to deliver it by Eight o'clock on Monday morning. The expense will be 225 dollars—If you can collect so much to indemnify me I will thank you so to do.

I am with respect, Sir, your obedient servant,

JONATHAN GOODHUE.

Printed at the Portsmouth Oracle-Office.

1815

---

month before news of the signing of the treaty had reached the capital. Jackson himself went on from this triumph to become the country's most popular hero since Washington.

### THE HARTFORD CONVENTION

If Prevost, before Plattsburg Bay, had hoped to detach New England from the United States and restore it to Britain, many New Englanders, men already soured by the whole tendency of Republican diplomacy, would have wished him luck. Besides Republican diplomacy, Republican expansionism, especially in the West, had also stirred the deepest misgivings in Yankee hearts. As early as January 4, 1811, during the opening stages of the debate over the admission of Louisiana as a state, the Massachusetts congressman Josiah Quincy told the House of Representatives that favorable action would make it "the duty of some to prepare definitely for a sep-

of cotton spindles in the region increased from 80,000 to 500,000 and looms to weave cotton cloth multiplied proportionately. Yankee industrialists, like Yankee merchants, put a high price on their products and not least on those most needed by the government for the war.

Their control of commerce and manufactures, in turn, gave Yankee capitalists control of the nation's money supply. For critical domestic goods as well as for those they imported, they demanded hard cash, thereby draining the rest of the country of its specie. Between 1811 and 1814 the banks of Massachusetts alone quadrupled their hoards of Spanish milled dollars and the other hard currency of the country. Yet of $40 million in long-term bonds floated by the federal government in this period, New Englanders subscribed less than $3 million.

New England was as niggardly with men as with money. She suffered for this after May 1814, when the British, as we have seen, extended the coastal blockade all the way to Maine and began raiding Yankee towns as they had earlier those to the south. New Eng-

land's persistent refusal to place her militiamen under federal orders left the government in Washington helpless to defend her in her new emergency. That she was herself largely to blame for her distress did not make her any more tolerant of the administration. Quite the contrary. The new pressures of the war on New England only made certain of her more extreme spokesmen the more insistent upon abandoning the Union altogether for British protection. Ironically enough, the widespread expectation that British success in New Orleans might then bring about the final separation of the West from the rest of the country only strengthened the resolve of many Yankees to flee the dissolving Union.

New England's intransigence came to a head in the dark days of October 1814, when

355

356

the Massachusetts legislature voted to call upon her sister states to send delegates to a convention to meet at Hartford, Connecticut, in December. Having gone this far with the zealots, the legislature issued a moderate statement of purposes: to consider their "public grievances and concerns," to strengthen their "defence against the enemy," and "to take measures, if they shall think proper, for producing a convention of delegates from all the United States, in order to revise the Constitution thereof." The legislature also placed at the head of the Massachusetts delegation the moderate George Cabot, who came out of retirement, as he said, "to keep the young hotheads from getting into mischief."

When the convention did assemble in secret session on December 15, it was found that only Massachusetts, Rhode Island and Connecticut had sent state delegations. These were accompanied by representatives from a few counties in Vermont and New Hampshire. The moderates, moreover, took command from the start and smothered the secessionist tendency.

At the conclusion of the Convention in January 1815, a "Report" was issued vigorously condemning the administrations of Jefferson and Madison in state-rights terms reminiscent of their own Virginia and Kentucky Resolutions of 1798. The Report also proposed the adoption of amendments to the Constitution for protecting New England, within the Union, from the rising majority in other sections. One amendment would have eliminated the "three-fifths" clause of the Constitution (see p. 253), thereby depriving the South of that part of its representation based on slaves. Another would have limited the presidency to one term and prohibited the election of successive presidents from the same state, i.e., Virginia. A series of additional amendments would have required a two-thirds majority in each house for the admission of new states, the "interdiction of commercial intercourse" with foreign nations, and declarations of war.

The Convention named a committee of three, headed by Harrison Gray Otis, a moderate of Massachusetts, to carry its Report to Washington and to present it to Congress. Promising to reconvene for more drastic action if Congress rejected its demands, the Convention closed just when the war was coming to an end.

A few days before the Hartford emissaries reached Washington early in February, the news of Jackson's victory at New Orleans and of the signing of the treaty of peace at Ghent (see p. 357) had arrived in the capital. Talk of sectional or state rights, let alone of secession, was out of the question at the moment of national celebration. The Hartford men stole away from the scenes of triumph, and New England leaders showed the good sense thereafter to forego the promised new meeting.

## III  *"Our Continent" Diplomacy*

### THE TREATY OF GHENT

The British, having dealt Napoleon his final blow, as they thought, in April 1814, launched their military offensive in America that summer (see p. 353) partly to gain a better position from which to dictate terms to the United States once they had settled accounts with her. When the peace commissioners of the two nations met formally for the first time in the Belgian town of Ghent in August 1814, the British were confidently awaiting reports of new victories in America and they confronted Madison's negotiators with the most exacting demands. Besides Gallatin, Bayard, and John Quincy Adams, who had been in Europe for more than a year (see p. 350), the American group included Henry Clay and his unstable satellite, Jonathan Russell. Although the British got nowhere in the end, their terms were well calculated to set the Americans at one another, especially Clay the westerner and Adams the Yankee, whose tempermental differences only sharpened their sectional ones.

The British "team" told the Americans at the start that they proposed to move the boundaries of Canada southward to give that province access to the Mississippi. They would also retain those parts of Maine that were still held by British troops. To keep American fur-traders and settlers out of the Northwest, moreover, the British suggested that an Indian buffer state be established in the fur-trapping region. At the same time, the British negotiators were to concede nothing on impressment or any other maritime issue, including the right of New Englanders—granted in 1783 but withdrawn at the outbreak of the War of 1812—to fish in Newfoundland and Labrador waters and to dry their catch on nearby uninhabited shores.

Britain's extravagant claims to the American West angered Clay, but not nearly so much as Adams's willingness to concede them if necessary in order to recover New England's fishing privileges. These privileges Clay, in turn, was ready to trade away for territorial demands of his own, consistent with the War Hawks' grand war aims. Although Gallatin kept the negotiations from foundering on the Americans' fierce antagonism toward one another, neither he nor his colleagues could force the British to back down on a single demand.

The British in London were also at odds among themselves, especially on the issue of continuing the war if need be to gain their territorial goals. But the Duke of Wellington impatiently warned them that the cost of a more conclusive victory in America would be greater than the people would bear. News of the British reversals at Niagara and Plattsburg Bay seemed to confirm his opinion, and the British expansionists finally gave ground. Britain at this time had begun to fall out with her recent allies at the Congress of Vienna where Napoleon's fate and that of his erstwhile empire were being decided. Her difficulties there made it all the more urgent for her to make peace if she could with the United States and perhaps eventually to seek her support in a new balance of power.

The British retreat at Ghent reminded the American negotiators that their own principal purpose was simply to make peace. On Christmas Eve, 1814, the two powers at last agreed to the treaty which the Senate promptly ratified when it reached that body the following February. This treaty left most issues precisely where they had been at the war's start, but it also provided for commissions to meet later to settle questions of boundaries, fisheries, and the terms of commercial intercourse.

John Quincy Adams characterized the Treaty of Ghent as "an unlimited armistice [rather] than a peace, . . . hardly less difficult to preserve than . . . to obtain." Congress agreed, and though devoid of funds, voted in March 1815 to set up a standing army of 10,000 men, to enlarge appropriations for West Point, and to spend $8 million for new warships.

Adams felt constrained to add to his earlier statement on the Treaty: "We have abandoned no essential right, and if we have left everything open for future controversy, we have at least secured our Country the power at her option to extinguish the war." In later months, Adams, Clay, and Gallatin were all to enlarge upon the salutary gains in national spirit earned by the successful confrontation of the greatest power in the world. In January 1816, for example, Clay challenged the House of Representatives:

> Let any man look at the degraded condition of this country before the war—the scorn of the universe, the contempt of ourselves—and tell me, if we have gained nothing by the war. What is our present situation? Respectability and character abroad; security and confidence at home; . . . our Constitution placed on a solid basis, never to be shaken. . . . Is there a man who could not desire participation in the national glory acquired by the war?

Like Adams, Clay spoke plainly of the uses to which this new spirit must be put. In the same speech in the House, he said:

> That man must be blind to the indications of the future, who can not see that we are destined to have war after war with Great Britain, until, if one of the two nations be not crushed, all grounds of collision shall have ceased between us.

358

New wars, as it turned out, were evaded, but many "grounds of collision" kept the threat of renewed hostilities alive.

COLLISION AND CONCILIATION
IN ANGLO-AMERICAN RELATIONS

About the events at sea leading to the war of 1812, Clay had observed at the time: "The real cause of British aggression was not to distress an enemy, but to destroy a rival." When the war ended, Americans rushed to replenish their supplies of European—mainly British—finery and other goods. Imports soared to record levels, and British manufacturers deliberately dumped goods in American markets at bargain prices. "It was well worth while," Henry Brougham told Parliament in defending this policy, "to incur a loss on the first exportation in order, by the glut, to stifle in the cradle those rising manufacturers in the United States which the war has forced into existence, contrary to the natural course of things." As petitions rolled into Congress demanding that such British aggression be checked, Clay led the fight for the first avowedly protective tariff in American history, which Congress passed and Madison signed in April 1816.

This tariff had the solid support of the country; even 16 congressmen from the South, which had few factories and which preferred to look abroad for manufactured goods, voted for the measure, although 35 southern congressmen opposed it. When the act failed to protect the new American manufactures, Clay said it was not because of the defects of the measure, which were many, nor because of smuggling, "which has something bold, daring, and enterprising in it," but because of Britain's "mean, barefaced, cheating, by fraudulent invoices and false denominations."

While the British thus forced themselves into American markets, they also kept Americans out of theirs. In July 1815, for example, a commercial treaty was at long last worked out between the two nations removing discriminations against the commerce of either party in the ports of the other. The stone in the shoe, however, was Britain's insistence that the precious West Indian trade be kept closed to Yankee ships. And closed it remained until Jackson forced it open in October 1830 (see p. 416).

The "armistice" of Ghent, meanwhile, soon spawned those "future controversies" that Adams had foretold. Article I of the treaty, for example, required that "any slaves or other private property . . . taken by either party from the other during the war, . . . shall be restored without delay." Americans claimed that as many as 3600 slaves taken by the British in raids in the Chesapeake region and around New Orleans were on ships of the Royal Navy at the time of the ratification of the Treaty. These, they said, must be paid for. The British demurred; they said the Treaty did not apply to slaves already aboard their ships. Eventually the Czar of Russia was asked to arbitrate. In 1826 he decided in favor of the Americans, and the British paid $1,200,000 to settle the claims.

The silence of the Treaty on impressment was certain to lead to new incidents, especially since the British continued after the war to search American vessels for British deserters on the Great Lakes themselves. On this issue, at last, controversy led to conciliation. When Madison learned that the British were building new frigates in Canada for lake service, he proposed to Foreign Secretary Lord Castlereagh that the building be abandoned and that both nations agree to keep naval ships off these waters. Castlereagh, as eager as the President to avoid a costly arms race, welcomed Madison's suggestion. In April 1817 Charles Bagot, the British representative in Washington, and Richard Rush, Madison's acting Secretary of State, worked out their famous agreement under the terms of which neither country would maintain more than four small armed vessels on the Great Lakes. Except for certain technical changes, the Rush-Bagot settlement was still in force 150 years later.

The successful demilitarization of the Great

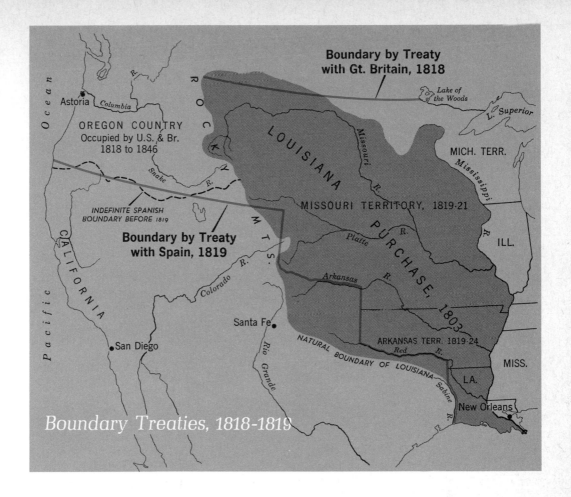

Boundary Treaties, 1818-1819

Lakes was a good omen for the settlement of the other boundary issues left to commissions by the Treaty. By 1818 four separate commissions had worked out the permanent boundary between the United States and Canada as far west as the "Great Stony [Rocky] Mountains." The peaceful settlement of the line this far was exceedingly gratifying to those concerned with America's "continental destiny." Knowledge of geography beyond the mountains was still vague, and Britain and the United States agreed to occupy the "Oregon Country" jointly. When settlement was extended to this region in the 1840s, America's "continental destiny" had become an obsession with many, and joint occupation became intolerable enough to inspire new talk of war (see Chapter Fifteen). The Maine boundary also remained an irritant for decades (see p. 471), while the issue of the fisheries continued to aggravate all other Canadian-American disputes until 1910.

### WEAKENING THE GRASP OF THE SPANISH AND THE INDIANS

The apparent improvement in Anglo-American relations arising from the peaceful negotiations over the Canadian boundary was endangered by events on the Spanish and Indian frontiers even before these negotiations were concluded. Trouble first occurred in the badlands situated between American West Florida and Spanish East Florida, the haunt of hostile Seminoles, discontented Creeks, and runaway slaves.

359

360

When violence in this wild region seemed to endanger settlers moving into Georgia after the war, the state asked the federal government to wipe out the disturbing elements. Early in 1817, General Jackson got the nod, or so he believed, to perform this service; and in his usual manner he performed it thoroughly, burning Indian villages and hanging Indian chiefs. Jackson also arrested, court-martialed, and executed two Britishers—an old Scottish trader, Alexander Arbuthnot, and a young adventurer, Robert Ambrister—who, he believed, had stirred up Indian discontent. He then marched on the Spanish in Pensacola, where the Seminoles had found a haven, ejected the governor, installed his own garrisons, and claimed the territory for the United States, as he had promised he would "in sixty days."

Many Britishers demanded war over the execution of Ambrister and Arbuthnot, to no purpose; while Spaniards, outraged over the invasion of their territory, made blustering gestures of their own. Meanwhile, Congress, where Jackson had powerful enemies, stormed over the uncontrollable General's arbitrary aggressions. The envious Clay and the self-righteous Secretary of War, Calhoun, both of whom saw in Jackson a threat to their presidential ambitions, urged that apologies be made to Britain and Spain. But Secretary of State John Quincy Adams held that Spain had got what she deserved for failing to keep order on American borders. Far from apologizing, Adams demanded that Spain pay the costs of Jackson's excursion. He also issued a virtual ultimatum to the Spanish minister in Washington, Luis de Onís, demanding that his country govern East Florida with a stronger hand or cede it to the United States.

Harassed by unrest at home and rebellion in Latin America (see p. 361), Spain realized that she could not strengthen her hold in Florida or anywhere else in America; before the United States simply took what she wanted, Spain agreed to negotiate. In the Adams-Onís Treaty of February 1819, she surrendered her remaining claims to West Florida, and ceded East Florida. In exchange, the United States agreed to assume, up to $5 million, the claims of American merchants who had lost ships and cargoes to Spain during the Napoleonic wars.

The Adams-Onís Treaty went beyond the Floridas to establish the boundary between the United States and Mexico all the way to the Pacific (see map, p. 359). Adams was disappointed in not getting Texas in the bargain; but the American interest here was only just awakening, and the Secretary of State, finding little support, did not press the issue. Revolution in Spain itself delayed approval of the treaty there until 1820; the United States Senate approved in February 1821.

For the time being, at least, Republican land-hunger was satisfied by the agreements with Britain and Spain on the northern and southern boundaries and by the acquisition of Florida from Spain. But before the lands within these generous borders could be settled, the Indians who still occupied them would have to be either subjugated or expelled. Tecumseh's death (p. 351) had deprived the northern tribes of their leader, and Britain's retirement from the Great Lakes area had removed their only remaining friend. The Indians' plight encouraged the United States to embark on an ambitious building program in this region. By 1822, older outposts like Fort Wayne and Fort Harrison in Indiana had been restored, and a string of new forts had been built along the Mississippi in Illinois and Wisconsin. This show of American force further cowed the Indians; in an effort to keep them from seeking any new allegiance with Canada, the government added a string of trading centers at which the braves could buy goods below cost. This stick-and-carrot policy gradually made the Indians in the Northwest Territory more tractable, and they at last agreed, in a series of new treaties, to move beyond the Mississippi.

In the Southwest, the red men had been overawed by Jackson's wartime victories and his ruthless subsequent assaults. Now the government offered them (in what was regarded as a humane move) the choice of taking up agriculture on the lands where they

*(Right) Henry Clay, age 44, and (far right) John C. Calhoun, age 40, by Charles B. King. (Both, details from portraits in the Collection of the Corcoran Gallery of Art.)*

lived, or of moving west. To the chagrin of the whites, most of the Indians preferred farming to abandoning their homes, and not until Jackson became president in 1829 were they forcibly ejected from their lands (see p. 409).

## THE MONROE DOCTRINE

In 1800, although she had yielded her exclusive claim to the Oregon country to Britain and Russia, and her vast territory of Louisiana to France, Spain still owned an immense New World empire ranging through nearly 100 degrees of latitude from Upper California to Cape Horn. Portugal, in turn, owned in Brazil a land soon to cover half of South America. Twenty-five years later, Spain's New World empire had been reduced to Cuba and Puerto Rico; Portugal's to nothing.

The immediate cause of this shattering collapse was Napoleon's successful invasion of Portugal in 1807 and of Spain in 1808. The Portuguese king and his family fled to Brazil and ruled there until called home in 1821, when the king's son was left behind to continue the monarchy in their New World land. Independence under the Portuguese heir was established in Brazil by 1823. The Spanish Bourbons suffered a less happy fate after Napoleon had placed his brother, Joseph, on their throne in 1808. The Spanish empire

was the personal possession of the Bourbons, and when the emperor fell, the colonies refused allegiance to the usurper. Revolts against the new administration began in Spanish America about 1810 and 1811, and the independence of the last of the new separate states was completed in 1824, when the Spanish viceroy of Peru capitulated.

The earliest uprisings in Spanish America had gained the blessing of President Madison who, like Jefferson and others, ached for the establishment of the American "system," preferably under United States control, throughout the Western Hemisphere. After Napoleon's downfall in 1814 and the restoration of the Bourbons, Spain made a serious effort to

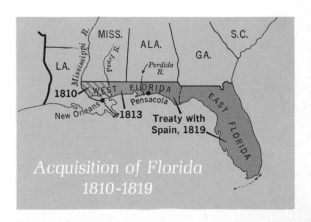

*Acquisition of Florida 1810-1819*

regain her New World lands. But she was successfully defied by such Latin-American patriots as José de San Martín, the founder of Argentina; Simón Bolívar, the founder of Venezuela; and Bernardo O'Higgins, the dictator of Chile.

When these new countries first sought formal recognition, the United States was negotiating for the purchase of Florida, and the new Monroe administration (see p. 364) was wary about affronting Spain. Clay, in Congress, took a bolder stand. He demanded as a point of honor that the American Republic embrace the new rebels against hateful monarchy. And more than honor was involved. Britain, from the first, had lent money to the Latin-American revolutionaries and was using their friendly disposition toward her to get in on the ground floor for trade and investment. It was high time, Clay thought, for the United States to combat the advantages already gained by the most hateful monarchy of all. Congress thought otherwise, however, and adopted a neutrality act in 1818. During the next few years, with the Florida treaty concluded and the Spanish-American revolutions farther advanced along the path of seemingly stable government, the United States did extend diplomatic recognition to some of the new nations.

The restoration of the Bourbons in Spain in 1814, besides heightening the revolutionary spirit in Spanish America, soon led to repression and revolution at home. By 1822 the "Holy Alliance," set up by the Congress of Vienna especially to combat the republican spirit in Europe, was ready to suppress the Spanish revolt. When, in 1823, France, the instrument of the Holy Alliance, did in fact invade Spain, Britain and the United States both believed that the invasion might easily reach across the Atlantic to suppress the revolutions in Spanish lands here. That spring, Canning, who had supplanted Castlereagh as British Foreign Secretary after the latter's suicide in 1822, "unofficially and confidentially" suggested to Richard Rush, now American minister in London, that their two countries declare to the world, for the benefit of France, that "we conceive the recovery of the [American] colonies by Spain to be hopeless." Canning innocently suggested further that they state that "we could not see any portion of them transferred to any other Power with indifference."

Canning's proposal was forwarded to Washington, where it arrived in October 1823, and immediately became the subject of debate in the Cabinet and of profound consideration by the retired Republican patriarchs, Jefferson and Madison. Jefferson, acknowledging that "Great Britain is the nation which can do us the most harm of any one," advised that "with her on our side we need not fear the whole world." He recommended accepting Canning's proposal. Madison concurred—and went even further. He proposed that the joint statement be extended to oppose French intervention in Spain and to support the current revolt of the Greeks against Turkey, a revolt that had won American sympathy.

Secretary of State John Quincy Adams was not so easily lulled. He feared that Canning was trying to lure the United States into a statement that would seem to be a pledge against future American acquisition of any territory still held by Spain—particularly Cuba. He urged that the United States, having freed herself from Britain in 1776 and made good her independent stature in 1815, should act in the Western Hemisphere alone. President Monroe yielded to Adams's arguments, and in his annual address to Congress on December 2, 1823, he used the words that have since been described as his "doctrine":

The political system of the allied powers [of Europe] is essentially different . . . from that of America. . . . We owe it, therefore, to candor and to the amicable relations existing between the United States and those powers to declare that we should consider any attempt on their part to extend their system to any portion of this hemisphere as dangerous to our peace and safety. . . . With the governments who have declared their independence and maintained it, and whose independence we have . . . acknowledged, we could not view any interposition . . . by any European power in any other light than as the manifestation of an unfriendly disposition towards the United States.

Latin America was not the only area of the Western Hemisphere in which European aggression worried Monroe's government. The Russians had been in Alaska for decades. In 1821, the ambitious Alexander I issued a decree declaring that "the pursuits of commerce, whaling, and fishery, and of all other industry on all islands, posts, and gulfs, including the whole of the northwest coast of America, beginning from Behring Straits to the 51° of northern latitude . . . is exclusively granted to Russian subjects." Nothing could have aroused Secretary Adams more; and he immediately advised the American minister in Russia that "the United States can admit no part of these claims."

To deter the Russians, Monroe added "as a principle," in his message to Congress, that the American continents "are henceforth not to be considered as subjects for future colonization by any European powers." The following April the American minister in Russia was able to advise his government that the Czar had agreed on 54°40′ as his southern boundary in North America.

Once Monroe had made his remarks (they were not known as the "Monroe Doctrine" until many years later), interested Latin Americans queried Secretary Adams on how the United States would implement the new policy in case of real need. For all his chauvinism, Adams had to admit that his government would fall back upon the British Navy, still mistress of the seas. Yet, if Monroe's message did little to buttress Latin America's security, it served to remind European reactionaries that the time had come to recognize the United States as a new force in world politics.

## IV *The Test of National Unity*

### MONROE'S ELECTION

James Monroe had been elected President of the United States in 1816 after gaining the nomination in the Republican caucus. The Randolph state-rights Republicans in the caucus had pressed the candidacy of William H. Crawford of Georgia, but Crawford himself did not oppose Monroe's nomination, and with Madison's support, Monroe became the Republican standard-bearer. His Federalist opponent was Rufus King of New York, whose selection was dictated by the desire of those New Englanders who still dominated the Federalist party to make it appear less sectional in character than it was. Monroe found the election easier to win than the nomination. He received 183 electoral votes to 34 for King, the last Federalist candidate in history, who carried only Massachusetts, Connecticut, and Delaware.

Born in 1758, Monroe early in life had become an admirer and follower of Jefferson. Later on he fancied himself a worthy competitor of Madison's. Lacking both the imagination of the "Sage of Monticello" and the intellectual energy of the scholar of "Montpelier," he was slower than either in divesting himself of his narrow localism. Yet, by refusing to join the die-hard state-rights men he kept himself available for regular Republican preferment. Monroe twice served as Governor of Virginia; on the national scene his major activity was in the field of diplomacy, which he capped by becoming Madison's Secretary of State in 1811. On the dismissal of John Armstrong in 1814 (see p. 353), Monroe also grasped the portfolio of Secretary of War and held two Cabinet posts simultaneously. The vigor of American military activity in the last phases of the War of 1812 reflected credit on Monroe's performance in the War Department and helped him to win both the coveted nomination and the election to the presidency in 1816.

Monroe had suffered many defeats during his long political career, some of them humiliating. Yet these setbacks failed to dampen his ambition or lower his self-esteem. Unlike many men jealous of power, he felt strong enough to surround himself with able associates. Indeed, his Cabinet probably was the strongest since that of Washington's first administration. After some early shuffling, it included Calhoun as Secretary of War; Crawford, a man of presidential caliber himself, as Secretary of the Treasury; and, as Attorney General, William Wirt, a Marylander who in Richmond, Virginia, had become one of the leading lawyers of the day. Monroe's most inspired stroke was the naming of the New Englander, John Quincy Adams, as Secretary of State—a selection that put the conduct of foreign affairs in the hands of an able diplomat and appeased Yankee feelings.

Shortly before his inauguration in March 1817, Monroe had been invited to visit New England by the editor of the *North American Review,* a journal that had been so determinedly Federalist during the war that it was often referred to as the "North Unamerican," but which was now ready to bury the hatchet. Monroe accepted the invitation and made a triumphal journey through the northeastern states. His visit was topped by a cordial reception in Boston, where, soon after, the *Columbia Sentinal* published the article "Era of Good Feelings," in which it noted with pleasure "all the circumstances . . . during the late Presidential Jubilee." By 1817, the Republicans had indeed shown so much concern for manufactures and the tariff, for an army and a navy, even for the chartering of a national bank (see p. 365), that the old issues seemed no longer to stand in the way of sectional reconciliation. Virginia and Massachusetts appeared to have made peace at last; and indeed Monroe was reelected in 1820 with but one electoral vote (from New Hampshire) cast against him.

## THE BOOM, THE BANK, AND THE BUST

The apparent conversion of the Republican agrarians to policies favorable to American commercial, industrial, and financial growth had been effected by the War of 1812. In 1813 Jefferson himself acknowledged that "manufactures are as necessary to our independence as to our comforts." To further the efforts of the bright young men who were seeking to promote manufactures and related activities, Jefferson favored subsidies, bounties, and patent laws as well as protective tariffs. Others, of course, took the same bent, with the same end in view. Their efforts seemed successful for a time; but once the War of 1812 ended, most of the "war babies" among American factories succumbed to British competition.

Britain's own postwar boom, however, soon sparked a non-industrial boom in the United States. The spurt in British textile manufacturing, for example, reflected in her massive exports to the United States, brought with it an enormous demand for southern cotton to feed her tireless machines. The end of the war also reopened European markets for southern tobacco. Poor European harvests in 1816 and 1817 added to the demand for American grain. These agricultural exports helped Americans pay for their record postwar imports of manufactures.

The boom in agriculture soon brought a boom in land speculation, especially in the West and Southwest, where population soared. By 1820, Ohio had become more populous than Massachusetts; and the entire West, with about 2,200,000 settlers, had more people than New England. Land, naturally, was in great demand, and the 300 or more state and "private" banks that had been established after the First Bank of the United States went out of existence in 1811 were available to help speculators sell it and settlers buy. By 1817, these banks had issued $100 million in paper money, much of it unnegotiable even in neighboring communities. Although these "facility notes," as they were called, helped newcomers get started and old-timers to expand, often enough they served only to create an obligation on which the banker could foreclose simply by withholding further "facilities" at his pleasure. "What," asked the journalist Hezekiah Niles, "is to be the end of such a business?—Mammoth fortunes for the *wise*, wretched poverty for the *foolish*. . . . SPECULATION in a Coach, HONESTY in the Jail."

By 1817, the Second Bank of the United States, chartered the year before, had entered the business picture. Back in 1814, financiers like John Jacob Astor and Stephen Girard, who had lent large amounts to the government to aid the war, had begun agitating for a new national bank to mobilize the country's financial resources. In 1815, Congress adopted a measure conforming to their plan, but Madison vetoed it. Once the war was over and imports began pouring in, more and more specie was drained from the country to supplement the agricultural exports used to pay for them. Much of the hard money that remained soon became tied up in land speculation, and by 1816 the government found itself hard pressed to meet its daily needs. Early in 1816, therefore, Secretary of the Treasury Alexander Dallas wrote a new bank bill tailored to the President's requirements. In April, this bill was passed over the opposition of New England, whose own banking system was the strongest in the land, and approved by Madison.

Like the first national bank, the Second Bank of the United States was chartered for 20 years as the sole depository for government funds. Its capital was placed at $35 million, three and a half times that of the earlier bank. Of this sum, the government was to subscribe one-fifth, or $7 million. Of the remainder, $7 million was to be subscribed in specie and $21 million in the form of securities of the United States. Five of the Bank's 25 directors were

*James Monroe, 1817, the second year of his administration. Portrait by Gilbert Stuart. (The Metropolitan Museum of Art, bequest of Seth Low, 1929.)*

to be appointed by the president of the United States; the rest by American stockholders. Foreign stockholders, who became numerous, were to have no voice in the Bank's affairs. The Second Bank had the right to establish branches in different parts of the country. Foreseeing competition, however, influential local bankers had persuaded some states to write into their constitutions provisions against "foreign banks" doing business within their borders.

Ill-managed from the first, the new Bank

365

of the United States proceeded to justify local fears by outdoing even the state banks in the lavishness of its loans. These were extended in the form of notes that were more acceptable than the notes issued by the local banks and thus tended to drive notes of local issue out of circulation. In retaliation, the injured bankers induced their state legislatures to try to tax out of existence both the branches and the notes of "the monster." In the summer of 1818, the Bank of the United States was at last ready with deflationary measures to control the boom. But these measures only made it as unpopular with the people as it remained with the local bankers. The sudden contraction of credit kept many debtors from making the payments due on their loans, and before 1819 ended, the boom collapsed.

Actually, the economic collapse was worldwide. The revival of European agriculture after the Napoleonic wars and the weakening of the postwar textile boom combined to create a glut both of wheat and cotton in world markets. But the depression was most severe in the United States and most devastating in the West.

The crisis prompted a number of states to abolish the useless and degrading practice of punishing debtors with imprisonment and to pass liberal bankruptcy laws and laws easing the settlement of contracts. Congress also came to the aid of the West with a new land act in 1820, which permitted a settler to buy an 80-acre homestead for $100 in cash. The next year Congress added a relief act to assist those people whom earlier credit provisions had got into trouble.

### THE NATIONALISM OF JOHN MARSHALL

Against this background of local self-assertion, business depression, and heightened conflict between debtors and creditors, John Marshall issued a series of historic Supreme Court decisions. We have already observed how, following his appointment in 1801, he had laid the basis in *Marbury* v. *Madison*

(1803) for the Court's power to declare acts of Congress unconstitutional (see p. 318), and how, in *Fletcher* v. *Peck* (1810), he had upheld the obligation of contracts against unilateral state interference (see p. 323).

In 1819 and succeeding years, Marshall had welcome opportunities to enlarge on his earlier opinions. Of sweeping importance was his decision in 1819 in *Dartmouth College* v. *Woodward,* which raised the question of whether a charter granted to the College in 1769 by George III and later acknowledged by the New Hampshire legislature could subsequently be changed by the legislature alone. Marshall decided that the charter was a contract and that certain action taken by the legislature without consulting the College had been taken unconstitutionally. Far more important than the College's gratification was the security Marshall's decision gave to business corporations; for it now appeared that their charters, defined as contracts, were substantially unchangeable, except with the consent of both parties.

A second decision in 1819, in *Sturges* v. *Crowninshield,* dealt with a New York State bankruptcy law. Marshall found that even though Congress was empowered to pass bankruptcy laws, the states could also enact them if Congress failed to exercise its powers. But insofar as the New York law sought to relieve a debtor of the obligation to pay his debt, Marshall found it in violation of the clause of the Constitution forbidding legislation that would impair contractual obligations. Marshall stuck to his guns eight years later in the case of *Ogden* v. *Saunders* (1827); but for the first and only time on the contract issue he failed to carry the Court with him. By a four-to-three vote, the Court upheld a New York bankruptcy law which relieved debtors of the obligation to pay up fully on debts contracted after the passage of the law, when its terms were known to debtors and creditors alike.

In confirming the supremacy of the federal government and the Supreme Court over state *legislation* on constitutional issues, Marshall's regime was a spectacular success. During his 34 years as Chief Justice, the Court acted no less than 13 times to set aside state laws as contrary to the Constitution. In *Martin* v. *Hunter's Lessee* (1816), the Court, speaking through Justice Joseph Story, asserted its supremacy over state *courts* as well in interpreting the Constitution. Five years later, in *Cohens* v. *Virginia* (1821), Marshall went out of his way to state this principle in the broadest possible terms.

Two other decisions in 1819 and 1824 clarified and broadened the powers of Congress over matters of decisive economic importance. In *McCulloch* v. *Maryland* (1819), the constitutionality of the national bank was questioned. This case grew out of an attempt by the state of Maryland to tax the Baltimore branch of the Bank of the United States out of existence. In broad language, Marshall found that the act by which the Bank had been created was constitutional: "Let the end be legitimate, let it be within the scope of the Constitution, and all means which are appropriate, which are plainly adapted to that end, which are not prohibited, but consist with the letter and spirit of the Constitution, are constitutional." This, one of the most famous sentences in American constitutional law, underpinned the broad interpretation of implied powers of Congress, for which Hamilton, among the Founding Fathers, had worked the hardest. As for the Maryland law taxing the Bank, Marshall found it unconstitutional. "The power to tax," he said, "involves the power to destroy." If states were permitted to nullify acts of Congress by attacking its agencies, they could "defeat and render useless the power to create." Hence states do not have the power to "retard, impede, burden, or in any manner control" the operation of constitutional laws passed by Congress to execute powers granted to the federal government.

Finally, in the case of *Gibbons* v. *Ogden* (1824), Marshall spoke out on the power of Congress to regulate commerce. New York had granted Robert Fulton and Robert R. Livingston a monopoly of steam navigation in state waters, and Aaron Ogden had bought from them the right to operate a ferry between New York and New Jersey. When Thomas Gibbons set up a competing ferry under a federal coasting license, Ogden tried to invoke the state-sanctioned monopoly to restrain him from running it. The original grant by New York encroached upon the exclusive right of Congress to regulate interstate commerce, but Marshall did not rest content simply with throwing out the New York monopoly. He went on to construe the term "commerce" so broadly as to include in it navigation within a state. And he excluded the states from acting on "commerce" when their acts came "into collision with an act of Congress."

It is frequently stated that Marshall, while the Republicans dominated the legislature and the executive, handed down Federalist law from the fortress he held for 34 years in the Supreme Court. But it is closer to the truth to say that, once his war with Jefferson had ended (see p. 312), Marshall gave all his energies to extending national power, just as Jefferson gave his to extending the national domain. Both were expansionists; the work of one complemented that of the other. Together they gave Americans of the oncoming Jacksonian era the limitless space and legal spaciousness within which they might seek their destinies unencumbered by local monopolists.

## THE MISSOURI COMPROMISE

The expansiveness of the postwar era was to be checked by the reopening of the slavery issue. Many Americans had feared such a happening for generations; yet as they had hidden the subject in the Constitution, so they had hidden it in their consciousness. When it emerged again during the controversy over Missouri in 1820, Jefferson himself wrote that, "like a fire bell in the night," the "momentous question . . . awakened and filled me with terror." And well it might.

Before the War of 1812, most western settlers had been southerners who moved through the mountain passes of Virginia to Kentucky and Tennessee and beyond. Often they carried slaves along with them. After the war, large numbers of Yankees also went West and "made" farms with their own hands. Some of them hated slavery with religious zeal, many more for its economic and social consequences. The planners of Jefferson's generation had forbidden slavery in the Northwest Territory. The first momentous clash over the extension of the "peculiar institution" took place just beyond, in the so-called Upper Louisiana Territory, whose settlers in 1818 applied for admission as a state under the name of Missouri.

The "enabling act" to grant Missouri statehood raised no problems in Congress until Representative James Tallmadge of New York, on February 13, 1819, shocked the South by offering an amendment to prohibit the introduction of any additional slaves into the new state. He proposed, further, that all children born of slaves in that region be freed when they reached the age of 25. The Tallmadge Amendment passed the House promptly by a narrow margin, reflecting the predominance of northern strength in that chamber, which itself reflected the greater population of the free states. The story in the Senate was different. Even though the free states outnumbered the slave states 11 to 10 at the time, a number of northern senators who had been born and brought up in the South voted with the large minority of southern senators and helped defeat the Tallmadge Amendment, 22 to 16.

The deadlock between House and Senate carried over to the next session, which got under way in December 1819. By then the situation had changed significantly. For one thing, the country had debated and divided on the issue. In October 1819 Madison re-

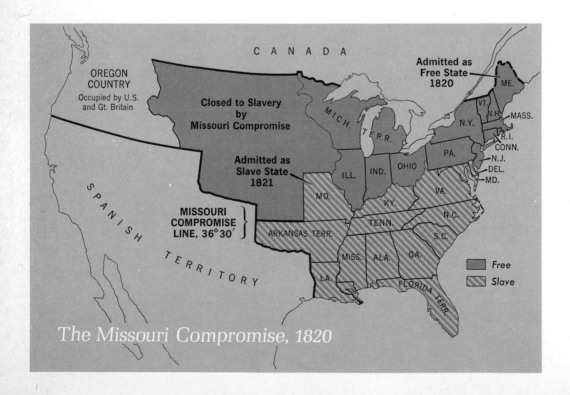

The Missouri Compromise, 1820

ceived a letter from a fellow-Virginian which expressed the rising tension: "Union must snap short at last," wrote this correspondent, "where Liberty ends, and Slavery begins. The Missouri Question is bringing on the Crisis." A second change was Alabama's application for statehood. There was no question about admitting Alabama as a slave state, and she was accepted as such on December 14, 1819. Alabama became the twenty-second state and established the balance between slave and free states at 11 each. Missouri, as a slave state, would thereby give the South a virtual veto in the Senate of all legislation enacted by the preponderantly northern House.

The northern majority in the House insisted on keeping Missouri closed to slavery. When the northeastern part of Massachusetts applied for admission to the Union as the independent state of Maine, however, some members of Congress, led by Henry Clay, grasped the chance to break the deadlock. Many in Maine did not relish their role. In a letter which, according to the historian Edward Channing, expressed a sentiment that was widespread in the North, one Maine inhabitant objected to his state being "a mere *pack-horse* to transport the odious, anti-republican principle of slavery into the new State of Missouri, against reason and the . . . great fabric of American liberty."

But the compromisers were not to be diverted by such objections. In a series of measures known as the "Missouri Compromise," they arranged for the temporary preservation of the balance of power in the Senate by admitting Missouri as a slave state and Maine as a free one. The most significant provision of the Compromise permitted slavery in Missouri, but prohibited it "forever . . . in all territory ceded by France to the United States . . . which lies north of 36°30′ . . . not included within the limits of [that] state." President Monroe hesitated to sign the compromise measures, indeed he was prepared to veto them, on the ground that the Constitution nowhere gave Congress the power to exclude slavery from a territory. But the unanimous urging of his Cabinet overcame his scruples and he signed the Missouri Compromise on March 6, 1820.

When Congress took up the matter of approving Missouri's new state constitution, as required by the admitting process, new trouble arose. This constitution provided that the state should never emancipate slaves without the consent of their owners; worse, it contravened the equal privileges and immunities clause of the federal Constitution by absolutely prohibiting the entry of free Negroes into the state.

Through the efforts of Henry Clay, Congress finally accepted the state constitution, but not before the so-called "Second Missouri Compromise" had been hammered out. This new compromise required the state legislature to guarantee that it would never deny any of the privileges and immunities of citizens of the United States inside the borders of Missouri. There the slavery issue rested for a generation, but the Missouri controversy intensified sectionalism and gradually submerged the focus on nationalism that the war generation had labored so hard to bring about.

# READINGS

Irving Brant, *James Madison* (6 vols., 1941–61), is the outstanding modern biography. S.K. Padover, *The Complete Madison* (1953), is less complete than it sounds, but offers a useful collection of Madison's writings. Adrienne Koch, *Jefferson and Madison: The Great Collaboration* (1950), is a respectful study. W.P. Cresson, *James Monroe* (1946), is a useful biography. On the internal conflicts of Monroe's administration, see the old biography by Carl Schurz, *The Life of Henry Clay* (2 vols., 1887); C.M. Wiltse, *John C. Calhoun, Nationalist 1782–1828* (1944); and Marquis James, *The Life of Andrew Jackson* (one vol. edition 1938).

Henry Adams's classic *History of the United States*, cited in Chapter Ten, remains the outstanding general account of the period that culminated in the War of 1812, and its treatment of the war itself is outstanding. The military parts have been extracted and published separately in H.A. De Weerd, ed., *The War of 1812* (1944). Another classic in American historical writing, essential to an understanding of this period, is F.J. Turner, *The Frontier in American History* (1920). Turner's *Rise of the New West* (1906) should also be read. Two books by George Dangerfield are unusually perceptive: *The Era of Good Feelings* (1952) and *The Awakening of American Nationalism 1815–1828* (1965).

J.W. Pratt, *Expansionists of 1812* (1925), persuasively develops the idea that the origins of the war had less to do with freedom of the seas than with American hunger for Canada and other territory. A.L. Burt, *The United States, Great Britain, and British North America* (1940), takes issue with Pratt's thesis. The quest for national prestige as a factor in bringing on the war is examined in three works: Reginald Horsman, *The Causes of the War of 1812* (1962); R.H. Brown, *The Republic in Peril: 1812* (1964); and N.K. Risjord, *The Old Republicans: Southern Conservatism in the Age of Jefferson* (1965). Michael Lewis, *A Social History of the Navy 1793–1815* (1960), provides rich background for British impressment practices. The issue as seen by Americans is well presented in J.F. Zimmerman, *Impressment of American Seamen* (1925). Three books by Bradford Perkins cover wartime diplomacy and its antecedents, using British sources: *The First Rapprochement: England and the United States 1795–1805* (1955); *Prologue to War . . . 1805–1812* (1961); and *Castlereagh and Adams . . . 1812–1823* (1964).

Besides De Weerd (above), good treatment of the war itself will be found in H.L. Coles, *The War of 1812* (1965), and F.F. Beirne, *The War of 1812* (1949). The Canadian side is recounted in C.P. Lucas, *The Canadian War of 1812* (1906), and J.M. Hitsman, *The Incredible War of 1812* (1966). On the war at sea, the most important work is A.T. Mahan, *Sea Power in Its Relations to the War of 1812* (2 vols., 1919). On the diplomacy of the war and the peace, S.F. Bemis, *John Quincy Adams and the Foundations of American Foreign Policy* (1949), is enlightening. F.L. Engleman, *The Peace of Christmas Eve* (1962), is more closely focused on the Treaty of Ghent. On the Hartford Convention, besides Henry Adams's and Dangerfield's books mentioned above, see Henry Adams, *Documents Relating to New England Federalism* (1877), and S.E. Morison, *Harrison Gray Otis 1765–1848: The Urbane Federalist* (1969).

Dexter Perkins, *A History of the Monroe Doctrine* (1955), is the standard account. For the British side, see C.K. Webster, *Foreign Policy of Castlereagh 1815–1822* (1925), and H.W.V. Temperley, *The Foreign Policy of Canning 1822–1827* (1925). R.A. Humphreys and John Lynch, *The Origins of the Latin American Revolutions 1808–1826* (1965), provides an excellent introduction to this subject and the literature on it.

An excellent account of the western Panic of 1819 can be found in vol. IV of Beveridge's *Life of John Marshall* (referred to in Chapter Seven), which also is best on the performance of the Court under Marshall in the period just after the Panic. A more intensive treatment is M.N. Rothbard, *The Panic of 1819, Reactions and Policies* (1962). On the Court, E.S. Corwin, *John Marshall and the Constitution* (1919), is short and authoritative. Much more detail is to be found in C.G. Haines, *The Role of the Supreme Court in American Government and Politics 1789–1835* (1960). On the Missouri Compromise, see Glover Moore, *The Missouri Controversy* (1953).

# TWELVE

The War of 1812 is often called America's "second war of independence," and there is much justice in that designation. When the war ended in 1815, all of 40 years had passed since Lexington and Concord. In those years the United States acquired territory far larger than all of western Europe, and she was soon to extend her holdings and her claims across the continent she coveted. After 1815, with France bled white in the Napoleonic struggles, with Spain forced to recede inward upon her troubled self, and with Britain soon to be preoccupied with the extension of her "second empire" eastward not westward, the United States became freer to organize her energies for the unwavering pursuit of wealth and welfare that was to become her hallmark in the virtual world she called her own.

Although hostile Britain still reigned in Canada, hostile Spain to the South and Southwest, and hostile aborigines in the open spaces between them, and although haughty monarchs overseas continued to view the United States as a pawn in their own power game, American involvement in foreign affairs gradually yielded to domestic questions. Among these, sectionalism overshadowed all others. Many issues, open or covert, obvious or obscure, lent their weight to pulling the country apart. Heaviest of all, perhaps, were those arising from the spectacular surge in economic growth, once the people turned to the discovery and development of their vast endowment in natural resources. Economic growth and its instrumentalities surely added to the strength of union too. But the Civil War disclosed the greater force of the sectional strains that had begun to rend the young nation, as we have seen, from the first moment of her independent existence.

# SECTIONAL STRAINS
# IN ECONOMIC GROWTH

## 1 Enterprise and Empire

**THE GRIP OF TRADITION**

In 1815, and indeed for several decades thereafter, the majority of white Americans in the South as well as in the North still lived on family farms, with all but a few of their needs supplied by the husbandry of men and boys, the spinning, stitching, baking, and brewing of women and girls. These people, or their forebears, had come to America in search of personal freedom based on economic independence. Although by their mere zealous occupation of the land they were the true emissaries of empire, they remained relatively unconcerned about economic enterprise or growth. Innovations in crops, tools, agricultural methods, and marketing techniques left most of them scornful and skeptical. They traded little and traveled less. Cultivating the land was to them a complete and gratifying way of life, which left them isolated from the ups and downs of the world and worldly affairs.

The fish of the sea supplied another great natural resource from which many Americans continued to eke out a fiercely independent existence long after the Revolution. In 1821, Timothy Dwight, reporting on his travels through New England, said of the fishing ports south of Boston: "The whole region wears remarkably the appearance of stillness and retirement; and the inhabitants seem to be separated in a great measure, from all active intercourse with their country." Fishermen in these ports went out, typically, like farmers, only for the day. Each had his own boat and brought back his catch for his family, though he might sometimes barter a surplus for grain, clothing, or equipment. At more active fishing centers like Newburyport and Beverly, and on Cape Cod, fishermen showed greater enterprise. Their voyages were longer and better organized. But here too the rule was that each man supplied his own gear and provisions in return for a share of the catch. The fisherman always preferred going out "on his own hook," a phrase that originated with these Yankees.

One specialized fishing occupation—whaling—ranked very high in value of product until kerosene supplanted whale oil as an illuminant after the Civil War. Until the War of 1812, just about every New England port had its whaling fleet, but after the war, Nantucket and New Bedford, Massachusetts, almost monopolized the industry. After 1820,

*Whaling was a hazardous life. Not only did the men have to battle the dangers of the sea, they had to contend with severe mistreatment by their captains. The whalemen in this woodcut from the 1840s are scrambling for a daily allotment of salt meat. (The Bettmann Archive.)*

New Bedford became the whaling center of the world, with perhaps a third of the international fleet. "New Bedford is not nearer to the whales than New London or Portland," wrote Emerson, "yet they have all the equipments for a whaler ready, and they hug an oil-cask like a brother."

The concentration of whaling activities in New Bedford added to the efficiency of operations; otherwise, whaling remained a conservative industry in which the only significant changes since colonial times were that voyages grew longer, captains crueler, and crews—paid, like fishermen, a share of the catch—more ruthlessly exploited. After 1820 no self-respecting American seaman would ship on a whaler. Innocent farm boys sometimes were lured on board by false and fancy promises, but many of them either mutinied or deserted at the first opportunity. Less rebellious hands often found themselves abandoned on some foreign shore by the captain, who thus avoided paying them their shares. On return voyages, crews were made up of men from every primitive island and backwater of civilization. Even Fiji islanders, and Polynesians like the harpooner Queequeg in Melville's *Moby Dick,* could be seen walking the streets of New Bedford after a whaler had put in.

In lumbering, as in farming, fishing, and whaling, few innovations were made in the first third of the nineteenth century. The industry grew, of course. Wood remained the great staple for commercial and domestic construction, for furniture making, and heating, and for power where streams were lacking. But until the railroads added their own huge demand for wood for fuel, ties, and rolling stock, and helped to settle the treeless prairies and the plains, lumbering remained the occupation of uncompromisingly individualistic loggers, who supplied timber to widely scattered and independently owned saw mills.

The Indians had taught the first settlers how to grow corn, harpoon whales, and girdle and kill trees before felling them. For more than two centuries, these basic techniques of farming, fishing, and lumbering spread unchanged as the country gradually expanded. Enterprises that specialized in making such other commodities as flour, leather goods, and ironware usually were organized locally and conducted according to time-tested methods by generation after generation in the same family. Such enterprises offered a living and a way of life; they were marked by stability rather than speculation, tradition rather than innovation. Until vast new markets were opened up by improved transportation, such enterprises continued to characterize the American economy, even if they did not portend its future.

## THE FUR TRADE
## AND THE CHINA TRADE

Even in the nineteenth century, no one in America was more isolated than the fur-trapper and trader. The fur-trader, Robert Glass Cleland writes, "started from frontiers at which more cautious pioneers were glad to stop . . . and wandered through the reaches of the outer West with all the freedom of the lonely wind." But, unlike the other primary occupations in America, the fur trade gave a new direction to American life, a new method to American business, and a new spirit to the American economy.

Fur—mink, otter, lynx, fox, and the ubiquitous beaver, as well as the coarser bear, wolf, deer, rabbit, muskrat, "coon," and "possum" —had been one of the first staples exported by the colonies. The finer pelts were used in hats, cloaks, and robes; the coarser ones in blankets for man and beast. The Indians, who did most of the actual trapping, traded their valuable furs for tinsel, shoddy, and drink. Consequently, from the start, profits had been large and competition keen. As early as 1700, overtrapping had depleted the fur-bearing animals in some areas, and in the next 50 years French traders from Canada and Spanish traders from Mexico, as well as the English colonists, had forced their way a thousand miles inland, far in advance of settlement.

Two thousand miles beyond even the farthest inland fur-trading post in the Mississippi Valley were the sea-otter waters off the Oregon coast. Sea captains from New England and New York, turning to the China trade immediately after the Revolution, discovered an eager market for the strikingly beautiful sea-otter skins (as well as for other domestic furs) among the wealthy mandarins of North China, where tastes were elegant, winters frigid, and dwellings unheated.

New Englanders, especially, were attracted to the sea-otter because it gave them a commodity to export in exchange for the tea, silk, spices, and cheap cottons ("nankeens") of the Orient, which were in such demand at home. By the early 1800s the sea-otter was nearing extinction. Profits from Chinese imports, however, had proved even greater than those from the sale of furs in China, and when the sea-otter supply failed, approximately at the outbreak of the War of 1812, the ship captains began to carry Hawaiian sandalwood to the Orient where it was used for incense in the joss houses. They also began to smuggle opium from the Dutch East Indies and neighboring islands into China to pay for tea. The leading New Englander in the China trade was Thomas Handasyd Perkins, who clung to it until the 1830s. The most active New Yorker in the trade was John Jacob Astor, who as early as 1800 had become the leading fur merchant in New York City.

The fur market in China had attracted land trappers and traders as well as sea captains, and following the return of Lewis and Clark from their trail-blazing expedition across the continent in 1806 (see p. 323), mountain men in quest of pelts and skins began to exploit the upper Missouri, the Yellowstone, the Green and other northwestern rivers, and the Colorado and the Gila in the southwestern desert. The farther trappers and traders reached out from their Mississippi base at St. Louis, however, the greater difficulty they found in carrying on their business. One reason for this was the hostility of the Plains Indians, with whom, it seemed, only large and well-armed expeditions could safely deal. Of more lasting importance was the fact that time and distance cost money; only well-financed organizations were able to send trappers and traders into distant fur-producing areas for a year or more at a time.

In 1809, a number of experienced St. Louis traders grasped the situation and pooled their funds in the Missouri Fur Company, a partnership. Other traders deeper in the West followed their lead; but it soon became evident that all of them suffered from undercapitalization and other evidences of inexperience in big business, and they quickly failed.

Trappers *by Alfred Jacob Miller, 1837. Miller, a city-bred artist, traveled west to the trappers' annual meetingplace in Wyoming and knew first-hand the Rocky Mountain trappers. (Walters Art Gallery, Baltimore.)*

Speeding their demise was Astor's American Fur Company, a corporation chartered by New York State in 1808 for 25 years and capitalized at $1 million.

In applying for the charter, Astor had stressed the patriotic aspects of his venture. His aim, he said, was to build a string of company posts along the route of Lewis and Clark to the Pacific, thereby saving the United States government the expense of maintaining its own posts in this wild territory, and hastening the day when it would be opened to settlement. Astor set up his enterprise as a corporation to give weight to this great national objective, which, as he suggested, could hardly

be won by a single individual. But as Astor's friend Washington Irving wrote, the entire "capital was furnished by [Astor] himself—he, in fact, constituted the company." He had simply played up the "sagacious and effective" idea that a group of responsible capitalists was behind the venture to justify his demand for a monopoly of the western fur trade.

Although New York refused to grant Astor the monopoly he petitioned for, the state did give him a corporate charter, on the basis of which he went ahead. In September 1810 he sent an expedition by sea to set up a trading post at the mouth of the Columbia River in Oregon, and in October he sent an overland expedition west from St. Louis. By the time the cross-country party arrived in Oregon early in 1812, the sea-going contingent had already landed and begun to build the settlement of Astoria.

Canadian fur-traders eyed Astor's maneuvers with growing hostility, and on the outbreak of the War of 1812 they decided to put an end to the American company. News of the war reached Astoria in January 1813, along with information that a British warship was headed toward the settlement. Since resistance would have been futile, Astor's men made the best deal they could by selling out to the North West Company, a Canadian enterprise, for $58,000. For a generation thereafter, the Canadians succeeded in barring American trappers and traders from Oregon and maintained their own monopoly of the region's fur.

But they did not succeed in stopping Astor. Once the War of 1812 was over, his American Fur Company, by means of efficient business methods and political maneuvers, set out to capture the fur trade east of Oregon. In 1816, at Astor's urging, Congress passed a law forbidding foreigners (i.e., Britishers) from engaging in the fur trade of the United States, except when licensed as employees of American traders. Subsequently, he got Governor Lewis Cass of Michigan Territory to issue licenses almost exclusively to his men. As Astor's agent wrote to him in 1817:

The Canadian Boatmen . . . are indispensable to the successful prosecution of the trade, their places cannot be supplied by Americans, who are far . . . too independent to submit quietly to a proper controul . . . and although the body of the Yankee can resist as much hardship as any Man, tis only in the Canadian we find that temper of mind to render him patient and docile and preserving. . . . It is of course your object, [concluded this wide-awake agent] to exclude every foreigner except those for whom you obtain licenses.

By such means, until the 1830s Astor's American Fur Company averaged about $500,-000 a year in profits. Then styles in Europe suddenly changed. "It appears that they make hats of silk in place of beaver," Astor observed during a European trip in 1834. By then, the fur reserves of the entire continent had almost become exhausted. The first natural resources to be exploited by the new business methods, they were the first to go.

The fur trade trampled and estranged the Indian, taught him to drink "firewater," and armed him with guns and ammunition. At the same time, it opened the path of empire "to that ocean," as Lewis and Clark said of the Pacific in 1805, "the object of all our labours, the reward of all our anxieties," and nurtured the China trade, which led to the start of continuous American settlement in Hawaii. The China trade also promoted the development of capitalism in New England and New York. It made Astor the first American millionaire, and his American Fur Company the first integrated corporation, rich in capital, strong in management, aggressive in competition, and active in politics.

### THE SANTA FE TRAIL

Less dramatic than the fur trade, and involving far fewer men and far less capital, was the trade across the Santa Fe Trail. Spain had established the isolated outpost of Santa Fe in the desert of New Mexico early in the seventeenth century, and had supplied it most laboriously from Vera Cruz, 1500 miles away.

The early efforts of Americans to trade at Santa Fe were frustrated by Spain's rigid colonial policy, which sternly excluded foreigners. Soon after Mexico won freedom from Spain in 1821, however, she opened the settlement to her northern neighbors, a step she later regretted and reversed (see Chapter Fifteen). The Santa Fe Trail, which ran westward from Independence, Missouri, through Kansas Territory (see map, p. 478), was surveyed by the American army in 1825. For the next 20 years, caravans of American farm wagons trekked across it, hauling all sorts of goods from the East and from Europe to be exchanged at fabulous profits for Spanish gold and silver.

The arrival of the caravan each year was a great event in the Spanish town. Gradually, some of the Americans settled in Santa Fe, and others, attracted by the fertile land bordering the eastern stretches of the trail, staked out farms along the way. When in 1844 Santa Anna, the Mexican leader, closed the trail, Americans viewed his act as interference with their rights and "destiny." The Santa Fe trade never engaged more than a couple of hundred persons a year. But, like the fur trade, it opened a new path across the continent, lured American businessmen into new country, and led to a political and territorial claim that eventually would be made good by the Mexican War.

## II *The Rise of the Middle West*

### THE EARLY SETTLERS

Well to the east of the fur-trappers and traders, but traveling over the trails they had marked through the wilderness, moved frontier families like that of Abraham Lincoln. Thomas Lincoln, the President's father, was the typical settler of the early nineteenth century, part backwoodsman, part farmer, part handyman-carpenter. Thomas had been born in the western Virginia hills in 1778. Four years later found the Lincolns in Kentucky, where Thomas grew up "a wandering

378

laboring boy," altogether without schooling. In 1806, he married the illiterate Nancy Hanks, who bore their son Abe in 1809. The Lincolns and the Hankses rarely stayed put for long, and by 1816 the whole tribe had reached Indiana, where they "squatted" the first year. For the whole of that time they occupied that "Darne Little half face camp," a three-sided wickiup before which a fire was kept burning around the clock. "We lived the same as the Indians," one of the Hankses said years later, " 'ceptin' we took an interest in politics and religion." After a year, they managed to build a typical log cabin, without floor, door, or window. A roof stuffed with mud and dry grass afforded their only protection from the rain. This remained their home for a decade before they pushed on to Illinois.

By 1816, more than a million people had trampled over the Lincolns' trail to set up households in the West. Most of them trav-

eled on foot, their possessions on their backs, in wheelbarrows, or saddled to a few scrawny cows that had been transformed into beasts of burden. Travelers from abroad noted the characteristic bluish complexion of these settlers, many of whom suffered from forest fever, milk sickness, and especially the swamp-bred ague (malaria). The land was cheap and fertile, but life was hard. "The rugged road, the dirty hovels, the fire in the woods to sleep by, the pathless ways through the wilderness, the dangerous crossings of the rivers" —why, asked the Englishman, William Cobbett, in 1817, did the settlers put up with all this? "To boil their pot in gipsy-fashion, to have a mere board to eat on, to drink whiskey or pure water, to sit and sleep under a shed far inferior to English cowpens, to have a mill at twenty miles' distance, an apothecary's shop at a hundred, and a doctor nowhere." Englishmen, confessed Cobbett, could never have survived such conditions. But Americans, as Jefferson said, found it "cheaper to clear a new acre than to manure an old one." So on into the West they moved.

Congressman Peter B. Porter of Buffalo,

*The arrival of a caravan of traders and settlers at Santa Fe after a long journey on the Trail from Independence, in the early 1840s. (The Bettmann Archive.)*

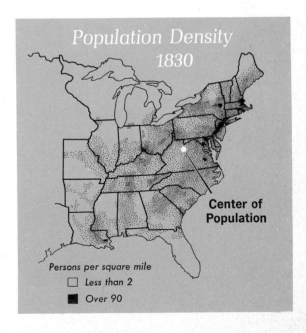

yet as respects most of the luxuries and many of the conveniences of life the people are poor. . . . The single circumstance of want of a market is already beginning to produce the most disastrous effect, not only on the industry, but on the morals of the inhabitants. Such is the fertility of their land that one-half of their time spent in labor is sufficient to produce every article which their farms are capable of yielding, in sufficient quantities for their own consumption, and there is nothing to incite them to produce more. They are therefore naturally led to spend the other part of their time in idleness and dissipation.

On the few occasions when these people might see a bit of money—from the chance sale of a hog or a horse to a newcomer who still had coin in his jeans—it would go east to buy salt for curing meat and fish, iron for muskets, lead for bullets, powder for the charge. Usually, though, they had a bundle of skins with which to pay for such necessities. Everything else the settlers wanted, they either made themselves or did without. They used up their capital instead of augmenting it, and even their boys, adept from childhood with rifle and rod, "lit out for the tall timber" on their own.

*Before the early settlers of the Middle West could cultivate their land it had to be cleared of trees. One method was to girdle and then burn the trees. Some of the timber was used for railings (as in the Lincoln legend) and firewood, but the ugly charred stumps remained in the fields. (Stokes Collection, New York Public Library.)*

New York, described the western country and the plight of the pioneers in 1810:

There is no better place where the great staple articles for the use of civilized life can be produced in greater abundance or with greater ease,

**Population Density 1830**

Center of Population

*Persons per square mile*
☐ Less than 2
■ Over 90

Eli Whitney, c. 1822, by the inventor-turned-artist Samuel F.B. Morse (Yale University Art Gallery, gift of George Hoadly), and his original cotton gin, 1793. (New Haven Colony Historical Society.)

## "KING COTTON" AND THE WEST

After 1815 the prospects of the West improved rapidly. The subjugation of the Indians, the departure of the British from their military posts and the Great Lakes, the disintegration of Spanish rule on the Gulf Coast all opened up new lands to permanent settlers. The government aided the pioneers by liberalizing its land-sale policies, and by showing more tolerance of "squatters." Two epochal developments then opened a growing market for western produce and supplied the means for reaching that market cheaply. The first was the phenomenal rise of King Cotton in the neighboring South (and large-scale sugar growing in Louisiana). The second was the introduction of the steamboat on western waters.

Before 1793, only fragile long-staple cotton, grown in a few selected areas, could be cleansed of its oily seeds at a reasonable cost. Thereafter Eli Whitney's gin, invented that year, made it practical to clean the green seeds from the hardier short-staple boll, which could be grown on almost any soil if the warm season were long enough. By 1816, 60 per cent of the nation's cotton crop was produced in South Carolina and Georgia, most of it in the piedmont region. By 1820, however, the land was used up as tidewater land had been earlier. The piedmont, said a traveler at this time, presented a scene of "dreary and uncultivated wastes . . . half-clothed negroes, lean and hungry stock, houses falling to decay, and fences wind-shaken and dilapidated." Turning their backs on this disheartening scene, cotton planters pushed west into Alabama and Mississippi. By 1830, their combined population exceeded 400,000, even though the large planters had been steadily buying up many small farms in the best cotton-producing areas. Sections of Tennessee, Arkansas, and Florida, suitable for cotton-planting also became heavily settled, as did the Louisiana sugar country.

The rapid growth of the new regions is reflected in the rising traffic at New Orleans.

In 1816 only 37,000 bales of cotton were shipped from this Mississippi port. By 1822, the figure was 161,000 bales, and by 1830, 428,000. Most of this cotton found its way to English textile factories, although some went to the Continent and increasing amounts to New England mills.

Until the beginning of the nineteenth century, South Carolina had exported considerable quantities of wheat and corn as well as cotton; and other southern states had exported horses, mules, and swine. Such diversity then disappeared. An English visitor observed in 1826:

> There is not a finer grazing country in the world than South Carolina; and were attention paid to the raising of cattle, sheep, goats, hogs, horses, mules, etc., this state might supply itself as well as the West India islands with these useful animals; but every other object gives place to cotton.

A year later, a traveler wrote of his visit to Louisiana:

> Corn, sweet potatoes, melons and all northern fruit, with the exception of apples, flourish here; though the planters find the great staples, cotton and sugar, so much more profitable than other kinds of cultivation that many of them calculate to supply themselves with provisions almost entirely from the upper country.

The Cotton Kingdom's growing need for food and work-animals gave the slack westerners the impulse they needed to lay down their rods and guns and to think seriously about farming. As markets and prices improved, many farmers hungered for more land and went into debt to acquire it as well as the seed, and tools, and other items needed to bring it into production. As land speculation spread, debt mounted, forcing the farmers to concentrate almost as single-mindedly as the planter on cash crops to meet their financial obligations. Southern specialization in cotton spurred western specialization in grain and meat and mules. The marvelous Mississippi River system conveniently tied the two sections together, and the steamboat tightened the knot.

## III   *The Growth of Intersectional Commerce*

### TRANSPORTATION PROBLEMS

In colonial America the ocean had afforded the easiest means of communication and trade. As farms and plantations spread along the eastern rivers, they too began to carry their share of people and goods. The progress of settlement in the West brought the Mississippi River system into the transportation network, and the steamboat made it the foremost inland carrier of all. The first steamboat on the western waters was *New Orleans,* built in 1811 by Robert Fulton, four years after his success with *Clermont* on the Hudson. As he had in New York, Fulton promptly won a monopoly of the carrying trade of the West which lasted, except for the competition of illicit interlopers, until 1824, when John Marshall, as we have seen (p. 367), in his momentous decision in *Gibbons* v. *Ogden,* dealt a death blow to all monopolies on interstate waters. By 1830, nearly 200 steamboats were plying the western rivers.

Keel-boat rates between Louisville and New Orleans had been about $5 per hundred pounds of freight. By 1820, steamboat rates for this trip had fallen to $2 per hundred pounds, and by 1842 competition had driven them down to 25 cents, still a profitable price since technological improvements had so greatly increased the carrying capacity and operating efficiency of the vessels. Western staples now were sped down to the levees of New Orleans for shipment overseas or for distribution by coastal vessels to the rest of the South and Southwest and even to the Northeast. Commodities from abroad or from the Northeast also were funneled into the booming port for transshipment inland.

The Mississippi system, however, was less hospitable than it seemed. The river itself

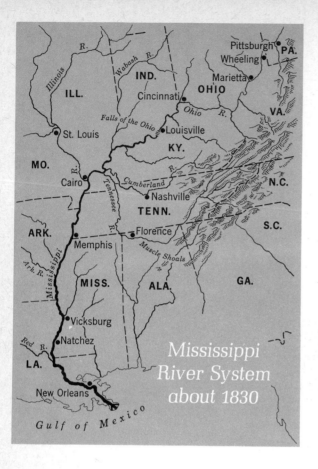

Mississippi
River System
about 1830

The difficulties of road transport, if anything, presented greater challenges than those on the rivers. From the earliest times, many Americans chose to settle far from neighbors on land several miles from water routes. And yet somehow they had to travel to the grist mills, tobacco warehouses, cotton gins, forges, country stores, county courts, and to the rivers themselves. As time went on, a crude network of roads spread across the sparsely settled countryside, often following old Indian trails and the paths of trappers and traders through dense, dank forests. Only a few of these roads were wide enough to accommodate wagons or carts. Moreover, they usually bristled with tree stumps. Spring floods and fall rains would transform them into muddy quagmires, while winter cold froze them into malevolent ruts.

As early as 1806, Congress chartered the "National Highway" to be built with federal funds, the greatest road-building enterprise of the early years of the Republic, but not until 1811 did the first crews begin to cut the road westward from Cumberland, Maryland. By 1818 it had been pushed as far as Wheeling, Virginia, on the Ohio River. The failure of Congress to provide additional money checked construction here, but work was resumed in 1825 and by mid-century the road had reached Vandalia, Illinois, its westernmost point.

The "National Highway" proved to be an efficient carrier. Other useful roads included the privately financed Lancaster Turnpike built in 1794 at a cost of $465,000 across the 62-mile stretch from Philadelphia to Lancaster, Pennsylvania. The tolls collected along the way more than paid for the cost of the enterprise, which proved profitable enough to encourage the construction of similar roads. By 1825, private companies, mostly in New England and the Middle states, built more than 10,000 miles of turnpikes. The best of them cost from $5,000 to $10,000 per mile, and state and local governments often helped defray the cost to the companies by buying their stock and by granting them the proceeds from the sale of government bonds.

Most of the turnpike companies, however,

and most of its tributaries teemed with snags, hidden banks, floating trees, whirlpools, and eddies, and pirates infested the entire system. Seasonal floods often swept both boat and boatmen to destruction, while summer droughts pinched the river channels into narrow ribbons, leaving many vessels stranded in the shallow water. So pernicious, indeed, was this hazard that most Mississippi traffic came to be bunched on the floodtides of spring and fall. This tactic eased the problems of navigation but raised new problems of marketing. During the floodtide seasons, produce now glutted the New Orleans wharves. Since it was costly to store the incoming crops and since, in any case, grain spoiled so quickly in the humid air of the Mississippi basin that shippers could not hold their produce off the market for long, they were obliged to accept the catastrophically low prices buyers offered.

were modest enterprises, and their short
stretches of road did little to improve the
sorry network of country paths. Their high
tolls, moreover, for the transportation of heavy
agricultural produce discouraged shippers,
who were always hardpressed for coin. By the
1830s, the management and maintenance of
the privately operated turnpikes had become
so costly, and the returns so scanty, that thousands of miles of turnpike either were abandoned or turned over to the states.

### THE CANAL BOOM

Turnpikes, clearly, would not enable New
York, Philadelphia, Boston, and the other eastern seaports to compete with New Orleans for
the growing trade of the West. These cities
turned instead to canals to link up the great
waterways with which nature had endowed
the American continent. But canals were even
harder and more expensive to build than turnpikes. They cost, not $5,000, but $20,000 a
mile; some cost as much as $60,000 and $80,-
000 a mile. They took not a year or two to

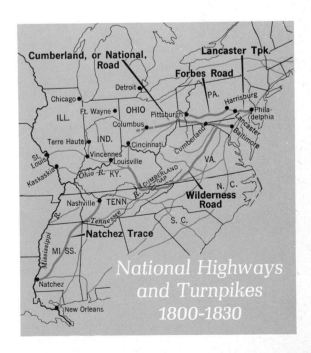

National Highways
and Turnpikes
1800-1830

384

build, but seven to ten years. Thus they presented new problems of finance and labor supply, and new problems of engineering and management.

In 1816 only three American canals ran as far as two miles, none as far as 30 miles. All told, the country boasted 100 miles of these artificial waterways. As early as 1810, the New York State legislature had appointed a committee to investigate the feasibility of digging a canal to the West, and in 1816 De Witt Clinton again raised the issue. So convincing were his arguments that even his political opponents voted for his project—a canal to connect the Hudson River with Lake Erie, 363 miles away. Clinton's canal was to have 83 locks, and was to cost over $7 million in state funds. Construction of the Erie Canal began in 1817, and by 1823 a 280-mile stretch was in operation from Albany to Rochester. The tolls that came pouring in from the traffic on this part of the canal were used to help finance the final leg to Buffalo, which was completed in 1825. In 1823, New York had also opened the Champlain Canal, connecting the Hudson River and Lake Champlain to the north. In 1825, returns from both projects exceeded $500,000, and over the next nine years the Erie paid back its total original cost of $7 million. Two figures tell the story of the Erie's success: It reduced freight rates between Buffalo and Albany from $100 to $15 a ton, and it reduced travel time from 20 to 8 days.

Spurred to action by New York's dramatic success, Boston, in 1825 induced the Massachusetts legislature to consider building a canal of its own into the interior, but the hilly Massachusetts terrain disheartened the promoters. When Boston did gain her entry to the West in 1842, it was by way of three railroads strung across Massachusetts to the eastern end of the Erie Canal. In 1826, Philadelphia won state approval for yet another scheme to tap the West, an undertaking even more ambitious than the one Boston had abandoned. This system included a main canal and railroad tracking, and was completed to Pitts-

burgh in 1834 at a cost of more than $10 million, all of it supplied by the state.

In 1827, Baltimore joined in the race for western business by announcing plans for the Chesapeake and Ohio Canal. The Maryland legislature thought the project visionary and refused to finance it, but work got under way with private and federal funds. The state legislators turned out to be right, for construction on the canal was brought to a halt by the broad southern mountains. In 1828, a private corporation began to lay track for the Baltimore and Ohio Railroad, the first successful line in America. But it was to be many years before the Baltimore and Ohio reached the Ohio River in the 1850s.

Westerners were as energetic as easterners in seeking ways to promote East-West trade, for they soon discovered that their rich soil could produce more wheat and corn, and that their corn could fatten more hogs, than the southern market could absorb. Moreover, westerners had grown weary of trying to cope with the hazards of river transportation. In the 1820s they turned a sympathetic ear to Henry Clay's program for high tariffs and "internal improvements," the first to promote the growth of eastern factory towns, the second to provide the means for opening these towns to western produce. "Internal improvements" would also mean that manufactured goods could be shipped more cheaply from the East than by way of New Orleans.

Clay's program never was adopted by Congress, but even without federal assistance Ohio and other western states soon embarked on their own ambitious canal and railroad programs. By 1837 Ohio boasted no less than 750 miles of canals, its most important one connecting Portsmouth on the Ohio River with Cleveland on Lake Erie, and, by the way of "Clinton's Big Ditch" and the Hudson River, with New York City. Indiana began building her canal system in 1827, and in the 1830s Illinois, Michigan, and Wisconsin all projected ambitious works which, though interrupted by the Panic of 1837 (see p. 421), eventually were carried to completion.

By 1840, some 3326 miles of canals, most of them in the North and West, had been constructed in the United States at a cost of $125 million. Private American investors were able to supply only a small fraction of this sum; federal and state subscriptions to the securities of private canal companies accounted for part of the balance; and more than half the total was provided directly by the states out of revenues or through the sale of state bonds abroad, mainly in England. The impact of the canals on the economy of the West was as great as expected. The South continued to be a valuable customer of the West, and the Ohio and Mississippi river systems continued to be heavily used. But the West's connection with the North and East became ever stronger as the canal system developed.

Travel over canals was much cheaper than

**Principal Canals, 1840**

over turnpikes, but for four months of the year the northern canal routes were frozen solid. Railroads finally freed shippers from the uncertainties of weather and from the medieval pace of oxen and tow horses. By 1840, 3328 miles of railroad had been built in the United States, almost exactly equal to the canal mileage. But only about 200 of these railroad miles could be found in the West. For some time after 1840, rivers, canals, and turnpikes continued to be the main channels of inland commerce.

### THE SPECTACULAR RISE OF NEW YORK CITY

In the competition for western trade, then, the East gradually outstripped the South. And in the East itself, New York City gradually pulled far ahead of the rival cities of Boston,

386

Philadelphia, and Baltimore. Nature was partly responsible for this success, for New York had a far greater hinterland market than Boston; the Hudson and Mohawk rivers gave her a far more serviceable water route to western markets than either Philadelphia or Baltimore enjoyed; and she was ideally situated for the coastal trade, since Boston was far to the north, and Philadelphia and Baltimore were too far upstream for easy access from the ocean. All these advantages in domestic commerce combined to make New York the best warehousing site for transatlantic trade as well. Competition, however, remained keen for a long time, and New York won its eventual supremacy through the enterprise shown by her businessmen in capitalizing on the advantages bestowed by nature.

The construction of the Erie Canal was the most rewarding accomplishment of the New Yorkers; but even before the canal was begun they had made other innovations. One was a modified auction system for disposing of imports—a scheme that assured merchants of a rapid turnover of goods for cash. Although auctions were held in many American ports, the common practice was to offer goods and then to withdraw them if the bids were unsatisfactory. But in New York City, after 1817, purchasers were assured that the highest bid would be accepted and that their purchases would be delivered as promised. New York soon became the favorite port on the seacoast for sellers and buyers who congregated there from all over the country.

Another innovation of the energetic New Yorkers was the development of transatlantic packets running on regular schedules between America and Europe, "full or not full." Until the introduction of this daring new procedure, ocean commerce waited upon the whims of the weather and the convenience of ship captains. New York's Black Ball Line, first in the world to operate on the new basis, dispatched *James Monroe* from New York on January 5, 1818, in the teeth of a snowstorm that would have been regarded as a valid excuse for delay by any ordinary vessel.

Even after the Black Ball Line began operations, irregularity of sailings continued to characterize most ocean shipping. The American merchant marine carried cargo around the world to the Levant, the Baltic states, Africa, and the East Indies, as well as to western Europe, China, and India. In an age without wireless communication shipowners themselves could not tell when a vessel might sight its home port, what it might be carrying, or what ports of call it might have touched. The shipowners of Boston in particular thrived on this old-fashioned world-wide carrying trade. Nevertheless, the so-called "Atlantic Shuttle" grew steadily in importance after 1820, when the American West began to feed industrial Europe, and the United States began to offer an expanding market for Old-World manufactures. And New York became most important among the "Shuttle's" ports. By 1828, New York's share of the American merchant marine was almost equal to the combined shares of Philadelphia, Boston, and Baltimore.

Dependable auctions and dependable sailings brought businessmen and goods flooding into New York. But the city's merchants still needed an adequate export staple to balance their trade. Western produce pouring into the city over the Erie Canal helped some, but in the 1820s New York's ambitious shippers began to sail right into New Orleans, Mobile, and other southern ports to pick up cotton to carry to Britain and the Continent. There they exchanged the cotton for manufactures and other goods, which they brought back to New York for distribution in the city and in the interior. Eventually they carried imports directly to the cotton ports themselves.

So successful were the New York merchants in this new trade that by 1830 it was estimated that 40 cents of every dollar paid for cotton went north—almost exclusively to New York—to cover the cost of freight tolls, insurance, commissions, and interest. In 1837, a convention in the South—called to promote the revival of direct trade with Europe—reminded southern merchants, "You hold the element

from which [the New York merchant] draws his strength. You have but to speak the word, and his empire is transferred to your own soil." But the word was not spoken. Two years later a similar convention declared that "the importing merchants of the South [had become] an almost extinct race, and her direct trade, once so great, flourishing, and rich, [had] dwindled down to insignificance."

## IV  *The Industrial Revolution*

### DIFFICULT BEGINNINGS

The expansion of commercial agriculture in the West, the rapid growth of western population, and the growing accessibility of western markets—all gave a strong impetus to the development of eastern industry. The concentration on cotton-planting in the South also made it a market for coarse textiles and other manufactures that it might otherwise have produced itself. Until western and southern markets were opened, however, factory industry had a hard time getting started in America.

Back in 1791, when Hamilton delivered his Report on Manufactures to Congress (see p. 282), he had written, "The expediency of encouraging manufactures in the United States . . . appears at this time to be pretty generally admitted." But he was too optimistic. In the first decades of the new nation's life, America had no surplus labor supply to man new factories, nor a surplus of capital. Cautious financiers chose to keep their money in the fruitful and accustomed paths of trade, shipping, and land-speculation. The Federalist swells of northern cities with their English commercial connections, or the Republican planters with their English commercial credit, counted their profits in pounds, shillings, and pence. Scorning goods manufactured at home,

387

they demanded English woolens, linens, china, cutlery, furniture, and tools. In 1791, Hamilton himself helped organize the Society for Establishing Useful Manufactures, a corporation capitalized at $1 million chartered by New Jersey. In the next few years, this corporation founded the city of Paterson, erected numerous buildings to house its works, smuggled in skilled British mechanics, and began manufacturing yarn, cloth, hats, and other commodities. By 1796, however, both the works and the town were moribund. A few similar undertakings suffered a similar fate.

Almost from the first days of colonization, America had had its own forges, blacksmith shops, flour mills, saw mills, paper factories, tanneries, and even some establishments for spinning woolen and linen fiber, and for finishing or "fulling" home-woven cloth. And as the settlers moved westward, they took their shops along. For some time, Pittsburgh served as a center for pioneers' supplies, especially metal farming implements too heavy to tote over the mountains from the East, and wagon-wheel rims to replace those that had worn out on the long journey west. By 1817, as many as 1280 workers were employed by the industries of Pittsburgh. In 1810, Lebanon, Ohio, with a population of only 300, boasted a wheelwright, three tan yards, four shoemaker shops, two blacksmith shops, two saddle shops, a nail-maker, and a hatter. But these usually were part-time enterprises carried on in cellars, spare rooms, or outbuildings by farmers and storekeepers, lawyers and doctors.

The first full-time factory in America to survive for more than a few years was the cotton-spinning plant of Almy & Brown, Providence merchants. Under the direction of an experienced Englishman, Samuel Slater, this factory began operations at Pawtucket in 1791. Nine children, working for wages of 12 to 25 cents a day, tended its 72 spindles under full-time supervision. Slater's, of course, was a tiny affair, and only Almy & Brown's well-established market connections kept the company afloat. After the outbreak of the Napoleonic Wars in Europe in 1799, Americans found it increasingly difficult to get British manufactures. To supply their needs, Slater's mill expanded operations and many hopeful imitators started up to enjoy a share of the market. Few of these enterprises were capitalized at more than $10,000; since their managers were inexperienced in keeping accounts, handling money and men, and exploiting markets, conservative banks would simply have nothing to do with them. They drew their labor from the poorest farm families in the area, often employing both the parents and their small children. The thread they spun was given out to home weavers to make into cloth. But Almy & Brown complained in 1809 that "a hundred looms in families will not weave as much cloth as ten . . . under the immediate inspection of a workman." Once the long war was over, most of the wartime mills shut down. The shining exception became one of the most profitable enterprises and laid the foundations for the industrial revolution in the United States.

### THE ENTRY OF BIG CAPITAL

This exception was the Boston Manufacturing Company of Waltham, Massachusetts, organized in 1813 by Francis Cabot Lowell, Patrick Tracy Jackson, and Nathan Appleton, great New England merchants. The Boston Manufacturing Company was as distinct a step forward in its day as Slater's mill had been 22 years before. The organizers, who had already demonstrated their ability to manage hazardous, large-scale enterprises, invested liberally in the new company. They poured $600,000 cash into it in the first six years, and held as much or more in reserve for operating and emergency expenses. They built the first wholly integrated cotton-manufacturing plant in the world; all operations were under one roof, from the unbaling of the raw cotton to the dyeing and printing of the finished cloth. They even established their own selling agencies, instead of depending on local jobbers as earlier companies had done.

The scale on which it operated, and its care-

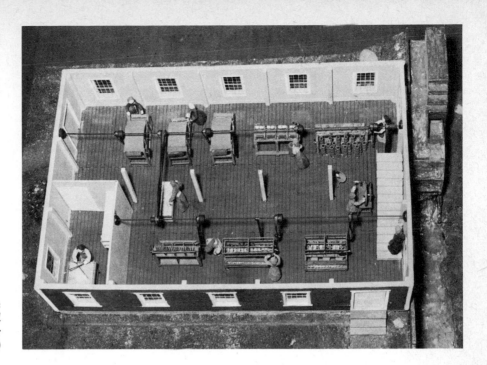

*Cut-away view showing the probable layout of Old Slater Mill. (Old Slater Mill Museum, Pawtucket.)*

fully integrated production methods enabled the Boston Manufacturing Company to eliminate middlemen and unsupervised domestic workers and to reduce the time spent in carrying goods from place to place for successive processing steps. The managers made their system even more economical by introducing power looms and power spindles and by giving constant attention to other improvements, from the design of water wheels and power-transmission systems to the fastness of dyes.

In another innovation, these New England merchants devised an original scheme for attracting and holding workers. Instead of employing children and parents from the immediate neighborhood, the Boston Manufacturing Company took on young women ranging in age from 18 to 22, and sheltered and fed them in newly constructed houses that made up a company town. Here, under the sharp eyes of the organizers, religion was cultivated, educational opportunities were made available in leisure hours, and cleanliness and hygiene were insisted upon. All these devices were calculated to attract a sturdy, ambitious, hard-working group of young women from re-

spectable farm families. And they succeeded in doing just that. Absenteeism was low and industrial discipline was easily imposed. The Boston Manufacturing Company did not begin operations until 1816 when the flood of British imports sank many struggling American mills. It proved an immediate and lasting success. In 1817, it earned a dividend of 12.5 per cent for its stockholders; thereafter, despite the Panic of 1819 (see p. 365), annual dividends rose even higher. By 1822, dividends totaling 104.5 per cent had been paid to the original investors.

### THE CORPORATION AND INDUSTRIAL PROGRESS

Around 1823 Harrison Gray Otis of Boston wrote: "There has been a curious 'revival' in the spirit of men . . . which is quite remarkable. Two years ago our sun had sunk never to rise again. . . . All is now reversed and [manufacturing] stocks as well as spirits have risen inordinately. . . . It is amazing to see what is done by the puff on one hand and the panic on the other." The opening up of the

389

West and the expansion of the Cotton Kingdom in the South spurred the general business upturn. The revolutions against Spain in Latin America (see p. 361) opened up the first foreign markets for American manufactured goods. After 1826, more and more such goods found their way to China to help pay for the tea that Americans drank in ever larger quantities.

All these changes were reflected in the expansion of the firms that had survived the depression and in the large numbers of new textile corporations that set up in business during the 1820s and 1830s. Some of these new companies were organized and chartered by the same group that had started the Boston Manufacturing Company. Between 1821 and 1835, these men, often referred to as the "Boston Associates," opened nine new companies in Massachusetts and southern New Hampshire, each specializing in a particular textile product on a large scale. More important, during and after the depression these men founded insurance companies and banks to maintain and concentrate their supply of capital, real-estate companies to take over the best factory sites, and water-power companies to control dams and dam sites and to harness the power of the great rivers. After 1823, Lowell on the Merrimack supplanted Waltham on the Charles as their main operating center.

The corporation had first been used as a legal device for securing a monopoly by means of a special charter. Astor employed it next as a symbol of prestige. The turnpike and bridge companies used the corporate form mainly as a means of accumulating capital through the sale of inexpensive shares to numerous subscribers. By the time the canal and railroad companies were being formed, the idea of limited liability had become well established in law and finance. Limited liability meant that the owners of corporation stock were liable for the obligations of the company only to the extent of their own investment, regardless of how large their personal fortunes might be. This protection helped to attract the capital required for costly, long-term projects.

The Boston Associates used the corporate form for all these purposes, and for certain new purposes of their own. In their hands, the corporation became a device by which a few able men, through the ownership of only a fraction of the total stock, could direct the

*Patrick Tracy Jackson, a cofounder of the Boston Manufacturing Company. He and Francis Cabot Lowell patented the Waltham loom. (Baker Library, Harvard University.)*

activities of many and varied businesses. The corporate form also made it possible for them to reside in Boston while actual operations were conducted in distant mill towns under the supervision of hired professional managers. Since corporate securities could be more easily disposed of than investments in partnerships or single-owner businesses, corporate enterprises could look forward to a long life, uninterrupted by the death or withdrawal of investors. Finally, stock holdings could easily be bought and sold or otherwise transferred without seriously affecting the financial structure of a business.

The cotton-textile industry became the proving ground for these new business techniques. It was the first mature American industry to be geared not to the individual craftsman but to the machine, to be financed not by the owner alone or by his bank, but by the accumulated private savings of numbers of people, and to be managed by hired professionals accountable to capitalists living in the great financial centers.

### THE EARLY LABOR MOVEMENT

The corporation gave a tremendous impetus to American economic and social progress, but almost from the outset it revealed a seemingly inherent tendency toward harshness in human relations. Before Samual Slater set up his first mechanized spinning plant in 1791, America had had many "spinning houses" and "spinning schools," the first of which appeared in Jamestown, Virginia, as early as 1646. These schools were opened to provide useful employment for the children of the poor. Slater's factory was modeled on these public institutions, and the children who worked for him were not abused. Many of Slater's imitators, however, were less charitable, especially when the heat of competition prompted the less efficient firms to make extravagant demands on their workers in a bid for survival. By 1810, few of the little spinning corporations scattered through southern New England retained any aspects of philanthropy.

A more striking deterioration in working and living conditions blighted the factories and factory towns of the Boston Associates and their imitators, especially after scrupulous

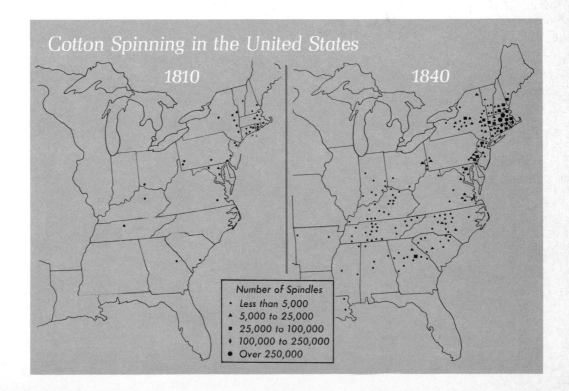

Cotton Spinning in the United States

1810    1840

Number of Spindles
·  Less than 5,000
▲  5,000 to 25,000
■  25,000 to 100,000
♦  100,000 to 250,000
●  Over 250,000

The mills of Lowell, Massachusetts, on the Merrimack River. The falls, with a drop of over 30 feet, produced the needed power. (Print Collection, New York Public Library.)

founders turned direct management over to outsiders whose efficiency was checked in Boston through the medium of financial reports. Here is the way an observer in Lowell described the factory routine in that city in 1846:

The operatives work thirteen hours a day in the summer time, and from daylight to darkness in the winter. At half past four in the morning the factory bell rings, and at five girls must be in the mills. A clerk placed as a watch, observes those who are a few minutes behind the time, and effectual means are taken to stimulate punctuality. This is the morning commencement of the industrial discipline (should we not rather say industrial tyranny?) which is established in these Associations of this moral and Christian community. At seven the girls are allowed thirty minutes for breakfast, and at noon thirty minutes more for dinner, except during the first quarter of the year, when the time is extended to forty-five minutes.

Some years earlier, in 1840, the reformer, Orestes Brownson, described the plight of Lowell girls who presumably had gone to work just long enough to accumulate a dowry or to add to the family income until they married:

The great mass wear out their health, spirits, and morals without becoming one whit better off than when they commenced labor. The bills of mortality in these factory villages are not striking, we admit, for the poor girls when they can toil no longer go home to die.

These conditions became particularly prevalent after the Panic of 1837 (see p. 421), when corporate managements cracked down on factory superintendents whose accounts showed too much red ink. But even before that panic, conditions had become so bad in some of the cotton factories that the girls were driven to strike. In February 1834 a thousand or more Lowell girls walked out in protest against a 15 per cent wage cut. "One of the leaders," reported the *Boston Transcript*, "mounted a stump, and made a flaming . . . speech on the rights of women and the iniquities of the 'monied aristocracy' which produced a powerful effect on her auditors, and they determined to 'have their way, if they died for it.'" Actually, the girls went back to work in a few days at the reduced wages—all but the leaders, who were discharged.

Other abortive strikes occurred in the 1830s, but the girls in the New England textile mills and the mill workers in other parts of the country lacked unions, funds, leadership, and organizational experience, and their pathetic rebellions almost always ended in failure.

One of the weapons the corporations used against strikers was the law itself. Until the decision of the Massachusetts Supreme Court in the case of *Commonwealth* v. *Hunt* in 1842, strikers were subject to prosecution for criminal conspiracy under the common law. The pretext for such prosecution lay in the idea that all labor combinations were organized to injure some person or persons. Judge Roberts made this point perfectly clear in a famous decision in a Pittsburgh labor trial in 1815:

In many cases of conspiracy the means employed have a semblance of being lawful. They are frequently such as would be lawful in an individual. For instance, you have a right to have your boots, your coat, or your hat made by whom you please. You may decline employing any particular shoemaker, tailor, or hatter at your pleasure: You may advise your neighbours not to employ a particular mechanic. But should you combine and confederate with others, to ruin any particular shoemaker, tailor, hatter, or other mechanic, or tradesman by preventing persons from employing him, this would be unlawful and indictable.

It was altogether legal, Judge Roberts explained, for a member of a theater audience to hiss a performer. "But if a number were to conspire, and confederate . . . to prevent him from exercising his profession, by hissing him off the stage, this would be . . . committing a public offence."

In Judge Roberts's terms labor organizations were illegal conspiracies *per se;* their mere existence menaced both employers and the workers who did not join up. This remained the prevailing attitude until Chief Justice Lemuel Shaw of the Supreme Judicial Court of Massachusetts ruled in 1842 that labor unions, even though they "may have a tendency to impoverish another, that is, to diminish his gains and profits," might nevertheless "be highly meritorious and public spirited." But even Justice Shaw left a wide opening for employers by declaring that if the objective of labor unions "be carried into

effect . . . by falsehood or force, . . . it may be stamped with the character of conspiracy." He permitted the supposition, however, that labor unions as such may be "to say the least, innocent," and granted them legal standing for the first time in American history.

Yet this improvement in the legal climate served chiefly to demonstrate that economic and social conditions, not the law, really underlay the workers' weakness. For a long time, the factory labor force simply remained too small in numbers to make much headway in an agrarian society that knew little and cared less about the problems of factory life.

Although little progress was made in organizing American industrial workers until the 1930s, the craft unions have had a much longer history. The crafts themselves—shoemaking, horseshoeing, carpentry, bricklaying, tailoring—reached far into the past. By the eighteenth century they were carried on by independent artisans who bought their own raw materials, fabricated them for their own customers, and set their own prices. Sometimes they employed journeymen who traveled from farm to farm to make shoes, repair houses and barns, and do other jobs beyond the capacity of the farm family. Below the journeymen ranked young apprentices, whose families contracted them out to artisans for as long as 20 years.

By the beginning of the nineteenth century, improvements in transportation had opened much larger markets to the artisans, some of whom gave up their hand work to become "merchant capitalists"—that is, businessmen who gathered up larger orders than one artisan and a few helpers could fill, and who employed artisans and journeymen to work for them. Others who had never been artisans also entered the different crafts as merchant capitalists. By the 1820s, competition among them had become so keen, they were forced to cut their craftsmen's wages. The craftsmen were further embittered by the loss of their independent status, and complained in addition that their specialized skills were being broken up into simpler tasks too often given to less well-trained workers who further depressed wage rates.

In protest against these conditions the first unions were formed in America. The Philadelphia shoemakers had organized as early as 1792, but not until the middle 1820s did other craftsmen, in defiance of the conspiracy law, turn to united action. In New York, Philadelphia, and other large centers, the craft unions combined in citywide organizations; and in 1834 six of these combinations joined forces in a "National Trades' Union." In the next three years craft union membership rose from 26,000 to 300,000. In these years, the unions conducted at least 175 strikes, many of them called to win improvements in working conditions, not merely to keep them from growing worse. In 1828, the Philadelphia unions organized the American Working Men's party to seek, by political means, such improvements as the ten-hour day for themselves and free public education for their children.

The business collapse of 1837 crushed the early craft-union movement. Some of the crafts, especially those in construction industries or in specialized fields like printing, managed to maintain a semblance of organization even in the worst years. The crafts subject to rising competition from factory production, however, tended to disappear, along with their unions and merchant capitalists. Workers who made cotton or woolen clothing, carpets, boots and shoes, and iron machinery and other hardware by hand simply could not survive in an environment marked by large-scale operations and mechanized techniques.

True, the United States was still many years away from becoming a mature industrial country unified by railroads, telegraph, telephone, automobiles, airplanes, and TV. But by 1830, migration to the cities had begun to compete seriously with migration to the West, and it was becoming clear that the Jeffersonian ideal of a society made up of independent and individualistic farmers spread over the whole continent, if not over the whole hemisphere, would never be realized.

# READINGS

Roger Burlingame, *The March of Iron Men* (1938), is a penetrating social history of American technology before the Civil War and provides an excellent introduction to the subject of this chapter. More conventional, but scholarly and comprehensive, is G.R. Taylor, *The Transportation Revolution 1815–1860* (1951). Taylor's book is part of a ten-volume *Economic History of the United States,* edited by Henry David and others. Two other volumes of this work are relevant here: C.P. Nettels, *The Emergence of a National Economy 1775–1815* (1962), and P.W. Gates, *The Farmers' Age: Agriculture 1815–1860* (1960). A brief presentation will be found in the early chapters of T.C. Cochran and William Miller, *The Age of Enterprise, A Social History of Industrial America* (1942). D.C. North, *The Economic Growth of the United States 1790–1860* (1961), is a careful appraisal of causes, which should be compared with Stuart Bruchey, *The Roots of American Economic Growth 1607–1861* (1965). W.P. Strassman, *Risk and Technological Innovation* (1959), and H.J. Habakkuk, *American and British Technology in the 19th Century* (1962), examine the machine process in relation to profits and labor productivity. Besides Gates, cited above, useful material on American agriculture in the early national period is available in L.B. Schmidt and E.D. Ross, eds., *Readings in Economic History of American Agriculture*

(1925), especially Part II. For contemporary material on other aspects of the economy, see G.S. Callender, ed., *Selections from The Economic History of the United States 1765–1860* (1909).

Herman Melville, *Moby Dick* (1851), is a great American novel that provides much fascinating and authentic whaling lore. E.O. Stackpole, *The Sea-Hunters* (1953), is authoritative on this subject, as are the chapters in S.E. Morison, *The Maritime History of Massachusetts 1783–1860* (1921). H.M. Chittenden, *The American Fur Trade of the Far West* (2 vols., 1902), while dated, remains the best comprehensive account. Bernard DeVoto, *Across the Wide Missouri* (1947), is excellent on the climax and decline of the trade. See also A.S. Morton, *A History of the Canadian West to 1870–71* (1938). A valuable biography of the main figure in the fur trade is K. W. Porter, *John Jacob Astor* (2 vols., 1931). On the Santa Fe trail, see Josiah Gregg, *Commerce of the Prairies* (1844).

L.D. Baldwin, *The Keelboat Age on Western Waters* (1941), is a good introduction to river transportation before the age of steam. J.T. Flexner, *Steamboats Come True* (1944), is a popular account of the development of new carriers. Unmatched on its subject is L.C. Hunter, *Steamboats on the Western Rivers* (1949). J.A. Durrenberger, *Turnpikes* (1931), is a scholarly work on the toll roads. Carter Goodrich, *Government Promotion of American Canals and Railroads 1800–1890* (1960), is outstanding. On the Erie Canal and related subjects, an excellent work is Nathan Miller, *The Enterprise of a Free People: Aspects of Economic Development in New York State during the Canal Period 1792–1838* (1962). Four other works are illuminating on the relations of the state and business enterprise in this period: Louis Hartz, *Economic Policy and Democratic Thought, Pennsylvania 1776–1860* (1948); Oscar and M.F. Handlin, *Commonwealth, A Study of the Role of Government in the American Economy, Massachusetts 1774–1861* (1947); J.N. Primm, *Economic Policy in the Development of a Western State: Missouri 1820–1860* (1954); and H.N. Scheiber, *The Ohio Canal Era: A Case Study of Government and the Economy 1820–1861* (1968). Volume II of Joseph Dorfman, *The Economic Mind in American Civilization* (5 vols., 1946–1959), is valuable for the thought behind the policies. Seymour Dunbar, *A History of American Travel* (4 vols., 1915), is a lavishly illustrated work. Excellent on ocean shipping, in addition to Morison, cited above, is R.G. Albion, *Square Riggers on Schedule* (1938). The same author's *The Rise of New York Port 1815–1860* (1939) is superb on New York's rise to greatness. Milton Reizenstein, *The Economic History of the Baltimore and Ohio Railroad 1827–1853* (1897), is a valuable study of the first railroad. For other works on railroad history, see Chapter Seventeen.

An excellent essay on Hamilton's industrial venture is, "The 'S. U. M.': The First New Jersey Business Corporation," by J.S. Davis, Jr. It is to be found in that author's *Essays on the Earlier History of American Corporations* (2 vols., 1917). Jeanette Mirsky and Allan Nevins, *The World of Eli Whitney* (1952), is a first-rate study of the emergence of the industrial spirit. C.F. Ware, *The Early New England Cotton Manufacture* (1931), presents all phases of America's first modern industry in scholarly fashion. An illuminating special study is Vera Shlakman, *Economic History of a Factory Town* (1935). Besides Davis, above, of special interest on the history of the corporation are E.M. Dodd, *American Business Corporations until 1860* (1954), and J.W. Cadman, Jr., *The Corporation in New Jersey 1791–1875* (1949). Volume I of V.S. Clark, *History of Manufacturers in the United States* (3 vols., 1928), is very informative on industrial developments. On pre-industrial developments, R.M. Tryon, *Household Manufactures in the United States 1640–1880* (1917), is invaluable. The best account of the early labor movement is in vol. I of J.R. Commons and others, *History of Labor in the United States* (4 vols., 1918–1935).

# THIRTEEN

When James Monroe left the White House in 1825, the age of the Founding Fathers had clearly ended. The new nation at last had won that standing and respect abroad which gave her the security she needed to direct the energies of her people toward the immeasurable opportunities beckoning at home. These opportunities were grasped with a will in all sections of the country (see Chapter Twelve), and their rewards had already fostered that great leveling tendency which was to culminate in widespread democratic reforms at the same time that they enlarged imperial hemispheric ambitions.

The Jeffersonians, the levelers and expansionists of the early national period, built their power by urging "the people," especially the people who had won a stake in the land, to vote. The philosophy that goes by the name of Jeffersonian Democracy assumed that nature had endowed the common man, the yeoman farmer, with enough good sense to vote for those among his betters who manifestly had his best interests in view. In the new age, governed by the philosophy called Jacksonian Democracy, one's "betters" seemed to have retreated to the backwaters of power or else to have been swallowed up in the strong surge toward equality, which open opportunity had favored. The Jacksonians, so-called, urged the people to seek office as well as to vote; careers in politics, as in business and the professions as well as on the land, were now open to talent no matter how coarse the garb it might be clothed in.

Few men were more coarsely clothed than "Old Hickory" himself. When friends hinted to the General early in the 1820s that he was "by no means safe from the presidency in 1824," he replied with his usual downright-

# GENERAL JACKSON
# AND HIS TIMES

ness: "No, sir, I know what I am fit for. I can command a body of men in a rough way; but I am not fit to be President." But after the people had twice elected him to the highest office, in 1828 and 1832, he acknowledged their superior authority. "Never for a moment," he said then, "believe that the great body of citizens of any State can deliberately intend to do wrong." If, nevertheless, by accident they or their duly elected representatives, in his opinion, did wrong, as President of all the people, he knew he was the man to set things right again.

Jackson's heroic past was irresistible to the new breed of career politicians, who, as one of them put it in 1823, "always bow to a 'rising sun,' and stand prepared to dance round the 'golden calf.'"

Once in office, moreover, Jackson's high and mighty posture only embellished his reputation with the people. Congress, the Supreme Court, the National Bank; the Indians, the British, and the French; the "interests" of the North, the "nullifiers" of the South, the "internal improvements" men of the West —all were to feel the sting of his wrath. With self-righteous zeal, Jackson slew imaginary dragons of inequality. Even on such a technical issue as the removal of the government's deposits from Biddle's bank (see p. 421), and

in such a formal missive as a communiqué to his Cabinet, he felt obliged to overextend his guardian hand.

The president repeats, that he begs the cabinet to consider the proposed measure as his own. . . . Its responsibility has been assumed, after the most mature deliberation and reflection, as necessary to preserve the morals of the people, the freedom of the press, and the purity of the election franchise.

"The morals of the people!" cried Henry Clay, when he learned of Jackson's statement. "What part of the Constitution has given to the president any power over 'the morals of the people?' None." And the same for "the freedom of the press" and the "purity of the franchise."

Jackson's zeal in searching out enemies of the people and his rhetoric in demolishing them enabled the politicians of his party to keep their idol in the public eye. Unfortunately for them, the politicians of Clay's own party borrowed Jacksonian methods to defeat Jackson's handpicked heir. In the election of 1840, when the Whigs mobilized Jackson's opponents in all sections behind another old hero, General William Henry Harrison, the full strength of "Jacksonian Democracy" for the first time really showed itself at the polls.

398

By broadening the scope of his office, Jackson helped give a new and lasting focus to democratic politics. By further refining the tactics of such politics, Jackson's opponents ultimately unseated his partisans.

## 1  *The Rise of the Common Man*

### THE DEMOCRATIC IMPULSE

On July 4, 1826, the fiftieth anniversary of the Declaration of Independence, the Jacksonian historian-to-be, young George Bancroft, said in a commemorative address:

We hold it best that the laws should favor the diffusion of property and its acquisition, not the concentration of it in the hands of the few to the impoverishment of the many. We give the power to the many in the hope and to the end, that they may use it for their own benefit.

At the time Bancroft spoke, a greater proportion of American citizens than ever before had acquired the power to vote, and to vote for candidates named by themselves. Between 1816 and 1821, six new states (all but Maine in the West or Southwest) entered the Union with constitutions that required no property qualifications for voting. But it was the older states, not those on the moving frontier, that had set the precedent and offered the example. As early as 1801, George Cabot of Massachusetts declared: "The spirit of our country is doubtless more democratic than the *form* of our government." According to the great Philadelphia architect, Benjamin H. Latrobe, writing in 1806, the "form" was already in the process of being made consistent with the spirit. "After the adoption of the Federal Constitution," wrote Latrobe, "the extension of the right of suffrage in the States to a majority of all the adult male citizens, planted a germ which had gradually evolved and has spread actual and practical democracy and political equality over the whole union."

The Vermont constitution of 1777, although containing other restrictive conditions, was the first explicitly to free the right to vote from property-holding or taxpaying qualifications, and this constitution remained intact when Vermont entered the Union in 1791. Kentucky in 1799, New Jersey in 1807, Maryland in 1810, Connecticut in 1818, then successively liberalized the franchise. Connecticut became a model for such northern states as Maine (one of the six new states), Massachusetts, and New York. As the New York *National Advocate* said in August 1821, "In Connecticut they disarmed the poorer classes by taking them into the body politic." New York followed suit that year (with further liberalizing constitutional amendments in 1826), after Maine and Massachusetts had acted in 1819 and 1820 respectively.

The South, generally, lagged behind the North and the West, and Virginia, despite the Jeffersonian tradition, lagged behind the rest of the South. In 1852 she became the last state in the Union to surrender the property test. Only a few years earlier, Louisiana significantly broadened the franchise by reducing her heavy taxpaying qualification. Elsewhere in the slave states, prompted in large part by the argument of Senator Morgan of Virginia, the more liberal example of Maryland already had been followed. "We ought," said Senator Morgan in 1829, "to spread wide the foundation of our government, that all white men have a direct interest in its protection." What Morgan meant specifically was protection against Negro slave revolts.

Besides Virginia and Louisiana, the only state that did not achieve virtual white male suffrage by 1840 was Rhode Island. Here, the state government still functioned under the colonial charter of 1663 according to which freeholders alone, now making up less than half of the adult males in the state, could vote. In 1841, the state administration rejected a proposed new "People's Constitution" with liberal franchise qualifications that had been drafted in orderly fashion and ratified by a large number of citizens. The determined reformers responded in 1842 by electing their own governor, Thomas W. Dorr, thereby creating a second government in Rhode Island.

*A self-made man of the frontier who had entered the ranks of the planter-slaveholder aristocracy, Jackson, portrayed here by his friend Ralph Earl in 1835, has the appearance of a nobleman. (New York Public Library.)*

Now the official regime declared the Dorr party in rebellion, imposed martial law, and called out the militia. When both sides appealed to President Tyler (see p. 426), he felt obliged under the United States Constitution (Art. IV, Sec. 4) to promise "protection" to the regular government "against domestic violence." After a Dorrite assault on the state arsenal failed (the extent of the "Dorr War"), Dorr surrendered. In 1844 he was tried and sentenced to life imprisonment, but the next year the sentence was withdrawn. In 1843, meanwhile, the official regime saw the light and accepted a new constitution liberalizing the franchise qualification.

The democratic spirit of the country failed to carry over to one significant class of the population—the free Negroes. As late as 1820, free Negroes were permitted by law to vote equally with whites in northern New England, in New York and Pennsylvania, and even in such southern states as Tennessee and North Carolina. This right, however, usually had arisen only from omissions in the law and was subject to every abuse until the law itself was tightened. As a delegate to the Pennsylvania constitutional convention of 1837 said on his way to the assemblage that would disfranchise the free Negro, "the people of this state are for continuing this commonwealth, what it always has been, a political community of white persons." By then, the free Negro's right to vote survived only in New England north of Connecticut. In Connecticut, after 1818, past Negro voters could continue to vote, but newly freed ones were disfranchised. In the other states where they once enjoyed the franchise free Negroes had been deprived of it, usually by the very same article which for the first time provided virtually full manhood suffrage for whites. No state entering the Union between 1819 and the Civil War permitted the free Negro to vote.

Loss of the franchise, moreover, was only one of the lengthening list of free Negro disabilities in the free as in the slave states. Consigned to miserable alley slums, confined

by curfews, beyond the pale of the judicial and educational systems, barred from all but the most menial urban occupations and from the land as well, he was "cast upon the world," as an Oregonian said even of his own distant commonwealth in the 1850s, "with no defense; his life, liberty, his property, his all, are dependent on the caprice, the passion, and the inveterate prejudices of not only the community at large but of every felon who may happen to cover an inhuman heart with a white face." By then, many western states would not even allow free Negroes in.

For the "political community of white persons," on the other hand, even more significant perhaps than the legal extension of the suffrage was the heightened interest of the common man in exercising that right. While proportions running up to 70 per cent of the electorate had voted earlier in hot local contests, presidential elections until 1828 seemed to have left most voters cold. Even in 1824, when Jackson himself first was a candidate, only 355,000 votes were counted, compared with 1,155,000 in 1828. In the following 20 years the number going to the polls rose by 250 per cent.

One reason for the voters' new interest was the gradual restoration of the two-party system after 1824 and sharper party differences on issues. Another was the voters' enlarged participation in actually naming the candidates. The old system of nominating presidential candidates by a "caucus," or meeting, of congressmen kept the inner-party clique in power. Rising politicians hated "king caucus," while to the public it seemed a symbol of aristocratic rule. The first break in the system came in 1824 when growing sectional differences made it difficult for the Republican congressional caucus to agree on a candidate and independent groups named men of their own. The credit for developing the modern method of nominating candidates by means of national conventions made up of delegates "fresh from the people," went to a short-lived minor party, the Anti-Masons, who held the first convention in 1830. The major parties adopted the innovation in time for the election of 1832 (see p. 418).

Still another institution gave way before the demand to bring government closer to the people. This was the old system under which, in most states, presidential electors had been chosen by the state legislatures. By 1828, all the states except Delaware and South Carolina had substituted for this sytsem the popular election of members of the electoral college. Jackson, as he often reminded his opponents, thus became the first President who could claim to have been elected directly by the voters, a claim not altogether justified since those named by the people to the electoral college retained personal discretion on just how they would cast their ballots. Governors also began to be popularly elected, and property qualifications for that office and others were swept away. Finally, in the 1840s state judges were being elected rather than appointed—an innovation that would have startled even the more democratic of the Founding Fathers.

## THE ELECTION OF 1824

If Jackson thought little of himself as presidential timber in 1824, the rising new politicians, party not public leaders, who saw in their power to control the popular vote a surer path to wealth and influence than office-holding, were eager to tie their fortunes to the General's coat tails. Among them were Amos Kendall of Kentucky and William B. Lewis of Tennessee, who later became part of Jackson's "Kitchen Cabinet." In 1824 they entered "Old Hickory" in the presidential sweepstakes.

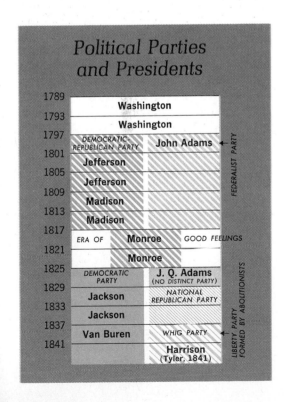

Jackson's opponents in 1824 were William H. Crawford of Georgia, the caucus candidate, who suffered a stroke during the campaign and was not a serious contender; John Quincy Adams of Massachusetts; and Henry Clay, now Speaker of the House.

Clay and Adams, although far apart in origins and temperament, both subscribed to Clay's celebrated "American System." Clay pictured an industrial East providing a growing home market for southern cotton and western grain and meat and an agricultural West and South providing an expanding market for eastern manufacturing enterprise. For the East he would supply protective tariffs; for the West and South "internal improvements" such as canals and railroads to lower transportation costs. Transactions between the sections would be facilitated by a stable credit system underwritten by a national bank. This plan, said Clay, would "place the confederacy upon the most solid of all foundations, [that] of common interest."

Just what Jackson stood for was less clear, even to himself. When pressed he said he was for a "judicious" tariff, which only caused Henry Clay to explode, "Well, by—, I am in favor of an injudicious tariff!" Jackson's stands were likely to be strongly personal. The biographer James Parton long ago successfully appraised Jackson's character:

. . . honest, yet capable of dissimulation; often angry, but most prudent when most furious; endowed by nature with the gift of extracting from every affair and every relation all the strife it can be made to yield; at home and among dependents, all tenderness and generosity; to opponents, violent, ungenerous, prone to believe the very worst of them . . . not taking kindly to culture, but able to achieve wonderful things without it.

Once he had overcome his humble North Carolina origins and made his mark as a lawyer in Tennessee, Jackson had never shown himself a "Jacksonian" democrat. His party affiliation was Jeffersonian; but his narrow state-rights views made it easy for him

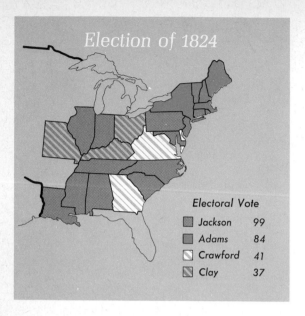

## Election of 1824

**Electoral Vote**

| | | |
|---|---|---|
| ▨ | Jackson | 99 |
| ▨ | Adams | 84 |
| ▨ | Crawford | 41 |
| ▨ | Clay | 37 |

to mingle with the powerful in the states, and not with the common man. His law practice placed him on the side of the "land barons" or "nabobs," and against the "leather shirts." He favored creditors over debtors, absentee landlords over squatters. Jackson shared with other westerners the willingness to judge men by their attainments, not by their social backgrounds. If this helped his backers to present him as the champion of the common man, so much the better for them all, even though the attainments of his friends were uncommon.

The hero of New Orleans did not disappoint the politicians. In the election of 1824 he won 153,000 popular votes to Adams's 108,000, Crawford's 46,000 and Clay's 47,000. In the electoral college, however, his 99 votes fell considerably short of the required majority, and the contest was thrown into the House of Representatives. Here Clay, having polled the lowest electoral total, was eliminated; yet he remained so placed as to be able to decide between Jackson and Adams by swinging his strong House following behind either man. Clay had no love for Jackson. "I cannot believe," he said, "that killing 2500 Englishmen at New Orleans qualifies [him] for the various difficult and complicated duties of the Chief Magistracy." After a private talk

with Adams, who sympathized with Clay's ideas on foreign policy as well as with his "American System," Clay swung his supporters to the Yankee. Thanks largely to Clay's influence, Adams was elected in the House, where the vital support of New York went to him by a single vote.

One of Adams's first presidential acts was to name Clay Secretary of State, and thereby, in the opinion of the age, as his successor. The Jackson men lost no time in charging that a "corrupt bargain" had been made at the Clay-Adams talk. Even had a bargain been made, there need have been nothing corrupt about it between men so sympathetic to one another's program. But "bargain and corruption" became the Jacksonians' slogan for the campaign of 1828, which they opened once they learned of their defeat in 1824. For four years they successfully manipulated public suspicion, and Adams's administration began, and ended, under this cloud.

### JOHN QUINCY ADAMS IN OFFICE

The alleged "deal" was not the only issue that haunted Adams in the White House. A sensitive and high-minded man, he regretted having to accept the Presidency with, as he said, "perhaps two-thirds of the whole people adverse to the actual result." Adams, nevertheless, was not to be deterred by popular symptoms from launching a program he considered right for the country. In his first annual message to Congress he displayed both his stubborn courage and his political ineptitude by making a sweeping argument for a strong national government vigorous in the use of its powers for national improvements directed from the top. Warned by Henry Clay and all but one of the rest of his Cabinet that, at a time when state-rights feelings were rising and sectional jealousies were strong, it was all but suicidal for a President—and a minority President at that—to launch upon such a course, Adams at least conceded that his program was a "perilous experiment."

Congress under the Constitution, Adams argued in his message, had the power to "provide for the common defense and general welfare." This power would justify "laws promoting the improvement of agriculture, commerce, and manufactures, the cultivation and encouragement of the mechanic and of the elegant arts, the advancement of literature, and the progress of the sciences, ornamental and profound." To refrain from exercising this power in the grand manner would be "treachery to the most sacred of trusts." Accordingly he called for the establishment of a national university, the financing of scientific expeditions, the building of astronomical observatories ("light-houses of the skies"), the promulgation of a uniform standard of weights and measures, reform of the patent laws, creation of a Department of the Interior, and the development of a large-scale program of internal improvements.

To suggest, as Adams thoughtlessly did, that the monarchical governments of Europe were doing something superior to democratic America in maintaining observatories only offered proof to his enemies that Adams was a monarchist at heart, one hardened in his attitudes by his long experience abroad. Adams's further suggestion that it would be shameful for Congress to be "palsied by the will of our constituents," was simply to seal the doom of his experiment from the outset.

A dozen years later, Adams explained that "the great effort of my administration" was to apply "all the superfluous revenue of the Union into internal improvement," and thereby provide employment for thousands while enriching the nation.

With this system in ten years from this day the surface of the whole Union would have been checkered over with railroads and canals. It may still be done half a century later and with the limping gait of State legislature and private adventure. I would have done it in the administration of the affairs of the nation.

Adams continued this explanation with an analysis of the defeat of his program:

When I came to the Presidency this principle of internal improvement was swelling the tide

John Quincy Adams by the English artist Thomas Sully. Although hard-working and well-meaning, the reclusive and religious Adams had a cold and introspective manner that prevented him from relating easily to the people. (Metropolitan Musuem of Art, Fletcher Fund, 1938.)

403

404

of public prosperity, till the Sable Genius of the South saw the signs of his own inevitable downfall in the unparalleled progress of the general welfare in the North, and fell to cursing the tariff and internal improvement, and raised the standard of free trade, nullification, and state rights.

In fact, many in the Middle states and the Middle West joined with the South in rejecting Adams's proposals. At the same time, many self-made men (Clay first coined this term to describe the rising manufacturers of Kentucky) were ranged on Adams's side. It is sometimes said that the President's paternalism dampened the spirit of such men; but Adams correctly identified his principal enemies and theirs as the state-rights men, the focus of that "mass of local jealousies," as one historian puts it, in the South as elsewhere.

Adams's own misguided morality must also bear part of the blame. Having made his too grandiose proposals to a lukewarm Congress in offensive rhetoric, he refused to use the power of the Presidency to push them through. He especially resisted the employment of presidential patronage to gain votes even for a program to which he was profoundly committed. During his entire term he removed but 12 civil servants from office and then only for fraud or malfeasance. No wonder he and his supporters were shocked later by Jackson's theory and practice of the "spoils system" (see p. 406).

Adams's comprehensive program for centralized economic development, and his failure to push it through, encouraged his state-rights opponents everywhere to mobilize their own machines behind the pleasingly vague and perfectly popular Jackson. His additional setbacks in Indian and foreign relations made their task all the easier. Adams's efforts to preserve the lands of the Creek Indians in Georgia, against the violent resistance of the state, its speculators, and its potential frontier settlers, proved most humiliating in their outcome. This confrontation led up to the case of *Worcester* v. *Georgia* (1832), which itself was to provide the occasion for Jackson's major victory over the Supreme Court (see p. 409).

Adams was no more successful in diplomacy. The United States had been invited to attend a congress of Latin-American republics in Panama in 1826 called by Simón Bolívar, the great South American liberator, to discuss common problems. Clay was particularly eager to have the United States represented, and Adams thought the congress might provide a first step toward the acquisition of Cuba. But when the President tactlessly agreed to send delegates without first consulting the Senate, his enemies there, led by Martin Van Buren and John Randolph, held up appropriations for the delegates' expenses, attacked one of the appointees as "an acknowledged abolitionist," and described the Latin-Americans as "an ignorant and vicious people." At the close of the Panama conference, no representative from the United States had made an appearance.

A more discouraging blow to national prestige resulted from Adams's clumsy and ill-timed negotiations with the British Foreign Secretary, George Canning. Adams had brought pressure on the British government to permit American ships to engage in direct trade with the British West Indies. But Canning was unyielding, and, in fact, imposed even more drastic restraints on American commerce. Adams's opponents added this failure to their already impressive list of campaign issues.

### THE ELECTION OF JACKSON

By the time of the congressional elections of 1826 Adams's program had gained for his followers the name of National Republicans, while his opponents became known as the Democratic Republicans. In those elections, for the first time in the history of the country, as Adams himself ruefully acknowledged, a President lost his majority in Congress after his first two years in office. When the new

Congress convened in December 1827, under Jacksonian leadership, its only purpose was to further Jackson's presidential prospects in 1828. When the Jackson men, led by the rising Van Buren of New York, placed their handpicked candidate in the Speakership of the House, Senator John Tyler commented that "the opposition party constitutes the *administration*. Upon it rests the responsibility of all legislative measures." Even Adams's Vice-president, Calhoun, although still a nationalist, went over to the Jacksonians and agreed to become their vice-presidential candidate. Very likely, Calhoun expected the 61-year-old Jackson not to run for a second term and to leave the succession to him.

The Jacksonian strategy was to woo support in all key or questionable states by means of legislative largesse. Beyond that, the Jacksonian press so blackened Adams's name that this austere Yankee intellectual, because of his long experience abroad, was made to seem "a very compost of European vices" and unfit for high office.

The campaign of 1828 marked a new high in electioneering activity and a new low in political dignity. Jackson's supporters introduced a rough-and-tumble carnival spirit into the presidential contest that persisted in later years. They paraded with hickory sticks to symbolize the toughness of "Old Hickory," and brandished hickory brooms to suggest the need for sweeping the rascals out. Feeling among the Jacksonians ran extraordinarily high. "Adams, Clay and Company—" ran a toast that was drunk in South Carolina, "Would to God they were like Jonah in the whale's belly; the whale to the devil; the devil in hell; and the door locked, key lost, and not a son of Vulcan within a million miles to make another." To top off their personal attacks on Adams, they accused the President of having purveyed an innocent American girl to the lust of Czar Alexander I while serving as United States minister to Russia years before.

Adams condemned the resort to abusive

smears, but he had backers who outdid the Jackson men in scurrility. They went so far as to brand Jackson an adulterer on a trivial technicality over his wife's divorce from her former husband almost 40 years earlier. Mrs. Jackson suffered intensely from such publicity and died shortly after the election. Jackson never forgave "those vile wretches who have slandered her" and, in his opinion, killed her.

The tactics of his supporters did Adams

405

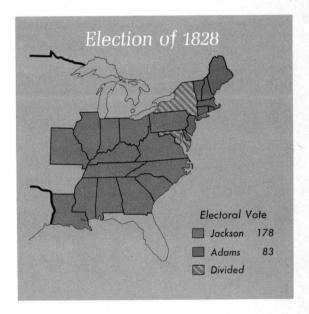

Election of 1828

Electoral Vote
- Jackson   178
- Adams      83
- Divided

no good whatever. Jackson's efforts to deal with issues, in turn, probably cost him votes. The principal issue was the protective tariff. By a tariff act in 1824, Congress had raised the duties on the leading manufactured goods. This act had won the support of the industrial Middle states and the Old Northwest, which continued to look eastward for markets for its agricultural surplus. New England, with big manufacturers of her own, yet still

406

heavily committed to commerce, had split on the measure. The cotton South, in turn, which had surrendered its hopes for manufacturing, overwhelmingly opposed it. Here was an alignment out of which Jackson's lieutenants, already heavily engaged in deals of all sorts, notably in granting federal public lands to politically doubtful states, might make more political hay. Their means was the tariff of 1828, whose object, as John Randolph said, was to encourage "manufactures of no sort but the manufacture of a President of the United States."

Because it raised the general level of the duties, southerners branded the tariff of 1828, "the tariff of abominations." But because it failed to protect woolens manufacturers while at the same time it raised duties on raw wool and other raw materials, the tariff of 1828 also distressed certain northern industrialists. By embracing the principle of protection, Jacksonians may have sought support among manufacturers in the forthcoming elections; but by writing a bill which manufacturers might help defeat, they may also have hoped for southern backing. If such was their plan it failed, for the bill passed, abominations and all.

Jackson survived the backfiring of the tariff scheme. As the hero of New Orleans, the champion of the common man, the most visible old soldier in the country for four solid years, he polled 647,000 votes. The surprise, if any, was that Adams, with 508,000 votes, was far from routed. In the electoral college Jackson won, 178 to 83. Despite the tariff catastrophe he carried the entire South. Only New England, Delaware, and New Jersey voted against him.

## II  *"Old Hickory" in the White House*

### THE HEAD OF THE GOVERNMENT

Jackson's inauguration attracted to Washington an immense crowd which seemed to

think, as Daniel Webster said, that "the country is rescued from some dreadful danger." The people surged through the still unpaved streets and pressed into the White House as if to make themselves equally at home as their hero.

In the White House itself the new chief was busily engaged with his personal friends in naming the official functionaries of his administration. Martin Van Buren emerged as Secretary of State. John McLean of Ohio, Adams's Jacksonian Postmaster-General was retained in his post and the post itself soon was raised to Cabinet level. One disappointed big fish said of the rest of the Cabinet that it reflected "The Millennium of the Minnows," and he was not far wrong. But it did not matter too much because Jackson's principal advisers, besides Van Buren, were in his private, not his public Cabinet. In addition to Kendall and Lewis (see p. 401), these advisers included the young nephew of Jackson's wife, Andrew Jackson Donelson, whom the President himself had raised, and such trusted western newspaper editors as Duff Green and Francis Preston Blair. Whatever these men or Jackson himself may have thought about the urgent new issues in national politics—the tariff, internal improvements, the bank, land and Indian policy—they all shared "Old Hickory's" feeling about the Presidency itself. Jackson's worst enemies wondered whether the arbitrary old General would turn out to be a tyrant, whether republican government was safe in his hands. These enemies eventually came together as Whigs (see p. 424) in defiance of "King Andrew I." Jackson did not, in fact, become a tyrant. But the first principle of his two administrations was the congenial one of executive supremacy: The President alone, elected by all the people, was the chief instrument of their will, as interpreted by himself.

Jackson's policy toward the executive civil service was consistent with his independent view of his high office. The President shocked the Adams men by discharging about 900 jobholders from among the 10,000 he found on the payroll. Actually, his party chieftains, having made many commitments in two campaigns, wanted more heads to roll, more places to fill; but Jackson restrained them. The Adams press made a great noise about the new "reign of terror," and the grim "purge" that was bloodying Washington's streets; but in the long run it was the President's gratuitous defense of the "spoils system," rather than the particular replacements themselves, that so firmly associated his name with it. Earlier Presidents had removed opposition partisans from office without raising many eyebrows. Jackson was the first to make the "spoils system" seem a social and moral as well as a political "reform."

The political aspect Jackson covered in his inaugural address. Conveniently closing his eyes to the deals made by his own promoters, he noted as "inscribed" by the recent election, "in characters too legible to be overlooked, the task of *reform*, which will require particularly the correction of those abuses that have brought the patronage of the Federal Government into conflict with the freedom of elections."

The social aspect Jackson dealt with in his first annual message to Congress in December 1829. In this message he proposed "a general extension of the law [passed in 1820] which limits appointments to four years," thereby furthering "that rotation which constitutes a leading principle in the republican creed, giving healthful action to the system." Such a law, he continued, in a style that was to become characteristic of his presidential pronouncements, would nullify the prevailing idea that "office is . . . a species of property, and government . . . a means of promoting individual interests, . . . an engine for the support of the few at the expense of the many." Jackson was ready to exclude judges, Cabinet officers, and diplomats "of the highest rank" from this egalitarian rule. Otherwise, "the duties of public offices" are "plain and simple," and plain and simple men could best perform them in the people's interest.

The moral aspect Jackson dealt with in his

*"Jackson is to be President, and you will be HANGED."*

In the War of 1812 Jackson's soldiers nicknamed him "Old Hickory" after "the toughest thing they could think of." Years later when an opponent expressed doubt over a threat by Jackson, one of the General's friends remarked, "I tell you . . . when Jackson begins to talk about hanging, they can begin to look for the ropes." (The Bettmann Archive.)

"Outline of Principles," according to which his heads of departments were to examine the "moral habits" of incumbents and to fire those lax in "private or public relations."

The four-year law Jackson suggested was not enacted; but he and his successors did so well without it in finding just rewards for party workers hungry for "the loaves and fishes" that the reform of Jackson's "reforms" eventually became the leading issue in American politics.

407

408

In his relations with Congress and the courts the new Chief Executive proved no less aggressive than in his attitude toward the "unfaithful" office holders he inherited.

Earlier Presidents had been largely content to administer the laws passed by Congress. But Jackson grasped the constitutional power given the executive to participate in making (or better, unmaking) the law as well as executing it. In his two terms Jackson vetoed more legislation than all former Presidents together. This would appear a remarkable record for one so openly attached to popular government; but Jackson, especially after his experiences in the election of 1824 (see p. 401), had come to regard Congress, in his usual vein, as the home of "aristocratical establishments" like the national bank, and his own office as the only popular bulwark against such "interests" as the new industrialists. In his inaugural address he promised that, "in administering the laws of Congress, I shall keep steadily in view the limitations as well as the extent of the Executive power." He did not necessarily mean the limitations of his own power, only the limitations on Congress in requiring the Executive to do what he did not wish to do. Jackson's vetoes usually were based on the specific constitutional point of unwarranted congressional invasions of state rights.

One of Jackson's most famous vetoes killed the so-called Maysville Bill of 1830, which would have required the federal government to subscribe to the stock of a private corporation promoted to build an "internal improvement" in Clay's state of Kentucky. Because the Maysville road would lie wholly within a single state, Jackson's stand was easier to take. He knew also that it would be strongly supported in such states as New York and Pennsylvania which had helped assure his election victory and which, having developed transportation systems at their own expense, were determined to keep the federal government from helping to construct competing systems farther west. He could expect support, too, from the South Atlantic states, increasingly committed to slavery and hence to the principle of state rights, the strongest constitutional bastion of slavery. These states were also increasingly opposed to protective tariffs on essential manufactures, which supplied the federal funds available for internal improvements.

Jackson, in his two administrations, approved unprecedented appropriations for river and harbor improvement bills and similar pork-barrel legislation sponsored by worthy Democrats in compensation for local election support. On the basis of this record a case has been made for the old General's genuine sympathy for federal aid to internal improvements of a national character, and hence for the exceptional nature of the Maysville veto, influenced, it is said, by strategic party considerations. But Jackson was eternally at pains to disavow any such interpretation and to make it clear that he believed federal aid to internal improvements of any sort an unconstitutional invasion of state prerogatives.

In his first annual message, Jackson told Congress that "the mode . . . hitherto adopted" for the "improvement of inland navigation and the construction of highways . . . has been deprecated as an infraction of the Constitution." He went on to propose, "that the most safe, just, and federal disposition which could be made of the surplus revenue would be its apportionment among the several states." He then proceeded to draw the general moral:

The great mass of legislation relating to our internal affairs was intended to be left where the Federal Convention found it—in the State governments. Nothing is clearer, in my view, than that we are chiefly indebted for the success of the Constitution under which we are now acting to the watchful and auxiliary operation of the State authorities. This is not the reflection of a day, but belongs to the most deeply rooted convictions of my mind. I can not, therefore, too strongly or too earnestly, for my own sense of its importance, warn you against all encroachments upon the legitimate sphere of State sovereignties.

In his Maysville veto message, Jackson reminded Congress that "the act which I am called upon to consider has, therefore, been passed with a knowledge of my views on this question." Such disrespect was intolerable to "Old Hickory," and the veto stuck. The more firmly to underscore the principle, Jackson, while he could not avoid approving additional funds for the extension of the National Road (see p. 382), as his predecessors since Jefferson all had done, destroyed the national character of the great project by turning over completed sections to the states in which they lay.

In asserting his independence of the Supreme Court also, Jackson put state rights first. His most famous stand against the Court came in 1832, following John Marshall's decision in *Worcester* v. *Georgia,* concerning Georgia's claims to sovereignty over Cherokee lands.

In 1803, as we have seen (p. 322), after Georgia ceded her western lands to the United States, the federal government agreed to quiet Creek and Cherokee title to the region. Federal action, however, was slow; and as cotton-growing spread in the state, the planters' patience ran out. The planters had the full sympathy of Georgia's militant Governor, George M. Troup, who in 1826 ordered a state survey of Creek lands with an eye to their prompt sale and settlement. When President Adams threatened to halt the survey with federal forces, Governor Troup said he would resist force with force. Civil war was averted only by the Creeks' own capitulation to the inevitable and their decision to move beyond the Mississippi.

The Cherokees, like the Creeks, had embraced the white man's ways, set up farms and factories, erected schools, and published a newspaper. In 1827, they decided to form an independent state on the American model. They also adopted a constitution under which this state would be governed. Georgia re-

sponded by nullifying all federal Indian laws and ordering the forcible seizure of Cherokee lands. When her courts next tried and convicted a Cherokee of murder, the Supreme Court of the United States ordered the conviction set aside; but Governor Troup and the state legislature ignored the federal government's "interference" and executed the prisoner. By then, Jackson had become President; and it was well-known in Georgia, as elsewhere, that his concern for the red men was as cold as his sympathy for the planters was warm.

Removal of Indian Tribes to the West

Unlike Adams, Jackson did nothing to assert federal authority over Georgia in Indian affairs. The Cherokees, however, did have friends who sought an injunction in the Supreme Court forbidding the extension of Georgia law over Indian residents and Georgia's seizure of Indian lands. In 1831, John Marshall, in the case of *Cherokee Nation* v. *Georgia,* denied the long-standing rule that the Indians were tantamount to "foreign nations" with whom the United States made treaties which federal courts were empowered to enforce. The Indians, he said, were "domestic

*Cherokee Indians of the period of the removal of the Cherokees to Oklahoma; drawing by George Catlin. (Courtesy of the New-York Historical Society, New York City.)*

Jackson is reported to have exclaimed, "John Marshall has made his decision, now let him enforce it."

Unfortunately for the Cherokees, the Jacksonian House of Representatives tabled the enforcement order introduced to restrain Georgia from evicting the Indians. This meant that no federal troops were made available to support Marshall's decision, and the spoliation of the Indian lands continued. By 1835, only a remnant of Indians still retained their lands, and after the subjugation of the Florida Seminoles (1835–42) millions of fertile acres were thrown open to white occupation. The Indians meanwhile made their trek westward over what became known, and rightly so, as the "trail of tears." A fourth or more of the red men died on the journey; officials overseeing them robbed them of their funds; what they had left went for burial rites. Of the Cherokee removal in particular, Emerson cried out that, "such a dereliction of all faith and virtue, such a denial of justice, and such deafness to screams for mercy were never heard of in time of peace . . . since the earth was made."

### THE WEBSTER-HAYNE DEBATE

While the head of the government in the White House was asserting his leadership of the whole nation and of all the people, the "heads of the sections" in Congress were clarifying their differences and sharpening their defenses. Many issues divided the slave from the free states, and the free West from the free East. And if agreements like the Missouri Compromise of 1820 from time to time cemented over sectional breaches, new developments in the rapidly expanding country broke them open again. Two of the most disruptive issues were public lands and protective tariffs, and the Webster-Hayne debate in the winter of 1830 plumbed the sectional depths of both.

From the 1820s on, the West had campaigned for cheap public lands (once the Indian title had been bought off and the

dependent nations," who could not sue in United States courts. He denied the injunction, but he asserted, nevertheless, that the United States alone, and no single state, had sovereignty over the red men and over the disposition of their lands. In 1832, Marshall had an opportunity to strengthen this opinion in the case of *Worcester* v. *Georgia*. One Samuel Worcester had been convicted by Georgia for occupying Cherokee land without having first obtained a state license to do so. Marshall reversed the conviction, and went on to say that the Cherokee nation was a legitimate political community, with clearly defined territories, where "the laws of Georgia can have no force, and which the citizens of Georgia have no right to enter" without Cherokee consent by law or treaty. Georgia herself boycotted the Court's proceedings. It was after this case that

aborigines themselves removed), and for protection for the "squatter" who claimed government land before it had officially been opened to settlement. The squatter who had improved his land during his illegal tenure demanded the right to buy it at the minimum rate when it was finally placed on the open market. But even the minimum rate of $1.25 an acre seemed excessive to many for whom Senator Thomas Hart Benton of Missouri became the spokesman. As early as 1824, Benton had proposed that the price of unsold government land be gradually reduced to 75 cents an acre and then to 50 cents. If no takers appeared even then, the land should be given away free. This proposal came to be known as "graduation," and it was the first formally to place a higher value to the nation as a whole on the work of the pioneer in opening up the country than on land-sale receipts to the Treasury.

Easterners regarded Benton's plan as one more scheme to tap their labor supply and force wage costs up; they also saw the quickening of western development as a further threat to their political strength in the nation. On the other hand, it was obvious that the continuation of land sales at the established prices would bring into the Treasury money enough to invalidate one of their principal arguments for high tariffs—the need for additional revenue to pay off the national debt and support government services. Easterners like John Quincy Adams had hoped that the chaotic growth of the American economy could be brought under the discipline of a central plan administered from the top; more particularly, they wanted the price of land kept up, and the proceeds distributed among the states to help them improve public education. When nothing came of this, they resorted to the rather desperate proposal that the West be closed to settlement altogether. In December 1829 Senator Samuel A. Foot of Connecticut offered a resolution to this effect, urging specifically that public-land surveys be stopped for a time and that future sales be limited to lands already on the market.

Senator Benton, speaking for the West, angrily denounced Foot's resolution as a manufacturer's plot. Spokesmen for the slave South, in turn, supported Benton in the hope that they could thereby aggravate the growing differences between the free East and the free West. The South's purpose was to lure the West away from the protective-tariff phase of the "American System," so much desired by eastern manufacturers.

Senator Robert Y. Hayne of South Carolina presented the South's case, but his most divisive remarks were derived from an antitariff essay published anonymously by Vice-president Calhoun in 1828 under the title of *Exposition and Protest*. According to Calhoun, the Tariff of 1828 (see p. 406) reduced the South to serfdom to northern industrialists. These men, he said, forced her to pay exorbitantly for their manufactures or for manufactured imports from Europe. At the same time, they goaded Europe into retaliating against American tariffs by raising their own against southern rice and cotton. "The tariff is unconstitutional and must be repealed," Calhoun wrote. "The rights of the South have been destroyed, and must be restored, . . . the Union is in danger, and must be saved." No free government, Calhoun argued, would permit the transfer of "power and property from one class or section to another." The tyranny of the majority could be met by the constitutional right of each state to nullify an unconstitutional act of Congress.

It was Hayne's introduction of Calhoun's nullification theory into his argument against Foot's resolution that moved Daniel Webster to reply to the South Carolinian in January 1830. The debate was prolonged, but Webster, stirred to make an especially noble effort by Hayne's provocative references to the New England Federalists' disloyalty to the Union during the War of 1812 (see p. 354), had the last word.

When Webster made his final reply, beginning on January 26, the Senate realized that the debate had moved from the merely troublesome issue of public-land policy to

412

the truly dangerous one of the underlying nature of the Union. The Union, said the "God-like Daniel," was not a mere compact among state legislatures; it was "the creature of the people." They had erected it; they alone were sovereign in it; their government, in its own right, was every bit as sanctified as the governments of the states. It was for the Supreme Court, not for the states, to decide whether laws passed by Congress were in keeping with the Constitution. If a single state had that right, the Union was dissolved and liberty itself was menaced. Webster closed his speech, which ran no less than four hours, with this remarkable rhapsody to the Union:

I have not allowed myself, Sir, to look beyond the Union, to see what might lie hidden in the dark recess behind. I have not coolly weighed the chances of preserving liberty when the bonds that unite us together shall be broken asunder. I have not accustomed myself to hang over the precipice of disunion, to see whether, with my short sight, I can fathom the depth of the abyss below; nor could I regard him as a safe counsellor in the affairs of this government, whose thoughts should be mainly bent on considering, not how the Union may be best preserved, but how tolerable might be the condition of the people when it should be broken up and destroyed. While the Union lasts, we have high, exciting, gratifying prospects spread out before us, for us and our children. Beyond that I seek not to penetrate the veil. God grant that in my day, at least, that curtain may not rise! God grant that on my vision never may be opened what lies behind! When my eyes shall be turned to behold for the last time the sun in heaven, may I not see him shining on the broken and dishonored fragments of a once glorious Union; on States dissevered, discordant, belligerent; on a land rent with civil feuds, or drenched, it may be, in fraternal blood! Let their last feeble and lingering glance rather behold the gorgeous ensign of the republic now known and honored throughout the earth, still full high advanced, its arms and trophies streaming in their original lustre, not a stripe erased or polluted, not a single star obscured, bearing for its motto, no such miserable interrogatory as "What is all this worth?"

nor those other words of delusion and folly, "Liberty first and Union afterwards"; but everywhere, spread all over in characters of living light, blazing on all its ample folds, as they float over the sea and over the land, and in every wind under the whole heavens, that other sentiment, dear to every true American heart,—Liberty *and* Union, now and for ever, one and inseparable!

Senator Benton called this effort "a fine piece of rhetoric misplaced," yet generations

of American schoolchildren soon were required to memorize it, and as grownups many of them recalled it most poignantly in the dark days 31 years after it was delivered, when Daniel Webster lay moldering in the dust and Lincoln tried to retrieve the Union from the abyss of secession and Civil War.

Senator Foot's resolution was lost sight of in the hubbub over the greater issues his proposal had brought more clearly into the open. Once the debate was over, the first question

*The eloquent senator from Massachusetts, Daniel Webster, about to reply to the urbane senator from South Carolina, Robert Y. Hayne (front row, hands in lap). Vice President Calhoun is at the extreme left and Senator Thomas Hart Benton is standing in the rear, his back against a pillar. This painting by George Peter Alexander Healy shows the intimacy of the chamber in which the Senate met until 1861. It later housed the Supreme Court. (Faneuil Hall, Boston.)*

413

414

everyone asked was, where does Jackson stand? Hayne was his close personal friend, a frequent visitor to the White House, the companion of his family. As early as January 28, publisher Duff Green, of the Kitchen Cabinet, appeared to have let the cat out of the bag, when he declared in his *United States Telegraph:* "The doctrine contended for by General HAYNE is too well understood and too firmly established . . . to be shaken." This opinion surely did no violence to Jackson's views as we have presented them up to this point of his administration. But still he kept his peace. A month passed before Webster and Hayne would release their polished-up speeches to the hungry press and people, a period during which pressure for a presidential statement mounted. Many Jacksonians accused Webster of hazardous demagoguery in attacking so fiercely the straw man of disunion. But once again, the man in the White House would go his own way. When he finally made up his mind to talk, he confronted not Hayne, the spokesman, but Calhoun, the philosopher behind the spokesman.

## NULLIFICATION

The doctrine of nullification was a curious lure for the South to choose to capture the heart of the West. Beyond the coastal tier of the 13 original commonwealths, each of which had asserted its own independence of Britain, all the new states were themselves created by the national government of the United States. They had never known independence; they had grown and flourished in and with the Union. Where they stood on the issue of nullification finally became clear enough to Jackson himself. And where the Union was involved he was with them. He was for state rights; about that there was to be no mistake. But he was for state rights *within* the Union of which he never forgot that he was President. There was to be no mistake about that either.

In April 1830, when the leading Democrats were gathered at a Jefferson birthday dinner,

"Old Hickory" looked Calhoun in the eye and proposed this toast: "Our Union—it must be preserved!" Before news of the toast was released, Hayne prevailed upon Jackson to soften the blow by inserting the word, "Federal" before "Union." But "Federal" or not, Calhoun was to be unrepentant. To Jackson's words, he rose to reply: "The Union—next to our liberty, the most dear." In the following months, old personal grudges and new personal conflicts produced a clean break between Jackson and Calhoun which profoundly influenced the developing sectional fight.

In the spring of 1830, through some of his advisers who disliked Calhoun, Jackson discovered that in 1818, when Calhoun was Secretary of War, he had favored punishing Jackson for his conduct during the Seminole War (see p. 359). Nervously Calhoun tried to explain himself in an embarrassed letter, but he only convinced the President of his lack of candor. "Understanding you now," wrote the unforgiving Jackson to his Vice-president, "no further communication with you on this subject is necessary." When Calhoun next attributed his misfortunes to Van Buren's machinations, the President viewed this as a blow at his trusted friend, and his break with Calhoun became final. At the same time the position of Calhoun's supporters in the Cabinet became untenable.

The split in the Cabinet was next intensified by a social dispute that rocked Washington. In 1829, Jackson's Secretary of War, John H. Eaton, had married the widow Margaret O'Neale Timberlake, an ex-barmaid and the daughter of a tavern-keeper. Eaton's name had been scandalously linked with hers before their marriage. When Mrs. Calhoun, followed by the wives of other Cabinet members, refused to receive Mrs. Eaton, Jackson did not hesitate to defend her, no doubt remembering the attacks on his own wife. Van Buren, a widower, took advantage of the situation to ingratiate himself all the more deeply with Jackson by acting cordially to the unconventional but charming wife of his colleague Eaton.

Realizing that the social atmosphere of the Cabinet would be a liability to the administration, however, Van Buren offered his resignation in the hope that it would enable Jackson to reorganize the whole Cabinet. This shrewd move relieved him from the charge that he was manipulating the administration in his own interests and further convinced other Jackson men of Van Buren's unselfish devotion. Eaton had also submitted his resignation, and Jackson now called for similar action by the remaining members. In appointing their successors, Jackson passed over the Calhoun men and chose a well-knit group of loyal backers. Van Buren was soon nominated as minister to Great Britain, and Eaton was appointed governor of Florida Territory.

It was obvious now that Jackson regarded Van Buren and not Vice-president Calhoun as his successor. More important, the make-up of the new Cabinet reflected the decline of Virginia and South Carolina in the Jacksonian party, which henceforth leaned heavily on a coalition comprising the newer states of the West and Southwest and the large Democratic states of Pennsylvania and New York.

Calhoun, nevertheless, still had a few volleys of his own to fire. As President of the Senate he was able to cast the tie-breaking vote by which Van Buren's nomination as minister to Britain was rejected 24–23. He also found a more significant occasion to press not only his defiance but his doctrine. Unfortunately for him, Jackson chose the same occasion to show who was boss. The South went largely with Calhoun; the free West and the free East clung to each other and to "Old Hickory."

The tariff, once more, provided the decisive issue. Receipts from the existing duties were so high that by 1830 the national debt had

*The Eaton scandal culminated in a special Cabinet meeting, satirized in this cartoon (Mrs. Eaton did not actually attend). Jackson judged her a "charming creature." (The Bettmann Archive.)*

been almost entirely paid off. Jackson believed protective (as against revenue) tariffs to be as unconstitutional as appropriations for internal improvements, and in his message of December 6, 1831, he urged Congress to revise the Tariff of 1828 downward. If he hoped to appease the discontented South by his proposal, he also sufficiently modified the requested reductions so as not to antagonize the industrial Northeast. On July 14, 1832, Congress passed a tariff bill that met Jackson's specifications. It hardly satisfied Calhoun, however, and the Vice-president rushed home from Washington to mobilize southern opposition.

The doctrine of nullification was reasserted. This time, moreover, in a series of dramatic steps, South Carolina moved to put Calhoun's theories into effect. A legislature overwhelmingly favorable to nullification was elected. This legislature then ordered the election of delegates to a special state convention. On November 19, 1832, this convention assembled and soon adopted by a vote of 136-26 an ordinance of nullification which declared the Tariffs of 1828 and 1832 void. The convention also (1) ordered the legislature to prohibit the collection of the duties in state ports after February 1, 1833; and (2) asserted that the use of armed federal forces to collect the duties would be followed by secession.

Jackson, more assertive than ever after his recent smashing success in the election of 1832 (see p. 421), replied on December 10 with his ringing Nullification Proclamation, which made his position plain:

> I consider . . . the power to annul a law of the United States, assumed by one State, incompatible with the existence of the Union, contradicted expressly by the letter of the Constitution, unauthorized by its spirit, inconsistent with every principle on which it was founded, and destructive of the great object for which it was formed.

Jackson warned that the laws of the United States compelled him to meet treason with force.

In February 1833 the Senate passed a "Force Bill" empowering the President to use the army and navy if rebellious South Carolina resisted federal customs officials. While the Force Bill was being debated, Henry Clay offered a new tariff bill calling for a gradual reduction of the 1832 duties. South Carolina leaders now waited to see what would happen to these two measures. They had already learned that other southern states had repudiated nullification and that a vigorous Unionist faction inside their own borders would continue to fight it.

On the day (March 2) that the Force Act became law, Jackson also signed Clay's Tariff of 1833. This tariff provided for a gradual reduction of duties until, by July 1, 1842, none would be higher than 20 per cent. It also lengthened the list of commodities that could be imported duty free. Even Calhoun, who had resigned as Vice-president in order to be named by the Carolina legislature for the Senate so that he could speak for his state there, voted for this bill. After its enactment, South Carolina showed her satisfaction by withdrawing her nullification ordinance. But she saved face by passing a new ordinance nullifying Jackson's Force Act. Since that act was now no longer needed, Jackson wisely ignored this empty formal defiance.

### "SHIRT-SLEEVE" DIPLOMACY

"Old Hickory" was as vigorous in asserting American rights in foreign relations as he was in projecting the rights of the Chief Executive at home. He appointed his diplomats, moreover, on the same basis as he appointed domestic spoilsmen, and their "shirt-sleeve" methods, at a time when diplomatic protocol was most strict, caused many a shock abroad.

It was Jackson's own handling of two longstanding issues, however, that brought the most satisfying results. By using the velvet glove approach, he at last persuaded Britain to open the British West Indian trade to American ships on the same basis that American ports would be opened to British ships engaged in the West Indian trade. This matter was settled in October 1830. By using the iron fist approach the following year, he also persuaded the French to agree to pay up American claims against them for ships and cargoes lost during the Napoleonic wars. When the French delayed making the actual payments, Jackson recommended to Congress that it vote reprisals on available French property. This recommendation was accompanied by such harsh words that the French demanded a formal apology. But Jackson retorted: "The honor of my country shall never be stained by an apology from me for the statement of truth and the performance of duty." The British at last undertook to mediate the dispute and the French eventually paid up in full.

Jackson was less vigorous and less provocative in his relations with Mexico over the issue of Texas independence, even though he personally favored both the initial independence of the Lone Star State and her eventual annexation by the United States.

## III *The Bank War*

### PARTY PREPARATIONS FOR 1832

With the defection of Calhoun and the intransigent state-rights men from the Jacksonian ranks, a new anti-Jackson coalition began to take form. The strength of this coalition was eventually to be found in the Whig party, largely Adamsite in its attitudes, but ready to unite for campaign purposes with all others opposed to Jackson's "presidential tyranny." As the elections of 1832 neared, this essentially conservative group was anxious to find some way of tapping the rising democratic sentiment of the country to which Jackson had so successfully appealed. Allegiance with an odd new political party—the Anti-Masonic party—seemed to offer the leaders of the anti-Jackson camp their opportunity.

Masonry had been widely condemned for its secrecy (a "horrid, oath binding system"),

which seemed to confirm its allegedly anti-democratic character. The fact that such a large proportion of established political leaders and judges were Masons suggested that Masonry constituted a kind of office-holding clique and a gigantic conspiracy against the common man. Moreover, many associated Masonry with free thought and found in it a threat to Christianity; others, excited by the rumor that alcohol was used with abandon in Masonic ceremonies, embraced Anti-Masonry almost as a temperance crusade.

All these anti-Masonic attitudes were brought into focus between 1826 and 1827 by the disappearance of a certain William Morgan, a stonemason and homespun intellectual of Batavia, New York. A Mason himself, Morgan had become embroiled in disputes with fellow members and threatened to write a book exposing the secrets of the society. One day in 1826 he was abducted by a group of unidentified men and never again seen. A year later, the body of a drowned man, washed ashore from Lake Ontario, was rather uncertainly identified as Morgan's. The latent suspicion that he had been murdered by a group of Masons now quickened into life, and an Anti-Masonic party soon was formed to make political capital of the new "enthusiasm." In the New York State elections in the fall of 1827, the new party carried several western counties and sent 15 members to the state assembly. The movement spread to other states and soon attracted anti-Jackson politicians on the make. Best of all, Jackson himself was a Mason.

Among those most determined to use anti-Masonic sentiment against Jackson was the hard-boiled Rochester editor, Thurlow Weed, who hoped to put Henry Clay into the White House in 1832. Embarrassingly enough, Clay too was a Mason. Moreover, he had as little use for Weed as for Jackson. Weed and his henchmen, Clay said in 1830, were "in pursuit of power . . . without regard to the means of acquiring it." The Anti-Masons at last found a candidate in the aged William Wirt of Maryland, and at their national con-

418

vention in Baltimore in September 1831—the first such convention in history, as we have said (p. 400)—named him their standard bearer. Wirt also was a Mason and he accepted this early nomination mainly with the hope of using it to strengthen his chances for being named by the National Republicans as well. But the latter, in their first national convention in Baltimore in December 1831, stuck with Clay. The Anti-Masons had adopted the convention system since they had no body of office holders to form a caucus; they made the most of this situation by stressing the democratic nature of the convention system as against the authoritarianism of Jackson. Not to be outdone, the Democrats, as the Jacksonians now formally called themselves, also held a nominating convention in Baltimore, in May 1832, where they named "Old Hickory" and "Little Van" by acclamation.

At the National Republican convention in Baltimore, Jackson was taken to task for his stand on internal improvements, Indian removal, and the tariff. But the principal target was his administration's unfriendly attitude toward the Second Bank of the United States. As it turned out, the Bank question overshadowed all other issues in the 1832 presidential campaign.

### PRESIDENT JACKSON V. PRESIDENT BIDDLE

For ten years prior to the election of 1832, the Second Bank had been managed by the able Philadelphian, Nicholas Biddle. A reformed Federalist, Biddle had been appointed a director of the Bank by President Monroe in 1819. In 1824 and 1828 he voted for Jackson himself. On becoming president of the Bank in 1823, Biddle had intensified the deflationary policies that his predecessor had introduced during the Panic of 1819 (see p. 365). Not only was Biddle cautious about issuing notes of his own Bank, but also by refusing to accept at face value the notes of state and local banks that had issued more

paper than their specie reserves warranted, he forced upon such banks an element of caution that they and their clients came to resent. Resentment lay deepest in the West, which, because it was growing faster than the rest of the country, felt most keenly the disregard of its financial needs by Biddle's watchdog policies.

*Nicholas Biddle, president of the Second Bank of the United States, after a painting by Rembrandt Peale. (The Bettmann Archive.)*

The Second Bank, in addition, had become an enormous institution, and its large capitalization, its far-reaching powers over the economy, and its privileged custodianship of the Treasury's deposits made it possible for critics to denounce it as a monopoly. No one attacked the Bank more vigorously on this score than Jackson's supporter, Senator Thomas H. Benton of Missouri. In February

1831 Benton introduced a resolution against rechartering the Bank and declaimed for several hours on the threat it represented to democracy: It was "the sole authority . . . to which the Federal Government, the State Governments, the great cities, corporate bodies, merchants, traders, and every private citizen, must, of necessity, apply, for every loan which their exigencies may demand." Skillfully Benton exploited the egalitarian feelings against the Bank: "It tends to aggravate the inequality of fortunes; to make the rich richer and the poor poorer; to multiply nabobs and paupers; and to deepen and widen the gulf which separates Dives from Lazarus." The Senate rejected Benton's resolution, but he had given a strong impetus to anti-Bank sentiment.

Benton's fear that the Bank was "too great and powerful to be tolerated in a government of free and equal laws" reflected a widespread conviction that this great agency, aside from its economic force, was corrupting political life. Its critics were aware, for example, that many congressmen had received low-interest loans and special services from the Bank. As a Bank lawyer, Webster was paid a substantial retainer which he was at pains to collect. News editors also received Bank favors, and their papers made considerable profit in circulating propaganda paid for by Biddle. In the Bank's defense it could be argued that most of the loans made to politicians and editors were sound enough, and that it would have been suicidal to refuse to do business with such influential men.

In addition to those who were troubled by the Bank's credit policies and possibly corrupt practices were those of the old Republican school who had never accepted its constitutionality. Among these Jackson himself ranked high. "You know my opinion as to the banks," he wrote William Lewis in 1820, "that the Constitution of our State, as well as the Constitution of the United States, prohibited the establishment of banks in any state." Thereafter Jackson seemed so often to have changed his mind that he became an

enigma to Biddle who desperately needed to understand him. In November 1829 Biddle had an interview with the old soldier in which Jackson set forth his old philosophy. Jackson handsomely acknowledged the Bank's services to the government, but he added:

I think it right to be perfectly frank with you—I do not think that the power of Congress extends to charter a Bank out of the ten mile square [District of Columbia]. I do not dislike your Bank any more than all banks. But ever since I read the history of the South Sea Bubble I have been afraid of banks.

Jackson added: "I have read the opinion of John Marshall [on the Bank's constitution-

419

*Thomas Hart Benton, senator from Missouri. (Library of Congress.)*

420

ality in *McCulloch* v. *Maryland,* 1819], . . . and could not agree with him."

Jackson's first annual message to Congress was under consideration among his advisers at the time of the Biddle interview. They urged him not to rock the boat, to say nothing about the Bank. But Jackson could not restrain himself. "My friend," he told one of them, "I am pledged against the bank." When the time came to submit this message in December, Jackson remained silent on the Bank almost to the end. Then he said it was not too soon for the issue of rechartering the Bank in 1836 to be submitted "to the deliberate consideration of the Legislature and the people." To assist them in their deliberations, he added: "Both the constitutionality and the expediency of the law creating this bank are well questioned by a large portion of our fellow-citizens." Two years later, in his message to Congress in December 1831, the President reaffirmed his views of the Bank "as at present organized."

Jackson himself, underestimating popular support for his position, would have preferred to keep the Bank out of the 1832 campaign, and his Secretary of State and Secretary of the Treasury were busy talking to Biddle's friends about certain renewal after the election if application were put off. But Webster and Clay, grossly overestimating public support for the Bank, urged Biddle to take the offensive against "Old Hickory" and petition Congress for a new Bank charter now. Biddle, increasingly confused in the political maelstrom, at last yielded to such seemingly authoritative advice, and on July 3, 1832, as forecast, the recharter bill passed both houses. Jackson, bedridden for the moment, grimly observed to his heir-apparent: "The Bank, Mr. Van Buren, is trying to kill me, *but I will kill it.*"

When the President's decision to veto this recharter bill was seen to be final, his most intimate White House advisers "prayed, begged, and entreated" him to make his veto "soft," so that the three million people in-cluded in the census of 1830 but as yet unrepresented in Congress might have a chance to ballot on the issue in the impending election. But Jackson dissented. For all his urging "deliberate consideration" upon them, Jackson felt he did not need the vote to know the people's mind. He would crush the "Monster" once and for all.

In his veto message of July 10, Jackson did not fail to note at the start that the recharter bill had come to him on the Fourth of July, and that he had considered it, "with that solemn regard to the principles of the Constitution which the day was calculated to inspire." Such consideration confirmed his old belief that, "some of the powers and privileges possessed by the existing bank are unauthorized by the Constitution, subversive of the rights of the States, and dangerous to the liberties of the people." If the Supreme Court, virtually to everyone else's satisfaction, disagreed, "the opinion of the judges has no more authority over Congress than the opinion of Congress has over the judges, and on that point the President is independent of both." Jackson went on to denounce the Bank as a monopoly operating to the advantage of the privileged few and open to the danger of control by foreign owners of its stock, a negligible possibility. His closing remarks were well suited to the coming election:

Distinctions in society will always exist under every just government. Equality of talents, of education, or of wealth cannot be produced by human institutions. In the full enjoyment of the gifts of Heaven and the fruits of superior industry, economy, and virtue, every man is equally entitled to protection by law; but when the laws undertake to add to these natural and just advantages artificial distinctions, to grant titles, gratuities, and exclusive privileges, to make the rich richer, and the potent more powerful, the humble members of the society—the farmers, mechanics, and laborers—who have neither the time nor the means of securing like favors to themselves, have a right to complain of the injustice of their Government.

Daniel Webster hastily prepared a brilliant and eloquent reply to Jackson's message—"a state paper," he said, "which finds no topic too exciting for its use, no passion too inflammable for its address and its solicitation." He expressed his bewilderment that "at the very moment of almost unparalleled general prosperity, there appears an unaccountable disposition to destroy the most useful and most approved institutions of the government." If Jackson's principles were followed, he solemnly warned, the Constitution would not survive "to its fiftieth year."

Biddle himself thought so little of Jackson's "manifesto of anarchy" that he had it circulated as pro-Bank propaganda. But Jackson swept the election with 687,000 votes to Clay's 530,000. In the electoral college it was Jackson by 219 to 49. Jackson, moreover, interpreted his triumph as a mandate to press on with his war against Biddle's "Hydra of corruption."

In this war Jackson had the often-wavering support of various groups in the country. In the early stages, he held the allegiance of old Bank enemies, substantial state bankers who had fought Biddle's unwelcome competition. More lasting in their support were the so-called "wild-cat bankers" of the West and the Southwest whose land-speculator clients were always demanding bigger and longer-term loans. A third group came to be represented by the "Locofocos" of New York, who got their name from the "locofoco" matches they used when party "regulars" shut off the lights after losing control of a Democratic meeting to these "radicals." The Locofocos were hard-money, middle-class business and professional men who opposed the Bank as they opposed all monopolies that seemed to block business opportunity.

As the war on the Bank grew warmer, the country's business leaders in all sections rallied to Biddle, while the ranks of the Jacksonians became strained. Jackson triumphed. But his victory was to prove very costly to the country as a whole.

Jackson's opening shot in the renewed battle with Biddle was to order the removal of government deposits from the Bank's branches on the grounds that Biddle's policies no longer insured the safety of the public's funds. He then ordered that these deposits and all new government revenue be placed in selected state institutions that became known as Jackson's "pet banks." These orders were more easily issued than carried out. The Secretary of the Treasury alone had the power to withdraw government deposits, and Jackson's Secretary was a friend of the Bank. Such obstacles did not long deter "Old Hickory." He fired two secretaries of the Treasury until he found in Roger B. Taney of Maryland the man who would do his bidding. Late in 1833 Taney began the removal of the deposits, and by the end of the year 23 state banks had been named to receive federal funds.

Even though his bid for a new charter had been beaten, Biddle did not take this new assault on his Bank with complacency. If the Bank was to be forced to close, it must begin to call in its loans and restrict its new business. Soon after the federal deposits had been removed, therefore, Biddle embarked on this policy with zeal. His object was to create a business panic so widespread that public opinion would force Jackson to reverse his stand on the charter. For some months in 1833 and 1834, a panic indeed seemed imminent. But once again Biddle miscalculated the political effects. To petitioners who began to press Jackson for help, the President insistently replied, "Go to Nicholas Biddle." In time, even segments of the business community appealed to Biddle to relent, and finally he gave in.

Relief over Biddle's capitulation promptly turned the near panic into a soaring boom, especially in the South and West where land was most in demand. The boom was fostered by the inflationary practices of the state banks which depended on federal deposits as reserves

422

for heavy speculative loans. By throwing millions of acres of public land on the market at this time, the administration further stimulated speculation.

The land boom caused an immediate demand for internal improvements, accompanied by reckless investments in turnpikes, canals, and railroads. Many of these projects were financed in part by foreign capitalists who would not risk their money in private American corporations but were willing to purchase state bonds, backed by state revenues, which many states now issued to support internal improvement schemes. The optimistic state programs were spurred on in the summer of 1836 when it became clear that the federal government was about to distribute to the states some of the $35 million Treasury surplus that had accumulated from tariff revenues and the sale of public lands. A measure sponsored by Henry Clay, and passed in June 1836, provided that all money in excess of $5 million in the Treasury on January 1, 1837, was to be apportioned during the year among the states in accordance with population. The measure passed in time to sustain the boom, but the surplus disappeared before payments could be completed. What dissipated the surplus was the collapse of the boom itself. This was speeded by another government measure, Jackson's "Specie Circular."

Like many of his supporters, Andrew Jackson was a hard-money man, greatly in favor of economic expansion yet fearful of speculation and debt. With speculation and debt rampant, on July 11, 1836, he issued his famous Circular, which required that all land purchased from the federal government after August 15 be paid for in silver or gold. Settlers, as distinguished from speculators, were permitted to use bank notes for an additional four months, provided their purchases were less than 320 acres.

This drastic reversal of policy abruptly checked land sales and sent prices plunging. In the spring of 1837, after Jackson had left office, stock and commodity prices also broke, and soon the Panic of 1837 was on in earnest.

Like other panics, that of 1837 was worldwide and had worldwide as well as American causes and effects. Especially hard hit were British investors in American securities and British banks engaged in financing American trade, mainly trade in cotton. Their calls on American merchants forced many to the wall.

The failure of Biddle's Bank, which had been operating since 1836 under a Pennsylvania charter, helped deepen the depression. After suspending activities twice, beginning in the fall of 1839, the Bank was finally turned over to trustees for liquidation in 1841. Biddle was charged with fraud but subsequently acquitted. In 1844, at the age of 58, he died a broken man, "waylaid and led astray by prosperity," as John Quincy Adams said after a visit with him, the victim not merely of his own arrogance, but of the bitterness of American politics and the curious state of American financial thought.

## IV  *Jackson's Legacy*

### THE CONCEPT OF THE PRESIDENCY

When the voters went to the polls in 1836 to choose Jackson's successor, the boom was still in full swing, and the surface prosperity helped sustain "Old Hickory's" popularity. He had checked nullification, had adopted a democratic and popular position in the Bank war, and had conducted foreign policy with notable success. The principal complaint against him was that of "executive usurpation," as his enemies called it. The fact that the Democratic candidate in 1836 was Jackson's handpicked heir, "Little Van," made the charge of autocracy the more telling.

No less an authority on the Constitution and the office of the Chief Executive than E. S. Corwin remarks that Jackson's Presidency was "no mere revival of the office—it was a remaking of it." In his own day, Henry Clay most bitterly attacked the "revolution, hitherto bloodless," as he told the Senate in December 1833, "but rapidly tending toward . . . the concentration of all power in the hands of one man." Clay and his friends were most deeply mortified by Jackson's manipulation of the power of appointment, in arrogant disregard of the Senate's rightful role. He had far exceeded presidential prerogatives, in their eyes, by requiring a Secretary of the Treasury to remove the government's deposits from Biddle's Bank to the "pet banks."

In 1834, at Clay's instigation, the Senate gave Jackson a taste of his own medicine by adopting, 26 to 20, the following unprecedented resolution:

*Resolved,* That the President, in the late Executive proceedings in relation to the public revenue, has assumed upon himself authority and power not conferred by the Constitution and laws, but in derogation of both.

Jackson responded promptly with an eloquent "Protest," which the Senate refused to enter in the journal of its proceedings. On their part, Jackson's supporters in the Senate waged a ceaseless battle for almost three years to have the censure resolution expunged from the record, and at last, in January 1837, they had their way. But in the process of the debate, Clay expressed the resentment of many of his fellow senators over what they regarded as Jackson's aggrandizement of his rights.

The Senate has no army, no navy, no patronage, no lucrative offices, nor glittering honors to bestow. Around us there is no swarm of greedy expectants, rendering us homage, anticipating our wishes, and ready to execute our commands. How is it with the President? Is he powerless? He is felt from one extremity to the other of this republic. By means of principles which he has introduced, and innovations which he has made in our institutions, alas! but too much countenanced by Congress and a confiding people, he exercises uncontrolled the power of the state. In one hand he holds the purse and in the other brandishes the sword of the country! Myriads of dependents and partisans scattered over the land are ever ready to sing hosannahs to him and to laud to the

skies whatever he does. He has swept over the government like a tropical tornado.

Others voiced the same judgment. "I look upon Jackson," wrote Chancellor Kent of New York, "as a detestable, ignorant, reckless, vain and malignant tyrant. . . . This American elective monarchy frightens me. The experiment, with its foundations laid on universal suffrage and our unfettered press, is of too violent a nature for our excitable people." In the Senate, Webster roared out this protest: "The President carries on the government; all the rest are sub-contractors. . . . A Briareus

*The Senate censure resolution of Jackson passed at Clay's instigation was a dramatic test of presidential versus senatorial power. Clay's success in preventing the recording of Jackson's protest inspired this contemporary cartoon, called "Symptoms of a Locked Jaw." (Courtesy of the New-York Historical Society, New York City.)*

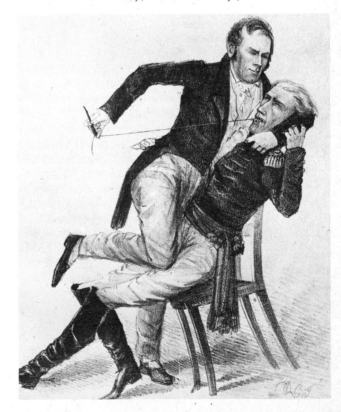

424

sits at the centre of our system, and with his hundred hands touches everything, controls everything." * The sentiments were exaggerated, but the transformation they complained of had, in fact, occurred.

### VAN BUREN'S ELECTION

Clay's theme became the keynote of the new Whig party, inheritors of National Republicanism, in the campaign against Van Buren. Consistent with this theme was the makeup of the Whig coalition—Jackson-haters from all sections of the country. The Whig party attracted old Adams men in New England, Clay men in the West, Anti-Masons in the Middle States, and disgruntled Democrats of Calhoun's stamp in the South. The party had money, brains, a lively press, and popular leaders. Its presidential strategy for 1836, however, was dictated by its apparent weakness in its first campaign, the congressional elections of 1834, when the Democrats captured 145 seats in the House to the Whigs' 98.

Realizing that they could not beat Jackson's chosen successor in 1836 if they entered into the usual two-sided contest, the Whigs decided to run a number of strong candidates who would appeal to different sections of the country: Webster to New England; William Henry Harrison of Ohio to the Middle States and the West; Judge Hugh L. White to Tennessee. South Carolina, where the presidential electors were still chosen by the state legislature, named the anti-Jacksonite Willie P. Mangum. The Whigs hoped to duplicate the situation of 1824, when the electoral votes were so divided that the election had been thrown into the House of Representatives. But Van Buren won out by a narrow margin. He received 762,000 votes to a total of 735,000

---

* Briareus, in Greek mythology, was one of the first children borne by Mother Earth after she emerged from Chaos—a semi-human giant of immense power with a hundred hands. Such allusions were not obscure to the college-educated men of Webster's generation.

for all his opponents combined. In the electoral college, Van Buren got 170 votes, Harrison 73, and the rest trailed. Harrison had shown enough popular appeal to make him a likely candidate for 1840.

### DEPRESSION PANACEAS

The problems facing Van Buren when he took office in March 1837 quickly became formidable. Financial panic was in full swing by May. Banks closed, prices of food and other necessities soared, factories shut down, and severe unemployment with all its attendant miseries gripped the North. Merchants and business leaders besieged Van Buren with petitions to relieve the distress by withdrawing Jackson's Specie Circular, which, they claimed, "had produced a wider desolation" than the cholera epidemic "which depopulated our streets." Conditions were just as bad in the South, where land and slaves fell sharply in value. Eventually the expansive West again became the worst sufferer of all.

Van Buren received plenty of conflicting advice on how to end the economic crisis. Biddle, for example, hinted that now was the time to restore the Bank of the United States. The conservative wing among the Democrats urged the President to recall the Specie Circular but to continue the state-bank system. The Locofocos proposed that the government go even farther than the Circular in its hard-money crusade. They also demanded that it remove public funds from all banks, so that United States fiscal operations might no longer be "embarrassed by the doings of speculators."

Van Buren favored the Locofoco approach to banks and throughout his administration sought to create an "Independent Treasury" system under which government specie and other funds would be placed in subtreasuries around the country and used to pay obligations in cash. The first Independent Treasury bill was presented in September 1837 to Congress, where it got a cool reception not only from

Whigs but from Democrats sympathetic to state-banking interests. Van Buren persisted until, in 1840, significant shifts having been made in the Democratic alignment, an Independent Treasury Act squeaked through. The administration margin was supplied by Calhoun and his southern followers who had returned to the Democratic fold from the Whig party to which Calhoun's feud with Jackson had driven them. This "divorce of bank and state" marked the peak of Locofoco hard-money influence in the Democratic party.

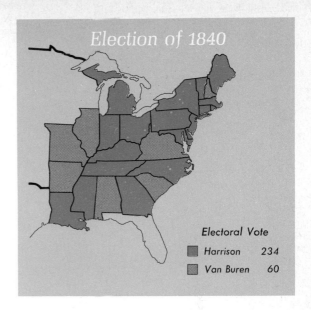

Election of 1840

Electoral Vote
Harrison 234
Van Buren 60

### TIPPECANOE AND TYLER TOO

As the election of 1840 drew near, Whig leaders scented victory. Clay had been defeated on the Bank issue in 1832 and had been by-passed in 1836 for strategic reasons; but now he hoped that the elusive prize would be his. This time, however, he failed to receive the support of Webster, who looked upon him as a rival. Having little hope of getting the nomination himself, Webster decided early in 1839 that the Whigs' only chance of victory lay with Harrison of Ohio, who had run so well in 1836, and he threw his influence on the side of the military hero. In the Whig convention at Harrisburg, Webster's supporters and the New Yorkers prevented Clay from turning his early plurality into a majority, and Harrison gained the nomination.

Though he called himself a "clod-hopper," Harrison was a promising candidate. His "victory" over Tecumseh at the Battle of Tippecanoe all of 30 years earlier (see p. 344)—transformed almost beyond recognition by the Whigs—his Virginia ancestry and western connections, and the vagueness of his political sentiments, all recommended him to the astute New York boss, Thurlow Weed. The selection of Harrison and his running-mate, John Tyler of Virginia, who it was hoped would strenghten the Whigs in the South, gave concrete expression to Weed's conviction that principles did not win elections. Granted, the

people could not be whipped into enthusiasm over Biddle's Bank, but they might respond to songs and slogans, ballyhoo and political revivalism.

Van Buren, again the Democratic standard-bearer, had already fallen from public favor as a result of the hard times, and the Whigs gleefully chanted their election slogan:

Little Van's policy, fifty cents a day and French soup;
Harrison's policy, two dollars a day and roast beef.

Whig orators regaled the voters with reports of a perfumed President living in undemocratic luxury at the taxpayers' expense. One campaign document, on the "Royal Splendor of the President's Palace," pictured Van Buren as a slothful and effeminate oriental potentate sampling French cookery from golden plates and resting after the turtle soup on a "Turkish divan." In contrast to this luxury, the Whigs pointed to the stern simplicity of "Old Tippecanoe." When a Baltimore newspaper taunted the Whigs by saying that Harrison would be perfectly satisfied with a log cabin and a good supply of cider, his managers capitalized on the slur and picked up the log cabin as a party symbol. "It tells of virtues," Thurlow Weed

425

*A Currier print of General Harrison at Tippe-canoe, published at the time of his campaign for the Presidency, 1840. His men are trying in vain to restrain him from riding up to the point of attack. (Courtesy Kenneth M. Newman, The Old Print Shop, N.Y.C.)*

declared, "that dwell in obscurity, of the privations of the poor, of toil and danger." The log cabin, this "emblem of simplicity," was far removed from Harrison's gentlemanly origins and habits of living, but the symbol helped to elect him. His popular majority was nearly 140,000 out of the 2,411,000 votes cast, and he won 234 electoral votes to Van Buren's 60.

The Whigs, by adopting the same tactics the Jacksonians had used against Adams in 1828, and by temporarily laying aside party and sectional feuds, had succeeded in electing their candidate. But at base they remained as divided as before. The central strength of the Whig party lay in a minority of conservatives

who were suspicious of unfettered democracy and of the foreign-born and the working classes. In order to succeed politically, however, these conservatives realized they had to lure into their party ranks some of the very people they distrusted. This they succeeded in doing extraordinarily well. Indeed, more significant than Harrison's margin of victory, or even his election, in 1840 was the size of the vote—40 per cent (far higher than the rate of population growth) above that in Jackson's day. Tens of thousands of new voters had become eligible under liberalized franchise laws; but more important was the extraordinary 78 per cent of the eligible voters that had turned out, compared to a maximum of 56 per cent in "Old Hickory's" campaigns. The persistence of the depression had presented a clear issue on which rival groups now arrayed under Democratic or Whig banners could rally their partisans. The new methods of campaigning (see p. 405) helped bring party appeals to the hearts and minds of the electorate.

Unfortunately for the Whigs, Harrison died after but one month in office. During that month he had humbly accepted the guidance of Webster and Clay. Of Clay, a New York newspaper correspondent had this to say at the time: "He predominates over the Whig Party with despotic sway. Old Hickory himself never lorded it over his followers with authority more undisputed, or more supreme." No doubt Clay hoped that John Tyler, on becoming President, would be as pliable as Harrison had promised to be, and that the real power of the administration would rest safe in his own hands. But Tyler, with the example of Jackson before him, was to be no cipher.

Tyler was a Whig only because he had followed Calhoun out of the Democratic party after the break with Jackson. A veteran of the Virginia legislature and of both houses of Congress, he had had many opportunities in the past to disclose his strong antitariff views, his antagonism to Biddle's Bank, his distaste for federal aid to internal improvements. Beyond these issues, he sided with Calhoun on nullification. The Whigs had named him for the Vice-presidency in order to attract southern anti-Jackson support; they paid dearly when this state-rights enthusiast became President under their banner.

On one matter Clay and Tyler were able to agree: Congress passed and the President signed in 1841 a measure repealing Van Buren's Independent Treasury Act. But when Clay pushed farther, he and his colleagues were unceremoniously rebuffed. In August 1841 Congress actually passed a bill creating a new national bank. When Tyler returned it with a firm veto, the Whigs, in September, adopted a new bank bill designed to satisfy Tyler's constitutional scruples. When Tyler vetoed this bill too, about 50 Whig congressmen met in caucus and read Tyler out of the party. Moreover, with the exception of Secretary of State Webster, who was busy with the negotiations that eventually led to the Webster-Ashburton Treaty (see p. 471), all the Cabinet members resigned. Tyler promptly named a new Cabinet which was southern, with two exceptions. Webster himself resigned in 1843 when his diplomatic work was done, and after a brief interval was replaced by Calhoun—evidence of the South Carolinian's unquestioned return to the Democratic party and confirmation of the party's becoming the standard-bearer of the slaveocracy.

### PRE-EMPTION: A FRONTIER TRIUMPH

Just before the Cabinet resigned, Tyler put his signature to a measure that marked a great victory for the West in the field of public-land policy. This was the Pre-emption Act of Sep-

tember 1841, adopted with bipartisan support.

Pre-emption meant that a settler who took up government land without authorization should have first chance to buy his land at the minimum price. Otherwise he would have to bid for his "own" land at competitive prices or be evicted from it when it was bought by others. During the 1830s pre-emption had been voted for short periods of time. Now it was enacted for an unlimited period. The principal provision of the Act of 1841 permitted any head of a family or single male adult—being a citizen or an alien having declared his intention of becoming a citizen—to pre-empt 160 acres of public land and then to pay the minimum price ($1.25 an acre) when the land was officially opened to settlement. Other provisions stated that 500,000 acres be given to each new state to support the construction of internal improvements; that 10 per cent of the revenues obtained from selling federal land were to be returned to the state in whose boundaries the land lay; that the rest of such revenues be distributed among the states in proportion to their representation in Congress. Another provision was included to meet the demands of southerners who feared that depletion of the Treasury would provide a good argument for the supporters of a high tariff: If tariff rates should ever exceed 20 per cent, the distribution of federal land revenues to the states was to cease. In August 1842 a tariff was enacted placing duties above the 20 per cent level and it explicitly repealed the distribution part of the Pre-emption Act. But pre-emption itself survived, the major triumph for the frontier until the Homestead Act of 1862 (see p. 618).

427

428

# READINGS

The spread of democratic political practices is best traced in Volume II of M. Ostrogorski, *Democracy and the Organization of Political Parties* (2 vols., 1902). Chilton Williamson, *American Suffrage, from Property to Democracy 1760–1860* (1960), provides a reliable analysis. On the free Negro and the franchise, see L.F. Litwack, *North of Slavery, The Negro in the Free States 1790–1860* (1961). Useful state studies include A.B. Darling, *Political Changes in Massachusetts 1824–1848* (1925); D.R. Fox, *The Decline of Aristocracy in the Politics of New York* (1919); and R.P. McCormick, *The History of Voting in New Jersey: A Study of the Development of Election Machinery 1664–1911* (1953). L.D. White, *The Jacksonians: A Study in Administrative History 1829–1861* (1954), is outstanding on the "spoils system" and its effects. P.P. Van Riper, *History of the United States Civil Service* (1958), is a good general account. On the types of men appointed to high office in the early republic, see S.H. Aronson, *Status and Kinship in the Higher Civil Service* (1964).

W.E. Binkley, *American Political Parties: Their Natural History* (1943), affords a good general introduction. R.P. McCormick, *The Second American Party System, Party Formation in the Jacksonian Era* (1966), clarifies a complicated subject. On particular parties other than Jackson's, the following are recommended: Charles McCarthy, *The Anti-Masonic Party* (1902); E.M. Carroll, *Origins of the Whig Party* (1925); and A.C. Cole, *The Whig Party in the South* (1913). C.S. Sydnor, *The Development of Southern Sectionalism 1819–1848* (1948), is excellent on nullification and other issues.

George Dangerfield, *The Era of Good Feelings* (1952) and *The Awakening of American Nationalism 1815–1828* (1965), afford well-written analyses of American politics leading up to the election of Jackson. Shaw Livermore, Jr., *The Twilight of Federalism: The Disintegration of the Federalist Party 1815–1830* (1962), stresses the survival of Federalist ideas and alignments despite the "disintegration." S.F. Bemis, *John Quincy Adams and the Union* (1956), is the standard work on the administration of the sixth President. A scholarly introduction to the organization of the Jacksonian party in the early 1820s is H.R. Stevens, *The Early Jackson Party in Ohio* (1957). R.V. Remini, *Martin Van Buren and the Making of the Democratic Party* (1959), is illuminating on New York's role. Remini's *The Election of Andrew Jackson* (1963) is the standard work.

F.J. Turner, *The United States 1830–1850* (1935), provides a classic introduction to Jacksonian democracy and its aftermath. See also Turner, *Rise of the New West 1819–1829* (1906). G.G. Van Deusen, *The Jacksonian Era 1828–1848* (1959), is a modern survey. The following offer varied points of view on Jacksonian democracy: E.C. Rozwenc, ed., *Meaning of Jacksonian Democracy* (1963); Arthur Schlesinger, Jr., *The Age of Jackson* (1945); Joseph Dorfman, *The Economic Mind in American Civilization 1606–1865* (2 vols., 1946); Richard Hofstadter, *The American Political Tradition* (1948); J.W. Ward, *Andrew Jackson, Symbol for an Age* (1955); Marvin Meyers, *The Jacksonian Persuasion: Politics and Belief* (1957); and Lee Benson, *The Concept of Jacksonian Democracy, New York as a Test Case* (1961).

Marquis James, *The Life of Andrew Jackson* (1938), is excellent reading. See also J.S. Bassett, *The Life of Andrew Jackson* (2 vols., 1925). Most useful on Van Buren besides Remini, above, is Holmes Alexander, *The American Talleyrand* (1935). J.C. Fitzpatrick, ed., *The Autobiography of Martin Van Bureau* (1920), tells what Van Buren wished to be told. Clement Eaton, *Henry Clay and the Art of American Politics* (1957), is sound and short. Carl Schurz, *Life of Henry Clay* (2 vols., 1887), remains valuable. C.M. Fuess, *Daniel Webster* (2 vols., 1930), is standard. The short biography, R.N. Current, *Daniel Webster and the Rise of National Conservatism* (1955), may also be recommended. C.M. Wiltse, *John C. Calhoun, Nullifier 1829–1839* (1949), is good on the man and his thought. This work may be supplemented by A.O. Spain, *The Political Theory of John C. Calhoun* (1951). W.W. Freehling, *Prelude to Civil War* (1966), provides the most intensive study of, in the words of its subtitle, "The Nullification Controversy in South Carolina 1816–1836." T.H. Benton, *Thirty Years' View* (2 vols., 1854–1856), offers an illuminating inside account. W.N. Chambers, *Old Bullion Benton, Senator from the New West* (1956), is a substantial biography. O.P. Chitwood, *John Tyler: Champion of the Old South* (1939), and Robert Seager II, *And Tyler Too* (1963), are best on this President.

On land and Indian policy, see R.G. Wellington, *The Political and National Influence of the Public Lands 1826–1842* (1914); Grant Foreman, *Indian Removal, The Emigration of the Five Civilized Tribes of Indians* (1932); Angie Debo, *The Road to Disappearance* (1941); and F.P. Prucha, *American Indian Policy in the Formative Years: The Indian Trade and Intercourse Acts 1790–1834* (1962).

A good short introduction to the Bank War (which is also treated in virtually all the Jacksonian books cited above), is G.R. Taylor, ed., *Jackson versus Biddle* (1949). Bray Hammond, *Banks and Politics in America: From the Revolution to the Civil War* (1957), is the most elaborate study. Volume 1 of Fritz Redlich, *The Molding of American Banking, Men and Ideas* (2 vols., 1947, 1951), is full of insight. T.P. Govan, *Nicholas Biddle, Nationalist and Public Banker 1786–1844* (1959), and R.C. McGrane, ed., *The Correspondence of Nicholas Biddle Dealing with National Affairs 1807–1844* (1919), give Biddle's side. On the Bank itself see R.C.H. Catterall, *The Second Bank of the United States* (1903), and W.B. Smith, *Economic Aspects of the Second Bank of the United States* (1953). R.C. McGrane, *The Panic of 1837* (1924), and W.B. Smith and A.H. Cole, *Fluctuations in American Business 1790–1860* (1935), are illuminating on the end of the boom.

# FOURTEEN

Reflecting on "Fenimore Cooper's White Novels" in his book, *Studies in Classic American Literature,* the English writer D. H. Lawrence asked the telltale question, "Can you make a land virgin by killing off its aborigines?" Toward the close of the nineteenth century, Americans were to grow less and less certain of the answer to this question; but the generation that came to manhood in the Age of Jackson had few if any doubts. Its greatest spokesmen salved the national conscience. Ours, said Emerson, "is a country of beginnings, of projects, of vast designs and expectations. It has no past; all has an onward and prospective look." "We," said Melville, "are the pioneers of the world; the advance guard sent on through the wilderness of untried things, to break a new path in the New World that is ours. In our youth is our strength; in our inexperience our wisdom."

Americans in this self-conscious age took ever greater pride in distinguishing their "system," as they came to call it—open, expansive, an Eden for the world's oppressed—from the closed system of declining Europe. And even before they had fulfilled what they long believed to be their rightful "destiny" to occupy the whole continental range from ocean to ocean (see Chapter Fifteen), their pretensions worked on Europe's fears. As early as 1824, following the bold assertions of the Monroe Doctrine (p. 362), no less a personage than Prince Metternich of Austria, the reigning head of the Holy Alliance formed to repress Europe's own republican tendencies, pointed the finger at the formidable new foe:

These United States of America, which we have seen arise and grow, and which during their too short youth already meditated projects which they dared not then avow, have suddenly

# AMERICA
# IN FERMENT

left a sphere too narrow for their ambition. . . . In their indecent declarations they have cast blame and scorn on the institutions of Europe most worthy of respect. . . . In fostering revolutions wherever they show themselves, in regretting those which have failed, in extending a helping hand to those which seem to prosper, they lend new strength to the apostles of sedition and reanimate the courage of every conspirator.

And yet questions beyond that posed by D. H. Lawrence remained to prod an ambitious people. Granted the virginity of the land and the rightness of their possession of it, what would Americans make of their wealth? And what would they make of their power? Would they succeed, as Horace Mann put it in 1842, in "converting material wealth into spiritual well-being"? The question of the character of the civilization which was to encompass the globe, if Americans had their way, kept the nation, and not merely its intellectuals, artists, and reformers, in continuous ferment.

## 1 *The American Temperament*

### A RESTLESS SOCIETY

All observers agreed that Americans worked harder, ate faster, moved around more, and

relaxed less than Europeans. In America, Tocqueville wrote in 1835,

a man builds a house in which to spend his old age, and he sells it before the roof is on, . . . he brings a field into tillage, and leaves other men to gather the crop, he embraces a profession and gives it up, he settles in a place, which he soon afterwards leaves, to carry his changeable longings elsewhere.

Nothing seemed finished in America. "Improvement," both personal and collective, was a national preoccupation. People were on the move, in transit, going from somewhere to somewhere. The symbol of the young republic might have been the locomotive that never ceased its labors, or the steamboat that moved up and down the rivers—and frequently blew up.

### AN OPTIMISTIC SOCIETY

In 1823 an anonymous writer listed some of the reasons for America's glorious prospects: "an extensive seacoast, abundantly provided with capacious ports and harbors"; "magnificent rivers" cutting across the country in every direction and providing the means for a "lucrative internal trade"; a tremendous water-power potential; "every variety of soil and climate,"

431

432

which made for self-sufficiency; inexhaustible supplies of timber, coal, iron, lead, and copper; "a capacity for raising cotton to supply the demand of the whole world"; a population "active, energetic, enterprising, and ingenious"; the freest, most liberal, and most cheaply administered government in the world; an insignificant public debt and light taxes; the absence of a nobility, and a citizenry free and independent; "abundant room for all the superfluous population of Europe."

America, set aside for a heavenly experiment, now looked forward to a golden age. In the words of one contemporary (1828):

A moral influence is withdrawing their subjects from the old and worn out governments of Europe and hurrying them across the Atlantic, to participate in the renovated youth of the new republic of the west; an influence which, like that of nature, is universal, and without pause or relaxation.

Cities burgeoned from squalid settlements, and factories hummed (as the boosters tiresomely repeated) where late "the whoop of the wild inhabitants" had sounded in the woods. Faith in the American future had actually sprung up before the Revolution, but after 1820 all signs seemed to confirm the prospects of "indefinite perfectibility." Economically, politically, and culturally, America prepared herself for the "golden day."

### A COMMERCIAL SOCIETY

American society was primarily a business society.

It will require but little reflection to satisfy us [wrote a spokesman for the mercantile and banking interests in 1838] that the resources of this country are controlled chiefly by the class which, in our own peculiar phraseology, we term "the business community"—embracing all those who are engaged in the great occupation of buying, selling, exchanging, importing and exporting merchandise, and including the banker, the broker, and under-writer.

Every American, declared the editor of a well-known commercial periodical, was in some sense a trader. The physician traded his "benevolent care," the lawyer his "ingenious tongue," the clergyman "his prayers." One principle motivated the commercial classes, another explained, a principle that enabled them to enrich the country as well as themselves:

Whether it be called avarice or the love of money, or the desire of gain, or the lust of wealth, or whether it be softened to the ear under the more guarded terms, prudence, natural affection, diligence in business, or the conscientious improvement of time and talents— it is still money-making which constitutes the great business of our people—it is the use of money which controls and regulates everything.

But even America's severest critics usually agreed that there was nothing mean-spirited or sordid, indeed that there was something large and even heroic, in this pursuit of wealth. Never was there to be greater opportunity for self-made men in America; and those who prospered often assumed the responsibilities that went with success. Public opinion regarded money as an "engine" of benevolence as well as a good in itself. Many merchants, like the public-spirited Abbott Lawrence of Boston, shared this view and supported humanitarian and cultural enterprises.

### AN IDEALISTIC SOCIETY

In spite of their insistence on the practical and the useful, even those Americans most triumphant in business competition felt the spiritual leavening of their conquests. In February 1853, his fortune having soared to $11 million, Cornelius Vanderbilt wrote to his friend, Hamilton Fish: "I have a little pride as an American to sail over the waters of England and France, up the Baltic and through the Mediterranean, without a reflection of any kind that it is a voyage for gain." When, later that year, "old Cornele" set out in his magnificent steamer, *North Star* (see p. 434), con-

*Joseph Yeager's aquatint of a procession of victuallers celebrating the slaughter of a special group of blue-ribbon cattle on March 15, 1821. The numbers, manners, and dress of the spectators gathered at the corner of Fourth and Chestnut Streets, Philadelphia, or leaning out of the sturdy houses to observe the parade, complete with flags and floats, give vivid evidence of the vigorous development of urban America at this time. (Philadelphia Museum of Art.)*

structed in the most extravagant way so "as to be a credit to our *Yankee Land,*" his fellow tycoon, James Gordon Bennett of the New York *Herald,* hailed the expedition. "Although it is solely a personal matter," Bennett said, "it partakes somewhat of a national character," one calculated to display "the refinement of those whose enterprise, industry and genius have placed them at the head of the social scale" solely through their own efforts.

Lesser Americans, with the world still to conquer, were themselves susceptible to every sort of evangelical appeal. This was pre-eminently the age of "Causes" to hasten on the new world acoming—of Hungarian independence, missionary crusades to Pacific islands and Africa and Asia, dietary panaceas, abolitionism, new religions and cults, pseudo-science, séances and exhibitions. Tocqueville found a "fanatical and almost wild spiritualism" rampant in America, and surmised that religious enthusiasm was probably natural in a society "exclusively bent upon the pursuit of material objects." A people who made so great a virtue of common sense, Tocqueville believed, were most prone to "burst the bonds of matter by which they are restrained" and "soar impetuously towards Heaven."

433

*Vanderbilt's* North Star, *length 278 feet, beam 38 feet, displacement 2500 tons—"a vessel," said the New York* Illustrated News, *"large enough to carry the armament of a British seventy-four." John Overton Choules, the Baptist pastor taken on to conduct religious exercises, wrote later: "There was discipline on board that ship, sir. Each man attended to his own business. The Commodore did the swearing and I did the praying. So we never disagreed." (The Granger Collection.)*

### A VIOLENT SOCIETY

Critics of American society had been quick to include the American penchant for the gun and the bowie knife in their canards. Between 1830 and 1860, they could find ample evidence for their charges in the American press and in popular literature. It was to be expected that violence would flourish under frontier conditions. Men who lived beyond the reach or protection of law were all potential criminals or victims, and the stories from the hinterlands (real or invented) told of stabbings and shootings, of ambuscades, river piracy, and deadly feuds. But by the 1840s, urban violence in the East was prevalent enough to attract the notice of reformers,

writers, and journalists. The slums of New York, Boston, and Philadelphia provided a lurid background for crimes that seemed to justify Jefferson's bias against cities as the boils and carbuncles on the body politic.

Prostitutes, thieves, and murderers might be explained, if not condoned, as the inevitable consequence of human wickedness or social injustice, but tolerance for lynch law did not meet with a comparable disapproval in the regions where it flourished. Whether lynchings or mobbings occurred in northern cities or in the still frontier-like areas of the South, the animus behind them was identical. "The victim," as David Brion Davis says, "was an alienated man, often the representative of a scapegoat group whose very existence infuriated a mob of righteous men." Between 1830 and 1860, groups of determined "regulators," sometimes including the most respectable men, inspired or enacted these social housecleanings without benefit of law. Undeterred by what one apologist of mob violence called the "sickish sensibility of mawkish philanthropy," they whipped, burned, tarred, exiled, or killed those whom they deemed vicious or subversive. Gamblers, Mormons, abolitionists, Roman Catholics, and Negroes among others during this ebullient period became the targets of these "righteous men."

## DEMOCRACY AND EQUALITY

In our government [declared an orator in 1840], we recognize only individuals, at least among whites; and in social life, the constant effort to do away with the castes produced by difference of fortune, education, and taste. The motto upon the flag of America should be "Every man for himself." Such is the spirit of our land, as seen in our institutions, in our literature, in our religious condition, in our political contests.

Democracy meant (to many, if not to all) social as well as political equality. To paraphrase Tocqueville again, men pounced "upon equality as booty" and clung to it "as some precious treasure."

Freedom-hungry immigrants, who were particularly impressed by American equalitarianism, swelled the ranks of democracy—to the traditional indignation of conservatives who felt that American privileges should not be granted so promiscuously. Here is a new citizen writing to his German friends in the late 1830s:

Our President walks across the street the same as I do—no Royal Highness or Majesty would ever do that. They do not even call him "Mister," since the word mister is never used in connection with a title in the English language. When talking to the President, you say simply: "How are you, President?" and he answers; "Thank you, how are you?"

Technically this newcomer was inaccurate, but spiritually he was already an American.

Yet even as patriots gave lip-service to equality, the increase in the number of factory workers as the industrial revolution got under way, and the growth of an urban population, weakened republican simplicity and intensified social distinctions. Although it is impossible to chart the fine gradations of rank and repute, successful planters, business leaders, bankers and lawyers still occupied the top rungs of society. Clergymen, physicians, and teachers, too, if they were patronized by the influential, might claim similar high standing. Below this privileged group ranged the rest of the white citizenry, with subtle distinctions among themselves.

Yet no fixed and artificial barriers prevented the mechanic or the clerk or the farmer—referred to in the press as the "bone and sinew" of the Republic—from rising rapidly. No class outside the South demanded special respect from another, and men of different degrees mingled indiscriminately in business and travel. Almost everyone had some stake in society, and despite the fears of conservatives the American people embarked on no wildly revolutionary course. Wrapped up in his daily affairs, and schooled to accept the ideas and prejudices of the majority, the citizen usually abided by the "empty phantom of public opinion," which was "strong enough to chill innovators and to keep them silent and at a respectful distance."

## INDIVIDUALISM AND COOPERATION

Much has been made, and correctly, of the pre-Civil War era as the heyday of individualism, of the self-propelled hero. But this was also a time of cooperation, of voluntary, not coercive "association." The achievements of the single man have come to overshadow the accomplishments of the group in American folklore, but when Tocqueville visited America he was immensely impressed by the fact that "the most democratic country on the face of the earth . . . carried to the highest perfection the art of pursuing in common the object of their common desires."

For the American to pool resources, both material and intellectual, and to throw in his lot with the community in which he worked and lived, simply seemed the most sensible thing to do at the time. A society of "lone wolves" would not have survived. Businessmen who joined together in companies in all the major lines of enterprise, very often to protect themselves against the competition of

436

foreign merchants, well understood this. Citizens hungry for culture set up libraries, art associations, and mutual improvement clubs, and immigrants formed societies with their fellow countrymen. Charitable, reform, fraternal, and benefit organizations sprang up naturally in a democracy where there was no ruling class with a tradition of social responsibility to supervise civic undertakings. "Many can accomplish what one cannot," said one organizer, defending his trespassing on individualism. But he was quick to add this qualification: "We mean to receive as much as we give, and we ask others to join us on that principle."

### SECTARIAN RIVALRY AND CENTRALIZING TENDENCIES

But if Americans poured their energies into countless organizations pulling in many directions at once, what was it, if anything, that held their society together? Many observers during the 1830s and 1840s were disturbed by the diffuseness of American activity, by the "lack of a common skeleton." Emerson, in 1847, noted America's "immense resources," but he was also struck by America's "village littleness." America, he concluded, "is great strength on a basis of weakness."

A major weakness in a country of churches was sectarian rivalry. Americans seemed to be the most religious of peoples and yet the one most afflicted by denominational discord. The United States had always provided a fertile soil for new sects, but in the 1830s and 1840s the splintering of dissenting churches, with each group claiming possession of the authentic faith, reached a peak of frequency and ferocity. The Baptists and Methodists, the fastest-growing denominations of the day, were most susceptible to schisms, but new cults sprang up everywhere and the competition for the souls of immigrants pouring into the Mississippi Valley was frequently unchristian. Doctrinal differences created a good deal of friction. Some denominations, moreover,

considered themselves socially superior to others, even in the sight of God, and such false pride only deepened religious conflict. Presbyterians, Congregationalists, Episcopalians, and Unitarians differed in theology and in church organization, but they all drew their membership from the well-to-do. Baptists, Methodists, Campbellites, and Universalists were held to be socially a cut below, while the immigrant and Free Negro churches lined the bottom.

Most Protestants, though they squabbled among themselves, shared a common hatred of the Roman Catholic Church. Even to sophisticated ministers like Lyman Beecher, the father of Harriet Beecher Stowe and president of Lane Seminary in Cincinnati, Catholicism still smacked of the sinister rites of the Inquisition and of political autocracy. The gullible readily swallowed crude fictions about Catholic atrocities and sensational "exposés" of Catholic depravity. Sometimes Catholics were insulted and attacked, their churches burned.

Anti-Catholic prejudice deepened after 1830 when immigration began to rise. Between 1830 and 1850, 2.5 million newcomers arrived, many of them Catholics from Ireland and Germany. In 1830, there were 500 Catholic priests in the United States and about 500,000 communicants. By 1850 there were 1500 priests serving 1,750,000 of their faith. In addition, the Church had established seminaries, schools, colleges, monasteries, convents, hospitals, and other parochial institutions. A Catholic press, starting with the *United States Catholic Miscellany,* in 1822, also had come into being, along with a Catholic Tract Society, founded in Philadelphia in 1827 to combat Protestantism and to promote the Church.

Yet despite America's social tensions and institutional rivalry, an inner unity—built on the general acceptance of democracy, private property, and Christian faith—bound the country together. True, the idea of the Union was to prove too weak to triumph over the

passions aroused by slavery, but the social fabric seemed tough enough to withstand every other strain.

An influential corps of ministers and lawyers who conducted their lives as though the Transcendental egoists and self-righteous reformers never existed, became the leading unifiers. Rejecting sectarianism and sectionalism, aristocracy and anarchy, they developed an ideology designed to integrate a people of diverse origins, upbringing, occupations, and interests.

One manifestation of this ideology took the form of religious collaboration in a revivalist movement to which most of the Protestant churches contributed. Powerful clergymen like Charles Grandison Finney (1792–1875) together with other evangelicals strove to redeem entire communities, to identify practical patriotism, and to cure the nation of its social blights. The revivalists offered salvation to all who wished to be saved. Many of them equated sin with social selfishness, and indifference toward benevolent enterprises like Sunday Schools, Home Missions, and temperance crusades as a sign of a "backslidden heart." Not all religious leaders went along

with Finney's advanced notions on the sinner's "natural ability" to attain grace any more than they shared his antislavery views. But under their assault even the orthodox began to question if not abandon the dark Calvinist belief in man's corrupt moral nature.

Lawyers performed a role analogous to that of the ministers. Between 1790 and 1830, such legal giants as James Kent and Joseph Story, aided by their persuasive fraternity, revised the popular image of the lawyer from pettifogger or creature of the rich to that of secular priest. Thereafter, the great figures of the antibellum period—Jackson, Webster, Clay, Calhoun, Stephen A. Douglas, and Lincoln, to name only a few—all were lawyers.

As the acknowledged articulators of national ideals, lawyers became the principal orators in this oratorical age. As conservatives, they guarded property against popular encroach-

437

438

ment. In the absence of a true aristocracy, Tocqueville found, the lawyers of America "form the highest political class, and the most cultivated circle of society. . . . If I were asked where I place the American aristocracy, I should reply without hesitation, that it is not composed of the rich, who are united together by no common tie, but that it occupies the judicial bench and the bar."

The model of the lawyer in this period was Daniel Webster. To his contemporaries he was a remarkable natural phenomenon, like Niagara Falls. No one declaimed about the Pilgrim Fathers or Bunker Hill more movingly or expressed so thrillingly the poetry of nationalism. Webster's reply to Hayne (see p. 412) symbolized to young Ralph Waldo Emerson "the beauty and dignity of principles." Later, Emerson came to regard Webster as admirable for Fourth of July celebrations but too much of an ancestor-worshiper:

He obeys his powerful animal nature;—and his finely developed understanding only works truly . . . when it stands for animal good; that is, for property. He believes, in so many words, that government exists for the protection of property. He looks at the Union as an estate, a large farm, and is excellent in the completeness of his defense of it. . . . Happily he was born late,—after independence had been declared, the Union agreed to, and the Constitution settled. What he finds already written, he will defend. Luckily that so much had got well-written when he came.

Emerson was less than fair in his dismissal of Webster, but he caught the great orator's essential nature as the unifying instrument of tradition. His standing even among those who had tired of his oratory, made to sound like buncombe by ceaseless repetition, perhaps became most evident in their vicious attacks upon him as a sort of god gone wrong when he accepted the Fugitive Slave Law of 1850 as part of the Compromise made hopefully to preserve the Union (see p. 494).

*Daniel Webster in his prime. Photo by Mathew Brady. (National Archives.)*

## II  *Writers and Society*

### PRECURSORS OF A NATIONAL LITERATURE

"Men of genius," according to a Boston critic in 1820, were "outlaws" because, "for the most part, they want that getting-along faculty which is naturally enough made the measure of man's mind in a young country, where every one has his future to make." And yet during the next three decades the United States experienced an intellectual flowering scarcely equaled by any other generation in American history. In 1802, when Washington Irving began to write, America had no literature and hardly a reading public. When he died, a year before the Civil War began, Emerson, Thoreau, Hawthorne, Poe, Melville, and Whitman had already struck off their masterpieces.

The achievements of these writers seem all the more remarkable when we consider the unpromising environment from which they sprang. Besides the prevailing hostility to genius in general there was the specific hostility to literature, and more particularly to American literature. After the Revolution, patriots had called for a national literature that would reflect the dawning greatness of the new nation, but such American poets as Timothy Dwight and Joel Barlow, who planned mighty epics, turned out only pale and unreadable imitations of English literary forms and deferred to English standards of taste. Among the would-be writers of this period, only the poet Philip Freneau (1752–1832), and the imaginative Philadelphia novelist Charles Brockden Brown (1761–1810) possessed more than a minor talent. For some time thereafter, the few Americans with literary interests preferred the easily obtainable works of popular British authors. Sir Walter Scott, Byron, Bulwer-Lytton, Mrs. Felicia Hemans, and Charles Dickens crowded American writers out.

American authors understood their neglect. America, they said, had no ancient traditions, no peasants, knights or kings, no ivy-covered castles, no Gothic churches, no legendary mist to stimulate their imagination. Washington Irving was only one of a long line of American writers who felt the charm of Europe, where the necessary romantic background was available.

I longed [Irving said] to wander over the scenes of renowned achievement,—to tread, as it were, in the footsteps of antiquity,—to loiter about the ruined castle,—to meditate on the falling tower,—to escape, in short, from the commonplace realities of the present, and lose myself among the shadowy grandeurs of the past.

American writers also had to reckon with the religiously inspired distrust of literature as Satan's snare. Fiction, it was said, "pampers and bloats the intellect with unwholesome food, and enfeebles and demoralizes all future exertions of the mind."

Yet the better-known American writers overcame or ignored these cultural handicaps and managed to attract a following of their own. Irving (1783–1859), an urbane New Yorker, was the first professional man of letters to win wide popularity at home and applause abroad. Irving lived much in Europe and wrote his best books about it. When still in his twenties, however, he wrote and published in America his *History of New York* (1809), a rousing burlesque of the early Dutch and later backwoods democrats, that had the whole country laughing. Irving's *History* ranks second in popularity among his works only to *The Sketch Book* (1819–20), an instantaneous success in Britain as in the United States, in which he made Rip Van Winkle and Ichabod Crane luminous American characters in the rural and village setting of his native state. In *A Tour on the Prairies* (1835) Irving evoked the charm of the landscape on the moving frontier.

Irving's friend and contemporary, William Cullen Bryant (1794–1878), grew up in the Berkshire Hills of Massachusetts, but he made his career in New York City as poet, newspaper man, and reformer. No lisping imitator of British sentiment, Bryant wrote of his native habitat in a way that won Emerson himself. It was Bryant, Emerson noted, who "subsidized every solitary grove and monument-mountain in Berkshire or the Katskills . . . every water fowl and woodbird . . . so that there is no feature of day or night in the country which does not, to the contemplative mind, recall the name of Bryant."

On the departure of his friend Thomas Cole, the painter and founder of the "Hudson River school" (see p. 450), for England in 1829, Bryant wrote in this characteristic vein:

Thine eyes shall see the light of distant skies;
  Yet, COLE! thy heart shall bear to Europe's strand

440

A living image of our own bright land,
Such as upon thy glorious canvas lies;
Lone lakes—savannas where the bison roves—
  Rocks rich with summer garlands—solemn
    streams—
  Skies, where the desert eagle wheels and
    screams—
Spring bloom and autumn blaze of boundless
  groves.
Fair scenes shall greet thee where thou goest—
  fair,
  But different—everywhere the trace of men,
  Paths, homes, graves, ruins, from the lowest
    glen
To where life shrinks from the fierce Alpine air.
  Gaze on them, till the tears shall dim they
    sight,
  But keep that earlier, wilder image bright.

An even more illustrious member of the New York group was the novelist James Fenimore Cooper (1789–1851). In Europe, where he lived and wrote for a number of years, Cooper truculently defended the government and institutions of his native land. In America, he berated his countrymen for bad manners, chauvinism, contempt for privacy, their slavish submission to public opinion. Cooper's upbringing among the landed gentry of New York did not block his early sympathy for Jackson and Jacksonian America. If his "democracy" soured in the last years of his life, his thoughtful depiction of republican government, *The American Democrat* (1838), remains one of the best political essays ever written by an American.

What first brought Cooper fame both in Europe and at home were his early "white novels," especially *The Pilot* (1823), a forerunner of many masterly tales of the sea. Of deeper interest today is the celebrated "Leatherstocking" series: *The Pioneers* (1823), *The Last of the Mohicans* (1826), *The Prairie* (1827), *The Pathfinder* (1840), and *The Deerslayer* (1841)—the romance of the white hunter, Natty Bumppo, among the Indians of the woods, the lakes, and the open country. Natty, in his first incarnation, was but a composite of some of the types Cooper had known during a boyhood spent in a pioneer

settlement in New York. In successive appearances, however, he grew into a mythic figure, a kind of forest philosopher-king mediating between white men and red, and immune both to the viciousness of civilization and the barbarism of the frontier. Cooper had by no means exhausted his talent after completing his wilderness saga, but he lost a good part of his audience when he turned from romance to social censure. Later critics like Mark Twain called attention to his literary offenses, but Cooper's tales still can be read for their clear portrayal of American character, the unique beauty of their settings, their grasp of the issues in the clashes of men of different colors on American soil.

A surer gauge of American taste in this early period of American literature is the phenomenal success of the New England poet Henry Wadsworth Longfellow (1807–1882), a milder writer than Cooper.

Born in Portland, Maine, and educated at Bowdoin College, Longfellow, like Irving and Cooper, had spent several years in Europe. He went there to prepare himself to become a professor of modern languages, first at Bowdoin and later (1836) at Harvard College. Sitting in his Cambridge study, Longfellow composed volume after volume of mellifluous verse that soon made him famous throughout the world. *Hyperion* (1839), *Evangeline* (1847), *Hiawatha* (1855), and *The Courtship of Miles Standish* (1858) delighted the largest audience, perhaps, that any American poet ever commanded. His sentimentality, his didacticism, his optimism, and his antiquarianism satisfied popular taste. If his Hiawatha smacked more of Cambridge, Massachusetts, than of the shores of Gitchie Gumee, and if the brawny "Village Blacksmith" was a Whig dream of a docile and respectful workingman, poems like "A Psalm of Life" expressed without irony the aspirations of middle-class America.

Let us, then, be up and doing,
  With a heart for any fate;
Still achieving, still pursuing,
  Learn to labor and to wait.

*Edgar Allan Poe presented this photo of himself to the widow Mrs. Sarah Helen Whitman, a minor poet, in 1848. They were engaged for a short time on the condition imposed by Mrs. Whitman that he renounce alcohol. He failed to uphold the bargain and the engagement was broken off, much to the relief of Mrs. Whitman's mother. After Poe's death a few months later, Mrs. Whitman wrote* Edgar Poe and His Critics, *an answer to his various detractors. (The Bettmann Archive.)*

Longfellow and his Boston and Cambridge associates belonged to the coterie of writers who contributed to what Van Wyck Brooks called, following the self-satisfied Yankees' own estimate of themselves, "The Flowering of New England." The emphasis placed by historians on this regional renaissance has partially obscured the intellectual and artistic activity of other sections. Yet, New England's "golden day" was real enough. No other area contained such a hive of industrious writers. Much of their culture was thin and bookish, and the great reputations once enjoyed by James Russell Lowell, Oliver Wendell Holmes, and John Greenleaf Whittier have deservedly shrunk. But the cumulative output of New England between 1830 and 1850

remains impressive, and the great names live on: Francis Parkman and William H. Prescott, historians; Ralph Waldo Emerson, and Henry David Thoreau, essayists and poets; Nathaniel Hawthorne, writer of romances and tales.

### EDGAR ALLAN POE

One Bostonian who did not relish Boston's appreciation of itself was Edgar Allan Poe (1809–1849). Although born in the "hub of the universe," a city he sarcastically referred to in later life as "Frogpond," Poe regarded himself as a Virginian. After the death of his actor parents during his infancy, Poe grew up in Richmond where his foster-father, John Allan, was a substantial merchant. He attended the University of Virginia until Allan's stinginess and Poe's own gambling debts forced him to leave. His subsequent career included a two-year hitch in the army, a nomination to West Point in 1830 and dismissal for gross neglect of duty in 1831. In between, he managed to publish two volumes of verse (*Tamerlane*, 1827, and *Al Aaraaf*, 1829), and after the West Point fiasco he became a professional man of letters.

Nothing could seduce Poe from this "most noble profession," as he once referred to it, but he spent the rest of his short life in the American Grub Street, writing and editing brilliantly for inferior men, and publishing poems, stories, and critical essays that brought him little. In his most productive year, 1843, Poe earned $300. The shabby and unrewarding years that he spent with the literary Bohemians of Philadelphia, Baltimore, and New York aggravated his natural instability. In 1836 he had married his 13-year-old cousin, Virginia Clemm. "I became insane," he wrote after her death ten years later, "with long intervals of horrible sanity." In 1849, Poe was found lying unconscious in a Baltimore street, and died in delirium at the age of 40.

Poe was no apostle of progress. Democracy displeased him, and he had no taste for middle-class truths. As a literary critic he per-

442

formed a tremendous service by attacking American provincialism in cruel reviews of bad books. His own poetry and fiction contained most of the weaknesses he detected in the writings of his inferiors: theatricality, bombast, and sentimentality. But in stories like "The Fall of the House of Usher," "The Imp of the Perverse," "The Black Cat," "The Man in the Crowd," and "The Premature Burial"—tales of murderers, neurotics, the near-insane—his vulgarity was redeemed by an extraordinary intelligence and intensity. The owner of the black cat who sorrowfully cuts out the eyes of his pet, the brother who entombs his sister alive, the lover who pulls out the teeth of his mistress while she sleeps in a cataleptic trance, all live in a tormented world far removed from Emerson's optimistic America. Yet Poe's very exoticism proved a tonic for the democratic culture he rejected. Had he been less unstable, he might have accomplished his dream of becoming the publisher of a successful popular magazine. As it was, Poe perfected, if he did not invent, the detective story, contributed significantly to the genre of science fiction (see his astonishing short novel, "The Narrative of Arthur Gordon Pym"), and profoundly influenced poets and critics of succeeding generations in Europe and America.

### EMERSON AND TRANSCENDENTALISM

The most universal literary figure of his generation was Ralph Waldo Emerson (1803–1882). Boston-born and Harvard-educated, he entered the ministry as his father and grandfather had done before him, but he resigned his pastorate in 1832 because church forms had become meaningless for him. Thereafter, he devoted himself entirely to writing and lecturing. *Nature* (1836), which contained in condensed form most of the themes he was to treat in his later works, was followed by two volumes of essays (1841, 1844), *Poems* (1847), *Representative Men* (1850), *English Traits* (1856), and *The Conduct of Life* (1860).

Half Yankee and half yogi, Emerson contained within himself the warring tendencies of his age. Part of him belonged to the practical American world of forms and banks and railroads, and no one celebrated more enthusiastically than he (see his essays on "Wealth," "Power," and "Napoleon") the deeds of powerful individualists. At the same time, Emerson was a mystic and an idealist who looked upon the external world as a passing show and detected an unchanging reality behind it. This shrewd and canny man declared himself to be "part and particle" of God and rejoiced in the unsettling effect his theories had on his countrymen.

Emerson, like many other Boston intellectuals of his day, had rebelled against the coldness and formality of the Unitarian faith which repudiated the harsh Calvinist doctrine of human depravity and a vengeful God but in the process became passionless. Emerson wanted to revive the old Puritan fervor without the rigidities of Puritan theology. Quakerism, with its doctrine of the inner light, its gentleness, and its humanitarianism, moved him deeply, and he was drawn to any philosophy that broke down the barriers between mind and matter. In Emerson's youth, the philosophy of the English materialist, John Locke, was still much in vogue. Locke had held that ideas did not arise spontaneously in the mind, but that they were implanted there by the impressions of the external world acting through the senses. This meant that spirit was subordinate to matter. Emerson's own disposition told him otherwise, and he found support for his idealism in the works of certain continental and Scottish philosophers, oriental poets and sages, and in English romantic poetry.

Transcendentalism, the philosophy associated with Emerson and his sympathizers, was not a systematic faith; it had no creed and could not be easily defined. To some, the word "transcendentalist" covered "all those who contend for perfect freedom, who look for progress in philosophy and theology, and who sympathize with each other in the hope that the future will not always be as the past." To the journalist and critic, Orestes Brownson, the only common bond shared by the transcendalists was their opposition "to the old school":

They do not swear by Locke, and they recognize no authority in matters of opinion but the human mind, whether termed the reason with some of them, or the soul with others. They have all felt that our old catechisms need revision, and that our old systems of philosophy do not do justice to all the elements of human nature, and that these systems can by no means furnish a solid basis for a belief in God, much less in Christianity. Some of them . . . *ignore* all philosophy, plant themselves in their instincts and wait for the huge world to come round to them. . . . Some of them reason . . . others merely dream.

Although vague in its outlines, transcendential doctrine was nobly formulated in Emerson's essays and lectures, in which he announced to his fellow Americans that they, too, could speak to God directly without the assistance of churches and creeds. He urged them to be self-reliant and to get their experience at first hand. Every object in the physical world had a spiritual meaning, and those who were capable of seeing that material things were the symbols of spiritual truths might understand nature's purpose. The ability to communicate with God, or the "Over Soul," was given to everyone, but only a small number of poets, scholars, and philosophers (Emerson called them men of "Reason") had developed this inborn capacity. From them, other men could learn that only the idea is real, that evil is negative (the mere absence of good), and that a kindly destiny awaited them.

These ideas Emerson expressed in fresh and audacious language. Even in his most abstract utterances, he used simple concrete words and homely illustrations:

The world of any moment is the merest appearance. Some great decorum, some fetish of

a government, some ephemeral trade, or war, or man, is cried up by half mankind and cried down by the other half, as if all depended on this particular up or down. The odds are that the whole question is not worth the poorest thought which the scholar has lost in listening to the controversy. Let him not quit his belief that a popgun is a popgun, though the ancient and honorable of the earth affirm it to be the crack of doom.

To an audience absorbed in material concerns, Emerson argued against the tyranny of *things* over the *spirit*, and he seemed to speak intimately to any person who read or heard him, encouraging every man to stand up against public opinion and be an individual:

443

*Ralph Waldo Emerson as a young man. (The Bettmann Archive.)*

444

What I must do is all that concerns me, not what the people think. This rule, equally arduous in actual and in intellectual life, may serve for the whole distinction between greatness and meanness. It is harder because you will always find those who think they know what is your duty better than you know it. It is easy in the world to live after the world's opinion, it is easy in solitude to live after our own; but the great man is he who in the midst of the crowd keeps with perfect sweetness the independence of solitude.

A number of Emerson's contemporaries tried to live according to his precepts: Henry David Thoreau as the transcendental adventurer of Walden Pond, Walt Whitman as the democratic poet, Theodore Parker as the minister-reformer, and others.

### THOREAU

Henry David Thoreau (1817–1862), like Emerson, his friend and mentor, was a graduate of Harvard College and a resident of Concord, Massachusetts. "He declined," Emerson later wrote of him, "to give up his large ambition of knowledge and action for any narrow craft or profession, aiming at a much more comprehensive calling, the art of living well." Throughout his life, Thoreau gave himself over to self-cultivation and self-exploration. His literary medium was the diary-like record of his intellectual experiences.

In *A Week on the Concord and Merrimack Rivers* (1849), *Civil Disobedience* (1849), and especially *Walden; or, Life in the Woods* (1854), Thoreau expressed his tart and unconventional opinions about literature, religion, government, and social relations. Many of the reformers were his friends, but he was never a "joiner"; he distrusted reform movements and tried to keep himself free from what he called "greasy familiarity." Good fellowship he once described as "the virtue of pigs in a litter, which lie close together to keep each other warm." "Not satisfied with

defiling one another in this world," he wrote, "we would all go to heaven together."

Like most transcendentalists, Thoreau was an unblushing egoist, but he wrote about himself, he said, because he did not know anyone else so well. Moreover, his own accounts of how he discovered the miraculous in the common were also suggestions for those men who led "lives of quiet desperation." He asked a generation geared to practicalities, what do the practicalities of life amount to? The immediate things to be done, he said, are trivial and can wait; the wealth of the world is less significant than one true vision.

The ways by which you may get money almost without exception lead downward. To have done anything by which you earned money *merely* is to have been truly idle or worse. . . . There is no more fatal blunderer than he who consumes the great part of his life getting his living . . . you must get your living by loving. . . . It is not enough to tell me that you worked hard to get your gold. So does the Devil work hard. . . . I believe that the mind can be permanently profaned by the habit of attending to trivial things, so that all our thoughts shall be tinged with triviality.

Thoreau advised his countrymen to simplify their private lives and to simplify their government, too, for he was a supreme individualist who regarded the organized state as a threat to true independence. Abolitionist, naturalist, poet, and rebel, and a down-to-earth but subtle writer—he attracted no great notice while he lived. In our day, *Walden* is justly considered a literary masterpiece, and its author—who discovered a universe in Concord—is regarded as one of the most original and challenging minds of the New England renaissance.

### WALT WHITMAN

The poet whose arrival Emerson had predicted in his essay "The Transcendentalist" (1842) was soon to appear. Emerson had written:

We have yet had no genius in America, with tyrannous eye, which knew the value of our incomparable materials, and saw, in the barbarism and materialism of the times, another carnival of the same gods whose picture he so admires in Homer. . . . Banks and tariffs, the newspaper and the caucus, Methodism and Unitarianism, are flat and dull to dull people, but rest on the same foundations of wonder as the town of Troy and the temple of Delphi, and are as swiftly passing away. Our log-rolling, our stumps and their politics, our fisheries, our Negroes and Indians . . . the northern trade, the southern planting, the western clearing, Oregon and Texas, are yet unsung. Yet America is a poem in our eyes; its ample geography dazzles the imagination, and it will not wait long for metres.

The "genius" Emerson demanded was Walt Whitman (1818-1892) born on Long Island and a life-long New Yorker. During his formative years, Whitman worked as schoolteacher, printer, carpenter, journalist, publisher, and editor. When *Leaves of Grass,* his first volume of poems, appeared in 1855, its undisguised references to the body and sex caused Whitman to be denounced as the "dirtiest beast of his age." The most friendly review, save the three reviews he wrote himself, described his verse as "a sort of excited compound of New England transcendentalism and New York rowdy." Emerson was the only eminent writer who immediately discerned Whitman's freshness and found (as he wrote to the poet) "incomparable things, said incomparably well." Whitman continued to revise and add to the *Leaves* until 1892, in addition to publishing other volumes of prose and verse, but the recognition he deserved came only after his death.

Whitman's poems, like Emerson's essays, embody the idea of progress, celebrate the innate goodness of man, and idealize nature; they insist on the spiritual reality underlying the material world. But Whitman was more passionately democratic than the New Englander, and he looked to the people rather than his own soul for his inspiration. Other poets, he said,

have adhered to the principle, and shown it, that the poet and the savant form classes by themselves, above the people, and more refined than the people, I show that they are just as great when of the people, partaking of the common idioms, manners, the earth, the rude visage of animals and trees, and what is vulgar.

This belief prompted him to write poems about Negroes and Indians, carpenters, coach-drivers, sailors, and trappers, felons and prostitutes, and above all, himself:

I celebrate myself, and sing myself,
And what I assume, you shall assume,
For every atom belonging to me as good belongs
    to you.
   . . . . . . .
The atmosphere is not a perfume, it has no taste
    of the distillation, it is odorless,
It is for my mouth forever, I am in love with it,
I will go to the bank by the wood and become
    undisguised and naked,
I am mad for it to be in contact with me.
   . . . . . . .
The boatmen and clam-diggers arose early and
    stopt for me,
I tuck'd my trowser-ends in my boots and went
    and had a good time;
You should have been with us that day round the
    chowder-kettle.
I saw the marriage of the trapper in the open air
    in the far west, the bride was a red girl,
Her father and his friends sat near cross-legged
    and dumbly smoking, they had moccasins
    to their feet and large thick blankets hang-
    ing from their shoulders,
On a bank lounged the trapper, he was drest
    mostly in skins, his luxuriant beard and
    curls protected his neck, he held his bride
    by the hand,
She had long eyelashes, her head was bare, her
    coarse straight locks descended upon her
    voluptuous limbs and rech'd to her feet.
   . . . . . . .
The butcher-boy puts off his killing-clothes, or
    sharpens his knife at the stall in the mar-
    ket, . . .
Blacksmiths with grimed and hairy chests environ
    the anvil, . . .

446

The negro holds firmly the reins of his four
  horses, the block swags underneath on its
  tied-over chain,
The negro that drives the long dray of the stone-
  yard, steady and tall he stands pois'd on one
  leg on the string-piece, . . .
I behold the picturesque giant and love him, and
  I do not stop there,
I go with the team also.
In me the caresser of life wherever moving, back-
  ward as well as forward sluing,
To niches aside and junior bending, not a person
  or object missing,
Absorbing all to myself and for this song.

In his poems, Whitman imagined ranks,
races, and civilizations commingling, and it

*Walt Whitman in 1854 when he was writing*
Leaves of Grass. (*Walt Whitman House, Camden.*)

was to be America's mission, he held, to promote this final fellowship of peoples. At home
he saw much in his generation to displease
him. His optimism was severely tested by the
Civil War, and his faith in America's manifest
destiny was shaken by the events after 1865
(see *Democratic Vistas*, 1871), but he did not
despair:

> Do I contradict myself?
> Very well then I contradict myself,
> (I am large, I contain multitudes.)

Whitman died believing that in the people
there existed "a miraculous wealth of latent
power and capacity."

### THE NAY-SAYERS

Emerson, like Whitman, made many
trenchant criticisms of American society, but,
like the New Yorker, he never flagged in his
optimism. As Emerson put it in his "Ode to
W. H. Channing":

> Foolish hands may mix and mar;
> Wise and sure the issues are.
> Round they roll till dark is light.

Some of his neighbors, however, were not
so sure. Nathaniel Hawthorne (1804–1864)
was one who could not slough off the pes-
simistic doctrines of his Puritan forefathers
on the irretrievable fall of man. The son of
a Salem shipmaster, Hawthorne attended
Bowdoin College with the more sanguine
Longfellow and grew up to be a robust, masculine person who held government jobs and
enjoyed human contacts. He was not the
recluse he has sometimes been painted, but
his ideas went against the grain of his age.
In his tales and sketches, and in his novels—
*The Scarlet Letter* (1850), for example—
Hawthorne painted a somber moral landscape
where men and women were devoured by
vices they were constrained to keep secret,
but which he exposed. These terrible facts of
life mocked the claims of progress. In his
works, schemes for human renovation

("Earth's Holocaust," "The Celestial Railway") come to nought; reformers, scientists, and secret probers are changed into monstrous villains thwarted in their search for perfection (see *"The Blithedale Romance,"* "Ethan Brand," and "Rappaccini's Daughter").

In 1852 Hawthorne wrote the campaign biography for his Bowdoin College classmate, Franklin Pierce, and earned the consulship at Liverpool for his pains. He remained abroad until the end of the decade, attracted and repelled by the European scene and anxious about the sectional conflict brewing at home. No friend of the Abolitionists, whom he accused of arrogating to themselves God's functions, his faith in an America unvexed by the issues they raised gradually weakened. In his last novel, *The Marble Faun* (1860), an outgrowth of his Italian travels, he treated once more the old theme of sin and redemption, but he already felt out of tune with the times and took no comfort in the thought that he had come closer to seeing the truth of the human condition than many of his optimistic friends. He died in the midst of a civil war he could neither understand nor wholeheartedly support.

Hawthorne's New York friend, Herman Melville (1819–1891), also clung to the idea of original sin. After his father's bankruptcy, Melville endured the humiliations of genteel poverty which were only deepened by teaching school. In 1841 he quit city life and sailed on a whaling ship to the South Seas. Three years of adventuring in the Pacific provided materials for his two best-selling books, *Typee* (1846) and *Omoo* (1847). His reputation declined after he stopped writing light-hearted sketches of Polynesian life and turned to his private conflicts.

An ardent nationalist and celebrator of "the great democratic God," Melville was too honest not to report discrepancies detected between American ideals and practices, appearance and reality. *Mardi* (1851), a huge and inchoate allegory, contains a chapter on the republic of Vivenza (America). Young and boastful Vivenza is convinced that its ocean-girded Eden can escape history, but Melville's spokesmen in the romance warn of a troubled future. Once the "wild western waste" has been occupied and the population "pressed and packed" like that of the Old World, then the "great experiment" may explode. Melville cautioned against a freedom that sanctioned barbarism, pronounced slavery "a blot, foul as the craterpool of hell," and predicted that "These South savannahs may yet prove battlefields." He was to be the somber observer of the war he envisaged and to write in *Battle-Pieces* (1866) some of the noblest poetry on this tragic episode.

In rejecting transcendental optimism, Melville reacted even more strongly than Hawthorne against Emerson's blandness. Evil, for Melville, resided not merely in the tainted heart, that "foul cavern," as Hawthorne called it; evil hung over the world like a curtain. In *Moby Dick* (1851), his finest novel, Melville struck through the "pasteboard mask" of life to confront this eternal menace. Ahab, a Yankee whaling captain, the lost hero of the novel, spends himself in pursuit of Moby Dick, a gigantic white whale that symbolized the beauty, the wickedness, and the mystery of nature. The pursuit fails; Ahab dies. If man were half-divine, as the transcendentalists insisted, according to Melville he nonetheless faced a tragic destiny. He was incapable of solving the ambiguities of the world. God remained unknowable, progress an illusion, the seeker only led on and deceived by what he saw and thought.

### THE NATIVE STRAIN

Whitman aside, with his common words ordinarily excluded from polite verse ("I reckon," "gallivant," "duds," "folks," "blab"), the leading authors of the antebellum period wrote in the accents and language of old England for a "high-brow" clientele. As a result, the "vulgar" prejudices of the average citizen found little expression in polite letters. Yet, as Whitman showed, an American vernacular, a native strain, had long been de-

448

veloping in the United States, especially among frontier settlers and the blacks. And along with it, there developed a mass of sub-literary publications—"dark and dingy pamphlets," penny magazines, song-books, camp-meeting hymn books, game-books, and parodies—patronized by many readers. These cheaply printed publications circulated everywhere, and by the 1820s, according to one contemporary, they were exercising "a direct influence upon the thoughts and opinions of the great reading mass of society." Yet only a literary revolution comparable to the Jacksonian political revolution could weaken the hold of the conservative taste-makers.

One prophet of the new democratic literature was a gifted Ohio physician, Dr. Daniel Drake, whose *Discourse on the History, Character, and Prospects of the West* (1834) brilliantly stated the claim for an authentic western literature. Drake invited his readers to look at nature afresh instead of through the eyes of the past. He envisaged a literature as colorful and energetic as western speech itself and as closely as possible derived from the thoughts and occupations of the people. The "great reservoir of spoken language," he said, would strengthen the written word. Western speech might be "inferior in refinement" to the mother tongue, but it was "superior in force, variety, and freshness." Drake had no qualms about a literature "tinctured" with utilitarian thoughts and terms. That was only to be expected:

The mechanic arts . . . modify the public mind; supply new topics for the pen; generate strange words and phrases, as if by machinery; suggest novel modes of illustration, and manufacture figures of speech by steam power.

Tocqueville had observed the American fondness for "immense and incoherent imagery," for "exaggerated descriptions and strange creations," and had explained it as a way in which the people compensated for their paltry activities. Drake was not disturbed by his countrymen's verbal incoherence and

like others looked especially fondly on oratory as helping to liberate the pen. For him oratory acted as an important "directive" force. No other literary form reached so many groups and classes or attained such a level of technical perfection. None succeeded so well in mingling the lofty with the useful, or made such effective use of national scenery, history, and biography.

Drake's enthusiasm for the native strain led later in the century to the native masterpieces of Mark Twain. But even earlier, between the 1830s and the 1850s, American writers had begun to put homely American words into the mouths of their lower-class characters. Davy Crockett, in his popular autobiography, complained of love-pangs in language that no conventionally romantic hero would ever use:

My heart would begin to flutter like a duck in a puddle; and if I tried to outdo it and speak, would get right smack up in my throat, and choke me like a cold potatoe—but I had hardly safety pipes enough, as my love was so hot as mighty nigh to burst my boilers.

Such talk could be heard where men gathered together to swap stories and anecdotes, in barrooms, river boats, and stage coaches, but not heretofore in books.

The accents of a masculine and unrefined American also began to be heard in such popular magazines as *William T. Porter's Spirit of the Times* (1831–61). This rowdy sporting and theatrical weekly enjoyed a huge circulation for that day (over 40,000 in the middle '40s) especially among jockeys, actors, artists, planters, doctors, and lawyers. People who enjoyed sports and fighting submitted their low-life sketches from every part of the country and recorded the humorous exploits of American backwoodsmen like Mike Fink and Davy Crockett, who had already begun to take on mythological proportions. Talented southern regional writers—Johnson J. Hooper, George W. Harris, and Joseph G. Baldwin were among the better ones—contributed stories of frontier rascality to Porter's paper. Hooper's rogue, Simon Suggs, acting on the frontier principle that "it is good to be shifty in a new country," symbolized the rough, boisterous, predatory settler of the pre-Civil War Southwest.

## III  *The Plastic and the Performing Arts*

### PAINTERS AND SCULPTORS

The division in American society between those who were preoccupied with "stern realities" and those who tried to keep the arts uncontaminated by "dirty facts" was felt by the would-be painter and sculptor as well as the author. The fine arts seemed particularly aristocratic to many sturdy democrats. *The North American Review* in 1825 described them as the products "of corrupt and despotic courts, the flatterers of tryranny, the panders of vice." The sculptor Horatio Greenough was not being facetious when he wrote to his friend and patron, James Fenimore Cooper, that "a man may be an artist without being ergo a blackguard and a mischievous member of society."

Strict moralists objected to painting and statuary even more strongly than they did to fiction. The Bible forbade the making of graven images and likenesses that dignified man rather than God. One influential Presbyterian minister put it this way:

All articles of furniture needed in domestic life; all necessary parts of philosophical apparatus; all vehicles of conveyance by land or sea can be fabricated without making the image or likeness of anything in heaven above or in the earth beneath. An artist may form a knife, a spoon, a table bureau and be not only an innocent but an estimable workman. But should he give to the handle of the knife the form of a serpent or fix his table to stand upon the feet of a bear or mount his bureau with the heads of

*Illustration from "Swallowing an Oyster Alive, a Story of Illinois—by a Missourian," from an issue of* William T. Porter's Spirit of the Times. *A "sucker" from Illinois on his first trip to St. Louis tasted his first "isters." The wag, center, tells him they're alive and will eat their way out of his body. Says the sucker, "O gracious!—what'll I do!—it's got hold of my innards already, and I'm dead as a chicken!—do somethin' for me, do—don't let the infernal sea-toad eat me afore your eyes." The wag then gives him a remedy— a bottle of hot sauce to be downed in one gulp! (Courtesy of the New-York Historical Society, New York City.)*

lions, he becomes, in my opinion, a transgressor of the moral law.

In an environment in which no utility could be found for the "meager productions of the pencil, the brush or the chisel," it is not surprising that Samuel F. B. Morse turned to invention after spending half his life as a

The Voyage of Life—Youth, *an elaborate allegory of aspiration painted by the English-born artist Thomas Cole in 1850, as one of a four-part series ranging from childhood to old age, commissioned by the New York banker, Samuel Ward, for his elaborate new house at 2 Bond Street, on the corner of Broadway. This house reputedly had the first private picture gallery in the City. (Munson-Williams-Proctor Institute, Utica, New York.)*

struggling artist, or that many American artists began their careers in the more practical roles of artisans and mechanics. The celebrated sculptor Hiram Powers (1805–1873), worked in a Cincinnati organ factory and made wax statues before turning to art as a career. Powers's mechanical ingenuity as well as his ability to model "busts remarkable for their perfect resemblance" accounted for his early reputation. But his most popular work, the "Greek Slave"—the statue that won him international fame—reveals only his pandering to popular notions of ideal form devoid of the fruits of his practical past.

Powers's work pleased the critics of the 1830s who only praised art that raised "the mind above the sordid interest of a merely material life." American artists were invited to contemplate native forests, rivers, and sunsets, which "inspired the soul of man with visions of the ideal, the beautiful, the immortal." The painter Thomas Cole (1801–1848) (see p. 439) became famous in this period for his romantic renditions of the Hudson River and Catskill Mountain regions dominated by "sweeping effects of storm cloud and streaming light to suggest the brooding presence of the Eternal." Asher Durand (1796–1886) and Thomas Doughty (1793–1856), contemporaries of Cole, painted America's scenic wonders in the same grand view. By 1860, a stronger school of landscape painters had emerged who caught the character of the horse Indians and early settlers on the Great Plains. Among the best were George Catlin (1796–

1872) and Alfred Jacob Miller (1810–1874).

A few iconoclasts tried to break down the unhappy distinction between the beautiful and the useful. Emerson argued that an object was beautiful if it had nothing superfluous about it and if it served the use for which it was made. Whitman celebrated the splendor of locomotives. Thoreau defended the functional house, and Horatio Greenough wrote at length about the beauty of sailing ships, bridges, and machinery:

The men who have reduced locomotion to its simplest elements, in the trotting wagon and the yacht *America,* are nearer to Athens at this moment than they who would bend the Greek temple to every use. I contend for Greek principles, not Greek things. If a flat sail goes nearest the wind, a bellying sail, though picturesque, must be given up. The slender harness, and tall gaunt wheels, are not only effective, they are beautiful for they respect the beauty of a horse, and do not uselessly tax him.

But views like these were not popular during the Jacksonian period and American artists who had gone to the Continent to study often grew resentful of the apathetic public on their return home.

A change in the national attitude toward the fine arts could be observed after 1840, when patronage in the larger cities offered new hope to talented and ambitious painters, sculptors, and architects. In the two decades before the Civil War, New York City, Philadelphia, and Boston built up their "academies" and "athenaeums," competing with each other for culture as they did for trade. Artists began to exhibit their work in private and public galleries; new schools of design appeared along with magazines devoted to the fine arts. Although the status of the artist did not change basically in the country as a whole, his mounting prestige in rich metropolitan areas and his new confidence in the prospects of an authentic native art, suggested a hitherto unsuspected cultural vitality.

The ordinary citizen, meanwhile, clearly derived more enjoyment from "a carnival of wild beasts" than from an exhibit of paintings. The one seemed to him genuine, the other pointless and dull. Artistic phenomena also had a vogue. Curious citizens trooped to exhibitions of huge panoramas, unwound from rollers, that presented with painstaking accuracy the Mississippi landscape or historical scenes like the landing of Lafayette. The depiction of native scenes sometimes attained lasting artistic merit, as in the works of John James Audubon (1785–1851), and the famous team of Currier and Ives. By fusing science and art, Audubon produced meticulous studies of American bird and animal life. Currier and Ives, meanwhile, flooded the country with gay lithographs of forest and farm, railroads, sleigh rides, and skating and boating scenes. Artists like William S. Mount (1807–1868), David G. Blyth (1815–1865), and George Bingham (1811–1879), the painter equivalents of the humorists and writers of tall tales, in turn, caught the atmosphere of minstrel shows, rowdy elections, and western river life. (See Mount painting, p. 453.)

### DRAMA AND MUSIC

If moralists had serious reservations about literature and the plastic arts, they felt even more strongly about the theater. Dramatic productions, as one of them declared, "lead the minds of youth from serious reflection, or if they reflect at all, their thoughts are employed on things which never had any existence but in the vain imagination of some distempered fancy like their own." Lay-preachers assailed the "vagabond profession" and the indecency of "displays of half-clad females." The most damning criticism of the theater was that it unfitted "mankind . . . for the common concerns of life."

But the theater seemed more vital than the fine arts and despite these objections it flourished. Audiences heard and applauded everything from Shakespeare to the broadest farce. New York remained the dramatic center, but cities in every section supported theaters. Famous stars like Edwin Forrest, James K.

452

Hackett, and Fanny Kemble won national reputations. But most popular of all were toe-dancers like the ravishing Fanny Elssler, burlesque and popular opera, and E.P. Christy's celebrated minstrel show.

Coming into vogue in the early 1820s, minstrelsy expropriated and formalized characteristic strains of Negro folk culture that had been flowing freely though the popular consciousness long before white entertainers in black-face commercialized them. Both foreign and American observers had often referred to the haunting chants and songs of the black man, his humor, his skill in extracting music and rhythms from primitive banjos, bones, and tambourines. As early as 1849, Bayard Taylor, poet and traveler, asserted that "Ethiopian melodies well deserve to be called, as they are in fact, the national airs of America. They follow the American race in all its migrations, colonizations, and conquests."

Many white minstrels who incorporated Negro tunes and themes into their comic or sentimental songs had heard them in the South and West. And not only the minstrel songs betray a Negro origin. The comic dances that figured in these shows also derived from the shuffles, shake-downs, and jigs performed in the plantation compounds. Friends of the Negro then and later interpreted the "comic nigger" of black-face as a racial slur and preferred the Spiritual as a truer and more dignified expression of Negro character. Yet black-face humor was double-edged—self-parody in part, but also covertly ridiculing white pretensions. The jaybird, turkey, crow, frog, bulldog, and fox enacted fables bearing closely on master-slave relations, with the master not infrequently discomfited. Denatured versions of these songs by popular song-writers of the day like Dan Emmett and, later, Henry C. Work, failed to capture the force and incisiveness of the originals sung at black camp-meetings. But even the act of borrowing Negro modes undercut the supposition of Negro inferiority. Perhaps it was not accidental that the appeal of minstrelsy coincided with the spread of emancipation sentiment, or that

Walt Whitman should see in the influence of the musical Negro dialects on English speech the possible basis for a native grand opera.

Foreigners might comment on the "barbarity" of American music, but between 1820 and 1860, along with the perfection of minstrelsy, instrumental and choral performances improved. Visiting artists from abroad successfully toured the country, and local musical societies in New York, Boston, and elsewhere offered orchestral and choral programs to appreciative if uncritical audiences. The ingratiating ballads of Stephen Foster (1826–1864), one of the first of a long line of northerners to romanticize the "sunny South," also were sung across the land; and opera, introduced about 1825, had some success in a few of the larger cities. Hymn-writers like Boston's Lowell Mason (1792–1872), composer of "Nearer My God to Thee" and "From Greenland's Icy Mountains," evoked a more genuine response and grew rich from the sales of their edifying songs.

## NEWSPAPERS AND MAGAZINES

"The influence and circulation of newspapers," wrote an astonished visitor to the United States about 1830, "is great beyond anything known in Europe. . . . Every village, nay, almost every hamlet, has its press." From 1801 to 1833, the number of newspapers rose from 200 to 1200; only 65 were dailies; most of the rest were weeklies, and competition in the larger cities grew ferocious. In 1830, New York City alone had 47 papers, only one daily among them claiming as many as 4000 subscribers. Enterprising editors reduced the price of their papers to a penny and sought to lure readers by featuring "robberies, thefts, murders, awful catastrophes and wonderful escapes."

Benjamin Day's New York *Sun* pioneered in the new sensationalism, but Day's rival, James Gordon Bennett of the *Herald*, soon surpassed him. Bennett played up the news value of New York society (he headlined his own marriage), and developed circulation

William Sidney Mount of Stony Brook, Long Island, was one of the leaders of the genre school of painting which appeared in the second quarter of the nineteenth century. In his horse-drawn mobile studio he traveled around Long Island painting people and events with a natural ease. An amateur musician, he once wrote, "I never paint on a picture, unless I feel in the right spirit," a spirit that animates his work *The Power of Music*, 1847. (*The Century Association; photo, John Pitkin.*)

techniques that were eagerly picked up throughout the country. New printing presses and improved delivery methods helped meet the rising demand. Advertising men kept up with the spirit of the times by substituting eye-catching copy and pictures for the old, staid announcements.

The press, as one reader pointed out, served as a kind of gutter that carried away "all the wanton vagaries of the imagination, all the inventions of malice, all the scandal, and all the corruptions of heart in village, town, or city." Yet the newspapers did more than pander to low tastes. "A newspaper," Tocqueville wrote, "is an adviser who does not require to be sought, but who comes of his own accord, and talks to you briefly every day of the Common weal." Each paper usually appealed to the prejudices and needs of particular groups. Mercantile interests, religious denominations, and political parties sponsored their own papers, and each editor rode his private hobby-horse. The best editors explained and interpreted pertinent issues, sometimes making demands upon their readers that

few modern editors would attempt. Often they supplemented commercial and political information with useful knowledge and succeeded in raising the level of popular culture.

Magazines also sprang up by the dozens in the middle decades, but few survived for long. With no generally accepted literary standards to rely upon, always in danger of offending the prudish, and yet aware of the "vulgar" preferences of their public, the harassed magazine editors had no way to turn. Delinquent subscribers were probably most responsible for the high mortality of periodicals, but the penny press and cheap imprints of pirated English books also reduced their audience. Almost every hamlet bravely launched a literary monthly or quarterly review, but only a few managed to carry on. *The North American Review* (Boston), *The Knickerbocker Magazine* (New York), *Graham's Magazine* (Philadelphia), and *The Southern Literary Messenger* (Richmond) achieved a national circulation. They printed pieces by Cooper, Poe, Bryant, Hawthorne, Holmes, and Longfellow, and by lesser figures, but they provided

453

454

only a meager outlet for American talent.

The "female" audience had its choice of *The Ladies Magazine,* edited by Sarah Josepha Hale, and *Godey's Lady's Book,* with which the former merged in 1836. *Godey's* did more than dictate fashions and rule over morals and manners. Miss Hale, literary editor of the magazine for many years, is best known as the author of "Mary's Lamb," but she published and reviewed intelligently the productions of leading American writers, paid for poems and articles (a significant innovation), and between 1837 and 1849 increased her magazine's circulation from 10,000 to 40,000. The success of *Godey's* and its imitators indicated that American women—the principal consumers of books and magazines—would soon dominate the cultural life of the nation. Their interest was indispensable, but it meant that women were able to impose a kind of petticoat tyranny over American letters and narrowly define the limits of propriety.

## IV  *Education: Formal and Informal*

### IN THE LOWER SCHOOLS

The religious spirit that had such a powerful effect on literature and the arts in America was felt even more strongly in education. One of the goals of organized religion had always been to create a Christian citizenry. Intellect without virtue, as the saying went, "makes a splendid villain"; what American leaders wanted was a "baptized intelligence." In many respects, education offered a secular kind of religious training. Most Americans favored Bible-teaching in the schools because, as the famous Presbyterian minister, Lyman Beecher, expressed it, the Bible gave no sanction "to civil broils, or resistance to lawful authority, but commands all men to follow peace, and to obey magistrates that are set over them, whatever the form of government may be."

The Bible would show European immigrants, "extensively infected with infidelity and Rationalism," that a "land of liberty is not a place to indulge in irreligion and license."

But despite the lip-service paid to Christian, democratic, and practical education, crusaders for free public schools faced an apathetic and often hostile populace. Men who could afford to educate their children in private academies saw no reason why they should be taxed to educate the children of the poor. The administrators of the private and parochial schools, farmers, and non-English-speaking groups joined the conservatives in fighting the free-school movement. They attacked it as a threat to individual liberty, as a radical innovation, as impractical nonsense. But the defenders of free public schools had strong arguments of their own: The extension of education would reduce poverty and crime, increase productivity, rectify social injustice, and preserve democratic institutions. Every class would benefit, according to one free-school advocate in 1832:

The man who is poor must see that this is the only way he can secure education for his children. The man in moderate circumstances . . . will have his children taught for a less sum than he pays at present. The rich man, who will be heavily taxed, must see that his course secures to the rising generation the only means of perpetuating our institutions, and the only guarantee that his children will be protected.

The leaders of the free-school movement—men like Horace Mann in Massachusetts, Henry Barnard in Connecticut, and Calvin Stowe in Ohio—hammered away with these arguments in widely circulated reports and articles based on thorough investigations, and finally won their battle. By 1860, most northern states had installed a tax-supported school program.

The free-school movement broke down one more vestige of caste in democratic America, but it did not work miracles. Education on all levels, in fact, continued to suffer from low salaries, poor physical equipment, primitive pedagogy, unmanageably large classes, and a short school term.

Throughout the period, educational reformers, classicists and anticlassicists, utilitarians and liberals, suggested a variety of schemes to raise the educational level. One focus of controversy was the Swiss educator Johann Heinrich Pestalozzi, who held that all education should proceed from the known to the unknown and the abstract. There was more point, his disciples argued, in teaching a child something about local geography than in making him memorize the rivers of Mesopotamia. Although Pestalozzi's ideas found some followers in America, rote memory drills prevailed.

Attempts by American schoolmasters to make education more interesting met stiff opposition. In defense of the critics, it must be acknowledged that many quacks flourished in the profession, and "painless" methods for acquiring a quick education were in vogue. One disgusted critic in 1829 complained that American youth learns

Latin and Greek by translations; they study French and Spanish, merely to say that they have studied them; they read history in abridgement, and biography in novels; they learn arithmetic by means of slips of paper, or little stories and counting their fingers; they carry to school large volumes of mineralogy, botany, or conchology; they learn composition by copying others' thoughts and language.

Such arguments were heard throughout the nineteenth century and into our own, but in the meantime, the quality of education improved enough for foreigners to comment on the exceptional literacy of the American public. The graded school with orderly upward progress made higher standards easier to impose; and improved teaching made the high standards easier to achieve.

Formal teacher-training came about largely through the work of Horace Mann, who established the first so-called "normal schools" for the preparation of teachers, and Henry Barnard, one of the founders of the American

*Classroom of the most prominent girl's school in Boston just before the Civil War. (Metropolitan Museum of Art, gift of I.N. Phelps Stokes and the Hawes Family, 1937.)*

Association for the Advancement of Education (1855) and editor of the influential *American Journal of Education.* Teachers' societies sprang up throughout the country, and educational periodicals disseminated advanced pedagogical methods.

Private academies were providing elementary and secondary education for girls by the 1840s. In 1833, Oberlin became the first coeducational college; in 1858, the University of Iowa, the first coeducational state university. For the most part, girls' seminaries concentrated on the ornamental accomplishments. The learned woman, or "blue-stocking," was considered a monstrosity:

If a young lady [declared a writer in 1833] speaks of anything with which the idea of study or research is associated, she is thenceforth looked upon, if not a pretender, at least as an unsexed woman. . . . We have a feeling . . . that a

455

456

learned woman does not fill her true place in the world. . . . It is thought more creditable for a young woman to possess accomplishments than wisdom—to be sentimental than learned—to *appear* than to *be*.

Yet schools like Mount Holyoke and Miss Emma Willard's Troy Female Seminary and Catharine Beecher's Hartford Female Seminary did attempt to provide a more substantial intellectual diet for their students.

There were few public high schools until 1840, but during the next two decades the number increased substantially, especially in Massachusetts, New York, and Ohio. Such schools offered a more practical kind of education than private schools and they were open to both girls and boys.

### IN THE COLLEGES

The number of so-called American "colleges" increased from 16 in 1799 to 182 in 1860. During these years 412 others started and died. Colleges, said a prominent educator in 1848,

rise up like mushrooms on our luxuriant soil. They are duly lauded and puffed for a day; and then they sink to be heard of no more. . . . Our people, at first, oppose all distinctions whatever as odious and aristocratical; and then, presently, seek with avidity such as remain accessible. At first they denounce colleges, and then choose to have a college in every district or county, or for every sect and party—and to boast of a college education, and to sport with high sounding literary titles—as if these imparted sense or wisdom or knowledge.

The multiplication of colleges resulted in part from the difficulties and expenses of travel, but sectarian rivalry and local pride were probably the principal causes. Religious control of institutions of higher learning was even more marked than on the elementary-school level. Each important denomination and many minor ones supported one or more colleges that helped to rekindle the spirit of piety. Most of these colleges, which students

might enter at 14 or 15, were hardly more than dressed-up academies. The so-called "universities" were hardly more than large colleges. Sometimes they included a theological or law department, but most professional schools in this period, law and medicine schools in particular, were separate institutions.

The curriculum in colleges and universities varied little throughout the country. Latin, Greek, mathematics, science, political economy, and moral philosophy offered a solid enough program, but teaching by rote was as common as in lower schools. Professors rarely were paid more than $1000 a year. Long hours and poor libraries, moveover, discouraged both research and publication. In 1839, only 18 college libraries held as many as 10,000 books, led by Harvard's 50,000 and Yale's 27,000.

Before the Civil War, a few notable professors found time to write and experiment, but in general the college atmosphere offered little stimulation. With sectarianism rampant and political issues explosive, no American college could live up to Jefferson's dream of a higher institution based "on the illimitable freedom of the human mind." Nondenominational colleges in particular were assailed as seats of atheism and aristocracy. Clearly, the "rise of the common man" by no means assured a more liberal education; indeed, it often bred intolerance and anti-intellectualism.

### THROUGH SELF-HELP

Philosophers of democracy like Franklin and Jefferson had insisted that only an educated electorate could sustain a republican government. Many, too busy or too old to go to school, continued to believe them. One institution designed to meet adult needs, especially in the towns and cities, was the mutual-improvement, or -benefit, society. Just as men voluntarily joined up in business, social, and political associations, it was believed that they could educate themselves by organizing cooperatives for study. During the 1830s and 1840s, many mutual-improvement societies, some with literary facilities, were formed.

An even more popular informal educational institution was the lyceum, which grew out of the proposals of an Englishman, Lord Henry Brougham, leader of the English Whigs and founder of the Useful Knowledge Society. In his *Political Observations Upon the Education of the People* (1825), which went through more than 30 editions in five years, Brougham called for a system of public lectures on the arts and sciences, the formation of discussion societies, the establishment of libraries for workingmen, and the publication of cheap books. His admirers in America, spurred on by a New Englander, Joseph Holbrook, soon put his recommendations into practice.

By 1835, lyceums could be found in 15 states, their activities coordinated by a national lyceum organization. By 1860, no less than 3000 lyceums had been set up, mainly in New England, New York, and the upper Mississippi Valley, where public-school sentiment was strong. The lyceums sponsored talks on every conceivable topic, with scientific and practical subjects arousing the greatest interest. Eminent men like Emerson addressed lyceum audiences on such themes as "Wealth" and "Power," and others of stature discoursed on the issues of the day.

The lyceums had their faults. They often "confounded knowledge of useful things with useful knowledge." The education they offered was likely to remain superficial and was often remote from the very classes for which it was theoretically designed. Yet lyceums helped to bridge the gulf between the learned minority and the community and spread the ideal of popular culture in a predominantly commercial society.

## v  *The Reformers*

### TEMPERANCE AND HUMANITARIANISM

The spirit of reform of which the free-school and lyceum movements were two reflections pervaded America during the ante-bellum era. It derived in part from the general optimism and also from faith in the power of cooperation to solve all problems and hurry progress on. Most reformers were religious people, motivated by an evangelical zeal to promote pet projects. Some were freakish and wild, insisting that salvation lay in the universal acceptance of reform in dress or diet, or in the abandonment of money. Some believed that the "social destiny of man" lay in new forms of communal society. But reform had its less visionary side as well. During the 1830s and 1840s, a number of men and women devoted their lives to stamping out specific social evils or to supporting particular causes: temperance, the treatment of the insane and the criminal, the education of the deaf, dumb, and blind, equality for women, world peace, and the abolition of slavery.

Until abolitionism aroused the country after 1830, the movement for "temperance" in the use of alcoholic beverages was the most intense reform activity of all. What caused the increasing consumption of liquor is hard to say, but the social scapegoats most frequently pointed to in this period were the excessive mobility of the American population, the attendant break-up of families and disruption of community life, the loneliness and fatigue of the farmer, and the long hours of the industrial worker newly arrived in the impersonal city from the country or from another country. In 1820, census-takers would not list distilling as a separate industry since almost everyone in rural areas engaged in it. In the cities, saloons were numbered in the thousands.

The agitation against drinking had been given a strong impetus by the publication in 1805 of Dr. Benjamin Rush's *Inquiry into the Effect of Ardent Spirits upon the Human Mind and Body*. But whereas Rush attacked drinking as bad for the health, the temperance reformers stressed its moral viciousness. This approach was promoted after 1810 by Lyman Beecher and his fellow evangelical preachers who, with the support of Bible and Tract societies and missionary boards, soon induced millions to take the pledge as "teetotalers." In

458

1826 the American Temperance Society was organized in Boston to coordinate the activities of hundreds of local groups. In 1833, when more than 2000 such groups were functioning, a stronger national organization was set up in Philadelphia as the United States Temperance Union. Three years later, with the affiliation of Canadian societies, its name was changed to the American Temperance Union.

One surviving example of teetotaling propaganda is Timothy Shay Arthur's *Ten Nights in a Bar-Room.* But the temperance crusaders went beyond persuasion to legislation. The first Prohibition law was enacted in Maine in 1846, and within five years 12 other states, all in the North, had adopted some kind of liquor control law. Many who supported such legislation were opposed to total prohibition and their quarrels with the teetotalers eventually weakened the movement. Yet the campaign against "demon rum" probably reduced the consumption of alcohol. It also offered a training ground for supporters of other reform movements.

One of the most salutary of these was the crusade for humane and effective treatment of the insane and feeble-minded, led by Dorothea Lynde Dix (1802–1887). In her *Memorial to the Legislature of Massachusetts* (1834), the result of painstaking investigation, Miss Dix depicted conditions in asylums throughout the state that were medieval in their barbarity. To the popular mind, insanity was a hideous moral regression into animality, and Miss Dix found that its victims were whipped and caged and neglected as if they were indeed dangerous beasts. In her fact-strewn and quietly effective summary, she omitted nothing: "The condition of human beings, reduced to the extremest states of degradation and misery, cannot be exhibited in softened language or adorn a polished page."

During the next 15 years, her influence extended into every section of the country. Eleven states established hospitals for the insane partly as a result of her work. Before

she died in 1887 she played an important part in establishing such hospitals in 21 other states.

## THE COMMUNITARIANS

In the early stages of the industrial revolution in America as in Britain and France, the condition of the workers often seemed so oppressive that leading industrialists themselves thought there must be some alternative to the barbarism around them, and substitutes for private capitalism won respectable and even conservative consideration. Cooperatives and, indeed, entire new cooperative communities were proposed by the most forward-looking, who, filled with the utopian spirit of the times, lectured to audiences and conducted short-lived community experiments until their bored, disillusioned, or offended disciples deserted them. Likewise, until the militant abolitionism of William Lloyd Garrison heightened feelings and hopes on the slave issue in the 1830s, the idea of black colonies and communities as an alternative to black bondage also attracted followers.

It is now fashionable to debunk the early nineteenth-century communitarians as escapists and nitwits, even as the precursors of twentieth-century totalitarianism. But in pointing out the obvious limitations of the utopian mentality, one need not throw out the baby with the bathwater. Early American communities, both religious and secular, were efforts to improve society, not escape it. Unlike the doctrinaire socialist, the communitarian believed in social harmony rather than in class warfare, in voluntary action rather than in compulsion.

The two most controversial community experiments during this period were inspired by Robert Owen, a successful manufacturer and industrial reformer from New Lanark, Scotland, and Charles Fourier, a French socialist. Robert Owen came to America in 1825 to found a community at New Harmony, Indiana, on a site that he had purchased from a group of German communitarians known as the Rappites. Owen believed that man was the product of his environment and that for a society to be happy and moral, its members must enjoy material equality. A number of gifted European scholars came to Owen's utopia, and for a time the community offered the best educational instruction in the country, but the rank and file had more than their share of human frailties. According to Timothy Flint, a missionary and novelist, New Harmony attracted.

the indolent, the unprincipled, men of desperate fortunes, moon-worshippers, romantic young men . . . those who had dreamed about earthly Elysiums, a great many honest aspirants after a better order of things, poor men simply desiring an education for their children.

A good many people wondered even in 1825 whether Owen's ideas could "keep alive that spirit of liberty and self-respect for one's own opinion, that so peculiarly belongs to the American people," and Owen's experiment did indeed fail after two years. But a large share of the failure of New Harmony can be attributed to the carelessness and imprecision of its founder. Though personally amiable and well-liked (he was one of the few socialists ever to address both Houses of Congress), Owen had the unhappy faculty of introducing irrelevant issues and needlessly antagonizing American prejudices. Owen's antireligious views provoked more abhorrence than his fluctuating economic opinions, which Owen always regarded as secondary to his main purpose: the establishment of a rational system of society. His denunciation of "MARRIAGE," as one along with "PRIVATE OR INDIVIDUAL PROPERTY" and "absurd and irrational SYSTEMS OF RELIGION," in his "TRINITY of the most monstrous evils that could be combined to inflict mental and physical evil," also got him into trouble. No instance of licentiousness was ever authenticated at New Harmony, but this did not save Owen himself from being classed by his critics with "whores and whoremongers," nor his community from being branded as "one great brothel."

The collapse of New Harmony in 1827 hastened the demise of Nashoba, the black community set up by the Owenite Englishwoman Frances Wright in 1826 in Shelby

*Owen's grandiose plan for New Harmony included public buildings and botanical gardens enclosed by a rectangle of members' dwellings. His dream never progressed much beyond the log cabin stage as seen in this steel engraving. (The Granger Collection.)*

460

County, Tennessee. Ironically, Nashoba was situated on 300 acres once forcibly taken from the Chickasaw Indians. From 50 to 100 slaves were to be brought here, hopefully to earn enough money to purchase their freedom while learning the attitudes and skills needed to sustain it. Miss Wright, however, soon imposed on Nashoba a full-scale communitarian scheme open to whites as well as blacks. She also went further than Owen in attacking marriage and religion, and one of her lieutenants proceeded to publish in a popular magazine accounts of the free sexual relationships there. Miss Wright defended these. If "the possession of the right of free action," she said, "inspire not the courage to exercise the right, liberty has done but little for us." Nashoba, however, could not long survive such revelations; yet its end was happier than that of many other communities in that Miss Wright sailed with Nashoba's slaves in January 1830 to Haiti, where their emancipation was effected.

Apparently the failure of Owen's experiments did little to reduce the persisting influence of his ethical, educational, and psychological theories. Later socialist communities, disavowing Owen's pet notions about religion and marriage, carried on the communitarian idea. In the 1830s, a resurgence of communitarian enterprise occurred which in some ways was an even more dramatic protest against the increasing impersonality of society.

Owenism had suggested free-thought and free-love to middle-class Americans. The doctrines of Fourier seemed less dangerous, and during the 1840s were espoused by a talented and respectable nucleus: Albert Brisbane, Fourier's chief propagandist; Parke Godwin, reformer and critic; Margaret Fuller, feminist, famed conversationalist, critic, and one-time editor of *The Dial,* the organ of the transcendentalists; George Ripley, founder of Brook Farm; and many others. Most of them eventually gave up their early radicalism, but for some years they spread Fourier's theories across the country.

The Fourierists (or "Fury-ites," as their enemies called them) regarded private capitalism as wasteful and degrading. If men would only abandon the competitive way and gather in *phalanxes,* or associated groups, they could transform the world of work into a paradise. What particularly appealed to the Fourierists, many of whom were New England transcendentalists, was the emphasis that Fourier put on practical idealism and the dignity of the worker.

Between 1840 and 1850, Fourier's followers organized more than 40 phalanxes in the United States. None was successful, but one at least became a lasting legend, the subject of Hawthorne's *The Blithedale Romance.* This was Brook Farm, organized by a group of transcendentalist intellectuals in 1841 and expressly converted to Fourierism in 1843–1844. More interested at first in the Oversoul than in their bank accounts, the Brook Farmers decided to demonstrate the possibility of combining the life of the mind with manual labor. ("After breakfast," Hawthorne noted in his diary, "Mr. Ripley put a four-pronged instrument into my hands, which he gave me to understand was called a pitch-fork; and he and Mr. Farley being armed with similar weapons, we all commenced a gallant attack upon a heap of manure.") The community, which never numbered more than 100, attracted about 4000 visitors a year. But its practical side proved less successful. In 1847 a fire ruined the already insolvent enterprise and it was abandoned.

Secular communities like Brook Farm failed because the volunteers had neither the knowledge nor the temperament to sustain them. But the communal settlements of the German sectarians—who brought with them a tradition of village cooperation, and who were skillful farmers held together by strong religious ties—showed time and again that the communitarian idea could be made to work. Yet Americans seemed too individualistic to sink their private ambitions in such projects.

## ABOLITION

From the 1830s on, one reform issue grew larger and more portentous until it overshadowed all the others: the antislavery cause, or abolition. Its origins reached back to the late seventeenth century, when humanitarian Puritans like Samuel Sewall and Roger Williams spoke out against the ownership of human chattels. The Quakers had long fought the buying and selling of slaves, and in the Revolutionary and post-Revolutionary eras liberals in every section had deplored slavery as a mortal disease. It was this conviction that inspired the American Colonization Society, founded in 1817 with private, state, and federal support, to establish Liberia in 1822 as a colony for ex-slaves. Unfortunately for the proponents of colonization, hardly more than a thousand free Negroes were transported to Africa between 1822 and 1830, and the others showed little desire to emigrate. By 1860 no more than 15,000 American blacks had settled outside the country. The failure of the colonization plan and the apparent ineffectiveness of those who believed in gradual emancipation encouraged the radical abolitionists to start their campaign for immediate emancipation.

In 1831, William Lloyd Garrison began publishing *The Liberator,* the first outright abolitionist periodical. Its appearance marked the beginning of the great antislavery offensive. Garrison was a Massachusetts journalist, neurotic and wayward yet gentle and humorous, tolerant on occasion yet uncompromising in his cherished beliefs. As with many of his followers, abolition was only one of Garrison's causes. He was an ardent worker for women's rights and international peace, a fervent opponent of capital punishment and imprisonment for debt. But after 1830 slavery absorbed him. He denounced slavery not because it was inefficient or undemocratic or unjust, but because it was sinful. The Constitution, which guaranteed slavery, he called "the most bloody

and heaven-daring arrangement ever made by men for the continuance and protection of a system of the most atrocious villainy ever exhibited on earth." And he publicly burned copies.

Garrison's vituperative attacks against the "Southern oppressors" did much to intensify antiabolition sentiment in the South, while his fanaticism frightened moderate antislavery people everywhere. His refusal to resort to political action also reduced his effectiveness. A different approach was taken by Theodore Dwight Weld of Ohio, who organized and directed the activities of the abolitionist societies in the Northwest. Weld preferred patient organization to flamboyant pronouncements, and his devoted followers, well versed in the techniques of revival meetings, converted thousands to the abolitionist cause. Before 1850, almost 2000 societies had been formed with a membership close to 200,000, and the talent and conscience of the North had rallied to the antislavery standard. John Greenleaf Whittier of Massachusetts became the bard of abolition, while Emerson, Thoreau, Whitman, Longfellow, and Melville all condemned slavery. Boston's eloquent Wendell Phillips thundered against it, as did reputable ministers like Theodore Parker and William Ellery Channing. Southerners like James G. Birney and the Grimké sisters renounced their slave property and joined the antislavery cause.

The abolitionists' strength lay in their unselfish dedication and their appeal to Christian principles. Their weakness lay in their reckoning insufficiently with the social barriers to be overcome by Negroes once they were declared free. Since the abolitionists denounced slavery as a sin as well as a social evil, they concentrated upon arousing the conscience of the country, not only to break the slave's shackles but to welcome him to the open society. "To be without a plan," cried one of Garrison's followers, "is the true genius and glory of the Anti-Slavery enterprise!" In his discussions of slavery, even Theodore Weld once said he had "always presented it as pre-eminently a

(Left) William Lloyd Garrison in 1850. (The Bettmann Archive) and (right) Wendell Phillips speaking against the Fugitive Slave Act on Boston Common in 1851. (The Granger Collection.) Phillips showed little interest in abolition until in 1835, outraged on seeing Garrison dragged through the streets, he gave up the practice of law, and devoted his life to the antislavery cause.

moral question, arresting the conscience of the nation. . . . As a question of politics and national economy, I have passed it with scarce a look or a word."

Such pronouncements reflected the abolitionist's conviction that the appeal to conscience must not be allowed to fail. If it failed, all would be lost. Practically all abolitionists abhorred the idea of violent revolution by the slaves, a fact seldom recognized in the South; nor did they envisage or want—as James Russell Lowell wrote in 1848—a civil war over slavery. Lowell did not, however, rule out the possibility:

No one can deplore more sincerely than we do an armed appeal for justice. But still more deeply do we lament the cause of it. Starvation and slaughter are both bad, but while you tolerate the one you are creating the necessity for the other. Are the atrocities of men driven to insurrection so horrible as the fact that society has allowed them to become capable of their commission. If violence be not the way of obtaining social rights, neither is it capable of maintaining social wrongs.

Once the war started, most abolitionists preferred to let the South go in peace in the hope that slavery would wither sooner there if the section were isolated from the rest of the world.

As the Civil War progressed, abolitionists gradually altered their stand and were in the forefront of those who helped convert the war into a struggle for emancipation (see p. 620). When emancipation finally did come, the abolitionists themselves had worked out a constructive program for weaning the ex-slave to full citizenship. But all that was in the future. In the mid-1830s even in the North, public opinion stigmatized the abolitionists as a band of misguided bigots whose activities on behalf of a people hopelessly inferior would destroy the Union if left unchecked. New

York, Boston, Philadelphia, Cincinnati, as well as Richmond and Charleston —towns and cities in every section—were swept by anti-Garrison riots and mobbings, in defiance, or with the connivance, of the local authorities. Garrison was dragged through the streets of Boston by an angry mob of "genteel ruffians," as he called them, and with the not so secret connivance of the "higher" classes; George Thompson, an English abolitionist, was howled down and threatened with bodily harm; Elijah Lovejoy, an antislavery editor in Alton, Illinois, was murdered by a mob in 1837.

Despite the stern repression of the abolitionists in the North and the constant assurances given to southern leaders that the majority of people in the free states detested the ideas of *The Liberator,* the South grew ever more uneasy (see Chapter Sixteen). It demanded penal laws against antislavery terrorists and threatened economic reprisals if they were not silenced. Southern postmasters confiscated suspected abolitionist literature. Southern fears of slave insurrection and resentment against atrocity stories in abolitionist propaganda made the South magnify the strength of the antislavery movement in the North. The intemperate response of the southerners, in turn, only increased northern antislavery sentiment. As the sectional conflict deepened, the dream of the millennium that had stirred the hearts of the reformers in the 1830s and 1840s faded away.

464

# READINGS

Alexis de Tocqueville, *Democracy in America* (1835), is a profound analysis of the period covered in this chapter. The new translation by George Lawrence (1966) is now preferred over the one by Henry Reeve issued immediately after the first French edition. G.W. Pierson, *Tocqueville and Beaumont in America* (1938), adds considerably to the understanding of Tocqueville's work. Useful and readable general accounts are A.F. Tyler, *Freedom's Ferment: Phases of American Social History to 1860* (1944); R.E. Riegel, *Young America 1830–1840* (1949); Meade Minnigerode, *The Fabulous Forties 1840–1850* (1924); and E.D. Branch, *The Sentimental Years 1836–1860* (1934). V.L. Parrington, *The Romantic Revolution in America 1800–1860* (1927) retains many merits. D.B. Davis, *Homicide in American Fiction 1798–1860* (1957), and Fred Somkin, *Unquiet Eagle: Memory and Desire in the Idea of American Freedom 1815–1860* (1967), are suggestive studies of the relation between social violence and literary reflection.

On individual writers, see Kay House, *Cooper's Americans* (1965); R.L. Rusk, *The Life of Ralph Waldo Emerson* (1949); J.W. Krutch, *Henry David Thoreau* (1948); A.H. Quinn, *Edgar Allan Poe* (1941); Mark Van Doren, *Nathaniel Hawthorne* (1949); Newton Arvin, *Herman Melville* (1950); and G.W. Allen, *The Solitary Singer: A Critical Biography of Walt Whitman* (1955). D.H. Lawrence, *Studies in Classic American Literature* (1923), is available in full, along with other penetrating literary studies, in the superb anthology, Edmund Wilson, ed., *The Shock of Recognition: The Development of Literature in the United States Recorded by the Men Who Made It* (1943). F.O. Matthiessen, *American Renaissance* (1941), is a brilliant interpretation of America's literary flowering. Lewis Mumford, *The Golden Day* (1926), is also revealing. R.W.B. Lewis, *The American Adam* (1955), treats of the theme of innocence in American literature. Leo Marx, *The Machine in the Garden* (1964), is concerned with innocence under pressure. On this theme see also Perry Miller, ed., *Margaret Fuller, American Romantic* (1963).

O.W. Larkin, *Art and Life in America* (1949), covers the history of painting and sculpture. Neil Harris, *The Artist in American Society: The Formative Years 1790–1860* (1968), is a searching analysis. Horatio Greenough's essays are conveniently collected in H.A. Small, ed., *Form and Function* (1957). On drama, music, and popular entertainment see A.H. Quint, *A History of the American Drama from the Beginning to the Civil War* (1923); O.S. Coad and Edwin Mims, Jr., *The American Stage* (1929); and J.T. Howard, *Our American Music, Three Hundred Years of It* (1946). C.M. Rourke, *American Humor* (1931), is full of insight. F.L. Mott, *American Journalism: A History of Newspapers in the United States* (1950 ed.), is standard, as is Mott's *A History of American Magazines* (5 vols., 1930–1968).

The literature on education is more extensive than exhilarating. Relevant for this chapter are S.L. Jackson, *America's Struggle for Free Schools: Social Tension and Education in New England and New York, 1827–1842* (1941), and Paul Monroe, *Founding of the American Public School System* (1940). Merle Curti, *The Social Ideas of American Educators* (1935), contains some excellent chapters. L.H. Tharp, *Until Victory: Horace Mann und Mary Peabody* (1953), is a readable biography of the leading education reformer. The history of colleges is well presented in Frederick Rudolph, *The American College and University* (1962). There are informative chapters in Richard Hofstadter and W.P. Metzger, *The Development of Academic Freedom in the United States* (1955). The best account of the lyceum movement is in Carle Bode, *The American Lyceum, Town Meeting of the Mind* (1956).

Leading books on special aspects of the reform movement include J.A. Krout, *The Origins of Prohibition* (1925); H.E. Marshall, *Dorothea Dix, Forgotten Samaritan* (1937); Albert Deutsch, *The Mentally Ill in America* (1937); Charles Nordhoff, *The Communistic Societies of the United States* (1875); Lindsay Swift, *Brook Farm* (1899); A.E. Bestor, *Backwoods Utopias: The Sectarian and Owenite Phases of Communitarian Socialism in America 1663–1829* (1950); and W.H. and J.H. Pease, *Black Utopia: Negro Communal Experiments in America* (1963). Religion and reform are treated in Perry Miller, *The Life of the Mind in America, from the Revolution to the Civil War* (1966); T.L. Smith, *Revivalism and Social Reform in Mid-Nineteenth Century America* (1957); C.S. Griffin, *Their Brothers' Keepers, Moral Stewardship in the United States 1800–1865* (1960); D.G. Mathews, *Slavery and Methodism, A Chapter in American Morality 1780–1845* (1965); and W.R. Hutchinson, *The Transcendentalist Ministers—Church Reform in the New England Renaissance* (1959).

P.J. Staudenraus, *The African Colonization Movement 1816–1865* (1961), is a scholarly monograph on efforts to settle the American Negro abroad. Of the many studies of antislavery and abolitionist activities, the most comprehensive is D.L. Dumond, *Anti-Slavery: The Crusade for Freedom in America* (2 vols., 1961). See also Martin Duberman, ed., *The Antislavery Vanguard, New Essays on the Abolitionists* (1965); Louis Filler, *The Crusade Against Slavery 1830–1860* (1960); G.H. Barnes, *The Anti-Slavery Impulse 1830–1844* (1933); Allan Nevins, *Ordeal of the Union* (2 vols., 1947); Laurence Lader, *The Bold Brahmins* (1961); and J.L. Thomas, ed., *Slavery Attacked: The Abolitionist Crusade* (1965). Truman Nelson, ed., *Documents of Upheaval, Selections from William Lloyd Garrison's* THE LIBERATOR *1831–1865* (1966), is valuable for this leading journal. S.M. Elkins, *Slavery* (1959), offers a critique of the abolitionist approach. J.M. McPherson, *The Struggle for Equality, Abolitionists and the Negro in the Civil War and Reconstruction* (1964), while covering a later period, is valuable for insights into the abolitionists' program. Biographical studies of such abolitionist leaders as Charles Sumner, J.G. Birney, William Lloyd Garrison, Theodore Parker, Wendell Phillips, Gerrit Smith, and Theodore Weld are rewarding. See also Readings for Chapter Sixteen.

# FIFTEEN

The struggle for power among the older sections of the country during the reign of "Old Hickory" did not obscure the beckoning opportunities in regions still to be encompassed in America's "empire for liberty."

Throughout the 1820s and 1830s, Americans were very much on the move not only into new states in the Louisiana Purchase but also deep into foreign territory beyond, all the way to the Pacific Coast and even to Pacific islands. Within little more than a quarter of a century thereafter, the unbroken expanse of the United States had been extended to its present limits, the annexation of Hawaii had been proposed, and the purchase of Alaska completed. Canada to the north and Cuba to the south, meanwhile, fed a craving for full hemispheric sovereignty that was curbed only with increasing difficulty once the slogan "Manifest Destiny" seemed to give the impetus of inevitability to America's explosive course.

The phrase Manifest Destiny became identified with expansionism only after 1845, but the idea of celestial design it embodied was much older. According to this idea, the "Father of the Universe," or the "Great Architect," had set aside the American continents and their island environs "for the free development of our yearly multiplying millions." No physical barrier, no foreign force, least of all what they often considered the sinister absolutism of the European system, could thwart the providential mission of the American people to extend *their* system across this hallowed land.

This vision of a mighty people on the march swelled an already inflated national rhetoric in the 1840s and 1850s and inspired often ridiculous oratorical displays couched in the

# MANIFEST DESTINY

current racist, imperialist, and mercenary idiom. But the rhetorical excesses of the Manifest Destiny school also derived in part from the prevalent optimistic idealism. New lands wrested from Indians and Mexicans, not to say Spaniards and Britons (as expansionists like Walt Whitman anticipated), by providing asylum and opportunity for the oppressed of Europe, would undermine world despotism, and by providing endless space for the full flowering of the American spirit, could only strengthen world democracy.

In this vein, Lewis Cass of Michigan told his fellow senators in February 1847:

In Europe . . . men are brought too much and kept too much in contact. There is not room for expansion. Minds of the highest order are pressed down by adverse circumstances, without the power of free exertion. . . . I trust we are far removed from all this; but to remove us further yet, we want almost unlimited power of expansion. That is our safety valve. The mightiest intellects which when compressed in thronged cities, and hopeless of their future, are ready to break the barriers around them the moment they enter the new world of the West, feel their freedom, and turn their energies to contend with the works of creation; converting the woods and the forest into towns, and villages, and cultivated fields, and extending the dominion of civilization and improvement over the domain of nature.

Practical politicians in charge of America's day-to-day diplomatic and military policies in the 1840s promoted more tangible objectives than the propagandists. They hoped to dominate northern Pacific waters and trade with the Orient, which they saw (and later generations continued to see) as the legitimate extension of the American West itself. The whole grand stretch of the Pacific Coast of North America afforded but three good locations for the necessary port facilities: the Strait of Juan de Fuca, leading into Puget Sound and then to disputed Oregon country; breathtaking San Francisco Bay inside Mexico's Californian Golden Gate; and the Bay of San Diego farther south, "as fine a bay for vessels under three hundred tons," said an American captain in the 1820s, "as was ever formed by Nature in her most friendly mood to mariners." American spokesmen from all sections of the country were in agreement on grasping these few fine anchorages and thereby keeping out rival powers, especially the rival who too proudly called herself Mistress of the Seas.

Much has been made in recent years of the force of these tangible objectives in effecting America's unparalleled expansion in this period, as against the vague vaporings of the Manifest Destiny enthusiasts. But it is safe to say that these tangible objectives themselves

467

468

gained in realism, as they gained in grandeur, for being promoted in the heady atmosphere of divine purpose which America's European rivals did not yet breathe.

## I Confrontations on the Canadian Border

### THE SEEDS OF SUSPICION

The westward surge of the American people and their star-spangled prognostications that their flag would soon wave from Patagonia to the North Pole only strengthened official British opinion (along with that of the rest of monarchical Europe) that the Yankees were a nation of bullies and braggarts who must be carefully watched and closely constrained.

Among the watchers in the 1830s and 1840s were the swarms of British travelers who made quick tours of the upstart land and reported it as dirty and swaggering and as shamelessly dollar-conscious as they thought it before they left home. These tours culminated in the visit of the famous "Boz," the still youthful Charles Dickens, in 1842, and the publication two years later of his novel, *Martin Chuzzlewit*.

Dickens's discontent with the United States was aggravated by his personal resentment against American publishers who pirated his enormously popular works. Deeper down he shared his countrymen's revulsion against the American states for repudiating their debts to British creditors after the Panic of 1837 (see p. 422). The American, Major Pawkins, Dickens writes in *Chuzzlewit*, "was a great politician; and the one article of his creed in reference to all public obligations involving the good faith and integrity of his country was, 'run a moist pen slick through everything, and start fresh.' This made him a patriot."

The soaring (Dickens said "spurious") spirit of American democracy—"we are a model of wisdom, and an example to the

*Charles Dickens at 31, the time of his first American visit. (The Granger Collection.)*

world, and the perfection of human reason, and a great deal more to the same purpose, which you may hear any hour in the day"— also angered many John Bulls, especially after Britain's First Reform Act of 1832 showed the force of the democratic spirit abroad. The American defense of slavery and assaults on abolitionists, after Britain had led the world in emancipating the Negroes in her colonies in 1833, only deepened the disenchantment with the American brand of liberty.

If Americans were to be watched and vilified within their very gates, they were to be constrained at the nearest vantage point outside, which was their Canadian border. The British, if possible, thought even less of their Canadian subjects than they did of the restless old rebels to the south, and for Canada itself as a paying colony they had learned to entertain the meagerest expectations. Yet Canada had her uses, "above all," wrote the future Colonial Secretary, E. G. Stanley, in 1824, "in case of [a third] war with the United States (no improbable future contingency)." In such an event, Stanley added, Canada "furnishes ample assistance in men, timber and harbours for carrying on the war, and that on the enemy's frontier." How seriously the British took the American menace is evidenced, beginning late in the 1820s, by their expenditure of millions of pounds (after the

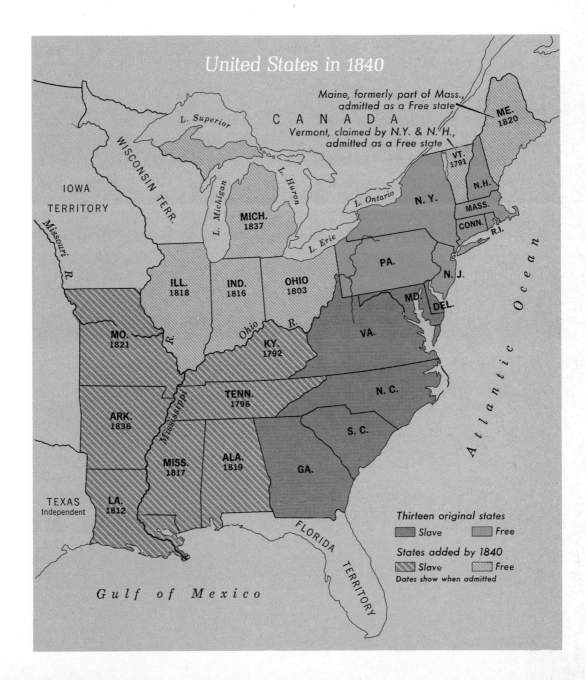

United States in 1840

Maine, formerly part of Mass., admitted as a Free state

Vermont, claimed by N.Y. & N.H., admitted as a Free state

ME. 1820

VT. 1791

N.H.

MASS.

CONN.

R.I.

N.Y.

PA.

N.J.

MD.

DEL.

VA.

N.C.

S.C.

GA.

WISCONSIN TERR.

IOWA TERRITORY

L. Superior

C A N A D A

L. Michigan

L. Huron

L. Ontario

L. Erie

MICH. 1837

ILL. 1818

IND. 1816

OHIO 1803

KY. 1792

MO. 1821

ARK. 1836

TENN. 1796

MISS. 1817

ALA. 1819

LA. 1812

TEXAS Independent

Missouri R.

Ohio R.

Mississippi

FLORIDA TERRITORY

Atlantic Ocean

Gulf of Mexico

Thirteen original states
Slave    Free

States added by 1840
Slave    Free
Dates show when admitted

470

Canadians themselves refused to be taxed for the purpose) in constructing the inland Rideau Canal as an alternative to the St. Lawrence waterway in case control of the latter ever fell to American invaders. The British spent millions more rebuilding the strategic citadel of Quebec.

### THE *CAROLINE* AFFAIR

Late in the 1830s and early in the 1840s three confrontations gave John Bull and Brother Jonathan welcome cause for honing up the weapons to be used beyond the war of words, if words failed. The first of these is known as "the *Caroline* affair."

In November and December 1837, inspired to a degree by the advance of the "great experiment" below the border, successive insurrections flared up in lower and upper Canada against the Crown. Loyal forces quickly suppressed these uprisings, but not before certain Americans had rallied to the rebels' cause. On the night of December 29, 1837, *Caroline,* a small American steamer engaged in ferrying supplies to the insurgents, lay moored on the New York side of the Niagara River. A party of loyal Canadian volunteers rowed across, routed *Caroline's* crew, set her afire, towed her out, and watched her sink. During the scuffle one American was killed.

The United States promptly demanded an apology for the British "invasion" of American territory. But the British replied that *Caroline,* by abetting the criminal conspiracy in Canada, had become fair game. They were on less tenable ground for having taken direct action without first formally protesting to American officials and giving them a chance to discipline their own citizens—an oversight which reflected the lifelong contempt of the British Foreign Secretary, Lord Palmerston, for American claims to nationhood. Further to rub it in, Queen Victoria knighted the Canadian officer who had led the boarding party.

Many Americans soon showed as little concern for protocol as Palmerston. While the stalemate over *Caroline* held, tens of thousands of backwoodsmen all along the border from Vermont to Michigan, many of them made jobless by the current business depression, joined together during the summer of 1838 in "Hunters' Lodges." Nominally secret, these well-armed organizations openly proclaimed their purpose, "to emancipate the British Colonies from British Thraldom." Each "Hunter" also swore an oath to "help destroy . . . every power, or authority of Royal origin, upon this continent, . . . So help me God!" Certain bands of "Hunters" soon crossed into Canada and engaged in futile skirmishes. But they misjudged the eagerness of most Canadians to throw off their yoke as Texans had recently thrown off that of Mexico, and were soon induced by General Winfield Scott, President Van Buren's persuasive emissary, to disband.

The *Caroline* affair might also have been allowed to die had not one of the alleged participants in the vessel's destruction, Alexander McLeod, been arrested by New York State authorities in November 1840 and charged with murder and arson. Palmerston now acknowledged that the raid had been officially planned to forestall American aid to the insurrectionists and demanded McLeod's release on the ground that any actions he may have taken were done under orders. McLeod's execution, Palmerston warned, would mean war.

New York's Governor William H. Seward insisted that McLeod face trial in the state courts, though he promised Secretary of State Webster that if convicted McLeod would be pardoned. Fortunately, McLeod was acquitted. Lest similar incidents occur, Webster, with presidential support, drafted a measure establishing federal jurisdiction in all cases involving aliens accused of committing acts under the direction of a foreign government. Congress passed this measure in August 1842.

### THE "AROOSTOOK WAR"

The Rideau Canal (see above), was not the only military-inspired transportation project of the British in Canada during these troubled times. The freezing of the St. Lawrence had hampered the movement of troops in putting down the Canadian insurrections of 1837, and the next year the British decided on the construction of an overland road from St. John on the Bay of Fundy in New Brunswick to Montreal and Quebec. In February 1839 work began on the proposed route in the rich Aroostook River valley where the conflicting claims of the State of Maine and the province of New Brunswick grew ever more roundly assertive as the value of the timber in the valley soared. When the "foreign" lumberjacks now once more entered the disputed area and began felling trees for the road project, the hastily mobilized Maine militia chased them out.

The "Aroostook War" was a bloodless affray; but during this second Anglo-American confrontation on the Canadian border, war-fever in Washington had grown even warmer than during the *Caroline* incident. Congress confirmed the gravity of the situation by appropriating $10 million for war purposes and authorizing President Van Buren to enlist 50,000 volunteers.

As it turned out, neither money nor men were needed, for in March 1839, General Winfield Scott again succeeded in smoothing things over at the scene. Scott, however,, could not eliminate the source of the trouble, which lay in the rankling vagueness of the frontier line. The scene of the "Aroostook War" had been in dispute since the end of the Revolution and soured Anglo-American relations until the Webster-Ashburton Treaty of 1842.

## THE CREOLE CASE

The third Anglo-American confrontation of this period, the *Creole* case of 1841, is related to the Canadian border only because it so strained Anglo-American relations on another touchy subject that it made the formidable border issues more difficult to settle. This confrontation arose out of an encounter on the high seas involving the slave trade.

In her attempts to destroy the slave traffic, especially after the emancipation of 1833, Britain had made treaties with many nations giving her navy even in peacetime the right to stop and search suspected merchantmen under all flags. Palmerston boasted that Britain had enlisted in the fight against the slave trade, "every state in Christendom which has a flag that sails on the ocean, with the single exception of the United States of North America." This was not entirely true; France, like the United States, had resisted Britain's assumption of holier-than-thou authority. But it suited Secretary Palmerston to point the accusing finger, and with some justice, for many slave ships escaped search and seizure simply by running up the Stars and Stripes in time.

Hard feeling aroused by Britain's affronts to the flag in the slave trade heightened American indignation in the *Creole* case. While carrying about 130 slaves from Virginia to New Orleans, the American vessel *Creole* was taken over by the blacks in a successful mutiny during which one white passenger was killed. The Negroes then sailed her to the British port of Nassau, in the Bahamas, and went ashore. Those not held for the killing were permitted to live in the Bahamas as free men, despite the protests of *Creole's* owners to local authorities and the efforts of American officials to reclaim them.

## THE WEBSTER-ASHBURTON TREATY

Behind each confrontation between Britain and her mettlesome former colonies throughout the nineteenth century lay the growing commercial and industrial rivalry of the two nations. This rivalry inspired Palmerston, the curmudgeon, to prick every Yankee pretension, and Americans to reply in kind. Palmerston's unremitting insults and attacks finally sickened even his own people and his colleagues in the Cabinet. When he fell with the Melbourne ministry in 1841, both nations breathed sighs of relief. Soon after, Lord Aberdeen, as the new Foreign Secretary, and

472

Webster, the American Secretary of State, arranged to meet in an attempt to improve Anglo-American relations. Aberdeen showed his goodwill by accepting Washington as the scene of negotiations and by appointing as his special envoy Lord Ashburton, the husband of an American heiress.

The principal subject of the Webster-Ashburton talks was the Canadian-American border. Webster ultimately compromised on the Maine boundary issue and reached an

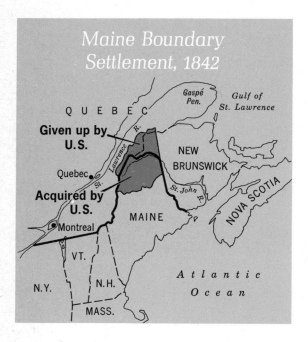

Maine Boundary Settlement, 1842

agreement that gave the United States approximately 7000 of the 12,000 square miles in question. The 5000 square miles granted to Britain were sufficient to protect the communications she so strongly desired between Quebec and New Brunswick. In return, she accepted the inaccurately surveyed boundary line running along the northern frontier of Vermont and New York and extending westward to Minnesota and Ontario. Agreement

here lessened the likelihood of conflict as settlement moved outward on the frontier. The line decided on, moreover, left the United States with the Mesabi iron ore deposits in northern Minnesota, unknown then, but of immense value later.

Webster enlarged the discussions by raising the question of the *Creole* incident, but Ashburton merely promised that henceforth British colonial authorities would not interfere with American vessels "driven by accident or violence" into British ports. The Americans, on their part, agreed to assist the British in patrolling the African coast and suppressing the slave-runners. Ashburton also refused to eat humble pie over the *Caroline* affair. He merely "regretted" that "some explanation and apology for this occurrence was not immediately made," and Webster had to make the best of the word "apology."

Extremists in Britain and America protested that their respective countries had suffered a diplomatic defeat in these negotiations, but the Webster-Ashburton Treaty, signed on August 9, 1842, was a model of compromise that paved the way for other peaceful settlements during the next two decades. Anglo-American relations were further improved in 1846 when Sir Robert Peel's government repealed the British Corn Laws and Polk's administration (see p. 480) pushed the Walker Tariff through Congress. The British measure opened her ports more freely to American wheat; the low duties in the Walker Tariff opened American markets more freely to British manufactures.

Canadian sentiment for annexation to the United States, however, continued strong, as did American sentiment (except in the South) for satisfying the Canadian feeling. The repeal of the Corn Laws particularly, by ending the favorable position enjoyed by Canadian wheat in Britain, fed the hopes of annexationists in Canada and in the United States, for Canadian growers now longed for free entry into the American market by means of the union of the two lands.

### LIMITATIONS ON SOUTHERN EXPANSION

The "manifest destiny" of Texas, and of the even more inviting warm empire beyond, had become far closer to realization by the time of the Webster-Ashburton Treaty than the destiny still reserved in optimistic American minds and hearts for the vast cold expanse of Canada. The speedier progress of Texas toward fulfillment in American terms stemmed largely from the unsatisfied, and as yet insatiable, land hunger of the South.

In the North, after the removal of the Sauk and Fox tribes in 1833, emigrants from Illinois, Indiana, Ohio, and Kentucky had begun to spill into the newly opened Iowa and Wisconsin country. By 1840, some 75,000 settlers had established themselves on the rich farmlands here, and smaller numbers, including lumbermen and trappers, were pushing into Minnesota. The small southern farmer, as well as the planter, had no such vast tracts at his disposal. By 1840, most of the best land on the southern Gulf plains was occupied by big planters and was being worked by slave gangs. After the admission of Arkansas in 1836, the only remaining prospective slave state under the provisions of the Missouri Compromise was the territory of Florida.

Immediately to the west of the last southern settlements lay the "permanent Indian frontier," established in the 1820s in much of present-day Oklahoma and Kansas, to hold forever, it was said, the displaced woods Indians of the East as well as the numerous hostile tribes native to the region. As late as the 1860s this Indian reserve was known as "the Great American Desert" and had little appeal to slaveholders whose "peculiar institution," in any case, was barred by law if not by nature from its northerly portion.

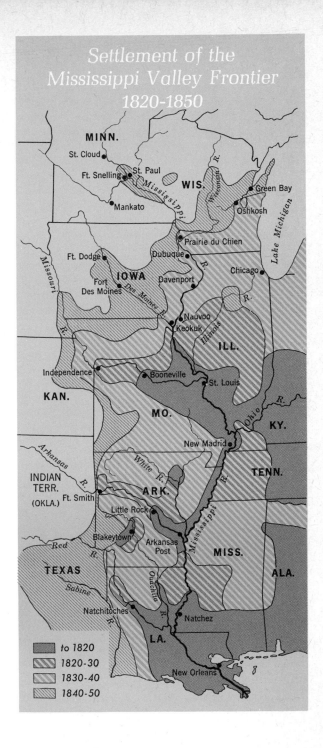

Settlement of the Mississippi Valley Frontier 1820-1850

to 1820
1820-30
1830-40
1840-50

474

South and west of the Indian range stretched Texas, recently become precariously independent of shaky Mexican regimes. Beyond Texas lay Mexico's vague and vaguely held California empire whose charms had so long and so lavishly been reported by far-ranging mountain men and mariners. Both Texas and California had ultimately to be fought for, but their fall to the United States seemed destined none the less.

Senator Robert J. Walker of Mississippi, Polk's promoter for the Presidency in 1844 on an aggressively expansionist platform (see p. 480), and then the power behind the throne, caught the spirit of the times in a letter to Democratic leaders across the country in January of the election year:

If the Creator had separated Texas from the Union by mountain barriers, . . . there might be plausible objections; but he has planed down the whole [Mississippi] valley, including Texas, and united every atom of the soil and every drop of the waters, . . . and marked . . . the whole for the dominion of one government and the residence of one people; and it is impious in man to attempt to dissolve the great and glorious union. . . . Who will desire to check the young eagle of America, now refixing her gaze upon our former limits, and repluming her pinions for the returning flight?

### THE LONE STAR REPUBLIC

In 1819, when she obtained Florida from Spain, the United States had surrendered her dubious claim, based upon the carefree geography of the Louisiana Purchase treaty, to the Mexican province of Texas in the state of Coahuila—much to the disgust of later frontier politcians like Senator Walker, who kept harping on "our former limits." American traders and military adventurers nevertheless continued the illicit commercial relations they had already established with the Mexicans despite Spain's many warnings. When Mexico, with the assistance of such traders and fighters, won her independence from Spain in 1821, she promptly put American commerce

on a legitimate footing and invited additional Americans to settle in Texas and develop the resources of the land.

Connecticut-born Moses Austin, who obtained a land grant from the Mexican government in 1820 after the Panic of 1819 had got him into serious financial difficulties in neighboring Missouri, pioneered the American colonization of Texas. Moses Austin died in 1821 and could not develop his tract, but in 1823 Mexico validated the grant for his son, Stephen, who carried through the first colonization program. Other American promoters, or *empresarios*, received concessions similar to the Austins'.

Mexican officials had hoped that the settlement of Texas by white Americans would protect their country from Indian raids and from possible aggression by the United States. But they soon realized they had miscalculated. Between 1820 and 1830, about 20,000 Americans with approximately 2000 slaves had crossed into Texas, largely from the lower Mississippi frontier. Most of them were law-abiding people, but rougher elements, particularly in eastern Texas, soon made the Mexicans subscribe to John Jay's old complaint that white frontiersmen were more troublesome than red Indians. The Texans, on their part, soon began to champ at their lack of self-government. As part of the state of Coahuila, Texas province was under the thumb of the Mexican-dominated state legislature. As early as 1826, after an *empresario* named Haden Edwards quarreled with the authorities over land titles, his brother, Benjamin, proclaimed the Republic of Fredonia and staged a rebellion that the Mexicans easily put down.

Offers by the United States to purchase Texas in 1827 only served to deepen Mexico's anxiety over Yankee expansionism. Mexico had complaints about Yankee independence as well. American settlers in Mexico had failed to become Catholics, as they were required to do by the terms of their invitation. They had ignored a Mexican prohibition against the slave trade by substituting a thinly disguised indenture system. Some, moreover, had slipped over into territory reserved by law for Mexicans.

In 1830 the Mexican government sent troops to occupy Texas, called a halt to further American immigration, and passed other restrictive measures, including the abolition of slavery itself. This change in policy angered the American Texans already aroused by the government's refusal to separate Texas from the state of Coahuila. In 1832 General A. L. de Santa Anna emerged as Mexico's strong man, instituted a centralist program, and three years later abolished all local rights. Early in 1836 he led an army of 6000 into Texas to bring the rebellious Americans to book. Confronted with Santa Anna's threat to exterminate them, Americans in Texas declared their independence on March 2, 1836, set up a provisional government under a constitution that sanctioned slavery, and appointed Sam Houston Commander-in-Chief of the few hundred men mobilized at Gonzales. Santa Anna already had the Alamo mission in San Antonio under siege and when it fell on March 6 he massacred the 187 defenders including the commander, William B. Travis, and such legendary figures as Davy Crockett and Jim Bowie. Three weeks later more than 300 were massacred at Goliad on surrendering to the Mexican General José Urrea.

Such brutal attacks led Houston to beat a steady retreat eastward until he reached the vicinity of San Jacinto creek. Here, on April 21, 1836, he suddenly turned on his unprepared pursuers. Fired up by the cry, "Remember the Alamo," Houston's force routed Santa Anna's army and took the dictator himself captive. On May 14, Santa Anna signed a treaty pledging Texan independence and fixing a vague boundary between Texas and Mexico. Although the Mexican Congress promptly repudiated the treaty, it could do nothing to reverse it.

### ANNEXATION EFFECTED

Sympathy for the Texas insurrectionists had been strong in the South and also in the Northwest, where their cause was identified with the struggles of the underprivileged. As one Ohio supporter declared in 1835:

The Texans are mostly composed of the poorer classes of society: men whom misfortunes have driven from our country; men who have gone there at the instance of the invitation of the Mexican Government, on the full assurance of the protection of that government; in the hope and expectation of being able to retrieve their shattered fortunes, and procure bread for their suffering families.

The Texas Revolution 1835-1836

Behind the boasts of the time about "the generous anglo-saxon blood" triumphing over the "blood thirsty barbarians of Mexico," was the widespread feeling that the Texans had fought the war of humanity and democracy.

Support for the Texans' cause, however, was less enthusiastic in the Northeast, especially among members of the Whig party, who viewed the Texans' request to enter the Union after they defeated Santa Anna as a slave-owners' plot. From five to seven states, it was pointed out, might be carved out of the huge

476

Texas domain, thus insuring southern control of Congress. Opponents of annexation protested so vehemently that President Jackson held off even recognizing the Lone Star Republic until just before he left office in 1837. Van Buren also withstood growing annexationist pressure, a policy that was to cost him dearly during Tyler's administration when his enemies in the South sought to unseat him as the titular head of the Democratic party, and thereby improve Calhoun's chances for the White House. In this strategy southern expansionists received enthusiastic support from western political leaders.

Denied admission to the United States and

menaced by unforgiving Mexico, the Lone Star Republic sought protection elsewhere. Britain liked the idea of an independent Texas that would export cotton and import British manufactured goods on a free-trade basis. Britain also opposed slavery. In December 1843 the British Foreign Secretary, Lord Aberdeen, was at pains formally to notify the United States that "it must be well known" to her "and to the whole world, that Great Britain desires, and is constantly exerting herself to procure the general abolition of slavery throughout the world," and "with regard to Texas, we avow that we wish to see slavery abolished there, as elsewhere." But slavery in Texas did not keep Britain from seeking permanent relations with her.

That Texas might link herself with Britain, a frightening prospect to northern businessmen, was even more frightening to slaveowners who felt that the abolition of slavery in Texas as a result of British pressure would encourage Negro insurrections in the slave states themselves.

*A woodcut depicting the annihilation of the Texan defenders of the Alamo. The principal figure is Davy Crockett, who joined the Texas forces shortly before this battle. The illustration is from* Davy Crockett's Almanac, *a publication devoted mainly to the humorous exploits of the Tennessee frontiersman and Congressman. (New York Public Library.)*

Sam Houston, now President of Texas, cleverly played upon American fears until the annexationists were ready to do almost anything to bring Texas into the Union before Britain succeeded in keeping her permanently out. President Tyler himself worked tirelessly to gain credit for annexation before his successor took office.

In April 1844 Tyler submitted a Texas statehood treaty to the Senate drawn up by Calhoun, whom he had just appointed Secretary of State. It was only on taking this office that Calhoun first learned of Lord Aberdeen's dispatch of the previous December and unfortunately for him he attached to the treaty proposal a letter he had just written in reply. In this letter, Calhoun defended southern slavery as a humane institution. He declared, furthermore, that Britain's abolitionist policy compelled the United States to absorb Texas out of self-protection.

Calhoun's little disquisition on the beauties of slavery delighted his disciples, but it insured the repudiation of the annexation treaty in the Senate by a vote of 36 to 16. Men who had been on the fence about Texas began to interpret annexation as a barefaced grab for slave territory. Tyler was chagrined by the Senate vote, but in February 1845, after expansionism had seemingly triumphed in the 1844 election (see p. 480), he succeeded in persuading both houses of Congress to pass a joint resolution favoring annexation. Such a resolution did not require the two-thirds majority in the Senate that an annexation *treaty* did under the Constitution, and it became effective on squeaking through the Senate 27 to 25. Texas now was offered statehood if she would agree to submit a proper constitution, assume her debts, and agree to the possible subdivision of her territory into not more than four states. In return, she would be permitted to keep her public lands and to retain slavery under the terms of the Missouri Compromise. Texas accepted this offer in October 1845, and on December 29 that year became the 28th state in the Union. Mexico, at the same time, recalled her minister in Washington.

*Daguerreotype of Sam Houston by Mathew Brady. (The Granger Collection.)*

III  *"Manifest Destiny" in the Far West*

### THE FUTURE OF OREGON

The future of Oregon as well as the future of Texas had reached a critical point as Americans rallied to their party standards for the presidential campaign of 1844.

Distant though it was from the mainstream of European and American politics and business, the Oregon country since the eighteenth century had been the scene and subject of competition among France, Spain, and Russia, as well as Britain and the United States. Early in the nineteenth century France and Spain both had surrendered their claims to the region; and in 1824, the Russians, expand-

477

478

ing southward from Alaska, had agreed to fix their own southern boundary at 54° 40′ (see p. 363). This left Britain and the United States free to settle ownership of the remainder of Oregon between themselves.

After John Jacob Astor's Pacific Fur Company was forced out of Oregon by the British North West Company in 1812 (see p. 376), Americans lost interest in Oregon for a generation. The British, on their part, feeling wholly secure in the region, made no effort to keep out those few adventurers from the United States who might find their way there. By the 1830s, however, American expansionists began to feel cramped even in their own vast territories and interest in Oregon revived. In 1832 and again in 1834, Nathaniel J. Wyeth, a merchant of Cambridge, Massachusetts, sent several expeditions to the region. Although financial failures, they served to

call attention once again to the feasibility of the overland route to the Northwest that had first been explored almost three decades earlier by Lewis and Clark.

Accompanying Wyeth to Oregon in 1834 was the first band of Methodist missionaries led by Jason Lee. The fertility of the soil in Oregon's Willamette Valley so captivated these men that its cultivation quickly took precedence over conversion of the Indians. By 1844, the home church in the East washed its hands of the enterprise, but the settlement in Oregon flourished. In the meantime, other denominations had followed the Methodists' lead. Marcus Whitman founded a Presbyterian mission near Fort Walla Walla in 1836, and in 1840 the Jesuits sent out Father De Smet, who founded a Catholic mission the next year.

The Protestants made little headway with

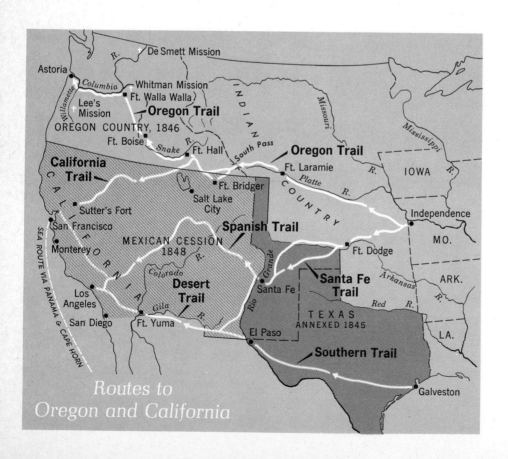

Routes to Oregon and California

the Indians of the Oregon region, whose resistance to the Gospel was sometimes rather
violent. Marcus Whitman, his wife, and 12
others in his mission were massacred in 1847
by a disgruntled tribe. Father De Smet, in
turn, found his principal difficulties with
French-Canadian priests who, with British
support, resisted American competition. The
missionaries' reports and letters, however, published regularly in the missionary press, kept
attention on Oregon's agricultural possibilities.
By 1843, "Oregon fever" was sweeping across
the Mississippi Valley frontier, and in that
year the first large migration, a thousand
strong, starting from Independence, Missouri,
under the leadership of Peter H. Burnett,
headed over the Oregon Trail to the new
country 2000 miles away. Hardly had they
arrived than American leaders in Oregon in
1843, in the face of aroused Canadian opposition, organized a provisional government,
while expansionists back east began to
thunder about America's right to the territory.

By 1843, the acquisition of Oregon had become almost a religious issue for the expansionists. Nor were they to be satisfied with a
boundary line at the 49th parallel, which had
been the limit of American claims in earlier
boundary discussions with Britain. They de-

manded all of Oregon up to the Russian
border. As the Democrats put it, in their campaign slogan for 1844, "54° 40′ or fight." The
issue, the expansionists said, had nothing to
do with "musty records and the voyages of old
sea captains." Even if Britain has both history
and law on her side, it was "our manifest
destiny to overspread and to possess the whole
of the continent which Providence has given
us for the development of the great experiment of liberty."

### THE ELECTION OF 1844

American bombast in the capital, brashness
in Texas, and bumptiousness on the Pacific
Coast naturally made expansion the leading
issue in the impending national elections. By
opposing the annexation of Texas, Van Buren
had forfeited his chance of renomination by
the Democrats. A majority in the convention
favored him, but the Calhoun men had
enough strength to invoke an old rule requir-

479

480

ing the vote of two-thirds of the delegates for the nomination, and Van Buren could not muster this much support. The deadlock that followed was broken when the tired delegates finally agreed on the first "dark-horse" candidate in American presidential history, James K. Polk of Tennessee. An ardent expansionist, Polk readily supported the aggressive Democratic platform plank, "the reoccupation of Oregon and the reannexation of Texas." When his followers cried "54° 40′ or fight," he did not attempt to quiet them.

Swiftly disposing of Tyler, the Whigs chose as their standard-bearer their idol, Henry Clay, on a platform that ignored the Texas question altogether. Unfortunately for Clay, the evasion did not pay off. Earlier, Clay and Van Buren, expecting the nominations of their respective parties, had agreed that both would oppose the immediate annexation of Texas. Clay at that time made public his famous "Raleigh Letter," explaining his position:

I consider the annexation of Texas at this time, without the assent of Mexico, as a measure compromising the national character, involving us certainly in war with Mexico, probably with other foreign powers, dangerous to the integrity of the Union, inexpedient in the present financial condition of the country, and not called for by any general expression of public opinion.

When Van Buren was rejected by the Democrats in favor of Polk, Clay tried, in his "Alabama Letters" of July, to retract his Raleigh statement. He would accept the admission of Texas, he said now, if it could be done "without dishonor, without war, with the common consent of the Union, and upon just and fair terms."

Clay's straddling of the Texas issue hurt him, especially in New York, where James G. Birney, the candidate of the antislavery Liberty party, with 15,800 votes, cut deeply enough into the Whig ranks to give that state's 36 electoral votes to the Democrats. Polk's electoral vote was 170 to 105 for Clay; his popular vote 1,337,000 to Clay's 1,299,000. The states west of the Appalachians went for Polk, except for Ohio, Tennessee, and Clay's own Kentucky. The Democrats enlarged their majority in the House and gained a majority in the Senate.

The election results were widely interpreted as a mandate for expansion, not least by Polk himself. Yet his triumph was hardly decisive, and some saw in the closeness of the vote a sign that expansionism would endanger national unity.

### A PEACEFUL SOLUTION

Although indeed a "dark horse," Polk was not so obscure as the Whig campaign dig— "Who is James K. Polk?"—was meant to imply. He was a well-tempered veteran of state politics in Tennessee, and before his election had served 14 years in the national House of Representatives, the last four (1835–1839) as Speaker. As President, Polk remained the solid Democrat he had always been. He opposed protection, and in 1846 signed the Walker Tariff which put the country back on low duties for revenue only. He opposed a national debt and meant to keep it low enough to be serviced (and reduced when possible) by the revenues available. He opposed banks and restored Van Buren's Independent Treasury System for handling federal funds. He gave nullifiers no comfort. Above all, he was as expansionist and isolationist as Jefferson.

In his inaugural address in March 1845, Polk asserted "the right of the United States to that portion of our territory which lies beyond the Rocky Mountains. Our title to the country of the Oregon," he said, "is 'clear and unquestionable,' and already are our people preparing to perfect that title by occupying it with their wives and children." Moreover, in his first annual message to Congress in December 1845, Polk stretched the Monroe Doctrine by making two assertions that are often called the Polk Doctrine: (1) "The people of *this continent* alone have the right to decide their own destiny"; (2) The United States cannot allow European states to prevent an independent state from entering the Union.

War with Britain over Oregon would have been foolhardy while war with Mexico over Texas still threatened. Polk was responsible enough to realize this and found a way to back down after the election was over and the 54° 40′ slogan had served its purpose. Polk had been reliably advised that Oregon above the 49th parallel was clearly ill-suited to agriculture. Below the 49th parallel, he said, lay "the entrance of the Straits of Fuca, Admiralty Inlet, and Puget's Sound, with their fine harbors and rich surrounding soils." A concession to Britain on the boundary, moreover, might speed America's effort to secure the even more valuable California ports.

Three times before, Britain had offered to divide Oregon at the 49th parallel, which in fact was a direct extension of the northern border of the United States westward from the Rockies. Britain herself now had reasons to try again. She was finding it increasingly difficult to keep unruly American elements out of Oregon. At the same time, the depletion of the supply of fur-bearing animals along the Columbia River gave her justification for getting out herself. British hostility to the United States and her aspirations, furthermore, had decreased with the reduction of American tariffs on British manufactures in 1846. Negotiations, therefore, were resumed in a conciliatory atmosphere, and on June 15, 1846, a treaty was signed that proved advantageous to both countries. The line drawn along the 49th parallel to Puget Sound and from there to the Pacific through the Straits of Juan de Fuca was simply an extension of the Canadian-American boundary that had been fixed in 1818 as far as the Rockies. The territory north of the Columbia, though it was clearly British by right of settlement, fell into the American sphere. Britain retained Vancouver Island and navigation rights on the Columbia River.

## THE MORMONS IN UTAH

While thousands of Americans from the North and the South were moving west to

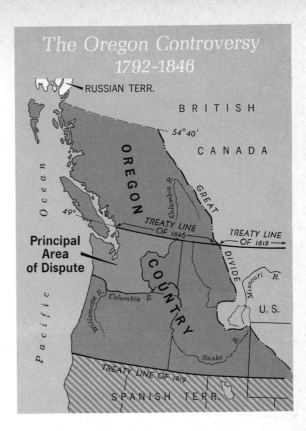

"perfect," as Polk said, American title to North America, one group moved west to escape the thralldom of American government. This group was the Mormons.

In 1823, Joseph Smith, a visionary from Vermont, claimed to have been led by angels to a place where "there was a book deposited, written upon gold plates," and "two stones in silver bows . . . deposited with the plates." The "possession and use of these stones," Smith wrote, "were what constituted Seers in ancient or former times; and . . . God had prepared them for the purpose of translating the book." As God's helper, Smith used the stones in revealing the Book of Mormon, a composite of mythology and prophecy which recalled an ancient legend that the Indians were descendants of the lost tribes of Israel and which enjoined Smith's followers to convert them from their heathenish ways.

On the basis of his revelation, Smith in 1830 founded the Church of Jesus Christ of the Latter-Day Saints and published his book.

481

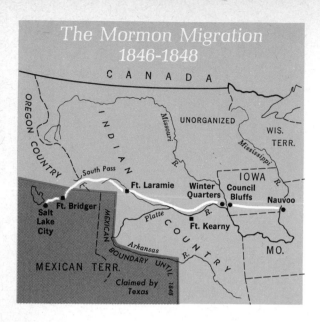

The Mormon Migration
1846-1848

Along with other Messianic movements of the times, Mormonism spread into the Western Reserve in Ohio, and there, at Kirtland, the distinctive pattern of Mormon community living—markedly similar to the seventeenth-century New England settlements centered on the church—first took shape.

Thereafter trouble dogged the Mormons. Following the Panic of 1837 financial difficulties in Ohio drove them to the frontier in Missouri; but within a year, scorned as a sect of thieving Yankee abolitionists and heretics, they were harried back across the Mississippi to Nauvoo, Illinois. Here they found peace until, following Joseph Smith's own example, the practice of plural marriages spread. Whether these marriages were "sealed for a time," that is, consummated in this life, or "sealed for eternity," that is, to be consummated in Heaven, or both, this practice alienated the monogamists of the sect and infuriated the non-Mormon inhabitants.

When the anti-Smith faction among the Mormons attacked him in their newly established newspaper in 1843, Smith and his friends smashed their press. For this offense, the civil authorities threw him and his brother Hyram into jail. Soon freed, they were jailed

*Salt Lake City, 1853. The Mormons called this broad barren plain Deseret, after the word from their scriptures meaning "land of the honeybee." Their brilliant leader Brigham Young is shown below, right. (Salt Lake: Stokes Collection, New York Public Library; Young: The Bettmann Archive.)*

again on a related charge and in 1844 were shot dead in their cell by members of an aroused mob. Joseph Smith's murder almost killed the Mormon movement. On the other hand, it also supplied the Mormon church with a martyr in whose name a new leader might rally its forces. Such a leader appeared in the person of Brigham Young, a loyal follower of Joseph Smith, who became the new "Lion of the Lord."

In 1842, Smith had envisaged a Mormon homeland "in the midst of the Rocky Mountains" and had even dispatched some of his followers to "investigate the locations of California and Oregon, and hunt out a good location, where we can . . . build a city in a day, and have a government of our own." Forced out of Illinois after the Prophet's assassination, in the winter of 1846 the Mormon host began their tortuous exodus westward, led by Young. On June 24, 1847, the first wave of Mormons entered the Salt Lake Valley—a Zion isolated on a barren Mexican plateau remote from the lands of the gentiles where (to quote a Mormon historian) the Saints had been "eternally mobbed, harassed, hunted, our best man murdered and every good man's life continually in danger." Here,

encircled by mountain and desert, the Mormon leaders created a theocracy superbly organized for survival.

The Salt Lake community was cooperative rather than competitive. Since its very existence depended on controlling the limited water supply brought in by the mountain streams, Young devised an irrigation system that distributed water equitably to the whole settlement. He and his advisers parceled out land in a manner reminiscent of the seventeenth-century New England town-planners. Between 1847 and 1857, they laid out 95 communities in which they closely regulated commerce and industry, and experimented in social planning. The Mormon state of Deseret (Congress later changed the name to Utah) was probably the most successful communitarian project in American history.

Remote as the "Saints" were, they soon found that they could not escape the American environment. In two years the American war with Mexico (see p. 487) brought Young's community once more under United States jurisdiction. Furthermore, the Mormon state lay athwart one of the routes to California and inevitably became involved in the American push to the Pacific. The Mormons were not the only people in the country who were governed by heavenly dictates. All Americans, it seemed, had the responsibility "to redeem from unhallowed hands a *land* above all others favored of heaven, and hold it for the use of a people who know how to obey heaven's behests."

### ON TO CALIFORNIA

California had been loosely held by Spain since the middle of the eighteenth century, when she opened a number of Franciscan missions, protected by small garrisons, for the double purpose of converting the Indians and preventing British and Russian penetration down the California coast. In theory, these missions were temporary establishments set up to teach the Indians agriculture and the household arts, and the Franciscans did succeed in

*The Carmel Mission, founded in 1771, one of a chain running from San Francisco to San Diego. Staffed by Franciscan friars, they were successful in their religious conversions, as well as in training and supervising the agricultural duties of the Indians who worked for them. The proud and vigorous "native Californian" (above right) is typical of the ranchers of the time. (Mission: M.H. de Young Memorial Museum; rancher: The Granger Collection.)*

Christianizing and training thousands of red men. After completing this task, the Franciscans were expected to move on to new fields and allow the regular clergy to take over. The mission lands would then be broken up and distributed to private owners. But who was to decide when each move was to be made? Anticlericals hungered for the lands from the start; and when Mexico won her independence from Spain early in the 1820s, officials and land-speculators pressed for distribution of mission property. By 1834 half the mission lands had passed into private hands, and the other half was soon lost to landsharks. At the outbreak of the Mexican War in 1846, the Indians had hopelessly degenerated and few signs of the missions remained.

During the preceding 25 years, American whalers from Nantucket and New Bedford had stopped at the California ports of Monterey and San Francisco, and New England traders had sailed there and farther south to

exchange everything from Chinese fireworks to English cartwheels for hides and tallow. These visitors year by year left behind them deserters and adventurers who, along with emigrants from the Oregon and Mississippi frontiers, began to acquire large tracts of California land and to monopolize commerce and industry.

Richard Henry Dana, Jr., whose classic *Two Years Before the Mast* (1840) contains the best account of California life in the 1830s, succumbed to the elegance and pride of the Mexicans encountered by these Yankee mariners, but he also saw the sources of their defenselessness against the interlopers. He found the Mexicans "an idle people" incapable of making anything, bad bargainers, and suspicious of foreigners. "Indeed," he wrote, "as far as my observation goes, there are no people to whom the newly invented Yankee word of 'loafer' is more applicable than to the Spanish Americans." For the interlopers themselves, the most helpful and knowledgeable figure on the coast was Thomas O. Larkin,

485

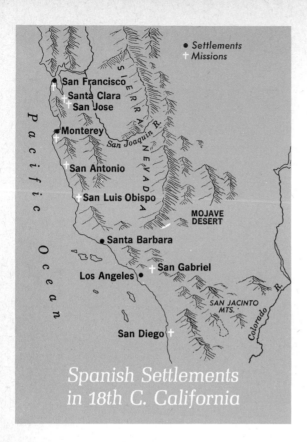

Spanish Settlements
in 18th C. California

cisco, all agreed, was the great prize, 20 times more valuable, thought Daniel Webster, than the whole of Texas. California's San Diego harbor, in turn, according to many observers, would prove far more important to American interests than any part of Oregon.

The United States, alas, had no claims to California except desire. During Jackson's and Tyler's administrations, the American government had tried to buy California, but these moves only deepened Mexican suspicions. In 1842 Daniel Webster sought British help in forcing Mexico to sell California in return for concessions to Britain in the Anglo-American dispute over Oregon, but he was rebuffed. In the same year, an American naval officer, Commodore Thomas ap Catesby Jones, who had been mistakenly informed in Peru that the United States and Mexico were at war and that the British were planning to seize California, sailed into Monterey and captured the city. When he discovered his mistake, he promptly apologized to the Mexicans, but the significance of this hostile gesture was plain enough.

In 1845, on learning that the government of General Herrera was in such desperate straits that it might be persuaded at last to sell California, President Polk hurriedly sent a representative, John Slidell, to Mexico City with another offer to buy, and with instructions to pay as much as $40 million for California and New Mexico if necessary. By then, however, United States and Mexican forces had already begun to make military passes at each other over Texas, and the recently installed Mexican regime would not even receive Slidell. The envoy wrote to Polk that nothing could be done with the Mexicans "until they shall have been chastised."

Autonomous action in California itself was still possible, especially since the canny Larkin had a plan all ready by which the United States would encourage a "spontaneous" rebellion of Spanish-speaking Californians favorably disposed to annexation. Nothing came of Larkin's scheme, but its feasibility was indicated by a spontaneous revolt of other Ameri-

who settled in Monterey in 1832 and later became a confidential agent of the American government. His counterpart in the interior was Captain John A. Sutter, who built a fort in the Sacramento Valley in 1839 and set up a small trading empire of his own (see map p. 478).

Although California had not been an issue in the 1844 campaign, it soon became identified in the popular mind with Oregon. No one was more eloquent in its praises than the witty Larkin, who described the pleasures of "hunting wild Deer and dancing with tame Dear." By the summer of 1845, talk about a mighty nation extending from sea to sea had become common, and expansionists warned Polk to take over California before the British stepped in. Polk himself aired plans for a transcontinental railroad to link the Golden Gate with the Mississippi Valley. San Fran-

cans in California north of San Francisco Bay where, on July 5, 1846, they set up an independent state with its own bear flag. On learning of the formal outbreak of war between the United States and Mexico, these rebels disestablished the "Bear Flag Republic" and joined the American forces.

## IV *The Mexican War and Its Legacy*

### A SHORT AND FRUITFUL WAR

With Texas wrenched from her and California obviously slipping away, Mexico, if only to save face, had to take a stand against her neighbor to the north. Her opportunity came early in 1846, when, on hearing from Slidell about the failure of his mission, Polk ordered General Zachary Taylor to occupy disputed territory on the southern boundary of Texas. Taylor had carried out his orders by the end of March. Such a show of force, thought Polk, might cause the Mexicans to reconsider their refusal to negotiate, but, failing that, it might cause an incident that would serve as an excuse for a declaration of war.

Mexico responded to Polk's strategy by sending up troops of her own, and on April 25, 1846, they clashed with Taylor's men. Polk had already prepared a war message and on May 11 he sent it to Congress. The shedding of American blood on what the United States claimed to be its own soil put Congress in a mood to act without lengthy debate. On May 13 Congress declared war by a vote of 40 to 2 in the Senate and 174 to 14 in the House.

New England antislavery spokesmen— James Russell Lowell, Theodore Parker, Ralph Waldo Emerson, and others—vigorously denounced the war. Polk, nevertheless, had hoped for formal bipartisan support, which he failed to win. His refusal openly to declare his war aims (the seizure of New Mexico and California) encouraged the Whigs in

both sections to attack his entire Mexican policy. To some northern Whigs, Polk, by forcing an unwilling people into war, was simply "attempting to consummate a scheme for the extension and strengthening of slavery and the Slave Power." Some southern Whigs themselves feared that the acquisition of the new territories would intensify old sectional controversies and destroy their party. But if the Whigs publicly castigated Polk, they did not obstruct the war and indeed began to make all the political capital they could out of the triumphs of two Whig generals, Zachary Taylor and Winfield Scott.

Within the Democratic party itself two strong factions fought Polk's policies from the beginning: the Van Burenites and the Calhounites. The Van Buren men, who had opposed Texas annexation, supported the war only under pressure of patriotism. They deplored its political consequences and saw only party suicide in the advancement it afforded for the presidential aspirations of victorious Whig generals. Calhoun and his followers agreed. And they were even more concerned with the effect of the war on the government's tariff policy. Would not the debts piled up by the war encourage the protectionists to demand higher tariffs on manufactures?

The moral and political dissatisfaction with the war was most in evidence in the Northeast, the most populous part of the country. This section supplied only 7930 recruits. Some 20,000 southerners and 40,000 westerners enlisted, however, and the war was quickly won.

Taylor captured Monterrey, Mexico, on September 24, 1846, and defeated a Mexican force of 15,000 men under General Santa Anna at Buena Vista on February 23, 1847. Lest one Whig general gain too much acclaim, Polk appointed another, General Scott, to lead an expedition against Mexico City, the enemy capital. Scott overcame tough resistance on landing at Vera Cruz and went on to take Mexico City on September 14, 1847. Farther west, an army under Colonel Stephen W. Kearny, starting from its base at Fort Leaven-

488

worth, Kansas, captured Santa Fe and pushed through to California. Commodore Robert F. Stockton and a battalion of troops under General John C. Frémont had already proclaimed the annexation of California in August 1846, but the Mexican rebels who had been fighting among themselves settled their differences and in September drove the Americans from southern California. When Kearny arrived at San Diego in December, he joined with American naval units under Stockton and with Frémont's men, to reestab-

# VOLUNTEERS!

## Men of the Granite State!
### Men of Old Rockingham!! the
strawberry-bed of patriotism, renowned for bravery and devotion to Country, rally at this call. Santa Anna, reeking with the generous confidence and magnanimity of your countrymen, is in arms, eager to plunge his traitor-dagger in their bosoms. To arms, then, and rush to the standard of the fearless and gallant CUSHING----put to the blush the dastardly meanness and rank toryism of Massachusetts. Let the half civilized Mexicans hear the crack of the unerring New Hampshire rifleman, and illustrate on the plains of San Luis Potosi, the fierce, determined, and undaunted bravery that has always characterized her sons.

Col. THEODORE F. ROWE, at No. 31 Daniel-street, is authorized and will enlist men this week for the Massachusetts Regiment of Volunteers. The compensation is $10 per month---$30 in advance. Congress will grant a handsome bounty in money and ONE HUNDRED AND SIXTY ACRES OF LAND.

Portsmouth. Feb. 2. 1847.

*(Right) While the Northeast seemed solidly against the war with Mexico, this call for volunteers in New Hampshire in 1847 showed that the "Granite State" was willing to send men below the Rio Grande at least to "put to the blush the dastardly meanness and rank toryism of [its neighbor] Massachusetts." (The Bettmann Archive.)*

*(Below) Amphibious assault on Vera Cruz under the command of General Winfield Scott, March 29, 1847. (The Bettmann Archive.)*

lish American rule. By January 13, 1847, all the Mexican forces in California had surrenderd.

When news of the victories at Buena Vista and Vera Cruz reached Washington, Polk decided to try to arrange a peace with the Mexican leaders. For this mission he chose the State Department's Spanish-speaking chief clerk, Nicholas P. Trist. Trist was instructed to demand the Rio Grande boundary and the cession of New Mexico and California, and was authorized to offer to pay American claims against Mexico and an additional sum of $15 million. The last provision was presumably meant to salve the American conscience by giving the annexations the character of a purchase.

Almost immediately after Trist arrived at Vera Cruz, he quarreled with General Scott, who resented the appearance of a State Department clerk whose authority exceeded his own. The two men soon became fast friends, however, to the alarm of the President, who had come to regard Scott as a serious political rival. When Trist's negotiations with Santa Anna broke down and the temporary armistice ended in August 1847, Polk ordered his emissary back to Washington. The President and his Cabinet now began to consider a prolonged occupation of Mexico, the annexation

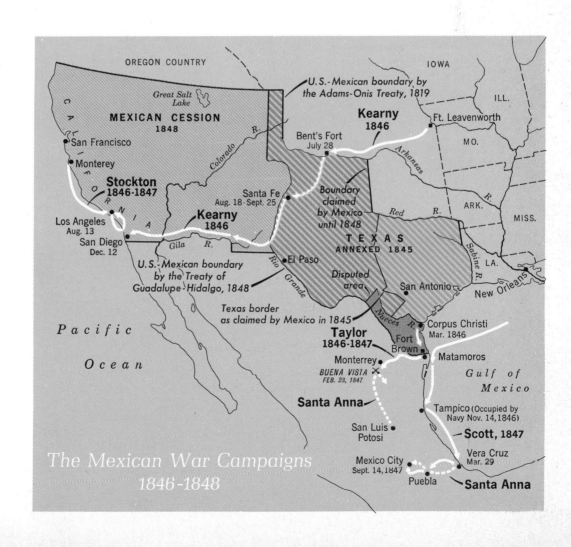

The Mexican War Campaigns 1846-1848

490

of New Mexico and California without payment, and a levy on the people of Mexico to pay the costs of occupation. There even was serious talk of a permanent annexation of all Mexico, an objective, strangely enough, opposed by southerners of both major parties. Antislavery men, they felt, would insist on keeping the annexed country free. Some, like Calhoun, also feared that the American government would become more centralized than ever in the effort to administer a conquered empire. Trist himself sympathized with these objections.

The rise to power of a moderate party in Mexico prompted Trist to ignore his instructions to return, and without authorization he pressed on with his negotiations. On February 2, 1848, he signed the Treaty of Guadalupe Hidalgo. In it he secured the Rio Grande boundary, Upper California, including the much-desired port of San Diego, and New Mexico. He agreed that the United States would assume Mexican obligations to Americans up to $3.25 million and would pay Mexico $15 million.

Astonishing as Trist's independent behavior was (Polk called him "an impudent and unqualified scoundrel"), the President nevertheless accepted the treaty and sent it to the Senate for approval. After all, it conformed to Trist's original instructions. Moreover, prolonged negotiations would surely raise vehement criticism in Congress, especially in the House, where the Whigs held a majority. The Senate on March 10, 1848, approved Trist's work by a vote of 38 to 14, most of the opposition coming from those who wanted all Mexico. The Treaty of Guadalupe Hidalgo added a magnificent 500,000 square miles to the continental domain of the United States. Although Trist failed to acquire a strategic 54,000 square miles along the southern New Mexico border, a strip of land that offered the best route for a railroad to the Pacific through the South, this oversight was corrected by the "Gadsden Purchase" of 1853 for $10 million.

## THE "FREE SOIL" ELECTION

As American soldiers stormed into Mexico, Ralph Waldo Emerson wrote in his journal: "The United States will conquer Mexico, but it will be as the man who swallows the arsenic, which brings him down in turn. Mexico will poison us."

The symptoms of this poisoning were swift to appear. As early as August 1846, David Wilmot, a free-soil Democrat from Pennsylvania, offered an amendment to an appropriation bill in the House, proposing that, "neither slavery nor involuntary servitude shall ever exist in any part" of the territory that might be acquired from Mexico. The House adopted the amendment; the Senate defeated it. But that was far from the end of the matter. The "Wilmot Proviso" was persistently added to bill after bill in Congress and was hotly debated there and in the country generally. At the same time, the admission of Iowa and Wisconsin to the Union was pending; Minnesota was soon to apply for statehood; and even the Oregon Territory was readying its petition. For all these inevitably free states to enter the Union while the South at the same time was to be deprived of slave states in the new territory won largely by her sons was an intolerable prospect to many southern spokesmen. But growing numbers of northerners saw in slavery an unmitigated evil that at least must be contained where it was.

Did Congress, indeed, have authority, to determine whether or not slavery might exist in territory obtained by the United States? Southerners who first raised this question replied that since the Constitution recognized and protected property in slaves, owners of such property could not lawfully be discriminated against by being prohibited to carry such property wherever they went, even across the Missouri Compromise line. But antislavery northerners replied that ever since 1789, when it confirmed the clause in the Northwest Ordinance of 1787 that excluded slavery from the

Northwest Territory, and especially in adopting the Missouri Compromise in 1820, Congress had exercised its prerogatives over property and territory as the Constitution (Art. IV, Sec. 3) plainly said it could.

A third position on the issue of extending slavery to the territories now appeared. This was "squatter sovereignty," or "popular sovereignty," a doctrine hopefully set forth by Lewis Cass of Michigan and Stephen A. Douglas of Illinois. They argued that there was a long-established precedent in America for communities to act as the best judges of their own interests. Let the new territories be set up with the question of slavery left open, and then permit the people to decide for themselves. Plausible enough, this doctrine nevertheless left disastrously vague precisely when a territory should decide this momentous question—after slaves had already been brought in or before, if free settlers had come before slave-owners? By leaving resolution of the question open to zealots of both camps, popular sovereignty also left it open to violence, which in fact broke out a few years later in Kansas (see p. 565).

By 1848 the issue of the extension of slavery to new territories had become so poisonous that both major parties, in preparing for the presidential campaign, shunned it. On taking office in 1845, Polk had pledged himself to but one term, and for the 1848 election the "regular" Democrats, at their convention in Baltimore, nominated Lewis Cass who ran on a platform that ignored slavery altogether. The "regular" Whigs, at their convention in Philadelphia, hoped to silence talk of all issues by nominating the "Hero of Buena Vista," General Zachary Taylor.

The watchword of the "regulars" in both parties was "party harmony." But they reckoned without the determined antislavery northern Democrats—in New York and New England they became known as "Barnburners," because they were said to be willing to "burn down" the Democratic "barn" in order to get rid of the proslavery "rats." The "regulars" also reckoned without the "conscience," as against the "cotton," Whigs. In August 1848 the antislavery Democrats and Whigs, who had bolted from the regular party conventions, met in Buffalo with other antislavery leaders and formed the Free Soil party, with the slogan, "Free soil, Free speech, Free labor, and Free men." They named as their standard-bearer Martin Van Buren, who had won their sympathy as he had lost that of the Democratic regulars, by his clear stand against the annexation of Texas.

The 1848 election itself aroused little popular enthusiasm. Neither Taylor nor Cass appealed particularly to his respective party, and Van Buren—despite his forthright repudiation of slavery—could not live down his reputation as a slippery fox. Moreover, he had no national political machine behind him. Horace Greeley dismissed Cass as a "pot-bellied, mutton-headed cucumber," but he supported Van Buren only as a lesser evil. Webster, after some hesitation, gave Taylor a cold endorsement. In the balloting, Taylor won 1,360,000 votes to Cass' 1,220,000. The Free-Soilers polled only 291,000 votes, but they absorbed enough Democratic support in New York to give that state's electoral vote to Taylor, and enough Whig support in Ohio and Indiana to give those states to Cass. The Free Soil party also elected nine congressmen to a divided House where they might hold the balance of power. Most important of all, the Free-Soilers had demonstrated the potential strength and disruptive power of a purely sectional party. Henceforth, there could be no slurring over of the slavery issue. Southern extremists now had fresh grounds on which to convince the moderates and Unionists in their states that a southern party must be formed to combat northern aggression against the "peculiar institution."

## THE COMPROMISE OF 1850

Sectional tensions relaxed for a moment when the news of gold in California spread

across the nation early in 1848. Americans of every class and occupation dropped whatever they were doing and headed for the Pacific Coast. Men from all over the world joined them. Some risked the perilous voyage around the Horn or the portage across Panama (see p. 539). Others took the overland route through Salt Lake City, thereby enriching the Mormons who sold supplies to the miners at fabulous prices. To Henry Thoreau, already launched on his own pilgrimage in Concord, the rush to California was a shocking reflection of American materialism. The "world's raffle," he called it:

What a comment, what a satire on our institutions! . . . And have all the precepts in all the Bibles taught men only this? . . . Is this the ground on which Orientals and Occidentals meet? Did God direct us to get our living, digging where we never planted,—and He would, perchance, reward us with lumps of gold?

By 1849, California had a population of over 100,000, and an inadequate military government to cope with it. Polk had retired before a deeply divided Congress could decide California's future. Taylor, the new President, blunt, well-intentioned, but politically inept,

recommended, on appeals from California leaders, that California, and New Mexico and Utah as well, draw up constitutions and decide without congressional direction whether or not slavery should be excluded. Congress, however, was in no mood to let the new President run things. This was especially true of proslavery spokesmen whose fears over antislavery decisions in the Far West were soon confirmed by the action of all three territories in writing constitutions which forbade slavery. These spokesmen, amidst talk of the certainty of secession, now prepared to take an uncompromising stand in Congress on all sectional issues. Should slave depots be banned in the District of Columbia? Should the Fugitive Slave Law be tightened? Must Texas, a slave state, yield part of its western land to the proposed free territory of New Mexico? Southern unity in defense of slavery had never been so strong.

President Taylor's reaction to the heightening crisis was simply to ask Congress, in December 1849, to avoid "exciting topics of sectional character." At a time when senators and representatives carried Bowie knives and Colt revolvers, and Washington newspapermen seriously discussed the possibility of bloody violence in the House, Taylor's request

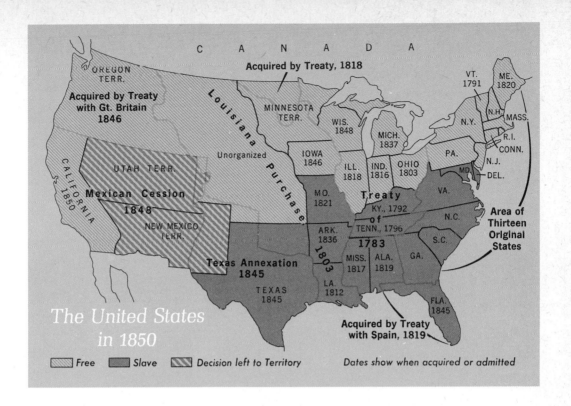

The United States in 1850

Acquired by Treaty, 1818

OREGON TERR.

Acquired by Treaty with Gt. Britain 1846

MINNESOTA TERR.

VT. 1791

ME. 1820

N.H.

MASS.

N.Y.

R.I.

CONN.

N.J.

Louisiana Purchase

WIS. 1848

MICH. 1837

PA.

MD.

DEL.

Unorganized

IOWA 1846

ILL. 1818

IND. 1816

OHIO 1803

CALIFORNIA 1850

UTAH TERR.

Mexican Cession 1848

NEW MEXICO TERR.

MO. 1821

Treaty

VA.

KY., 1792

of

N.C.

ARK. 1836

TENN., 1796

1783

S.C.

Texas Annexation 1845

MISS. 1817

ALA. 1819

GA.

Area of Thirteen Original States

TEXAS 1845

LA. 1812

FLA. 1845

Acquired by Treaty with Spain, 1819

▨ Free   ▤ Slave   ▧ Decision left to Territory        Dates show when acquired or admitted

*Henry Clay, shortly before the controversy over the Compromise of 1850; after a daguerreotype by Mathew Brady. (The Bettmann Archive.)*

was tantamount to abdication. Clearly the South had no intention of allowing California to enter the Union as a free state unless it received important concessions. The South would secede rather than accept the Wilmot Proviso.

Fortunately there remained more realistic leaders than the President, yet men who put the Union first and the section second. Their spokesman was Henry Clay, 73 years old now, but still a powerful and persuasive orator who understood the truly desperate mood of the South. On January 29, 1850, Clay offered the following resolutions in the Senate: (1) that California be admitted as a free state; (2) that the territorial governments set up in Utah and New Mexico decide for themselves whether slavery should be permitted or abolished; (3) that the western boundary of Texas be fixed so as to exclude "any portion of New Mexico"; (4) that in return for this concession, the United States would assume that portion of the public debt of Texas contracted before annexation; (5) that slavery within the

493

494

District of Columbia would not be abolished without the consent of Maryland and the residents in the District, and "without just compensation to the owners of slaves within the District"; (6) that slave-trading be prohibited in the District of Columbia; (7) that a stricter fugitive slave law be adopted; and (8) that "Congress has no power to promote or obstruct the trade in slaves between the slave-holding States."

The battle for the Compromise of 1850 was one of the most bitterly contested in congressional history. Arrayed against Clay were: (1) the angry and suspicious President Taylor, firm in his conviction that California must be admitted to the Union without any reservations, and prepared to treat even moderate and Union-loving southerners as traitors if they protested; (2) fiery secessionists like Jefferson Davis (Mississippi), Robert Barnwell Rhett (South Carolina), and Louis T. Wigfall (Texas)—contemptuous of compromise and certain that Clay's plan was simply a disguise for the ambitions of a brutal North; (3) extreme antislavery men and radical free-soilers like William H. Seward (New York), Salmon P. Chase and Joshua Giddings (Ohio), and Charles Sumner (Massachusetts), who stood pat on the Wilmot Proviso and placed the law of Congress, and the Constitution, below the "Higher Law"—the law of God—under which slavery could never be justified.

But Clay's resolutions were broad and conciliatory enough to win over reasonable men, North and South, and devout Unionists in every section. Among the staunchest of the Unionists was Daniel Webster, who, in a moving speech in the Senate on March 7, 1850, brooked the wrath of his fellow Yankees by supporting even Clay's proposal for stricter enforcement of the Fugitive Slave Law. Massachusetts humanitarians accused Webster of making another bid for the Presidency and never forgave him. They talked of him as a fallen and tarnished hero who with other "deformed, mediocre, sniveling, unreliable, false-hearted men . . . insulted and betrayed"

their country. Theodore Parker, the radical Boston clergyman, could find no words strong enough to show his disapproval of what Webster had done:

When he will do such a deed, it seems to me that there is no such life of crime long enough to prepare a man for such a pitch of depravity; I should think he must have been begotten in sin, and conceived in iniquity . . . that the concentration of the villainy of whole generations of scoundrels would hardly be enough to fit a man for a deed like this.

Webster himself had underestimated northern revulsion against returning fugitive slaves and free-soil hatred of the whole plantation system. But for the moment at least, his efforts strengthened the Unionists' position to which other eloquent men rallied. Outstanding among them was Stephen A. Douglas, who brought many in Congress around to the view that the Southwest was unsuitable for slave labor. After the aged Clay had been forced to retire from the fray exhausted, Douglas whipped the Kentuckian's resolutions through. Five separate measures made up the Compromise of 1850. Their adoption became certain when President Taylor, unyielding in his opposition, died suddenly early in July 1850 and was succeeded by the moderate Vice-president, Millard Fillmore, a free-soiler who nevertheless favored the Compromise.

Under the provisions of the Compromise of 1850, California entered the Union as a free state, and the western boundary of Texas was fixed where it is today, at the 103rd meridian. Texas received $10 million for giving up her claims to New Mexico. Two new territories, New Mexico and Utah, were created, with the proviso that the question of slavery be left for the people to decide in their constitutions at the time of their becoming states. Slave-trading, but not slavery, was prohibited in the District of Columbia. Finally, a severe fugitive slave law was passed, with many northern congressmen abstaining from voting.

Several northern states, beginning with

Vermont in 1850, virtually nullified the fugitive slave law by enacting new "personal liberty laws" enabling alleged fugitives to have legal counsel, jury trials, and other means of defending their freedom. Northern Negroes themselves also took up the defense of fugitives. Negroes, they said, had for too long been characterized as meek and yielding. "This reproach must be wiped out," declared the free Negro leader Frederick Douglass, "and nothing short of resistance on the part of the colored man, can wipe it out. Every slavehunter who meets a bloody death in his infernal business, is an argument in favor of the manhood of our race."

### THE ELECTION OF 1852

The nation as a whole, nevertheless, exulted when news of the Compromise became

*Frederick Douglass in 1854, at age 35. (The Granger Collection.)*

known, and in the first presidential election after the Compromise the national yearning for sectional tranquility and moderation seemed to persist. In this election, in 1852, Franklin Pierce, the Democratic candidate, easily defeated General Scott, now the Whig candidate, running up a popular plurality of 214,000 votes and a margin of 254 to 42 in the electoral college. The Free Soil candidate, John P. Hale, won only half as many votes as Van Buren in 1848, as northern Democrats in particular returned to the fold.

But in the long run the issue of slavery and its extension could not be compromised, and civil war loomed as the Manifest Destiny of the nation all the more certainly as the Manifest Destiny of continentalism was pursued. An ominous sign of trouble ahead was the breaking up of the Whig party following the deaths of such staunch Unionists as Webster and Clay in 1852. The party, said Schuyler Colfax in Indiana, "seems almost annihilated by the recent elections." Thurlow Weed in New York was disposed to agree. "There may be no political future for us," he lamented. Once-loyal southern Whigs felt that this was precisely what any party deserved that accepted the guidance of a Seward. The New York Free-Soiler's influence, declared Robert Toombs of Georgia, was a permanent threat to the "peace and security" of the South. "We can better purchase them by the destruction of the Whig party than of the Union. If the Whig party is incapable of rising to the same standard of nationality as the motley crew which opposes it under the name of the Democracy it is entitled to no resurrection. —It will have none." Whig strength was declining in the South precisely because the party had traditionally represented a national rather than a sectional outlook. And yet it had never possessed the drive and vitality of Jacksonian Democracy. In Emerson's words, the Whig party was "tame and weak:"

Instead of having its own aims passionately in view, it cants about the policy of a Washington or a Jefferson. It speaks to expectation, and not

496

the torrent of its wishes and needs, waits for its antagonist to speak that it may have something to oppose, and, failing that, having nothing to say is happy to hurrah.

The Democrats still stood as a great national party, to which, indeed, many southern Whigs were now drawn. The rest of the Whigs would soon form the backbone of a new *northern* party to be called the Republi-can party (see p. 569). Politics, moreover, was not the only realm of sectional division. The slave South had become profoundly con-scious of its differences from the burgeoning North and West in all phases of life. These sections, in turn, developed a sense of their own individuality which grew clearer and stronger as the South felt impelled to stress its distinctive culture.

# READINGS

General accounts of continentalism are available in the diplomatic histories cited in our general bibliography. On British and Canadian relations, see H.C. Allen, *Great Britain and the United States* (1955); H.T. Manning, *The Revolt of French Canada 1800–1835* (1962); and A.B. Corey, *The Crisis of 1830–1842 in Canadian-American Relations* (1941). The story is carried further in D.F. Warner, *The Idea of Continental Union, Agitation for the Annexation of Canada to the United States 1849–1893* (1960).

An excellent review of the expansionist period may be found in R.A. Billington, *The Far Western Frontier 1830–1860* (1956), and more generally in the same author's *Westward Expansion* (1967). Albert Weinberg, *Manifest Destiny* (1935), is comprehensive on the expansionist spirit. H.N. Smith, *Virgin Land* (1950), is an imaginative study of Ameri-cans' conception of the West and its place in their destiny. Three books by Frederick Merk reflect a lifetime of study: *Manifest Destiny and Mission in American History: A Reinter-pretation* (1963); *The Monroe Doctrine and American Expansionism 1843–1849* (1966); and *The Oregon Question* (1967), a collection of penetrating "Essays in Anglo-American Diplomacy and Politics." N.A. Graebner, *Empire on the Pacific* (1955), stresses the com-mercial side of expansionism. F.P. Prucha, ed., *Army Life on the Western Frontier* (1958), is illuminating on the western forts and the peacetime army as seen, as its subtitle says, in "Selections from the Official Reports made between 1826 and 1845, by Colonel George Croghan," The Inspector-General. Prucha's monograph, *The Sword of the Republic: The United States Army on the Frontier 1783–1846* (1969), is authoritative. Bernard DeVoto, *The Year of Decision* (1943), is a fine popular history of the events of 1846.

E.C. Barker, *Mexico and Texas 1821–1835* (1928), offers a good account of the begin-nings of American interest; W.C. Binkley, *The Texas Revolution* (1952), carries the narrative further along. R.N. Richardson, *Texas, the Lone Star State* (1943); Stanley Siegel, *A Political History of the Texas Republic 1836–1845* (1956); and E.D. Adams, *British Interests in Texas* (1910), are informative on special subjects. More comprehensive older works include G.L. Rives, *The United States and Mexico 1821–1848* (2 vols., 1913), and two books by J.H. Smith, *The Annexation of Texas* (1911), and *The War with Mexico* (2 vols., 1919). A good shorter history of the war is A.H. Bill, *Rehearsal for Conflict: The War With Mexico 1846–1848* (1947).

C.J. Brosnan, *Jason Lee: Prophet of the New Oregon* (1932), and C.M. Drury, *Marcus Whitman, Pioneer and Martyr* (1937), supply the missionary background. Francis Parkman's classic, *The California and Oregon Trail* (1849), is better known through many modern editions simply called *The Oregon Trail*. A well-written modern work is David Lavender, *Westward Vision: The Story of the Oregon Trail* (1963). D.O. Johansen and C.M. Gates, *Empire of the Pacific: A History of the Pacific Northwest* (1957), is among the best general accounts. R.G. Cleland, *Early Sentiment for the Annexation of California* (1915), may be supplemented by Cleland's *From Wilderness to Empire: A History of California 1542–1900* (1944), and J.W. Caughey, *California* (1953).

Wallace Stegner, *The Gathering of Zion: The Story of the Mormon Trail* (1964), is a stirring account. Nels Anderson, *Desert Saints: The Mormon Frontier in Utah* (1942), is outstanding. L.J. Arrington, *Great Basin Kingdom: An Economic History of the Latter-day Saints 1830–1900* (1958), is best on the material side of Mormon history. T.F. O'Dea, *The Mormons* (1957), is a detached and informative discussion of Mormon history and doctrine. Fawn Brodie, *No Man Knows My History: The Life of Joseph Smith* (1945), and Preston Nibley, *Brigham Young, the Man and His Work* (1936) are illuminating biographies of the Mormon leaders.

Allan Nevins, *Ordeal of the Union* (2 vols., 1947), offers a scholarly survey of the politics of this period. It may be supplemented by two older works, W.E. Dodd, *Expansion and Conflict* (1915), and volumes V and VI of Edward Channing, *A History of the United States* (6 vols., 1905–1925). J.H. Silbey, *The Transformation of American Politics 1840–1860* (1967), is an anthology revealing underlying forces in party realignments. T.C. Smith, *The Liberty and Free-Soil Parties in the Northwest* (1897), is still valuable. J.T. Carpenter, *The South as a Conscious Minority* (1930), and A.O. Craven, *The Growth of Southern Nationalism 1848–1861* (1953), are good on the slave section's position. Holman Hamilton, *The Compromise of 1850* (1964), offers a scholarly analysis. Strong Negro comment on the Compromise and on the events preceding it will be found in the pertinent sections of Herbert Aptheker, ed., *A Documentary History of the Negro People in the United States* (1951).

Numerous biographies also supply invaluable background: C.G. Sellers, Jr., *James K. Polk: Jacksonian 1795–1843* (1957) and *James K. Polk: Continentalist 1843–1846* (1966); Allan Nevins, ed., *Polk: The Diary of a President 1845–1849* (1952); Holman Hamilton, *Zachary Taylor* (2 vols., 1941, 1951); R.J. Rayback, *Millard Fillmore: Biography of a President* (1959); F.B. Woodford, *Lewis Cass, The Last Jeffersonian* (1950); G.F. Milton, *Eve of Conflict: Stephen A. Douglas and the Needless War* (1934); G.M. Capers, *Stephen A. Douglas, Defender of the Union* (1959); C.B. Going, *David Wilmot, Free-Soiler* (1924); A.J. Beveridge, *Abraham Lincoln* (2 vols., 1928); U.B. Phillips, *The Life of Robert Toombs* (1913); and the lives of Clay, Calhoun, and Webster cited in Chapter Eleven.

# SIXTEEN

The challenge of the South, the persistent discrepancies between its values and its condition, its longings and its impotence, is older than the Union. These discrepancies grew especially harsh after 1820 when industrialism under a regime of free labor captured the spirit of the country and the Western world while the South with its slaves clung only the more compulsively to plantation and subsistence agriculture.

For a time, while the open land lasted in the South and industrialism elsewhere often was convulsed by its own growing pains, southern spokesmen successfully deluded themselves with dreams of grandeur sweetly nourished by the elevation slavery gave even to the crudest planter's ego and by the immense role of King Cotton in the industrial revolution itself. The growing differences, and the growing rivalry, between the slave states and the rest of the country in this period evoked enough interest to multiply the number of inquisitive visitors to the South, and her leaders remained confident enough to let them in. Many of them learned, indeed from troubled southerners themselves, that nineteenth-century cotton, like eighteenth-century tobacco, was in fact keeping the South a colony, not a kingdom, one characteristically producing raw materials for the enrichment of distant carriers and processors. They found, also, that slavery was making the section a pariah in a democratic age, one shunned by most newcomers to the country. The increasingly hostile reports of these visitors, their savage exposure of the dream of white excellence built upon black thralldom, caused the South as early as the 1830s to turn ever more self-consciously inward, to ravel up the many and varied strands of her own culture,

# THE SOUTHERN
# NATION

and with fierce intransigence to see to the defenses of her "peculiar institution" and its fruits.

Richard Hildreth, the New England historian, visited the South late in the 1830s and in 1840 published his book, *Despotism in America; or An Inquiry into the Nature and Results of the Slave-Holding System in the United States*. Within the "great social experiment of Democracy" in America, he found in the South, "another experiment, less talked about, less celebrated, but not the less real or important, to wit, the *experiment of Despotism*. . . . The Southern States," he wrote, "are Aristocracies; and aristocracies of the sternest and most odious kind." Hildreth anticipated certain modern scholars who have found the slave systems of Brazil and Spanish America more humane than that in the United States. After examining these systems and others, he concluded that slavery in the South, "is a far more deadly and disastrous thing, more fatal to all the hopes, the sentiments, the rights of humanity, than almost any other system of servitude which has existed in any other community."

Hildreth saw only two classes in the southern aristocracies, the privileged planters and all lesser whites who aspired to planter status

on the one hand, and their "hereditary subjects, servants and bondsmen" on the other. "Extremes meet," he added. "Ferocity of temper, idleness, improvidence, drunkenness, gambling—these are vices for which the masters are distinguished, and these same vices are conspicuous traits in the character and conduct of slaves."

This was the image of Dixie that was also spread in the abolitionist tracts of the day. Some in the South undertook to expose the excessive simplicity of the image and thereby discredit and destroy it. The section's most aggressive defenders, however, following the lead of Calhoun himself, preferred an equal simplicity and meeting of extremes the better to convey an alternative image of their own. In January 1838, Calhoun told Congress:

This agitation [against the slave system] has produced one happy effect at least; it has compelled us in the South to look into the nature and character of this great institution, and to correct many false impressions that even we had entertained in relation to it. Many in the South once believed that it was a moral and political evil; that folly and delusion are gone; we see it now in its true light, and regard it as the most

499

500

safe and stable basis for free institutions in the world.

Calhoun continued:

It is impossible with us that the conflict can take place between labor and capital, which makes it so difficult to establish and maintain free institutions in all wealthy and highly civilized nations where such institutions as ours do not exist. The Southern States are an aggregate, in fact, of communities, not of individuals. Every plantation is a little community, with the master at its head, who concentrates in himself the united interests of capital and labor. . . . These small communities aggregated make the State [in which] labor and capital [are] equally represented and perfectly harmonized. The blessing of this state of things extends beyond the limits of the South. It makes that section the balance of the system; the great conservative power, which prevents other portions, less fortunately constituted, from rushing into conflict. . . . Such are the institutions which these deluded madmen are stirring heaven and earth to destroy, and which we are called on to defend by the highest and most solemn obligations that can be imposed on us as men and patriots.

Recent historians have returned to the view that the structure of southern society before the Civil War was in fact more complex than Hildreth's hell or Calhoun's heaven. All authorities now concede that aristocratic planters were few and that many slaves enjoyed adequate creature comforts. They add that the "poor white trash," who once were lumped indiscriminately with all nonslaveholding whites, were but a small minority reduced by disease to what subsistence they could scratch from otherwise unwanted land, eked out by fish and game; and that the statistically "average" southerner was an independent "yeoman" farmer who worked his own quarter-section, more or less, with the help of his family, all perhaps laboring side by side with their one or two Negro "hands." This independent yeoman is especially celebrated in the work of Frank L. Owsley, whose influential studies of *Plain Folk of the Old South* are devoted to making the slave section seem in fact an agrarian utopia. Other historians have rediscovered the Creoles of Louisiana and neighboring states, the mountaineers of Appalachia and the Ozarks, the "crackers" of the piney woods. Still others recall that the South had its professional class, doctors, lawyers, editors, teachers, and its urban and even its industrial centers. These urban enclaves were dominated, of course, by the cotton trade, but they also were active in the manufacture of sugar and tobacco products and of the textiles and ironware that were to serve the Confederacy so surprisingly well during the Civil War.

And yet, as that war forcibly reminds us, the simpler picture probably remains the more valid and more realistic one. Creoles, crackers, and mountaineers, commercial and industrial workers, trained professionals, were but marginal groups in the Old South. The average yeoman, moreover, decided neither his own fate nor the fate of his section. It was the planter, in an increasingly unfriendly universe, and his "niggers" bereft of their manhood, who set off the South from the rest of the country and from more and more of the world. The old Virginians knew this and regretted it. As the hateful system spread itself, the romantic fiction of Old Dominion cavaliers helped cloak the crude violence of frontier life. The "Great Revival" in religion, from which abolitionism itself took fire (see p. 437), also burned through the South and Southwest and spawned many lasting reforms, especially against whiskey drinking and its attendant degradation. To many northerners newly admitted to the "mighty Baptism of the Holy Spirit," no greater sin could be found in Christendom than pride of pigment, property in men, the enslavement of one Christian brother by another. To many southerners, the word of the Lord placed the black sons of Ham in everlasting bondage. Fundamentalism in religion reinforced the slave foundations of southern life.

501

# I *The White People of the South*

## DIXIE LAND

No one knew of the South as "Dixie" until Dan Emmett, a blackface minstrel out of Mount Vernon, Ohio, sang the new song of that name in a New York City theater in 1859. Two years later the band played "Dixie" at Jefferson Davis's inauguration as first President of the Confederacy, and it then became the unofficial anthem of the southern republic. No one knows just where the term "Dixie" came from. One of the more dubious derivations is one of the most suggestive—that is, that it was a corruption of the name of Jeremiah Dixon who surveyed the Mason-Dixon line. The Mason-Dixon line helped settle the boundary between Pennsylvania and Maryland in the 1760s. Its extension westward, roughly along the Ohio River, also helped settle the northern boundary of Dixie. Above that boundary slavery had been put well on the way to extinction around the turn of the nineteenth century (see p. 217). Below that boundary slavery existed in all the 16 states and neighboring territories. Dixie was the land of slavery. It was also, as the song says, "the land of cotton."

There are many parts of the South where the growing season is too short for cotton, where the weather is too cold for rice, where it snows every winter and even beasts need sheltering barns. Yet the characteristic and distinguishing feature of the southern climate is the prevailing heat—*90° in the Shade* Clarence Cason titled his moving book on the South published in 1935, one of the early works of our time to expose the fiction and frailties of the utopian legend. A slightly later (1941) and more penetrating book is W.J. Cash's history of *The Mind of the South,* in which the weather also evokes the perceptive prose: "If the dominant mood is one of sultry reverie," writes Cash,

the land is capable of other and more sombre moods. . . . There are days when the booming of the wind in the pines is like the audible rushing of time—when the sad knowledge of the grave stirs in the subconsciousness and bends the spirit to melancholy. . . . And there are other days . . . when the nerves wilt under the terrific impact of sun and humidity, and even the soundest grow a bit neurotic. . . . There are other days, too, when . . . hurricanes break forth with semi-tropical fury; days when this land which, in its dominant mood, wraps its children in soft illusion, strips them naked before terror.

If the weather drew the characteristic southerner outdoors, the terrain and what it held helped keep him there. All across the Cotton Kingdom were the densest forests in the world; as late as 1860 a large part of the slave's labor was given to clearing new land to let in the sunshine as well as to prepare fields for cultivation. The forests rewarded the hunter with ample and varied game. The Kingdom was also exceedingly well endowed with navigable streams to carry cotton and other staples to export centers, and with thousands of smaller brooks and creeks and rivulets, lakes and ponds, to feed the marshes and water the earth. These waterways rewarded the fisherman with ample and varied fare. "His leisure," writes Cash,

left the Southerner free to brood as well as to dream—to exaggerate his fears as well as his hopes. And if for practical purposes it is true that he was likely to be complacently content with his lot, and even though it was the lot of white-trash, it is not yet perfectly true. Vaguely the loneliness of the country, the ennui of long burning empty days, a hundred half-perceived miseries, ate into him and filled him with nebulous discontent and obscure longing. Like all men everywhere, he hungered after a better and a happier world.

A more concrete ambition also stirred the southerner's soul, like that of enterprising busi-

nessmen everywhere in America. The Cotton Kingdom was not extended in a single generation from South Carolina to Texas by men content to brood and dream at home. No better cotton land existed anywhere than in the Red River Valley of northern Louisiana and Texas. A typical Red River planter, accosted one day on a steamboat by a representative of the Education Society selling a "Bible Defence of Slavery," shouted: "Now you go to hell! I've told you three times I didn't want your book. If you bring it here again, I'll throw it overboard. I own niggers; and I calculate to own more of 'em, if I can get 'em, but I don't want any damn'd preachin' about it."

Yet southern society was more homogeneous than northern, more settled and conservative in its ways, and less exposed to social and intellectual ferment. To the novelist John De Forest, who lived with the "Southrons" immediately after the Civil War, they seemed as different from the people in New England as the Spartans were from the Athenians. "They are more simple than us," he wrote, "more provincial, more antique, more picturesque; they have fewer of the virtues of modern society, and more of the primitive, the natural virtues." The violence of white southern life has perhaps been exaggerated, but the "Arkansas toothpick" (as the Bowie knife was sometimes called) became one of the principal instruments for settling differences in the rougher sections, and even in the older and more settled regions the code of honor prevailed.

The history of the Tillmans, a South Carolina family, is a saga of violence. Benjamin Ryan Tillman, the first, was an industrious but lawless planter who gambled as hard as he worked, killed a man in 1847, and died of typhoid fever two years later, aged 46. His wife, Sophia, a commanding, efficient woman, bore him three daughters and seven sons. Thomas, the oldest son, was killed in the Mexican War. The second, George Dionysius Tillman, might have served as the hero of a Faulkner novel. (Faulkner speaks of the "glamorous fatality" of southern names.) This erratic and intelligent young man spent a year at Harvard, read law, and served in the state legislature. On two separate occasions, he fought and wounded his opponent; shortly after, he killed a third man during a card game. George fled the country, filibustered in Cuba, and returned in 1858, repentant, to spend two luxurious years in the local jail. Another son, handsome and ill-tempered, was killed by two brothers whose family he had insulted, and still another son was slain over some domestic quarrel.

Despite such open violence, travelers found the people hospitable and friendly until the virus of suspicion spread.

## THE SOUTHERN CASTES

In 1850, about 6,185,000 white people lived in the South, of whom only 350,000 owned slaves. With their families, this group probably made up less than a third of southern whites. Most of them owned but one or two slaves, only a small number as many as ten. A mere 8000 planters owned 50 or more slaves, 254 owned 200 or more, and only 11 in the entire South owned 500 or more. The cotton kings, whose vast holdings and splendid mansions figure so prominently in southern romances, never amounted to more than 1 per cent of the white population.

No doubt a conspicuous number of the large-planter caste lived the high life of saber-rattling, fire-breathing "cavaliers." But they were likely to be more worrisome than wonderful even to their own families. In their youth, sons of the well-to-do often were sent West with the hope that they might settle down under the cares of plantations of their own. Many did; but many more only found broader scope for recklessness and violence to match the rough and somber environment. Those who, like our Red River planter, were determined to develop their priceless natural endowment, spent many years in crude surroundings. The saw mill itself came late to Alabama, Mississippi, and Louisiana, and even in the 1840s and 1850s wealthy planters continued to live in the typical "two pen" log houses, with crevices between the unhewn logs to let in the only light along with the rain and the wind.

In the older South many of the gentry lived well, and some extravagantly. But most of them also bore the cares that went with ownership of property and had little time to enjoy anything more than the simple pleasures of rustic society. Hunting, horse-racing, card-playing, visiting, and perhaps an annual summer pilgrimage to the mountains or the sea to escape the heat, pretty well exhausted their recreations.

What one southern writer, John Pendleton Kennedy, referred to as "the mellow, bland, and sunny luxuriance" of old-time Virginia society is delineated in the pages of his *Swallow Barn, or a Sojourn in the Old Dominion* (1832), and in Susan Dabney Smedes's engaging account of her father, Thomas S. G. Dabney of Virginia and Mississippi, the *beau ideal* of the southern planter. Humane, upright, generous, and courteous, such hard-working and practical gentlemen as Dabney were most deeply involved with sick slaves, the price of cotton, and unreliable overseers. Subjects too unliterary for southern romancers, they make up the meat of plantation diaries and account books, with their records of hazards, anxieties, and disappointments. "Managing a plantation," Mrs. Smedes observed, "was something like managing a kingdom. The ruler had need of great store, not only of wisdom, but of tact and patience as well." Nor did the planter's wife escape irksome domestic duties.

To the two-thirds of the southern white families who owned no slaves at all one should add those who worked their small holdings side by side with a black helper or two to find the true proportion of "plain folk" in the antebellum South. The farms of these "average" yeomen might be discovered tucked away among the large plantations in the cotton and tobacco country, but they predominated in the upland South—in eastern Tennessee, western North Carolina, northern Georgia, Alabama, and Mississippi. Here, while some produced the southern staples, most of the plain folk grew subsistence crops—grains and cereals, sweet potatoes, sorghum cane—or raised live-

503

A double log cabin on an Alabama plantation, typical of those occupied by yeoman farmers. (Library of Congress.)

stock. The plain folk also included the store-keepers, the mechanics, and other artisans in southern villages and towns.

Seen through the candid but critical eyes of Frederick Law Olmsted, the Connecticut Yankee who traveled through the southern hinterlands in the early 1850s, the living standards of the yeoman whites seemed distinctly low when compared with those of northern farmers. And yet, though Olmsted complained of wretched cookery, vermin-filled beds, and rude manners, he also noted that the white farmers in general presented a picture of a sturdy, proud, and friendly people. "If you want to fare well in this country," he was told in northern Alabama, "you stop to poor folks' housen; they try to enjoy what they've got while they ken, but these yer big planters they don' care for nothing but to save." Riding through an area of thin sandy soil, Olmsted reported that it was

thickly populated by poor farmers. Negroes are rare, but occasionally neat, new houses, with other improvements, show the increasing prosperity of the district. The majority of dwellings are small log cabins of one room, with another separate cabin for a kitchen; each house has a well, and a garden enclosed with palings. Cows, goats, mules and swine, fowls and doves are abundant. The people are more social than those of the lower country, falling readily into friendly conversation. . . . They are very ignorant; the

agriculture is wretched and the work hard. I have seen three white women hoeing field crops today. A spinning-wheel is heard in every house . . . every one wears home-spun. The negroes have much more individual freedom than in the rich cotton country, and are not infrequently heard singing or whistling at their work.

Among such farmers, as one who grew up among them in Mississippi reported, "people who lived miles apart, counted themselves as neighbors, . . . and in case of sorrow or sickness, or need of any kind, there was no limit to the ready service" they rendered one another. Such social activities as might bring them together centered on the church, the county court, the market towns and the village taverns.

The "bottom sill" of southern white society was the so-called "poor white trash." Perhaps as much as the Negro himself, the "poor whites" were the victims of slavery. Their illiteracy, their disdain for manual labor, and their prejudices were in large measure the result of slavery. Such was the conclusion of one embittered southerner, Hinton Rowan Helper, a Negro-hater who turned abolitionist to save the South from itself. His sensational and propagandistic book, *The Impending Crisis of the South: How to Meet It* (1857), made slavery "the root of all the shame, poverty, ignorance, tyranny and imbecility of the

504

South." Although Helper's widely publicized analysis distorted the southern picture, it contained some uncomfortable truths about white people that were hardly answered by calling its author a "miserable renegade."

On the "poor whites," the discerning Olmsted wrote:

They are said to "corrupt" the negroes, and to encourage them to steal, or to work for them at night and on Sundays, and to pay them with liquor, and to constantly associate licentiously with them. They seem, nevertheless, more than any other portion of the community, to hate and despise the negroes.

## II *The Life of the Southern Negro*

### THE BLACK POPULATION

Slavery took root in the South because black Africans provided a cheap and available labor force to cultivate the staple crops. By the time Congress closed the slave trade in 1808, about 1,160,000 slaves were owned in the southern states. Others were subsequently smuggled in from Africa (one estimate places the number at about 270,000 between 1808 and 1860); but most of the slaves who were

transported to the newly opened lands in the Southwest came from slave populations of the older states. Between 1830 and 1850, Virginia alone, in what had become a profitable business, exported close to 300,000 Negroes, South

505

**N. B. FOREST,
DEALER IN SLAVES,
No. 87 Adams-st, Memphis, Ten.,**

HAS just received from North Carolina, twenty-five likely young negroes, to which he desires to call the attention of purchasers. He will be in the regular receipt of negroes from North and South Carolina every month. His Negro Depot is one of the most complete and commodious establishments of the kind in the Southern country, and his regulations exact and systematic, cleanliness, neatness and comfort being strictly observed and enforced. His aim is to furnish to customers A. 1 servants and field hands, sound and perfect in body and mind. Negroes taken on commission.          jan21

*(Above) A newspaper advertisement of the early 1850s offering tidewater and piedmont slaves for sale in one of the great slave markets of the West. (The Bettmann Archive.) Antebellum slave quarters (below) on Edisto Island, South Carolina. This photograph of 1862 shows Union soldiers in uniform and young blacks in campaign caps during one of the first Reconstruction experiments on Confederate territory occupied early in the Civil War. (Courtesy of the New-York Historical Society, New York City.)*

Carolina about 170,000. On the eve of the Civil War about 3,800,000 slaves lived in Dixie, a mere 200,000 free Negroes.

The slave population in the antebellum South was far from evenly distributed (see map, p. 512). In southern Appalachia and the Ozarks where the land was unsuited to staple crops, slaves were a rarity. In areas better suited to the plantation method of production —the tobacco regions of the Chesapeake, the rice flats of coastal South Carolina and Georgia, the sugar fields of Louisiana and Texas, and above all the Cotton Kingdom of the middle and lower South—slaves were numerous. In some counties and parishes in these areas slaves made up as much as three-fourths of the total population. The 1850 census estimated that out of the 2,500,000 blacks engaged in agriculture in the South, no less than 1,815,000 were employed in growing cotton. Tobacco occupied 350,000; sugar 150,000; rice 125,000; and hemp 60,000.

The heaviest concentration of slaves and cotton could be found in the prize lands of the South: in the "Black Belt" that stretched across central Alabama into northwest Mississippi; in the flood plains of the Mississippi River; and in parts of southern Texas that drained into the Gulf of Mexico. By 1850, the Black Belt had become the greatest cotton-growing region in the world. And here it was that the slave system could be studied in its most mature form. Labor on plantations of from one to two thousand acres (the most efficient size) was reduced to a series of routine operations with the slaves divided into plow and hoe gangs under the direction of "drivers" and "overseers." Relations between master and slave were of necessity more impersonal on the large plantations than on the small ones, and discipline was more severe. The well-run plantation "factories," which often became self-sufficient units producing corn, peanuts, and livestock in addition to cotton, were serviced by slave carpenters, masons, and weavers, as well as field hands.

Few free Negroes lived in the South's agricultural regions, but among them were some who themselves had become great planters and slaveowners. Such Negro "kings" were especially conspicuous on the frontier in Mississippi, Alabama, and Louisiana before the period of "ultraism" in white supremacy following upon the onset of the abolitionist crusade; and they were treated as gentlemen among gentlemen. In the cities, too, free Negro businessmen owned slaves whom they hired out for all sorts of urban tasks.

In the first quarter of the nineteenth century, slaves made up at least 20 per cent of the urban population of the South; in places like New Orleans and Richmond they were more numerous; and in Charleston, South Carolina, they outnumbered whites. Thereafter the slave population of southern cities declined. By 1848 it was said that "slavery exists in Louisville and St. Louis only in name." Two reasons were offered by contemporaries for the falling off in urban slaves: "The first is a dense population . . . the next is the intelligence of slaves." Among blacks, as among whites, cities offered a stimulating environment far different from the isolation of plantation life. To be remunerative, city slaves had to be hired out singly or in small numbers, not in gangs under overseers. Thus, flight or mere disappearance could be more easily effected, and with his skills learned as a slave a Negro could make a living as a free man.

Even so, at the outbreak of the Civil War, approximately 500,000 slaves were living in southern cities and towns as servants or artisans or were engaged in such nonagricultural pursuits as cutting wood for steamboats, lumbering, mining, iron-manufacturing, and construction.

### THE SLAVE'S WORLD

"The first black men in the American midlands—not counting a few who were brought in chains to work the salt mines—were fugitives and wanderers. They came thrashing the wilderness grass like frightened animals," write Arna Bontemps and Jack Conroy in their

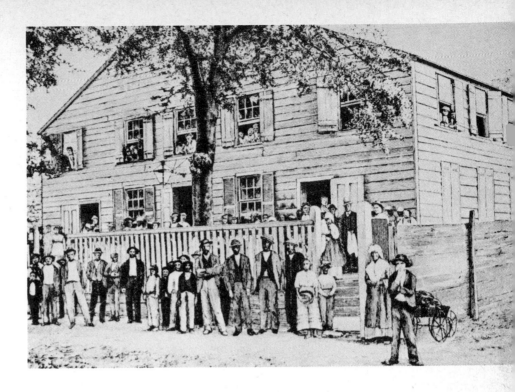

Southern urban Negroes before the First Negro Baptist Church, Savannah, Georgia. The congregation was established in 1779.

book on Negro migrations, *Any Place But Here,*

and at night they cast their aching, exhausted bodies on the ground and slept. In the morning they rose up, filled their lungs with the free air of God's country, and swore it was different from the air of bondage. The difference, they reasoned soberly, was exactly the difference between night and day. . . . The air made the difference. That's why folks always talked about going North and breathing the free air. Many such folks came to Illinois . . . and some stayed put, but others moved on [to Canada and to California.]

No one knows how many slaves took the path of the "underground railroad" toward freedom, nor how many died before reaching their goal. Estimates range as high as 100,000 successful escapees, most of them moving out after the onset of the abolitionist campaign in 1830. Peak traffic on this "railroad" was reached in the 1850s when the Fugitive Slave Law (see p. 494) deepened northern antagonism to the slave system and drew more and more whites to assist the flying blacks. Most of the "conductors" on this railroad, however, were Negroes who had earlier made good their escape from the South or who had been born free in the North and who used their freedom to help others retrieve their humanity. The number of active workers on the underground railroad has been placed as high as 3200, but many more surely gave a meal and refuge to the trembling "passengers."

Running away was always part of the slave's dream and the slave system. Flight was one of the principal actions that made the slave such a "troublesome property" to the master. With the development of the underground railroad, when flight became a systematically organized attack on the entire order of slavery, southern rulers responded with even harsher repression and punishment than before.

Certain bondsmen, as we have seen, escaped the drudgery of the field gang; and the lot of others might vary according to their age and sex, the region in which they worked, the character and disposition of their masters, and their own temper and personality. Yet all

507

A slave auction at the Richmond market in 1856. (New York Public Library, Schomburg Collection.)

slaveowners, in the nineteenth as in the eighteenth century (see p. 99), were bound by the system under which black men and women were their chattels in an environment of violence and mutual fear and dread. House servants usually found life easier than field hands; but the death of a humane master might result in his servants' being put out to the land when least prepared for its burdens. Some gifted slaves were rewarded with positions of trust and responsibility and responded with loyalty and devotion to their masters for affectionate treatment. Yet even the kindliest slaveholder, either as buyer or seller, sometimes felt obliged to break up Negro families, which themselves had no standing under the law.

Of all the institutions of slavery, the slave market was perhaps the worst, for white and black alike. Lincoln, in 1854, reminded the South that "the great majority" there as in the North, "have human sympathies, of which they can no more divest themselves than they can of their sensibility to physical pain." The one who tried those sympathies to the utmost was "a sneaking individual, of the class of native tyrants, known as the 'SLAVE-DEALER.'" Lincoln went on:

He watches your necessities, and crawls up to buy your slave, at a speculating price. If you cannot help it, you sell to him; but if you can help it, you drive him from your door. You despise him utterly. . . . Your children must not play with his; they may rollick freely with the little negroes, but not with the "slave dealer's" children. . . . It is common with you to join hands with the men you meet; but with the slave dealer you avoid the ceremony—instinctively shrinking from the snaky contact. Now why is this? You do not so treat the man who deals in corn, cattle or tobacco.

On some plantations where the "task" system was employed, a slave might complete his assigned work by early afternoon and spend the rest of the day as he chose. Progressive planters sometimes gave their slaves incentive payments and also encouraged them to cultivate truck gardens and to raise pigs and chickens for their own consumption or for sale. Holidays and entertainments alleviated the drudgery on some plantations, and where work became too exacting slaves developed their own slow-down techniques. Yet such situations were exceptional, even in the upper South where the "institution" is said to have been less vicious than elsewhere in the United States.

The main attraction and advantage of the slave system to the slaveowner was the uniformity that could be imposed upon masses of labor engaged in routine and repetitive tasks. Whether kindly used or ferociously abused, the slave remained but a species of property valued primarily for the work that could be extracted from him. Frederick Douglass, a house servant who had been taught to read and write, yet who fled from slavery in Maryland in 1838 and gave the rest of his life to the pursuit of freedom and equality for other blacks, spoke from experience when he wrote of slavery as, "perpetual unpaid toil; no marriage, no husband, no wife, ignorance, brutality, licentiousness; whips, scourges, chains, auctions, jails and separations; an embodiment of all the woes the imagination can conceive."

The poet Paul Laurence Dunbar of Dayton, Ohio, son of a fugitive slave and friend of Douglass, wrote in "Life":

A crust of bread and a corner to sleep in,
A minute to smile and an hour to weep in,
A pint of joy to a peck of trouble,
And never a laugh but the moans come double:
    And that is life!

A crust and corner that love makes precious,
With the smile to warm and the tears to refresh
    us:
And joy seems sweeter when cares come after,
And a moan is the finest of foils for laughter:
    And that is life!

On the characteristic plantation of the Cotton Kingdom, where the vast majority of slaves lived and worked, the routine hardly varied from day to day and year to year, only a break on July 4th and at most a week at Christmas relieving the tedium. The day's work ran, as the saying went, from "can see, 'til can't." Solomon Northrup, a free Negro who had been kidnapped and compelled to toil for 12 years in the Red River region of northern Louisiana, began his work in the cotton fields as soon as it was light. He and his fellow slaves got 10 to 15 minutes at noon to eat their rations of cold bacon, and then often worked until after dark. Their assigned "task" in the harvest season would be a certain weight of cotton to pick. Those who failed to "tote" their quotas to the gin house were thrashed; those who exceeded their quotas under the whip in the field were assigned an extra measure thereafter. Each Sunday Northrup received his weekly food allowance: "three and a half pounds of bacon, and corn enough to make a peck of meal." Occasionally he was given a sprinkling of salt, but no coffee, tea, or sugar. In his log cabin, open to the wind and rain, he slept on "a plank 12 inches wide and 10 feet long," with a "stick of wood" for a pillow and a coarse blanket for his bedding.

Slave gangs like Northrup's worked the long day under the eye of the overseer whose job it was to get out the crop. Obviously it was to the slaveholder's advantage to protect his slave property against excessive work and barbarous punishment; but it required the nicest judgment to maintain a balance between laxness and severity in the management of involuntary workers, and overseers with such judgment were hard to come by. The lash, applied by the overseer himself or his Negro "driver" (a slave assigned as a kind of foreman to keep the hands on the job) was more commonly resorted to than other inducements.

Abolitionists sometimes exaggerated the brutalities of slavery, but they did not have to invent stories of whippings, brandings, mutilations, and murder. The custom of flogging recalcitrant Negroes was widespread. Some planters set their dogs on runaway slaves, and hundreds of authentic records testify to the brutal punishment of Negroes who struck white men or who committed misdemeanors. Some were burned alive; others were starved, shot, or hanged. Slave-owners who killed their slaves often escaped punishment, for Negro witnesses were not permitted to testify against white men in court.

The claim that Negro slaves were contented, that their happy-go-lucky temperament enabled them to adjust to their menial position, and that they did not respond to bondage as white men would have done is contradicted by documented evidence. Many tried to buy their freedom, and a few succeeded. Failing this, even those who had been treated kindly would run away. Slaves often feigned sickness, mutilated themselves, simply loafed, and sometimes openly rebelled to escape forced labor. The fear of slave revolts in the antebellum period as earlier kept the South on edge, even though in most cases anxiety proved unwarranted.

Allusions to "horrible and barbarous massacres" plotted by blacks, as we have seen (p. 99), go back to the early colonial period. The first widely publicized one in the nineteenth century was the so-called Gabriel Conspiracy. Gabriel's abortive uprising in Henrico County, Virginia in 1800 (more than 1000 slaves were allegedly implicated) was betrayed by black informers. Twenty-two years later, Denmark Vesey, a freedman living in Charleston, planned and organized a far-reaching insurrection. His revolt was also betrayed by slaves, and Vesey and over 30 of his followers were executed. By far the most sensational slave revolt—certainly the one that produced the loudest reverberations—was engineered by a Virginia Negro preacher named Nat Turner in 1831. Believing himself to be divinely appointed, Turner launched his squads on a 48-hour rampage which ended in the death of 57 whites and about 100 blacks. What Turner hoped to accomplish after he had killed every white person (children and women included) in Southampton County was never disclosed; but his "deep and deadly"

plot shocked the country as had no previous one. According to the reporter who interviewed Turner in prison, the "contriver" was neither ignorant nor cowardly, nor was his object "to murder and rob for the purpose of obtaining money to make his escape." Turner did not drink or smoke. Not only could he read and write, but he also displayed a "natural intelligence and quickness of apprehension" that struck this reporter as remarkable. He could only attribute Turner's actions to "warped and perverted" influences.

Turner's was the last of the organized slave revolts, but insurrection panics occurred a number of times between 1831 and 1860, and "reports of Negro plots" provided sensational material for jittery southern newspaper editors. Riding night patrols was one task even irresponsible planters took seriously, whiskey often bucking them up against the terrors of darkness. In the towns and cities, police costs "for the purpose of 'keeping down the niggers'," as one traveler reported, made up the largest municipal budget item. Olmsted wrote that in nearly every southern city he visited, "you come to police machinery such as you never find in towns under free governments: citadels, sentries, passports, grapeshotted cannon, and daily public whippings . . . for accidental infractions of police ceremonies."

Well-treated slaves like Nat Turner belied the notion that gentleness would attach the slave to his master. The religious language in which rebel exhorters addressed their followers convinced many planters that Bible reading— indeed, reading of any kind—was potentially incendiary. They blamed abolitionist propaganda, of course, for slave unrest, and "free people of colour" also came increasingly under disfavor following the discovery or reports of slave revolts. Their presence alone, it was felt, exacerbated slave discontent.

All the same, the slave's passion for freedom usually was balanced by a realization of the futility in trying to achieve it. News traveled fast among the slave population, and reports of repressions and bloody reprisals carried a disheartening message. As Kenneth Stampp asserts: "In truth, no slave uprising ever had a chance of ultimate success, even though it might have cost the master class heavy casualties." Until his emancipation the black slave had to seek to alleviate the system or to sabotage it. He might do the first by accommodating himself to his master's demands and playing the role of the faithful servant; or by seeking ways to work without rigid supervision. Slaves hired out for their special skills—especially urban slaves—enjoyed a certain amount of mobility, often managed to keep a little of the money they earned for their owners, and acquired what many slaveholders regarded as the baneful and pernicious habit of self-reliance. Slaves fated to spend their days under the "domestic control of the master" might express their hatred of slavery by fooling white people, chanting subversive messages in the form of spirituals, running away, or by adopting other forms of planned incapacity. Even in an environment where independence was systematically and ruthlessly repressed and every effort made to keep the slave in intellectual darkness, men and women of ability emerged from the slave's world as living refutations of ethnic prejudice.

## III  *The Plantation System*

### MINOR SOUTHERN STAPLES

The southern economy lagged behind that of the North for some reasons that had nothing to do with slavery. The North had a more invigorating climate, more varied natural resources, better harbors. But it was the single-crop system, the gang-labor system, the slave system, that kept the South from making the most of its own natural endowment.

The first southern agricultural staple was tobacco, and the first slave-labor plantations were devoted to growing the leaf in tidewater Virginia and Maryland (see p. 56). After 1800, tobacco culture spread westward across the upper South, and by mid-century this newer area was raising more tobacco than the old. In the 1850s, however, Virginia, North Carolina, and Maryland made such a spectacular comeback in tobacco production that seven of the ten leading tobacco counties in the entire country were in those three states. The source of their new prosperity was the discovery in 1839 by a slave, Stephen, employed as an overseer and blacksmith on a North Carolina plantation, of a way of curing a type of tobacco, the "Bright Yellow Tobacco," that grew better on the poor sandy soil of the Roanoke Valley and inland Maryland than on the worn-out soil of the tidewater. Great plantations again became the rule in the Old Dominion and her neighbors, and the grim business of breeding slaves for the Southwest declined. But compared to cotton, tobacco remained a minor southern crop, and the tobacco revival did not bring general prosperity even to the three leading states. In 1860, only 36 per cent of Virginia land and 27 per cent of land in North Carolina was "improved," compared to 68 and 61 per cent for New York and Pennsylvania.

Although the chief beneficiaries of the bright-tobacco boom were great slaveholders, tobacco was also grown by a large number of small farmers. Small farmers were the main producers of another minor crop, hemp, which became a staple in Kentucky and Missouri. Only rich planters, on the other hand, could embark on the production of rice and sugar, the South's two other important minor staples. In 1860, indeed, not even the Gulf states of the Cotton Kingdom could match the rice regions of South Carolina and Georgia in the relative density of their slave populations and the scale of their plantations. The only estate of more than 1000 slaves in the entire South was in the South Carolina rice country. Besides South Carolina and Georgia, rice was produced in lowland regions in Louisiana, Texas, and Arkansas. Because rice plantations were usually situated in hot marshy districts, their owners normally spent the spring and summer in more salubrious spots to escape

512

malaria. Under hard-driving overseers, their blacks fared badly. Cholera and yellow fever, as well as malaria, thinned their ranks.

Cane-sugar planting gained a great impetus after 1822, when steam-engines were introduced to crush the cane. The cost of machinery for a sugar plantation might run as high as $14,000, and the harvesting of cane called for intensive periods of the hardest labor by gangs of slaves. Only owners of the large plantations in the rich delta lands of Louisiana and the alluvial soil regions of southeastern Texas and coastal Georgia could afford the cost of sugar-milling equipment, but even they were able to compete with the more favorably situated West Indian producers only because of the high tariff on imported sugar.

### THE COTTON KINGDOM

As early as 1820, the South's cotton crop had become more valuable than all its other crops combined. By 1835 the Cotton Kingdom itself had spread more than a thousand miles from South Carolina and Georgia all the way to Texas and ranged some six or seven hundred miles up the Mississippi Valley. In 1859, the United States produced a record cotton crop of 5,387,000 bales, two-thirds of it grown in the Gulf states. At that time, cotton accounted for two-thirds of the *nation's* exports.

With a little capital, small acreage, and a few slaves, a cotton farmer could still make a profit. Cotton could survive rough handling when it was shipped to market, and it did not spoil—important considerations where roads were bad and transportation facilities often were lacking or subject to delay. Much of the American cotton crop, even on the frontier, was in fact grown by small farmers; yet cotton, with its huge market and great adaptability to slave-gang labor, was the ideal staple for the slave-owning planters who spread over the virgin lands of the Southwest. By 1860, slave-owning cotton growers pro-

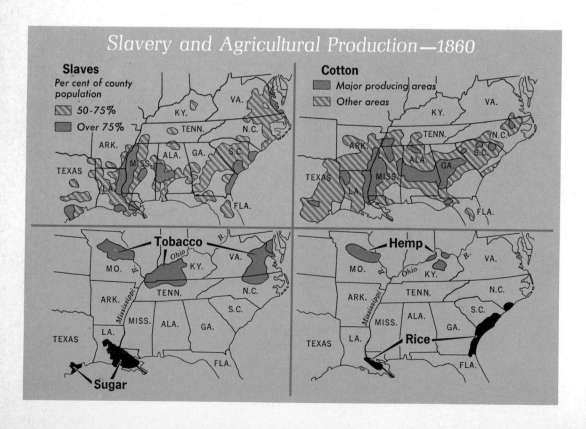

Slavery and Agricultural Production—1860

duced more than 93 per cent of the Mississippi crop.

Where land was plentiful and cheap and labor dear, the essence of good plantation management was high production per slave, not per acre. Under effective overseers and gang bosses, the more slaves a planter had, the greater his margin of success was likely to be. It was this circumstance that helped put such great pressure on overseers and on the slaves themselves. Good overseers were hard to find and to keep; the most successful planters were those who kept a close eye on all their affairs and even dispensed with overseers when they could. Large-scale operations gave big planters other advantages as well. Necessities that they could not grow or make on the plantation they could purchase in large quantities at wholesale rates. They could also market their crops more efficiently. Wealthier planters, moreover, were more likely to be interested in conserving the soil, more willing to experiment with new agricultural techniques.

### PROFITS AND PENALTIES OF THE PLANTATION SYSTEM

Those who argue—as many did in the South as well as the North before 1860, and as many continue to argue today—that slave labor was more costly in cotton-growing than free labor would have been and that slavery would have disappeared eventually if left alone, have tended to make a mere bookkeeping problem of a profound social issue. It is true that only exceptional cotton plantations earned large profits, even on the virgin soil of the Gulf area. It is also true that such profits as were earned were menaced by high slave mortality and the cost of maintaining aged slaves and slave children. Despite efforts to quicken their incentive, moreover, slaves proved to be reluctant workers, while solicitude for their welfare proved insufficient to prevent them from misusing tools and damaging equipment. To make matters worse, the cost of prime male field hands jumped in the 1840s and 1850s from $1000 to $1200 or more. The planter

necessarily found that a heavy proportion of his capital was tied up in slaves. But he was no more motivated on that account to abandon slavery than Queen Victoria was motivated to abandon monarchy because of the rising cost of soldiers.

If slavery was in fact an economic disadvantage to the cotton South, it need not bear all the responsibility for southern economic backwardness. Even in antebellum days men like Edmund Ruffin of Virginia argued that southern soil exhaustion, for example, was only indirectly connected with the unchanging routines of slave gangs. Soil exhaustion, they said, was primarily the result of short-sightedness, itself encouraged by the easy availability of new land; and of ignorance, promoted by widespread white illiteracy and indifference to technology. But even these men acknowledged that the plantation system itself discouraged widespread education even in agricultural processes, and that slavery induced an indifference to technological innovation.

Would slavery have persisted after the lands suitable for staple crops had been used up? Many southerners and northerners believed that nature had confined slavery to a restricted area and that the institution on that account would not outlast the century. Lincoln and others in the North who, in the political arena, so strongly opposed the extension of slavery to new territories (see Chapters Fifteen and Eighteen) obviously did not share this belief. Nor did those in the South who so pertinaciously opposed restrictions on free expansion of the institution. It has been argued, moreover, by Lewis C. Gray, the leading historian of antebellum agriculture in the South, that the expansion of the railroads would have brought fresh lands into easy reach of the migrating planter, and that industry might well have absorbed the surplus slave population. Although slaves, as we have seen (p. 511), did in fact work in southern industries and in other urban occupations, the growing need to defend the slave system and the plantation system from attack by the industrial North drained such incentive as there might

*"A Cotton Plantation on the Mississippi River," a Currier and Ives print from a painting by W.A. Walker. (Museum of the City of New York.) The picked cotton was dumped into primitive presses in the fields (below) to form bales for easy shipment. (The Bettmann Archive.)*

have been among the great planters really to develop a dynamic industrial regime in their own area. The need to justify the slave system and the plantation system in its own terms, indeed, helped dissipate the profits that were made on the land and turned the proud Cotton Kingdom into a disenchanted colony of industrial and commercial Britain and the North.

## THE COLONIAL STATUS OF THE KINGDOM

Southerners were perfectly familiar with the invidious contrasts drawn by their own representatives between the busy, contented North—enterprising, public-spirited, prosperous—and the indolent, poverty-stricken southern country. Many of them nevertheless feared the effects of introducing factories into an agrarian slave society. Some felt (though there was evidence in some southern factories to the contrary) that a Negro working in a factory was already half-free; others believed that blacks were not capable of mastering machinery. Many, moreover, harbored the old distrust of cities that Jefferson had expressed so vividly in his *Notes on Virginia*.

In spite of all these doubts and apprehensions, a favorable attitude toward manufacturing developed during the 1820s and 1830s when tariff controversies made the South acutely conscious of its dependence on northern industry. Georgians and Virginians petitioned their legislators to encourage planters to build their own factories to employ the hitherto unproductive poor whites, and thereby to restore the glory of the South by keeping her wealth at home.

Not until the 1840s, however, did the arguments for building up southern manufactures begin to take hold. This decade was a time of falling cotton prices and economic stagnation in the South Atlantic states, and the people were in the mood to listen to a thoughtful Charleston businessman, William Gregg. His *Essays on Domestic Industry* (1845)—written after a tour of the New England mills—pointed the way to an economic and moral rehabilitation of the poor whites through industrial employment. Gregg's proposals, embodied in his own model factories run along the lines of the Lowell plan (see p. 390), contained nothing offensive to southern prejudices. Gregg did not advocate the use of slave labor for manufacturing. Nor did he demand tariff protection, for the coarse variety of cotton cloth produced in the South did not compete with foreign textiles. His program was applauded by the growing number of southern nationalists (already looking ahead to southern independence) who wanted a strongly industrialized South when the great day arrived. Another influential group backed the industrial program for precisely opposite reasons: They hoped that factories would make the South prosperous and that prosperity would remove the chief cause of animosity between the sections.

Yet little came of Gregg's work. Between 1850 and 1860, the number of industrial workers in the South rose only from 165,000 to 190,000. On the eve of the Civil War, the South was producing less than 10 per cent of the nation's manufactured goods. In 1860, the Lowell mills alone operated more spindles than all the cotton-spinning factories of the South combined.

The South showed an even greater aversion to commerce than to manufacturing, with even stiffer penalties for producers of staple crops that had to be marketed abroad and carried to their purchasers. The planter relied on commission merchants, or "factors," to sell his crops. These factors, who resided in port cities or in interior market towns, shipped the produce northward or directly to Europe for a commission. They also sold supplies to the planter, advised him when to sell his crop, bought slaves for him, and performed personal services. Frequently, the planter fell so deeply in debt to his factors that they could dictate the kind of crop they wanted consigned to them for payment. The factor system therefore increased the concentration on cotton, since this was the safest cash crop, and restricted the most lucrative commercial activity to the seaboard cities and to a few river towns like Memphis.

Many factors were New Englanders, backed by New York capital. They were often criticized by planters for charging high brokerage fees—up to $2\frac{1}{2}$ per cent for selling a crop and from $2\frac{1}{2}$ to 10 per cent for buying supplies. A more valid reason for the planters' constant indebtedness was the business organization that permitted New York commercial interests to tap the profits from southern exports (see p. 386). By the 1850s about 40,000 American seamen were employed in the cotton-carrying trade, but few of them were southerners on southern ships. At the numerous commercial conventions held in the South between 1830 and 1860, the southern imagination was fired with rhetorical visions of teeming cities, happy artisans, and bustling marts, all the rewards of recapturing the cotton-carrying trade. But the steamship lines that were to provide direct communication with Europe, the railroads that were to tap the western markets, the trade that was to spring up with South America, and the cotton factories that were to turn New England into a desert, rarely passed beyond the rhetorical stage.

### THE ROOTS OF SOUTHERN LOYALTY

Profitable as slavery may have been to a few thousand planter families at most, it was socially disastrous for the South. "It may seem a paradox, and yet it is true," declared a North Carolinian in 1853, "that a community of planters may grow rich while they are impoverishing and depopulating their country." Slavery discouraged diversity in agriculture, accelerated the flow of southern yeomanry to the free-soil states, and created an illusory prosperity based on the ownership of land declining in fertility and of slaves rising in cost.

For the Negro, the physical and psychic injuries that resulted from his enforced servitude were obviously immense and lasting. The penalties that slavery imposed upon many slave-owners were almost as disastrous, though less obvious and less physically trying. The possession of such complete authority over human chattels brought out the worst in many slave-owners, not merely among the perverse and the depraved but in many well-meaning men and women as well. The barbarism of the institution affected even the most well-intentioned of the planters, and tempted them into practices that left a legacy of guilt. The very zeal with which they volunteered unconvincing justifications for black servitude suggests that they were frequently far from easy in their minds, and privately they often confessed as much. A few slave-owners publicly acknowledged their spiritual discomforts, as the following extract from the will of a North Carolinian who emancipated his slaves makes clear. He gave four reasons for his action:

Reason the first. Agreeably to the rights of man, every human being, be his or her colour what it may, is entitled to freedom. . . . Reason the second. My conscience, the great criterion, condemns me for keeping them in slavery. Rea-

son the third. The golden rule directs us to do unto every human creature, as we would wish to be done unto. . . . Reason the fourth and last. I wish to die with a clear conscience, that I may not be ashamed to appear before my master in a future World.

And yet the allegiance of the vast majority of southerners to the slave system and the plantation system after 1830 only deepened. Their attachment to the "peculiar institution," of course, varied according to class, region, and occupation, but the following considerations help to explain why slavery received such overwhelming support in the decades preceding the Civil War:

1. *Fear of becoming a white minority.* The heavy concentration of Negro slaves in parts of the South created a serious problem in race relations. Antislavery northerners, southern spokesmen declared, living in states where blacks comprised only a tiny fraction of the population, had no inkling of what it was like to live in South Carolina or Mississippi where blacks outnumbered whites. The total Negro population of the 16 free states in 1850 was under 200,000. In 1860, each of five southern states had twice that number of Negroes.

2. *The Negro unfit for freedom.* It was widely held in the South that the Negro would only be harmed by abolition. And this conclusion was strenghtened by reports about the condition of free Negroes in the North. Everywhere in the free-soil states, even in the centers of abolition, as we have seen (p. 399), Negroes were abused and discriminated against politically, economically, and socially, and then blamed for their low condition as though the reasons were congenital. In the South, free Negroes were often worse off, especially after the growing fear of slave revolts made them objects of suspicion.

3. *The anti-Negro sentiments of white laborers.* White workers in southern cities, like most northern workingmen, did not want to see slavery abolished. Negro competition, whether slave or free, threatened their security, and they often refused to work with

Negroes, who underbid them or who demeaned their social position by the mere fact of competing against them. Race prejudice was particularly strong among immigrant groups, like the Irish, who performed menial jobs too dangerous for high-priced slaves.

4. *The social ambitions of the small planter.* Small planters, linked to the gentry either by kinship or common interest, felt that their chances of rising in the world would be jeopardized by abolition. They, and many yeoman farmers too poor to own slaves, looked forward to the time when they would be masters of larger plantations. Hence, antiabolition sentiment was strong in many areas where the slave population was small.

5. *The "poor white" committed to racial inequality.* Finally, the impoverished southern whites, disease-ridden and shiftless, fanatically supported slavery as a way of preserving what little status they had. When the time came, they fought for slave property and for a slave-owning class that looked upon them with contempt.

## iv *The Mind of the South*

### LIMITATIONS ON THE REFORM SPIRIT

The antebellum South produced some admirable types, but opinions have differed widely over the range and depth of its culture. Measured by conventional standards—illiteracy rates, public schools, museums, the fine arts, and publishing—the South lagged behind the North. To the Bostonian Henry Adams, the southerners he met at Harvard between 1854 and 1858 seemed incredibly archaic, sunk in a simplicity beyond the comprehension of the most unsophisticated New England student. "Strictly, the Southerner had no mind; he had temperament," Adams wrote later in his celebrated *Education.* "He was not a scholar; he had no intellectual training; he could not analyze an idea, and he could not even conceive of admitting two."

Adams's sweeping generalization was provincial enough. Calhoun, a brilliant though somewhat doctrinaire analyst, more ingenious than profound, was one of a number of acute thinkers in the South who reasoned only too well. But the claim of impassioned proslavery men that the South had erected a superior culture on a slave base was no less mistaken. Intellectual novelties were not welcomed in the South, and the arts won little encouragement; old ways and old ideas retained their hold longer in this agrarian society, and intellectual pursuits were largely confined to an upper-class minority. There was no counterpart, for example, of the educated New England rustic or the self-taught Yankee artisan. An agricultural people was more likely to produce soldiers, orators, and politicians than artists and poets.

Although the South had no industrial revolution, no literary renaissance, it did pass through a period of social and political ferment between 1820 and 1860. Again, reform movements did not explode violently in a society that was still instinctively reactionary, and "isms" did not flourish in the southern atmosphere. The fundamentalist temper of the old South discouraged liberal and transcendental religious speculation as well as the yeasty fads and visionary doctrines that flourished in the North. So-called "northern fanaticism," much exaggerated by fiery southern patriots, could not take root in a society where both clergy and press remained constantly alert to "socialism, or to social equality, nihilism, communism, or to infidelity in any of its shapes or shades." Because few European immigrants settled in the South, alien ideas usually arrived by way of the North. In the southern mind, all "isms"—feminism, transcendentalism, Fourierism, and the rest—became tinged with abolitionism, a tinge that was sound enough, since northern abolitionists like Garrison, Theodore Parker, Theodore Weld, and Horace Greeley *were* interested in the whole range of reform programs. But the South spurned extravagant reforms for other reasons as well. Feminism outraged the southern ideal of womanhood. Experiments like

518

Frances Wright's plantation in Nashoba, Tennessee, where Negroes and whites were to live happily together, failed completely (see p. 459). Some southern mavericks—notably the aristocratic Grimké sisters, Angelina and Sarah, of Charleston—turned abolitionist or succumbed to other enthusiasms, but they were among the exceptions.

Yet the repudiation of Yankee intellectual notions and panaceas did not mean that the South was wholly immune to the humanitarian influences that touched most Americans in the 1830s and 1840s. The rise of evangelical religion was accompanied by a concerted effort to check frontier brutality and to discipline breaches of moral conduct. In the South, as elsewhere, criminal codes were humanized, prisons were improved, and treatment of the insane was made more scientific. Dorothea L. Dix was one Yankee reformer whom the South loved and cherished for her work on behalf of the mentally ill. Her visit to Tennessee and North Carolina in 1847–48 brought immediate action, and the asylum that was opened in Raleigh, North Carolina, in 1853 bore her name. During the same period, schools for the deaf patterned after northern models were established in a number of southern states. Perhaps the most enthusiastically supported reform movement in the prewar South was the temperance cause. Backed by religious and political leaders, temperance societies sprang up everywhere to the accompaniment of parades and petitions and the publicized testimony of reformed drunkards.

### ANTISLAVERY SENTIMENT

Until the antislavery crusade in the North gathered momentum in the early 1830s, a number of southerners criticized slavery or apologized for it, and looked forward to its ultimate extinction. Many years before slavery aroused the humanitarian zeal of the North, southern men and women who knew slavery at first hand had listed its baneful effects on the whites. In the eighteenth century, William Byrd II complained that slaves by their very

presence "blow up the pride and ruin the industry of the white people who, seeing a rank of poor creatures below them, detest work for fear it should then make them look like slaves." During the Revolutionary period, southern leaders like Washington, Jefferson, Madison, and Patrick Henry were well aware of the incongruity of slavery in a Republic dedicated to the principles of the Declaration of Independence, although they did little about it.

A later generation of southerners dominated the American Colonization Society, dedicated to transplanting freed slaves oversees, which was headed by George Washington's nephew. In Virginia, abolition was seriously argued in 1829, when a new state constitution was being drafted, and again in the legislature of 1831–32. The second debate followed on the heels of Nat Turner's insurrection.

The southern antislavery group not only played up the constant threat of slave revolts but also raised many of the arguments against slavery that northern abolitionists were later to use: that slavery was wedded to the destructive one-crop system so injurious to the land, that the presence of slaves discouraged immigration to the South, that slavery kept the South poor. "Wherefore, then, object to slavery?" asked one of the delegates to the Virginia Constitutional convention in 1832.

Because it is ruinous to the whites, retards improvements, roots out an industrious population —banishes the yeomanry of the country—deprives the spinner, the weaver, the smith, the shoemaker, the carpenter, of employment and support.

Southern attitudes toward slavery grew in illiberality starting as early as 1793, when Whitney's cotton gin gave the South a strong new reason for expanding the plantation and the slave systems (see p. 380). The abolitionist crusade in the North and the awareness of antislavery opinion in Europe also made the South increasingly sensitive to criticism and more eager to provide slavery with an ideological as well as a material defense.

## THE DEFENSE OF SLAVERY

During the 1830s, the proslavery forces in the South launched their counterattack first against the southerners opposed to slavery and then against the northern emancipationists. In order to combat abolitionist exaggerations and present slavery as an idyllic and humane institution, they felt obliged to demonstrate that slavery was sanctioned by religion, political economy, science, and culture. Southern professors, ministers, jurists, scientists, and journalists had to justify slavery constitutionally and show that it fostered a genuine and classical form of democracy distinct from the "mongrelized" industrial democracy of the North.

A spate of books and pamphlets was written to prove that the Bible authorized slavery, that the Negro belonged to a degraded race, that he was physiologically as well as morally inferior to whites, that men were not born free and equal, and that talk about inalienable rights was so much nonsense. George Fitzhugh's *Sociology for the South; or The Failure of Free Society* (1854), and *Cannibals All! or Slaves Without Masters* (1857) managed to include most of the familiar arguments of the day.

The slave system, as it appeared in Fitzhugh's artful descriptions, was a kind of benevolent socialism. In the South, he claimed, capital and labor were not divorced, thus following Calhoun's prized lead. The fierce exploitation of one class by another, which characterized the cruel and cannibalistic laissez-faire economy of the North, was blessedly absent. He contrasted the hideous conditions in northern and British industrial cities and the miseries of the white slave or "hireling" with the blissful life of the plantation Negro, nurtured and guarded from cradle to grave. Northern capitalism, he declared, led to the impoverishment of the masses and to revolution. No such danger threatened the South. Fitzhugh even called on northern conservatives to accept slavery as a fact, to join the planters in maintaining a stratified society, and to repress the social upheavals in the free states that Fitzhugh attributed directly to unregulated capitalism.

Fitzhugh's extreme views were presented in his exuberant style and made an impression in the North that only fostered misunderstanding. Everyone's attention focused on slavery, some seeing it as a curse and some as a blessing, but other problems that were just as important in understanding the ills and promise of the South were obscured. It was convenient for the northerner to ascribe soil exhaustion, illiteracy, and economic instability to slavery alone, just as it was convenient for the southerner to attribute the social and economic backwardness of his region to greedy northern middlemen and to high tariffs.

## EDUCATION

The extension of the suffrage just before the abolitionist campaign got under way went further in the North than in the South (see p. 398), but even in the slave section it raised the specter of an "ignorant and debased" electorate. Public education in the slave states was almost nonexistent, and its advocates faced even greater obstacles than did northern educational reformers. Even a Horace Mann could not have made much headway in the thinly populated rural areas of the South where rich planters resisted taxation for public schools while those who would have benefited from them felt they bore the stigma of charity. Until the 1840s, private rural elementary schools and academies sufficed for those with the interest and income to attend. Some 2700 academies could be found in the South by 1850, more than double the number in New England and 600 more than in the Middle states. But the quality of education they provided fell below the standards of northern schools, and students were few. The 1850 census showed 20 per cent of southern whites illiterate as against 3 per cent in the Middle states and 1 per cent in New England.

Southern higher education compared more favorably with that in the North but, even after abolitionism had soured them on northern ideas, southern families who could afford it continued to send their sons to Princeton, Harvard, Yale, and the University of Pennsylvania rather than to their own state universities and denominational colleges. At the same time, a greater percentage of young southerners than northerners was receiving college training. In 1860, for example, when the northern population was $2\frac{1}{2}$ times that of the white population of the South, each section counted about 26,000 college students. Most southern colleges, to be sure, were less richly endowed with funds or facilities than those in the North. But the University of Virginia, South Carolina College, and briefly, Transylvania, measured up to the standards of the best above the Mason-Dixon line.

As antinorthern sentiment intensified in the 1840s and 1850s, southern leaders made strenuous efforts to throw off the intellectual yoke of the Yankees. Conventions passed resolutions urging that southern youth be educated at home by native teachers, and that textbooks coincide with "the educational wants and the social condition of these States, and the encouragement and support of inventions and discoveries in the arts and sciences, by their citizens." It was particularly galling for southern students to be given biased northern texts. One book, for example, spoke of the upper-class southerner's addiction to drinking and gambling. Another described slavery as "that stain on the human race, which corrupts the master as much as it debases the slave." Agitation against importing poisonous alien doctrines, however, apparently did not halt the sale of northern books in the South nor keep significantly larger numbers of southern students from northern schools.

### RELIGION IN THE SOUTH

The political and religious liberalism so marked in the Jeffersonian South (see p. 518) declined after 1825 when the skeptical spirit fostered by the Enlightenment among the aristocracy gave way to the fundamentalism of the common man. The great religious revivals in the early 1800s converted thousands to the Methodist and Baptist faiths, and ministers of the evangelical denominations now assumed a powerful influence over the raw democracy. From southern pulpits came denunciations against infidelity and abolitionism. The atheist, the Deist, the Unitarian (all often lumped together) were regarded by the fundamentalists as subversive. In 1835, a North Carolina constitutional convention voted to exclude Jews, atheists, and skeptics from public office. Six years later, a Georgia court held the testimony of Universalists (who did not believe in hell-fire) invalid.

Such evidences of intolerance were by no means confined to the South. Heresy hunts and anti-infidel crusades occurred in the North and West at the time, but in the South the skeptical minority had to keep silent. During Jefferson's lifetime, Deist and Unitarian opinion found expression in the southern disciples of the English scientist Joseph Priestley and of the revolutionary political philosopher Thomas Paine. Jefferson himself had tried to obtain a professorship at the University of Virginia for the free-thinking Dr. Thomas Cooper. He failed, but Cooper served as president of South Carolina College between 1821 and 1834. His political views endeared him to the South Carolinians, for he vigorously upheld the southern position on slavery, state rights, and the tariff. But his attacks against the clergy and against Biblical literalism became too extreme to be condoned. His successor, J. H. Thornwell, not only stoutly championed slavery as ordained by God but also struck mighty blows against infidelity. Conservative Presbyterians captured lost ground in Kentucky when they ousted the liberal Unitarian Horace Holley from the presidency of Transylvania University in 1827. Unitarianism soon practically disappeared from the South. The Episcopal and Presbyterian churches appealed to the gentility of the tidewater, but elsewhere, those whom the frontier preacher described as "profane sinners, downright skeptics, and God-defying wretches" were either converted or silenced.

## LITERATURE

No literary flowering occurred in the South that was in any way comparable to New England's during the antebellum period, although a number of talented writers published fiction, poetry, and essays of high quality. Even Edgar Allan Poe, often considered the South's greatest writer, was, as we have seen (p. 441), born in Boston. The distinguished modern Virginia novelist Ellen Glasgow felt that Poe was a "distillation of the Southern":

The formalism of his tone, the classical element in his poetry and in many of his stories, the drift toward rhetoric, the aloof and elusive intensity—all these qualities are Southern. And in his more serious faults of over-writing, sentimental exaggeration, and lapses now and then, into a pompous or florid style, he belongs to his epoch and even more to his South.

Yet Poe's literary domain was the landscape of the mind, not the section; and his "southernism" is more often denied or ignored. Such contemporaries of his as the South Carolinian William Gilmore Simms, moreover, reflected more of his literary faults than his virtues.

Southern writers were exposed to the same romantic currents that fostered the literary renaissance in the North. They too had to combat the national indifference to literature and contempt for the writer, but conditions peculiar to their section magnified the problems of the southern authors.

So long as the older and better-educated families dominated southern culture, literary tastes and standards were those of cultivated amateurs who believed professional writing to be unsuitable for gentlemen. They enjoyed biography and history and shared the national enthusiasm for British authors, but they gave little practical encouragement to their own writers. The "highbrows" of Charleston, according to the poet Paul Hamilton Hayne, who grew up among them, were great devotees of the classics but read little else. They might admire their distinguished townsman, Simms, but they did not buy enough of his books to please him. "The South," Simms wrote to a friend in 1847,

don't care a d—n for literature or art. Your best neighbor & kindred never think to buy books. They will borrow from you & beg, but the same man who will always have wine, has no idea of a library. You will write for & defend their institutions in vain. They will not pay the expense of printing your essays.

Northern writers, to be sure, faced similar difficulties but not to the same degree. When, for patriotic reasons, southern writers published in the South, their books sold poorly. Well-written magazines like the *Southern Literary Messenger* might praise their works, but only the approval of northern periodicals had cash value. Southern writers resented their dependence on northern publishers, periodicals, and critics who, they felt, puffed Yankee mediocrities while ignoring southern genius. Without northern publishers and audiences, however, such popular writers as Poe and Simms would have fared even more poorly than they did. Simms's conclusion about his countrymen seems just: "We are not, in fact, a reading people. We are probably, at best, only the pioneers for those, who will atone to letters and the arts hereafter, for our grievous neglect." The brilliant spurt of southern letters in our own century has borne out the prophecy.

As sectional animosities deepened, southern writers found themselves in a dilemma. According to the Charleston poet Henry Timrod, any truthful account of the South antagonized northern readers, while southern readers were quick to detect any lapse in local pride. Writers were expected to fight with their pens to uphold the southern gospel against such intellectual incendiaries as Emerson.

522

His name [declared a critic in the *Southern Literary Messenger*] is like a rag-picker's basket full of all manner of trash. His books are valuable, however, for the very reason they are no earthly account. They illustrate the utter worthlessness of the philosophy of free society. Egoism, or rather Manism (if we may coin a word,) propounded in short scraps, tags, and shreds of sentences may do well for a people who have not settled opinions in politics, religion or morals, and have lived for forty years on pure fanaticisms. We of the South require something better than this no-system. Your fragmentary philosopher, of the *Emerson* stamp, who disturbs the beliefs of common folk . . . is a curse to society.

In the light of these peculiar circumstances, what can be said of the literary achievements of the Old South? Taken as a whole, southern writers did not depict the agrarian society as accurately or as fully as they might have. Nowhere is slavery or the Negro treated meaningfully. Simms, the section's most prolific novelist, contributed his full share of wooden heroes, whose lips curl and whose eyes flash, and of doll-like ladies who speak in stilted phrases. But at least his low-life characters, his traders, tavern-keepers, and poor whites, are real. He was the only southern novelist before the war who wrote convincingly of the yeomanry and the riffraff. His novels, loose and careless in style, nevertheless capture the violence and gustiness of the southern frontier. His fondness for brutal detail makes him seem at times a precursor of the twentieth-century school of southern naturalists.

The plain people of the South are also graphically portrayed in the sketches of southern humorists, journalists, doctors, sportsmen, lawyers. They wrote of frolics, quilting parties, horse-swaps, gander-pullings, camp-meetings, and fights. Their "tall tales" provide a vivid panorama of the frontier South. Poe praised as masterpieces of reporting Augustus Baldwin Longstreet's colorful descriptions of rural Georgia. The Cumberland Mountain country inspired another frontier humorist, George Washington Harris.

## A "CONSCIOUS MINORITY"

After 1831, abolitionist assaults against slavery heightened the southerners' sense of isolation and drove their public men and their intellectuals into truculent defense of southern institutions. Against such biting attacks as Theodore Weld's *American Slavery as It Is* (1839) and its fictional counterpart, Harriet Beecher Stowe's *Uncle Tom's Cabin* (1852), the South replied with proslavery arguments, fiery proclamations in defense of state rights, and a rallying of public opinion against anyone in Dixie whose loyalty to southern ideals was suspect. "Unreliable" professors were removed from southern colleges; free discussion of slavery was quashed; newspapers kept silent on the dangerous subject.

Calhoun's career symptomized the southern shift from nationalism to sectionalism. Starting as an ardent defender of positive government, a constitutional "loose constructionist," he ended as the apostle of nullification after becoming convinced that northern industrial interests were enslaving the agrarian South.

Calhoun loved the Union too much to advocate secession, and yet he grew convinced that existing constitutional safeguards could not protect a minority from a rapacious majority capable of taxing it out of existence. In his posthumously published reflections, *A Disquisition on Government* (1851) and *Discourse on the Constitution and Government of the United States* (1851), Calhoun proposed his theory of "concurrent majorities," which would grant any interest group (in effect, a section like the South) the right to veto an act passed by the majority (in effect, Congress). Calhoun's solution, in other words, was nothing less than a rationale for minority veto of a majority act. It was a device whereby a section that was out of power could protect its property against a section that was in power "by dividing and distributing the powers of government."

Like his northern opponents, Calhoun was

"Sun of Intellectual light & liberty,
stand ye still, in masterly inactivity,
that the Nation of Carolina may continue
to hold negroes & plant Cotton till the
day of Judgment!"

*In this cartoon, published in 1848, the sun represents the abolitionist press and Calhoun, as Joshua, is issuing his command for the sun to stand still. (The Granger Collection.)*

often misinformed, unrealistic, and parochial in his thinking, but his clearly reasoned speculations pointed up the threat of majority tyranny in a democracy. Unfortunately, he spoke in behalf of slaveowners and did not carry over his defense of political minorities to intellectual minorities. He shared a large part of the responsibility for the throttling of independent opinion in the ante-bellum South. His appeal to southern honor, his inflammatory speeches on southern wrongs, kept the South constantly agitated, and after his death in 1850 his devoted followers kept the emotional fires burning.

524

# READINGS

F.B. Simkins, *A History of the South* (1963), and W.B. Hesseltine, *The South in American History* (1960), are two useful surveys of southern life. Clement Eaton, *A History of the Old South* (1949), offers a more detailed survey up to the Civil War. Eaton's *The Growth of Southern Civilization 1790–1860* (1961) deals more comprehensively with the period of this chapter. W.E. Dodd, *The Cotton Kingdom* (1919), and R.S. Cotterill, *The Old South* (1939), are stimulating short analyses. C.S. Sydnor, *The Development of Southern Sectionalism 1819–1848* (1948); A.O. Craven, *The Growth of Southern Nationalism 1848–1861* (1953); and Allan Nevins, *Ordeal of the Union* (2 vols., 1947), contain richly documented analyses of many aspects of southern life.

E.D. Genovese, *The Political Economy of Slavery* (1965), is a broad analysis of the southern economy. E.Q. Hawk, *Economic History of the South* (1934), while dated in some respects, contains useful information. L.C. Gray, *History of Agriculture in the Southern United States to 1860* (2 vols., 1933), the standard work, may be supplemented with the chapters on the South in P.W. Gates, *The Farmer's Age: Agriculture 1815–1860* (1960). See also J.C. Sitterson, *Sugar Country, The Cane Sugar Industry in the South 1753–1950* (1953), and J.C. Robert, *The Story of Tobacco in America* (1952). For other aspects of southern economic life see Broadus Mitchell, *William Gregg, Factory Master of the Old South* (1928); L.E. Atherton, *The Southern Country Store 1800–1860* (1949); R.E. Russel, *Economic Aspects of Southern Sectionalism 1840–1861* (1924); and U.B. Phillips, *A History of Transportation in the Eastern Cotton Belt* (1908). Illuminating "Sources and Readings" will be found in Stuart Bruchey, *Cotton and the Growth of the American Economy 1790–1860* (1967), and H.D. Woodman, *Slavery and the Southern Economy* (1966).

F.L. Olmsted's indispensable record of his travels in the South is presented in the excellent modern edition by A.M. Schlesinger, *The Cotton Kingdom* (1953). Volume II of W.S. Tryon, ed., *A Mirror for Americans, Life and Manners in the United States 1790–1870* (3 vols., 1952), presents the reports of other travelers in the region. H.R. Floan, *The South in Northern Eyes, 1831–1861* (1958), is a useful monograph. Other revealing glimpses of southern life may be found in J.P. Kennedy, *Swallow Barn, or a Sojourn in the Old Dominion* (1832); Susan D. Smedes, *Memorials of a Southern Planter* (1887); F.B. Simkins, *Pitchfork Ben Tillman* (1944); J.H. Franklin, *The Militant South 1800–1861* (1956); and Everett Dick, *The Dixie Frontier* (1948). F.L. Owsley, *Plain Folk of the Old South* (1949), has been most influential in emphasizing the yeoman as against the plantation tradition. The lasting costs of this emphasis are examined in W.H. Nicholls, *Southern Tradition and Regional Progress* (1959).

Modern reading on slavery must begin with W.D. Jordan, *White Over Black* (1968). J.H. Franklin, *From Slavery to Freedom: A History of American Negroes* (1967), is the standard account. Two general works by August Meier and E.M. Rudwick are also recommended: *From Plantation to Ghetto* (1966), an authoritative short survey, and *The Making of Black America* (1969), a comprehensive anthology of "Essays in Negro Life and History." Allen Weinstein and F.O. Gatell, eds., *American Negro Slavery: A Modern Reader* (1968), also offers informative selections. B.A. Botkin, ed., *Lay My Burden Down* (1945), is a revealing "Folk History of Slavery" as told by surviving former slaves in the 1930s. Two older works by U.B. Phillips, *Life and Labor in the Old South* (1929), and *American Negro Slavery* (1918), should be contrasted with K.M. Stampp, *The Peculiar Institution: Slavery in the Ante-Bellum South* (1956). R.B. Flanders, *Plantation Slavery in Georgia* (1933), and C.S. Sydnor, *Slavery in Mississippi* (1933), are good state studies. Frederic Bancroft, *Slave Trading in the Old South* (1931), is excellent on the domestic slave trade. A.H. Conrad and J.R. Meyer, *The Economics of Slavery* (1964), is a study in "econometric history." H.D. Woodman, "The Profitability of Slavery: A Historical Perennial," in *Journal of Southern History*, XXIX, No. 3 (August 1963), affords a documented survey of studies of this subject from the 1840s to the 1960s.

From the thin literature on the free Negro, the following may be cited: L.P. Jackson, *Free Negro Labor and Property Holding in Virginia 1830–1860* (1942), and C.H. Wesley, *Negro Labor in the United States* (1927). R.C. Wade, *Slavery in the Cities, The South 1820–1860* (1964), is a scholarly monograph on a neglected subject. Frank Tannenbaum, *Slave and Citizen, The Negro in the Americas* (1947), and S.M. Elkins, *Slavery, A Problem in American Institutional and Intellectual Life* (1959), afford comparisons of southern slavery with the institution in other American lands. Herbert Aptheker, *American Negro Slave Revolts* (1943), is standard. On the underground railroad see Larry Gara, *The Liberty Line* (1961). Aptheker, ed., *A Documentary History of the Negro People in the United States* (1951), is a painstaking anthology of the Negro's own words from colonial times to 1910. Benjamin Quarles, ed., *Narrative of the Life of Frederick Douglass, An American Slave, Written by Himself* (1960), is a moving document.

W.J. Cash, *The Mind of the South* (1941), is a penetrating study of illusion and reality in southern life and literature, exceptionally well written. W.R. Taylor, *Cavalier and Yankee: The Old South and American National Character* (1961), probes the conflict of attitudes that helped bring about the Civil War. F.P. Gaines, *The Southern Plantation: A Study in the Development and Accuracy of a Tradition* (1924), confronts southern romanticism with certain aspects of realism. Other challenges to southern thinking are examined in R.G. Osterweis, *Romanticism and Nationalism in the Old South* (1949), and J.T. Carpenter, *The South as a Conscious Minority* (1930). Clement Eaton, *Freedom of Thought in the Old South* (1940), is a broader commentary on southern culture than its title suggests. D.R. Fox, *Ideas in Motion* (1935), contains an illuminating essay, "Cultural Nationalism in the Old South." E.L. McKitrick, ed., *Slavery Defended: The Views of the Old South* (1963), is a valuable anthology of the writings of the proslavery apologists. This subject is dealt with in W.J. Jenkins, *Pro-Slavery Thought in the Old South* (1935), and Harvey Wish, *George Fitzhugh: Propagandist of the Old South* (1943). H.C. Bailey, *Hinton Rowan Helper, Abolitionist-Racist* (1965), is a penetrating study of the author of *The Impending Crisis of the South and How to Meet It* (1857), the most controversial contemporary account of slavery and the southern white population. J.B. Hubbell, *The South in American Literature 1607–1900* (1954), is a comprehensive history. Edmund Wilson, *Patriotic Gore, Studies in the Literature of the American Civil War* (1962), is a masterly analysis of expression in both sections. The *Letters* of William Gilmore Simms (1952–1955), are full of interesting material on the southern writer. V.W. Brooks, *The World of Washington Irving* (1944), contains several perceptive chapters on the South. S.L. Gross and J.E. Hardy, eds., *Images of the Negro in American Literature* (1966), is a revealing collection of essays. See also Readings for Chapters Three, Fourteen, and Eighteen.

# SEVENTEEN

At the end of 1854, after a decade of unprecedented expansion, a brief depression befell the American economy. The stock market crashed, tens of thousands of factory workers were thrown out of work, prices of western produce tumbled, and land values collapsed. The depression was short-lived, but the recovery that began in 1855 raised the speculative fever to such a pitch that a new and more resounding crash occurred in 1857. All sections of the country suffered except the South, and all sectors of the economy were depressed except the culture of cotton. "The wealth of the South" announced that section's leading economist, J.D.B. DeBow of New Orleans, "is permanent and real, that of the North fugitive and fictitious."

Never was thinking more wishful or more wrong. The South's economy, though prosperous, lacked the vitality and variety of the North's; and the ups and downs in northern production reflected the dynamism of industry that would soon make the United States the richest country in the world. Perhaps we should speak of industrial*ism* rather than of industry alone, for it was the spirit of machine production that was at work—a spirit that was to pervade commercial agriculture and steamboating and railroading as well as the factories.

## I   Peopling the "Middle Border"

Mechanized agriculture first became widespread in the United States on the free family farms of the northern prairies and the eastern edges of the unforested Great Plains. This fertile country, Hamlin Garland's "Middle

# THE EXPANSIVE

# NORTH

Border," stretched from upper Indiana and Illinois northward to central Wisconsin and Minnesota, and westward through Iowa and upper Missouri to the eastern townships of Kansas and Nebraska. Even more than the southern coastal plains, this level, lush terrain invited the large-scale corporate type of farming that characterizes much of the area in the twentieth century. At the outset, however, most of its settlers were independent small farmers from the neighboring states to the east or immigrants from the British Isles and the continent of Europe.

Driven by debt during the world-wide depression of the early 1840s, tens of thousands of farm families in the Ohio Valley and the country bordering Lake Erie and Lake Michigan sold their cleared and cultivated homesteads to newcomers with capital. Drawn by the government's liberalized land policy (see p. 427) to try again on the distant frontier, they settled there in such numbers that Iowa became a state in 1846, and Wisconsin in 1848. By 1860, hundreds of thousands of other farm families, including "shoals" of Yankee abolitionists, had helped to treble the population of these new states. Minnesota had grown large enough for statehood by 1858, and the admission of Kansas was delayed until 1861 for political reasons, not for lack of population. Nebraska and even the Dakotas to the north were also becoming inhabited.

During this period, economic distress, accompanied by political repression and religious persecution, had spread across Europe once again. Among the worst sufferers were the Irish Catholics, who were especially hard hit by the potato crop failure and the famine that followed in 1845 and 1846. In the decade that ended with the business panic of 1854, about 1,300,000 Irish had fled the Emerald Isle for the United States. Their love of the Old Country ran deeper than that of the Ulstermen of the eighteenth-century (see p. 93); yet for all their attachment to the "old sod," they were usually too poor even to move inland from the coastal cities in which they landed. Some of them did travel west as laborers with canal and railroad-building crews, and of these a few eventually were drawn back to the soil. Second in numbers to the Catholic Irish were the 940,000 Germans who arrived during this decade to augment the German population long here (see p. 87). The decade's immigrant Englishmen, Welshmen, and Scots numbered about 375,000. A few thousand Scandinavians also came, the heralds of a large migration later in the nineteenth century, along with small contingents of Dutch, Swiss, Belgians, French, and Czechs.

528

All told, between 1844 and 1854 almost three million immigrants braved the Atlantic crossing to America. The voyage in filthy steerage quarters was not as bestial as in the eighteenth century; yet on some immigrant ships 10 per cent of the passengers died mainly from diseases contracted during the journey. Most of the newcomers shunned the land of cotton, although some of the thousands who were crowded into cotton ships on the return voyages from English ports remained in New Orleans where they were landed. Others transferred their few belongings to Mississippi River steamboats (where travel conditions were hardly better than those encountered on the ocean) and proceeded north to nonslave country.

A majority of the immigrants were young, unmarried adults, who, as industrial and construction workers, farmers, farm-laborers, or domestic servants, immediately swelled the working force of the free section. Others

came as before in family groups, among them independent, outspoken middle-class businessmen, lawyers, doctors, scientists, and journalists, who brought new skills, new learning, and new leadership to western cities like Cincinnati and St. Louis, and to aspiring frontier towns like Chicago and Des Moines. More numerous than these urban settlers were rural "reading families," who were readily identified by their bookish preparation for life in the New World. Such families were devoted to the Bible and often were led to America by their old-country pastors. By 1860 they made up 30 per cent of the population of Wisconsin and Minnesota and were almost as numerous in the other states that comprised the Middle Border.

So determined were these religious newcomers to preserve their old way of life in the wilderness that they sometimes segregated themselves in a "New Germany," a "New Norway," or a "New Bohemia." But many

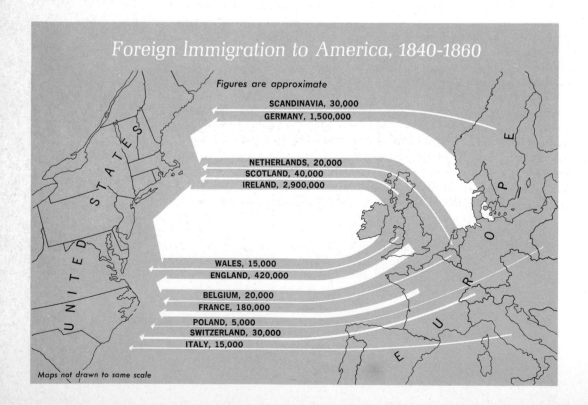

Foreign Immigration to America, 1840-1860

Figures are approximate

SCANDINAVIA, 30,000
GERMANY, 1,500,000

NETHERLANDS, 20,000
SCOTLAND, 40,000
IRELAND, 2,900,000

WALES, 15,000
ENGLAND, 420,000

BELGIUM, 20,000
FRANCE, 180,000
POLAND, 5,000
SWITZERLAND, 30,000
ITALY, 15,000

UNITED STATES

EUROPE

Maps not drawn to same scale

In this English wood engraving of 1857, the ships "Nimrod" and "Atilone" are loading passengers at Cork bound for Liverpool. There the Ulstermen transferred to trans-Atlantic steamers. (The Granger Collection.)

soon caught the vision of a brighter future, and their commitment to the homeland and to the past grew dimmer with the passing years. "The prairies," said the son of one of the English immigrants of the 1850s, "possessed a charm created by beauty instead of awe." The Illinois landscape, he recalled, "was an inspiration," and the land of Iowa and Kansas "sloped upward to the West, giving to the mind an ever-increasing sense of hope and power."

So long as the cotton planters kept their labor system to themselves, away from the Lord's free soil, these western pioneers as a rule opposed any meddling with the institution of slavery. Their own labor supply came from their large families; they kept their sons and daughters on the land, and invested in machines to multiply their productivity. The religious mysticism and pseudo-science of the times fed the belief that iron poisoned the earth, and some of these settlers were as wary of iron and steel implements and machines as of abolition. But they could not long withstand the competitive force of innovation and the sweeping tide of progress.

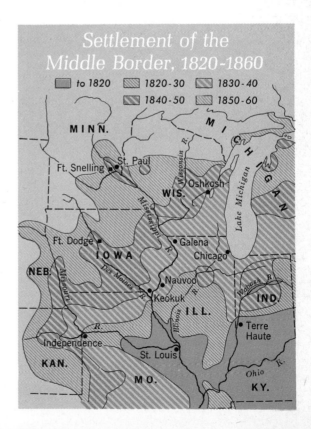

530

## II  *The Agricultural Revolution*

### BREAKING THE SOD

For most of the decade and a half before the Civil War, the settlement of the free West ran well ahead of the railroads. Pioneer families traveled on foot, in wagons, and in boats on the rivers and the Great Lakes. Groups of families sometimes settled a particular region, but even here the whole territory was so vast that farms were often a day's travel or more apart. One reason for choosing isolated sites was the settler's habitual suspicion of intruders. More important was his hope of adding more land to the quarter-section with which he usually started.

Having prayerfully picked his land and registered it at the nearest land office, a farmer would build a one-room log cabin or, in tree-less country, a hut constructed of slabs of sod and a barn of the same material. Meanwhile, he would turn his few sheep, cows, and oxen out to graze on the wild buffalo grass and fence them off as best he could from the kitchen vegetable garden—the care of which became one of the many responsibilities of his wife. Once he had fenced in his main fields, at a cash outlay of $1 or $1.25 an acre, he would begin the laborious round of cultivation. At this point the pioneer would discover that the plow he had carried with him from the East, though it took two men to handle and four oxen to pull, would hardly scratch the heavily matted, grass-rooted virgin soil. So at a further cost of $1.75 to $2.50 an acre, he would have to hire professional "breakers," teams of men with huge plows drawn by 6 to 12 oxen, who would cut the first shallow furrows on the prairies and the plains. In these furrows, in holes dug deeper with axes, the farmer would plant his Indian corn, and some pumpkins and beans to eke out the produce of the kitchen garden. In subsequent seasons, the farmer and his family would be able themselves to plow and plant the land first broken by the professional teams.

*"Breakers" with their team of oxen working on the tough prairie sod. (The Bettmann Archive.)*

北亞墨利加人物

ペルリ像

*A contemporary Japanese woodcut artist depicted Commodore Matthew Perry, at the time of his visit to Japan, as the Yankee equivalent of a shogun. (National Portrait Gallery, Washington, D.C.)*

An acre or an acre and a half a day—perhaps 40 acres of a 160-acre quarter-section in the planting, and harvesting, season—was the most the pioneer could hope to put under cultivation with his available ox-power and equipment. But men who had moved their families to the prairies and the plains with the idea simply of re-establishing an independent way of life based on self-help and Christian charity were quite satisfied to do as well as this. In the belief, cherished in the United States, that the tiller of the soil was of all creatures closest to God—a belief that had given a Christian base to the Jeffersonian ideal of a democracy of farmers—they tended to resist rapid changes that promised nothing more than greater material reward for their labors.

And yet the sheer fertility of the Border's soil, superficially cultivated though it was by backward methods and outmoded tools, soon inundated the pioneers with surplus crops. Many of them welcomed an opportunity to market their produce for cash. And even the more idealistic always needed money to pay old debts, to purchase bare necessities like salt, ammunition, harness, and boots, and to maintain their wagons and equipment. Every farmer, or at least every farmer's wife, aspired to move on from the crude log cabin or musty sod hut to a neat frame dwelling with proper furniture and a touch of color in a table covering, a window curtain, or a picture on the wall. Such "improvements" required money, and until the crash of 1857 money was crying to be made. The crash, indeed, reminded many of how deeply they had sunk into the sin of covetousness, and in 1858 a new sweep of revivalism in the West recalled backsliders —for a time at least—to religion and church.

### EXPANDING MARKETS

For all the Christian traditionalism of the "New Germanys" and the "New Norways," and the terrifying isolation of the American settlements, the prairie farmers in this Age of Progress were in fact the vanguard and support of a world-wide business surge. In Europe, industrialism was spreading, the last serfs were being freed from their ties to the land, cities were growing rapidly, tariffs on agricultural imports were coming down, the exchange of currencies was being simplified. Accompanying these social changes were the revolutions, famines, and wars that cast so many immigrant families onto American shores in search of asylum and a fresh start. These circumstances taken together created a lively demand for foodstuffs which the virgin American West, manned so largely by the immigrants themselves, could quickly supply.

Nor was the business ferment restricted to Europe. After 1844, American ships and the vessels of other nations enjoyed new rights in the treaty ports of China; in 1854, Commodore Matthew Perry, with a fine show of American naval power, opened up the "Hermit Kingdom" of Japan to American trade; in 1856, Siam (modern Thailand) broadened the privileges accorded 20 years before to United States exporters; and all this stirring in the Pacific warmed American interest in salubrious Hawaii. The Orient never became a market for the produce of American farms, but Oriental trade in other goods helped transform the American merchant marine into the largest fleet in the world and its home ports into booming metropolises. In these metropolitan centers, as in the great cities of Europe, landless multitudes were clamoring to be fed.

In the West itself the farmers also were finding markets at government frontier forts, among the loggers who had recently opened up the north woods of Wisconsin and Minnesota, and among the lead miners who, after the 1830s, extended their operations from Galena, Illinois, into neighboring Wisconsin and Iowa. Gold-mining camps farther west even than the organized frontier settlements had also begun to look to the nearest farmers for flour and meal.

From the beginning of the westward movement, corn was always the frontier farmer's first marketable crop. Easily converted into fattened hogs (which were commonly turned loose in the corn fields to "hog down" the ripened ears), corn could be made to walk to market when other transportation was lacking. Corn also served as suitable winter feed for beef cattle, which could be walked even farther than hogs. For human consumption, corn was distilled into a potable and packageable "likker," or it was eaten off the cob, baked into bread, and prepared in many other ways. In the famine years of the late 1840s, even the hungry Irish brought themselves to eat American corn; but they and other Europeans never developed a taste for it, and corn failed to become a stable or significant export. In the United States, on the other hand, corn bread and corn-fed pork made up the bulk of the national diet.

As late as 1849, Tennessee and Kentucky had led in the production of corn-fed hogs. Ten years later these states had fallen behind Indiana and Illinois. In the production of corn itself, Illinois by then had risen to first place; Missouri had passed Tennessee and Kentucky; and Iowa, Kansas, and Nebraska were making noticeable inroads on the market. American corn production reached 838 million bushels in 1859, an increase of 40 per cent in ten years, and the Middle Border states accounted for most of the gain.

Wheat was far more selective than corn in soil and climate, and even in suitable latitudes it grew best on land that had already produced a corn crop. In 1849, Pennsylvania, Ohio, and New York were the leading wheat states. By 1859, though the country's total wheat production had soared 75 per cent to a record 173 million bushels, each of these three states produced less wheat than it had a decade earlier. Illinois, Indiana, and Wisconsin had moved to the head of the wheat states; and in succeeding decades, reflecting the momentum of the westward surge of wheat-growing, first Iowa, then Minnesota, then Kansas, and then the Dakotas entered the ranks of the leaders.

Acre for acre, wheat paid better than corn, over which it had advantages both in marketing and production. Unlike corn, wheat was eaten all over the world. Less bulky than corn in relation to value, it could bear high transportation costs more easily, and it also withstood shipment more successfully. Finally, on the open prairies and plains, where land was plentiful and hired labor scarce, wheat production responded magnificently to improved tools and labor-saving machinery.

## MECHANIZED FARMING

The western farmer's first need in the way of equipment was a new plow. Back in 1837, John Deere, an Illinois blacksmith, had produced the first American steel plow, and by 1858, after making many improvements on his original design, he was manufacturing 13,000 a year. Light enough for a strong man to sling over his shoulder, the Deere plow nevertheless was the first to cut deep, clean furrows in the prairie sod. Nor did it take bovine strength to draw it, and the weaker but faster-moving horse began to supplant the ox on western farms. So great was interest in plow improvement that by the time of the Civil War 150 varieties of plows were on the market, and experimenters were working on steam-powered "plowing engines" that could cut as many as six furrows at once.

Even more striking improvements were being made in machines especially designed for wheat-growing. Cyrus Hall McCormick of Virginia (in 1834) and Obed Hussey of Ohio (in 1833) had patented practical steel-tooth reapers in the early days of the westward movement. With McCormick's horse-drawn machine a single man could do the work of five men equipped with scythes. Sales lagged, however, until McCormick (while Hussey languished in the East) moved his plant to Chicago in 1848 and hurried his demonstrators off to the western frontier. Ten years later, by means of the "American System," as admiring Europeans had begun to call the assembly of interchangeable parts, McCormick was manufacturing 500 reapers a month and was still failing to keep up with the demand.

At first, entire neighborhoods had to be mobilized to harvest the vast quantities of wheat the new reapers could cut down. But in the 1850s progress was being made in the design of mechanical wheat-binders, which in the next decade would eliminate much of the harvesting army. In the 1850s, mechanical threshers were already in use, and, according to the census report of 1860, they were 60 per cent more efficient than "the old flail mode."

In 1800, the average American farmer had spent about $15 to $20 for his tools, and the equipment the emigrants toted west in the 1840s was worth little more. By 1857, *Scientific American* was recommending that every farmer with 100 acres of land should have

machinery worth about $600. Although many wheat farmers got along with less, the expansion of wheat production could not have occurred had not most of the farmers sloughed

533

*Page from an almanac, 1871. Books of this sort still enjoy a wide circulation in rural areas of the United States, the* Farmer's Almanac *being just one example of many still thriving. The Deere advertising states, "many followers and imitators, but no successful competitor for thirty years." (The Bettmann Archive.)*

THE JOHN DEERE **MOLINE PLOW**

HAS HAD

Many followers and imitators, but no successful competitor for thirty years. Ask the older farmers how it is.

**DEERE, MANSUR & CO.**

## JUNE.

| Day of Mo. | Day of Wk. | SUN Rises and Sets. H. M. | MOON Rises and Sets. H. M. |
|---|---|---|---|
| 1 | T | 4 39r | 1 31 |
| 2 | F | 7 18s | 1 53 |
| 3 | S | 4 39r | 2 17 |
| 4 | S | 7 19s | 2 45 |
| 5 | M | 4 38r | 3 16 |
| 6 | T | 7 20s | rises |
| 7 | W | 4 37r | 8 28 |
| 8 | T | 7 21s | 9 15 |
| 9 | F | 4 37r | 9 56 |
| 10 | S | 7 21s | 10 31 |
| 11 | S | 4 37r | 11 1 |
| 12 | M | 7 22s | 11 27 |
| 13 | T | 4 37r | 11 51 |
| 14 | W | 7 23s | morn |
| 15 | T | 4 37r | 0 13 |
| 16 | F | 7 24s | 0 34 |
| 17 | S | 4 38r | 0 59 |
| 18 | S | 7 25s | 1 29 |
| 19 | M | 4 38r | 2 4 |
| 20 | T | 7 25s | 2 50 |
| 21 | W | 4 38r | sets |
| 22 | T | 7 26s | 8 47 |
| 23 | F | 4 39r | 9 35 |
| 24 | S | 7 26s | 10 25 |
| 25 | S | 4 39r | 10 43 |
| 26 | M | 7 26s | 11 10 |
| 27 | T | 4 40r | 11 34 |
| 28 | W | 7 26s | 11 57 |
| 29 | T | 4 41r | morn |
| 30 | F | 7 26s | 0 20 |

**MOON'S PHASES.**

| | D. | H. | M. |
|---|---|---|---|
| Full Moon | 6 | 7 | 27—A |
| Last Quarter | 14 | 10 | 4—A |
| New Moon | 21 | 5 | 7—A |
| First Quarter | 28 | 10 | 4—M |

### Sugar-Cured Beef.

Make a brine of eight pounds of the best salt, three ounces of saltpetre, and a quart of molasses, or three pounds of sugar for each one hundred pounds of beef, and you will have a pickle for salting that will always enable you to eat corned beef of the first quality; but it will not usually keep longer than the middle of May. If preserved beyond this time the beef should be repacked the brine scalded, skimmed and returned to the meat with the addition of a little more salt. Beef should always be kept as cool as possible, even frozen to be nice.

### Excellent Interest Rules.

For finding the interest on any principal for any number of days. The answer in such a case being in cents, separate the two right hand figures of the answer to express it in dollars and cents:

Four per cent.—Multiply the principal by the number of days to run; separate right hand figure from product, and divide by nine.

Five per cent.—Multiply by the number of days, and divide by seventy-six.

Six per cent.—Multiply by the number of days; separate right hand figures, and divide by six.

Eight per cent.—Multiply by the number of days, and divide by forty-five.

Nine per cent.—Multiply by the number of days; separate right hand figure, and divide by four.

Ten per cent.—Multiply by the number of days; separate right hand figure, and divide by three.

*Cyrus Hall McCormick's horse-drawn mechanical reaper. The arms of the rotating spindle bent the wheat against the cutting knife and dropped it onto an attached platform. (International Harvester, Chicago.)*

off their traditional methods and adopted mechanized techniques. By the time of the Civil War, about $250 million was invested in farm implements and machines, an average of about $120 for each farm in the country. On the extensive wheat farms of the prairies and the plains, the average investment was much higher.

### FARMING AS A BUSINESS

Once the western farmer had committed himself to machinery, he found his life greatly altered. The most disturbing change came from his discovery that he was suddenly in the grip of forces over which he had little control. His principal machines, for example, such as reapers and threshers, could speed the production of wheat but they could be used for little else when the wheat market fell off, as it did in 1854. The fact that he usually purchased these machines on credit further narrowed the farmer's range of choice, for his debt eventually had to be paid in cash, and wheat, the specialty of the new machines, was also the cash crop *par excellence*. Falling wheat prices simply forced him to grow more wheat than ever in order, at lower prices, to get as great an *aggregate* cash return as before. But increasing his wheat production

often meant breaking or buying new land, either of which would plunge him still more deeply into debt. Then he would need still larger wheat crops in order to acquire the cash to maintain the payments on his larger obligations.

The continuous round of specialization, mechanization, and expansion in the free West gave a momentum to wheat production that was a priceless boon to the world. Other aspects of wheat-growing on the prairies and the plains, however, were hardly boons to the farmer. In some years, frost, hail, and other visitations far more severe than in the East destroyed much of the crop before it could be harvested. Even in the best growing seasons, moreover, the servicing of broad new markets seemed to involve an endless spiral of new charges. The steps between the wheat-grower and the ultimate urban consumer, for example, seemed to multiply disastrously with distance. All along the line, weighers, graders, storage-elevator operators, rail and water carriers, warehouses, local haulers, insurers, moneylenders, and speculators—the whole urban apparatus of finance and distribution—mysteriously placed a hand on the farmer's fate, and worse, in the farmer's pocket.

The world-wide collapse of prices in 1857 staggered the wheat farmer. His debts went unpaid, the threat of foreclosure and indeed foreclosure itself soured his prospects, and his mind turned once more to the free frontier. In 1858, western wheat farmers began attending meetings other than religious revivals, and from these meetings arose broad denunciations of conspiratorial "trading combinations," monopolistic elevator and railroad operators, and grasping moneylenders. The farmer's special place in God's plan received renewed publicity, and farmers were urged to "assert not only their independence but their supremacy" in society. Vague proposals also began to be made for farm cooperatives and for state and federal control of railroads and other big businesses.

Out of it all, before the Civil War, came a stronger demand for two specific programs. One, a favorite among educational and agricultural reformers, was for agricultural colleges to educate farm youth in the science of agriculture and to afford them broader educational opportunities as well. These colleges were to be set up by the federal government and financed by federal land grants. The second demand, with a far broader backing among farmers, was for free homesteads—free of payment and free of slaves—on the remainder of the public domain. Over southern opposition, Congress enacted a land-grant college bill in 1859, only to have President Buchanan veto it. In June 1860 he vetoed a homestead bill that would have made western

lands available at 25 cents an acre. In the elections later that year, the farmers of the West, crying the slogan "Vote Yourself a Farm," helped carry the country for Lincoln, even though they were aware that his policy of no extension of slavery to the territories could carry the nation to war.

### THE AGRICULTURAL REVOLUTION IN THE EAST

Right up to the outbreak of the Civil War southern planters remained active customers of the western farmers, but the great bulk of western grain and meat flowed to the Northeast. So great did this volume become that the agricultural revolution in the West forced upon the East an agricultural revolution of its own.

Let the West "supply our cities with grain," William Buckminster of Massachusetts had said in 1838:

> We will manufacture their cloth and their shoes. [Our farms] shall find employment in furnishing what cannot so well be transported from a distance. Fresh meats, butter, hay, and the small market vegetables must be supplied by the farmers of N. England.

What Buckminster had foreseen developed with a rush in the following 20 years—not only in New England but also on the more

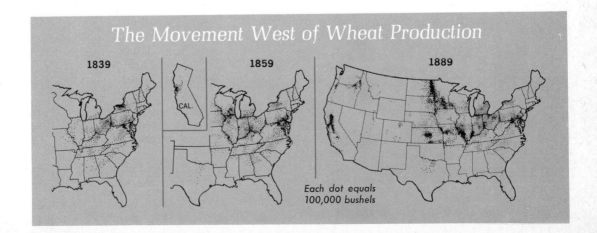

## The Movement West of Wheat Production

1839    1859    1889

CAL.

Each dot equals 100,000 bushels

friendly soil of other eastern states. Two foodstuffs that Buckminster failed to enumerate became the most profitable of all—milk and fruits.

Dairying, once a routine chore in most households, had become big business by 1850. In that year, the Harlem Railroad brought about 25 million quarts of milk into New York City. Every other sizable city in the East had developed its own "milk shed," a nearby expanse of pasture land where carefully bred and carefully tended herds of cows were reared especially for milk production.

Fruit orchards were as common as pastures in the East. But after 1840, the growing of apples and peaches was expanded and brought under scientific care. Strawberries, blackberries, and many varieties of melons added interest and nourishment to the urban American's diet. The tin canister, or the "tin can," an English invention for packaging perishables, became widely used by American fruit and vegetable merchants in the late 1840s, greatly enlarging the market for their products and even extending it to men at sea.

A revival of scientific farming in the East furthered the agricultural revolution in that section. An earlier scientific farming movement, which had been restricted to gentlemen farmers, had died in the 1830s. But after 1845, when success or failure hinged increasingly on special knowledge and up-to-date processes, eastern dirt and dairy farmers took a keen interest in information about climate, soils, fertilizers, methods of cultivation, and the idiosyncrasies of different crops. Agricultural associations, fairs, magazines, books, courses, and schools all multiplied in the East in the 1840s and 1850s.

Railroad and water routes between the East and the West encouraged each section to produce specialties of its own. Railroads and water routes *in* the East and especially in New England so covered the land that farmers in this section could specialize in perishables with the assurance that their produce would be speeded to city markets.

## III *The Peak of Water Transportation*

### THE REVIVAL OF FOREIGN TRADE

When the Civil War began, the railroad dominated the economy of the free North and exercised a powerful influence on the welfare of the entire nation. But the railroad had to fight for ascendancy, and during the period of its rise other avenues of exchange and other forms of transport were helping to build up the country.

One of the most important commercial developments of the 1840s and 1850s was the revitalization of America's foreign trade. During the depression that followed the crash of 1837, foreign trade had fallen to a point well below the level even of the early years of the Republic. In 1843, combined imports and exports were only $125,250,000, a trough never touched in the preceding 30 years. Then began an almost continuous rise to a record $687,200,000 in 1860. In almost every year during this period, imports exceeded exports. Eighty per cent of the half-billion dollars in gold taken from the California mines before 1857 was sent abroad to make up the difference. The rapidly increasing export of western wheat and flour helped keep the imbalance within reasonable limits.

The revival of foreign trade had a tremendous effect on immigration. Without the vast fleets of merchantmen that plied the Atlantic between Europe and America, the millions of newcomers to the United States in the late 1840s and in the 1850s could never have found passage to the New World. Seventy-five per cent of American commerce, and an even greater proportion of the immigrant traffic, was carried in American sailing ships.

The average westward crossing by sail from Liverpool, England, to New York took about 33 days. Steamships, which had been used in ocean commerce since 1838, could make this crossing in the 1850s in 10 to 15 days. But they were unreliable and excessively costly to operate. As late as 1899, all ocean steamships carried sails for auxiliary or emergency power. By 1860, only a tiny fraction of the world's ocean commerce had been captured by steamships, most of which were British.

## THE SURGE OF DOMESTIC COMMERCE

In the 15 years before the Civil War, American domestic commerce far surpassed even the record foreign trade both in volume and rate of growth. The vitality of foreign trade itself contributed significantly to this development, for the mere collection at American ports of commodities for export created a great deal of business for home carriers. Similarly, the need to distribute to the interior the increasingly voluminous imports landed at a few great coastal cities added steadily to the demand for domestic transportation.

But domestic commerce was far more than an adjunct of foreign trade. As the American population grew—and it grew with phenomenal rapidity in the free North in the 1840s and 1850s—the home market naturally expanded. As different regions began to specialize in particular commodities, the need for exchange among them increased. Exchange itself was made easier by the gold being mined in California and by the improved credit facilities of the expanding banking system. Between 1851 and 1860, money in circulation in the United States, including specie and banknotes, rose 9 per cent per capita. But the importance of this increase to trade was even greater than this figure indicates, for the telegraph and the railroads were now speeding up business transactions and accelerating the collection of bills. This meant that the actual money in circulation could be used many more times in a single year than heretofore; and, since the amount of money itself was rising rapidly, the whole pace of domestic commerce quickened. Between 1843 and 1860,

while American foreign trade grew five and a half times, domestic trade grew ten times. By 1860, domestic carriers were hauling goods worth at least 15 times the combined value of exports and imports, or about $10 billion worth a year.

## THE CLIPPER SHIP ERA

Before the railroad boom of the 1850s, domestic commerce was almost monopolized by water carriers; and of these carriers the oldest and for a long time the most successful were the coastal sailing ships. In 1852, the value of goods carried by American coastal vessels (the coastal trade was closed by law to foreign ships) was three times the value of goods hauled by the railroads and canals combined.

The most glamorous period of coastal commerce was the era of the clipper ship, the boldest commercial sailing vessel ever built. The designers of the clippers, among whom Donald McKay in East Boston, Massachusetts, was the unchallenged master, drew out the ordinary three-masted packet ships to extraordinary lengths and then reduced the ratio of beam to length so drastically that traditional shipbuilders were dazed. The result was the most graceful hull that ever took to the sea. The hulls were topped with the tallest masts available and the largest spread of canvas ever to challenge a captain's courage. The captains themselves were selected from among the most relentless "drivers" of the day. Probably the most famous of the clipper ships was McKay's aptly named *Flying Cloud*. Launched in the summer of 1851, she made a day's run of 374 miles during her maiden voyage—"the fastest day's run," writes the historian Robert G. Albion, "yet made by a ship—nearly forty miles better than any steamship travelled in a single day up to the Civil War." Yet McKay soon outdid himself. In 1854, his *Lightning* flew 436 miles in one 24-hour stretch on her maiden voyage.

The first genuine clippers were built early in the 1840s in an attempt to shorten the seem-

*The full-rigged Boston-built clipper ship "Flying Cloud," loading at her wharf in New York. A newspaper description of 1857: "She is 230 feet long on deck, has 41 feet extreme breadth of beam, 21 feet depth of hold. . . . Not only is she the longest and largest clipper ship in the world, but she has the sharpest ends, and is considered by all who have seen her, as possessing great beauty of model. . . . For symmetry and beauty, the marine of no other nation can compare with these." (The Granger Collection.)*

ingly endless voyage to the Orient, where trade, as we have seen (p. 531), had taken a promising turn. From China and India, clippers sometimes sailed to Liverpool and London, where the astonished British ordered such ships for themselves to be built in America for the Atlantic run. But the clippers really came into their own with the growth of California gold mining after 1850. Since the clippers' designers had sacrificed cargo space for speed, their owners had to charge higher rates for their limited cargoes than most shippers could afford. To the California adventurers, however, money was no obstacle and speed was all-important. Conventional sailing ships arriving at San Francisco in the summer of 1850 from Boston and New York had averaged 159 days for the journey around the Horn. The next summer, *Flying Cloud* arrived from New York after a voyage of 89 days, 21 hours, a record that stood until she herself reduced it by 13 hours three years later. It was for this run that most of the great clipper ships were built.

Unfortunately for the clippers, they were beaten at their own game just about the time they seemed to have perfected it. Even before the gold rush to California, New York steamship operators had organized an alternate route by which the trip to the West Coast could be completed in five weeks or less, as against the clippers' best time of three months. This route involved an Atlantic run to Panama, a portage across the Isthmus, and then a Pacific run north again in another steamship to American ports. At first this route was meant to serve the settlers of Oregon, but by the time the initial voyage was made, in January 1849, news of the California gold discoveries had swept through the country, and San Francisco supplanted Oregon as the main destination.

The difficulty with this short cut to the West Coast was the Panama portage, a nuisance that discouraged many travelers and made the handling of heavy freight impossible. Even so, enough profit was made by the New York entrepreneurs to attract the interest of Cornelius Vanderbilt, the richest man in the country, who had made his fortune as a ship operator. In 1851, Vanderbilt launched a competing line to the West Coast, using a Nicaragua instead of a Panama portage. In 1855, Vanderbilt, in turn, was challenged by still other New Yorkers bold enough to try to dislodge him from Nicaragua by supporting William Walker in his successful effort to take over the government of that country.

Vanderbilt promptly retaliated by hiring agents to raise a force among neighboring Central American states with which to overwhelm Walker's government. The conflict between the two camps effectively closed the Nicaraguan route.

Events in Panama, meanwhile, greatly improved the competitive position of the original steamship operators. There, in 1855, after many engineering difficulties had been overcome, an efficient railroad was opened across the Isthmus. This railroad and its affiliated steamships virtually monopolized traffic to the West Coast until 1869, when the first transcontinental railroad was opened across the United States. Long before that, many of the surviving clippers, their magnificence quite tarnished, had sunk to the status of tramps sailing random routes with random cargoes under alien flags.

Sea-going commerce to California by sail or steam effectively tied the East and West coasts to each other and made a single, throbbing organism of the free states. It also sharpened the interest of northern businessmen in faster east-west carriers of heavy freight.

In response to this interest Congress, in 1853, instructed the army to survey potential routes for a transcontinental railroad. This decision stirred a hornet's nest of sectional controversy over the location of the first cross-country line, and not until the South left the Union in 1861 were the first transcontinentals chartered. By 1853, however, many lesser railroads and highways as well as the western river systems had begun to meet the expanding needs of inland commerce. They proved so successful that the coastal carrying trade, inescapably rigid and roundabout in its routes, suffered a precipitous decline. At the outbreak of the Civil War, the coastal vessels were reduced to carrying cotton from New Orleans or Mobile directly to New England, the last remnant of a once-thriving commerce to which (with the unsavory exception of cotton-smuggling during the conflict) the war itself also put an end.

### THE STEAMBOAT CRISIS

The early success of coastal shipping can be attributed in large part to the great volume of goods brought down to Atlantic and Gulf ports over the navigable rivers with which the United States was so lavishly endowed. Most of the river traffic moved through the Ohio and Mississippi river systems (see p. 381), which profited both from the expansion of the free Northwest and the extension of cotton culture into the Southwest. All told, about 750 steamboats plied the western rivers in the 1850s, and the traffic they carried climbed to its historic peak in that decade. The boom probably was most spectacular on the upper Mississippi, where sleepy St. Paul became transformed into a bustling port by settlers sending first furs, then lumber, and then wheat, downstream. The bulk of river commerce was increased by an immense traffic in passengers, many of them immigrants heading west, but most of them native Americans characteristically on the go.

If the coastal trade suffered from having to traverse great distances over roundabout routes, the river trade suffered from the inflexibility of the main streams. Rivers could not be relocated to accommodate the inland settlers. River commerce reached its peak about 1851; but even then, so great had the total of domestic commerce become that the rivers carried but one-twentieth of it. By 1851, the upstart canals and the rising railroads each carried goods worth three times those transported on all the rivers of the country. The relative share of rivers in the commerce of the West, where other means of transportation were less developed than in the East, was no doubt much greater; but the fight to maintain this share proved less successful each year.

In order to compete with the railroads and canals, river men began cutting their rates to the bone. That was bad enough, but as they engaged in fierce competition among themselves for a worthy share of the traffic saved by rate-cutting, they also saddled themselves with

suicidal rising costs. Never was western steamboat travel so speedy, so luxurious, so gilded with gaudy inducements as it was in the middle 1850s. But the river men themselves grew only more and more depressed. In days gone by, races between the river boats had been one of the joys of competition and had lent sparkle and spirit to river life. But now the grim competitors sought literally to knock one another out, and collisions, explosions, and fires took a sharply rising toll of property and lives.

### COMPLETING THE CANALS

When canals between the East and the West were first built, the river men hoped that the new artificial waterways would serve as feeders to hungry river craft, just as the natural rivers fed the coastal carriers. And in many eastern states the canals actually did perform this function. None, of course, performed it better than the Erie Canal, which poured a flood of western commodities into boats standing ready at Albany to carry them down the Hudson River to New York harbor.

And yet in the long run the Erie, in concert with the Ohio canals and others completed in the West before 1837, took trade away from the western rivers. By 1838, Buffalo, at the Erie's western end, was receiving more grain and flour annually than New Orleans. And once western canal construction had begun in the 1840s (there was little more canal building in the East after 1837), virtually every project was aimed at swinging more and more of the western trade away from the Mississippi system toward the North and the East.

In 1846 the newly completed Miami and Erie Canal began to suck Cincinnati's commerce away from the Ohio River and to route it north to Toledo on Lake Erie. In 1853, the Wabash and Erie Canal reached even farther down the Ohio to tie Evansville, Indiana, to Toledo. In 1848, Illinois completed the Illinois and Michigan Canal, linking Chicago on Lake Michigan with La Salle on the Illinois River. This river, which joined the Mississippi north of St. Louis, quickly siphoned off so much of the Mississippi traffic that by 1850 Chicago had roared to greatness as a port even though the city was still without a single railroad connection.

Much of the canal-boat traffic originated right in the vigorous market towns that sprang up along the canal routes. By reversing the direction of southbound traffic on the Ohio, the Illinois, and the northern Mississippi, the canals transformed these once-proud rivers into humble feeder streams. By supplying commodities for the canal boats, the carriers on these rivers managed to compensate somewhat for the sharp decline in volume of their downstream runs.

In the 15 years before the Civil War, a struggle for control of western commerce occurred between the Mississipi River system and the Great Lakes—a struggle that paralleled the rivalry of the free states and the slave for control of the West itself. By the 1850s, the canals had swung the victory irrevocably to the Lakes. Two canals, one of which was foreign-built and neither of which was in any way associated with the great north-south river system, added to the Lakes' supremacy. The first was the Welland Canal, which circumvented Niagara Falls. Built by the Canadian government, this canal joined Lake Erie with Lake Ontario, and thence by way of the St. Lawrence River connected the Northwest with the East at Quebec. In the late 1850s, vessels laden with western goods were beginning the voyage from Chicago all the way to Liverpool, England, over this route.

The second Great Lakes canal was the Saulte-Ste. Marie, popularly known as the Soo Canal. This one was needed to bypass turbulent St. Mary's Falls, which blocked the passage of ships between Lake Superior and Lake Huron. After two years of incredible construction feats under the guidance of engineer Charles T. Harvey, the Soo was opened in April 1855, just in time to catch the massive flow of iron ore from the Marquette range of northern Michigan to the mills of Pittsburgh, Cleveland, and Chicago. Northern wheat also found a convenient outlet through the Soo.

The value of goods carried by Great Lakes vessels, which was estimated at $150 million in 1851, quadrupled in the next five years. This increase reflected the growth of the canals that were diverting traffic away from the South, but it also reflected the rise of the western Great Lakes country itself as a power and a prize.

## IV *The Triumph of the Railroad*

### MENTAL AND TECHNICAL OBSTACLES

The striking extension of the canal system in the late 1840s and the 1850s serves to remind us today that the railroad was not so obvious an improvement over other means of inland transportation as we might suppose. Practical steam locomotives had been invented in England and the United States years before 1829, when their commercial feasibility was first established. But as late as 1848 the directors of the Pennsylvania Railroad declared that "railroads must be used exclusively for light freight."

Before the coming of the railroad, most means of transportation had been easily available to the individual shipper. The farmer could drive his wagon, his pigs, and his cattle over the public roads; he could sail his own boat on the rivers or the sea. Such freedom was impossible on fixed track, but when railroad traffic was first placed under strict control, railroad managers were roundly condemned as undemocratic. Even without the chaos of random individual traffic, the scheduling of railroad trains presented formidable problems until systems of operation were devised late in the nineteenth century that functioned with reasonable safety.

Efficient railroad equipment and construction methods also were slow in coming. Even after steam locomotives had been proved practical, sails were used to propel the cars over some lines, and horses were still being used in the middle 1840s. One of the persistent problems of steam locomotion was how to generate enough power for the engine to pull a string of cars as well as to move itself. Power could be increased only by adding to the locomotive's weight, and heavier locomotives intensified several related problems, novel in themselves, such as the construction of road beds, the laying of track, and the strengthening of bridges to withstand the mounting burdens. The limits of grades and curves were

was disrupted whenever a rail had to be replaced. Worse, the need for a replacement often became apparent only after the broken track had wrecked a speeding train.

Just how much space to leave between the parallel rails was an issue that took longer to settle than the manufacture of the rails themselves. As late as 1865, eleven different gauges of track—usually carefully devised by state and local railroad promoters to keep the rolling stock of competitors from passing over their lines—marred the continuity of the railroad

*The first locomotive built in the United States for actual service on a railroad. Built in New York City for the South Carolina Railroad, the "Best Friend" made its first excursion trip, depicted here, on January 15, 1831. (Library of Congress.)*

other questions answered only after the loss of many lives through accidents.

Early railroad builders had great difficulty in determining the most desirable material for rails, a problem not settled until the perfection of the steel rail in the 1870s. Until then rails usually were made of wrought iron. With a cross section that looked like an inverted "T," the broad base of the rail was attached to wooden ties by means of spikes. Compared to a steel rail's life of 15 years or more, wrought iron rails on busy routes seldom lasted longer than three *months,* and service

system in the North. Even "through" shipments often had to be transferred from car to car before they arrived at their destination, and changing trains was one of the many nuisances of passenger travel.

Yet the American railroad network, 30,000 miles long in 1860, had become one of the marvels of the world. In that year, American passenger trains sped along at more than 20 miles an hour, though only at mortal peril to travelers, and freight trains averaged about 11 miles an hour.

### RAILROADS IN THE EAST

Of the 3328 miles of railroad track in the United States in 1840, a meager 200 miles lay rusting in the West, mute testimony to the debts and disappointed hopes of Michigan,

Indiana, and Illinois (see p. 422). The rest of the mileage was shared almost equally by the Northeast and the old South. No railroad linked these two sections south of Washington, and neither section had succeeded in thrusting a line across the Appalachian barrier to the Ohio or Mississippi valleys. The 1470 miles of existing track in the South in 1840 included the Baltimore and Ohio, which had made the most determined effort to reach the West by rail but had fallen far short of its goal.

In 1840, there were 1670 miles of railroad track scattered through every state of the Northeast except Vermont. Pennsylvania, with about one-third of all the northern railroad mileage, was the nation's leader. But most of Pennsylvania's track had been laid in the northeastern part of the state, where small lines, privately built, had begun to haul anthracite to barges on nearby rivers and canals. The state government was determined to protect its canal system to the West—so determined, in fact, that even when the legislature did grant a charter in 1846 to the privately financed Pennsylvania Railroad Company, permitting it to build a line from Harris-

burg west to Pittsburgh, the new company was required to pay the state's canal administration 3 cents for each ton-mile of freight hauled.

Second to Pennsylvania in railroad mileage in 1840 was New York State, most of whose lines were located in the Albany-Troy-Schenectady region at the eastern end of the Erie Canal, or west of that region roughly parallel to the canal itself. By 1842, seven different railroads strung across the state offered a kind of through route between Albany and Buffalo, but these roads cooperated poorly at best. Until 1851 New York, as eager as Pennsylvania to protect its canal investment, forbade the railroads to carry any freight except when the Erie Canal was frozen over or otherwise closed to navigation. In 1840, New York City had only one tiny railroad, the New York and Harlem, which connected the metropolis with

*A Baltimore and Ohio special train crossing a wrought iron truss bridge, at North Branch, Maryland, in June 1858. Wrought iron, which replaced cast iron for bridge construction in the 1850s, ensured greater safety (The Granger Collection.)*

544

the independent town of Harlem seven miles to the north.

Boston's thriving capitalists, ever on the lookout for new investment opportunities (see p. 390), did not allow Massachusetts to lag for long in railroad construction. By 1850 almost every town in the state with 2000 persons or more was served by trains. Boston became the hub of the whole New England railroad network, and, more important, rail connections with the Welland and Erie canals now made her a vigorous competitor for western trade. To further this trade, in the late 1840s Boston capitalists under the leadership of John Murray Forbes began investing heavily in railroads in distant western cities.

Baltimore was as free as Boston from the prior claims of a state canal system to western traffic. In 1842 the promoters of the Baltimore and Ohio Railroad began gathering new capital with an eye to pushing their road over the mountains to Wheeling, Virginia, on the Ohio River. The B&O actually reached Wheeling in 1853.

The enterprise of Boston and Baltimore in extending their railroads toward the West jolted Pennsylvania and New York out of their complacent confidence in canals. The Pennsylvania Railroad was opened from Philadelphia to Pittsburgh in December 1852, months before the B&O itself reached Wheeling. Five years later, the Pennsylvania bought out the state canal system and the short railroad lines the state had built to feed the canals with traffic. Henceforth, the Pennsylvania Railroad was to dominate the transportation structure of the commonwealth and thus much of its economic and political life.

New York City gained its first western rail connection in 1851 when the Hudson River Railroad was opened all the way to the Erie Canal at East Albany. Two years later, under the direction of Erastus Corning, an iron manufacturer and former mayor of Albany, the seven independent railroads strung from Albany to Buffalo were consolidated into the New York Central Railroad. In conjunction with the Hudson River Railroad, the Central could offer a continuous water-level route from New York to the West. A few years later, a second New York railroad, the Erie, was opened all the way from Jersey City to Buffalo, thereby becoming the fourth great eastern road in competition for east-west traffic.

By March 1852 some 10,800 miles of railroad (about three times the mileage of a decade earlier) had been completed in the United States, and an additional 10,900 miles were under construction. Most of the completed roads were either in the Northeast or else connected that section with waterways beyond the Appalachians. With few exceptions these railroads originated in the great cities and ran through hundreds of miles of rich and populous territory; clearly they promised to return ready profits to investors. Although most of the roads were assisted by state and local governments, they could be and were financed largely by the sale of corporation stock to private investors.

## RAILROADS IN THE WEST

Most of the railroads built during the 1850s were in the West—in Ohio, Indiana, Illinois, Missouri, Michigan, Iowa, and Wisconsin. By 1860, these states, with 11,000 miles of track, had more railroads than the middle states and New England combined. The western roads faced entirely different conditions from those in the East, for private investment capital was scarce beyond the mountains, population was sparse, and corporation stock difficult to market.

Before 1850, the federal government had given about 7 million acres of the national domain to road and canal companies to assist them in building transportation facilities in thinly settled areas. The recipients of these land grants could sell or mortgage the property in return for the cash they needed for construction and for operational expenses in the first few years. Congress made the first land grant for railroad construction in 1850, for the benefit of a system of railroads to run

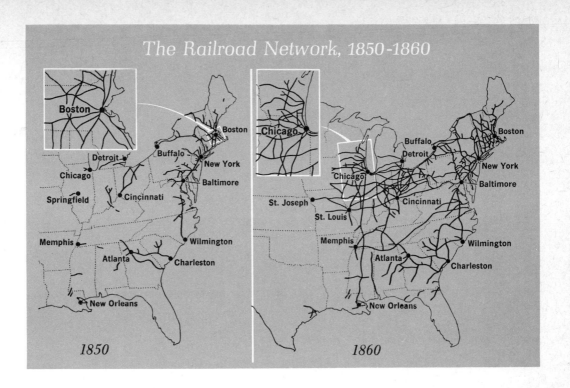

## The Railroad Network, 1850-1860

**1850**

**1860**

north and south from Chicago to Mobile, Alabama. Congressman Stephen A. Douglas of Illinois whipped this legislation through with the help of southern votes attracted by the Mobile terminal. Actually, Congress granted the land to the states that would be crossed by the railroads (except Tennessee and Kentucky, where the federal government owned no land) with the understanding that the states in turn would give the land to the companies that were chartered to build and operate the lines. All told, the first grant ran to 3,736,000 acres, 2,500,000 of them in Illinois, the only state to complete its part of the new system.

In the legislation authorizing this land grant, Congress had provided for a 200-foot-wide right-of-way, and had also relinquished the even-numbered sections (640 acres) of land to a depth of six miles on either side of the line. The government retained the intervening odd-numbered sections for sale at a later date. This grant served as the model for most subsequent grants of western lands, though some railroads were to receive their lands directly, instead of by way of the state governments. By 1860, Congress had granted 18 million acres in 10 states for the benefit of 45 different railroads. With these lands as collateral, the roads were able to market first-mortgage bonds through Wall Street investment bankers to American and foreign investors. During the 1850s, indeed, the issues of such bonds became so voluminous that many New York mercantile firms, especially those with connections abroad, gave up handling goods and became investment bankers specializing in the distribution of railroad securities. The invention of the first-mortgage bond and the development of investment banking were as important as iron and steel in speeding the development of the western railroads and the West itself. In this connection the Illinois project was pivotal.

In 1851, the Illinois state legislature became the scene of a heated contest among the financial interests struggling for possession of the federal land grant and for the privilege of constructing the new north-south railroad. The victors were a group of New York capi-

545

# THE FINEST FARMING LANDS

## CORN — COTTON — FRUITS & VEGETABLES
### EQUAL TO ANY IN THE WORLD!!!
MAY BE PROCURED

# AT FROM $6 TO $12 PER ACRE,

Near Markets, Schools, Railroads, Churches, and all the blessings of Civilization.

## 1,200,000 Acres in Farms of 40, 80, 120, 160 Acres and upwards, in ILLINOIS, the Garden State of America.

*The Illinois Central Railroad Company offer, on LONG CREDIT, the beautiful and fertile PRAIRIE LANDS lying along the whole line of their Railroad, 700 MILES IN LENGTH, upon the most Favorable Terms for enabling Farmers, Manufacturers, Mechanics, and Workingmen, to make for themselves and their families a competency, and a home they can call Their Own.*

### ILLINOIS
Is about equal in extent to England, with a population of 1,722,666, and a soil capable of supporting 20,000,000. No State in the valley of the Mississippi offers so great an inducement to the settler as the State of Illinois. There is no part of the world where all the conditions of climate and soil so admirably combine to produce those two great staples, CORN and WHEAT.

### CLIMATE.
Nowhere can the industrious farmer secure such immediate results from his labor as on these deep, rich, loamy soils, cultivated with so much ease. The climate from the extreme southern part of the State to the Terre Haute, Alton and St. Louis Railroad, a distance of nearly 200 miles, is well adapted to Winter

### WHEAT, CORN, COTTON, TOBACCO,
Peaches, Pears, Tomatoes, and every variety of fruit and vegetables are grown in great abundance, from which Chicago and other Northern markets are furnished from four to six weeks earlier than their immediate vicinity.

### THE ORDINARY YIELD
of Corn is from 50 to 80 bushels per acre. Cattle, Horses, Mules, Sheep and Hogs are raised here at a small cost, and yield large profits. It is believed that no section of country presents greater inducements for Dairy Farming than the Prairies of Illinois, a branch of farming to which but little attention has been paid, and which must yield sure profitable results.

### AGRICULTURAL PRODUCTS.
The Agricultural products of Illinois are greater than those of any other State. The Wheat crop of 1861 was estimated at 35,000,000 bushels, while the Corn crop yields not less than 140,000,000 bushels, besides the crop of Oats, Barley, Rye, Buckwheat, Potatoes, Sweet Potatoes, Pump-

kins, Squashes, Flax, Hemp, Peas, Clover, Cabbage, Beets, Tobacco, Sorghum, Grapes, Peaches, Apples, &c., which go to swell the vast aggregate of production in this fertile region. Over Four Million tons of produce were sent out of Illinois during the past year.

### CULTIVATION OF COTTON.
The experiments in Cotton culture are of very great promise. Commencing in latitude 39 deg. 30 min. (see Mattoon on the Branch, and Assumption on the Main Line), the Company owns thousands of acres well adapted to the perfection of this fibre. A settler having a family of young children can turn their youthful labor to a most profitable account in the growth and perfection of this plant.

### THE ILLINOIS CENTRAL RAILROAD
Traverses the whole length of the State, from the banks of the Mississippi and Lake Michigan to the Ohio. As its name imports, the Railroad runs through the centre of the State, and on either side of the road along its whole length lie the lands offered for sale.

### CITIES, TOWNS, MARKETS, DEPOTS.
There are ninety-eight Depots on the Company's Railway, giving about one every seven miles. Cities, Towns, and Villages are situated at convenient distances throughout the whole route, where every desirable commodity may be found as readily as in the oldest cities of the Union, and where buyers are to be met for all kinds of farm produce.

### EDUCATION.
Mechanics and working men will find the free school system encouraged by the State, and endowed with a large revenue for the support of the schools. Children can live in sight of the school, the college, the church, and grow up with the prosperity of the leading State of the Great Western Empire.

**For Prices and Terms of Payment,**
*ADDRESS LAND COMMISSIONER, Ill. Central R. R. Co., Chicago, Ill.*

*An advertisement widely used by the Illinois Central once it had won its land grant. The railroad's Land Department had an annual advertising budget of about $11,000, and in addition employed a number of agents in America and abroad. These men paid special attention to local pastors, who often permitted them to address congregations in their churches to induce entire religious bodies to move west along the railroad. (Courtesy Illinois Central Railroad.)*

talists allied with the Bostonian, John Murray Forbes, who called their company the Illinois Central. Construction soon got underway and by 1858 Chicago at last was linked by rail with the Mississippi at Galena to the west and Cairo to the south. Forbes had interests in other western railroads, among them the Michigan Central, which linked Detroit with Chicago. Two years later, Chicago was also reached by the Lake Shore and Michigan Southern, which paralleled the Michigan Central across the state.

The next step in western railroad expansion was to push the rails across the Mississippi. By 1856 Forbes and his associates had integrated and constructed various lines to form the Chicago, Burlington & Quincy Railroad, the first to penetrate the state of Iowa from the east. By tying this line to the Michigan Central, and by making arrangements be-

tween the Michigan Central and Corning's New York Central, Forbes by 1856 was able to offer service all the way from New York City to Burlington, Iowa. Not to be entirely outdone, the Michigan Southern promoters soon tied their line with the Erie and other railroads to complete a system running from Jersey City through Chicago to Rock Island, Illinois, on the east bank of the Mississippi just across from Davenport, Iowa.

In 1851 Chicago did not have a single railroad connection with another city. By 1856, it had become the nation's largest railroad center. Almost 2500 miles of track radiated

*Grain elevators at the depot of the Illinois Central Railroad in Chicago, 1858. Grain was brought by rail from the prairies into Chicago, stored, and then transported East. (Harper's Weekly.)*

548

out from the city into the East, the South, and the West, tapping the traffic of 150,000 square miles. By 1860, a total of 5000 miles of track extended Chicago's connections from the Atlantic all the way to the Missouri River at St. Joseph, Missouri. The Mississippi River had been bridged in twelve places, nine of them served by roads connecting with Chicago, a mere three with St. Louis.

All over the West the railroad knocked out the canal systems and decimated river traffic. Railroad trains were faster than canal barges or steamboats. Moreover, railroad spurs could be laid directly to factory doors and warehouses. The competitive practices of railroad managers hastened their triumph. Where they encountered water rivals, the railroads cut their rates even below cost to capture the available traffic. They recouped the losses on such runs by charging all the traffic would bear at noncompetitive terminals.

And yet two waterways survived railroad competition. One was the Great Lakes route, over which heavy freight like wheat and iron ore could still be carried more efficiently than it could by freight trains. The other was the Erie Canal. The continued use of these two waterways reflected the massive volume of the east-west trade, which needed every carrier available to meet the demands of the rising population of the western farms and the eastern cities. As for the east-west railroads themselves, the census of 1860 reported, "So great are their benefits that, if the entire cost of railroads between the Atlantic and the western States had been levied on the farmers of the central west, their proprietors could have paid it and been immensely the gainers."

## v  *The Advance of Northern Industry*

### INDUSTRY AND THE UNION

"Could the Union endure?—that," writes Allan Nevins, "was the anxious, all-pervading question that faced the politicians" of the 1850s. "Could a truly national utilization of the country's resources be achieved?—that was the major question confronting business leaders." The steamboat and clipper-ship operators, and the canal- and the railroad-builders, had done everything they could to further this "truly national utilization." But by drawing the East and the West closer together, they seemed only to broaden the chasm between the free states and the slave. The spread of manufacturing in the free states, and the southern states' continued concentration on cotton-growing and other staples, made still clearer the profound differences in their ways of life.

In the 1850s southern businessmen—merchants, land-speculators, manufacturers, and railroad promoters—sometimes saw that their section's future lay in joining the "truly national" development of the country. Some of the richest planters themselves were investing their fluid capital in northern lands, northern mines, and northern railroads. But these southerners, who were among the last to yield to their section's secessionist agitators, remained but a corporal's guard in an overwhelmingly agrarian society. The southern leaders decried the fact that as cotton-planting flourished, their section's entire economy grew more and more dependent on northern textile factories for markets, on northern ships to carry cotton to factories abroad, and on northern bankers and brokers to finance cotton transactions. At the same time, they made a virtue of southern character, which, they said, saved men from the demeaning industrial and commercial pursuits.

Northern businessmen, in turn, often valued their southern business connections. Almost without exception they deplored the abolitionist campaign in their own section and were among the last to yield to the cry for war once the South had left the Union. Yet few northern businessmen, uncoerced, would restore to embittered New Orleans or St. Louis the commerce that New York and Chicago had captured by enterprise and energy. Fewer still would grant the slaveocracy the first transcontinental railroad or the western lands it would traverse. Southerners might take part in the country's development, and welcome. But they could not be allowed to forestall it or fence it in.

In the 1850s, the North was almost unanimous in the belief that the country's growth would proceed apace even if the South should desert the Union. In the North in the 1850s, writes Nevins, "the underlying forces of the industrial revolution were simply irresistible." Among them he notes the country's natural resources, the movement of immigrants into the labor force, the energy and inventiveness of the people, the flow of capital from California gold mines and from abroad, government friendliness to industrial objectives as shown in tariff policies, low taxes, and subsidization of transportation. All these, he writes, "combined like a chain of bellows to make the forge roar."

### INDUSTRY AND THE LAND

And yet even in the North the roar of industry had only begun to be heard. As late as 1860, the richest northerners were, with few exceptions, merchants rather than industrialists. Among them were H. B. Claflin, who had built up a great wholesale drygoods business on the modern principle of mass sales at low unit profits; A. T. Stewart, one of the creators of the American department store, whose retail emporium later became John Wanamaker's in New York; and Charles L. Tiffany, who made his fortune selling jewelry and silverware to other rich merchants. China traders like John Murray Forbes and importers like George Griswold, Jonathan Sturges, and Morris Ketchum, not industrialists, also supplied much of the early enterprise and capital for railroad building in the United States.

The stock-in-trade of all these men had been manufactured goods not from American factories or handicrafters but almost exclusively from abroad. The limits of industrial progress in the United States before 1860 are indicated by the urgent missions the North itself had to send to Europe at the outbreak of the Civil War to purchase arms and woolen cloth for uniforms. These purchases, like the imports brought in before the war, were paid for largely by the export of our vast agricultural surpluses, whose value even during the years of "irresistible" industrial progress was increasing at a faster rate than the value of manufactured goods.

The first fairly accurate census of American manufactures was taken in 1850. The results were doubly dramatic, for they showed (1) that the annual output of American industry had just passed $1 billion in value, and (2) that this figure was a few million dollars more than the value of all agricultural products, including cotton. In the next ten years, as the Census of 1860 showed, American manufacturers had pushed their production almost to $2 billion. (The exact figure was $1,885,-862,000.) Yet by 1860, agriculture seems to have regained the lead it had lost ten years earlier, for agricultural commodities were now valued at $1,910,000,000.

The growth of manufacturing and the growth of agriculture, of course, reinforced each other. As the industrial cities grew, their landless populations provided expanding markets for farm products; and as the number of farms increased, farm families provided an expanding market for domestic manufactures. Yet it is remarkable how closely related to the land large segments of American manufacturing still remained. One of the great industries of 1860 was the making of lumber from the virgin forests that still covered much of the nation's land. Lumber production that year was evaluated by the census at $105 million, about equal to the value of cotton-textile production itself. Far higher than either in value were the flour and meal produced by the milling industry, whose output in 1860 the census for that year put at nearly $250 million— more than one-eighth of the nation's entire industrial production. The distilling of spirits, the brewing of beer, the tanning of leather,

550

and the packing of meat also were growing rapidly.

All these industries were represented in the cities of the East, but it was the factories of the West that produced the greatest volume. The scale of their operations, moreover, was not their only modern characteristic. By the 1850s, many lumber mills had begun to *specialize* in the production of barrel staves or shingles or railroad ties, and employed single-purpose machines for the work. Specialization and mechanization appeared in other industries as well, paritcularly meat-packing, which, in addition, developed to a high degree the modern principle of using by-products. The hams and shoulders of hogs, for example, were packed as meat. The rest of the flesh then was rendered into oil for sale as a lubricant and shortening. The hog's bristles were used for brushes, the blood for chemicals, the hooves for glue. What remained of the animal was then ground into fertilizer.

Another modern feature of meat-packing was the use of inclined tables down which each carcass would slide past a stationary worker responsible for removing a particular part. This "continuous-flow" method remains one of the principles of modern assembly-line technique in many industries, even those run by computers. One of the great industries of the West was the manufacture of agricultural machinery, in which mass production based on the assembly of interchangeable metal parts was perhaps more advanced than in any other industry in the world.

### PROGRESS IN INVENTION

At the 1851 "world's fair" held at the Crystal Palace in London, few exhibits won greater admiration than the display of American farm devices. Everything from road-scrapers and sausage-stuffers to currycombs and hayrakes "bore off the palm" for their "ingenuity, utility, and cheapness." Few of these inventions were ever patented, and we know hardly any of the inventors' names.

Nonagricultural inventions still were far less numerous than agricultural ones, but they helped swell the number of patents issued by the United States Patent Office each year after it was opened in 1790. In 1835, a record number of patents, 752, were issued; in 1860, 4700 were granted. Most, no doubt, went to the actual inventors of the devices, but some went to those who only promoted their ideas.

One of the great inventions of the nineteenth century was the electric telegraph, for which Samuel F.B. Morse, a painter, received the first American patent in 1840. But Morse's contribution to the telegraph, which was per-

*Joseph Henry in his official photograph as Smithsonian Institution director. Besides discovering the principle of the telegraph, he found a way of producing induced current (the unit of induction physics is called a* henry*), discovered the oscillatory nature of electrical discharge, and began the practice of issuing weather reports. (The Granger Collection.)*

fected for commercial use in the United States in 1844, had more to do with promotion than with mechanics. Back in 1831, Joseph Henry, one of America's most brilliant scientists and later the first director of the Smithsonian Institution in Washington, rang a bell by an electric impulse transmitted over a mile of wire. This accomplishment was based on knowledge of electricity that had taken a century to accumulate—knowledge with which Morse had scarcely a nodding acquaintance. In 1837, Henry made his idea available to an English inventor, Charles Wheatstone, who proceeded to furnish his homeland with practical telegraph service. The principal American contribution to telegraph operation was the "Morse Code," but Morse himself designed neither the apparatus nor the alphabet, for which much of the credit belongs to his partner, Alfred Vail.

It was Morse, however, who prodded Congress into contributing financially to the telegraph's development in 1843. With government money, Morse staged the famous tableau on May 24, 1844, in the Supreme Court Chambers in Washington, when he sent the message, "What hath God wrought?" to Vail in Baltimore, who then returned it. This demonstration aroused great public interest in the telegraph, and companies began bidding for the rights to use it. By 1860, 50,000 miles of telegraph wire had been strung in the United States, and the next year a transcontinental service was opened.

In England, the telegraph was first used to control railroad traffic, an application that came later in the United States. The first use to which Americans put the telegraph was the transmission of business messages and public information. Its effect on the newspaper business was enormous. The "penny press" already dominated American journalism, and printing machinery had been developed that could produce 1000 newspapers an hour. But with news telegraphy the demand for newspapers leaped so sharply that presses were wanted that could turn out at least 10,000 papers an hour. This

resounding volume was achieved in 1847 by the cylindrical press developed by Richard March Hoe. Steady improvement thereafter in presses and other printing equipment enabled publishers to keep pace with the people's growing appetite for "hot news," advertising, and printed entertainment.

Two industrial patents merit special notice: (1) the vulcanization of rubber, and (2) the sewing machine. "India" rubber (most of which came from South America, though the East Indies supplied some) had a unique imperviousness to rain, snow, and mud, but when exposed to heat it melted, grew sticky and collapsed. Finally, after years of effort, Charles Goodyear, a stubborn, sick, impoverished Yankee, hit on just the right mixture of raw rubber, chemicals, and heat that would yield a stable product at all ordinary temperatures. Goodyear patented his process, called "vulcanization," in 1844. A profitable rubber-goods industry was quickly developed by men licensed by Goodyear, but the inventor himself died in 1860 leaving debts of $200,000.

Before the automobile, rubber was used mainly in the boot and shoe industry—one that soon gained further impetus from the sewing machine patented by Elias Howe in 1846. Howe's invention aroused little interest in America until 1851, when Isaac Merritt Singer entered the picture. Singer, a clever inventor in his own right, made many improvements on Howe's original machine, but his largest contribution to its success was his invention of installment selling, an idea he made popular through mass advertising. Having worked up an impressive demand for sewing machines, Singer proceeded to mass-produce them by assembly-line methods. By 1860, a total of 110,000 sewing machines had been manufactured, largely for home use but for factories as well. Almost all boots and shoes were now factory-sewn. The sewing machine also made factory-sewn clothing practical, cheap, and popular.

The perfection of new machines often led

552

to the development of entirely new industries —some for the manufacture of the new devices, others for their employment. In the older industries, such as the manufacture of cotton and woolen goods, spectacular new inventions were no longer to be looked for. Even so, as Victor S. Clark, the historian of American manufactures, suggests, a continuous round of invention greatly speeded up production and turnover:

At the opening of the [nineteenth] century, the owner of a factory thought that he had done well if from the day he purchased his cotton or wool to the time he sold his goods no more than a year elapsed. Within a few years machinery had so accelerated manufacturing that in its ordinary course goods often reached buyers a few days after the raw material from which they were made was received at the factory.

The acceleration of the industrial pace was more marked in the cotton-goods industry than in woolens. But in both, new machines like the Crompton loom, which permitted the weaving of patterns, and new applications of chemistry, which led to improved dyes of many colors, added to the variety of factory-made cloth. Middle-class consumers now had a wide range of styles and qualities to choose from at prices importers no longer could match. Women became increasingly conscious of fashion, and began to feel that they had to follow the annual shifts in style if they were to keep up with the Joneses. By 1860, the cotton-goods industry ranked second only to grain milling in value of product. This category, of course, included the value of the raw materials. In "value *added by manufacture,*" the cotton-textile industry ranked as the nation's leader.

### THE IRON INDUSTRY

The whole cycle of invention from the simple steel plow to the Hoe press and the sewing machine gave a great boost to the American iron industry. New reapers and threshers, rakes and seed drills, were fabricated from iron and steel parts. By 1860, about 3500 steamboats had been built for the western rivers alone, and all of them required boil-

*This hoopskirt manufactory provided "healthy and lucrative" employment to about 1000 girls. By striving to excel (note motto on back wall) the girls were able to turn out almost 90,000 skirts per month; the weekly wage was four dollars. (Harper's Weekly.)*

W. S. & C. H. THOMSON'S SKIRT MANUFACTORY.

ers made of iron sheets—as well as boilers to replace those that blew up. The hulls of the clipper ships were themselves reinforced with iron forms. The telegraph was strung entirely with iron wire until copper began to replace it in the 1860s. By 1846, John A. Roebling, the future builder of the Brooklyn Bridge, had begun to use wire rope in bridge suspension. Four years later, James Bogardus, an imaginative New Yorker, erected the world's first completely cast-iron building. Cast iron buckled under strain; but when wrought-iron beams began to be rolled for building construction, the invention of the skyscraper was in the offing. The first wrought-iron building was New York's Cooper Union, designed by F.A. Petersen and erected in 1854. In machinery for the manufacture of textiles and for other industries, and for machines that made machines, iron was indispensable.

By far the biggest single user of iron in the 1850s was the railroad—for rails, locomotives, wheels, axles, and hundreds of other parts of the railroad's stationary equipment and rolling stock. The railroads, moreover, had by far the most extensive machine shops in the country, which not only made parts and repairs but also turned out their own iron and steel tools and machinery.

In the refining of iron ore and the manufacture of iron products, as in so many other industrial processes, heat is the key element. One of the fundamental changes in iron manufacture after 1840 was the rapid shift in fuel from wood and charcoal (half-burned wood) to anthracite and coke (half-burned soft coal). Far greater temperatures could be attained with these new combustibles, and the rate of production was boosted to still higher levels. A second great change was the widespread use of rolling mills, in place of the hand forge, for shaping iron forms. Improvements in iron-making were reflected in a four-fold increase in the production of pig iron in the two decades between 1842 and 1860, when its annual volume stood at 920,000 tons.

Dramatic as all these developments seem,

the American iron industry in the 1850s developed very slowly in comparison with progress abroad. In 1860, the United States was mining less iron ore and manufacturing less pig iron than Britain had been 20 years earlier. Britain's coal production in 1860 was five times the output of United States mines, and even little Belgium mined 60 per cent as much coal as Americans did. In 1856, Abram Hewitt, America's leading iron manufacturer, observed: "The consumption of iron is a social barometer by which to estimate the relative height of civilization among nations." But America's consumption of iron merely suggested that the country had a long way to go to catch up with the other industrial nations of the day.

Certain scattered incidents underline the immaturity of the industrial spirit. In 1829, drillers had brought in an oil gusher in Kentucky; but it only terrified and angered the workmen, who had been looking for salt. Two years later, Joseph Henry had worked out the essentials of the electric dynamo; but many decades were to pass before his "philosophical toy," as he called his electromagnetic machine, found practical employment. In 1847, William Kelly, a Kentucky ironmaster, had discovered the essential process for the mass production of steel; but scarcely anyone was apprised of his discovery until an Englishman, Henry Bessemer, successfully sought American patents in 1856 for a similar process and the machinery for its use. Even so, another 15 years passed before Bessemer steel was being produced in large commercial quantities in the United States.

## VI *Industry and Society*

By 1860, invention and industry had begun to transform the face of America and the character of its people. But the majority of farmers and the commercial elements in the cities misjudged—and with good reason—both the force and the imminence of the revolution that was taking place. Three years before, in 1857, the country had suffered a severe economic decline. But there had been panics in the past, notably in 1819 and 1837, so there was nothing particularly remarkable in the occurrence of yet another one.

Still, the crash of 1857 had certain peculiarities that should have given a hint of the extraordinary changes in the United States in the preceding 20 years. By 1857, the number of factory workers had risen to 1.3 million, and together with construction workers they made up an industrial labor force of almost 2 million persons, nearly three times that of 1837. Unemployment following the crash thus was far more widespread than ever before. The harshness of the depression years was aggravated by the urban family's total lack of preparation for them. Even when fully employed and receiving regular wages, the members of the new industrial proletariat endured the worst working and living conditions yet found in white America. Factories had become centers of petty tyrannies ruled by foremen under unremitting pressure to keep the hands busy and the rebellious away. In the ranks, back-breaking tasks and long hours helped quench the spark of leadership, and efforts to form unions and gain reforms were pitiful. Bad as working conditions were, living conditions in the segregated slums of industrial cities were worse. Housing alone was so miserable that many workers preferred to put in the long hours in the factories, sheltered and among friends, than to spend their time at home. Under these circumstances, the crash, depriving hundreds of thousands of work, proved unprecedentedly brutal.

Other telltale features of the crash of 1857 were not so apparent to contemporaries. In the 1850s, as in the 1830s, large amounts of money and great reserves of credit had been drawn to land-speculation. The number of banks in the country had grown rapidly and their loans for this purpose had grown even faster. These circumstances confirmed conservatives

in their belief that little had changed in 20 years, and that fools were parted from their fortunes as before. By 1857, however, overinvestment in productive facilities had become as important as overinvestment in land in bringing about the stringency of funds that led to the crash and deepened the depression that followed. By then more than a billion dollars had been invested in manufacturing and another billion in railroads, two-thirds of it during the seven years just preceding the crash.

The source of funds for these investments introduced another new element, which was to grow in importance—speculation in corporate stocks and bonds. Securities often were bought with mere token down-payments eked out with high-interest loans from New York banks. These banks, in turn, often paid interest to depositors, among whom so many other banks were included that, in the late 1850s, 70 per cent of the entire country's bank reserves were on deposit in New York. In times of financial emergency, country banks sought to withdraw some of their funds from the metropolis. To satisfy their country bank depositors the New York banks would have to call in the loans made with the country deposits. Such calls were almost certain to embarrass city security speculators and drive many of them into bankruptcy. Their failures, in turn, would leave their creditor-banks insolvent or nearly so.

On August 24, 1857, the New York branch of the Ohio Life Insurance and Trust Company, Ohio's leading bank, was forced to close its doors after discovering that its treasurer had embezzled most of its funds. The parent bank in Ohio soon failed, causing runs on many New York banks. By October 13 all but one of these had closed, as had most of the banks in the country.

Fortunately, industrialists and financiers learned valuable lessons from the latest financial breakdown. In the 1850s, as we have said (p. 549), most leading businessmen still were merchants, many of whom hoped, like the diarist Philip Hone, to earn enough by 40 to retire to the good things of life. But the representative businessmen with the future on their side now were industrial corporation executives, often administrators for absentee owners or scattered stockholders. Confronted with the high daily toll of overhead costs, they became alert to rapid changes in technology, markets, and sources of raw materials, and sensitive to the nuances and rumors of the money markets. Such men no longer looked for profits in the lucky voyage or the fortunate speculation or the simple soundness and progress of the country. Profit would come henceforth from strict attention to management, from cautious financing, careful bookkeeping, enhancement of labor productivity, adaptability to changing markets. Profits promised to grow enormously beyond the dreams of speculative avarice; but they were likely to be made up of mountains of pennies and fractions of pennies, which were just as likely to disappear unless constant attention was given to such insignificant sums.

The lure of speculation did not die; unsettled conditions during the Civil War, and the expansion of the country after the war ended, created a speculator's paradise. But American industrialists had learned something of the industrial discipline; and the North, and ultimately the nation, were the stronger for it.

# READINGS

Most of the books suggested for Chapter Twelve are important for this chapter as well and the reader is referred to the listing there. On the northern economy, in addition, we may recommend here, Allan Nevins, *Ordeal of the Union* (2 vols., 1947), especially Volume II. On American material well-being, E.W. Martin, *The Standard of Living in 1860* (1942), is informative. Technical but often accessible essays are available in The National Bureau of Economic Research, *Trends in the American Economy in the Nineteenth Century* (1960).

The writings of Hamlin Garland on the Middle Border are full of interest. The reader might start with *A Son of the Middle Border* (1917). A moving account of pioneer life in Illinois is Francis Grierson, *The Valley of Shadows* (1948). Leo Rogin, *The Introduction of Farm Machinery, in Its Relation to the Productivity of Labor in Agriculture in the United States During the Nineteenth Century* (1931), C.H. Danhof, *Change in Agriculture, The Northern United States 1820–1870* (1969), and the early chapters of A.G. Bogue, *From Prairie to Corn Belt: Farming on the Illinois and Iowa Prairies in the Nineteenth Century* (1963), are especially illuminating. On the relation of the farmer to God and the soil, see H.N. Smith, *Virgin Land* (1950).

For the immigrants, M.L. Hansen, *The Atlantic Migration 1607–1860* (1940), is indispensable. Somewhat less formal is the same author's *The Immigrant in American History* (1940). A more general account is Carl Wittke, *We Who Built America* (1967). The background for the German immigration of the mid-nineteenth century is well depicted in Mack Walker, *Germany and the Emigration 1816–1885* (1964). For the Irish, see George Potter, *To the Golden Door* (1960), and Cecil Woodham-Smith, *The Great Hunger* (1962); for the British, see W.S. Shepperson, *British Emigration to North America, Projects and Opinion in the Early Victorian Period* (1957).

On American trade the best general survey is E.R. Johnson and others, *History of Domestic and Foreign Commerce of the United States* (2 vols., 1915). Roger Pineau, ed., *The Japan Expedition 1852–1854: The Personal Journal of Commodore Matthew C. Perry* (1969), is illuminating on the opening of the "hermit kingdom." A thorough compendium of shipbuilding and shipping is J.G.B. Hutchins, *The American Maritime Industries and Public Policy 1789–1914* (1941). The leading works on the clipper ships are A.H. Clark, *The Clipper Ship Era, 1843–1869* (1910), and C.C. Cutler, *Greyhounds of the Sea* (1930). One of the best business biographies, and relevant to shipping as well as railroads, is W.J. Lane, *Commodore Vanderbilt* (1942). An excellent study of another New Yorker is I.D. Neu, *Erastus Corning, Merchant and Financier, 1794–1872* (1960). L.C. Hunter, *Steamboats on the Western Rivers, An Economic and Technological History* (1949), is invaluable. Most comprehensive on the canals is Carter Goodrich, *Government Promotion of American Canals and Railroads 1800–1890* (1960).

An excellent introduction to railroad history is F.A. Cleveland and F.W. Powell, *Railroad Promotion and Capitalization in the United States* (1909). More technical are R.W. Fogel, *Railroads and American Economic Growth: Essays in Econometric History* (1964), and Albert Fishlow, *American Railroads and the Transformation of the Ante-Bellum Economy*

(1965). A.D. Chandler, Jr., *Henry Varnum Poor: Business Editor, Analyst, and Reformer* (1956), stresses the role of management in railroad development. Exceedingly thorough on the theme indicated by their titles are L.H. Haney, *A Congressional History of Railways in the United States to 1850* (1908) and the same author's *A Congressional History of Railways in the United States 1850–1887* (1910). The major work on New England railroads is E.C. Kirkland, *Men, Cities and Transportation 1820–1900* (2 vols., 1948). Other useful railroad histories include F.W. Stevens, *The Beginnings of the New York Central Railroad* (1926); G.H. Burgess and M.C. Kennedy, *The Pennsylvania Railroad Company 1846–1946* (1949); and two books by Edward Hungerford, *The Story of the Baltimore and Ohio Railroad 1827–1927* (2 vols., 1928), and *Men of Erie* (1946). Two first-rate books on railroads and western lands are P.W. Gates, *The Illinois Central Railroad and Its Colonization Work* (1934), and R.C. Overton, *Burlington West* (1941). R.R. Russel, *Improvement of Communication with the Pacific Coast as an Issue in American Politics 1783–1864* (1948), affords an illuminating introduction to the transcontinentals. T.C. Cochran, *Railroad Leaders, 1845–1890: The Business Mind in Action* (1953), fulfills the promise of its subtitle.

On the iron industry, in addition to V.S. Clark (see Chapter Twelve), E.C. Mack, *Peter Cooper, Citizen of New York* (1949), and Allan Nevins, *Abram S. Hewitt, with Some Account of Peter Cooper* (1935), are informative. Harlan Hatcher, *A Century of Iron and Men* (1950), affords a readable introduction to the exploitation of western iron resources. Waldemar Kaempffert, ed., *A Popular History of American Invention* (2 vols., 1924), is very informative. An important book on a badly neglected figure is Thomas Coulson, *Joseph Henry, His Life and Work* (1950). R.L. Thompson, *Wiring a Continent: The History of the Telegraph Industry in the United States 1832–1866* (1947), is useful on one of the major applications of Henry's work. D.H. Calhoun, *The American Civil Engineer, Origins and Conflict* (1960), is a substantial study. On the conditions of labor, a basic account is Norman Ware, *The Industrial Worker 1840–1860* (1924). Worth reading too is C.M. Green, *Holyoke, Massachusetts, A Case History of the Industrial Revolution in America* (1939). On banking and the money market, see M.G. Myers, *The New York Money Market* (1931); L.H. Jenks, *The Migration of British Capital to 1875* (1927); and *Henry Varnum Poor* by A.D. Chandler, Jr., referred to above. Much the best account of the ups and downs of economic life is W.B. Smith and A.H. Cole, *Fluctuations in American Business 1790–1860* (1935). G.W. Van Vleck, *The Panic of 1857* (1943), offers a readable analysis.

# EIGHTEEN

At the beginning of the 1850s the North and the South, like two bellicose nations, warily eyed each other. Responsible statesmen, of whom there were too few in either section, tried desperately to find ways of reconciling sectional differences, but powerful forces seemed to defeat their every effort.

The most divisive force, of course, was slavery. Northern abolitionists, and growing numbers of others in the North, looked upon slavery as a sin, one all the worse for its menace to the Union. To southerners, slavery had become the keystone of their civilization, the agency of their material well-being. If all the world was right about slavery and had put it on the road to extinction, all the more tenaciously would the South, and a few outlying centers of the institution like Cuba and Brazil, defend it.

While abolitionists in the North and fire-eaters in the South heated the atmosphere, businessmen and promoters and the ordinary citizens of both sections continued to follow the main chance—to settle the land, to speculate, to seek profits from services and supplies to one another—overlooking sectional differences or sectional aims whenever possible. Moral issues often seemed secondary to them, but they could not go far along their own paths without encountering the moral combatants. In the promotion of railroads, the organization of territories, the settlement of disputed areas such as Kansas, businessmen plunged ahead. But others in the North and the South, full of the sense of their own righteousness and often heedless of the slave himself, also held their own fatal course.

In the past, political leaders had been able to mediate between the sections whenever the slavery issue threatened to upset

# A DECADE
# OF FAILURE

the sectional balance. The Federal Convention of 1787, for example, had devised the "three-fifths compromise," and had put off for 20 years Congress's power to prohibit further slave importations. The next generation had negotiated the Missouri Compromise. Most recently, the great leaders who were just passing from the scene had exerted themselves to the utmost to bring about the Compromise of 1850. In the next decade compromise after compromise was attempted, even as late as 1861. But the bonds of the Union had become too frayed by sectional friction, the opposition of North and South too sharply honed by argument, and all compromise efforts failed.

## I *The Slave Issue Confronts Pierce*

### HUNTING FUGITIVES

Franklin Pierce of New Hampshire took office as the 14th President of the United States on March 4, 1853. A "vain, showy, and pliant man," as a contemporary commentator said, Pierce quickly showed those qualities which made his administration quail before the contesting forces, free and slave, that sought to dominate the country.

Most Americans in 1853, including the President, still hoped that the Compromise of 1850 would stifle the agitation over slavery once and for all. But extremists did their best to keep the issue burning. The North had gagged particularly on the provision in the Compromise of 1850 requiring the return of fugitive slaves to the owners, and many northern states deliberately hampered the recovery of runaways. Actually, the number of slaves who managed to escape was infinitesimal, but the South regarded the northerners' cooperation with the fugitives as one more proof of the free section's conspiracy against southern institutions. Even those northerners who disliked blacks as much as they respected property, now began to condemn slavery as a stench to the whole nation and to look forward to the time, as Lincoln put it later, when "the hateful institution, like a reptile poisoning itself, will perish by its own infamy."

The person who singlehandedly did more than any other American to deepen hatred of slavery was the novelist Harriet Beecher Stowe. A New Englander who had lived close to slavery in the border city of Cincinnati, Mrs. Stowe wrote *Uncle Tom's Cabin* (1852) in the belief that once the South recognized the

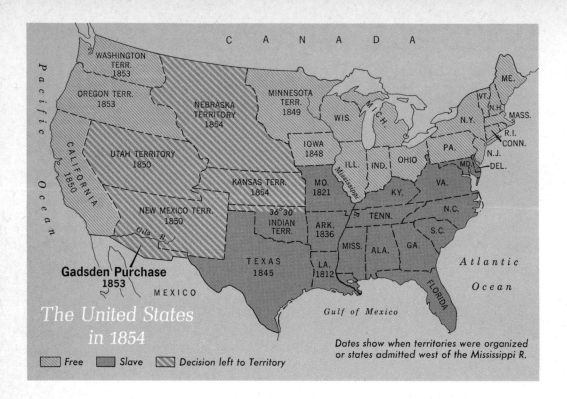

**The United States in 1854**

CANADA

WASHINGTON TERR. 1853
OREGON TERR. 1853
NEBRASKA TERRITORY 1854
MINNESOTA TERR. 1849
WIS.
MICH.
ME.
VT.
N.H.
MASS.
N.Y.
R.I.
CONN.
PA.
N.J.
DEL.
MD.

UTAH TERRITORY 1850
IOWA 1848
ILL. IND. OHIO
VA.
KY.

CALIFORNIA 1850
KANSAS TERR. 1854
MO. 1821
N.C.
TENN.
S.C.

NEW MEXICO TERR. 1850
36°30′
INDIAN TERR.
ARK. 1836
MISS. ALA. GA.
Gila R.

Gadsden Purchase 1853
MEXICO
TEXAS 1845
LA. 1812
FLORIDA

Pacific Ocean

Atlantic Ocean

Gulf of Mexico

Mississippi

Dates show when territories were organized or states admitted west of the Mississippi R.

☐ Free  ■ Slave  ▨ Decision left to Territory

sinfulness of the "peculiar institution," the Negroes would be freed. She felt no malice toward the slave-owners. The villain of her novel, Simon Legree, was a Yankee. Her most eloquent spokesman against slavery was a humane southern planter. The sensational incident, humor, and pathos of *Uncle Tom's Cabin* appealed to a vast audience in the North, especially women, who responded with tears to the episodes of Negro mothers forcibly separated from their children. Southern matrons also wept at those passages.

Mrs. Stowe's novel sold 300,000 copies in its first year, and its stage version became a smash hit. One young southerner, after reading the novel in 1853, observed that it

greatly tended . . . to influence one-half of the nation against the other, to produce disunion and to stir up a civil war. . . . Can any *friend* of the human race, or any *friend* of the Negro desire such an issue?

Northern resistance to the Fugitive Slave Law was quickened by *Uncle Tom's Cabin*, and slave-owners pursuing runaways into free

states often were glad to get home safely even without their quarry. In Chicago, Detroit, Boston, and elsewhere, federal officers trying to reclaim fugitive slaves were menaced by mobs.

### THE OSTEND MANIFESTO

The South considered the incitement of runaways and the breakdown of the Fugitive Slave Law as clear violations of its constitutional property rights and sought countermeasures. A vociferous minority demanded the reopening of the African slave trade. A more influential group, supported by Pierce himself, sought the acquisition of Cuba, the slave-packed "pearl of the Antilles."

Cuba, like the rest of the Western Hemisphere, had been eyed by American expansionists for decades. In 1848 President Polk had offered Spain $100 million for the island, but was haughtily turned down. Three years later, although alarmed by two filibustering expeditions from the American mainland, launched by Cuban rebels against Cuba, Spain

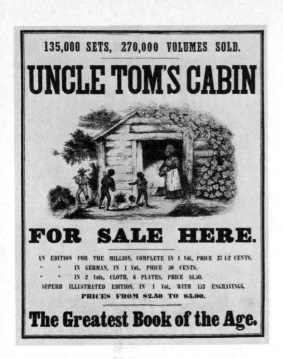

*An early poster advertising* Uncle Tom's Cabin *in various editions, including one in German for the strong antislavery immigrants of '48. (Courtesy of the New-York Historical Society, New York City.)*

again rejected offers of purchase. In 1854, a naval incident at Havana in which, on a mere technicality, Spanish officials seized an American merchant vessel, gave Pierce an excuse to press the question once again, even though it was plain that a war with Spain over Cuba —given the excited state of popular feeling in the United States—would split the country and the Democratic party.

Before sitting down with Spanish representatives, Secretary of State William L. Marcy asked Pierre Soulé, the American minister in Madrid, to discuss the problem of Cuba with James Buchanan, the American minister in London, and John Y. Mason, the American minister in Paris. The three diplomats met at Ostend in Belgium, and on October 15, 1854, sent a confidential dispatch to Marcy recommending that the United States offer $120 million for Cuba. If the offer was rejected, they added, "by every law, human and divine," the United States "shall be justified in wresting [the island] from Spain," on the ground that Spain's control of it gravely endangered "our internal peace and the existence of our cherished Union."

The diplomats were merely advising Marcy to do what he already contemplated; what he had hoped for from them was not this incendiary avowal of his own plans, but an estimate of how the European powers would react to them. When Pierce's enemies in the House of Representatives insisted on the publication of the confidential dispatch, what became known as "The Ostend Manifesto" was out of the pot. Free-soilers denounced it vigorously—the New York *Tribune* called it a "Manifesto of Brigands"—and Marcy had to repudiate its proposals.

Quite possibly enough public support could have been mustered by the Pierce administration to annex Cuba had not Congress, some months before the Ostend Manifesto, passed a momentous measure which, in the words of a New York paper, "has forever rendered annexation impossible." This was the Kansas-Nebraska Act, which, by reopening the question of slavery in the western territories, strengthened northern determination to check the spread of slavery anywhere, *"come what may,"* as this New York paper put it.

### THE KANSAS-NEBRASKA ACT

Nebraska country, a veritable empire ranging west of the 95th meridian all the way to Oregon Territory and north to the Canadian border, stood athwart the aspirations of the contending older sections of the country for two reasons: (1) Its southern part bordered the slave state of Missouri, but slaveholders were forbidden to extend slavery there by the Missouri Compromise of 1820; (2) this segment and the area north of it to the Great Bend of the Missouri River which now forms the eastern boundary of the State of Nebraska, also lay just beyond the "Permanent Indian Frontier" (see p. 473). Here, in the words of Stephen A. Douglas, and the italics are his, the Indians, by treaty, had been guaranteed "perpetual occupancy, *with an express condition that* [the land] *should never be incorporated within the limits of a territory or state of the Union.*" This "barbarian wall," Douglas continued, "was to have been a colossal monument to the God terminus saying to christianity, civilization and Democracy, 'thus far mayest thou go, and *no* farther.'"

As early as the congressional session of 1843–44, "with a direct view of arresting the further progress of this savage barrier to the extension of our institutions," Douglas, then a freshman member of the House of Representatives from Illinois, had introduced the first bill to break the Indian treaties and organize the Territory of Nebraska. "From that day to this," Douglas wrote in December 1853, when he had risen to the chairmanship of the Committee on Territories in the Senate, "I have taken care always to have a bill pending when Indians were about to be located in that quarter." Others, meanwhile, led by Senator David R. Atchison of Missouri, who vowed he would see Nebraska "sink in hell" before allowing it to be organized as a free territory, also had bills at hand to forestall any measure aimed at keeping slavery out.

Much else had risen besides Douglas himself by 1853, including his own aspirations for the Presidency and the fever of the sectional conflict. The sectional conflict itself was intensified by the growing rivalry between North and South for the first transcontinental railroad.

By 1853, Douglas had become the leading spokesman for the construction of the first transcontinental over a northern route that would link the Pacific coast with his beloved Chicago, where he owned much real estate. But he was not selfish about that. "Continuous lines of settlement," he said then,

with civil, political and religious institutions all under the protection of law, are imperiously demanded by the highest national considerations. These are essential, but they are not sufficient. No man can keep up with the spirit of this age who travels on anything slower than the locomotive, and fails to receive intelligence by lightning. We must therefore have Rail Roads and Telegraphs from the Atlantic to the Pacific, through our own territory. Not one line only, but many lines. . . . The removal of the Indian barrier and the extension of the laws of the United States in the form of Territorial governments are the first steps toward the accomplishment of each and all of those objects.

For these purposes, Douglas reported his fourth and fateful Nebraska bill to the Senate on January 4, 1854.

Douglas's report was deliberately vague and crafty. He specifically undertook to apply in Nebraska—part of the Louisiana Purchase north of 36° 30′—the "popular sovereignty" provisions applied in the Mexican cessions of Utah and New Mexico by the Compromise of 1850 of which he was so proud (see p. 494). He would not, however, expressly repeal the Missouri Compromise, which specifically forbade slavery in Nebraska but not in Utah and New Mexico. Some "eminent statesmen," Douglas's report said, thought the Missouri Compromise was unconstitutional. But the Committee on Territories was "not now prepared" to make recommendations "as to the legal points involved." If they never came up, so much the better. On one unfortunate provision of the Compromise of 1850, nevertheless, the committee was prepared to make a recommendation: that in Nebraska, as in all other territories and states, the Fugitive Slave Law must be enforced.

Douglas's tactic has been called "astute." If, as his committee said, it hoped by this means to hasten the progress of the Great West while avoiding a repetition of "the fearful struggle of 1850," no doubt it was a supportable gambit and possibly the only one that offered any prospect of success. But its evasions also offered too attractive an invitation to the committed spokesmen of the contending sections to make the "legal points" Douglas so conspicuously had passed up. They lost little time in doing so, and in an especially incendiary manner because of the committee's shilly-shallying on freedom while standing firm on the return of fugitive slaves.

Douglas's report of January 4 ordinarily would have been only a routine step by which to place his Nebraska bill before the Senate in preparation for a full-dress debate at some future date. This date, as it happened, was to be January 24, but it was not until January 30 that formal debate began. By then, the bill had already been bitterly argued in and out of Congress and had been so fatally altered under sectional pressure that Douglas himself is said to have predicted that in its latest form it would raise "the hell of a storm."

Three critical alterations were made in the bill, two of them outright victories for the slave section, and the third, one which the South hoped to turn to advantage.

As originally written it seemed that the bill did not necessarily deprive Congress of its constitutional power to "make all needful Rules and Regulations respecting the Territory . . . belonging to the United States," including those respecting slavery. If, as the bill said, the constitution of a new state in the territory itself permitted slavery, Congress appeared still to have the power to accept or reject this constitution during the admission procedure. Under unyielding pressure from Senator Atchison and his southern colleagues, who perceived this loophole, Douglas was forced to correct what he lamely called this "clerical error" in the bill. His correction explicitly took the power over slavery from Congress and gave it, "in the Territories and in the new States to be formed therefrom, . . . to the people residing therein, through their appropriate representatives." This change left Nebraska open to slaveholders, regardless of Congress or of the Missouri Compromise.

Once he had thus enlarged the area of application of the principle of "popular sovereignty," whose ambiguities had already become anathema to many in the North (see

p. 491), Douglas was next forced specifically to concede, in the bill, that the Missouri Compromise was henceforth to be "inoperative and void." It was "inconsistent," the bill now said, "with the principle of nonintervention by Congress with slavery in the States and Territories, as recognized by the legislation of 1850 commonly called the Compromise Measures."

Douglas's third concession revolved around the railroad issue. It was clear to all that Congress at this time would help build no more than one transcontinental line. A government-sponsored survey in 1853 had shown that a southern route along the Mexican border offered the fewest physical obstacles for the construction of such a line. The Gadsden Purchase from Mexico, in fact, had been made explicitly for possible railroad use (see p. 490). Atchison's prosouthern group in Missouri, at

563

*A rare daguerreotype of Stephen A. Douglas at the outset of his Congressional career by Mathew Brady. (Library of Congress.)*

EIGHTEEN *A Decade of Failure*

564

the same time, advocated a central route originating in St. Louis. They would not even consider supporting any transcontinental, including their own, which passed through territory forever closed to slavery. Fearful of their strength, and fearful that the southern part of Nebraska bordering Missouri would indeed fall to slavery, a group of Iowa congressmen urged Douglas to divide Nebraska into two territories to insure the passage of the transcontinental through the free valley of the Platte in the more northerly part. Douglas had said of the whole of Nebraska, "in that climate . . . it is worse than folly to think of its being a slaveholding country." Although skeptical of the Iowans' fears concerning slavery in this region, he felt constrained to concede their request as he had conceded those of their enemies. His bill was altered to divide Nebraska into two territories, Nebraska and Kansas. And Kansas was immediately marked for slavery by the South.

These three alterations in fact make up the substance of the Kansas-Nebraska Act as finally passed on May 30, 1854. The first transcontinental was itself to remain a will-o'-the-wisp for ten more years. But the law was readied for the belated extension of slavery into new country and for another dislodgment of the aborigines from it.

In the Senate, which was less subject than the House to political storms, the Kansas-Nebraska Act passed, 37 to 14. In the House, which in 1854 was up for election, the bill had much harder going before it squeaked through, 113 to 100. Every one of the 45 northern Whigs in the House voted against the bill. This group received the support of almost half the northern Democrats, thereby fracturing the principal *national* party, on whose unity Douglas himself had staked his own future as well as that of the Union. A solid bloc of southern Democrats and half the northern Democrats, on the other hand, together with the majority of the *southern* Whigs, had put the measure across. Thus the Whig party was split as well.

It took southerners outside of Congress a

little time to grasp the value of their coup. One paper declared that the Kansas-Nebraska Act was "barren of practical benefit." Others gradually came to see it as "a measure . . . just in regards to the rights of the South, . . . and reasonable in its operations and effect." In Missouri it was said that Kansas must be a slave state because "it is suited and adapted only to slave labor," and because "we have both the numerical and moral strength to make it so." Howell Cobb of Georgia, sending Douglas his congratulations on the measure, declared that "he who dallies [in support of it] is a dastard and he who doubts is damned."

One reason for the South's growing truculence was the "mad ferocity" with which many in the North had begun to assault the measure from the start. The repeal of the Missouri Compromise, in particular, sent a thrill of excitement through the people. Lawyer Lincoln himself wrote in his third-person autobiographical sketch that by 1854, "his profession had almost superseded the thought of politics in his mind, when the repeal of the Missouri Compromise aroused him as he had never been before." Perhaps the most influential attack, written while Douglas's draft was still undergoing alteration, but not widely published until after the act's adoption, was the "Appeal of the Independent Democrats in Congress to the People of the United States," the work mainly of Senators Salmon P. Chase of Ohio and Charles Sumner of Massachusetts, but also signed by other members. The "Appeal," one of the first sitmulants for the formation of the Republican party (see p. 569), branded the Kansas-Nebraska Act a

criminal betrayal of precious rights; as part and parcel of an atrocious plot to exclude from a vast unoccupied region immigrants from the Old World and free laborers from our own States, and convert it into a dreary region of despotism, inhabited by masters and slaves.

That they did not intend to let this "betrayal" pass is clear from their other statements. "They celebrate a present victory," said Chase when the act passed the Senate, "but the echoes they awake will never rest till slavery itself shall die." Sumner added: The act was "at once the worst and the best which Congress ever enacted. It is the worst bill, inasmuch as it is a present victory of Slavery. . . . It is the best bill, . . . for it annuls all past compromises with Slavery, and makes all future compromises impossible. Thus it puts Freedom and Slavery face to face, and bids them grapple. Who can doubt the result?"

When Douglas himself attempted to speak in defense of his act, even in his home base in Chicago, he was hooted off the platform by members of his own party and menaced by crowds in the streets.

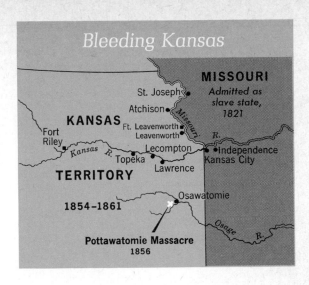

Bleeding Kansas

## "BLEEDING KANSAS"

The Kansas-Nebraska Act failed its first test in the new territory of Kansas. Under the theory of "popular sovereignty," did a new territory have the power to prohibit or legalize slavery before framing its constitution and before seeking statehood? According to Douglas, it did. According to southern spokesmen, it did not. No territory could decide this question, southerners said, until it became a state. So long as it was still a territory it could not keep slaves out. As settlers moved into Kansas, the issue passed beyond debate.

Most of those who settled in Kansas after the organization of the territory were slaveless farmers from adjacent states. Along with them, as in all other frontier settlements, came the characteristic body of rovers and opportunists bent on bleeding the newcomers. These men were indifferent to slavery, and indifferent to politics except as it offered patronage and prey. As a cover for their unsavory activities, they were no doubt callous enough to keep the controversy over slavery boiling.

Others, however, also helped turn Kansas into a battleground. To "beard oppression in its very den," as they said, the New England Emigrant Aid Company and similar associations organized in the North between 1854 and 1855 financed the migration of more than a thousand right-thinking Yankees to Kansas to see that the new settlers voted correctly when the issue of free soil or slavery came up, and to participate in the vote themselves. To support their mission, boxes of "Beecher's Bibles" were sent to them. Henry Ward Beecher, a vigorous antislavery clergyman, had preached that rifles might have stronger effect than the Bible on the pro-slavery camp, and he was taken at his word. Missourians, led by the ubiquitous Senator Atchison, viewed this activity as part of an abolitionist plan to use Kansas as a launching pad for an assault on slavery in the entire Southwest. To forestall these Yankee "serfs," "paupers," and "cutthroats," as they called them, hot-headed Missourians—"bar-room rowdies," "blacklegs," and "border ruffians," said the Yankees, returning the compliments—as well as hundreds from Alabama, Georgia and South Carolina, also poured into Kansas, determined to pack the first Kansas territorial legislature with pro-slavery men.

On election day, March 30, 1855, slightly more than 2000 Kansans were registered to vote, but over 6000 ballots were cast, most of them by Missourians who had come into Kansas for this day only. Andrew H. Reeder, a Pennsylvania Democrat who had been appointed governor of the Kansas Territory by Pierce, tried to disqualify eight of the 31 mem-

565

The rude six-room cabin which served as the Governor's mansion at Lecompton, Kansas (Harper's Weekly.) Dr. Charles Robinson (later governor of the state) was the featured speaker at the Free Kansas meeting of 1855 advertised in the poster at left. (The Bettmann Archive.)

## KANSAS a FREE STATE.

## Squatter Sovereignty VINDICATED! NO WHITE SLAVERY!

The Squatters of Kansas who are favorable to FREEDOM OF SPEECH on all subjects which interest them, and an unmuzzled PRESS: who are determined to do their own THINKING and VOTING independent of FOREIGN DICTATION, are requested to assemble in

## MASS MEETING

at the time and places following to wit:

The following speakers will be in attendance, who will address you on the important questions now before the people of Kansas.

## DR. CHAS. ROBINSON,

J. A. Wakefield, C. K. Holliday, M. F. Conway, W. K. Vail, J. L. Speer, W. A. Ela, Josiah. Miller, O. C. Brown, J. K. Goodin, Doct. Gilpatrick, Revs. Mr. Tuton and J. E. Stewart, C. A. Foster, J. P. Fox, H. Bronson, G. W. Brown, A. H. Malley and others.

## TURN OUT AND HEAR THEM!

bers who had been elected irregularly, but Pierce himself refused to back his governor. Over Reeder's vetoes, the new legislature passed a series of savagely repressive laws that, among other punishments, prescribed the death penalty for aiding a fugitive slave. Simply to question the legality of slavery in Kansas carried a sentence of two years at hard labor.

But the free-soilers in Kansas were not intimidated. When Pierce eventually sent William Shannon to replace the uncooperative Reeder, the free-soilers sent Reeder to Congress as their territorial delegate. In the fall of 1855 they met in Topeka and drew up their own constitution. In January 1856, they elected their own legislature and Charles Robinson as governor.

With two rival administrations, Kansas was ripe for war. And in May 1856, while Pierce hesitated, war came. At that time a force of proslavery men led by a United States marshal raided the Kansas town of Lawrence in search of some free-soil leaders who had been indicted for treason by the proslavery legislature. Fortified by alcohol, the raiders burned down the hotel, destroyed homes, and smashed free-soil printing presses.

This celebrated "sack of Lawrence," blown up to horrendous proportions by northern newspapers, took two lives and spawned a bloodier sequel. John Brown, of Osawatomie, Kansas, a fanatical abolitionist who was soon to become better known, gathered six followers, rode into the proslavery settlement at Pottawatomie Creek, and wantonly hacked five men to death. He acted, so he said, under God's authority. But his sacred vendetta started a guerrilla war in which over 200 persons were killed.

Violence over Kansas, moreover, had already spread from the territory to the very halls of Congress. On May 19, 1856, shortly after the "sack of Lawrence," but before news of the incident reached Washington, Charles Sumner of Massachusetts rose to speak in the Senate in favor of the free-soil constitution of Kansas. His speech lasting all of two days flailed away at the "harlot slavery," and especially at the "murderous robbers" of Missouri, "hirelings picked from the drunken spew and vomit of an uneasy civilization." But Sumner aimed his choicest epithets at Senator Andrew P. Butler of South Carolina, and drove Butler's nephew, Preston Brooks, congressman from South Carolina, to avenge his uncle, his state, and his section. Two days after his speech, as Sumner sat at his desk in the Senate chamber, Brooks beat him repeatedly over the head with a cane and injured him so severely

*The account of the assault on Senator Sumner by Representative Brooks on May 22, 1856 (illustrated above) as reported the following day in the* New York Herald *via magnetic and printing telegraph. (Top: The Granger Collection; Bottom: Courtesy of the New-York Historical Society, New York City.)*

## THE LATEST NEWS.

### BY MAGNETIC AND PRINTING TELEGRAPHS.

**Assault on Senator Sumner in the Senate Chamber.**

WASHINGTON, May 22, 1856.

About half past one, after the Senate adjourned, Col. Preston S. Brooks, M. C., of South Carolina, approached Senator Sumner, who was sitting in his seat, and said to him—

Mr. Sumner, I have read your speech against South Carolina, and have read it carefully, deliberately and dispassionately, in which you have libelled my State and slandered my white haired old relative, Senator Butler, who is absent, and I have come to punish you for it.

Col. Brooks then struck Senator Sumner with his cane some dozen blows over the head. Mr. Sumner at first showed fight, but was overpowered. Senator Crittenden and others interfered and separated them.

Mr. Keitt, of South Carolina, did not interfere, only to keep persons off.

Senator Toombs declared that it was the proper place to have chastised Mr. Sumner.

The affair is regretted by all.

The stick used was gutta percha, about an inch in diameter, and hollow, which was broken up like a pipe-stem.

About a dozen Senators and many strangers happened to be in the chamber at the moment of the fight. Sumner, I learn, is badly whipped. The city is considerably excited, and crowds everywhere are discussing the last item. Sumner cried—"I'm most dead! oh! I'm most dead." After Sumner fell between two desks, his own having been overturned, he lay bleeding, and cried out—"I am almost dead—almost dead!"

that Sumner remained an invalid for the next three and a half years. The assault on Sumner by "Bully" Brooks, together with the news from Kansas, came unfortunately just when preparation were being made for the presidential campaign in 1856.

### A NEW PARTY ALIGNMENT

The decline of the Whig party had set in even before the election of 1852 (see p. 495), and the party's defeat in the presidential campaign that year speeded its breakup. Events during Pierce's administration, in turn, so aggravated sectional strife that the foundations of his own party, the Democrats, also crumbled. Their old allegiances broken, politicians and their followers looked anxiously for new homes.

Out of the troubles of the old intersectional parties rose a new third party, the American party, a composite of anti-Catholic and anti-foreign groups whose origins dated back to the early 1840s. Stemming from "The Order of the Star-Spangled Banner," the American party raised its patriotic standard in the late months of 1852. *"Americans must rule America,"* said its leaders. In its first published platform in 1856, it urged "a change in the laws of naturalization, making a continued residence of twenty-one years, . . . an indispensable requisite for citizenship," and hence for the franchise. "Whether of native or foreign birth," it added, "no person should be selected for political station who recognizes any . . . obligation of any description to any foreign prince, potentate, or power."

The American party was itself so fearful of its own biases that it placed its members under strict regulations requiring them to pretend to "know nothing" when pressed for information. Thus they soon became known as the "Know Nothings." Plain snobbery and the spell of cabalistic hand-clasps and mystifying passwords no doubt added to the party's ranks. But the Know Nothings also made a more rational appeal to so broad a spectrum of the population that they saw themselves supplanting the Democrats as the great national party while the opposition shriveled up as the sectional party of the South.

The old Whigs in the cities, North and South, formed the foundation of American party ranks. But many Democrats, sick of the corruption of their own party machines under leaders who virtually owned the immigrant vote, also welcomed the chance to shift their allegiance. Native-born laborers, fearful of immigrant pressure on their wages; Protestants, alarmed by the increase of adherents of the Papacy; temperance reformers who associated Catholics with grog shops—all seemed eager to join up.

Nor were country contingents lacking, especially in the South. In upland North Carolina, for example, the old Whigs, who hated the Democratic slaveowners, became Know Nothings almost to a man. And even Democratic aristocrats found solid value in the movement. "Foreignism," said Congressman William Smith of Virginia,

brings 500,000 who settle annually in the free states with instincts against slavery, making fifty representatives in ten years to swell the opposition to the South. . . . The effect of Know Nothingism is to turn back the tide of immigration and our highest duty to the South is to discourage immigration.

But the new party won stanch enemies as well, among them the aroused Abraham Lincoln who was slower than most to disown his long Whig allegiance. Lincoln wrote in 1855:

I am not a Know-Nothing. That is certain. How could I be? How can anyone who abhors the oppression of negroes be in favor of degrading classes of white people? Our progress in degeneracy appears to me to be pretty rapid. As a nation, we began by declaring that *'all men are created equal.'* We now practically read it "all men are created equal *except negroes.*" When the Know-Nothings get control, it will read "all men are created equal except negroes *and foreigners and Catholics.*" When it comes to this I should prefer emigrating to some country where they make no pretense of loving liberty—to Russia, for instance, where despostism can be taken pure, without the base alloy of hypocrisy.

Like the two major parties, the American party could not avoid a split over slavery and when, in 1854, its national convention voted to support the Kansas-Nebraska Act, most of its following in the South returned to the Democrats, while many northeastern Know Nothings soon joined the new Republican party.

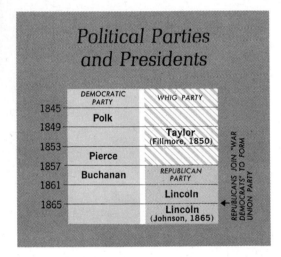

ery was so strong that they had refused to join their party's condemnation of the Wilmot Proviso (see p. 490). Northern Democrats who rejected all further compromise with the South also joined, as did outright Abolitionists, and a considerable number of German immigrants, who might have been deterred by the Know Nothing contingent, but whose opposition to the extension of slavery proved stronger than their distaste for teetotalers and nativists.

Although the Republicans opposed the extension of slavery, it is doubtful that more than a small minority of them had any humanitarian interest in the well-being of the Negro. What most Republicans wanted was free soil, not freed slaves; the welfare of the common white man, rather than the advancement of the black.

## II   *Buchanan's Ordeal*

### THE ELECTION OF 1856

Franklin Pierce actively sought renomination for the Presidency in 1856, and to improve his chances as the conventions approached he made complaisant gestures toward the South, as we have seen, in Kansas as well as Cuba. These backfired, however, and even many southern Democrats no longer could stomach his incompetence. Democratic leaders, at the same time, dared not nominate Douglas, whose successes, as in the adoption of the Kansas-Nebraska Act, proved even more damaging to the party than Pierce's failures. Instead they named a veteran of 40 inconsequential years in politics, the conservative Pennsylvanian, James Buchanan, who as minister to Britain, had been out of the country and distant from the party squabbles of Pierce's administration.

"Old Buck" was soon to be despised as a "Doughface," a northern man with southern principles. Temperamentally unsuited for leadership in a time of crisis, he was never-

The Republican party came into being almost spontaneously in 1854. It has numerous alleged "birthplaces," but no single leader or group can claim sole credit for its organization. One firm principle brought its members together: the determination to keep slavery out of the territories and the conviction that Congress had the right to do so. At the same time, like most other major parties in American history, its composition was mixed. Besides the Know Nothings, Free-soilers, of course, flocked to Republican ranks, as did "conscience Whigs"—those, that is, whose dislike of slav-

theless an honest man and a lover of the Union. The efficient Democratic machine, moreover, brought him home ahead of his Republican opponent, the glamorous soldier-explorer John C. Frémont. The expiring American party's candidate, ex-President Millard Fillmore, finished a poor third.

Although Buchanan won 174 votes in the electoral college, to Frémont's 114 and Fillmore's 8, his popular vote came to only 45 per cent of the ballots cast. Nor did the sectional character of the vote augur well for the country. New England, stung by the Kansas-Nebraska Act and increasingly hostile to slavery, voted overwhelmingly (61.7 per cent) for Frémont. Frémont also won New York. Had he captured Pennsylvania and Illinois, the Republicans would actually have taken the election. Hence what solace the South found in the Democratic victory hardly compensated for the extraordinary Republican show of strength.

### THE CASE OF DRED SCOTT

Buchanan was in office only a few days when faced with the first great crisis of his administration. The trouble arose over the Supreme Court decision in the case of *Dred Scott* v. *Sandford,* which confirmed the southern contention that Congress had no right under the Constitution to exclude slavery from the territories.

Dred Scott, a slave, had been taken by his master in 1834 from Missouri to the free state of Illinois, and from there to the Wisconsin Territory where he stayed until his return to Missouri several years later. The anti-slavery group who backed his suit for freedom hoped to prove that Dred Scott's sojourn in free Illinois and in a territory where slavery was illegal under the Missouri Compromise had made him a free man. Scott lost his suit in the Missouri Supreme Court. His ownership, meanwhile, had passed into the hands of a New York citizen named Sandford, against whom Scott brought suit for his freedom in the United States Circuit Court. The case had

been taken out of the Missouri courts and into the federal courts on the constitutional ground that it was an action between citizens of different states.

The *Dred Scott* case finally reached the Supreme Court in May 1856 and was decided March 6, 1857. The justices might simply have dismissed it on the grounds that Scott was not a citizen of Missouri or of the United States and hence was not entitled to sue in the federal court. Or, falling back on an earlier Supreme Court decision, *Strader* v. *Graham* (1850), they might have ruled that Scott's residence in a free state only suspended his slave status temporarily. But the Court knew that Buchanan was expecting it to resolve the thorny issue of the status of slavery in the territories, with which neither the executive nor legislative departments had had any success. Buchanan had even gone so far as to indicate his expectation to Justices Catron and Grier while the case was pending; and on receiving their agreement, he had stated in his inaugural address two days before the decision: The issue of slavery in Kansas "is a judicial decision which legitimately belongs to the Supreme Court of the United States before whom it is now pending, and will, it is understood, be speedily and finally settled."

No fewer than eight of the nine justices on the Supreme Court wrote separate opinions on different aspects of the *Dred Scott* case. In speaking for the Court for more than two hours, Chief Justice Taney spent half his time arguing that since Negroes had been viewed as inferior at the time the Constitution was adopted, its framers did not intend to include them within the meaning of the term "citizens." Therefore, the right of citizens of different states to sue in the federal courts could *never* apply to a former slave or descendant of a slave. Only two justices would concur in Taney's rank racial concepts and *ex parte* perversions of history. These two and four others joined Taney in finding that Scott, even had he become free, had reverted to slavery on his return to the slave state of Missouri under whose laws his status was to be determined. By those laws he was a slave; because he was a slave and not a citizen, he had no right to sue in a federal court.

Five justices joined the Chief Justice in plunging further. The slave, they said, is property, pure and simple. According to the Fifth Amendment to the Constitution, "No person shall be . . . deprived of life, liberty, or property without due process of law." The prohibition against taking slave property into the territories they found to be a violation of this clause. "No word can be found in the Constitution," Taney observed, "which gives Congress a greater power over slave property, or which entitles property of that kind to less protection than property of any other description." Thus Congress had no right under the Constitution to exclude slavery from the territories and the Missouri Compromise was, and always had been, unconstitutional.

The Kansas-Nebraska Act, as we have seen (p. 563), had already declared the Missouri Compromise "inoperative and void." If, as the Court now held, the attempt of the Compromise to legislate slavery out of the territories was also unconstituional, then the fundamental objective for which the Republican party had been formed was unconstitutional. Even the Douglas Democrats were troubled about the decision. They saw that if Congress did not have the power to exclude slavery from the territories, then neither did any territorial legislature which existed by congressional authorization, and Douglas's program for "popular sovereignty" in the territories was dead.

Buchanan had been so confident of this agreeable settlement that he had gone on to say of the Court in his inaugural: "To their decision, in common with all good citizens, I shall cheerfully submit." But the New York *Tribune* accurately reflected northern opinion in its response to the President: "You may 'cheerfully submit,' of course, you will . . . But no man who really desires the triumph of Freedom over Slavery in the Territories will do so. . . . Happily this is a country in which the People make both laws and Judges, and

they will try their strength on the issue here presented."

In June 1857, as part of his continuing campaign against Douglas's "popular sovereignty" position, Lincoln said of the *Dred Scott* decision:

> If this important decision had been made by the unanimous concurrence of the judges, and without any partisan bias, and . . . had been in no part, based on assumed historical facts which are not really true; or, if . . . it had been before the court more than once, and had there been affirmed and re-affirmed through a course of years, it then might be, perhaps would be, factious, nay, even revolutionary, to not acquiesce in it as a precedent.
>
> But when, as it is true, we find it wanting in all these claims to the public confidence, it is not resistance, it is not factious, it is not even disrespectful, to treat it as not having yet quite established a settled doctrine for the country.

### THE SECTIONAL RIFT WIDENS

The baleful issue of slavery in the territories was most comprehensively examined during the contest for the Illinois senatorial seat in 1858. In July that year, the rising Republican candidate, Abraham Lincoln, challenged his Democratic opponent, "the little giant," Stephen A. Douglas, to a series of joint debates. Before the Lincoln-Douglas debates began, however, two events in 1857 and 1858 soured the hopes of the South as much as the *Dred Scott* decision had sweetened them.

The first of these events was the business panic of August 1857 (see p. 554). The sudden collapse of the free economy did allow southern spokesmen to point with pride to the apparent stability and success of the slave system. But the depression following the actual panic aligned all the more strongly with the antislavery Republican party (1) free businessmen (and the workers they employed), who favored the Republican plank for high tariffs to stimulate free industry and industrial employment; and (2) free farmers,

571

who endorsed the Republican plank for free homesteads. Southern planters, as fearful of high tariffs and free land as of the Republican party itself, thus grew all the more determined to preserve for their section, if only for political advantage, all the western territories not yet lost to slavery.

The second event was the state constitutional convention at Lecompton, Kansas, in October 1857. Here, proslavery delegates named in a rigged election not only wrote a constitution explicitly guaranteeing slavery, but prudently, from their point of view, refused to permit the electorate as a whole to vote on it. Under severe pressure they did offer the electorate a proposition which restricted the entry of new slaves but which protected slave property already in the state. The dominant antislavery voters abstained from balloting on this proposition and the proslavery party thereby carried it.

Governor Robert J. Walker, a Buchanan appointee, presented the President himself with the demand that all Kansas be allowed in an honest election to vote on the Lecompton Constitution. But Buchanan, leaning heavily in the direction of southern Democratic strength, affirmed the validity of the vote on the slavery proposition and the validity of the constitution as well, and laid the latter before Congress as the document on which admission of Kansas as a state should be determined. Walker immediately resigned. Senator Douglas fought the entry of Kansas on Buchanan's terms, but the bill accepting the Lecompton Constitution won in the Senate. In the House, however, "Douglas Democrats" in favor of honest "popular sovereignty" joined with Republican congressmen to defeat it.

The stalemate was broken in May 1858, when Congress passed the English Bill, which would give Kansas statehood immediately together with a federal land grant should her voters decide to accept the Lecompton Contitution, or which would continue territorial status should they reject it. Given the chance, Kansans overwhelmingly rejected the Lecompton Constitution, 11,812 to 1926. Here the matter rested until 1861, when Kansas entered the Union as a free state.

## THE LINCOLN-DOUGLAS DEBATES

The Illinois state Republican convention that was to nominate Lincoln as its senatorial candidate to run against Douglas met in Springfield on June 16, 1858. Here is how Lincoln described himself about this time: "It may be said I am, in height, six feet four inches, nearly; lean in flesh, weighing on average one hundred and eighty pounds; dark complexion, with coarse black hair and gray eyes. No other marks or brands recollected." Lincoln was clean-shaven during this period. His lank frame, careless dress, and seamed yet sensitive face were not so well known as they soon would be, but in Illinois he was already a popular figure, a prosperous lawyer and Whig leader who had served a term in the United States House of Representatives. In his speech accepting the senatorial nomination, he observed that the slavery issue had grown worse each year. "In my opinion," he said, "it will not cease until a crisis shall have been reached and passed. 'A house divided against itself cannot stand.'"

This address, subsequently known as the "House Divided" speech, was carefully studied by Senator Douglas and furnished the basis for his attacks against Lincoln in the seven Lincoln-Douglas debates that followed. Douglas, who admired Lincoln personally, stigmatized him during the debates as a sectionalist whose "house divided" philosophy would end in "a war of extermination." Why, Douglas asked, did the Republicans say that slavery and freedom could not peaceably coexist? Lincoln replied that his party did not propose to interfere with slavery where it existed, nor did he wish to enforce social equality between black and white, as Douglas alleged. But, in keeping with the Republican program, he flatly opposed any further extension of slavery.

In the debate at Freeport, Illinois, Lincoln

asked Douglas a momentous question: "Can the people of a United States territory, in any lawful way, against the wish of any citizen of the United States, exclude slavery from its limits prior to the formation of a State constitution?" To answer this question, Douglas either had to abandon his popular sovereignty concept or defy the *Dred Scott* decision. If the people could not exclude slavery, popular sovereignty meant little. If they could exclude it, popular sovereignty was as much in conflict with the *Dred Scott* decision as the Republican principle of congressional exclusion. Douglas answered that the people of a territory could take this step, in spite of the *Dred Scott* decision. Slavery could not exist for a day, he explained, if the local legislature did not pass the necessary laws to protect and police slave property. Therefore, merely by failing to arrange for slavery, a territorial legislature, without formally barring it, could make its existence impossible.

Douglas's realistic answer broadened the opposition to him in the South, and widened the split in the Democratic party, as Lincoln had expetced. Douglas won the senatorial election in the state legislature despite Lincoln's popular plurality, since inequalities in apportionment permitted Douglas men to dominate. But the war between Douglas and Buchanan's administration left the Democratic party more divided than ever.

### JOHN BROWN'S RAID

The most portentous event in the sectional struggle was John Brown's raid on the federal arsenal at Harpers Ferry, Virginia, Sunday, October 16, 1859. Brown and his 17 men actually captured the arsenal with millions of dollars worth of arms, and that night he sent a detachment to take nearby planters, with some of their slaves, as hostages. This mission ac-

*Abraham Lincoln at 50, on the eve of becoming President. (Library of Congress.)*

574

complished, he awaited news of the slave uprisings he hoped would follow. "When I strike the bees will swarm," Brown had told Frederick Douglass and others.

By dawn, Monday, instead, news of his own exploit had spread across the countryside and hastily gathered militia counterattacked. Dangerfield Newby, a free Negro—his wife and seven children still slaves in Virginia—was the first of Brown's raiders to die. Brown's two sons also were mortally wounded that day, along with others. Before the day ended, Brown and his survivors had been trapped in the arsenal. Exaggerated stories of the adventure by now reached Washington, and Buchanan quickly ordered the nearest federal troops to the scene. He also dispatched Colonel Robert E. Lee and Lieutenant J.E.B. Stuart from the capital to take charge, Lee being placed in command. On Tuesday, October 18, having rejected Brown's truce terms, Stuart led the attack on the arsenal and soon regained it, taking Brown and five others prisoners, leaving ten of Brown's men dead.

Eminent northern reformers, while they did not incite Brown to violence, had known of his project and provided him with money and weapons, ostensibly intended for antislavery partisans in Kansas. Such collaboration only aggravated the fury of the reaction in the South where, at some other time, Brown's exploit might have been passed off as the act of an unbalanced mind. Throughout the South, instead, vigilante groups now beat up and banished anyone who was suspected of antislavery sympathies, and dangerous books were publicly burned. Governor Wise of Virginia did nothing to calm the excitement in his state. In New York, Boston, and elsewhere, meanwhile, huge meetings organized by northern conservatives attacked Brown and his methods. Seward, Lincoln, Douglas—men of all parties—joined in the condemnation. But when Wise rejected the plea of Brown's relatives and friends that the raider was insane and ordered him hanged, he insured Brown's martyrdom. Brown's bravery and dignity on

the scaffold touched millions of people who had abhorred his deeds.

Now, if it is deemed necessary that I should forfeit my life for the furtherance of the ends of justice, and mingle my blood further with the blood of my children and with the blood of millions in this slave country whose rights are disregarded by wicked, cruel, and unjust enactments, I say, let it be done.

So spoke John Brown. His demeanor prompted one conservative New Yorker to confide in his journal: "One's faith in anything is terribly shaken by anybody who is ready to go to the gallows condemning and denouncing it." The deification of John Brown that followed was partly the work of American writers like Emerson and Thoreau, who converted a brave monomaniac into an "angel of light." After the execution, as Thoreau observed, John Brown became "more alive than ever he was."

By convincing many in the South that the entire North was implacably hostile to slavery, the John Brown episode weakened further the frayed ties that held North and South together. "I have always been a fervid Union man," wrote a North Carolinian shortly after Brown was hanged, "but I confess the endorsement of the Harpers Ferry outrage . . . has shaken my fidelity and . . . I am willing to take the chances of every probable evil that may arise from disunion, sooner than submit any longer to Northern insolence and Northern outrage."

## III  *No Compromise*

### LINCOLN'S ELECTION

The months before the presidential campaign of 1860 were packed with dramatic incidents, political and otherwise. In 1859, a few American intellectuals were reading a disturb-

*The John Brown legend persisted into the twentieth century, inspiring such works as Stephen Vincent Benet's Pulitzer prize-winning* John Brown's Body *and this work,* John Brown Going to His Hanging *done by the Negro folk artist Horace Pippin in 1930 (Pennsylvania Academy of Fine Arts.)*

ing book by an English naturalist named Charles Darwin (*The Origin of Species*), which showed how new species had been evolved by natural selection rather than by special acts of God. Ordinary people were absorbed in such matters as the visit by a delegation from Japan (celebrated in verse by Walt Whitman), an Anglo-American prize fight that was stopped in the 37th round, the docking of a new British "Leviathan," *Great Eastern,* the arrival of the Prince of Wales, and the collapse of a factory in Lawrence, Massachusetts, which killed or injured hundreds of workers. But politics overshadowed all other concerns as Republicans and southern Democrats sought to capture the speakership of the House for their respective parties. In the contest, some congressmen rose to speak armed with pistols as protection against attack.

In April 1860 the Democratic national convention assembled at Charleston, South Carolina, the very heartland of secession sentiment. Southern extremists had resolved to insist on a plank in the party platform declaring that neither Congress nor a territorial government could abolish slavery or impair the right to own slaves. Northern Democrats, hoping to nominate Douglas, without irretrievably alienating the Southerners, were willing to accept the ruling of the Supreme Court in the *Dred Scott* case; but they were equally firm for popular sovereignty. "We cannot recede from this doctrine," a spokesman for Douglas in-

EIGHTEEN *A Decade of Failure*

sisted, "without personal dishonor, and so help us God, we never will abandon this principle." When it became evident that the plank advocating federal protection of slavery in the territories could not be adopted, most of the delegates from eight southern states withdrew. Their departure made it impossible for Douglas to get the two-thirds of the ballots needed to win the nomination, and the convention adjourned.

On June 18 the Democrats reconvened in Baltimore. When the southern delegates bolted once more, this convention went ahead to nominate Douglas on a popular-sovereignty platform. The southerners then met independently in Baltimore on June 28 and chose John C. Breckinridge of Kentucky, himself a moderate, to represent their position on slavery in the territories. With two Democrats in the field, the last unionist bond—a great political party with large followings in both North and South—had broken.

The Republicans, buoyed up by the Democratic fiasco at Charleston, met in Chicago on May 16. Their most impressive leader was William H. Seward of New York. But Seward had a perhaps undeserved reputation as an extremist because he once had spoken of the "irrepressible conflict" between North and South. The unsavory reputation of his backer, the political boss Thurlow Weed, and the rowdy actions of Weed's henchmen at the convention, also handicapped him. Two other possibilities were Salmon P. Chase of Ohio and Edward Bates of Missouri. The former's reputation for radicalism exceeded even Seward's, the latter's flirtation with the Know Nothings had alienated the German vote. The disabilities of these favored candidates opened the way for Abraham Lincoln, strongly supported by the powerful Illinois and Indiana delegations and acceptable to both East and West. Six weeks before the convention Lincoln had written to a friend: "My name is now in the field; and I suppose I am not the *first* choice of a very great many. Our policy, then is to give no offense to others—leave them in a mood to come to us, if they shall

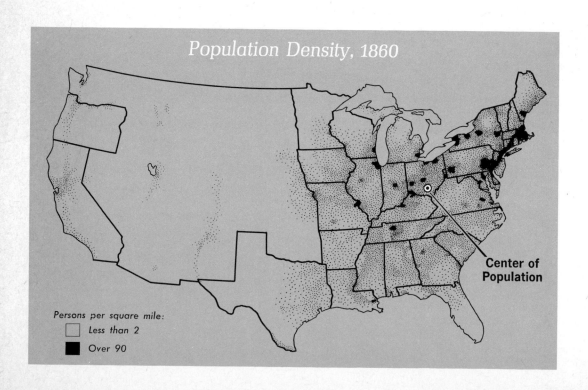

Population Density, 1860

Center of Population

Persons per square mile:
Less than 2
Over 90

be impelled to give up their first love." This strategy paid off when the Pennsylvania and Ohio delegations threw their strength to Lincoln instead of Seward, and on May 18 Lincoln was nominated.

The Republican platform made a shrewd appeal to powerful economic interests and at the same time sounded a high moral tone. It included planks for a protective tariff, free homesteads, a Pacific railroad, and the rights of immigrants. "The normal condition of all the territory of the United States," it said, "is that of freedom, . . . and we deny the authority of Congress, of a territorial legislature, or of any individuals, to give legal existence to slavery in any territory of the United States." Practical politicians knew that to win the election, Pennsylvania and either Illinois or Indiana would have to go Republican. The tariff was a bid to the iron interests in Pennsylvania; Abraham Lincoln was a lure to the Indiana Hoosiers and the men of Illinois. But a resolution (passed over powerful conservative opposition) calling for a reaffirmation of the Declaration of Independence indicated the idealism of the rank-and-file Republicans if not of the convention managers.

The campaign was further complicated by the nomination of a fourth-party candidate a few weeks before Lincoln's victory at Chicago. On May 9, the Constitutional Union party assembled in Baltimore. This new party, composed of the conservative remnants of defunct parties, appealed only to fading loyalties, especially among old-line Whigs in the border states. It chose John Bell of Tennessee for President and Edward Everett of Massachusetts as his running-mate. The Union party called upon the people "to recognize no political principle other than the Constitution of the country, the Union of the states, and the enforcement of the laws."

The 1860 election presented the remarkable picture of a divided nation simultaneously carrying out two separate contests for a single office: one between Breckinridge and Bell in the South, the other between Lincoln and

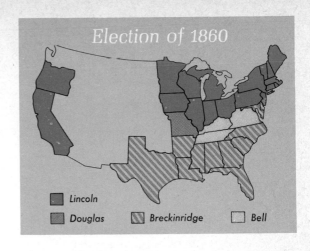

Election of 1860

Lincoln
Douglas
Breckinridge
Bell

Douglas in the North. Ten southern states did not even place Lincoln's name on the ballot. Of his 1,866,000 popular votes, Lincoln won a meager 26,000 in the entire South. Douglas, although acknowledged as a candidate, also ran poorly there. In the North, at the same time, Breckinridge, the other Democrat, and Bell, the Constitutional Unionist, made no headway. Only in Missouri, California, and Oregon could the election be described as a contest between more than two of the four parties. In Missouri, where Douglas won by a bare 140 ballots, all four candidates ran pretty evenly. Douglas and Breckinridge also made good showings in the Pacific states. Lincoln carried California by 643 and Oregon by 264 out of 119,000 and 13,000 votes respectively.

Although sectional loyalties proved decisive in the 1860 election, the significance of the unionist vote in the South must not be overlooked. Bell won Kentucky, Tennessee, and Virginia; he barely lost Maryland and Missouri. Breckinridge had a clear majority in only seven southern states and in his sole campaign speech flatly denied that he was a disunionist or had any disunionist connections. Nevertheless, although Lincoln had a decisive majority in the electoral college, he carried less than 40 per cent of the popular vote, and none could deny that a sectional candidate had become President of the United States.

# CHARLESTON MERCURY

## EXTRA:

Passed unanimously at 1.15 o'clock, P. M., December 20th, 1860.

### AN ORDINANCE

*To dissolve the Union between the State of South Carolina and other States united with her under the compact entitled " The Constitution of the United States of America."*

We, the People of the State of South Carolina, in Convention assembled, do declare and ordain, and it is hereby declared and ordained,

That the Ordinance adopted by us in Convention, on the twenty-third day of May, in the year of our Lord one thousand seven hundred and eighty-eight, whereby the Constitution of the United States of America was ratified, and also, all Acts and parts of Acts of the General Assembly of this State, ratifying amendments of the said Constitution, are hereby repealed; and that the union now subsisting between South Carolina and other States, under the name of " The United States of America," is hereby dissolved.

# THE UNION IS DISSOLVED!

*Broadside issued by the* Charleston Mercury *at the moment the secession decision was made. (The Granger Collection.)*

## THE DEEP SOUTH MOVES OUT

Southern leaders had repeatedly warned after Lincoln's nomination that a Republican victory would be followed by secession—for,

as the governor of South Carolina put it, the election of a sectional northern candidate would "inevitably destroy our equality in the Union, and ultimately reduce the Southern states to mere provinces of a consolidated despotism, to be governed by a fixed majority in Congress hostile to our institutions and fatally bent upon our ruin."

These expectations perhaps supply the best answer to the question, Why did the South move out? During the 1850s, three free states —California, Minnesota, and Oregon—had been added to the Union, but no slave state had come in. The North, growing visibly and rapidly in wealth and population, had also linked itself firmly with the West by railroad connections. It was winning the new territory. Would it not ultimately become strong enough to act directly against slavery and destroy the civilization of the Old South.

An informed southerner could hardly have imagined that the election of Lincoln would lead to immediate abolition in states where slavery had always been legal. Lincoln denied any such intention. His party, moreover, controlled neither the Senate nor the Supreme Court, which was still composed, as in the days of the *Dred Scott* case, of five southern and four northern justices. Many southerners, of course, were not well informed and looked upon Lincoln as nothing but "the daring and reckless leader of Abolitionists." To understand secession, it is also important to understand that, aside from its more profound motivations, few men in the South anticipated its melancholy aftermath. It was by no means certain that the North would go to war to keep a reluctant South in an unhappy Union. The old South Carolina nullifier, Robert Barnwell Rhett, told a Charleston audience that if secession produced a war, he would eat the bodies of all who were slain in the struggle. And if war came, why should not the South win, and quickly? Many southerners imagined that the will to fight in the crass commercial civilization of the North would be weak. For success they also looked to the sympathy of foreign aristocrats, the commercial power of "King Cotton," and to pro-southerners in the North who would sap its spirit.

Secession also had positive lures. No longer would the South be drained of its resources by paying taxes and tariffs that chiefly benefited the North. No longer would it pay tribute to northern banking and shipping interests. Perhaps the slave trade would be reopened and more cheap labor brought in. Cuba, Santa Domingo, Mexico, even territories in Central America, beckoned enterprising planters.

On December 20, 1860, South Carolina at last took the initiative to bring such thinking to fruition. A convention formally repealed the state's ratification of the Constitution and withdrew from the Union. By February 1, 1861, six other commonwealths—Mississippi, Florida, Alabama, Georgia, Louisiana, and Texas—had reluctantly followed her example. In almost every case, even in the deep South, the momentous step was taken over articulate

opposition ready to give Lincoln a chance to show whether he would really enforce the Fugitive Slave Act and meet other southern demands.

Perhaps the most important debate took place in Georgia, whose wealth, geographical position, western connections, and railroad communications made her allegiance essential to the secessionist cause. In men like Herschel V. Johnson, Benjamin H. Hill, and Alexander H. Stephens, the Georgia moderates had able spokesmen; and in the northern hill country and pine-barren areas, inhabited by small farmers and stock-raisers, unionist sentiment was strong. But the rich cotton-planters in the Savannah River Valley and the urban Georgians led by such extremists as Senator Robert Toombs, Governor Joseph E. Brown, and Howell Cobb carried the day. Secessionist delegates at the state convention defeated by a vote of 164 to 133 the proposal to postpone action until a convention of slave-holding states had presented southern demands to the

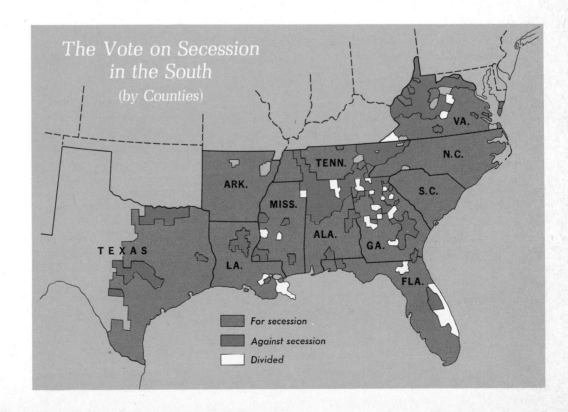

### The Vote on Secession in the South
(by Counties)

VA.

N.C.

TENN.

ARK.

S.C.

MISS.

ALA.

GA.

TEXAS

LA.

FLA.

☐ For secession
☐ Against secession
☐ Divided

580

North. Fatalistically accepting defeat, a number of moderates then voted with the secessionists to take Georgia out of the Union, January 19, 1861.

As in Georgia, cooperationist sentiment in Alabama centered in the relatively slaveless sections in the northern counties. Secessionists in the state convention outnumbered the unionists 54 to 46, thus assuring secession on January 11, 1861, but 33 of the delegates refused to sign the secession ordinance without a state plebiscite and blamed the extremists for refusing to consult with other southern states before voting.

Unionism had strong advocates in both Louisiana and Texas, but here, too, the disunionists cleverly circumvented the opposition. Even though secession went against the best interests of the Louisiana sugar planters (who benefited from tariff protection) and the New Orleans merchants (who traded with the North), the voters elected a majority of pro-secession delegates to the state convention. Cooperationist delegates, representing for the most part the small farmers, lost their plea to submit the secession ordinance to the electorate by a vote of 84 to 33. In Texas, Governor Sam Houston—an uncompromising unionist—blocked secession efforts for a while by refusing to call the legislature into session. "You may," he warned a Galveston crowd, "after the sacrifice of countless thousands of treasure and hundreds of thousands of precious lives, as a bare possibility, win Southern independence, if God be not against you; but I doubt it." This was a brave stand, but the disunionists nevertheless forced Houston to call a state convention. Houston's unionist followers boycotted the meeting, which, without them, voted to submit the secession ordinance to a plebiscite, the only one held in the lower South. In this dramatic test the secessionists carried the ordinance by a smashing majority of more than three to one.

Pockets of unionism persisted in the lower South. Yet by the spring of 1861 the majority of southerners of all classes appeared ready to secede. Older men naturally were more cautious about making the break. "It was disgusting to me," wrote an Alabama father to his secessionist son, "to think that I had Raised a child that would Cecede from under the government that he was born and raised under. . . . Tha have got you puft up with Cecessionism as tight as a tode I dont See what you nede to Care for you hant got no Slaves." His son replied as most young firebrands would: "Henry Bell Is my Name and fite I will before I will submit to black republican princibles lose my life I will first."

On February 4, 1861, with seven states having seceded, but with Texas absent, delegates from six states met at Montgomery, Alabama, to form a new government, which they called the Confederate States of America, to adopt a new flag, the "Stars and Bars," and to write a new constitution.

## A FEDERAL VACUUM

Secession, which had begun promptly with Lincoln's victory, took place while Buchanan was still in the White House. Thus, at the moment of greatest urgency, the country had a "lame-duck" president, one without the will or the power to make commitments. Although Buchanan declared that secession was unconstitutional, he also argued that Congress had no power under the Constitution to prevent it!

While Buchanan talked of conciliation, others sought to do something about it. Significantly, the two main compromise efforts came from the border states, where men knew that if secession were followed by war their land would become a battleground.

The most seriously considered of the compromise proposals was the Crittenden Plan, drawn up on December 18, 1860, two days before South Carolina's formal departure from the Union. This plan, put forward by Senator John J. Crittenden of Kentucky, offered these constitutional amendments: (1) Slavery was to be barred in the territories north of the line 36° 30′. (2) But it was to be established and maintained under federal protection every-

*"The inauguration of the Hon. Jefferson Davis as President of the provisional government of the new Southern Confederacy of America" at Montgomery, Alabama, on February 18, 1861; as depicted in an English newspaper. (The Granger Collection.)*

where south of that line. (3) Future states were to come in as they wished, slave or free. (4) The Fugitive Slave Law was to be enforced, and compensation paid by the federal government when enforcement failed because of the action of northerners. (5) The Constitution was never to be amended so as to authorize Congress to interfere with slavery in any state or the District of Columbia.

This comprehensive program failed to win either northern or southern support. Southern leaders would not accept it unless it was endorsed by the Republican party. Lincoln himself, though he favored enforcement of the Fugitive Slave Law and would accept an amendment protecting slavery where it then existed, was wholly opposed to any compromise on the exclusion of slavery from the territories. To a friend in Congress he wrote: "Entertain no proposition for a compromise in regard to the extension of slavery. The in-

stant you do they have us under again: all our labor is lost, and sooner or later must be done over."

The second compromise effort was made by Virginia. On the very day the Confederacy was being organized in Montgomery, Alabama —February 4, 1861—a peace convention called by Virginia assembled in Washington itself. Twenty-one states, free and slave, dutifully sent representatives, but the best they could offer were the discredited Crittenden proposals.

## IV  *The Final Failure*

### LINCOLN'S INAUGURAL

When, on March 4, 1861, Abraham Lincoln stood up to take the oath of office, secession

581

582

was an accomplished fact. A Southern Confederacy had been formed and important federal properties had fallen into the hands of rebel states. Yet a far greater territory than the then existing Confederacy remained very much at issue. The upper South—Virginia, Maryland, North Carolina, even Delaware— was riven by conflict as individuals, families, neighborhoods, and entire regions wrestled with their awful alternatives. Farther west, in the more authentic border states of Tennessee, Kentucky, Arkansas, and Missouri, genuine battles were fought before allegiance to the North or the South could be established. In all these states the President's inaugural address had been almost too long awaited, and his words when received were pounced upon like Nevada nuggets and minutely assayed for their true value.

Early in his oration Lincoln stressed the perpetuity of "the more perfect Union" established by the Constitution, and then followed his sharpest words to the rebels:

It follows from these views that no State upon its own mere motion can lawfully get out of the Union; that resolves and ordinances to that effect are legally void; and that acts of violence, within any State or States, against the authority of the United States, are insurrectionary or revolutionary, according to circumstance.

"The mails, unless repelled," Lincoln declared, "will continue to be furnished in all parts of the Union. So far as possible, the people everywhere shall have that sense of perfect security which is most favorable to calm thought and reflection."

The President was as conciliatory as his office and his nature allowed. He had, he said, neither the right nor the inclination "to interfere with the institution of slavery in the States where it exists." As Chief Executive, he was bound to enforce federal regulations, including those requiring the return of fugitive slaves, in all the states. He even went so far as to say that he had no objections to a proposed constitutional amendment guaranteeing that "the Federal Government shall never

interfere with the domestic institutions of the States"—including slavery. Other constitutional obligations, which "I deem to be only a simple duty on my part," required that he "hold, occupy, and possess the property and places belonging to the Government, and to collect the duties and imposts" in every American port. But in performing these acts, "there needs be no bloodshed or violence; and there shall be none, unless it be forced upon the national authority."

In your hands, my dissatisfied fellow-countrymen, and not in mine [Lincoln reminded the intransigents near the end of his address], is the momentous issue of civil war. The government will not assail you. You can have no conflict, without being yourselves the aggressors. You have no oath registered in Heaven to destroy the government, while I shall have the most solemn one to "preserve, protect, and defend" it.

But Lincoln could not stop on a note of iron, and added this famous, eloquent paragraph:

I am loath to close. We are not enemies, but friends. We must not be enemies. Though passion may have strained, it must not break, our bonds of affection. The mystic chords of memory, stretching from every battlefield and patriot grave to every living heart and hearthstone all over this broad land, will yet swell the chorus of the Union when again touched, as surely they will be, by the better angels of our nature.

Few if any inaugural orations in our history bore the burden of Lincoln's first. Few if any played so deliberately for time. In the terrible economic crisis of 1933, Franklin D. Roosevelt caught the public mood when he declared in *his* inaugural address, "In their need [the people of the United States] have registered a mandate that they want direct, vigorous action." But Lincoln, though pressed by zealots of every political creed, electrified the nation by putting action off:

My countrymen, one and all, think calmly and well upon this whole subject. Nothing valuable can be lost by taking time. If there be an object to hurry any of you in hot haste to a step which you would never take deliberately, that object will be frustrated by taking time; but no good object can be frustrated by it.

### SUMTER FALLS

And yet there was action, precipitate action indeed, required of the President himself. One of his most urgent problems was what to do about "occupying and possessing" federal forts on Confederate soil, notably the garrison under Major Robert Anderson at Fort Sumter in Charleston harbor. In a special message of January 8, 1861, Buchanan had refused to recognize the legality of secession and had threatened to meet with force any effort to obstruct federal authorities or to seize federal property. Undaunted, South Carolina fired on a federal ship as it attempted to land supplies, men, and arms at Fort Sumter on January 9. The vessel returned without completing its mission, and Buchanan made no reprisal. In the next two months, the Confederacy had seized federal forts, post offices, and customhouses throughout the South, leaving under federal control only Fort Sumter and three other forts off the cost of Florida. On March 5, the day after Lincoln's inauguration, he was given a letter from Major Anderson, reporting that Fort Sumter could be held only with the immediate aid of 20,000 men, a large naval force, and ample provisions.

Anderson, in effect, recommended evacuation. But if Lincoln retreated, as his Secretary of State, Seward, and his military advisers suggested, he would have taken the first step toward recognizing the power if not the legality of the Confederacy. If, on the other hand, he attempted by force to strengthen Sumter, he would risk blood-letting and would appear as the aggressor. Sensing that there would be popular support for forcing a decision, the President took action that involved neither of these alternatives. He undertook to provision Fort Sumter peacefully, and notified the South Carolina authorities that he had dispatched an expedition carrying supplies for this purpose. "If such attempt be not resisted," he wrote Governor Pickens, "no effort to throw

in men, arms, or ammunition will be made without further notice, or in case of an attack upon the Fort."

Lincoln's decision shifted the burden to Confederate authorities. If they permitted Sumter to be provisioned, the fort would stand indefinitely in the mouth of one of their few good harbors, a threat to their prestige throughout the world. If they attacked a peaceful expedition bringing food, *they* would have fired the first shot.

When requested by the southern general, Pierre G. T. Beauregard, to surrender Sumter before the supply ships arrived, Major Anderson promised to evacuate by April 15, unless he was relieved or ordered to remain. But the Confederates dared not risk so long a delay. They gave Anderson until 4 A.M. April 12 to capitulate. At 4:30 A.M. the batteries on the Charleston shore began their 34-hour bombardment. Lincoln's provisioning flotilla lay in the vicinity of the fight, but without the support of *Powhatan,* the navy's most powerful warship, which had failed to escort the supply vessels as a result of official bungling, no provisions could be landed. When Anderson at last ran down the flag on the afternoon of April 13, Sumter was virtually consumed in flames and her ammunition gone. Only then did the federal ships approach, with Confederate permission, to take off the defenders. Remarkably, not a man had been hit on either side during the engagement. But a war that was to overshadow even Napoleon's campaigns in casualties had begun.

Before Sumter, northern opinion had divided sharply on the proper response to secession. Radical abolitionists like Garrison, Phillips, and the poet John Greenleaf Whittier thought that it would be futile to enforce union "where one section is pinned to the residue by bayonets." For once, the business community, still suffering the effects of the Panic of 1857 and concerned over collecting southern debts and holding southern markets, fully agreed with abolitionist policy to let the "erring sisters go in peace." Bellicose northerners, on the other hand, spoke early and often. "If South Carolina is determined

584

upon secession," warned *The New York Times,* "she should take the plunge with her eyes open. She must face the consequences—and among them all, the most unquestionable is war . . . there is no possibility of escaping it." Once the plunge had been taken, many northern newspapers advocated immediate coercive action and threatened the South with the "full power of government." "Artful politicians—rich merchants and speculators, whose god is money, will counsel peace, regardless of principle," wrote one constituent to his congressman. "See that you yield not to their solicitation."

Detestation of disunion was especially widespread in the Northwest, where freedom for white men on the land was the very watchword of the Lord, and the free use of the Mississippi from its source in Minnesota to its mouth below New Orleans the foundation of economic life. No section uttered "Amen" more appreciatively to Lincoln's March 4 dictum, "Physically speaking, we cannot separate." After Sumter, peace partisans still were heard here and there in the North. But with the Confederacy branded before the world as the aggressor, it became easier than before to portray hostilities as a *defense* of the Union. Lincoln's call on April 15 for 75,000 three-month volunteers met with overwhelming response everywhere. Walt Whitman in Manhattan, whose *Drum Taps* establish him as the Union poet of the war, caught the new surge of spirit:

Forty years had I in my city seen soldiers parading,
Forty years as a pageant, till unawares the lady of this teeming turbulent city,
Sleepless amid her ships, her houses, her incalculable wealth,

*Interior view of Fort Sumter as photographed by S.R. Seibert at the time of the Civil War. (Library of Congress.)*

With her million children around her, suddenly,
At dead of night, at news from the south,
Incens'd struck with clinch'd hand the pavement.
A shock electric, the night sustain'd it,
Till with ominous hum our hive at daybreak
    pour'd out its myriads.

From the houses then and the workshops, and
    through all the doorways
Leapt they tumultuous, and lo! Manhattan arming.

### THE UPPER SOUTH
### AND THE BORDER DECIDE

One man who examined Lincoln's inaugural address with consummate care was the Virginia lawyer Jubal Anderson Early, who wrote on the day following the speech:

*Thomas Nast clearly captured the cheering, flag-waving throngs as New York's Seventh Regiment marched down Broadway on April 19, 1861. (The Granger Collection.)*

I do not approve of the inaugural of Mr. Lincoln . . . ; but sir, I ask . . . if it were not for the fact that six or seven states of this Confederacy have seceded from the Union, if the declaration of President Lincoln that he would execute the laws in all the states would not have been hailed throughout the country as a guarantee that he would perform his duty? . . . I ask why it is that we are placed in this perilous condition? And if it is not solely from the action of these states that have seceded from the Union without having consulted our views?

585

Early was not without sympathizers in Virginia. The Old Dominion, with more than 1.5 million people in 1860, was by far the largest and wealthiest of the slave states. On January 14, 1861, her legislature had voted to call a convention on secession; but not even a special delegation from the hot-heads farther south could sway this convention's unionist majority. As late as April 4, the very day Lincoln had decided to provision Sumter with armed support if needed, the Virginia convention rejected a proposition to draw up a secession ordinance by the resounding vote of 88 to 45. Four days later it sent a three-man mission to Lincoln in Washington, searching for grounds of conciliation to the very end.

It is sometimes said that South Carolinians, aware that a Confederacy without Virginia would be a tragic sham, hastened the bombardment of Sumter to force the Old Dominion's hand in taking up arms to defend the South against the expected retaliation from the North. It is also said that Lincoln, to preserve Virginia for the Union, at one point seriously contemplated letting Sumter go. "A State for a fort," he is reported to have told two unofficial visitors from the Virginia convention, "is no bad business." By April 13, however, the time for bargaining had passed. To the official Virginia mission that day, Lincoln declared: "I shall hold myself at liberty to repossess, if I can," all federal forts and stations grasped by the Confederacy. "I shall to the extent of my ability repel force with force."

On April 14, in session with his Cabinet, Lincoln framed the fateful proclamation declaring that "combinations too powerful to be suppressed" by ordinary means existed in the seven Confederate states, and calling "forth the militia of the several States of the Union, to the aggregate number of seventy-five thousand, in order to suppress such combinations." On April 15 this proclamation was received with hosannas throughout the embattled North. Throughout the upper South and the border states it came like the toll of death. Should Virginia and the rest answer the President's call and yield their militia to the Union cause? Should they stand by while the deep South was invaded by southern men and arms?

More than Lincoln's election, more than his inaugural, more even than the attempt to provision Sumter itself, Lincoln's proclamation of April 15 sealed the issue of war and peace. On April 17 the Virginia convention at last passed its ordinance of secession 88 to 55. One week later it leagued the Old Dominion with the Confederacy and put its armed forces at the service of the Stars and Bars. On May 21, the provisional Confederate government named Richmond its permanent capital and prepared to move from Montgomery in June. No one—except Lincoln and the Virginia mountaineers—seemed to care that Virginia law required public approval by referendum of any secession ordinance, and that the people had not yet been heard from. Such a referendum was set for May 23, and on that day Virginians—at least eastern Virginians—did what was expected of them. Only then did the President acknowledge all hope gone: "The people of Virginia have thus allowed this giant insurrection to make its nest within her borders; and this government has no choice left but to deal with it where it finds it." Only then were the federal mails cut off from Confederate routes. Secession was now complete in Virginia, even to the point where the western counties were organizing to secede themselves from the new Confederate state.

On April 19 Lincoln had supplemented his proclamation calling out the militia with an order to the navy to blockade the ports of the first seven Confederate states. On April 27 he extended the blockade to Virginia and North Carolina. The Supreme Court was later to rule that the war legally began with these blockade orders, which officially recognized that a state of "belligerency" existed between two powers. Lincoln himself never accepted this idea; he never recognized the Confederacy as a nation, nor secession as anything but "insurrection."

Virginia ranks among the Confederacy's greatest conquests, one enhanced by the satellites and stragglers that now quickly took the same path. North Carolina's governor declared that his state would not be a party "to this war upon the liberties of a free people," and on May 20 a convention called by the legislature unanimously voted to secede. In Tennessee, the governor and legislature took the state into the Confederacy even before the people ratified this decision on June 8 by a vote of 104,913 to 47,238. Arkansas sharply repudiated Lincoln's request for troops and vowed, in her governor's words, to defend "to the last extremity, their honor, lives, and property, against Northern mendacity and usurpation." In March the Arkansas convention had rejected secession, but on May 6 approved it.

Unionist regions, nevertheless, could still be found in the upper South and on the border. Like the western Virginians, the yeomen of eastern Tennessee would probably have rejoined the Union had Confederate troops not prevented them. Four indecisive slave states, moreover—Kentucky, Missouri, Maryland, and Delaware—were retained by the Union. Maryland's strategic position forced Lincoln to take strong unconstitutional measures against prosouthern agtiators there, and with the show of federal force the secessionist spirit in Maryland subsided. Rich and populous Kentucky maintained a precarious neutrality until September 1861, when the legislature voted to remain loyal to the Union. Kentucky volunteers for the Confederates numbered about 35,000, and approximately 75,000 fought with the Federals. In Missouri the division between prosouthern and pronorthern supporters flared up into a small civil war, but only 20,000 Missourians fought with the South as against 100,000 who joined the Union armies.

# READINGS

The most comprehensive survey of this fateful decade, and excellent reading, is to be found in Allan Nevins, vol. II, *Ordeal of the Union* (2 vols., 1947), and *The Emergence of Lincoln* (2 vols., 1950). A.O. Craven, *The Growth of Southern Nationalism 1848–1861* (1953), and H.C. Hubbart, *The Older Middle West 1840–1880* (1936), are rich in sectional materials. A.C. Cole, *The Irrepressible Conflict 1850–1865* (1934), is illuminating on the social history of the antebellum decade as well as the war years. Craven, *The Coming of the Civil War* (1942), and *Civil War in the Making 1815–1860* (1959); R.F. Nichols, *The Disruption of American Democracy* (1948); H.H. Simms, *A Decade of Sectional Controversy* (1942); and Bruce Catton, *The Coming Fury* (1961), offer differing explanations of the sectional schism. D.L. Dumond, *Anti-Slavery Origins of the Civil War* (1939), is a short and incisive analysis, elaborated by the author in *Anti-Slavery: The Crusade for Freedom in America* (2 vols., 1961). Two general books on the Civil War also discuss events that led up to it: J.G. Randall and David Donald, *The Civil War and Reconstruction* (1961 ed.); and Clement Eaton, *A History of the Southern Confederacy* (1954). Volume VI of Edward Channing, *A History of the United States* (6 vols., 1905–1925); and volumes I and II of J.F. Rhodes, *History of the United States 1850–1877* (7 vols., 1906), should not be neglected because of their age.

American expansionism is the 1850s is thoroughly analyzed in Nevins's *Ordeal* (cited above). Douglas and his ideas are well presented in R.W. Johannsen, ed., *The Letters of Stephen A. Douglas* (1961), and G.M. Capers, *Stephen A. Douglas, Defender of the Union* (1959). Also valuable is Basil Rauch, *American Interest in Cuba 1848–1855* (1948). To Nevins's summary of the Kansas-Nebraska issue should be added two books by J.C. Malin: *John Brown and the Legend of Fifty-Six* (1942) and *The Nebraska Question 1852–1854* (1953). Also important are P.W. Gates, *Fifty Million Acres: Conflicts over Kansas Land Policy 1854–1890* (1954), and C.V. Woodward's essay on John Brown in Daniel Aaron, ed., *America in Crisis* (1952). Edward Stone, ed., *Incident at Harpers Ferry* (1956), is an excellent collection of contemporary material on John Brown's last act. On Brown and others in the rival sections, Arnold Whitbridge, *No Compromise! the Story of the Fanatics Who Paved the Way to the Civil War* (1960), is illuminating.

For parties and politics, the general works cited above are sufficiently detailed, but the following are also recommended: R.F. Nichols, *Franklin Pierce* (1931); P.G. Auchampaugh, *James Buchanan and His Cabinet on the Eve of Secession* (1926); for the Know-Nothing movement, R.A. Billington, *The Protestant Crusade, 1800–1860* (1938), and W.D. Overdyke, *The Know-Nothing Party in the South* (1950); for the background and origins of the Republican party, A.W. Crandall, *The Early History of the Republican Party 1854–1856* (1930); J.A. Isely, *Horace Greeley and the Republican Party 1853–1861* (1947); and M.B. Duberman, *Charles Francis Adams* (1961). David Donald, *Charles Sumner and the Coming of the Civil War* (1950), is an outstanding modern biography. C.B. Swisher, *Roger B. Taney* (1935), is excellent on Dred Scott, as is Nevins's analysis in *Ordeal* (cited above). See also Vincent Hopkins, *Dred Scott's Case* (1951). Valuable background material will be found in Charles Warren, vol. II, *The Supreme Court in United States History* (2 vols., 1922). G.W. Van Vleck, *The Panic of 1857: An Analytical Study* (1943), is good on that crisis.

The story of Lincoln's emergence is well presented in short compass in D.E. Fehren-bacher, *Prelude to Greatness, Lincoln in the 1850's* (1962). See also B.P. Thomas, *Abraham Lincoln* (1952). A.J. Beveridge, *Abraham Lincoln 1809–1858* (2 vols., 1928), and Carl Sandburg, *Abraham Lincoln, the Prairie Years* (1-vol. ed., 1929), are classic studies. The Lincoln-Douglas debates are presented in full in P.M. Angle, ed., *Created Equal* (1958). A stimulating analysis is H.V. Jaffa, *Crisis of the House Divided* (1959). R.H. Luthin, *The First Lincoln Campaign* (1944), is authoritative.

Secession itself is the theme of D.L. Dumond, *The Secession Movement 1860–1861* (1931); U.B. Phillips, *The Course of the South to Secession* (1939); G.H. Knoles, ed., *The Crisis of the Union 1860–1861* (1965); and R.A. Wooster, *The Secession Conventions of the South* (1962). Ollinger Crenshaw, *The Slave States in the Presidential Election of 1860* (1945), adds an important link to the story. For Lincoln's role, see David Potter, *Lincoln and His Party in the Secession Crisis 1860–1861* (1942). K.M. Stampp, *And the War Came: The North and the Secession Crisis 1860–1861* (1950), analyzes the northern position in general. R.N. Current, *Lincoln and the First Shot* (1963), deals in detail with the Sumter alternatives. P.S. Foner, *Business and Slavery: The New York Merchants and the Irrepressible Conflict* (1941), contains useful information. For a private view of the crisis, *The Diary of George Templeton Strong* (4 vols., 1952), splendidly edited by Allan Nevins and M.H. Thomas, is strongly recommended.

# NINETEEN

Beat! beat! drums!—blow! bugles! blow!
Make no parley—stop for no expostulation,
Mind not the timid—mind not the weeper or
prayer,
Mind not the old man beseeching the young
man,
Let not the child's voice be heard, nor the
mother's entreaties,
Make even the trestles to shake the dead
where they lie awaiting the hearses,
So strong you thump O terrible drums—so
loud you bugles blow.
(Walt Whitman, "Beat! Beat! Drums!" 1861)

A Confederate general, writing when the Civil War was over, said: "Aggrieved by the action and tendencies of the Federal Government, and apprehending worse in the future, a majority of the people of the South approved secession as the only remedy suggested by their leaders. So travelers enter railway carriages, and are dragged up grades and through tunnels with utter loss of volition, the motive power, generated by fierce heat, being far in advance and beyond their control."

Secession, whether or not a majority in the South did in fact approve it, led directly to the war. It was not to be so easy to sever the Union as southern leaders might suppose —to tear away a third of its occupied land, to set artificial barriers against the course of its rivers, to defy its sovereign laws, to thwart at one stroke its grand continental aspirations and its great experiment in republican government. The South was not to be allowed to depart in peace. "Beat! beat! drums!—blow! bugles! blow!"

And yet, from the start of the war a pall seemed to lie on both combatants. The Civil

# CIVIL WAR

War became the longest and deadliest war ever fought on this continent. Even some of its earlier engagements were marked by a shockingly high toll in lives. Nevertheless, the war was amazingly slow in gaining direction, agonizingly slow to those on both sides whose most fervent wish was that, once begun, it might soon be over.

And when it was over, little indeed seemed to have been secured by the slaughter. Not that, in the judgment of history, nor even in the judgment of the times, it was in vain. Lincoln made that clear in the Gettysburg Address: "from these honored dead we take increased devotion to that cause for which they gave the last full measure of devotion—that . . . this nation, under God, shall have a new birth of freedom—and that government of the people, by the people, for the people, shall not perish from the earth." The war pointed the way "for us the living," as Lincoln said, to dedicate themselves to "the unfinished work which they who fought here have thus far so nobly advanced." And yet "the living" were to stride but a very short distance forward with this task, and then only to turn back; and their descendants for a century would leave the "unfinished work" untouched.

The war was not soon forgotten in the North; the Republican party itself was to live for generations on Lincoln's and Grant's success. But with the Union forcibly restored, with the land made free not slave, the people of the North resumed, all the more passionately after the four hateful years of delay, the development of the resources of the land which the war had so rudely interrupted. The pursuit of the immense private wealth the land would yield, and the many new problems arising from that pursuit, engrossed their attention, along with the heady progress of their country among the imperial powers of the world.

The people of the South, although checked momentarily by the zeal of Radical Reconstruction, were left freer, by the North's pre-occupations, to retrieve and restore the scattered fragments of their lives. "The Lost Cause" became an inspiration, an eternal light. Surrender need not mean submission. Their own glorious dead might be redeemed. "The Past!" cried Tom Watson of Georgia, a leader of the postwar generation, "There lies our brightest and purest hopes, our best endeavors, our loved and lost. . . . Come back to us once more, Oh dream of the old time South!"

1 *Enemies Face to Face*

### THE QUESTION OF MANPOWER

In April 1861, about 22 million persons lived in loyal states and territories. Nine million (5.5 million whites and 3.5 million Negroes) lived in "Secesh" country. But Union superiority in manpower was not so great as the gross figures suggest.

Half a million persons, scattered from Dakota to California, could make no substantial contribution to Union strength. On the contrary, every year during the Civil War, Union regiments were sucked into the Wild West to wage a desperate war against the Indians.

Hundreds of thousands of Americans in loyal border states and millions more in southern Ohio, Indiana, and Illinois, moreover, favored the Confederacy and worked or fought for southern independence. Even such hotbeds of abolitionism as Massachusetts, Vermont, Michigan, and Wisconsin—and indeed every northern state—furnished men for the southern cause. Many southerners, of course, clung to the old flag and the Union. "Old Fuss and Feathers," General Winfield Scott, the ancient head of the armed forces of the United States at the outbreak of hostilities, was one Virginian who had no need to search his soul, as did Robert E. Lee, to decide where his allegiance lay. He "had fought 50 years under the flag," Scott told Senator Douglas, "and would fight for it, and under it, till death." The great Lee's nephew, Admiral Samuel P. Lee, served the Union navy throughout the war. So did Admiral David Porter Farragut, born in Tennessee, raised in New Orleans, twice married to women of Norfolk, Virginia, where he lived until April 18, 1861. Such instances can be multiplied many times; in every commonwealth in the South (as in the North) there were enclaves of enemy sympathizers, and thousands of southerners defected to the Union side. But there is little doubt that more Federals than Confederates "crossed over."

Certain other considerations, when it was seen that the North really meant to fight, may also have tempered southern discouragement in the face of apparently overwhelming Union numbers. One was superior officer personnel. For 20 years before Lincoln's inauguration, a southern clique headed by General Scott ruled the army. Under this regime, many northern West Pointers, including Sherman and Grant, found little opportunity for advancement and resigned their commissions early in life for civilian careers. Virtually all the young officers pushed up the ladder by Scott were southerners, and most of them, unlike Scott, embraced the Confederate cause.

A second comfort to the South was its confidence in cotton, largely produced by slaves. Secession leaders expected to exchange their famous staple for all the foreign manufactures they needed without sacrificing fighting men to factory work. A third consideration reinforced the second. The South's vaunted military tradition—which meant, practically speaking, that white men of all classes were trained from childhood to the horse, the hunt, and the use of firearms—had left southern women with the drudgery of running the small family farms and even some of the large plantations. When the men went off to "hev a squint at the fighting," the women redoubled their efforts in raising dirt crops, cattle and swine.

A fourth, and the most important, consideration was strategic. Throughout the fighting, the men in gray defended short "interior" lines against invaders who were forced to traverse and protect long avenues of communication and to attack on a broad periphery. The Confederacy, moreover, had no need to divert "effectives" to such tasks as garrisoning captured cities and holding subjugated territory. "Owing to the character of the conflict," concludes the historian Edward Channing, "instead of two or three Northern soldiers for

every Southern one, there should have been five or six at least."

By the end of the war, from its 1.5 million white men of fighting age, the South had enlisted about 900,000. Thousands of slaves performed fatigue duty and other tasks for the services, but no blacks except such as might pass for whites were armed. Rebel forces reached their numerical peak at the start of 1864, when some 480,000 were in uniform.

From its 4 million white men of fighting age, the Union enrolled approximately 2 million, nearly half of them toward the end of the war. In addition, after 1862, about 200,000 Negroes, most of them former slaves from border states or occupied Confederate territory, were enlisted in the Union army (and to a small extent in the Union navy), many

"As in 1800 and 1850, so in 1860," wrote Henry Adams in his Education, recounting his return to Washington just after Lincoln's election, "the same rude colony was camped in the same forest, with the same unfinished Greek temples for work rooms, and sloughs for roads. "The Government," he added, "had an air of social instability and incompleteness that went far to support the right of secession in theory as in fact; but right or wrong, secession was likely to be easy where there was so little to secede from." (The Granger Collection.)

of them forcibly and under discriminatory conditions in pay and quarters. Congregated in their own regiments, mainly under white officers who resented such assignments, they nevertheless performed hearteningly well in

593

594

the opinion of those who had their capacity for freedom in mind.

During the first two years of fighting, the Union armies probably outnumbered the Confederates by no more than three to two. During the last two years, Union superiority grew to two to one. In a short war, northern numerical superiority would have availed little. Nothing shows this more convincingly than Lee's nearness to complete triumph after the Second Battle of Bull Run in August 1862 (see p. 614). The Confederacy may have been deterred from pressing its deadly advantage at this time and on other occasions by an awareness of its own limited manpower. In any case, such irresolution played directly into the hands of the enemy. As the war drew itself out, and as generals were found with the determination to take advantage of the disparities in their favor, northern numerical strength became a psychological as well as a physical weapon. During the closing years of the con-

flict, the Union armies, massed at last against critical strongholds, suffered terrible casualties but seemed to grow stronger with every defeat. By the same token, Confederate frustration as well as Confederate losses sapped the southern will to fight.

### THE QUESTION OF MACHINES

The fact that the Civil War stretched over years instead of months magnified every other material advantage of the North—in money and credit, factories, food production, transport. It took precious time to redirect the free economy of the North to the requirements of the battlefield, especially as these requirements were persistently underestimated because of wishful thinking about the likely duration of the war. But the South, with its intense concentration on cotton-growing even at the expense of foodstuffs, found it more difficult than the North to convert to a war footing.

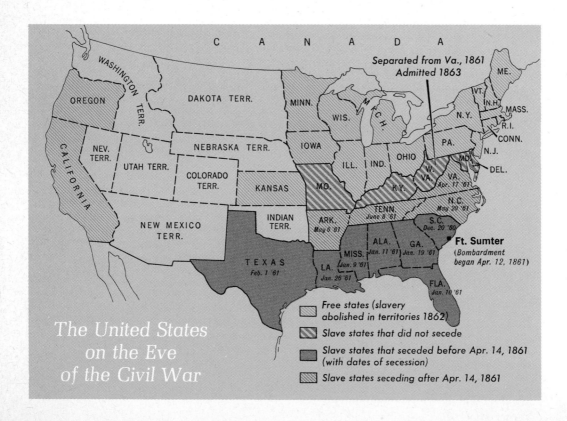

The United States
on the Eve
of the Civil War

Free states (slavery abolished in territories 1862)

Slave states that did not secede

Slave states that seceded before Apr. 14, 1861 (with dates of secession)

Slave states seceding after Apr. 14, 1861

Production at the Tredegar Iron Works before the war compared favorably with that of the best iron foundries in the North. In this wood engraving from 1861 the foundry has become an armory, where as shown in the sketch below, gun carriages were being made by hand. (The Granger Collection.)

Abominable roads and poorly built railroads which bypassed many strategic centers magnified every difficulty. Texas and Arkansas, the Confederacy's leading food-growing states, had no train connections whatever with the rest of the South.

As the war lengthened, southern troops suffered miserably from short rations and ragged clothing, especially the paucity of shoes. Their shelter in winter months, whose severity came as a shock to many from the North, was usually nominal. Yet the Confederacy was never so lacking in basic materials of war—small arms, artillery, ammunition, and horses—that it could not carry out whatever actions its strategy or its predicament required. Every rural home in the South had its weapons, and some estimates place as high as 5 million the number of such private arms available for the cause. Large quantities of munitions also were garnered from captured federal forts and federal positions. To these were added imports run through the blockade (see p. 586). Under the brilliant administration of its chief of ordnance, Josiah Gorgas, a Pennsylvanian who had long since adopted the sentiments of his Alabaman wife, the Confederacy also developed its own munitions plants to supplement the output of the giant Tredegar Iron Works in Richmond, itself directed by its president, the Virginian, Joseph R. Anderson, a West Point graduate.

General Beauregard put the South's situation most clearly:

No people ever warred for independence with more relative advantages than the Confederates; and if, as a military question, they must have failed, then no country must aim at freedom by means of war. . . . The South, with its great material resources, its defensive means of mountains, rivers, railroads, and the telegraph, with the immense advantage of the interior lines of war, would be open to discredit as a people if its failure could not be explained otherwise than by mere material contrast.

Beauregard placed most of the blame for the South's defeat on the failure of President Davis and the civilian command to follow up strategic victories in the field with bold and comprehensive campaigns. Lee's official wartime correspondence strongly confirms Beauregard's conclusion.

## II *The Civilian Commands*

### THE CONFEDERATE CONSTITUTION

When the delegates from the first seceding states met at Montgomery, Alabama, in February 1861 to draft a frame of government for the new southern republic (see p. 580), they had hoped, by not departing too greatly from the familiar federal document, to attract their as yet uncommitted neighbors in the upper South and on the "border." In squelching democratic extremists, they also had their eye on the good opinion of the conservative states of Europe. Because so many of the South remained more firmly opposed than ever to surrendering state rights to a central government, certain weaknesses so successfully fought in 1787 nevertheless crept into the Confederate version.

Nothing was said in the new constitution of the right of secession, which, in southern opinion, was sufficiently sanctioned in the older document. The very preamble of the new constitution, however, declared that it was established, not by "We, the people," the clarion cry of the Union, but by "the people of the Confederate states, each state acting in its sovereign and independent character." While the new Congress was granted the power "to . . . provide for the common defense," no mention was made of promoting the "general welfare." Tariffs "to promote or foster any branch of industry," and appropriations "for any internal improvement intended to facilitate commerce," were forbidden, in true agrarian style. "The judicial power of the Confederate States" was placed in a Supreme Court and certain lower tribunals. But no Supreme Court ever was set up. The old federal district courts, indeed, continued to sit in the Confederacy, often under their old judges who applied the old rules and precedents, each as he saw fit. The President's term, optimistically, was extended to six years; but whatever advantage in stability was sought by this change was vitiated by the provision barring his re-election. The Confederate President soon became a lame-duck with little political leverage or allegiance. A more salutary innovation permitted the Congress to grant Cabinet members seats on the floor of either house with the privilege of discussing measures relating to their departments.

The new constitution contained provisions designed to make it a weapon as well as a vehicle of government. Of course, it "recognized and protected . . . the right of property in negro slaves." Yet it explicitly prohibited "the importation of negroes . . . from any foreign country." As a sop to Virginia and other slave-breeding states not yet in the Confederacy, it excluded the slave-holding states of the United States from this prohibition. But as a manifest threat to such states, it empowered the Confederate Congress, when it wished, to include in the ban "any State not a member of . . . this Confederacy."

### JEFFERSON DAVIS'S ADMINISTRATION

The Montgomery Constitutional Convention named Jefferson Davis of Mississippi provisional President, and Alexander H. Stephens of Georgia provisional Vice-president. Neither man sought nor wanted his job, but in the first Confederate elections in November 1861, the voters confirmed the convention's choices.

Like so many Mississippians, Jeff Davis was born out of the state, in Kentucky. A West Pointer of the class of 1828, at heart he was a soldier hungry for honor in the field. In 1846, he had resigned his seat as a Democratic congressman to lead his regiment of "Mississippi Rifles" in one grand stand at Buena Vista. This exploit convinced him perhaps more than it did the Mexicans that he was born to generalship, an opinion that was to be of no help to Confederate officers. From 1847 to 1851, and again from 1857 to 1861, Davis served in the Senate, and during the whole of Pierce's administration was Secretary of War. In the Senate, his ardent expansionism was tempered somewhat by his vision of a united nation dominated by the South. Much as he wanted new territories, he became one of the bitterenders, one of a mere ten, against the admission of California as a free state under the Compromise of 1850. His strong southern chauvinism soon linked him with the anti-Douglas wing of the Democratic party. But he was no fire-eater, and while sympathetic to secession, he had hoped that the South could take the plunge united and not be harried into the fatal step piecemeal by headstrong individual commonwealths like South Carolina.

Ill health may have accounted for Davis's testiness as President. But his frequent quarrels with subordinates also arose from their incompetence and even hostility. Vice-president Stephens, especially, although he stayed home in Georgia most of the time, was a thorn to his harassed commander-in-chief.

A wizened little scholar wracked by rheumatism and neuralgia, Stephens yearned only for the solitude of the study. The convention named him mainly to appease his state for refraining from pushing the vainglorious Howell Cobb and for withdrawing Robert Toombs, her hard-drinking favorite son. As a

stickler for state rights, Stephens complained on every exercise of presidential power that Davis was becoming a despot with Bonapartist ideas of grandeur. Saddest of all, Stephens had been certain from the start that not even a Bonaparte could establish a free Confederacy, and his pessimism became contagious.

Davis's Cabinet scarcely made up in strength for the Vice-president's weakness. Either because Davis would not appoint them or because they would not serve one so careless of state rights, great planters were conspicuous by their absence. Many of them, of course, preferred to serve in the field. Fourteen different men filled the six Confederate Cabinet posts during the life of the southern republic.

*From an early daguerreotype: Jefferson Davis and his second wife, Varina Howell Davis, whom he married in February 1845. He seemed to her, as she said during the inauguration ceremonies, "a willing victim, going to his funeral pyre." That evening, during the President's reception, she remarked, "Thus my husband entered his martyrdom." (Brady-Handy Collection, Library of Congress.)*

Such turnover alone would have forced the President to lean increasingly on the few familiar figures about him; and of these Judah P. Benjamin, a brilliant New Orleans lawyer who served through the whole ill-fated administration, first as Attorney-General, then as Secretary of War, and finally as Secretary of State, was by far the ablest. Benjamin's task was made none the lighter by the ceaseless slander of his character by newspapers and legislators from 1862 on. His determination to make the Confederacy face up to the grim reality of its financial, economic, and diplomatic predicament earned him the appellation "the hated Jew."

The Confederate Congress, more stable in personnel than the Cabinet, was no more responsible. Three distinct congresses held office during the life of the Confederacy. Many men served in all three, and as conditions worsened they came to grate so on one another's nerves that the more truculent brandished guns and

*Judah P. Benjamin, Davis's sturdiest supporter. (Brady-Handy Collection, Library of Congress.)*

Bowie knives, in addition to the traditional horsewhips and canes, to cut short distasteful harangues. As federal forces occupied "Secesh" territory, irresponsibility increased, for many legislators found themselves representing lost constituencies which could not vote them out.

Davis was especially hard pressed by state-rights enthusiasts who saw almost no justification for any central government at all. William L. Yancey, the Alabama fire-eater, entered the Confederate Senate in 1862 and remained there until his death the following year, never letting an occasion pass to belabor the administration. His attacks grew especially scathing when he learned that Alabama brigades were to be placed under the command of "foreign" officers, and reached apoplectic levels when his son, Dalton, was denied a commission by the President. The South's military genius was paraded daily in the legislative halls where Davis's strategy came under ever harsher scrutiny. Military reverses, of course, raised the fever of the malcontents to delirious heights, to which the famed oratorical genius of the Old South proved equal. Such reverses also heightened opposition to Davis's program for mobilizing the South's men and resources. Widely deemed useless for anything else, the central government of the Confederacy eventually proved a heaven-sent scapegoat for a chagrined and bewildered people. Within the central government, Davis's brow offered the most glittering target.

### LINCOLN AS PRESIDENT

By temperament and character, Lincoln was far better fitted than Davis for presidential responsibility during "the brothers' war." Patient as a possum, tolerant, flexible, and crafty, Lincoln had a genius for giving men enough rope to hang themselves. If they escaped the noose, so much the better. Once, early in the war when he was snubbed by the priggish McClellan, Lincoln told his outraged associates that he would hold the General's horse if he would only bring Union victories. Mc-

Clellan failed, repeatedly, and eventually he went. When Lincoln offered the General's great friend and advocate, Edward M. Stanton, the office of Secretary of War, McClellan asked Stanton, "What are you going to do?" "I am going to make Abe Lincoln President of the United States," rasped the rough Ohio diamond. "No man in American history," Secretary of State Seward warned the President about Stanton, "has treated another so brutally as he has treated you." Lincoln smoothed the appointment over with a story:

There is a Methodist minister I know out in the West. He gets worked up to so high a pitch of excitement in his exhortations that they have to put bricks in his pockets to keep him down. We may be obliged to serve Stanton in the same way, but I guess we'll let him jump a while first.

The bricks came down on the "black terrier" fairly early in the game. But Lincoln knew a first-rate Secretary of War when he saw him, and knew as well how to keep him in leash with the pack.

Nathaniel Hawthorne, who met the President in 1862, recognized the artful manipulator and long-headed political strategist behind the mask of "Honest Abe":

The whole physiognomy is as coarse a one as you would meet anywhere in the length and breadth of the States; but withal, it is redeemed, illuminated, softened, and brightened by a kindly though serious look out of his eyes, and an expression of homely sagacity, that seems weighted with rich results of village experience. A great deal of native sense; no bookish cultivation, no refinement; honest at heart, and thoroughly so, and yet, in some sort, sly—at least, endowed with a sort of tact and wisdom that are akin to craft, and would impel him, I think, to take an antagonist in flank, rather than to make a bull-run at him right in front.

Throughout his term, the President was savagely handled by most newspapers and abused by politicians of his own and other parties. Nor was he popular with the electorate. But Lincoln took the verbal abuse, it seemed, with a kind of wry satisfaction in his critics' scratching for barbs. Even to men who knew him longest he remained something of a mystery, enlivening meetings with the earthiest kind of stories and yet melancholy, aloof, in counsel with his inner self. "The only ruler I have is my conscience," he once blurted out in a rare show of pique, "and these men will have to learn that yet." His law partner, William H. Herndon, considered him a "sphinx . . . incommunicative—silent—reticent—secretive—having profound policies—and well laid—deeply studied plans."

According to Republican Senator John Sherman of Ohio, Lincoln peppered his Cabinet with men intensely jealous of one another, "as by that means he would control rather than be controlled by it." In any case, a coalition of many interests had made Lincoln's election possible, and, like it or not, he could not ignore their claims on high office. The President himself seldom acted until he felt that the groundswell of public opinion would sustain him, a point he reached by a process of divination to which his contentious associates contributed much by their discussions, but how much and in what way precisely they could not tell.

Nor was he always right, especially in simply taking time. Lincoln's lapses encouraged the ambitious egotists around him—Secretary of State Seward, for example, and Secretary of the Treasury Chase—each to strive to assume "a sort of dictatorship for the national defense" in order to fill the vacuum they found in presidential power. But all learned sooner or later, as Seward acknowledged after an early brush with the rail-splitter's own ego, that "the President is the best of us. There is only one vote in the Cabinet and it belongs to him. Executive ability and vigor are rare qualities, but he has them both."

No permanent civil service existed when the Civil War began; the victorious ticket ordinarily swept out the workers of the previous administration and filled their places with its own favorites. This practice became all the more justified in 1861, for the Republicans

600

found the government honeycombed with secessionists. "Honest Abe" took full advantage of this excuse to satisfy the "host of ravenous partisans from Maine to California" who were clamoring for jobs. No President, not even Jackson, cleaned house so indiscriminately. Few, on the other hand, chose replacements with such care. Lincoln labored so painstakingly in selecting loyal Republicans that idealistic critics accused him of frittering away his time with low politics while the nation was splitting apart. His justification was that patronage was the cement of the Republican party, which alone held the North together.

For all his compromises Lincoln did not lower the tone of the domestic civil service, and in making his foreign appointments he undoubtedly raised the level of the recent past. The experienced diplomat Charles Francis Adams, son of John Quincy, was named minister to Great Britain. Other distinguished posts overseas were filled by such eminent Americans as the historians John L. Motley and Richard Hildreth, and the German-American leader Carl Schurz.

### DISUNITY WITHIN THE UNION

In reality, throughout the war the North remained as bitterly divided as the South. Extremes sometimes met in opposition to the administration. Many dedicated abolitionists, for example, were also dedicated pacifists. In addition, they had preached "disunion" as vigorously as Calhoun. Their argument, that by sloughing off the slave section the Union itself would be purified (a goal somewhat different from their most widely advertised one), fed on the fond hope that in an isolated South slavery would wither away. Now these abolitionists demanded that the rebels be allowed to depart in peace, slaves and all. "Peace" was also the goal of many Democrats, often called "Copperheads," who spared Lincoln no abuse but who saved their heaviest fire for the abolitionists themselves.

As the war proceeded and congressional

support for emancipation grew, partly as a result of continued abolitionist agitation, most abolitionists eventually embraced the fight to the finish. Many, indeed, came to fear an early end to the conflict lest it lead to a compromise peace, with the "peculiar institution" still intact in the South. As the Confederacy's chances declined, on the other hand, the "Copperheads" grew shriller in their demands for compromise and more active in obstructing Union enlistments, while encouraging northerners to fight for the slave power.

Copperhead sentiment was strongest in southern Ohio, Indiana, and Illinois, Ohio supplying, in ex-congressman Clement L. Vallandigham, the acknowledged leader of the faction in this region. Arrested early in May 1863 on a charge of declaring sympathy for the enemy, Vallandigham was summarily tried by a military commission, found guilty, and jailed. While his friends sought a reversal of the verdict in more formal courts, Lincoln, mingling mercy with humor, had Vallandigham released and banished to the Confederacy. From there he fled to Canada by ship and soon showed up again in Ohio where, with no further official notice, he resumed his earlier course. In the closing years of the war, rumors were rife of traitorous plots by secret Copperhead societies, but these groups, largely made up of the ill-educated and untrained, never constituted an effective fifth column.

As abolitionists gradually came around to conceding the rightness of the fighting, they also threw their support to the faction within the Republican party most in sympathy with emancipation as the objective of the war. This faction became known as the "Radicals." The "Regulars," or "Conservatives," sought only to suppress the "insurrection" and to restore the Union for the white men regardless of the freedom and progress of the black. The split between the Radicals and Conservatives widened as the war proceeded and had far deeper consequences than that between the Republican party as such and the dissidents outside.

Lincoln who never ceased to fear offending

the slaveholders of the loyal border states, likewise never disavowed his Conservative leanings. No one, indeed, put the Conservative case better than he in a remarkable letter written in August 1862 to the most influential newspaper publisher in the Union, Horace Greeley of the New York *Tribune*:

As to the policy I "seem to be pursuing," as you say, I have not meant to leave any one in doubt.

I would save the Union. I would save it the shortest way under the Constitution. The sooner the National authority can be restored, the nearer the Union will be "the Union as it was." If there be those who would not save the Union unless they could at the same time destroy Slavery, I do not agree with them. My paramount objection in this struggle is to save the Union, and is not either to save or destroy slavery. If I could save the Union without freeing any slave, I would do it; and if I could save it by freeing all the slaves I would do it; and if I could do it by freeing some and leaving others alone, I would also do that. What I do about Slavery, and the colored race, I do because I believe it helps to save this Union; and what I forbear, I forbear because I do not believe it would help save the Union.

Lincoln closed this missive with a characteristic expression of his humanity, which was not necessarily shared by the Conservative camp and which helps explain the President's own continued tolerance of the Radicals, to whom he harkened at least as patiently as to others. "I have here stated my purpose," he wrote Greeley, "according to my view of official duty, and I intend no modification of my oft-expressed personal wish that all men, everywhere, could be free."

In contradistinction to the Conservatives, the Radicals fought the war not only to free the slaves but to impose the "permanent dominion" of free institutions on the slaveocracy. Radicals differed on many issues of the day —on the tariff, the homestead law, federal subsidies to transcontinental railroads, currency policy. But overriding such mundane concerns was their belief in themselves as

a divine instrument to bring about the downfall of the enemy—"to lay low in the dust under our feet, so that iron heels will rest upon it, this great rebel, this giant criminal, this guilty murderer, that is warring upon the existence of the country." By their cannonading criticism of Lincoln's tentative if not timid conduct of the war, they early earned the epithet "Vindictives," which was not unacceptable to them.

The Radicals boasted a formidable array in both houses of Congress, led in the Senate by Sumner of Massachusetts, Wade of Ohio, and Chandler of Michigan, and in the House by the most vindictive Radical of all, Thaddeus Stevens of Pennsylvania, chairman of the regal Ways and Means Committee. Born and bred on the Vermont frontier, Stevens had made his career in Pennsylvania, where he owned extensive iron works. There, in 1837, he refused to sign the new constitution, to the writing of which he had contributed a great deal, because the convention had rejected his demand that Negroes as well as whites be given the suffrage. He had seen much of slavery in those parts of Maryland that adjoined his Pennsylvania haunts and he early denounced it as "a curse, a shame, and a crime." A lawyer as well as a businessman, Stevens defended fugitive slaves without a fee and usually secured their freedom. The Civil War crowned a political career notable for its ups and downs. After the war Stevens's determination that the slaveocracy should never rise again made him for a time the most powerful figure in the country (see Chapter Twenty).

## LINCOLN'S "DICTATORSHIP"

Lincoln allowed nearly a whole year to pass after the first shocking act of secession before he would acknowledge, and even then not fully, that the awful chasm between the two sections could be closed only by the dead of both. He hated bloodshed. Determined to get the war over as expeditiously as possible, he nevertheless was reluctant even to begin the fighting. As late as December 3, 1861, he told

602

Congress: "I have been anxious and careful that the inevitable conflict . . . shall not degenerate into a violent and remorseless revolutionary struggle."

Lincoln's refusal to be harried into catastrophe, throughout the war and during the first stages of Reconstruction as well, kept the Radicals continuously on edge. Secretary of the Treasury Chase, the leading Radical in the Cabinet, set the tone when he complained to a friend early in the administration that Lincoln had "merely the general notion of drifting, the Micawber policy of waiting for something to turn up." Actually, no President in American history ever earned the epithets "despot," "tyrant," "dictator," more justly than Lincoln did between April and July 1861, when he was readying the Union for survival while leaning away from the abyss of war.

With Congress cooling its heels at home (against the wishes of many members who wanted their special session to begin in March when the President was inaugurated, and not in July, as he had designated), Lincoln on May 3, without presidential precedent or legislative authority, issued a call for 40 regiments of three-year United States volunteers to supplement the state militias he had called out in April (see p. 586). On no firmer constitutional grounds, he ordered a rapid expansion of the fleet to enforce his April 19 and April 27 proclamations blockading rebel ports (see p. 586), proclamations which themselves were considered by many, including a majority of the Supreme Court, as usurpations of Congress's power to declare war. The Constitution states: "No money shall be drawn from the Treasury, but in Consequence of Appropriations made by Law." Without any law, Lincoln ordered Chase to scratch for funds to pay for these increases in the armed forces and for other mysterious "military and naval measures necessary for the defense and support of the government," and Chase obliged.

Only legalists and political enemies complained of these military and monetary stratagems. Much more widely opposed were Lincoln's invasions of personal privacy and his overrunning of traditional safeguards of personal rights in the Union's emergency. On April 20, at a time when, as Secretary Stanton explained later, "every department of the government was paralyzed with treason," Lincoln ordered United States marshals in major northern cities to seize copies of all telegrams sent and replies received during the past 12 months. The Post Office was granted extraordinary powers to examine all mail suspected of giving aid or comfort to the enemy. Secret State Department agents were stationed in all major ports to examine questionable passports and, merely on suspicion, to arrest travelers entering and leaving the country. In such ports and elsewhere, military commanders also were empowered to make summary arrests without warrants and "in the extremest necessity," in Lincoln's words, to suspend the writ of habeas corpus. Under this edict and even harsher later ones, at least 15,000 Americans were jailed, and despite Lincoln's characteristic clemency, many remained in jail until the war's end without ever having been faced with their accusers or informed of the charges against them.

But even these high-handed measures were mild compared with Lincoln's militancy in Maryland, Kentucky, and Missouri, where the most anguished cries of dictatorship arose. These border states (along with Delaware) had refused to follow Virginia into the Confederacy (see p. 587). But (unlike Delaware) they denied the federal government the use of their state militias, as called for on April 15, and instead had declared their individual "armed neutrality."

Each of these states had immense strategic importance. Maryland virtually surrounded Washington and, with Virginia gone, could make the national capital the captive of the Confederacy. Baltimore, Maryland's leading port and railroad center, was also Washington's main link with the outside world. Kentucky, in turn, controlled the use of the Ohio River; Missouri, with Kentucky, controlled the use of the Mississippi. At the confluence of these two great streams stood the town of Cairo,

Illinois, the terminous of the Illinois Central Railroad. Ascendancy here meant domination of the length and breadth of the Mississippi Valley—the very spinal column of the nation.

Even more than strategy was involved. The "mystic chords of memory" to which the President had referred in his inaugural address must have recalled to millions how their forebears on the frontier had made the free and uninterrupted use of the Mississippi from its source to its mouth a sacred principle for which many had died. Few could have felt the worth and meaning of this territory more deeply than Abe Lincoln. The nation's heartland, it and it alone had nourished the President's soul and sinew, had made him the peculiarly American person he was. It was unthinkable that the majestic valley and its river should be severed or surrendered. "An arming of those states," Lincoln told Congress in July, "to prevent the Union forces passing one way, or the disunion the other, over their soil . . . would be disunion completed, . . . for under the guise of neutrality it would tie the hands of Union men and freely pass supplies . . . to the insurrectionists, which it could not do as an open enemy. [Moreover], it recognized no fidelity to the Constitution, no obligation to maintain the Union."

Maryland, because of its proximity to Washington, was the first of the "neutrals" to feel Lincoln's heel. After a riot in Baltimore on April 15, 1861, between Massachusetts troops bound for Washington and secessionist-minded citizens, Lincoln sent a force into Maryland under Brigadier-General Benjamin F. Butler with orders to take all necessary measures to forestall the state authorities from arming the people against the Union, "even, if necessary, to the bombardment of their cities." Butler, a notorious "problem on two legs," soon roughly rounded up and jailed the mayor of Baltimore, 19 members of the state legislature, and other citizens. Butler engaged in so much other inflammatory activity that Lincoln felt obliged to recall him. But Lincoln did not undo the General's work; and Maryland, especially the secessionist eastern sector, was held

to the Union side throughout the war chiefly by uninvited Union forces.

"I hope I have God on my side," Lincoln said, "but I must have Kentucky." By the time Kentucky formally declared her neutrality on May 24, 1861, Simon Bolivar Buckner, the commander, had molded the state militia into an effective army of 61 companies. Buckner's Confederate sympathies had already aroused suspicion, and another Kentuckian, a former naval lieutenant, William Nelson, went to Lincoln for permission to organize and arm a countervailing loyal force. Nelson's mission was successful and, under cover of night, he soon had 10,000 "Lincoln rifles" distributed among his "home guard." By June 1861, Union sentiment in the Kentucky legislature was so strong that funds requested by Buckner were voted for Nelson instead. By then, too, Lincoln had ordered the establishment at Danville, Kentucky, of a Union recruiting camp to offset camps the Confederates had set up on Kentucky's border in Tennessee.

The delicate balance held in Kentucky until September 4, 1861, when General Leonidas Polk, unnerved by the growing unionism Lincoln had patiently nourished, ordered his rebel forces to occupy the strategic town of Columbus on the Mississippi (see map, p. 609). When Polk's men moved in, the recently commissioned Ulysses S. Grant swung over from Cairo, Illinois, to occupy Paducah, Kentucky, on the Ohio. Davis tried to recall Polk's forces and retrieve his hasty step. But it was too late. Kentucky declared her allegiance to the Union (although a separate convention of Confederate volunteers voted in November to join Kentucky to the South), and was held thereafter, but only at great cost.

Unlike Maryland, which had a Unionist governor, and Kentucky, which had a Unionist legislature, Missouri's government was wholly Confederate in temper. Here Lincoln went so far as to sanction the establishment of a revolutionary Union government which, throughout the great war, carried on a local civil war with the secessionist regime it had

603

604

unseated. Thousands were killed in Missouri even before the first battle of Bull Run in July 1861.

In still a fourth area, western Virginia, traversed by the Baltimore and Ohio Railroad, Washington's principal link with the West, Lincoln early took advantage of Union sentiment to create a Union bulwark. His agent here was General George Brinton McClellan, who, in June 1861, drove Virginia state forces from the western mountain passes and restored service on the B&O which these forces had disrupted. Local civil war persisted in Virginia until 1865; but the western counties—and after 1863, the new state of West Virginia as such—remained a firm part of the Union-held border stretching from the Atlantic to the Mississippi.

McClellan reported his successes in western Virginia in such resounding language that he became the first Civil War soldier to win official citation by Congress. After the Union rout at Bull Run (see p. 606), it was to this officer, largely on his literary performance, that the country turned three times for safety —each time to suffer twinges of regret.

*General Winfield Scott at 75, veteran of the War of 1812 and the Mexican War. Photo by Mathew Brady. (National Archives.)*

## III  *"Forward to Richmond!"*

### THE FIRST BATTLE OF BULL RUN

Lincoln's principal military adviser in the early months of the war was the General in Chief of the United States Army, Winfield Scott—"magnificent as a monument and nearly as useless," as an ungenerous critic described him in 1861. Born in 1786, Scott was a year older than the Constitution itself. Once towering six feet four-and-a-quarter inches, and vain enough "to insist on the fraction," he was now "swollen and dropsical." Visited midday on one occasion in May 1861 by Radical Senator James W. Grimes of Iowa and other representatives of that state, Scott dozed off during the meeting. Grimes stormed out to complain bitterly to the President about the

old imbecile who, if not soon removed, would see the Union buried before himself. "You stirred up Grimes to swear in madness over the incapacity of our General," Lincoln remarked to Iowa Congressman Josiah B. Grinnell later that day. "Now, candidly, did he color it?" Grinnell laughed. "He did sleep, and we retreated, not on bugle-call, but he snored us out in prologue."

Yet difficult as he sometimes found it to keep his eyes open, Scott was one of the few leaders wide awake to the fact that the Union must prepare for a long struggle. Scott, moreover, was prefectly clear-headed about the uses to which he would put the many months he wanted. Clamp a vise of steel on the border states, he said; master the whole course of the Mississippi; screw down the blockade on every rebel port on the Atlantic and the Gulf. Then, when the enemy had begun to writhe under pressure, speed his inevitable end by marching in the overpowering armies for whose preparation all earlier steps would have gained the necessary time.

Lincoln's early success in thwarting the neutrality of the border states provided a favorable start in carrying through Scott's plan on the land. The early success of Secretary of the Navy Gideon Welles in making Lincoln's "paper blockade" of April 19 effective (see p. 602) further improved prospects on the water. In a few months all but a few rebel seaports were closed in, and the South's foreign trade had been cut at least 80 per cent.

Jefferson Davis, as revolted as Lincoln by the likelihood of bloodshed and reluctant to surrender the fantasy that the South would be permitted peacefully to sever the Union, had a war plan of his own that played right into Scott's hands.

The South, Davis said, had seceded to get away from, not to conquer, the North. He saw a perfect "natural frontier" stretching along the Mason and Dixon Line onward to the Black Hills of the Dakotas. Plant along this sweeping border, within which the Confederacy would have ample room for growth, a forest of impregnable forts. Then look to the naval power of Britain and France—hungry as these countries must quickly become for the cotton that was King of the Universe—to unlock southern ports, free southern trade, and protect independent southern commerce. As early as March 16, 1861, almost a month before Beauregard's bombardment of Fort Sumter, Davis, in one of his first steps as President, had sent three commissioners to Europe to carry out this "cotton diplomacy." Their initial goal was to arrange for massive munitions and supplies needed immediately by the Confederacy. How Lincoln's own commissioners foiled this mission, except in one significant respect (see p. 618), may have been a straw in the wind. Far more than cotton, with which she had filled her warehouses in anticipation of the war, Britain in particular in 1861 needed wheat. Wheat could be purchased else-

where, but the Union's ability to pay with massive wheat exports for the munitions and supplies her own envoys ordered in large quantities in the early years of the war made it difficult for Davis's agents to do business.

In the end, the Civil War was to be fought out as the confrontation of Davis's defensive plan, full of holes from the start though it was, and Scott's aggressive "anaconda," painfully slow though it proved to mount.

Both strategies, however, had their enemies from the outset. Many Confederate leaders, General Beauregard among them, urged a relentless Confederate offensive without delay. This camp banked on the supposed superior valor of southern troops and on the less satisfying realization that if the South did not win quickly she was not likely to win at all.

The most popular Union plan seemed to count on just such rebel strategy as Beauregard proposed. In June 1861 the main rebel army under Beauregard himself was stationed at Manassas Junction in Virginia, a critical railroad crossing between Washington and Richmond. Wipe out this army, sweep triumphantly down to the rebel capital, and crush the insurrection in one stroke—that was the siren plan to which Lincoln himself, nursing his own fantasy of a "ninety-day war," remained for some time trustingly drawn.

Each morning during the week preceding the return of Lincoln's Congress to Washington for its special session, Horace Greeley flaunted on the editorial page of his nationally read New York *Tribune,* "Forward to Richmond!" Then, on July 4, the day Congress opened, the *Tribune* cried: "Forward to Richmond! Forward to Richmond! The Rebel Congress must not be allowed to meet there on the 20th of July. By that date the place must be held by the National Army."

Thereafter, Radical demands mounted for "action—crushing, irresistible, overwhelming." The President may have done wonders; indeed, in some respects, too much. But the essential thing remained undone: to engage the enemy and destroy him. A touch of hysteria magnified the pressure. The Confederacy,

## First Bull Run July 21, 1861

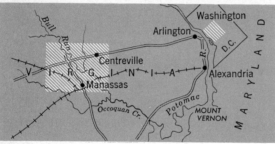

yell," first heard here, halted the Union offensive.

In the afternoon, Confederate reinforcements under General Joesph E. Johnston arrived from the Shenandoah Valley where the rebels were to maintain a force for most of the war like a gun at Washington's back. McDowell, disappointed at not receiving reinforcements of his own, soon deemed it the better part of valor to retire. Fashionable ladies and congressmen and correspondents who, in a holiday mood, had set out with the Federals to see the rebels crushed, were engulfed in the retreat as it became a headlong scramble of innocent youth homeward. Some of McDowell's men, their three-months' service over, kept going all the way to New York, New Hampshire and Maine, where they first had volunteered.

In the presence of a congressional delegation in the White House after the battle, General Scott told the President: "Sir, I am the greatest coward in America. I deserve removal because I did not stand up, when the army was not in condition for fighting, and resist it to the last." "Your conversation seems to imply," Lincoln remarked, "that I forced you to fight this battle." Scott, who had been the associate of every President since Jefferson, replied, "I have never served a President who has been kinder to me than you have been."

Recriminations also were rife in the South. "Give me 10,000 fresh troops, and I will be in Washington tomorrow," "Stonewall" Jackson is reported to have stated after Bull Run. But President Davis clung to his defensive plan and Washington, if indeed it was in mortal danger, was saved.

### "ALL QUIET ON THE POTOMAC"

In his opening message to the new Congress on July 4, 1861, Lincoln had reviewed the record of his autonomous four months. "Of all that which a President might constitutionally and justifiably do in such a case," he

everyone said, was gathering a rebel host for its own assault on Washington. "Why don't they come?" was the anxious questions on every tongue. At last, on July 16, with the "three-months men" nearing the end of their service, General Scott, on Lincoln's authorization, ordered General Irvin McDowell to move.

McDowell's 30,000 were green as saplings, but Beauregard's force, estimated at 24,000, was no more seasoned. As McDowell marched southward, Beauregard probed northward to meet him on suitable terrain. By July 20 he had settled in on the southern side of the little stream of Bull Run, and there, the next morning, the Federals found him. By noon a Union triumph seemed certain. Then General Thomas J. Jackson's "stonewall" stand in one sector, followed by a succession of counterattacks, their fury embellished by the "rebel

said, "everything was forborne without which it was believed possible to keep the government on foot." When three days later, however, a joint resolution was introduced seeking to validate the President's extralegal acts in Congress's absence, the majority laid the resolution aside. Even those members who sympathized with Lincoln's conduct refused to sanction, *post facto,* an invasion of their powers when they themselves deliberately had been left out in the cold. Congress would not even vote Lincoln the men and money he requested, "the legal means for making this contest a short and decisive one," until after the debacle of Bull Run. Only on August 5, the day before the session closed, and then merely as a rider to an army pay bill, would both houses vindicate Lincoln's military steps. His suspensions of habeas corpus never was approved.

On August 6, the last day of the session, the Radicals pushed through Congress a portentous measure of their own which Lincoln, fearful of driving the South to vengeful retaliation, said he "had some difficulty in consenting to approve." This was the so-called First Confiscation Act (a second was to be passed in July 1862; see p. 622), making it the duty of the President to seize all property used in aiding the insurrection. Hateful as it was to the Radicals to identify Negroes as property, the act nevertheless included as subject to forfeit all slaves employed in building fortifications and in other military and naval work. Lincoln did sign the measure. "This government will be preserved," cried Congressman Hickman of Pennsylvania in approval, "and the gallows will eventually perform its service."

But the rebels had to be caught before they could be hanged. Immediately after Bull Run, Lincoln relieved McDowell, created a new Division of the Potomac, and placed McClellan, then a cocky 34 years of age, at its head. "All tell me that I am held responsible for the fate of the nation," the new commander wrote to his wife. A few days later, with his characteristic flourish, he added the telltale plan: "I shall carry this thing *en*

*grande* and crush the rebels in one campaign." Under the paralyzing pull of Richmond, on the one hand, and the paralyzing fear for Washington's safety on the other, the "anaconda" policy was on its way toward official oblivion. By November 1, Scott himself, outgeneraled in the struggle for power in the capital, retired. McClellan, who had his hand in everything, including the overthrow of his old chief, was elevated to Scott's place. At the same time, this General's officious buzzing about in nonmilitary affairs, against the background of the prolonged inactivity of the army

*Major General George Brinton McClellan, at 34 General in Chief—a position he held for only five months. (National Archives.)*

608

he was readying, soon caused confidence in him, and indeed in Lincoln on his account, to curdle.

McClellan's task on taking charge of the Division of the Potomac was unenviable. The remnants of McDowell's force—"It could not properly be called an army," said McClellan —were much the worse for having tasted the demoralization of defeat. The large new levies voted by Congress, in turn, arrived slowly. Washington, moreover, lay ominously open to the enemy, its lack of a protective shield of forts perhaps justifying McClellan in his unwillingness to depart. If the young commander needed still another reason for not lunging hastily at the rebels, he found it in the nightmare of a second Bull Run, one all the more perturbing in view of the huge Confederate armies he himself conjured up on Washington's threshold.

McClellan's orders were, in the vicinity of the anxious capital, to forge the Army of the Potomac into a mighty sword and with it to bring the rebels to their knees. He was, in fact, a masterly organizer and conditioner. His failing was his pride in smart execution of the drill, his exasperating reluctance to risk his beauties in battle. By the time Congress reconvened for its regular session on December 2, 1861, McClellan was still grandly housed in Washington, still marching his men, and beginning to tax even Lincoln's patience. Although the rebels were making restless forays nearby, and in one of them, at Ball's Bluff in October, had trapped and slaughtered a federal force sent by McClellan to see what was up, "Forward to Richmond!" was forgotten by the press and the people. Although rebel batteries also were making the Potomac River untenable for commercial vessels, "All Quiet on the Potomac" had become the derisive Union slogan of the day.

Little more than two weeks after Congress reconvened, the Radicals, their ranks augmented in the legislature by the apparent indolence of the executive, succeeded in establishing a Joint Committee on the Conduct of the War, with wide powers of investigation.

Conservatives decried this "attempt on the part of the legislative branch to direct or supervise the military movements of the administration." The Radicals denounced them as "the diluted spawn of pink-eyed patriots." It was the "bounden duty" of Congress, they said, to scrutinize "executive agents," including generals who made a practice of returning fugitive slaves and were otherwise retrograde on "the Negro question." McClellan, well-known for his "softness" on slavery, soon became the Committee's pet target and hence doubly Lincoln's concern. Radical suspicions grew that he was in fact more unwilling than unready to fight the rebels, a view the President, although still dreading the onset of a war to the finish, dared not allow to be confirmed.

At last, on January 27, 1862, his patience spent, Lincoln issued General Order No. 1, naming Washington's Birthday, February 22, as "the day for a general movement of the land and naval forces of the United States against the insurgent forces." But even this unmistakable command went unheeded by McClellan. "In ten days I shall be in Richmond," he boasted on February 13. But not until April did he move.

### COMING TO GRIPS IN THE WEST

While Washington remained preoccupied with the long quiet on the Potomac, the war was far from quiet in the West, where subordinate Union officers had taken things more or less into their own hands. One such officer was the rough Republican firebrand Nathaniel Lyon, who earlier had forced the removal of his chief in St. Louis for his southern sympathies.

Lyon's efforts to rid divided Missouri of rebel troops were checked on August 10, 1861, when, outnumbered two to one, he lost a bitterly fought engagement at Wilson's Creek in the southwestern corner of the state. Lyon was killed in this battle, and his new chief, the flamboyant John C. Frémont, for failing to support him with men and supplies, was blamed for his death as well as his defeat. In

November, Frémont was replaced in command of the Department of the West by General Henry W. Halleck, "Old Brains" to his cronies, but characterized by McClellan as "the most hopelessly stupid [man] I have encountered in high position."

Regular Confederate forces held on in southwestern Missouri until March 1862, when General Samuel R. Curtis, serving under Halleck, chased them into Arkansas and on March 8 defeated them at Pea Ridge. In southeastern Missouri, General John Pope drove the rebels from New Madrid on March 13, and from heavily fortified "Island No. 10" in the Mississippi on April 7, thereby opening the great river all the way to Memphis.

In neighboring Kentucky, Confederate General Albert Sidney Johnston, having seized Bowling Green in mid-September 1861 and made it his headquarters, labored all fall to firm up a line across the southern range of the state from the Mississippi almost to Virginia. If he could not advance farther into Kentucky, Johnston, if he were lucky, planned at least to protect Tennessee and the heartland of the deep South she guarded.

The western anchor of Johnston's line was Columbus, Kentucky, where Polk had established his rebel camp on September 4. Bowling Green held down the center. The eastern end lay in the vicinity of the Cumberland Gap. Johnston could not establish his line without some successful skirmishing with federal parties, but the first real fighting of the war in Kentucky was bad news for him. On January 19, 1862, Union General George H. Thomas, having earlier unnerved his superior, General Don Carlos Buell, with experimental advances toward Tennessee, caught one of Johnston's outlying contingents just above Mill Springs on the Cumberland River. The rebels tried to shoot their way out, but Thomas quickly gained the initiative and sent them flying while his own men gathered up abandoned Confederate munitions, horses, and mules.

Mill Springs undid Johnston's line in the east. It was followed up on February 6 (after

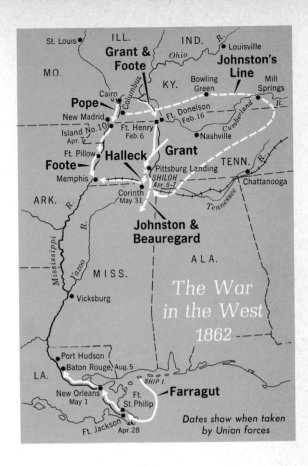

a month of hard petitioning for Halleck's approval) by the triumph of Commodore Andrew H. Foote, directing a flotilla of gunboats under Grant's command, at Fort Henry on the Tennessee River. On February 16 (with no authorization from Halleck at all) Grant's and Foote's combined operation took nearby Fort Donelson on the Cumberland. The loss of Fort Henry cut Johnston's communications between Bowling Green and Columbus and prompted him to quit his Kentucky line. The loss of Fort Donelson prevented him from taking a stand even in Tennessee. It was at Donelson that Grant made the demand on Johnston's subordinate, Simon Bolivar Buckner, which caught the fancy of the North: "No terms but immediate and unconditional surrender." The rebels had suffered a terrible setback, and the Federals had found a fighter able to make them look for more of the same.

609

610

Yet all the worst fighting lay ahead for both sides.

In his *Personal Memoirs* Grant wrote, "immediately after the fall of Fort Donelson the way was opened to the National forces all over the Southwest without much resistance." The way was closed because no "one general who would have taken the responsibility had been in command." Grant himself was relieved of duty by the confused Halleck on March 4, and while his army was broken up for tactical operations here and there (including those of Pope in southeastern Missouri), "the enemy," Grant added, gained time "to collect armies and fortify his new positions."

During the month following Donelson, Albert Sidney Johnston was left free to lead his men across the whole of Tennessee to the strategic railroad center of Corinth, Mississippi. Trailing along behind, Buell mopped up in Tennessee. When Grant resumed command on March 17, he found most of his force at Pittsburg Landing on the Tennesse River, just above Tennessee's southern boundary opposite Corinth. Before pushing south once more against Johnston, Grant decided to await Buell's arrival. But Johnston took the offensive himself before Buell showed up.

On April 6, Johnston led the attack on Grant's exposed encampment at Shiloh, southwest of Pittsburg Landing, and with the advantage of surprise pushed the Federals back to the Tennessee River. There Buell's vanguard appeared and helped stiffen Union resistance. Johnston was killed the first day, and on the next, the combined armies of Grant and Buell drove off the shaken rebels, now led by General Beauregard. Halleck soon appeared to take personal command of pressing the Union counteroffensive into Corinth. But he procrastinated for weeks as usual, and while his strength persuaded Beauregard, at the end of May, to abandon Corinth, the rebels got away again with their army intact.

Neither side could take much satisfaction from the bloody Shiloh engagement (the Federals lost 13,000 of 60,000 men; the Confederates almost 11,000 of 40,000), yet it gave

each a healthier respect for the other. When Grant saw that the rebels here "not only attempted to hold a line farther south, . . . but assumed the offensive and made such a gallant effort to regain what had been lost, then, indeed," he wrote in his *Memoirs*, "I gave up all idea of saving the Union except by complete conquest." Robert E. Lee, in turn, still cooling his heels in Richmond as a presidential adviser, warned Davis that unless he outdid himself to hold the lower Mississippi and keep the Confederacy from being split, Grant's "complete conquest" would not be far off.

Lee's warning was underscored soon after Shiloh by more decisive Union operations farther west. At the end of April a Union fleet led by Captain David G. Farragut smashed through Confederate fortifications below New Orleans and forced that great Mississippi port to surrender. Baton Rouge fell soon after to a force under General Butler. In the meantime, Foote's formidable flotilla had come pushing down the Mississippi to Memphis where it destroyed a Confederate fleet. Between Memphis and New Orleans only Vicksburg, Mississippi, and Port Hudson, Louisiana, now blocked Union control of the mighty river, the outermost border of the "anaconda" plan.

## THE PENINSULAR CAMPAIGN

Union operations in the West early in 1862 received only the barest notice in Washington, where protection of the capital and preparation of the *"en grande"* assault on Richmond were the main concerns.

Lincoln, who had taken to studying books on military strategy to compensate for the manifest inadequacy of his advisers, had formed very definite opinions about how Richmond might be taken. In short, he was for a new direct frontal attack, which would have had the advantage of keeping the Army of the Potomac between the Confederates and Washington itself. Largely because he had not been consulted about it, McClellan opposed Lincoln's plan. The Confederate capital, the General argued, should be approached by way of the peninsula formed by the York River (on the north) and the James River (on the south). The peninsular plan involved a hazardous combined sea-and-land operation dangerously distant from Washington. To the normal difficulties of such an operation were added in this instance Confederate control of the Norfolk navy yard at the mouth of the James.

In March 1862, just as they had tried to close the gap in Davis's perimeter in Kentucky, the Confederates had in Norfolk tried to break the Union's blockade on the Atlantic. For this purpose, Confederate engineers had transformed the wreck of the old United States frigate *Merrimac*, found in Norfolk Harbor, into a freakish man-of-war—an iron-plated fortress which they renamed *Virginia*, a vessel too unseaworthy to venture into open water but capable of floating safely in the calm off Hampton Roads. Anchored there were five wooden Union warships on blockade duty. On March 8, 1862, *Virginia* floated down to attack them. Impervious to the heavy fire from the Union ships, *Virginia* destroyed or damaged three of the largest before engine trouble forced her to withdraw.

The Confederacy was jubilant over the victory. In Washington, the proclivity to panic was never more apparent. Both reactions, however, proved premature. When *Virginia*, her running gear patched up, returned the next day to finish off the last of the wooden Union ships, she found herself confronted by an even more fantastic craft than herself. This was the famous *Monitor*, the "cheese-box on a raft," designed by the imaginative Swedish-born inventor, John Ericsson. On March 9, *Monitor* met the much larger *Virginia* off Hampton Roads. Neither ironclad could sink the other and in the end *Virginia* retreated upstream. She had failed to open a permanent breech in the Union blockade, but on the James she still remained a menace to any Union advance.

Could McClellan rely on Union naval support while *Virginia* menaced Chesapeake Bay? Lincoln thought not. Thankful, however, that

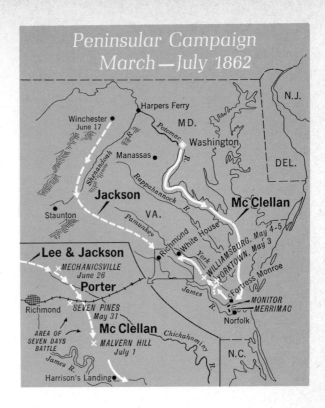

Peninsular Campaign
March—July 1862

McClellan at last proposed to move, Lincoln let him have his way. But Lincoln insisted that McClellan surrender to the President himself his overall command, retaining leadership only of his new Army of the Potomac, and that he leave behind under other generals a part even of this army to guard the capital.

The first contingents of McClellan's force —all told, 110,000 strong—were landed successfully on the peninsula on April 4, 1862. Yorktown, the first Confederate stronghold on the way to Richmond, might have been overrun in a day. McClellan, still fearful of a new Bull Run, took a month to level and enter the town. Almost another month was lost while the General, vainly awaiting expected reinforcements, was led slowly up the peninsula by wily "Joe" Johnston who had a rendezvous with reinforcements of his own. What kept McClellan's reinforcements away was "Stonewall" Jackson's brilliant foray up the Shenandoah Valley, where, as Lincoln had anticipated, he menaced Washington from

611

the rear. Jackson's masterly campaign won grudging admiration even from the northern press. The New York *Mercury* described him as "no mortal man," and remarked that his "abstemiousness enables him to live for a fortnight on two crackers and a barrel of whisky." Having unnerved the Union capital sufficiently to force Lincoln to keep even a stronger army there than he had planned, Jackson dashed back to the main front to lend his strength to Johnston.

Before Jackson arrived, McClellan had been drawn to within five miles of Richmond where, on May 31, he narrowly averted disaster at Seven Pines. "Joe" Johnston was badly wounded in this battle, and McClellan might have taken advantage of the Confederates' ill-luck to press on. Instead, he left 25,000 men under General Fitz-John Porter in the vicinity of Richmond and returned with the rest to his base at the town of White House, some 20 miles to the east. Here he waited once again, in expectation of the still more

men he had requested to oppose the vast host that he imagined stood before the Confederate capital. While McClellan waited, on June 1 Lee at last was returned to the field as the wounded Johnston's replacement. On taking charge, he gave his troops the name "The Army of Northern Virginia," his only command until Davis, in February 1865, named him General in Chief of all the forces of what by then had become "The Lost Cause."

An illustrious member of an illustrious Virginia family, Lee had attended West Point and served with distinction in the Mexican War. After Sumter, Winfield Scott had offered him the leadership of the Union armies but Lee had refused—not because he was an enthusiastic advocate of either slavery or secession, but because he was a loyal son of Virginia. A southern admirer described him at the time he made this great decision: "As he stood there, fresh and ruddy as a David from the sheepfold, in the prime of manly beauty and the embodiment of a line of heroic and patriotic fathers and worthy mothers, it was thus I first saw Robert E. Lee. . . . I had before me the most manly and entire gentleman I ever saw."

Lee possessed the capacities as well as the appearance of a hero. His many admirers regarded him as the greatest military genius of the war—as an inspired commander who performed miracles with undermanned and poorly equipped armies. His soldiers themselves came to look upon him as a man "above his race" who "communed with the angles of Heaven." Some military historians have argued that Lee was so concerned with defending his native state that he never developed a coordinated over-all strategy. But Virginia's front for too long was all he was vouchsafed and he used it, with his forays into the North itself (see pp. 614, 625), as the most effective means of relieving Union pressure elsewhere. Other writers point to Lee's failure to provide adequate supplies for his armies, which kept him from exploiting his victories; his habit of giving too much independence to his generals in the field; and his practice of taking on staggering burdens of staff work that he should have delegated to others. So long as he could draw on brilliant corps commanders, however, Lee's confidence was rarely misplaced. In the later stages of the war—particularly after the loss of "Stonewall" Jackson, at Chancellorsville in May 1863 (see p. 625)—the caliber of his junior officers declined.

Soon after he had taken the field, Lee learned of how McClellan had split his army. Lee immediately formed a plan to send a small force "looking numerous and aggressive" to intimidate the susceptible General, while he himself moved in to crush Porter. This accomplished, Lee hoped to outflank McClellan and cut his main force to pieces.

Unfortunately for Lee, Porter and McClellan were prepared. Lee's "eye" in spying out McClellan's position was his dashing cavalry chief, "Jeb" Stuart. It was Stuart's nature to improve any opportunity for showmanship. In a marvelous manifestation of contempt for

Robert E. Lee as a young officer. (Library of Congress.)

the enemy—and of foolish disregard of the risk for his own cause—for three days (June 12–15, 1862) he drove his worthies completely around the idling Federals and, unscathed, brought Lee the wanted information. His exploit also alerted the Union invaders. McClellan regrouped his forces and surprised the Confederates with his mobilized strength. Having done this much, however, he turned again to the strategy of retreat. In the Seven Days' Battle, between June 26th and July 1, McClellan inflicted very heavy losses on Lee's advancing troops, but his own sorry objective was Harrison's Landing on the James River where the Union navy, if necessary, could evacuate his men.

### SECOND BULL RUN AND ANTIETAM

Lincoln visited McClellan at Harrison's Landing on July 9. When McClellan proposed that he renew the assault on Richmond, Lincoln vetoed the suggestion. In fact, under Radical pressure, he called off the whole Peninsular Campaign and decided to bring back McClellan's army. Once again he placed this army with all the Union forces under a military leader. That he appointed Halleck as the new chief is often considered a serious blunder, but there is no evidence that anyone else who seemed eligible would have been better.

Lee, relieved of pressure from McClellan's large force, now left a small group to watch over the Federals' withdrawal and took his own army on a new advance northward. To meet him Halleck assigned the rash and boastful Pope who had been fighting Jackson in the Shenandoah Valley. As Pope moved slowly southward from the vicinity of Bull Run toward the strategic town of Gordonsville, he was intercepted by Jackson and defeated, August 9, at Cedar Mountain. Lee and Jackson then gradually maneuvered him northward once more and forced him to take a stand again near Manassas. On August 29–30 the two armies clashed in their full might in the momentous Second Battle of Bull Run, and Pope, completely outgeneraled, was routed with the loss of 16,000 out of 75,000 troops. Lee lost 9,000 of his 48,000. Halleck must bear some of the onus for this stunning new disaster. When reinforcements for Pope might have averted defeat, Halleck had refused to issue the orders that would have given Pope the unified command of a larger force than he had.

This fresh setback left the Union soldiers bitter and discouraged. "So long as the interests of our country are entrusted to a lying braggart like Pope," one of them wrote home, "we have little reason to hope successfully to compete with an army led by Lee, Johnston, and old 'Stonewall' Jackson." In June 1862 McClellan had been on Richmond's threshold, three strong Union armies appeared to have control of the Shenandoah Valley, and western Virginia was in Union hands. Now, at the end of August, as Douglas S. Freeman says,

"the only Federals closer than 100 miles to Richmond were prisoners . . . and men . . . preparing to retreat." In desperation, Lincoln again entrusted McClellan with temporary command of the disorganized army in the East. "If he can't fight," Lincoln said, "he excels in making others ready to fight."

Lee, meanwhile, characteristically pressed the attack, hoping for the first time to penetrate the North. Across his path lay the refurbished federal arsenal at Harpers Ferry, Virginia, with 10,000 men, and munitions and supplies much needed by his own ragged and hungry troops. If he could take the arsenal and move from there into Maryland, he might win new recruits in this and other border states with which to move on to Pennsylvania. France and Britain then might recognize the southern republic and actively intervene on its behalf. McClellan at the same time would be driven to defensive activity with a still demoralized force backed by a disheartened citizenry.

On September 9 Lee boldly ordered the division of his army, one part under Jackson to move on Harpers Ferry, the rest, under General James Longstreet, to push toward Hagerstown, Maryland. Harpers Ferry, to Lee's discomfort, held out until September 15; by then it was clear, as well, that Maryland would not rally to the southern invaders. In the meantime, an unlucky accident, on September 13, helped make certain the frustration of Lee's project. On that day a Union officer picked up on the road a dispatch (wrapped around three cigars) from Lee to one of his generals disclosing how Lee had split up his force. Here was McClellan's chance to crush the enemy before he could regroup. McClellan's 70,000 men at Frederick, Maryland, outnumbered Lee's entire force by almost two to one. His natural hesitancy, however, and Halleck's fear of a trap, held him back until September 17, and by then the triumphant Jackson had rejoined Lee. At last, the Federals stormed across Antietam Creek, near Sharpsburg, Maryland, and nearly engulfed the Confederate lines, but then McClellan faltered. He lacked, according to one of his Confederate opponents, "that divine spark which impels a commander, at the accepted moment, to throw every man on the enemy and grasp complete victory." Instead, he permitted the exhausted enemy to slip back across the Potomac. In the one-day battle 25,000 men, divided almost equally between the two rivals, were lost.

Antietam has been called, "a defeat for both armies." But the Union, at least, had repulsed an invasion on which the South had spent perhaps too much. "Our maximum strength has been mobilized," Jefferson Davis told his Secretary of War after the battle, "while the enemy is just beginning to put forth his might."

## IV  *The Civilian Response*

### CONFEDERATE WAYS AND MEANS

The brutal, inconclusive engagement at Antietam was an appropriate symbol of the course of the whole war. Under the stress of political demands or military expediency, both sides seemed long since to have forgotten their high hopes and grand strategies, and the conflict had devolved into a series of separate engagements, one more violent than another. In the North, Scott's anaconda plan was scarcely more than a memory to most of those charged with the responsibility of restoring the Union. Richmond had become the prime target, and Richmond remained more distant than ever in a military sense. Davis's defensive and diplomatic tactics, on the other hand, had brought the Confederacy little but frustration, Lee's belated offensives little but death. Naturally the civilian fronts bent under the pressure of the aimless slaughter.

One manifestation of civilian discontent was the mounting criticism of the conduct of the war. To check it in the Confederacy, Davis, on February 27, 1862, prevailed upon his Congress to enact the first Confederate law

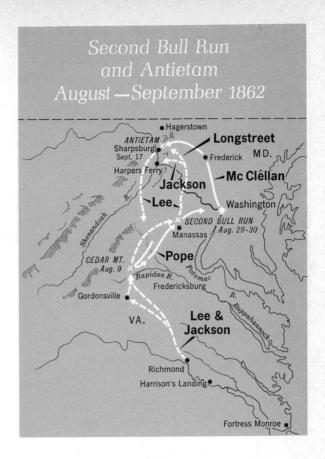

Second Bull Run and Antietam August—September 1862

granting the executive power to suspend the writ of habeas corpus and to impose martial law. But so intense had state-rights sentiment become in the South, that no sooner were Davis's critics locked up under Confederate authority than state authorities released them. Southern editors were frequent victims of the regime. Yet criticism would not be stilled.

The military stalemate was even more acutely felt by those charged with maintaining the resources and manpower of the fighting forces. The manpower problem on both sides was aggravated by the disposition of the enormous number of captives taken on the battlefields. Unwilling to recognize the Confederacy as a nation, the Union was reluctant from the start to make the normal wartime exchange of prisoners. Later on, when Grant determined that his main objective was to destroy the Rebel armies, the refusal to release men who might fight again hardened.

615

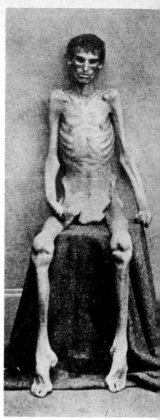

*Few deny that Union prisoner-of-war camps had their brutal and inhuman aspects, varying in intensity with the character of officers, guards, and inmates. Yet with the collapse of the southern economy near the war's end, the conditions at Confederate camps, with least claim on rebel resources, became indescribable and a scandal in the North. Most notorious was Camp Sumter in Andersonville, Georgia, opened early in 1864. Nearly one-third of those sent there died in a few*

*months, some by suicide. For the rest, in the words of Confederate surgeon Joseph Jones, it became a "gigantic mass of human misery." Many men went naked; no shelter was provided in the open stockade until healthy latecomers built the huts shown here; a small stream, the only water source, ran through the open latrines. The figure on the right shows one of the "living dead men" among those released at the end of the war. (Library of Congress.)*

Confederate refusal, at the same time, to treat captive Negro troops as soldiers, not slaves, helped justify Union policy. Even so, during the War the Union paroled more than half of the 460,000 captives taken; the Confederacy less than 10 per cent of its 210,000 Union prisoners. Despite the apparently generous Union parole policy, as early as April 1862, the Confederate Congress was obliged to enact the first conscription act in American history, calling up for three years' service all

white men 18 to 35. Later acts raised the age limit to 50. But anyone could escape the draft by paying for a substitute, and occupational exemptions were numerous. Evasion, moreover, had the support of certain state-rights governors who ran their commonwealths like private satrapies dissociated from the capital.

The poor showing reflected in southern draft statistics veils the true serviceability of the conscription acts. "Conscript" became such a brand of opprobrium that many youths hastened to volunteer before their age group was called, and they more than the conscripts themselves maintained Confederate military manpower. On the other hand, the draft acts' official sanction of the purchase of substitutes seemed to confirm the disheartening slogan, "a rich man's war and a poor man's fight." Desertions soared to well over 100,000—only a third, perhaps, of Union desertions, but much more keenly felt. As the Confederate economy foundered, and as disheartening letters to the front revealed the plight of the home folks, many of the men saw no disgrace in leaving the lost cause to succor their suffering families. If not they, who would? Surely not the rising race of speculators—the "little whipper-snapper blear-eyed . . . wretches," in the lexicon of a Richmond editor, "who would bottle the universal air and sell it at so much a bottle."

Symptoms of economic difficulties could be detected in the South even during the first year of the war. Loans in specie were virtually impossible to make in a country where wealth was traditionally tied up in land and slaves. By 1862 the Confederacy was trying "produce loans" by which planters were expected to pay in cotton and other commodities for Confederate bonds. But these loans had two drawbacks. Many planters would not surrender their commodities for government paper; and when they did, the government found it as hard as its citizens to transform commodities into cash.

The Confederacy had little better luck with taxes, and like other governments frustrated in the quest for gold, it began to print paper money in 1861. Before the end of the war a billion dollars' worth of these notes had been issued by Davis's government, and another billion by southern states and cities. By 1864 a dollar in Confederate paper was worth, on average, a cent and a half in specie. Prices naturally soared, thus encouraging speculation and hoarding. Food was especially hard to obtain; and widespread famine, made more difficult to fight by the breakdown of trans-

portation, hurt Confederate morale even more than setbacks in the field.

### THE FAILURE OF SOUTHERN DIPLOMACY

Confederate difficulties at home were aggravated by the collapse of southern diplomacy abroad, after some early successes.

The ruling classes in Europe had no love for slavery, but as aristocrats they feared popular government as practiced in the United States and would have been pleased with the failure of the "American experiment." Britain and France in particular had hastened early in 1861 to recognize the Confederacy's independent status as a belligerent power if not as a sovereign government. Britain, moreover, made warlike gestures at Lincoln's administration in November 1861, after a Union cruiser stopped the British mail steamer *Trent* on the high seas and removed two Confederate diplomats, Mason and Slidell, on their way to London and Paris. War was averted when Secretary of State Seward heeded British representations and released the two rebels. But Britain followed up the *Trent* episode by dispatching 8000 troops to Canada.

Confederate hopes for foreign military assistance, sanguine after the *Trent* affair, were scotched by the check Confederate forces received a year later at Antietam. When Lincoln, moreover, took this occasion to announce an emancipation proclamation (see p. 623), the surge of Union sentiment among foreign middle- and working-class elements made it even more unlikely that foreign rulers would risk discontent at home by again backing the wrong horse in America. Early in November 1862, the British government rejected the last French approach to intervene in the war and thereafter resisted all Confederate pleadings as well.

Britain's willingness to build sea-raiders for the Confederacy, however, seemed to invalidate her official policy of nonintervention. International law permitted neutrals to build nonnaval craft for belligerents, but it forbade such craft to be "equipped, fitted out, or armed" for fighting. British shipbuilders evaded this restriction by allowing apparently inoffensive hulls to "escape" to obscure and unpoliced ports, there to take on guns and munitions. All told, 18 of these "brigands of the sea" (*Alabama* was the most successful of them) preyed on northern shipping.

In July 1862 Charles Francis Adams, the Union minister in Britain, protested in vain against the "escape" of *Alabama*. By 1863, however, Union threats to loose a "flood of privateers" against Britain's nominally neutral trade had the desired effect. No new Confederate raiders were launched; but the American merchant marine did not recover until World War I from the blows of those already at sea, and American claims against the British for the raiders' wartime damages became a hot political issue after 1865.

By 1863 an air of caution had taken hold in France as well, where Napoleon III had dreams of reinstating a monarchy in Mexico, to which the Confederates might look for help. Maximilian of Austria, a puppet of Napoleon's actually was placed at the head of Mexico's government soon after French army units had taken over Mexico City in June 1863. But thereafter he received scant French support, and when Maximilian was captured and executed by Mexican rebels in June 1867, the French acquiesced quietly in his extinction.

### THE NORTH IN WARTIME

The conduct of the war, of course, was the overwhelming civil as well as military responsibility of Lincoln's government. Yet the Republican party had also made many civil commitments that had nothing to do with the war, and many in the party's leadership were eager to meet these commitments while the South was out of the Union and unable any longer to obstruct federal fostering of industrial growth.

Thus the Republican Congress soon enacted the following measures: (1) In 1861 it passed the Morrill Tariff, which lifted duties to their 1846 levels. The protective tariff was steadily raised throughout the war, and once the war was over duties continued to soar. Payment of the war debt incurred in restoring the Union became one of the sacred arguments for postwar protectionism and covered its worst abuses. (2) In 1862 the Republican Congress voted to build the long-debated transcontinental railroad over a central route and to help finance it with lavish grants of public lands and generous cash loans. (3) In 1863, with revisions in 1864, Congress created a national banking system congenial to northern capitalists.

Nor did Republican leaders neglect their strong free-soil supporters. The Homestead Act passed in May 1862 made available to adult "citizens of the United States" (meaning whites) and to those who declared their intention of becoming citizens, 160 acres of the public domain. The land itself was free of charge, but prompt "settlement and cultivation" of the land was required by the act. Only men who had borne arms against the United States were explicitly excluded. Farmers also benefited from the Morrill Land Grant Act of July 1862, the result of a long campaign led by Jonathan B. Turner, an Illinois educational and agricultural reformer. This act donated public lands to the states and territories to support colleges where agriculture, the mechanical arts, and military science become the staples of the curriculum.

The impact of these legislative measures was to be felt far into the future. During the war years, following a short depression in 1861–1862 caused by the loss of $300 million in uncollectible southern debts and uncertainty about the war's duration, financing, and success, the North enjoyed a substantial boom. Historians have questioned the role of the war in stimulating general economic growth in the North; but it cannot be denied that the splurge of government war buying in particular gave a great impetus to the expansion and mechanization of agriculture, the production of shoes and other apparel, and the manufacture of munitions. "Shoddy" millionaires made fortunes foisting off on the government much useless material. Other millionaires of the future—Rockefeller, Carnegie, Mellon, Morgan—all laid the foundations of their huge fortunes in wartime business activity. Even if industrial growth was spotty, large amounts of capital for postwar business expansion accumulated in private hands.

Wartime prosperity had its harsh aspects, of course. Industrial wages, for example, rose far more slowly than living costs, causing much hardship in cities where food speculators flourished. Families living on fixed incomes were especially hurt by the wartime inflation. Yet few northerners suffered the privations that became all but universal in the Confederacy.

Despite the boom, Lincoln's government had a difficult time financing the war, partly because it failed to realize how long the war would last. Secretary of the Treasury Chase's monetary doctrines did not help matters. Chase distrusted debt and paper money, but when the heavy excise taxes and even the income tax imposed in 1861 at his behest failed to provide the needed revenue, he was compelled to resort to both. As the military situation worsened, however, he found the Union bankers less and less willing to accept government bonds in exchange for loans. When he next tried to borrow directly from the public he failed, until, in October 1862, he named his friend, the private banker Jay Cooke, as treasury agent in charge of bond sales. Cooke soon mounted a publicity campaign which, according to Senator John Sherman, reached "the people in every household from Maine to California." By this means, in a little over a year, he disposed of $500 million in bonds to almost a million persons.

Cooke's later campaigns were less successful. In any case, the government needed more revenue than could be raised by borrowing, and in 1862 Secretary Chase was obliged to turn to the printing of paper money. That year and the next, the Treasury issued certificates soon known as "greenbacks," to the

amount of $450 million. Unsupported by gold, these certificates nevertheless were made legal tender for domestic debts. By the summer of 1864, when Union armies were still in straits, the greenbacks had fallen in value to their low of 39 cents on the gold dollar. Thereafter Union bonds began to sell well again, no more paper money was issued, and the greenbacks' value rose. The question of the continued circulation of the greenbacks became a heated political question after the war.

Despite the sizable emigration from Europe to the North during the war, shortages of manpower hurt the Union military effort at certain junctures almost as much as they hurt the Confederacy. By March 1863 conscription could no longer be put off, and on the 3rd of that month, almost a full year after the Confederacy's measure, Congress voted the first Union draft. Far from helping the manpower situation, the wording of the act lit a torch to inflammable social discontent. One of its provisions permitted a man to escape military service simply by paying a fee of $300 to the authorities, leaving them with the responsibility of finding substitutes ready to serve for a bounty. Clearly the poor were going to be saddled with the rich man's duty in a fight that would only elevate the black worker.

Minor riots protesting the discriminatory measure occurred in Rutland, Vermont; Portsmouth, New Hampshire; and Wooster, Ohio. In Boston, several would-be rioters were shot dead after stoning troops there. Democratic Governor Horatio Seymour of New York helped turn the protest in New York City into a violent disturbance of major proportions by denouncing the constitutionality as well as the unwisdom of the draft on the eve of the first drawing of names, July 11. On July 12, the City's papers printed the names of early draftees, and the next day, and for three days following, mobs reaching 50,000 in number so terrorized New York that federal troops had to be withdrawn from the battlefield to quell the violence. The leading perpetrators were poor Irish-American workingmen, themselves heavily discriminated against for their Cathol-

620

icism. Some of them were striking longshoremen whose jobs the City's free Negroes had filled. Competition for work among poor Irish and poor blacks in New York and other ports had long been intense and violent. Now, the Negroes, their churches, and their homes became the principal targets of the rioters.

While damage claims are said to have exaggerated the extent of property damage in New York City, fires roaring out of control are estimated to have destroyed buildings worth $1.5 million. At least a dozen people were killed and hundreds wounded during the riots. As in the Confederacy, the Union draft furnished comparatively few soldiers. But by prompting tens of thousands of young men to enlist voluntarily to avoid the brand of "conscript," it helped build up the fighting forces.

## THE PROGRESS OF EMANCIPATION

If Lee, before Antietam, and again before Gettysburg (see p. 624), yearned to end the war's hateful slaughter by breaking the North's morale through invasion, Lincoln, as the dreary reports from the battlefields indicated no release from the dreadful stalemate, yearned to end it through political action. That, no doubt, is what he meant when he said that "military necessity" required the Emancipation Proclamation of January 1,

*Mob lynching a Negro on Clarkson Street, during the New York City draft riots. A wood engraving from a contemporary English newspaper. (The Granger Collection.)*

1863. "Military necessity" was a phrase that the pertinacity of the abolitionists themselves first made popular and palatable as the proper ground for emancipation. It also offered, in Lincoln's eyes, perhaps the only constitutional justification for the Proclamation. But he used the phrase for more than merely expedient or technical reasons.

From the day he took office Lincoln had "struggled," as he said, against every kind of pressure, religious, journalistic, political, personal, to declare the slaves free without compensating their owners and without undertaking to "colonize" freed Negroes outside the country. Even had he sympathized with such demands, he felt too keenly the sensitivity of the border states within the Union, where slavery still persisted, not to speak of northern sentiment in general, to yield to them. During the early months of the war such bold antislavery generals as Benjamin F. Butler, John C. Frémont, and David Hunter, in pursuing their duties as they understood them, had threatened, and in certain cases had effected, the emancipation of slaves in the areas of their commands. They had even enlisted freed Negroes in their fighting forces. Lincoln

*"Come and join brothers." To induce Negroes to join the Union army many such recruiting posters were published. Another declared: "If we value Liberty, if we wish to be free in this land, if we love our country . . . we must strike NOW while the Country calls: must rise up in the dignity of our manhood, and show by our own right arms that we are worthy to be freemen." (Schomberg Collection, New York Public Library.)*

countermanded their actions and rebuked them for their precipitancy. "On the news of General Frémont having actually issued deeds of manumission" in Missouri in August 1861, Lincoln declared, "a whole company of our volunteers threw down their arms and disbanded." He added that "the Kentucky legislature would not budge [in the direction of loyalty] till that proclamation was modified."

As the fighting spread in the border states and in the South itself, and increasing numbers of blacks sought the security of Union lines, the generals in the field still were left more or less to their own discretion in dealing with them until in March 1862 Congress adopted "an additional article of war" forbidding officers, on pain of dismissal from the service, from using any of their forces to return fugitive slaves to their owners. In August 1862 the War Department issued the first specific authorization for the recruitment of fugitive slaves as soldiers. This authorization, although of very limited application, was accompanied by the request that it "must never see daylight because it is so much in advance of public opinion." In itself, however, it reflected a further liberalization of feeling which led, after January 1863, to the open enrollment of black regiments.

Following the "First Confiscation Act" of August 1861 (see p. 607), Congress also added more steps to the ladder of freedom independent of the armed forces. In April 1862 it passed and Lincoln signed a measure abolishing slavery in the District of Columbia. Under this act, former owners were to be paid, on the average, $300 per slave. In June that year Congress, with Lincoln's consent, also abolished slavery in United States territories, with no compensation granted. In July, Congress adopted the so-called "Second Confiscation Act," providing for the conviction for treason of all persons engaged in rebellion, "or who shall in any way give aid . . . thereto," and including as among its penalties the stipulation that "all slaves" of such persons "shall be forever free of their servitude." Lincoln prepared a veto message explicitly rejecting this bill on the grounds of the unconstitutionality of the word "forever." According to the Constitution, he pointed out, "no attainder of treason shall work corruption of blood, or forfeiture, except during the life of the person attainted." This was a technicality under the circumstances, and when Congress, equally technical, formally acknowledged that "forfeiture" was not meant to extend beyond the life of the guilty, Lincoln withheld his veto and signed the act. His proposed veto message, nevertheless, revealed the progress of his own thinking. In it he had observed:

It is startling to say that congress can free a slave within a state; and yet if it were said the ownership of the slave had first been transferred to the nation, and that congress had then liberated him, the difficulty would at once vanish. . . . I perceive no objection to Congress deciding in advance that they shall be free.

Union generals had dealt with slavery mainly by emergency measures. Congress had dealt with its under the whip of Radical opinion. When he signed the Second Confiscation Act on July 17, 1862, Lincoln had already failed in his own first effort as Chief Executive to use emancipation as an instrument to end the war and restore the Union. This effort was made in March 1862, when he proposed to Congress that both houses adopt a joint resolution offering to "any state which may adopt gradual abolishment of slavery, . . . pecuniary aid . . . to compensate" it for the "change of system." His object was to wean the border states from their attachment to the "institution." In his message to Congress, Lincoln explained his thinking:

The leaders of the existing insurrection entertain the hope that this government will ultimately be forced to acknowledge the independence of some part of the disaffected region, and that all the slave States north of such part will then say, "the Union for which we have struggled being already gone, we now choose to go with the Southern section." To deprive them of this hope substantially ends the rebellion, and the initiation of emancipation completely deprives them of it as to all the States initiating it.

In Congress, border state votes helped defeat Lincoln's proposal. On July 12 the President invited border state representatives to the White House in an effort to change their minds. "If you had voted for the resolution," he told them, "the war would now be substantially ended." He urged them to reconsider in preparation for the next Congress. But within 48 hours their spokesmen returned and told Lincoln the majority among them felt that his plan would not "lessen the pressure for 'unconstitutional' emancipation by proclamation of the remaining three million slaves in the seceded states, which [they] were unwilling to approve."

Having lost his appeal to the border states to free their slaves and save the Union, Lincoln, as a last peaceful recourse, now decided to admonish the slave states to return to the Union or see their slaves freed. For this purpose he immediately began work on his so-called preliminary emancipation proclamation which he was prevailed upon by the Cabinet to withhold from the public at least until word from the battlefield improved. He was unwilling to wait beyond Antietam, which, on September 17, 1862, saw the frustration of Lee's war-ending effort (see p. 614). Thus, on September 22 he read to the Cabinet a new draft of a proclamation. Secretary Chase recorded the President's words in his diary:

I think the time has come now. I wish it were a better time. I wish that we were in a better condition. The action of the army against the rebels has not been quite what I should have best liked. But they have been driven out of Maryland, and Pennsylvania is no longer in danger of invasion. When the rebel army was at Frederick, I determined, as soon as it should be driven out of Maryland, to issue a Proclamation of Emancipation such as I thought most likely to be useful. I said nothing to any one; but I made the promise to myself, and (hesitating a little)—to my Maker. The rebel army is now driven out, and I am going to fulfill that promise.

On September 23, the papers published this preliminary emancipation plan. In it, Lincoln said that at the next meeting of Congress in December he would recommend the enactment "of a practical measure" offering to *all* slave states not then in rebellion against the United States and having "voluntarily adopt[ed] immediate, or gradual abolishment of slavery within their limits," the same type of "pecuniary aid" as he had offered the border states in March. He also promised to continue his efforts to "colonize persons of African descent, with their consent." On January 1, 1863, the September proclamation went on, he would designate which states still were in rebellion, and in them, "all persons held as slaves . . . shall be then, thenceforward, and forever free," with no compensation whatever. Moreover, "the military and naval authority" of the United States would make no effort to suppress any efforts slaves may then make to effect their freedom; on the contrary, this authority would do whatever necessary to protect it.

Conservatives in the North, sick of the military stalemate and fearful that any tampering with slavery would only prolong the South's resistance, registered their disapproval of the preliminary emancipation proclamation in the fall elections of 1862, when the Democrats cut deeply into the Republican majority in the House and won the governorship in New York. The Radicals, on the other hand, deplored Lincoln's tortuous and tolerant maneuverings and demanded that he get on with the "revolutionary struggle" he abhorred.

Lincoln, nevertheless, held to his deliberate course. Following the elections, in accordance with his preliminary emancipation plan, he urged Congress in his second annual message on December 1, 1862, to adopt an amendment to the Constitution providing that each slave state which abolished slavery "any time before the 1st day of January, 1900, shall receive compensation from the United States"; but only those not in rebellion against the United States on January 1, 1863, might participate in this offer. Lincoln's urging fell on deaf ears. Indeed, in mid-December, following the Union military disaster at Fredericksburg (see p. 624), Senator Sumner led a congressional delegation to the White House demanding that Secretary of State Seward, McClellan's friend, be dropped, and a further shuffling of the Cabinet. Lincoln's friend, Senator Browning, advised the President that the goal was to transform his Cabinet into a thoroughly Radical body which would run the war from the Executive Department the way the Committee on the Conduct of the War, in Congress (see p. 608), wanted it run. Lincoln turned the tables on the visitors, got Chase's resignation instead of Seward's, and cried, "Now I can ride!"

624

On January 1, 1863, his "full period of one hundred days" of grace gone by with no takers among the rebellious commonwealths (they, in fact, viewed the proclamation as little short of an invitation to slave revolts and a servile war), Lincoln issued his final proclamation:

I, Abraham Lincoln, . . . in time of actual armed rebellion against the . . . United States, and as a fit and necessary war measure for suppressing said rebellion, do . . . order and declare that all persons held as slaves within . . . states and parts of states wherein the people . . . are . . . in rebellion . . . are and henceforward shall be free. . . . And I hereby enjoin upon the people so declared to be free to abstain from all violence, unless in necessary self-defense. . . . And I further declare . . . that such persons . . . will be received into the armed service of the United States.

"I know very well," Lincoln told Sumner at this time, "the name connected with this document will never be forgotten." The Proclamation neither freed any slaves nor shortened the war. But it insured the death of slavery when the war would be won. In his message to Congress in December 1862, Lincoln said, "in *giving* freedom to the *slave, we assure* freedom to the *free*." The last months of 1862, politically trying to Lincoln's administration, were to be tragic for the Union armies. But the South and the world knew there could no longer be any surrender to slavery.

## v *Gettysburg, Vicksburg, and Atlanta*

### THE LONG ROAD TO GETTYSBURG

After Antietam (see p. 615), McClellan held Lee at his mercy but withstood every demand that he move until Lincoln, observing in utter disgust that McClellan had the "slows," removed him in November. As before, his replacement at the head of the still formidable Army of the Potomac, General Ambrose E. Burnside, proved much worse.

Burnside guilelessly tried to steal a march on Lee while mounting still another frontal assault on Richmond. As might have been expected, Lee turned the tables on his opponent. Their brutal meeting took place at Fredericksburg, Virginia, on December 13, after Lee with 70,000 men had been given a month to set up impregnable defenses on the surrounding heights. Six times Burnside ordered the full force of his 125,000 men against this barrier. Six times his gallant lines were cut to pieces. Burnside was eager to keep up the dreadful assault—"There was a great stubbornness in him," writes Bruce Catton, "a great stubbornness and nothing more"—but his more merciful subordinates persuaded him to withdraw after he had lost more than 12,000 of his best men (see illustration, pp. 626–627).

In January 1863 Lincoln relieved Burnside and turned the eastern command over to "Fighting Joe" Hooker, an intriguer and blusterer who once had declared that the country needed a dictator in the President's place. "What I now ask of you is military success," Lincoln told Hooker, "and I will risk the dictatorship." By springtime, the Army of the Potomac was up to 130,000 men and again in splendid trim. "My plans are perfect," Hooker boasted, "and when I start to carry them out, may God have mercy on General Lee, for I will have none."

Hooker recognized that Lee's army of 60,000, still safe in its Fredericksburg entrenchments, remained too formidable to be taken by frontal assault. He decided to feign such an assault, repeating Burnside's disastrous maneuver, while actually bringing his main force around to strike at Lee's undefended rear. On April 27, the Federals carried out the first part of the plan to perfection. Drawn from their Fredericksburg entrenchments by the new Union activity, Lee's heavily outnumbered forces encountered Hooker at Chancellorsville, a small crossroads settlement to the west. Seizing the initiative, Lee split up his troops, dispatching "Stonewall" Jackson to roll up Hooker's vulnerable right flank while Lee himself attacked the Union front. On May 2, Jackson descended on the unprepared Federals and completely demoralized them. He also demoralized Hooker who might have counter-attacked successfully and destroyed the divided Confederates but who instead, against the entreaties of his corps commanders, decided to run. On May 5, having lost more than 17,000 men, Hooker recrossed the Rappahannock northward toward Washington. "My God, my God," Lincoln is reported to have cried out on learning the news, "What will the country say! What will the country say!"

Chancellorsville, following Fredericksburg, marked the peak of Confederate success in the eastern theater. Military historians call it "Lee's masterpiece," but it was to prove a disastrous triumph. The battle cost Lee 12,000 men. It also took the life of his flaming field commander, "Stonewall" Jackson. Worse still, it opened up to Lee what he saw as the opportunity—the very last such opportunity —to win the war with one blow: to surge northward once more, to bring bloodshed and destruction to Pennsylvania and Ohio, to dissolve the last shreds of Union morale and Union resistance. For this purpose he demanded of Davis every possible man of the quarter-million or more the Confederacy had fully under arms at the time. Davis would allow him no more than those he had in his Virginia command. Davis was not without justification. Simultaneously with the ever more vicious engagements in the East, the pace of the war was also rising in the West (see p. 630). Men were needed there too. Lee, who had come to believe the West irrelevant to final success, ignored his setback at the President's hands. Move he would, and move he did. "General Lee," one of his lieutenants said at this time, "believed that the Army of Northern Virginia, as it then existed, could accomplish anything." He was wrong.

Lee began his fateful march toward Harrisburg, Pennsylvania, on the strategic Susquehanna River, on June 3, 1863. Up ahead he sent his Second Corps under General Rich-

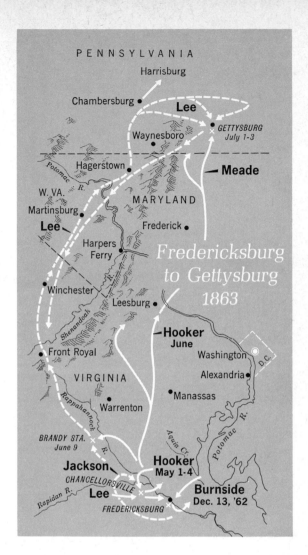

Fredericksburg to Gettysburg 1863

ard S. Ewell, who had fallen heir to most of Jackson's men. Then came the First Corps under Longstreet, and finally the Third Corps under A. P. Hill, the last to abandon the Rappahannock entrenchments. Ordered to cover the whole long thin line of march was the consolidated cavalry under unpredictable "Jeb" Stuart. Hooker, unchastened, thought he detected in Lee's departure yet one more, one more chance to move on Richmond. But Lincoln, grown wiser with the years, undertook to set him straight: "Lee's army, not Richmond, is your true objective point. If he comes toward the upper Potomac, follow on his flank

625

Behind the Union Lines at Fredericksburg as sketched by Thomas Nast. Troops ready to be called into battle view with foreboding the appalling conditions at the improvised field hospital. Amputated limbs lay under the table where a surgeon performs an operation. The whiskey on the table was the only anaesthetic available. (Harper's Weekly.)

*Tempered, tired, with a lean and hungry look, these Rebel soldiers were taken at Gettysburg. (Library of Congress.)*

and on his inside track, shortening your lines while he lengthens his."

Lee's army moved steadily up the familiar Shenandoah Valley, past already historic Harpers Ferry, across the Potomac into Maryland. Hooker's army beat a roughly parallel path between the Valley and Washington. Here and there, as they marched through Maryland, the enemies made contact, the cavalry of each, the "eyes" of the army, engaging in numerous indecisive skirmishes as they tried to keep the "feel" of one another. At Brandy Station, Virginia, on June 9, Hooker's Pleasanton and Lee's Stuart engaged in the biggest cavalry fight in American history before each proceeded once more on his way. By June 23, Ewell's advance Corps had reached Chambersburg, Pennsylvania, and was soon to push on to within ten miles of Harrisburg—the deepest penetration of the war. Stuart, that same day, thoughtlessly sallied to within four miles of Washington, where he cut off a Union wagon train, diverting to Lee supplies the Confederates much needed. Disastrously for Stuart, on June 25, Hooker got between him and Lee, and Lee's "eyes" were lost. Two days later, Lee's entire army had entered Pennsylvania, using Chambersburg as its base, but Lee no longer knew where Hooker was. Worried about his communications, Lee called Ewell nearer "home," abandoned the Harrisburg objective, and prepared for the showdown.

As it happened, even had he had his "eyes," Lee would not have been able to find "Fighting Joe." With battle impending, Hooker managed to get into an altercation with Halleck, still, unaccountably, General-in-Chief of the Union armies, and on June 28 he was replaced by "the old snapping turtle," George Gordon Meade.

On June 30, while Lee and Meade were seeking contact at some favorable point, a group of A. P. Hill's men entered the crossroads town of Gettysburg, Pennsylvania, looking for shoes and other supplies. There to greet them was Union cavalry under John Buford, Meade's most northerly watch. Heavily outnumbered, Buford sent word for help and then fought for all he was worth. Word of the encounter quickly reached Lee and Meade, and on July 1 the Battle of Gettysburg began in earnest.

Pouring into Gettysburg from the north, Ewell and Hill swept through the town, slaughtering the hastily mobilized Federals under Winfield Scott Hancock. But Hancock rallied his regiments quickly, led them to the lee of Cemetery Ridge just below Gettysburg, and there holed in while lookouts anxiously watched "the masses of blue coats toiling forward." At the end of the day Meade's men reached Cemetery Ridge in force. Parallel to Cemetery Ridge, to the west, across a mile-wide valley where "the fields were yellow with the golden harvest," lay Seminary Ridge, which the Confederates hastened to make their own.

The setting was almost perfect for a fight to the death. Cemetery Ridge had a peculiar shape, often compared to a fish hook. Longstreet, whose every instinct rebelled against assailing this redoubtable elevation, urged Lee to outflank it on the south, interpose his army between Meade and Washington, and force the Federals to attack him. This may have been more easily advised than accomplished; in any case, Lee knew that he and his men had come this far to advance farther and not to retreat or maneuver, and on July 2 he ordered the assault to begin.

The fighting on July 2 did not start until very late in the afternoon. Then it was fierce but indecisive. The next day Lee renewed the attack. Once more, on the morning of July 3, Ewell's men breasted the slopes of Culp's Hill on the northeasterly end of Cemetery Ridge, fought valorously, yet were repulsed. Still farther east, and unknown to most of the soldiers on the Ridge, Stuart's cavalry was making its own fierce effort to break into the Union rear and prepare a path for encirclement. But Stuart, too, was repulsed. Would Lee dare drive up the middle? Meade thought he would and decided to wait. At one o'clock a terrific artillery barrage began to rake the Union positions, and through the smoke Union men saw the Confederate preparations for Pickett's suicidal charge. The artillery had done little damage. When General George E. Pickett and his Virginians—supported by Pettigrew, Wilcox, and Trimble—15,000 troops in all, at last poured forth across the valley heading for the center of Cemetery Ridge, the big Union guns opened fire. Many rebels fell, but more came on. Gradually Pickett's flanks dissolved; then his main body came into infantry range and was picked to pieces; some dauntless men even scaled the Ridge but there they were surrounded and subdued.

The greatest battle of the war had ended, but the war itself would go on. Union casualties at Gettysburg are estimated at 23,000; Confederate casualties at 28,000. "Call no council of war. . . . Do not let the enemy escape," Halleck, at Lincoln's instructions, wired the victorious Meade. But Meade called

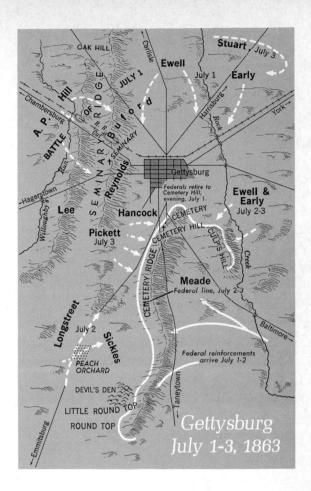

Gettysburg
July 1-3, 1863

a council of war while Lee made good his retreat. "Our army held the war in the hollow of its hand," Lincoln said later, "and would not close it." In a restrained but bitter letter to Meade (which he decided not to send), Lincoln wrote:

You stood and let the river run down, bridges be built, and the enemy move away at his leisure without attacking him. Again, my dear General, I do not believe you appreciate the magnitude of the disaster involved in Lee's escape.

Many months after the memorable battle, the bodies of thousands who there "gave their lives" still lay unburied. The degrading sight led to a call for a national cemetery in their honor. It was at the dedication ceremonies for this cemetery, on November 19, 1863, that

629

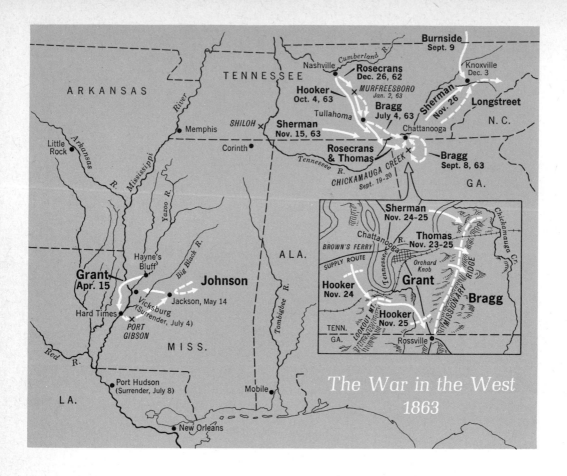

The War in the West
1863

Lincoln delivered the Gettysburg Address, promising "that these dead shall not have died in vain."

### GRANT IN THE WEST

On July 4, 1863, on the heels of the victory at Gettysburg, came the thrilling report of as great a Union triumph in the West. Grant had taken Vicksburg, "the Gibraltar of the Mississippi."

Operations to crack Vicksburg had begun in May 1862, but all efforts to take it from the north had failed. In 1863, Grant decided to strike from the more vulnerable southern and western approaches. He transported his troops across the Mississippi above Vicksburg and marched them down the western shore to a point south of the city, where transport ships that had run through the batteries of the fortress ferried them across to the eastern shore. Abandoning their supply trains, Grant's troops sped ahead, living off the country. Once he had eliminated the Confederate concentration at his rear in Jackson (May 14), Grant turned back toward Vicksburg, which, after a harrowing siege, capitulated July 4. On July 8, Port Hudson, the last Confederate stronghold on the Mississippi, also surrendered. Then it was that Lincoln wrote his memorable words: "The Father of Waters again goes unvexed to the sea."

After Vicksburg, one Confederate army and part of the Confederacy itself were isolated west of the Mississippi, but another Confederate army under General Braxton Bragg was still operating in central Tennessee. Late in June 1863, after months of shilly-shallying,

General William Rosecrans had begun his pursuit of Bragg southeasterly from Murfreesboro and by July 4 had forced him all the way across the Tennessee River into the strategic rail center of Chattanooga. A month of additional delay followed before Rosecrans crossed the river himself southeast of the city and, after further maneuvering on both sides, finally confronted Bragg, on September 19 at Chickamauga Creek. Here, only the deadly defensive action of General George H. Thomas averted a complete Union rout, and Rosecrans was now himself bottled up in Chattanooga, which had become useless to blue and gray alike.

Grant, who in October had been put in command of the Union armies operating between the Alleghenies and the Mississippi, now ordered Thomas to take over from Rosecrans and moved swiftly to raise the siege. Two corps from the Army of the Potomac under Hooker sped westward by rail to Nashville, then hastened toward Chattanooga. At the same time, General William T. Sherman marched his army eastward from the Mississippi. Grant himself arrived late in October to take personal charge. On November 25, with Thomas's troops, 18,000 strong, scaling Missionary Ridge, the seemingly impregnable anchor of Bragg's position, the Confederate center was broken in spectacular fashion, and Bragg was forced to retire. Sherman moved on to relieve the Union army penned up at Knoxville, and succeeded in liberating all pro-Union Tennessee. The Confederacy now was split north and south as well as east and west, and lay open to Sherman's march to the sea.

## LINCOLN'S GENERAL

Grant's performance as supreme commander in the West could not have been in more striking contrast to the dreary plodders who had so far made a brutal shambles of the war elsewhere. No longer would Lincoln, yearning for a leader, have to review the same disheartening circle—the McDowells, McClellans, Frémonts, Burnsides, Hallecks, Hookers, and Meades. On February 26, 1864, Congress revived the highest office in the army, that of lieutenant-general. On March 1, Lincoln named Grant to the post, and on the 2nd the Senate confirmed the nomination. By March 9 Grant had arrived in Washington for the first time for his initial meeting with Lincoln.

Grant possessed none of the glamor that surrounded so many of the colorful Confederate and Union prima donnas. A stubby, nondescript man, carelessly dressed, taciturn, shy, he seemed the very antithesis of the splendid soldier. One of Grant's devoted officers, General Horace Porter, wrote of him that "he never carried his body erect, and having no ear for music or rhythm, he never kept step to the airs played by the bands, no matter how vigorously the bass drums emphasized the accent." In battle, Grant moved swiftly, nevertheless, and in the words of one of his Confederate opponents, he had the "disagreeable habit of not retreating before irresistible veterans." His own "art of war" best sums up his military theory: "The art of war is simple enough. Find out where your enemy is. Get him as soon as you can. Strike at him as hard as you can and keep moving on."

His commission as supreme commander of all Union forces received, Grant got right down to work on the victory program. In the West his forces held all important communication centers and could lay waste the interior of the Confederacy from Mississippi to Virginia. In the East, back in the vicinity of Fredericksburg, Lee had rebuilt the army he had been allowed to salvage at Gettysburg into a formidable force, once again capable of menacing Washington. Grant's plan was for the Army of the Potomac, itself rebuilt and now directly under himself and Meade, so to occupy Lee's army that it could not link up with any other rebel force—and to bleed it daily in the bargain. While the Army of the Potomac thus was to cling to the Confederacy's leg, as it were, Sherman's army was to push eastward from Tennessee into Georgia and take Atlanta, skinning the Confederacy's body

632

as it went. Franz Sigel, at the same time, was to operate in the Shenandoah Valley and protect Washington from that direction; while still another army, under "Ben" Butler at Fortress Monroe, was to repeat McClellan's peninsular maneuver and strike at Richmond, which Lee was to be kept from defending.

The first reports of Grant's campaign were disheartening. As the Army of the Potomac, on May 4, 1864, marched south across the Rapidan from Culpeper, Virginia, where it had been encamped since its return from Gettysburg, it was met, rather earlier than Grant had planned, by Lee's heavily outnumbered force on the grim terrain of the "Wilderness." So thick was the forest, the fighters on either side could only be detected by the smoke of rifles. The woods quickly caught

fire and wounded men were trapped in the flames and burned to death. After two days of gruesome fighting, neither army had gained an advantage, and cynical Union veterans expected they would now retreat. Instead, Grant advanced inexorably, forcing Lee southward toward Spotsylvania in fierce hand-to-hand fighting. There, on May 10, Union and Confederate troops struggled blindly at "the Bloody Angle," a bend in Lee's line, where there occurred (to quote one of the participants), "the most terrible twenty-four hours of our service in the war." By midnight the rebel lines had been cracked, but at the cost of 7000 Union casualties. Despite the shocking losses, Grant kept advancing, and this fact alone had a tonic effect on the morale of his army. According to Charles Francis Adams, Jr., who

*Mathew Brady captured the worn look of a man who has borne a tremendous responsibility. This photo, taken after Vicksburg, shows Grant in Washington to receive his third star from Lincoln. (GAF Corporation.)*

served with Meade during the Wilderness campaign, "this Army [is] now just on its second wind, and more formidable than it ever was before." As events turned out, it needed to be.

By the end of May, Grant had re-established contact with Lee's army at Cold Harbor, Virginia, and on June 1 and 3 he ordered suicidal assaults against the entrenched Confederates. After a momentary success, the attack was savagely repulsed. "Our men have, in many instances, been foolishly and wantonly sacrificed," a Union staff officer wrote home. "Assault after assault has been ordered upon the enemy's entrenchments when they knew nothing about the strength or position of the enemy."

The enormous federal casualties in the Wilderness and at Cold Harbor—Grant is said to have lost a colossal 55,000 men in this first month of his campaign—aroused strong resentment in the North, and newspapers began to speak of Grant, like Burnside, as "the butcher." But Lincoln stood by this General:

"I have just read your dispatch," he wrote to Grant after Cold Harbor. "I begin to see it. You will succeed. God bless you all." Grant himself, however, had begun to have second thoughts. On June 12, he decided to disengage his army from Lee's, to swing down to the peninsula, and with Butler's assistance to get at Richmond once more from the South. Butler botched his orders sufficiently for the rebels to block Grant at Petersburg, 20 miles below Richmond, long enough for Lee to move his own forces to this front. Nine months later, in March 1865, Grant's siege of Petersburg still was on.

In July 1864, to help lift this siege, Lee sought to re-enact "Stonewall" Jackson's old diversion of 1862: to menace Washington by

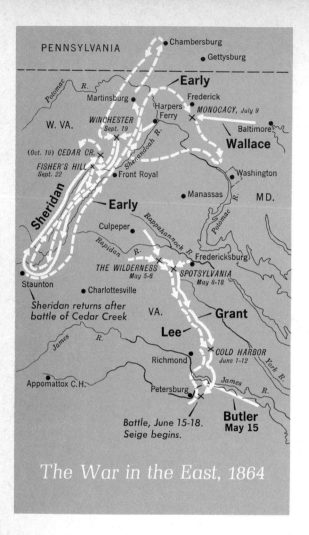

PENNSYLVANIA

• Chambersburg
• Gettysburg

**Early**
Martinsburg
Frederick
W. VA.
Harpers
Ferry
MONOCACY, July 9
WINCHESTER
Sept. 19
Baltimore
(Oct. 19) CEDAR CR.
**Wallace**
FISHER'S HILL
Sept. 22
Front Royal
Washington
Sheridan
• Manassas
MD.
**Early**
Culpeper
Rappahannock R.
R.
Staunton
Rapidan
• Charlottesville
THE WILDERNESS
May 5-6
R.
Fredericksburg
SPOTSYLVANIA
May 8-18
VA.
**Grant**
Sheridan returns after
battle of Cedar Creek
James R.
**Lee**
COLD HARBOR
June 1-12
York R.
Appomattox C.H.
Richmond
Petersburg
James R.
Battle, June 15-18.
Seige begins.
**Butler**
**May 15**

The War in the East, 1864

way of the Shenandoah Valley. By July 11, the rebels under General Jubal Early, after being checked at Monocacy for 24 hours by a raw force under General Lew Wallace two days earlier, actually entered the District of Columbia. On July 13, on learning that Grant had at last released a sizable contingent to protect the capital, Early decided to return to the valley and create more havoc there. Early's success led to the replacement of Sigel with Grant's top cavalryman, General Philip Sheridan, who took command in the valley on August 7. Grant's orders to Sheridan said, "Nothing should be left to invite the enemy to return. . . . If the war is to last another year we want the Shenandoah Valley to re-

main a barren waste." By March 1865 Sheridan had carried out these orders with the thoroughness of a Sherman. "A crow would have had to carry its rations," he said, "if it had flown across the valley." Sheridan then joined Grant for the Richmond campaign.

Since May 1864 Sherman himself, with three veteran armies in the West, had been slowly forcing the redoubtable Joseph E. Johnston toward Atlanta. On September 3 Sherman wired Washington, "So Atlanta is ours, and fairly won." On November 16, having left Atlanta, as he said, "smouldering and in ruins," Sherman and his "bummers" began their "picnic" march to the sea (see map, p. 636). "To realize what war is," Sherman said, "one should follow in our tracks."

## VI  To Appomattox

### THE ELECTION OF 1864

Sherman's victory at Atlanta in September 1864 had more than military significance. Early in the year the politicians had begun to prepare for the presidential elections in November and Lincoln, for the good of the Republican party, had been urged not to seek renomination. By the time of the party convention at Baltimore in June, however, his Radical opponents had failed to agree among themselves on a candidate and his loyal backers put him across. To bolster the ticket they named the "War Democrat," Andrew Johnson of Tennessee for Vice-president. In fact Lincoln and Johnson ran under a "Union party" label.

When the Democrats met at Chicago in August, a hodgepodge (to quote Gideon Welles) of "Whigs, Democrats, Know-Nothings, Conservatives, War men and Peace men, with a crowd of Secessionists and traitors to stimulate action," promptly chose General McClellan for President after the bid of Governor Seymour of New York fizzled out. The "war failure" plank in the Democratic platform, drafted by the "Copperhead" Vallandigham, declared that four years of war had not restored the Union, that hostilities should cease, and that the "Federal Union of the States" should be re-established on the old basis. This was nothing less than an armistice offer. McClellan, after serious soul searching, decided to reject this plank and to commit himself to continuing the war until the southerners agreed to rejoin the Union. At the same time, some of Lincoln's advisers had begun to press him to make peaceful overtures to Richmond.

Sherman's victory at Atlanta did a great deal to check peace talk in the North, and the rising confidence in the administration was shown in many local elections in October, when most Democrats went down to defeat. Lincoln's own renewal of confidence was rewarded by his winning 55 per cent of the popular vote in November. His electoral vote was 212 against McClellan's 21. The Republicans also won control of Congress and most of the state governments. Victory, not negotiated peace, now became the military theme as well.

**THE END IN SIGHT**

While Sherman and his men were gouging their way through Georgia, George Thomas and his subordinate, John Schofield, had been left to clean up in the West. Their objective was the Confederate Army commanded by General John Bell Hood, who had replaced "Joe" Johnston just in time to yield Atlanta to Sherman. Having saved his army then, Hood lost little time turning back to try to regain Tennessee, but on December 15 Thomas annihilated Hood at Nashville in one of the most crushing defeats of the war. Five days later Savannah fell to Sherman in Georgia. By his own estimate, Sherman's invasion had cost Georgia some $100 million in military resources, $80 million of it "simple waste and destruction."

From Savannah, in February 1865, Sherman headed north toward the "hellhole of secession," South Carolina, where, as he said,

"the devil himself could not restrain his men." By February 17, the "pitiless march" had brought him to Columbia, South Carolina's capital, and soon, whether by accident or design, one of the most beautiful cities in the country was being consumed in flames. Charleston, outflanked by Sherman, was occupied the next day by Union forces blockading the harbor after the defending rebels had fled. Sherman, meanwhile, pounded on into North Carolina, where on February 22 Wilmington, the very last of the Atlantic ports of the blockade-runners, was evacuated, like Charleston, by the rebel defenders and taken by Union harbor contingents.

On March 19 Sherman's progress was checked at Bentonville, North Carolina, by a considerable force commanded, once again, by Joseph E. Johnston, whom Lee had restored to service. Johnston yielded Bentonville to Sherman's larger army after a fight, but the contact with the Confederates convinced Sherman that it would be best to leave Richmond and Lee to Grant and Sheridan while he kept the capable Johnston away.

Gettysburg, Vicksburg, Atlanta, the humiliating failure of cotton diplomacy, the bruising wall of the blockade—none of these had quite managed to dissipate the Confederacy's material capacity for war. But before Sherman's devastation the southern spirit drooped. As early as September 1864 Davis acknowledged that "two thirds of our men are absent . . . most of them absent without leave." Soon after, he began negotiations for a peace conference on terms capable of "firing the Southern heart." But no such terms remained. On February 3, 1865, on a Union steamer in Hampton Roads, occurred the extraordinary conference between Lincoln—ready always for peace *and* union—and Vice-president Stephens, carrying Davis's terms of peace and independence. There was no chance that they could agree. "Davis," Lincoln said, "cannot voluntarily reaccept the Union; we cannot voluntarily yield it." The conference came to naught.

On February 9, 1865, in what was to be

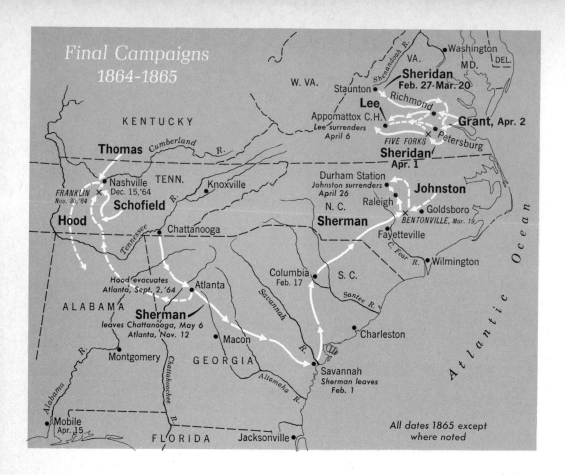

Final Campaigns
1864-1865

W. VA.

VA. • Washington
MD. DEL.

Sheridan
Feb. 27-Mar. 20

Staunton •

Lee
Appomattox C.H.
Lee surrenders
April 6

Richmond

Grant, Apr. 2

Petersburg

FIVE FORKS
Sheridan
Apr. 1

KENTUCKY

Thomas    Cumberland    R.

• Nashville    TENN.    • Knoxville
Dec. 15, '64

FRANKLIN ✕
Nov. 30, '64

Schofield

Hood

• Chattanooga

Durham Station
Johnston surrenders
April 26

N. C.    • Raleigh

Sherman

Johnston

• Goldsboro
BENTONVILLE, Mar. 19 ✕

Atlantic Ocean

• Fayetteville

C. Fear R.

Columbia
Feb. 17

S. C.

Santee R.

• Wilmington

Hood evacuates
Atlanta, Sept. 2, '64    • Atlanta

ALABAMA

Sherman
leaves Chattanooga, May 6
Atlanta, Nov. 12

• Macon

Savannah    R.

• Charleston

Montgomery •

GEORGIA

Altamaha R.

Savannah
Sherman leaves
Feb. 1

R.

Alabama    R.

• Mobile
Apr. 15

FLORIDA    • Jacksonville

Chattahoochee    R.

All dates 1865 except
where noted

his last public address, Secretary of State Benjamin reviewed the desperate straits into which Lee's proud forces had sunk and proposed to retrieve the situation by enrolling all slaves "who might volunteer to fight for their freedom." The next day a measure for black enlistments was introduced into the Confederate Congress; but six stormy weeks were spent eviscerating it. To arm slaves was to propose terror enough; to encourage enlistment with the promise of emancipation was unthinkable. The measure as finally passed offered the Negro nothing, and came far too late to lift Lee's sinking heart.

By the end of March 1865 Lee and Grant had been facing each other before the railroad junction of Petersburg for nine cruel months. Opportunity after opportunity had been lost by the Federals to crack the Confederate defenses and crash into Richmond; yet Grant had been making progress nonetheless. As he

gradually extended his lines to cut off Petersburg's communications with the rest of the Confederacy, he forced Lee to attenuate his own lines in order to guard his flanks. This was a tactic that Lee's depleted army could only carry out for so long before becoming attenuated to death. By the end of March the once nearly even opponents numbered 115,000 Federals to 54,000 "rebs." The time had come for Lee to pull out of his hateful trenches while he still had so formidable a force, try to join up with Johnston in North Carolina, and carry on the war from there.

Under cover of darkness on April 2, the Confederate exodus began. On April 3, while Davis and his government fled from their capital, exposed at last by the evacuation of the Petersburg front, contingents of Grant's army poured into Richmond. Grant and Sheridan themselves pursued Lee. On April 7, his path to North Carolina irretrievably sealed off,

Lee asked for terms. On April 9, impeccable in a new uniform, he met the mud-spattered Grant in the McClean farmhouse at Appomattox Court House, a village some 95 miles west of Richmond. "Give them the most liberal terms," Lincoln had ordered Grant and Sherman.

Let them have their horses to plow with, and, if you like, their guns to shoot crows with. I want no one punished; treat them liberally all round. We want those people to return to their allegiance to the Union and submit to the laws. Again I say, give them the most liberal and honorable terms.

Grant complied. On April 26 "Joe" Johnston surrendered his army to Sherman at Durham Station, North Carolina. On May 10 the fleeing Davis was caught in Georgia, imprisoned for two years, released, and permitted to retire.

**LINCOLN'S DEATH**

When news of Richmond's fall reached Washington on April 3, the city exploded with joy, and for the next 11 days the holiday mood continued. Then, on April 14, Good Friday, Lincoln was shot by the mentally unbalanced John Wilkes Booth as the President sat in his box at Ford's Theatre in Washington watching a performance of *Our American Cousin*. At 7:20 the next morning he died.

Lincoln had charged the nation to act "with malice towards none; with charity for all." He had acknowledged the guilt of the North as well as the South for "the bondsman's two hundred and fifty years of unrequited toil." At first Robert E. Lee would not credit the news of Lincoln's death. Then, on that Sunday, he told a visitor that he had "surrendered as much to [Lincoln's] goodness as to Grant's artillery." Now Lincoln and "goodness" had been removed from the scene, with what consequences Herman Melville foretold when he wrote in "The Martyr":

He lieth in his blood—
  The father in his face;
They have killed him, the Forgiver—
  The Avenger takes his place. . . .


There is sobbing of the strong,
  And a pall upon the land;
But the People in their weeping
  Bare the iron hand:
Beware the People weeping
  When they bare the iron hand.

637

*The last photograph of Abraham Lincoln, taken four days before he was assassinated. (Library of Congress.)*

# READINGS

The best modern study of the Civil War era is that by Allan Nevins. In addition to the prewar volumes cited for Chapter Eighteen, see the two volumes under the general title *The War for the Union: The Improvised War 1861–1862* (1959) and *War Becomes Revolution 1862–1863* (1960). J.F. Rhodes, *History of the United States, 1850–1877* (7 vols., 1906) remains invaluable for many special subjects. A shorter scholarly survey is J.G. Randall and David Donald, *The Civil War and Reconstruction* (rev. ed., 1961). The strong national feeling in the North is well documented in G.M. Frederickson, *The Inner Civil War: Northern Intellectuals and the Crisis of the Union* (1965). M.M Boatner III, *The Civil War Dictionary* (1959), is an invaluable reference work.

Northern industrial potential is measured in E.D. Fite, *Social and Industrial Conditions in the North during the Civil War* (1910). Lincoln's interest in industry is the subject of R.V. Bruce, *Lincoln and the Tools of War* (1956). J.C. Schwab, *The Confederate States of America* (1901), covers financial and industrial matters in the South. See also F.E. Vandiver, *Ploughshares into Swords: Josiah Gorgas and Confederate Ordnance* (1952). Thomas Weber, *The Northern Railroads in the Civil War 1861–1865* (1952), and R.C. Black III, *The Railroads of the Confederacy* (1952), are scholarly accounts. Ralph Andreano, ed., *The Economic Impact of the American Civil War* (1962), and D.T. Gilchrist and W.D. Lewis, eds., *Economic Change in the Civil War Era* (1965), present stimulating essays on the war and industrial growth. E.P. Oberholtzer, *Jay Cooke, Financier of the Civil War* (2 vols., 1907), is good on bond sales. W.C. Mitchell, *A History of the Greenbacks* (1903), is the classic account. A more general modern analysis is R.P. Sharkey, *Money, Class & Party, An Economic Study of Civil War and Reconstruction* (1959).

Clement Eaton, *A History of the Southern Confederacy* (1954), is the best general survey. See also E.M. Coulter, *The Confederate State of America 1861–1865* (1950); and C.P. Roland, *The Confederacy* (1960). A.D. Kirwan, *The Confederacy* (1959), is a "social and political history in documents." A.H. Stephens, *Recollections* (1910), offers a remarkable inside view by the Confederate Vice-president. On the Confederate President and his administration, see Hudson Strode, *Jefferson Davis, American Patriot* (1955) and *Jefferson Davis: Confederate President* (1959); and R.W. Patrick, *Jefferson Davis and His Cabinet* (1944). F.L. Owsley, *State Rights in the Confederacy* (1925), is a valuable monograph.

Of the many books on Lincoln as President, Carl Sandburg, *Abraham Lincoln: The War Years* (4 vols., 1939), remains preeminent. The following also are recommended: J.G. Randall, *Lincoln, the President: Springfield to Gettysburg* (4 vols., 1945–1955)—the last volume was completed by R.N. Current after Randall's death; and B.P. Thomas, *Abraham Lincoln* (1952), a one-volume life. R.P. Basler, ed., *The Collected Works of Abraham Lincoln* (9 vols., 1953–1955), offers information and insights not available elsewhere. David Donald, *Lincoln Reconsidered* (1956), is illuminating. On Lincoln and his Cabinet see *The Diary of Gideon Welles* (3 vols., 1911); David Donald, ed., *Inside Lincoln's Cabinet: The Civil War Diaries of Salmon P. Chase* (1954); and B.P.

Thomas and H.B. Hyman, *Stanton: The Life and Times of Lincoln's Secretary of War* (1962). Lincoln's troubled relations with his party are discussed in D.M. Potter, *Lincoln and His Party in the Secession Crisis* (1942); T.H. Williams, *Lincoln and the Radicals* (1941); H.J. Carman and R.H. Luthin, *Lincoln and the Patronage* (1943); and H.B. Hesseltine, *Lincoln and the War Governors* (1948). Copperheadism is described in Wood Gray, *The Hidden Civil War* (1942), and F.L. Klement, *The Copperheads in the Middle West* (1960). J.G. Randall, *Constitutional Problems under Lincoln* (1926), offers a rigorous examination. The role of the abolitionists during the war is presented in J.M. McPherson, *The Struggle for Equality, Abolitionists and the Negro in the Civil War and Reconstruction* (1964). F.M. Brodie, *Thaddeus Stevens* (1959), and David Donald, *Charles Sumner* (1961), are outstanding on the leading Radicals. J.H. Franklin, *The Emancipation Proclamation* (1963), is the leading monograph on that document. The diplomatic aspects of the war are covered in the general war histories. See also F.L. Owsley, *King Cotton Diplomacy* (1931), and M.B. Duberman, *Charles Francis Adams* (1961), on the Union minister in London.

A vast literature exists on the military aspects of the Civil War. Moving and authoritative accounts of the Union army in the East may be found in four books by Bruce Catton: *Mr. Lincoln's Army* (1951); *Glory Road* (1952); *A Stillness at Appomattox* (1954); and *This Hallowed Ground* (1956). Also recommended are Catton's *Centennial History of the War* (3 vols., 1961–1965) and K.P. Williams, *Lincoln Finds a General: A Military History of the Civil War* (4 vols., 1949–1956). T.H. Williams, *Lincoln and His Generals* (1952), treats an important phase. A classic account of the campaigns is *The Personal Memoirs of U.S. Grant* (2 vols., 1885–1886). See also Lloyd Lewis, *Captain Sam Grant* (1950), and its sequels by Bruce Catton, *Grant Moves South* (1960) and *Grant Takes Command* (1969). W.T. Sherman, *Memoirs* (2 vols., 1886), may be supplemented by Lloyd Lewis, *Sherman, Fighting Prophet* (1932). W.W. Hassler, Jr., *General George B. McClellan, Shield of the Union* (1958), is a sympathetic study. R.S. West, Jr., *Mr. Lincoln's Navy* (1957) is a good account.

D.S. Freeman, *R.E. Lee, A Biography* (4 vols., 1934–1935) and *Lee's Lieutenants* (3 vols., 1942–1944), are authoritative. An outstanding one-volume life is Clifford Dowdey, *Lee* (1965). Dowdey and L.H. Manarin, eds., *The Wartime Papers of R.E. Lee* (1961), is a rich collection. G.R.F. Henderson, *Stonewall Jackson and the American War* (2 vols., 1898), and Burke Davis, *Jeb Stuart* (1957), are also valuable. Many biographies celebrate other generals on both sides. For the ordinary man's role in the war, see H.S. Commager, ed., *The Blue and the Gray: The Story of the Civil War as Told by Participants* (2 vols., 1950); and B.I. Wiley, *The Life of Johnny Reb* (1943) and *The Life of Billy Yank* (1952). On the war and the Negro see Benjamin Quarles, *The Negro in the Civil War* (1953); T.W. Higginson, *Army Life in a Black Regiment* (1870); D.T. Cornish, *The Sable Arm: Negro Troops in the Union Army 1861–1865* (1958); B.I. Wiley, *Southern Negroes 1861–1865* (1938), as well as W.L. Rose, *Rehearsal for Reconstruction* (1964).

Wartime Washington is colorfully described in Margaret Leech, *Reveille in Washington 1860–1865* (1941), and C.M. Green, *Washington, Village and Capital 1800–1878* (1962); wartime Richmond, in A.H. Bill, *The Beleaguered City: Richmond 1861–1865* (1946), and L.H. Manarin, ed., *Richmond at War: The Minutes of the City Council 1861–1865* (1967). Southern civilian life is presented in B.I. Wiley, *The Plain People of the Confederacy* (1943), and C.H. Wesley, *The Collapse of the Confederacy* (1937). The reader should not miss Whitman's *Drum-Taps* (1865) and *Specimen Days* (1875), and Melville's *Battle-Pieces and Other Aspects of the War* (1866).

# TWENTY

Most of the wars of the nineteenth century, once the great Napoleonic struggle had ended, were waged for limited objectives, by professional forces, between nations that rarely questioned one another's sovereignty. The wars between the United States and Mexico and the United States and Spain (1898) were such wars. The American Civil War also began as a war for limited objectives, but with the question of sovereignty at its very heart. And it soon engaged an entire people in a struggle for survival. Confederate Vice-president Alexander H. Stephens made this clear when he said in 1863: "A large majority in both sides are tired of the war; want peace. . . . But we do not want peace without independence, so they do not want peace without union." For the Confederacy to succeed, the Union had to be destroyed. For the Union to survive, the Confederacy had to be obliterated. The Union survived. The men in blue, said one disillusioned southerner late in 1865, "destroyed everything which the most infernal Yankee ingenuity could devise means to destroy; hands, heart, fire, gunpowder, and behind everything the spirit of hell, were the agencies which they used."

Two days after Appomattox, three days before his assassination, Lincoln, on April 11, 1865, said of the South:

Unlike the case of a war between independent nations, there is no organized organ for us to treat with. No one man has authority to give up the rebellion for any other man. We must simply begin with, and mould from, disorganized and discordant elements.

Lincoln's view of the realities of the southern situation was consistent with his whole theory of secession, rebellion, and reconstruction.

# THE

# RECONSTRUCTED

# UNION

Lincoln held from the outset that the Union was indestructible and that states could not break away from it even though their people might rebel. Rebellious citizens could be restored to citizenship by presidential pardon and then could set about manning new governments in states which themselves had never been defunct. This view became the foundation of Lincoln's program for reconstruction by the *executive* department. At his very last Cabinet meeting before his assassination, according to his Navy Secretary, Gideon Welles, Lincoln had called it "providential" that "the rebellion was crushed just as Congress had adjourned. . . . If we were wise and discreet," he added, "we should reanimate the States and get . . . the Union reestablished before Congress came together in December."

In designing his program, Lincoln calculatingly closed his eyes to one overwhelming fact: the war, besides devastating parts of the South, had washed away the slave foundations of southern society. The Radicals knew this very well; in fact its accomplishment had been their central objective. After the war, they aimed to rebuild southern society around the equality of freedman and white, come what may. Lincoln's Radical Secretary of the Treasury, Salmon P. Chase, stated it clearly to the President: "This way is recommended by its

simplicity, facility, & above all, justice. It will be, hereafter, counted equally a crime & a folly if the colored loyalists of the rebel states shall be left to the control of restored rebels, not likely, in that case, to be either wise or just, until taught both wisdom and justice by new calamities." According to Radicals in Congress, the rebel states had forfeited all connection with the Union and were reduced to the status of territories. In seeking statehood once again, they came under the jurisdiction, not of the executive but of the *legislative* department in whose hands territorial affairs lay.

Lincoln, an ex-Whig, had not forgotten the strength this nationalist party had found among business leaders and professional men in the Old South. By his policy of "malice toward none; charity for all," as he said in his second inaugural in March 1865, he hoped to draw surviving southern Whigs to the Republican standard. By entrusting the freedman's fate to these new "Republicans," the party would be strengthened nationally. If he could swing his old project of Negro colonization overseas, a project he never surrendered (see p. 649), so much the better. The Radicals, on the other hand, saw the southern Negro vote as the only means of gaining that section for the Republicans and insuring their

641

642

party's national character and strength. To protect the freedman from southern pressure, the Radicals also tried to develop an educational program to nourish his mental independence and a land program to support his economic liberty.

The conflict between the conservative executive and the Radical legislators, clearly joined during the war, reached its climax in the impeachment proceedings in Congress against President Andrew Johnson in 1868. Thereafter, for almost a decade, the Radicals ruled both the South and the nation, gradually fatiguing themselves and the people with what seemed more and more a thankless and degrading task. Many Radicals and their sympathizers failed to recognize the depth of the problem they had undertaken in trying to win political independence and social equality for the freedman. Color was one overweening obstacle. Race, in so far as it was distinguishable from color (as it was in the case of the deep prejudice against the Irish), was another. A third was the vogue of "Social Darwinism," with its emphasis on "natural selection" in effecting the "survival of the fittest." Leading Radicals who were determined to overcome their color and race prejudices in order to give the ex-slave his chance in a free society saw no reason to run against the best scientific thinking of the day to gain their objective. "Now, we totally deny the assumption," said *The Nation* magazine, founded in 1865 explicitly to assist the freedman, "that the distribution of other people's land to the negroes is necessary to complete the work of emancipation." Once free, *The Nation* held, the Negro's survival must be determined by his own enterprise.

The failure of Radical Reconstruction is no indication that Lincoln's alternative was preferable. The evidence is overwhelming that the South's attitude toward the ex-slave was as unregenerate just after the war as it was after Radical Reconstruction was formally abandoned in 1877. A Virginia judge reported the observation of a friend of his in 1866: "Sooner than see the colored people raised to a legal and political equality, the Southern people would prefer their total annihilation." The judge added, "I regarded him [the friend] as well informed and almost as candid a man as we have." Radical Reconstruction postponed the legal and political annihilation of the freedman for a decade, and it laid the legal and political foundation for the improvement of his condition when he found his own leaders in the twentieth century.

## 1 *The Conquered Section*

The Civil War ravaged the fighting families of the North as well as the South; and it was difficult even for the most conciliatory Unionist to forget for long "the patriot hosts that had fallen on fearful battlefields." Yet the North, as Whitman stated it, had its great compensation:

> The ship is anchor'd safe and sound, its
> voyage closed and done,
> From fearful trip the victor ship comes in
> with object won;
> Exult O shores, and ring O bells!

The North had more mundane compensations as well on which to build a mighty future. Its $4 billion in direct wartime expenditures gave a fillip to business enterprise, an impetus to industry (see p. 618). The prosperity did not extend to all lines of business. The cotton textile industry, for example, broke down; the merchant marine and the shipbuilding industry suffered losses from which they did not recover until the wars of the twentieth century; railroad-building was sharply retarded. Yet, as John Sherman wrote in 1865 to his brother, General William T. Sherman, wartime expenditures by the federal government lifted the hopes of businessmen in the North. "The close of the war," he said, "with our resources unimpaired gives an elevation, a scope to the ideas of leading capitalists, far higher than anything ever undertaken in this country before. They talk of millions as confidently as formerly of thousands."

Direct Confederate expenditures for the war exceeded $2 billion, and expenditures by the individual southern states added many millions more to the total cost. But in the South, by contrast, these outlays became an utter loss. A few southerners managed to accumulate capital during the war—some by running cotton through the northern blockade or by preying profitably on Yankee shipping, others by demanding gold or goods from their neighbors instead of Confederate paper money in payment for food, clothing, and farm supplies. But most southerners were impoverished. The planters' $2.5 billion investment in slaves had vanished. Their land, worth $1.5 billion in 1860, was evaluated at but half that amount ten years later. The section's $1 billion in banking capital had been wiped out; and

worse, the credit system on which the staple planters had been dependent for all essential purchases was paralyzed. At the end of the war, each of the boys in blue went home at government expense with about $235 in his pocket and with every hope of returning to the fruitful land, to business, or to school. The boys in gray turned homeward with their pockets empty, their prospects grim. Some of Lee's soldiers, writes Dixon Wecter, "had to ask for handouts on the road home, with nothing to exchange for bread save the unwelcome news of Appomattox."

Fighting had occurred only in a relatively

643

*The triumphal march through Washington of the returning troops as seen in* The Grand Review of the Glorious Army of the Potomac, *May 1865, from a painting by James E. Taylor. (National Archives.)*

644

few sections in the South, but in these areas the destruction was likely to be complete. Writing in September 1865 of Columbia, South Carolina, believed by many to have been the most beautiful city in North America, a traveler said it was "a wilderness of ruins. . . . Not a store, office, or shop escaped [the burning]; and for a distance of three-fourths of a mile on each of twelve streets there was not a building left."

Nor had rural areas escaped. Five years after the war an English traveler described the Tennessee Valley country:

The trail of war is visible throughout the valley in burnt-up gin-houses, ruined bridges, mills, and factories . . . and in large tracts of once cultivated land stripped of every vestige of fencing. The roads, long neglected, are in disorder, and . . . in many places . . . impassable.

*The devastation that was once Columbia, South Carolina. (Brown Brothers.)*

Southern river ports and coastal harbors were put out of commission. Levees were destroyed or neglected, and floods washed out miles of farm land.

But the South lost even more in nonmilitary damage.

Weak their hearts from too much sorrow,
Weak their frames from want and toil . . .

So ran the lament of southern women left with responsibility for land, buildings, tools, and machinery when even the boys ran off to fight. Every third horse and mule had died, wandered off, or been taken by Union or Confederate foragers, so that after the war men and women often harnessed themselves to the old plows in order to prepare their fields for planting. Southern factories, in turn, frequently had to be forsaken for want of the materials to make even simple repairs; gradually they fell into irretrievable decay.

In the disorganization of southern life, few

*In the typical makeshift contraband camp—the one shown above was in Richmond, 1865—the Negroes lived in squalor, ignorant of the means to combat disease. Nonetheless former slaves and runaways continued to head northward to encampments by horse and wagon (right)—or, more likely, on foot. (The Granger Collection.)*

suffered more than the ex-slaves. The problem of free and footloose blacks had been forced upon the Union armies and the Union government at the very outset of the war, as Negro families in both the border states and the Confederacy fled to the shelter of the Union lines. Land-hunger probably gave the greatest impulse to the freedman's wandering. As early as 1862, in debates over the Confiscation Acts by which Congress threatened the rebels with conviction for treason and the emancipation of their slaves, Radicals in Congress had talked seriously of establishing freed Negroes on land captured by Union forces. Subsequently, on taking over conquered territory, certain Union generals made land available to ex-slaves on easy terms. Since many of the black farmers did well, others grew eager for land of their own, but little ever came of their aspirations. Eventually, thousands of Negroes were corralled in Union "contraband camps,"

so flimsy, filthy, and crowded that death from epidemics, exposure, and crime soon claimed one of every four inmates. Private philanthropy, first organized in the North in 1862, supplemented these early official measures with somewhat happier results.

When the Emancipation Proclamation of January 1, 1863, sharply focused attention on the plight of free Negroes, Congress began to consider bills to establish a bureau for their care. Not until March 3, 1865, however, did Congress create, as part of the War Department, the Bureau of Refugees, Freedmen, and Abandoned Lands—or, simply, the Freedmen's Bureau. This agency, which was to operate for only one year after the end of the war, was authorized to issue "provisions, clothing and fuel . . . for . . . destitute and suffering refugees and freedmen." The commissioner at its head was empowered to set aside land within the Confederacy which "shall have been abandoned" or confiscated, and to assign at a fair rent "to every male citizen, whether refugee or freedman . . . not more than forty acres of such land."

At first, the Freedmen's Bureau did nobly. But once the full flush of liberty struck the former slaves, the rate of migration soared and the Bureau became so hard-pressed merely to sustain life that the land program languished. In the summer of 1865, more than 20,000 blacks flocked into Washington, D.C. Greater numbers congregated in Charleston, New Orleans, Memphis, and other southern cities. Their resources sorely diminished by the war, these cities could do little for the newcomers but increase the number and size of their already overtaxed "contraband camps." Death and disease rates soared; during the first two postwar years in some camps a third of the ex-slaves died.

White farmers and planters often fared little better than the blacks. Famine struck many parts of the South as early as 1862, and the disruption of the transportation system prevented people in the more fortunate areas from sending food to their starving neighbors. By 1865, the statewide systems of relief set up during the war years in all the Confederate commonwealths had collapsed in the general ruin. Moreover, the 1865 harvest was extremely lean, so that, as one official of the Freedmen's Bureau reported, it was "a common sight, an every-day sight . . . , that of women and children, most of whom were formerly in good circumstances, begging for bread from door to door." In the first four years after the war the Freedmen's Bureau alone issued almost 21 million rations, 6 million of them to impoverished whites.

Perhaps the heaviest blow to the South was the moral cost of war and defeat. The losses in youth and talent hurt beyond measure. Among the survivors, purpose, morale, and aspiration drooped. In Georgia, in 1865, one reporter noted that "aimless young men in gray, ragged and filthy, seemed, with the downfall of the rebellion . . . to have lost their object in life." Mississippi alone, it was estimated, had 10,000 orphans. As late as 1879, a journalist remarked that the migrants who were leaving the Old South for Texas had "no progress in them, no love for adventure, no ambition." Those who stayed behind, though often the most stable persons in the community, were often the most discouraged. "These faces, these faces," cried a northern observer in 1873 on a visit to New Orleans: "One sees them everywhere; on the street, at the theater, in the salon, in the cars; and pauses for a moment struck with the expression of entire despair."

The war crippled all social agencies in the South. Church buildings were demolished, their congregations scattered. Schools and colleges simply ceased to exist. Policemen, sheriffs, courts, judges—the instruments of law enforcement—could scarcely be found. Heartless bands led by ex-Confederate guerillas like Jesse and Frank James roamed the countryside, refusing to give up the war against the victors and their society. "Our principal danger," said one observer, "was from lawless bands of marauders. . . . Our country was full of highwaymen . . . the off-scourings of the two armies and of the suddenly freed negro population."

Not until 1877 did the South produce a cotton crop as large as that of 1860, and not until 1879 did cotton exports to England reach the level of 1859. Much is sometimes made of postwar southern industrialism in smoothing the "road to reunion." Yet as late as 1900, the so-called industrialized New South actually produced a smaller proportion of American manufactures than did the Old South in 1860.

## II *Presidential Reconstruction*

### LINCOLN'S COMMITMENT

Many of those who, like Lincoln, closed their eyes to the inescapable challenge of the slaveless South were encouraged to do so by the official Union objective in the war, to which Lincoln himself adhered to the end of his life. This objective was set forth as follows in the Crittenden Resolution adopted by the House on July 22, 1861, with but two dissenting votes:

This war is not waged . . . for any purpose of . . . overthrowing or interfering with the rights or established institutions of . . . the Southern States, but to defend and maintain the supremacy of the Constitution and to preserve the Union, with all the dignity, equality, and rights of the several States unimpaired; and . . . as soon as these objects are accomplished the war ought to cease.

Three days after the House acted, the Senate, with but five dissenting votes, adopted the virtually identical Johnson Resolutions.

True to the Crittenden criteria, Lincoln in 1862, when much of Tennessee, Louisiana, and North Carolina had fallen to Union arms, hastened to appoint military governors to shepherd these states back to the shelter of the Constitution. These governors were simply to pave the way for the re-establishment in their states of "such a republican form of State government, as will entitle the State . . . to be protected . . . by the United States against invasion and domestic violence," as the United States Constitution (Art. IV, Sec. 4) prescribed, and nothing more.

One of Lincoln's shining virtues was his flexibility; and many of those who mourn his passing at the very moment when the recon-struction of the South had to be undertaken in earnest see in his loss the cause of subsequent extremism in the North and South alike. Lincoln showed his flexibility in December 1863, when Arkansas and certain other rebel states seemed on the verge of capitulation and a more general reconstruction program was required. On December 8 he issued his "Proclamation of Amnesty and Reconstruction," which became known as Lincoln's "ten per cent plan." By then, under mounting Radical pressure, Congress had passed the Second Confiscation Act and other antislavery measures (see p. 622), and Lincoln himself had issued the Emancipation Proclamation. Lincoln adapted the terms of his new proclamation to these *political* realities.

The "ten per cent plan" excluded from participation in southern politics all high military and civil officers of the Confederacy or its states and any others who had attempted to return black prisoners of war to slavery. To all other Confederates who would take an oath of loyalty to the Constitution and "solemnly swear" to "abide by all acts of Congress passed during the existing rebellion with reference to slaves, . . . and faithfully support all proclamations of the President . . . having reference to slaves," a general amnesty would be granted by the President and any confiscated property other than slaves would be restored. As soon as 10 per cent of a state's *1860 electorate* had taken the oath and sworn allegiance to the Union, that state, having thereby gained Executive recognition, could proceed to write a new constitution, elect new state officers, and send members to the United States Congress. The House and Senate, of course, were to retain their constitutional privilege of seating or rejecting such members.

Other provisions of this proclamation, at the same time, disclose how *in*flexible Lincoln was to remain on the *social* realities of the emancipation measures. The "ten per cent" proclamation, for example, assured the states to which it applied, "that any provision" they may make "in relation to the freed people of such State, . . . which may yet be con-

648

sistent with their present condition as a laboring, landless, and homeless class, will not be objected to by the national Executive." The proclamation backed down still further: "It is suggested as not improper," Lincoln said, that "subject only to modifications made necessary" by emancipation, "in constructing a loyal State government, . . . the general code of laws, as before the rebellion be maintained." This was nothing short of an invitation to the reconstructed states to adopt such inflammatory "Black Codes" as those they did in fact adopt in 1865 and 1866 (see p. 653).

Two further observations on Lincoln's proclamation are in order: (1) He was at pains in it to reassure all states that had remained loyal to the Union that the congressional antislavery measures and the Emancipation Proclamation did not yet apply to them. (2) He was also at pains to notify these and the rebel states that Congress could repeal or modify its antislavery measures, and that the Supreme Court could nullify them and the Emancipation Proclamation.

To make congressional repeal more difficult, Supreme Court nullification impossible, and emancipation itself more general, two Radical congressmen, only a few days after Lincoln's "ten per cent" proclamation, introduced in the House a proposal for an amendment to the Constitution which would forever abolish slavery throughout the United States. A few months later, the Senate joined the House in considering a joint resolution to submit such an amendment to the states. The resolution passed the Senate in April 1864 by 38 to 6. In June, the House voted for it, 93 to 65, with 23 abstentions. Lacking the two-thirds majority needed in the House, the joint resolution failed.

This action by a Congress in which the South was wholly unrepresented only confirmed Lincoln's skepticism about northern concern for the freedman's welfare. The proposed amendment promptly became a leading issue in the presidential campaign of 1864, the Republican platform declaring that year that "slavery . . . must be, always and everywhere, hostile to the principles of Republican Government," and committing the party to "such an amendment as shall terminate and forever prohibit [its] existence . . . within the limits of the jurisdiction of the United States." Yet in August 1864, during the campaign, Lincoln told a conservative critic, "If Jefferson Davis wishes to know what I would do if he were to offer peace and reunion, saying nothing about slavery, let him try me."

Lincoln interpreted his re-election by a large majority in November 1864 as a demand for the amendment, and in the lame-duck Congress that met in December his effective logrolling among House Democrats won over enough votes to the Radical side to squeeze out the bare two-thirds margin by which that chamber approved the proposal on January 31, 1865 and allowed it to be sent to the states, the Senate's earlier approval having carried over. Yet a mere three days later, Lincoln, according to his old Whig friend, Alexander H. Stephens, told a peace delegation headed by the Confederate Vice-president, that in his opinion the Emancipation Proclamation freeing the slaves of the South "was a war measure, and . . . as soon as the war ceased, it would be inoperative for the future. It would be held to apply only to such slaves as had come under its operation while it was in active exercise." At that time, at least 3 million slaves still were in bondage in the Confederacy.

The Thirteenth Amendment was ratified in December 1865 by the required 27 states, including eight formerly of the Confederacy, which Congress, for other purposes, did not even recognize as states (see p. 657). The leading Radical in the Senate, Charles Sumner of Massachusetts, believed that the unprecedented second section of the Thirteenth Amendment—"Congress shall have power to enforce this article by appropriate legislation" —meant that Congress could enfranchise the ex-slave if, in its judgment, the Negro required the right to vote in order to preserve his freedom. Not many, as yet, even among the Radicals, went along with the Senator. In his last public address on April 11, 1865, Lincoln dallied with the idea "that the elective franchise" might be "now conferred on the very intelligent" among the colored men, "and on those who serve our cause as soldiers." But for "the great mass of Negroes," as Kenneth M. Stampp writes, "he never abandoned his hope that they could be persuaded to leave the country." One of Lincoln's last efforts at overseas colonization was one of the most disastrous. This occurred early in 1864 when he won the reluctant approval of the government of Haiti to allow certain northern promoters to settle hundreds of freedmen on an island off the Haitian coast. A virtual return to slave conditions under the most ruthless exploitive methods killed half the victims before the rest were brought home.

### THE CONGRESSIONAL RESPONSE

Very early in the war, Senator Sumner observed that, "Mr. Lincoln's administration acted in superfluous good faith with the Rebels." As the war proceeded, Sumner found few reasons to change his mind; and as the end neared, he meant to see to it that Lincoln's policy did not cost the Union the fruits of victory. Sumner was one of the five Senators who had refused to vote for the Johnson Resolutions in July 1861, defining the limited purposes of the war (see p. 647). His alter ego in the House, Thad Stevens of Pennsylvania, had cast one of the two votes against the similar Crittenden Resolution. To these determined men, the war had been fought to free and elevate the slaves. They were not opposed to the "constitutional" reconstruction of the Union as these Resolutions prescribed, but they had further terms which they would not surrender even if reconstruction itself were sacrificed.

Stevens had championed the black man all his life (see p. 601) and was determined that his ideas of social equality, though advanced even for the North, be forced upon the proud planters.

The whole fabric of southern society [he declared] *must* be changed. . . . The Southern states have been despotisms, not governments of the people. It is impossible that any practical equality of rights can exist where a few thousand men monopolize the whole landed property. . . . If the South is ever to be made a safe republic let her lands be cultivated by the toil of the owners or the free labor of intelligent citizens. This must be done even though it drive her nobility into exile. If they go, all the better.

Surely the crimes of the South, said Stevens, "are sufficient to justify the exercise of the extreme rights of war—'to execute, to imprison, to confiscate.'" And Sumner added his insistent voice: "If all whites vote, then must all blacks. . . . Without them the old enemy will reappear, and . . . in alliance with the Northern democracy, put us all in peril again."

If Lincoln had a reconstruction plan for restoring the southern states but none for elevating the southern Negro, Sumner and Stevens had a plan for the Negro, but none that they openly championed at first for the southern states. Their principal early goal was to slow down political reconstruction so that southern congressmen would not soon reappear in Washington and exert political influence. In this objective they had the support of many conservative Republicans who were fearful that northern and southern Democrats would close ranks as before the war and overturn Republican economic legislation.

The Radical leadership did not offer an alternative to Lincoln's "ten per cent" plan of December 1863 until July 4, 1864, when Congress, on the last day of the session, adopted the Wade-Davis bill. This bill would have made reconstruction of the South by southerners impossible. It required a *majority* of citizens, not just ten per cent, to swear loyalty to the Union before an acceptable state government could be established in a seceding state. This majority, moreover, had to swear not only that it would be loyal in the future but that it had been consistently and continuously loyal in the past. The bill also prescribed that new state constitutions in the South must

650

abolish slavery, repudiate state debts, and disfranchise ex-Confederate leaders. Sumner tried to get the Senate to write into the bill a provision requiring the extension of the franchise to all male citizens regardless of color, but he gave up the idea when he saw that it would cost votes needed to insure the bill's passage.

The Radical strategists hoped by this bill to commit the Republican party to the Radical reconstruction program in the 1864 presidential campaign. Lincoln attempted to forestall them by permitting the Wade-Davis bill to die by a pocket veto and issuing a proclamation justifying his action. Lincoln said rebel states might follow Wade-Davis provisions if they wished, but he refused to make them mandatory. The Radicals replied with the Wade-Davis Manifesto of August 1864. "The President," it declared, "by preventing this bill from becoming a law, holds the electoral votes of the Rebel States at the dictation of his personal ambition. . . . A more studied outrage on the legislative authority of the people has never been perpetrated."

Most of the Radical leaders supported Lincoln in the 1864 campaign because they did not want to smash the Republican party machinery which they hoped soon to control. Once the election was over, they again resumed their own bent. In January 1865, as we have seen, they adopted the Thirteenth Amendment (p. 648). In February, Congress refused to admit members from Louisiana which Lincoln had declared "reconstructed" under his "ten per cent" plan. On March 3, it created the Freedmen's Bureau with, among other things, its power over abandoned or confiscated land (see p. 646). The next day, Congress went home, with the Radicals determined to keep up the steam in their boilers

*(Top) Thaddeus Stevens at 74. A Mathew Brady photograph of 1866. (National Archives.) The lithograph (bottom) shows Charles Sumner at age 61 in 1872. (The Granger Collection.)*

and blow their whistles every day. "There's ample public opinion to sustain your course," Wendell Phillips, the abolitionist, admonished Sumner; "it only needs a reputable leader to make this *evident* . . . We have six months to work in . . . & if you'll begin an agitation —we will see that it reaches the Senate room."

### ANDREW JOHNSON CARRIES ON

When Lincoln died on April 15, 1865, Andrew Johnson, 56 years old, became President of the United States. Born, like Lincoln, into the direst poverty, Johnson never succeeded in outgrowing his self-pity. Early in his political career this attitude had taken the form of aggressive dislike for the nobby cotton planters, and a good deal of Johnson's almost unbroken success at the polls in nonslaveholding eastern Tennessee may be attributed to his ability as a stump speaker in rousing the poor farmers against the plantation class.

Johnson won his first elective office—as alderman of Greenville, Tennessee—at the age of 20. Thereafter, he served successively as mayor, member of the state House and Senate, United States congressman, governor of Tennessee, and United States senator. Of all the southern senators in 1861, Johnson alone had refused to abandon his seat. While still a senator, in March 1862, he was appointed by Lincoln as military governor of Tennessee and succeeded in restoring civil government to that state before the threat of Confederate re-entry was ended. Under his regime, Tennessee became a kind of laboratory for Lincoln's reconstruction policy and Johnson's success there earned him the nomination of the Republican (Union) party for the Vice-presidency in 1864, even though he had been a dedicated Jacksonian Democrat all his life.

During the 1864 campaign, Johnson made himself attractive to many Radicals by his characteristic denunciations of the rebel leaders. They have "ceased to be citizens," he cried. They have become "traitors." Traitors, he went on, must not only be punished; they "must be impoverished." Within ten days of

Lincoln's death, Senator Chandler of Michigan declared that Johnson "is as radical as I am and as fully up to the mark." In May, Carl Schurz himself reported that, "The objects he aims at are all the most progressive friends of human liberty can desire." "Johnson, we have faith in you," exclaimed the jubilant Ben Wade of Ohio. "By the gods, there will be no trouble now in running this government."

Others, however, suspicious of Johnson's southern background and political past, held back. Congressman George W. Julian of Indiana, an old abolitionist, recalled that early

651

*President Andrew Johnson photographed by Brady in 1865. (The Granger Collection.)*

652

in the war, Johnson had been as energetic a Negro colonizer as Lincoln. Julian acknowledged Johnson's hatred of the planters; but he recognized that as one of the yeoman class he was also "as decided a hater of the negro . . . as the rebels from whom he separated." Julian also feared the state-rights bent of Johnson's Jacksonian philosophy.

Julian and others, nevertheless, were willing to give Johnson a chance. If he failed them, they would know how to deal with him. Johnson had no claims on Republican party allegiance. What small hold he may have had on the people, he sacrificed by the disaster of his inauguration as Vice-president. Exhausted and ill, Johnson had agreed to attend the ceremonies only on Lincoln's urging. On the morning of the inauguration he unfortunately tried to buck himself up for the great occasion by taking a little too much to drink. His inauguration speech grew more and more garbled until, at last, nearby officials cut in, administered the oath of office and led him compassionately away. Once President on his own, moreover, Johnson, foolishly perhaps, took over Lincoln's Cabinet intact, with its strong Radical contingent led now by Secretary of War Stanton, who by nature would let no opportunity pass to embarrass his new chief.

Thus armed, the Radicals confronted the future optimistically. But Johnson moved more swiftly and independently than they anticipated. Early in May 1865 he recognized Lincoln's "ten per cent" governments in Louisiana, Tennessee, Arkansas, and Virginia. He next appointed military governors in the seven states that had not yet complied with Lincoln's "ten per cent" plan. On May 29 he offered executive amnesty to citizens of these states except high Confederate military and civil officers, and citizens with more than $20,000. These people had to make personal application for amnesty to the President. The "whitewashed" electorate—that is, those who benefited by the amnesty offer—were then to elect members to a constitutional convention in each state, which would abolish slavery,

rescind the state's secession ordinance, adopt the Thirteenth Amendment, repudiate the state war debt, and call an election for a new state government. The suffrage for this election was to be determined by each state rather than by Congress. The Negro, clearly, would not get the ballot in the South any more than in most states in the North.

By the winter of 1865, all the seceding states but Texas had complied with Johnson's terms, and their sincerity was confirmed by the reports of investigators Johnson had sent to find out if the South actually did accept the judgment of arms. One investigator, however, Carl Schurz, found that "there is as yet among the southern people an *utter absence of national feeling* [Schurz's emphasis] . . . and a desire to preserve slavery in its original form as much and as long as possible." Johnson received this report with "great coldness," and only at Sumner's urging did Schurz decide to make it public. Few deny today that of all Johnson's emissaries, Schurz was the one who was right, and that southern extremism was plainly evident even before Radical Reconstruction began.

For all his yeomen animosity to the southern Old Guard, Johnson no doubt also had a sneaking admiration for them, if not a sneaking servility in their presence. His personal grants of amnesty, in any case, exceeded all bounds and the whitewashed voters soon proceeded to elect suddenly available ex-Confederate generals as governors, ex-Confederate solons as United States senators, ex-Confederate war heroes as local legislators. Other candidates, as a correspondent from Alabama informed Johnson, were cried down as "traitors to the South" and were routed at the polls. In some states, moreover, the secession ordinances were merely repealed, not repudiated. In others a reluctance to renounce the rebel debt was accompanied by a determination to resist taxation for redemption of the Union debt. The Georgia constitutional convention, in turn, was not alone in pressing claims for compensation as its price for "acquiescence" in a "war measure" like the Emancipation

Proclamation. In ratifying the Thirteenth Amendment, Johnson's reconstructed states were no less stiff-necked. Almost as a unit they warned Congress to keep hands off "the political status of former slaves, or their civil relations," to quote the South Carolina legislature. In the "Black Codes" adopted in 1865 and 1866 by all the reconstructed states but Tennessee, the freedman's "political status" was nullified simply by being ignored.

### THE BLACK CODES

Some alterations in the civil and criminal codes of the southern states and communities clearly were called for, as Lincoln had said, to meet the new southern social conditions. But the spirit in which the Black Codes were adopted would have given any fair-minded person pause. The Black Code of Mississippi, harsh though it was, was not the harshest. Adopted November 20, 1865, it opened as follows, with italics in the original:

*Under the pressure of federal bayonets, urged on by the misdirected sympathies of the world in behalf of the enslaved African,* the people of Mississippi have abolished the institution of slavery. . . . We must now meet the question as it is, and not as we would like to have it. . . . The negro is free, whether we like it or not. . . . *To be free, however, does not make him a citizen, or entitle him to social or political equality with the white man.* But the constitution and justice do entitle him to protection and security in his person and property, both real and personal.

British practice after the emancipation of slaves in the West Indies and northern practice in legislating for free Negroes served the southern states as models for explicit provisions, but substantial parts of their old slave codes also were re-enacted.

The Black Codes usually granted Negroes the right to sue, to give evidence in court, to go to school, to have marriages sanctified, and to have apprenticed children protected by the state. But nowhere could Negroes hold office, vote, serve on juries, or bear arms. In some states, the codes permitted blacks to own property, to work at any jobs they could hold down, and to quit a job freely. But in most states, they were prohibited from working as artisans, mechanics, and in other capacities where they competed with white labor; and they could not leave their jobs except under stated conditions. At the same time, as the Mississippi code put it, the law "shall not be construed as to allow any freedman, free negro or mulatto to rent or lease any lands or tenements." The code of a parish in Louisiana stated: "Every negro is required to be in the regular service of some white person, or former owner, who shall be held responsible for the conduct of said negro."

The vagrancy laws were the most oppressive provisions of the codes. In Georgia, for example, the law said that "all persons wandering or strolling about in idleness, who are able to work and who have no property to support them," might be picked up and tried. If convicted, they could be set to work on state chain gangs or contracted out to planters and other employers who would pay their fines and upkeep for a stated period.

The Black Codes, said the Radical Schurz, are "a striking embodiment of the idea that although the former owner has lost his individual right of property in the former slave, 'the blacks at large belong to the whites at large.'" The conservative Gideon Welles at the same time recorded in his diary: "The entire South seem to be stupid and vindictive, know not their friends, and are pursuing just the course which their opponents, the Radicals, desire. I fear a terrible ordeal awaits them in the future."

## III  *Congress and the South*

### THE STORM BREAKS

When Congress met in December 1865, it was faced with Johnson's executive coup and the South's disquieting response to it. Stevens improved the opportunity thus offered when he said, "Let all who approve of our [principles] . . . tarry with us. Let all others go with copperheads and rebels. Those will be the opposing parties."

As their first move, the Radicals set up the Joint Committee of Fifteen—six senators and nine representatives—to scan the qualifications of the men elected in the southern states and to review the whole presidential reconstruction plan that had brought such "traitors" to the very threshold of Congress. These men were never permitted to take their seats. Without them, Congress proceeded early in 1866 to enact a bill continuing the Freedmen's Bureau, which was gradually becoming an instrument of Radical policy. Johnson, believing that the future care of the freedmen had better be left to the state legislatures, vetoed the bill. "A veto at that time," said young Representative Shelby M. Cullom of Illinois, "was almost unheard of. . . . It came as a shock to the country." The Radicals succeeded in overriding the veto in the House, but failed in the Senate.

In March 1866 Johnson vetoed a civil-rights bill which forbade states to discriminate among their citizens on the basis of color or race, as they had in the Black Codes. But by now a sufficient number of conservative senators were ready to join the Radicals in defense of congressional prerogatives, if not of Radical principles and both houses overrode the President. A few months later, in July 1866, the Radicals pushed through a second Freedmen's Bureau bill over Johnson's veto.

The Radicals were showing their parliamentary mettle as well as their political policy. The real test developed over the Fourteenth Amendment, perhaps the most far-reaching one ever added to the Constitution. When the Republicans introduced this amendment in June 1866, they were concerned over the constitutionality of coercing the states under the Civil Rights Act and the danger that another Congress might repeal this act. A civil-rights amendment would set the constitutionality

issue at rest and would also make repeal more difficult.

The amendment's opening section for the first time defined citizenship in the United States as distinct from citizenship in a state. By identifying as citizens "all persons born or naturalized in the United States," it automatically extended citizenship to American-born Negroes. (Some years later, to check state regulation, the courts held that the amendment also extended United States citizenship to such "legal persons" as business corporations. The amendment forbade any state from abridging "the privileges and immunities" of United States citizens, and further impinged on state power by declaring that no state shall "deprive any person of life, liberty or property, without due process of law," nor "deny to any person within its jurisdiction the equal protection of the laws."

The second section of the amendment did not give Negroes the vote, but it penalized a state for withholding it by reducing its representation in Congress in the same proportion that those deprived of the vote bore to the "whole number of male citizens twenty-one years of age in such State." Northern as well as southern states, of course, were subject to the penalty, but in no northern state was the colored population large enough to bring about a reduction in representation in case Negro suffrage continued to be withheld. By 1866, only six northern states had enfranchised Negroes.

Third, the amendment disqualified from office, unless Congress specifically lifted the disqualification by a two-thirds vote, all Confederates who before the war had taken a federal oath of office. Finally, the amendment guaranteed the Union debt and outlawed the Confederate debt and any claims for compensation for loss of slaves.

At the time the Fourteenth Amendment was proposed many in the South as well as in the North hoped that it would provide "the final condition of restoration," as a Boston paper put it; that it would in effect be a lasting "treaty of peace" re-establishing the Union.

The leading Radicals, however, thought it too full of compromises and hoped to stiffen its provisions later on. No one backed Negro suffrage more fervently than Stevens. Yet in speaking in favor of the amendment in Congress, Stevens said:

In my judgement we shall not approach a measure of justice until we have given every adult freedman a homestead on the land where he was born and toiled and suffered. Forty acres of land and a hut would be more valuable to him than the immediate right to vote. Unless we give them this we shall receive the censure of mankind and the curse of Heaven.

But Stevens himself acknowledged even of the indirect suffrage provisions of the Fourteenth Amendment, let alone its failure to insure the freedman's economic independence: "I believe it is all that can be obtained in the present state of public opinion."

Susan B. Anthony and other agitators for woman's suffrage at this time argued that by their contributions to victory in the Civil War women at last had earned the right to vote. They fought valiantly to have the word "male" deleted from the franchise provisions of the Fourteenth Amendment (and soon to have the word "sex" added to "race, color, or previous condition of servitude" in the Fifteenth Amendment). But Radical leaders, believing that merging women's rights with Negro rights would weaken the chances of both, resisted the women's campaign. Not until the end of another war, World War I, would women's political equality with men be acknowledged.

The Radicals demanded that southern states ratify the Fourteenth Amendment to regain representation in Congress. Johnson advised the states not to ratify, and by mid-February 1867, all but Tennessee—that is, 10 of the 11 ex-Confederate states—had followed his advice. Legally, the amendment was dead. At

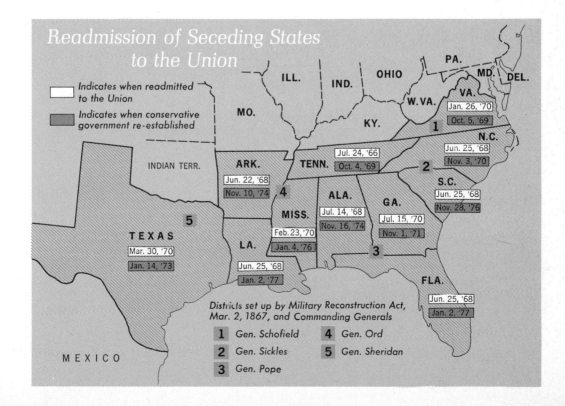

**Readmission of Seceding States to the Union**

☐ Indicates when readmitted to the Union
▨ Indicates when conservative government re-established

*Districts set up by Military Reconstruction Act, Mar. 2, 1867, and Commanding Generals*

1  Gen. Schofield
2  Gen. Sickles
3  Gen. Pope
4  Gen. Ord
5  Gen. Sheridan

VA. Jan. 26, '70 / Oct. 5, '69
TENN. Jul. 24, '66 / Oct. 4, '69
N.C. Jun. 25, '68 / Nov. 3, '70
ARK. Jun. 22, '68 / Nov. 10, '74
ALA. Jul. 14, '68 / Nov. 16, '74
GA. Jul. 15, '70 / Nov. 1, '71
S.C. Jun. 25, '68 / Nov. 28, '76
MISS. Feb. 23, '70
LA. Jun. 25, '68 / Jan. 2, '77
TEXAS Mar. 30, '70 / Jan. 14, '73
MISS./LA. Jan. 4, '76
FLA. Jun. 25, '68 / Jan. 2, '77

TWENTY *The Reconstructed Union*

656

the time of the adoption of the Thirteenth Amendment, Congress had agreed that the 11 as yet unreconstructed states should be counted as part of the Union for purposes of ratification, making 37 states in all. The same 37 were to vote on the Fourteenth Amendment, which could thus be defeated (according to the constitutional provision requiring approval by three-fourths of the states) by 10 commonwealths. For good measure, Delaware and Kentucky, in addition to the 10 ex-Confederate states, had also rejected the amendment by this time, making 12 rejections in all. When the last of the southern rejections had arrived, James A. Garfield of Ohio declared: "The last one of the sinful ten has at last with contempt and scorn flung back into our teeth the magnanimous offer of a generous nation. It is now our turn to act."

### THE RADICAL SURGE

The Fourteenth Amendment had been rejected in most of the ex-Confederate states while the congressional elections of 1866, the first national elections since the close of the war, were taking place. The amendment had drawn the issue clearly between the President and Congress. Between August 28 and September 15, Johnson made his unfortunate "swing around the circle," visiting key cities on behalf of congressional candidates who favored his policy. Many people considered such campaigning unseemly for a President, and all the more so in Johnson's case, since he was often indiscreet as an impromptu political speaker. The more he talked, the more the Radicals made fun of him. Fodder for the Radicals' own campaign was supplied by violence in the South, which reached its peak during a riot in New Orleans on July 30 over Radical efforts to force Negro suffrage on the state of Louisiana. Blacks and whites clashed and 41 persons were killed.

The Radicals used such incidents to pound home the intransigence of the Confederates. As if to underscore the need for vigilance, Union veterans completed the organization of

the Grand Army of the Republic just before the elections, and in November 1866 the G.A.R. held its first national encampment in Indianapolis. The Radicals made a big play for the soldier vote. They also reminded businessmen what a threat to high tariffs, hard money, and the national debt the South's return to national power would be. Stung by the South's rejection of the Fourteenth Amendment, the Radicals worked hard for a sweeping victory that they might interpret as a mandate for even severer measures. Indeed, they sought to win enough seats to give them two-thirds majorities in both houses so as to insure the enactment of their bills over presidential vetoes. Nor were they disappointed. They carried the Senate with 42 Republican seats to 11 for the Democrats, and the House 143 to 49.

So convincing was the Radicals' victory that even before the new Congress met they were able to marshal all the votes they needed to proceed with a virtual revolution in the government. Ordinarily, the new Congress would not have convened until December 1867, unless called into special session by the President. But on January 22, 1867, the old Congress took it upon itself to call the new Congress into session on March 4, the day the old Congress was required by law to adjourn. Having insured Congress's uninterrupted presence in Washington the Radicals moved to concentrate all power in congressional hands.

Their initial and most comprehensive measure was the so-called First Reconstruction Act, which was passed over Johnson's veto on March 2, 1867 (supplementary Second, Third, and Fourth Reconstruction Acts elaborated its language and filled out its enforcement machinery). By the terms of this act, all existing southern state governments except that of Tennessee, which had been accepted back into the Union in 1866 were declared illegal. The South was organized into five military districts, each under a general to be named by the President. Each general was to have an armed force at his command to help

*Federal troops, under the command of General Sheridan, summoned to New Orleans as a result of the rioting. Here, they march up St. Charles Street past the St. Charles Hotel (center). (Harper's Weekly.)*

him maintain martial law if necessary. The general's main task was to call a new constitutional convention in each state, the delegates to be elected by universal adult male suffrage, black and white. Although the Fourteenth Amendment had been dead for nearly a month, the act explicitly cited its provisions to indicate those in the "said rebel states" who were to be excluded from serving as or voting for delegates.

Once manned, the new conventions would proceed to establish state governments in which Negroes could vote and hold office. Once in operation, these governments were to ratify the arbitrarily revived Fourteenth Amendment as a condition for their return to the Union and the acceptance of their representatives by Congress.

By June 1868 all but three states—Mississippi, Texas, and Virginia—had been "reconstructed" by Congress in time to participate in the presidential elections that year, though in some of them armed forces remained to protect Republican rule for as long as ten years more. In July 1868 Secretary Seward announced the completion of ratification of the Fourteenth Amendment, but only after Congress a week earlier by a joint resolution wholly unsanctioned by the supreme law of the land had declared the amendment part of the Constitution. The three recalcitrant states were re-admitted in 1870. In that year, Georgia, whose reconstruction had been suspended because of the expulsion of black members from her legislature, was also re-admitted for the second time.

The Radicals' next step was to protect their program from the Supreme Court. In the case of *ex parte Milligan* (1866), which arose over Lincoln's suspension of habeas corpus in Indiana during the war, the Supreme Court had held that if military rule "is continued *after* the courts are reinstated, it is a gross usurpation of power." When the First Reconstruction Act was passed southern courts were open, and by establishing military rule the act deliberately defied this decision. When, in *ex parte McCardle,* the constitutionality of the First Reconstruction Act was challenged, the Radicals attached a rider to a minor bill, withdrawing appellate jurisdiction from the Court in habeas corpus matters. Johnson vetoed the whole bill, but the withdrawal provision was then passed over his veto, in March 1868. The Court had already put *ex parte McCardle* on its schedule but, against the judgment of two justices, the majority yielded to the Radicals, allowed the case to be quashed, and the First Reconstruction Act survived.

Having successfully defied the Supreme Court, the Radicals next set about eliminating the Executive. Two measures had been passed at the same time as the First Reconstruction Act, in March 1867, with this end in view. The first, the Tenure of Office Act, declared that the President could not remove federal officers who had been appointed with the consent of the Senate without first getting the Senate's consent to their removal. The second, the Command of the Army Act, forbade the President to issue orders to the army except through the General of the Army, General Grant. These measures left the President at the mercy of Radical office-holders and divested him of his constitutional role as Commander-in-Chief. But the Radicals were not satisfied.

After almost a full year of investigation in 1867, the House Judiciary Committee, in November, though failing to draw up any list of Johnson's "high crimes and misdemeanors," had voted by a bare 5-to-4 majority to recommend to the whole chamber that the President be impeached and haled before the Senate for trial. The committee's grounds were simply that the President's offenses were all referable "to the one great overshadowing purpose of reconstructing the . . . rebel States in accordance with his own will, in the interests of the great criminals who carried them into rebellion." This charge proved too vague for the whole House to swallow, and in December 1867 it rejected the committee's recommendation 57 to 108. By attempting to remove Secretary of War Stanton, the remaining Radical in his Cabinet, and thereby also to test the validity of the Tenure of Office Act, Johnson soon gave his congressional enemies a second chance.

On February 21, 1868, Stanton was formally removed. Three days later, a new impeachment resolution came before the House, this one reported out not by the Judiciary Committee, but by the Committee on Reconstruction, of which Stevens was chairman. Once more no bill of particulars was leveled at the Chief Executive; yet the House now voted for impeachment, 126 to 47, and only then promised the Senate in due time "to exhibit particular articles of impeachment . . . and make good the same." By March 2, eleven "particular articles" had been drawn up, all but one of them referring to the Tenure of Office Act. The exception was the notorious "Butler article," number 10, which charged Johnson with "inflammatory, and scandalous harangues" calculated to bring Congress into disgrace, but which mentioned no law that had thereby been violated.

On March 5, Chief Justice Chase solemnly organized the Senate as "a court of impeachment for the trial of the President of the United States," but proceedings did not seriously get underway until March 13. That bad penny, Ben Butler, took the lead for the prosecution and promptly turned the affair into "a solemn theatrical fiasco," to use the words of James Schouler. An effort was even made to implicate Johnson in Lincoln's assassination; and while most of the other charges had no better foundation, Johnson escaped conviction only by the barest margin. The trial drew out for more than two months. But when, on May 16 and again on May 25, seven Republicans showed their determination to desert the Radical leadership, the Radicals' game was up. These seven, together with 12 Democrats, made 19 against Johnson's removal. Thirty-five voted for it, one short of the two-thirds needed to carry. "The single vote by which Andrew Johnson escaped conviction," concludes the historian William A. Dunning, "marks the narrow margin by which the Presidential element in our system escaped destruction."

### THE ELECTION OF 1868

In the presidential election of 1868, the Radicals succeeded in getting General Grant nominated by the Republicans. Grant had no known political principles, although in 1856 he had voted for the Democrat, Buchanan, and in 1860 he had favored Douglas. Johnson himself had such faith in the General that at one point in his controversies with Stanton, in August 1867, he had suspended the Secretary and had named Grant acting head of the War Department. At that time, Johnson had already decided to remove Stanton altogether. Anticipating senatorial objections, he had arranged with Grant either to cling to the office even if the Senate upheld Stanton's claims, or to inform Johnson beforehand of his desire to quit so that the President might appoint someone who would keep Stanton out. Grant must have misunderstood, for he held the place until the Senate upheld Stanton and then yielded the office to the suspended Secretary. Johnson naturally felt he had been betrayed and his personal relations with Grant deteriorated. The General, meanwhile, his own ambitions fired by Radical flattery and by the people's undiminishing acclaim whenever he appeared in public, became easy game for Johnson's political enemies.

On his war record Grant appeared a certain winner, and that was enough for the Radicals. Johnson himself sought the Democratic nomination, but the party turned instead to an untainted if unenthusiastic northerner, former governor Horatio Seymour of New York.

The Democrats tried to make a campaign issue of cheap money. In 1866 Congress had provided for the gradual retirement of the greenbacks issued during the war, and in the following two years almost $100 million worth had been withdrawn from circulation. Although the greenbacks had fluctuated widely in value, they always held below the value of gold and hence were popular with long-term debtors like farmers who wanted cheap money with which to pay their fixed mortgage obligations. To curry favor with the farmers of the West, the Democrats now adopted a platform plank advocating the reissuance of the retired greenbacks to redeem war bonds which did not specifically require redemption in gold. Since the author of this plank was George H. Pendleton of Ohio, the party's vice-presidential candidate in 1864 and an early aspirant for the presidential nomination in 1868, this "soft money" proposal became known as the "Ohio Idea."

The Republicans scotched the Ohio Idea in the strongly Union-minded West by reminding the farmers, in difficulties though they were because of the falling off of the wartime demand for foodstuffs and fibers, that redemption of war bonds in anything but gold smacked of rebel repudiation of a sacred debt that had been contracted to preserve the Union. At the same time, the Republicans promised businessmen that they would extend redemption "over a fair period" so as not to disturb the business credit structure, and that when the time came, all bondholders would be paid in gold. Having thus dealt with the complex problem of money, the Radicals proceeded to keep before the public the main political issue—Radical Reconstruction.

In the elections of 1866, the Republicans had had great success "waving the bloody shirt," a tactic by which they reviled the Democratic party as the standard-bearer of rebellion, Negro repression, and financial repudiation. "In short," cried Oliver P. Morton, the Radical governor of Indiana, in a typical "bloody shirt" foray, "the Democratic party may be described as a common sewer and loathsome receptacle, into which is emptied every element of treason North and South, and every element of inhumanity and barbarism which has dishonored the age." In 1868, and in subsequent elections, such tirades served as the staple of Republican oratory. Practical Republican electioneering was handled by the Union League clubs which had been organized in the North in 1862 to spread Union propaganda. Gradually they extended their wartime activity to captured southern territory. By 1868, more than 80 chapters of the League were operating in South Carolina alone, where estimates indicate that most of the Negroes in the state were enrolled as members. "I can't read, and I can't write," one Negro said. "We go by [League] instructions."

Yet the Republican campaign did not overwhelm the opposition. In 1868, against a weak opponent, Grant was elected with a popular plurality of a mere 310,000. Had the Union League not helped deliver the votes of about 700,000 freedmen in the seven hastily reconstructed southern states, Grant might have had no plurality at all.

The part that Negroes played in winning the election—or rather the fact that Negroes in certain states such as Louisiana and Georgia had been prevented from casting what might have been much-needed Republican votes—led Radicals to attempt to strengthen the Fourteenth Amendment's protection of black suffrage. When Congress convened early in 1869, it promptly passed the Fifteenth Amendment, which provided that: "The right of citizens of the United States to vote shall not be denied or abridged by the United States or by any State on account of race, color, or previous conditions of servitude." This amendment, sent to the states in February 1869, was declared ratified in March 1870.

"The agitation against slavery," declared *The Nation*, "has reached an appropriate and triumphant conclusion." But many retained doubts about *The Nation's* own conclusion. During the congressional debate on the amendment, Oliver P. Morton, now in the Senate, accurately forecast the future:

This amendment leaves the whole power in the States just as it exists now except that colored men shall not be disfranchised for the three reasons of race, color, or previous condition of slavery. . . . Sir, if the power should pass into the hands of the Conservative or Democratic population of those southern States, if they could not debar the colored people of the right of suffrage in any other way they would do it by an educational or property qualification . . . and thus this amendment would be practically defeated in all those States where the great body of colored people live [see p. 679].

## iv The Day of the Carpetbagger

### REVISIONS IN THE RADICAL CAMP

When Grant accepted the Republican nomination in May 1868, he wrote, "Let us have peace." Many men, recalling his magnanimous surrender terms to Lee, thought that the severity of Radical Reconstruction might now be softened. The death of Stevens in August 1868, the defeat of Ben Wade for the Senate later that year, and Sumner's decline soon after (see p. 666) gave substance to this hope.

But Grant's administration was easily dominated by such surviving Radicals as Senators Zachariah Chandler of Michigan, Simon Cameron of Pennsylvania, and Roscoe Conkling of New York. These men were untinged by the abolitionist idealism that had marked the Stevens-Sumner leadership, but they had ample partisan reasons—chief among them the wish to protect wartime tariff, railroad, and banking legislation from attack by returning southerners—for keeping ex-Confederates disfranchised and colored voters safe in the Republican camp. In pursuing their aims in the defeated section they had the help of Radical "carpetbaggers" who had begun to go South right after the war to show what northern "brains and sinew" could accomplish. The number of carpetbaggers soared after the adoption of the First Reconstruction Act in March 1867 (see p. 657), when, under the protection of the military, they virtually took charge of politics. In the seven states reconstructed in 1868, 10 of 14 United States senators, 20 of 35 congressmen, and four governors were carpetbaggers. The others, with few exceptions, were "scalawags"—southerners who rode to office on Radical coattails but eventually broke with the carpetbaggers on the race issue. The few exceptions were Negroes.

### CARPETBAGGERS AS REFORMERS

Many carpetbaggers, especially the early ones, were genuine reformers who tried to help the freedmen become useful citizens, economically independent and politically and legally the equal of whites. Often enough the objectives of the reformers were not in conflict with those of the self-seekers who came later, and under carpetbag rule political and social advances were made in the South which benefited both races.

Many of these gains grew out of the provisions of the new southern state constitutions written by the "black and tan" conventions, as southerners branded the assemblages called by the Radical generals. These constitutions, unlike most of those in the North itself, had given the Negro the right to vote and hold office even before the Fifteenth Amendment was ratified. They also eliminated property qualifications for voting and office-holding among whites as well as blacks, and more fairly apportioned representation in state legislatures and in Congress. These constitutions also abolished imprisonment for debt and other archaic social legislation. Above all, for the first time in many southern states, they provided for public schools—for whites and blacks.

Next to giving the vote to Negroes, nothing offended the South more than Radical efforts to give them schooling. The slogan, "School-

661

*Carpetbagger assuring that a Negro votes the Radical Republican ticket in the first municipal election held in Richmond after the war.* (Harper's Weekly.)

ing ruins the Negro," expressed the general belief. As early as July 1865 Carl Schurz had noted instances of Negro schools being burned and of teachers and students being threatened. Yet by 1877, 600,000 blacks were enrolled in southern elementary and secondary schools; and several colleges and universities, including Fisk, Howard, and Atlanta, and the Hampton Institute in Virginia, had been established by the Freedmen's Bureau and northern church and philanthropic agencies. Night schools for adults also flourished. "The great ambition of the older people," said Booker T. Washington, "was to try to learn to read the Bible before they died."

The ballot, though at first misused, was a notable step forward for the freedman. Office-holding, though also abused, was another significant advance, but it was not so widespread as the term "black reconstruction" might imply. Only in South Carolina, in 1868, did Negro legislators outnumber whites, 88 to 67, but the sessions were not controlled by the Negroes. In other state legislatures, blacks made up sizable minorities, but the white politicians always dominated the proceedings. One mulatto, P.B.S. Pinchback, became lieutenant-governor of Louisiana. Several Negroes became congressmen and two became United States senators. Others gained administrative posts, in which they did well.

### CORRUPTION AND REACTION

Many southern leaders actually found little fault with the Radicals' tariff, railroad, and money policies, and felt that the Republicans could trust the South sufficiently to give its spokesmen a voice in national affairs once again. Southern whites also felt that by 1868 they had made every concession that a vanquished nation (as they thought of themselves) ought to have been asked to make by the victors in the late war. The South had disbanded the remnants of its army, repudiated the Confederate debt, renounced secession as a constitutional device, and accepted the Thirteenth Amendment abolishing slavery. None of these concessions had been made gracefully, but they had been made. When the Radicals began to court the Negro vote to insure protection for their national legislative program, southerners balked at what they called "barbarization of the South," and prepared, if not to resume the war, at least to promote violence and terror to thwart the Radicals' plan.

The mere existence of the carpetbag governments within their borders seemed insulting and shameful to many southeners. Carpetbag corruption made the affront even harder to bear, even though it was not as bad as it has been painted. Between 1868 and 1874, the bonded debt of the 11 Confederate states grew by over $100 million. But this enormous sum was not itself evidence of crime. To raise money, the southern states had to sell bonds in the North, where southern credit was so poor that investors often demanded a 75 per cent discount from the bond's face value. Thus for every $100 worth of bonds sold, a southern state might actually receive only $25. Many of the social and humanitarian reforms of the Reconstruction legislatures, moreover, were costly, as was the relief extended to the starving and homeless of both races.

Nevertheless, much of the debt was corruptly incurred, though not necessarily by carpetbaggers. A large part of it was piled up through the sale of state bonds to back southern-sponsored railroad enterprises that never built a mile of track, or to aid companies that merely distributed as profit the money they received. Carpetbaggers were more likely to busy themselves with more traditional forms of graft. A considerable portion of the debt was created, for example, by politicians who won large contracts for construction or printing, and then supplied little of the services or goods that the contracts called for. Public funds also were spent for personal furniture, homes, carriages, jewelry, liquor, leather goods, and other amenities. But such conspicuous corruption probably cost the least.

*A contemporary northern impression of a school established by the Freedmen's Bureau and attended by both young and old. (The Bettmann Archive.)*

Taxes to pay for carpetbag government expenditures and to service the rapidly growing debt fell most heavily on the oppressed planters, who before the war had been able to pass taxes on to other groups in the South. Business firms escaped with small levies, and personal taxes were low and could easily be evaded.

The growing public debt and the unequal taxation aroused the ire of the former leaders of the South. But the majority of the people complained most bitterly about the gross conduct, the bizarre legislative sessions, the flamboyant or slovenly dress, and the posturing of the new political leaders, black and white. Negro militia roamed the southern countryside and sometimes shot up city streets. Negro legislatures were something rare on the face of the earth, and travelers came from Europe and the North to watch them in action. What the visitors expected to find in a society so recently upended is not clear, but their reactions often matched the horror of the southerners themselves. Rubbed into the unhealed sores of the war, this kind of "reconstruction" completed the moral rout of the South. Sidney Lanier, the poet, said during this period in a letter

north, "Perhaps you know that with us of the young generation in the South, since the war pretty much the whole of life has been merely not dying."

To combat carpetbag rule and the Negro vote on which it rested, thousands even of the most respectable elements in the South banded together in the Ku Klux Klan, the Knights of the White Camelia, and other secret groups. Between 1867 and 1869, hooded or otherwise incognito, they roamed the land, shot, flogged, and terrorized Negroes and their supporters, burned homes and public buildings, attacked Reconstruction officials, and, under the guise of keeping order (which, indeed, sometimes needed keeping), perpetrated other acts of violence dedicated to the maintenance of white supremacy. After 1869, some of these white organizations engaged in such random pillage and murder that the respectable elements abandoned them in horror. But the organizations themselves persisted.

663

*Engraving after a photograph of Ku Klux Klansmen in the disguises they wore when captured in 1871 after the attempted murder of a family. The despicable acts committed by these bands not only drove away the respectable element in the movement but actually moved the counsel for the defense at a KKK trial to say, "I have listened with horror to some of the testimony which has been brought before you. The outrages proved have been shocking to humanity; . . . they violate every obligation which law and nature impose upon me." (The Granger Collection.)*

## RADICAL REPRISALS AND RETREATS

The Radical leadership in Congress did not permit the activities of the violent white organizations to go unchallenged. In May 1870 they passed a Force Act designed to strengthen the protection of Negro voting rights by imposing heavy fines and jail sentences for offenses under the Fourteenth and Fifteenth amendments. This act also gave federal courts controlled by carpetbaggers, rather than southern state courts, original jurisdiction in all cases arising under these amendments.

In spite of the Force Act, the Democrats made substantial gains in the congressional elections of 1870, and by the following year southern whites had recaptured the state governments of Tennessee, Virginia, North Carolina, and Georgia. Attributing these successes to violence, the Radicals next forced through Congress the Ku Klux Klan Act of 1871. This act gave federal courts original jurisdiction in all cases arising out of conspiracies or terrorism against freedmen. It also empowered the President to suspend habeas corpus in any terrorized community, to declare martial law, and to send in troops to maintain order.

Within a short time, about 7000 southerners were indicted under these two acts, and although few were convicted or even tried, the personal harassment served to smother white political activity. In October 1871, to convince remaining skeptics that the Radicals still meant business, Grant declared nine counties of South Carolina, where the Klan was especially active, to be again in rebellion and placed them under martial law. An investigation by a congressional committee presently placed its seal of approval on the President's militancy.

The South Carolina episode marked the peak of forceful repression of southern whites. In May 1872 Congress passed a liberal Amnesty Act which restored voting and office-holding privileges to all white southerners with the exception of a few hundred of the highest surviving Confederate dignitaries. In the same year, the Freedmen's Bureau, the protector of Negro rights, was permitted to expire.

No doubt the coming presidential election in November 1872 led the Radicals to make these concessions. Testimony offered at the few trials of persons indicted in South Carolina and elsewhere under the Force Act and the Ku Klux Klan Act had cast doubt on the efficacy of the Radicals' program. The severe political and social disabilities fastened upon the southern states seemed clearly to have retarded their recovery. Evidence inadvertently publicized by the congressional committee's own report supported the trials' disclosures. To many in the North it now appeared that carpetbaggers were using the black vote simply to sustain their own corruption and oppression. Increasingly disgusted by Radical excesses in their own section—now roundly condemned under the unedifying epithet, "Grantism"—they were ready to call a halt to such excesses in the South. By buoying up the white South while jettisoning the blacks, the tarnished General's Radical backers hoped to preserve Grantism in Washington a while longer.

## v  *Radical Republicanism in the North*

### GRANTISM

On observing the Washington scene early in 1869, young Henry Adams, grandson and great-grandson of early presidents, remarked that "the progress of evolution from President Washington to President Grant was alone evidence enough to upset Darwin." An organism as simple as U.S. Grant, thought Adams, "had no right to exist. He should have been extinct for ages."

In fact, however, Grant, as President, was no throwback but very much a product of his time. A failure in business himself, he became infatuated with business success. He wanted to make A.T. Stewart, the department store king and a lavish contributor to his campaign fund, Secretary of the Treasury; but it was discovered that a law of 1789 forbade persons engaged in commerce to hold that post. The Senate stubbornly refused Grant's request to except Stewart from the law, and the nominee's name had to be withdrawn. In Washington, Grant was frequently entertained by Henry Cooke, whose business it was to report to his financier brother, Jay, what he could

learn at the nation's capital. Fond of the horse-racing at Saratoga Springs, New York, Grant, in the summer of 1869, accepted the use of Commodore Vanderbilt's private railroad car to travel there. He once described Jim Fisk as "destitute of moral character"; yet, as President, he saw nothing wrong in using Fisk's sumptuous boats, dining publicly with Fisk and Gould, and otherwise enjoying the hospitality of the Erie looters while making them privy to the country's financial affairs.

Grant's political appointments were hardly likely to keep the President's businessman associates from using the information they collected from him. In making his appointments, the President, understandably, turned first to his old army friends, most of whom were as politically innocent as their chief. Grant's White House staff, it was said, had "nothing but uniforms." General Horace Porter became Grant's private secretary. The assistant secretary, in the key position of making up Grant's daily visitor list and controlling access to the President, was his former military aide, the foppish Colonel Orville E. Babcock. These men dominated Grant's "Kitchen Cabinet." With three exceptions, his regular Cabinet was made up of men who frightened people by their very obscurity. The three exceptions were Secretary of State Hamilton Fish, who served through Grant's two administrations; and Secretary of the Interior Jacob D. Cox, and Attorney-General Ebenezer Rockwood Hoar, both of whom were supplanted in a little over a year by more pliant souls.

The Kitchen Cabinet made most of the decisions on the appointment of federal jobholders, among whom Grant's relatives and neighbors, and retainers of the Kitchen Cabinet itself, were numerous. Federal patronage had grown enormously with the growth of government activity during and after the war, and in dispensing it men like Babcock (on the example of the President himself) often ignored the tradition of consulting the party's senators from the various states. This practice angered senatorial leaders and quickly cost Grant any chance he had for the support of

666

such senators as Sumner and Schurz, and Lyman Trumbull of Illinois, an old favorite of Lincoln's. Alienated also were some of the less-principled patronage-mongers in Republican states like New York and Pennsylvania, who resented being shortchanged on political jobs in favor of Babcock's Radical Republican cronies, men as dishonest as themselves. Schurz and Trumbull were among the leaders of the movement for federal civil-service reform, which the enormous wartime rise in patronage had inspired. It was their aim to place federal job-holding on a merit basis, with candidates selected by objective examinations. But the patronage-mongers found it easy to mobilize congressional opposition whenever civil-service legislation loomed.

Even worse than Grant's handling of major appointments and patronage in the ranks was the way he allowed himself and his great office to be used by the corruptionists who surrounded him. One of the most unsavory incidents occurred only a few months after Grant's inauguration. This was "Black Friday," September 24, 1869, when Grant's long overdue action in releasing $4 million in government gold to New York banks broke a gold corner that Jim Fisk and Jay Gould had planned by earlier persuading the financially innocent President not to release any government gold that fall. Fisk and Gould were foiled, but not before many speculators and others who needed gold in their business transactions had been ruined.

"Black Friday" occurred in the midst of negotiations over the annexation of Santo Domingo (now the Dominican Republic), for which other of Grant's cronies had won his pledge "privately to use all his influence." An island exceedingly rich in minerals, timber, and fruit, Santo Domingo had won its independence from Spain in 1865. Among those who now hungrily eyed the island were a couple of discreditable Massachusetts promoters who, like so many of the kind, got Orville Babcock's ear. On visiting Santo Domingo late in 1869, Babcock was able to negotiate a treaty of annexation. When Attor-

ney-General Hoar denounced Babcock's treaty-making as illegal, Grant removed Hoar from office. When Charles Sumner, Chairman of the Senate Foreign Relations Committee, then denounced the entire "deal," the Senate defeated Babcock's treaty in 1870. Grant's senatorial friends retaliated the next year by stripping Sumner of his committee post and practically reading him out of the Republican party.

## LOBBIES AND LEGISLATION

Grant, no doubt, was simply used by the corruptionists. As a victorious general he had become accustomed to receiving the lavish patronage of the rich. Before his candidacy for the Presidency, a group of millionaires headed by A.T. Stewart had presented him with a fully furnished mansion in Philadelphia. Another group, including Hamilton Fish, had helped pay off the $100,000 mortgage on Grant's Washington home. Still a third group, made up of "fifty solid men of Boston," had equipped this home with a $75,-000 library. Many of these men had made fortunes on war contracts, but in Grant's eyes they had also contributed handsomely to winning the war. Now they were sustaining the postwar boom. What of it if their accomplishments were abetted by special-interest legislation forced through Congress? No one in the postwar epoch could be pure and progressive at the same time.

To those who would point a finger, moreover, Grant could reply that he had inherited a government already far gone in corruption. The competition for war contracts and the fight for other wartime legislation covering protective tariffs, land grants, and the money system, had made lobbying a full-time occupation. Men like John Lord Hayes, who represented the woolen manufacturers, and James M. Swank, who spoke for the iron and steel interests, spent almost all their time cultivating legislators in wartime Washington and actually prowled the floor of the House to keep their congressmen in line. Just before concluding four years in Congress in 1873, Job Stevenson of Ohio told his colleagues that "the House of Representatives was like an auction room where more valuable considerations were disposed of under the speaker's hammer than in any other place on earth."

Few political plums were more valuable than the tariff, which by 1870 had become "a conglomeration of special favors." The situation is indicated in this comment by General Robert C. Schenck, representative from Ohio from 1863 to 1871: "Sitting here as a friend of protective tariffs for eight years, I have voted aye or nay as those who got up the tariff bills have told me."

The railroads also shared in congressional handouts. The last federal land grant for railroad-building was made in 1871, by which time the total distributed to the roads directly or through the states came to 160 million acres, valued conservatively at $335 million. The roads also had received lavish government loans. After the Union Pacific and Central Pacific railroads had obtained their loans, Congress annually considered legislation that would have provided for their eventual repayment. The transcontinentals fought this legislation stubbornly and successfully. It was on one such occasion, in the session of 1867–68, that Congressman Oakes Ames distributed shares in the Crédit Mobilier, the construction company that built the Union Pacific Railroad, among senators and representatives "where they will do the most good to us." The revelation of Oakes' action on the eve of the presidential election of 1872 simply added one more scandal to the Republican record under Grant.

Nor were northern financers left out of the "Great Barbecue," as Grant's regime has been called. In March 1869, in fulfilling Republican promises, both houses of Congress adopted a resolution pledging the government to redeem the entire war debt in gold or in new gold bonds. This pledge, and the laws soon passed to carry it out, sent the value of war bonds soaring and brought substantial profits to speculators. These laws, it should be said, proved salutary as far as the government's credit was concerned. Forced during the war to offer interest as high as 6 per cent, the victorious national government was soon able to borrow for as little as 2½ per cent. Yet the new laws permitted the Secretary of the Treasury to issue new bonds more or less at his pleasure, and rumors, hot tips, and cloakroom gossip about Treasury activities flowed between Washington and New York and other financial centers. Even the men closest to the government were not above sending out "sure things" over the telegraph to their financial friends around the country, in order to get a share of investment projects that ordinarily would have been much too rich for them. Enemies and innocent bystanders, on the other hand, often were hurt. Wall Streeters in the early 1870s openly charged that the Secretary of the Treasury, George S. Boutwell, frequently made moves "conspicuously more advantageous to certain 'friends of Government' among speculators . . . than to men engaged in legitimate business."

### THE ELECTION OF 1872

One feature of the 1872 campaign was the "Liberal Republican" movement under the leadership of Carl Schurz and B. Gratz Brown. This movement had begun years earlier in Missouri as an effort to dislodge the corrupt Radical regime there. Following Schurz's election to the Senate by the Missouri legislature in 1868, Brown, a veteran Radical senator himself but like Schurz alienated now from the national leadership, was elected governor of the state in 1870. The size of his majority in this election encouraged the two Missourians to transform their state movement into a national one, with "Grantism" and Grant himself as their targets.

Since the worst of the corruption in Grant's first administration was not revealed to the public until after the election of 1872, Schurz and Brown and their friends could not use it in their efforts to withhold the regular Republican nomination from the General and name a reform candidate. On May 1, 1872, therefore, the reformers assembled in Cincinnati, organized a new national party, the Liberal Republican party, and wrote a platform with

*The Liberal Republican leader Carl Schurz (right) as Secretary of the Interior under President Hayes. The political cartoon below, "A Modern Belshazzar: People's Handwriting on the Wall," appeared in* Leslie's Illustrated Weekly. *Under a canopy labeled "Despotism," the drunken President is being served some "second term" by his chief sycophant, Roscoe Conkling. Immediately to the left of Conkling is Senator Morton and below him Congressman Butler. On Grant's left, with pompadour, is Hamilton Fish and on Grant's right, under his arm, is his Vice-president-to-be, Henry Wilson. The rotund gentleman at lower left is Winfield S. Hancock. James G. Blaine is at the extreme lower right and above him is John A. Logan. In the crowd, wearing glasses, is Carl Schurz. (Both, the Granger Collection.)*

special emphasis on civil-service reform. Old-line Republicans like Senators Sumner and Trumbull, ex-ambassador Charles Francis Adams, and ex-cabinet members Cox and Hoar, all victims, as we have seen, of the Chandler-Conkling type of Radical political brutality, rallied to the new standard. They were joined by such newly influential independent journalists as Godkin of *The Nation* and George W. Curtis of *Harper's Weekly,* and, in the Middle West, Horace White of the Chicago *Tribune* and Murat Halstead of the Cincinnati *Commercial.* All were Republicans who felt that the party of free soil and free men had clearly become the party of adventurers. Unfortunately for them, Liberal Republican ranks were promptly infiltrated by many other less dedicated angry men: businessmen who had been victimized by Radical grafters and political hacks who had lost out in contests for patronage and simply sought a vehicle for revenge. Many northern Democrats also joined the movement, hoping thereby to cast off the treasonous label of their own party and win their way back to positions of power.

At the Cincinnati convention the irreconcilable differences in this motley array became apparent from the start and the leaders were forced to choose a compromise candidate, Horace Greeley, with B. Gratz Brown as his running mate. Greeley was a strange choice. As befitted a man who had long been an abolitionist, Greeley remained an outspoken Radical. Worse, he was a staunch high-tariff man, an enemy not only of free trade, but of foreign relations of any kind. Worse still, as editor for more than 30 years of the New York *Tribune* he had supported so many contradictory political positions that he had become universally known as a crackpot. Greeley's nomination made a travesty of the whole Liberal Republican campaign. So roundly was the candidate denounced in the press that he declared at one point that he did not know whether he was running for the Presidency or the penitentiary.

If Greeley's nomination was a misfortune for the Liberal Republicans, it was a tragedy for the Democratic party. This party's only chance to regain national power was to support Grant's opponents. Yet Grant's opponents had nominated the man who in 1866 in the *Tribune* had publicly branded the Democrats as "the traitorous section of Northern politics." The Democrats eventually swallowed their pride and at their convention in Baltimore in July named Greeley as their own standard-bearer. This move made the election contest easy for Grant, who had been nominated without opposition at the regular Republican convention in Philadelphia in June. The General won by a majority of 763,000 and carried all but six states. His share of the popular vote, 55.6 per cent, made his the most decisive victory since Andrew Jackson's in 1828.

### GRANT'S SECOND TERM

During Grant's campaign in 1872, Roscoe Conkling told a receptive New York audience: "If the name and the character of the administration of Ulysses S. Grant have been of value to the nation, no one knows it so well as the men who represent the property, the credits, the public securities and the enterprise of the country." These men truly were in debt to the Republican party, and as a group were to become its strongest backers over the years. Yet even many of them had begun to grow restless over the ceaseless exactions of the Radical Republicans who controlled the party, Conkling himself being a particularly nasty thorn in their flesh.

The outright scandals of the administration in turn soon soured many more Republicans and fostered the Democratic revival. The first major Grant scandal, the Crédit Mobilier affair (see p. 667), broke while the 1872 campaign still was in progress. After the business crash of 1873, each new revelation struck with added force, and once the Democrats captured the House in 1874, revelations and prosecutions snowballed.

Two affairs hit close to Grant himself. One was the uncovering of the "Whiskey Ring" in

670

St. Louis, which had defrauded the government of millions of dollars in internal revenue charges. Deeply involved in this, as in other frauds, was Grant's ubiquitous assistant secretary Orville Babcock, whom the President saved from imprisonment only by incessantly interfering in his trial. The second affair led to the impeachment of Grant's third Secretary of War, W. W. Belknap, who, since his appointment in 1870, had been "kept" by traders in Indian Territory under his jurisdiction. When his impeachment appeared imminent, Belknap had taken the precaution to offer his resignation to the President, which Grant, with charcteristic loyalty to his betrayers, accepted "with great regret." The House proceeded with Belknap's impeachment despite

*"The Union as it Was." Wood engraving, after Thomas Nast, depicting the plight of the southern black at the hands of the white "redeemers." Many Negroes were so discouraged by their treatment in the 1870s that they fled North in a vain attempt to gain the advantages of freedom. (Library of Congress.)*

his resignation; but the Senate, more a stickler for forms, allowed the Secretary's friends to forestall conviction on the grounds that that body no longer had jurisdiction.

The ultimate outrage to both the reformers and the public was the "Salary Grab Act" of 1873 by which congressmen raised their own salaries 50 per cent from $5000 to $7500 and made the raise retroactive for two years, thereby voting themselves a virtual gift of $5000. The act also raised the salaries of the President, the Cabinet, and Supreme Court justices.

While his cronies were undermining Republican strength in the North, Grant, by persisting in the forbearance evident before the election of 1872 (see p. 664), was helping to enhance Democratic strength in the South. In particular, he refused any longer to call upon the army for additional support for troubled Republican regimes. Encouraged by Grant's turnabout, southern leaders in states still under carpetbag rule became more determined than ever to "redeem" their states through their own efforts.

In communities where Negroes were a majority or nearly so, these efforts revolved around the so-called Mississippi Plan which operated openly with full white support and thus proved more effective than the covert Klan. The aim of the Mississippi Plan was to force all whites into the Democratic party while at the same time forcing Negroes to desist from political action. Where persuasion failed, violence was used against both groups by such well-armed, semimilitary enforcement agencies as Rifle Clubs, White Leagues, and Red Shirts. Whites who resisted were virtually driven from their homes and from their communities. Recalcitrant black sharecroppers, in turn (see p. 675), were denied credit by southern merchants, evicted from their land, denied other employment, and assaulted and murdered. Many blacks themselves had had their fill of northern domination and some proved willing to cooperate with their new masters. "Redemption" was also accelerated by the growing inability of the carpetbaggers to make their scalawag collaborators get along with black officials. Quarrels with Negroes led more and more scalawags to cast their lot with the "white supremacy" advocates. After the Panic of 1873 depressed northern business, capitalists looking south for investment opportunities also aided the white "redeemers."

As the election of 1876 neared, the national administration began to have second thoughts about revived Democratic strength. To counteract it, the House, in February 1875, passed a new Force Bill. During the debate on the measure, it was said that the 138 "electoral votes of the reconstructed States rightfully belong to the Republican party," and "if the bill now pending . . . becomes a law it will secure these votes to that party, and otherwise they will be lost." The Senate was not impressed by this threat and rejected the bill. At the same time, however, it joined the House in adopting a new Civil Rights Act which Grant signed on March 1. This act recognized "the equality of all men before the law," and imposed stiff penalties for denying any citizen "full and equal enjoyment of . . . inns, public conveyances, . . . theaters, and other places of public amusement." Penalties also were placed on the denial of equal rights to serve on juries.

Eight years later, in the momentous *Civil Rights Cases* of 1883, the Supreme Court declared much of the Civil Rights Act unconstitutional, ruling that the federal government had no jurisdiction over discrimination practiced by private persons or organizations. Later on the Court sanctioned state segregation laws requiring separate public facilities for whites and blacks. In *Plessy* v. *Ferguson* in 1896, the Court decided that the Negro's equal rights under the Fourteenth Amendment were not abrogated if the separate facilities on railroads were themselves equal. In *Cumming* v. *County Board of Education* in 1899, the Court extended the philosophy of "separate but equal" to schools. These decisions ruled until the desegregation decisions of the 1950s and 1960s.

## VI  *The Extension of White Supremacy*

### THE ELECTION OF 1876

The approach of the national nominating conventions in 1876 found the Grand Old Party, as the Republicans had taken to calling themselves, split more deeply than ever over the growing issue of corruption. The "Stalwarts," the hard-core political professionals closest to Grant, wanted the General to run for still a third term in order to insure the wherewithal for party machines and party workers. These men put politics first; if business wanted favors, it would have to continue to come to them and pay up. The "Halfbreeds" —the name was given in contempt by the Stalwarts to those Republican reformers who had not deserted to the Liberal Republicans in 1872—lined up behind their acknowledged leader, the "Plumed Knight," Congressman James G. Blaine of Maine.

Unluckily for the "Halfbreeds," Blaine's candidacy was undermined by the dramatic disclosure early in 1876 of his shady relations with the Union Pacific Railroad while serving as Speaker of the House during the preceding five years. Blaine might still have won the nomination. Although he labored under the handicap of having no war record, his well-publicized hostility to Britain made him attractive to Irish voters and his astuteness as a campaigner was admitted by all. He blundered, however, in denouncing the Stalwarts as "all desperate bad men, bent on loot and booty." When the Republican convention met in Cincinnati in June, Conkling and the old guard exacted the penalty. Balked in their attempts to renominate Grant, they threw their support to Rutherford B. Hayes, the reform governor of Ohio.

Eastern, western, and southern Democrats differed on many important issues such as money policy, the tariff, and federal subsidies

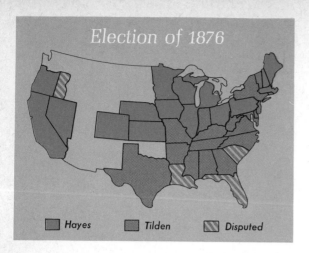

## Election of 1876

■ Hayes　　■ Tilden　　▨ Disputed

for internal improvements. But hunger for the spoils of the Presidency, long denied them, led them to close ranks at their June convention in St. Louis behind Samuel J. Tilden, a rich corporation lawyer and hard-money man who had won a national reputation as a reform governor of New York. Tilden's strongest claim on the nomination was his success, in 1872, in sending "Boss" Tweed, the notorious head of Tammany Hall, the leading Democratic club in New York City, to the penitentiary. During the preceding three years, the Tweed Ring had looted the city government of no less than $100 million.

Republican scandals, the hard times followed the business crash of 1873, and the rising demand for reform all seemed to work to the Democrats' advantage, so much so that Hayes himself privately forecast his defeat. No one was certain, however, how the "redeemed" white South would vote. Many of the new southern leaders were former Whigs to whom Lincoln had looked so optimistically. They had never been comfortable in the Democratic party, into which secession and the war had forced them. As harbingers of a new industrialized and business-minded South, they often found the Republican economic policies more attractive than Democratic economic programs, and they especially resented the failure of northern Democrats to support land grants and other federal subsidies to southern railroads.

The attitudes of the Whiggish southern

Democrats were not lost on Hayes's political managers who were eager to create a southern Republican wing to offset the losses the party had suffered through corruption in the North and repression of the Negro in the South. One group in particular caught their eyes, a group made up of southerners who, along with powerful northern railroad interests led by Tom Scott of the Pennsylvania, were seeking federal subsidies for a new transcontinental line to link Texas with the Pacific. No political bargains were struck between Hayes's managers and the railroad cabal, but it was understood that if Hayes won the Presidency, the government might look kindly on supporting "internal improvements of a national character."

First reports of the election results seemed definite enough. The Democratic candidate, Tilden, had a plurality of 250,000 votes, and the press proclaimed him the new President. But Republican strategists suddenly awoke to the fact that the returns from Louisiana, Florida, and South Carolina, the three states where carpetbagger control was still supported by military contingents, had not yet come in because of election irregularities. These states, together with Oregon (one of whose three electoral votes was claimed by the Democrats on a technicality), held a total of 20 disputed electoral votes. Tilden needed but one of these votes to win; Hayes needed all 20 to gain the 185 electoral votes required for election. Although both parties had resorted to the most bare-faced skullduggery, evidence available now indicates that Tilden deserved Florida's four electoral votes and Hayes the others. In 1876, however, Congress had to decide which of the double sets of returns from the three states should be accepted, the Democratic count or the Republican.

Amidst renewed talk of insurrection, the two parties agreed to decide the election by turning the problem over to a commission of five representatives, five senators, and five Supreme Court justices. One of the justices, David Davis, presumably was independent in politics; the remaining fourteen members of the commission were equally divided between

Democrats and Republicans. Unfortunately for Tilden, Davis quit the commission before it met and was replaced by a Republican justice. The Republican majority of eight then voted unanimously for Hayes.

One step that helped placate the South was a Republican pledge to grant subsidies to southern railroads. In exchange, southern leaders, Democrats though they nominally were, and Democratic though the new House of Representatives was to be, agreed to vote for a Republican, James A. Garfield, as Speaker—a position through which the whole course of legislation could at that time be controlled.

### THE "SOLID SOUTH"

Very soon after Hayes's inauguration it became clear to the South that the new administration would fail to fulfill its promise of railroad subsidies. Unfortunately, one reason for the Republican defection on this score was the failure of southern leaders in the House to deliver enough Democratic votes to give the promised speakership to Garfield. Thus the compromise by which the talk, at least, of the resumption of armed conflict was quieted, broke down almost at its first test. At the time the agreements leading to Hayes's victory had been made, northern Republican newspapers had written warmly of the South's return to statesmanship and nationalism. By 1877 they had reverted to the old theme of an unreconstructed South: "The spirit of rebellion still lives and is liable at any moment to be entrenched again in arms." At the same time, Stalwarts refurbished the bloody shirt that had carried them to so many electoral victories in the recent past.

Hayes refused for a time to be stampeded by the resurgent northern Stalwarts; but he soon learned to withstand as well the southern sectionalists he had courted. He showed his mettle against the Stalwarts by giving control of the distribution of party patronage to Liberal Republican leaders who were promoting civil-service reform. He also named northern reformers and even an ex-Confederate Democrat to his Cabinet. By the end of April 1877, moreover, Hayes had fulfilled his campaign pledge to remove the last of the federal troops from the South. When he did so, the last Radical state governments collapsed.

As soon as southern Democrats took advantage of their friend in the White House, however, by crushing the Negro voters in the congressional elections of 1878, Hayes fought off all southern efforts in Congress to repeal the Force Act of 1870, even though the Supreme Court in *United States* v. *Reese,* in 1876, had already drained the act of much of its power to protect the freedman's franchise.

The Radicals had hoped to sustain their program for the nation and for the South by making the South solid for the Republican Party. But they succeeded only in making the South solidly Democratic. For the next 75 years, with the sole exception of the election of 1928, the "Solid South" was to deliver the section's electoral vote to the Democratic presidential candidate.

### THE ECONOMIC UNDERTOW

While the Radicals tried to reconstruct the Union by extending to the conquered section the familiar political privileges of freedom, their failure to buttress political with economic gains had given southerners themselves a better opportunity to reconstruct their *section* by restoring the familiar economic disabilities of slavery. The Radicals' failure, in particular, to distribute land to the freedmen left the national government with no instrument but force to protect the political rights of its charges; but force was a wearing and costly instrument, wearing as much on those who had to pay for it and to bear the responsibility of its abuse as on those constrained and abused by it. When the policy of force was given up, the bitter fruits of the freedmen's economic dependency were harvested. The economic plight of the South and its people, colored and white, was worsened by many other federal policies, although a few were ameliorative.

674

One of the first economic needs of the South after the war was the restoration of markets and transportation, and here the federal government lent a helping hand. By July 1865 all restrictions on the exchange of commodities between the former enemies were withdrawn and the blockade of Confederate ports was terminated, thus allowing goods to move north and south and across the sea. Soon after, the federal government returned southern railroads it had taken over—many of them in better condition than before the war. River transport was at least as important to the South as railroads, but 20 years of Republican rule were to pass before the South got a fair share of river- and harbor-improvement funds, and many navigable streams long remained unusable for commerce. As for wagon roads, the South was left to its own devices, with the characteristic result that roads were rebuilt more with an eye to horse racing than to hauling.

The South's need for capital was as urgent as that for markets and transport. Many planters had hoped to raise the money with which to restore land, buildings, and equipment to their former productivity by selling at the incredibly high prices of 1865 the stores of cotton they had built up during the war, presumably for export. But these hopes were quickly dashed. Ordered, at the end of hostilities, to confiscate all Confederate government assets, federal Treasury agents indiscriminately raided private as well as public warehouses and kept much of their loot. The Treasury eventually paid some 40,000 southerners $30 million for their losses, but this was only a fraction of what was taken and in any case came too late to help in the first postwar years. Confiscatory federal taxes further depleted southern capital. In three years following the war, a so-called revenue tax on cotton alone took $68 million from the South—far more than the total amount spent on relief and reconstruction by all northern agencies.

Before the war, most of the large southern plantations had been heavily mortgaged. After the war, creditors, hard-pressed themselves, began demanding payments of interest and principal. The fear of imminent foreclosure stirred some planters to an unwonted show of activity, but the federal confiscation and confiscatory taxes checked them. Some southern planters fended off the day of judgment by selling off part of their land in order to finance cultivation of the rest. Others leased out acreage for money rent. But obviously there was not money enough available to sustain these expedients for long. The upshot was the re-enactment of the familiar routine of the prewar South, by which planters paid no wages for labor while their workers paid no rent for land. Instead, each was to share in the *forthcoming* crop. That was the rub.

In order to get this crop into the ground both parties to the arrangement had to borrow. Since they had no other security, they had to give a first lien on what they hoped to produce. Only against this *forthcoming* collateral would the supply merchant advance the required seed, fertilizer, and equipment, as well as food and clothing. For his own stock-in-trade, the local merchant had to seek credit from northern suppliers. Risks in the South were so great that these suppliers demanded high prices for the goods they sold directly and high interest for the credit they extended. In addition, oppressive fees were charged for transportation, insurance, and other commercial services. All these charges the merchant passed on to the landlords and croppers whose liens he held. The merchant also added his own profit and perhaps a generous tithe to reward himself for his literacy at the expense of borrowers who could not read his books. Under this regime, the South became more firmly chained to northern creditors than ever, while the cropper was enslaved to the merchant.

The South drifted the more deeply into the sharecropping and crop-lien systems because they offered a solution to the problem of labor as well as capital. Immediately after the war, many planters tried to hold on to their newly freed workers by offering them keep and cash. To protect the Negroes from being packed off as soon as the crops were in, the Freedmen's Bureau insisted, often over the objections of the suspicious freedmen themselves, that the working arrangements be confirmed by written contracts. In the hope that the Negroes would stay at least until the harvest was over, the planter usually was willing to sign. The Black Codes, in turn (see p. 653), made it dangerous for the ex-slave to wander. A typical contract stipulated that the planter pay wages of $10 to $12 a month, less the cost, determined by the planter, of "quarters, fuel, healthy and substantial rations." In exchange, the freedman agreed "to labor . . . faithfully . . . six days during the week, in a manner customary on a plantation."

The wage system failed on the plantations largely because, as before, there was too little money. For what money there was, moreover, the planter usually found good prior uses. "The freedmen have universally been treated with bad faith," wrote General W. E. Strong from Texas in 1866, "and very few have received any compensation for work performed." The Negro himself often did not help matters. Emancipated, he quickly learned to resent working "in a manner customary on a plantation."

Sharecropping gradually stabilized labor relations in the cash-poor South. It also helped preserve the plantation system. Under sharecropping, the land was divided into many small "holdings" which gave the illusion of small independent farms, and indeed did represent a significant upward step for the freedman relieved of the gang labor of the slave system. But many small holdings together actually formed parts of single plantations, which, through foreclosures, gradually fell to the supply merchants or their own creditors. These businessmen helped liquidate the survivors of the old planter caste, but they themselves gained much gratification from becoming great landowners. Besides strengthening the tendency toward land monopolization, the credit system also furthered the concentration on cotton, the great cash crop. Lest the crop

fail, moreover, the businessman-planter assumed a degree of supervision over the life of the cropper and his family that old-time overseers would hardly have felt worthwhile.

During the late 1860s and early 1870s, the cotton crop never reached the prewar levels of 3.5 to 4 million bales and prices held at 15 cents a pound or more. Under the sharecropping system, overproduction soon became the rule and cotton prices tumbled. By 1890, the South was growing 8.5 million bales, and the price had fallen to 8.5 cents. In 1894, production reached a record high of 10 million bales, and the price sank to a record low of $4\frac{1}{2}$ cents. Falling prices and mounting debts sapped whatever spirit of enterprise had survived the social conflicts and legalized abuses of the time.

### THE WHITE FARMER IN THE "NEW SOUTH"

At the outbreak of the Civil War, eight times as many Negroes as whites had been employed in growing cotton, most of them concentrated on the newer plantations of the rich Gulf plain and the Mississippi Valley. After the war, many of these Negroes had become sharecroppers and continued to work these once excellent lands. Many of them found it easier than the old slaveless yeoman farmers to adjust to the inertia of the new system. Their lingering servility, in turn, recommended them to the landowner and the merchant. White croppers were likely to be "ornery." They also tended to look down upon the new businessman "planters" as worse by far than their Damnyankee models, as parvenus usurpers, betrayers of the Lost Cause. This attitude only sharpened the parvenu's hunger for black "help" to authenticate the new plantation life. "White labor," said an Alabama planter in 1888, "is totally unsuited to our methods, our manners, and our accommodations." Another in Mississippi said, "Give me the nigger every time. . . . We can boss him, and that is what we southern folk like."

The devastation of the war, however, also soon caught up with the white farmer, as it

676

had with the great planter. It was not long before he too needed credit from the local merchants to get his land back into production and his home and barns repaired. And, as in the case of the croppers, the merchants dictated that the white farmers also grow nothing but cotton. At first, the white farmers gave the merchant a lien on their forthcoming crops. As debts mounted, the merchant demanded a mortgage on the farmer's land as well; and as the cotton market deteriorated, the merchant ultimately foreclosed. Some white farmers managed to beat the trend and became large landowners and even merchants. But most of them went under.

The independent white farmers had learned early to look on sharecropping as a Negro institution. When they lost their land, they tried working as tenants on rented land, but lack of cash eventually forced them into sharecropping—"like victims of some horrid nightmare," said the imaginative Tom Watson of Georgia, "powerless—oppressed—shackled." Those who refused to give up their independence were relegated to the poorest land, from which their offspring began drifting to the towns. By the 1880s, many white farmers had lost virtually everything but their pride of race. It was to restore employment and ambition to white farm youth that the idea of the "New South" was born—a South in which the Negro "hands" would "keep their place" growing cotton and tobacco in the hot sun while the whites found remunerative work in textile and tobacco factories, iron and steel mills, and other industrial enterprises.

The movement to save the South through industrialism took on the guise of a crusade. After 1880, white doctors, preachers, lawyers, professors, and a veritable army of old generals and colonels gave their names and reputations, their energy and their capital to the mission. The textile industry, already restored continued to grow most rapidly, but during the depression of the mid-1880s, southern iron began to compete successfully with Pittsburgh's, the North Carolina tobacco manufacturing industry responded optimistically to the

new fad of cigarette smoking, and a bit later the cottonseed-oil manufacturing industry spurted upward. Another and more important goal of the crusade was to draw northern capital southward. It was to this goal that Henry Grady, publisher of the powerful *Atlanta Constitution,* gave most attention. Invading the North to recruit capital, management, and men, Grady told the barons of the New England Club in New York: "We have wiped out the place where Mason and Dixon's line used to be. . . . We are ready to lay odds on the Georgia Yankee as he manufactures relics of the battle-field in a one-story shanty and squeezes pure olive oil out of his cotton-seed, against any down easterner that ever swapped wooden nutmegs for flannel sausages in the valleys of Vermont."

In the 1880s northern capital had good reason for looking hopefully to the South. "The South," Chauncey M. Depew, the railroad lawyer and politician, told the Yale alumni, "is the Bonzana of the future. We have developed all the great and sudden opportunities for wealth . . . in the Northwest States and on the Pacific Slope." In the South lay "vast forests untouched; with enormous veins of coal and iron. . . . Go South, Young Man." There were still other inducements. "Long hours of labor and moderate wages will continue to be the rule here for many years to come," promised the *Southern Manufacturers' Record.* An Alabama publicist in 1886 offered this additional security: "The white laboring classes here are separated from the Negroes . . . by an innate consciousness of race superiority. This sentiment dignifies the character of white labor. It excites a sentiment of sympathy and equality on their part with the classes above them, and in this way becomes a wholesome social leaven."

Unfortunately for the promoters of the New South, as late as 1900 fewer than 4 per cent of the people in the important textile state of South Carolina were as yet engaged in manufacturing, while 70 per cent remained in agriculture. The ratios in the rest of the South were little different. And what did the white

(Left) Celebration of the adoption of the standardized northern railroad gauge in the South (The Granger Collection) and (right) wealthy Northerners promenading in St. Augustine, Florida during a winter season in the 'eighties. (Harper's Weekly.) This image of Reconstruction promoted in the 1880s by big business wealth in the North and big business aspirants in the South faded away in the 1890s when southern Democrats turned more compulsively to the race relations of the past and northern Republicans discovered that they had become the majority party no longer in need of the Negro's or the southern white's vote in the future.

industrial family gain? "Their power," writes a critic of the factory owners, "was peculiarly Southern. Unconsciously copying the planters, they established their workers in villages which resembled the slave quarters of old." In return for this "benevolence" they received a "feudal obedience."

And as for the agrarian South? In 1888, young Tom Watson wrote in his journal: "Mr. Grady thinks that 'Plenty rides on the springing harvest!' It rides on Grady's springing

677

678

imagination. . . . In Grady's farm life there are no poor cows . . . lands all 'Rich—Richer —Richest.' Snowy Cotton, rustling corn. In reality—barren wastes, gullied slopes—ruined lowlands. . . . Gin houses on crutches. Diving down in the grass for cotton." In notes for a speech which Grady's *Constitution* would not print, Watson jotted: " 'New South' idea. If it means apology, abject submission— sycophancy to success—perish the thought. . . . Shame to Southern men who go to Northern Banquets and Glory in our defeat. . . . Unpaternal, patricidal."

### THE CLOSED SOCIETY

While the Supreme Court's decision in the *Civil Rights Cases* of 1883 opened the way for social segregation under the law in the South, and the "separate but equal" decisions extended the legality of such segregation to educational institutions, Negro voting in many parts of the South survived the end of Radical Reconstruction in 1877 and the violence of the white supremacists (see p. 670). One reason for this was the heavy concentration of Negroes in the old plantation districts; another was that, in many localities where they did not actually make up a majority of the electorate, they were sufficiently numerous to hold the balance of power when white voters split, as they often did on important local issues. When these splits occurred, even though their own interests might be closer to those of the small white farmers, the Negroes usually were courted with success by the ruling conservatives, or Bourbons. Perhaps the successors to the old masters indeed knew how to manage their colored hands. In any case, their tactics, when they wanted the black vote, also included economic intimidation in the form of threats of loss of land, credit, or jobs; and economic and other inducements such as bribes and fiery libations. When intimidation and inducement failed, open resort was had to crude election frauds. All these expedients came to be used against vulnerable whites as well.

In the late 1880s and early 1890s, when agricultural depression caused discontented staple farmers to organize in the Populist movement and to pit their strength against conservative business and political leaders, it seemed possible in the South that poor white and Negro farmers might join together politically to unseat the Bourbons. Populist leaders like Tom Watson now began to preach cooperation among poor croppers regardless of race. Only in North Carolina, however, were the Populists able, by joining with the Republicans still to be found there, to defeat the Bourbon Democrats. In 1894 the Populists won control of the state legislature, captured a majority of the state's congressional seats, and elected both United States senators. In 1896 they retained control of the state legislature and also won the governorship. Most colored voters supported them in these elections and they rewarded hundreds of Negroes with jobs.

North Carolina promptly became the target of the entire South, which rallied to the support of the Democratic party in the state and helped it violently to dislodge the biracial Populists in the election of 1898. Elsewhere in the South. Negro support of the hated Bourbons, even at the peak of Populism's highly emotional appeal, only intensified the small farmers' antipathy toward the Negro himself, and their racism and resentment of Bourbonism both ran amuck.

In order to restore some stability to white unity after they had thwarted the Populist challenge, the Bourbons displayed a growing willingness to sacrifice what remained of those Negro prerogatives which had served themselves so well. They were the more strongly motivated to do so by their own profound revulsion from the corruption and violence that increasingly marred southern elections as differences among white voters widened. By appealing, at the same time, to the small farmers' deepened commitment to white supremacy, the Bourbons hoped to induce them to sacrifice some of their own prerogatives for the cause, and thereby offset Bourbon losses in Negro voting strength.

The small farmers proved very reluctant to be induced; yet, after making some genuine concessions, sometimes simply by legislation, sometimes by constitutional amendments, but most frequently by wholly new constitutions, the Bourbons carried the day after all. Their concessions included such Populist demands as railroad regulatory commissions and paid public appraisers of corporation property so that it might more rewardingly be taxed. But the stormiest issue was the central one of the suffrage, and the broadest concessions were made here. These took such forms as the notorious "understanding" tests, "grandfather" clauses, "veterans" privileges, and "good character" provisos, all to be administered by Democratic registration boards and similarly "discreet" election officials. As the Chairman of the Judiciary Committee of the Louisiana Constitutional Convention of 1898, Thomas J. Semmes, said of the grandfather clause adopted there, by this means ". . . every white man . . . although he may not be able to read and write, although he does not possess the property qualifications, may, notwithstanding, if he register himself pursuant to this ordinance of the Constitution, be thereafter entitled to vote."

Such were the sieves—and there were others, such as long residence requirements and disqualifications for the pettiest of crimes, that were especially effective against peripatetic and sufficiently provoked Negroes—that were to trap the Negro aspirant but let the white man through. Because these measures "did not on their face discriminate between the races," as they were forbidden to do by the Fifteenth Amendment, but rather "swept the circle of expedients" remaining, the Supreme Court itself, in the case of *Williams* v. *Mississippi,* April 25, 1898, held them to be "within the field of permissible action under the limitations imposed by the Federal Constitution."

Nevertheless, there were catches for the whites as well. One of them was the time limit often placed on the escape provisions. As Semmes said of the white man's grand-

father clause, "If he doesn't choose to register between now and the last of September next, he loses the privilege conferred upon him, and thereafter he can only vote provided he possesses the qualifications which I have just mentioned—the property or education. That is the temporary clause." The property qualifications, in turn, were uniformly high, while the education clauses could be enforced stringently enough to discourage respectable illiterates from exposing their limitations in schooling to their neighbors. Another effective catch was the poll tax usually imposed by the new regulations. This tax was cumulative from year to year. Since little effort would be made to collect it, it often mounted up. The only penalty for non-payment might be the loss of the right to vote, a loss the more stoically borne as the amount soared.

The small farmers had been so certain that any means of disfranchising the Negro under the Fourteenth and Fifteenth Amendments would necessarily disfranchise themselves that they vigorously fought even the calling of the new constitutional conventions. So certain were the Bourbons, in turn, that the escape clauses for the whites would prove unsatisfactory to these farmers that, except in Alabama, they declared the new fundamental laws adopted without submitting them to referendums. Both groups were proved right. In state after state, following Mississippi's example of 1890, as the new suffrage laws were adopted, Negro voting virtually ceased, white voting also fell off, and small Democratic oligarchies gained control of political machinery. Such control insured Bourbon domination of most social institutions in the South and kept them lily white.

By returning their friends to Congress year after year, the Bourbon Democrats also gained extraordinary power in major House and Senate committees, where seniority ruled and the life and death of legislation often was at stake. This was especially true during Democratic administrations which they themselves helped elect by delivering the "Solid South" to the party.

# READINGS

The best introduction to the Reconstruction period is K.M. Stampp, *The Era of Reconstruction 1865–1877* (1965). R.W. Patrick, *The Reconstruction of the Nation* (1967), and J.H. Franklin, *Reconstruction After the Civil War* (1961), are able surveys. See also Franklin's standard history of Negro Americans, *From Slavery to Freedom* (1967). J.G. Randall and David Donald, *The Civil War and Reconstruction* (1961), is a comprehensive study with special emphasis on constitutional issues. Donald, *The Politics of Reconstruction 1863–1867* (1965), is illuminating on early policies. W.L. Fleming, *Documentary History of Reconstruction* (2 vols., 1906), is a comprehensive collection. R.N. Current, ed., *Reconstruction 1865–1877* (1965), and J.P. Shenton, ed., *The Reconstruction, a Documentary History 1865–1877* (1963), are useful short anthologies. Other general works from various points of view include: W.A. Dunning, *Reconstruction, Political and Economic 1865–1877* (1907); W.L. Fleming, *The Sequel of Appomattox* (1919); and E.M. Coulter, *The South During Reconstruction 1865–1877* (1947). W.J. Cash, *The Mind of the South* (1941), is as stimulating on this period as on others. P.H. Buck, *The Road to Reunion 1865–1900* (1937), is a unique study of influences tending, with too little success, to reunite the sections. W.E.B. Du Bois, *Black Reconstruction in America 1860–1880* (1935), is a classic by a leading Negro intellectual. Robert Cruden, *The Negro in Reconstruction* (1969), is illuminating if less ambitious. Otis Singletary, *The Negro Militia and Reconstruction* (1957), gives a glimpse of the violence of the times. Much valuable material on this subject will be found in Herbert Aptheker, *A Documentary History of the Negro People in the United States* (1951).

The following may be suggested from a long list on the South just after the war: Whitelaw Reid, *After the War, A Tour of the Southern States 1865–1866* (1965 ed.); Sidney Andrews, *The South since the War* (1866); and J.T. Trowbridge, *The South* (1866). Travelers' accounts later in the Reconstruction period include Robert Somers, *The Southern States since the War 1870–1871* (1871), and Edward King, *The Southern States* (1875). J.W. De Forest, *A Union Officer in the Reconstruction* (1948), is a revealing report.

Reconstruction of the South really began with the movement southward of northern troops. The Lincoln biographies cited in the Readings for Chapter Nineteen cover much of his program. Early reconstruction efforts are examined in W.L. Rose, *Rehearsal for Reconstruction, The Port Royal Experiment* (1964), and Joel Williamson, *After Slavery, The Negro in South Carolina during Reconstruction 1861–1877* (1965). J.E. Sefton, *The United States Army and Reconstruction 1865–1877* (1968), is a comprehensive monograph. E.L. McKitrick, *Andrew Johnson and Reconstruction* (1960), a critical modern account, may be supplemented by such older works as G.F. Milton, *The Age of Hate: Andrew Johnson and the Radicals* (1930), and H.K. Beale, *The Critical Year: A Study of Andrew Johnson and Reconstruction* (1930). LaWanda and J.H. Cox, *Politics, Principle and Prejudice 1865–66* (1963), emphasizes Johnson's role in efforts to restore the Democratic party in the North.

681

T.II. Williams, *Lincoln and the Radicals* (1941), offers a starting point for the study of Stevens, Sumner, and company. F.M. Brodie, *Thaddeus Stevens, Scourge of the South* (1959), is the leading biography. Moorfield Storey, *Charles Sumner* (1900), will serve until David Donald brings his modern life of the Senator to the Reconstruction period. J.M. McPherson, *The Struggle for Equality, Abolitionists and the Negro in the Civil War and Reconstruction* (1964), is an outstanding monograph on certain sources of Radical thinking. B.B. Kendrick, ed., *The Journal of the Joint Committee of Fifteen on Reconstruction* (1914), elaborates this theme. Illuminating monographs on the Fourteenth Amendment include J.B. James, *The Framing of the Fourteenth Amendment* (1956), and Jacobus tenBroek, *The Antislavery Origins of the Fourteenth Amendment* (1951). On the Fifteenth Amendment, see William Gillette, *The Right to Vote, Politics and the Passage of the Fifteenth Amendment* (1965). Paul Lewinson, *Race, Class and Party, A History of Negro Suffrage and White Politics in the South* (1932), is an able study of its subject from 1860 to 1930. S.D. Smith, *The Negro in Congress 1870–1901* (1940), is a scholarly account. G.R. Bentley, *A History of the Freedman's Bureau* (1955), is best on that agency. V.L. Wharton, *The Negro in Mississippi 1865–1890* (1947), is a model study; among other such special accounts the following may be noted: A.A. Taylor, *The Negro in Tennessee 1865–1880* (1941), and G.B. Tindall, *South Carolina Negroes 1877–1900* (1952).

Allan Nevins, *Hamilton Fish: The Inner History of the Grant Administration* (1936), is the definitive account. See also Matthew Josephson, *The Politicos 1865–1896* (1938). Horace Greeley, *Recollections of a Busy Life* (1868), supplies first-hand background on the Liberal Republican campaign. See also E.D. Ross, *The Liberal Republican Movement* (1919), and C.M. Fuess, *Carl Schurz, Reformer* (1932).

Four outstanding works by C.V. Woodward offer the best introductions to the demise of the Reconstruction spirit: *Reunion and Reaction: The Compromise of 1877 and the End of Reconstruction* (1951), *Origns of the New South 1877–1913* (1951), *Tom Watson, Agrarian Rebel* (1938), and *The Strange Career of Jim Crow* (1966 ed.). V.O. Key, Jr., *Southern Politics in State and Nation* (1949), is a brilliant study in depth of the "redeemers" legacy. On sharecropping and related subjects, see the relevant chapters in F.A. Shannon, *The Farmers Last Frontier: Agriculture 1860–1897* (1945). Theodore Saloutos, *Farmer Movements in the South 1865–1933* (1960), is excellent on organized protest and self-help. R.B. Nixon, *Henry W. Grady: Spokesman of the New South* (1943), is a useful introduction to the industrial spirit. Broadus Mitchell, *The Rise of Cotton Mills in the South* (1921), shows the community character of the movement. R.W. Logan, *The Negro in American Life and Thought, The Nadir 1877–1901* (1954), is a detailed study of the abandonment of Radical goals, north and south. For the Negro reaction see August Meier, *Negro Thought in America 1880–1915* (1963). J.A. Isely, *Horace Greely and the Republican Party 1853–1861* (1947), and R.F. Durden, *James Shepherd Pike, Republicanism and the American Negro 1850–1882* (1957), are informative on early party attitudes. Outstanding on the party's later attitudes are S.P. Hirshon, *Farewell to the Bloody Shirt: Northern Republicans & the Southern Negro 1877–1893* (1962), and V.P. De Santis, *Republicans Face the Southern Question—The New Departure Years 1877–1897* (1959). A.W. Tourgée, *A Fool's Errand* (1879); L.H. Blair, *A Southern Prophecy, The Prosperity of the South Dependent upon the Elevation of the Negro* (1889; modern ed., 1964); and Arlin Turner, ed., *The Negro Question, A Selection of the Writings on Civil Rights in the South by George W. Cable* (1958 ed.), foreshadow some modern ideas.

# APPENDIX

## General Reading

The works cited below are provided, first, to acquaint the student with the nature of the historical discipline and related fields, and second, to direct him to useful histories, reference and source books, and periodicals in American history.

### HISTORY AND RELATED DISCIPLINES

A.S. Eisenstadt, *The Craft of American History* (2 vols., 1966), is an outstanding collection of essays on interpreting the American past. John Higham, ed., *The Reconstruction of American History* (1962), presents critical assessments of the treatment of major topics. B.J. Bernstein, ed., *Towards a New Past: Dissenting Essays in American History* (1968), is more polemical. Economics, political science, and sociology rank high among the social sciences most useful in the study of history. Penetrating introductions to them will be found in the short, scholarly volumes in the following: Otto Eckstein, ed., *Foundations of Modern Economics Series* (1964– ); R.A. Dahl, *Foundations of Modern Political Science Series* (1963– ); and Alex Inkeles, ed., *Foundations of Modern Sociology Series* (1964– ). Modern critiques of these and other academic disciplines will be found in Theodore Roszak, ed., *The Dissenting Academy* (1968). E.R.A. Seligman and Alvin Johnson, eds., *Encyclopaedia of the Social Sciences* (15 vols., 1930–1935), remains invaluable. On the relation of other sciences to history, see, for example, W.T. Jones, *The Sciences and the Humanities: Conflict and Reconciliation* (1965), and Gerald Holton, ed., *Science and Culture, A Study of Cohesive and Disjunctive Forces* (1965).

### REFERENCE WORKS AND PERIODICALS

Oscar Handlin and others, eds., *The Harvard Guide to American History* (1954), is the most comprehensive bibliographic source, which may be updated by our own chapter Readings. Allen Johnson and Dumas Malone, eds., *Dictionary of American Biography* (22 vols., 1928–1958), and J.T. Adams and R.V. Coleman, eds., *Dictionary of American History* (6 vols., 1940), are comprehensive works on the lives of outstanding Americans and the stories of leading events. J.G.E. Hopkins, ed., *Concise Dictionary of American Biography* (1964), is a one-volume abridgement of Johnson and Malone, and T.C. Cochran and Wayne Andrews, eds., *Concise Dictionary of American History* (1962), is a one-volume abridgement of Adams and Coleman. R.B. Morris, ed., *Encyclopedia of American History* (1965), is a dependable summary, with a supplement of 400 biographies. W.L. Langer, ed., *Encyclopedia of World History* (1968), is superb.

United States Department of Commerce, *Historical Statistics of the United States* (1957), with *Continuation to 1962* (1965), is immensely useful for quantitative information. For maps, see C.O. Paullin, *Atlas of the Historical Geography of the United States* (1932), and, by the editors of *American Heritage, The American Heritage Atlas of United States History* (1966). Invaluable for its fine text as well as for its excellent military maps is Brig. Gen. V.J. Esposito, ed., *The West Point Atlas of American Wars 1689–1953* (2 vols., 1959). R.H. Brown, *Historical Geography of the United States* (1948), is outstanding for the physical environment.

The *American Historical Review,* although devoted to all fields of history, gives much space to research and reviews in American history. Strictly American history periodicals include: *The Journal of American History* (until 1964, *The Mississippi Valley Historical Review*), *The Journal of Southern History, The William and Mary Quarterly,* and *The Pacific Historical Review.* The *American Quarterly* is published by the American Studies Association. The following journals often carry articles and reviews important for American history: *The Journal of Economic History; Political Science Quarterly; American Political Science Review; American Sociological Review;* and *American Journal of Sociology.*

## COLLECTIONS OF SOURCES

H.S. Commager, ed., *Documents of American History* (2 vols., 1968), is a massive collection of public documents, invaluable for its coverage. William Miller, ed., *Readings in American Values, Selected and Edited from Public Documents of the American Past* (1964), is more selective. C.L. Ver Steeg and Richard Hofstadter, *Great Issues in American History: From Settlement to Revolution 1584–1776;* and Richard Hofstadter, ed., *Great Issues in American History: From Revolution to the Civil War 1765–1865,* and *From Reconstruction to the Present Day 1864–1969* (1969), focus on major controversies. A.F. Davis and H.D. Woodman, eds., *Conflict or Consensus in Early American History* (1968), offers selections from major secondary studies from the first settlements to the Civil War. The same period is covered, with primary as well as secondary materials, in Paul Glad and others, eds., *The Process of American History* (vol. I, 1969). The following series offer a wide selection of contemporary materials in short well-edited paperbacks: *Spectrum* (Prentice-Hall); *The American Heritage* (Bobbs-Merrill); *Anvil* (Van Nostrand); and *Documents in American Civilization* (Anchor). The Amherst series, *Problems in American Civilization* (Heath), are well-edited paperbacks, presenting opposing scholarly treatments of major issues. Sidney Fine and G.S.

Brown, eds., *The American Past, Conflicting Interpretations of Great Issues* (2 vols., 1965), is a useful anthology of journal articles.

Substantial collections of materials in more specialized fields include: K.H. Porter and D.B. Johnson, eds., *National Party Platforms 1840–1960* (1961); W.A. Williams, ed., *The Shaping of American Diplomacy* (1956); J.R. Commons and others, eds., *Documentary History of American Industrial Society* (10 vols., 1910–1911); Edith Abbott, ed., *Historical Aspects of the Immigration Problem, Select Documents* (1926); Elizabeth Donnan, ed., *Documents Illustrative of the History of the Slave Trade to America* (4 vols., 1930–35); and A.D. Chandler, ed., *The Forces in American Economic Growth Series* (5 vols., 1964–1967). Moses Rischin, ed., *The American Gospel of Success* (1965), is an excellent collection on ascent and aspiration. Herbert Aptheker, *A Documentary History of the Negro People in the United States* (1951), affords valuable testimony to 1910. August Meier and Elliott Rudwick, eds., *The Making of Black America* (1969), is an outstanding collection of secondary materials. Staughton Lynd, *Nonviolence in America: A Documentary History* (1966), breaks new ground. Oscar Handlin, ed., *This Was America* (1949), is an illuminating collection of foreign commentary. Richard Hofstadter and Wilson Smith, eds., *American Higher Education* (2 vols., 1961), is comprehensive. F.O. Matthiessen, *The Oxford Book of American Verse* (1950), is a fine anthology.

## COMPREHENSIVE GENERAL WORKS

H.S. Commager and R.B. Morris, eds., *The New American Nation Series* (1954–        ), on its completion, will afford the most comprehensive modern treatment of American history, rich in bibliography. By 1969 twenty volumes had been issued. Other useful multi-author series include A.M. Schlesinger and D.R. Fox, eds., *A History of American Life* (13 vols., 1927–1948); Allen Johnson, ed., *Chronicles of America* (50 vols., 1918–1921, with 6 additional volumes edited by Allan Nevins, 1950–1951); D.J. Boorstin, ed., *The Chicago History of American Civilization* (1956–        ), offering short works on special periods and topics.

C.A. and M.R. Beard, *The Rise of American Civilization* (1927), *America in Midpassage* (1939), and *The American Spirit* (1942), al-

684

though somewhat dated, remain valuable for their sweep and insight. D.J. Boorstin, *The Americans: The Colonial Experience* (1958) and *The Americans: The National Experience* (1965), are the first two volumes of a history in progress. Older comprehensive works by single authors, still of value, include George Bancroft, *History of the United States* (10 vols., 1834–1875), to the end of the Revolution, and Edward Channing, *History of the United States* (6 vols., 1905–1925), to the end of the Civil War. For the Middle Period, see J.F. Rhodes, *History of the United States From . . . 1850 to 1877* (7 vols., 1906), and Allan Nevins's 10-volume work in progress, of which 6 volumes from 1847 to 1863 had been published by 1969.

### POLITICAL AND CONSTITUTIONAL HISTORY

A.H. Kelly and W.A. Harbison, *The American Constitution, Its Origins and Development* (1963), is an outstanding history from the early English background through the civil rights controversies of the 1960s, rich in bibliography. J.M. Smith and P.L. Murphy, eds., *Liberty and Justice: A Historical Record of American Constitutional Development* (2 vols., 1958), is a useful anthology. Charles Warren, *The Supreme Court in United States History* (2 vols., 1937), is standard for the nineteenth century. R.G. McCloskey, *The American Supreme Court* (1960), is a short modern history. E.S. Corwin, ed., *The Constitution of the United States of America, Analysis and Interpretation* (1953), is an invaluable annotated edition that traces Supreme Court decisions on every section.

On the executive, see E.S. Corwin, *The President, Office and Powers* (1957). N.J. Small, *Some Presidential Interpretations of the Presidency* (1932), is a revealing monograph. *Inaugural Addresses of the Presidents of the United States* (an anonymous government publication, 1961), and A.M. Schlesinger, Jr., and Fred Israel, eds., *The State of the Union Messages of the Presidents* (3 vols., 1966), are helpful collections. G.B. Galloway, *History of the House of Representatives* (1962), and G.H. Haynes, *The Senate of the United States* (2 vols., 1938), cover the legislature. Leonard White, *The Federalists* (1948), *The Jeffersonians* (1951), *The Jacksonians* (1954), and *The Republican Era 1869–1901* (1958), are excellent on administra-

tive history. W.E. Binkley, *American Political Parties: Their Natural History* (1963), may be supplemented by Richard Hofstadter, *The Idea of a Party System* (1969); R.F. Nichols, *The Invention of American Political Parties* (1967), and W.N. Chambers and W.D. Burnham, eds., *The American Party System, Stages of Development* (1967). Richard Hofstadter, *The American Political Tradition* (1948), and Louis Hartz, *The Liberal Tradition in America* (1955), offer interpretations.

### DIPLOMATIC AND MILITARY HISTORY

Alexander DeConde, *A History of American Foreign Policy* (1963), is an outstanding text. J.W. Pratt, *A History of United States Foreign Policy* (1965); and R.W. Leopold, *The Growth of American Foreign Policy* (1962), are also useful. S.F. Bemis, ed., *American Secretaries of State and Their Diplomacy* (10 vols., 1927–1929), contains scholarly essays on all the holders of that office during the period of this volume. The best collection of treaties in convenient form is W.M. Malloy, ed., *Treaties, Conventions, International Acts, Protocols, and Agreements between the United States and Other Powers 1776–1937* (4 vols., 1910–37).

R.F. Weigley, *History of the United States Army* (1967), is definitive on military institutions and ideas. Marcus Cunliffe, *Soldiers and Civilians: The Martial Spirit in America 1775–1865* (1968), stresses the conflict of professional and amateur soldiers. S.E. Ambrose, *Duty, Honor, Country: A History of West Point* (1966), is outstanding on the main source of professionals. Harold and Margaret Sprout, *The Rise of American Naval Power 1776–1918* (1942), and R.D. Heinl, Jr., *Soldiers of the Sea, the U. S. Marine Corps 1775–1962* (1962), are the leading surveys. *The West Point Atlas of American Wars* (cited above, under Reference Works), is outstanding for military engagements. These are also stressed in Department of the Army ROTC Manual, *American Military History 1607–1953* (1956), an authoritative short account. Walter Millis, *Arms and Men, A Study of American Military History* (1956), is a critical survey. Millis, ed., *American Military Thought* (1966), is a valuable anthology. Louis Smith, *American Democracy and Military Power* (1951), and A.A. Ekirch, Jr., *The Civilian and the Military*

(1956), deal historically with problems indicated by their titles.

## THE FRONTIER, THE WEST, AND THE SOUTH

R.A. Billington, *Westward Expansion* (1967), is a well-organized history of the moving frontier, with an up-to-date bibliography. F.J. Turner, *The Frontier in American History* (1920), and *The Significance of Sections in American History* (1932), are classic studies. R.M. Robbins, *Our Landed Heritage* (1942), affords a good general account of the disposal of the public domain. Marshall Harris, *Origin of the Land Tenure System in the United States* (1953), is authoritative on early methods. On the Indians and related subjects, three works from a growing literature may be cited, in addition to those in relevant chapter Readings: R.H. Pearce, *The Savages of America, A Study of the Indian and the Idea of Civilization* (1953); W.E. Washburn, ed., *The Indian and the White Man* (1964); and A.M. Josephy, Jr., *The Indian Heritage of America* (1968). W.D. Wyman and C.B. Kroeber, *The Frontier in Perspective* (1957), is made up of essays on frontiers from Roman times onward, including the American frontier.

Many works on the distinctive South are cited in chapter Readings, especially for Chapter Sixteen. W.H. Stephenson and E.M. Coulter, eds., *A History of the South* (10 vols., 1947–1967), is an outstanding series. Valuable one-volume books covering the range of southern history include F.B. Simkins, *History of the South* (1963); W.B. Hesseltine, *The South in American History* (1960); W.J. Cash, *The Mind of the South* (1941); and J.B. Hubbell, *The South in American Literature 1607–1900* (1954).

## ECONOMIC HISTORY

The Readings for Chapters Twelve and Seventeen should be consulted first for works on this topic. Of the numerous general surveys, the following may be suggested here: E.C. Kirkland, *A History of American Economic Life* (1951), in the narrative tradition, and R.M. Robertson, *History of the American Economy* (1964), in the analytic tradition. Henry David and others, eds., *The Economic History of the United States,*

(1945–    ), is a projected 10-volume work by leading scholars, of which all but the first and last volumes had been published by 1969. D.R. Dewey, *Financial History of the United States* (1934), remains a standard work. Bray Hammond, *Banks and Politics in America, From the Revolution to the Civil War* (1957), is more analytical. On the tariff, F.W. Taussig, *The Tariff History of the United States* (1931), is standard, but valuable also is F.W. Stanwood, *American Tariff Controversies in the Nineteenth Century* (2 vols., 1903). On taxation, Sidney Ratner, *American Taxation* (1942), is detailed. The standard work on labor history is J.R. Commons and others, *History of Labor in the United States* (4 vols., 1918–1935). J.G. Rayback, *A History of American Labor* (1959), is a sound one-volume work.

E.E. Edwards, "American Agriculture: The First Three Hundred Years," in the *1940 Yearbook of Agriculture,* published by the Department of Agriculture, is an excellent short account. M.R. Benedict, *Farm Policies of the United States 1790–1950* (1953), is good on issues and legislation. V.S. Clark, *History of Manufactures in the United States* (3 vols., 1929), is standard. Roger Burlingame, *March of the Iron Men* (1938), is the best introduction to the history of technology. On commerce, transportation, and travel, the following are outstanding: E.R. Johnson and others, *History of Domestic and Foreign Commerce of the United States* (2 vols., 1915); B.H. Meyer and others, *History of Transportation in the United States before 1860* (1917); and Seymour Dunbar, *History of Travel in America* (4 vols., 1915).

T.C. Cochran and William Miller, *The Age of Enterprise, A Social History of Industrial America* (1942), is a general interpretation from 1800 to the New Deal. Joseph Dorfman, *The Economic Mind in American Civilization* (5 vols., 1946–1959), is a wide-ranging history of political-economic thought.

## SOCIAL AND URBAN HISTORY

M.R. Davie, *World Immigration* (1949), is a history of the movement of peoples since colonial times. Carl Wittke, *We Who Built America* (1967), is a general survey of the immigrant in the United States. M.L. Hansen, *The Atlantic*

*Migration 1607–1860* (1940), is a valuable study of the "old" newcomers. See also the Readings for Chapters Three and Seventeen. The leading general history of the Negro in Africa and America, with full up-to-date bibliographies, is J.H. Franklin, *From Slavery to Freedom: A History of American Negroes* (1967). See also Benjamin Quarles, *The Negro in the Making of America* (1964), and August Meier and E.M. Rudwick, *From Plantation to Ghetto, An Interpretive History of American Negroes* (1966). Anti-immigrant prejudice and its consequences are traced in R.A. Billington, *The Protestant Crusade 1800–1860* (1938). Valuable for anti-white as well as anti-Negro feelings is T.F. Gossett, *Race, The History of an Idea in America* (1963). Once again, W.D. Jordan, *White over Black, American Attitudes Toward the Negro 1550–1812* (1968), transcends its specific period. See also William Stanton, *The Leopard's Spots, Scientific Attitudes Toward Race in America 1815–1859* (1960).

Urban life in America before the middle of the nineteenth century is barely touched on in such general works as C.M. Green, *The Rise of Urban America* (1965), and *American Cities in the Growth of the Nation* (1957). More valuable are such scholarly accounts of particular times and places as: Carl Bridenbaugh, *Cities in the Wilderness* (1938), *Cities in Revolt* (1955), and *Rebels and Gentlemen: Philadelphia in the Age of Franklin* (1942); D.B. Rutman, *Winthrop's Boston, A Portrait of a Puritan Town 1630–1649* (1965); C.M. Green, *Washington, Village and Capital 1800–1878* (1962); R.G. Albion, *The Rise of New York Port 1815–1860* (1939); and R.C. Wade, *The Urban Frontier: The Rise of Western Cities 1790–1830* (1959), and *Slavery in the Cities: The South 1820–1860* (1964).

H.W. Farnam, *Chapters in the History of Social Legislation in the United States to 1860* (1938), is invaluable on a whole range of social issues. On selected special subjects, see A.W. Calhoun, *A Social History of the American Family* (3 vols., 1917–1919); Dixon Wecter, *The Saga of American Society* (1937); I.G. Wylie, *The Self-Made Man in America* (1954); F.R. Packard, *History of Medicine in the United States* (2 vols., 1931); Blake McKelvey, *American Prisons* (1936); F.R. Dulles, *America Learns to Play* (1940); and A.M. Schlesinger, *Learning How to Behave* (1946).

## INTELLECTUAL AND CULTURAL HISTORY

The Readings for Chapters Four and Fourteen should be consulted first on this topic. V.L. Parrington, *Main Currents in American Thought* (3 vols., 1927–1930), though much criticized, remains a useful work. Merle Curti, *The Growth of American Thought* (1964), is comprehensive. R.H. Gabriel, *The Course of American Democratic Thought* (1956), covers the period since 1815. H.W. Schneider, *A History of American Philosophy* (1946), is the standard work. R.E. Spiller and others, *Literary History of the United States* (3 vols., 1943), is an exhaustive survey. The third volume is wholly bibliographical. Van Wyck Brooks, *Makers and Finders* (5 vols., 1936–1952), on writers from 1800 to 1915, is rich in background. Marcus Cunliffe, *The Literature of the United States* (1954), is a sound one-volume account. Constance Rourke, *American Humor* (1931), is a brilliant study of national character.

Leading books in special fields of art include: Richard McLanathan, *The American Tradition in the Arts* (1968); O.W. Larkin, *Art and Life in America* (1949); E.P. Richardson, *Painting in America, The Story of 450 Years* (1956); James Burchard and Albert Bush-Brown, *The Architecture of America, A Social and Cultural History* (1966); Wayne Andrews, *Architecture, Ambition and Americans* (1955); and J.M. Fitch, *American Building* (1948).

The standard works on journalism are F.L. Mott, *American Journalism* (1950), and *A History of American Magazines* (5 vols., 1930–1968). Merle Curti, *Social Ideas of American Educators* (1935), is a thoughtful introduction. E.P. Cubberley, *Public Education in the United States* (1934), remains most useful on its subject. On the higher learning, see Richard Hofstadter and Walter Metzger, *Academic Freedom in the United States* (1955), which goes well beyond the scope of its title, and Laurence Veysey, *The Emergence of the American University* (1965). Winthrop Hudson, *Religion in America* (1965), is a leading general work. S.E. Mead, *The Lively Experiment, The Shaping of Christianity in America* (1963), is a penetrating short analysis. E.B. Greene, *Religion and the State* (1941), and J.F. Wilson, *Church and State in American History* (1965), afford good introductions to that issue.

## *The Declaration of Independence*

When in the course of human events, it becomes necessary for one people to dissolve the political bands which have connected them with another, and to assume, among the powers of the earth, the separate and equal station to which the laws of nature and of nature's God entitle them, a decent respect to the opinions of mankind requires that they should declare the causes which impel them to the separation.

We hold these truths to be self-evident, that all men are created equal; that they are endowed by their Creator with certain unalienable rights; that among these, are life, liberty, and the pursuit of happiness. That, to secure these rights, governments are instituted among men, deriving their just powers from the consent of the governed; that, whenever any form of government becomes destructive of these ends, it is the right of the people to alter or to abolish it, and to institute a new government, laying its foundation on such principles, and organizing its powers in such form, as to them shall seem most likely to effect their safety and happiness. Prudence, indeed, will dictate that governments long established, should not be changed for light and transient causes; and, accordingly, all experience hath shown, that mankind are more disposed to suffer, while evils are sufferable, than to right themselves by abolishing the forms to which they are accustomed. But, when a long train of abuses and usurpations, pursuing invariably the same object, evinces a design to reduce them under absolute despotism, it is their right, it is their duty, to throw off such government and to provide new guards for their future security. Such has been the patient sufferance of these colonies, and such is now the necessity which constrains them to alter their former systems of government. The history of the present King of Great Britain is a history of repeated injuries and usurpations, all having, in direct object, the establishment of an absolute tyranny over these States. To prove this, let facts be submitted to a candid world:—

He has refused his assent to laws the most wholesome and necessary for the public good.

He has forbidden his governors to pass laws of immediate and pressing importance, unless suspended in their operation till his assent should be obtained; and, when so suspended, he has utterly neglected to attend to them.

He has refused to pass other laws for the accommodation of large districts of people, unless those people would relinquish the right of representation in the legislature; a right inestimable to them, and formidable to tyrants only.

He has called together legislative bodies at places unusual, uncomfortable, and distant from the depository of their public records, for the sole purpose of fatiguing them into compliance with his measures.

He has dissolved representative houses, repeatedly for opposing, with manly firmness, his invasions on the rights of the people.

He has refused, for a long time after such dissolutions, to cause others to be elected; whereby the legislative powers, incapable of annihilation, have returned to the people at large for their exercise; the state remaining, in the meantime, exposed to all the danger of invasion from without, and convulsions within.

He has endeavored to prevent the population of these States; for that purpose, obstructing the laws for naturalization of foreigners, refusing to pass others to encourage their migration hither, and raising the conditions of new appropriations of lands.

He has obstructed the administration of justice, by refusing his assent to laws for establishing judiciary powers.

He has made judges dependent on his will alone, for the tenure of their offices, and the amount and payment of their salaries.

He has erected a multitude of new offices, and sent hither swarms of officers to harass our people, and eat out their substance.

He has kept among us, in time of peace, standing armies, without the consent of our legislatures.

He has affected to render the military independent of, and superior to, the civil power.

He has combined, with others, to subject us to a jurisdiction foreign to our Constitution, and unacknowledged by our laws; giving his assent to their acts of pretended legislation:

For quartering large bodies of armed troops among us:

For protecting them by a mock trial, from punishment, for any murders which they should commit on the inhabitants of these States:

For cutting off our trade with all parts of the world:

For imposing taxes on us without our consent:

For depriving us, in many cases, of the benefit of trial by jury:

For transporting us beyond seas to be tried for pretended offences:

For abolishing the free system of English laws in a neighboring province, establishing therein an arbitrary government, and enlarging its boundaries, so as to render it at once an example and fit instrument for introducing the same absolute rule into these colonies:

For taking away our charters, abolishing our most valuable laws, and altering, fundamentally, the powers of our governments:

For suspending our own legislatures, and declaring themselves invested with power to legislate for us in all cases whatsoever.

He has abdicated government here, by declaring us out of his protection, and waging war against us.

He has plundered our seas, ravaged our coasts,

burnt our towns, and destroyed the lives of our people.

He is, at this time, transporting large armies of foreign mercenaries to complete the works of death, desolation, and tyranny, already begun, with circumstances of cruelty and perfidy scarcely paralleled in the most barbarous ages, and totally unworthy the head of a civilized nation.

He has constrained our fellow citizens, taken captive on the high seas, to bear arms against their country, to become the executioners of their friends, and brethren, or to fall themselves by their hands.

He has excited domestic insurrections amongst us, and has endeavored to bring on the inhabitants of our frontiers, the merciless Indian savages, whose known rule of warfare is an undistinguished destruction of all ages, sexes, and conditions.

In every stage of these oppressions, we have petitioned for redress, in the most humble terms; our repeated petitions have been answered only by repeated injury. A prince, whose character is thus marked by every act which may define a tyrant, is unfit to be the ruler of a free people.

Nor have we been wanting in attention to our British brethren. We have warned them, from time to time, of attempts made by their legislature to extend an unwarrantable jurisdiction over us. We have reminded them of the circumstances of our emigration and settlement here. We have appealed to their native justice and magnanimity, and we have conjured them, by the ties of our common kindred, to disavow these usurpations, which would inevitably interrupt our connections and correspondence. They, too, have been deaf to the voice of justice and consanguinity. We must, therefore acquiesce in the necessity which denounces our separation, and hold them, as we hold the rest of mankind, enemies in war, in peace, friends.

We, therefore, the representatives of the United States of America, in general Congress assembled, appealing to the Supreme Judge of the world for the rectitude of our intentions, do, in the name, and by the authority of the good people of these colonies, solemnly publish and declare, that these united colonies are, and of right ought to be, free and independent states: that they are absolved from all allegiance to the British Crown, and that all political connection between them and the state of Great Britain is, and ought to be, totally dissolved; and that, as free and independent states, they have full power to levy war, conclude peace, contract alliances, establish commerce, and to do all other acts and things which independent states may of right do. And, for the support of this declaration, with a firm reliance on the protection of Divine Providence, we mutually pledge to each other our lives, our fortunes, and our sacred honor.

## The Constitution of the United States of America

We the people of the United States, in order to form a more perfect union, establish justice, insure domestic tranquility, provide for the common defense, promote the general welfare, and secure the blessings of liberty to ourselves and our posterity, do ordain and establish this Constitution for the United States of America.

### ARTICLE I

*Section 1.* All legislative powers herein granted shall be vested in a Congress of the United States, which shall consist of a Senate and House of Representatives.

*Section 2.* 1. The House of Representatives shall be composed of members chosen every second year by the people of the several States, and the electors in each State shall have the qualifications requisite for electors of the most numerous branch of the State legislature.

2. No person shall be a representative who shall not have attained to the age of twenty-five years, and been seven years a citizen of the United States, and who shall not, when elected, be an inhabitant of that State in which he shall be chosen.

3. Representatives and direct taxes [1] shall be apportioned among the several States which may be included within this Union, according to their respective numbers, which shall be determined by adding to the whole number of free persons, including those bound to service for a term of years, and excluding Indians not taxed, three fifths of all other persons. [2] The actual enumeration shall be made within three years after the first meeting of the Congress of the United States, and within every subsequent term of ten years, in such manner as they shall by law direct. The number of representatives shall not exceed one for every thirty thousand, but each State shall have at least one representative; and until such enumeration shall be made, the State of New Hampshire shall be entitled to choose three, Massachusetts eight, Rhode Island and Providence Plantations one, Connecticut five, New York six, New Jersey four, Pennsylvania eight, Delaware one, Maryland six, Virginia ten, North Carolina five, South Carolina five, and Georgia three.

4. When vacancies happen in the representation from any State, the executive authority thereof shall issue writs of election to fill such vacancies.

5. The House of Representatives shall choose their speaker and other officers; and shall have the sole power of impeachment.

*Section 3.* 1. The Senate of the United States shall be composed of two senators from each State,

---

[1] See the 16th Amendment.

[2] See the 14th Amendment.

chosen by the legislature thereof,[3] for six years; and each senator shall have one vote.

2. Immediately after they shall be assembled in consequence of the first election, they shall be divided as equally as may be into three classes. The seats of the senators of the first class shall be vacated at the expiration of the second year, of the second class at the expiration of the fourth year, and of the third class at the expiration of the sixth year, so that one third may be chosen every second year; and if vacancies happen by resignation, or otherwise, during the recess of the legislature of any State, the executive thereof may make temporary appointments until the next meeting of the legislature, which shall then fill such vacancies.[4]

3. No person shall be a senator who shall not have attained to the age of thirty years, and been nine years a citizen of the United States, and who shall not, when elected, be an inhabitant of that State for which he shall be chosen.

4. The Vice President of the United States shall be President of the Senate, but shall have no vote, unless they be equally divided.

5. The Senate shall choose their other officers, and also a president pro tempore, in the absence of the Vice President, or when he shall exercise the office of the President of the United States.

6. The Senate shall have the sole power to try all impeachments. When sitting for that purpose, they shall be on oath or affirmation. When the President of the United States is tried, the chief justice shall preside: and no person shall be convicted without the concurrence of two thirds of the members present.

7. Judgment in cases of impeachment shall not extend further than to removal from office, and disqualifications to hold and enjoy any office of honor, trust or profit under the United States: but the party convicted shall nevertheless be liable and subject to indictment, trial, judgment and punishment, according to law.

*Section 4.* 1. The times, places, and manner of holding elections for senators and representatives, shall be prescribed in each State by the legislature thereof; but the Congress may at any time by law make or alter such regulations, except as to the places of choosing senators.

2. The Congress shall assemble at least once in every year, and such meeting shall be on the first Monday in December, unless they shall by law appoint a different day.

*Section 5.* 1. Each House shall be the judge of the elections, returns and qualifications of its own members, and a majority of each shall constitute a quorum to do business; but a smaller number may adjourn from day to day, and may be authorized to compel the attendance of absent members, in such manner, and under such penalties as each House may provide.

2. Each House may determine the rules of its proceedings, punish its members for disorderly behavior, and, with the concurrence of two thirds, expel a member.

3. Each House shall keep a journal of its proceedings, and from time to time publish the same, excepting such parts as may in their judgment require secrecy; and the yeas and nays of the members of either House on any question shall, at the desire of one fifth of those present, be entered on the journal.

4. Neither House, during the session of Congress, shall, without the consent of the other, adjourn for more than three days, nor to any other place than that in which the two Houses shall be sitting.

*Section 6.* 1. The senators and representatives shall receive a compensation for their services, to be ascertained by law, and paid out of the Treasury of the United States. They shall in all cases, except treason, felony, and breach of the peace, be privileged from arrest during their attendance at the session of their respective Houses, and in going to and returning from the same; and for any speech or debate in either House, they shall not be questioned in any other place.

2. No senator or representative shall, during the time for which he was elected, be appointed to any civil office under the authority of the United States, which shall have been created, or the emoluments whereof shall have been increased, during such time; and no person holding any office under the United States shall be a member of either House during his continuance in office.

*Section 7.* 1. All bills for raising revenue shall originate in the House of Representatives; but the Senate may propose or concur with amendments as on other bills.

2. Every bill which shall have passed the House of Representatives and the Senate, shall, before it become a law, be presented to the President of the United States; If he approves he shall sign it, but if not he shall return it, with his objections, to that House in which it shall have originated, who shall enter the objections at large on their journal, and proceed to reconsider it. If after such reconsideration two thirds of that House shall agree to pass the bill, it shall be sent, together with the objections, to the other House, by which it shall likewise be reconsidered, and if approved by two thirds of that House, it shall become a law. But in all such cases the votes of both Houses shall be determined by yeas and nays, and the names of the persons voting for and against the bill shall be entered on the journal of each House respectively. If any bill shall not be returned by the President within ten days (Sundays excepted) after it shall have been presented to him, the same shall be a law, in like manner as if he had signed it, unless the Congress by their adjournment prevent its return, in which case it shall not be a law.

3. Every order, resolution, or vote to which the concurrence of the Senate and the House of Representatives may be necessary (except on a question of adjournment) shall be presented to the President of the United States; and before the same shall take effect, shall be approved by him, or being disapproved by him, shall be repassed by two thirds of the Senate and House of Representatives, according to the rules and limitations prescribed in the case of a bill.

*Section 8.* The Congress shall have the power

---

[3] See the 17th Amendment.
[4] See the 17th Amendment.

1. To lay and collect taxes, duties, imposts, and excises, to pay the debts and provide for the common defense and general welfare of the United States; but all duties, imposts, and excises shall be uniform throughout the United States;

2. To borrow money on the credit of the United States;

3. To regulate commerce with foreign nations, and among the several States, and with the Indian tribes;

4. To establish an uniform rule of naturalization, and uniform laws on the subject of bankruptcies throughout the United States;

5. To coin money, regulate the value thereof, and of foreign coin, and fix the standard of weights and measures;

6. To provide for the punishment of counterfeiting the securities and current coin of the United States;

7. To establish post offices and post roads;

8. To promote the progress of science and useful arts, by securing for limited times to authors and inventors the exclusive right to their respective writings and discoveries;

9. To constitute tribunals inferior to the Supreme Court;

10. To define and punish piracies and felonies committed on the high seas, and offenses against the law of nations;

11. To declare war, grant letters of marque and reprisal, and make rules concerning captures on land and water;

12. To raise and support armies, but no appropriation of money to that use shall be for a longer term than two years;

13. To provide and maintain a navy;

14. To make rules for the government and regulation of the land and naval forces;

15. To provide for calling forth the militia to execute the laws of the Union, suppress insurrections and repel invasions;

16. To provide for organizing, arming, and disciplining the militia, and for governing such part of them as may be employed in the service of the United States, reserving to the States respectively, the appointment of the officers, and the authority of training the militia according to the discipline prescribed by Congress;

17. To exercise exclusive legislation in all cases whatsoever, over such district (not exceeding ten miles square) as may, by cession of particular States, and the acceptance of Congress, become the seat of the government of the United States, and to exercise like authority over all places purchased by the consent of the legislature of the State in which the same shall be, for the erection of forts, magazines, arsenals, dockyards, and other needful buildings; and

18. To make all laws which shall be necessary and proper for carrying into execution the foregoing powers, and all other powers vested by this Constitution in the government of the United States, or any department or officer thereof.

*Section 9.* 1. The migration or importation of such persons as any of the States now existing shall think proper to admit, shall not be prohibited by the Congress prior to the year one thousand eight hundred and eight, but a tax or duty may be imposed on such importation, not exceeding ten dollars for each person.

2. The privilege of the writ of habeas corpus shall not be suspended, unless when in cases of rebellion or invasion the public safety may require it.

3. No bill of attainder or ex post facto law shall be passed.

4. No capitation, or other direct, tax shall be laid, unless in proportion to the census or enumeration hereinbefore directed to be taken.[5]

5. No tax or duty shall be laid on articles exported from any State.

6. No preference shall be given by any regulation of commerce or revenue to the ports of one State over those of another: nor shall vessels bound to, or from, one State be obliged to enter, clear, or pay duties in another.

7. No money shall be drawn from the treasury, but in consequence of appropriations made by law; and a regular statement and account of the receipts and expenditures of all public money shall be published from time to time.

8. No title of nobility shall be granted by the United States: and no person holding any office of profit or trust under them, shall, without the consent of the Congress, accept of any present, emolument, office, or title, of any kind whatever, from any king, prince, or foreign State.

*Section 10.* 1. No State shall enter into any treaty, alliance, or confederation; grant letters of marque and reprisal; coin money; emit bills of credit; make any thing but gold and silver coin a tender in payment of debts; pass any bill of attainder, ex post facto law, or law impairing the obligation of contracts, or grant any title of nobility.

2. No State shall, without the consent of the Congress, lay any imposts or duties on imports or exports, except what may be absolutely necessary for executing its inspection laws: and the net produce of all duties and imposts laid by any State on imports or exports, shall be for the use of the treasury of the United States; and all such laws shall be subject to the revision and control of the Congress.

3. No State shall, without the consent of the Congress, lay any duty of tonnage, keep troops, or ships of war in time of peace, enter into any agreement or compact with another State, or with a foreign power, or engage in war, unless actually invaded, or in such imminent danger as will not admit of delay.

## ARTICLE II

*Section 1.* 1. The executive power shall be vested in a President of the United States of America. He shall hold his office during the term of four years, and, together with the Vice President, chosen for the same term, be elected, as follows:

2. Each State shall appoint, in such manner as the legislature thereof may direct, a number of electors, equal to the whole number of senators and representatives to which the State may be entitled

[5] See the 16th Amendment.

in the Congress: but no senator or representative, or person holding an office of trust or profit under the United States, shall be appointed an elector.

The electors shall meet in their respective States, and vote by ballot for two persons, of whom one at least shall not be an inhabitant of the same State with themselves. And they shall make a list of all the persons voted for, and of the number of votes for each; which list they shall sign and certify, and transmit sealed to the seat of the government of the United States, directed to the president of the Senate. The president of the Senate shall, in the presence of the Senate and House of Representatives, open all the certificates, and the votes shall then be counted. The person having the greatest number of votes shall be the President, if such number be a majority of the whole number of electors appointed; and if there be more than one who have such majority, and have an equal number of votes, then the House of Representatives shall immediately choose by ballot one of them for President; and if no person have a majority, then from the five highest on the list the said House shall in like manner choose the President. But in choosing the President, the votes shall be taken by States, the representation from each State having one vote; a quorum for this purpose shall consist of a member or members from two thirds of the States, and a majority of all the States shall be necessary to a choice. In every case, after the choice of the President, the person having the greatest number of votes of the electors shall be the Vice President. But if there should remain two or more who have equal votes, the Senate shall choose from them by ballot the Vice President.[6]

3. The Congress may determine the time of choosing the electors, and the day on which they shall give their votes; which day shall be the same throughout the United States.

4. No person except a natural born citizen, or a citizen of the United States, at the time of the adoption of this Constitution, shall be eligible to the office of President; neither shall any person be eligible to that office who shall not have attained to the age of thirty-five years, and been fourteen years a resident within the United States.

5. In case of the removal of the President from office, or of his death, resignation, or inability to discharge the powers and duties of the said office, the same shall devolve on the Vice President, and the Congress may by law provide for the case of removal, death, resignation or inability, both of the President and Vice President, declaring what officer shall then act as President, and such officer shall act accordingly, until the disability be removed, or a President shall be elected.

6. The President shall, at stated times, receive for his services a compensation, which shall neither be increased nor diminished during the period for which he shall have been elected, and he shall not receive within that period any other emolument from the United States, or any of them.

7. Before he enter on the execution of his office, he shall take the following oath or affirmation:—"I do solemnly swear (or affirm) that I will faith-

fully execute the office of President of the United States, and will to the best of my ability, preserve, protect and defend the Constitution of the United States."

*Section 2.* 1. The President shall be commander in chief of the army and navy of the United States, and of the militia of the several States, when called into the actual service of the United States; he may require the opinion, in writing, of the principal officer in each of the executive departments, upon any subject relating to the duties of their respective offices, and he shall have power to grant reprieves and pardons for offenses against the United States, except in cases of impeachment.

2. He shall have power, by and with the advice and consent of the Senate, to make treaties, provided two thirds of the senators present concur; and he shall nominate, and by and with the advice and consent of the Senate, shall appoint ambassadors, other public ministers and consuls, judges of the Supreme Court, and all other officers of the United States, whose appointments are not herein otherwise provided for, and which shall be established by law: but the Congress may by law vest the appointment of such inferior officers, as they think proper, in the President alone, in the courts of law, or in the heads of departments.

3. The President shall have power to fill up all vacancies that may happen during the recess of the Senate, by granting commissions which shall expire at the end of their next session.

*Section 3.* He shall from time to time give to the Congress information of the state of the Union, and recommend to their consideration such measures as he shall judge necessary and expedient; he may, on extraordinary occasions, convene both Houses, or either of them, and in case of disagreement between them with respect to the time of adjournment, he may adjourn them to such time as he shall think proper; he shall receive ambassadors and other public ministers; he shall take care that the laws be faithfully executed, and shall commission all the officers of the United States.

*Section 4.* The President, Vice President, and all civil officers of the United States, shall be removed from office on impeachment for, and conviction of, treason, bribery, or other high crimes and misdemeanors.

ARTICLE III

*Section 1.* The judicial power of the United States shall be vested in one Supreme Court, and in such inferior courts as the Congress may from time to time ordain and establish. The judges, both of the Supreme and inferior courts, shall hold their offices during good behavior, and shall, at stated times, receive for their services, a compensation, which shall not be diminished during their continuance in office.

*Section 2.* 1. The judicial power shall extend to all cases, in law and equity, arising under this Constitution, the laws of the United States, and treaties made, or which shall be made, under their authority;—to all cases affecting ambassadors, other public ministers and consuls;—to all cases of admiralty and

---

[6] Superseded by the 12th Amendment.

maritime jurisdiction;—to controversies to which the United States shall be a party;[7]—to controversies between two or more States;—between a State and citizens of another State;—between citizens of different States;—between citizens of the same State claiming lands under grants of different States, and between a State, or the citizens thereof, and foreign States, citizens or subjects.

2. In all cases affecting ambassadors, other public ministers and consuls, and those in which a State shall be party, the Supreme Court shall have original jurisdiction. In all the other cases before mentioned, the Supreme Court shall have appellate jurisdiction, both as to law and fact, with such exceptions, and under such regulations as the Congress shall make.

3. The trial of all crimes, except in cases of impeachment, shall be by jury; and such trial shall be held in the State where the said crimes shall have been committed; but when not committed within any State, the trial shall be at such place or places as the Congress may by law have directed.

*Section 3.* 1. Treason against the United States shall consist only in levying war against them, or in adhering to their enemies, giving them aid and comfort. No person shall be convicted of treason unless on the testimony of two witnesses to the same overt act, or on confession in open court.

2. The Congress shall have power to declare the punishment of treason, but no attainder of treason shall work corruption of blood, or forfeiture except during the life of the person attainted.

### ARTICLE IV

*Section 1.* Full faith and credit shall be given in each State to the public acts, records, and judicial proceedings of every other State. And the Congress may by general laws prescribe the manner in which such acts, records and proceedings shall be proved, and the effect thereof.

*Section 2.* 1. The citizens of each State shall be entitled to all privileges and immunities of citizens in the several States.[8]

2. A person charged in any State with treason, felony, or other crime, who shall flee from justice, and be found in another State, shall on demand of the executive authority of the State from which he fled, be delivered up to be removed to the State having jurisdiction of the crime.

3. No person held to service or labor in one State under the laws thereof, escaping into another, shall, in consequence of any law or regulation therein, be discharged from such service or labor, but shall be delivered up on claim of the party to whom such service or labor may be due.[9]

*Section 3.* 1. New States may be admitted by the Congress into this Union; but no new State shall be formed or erected within the jurisdiction of any other State; nor any State be formed by the junction of two or more States, or parts of States, with-

out the consent of the legislatures of the States concerned as well as of the Congress.

2. The Congress shall have power to dispose of and make all needful rules and regulations respecting the territory or other property belonging to the United States; and nothing in this Constitution shall be so construed as to prejudice any claims of the United States, or of any particular State.

*Section 4.* The United States shall guarantee to every State in this Union a republican form of government, and shall protect each of them against invasion; and on application of the legislature, or of the executive (when the legislature cannot be convened) against domestic violence.

### ARTICLE V

The Congress, whenever two thirds of both Houses shall deem it necessary, shall propose amendments to this Constitution, or, on the application of the legislatures of two thirds of the several States, shall call a convention for proposing amendments, which in either case, shall be valid to all intents and purposes, as part of this Constitution, when ratified by the legislatures of three fourths of the several States, or by conventions in three fourths thereof, as the one or the other mode of ratification may be proposed by the Congress; Provided that no amendment which may be made prior to the year one thousand eight hundred and eight shall in any manner affect the first and fourth clauses in the ninth section of the first article; and that no State, without its consent, shall be deprived of its equal suffrage in the Senate.

### ARTICLE VI

1. All debts contracted and engagements entered into, before the adoption of this Constitution, shall be as valid against the United States under this Constitution, as under the Confederation.[10]

2. This Constitution, and the laws of the United States which shall be made in pursuance thereof; and all treaties made, or which shall be made, under the authority of the United States, shall be the supreme law of the land; and the Judges in every State shall be bound thereby, any thing in the Constitution or laws of any State to the contrary notwithstanding.

3. The senators and representatives before mentioned, and the members of the several State legislatures, and all executive and judicial officers, both of the United States and of the several States, shall be bound by oath or affirmation to support this Constitution; but no religious test shall ever be required as a qualification to any office or public trust under the United States.

### ARTICLE VII

The ratification of the conventions of nine States shall be sufficient for the establishment of this Constitution between the States so ratifying the same.

---

[7] See the 11th Amendment.
[8] See the 14th Amendment, Sec. 1.
[9] See the 13th Amendment.

[10] See the 14th Amendment, Sec. 4.

Done in Convention by the unanimous consent of the States present the seventeenth day of September in the year of our Lord one thousand seven hundred and eighty-seven, and of the independence of the United States of America the twelfth. In witness whereof we have hereunto subscribed our names.

[Names omitted]

\*   \*   \*

*Articles in addition to, and amendment of, the Constitution of the United States of America, proposed by Congress, and ratified by the legislatures of the several States, pursuant to the fifth article of the original Constitution.*

### AMENDMENT I [First ten amendments ratified December 15, 1791]

Congress shall make no law respecting an establishment of religion, or prohibiting the free exercise thereof; or abridging the freedom of speech, or of the press; or the right of the people peaceably to assemble, and to petition the government for a redress of grievances.

### AMENDMENT II

A well regulated militia, being necessary to the security of a free State, the right of the people to keep and bear arms, shall not be infringed.

### AMENDMENT III

No soldier shall, in time of peace be quartered in any house, without the consent of the owner, nor in time of war, but in a manner to be prescribed by law.

### AMENDMENT IV

The right of the people to secure in their persons, houses, papers, and effects, against unreasonable searches and seizures, shall not be violated, and no warrants shall issue, but upon probable cause, supported by oath or affirmation, and particularly describing the place to be searched, and the persons or things to be seized.

### AMENDMENT V

No person shall be held to answer for a capital, or otherwise infamous crime, unless on a presentment or indictment of a grand jury, except in cases arising in the land or naval forces, or in the militia, when in actual service in time of war or public danger; nor shall any person be subject for the same offense to be twice put in jeopardy of life or limb; nor shall be compelled in any criminal case to be a witness against himself, nor be deprived of life, liberty, or property, without due process of law; nor shall private property be taken for public use, without just compensation.

### AMENDMENT VI

In all criminal prosecutions, the accused shall enjoy the right to a speedy and public trial, by an impartial jury of the State and district wherein the crime shall have been committed, which district shall have been previously ascertained by law, and to be informed of the nature and cause of the accusation; to be confronted with the witnesses against him; to have compulsory process for obtaining witnesses in his favor, and to have the assistance of counsel for his defense.

### AMENDMENT VII

In suits at common law, where the value in controversy shall exceed twenty dollars, the right of trial by jury shall be preserved, and no fact tried by a jury shall be otherwise reëxamined in any court of the United States, than according to the rules of the common law.

### AMENDMENT VIII

Excessive bail shall not be required, nor excessive fines imposed, nor cruel and unusual punishments inflicted.

### AMENDMENT IX

The enumeration in the Constitution of certain rights shall not be construed to deny or disparage others retained by the people.

### AMENDMENT X

The powers not delegated to the United States by the Constitution, nor prohibited by it to the States, are reserved to the States respectively, or to the people.

### AMENDMENT XI [January 8, 1798]

The judicial power of the United States shall not be construed to extend to any suit in law or equity, commenced or prosecuted against one of the United States by citizens of another State, or by citizens or subjects of any foreign State.

### AMENDMENT XII [September 25, 1804]

The electors shall meet in their respective States, and vote by ballot for President and Vice President, one of whom, at least, shall not be an inhabitant of the same State with themselves; they shall name in their ballots the person voted for as President, and in distinct ballots the person voted for as Vice President, and they shall make distinct lists of all persons voted for as President and of all persons voted for as Vice President, and of the number of votes for each, which lists they shall sign and certify, and transmit sealed to the seat of the government of the United States, directed to the President of the Senate;—The President of the Senate shall, in the presence of the Senate and House of Representatives, open all the certificates and the votes shall then be counted;—The person having the greatest number of votes for President, shall be the President, if such number be a majority of the whole number of electors appointed; and if no person have such majority, then from the persons having the highest numbers not exceeding three on the list of those voted for as President, the House of Representatives shall choose immediately, by ballot, the President. But in choosing the President, the votes shall be taken by States, the representation from each State having one vote; a quorum for this purpose shall consist of a member or members from two thirds of the States, and a majority of all the States shall be necessary to a choice. And if the House of Representatives shall not choose a President whenever the right of choice shall devolve upon them, before the fourth day of March next following, then the Vice President shall act as President, as in the case of the death or other constitutional disability of the President. The person having the greatest number of votes as Vice President shall be the Vice President, if such number be a majority of the whole number of electors appointed, and if no person have a majority, then from the two highest numbers on the list, the Senate shall choose the Vice President; a quorum for the purpose shall consist of two thirds of the whole number of Senators, and a majority of the whole number shall be necessary to a choice. But no person constitutionally ineligible to the office of President shall be eligible to that of Vice President of the United States.

AMENDMENT XIII [December 18, 1865]

*Section 1.* Neither slavery nor involuntary servitude, except as a punishment for crime whereof the party shall have been duly convicted, shall exist within the United States, or any place subject to their jurisdiction.
*Section 2.* Congress shall have power to enforce this article by appropriate legislation.

AMENDMENT XIV [July 28, 1868]

*Section 1.* All persons born or naturalized in the United States, and subject to the jurisdiction thereof, are citizens of the United States and of the State wherein they reside. No State shall make or enforce any law which shall abridge the privileges or immunities of citizens of the United States; nor shall any State deprive any person of life, liberty, or property, without due process of law; nor deny to any person within its jurisdiction the equal protection of the laws.
*Section 2.* Representatives shall be apportioned among the several States according to their respective numbers, counting the whole number of persons in each State, excluding Indians not taxed. But when the right to vote at any election for the choice of electors for President and Vice President of the United States, representatives in Congress, the executive and judicial officers of a State, or the members of the legislature thereof, is denied to any of the male inhabitants of such State, being twenty-one years of age, and citizens of the United States, or in any way abridged, except for participating in rebellion, or other crime, the basis of representation therein shall be reduced in the proportion which the number of such male citizens shall bear to the whole number of male citizens twenty-one years of age in such State.
*Section 3.* No person shall be a senator or representative in Congress, or elector of President and Vice President, or hold any office, civil or military, under the United States, or under any State, who having previously taken an oath, as a member of Congress, or as an officer of the United States, or as a member of any State legislature, or as an executive or judicial officer of any State, to support the Constitution of the United States, shall have engaged in insurrection or rebellion against the same, or given aid or comfort to the enemies thereof. But Congress may by a vote of two thirds of each House, remove such disability.
*Section 4.* The validity of the public debt of the United States, authorized by law, including debts incurred for payment of pensions and bounties for services in suppressing insurrection or rebellion, shall not be questioned. But neither the United States nor any State shall assume or pay any debt or obligation incurred in aid of insurrection or rebellion against the United States, or any claim for the loss or emancipation of any slave; but all such debts, obligations, and claims shall be held illegal and void.
*Section 5.* The Congress shall have power to enforce, by appropriate legislation, the provisions of this article.

AMENDMENT XV [March 30, 1870]

*Section 1.* The right of citizens of the United States to vote shall not be denied or abridged by the United States or by any State on account of race, color, or previous condition of servitude.
*Section 2.* The Congress shall have power to enforce this article by appropriate legislation.

AMENDMENT XVI [February 25, 1913]

The Congress shall have power to lay and collect taxes on incomes, from whatever source derived, without apportionment among the several States, and without regard to any census or enumeration.

AMENDMENT XVII [May 31, 1913]

The Senate of the United States shall be composed of two senators from each State, elected by the people thereof, for six years; and each senator shall have one vote. The electors in each State shall have the qualifications requisite for electors of the most numerous branch of the State legislature.
When vacancies happen in the representation of any State in the Senate, the executive authority of such State shall issue writs of election to fill such vacancies: *Provided,* That the legislature of any State may empower the executive thereof to make temporary appointments until the people fill the vacancies by election as the legislature may direct.
This amendment shall not be so construed as to affect the election or term of any senator chosen

before it becomes valid as part of the Constitution.

### AMENDMENT XVIII [11] [January 29, 1919]

After one year from the ratification of this article, the manufacture, sale, or transportation of intoxicating liquors within, the importation thereof into, or the exportation thereof from the United States and all territory subject to the jurisdiction thereof for beverage purposes is thereby prohibited.

The Congress and the several States shall have concurrent power to enforce this article by appropriate legislation.

This article shall be inoperative unless it shall have been ratified as an amendment to the Constitution by the legislatures of the several States, as provided in the Constitution, within seven years from the date of the submission hereof to the States by Congress.

### AMENDMENT XIX [August 26, 1920]

The right of citizens of the United States to vote shall not be denied or abridged by the United States or by any State on account of sex.

Congress shall have the power to enforce this article by appropriate legislation.

### AMENDMENT XX [January 23, 1933]

*Section 1.* The terms of the President and Vice President shall end at noon on the 20th day of January, and the terms of Senators and Representatives at noon on the 3d day of January, of the years in which such terms would have ended if this article had not been ratified; and the terms of their successors shall then begin.

*Section 2.* The Congress shall assemble at least once in every year, and such meeting shall begin at noon on the 3d day of January, unless they shall by law appoint a different day.

*Section 3.* If, at the time fixed for the beginning of the term of President, the President-elect shall have died, the Vice President-elect shall become President. If a President shall not have been chosen before the time fixed for the beginning of his term, or if the President-elect shall have failed to qualify, then the Vice President-elect shall act as President until a President shall have qualified; and the Congress may by law provide for the case wherein neither a President-elect nor a Vice President-elect shall have qualified, declaring who shall then act as President, or the manner in which one who is to act shall be selected, and such person shall act accordingly until a President or Vice-President shall have qualified.

*Section 4.* The Congress may by law provide for the case of the death of any of the persons from whom the House of Representatives may choose a President whenever the right of choice shall have devolved upon them, and for the case of the death of any of the persons from whom the Senate may choose a Vice President whenever the right of choice shall have devolved upon them.

[11] Repealed by the 21st Amendment.

*Section 5.* Section 1 and 2 shall take effect on the 15th day of October following the ratification of this article.

*Section 6.* This article shall be inoperative unless it shall have been ratified as an amendment to the Constitution by the legislatures of three-fourths of the several States within seven years from the date of its submission.

### AMENDMENT XXI [December 5, 1933]

*Section 1.* The Eighteenth Article of amendment to the Constitution of the United States is hereby repealed.

*Section 2.* The transportation or importation into any State, Territory, or possession of the United States for delivery or use therein of intoxicating liquors in violation of the laws thereof, is hereby prohibited.

*Section 3.* This article shall be inoperative unless it shall have been ratified as an amendment to the Constitution by conventions in the several States, as provided in the Constitution, within seven years from the date of the submission thereof to the States by the Congress.

### AMENDMENT XXII [March 1, 1951]

No person shall be elected to the office of the President more than twice, and no person who has held the office of President, or acted as President, for more than two years of a term to which some other person was elected President shall be elected to the office of the President more than once.

But this article shall not apply to any person holding the office of President when this article was proposed by the Congress, and shall not prevent any person who may be holding the office of President, or acting as President, during the term within which this article becomes operative from holding the office of President or acting as President during the remainder of such term.

This article shall be inoperative unless it shall have been ratified as an amendment to the Constitution by the legislatures of three-fourths of the several States within seven years from the date of its submission to the States by the Congress.

### AMENDMENT XXIII [March 29, 1961]

*Section 1.* The District constituting the seat of Government of the United States shall appoint in such manner as the Congress may direct:

A number of electors of President and Vice President equal to the whole number of Senators and Representatives in Congress to which the District would be entitled if it were a State, but in no event more than the least populous State: they shall be in addition to those appointed by the States, but they shall be considered, for the purposes of the election of President and Vice President, to be electors appointed by a State; and they shall meet in the District and perform such duties as provided by the twelfth article of amendment.

*Section 2.* The Congress shall have power to enforce this article by appropriate legislation.

AMENDMENT XXIV [January 23, 1964]

*Section 1.* The right of citizens of the United States to vote in any primary or other election for President or Vice President, for electors for President or Vice President, or for Senator or Representative in Congress, shall not be denied or abridged by the United States or any State by reason of failure to pay any poll tax or other tax.

*Section 2.* The Congress shall have power to enforce this article by appropriate legislation.

AMENDMENT XXV [February 10, 1967]

*Section 1.* In case of the removal of the President from office or of his death or resignation, the Vice President shall become President.

*Section 2.* Whenever there is a vacancy in the office of the Vice President, the President shall nominate a Vice President who shall take office upon confirmation by a majority vote of both Houses of Congress.

*Section 3.* Whenever the President transmits to the President pro tempore of the Senate and the Speaker of the House of Representatives his written declaration that he is unable to discharge the powers and duties of his office, and until he transmits to them a written declaration to the contrary, such powers and duties shall be discharged by the Vice President as Acting President.

*Section 4.* Whenever the Vice President and a majority of either the principal officers of the exec-utive departments or of such other body as Congress may by law provide, transmit to the President pro tempore of the Senate and the Speaker of the House of Representatives their written declaration that the President is unable to discharge the powers and duties of his office, the Vice President shall immediately assume the powers and duties of the office as Acting President.

Thereafter, when the President transmits to the President pro tempore of the Senate and the Speaker of the House of Representatives his written declaration that no inability exists, he shall resume the powers and duties of his office unless the Vice President and a majority of either the principal officers of the executive departments or of such other body as Congress may by law provide, transmit within four days to the President pro tempore of the Senate and the Speaker of the House of Representatives their written declaration that the President is unable to discharge the powers and duties of his office. Thereupon Congress shall decide the issue, assembling within forty-eight hours for that purpose if not in session. If the Congress, within twenty-one days after receipt of the latter written declaration, or, if Congress is not in session, within twenty-one days after Congress is required to assemble, determines by two-thirds vote of both Houses that the President is unable to discharge the powers and duties of his office, the Vice President shall continue to discharge the same as Acting President; otherwise, the President shall resume the powers and duties of his office.

## Admission of States to the Union, 1787–1876

| | | | | | | | | |
|---|---|---|---|---|---|---|---|---|
| 1. | *Delaware* | Dec. 1, 1787 | 14. | *Vermont* | Mar. 4, 1791 | 27. | *Florida* | Mar. 3, 1845 |
| 2. | *Pennsylvania* | Dec. 12, 1787 | 15. | *Kentucky* | June 1, 1792 | 28. | *Texas* | Dec. 29, 1845 |
| 3. | *New Jersey* | Dec. 18, 1787 | 16. | *Tennessee* | June 1, 1796 | 29. | *Iowa* | Dec. 28, 1846 |
| 4. | *Georgia* | Jan. 2, 1788 | 17. | *Ohio* | Mar. 1, 1803 | 30. | *Wisconsin* | May 29, 1848 |
| 5. | *Connecticut* | Jan. 9, 1788 | 18. | *Louisiana* | Apr. 30, 1812 | 31. | *California* | Sept. 9, 1850 |
| 6. | *Massachusetts* | Feb. 6, 1788 | 19. | *Indiana* | Dec. 11, 1816 | 32. | *Minnesota* | May 11, 1858 |
| 7. | *Maryland* | Apr. 28, 1788 | 20. | *Mississippi* | Dec. 10, 1817 | 33. | *Oregon* | Feb. 14, 1859 |
| 8. | *South Carolina* | May 23, 1788 | 21. | *Illinois* | Dec. 3, 1818 | 34. | *Kansas* | Jan. 29, 1861 |
| 9. | *New Hampshire* | June 21, 1788 | 22. | *Alabama* | Dec. 14, 1819 | 35. | *West Virginia* | June 19, 1863 |
| 10. | *Virginia* | June 25, 1788 | 23. | *Maine* | Mar. 15, 1820 | 36. | *Nevada* | Oct. 31, 1864 |
| 11. | *New York* | July 26, 1788 | 24. | *Missouri* | Aug. 10, 1821 | 37. | *Nebraska* | Mar. 1, 1867 |
| 12. | *North Carolina* | Nov. 21, 1789 | 25. | *Arkansas* | June 15, 1836 | 38. | *Colorado* | July 1, 1876 |
| 13. | *Rhode Island* | May 29, 1790 | 26. | *Michigan* | Jan. 26, 1837 | | | |

## Justices of the United States Supreme Court, 1789–1877

| Name (Chief Justices in Italics) | Service (Term) | (Years) | Name (Chief Justices in Italics) | Service (Term) | (Years) |
|---|---|---|---|---|---|
| *John Jay* (N.Y.) | 1789–1795 | 6 | James M. Wayne (Ga.) | 1835–1867 | 32 |
| John Rutledge (S.C.) | 1789–1791 | 2 | *Roger B. Taney* (Md.) | 1836–1864 | 28 |
| William Cushing (Mass.) | 1789–1810 | 21 | Philip P. Barbour (Va.) | 1836–1841 | 5 |
| James Wilson (Pa.) | 1789–1798 | 9 | John Catron (Tenn.) | 1837–1865 | 28 |
| John Blair (Va.) | 1789–1796 | 7 | John McKinley (Ala.) | 1837–1852 | 15 |
| James Iredell (N.C.) | 1790–1799 | 9 | Peter V. Daniel (Va.) | 1841–1860 | 19 |
| Thomas Johnson (Md.) | 1792–1793 | ½ | Samuel Nelson (N.Y.) | 1845–1872 | 27 |
| William Paterson (N.J.) | 1793–1806 | 13 | Levi Woodbury (N.H.) | 1845–1851 | 6 |
| *John Rutledge* (S.C.)[1] | 1795–1795 | | Robert C. Grier (Pa.) | 1846–1870 | 24 |
| Samuel Chase (Md.) | 1796–1811 | 15 | Benjamin R. Curtis (Mass.) | 1851–1857 | 6 |
| *Oliver Ellsworth* (Conn.) | 1796–1800 | 4 | John A. Campbell (Ala.) | 1853–1861 | 8 |
| Bushrod Washington (Va.) | 1798–1829 | 31 | Nathan Clifford (Maine) | 1858–1881 | 23 |
| Alfred Moore (N.C.) | 1800–1804 | 4 | Noah H. Swayne (Ohio) | 1862–1881 | 19 |
| *John Marshall* (Va.) | 1801–1835 | 34 | Samuel F. Miller (Iowa) | 1862–1890 | 28 |
| William Johnson (S.C.) | 1804–1834 | 30 | David Davis (Ill.) | 1862–1877 | 15 |
| Brock. Livingston (N.Y.) | 1806–1823 | 17 | Stephen J. Field (Calif.) | 1863–1897 | 34 |
| Thomas Todd (Ky.) | 1807–1826 | 19 | *Salmon P. Chase* (Ohio) | 1864–1873 | 9 |
| Joseph Story (Mass.) | 1811–1845 | 34 | William Strong (Pa.) | 1870–1880 | 10 |
| Gabriel Duval (Md.) | 1811–1835 | 24 | Joseph P. Bradley (N.J.) | 1870–1892 | 22 |
| Smith Thompson (N.Y.) | 1823–1843 | 20 | Ward Hunt (N.Y.) | 1872–1882 | 10 |
| Robert Trimble (Ky.) | 1826–1828 | 2 | *Morrison R. Waite* (Ohio) | 1874–1888 | 14 |
| John McLean (Ohio) | 1829–1861 | 32 | John M. Harlan (Ky.) | 1877–1911 | 34 |
| Henry Baldwin (Pa.) | 1830–1844 | 14 | | | |

[1] Appointed and served one term, but not confirmed by the Senate.

## Presidents, Vice-Presidents, and Cabinet Members, 1789–1881

| President | | Vice-President | | Secretary of State | | Secretary of Treasury | |
|---|---|---|---|---|---|---|---|
| 1. George Washington<br>Federalist | 1789 | John Adams<br>Federalist | 1789 | T. Jefferson<br>E. Randolph<br>T. Pickering | 1789<br>1794<br>1795 | Alex. Hamilton<br>Oliver Wolcott | 1789<br>1795 |
| 2. John Adams<br>Federalist | 1797 | Thomas Jefferson<br>Democratic-<br>Republican | 1797 | T. Pickering<br>John Marshall | 1797<br>1800 | Oliver Wolcott<br>Samuel Dexter | 1797<br>1801 |
| 3. Thomas Jefferson<br>Democratic-<br>Republican | 1801 | Aaron Burr<br>Democratic-<br>Republican<br>George Clinton<br>Democratic-<br>Republican | 1801<br><br><br>1805 | James Madison | 1801 | Samuel Dexter<br>Albert Gallatin | 1801<br>1801 |
| 4. James Madison<br>Democratic-<br>Republican | 1809 | George Clinton<br>Independent-<br>Republican<br>Elbridge Gerry<br>Democratic-<br>Republican | 1809<br><br><br>1813 | Robert Smith<br>James Monroe | 1809<br>1811 | Albert Gallatin<br>H. W. Campbell<br>A. J. Dallas<br>W. H. Crawford | 1809<br>1814<br>1814<br>1816 |
| 5. James Monroe<br>Democratic-<br>Republican | 1817 | D. D. Thompkins<br>Democratic-<br>Republican | 1817 | J. Q. Adams | 1817 | W. H. Crawford | 1817 |
| 6. John Q. Adams<br>* | 1825 | John C. Calhoun<br>* | 1825 | Henry Clay | 1825 | Richard Rush | 1825 |
| 7. Andrew Jackson<br>Democrat | 1829 | John C. Calhoun<br>Democrat<br>Martin Van Buren<br>Democrat | 1829<br><br>1833 | M. Van Buren<br>E. Livingston<br>Louis McLane<br>John Forsyth | 1829<br>1831<br>1833<br>1834 | Sam D. Ingham<br>Louis McLane<br>W. J. Duane<br>Roger B. Taney<br>Levi Woodbury | 1820<br>1831<br>1833<br>1833<br>1834 |
| 8. Martin Van Buren<br>Democrat | 1837 | Richard M. Johnson<br>Democrat | 1837 | John Forsyth | 1837 | Levi Woodbury | 1837 |
| 9. William H. Harrison<br>Whig | 1841 | John Tyler<br>Whig | 1841 | Daniel Webster | 1841 | Thos. Ewing | 1841 |
| 10. John Tyler<br>Whig and<br>Democrat | 1841 | | | Daniel Webster<br>Hugh S. Legare<br>Abel P. Upshur<br>John C. Calhoun | 1841<br>1843<br>1843<br>1844 | Thos. Ewing<br>Walter Forward<br>John C. Spencer<br>Geo. M. Bibb | 1841<br>1841<br>1843<br>1844 |
| 11. James K. Polk<br>Democrat | 1845 | George M. Dallas<br>Democrat | 1845 | James Buchanan | 1845 | Robt. J. Walker | 1845 |
| 12. Zachary Taylor<br>Whig | 1849 | Millard Fillmore<br>Whig | 1849 | John M. Clayton | 1849 | Wm. M. Meredith | 1849 |
| 13. Millard Fillmore<br>Whig | 1850 | | | Daniel Webster<br>Edward Everett | 1850<br>1852 | Thomas Corwin | 1850 |
| 14. Franklin Pierce<br>Democrat | 1853 | William R. D. King<br>Democrat | 1853 | W. L. Marcy | 1853 | James Guthrie | 1853 |
| 15. James Buchanan<br>Democrat | 1857 | John C. Breckinridge<br>Democrat | 1857 | Lewis Cass<br>J. S. Black | 1857<br>1860 | Howell Cobb<br>Philip F. Thomas<br>John A. Dix | 1857<br>1860<br>1861 |
| 16. Abraham Lincoln<br>Republican | 1861 | Hannibal Hamlin<br>Republican<br>Andrew Johnson<br>Unionist | 1861<br><br>1865 | W. H. Seward | 1861 | Salmon P. Chase<br>W. P. Fessenden<br>Hugh McCulloch | 1861<br>1864<br>1865 |
| 17. Andrew Johnson<br>Unionist | 1865 | | | W. H. Seward | 1865 | Hugh McCulloch | 1865 |
| 18. Ulysses S. Grant<br>Republican | 1869 | Schuyler Colfax<br>Republican<br>Henry Wilson<br>Republican | 1869<br><br>1873 | E. B. Washburne<br>Hamilton Fish | 1869<br>1869 | Geo. S. Boutwell<br>W. A. Richardson<br>Benj. H. Bristow<br>Lot M. Morrill | 1869<br>1873<br>1874<br>1876 |
| 19. Rutherford B. Hayes<br>Republican | 1877 | William A. Wheeler<br>Republican | 1877 | W. M. Evarts | 1877 | John Sherman | 1877 |

* No distinct party designations.

| Secretary of War | Attorney-General | Postmaster-General † | Secretary of Navy | Secretary of Interior |
|---|---|---|---|---|
| Henry Knox 1789<br>T. Pickering 1795<br>Jas. McHenry 1796 | E. Randolph 1789<br>Wm. Bradford 1794<br>Charles Lee 1795 | Samuel Osgood 1789<br>Tim. Pickering 1791<br>Jos. Habersham 1795 | Established<br>April 30, 1798. | Established<br>March 3, 1849. |
| Jas. McHenry 1797<br>John Marshall 1800<br>Sam'l Dexter 1800<br>R. Griswold 1801 | Charles Lee 1797<br>Theo. Parsons 1801 | Jos. Habersham 1797 | Benj. Stoddert 1798 | |
| H. Dearborn 1801 | Levi Lincoln 1801<br>Robert Smith 1805<br>J. Breckinridge 1805<br>C. A. Rodney 1807 | Jos. Habersham 1801<br>Gideon Granger 1801 | Benj. Stoddert 1801<br>Robert Smith 1801<br>J. Crowninshield 1805 | |
| Wm. Eustis 1809<br>J. Armstrong 1813<br>James Monroe 1814<br>W. H. Crawford 1815 | C. A. Rodney 1809<br>Wm. Pinkney 1811<br>Richard Rush 1814 | Gideon Granger 1809<br>R. J. Meigs, Jr. 1814 | Paul Hamilton 1809<br>William Jones 1813<br>B. W. Crowninshield 1814 | |
| Isaac Shelby 1817<br>Geo. Graham 1817<br>J. C. Calhoun 1817 | Richard Rush 1817<br>William Wirt 1817 | R. J. Meigs, Jr. 1817<br>John McLean 1823 | B. W. Crowninshield 1817<br>Smith Thompson 1818<br>S. L. Southard 1823 | |
| Jas. Barbour 1825<br>Peter B. Porter 1828 | William Wirt 1825 | John McLean 1825 | S. L. Southard 1825 | |
| John H. Eaton 1829<br>Lewis Cass 1831<br>B. F. Butler 1837 | John M. Berrien 1829<br>Roger B. Taney 1831<br>B. F. Butler 1833 | Wm. T. Barry 1829<br>Amos Kendall 1835 | John Branch 1829<br>Levi Woodbury 1831<br>Mahlon Dickerson 1834 | |
| Joel R. Poinsett 1837 | B. F. Butler 1837<br>Felix Grundy 1838<br>H. D. Gilpin 1840 | Amos Kendall 1837<br>John M. Niles 1840 | Mahlon Dickerson 1837<br>Jas. K. Paulding 1838 | |
| John Bell 1841 | J. J. Crittenden 1841 | Francis Granger 1841 | George E. Badger 1841 | |
| John Bell 1841<br>John McLean 1841<br>J. C. Spencer 1841<br>Jas. M. Porter 1843<br>Wm. Wilkins 1844 | J. J. Crittenden 1841<br>Hugh S. Legare 1841<br>John Nelson 1843 | Francis Granger 1841<br>C. A. Wickliffe 1841 | George E. Badger 1841<br>Abel P. Upshur 1841<br>David Henshaw 1843<br>Thos. W. Gilmer 1844<br>John Y. Mason 1844 | |
| Wm. L. Marcy 1845 | John Y. Mason 1845<br>Nathan Clifford 1846<br>Isaac Toucey 1848 | Cave Johnson 1845 | George Bancroft 1845<br>John Y. Mason 1846 | |
| G. W. Crawford 1849 | Reverdy Johnson 1849 | Jacob Collamer 1849 | Wm. B. Preston 1849 | Thomas Ewing 1849 |
| C. M. Conrad 1850 | J. J. Crittenden 1850 | Nathan K. Hall 1850<br>Sam D. Hubbard 1852 | Wm. A. Graham 1850<br>John P. Kennedy 1852 | A. H. Stuart 1850 |
| Jefferson Davis 1853 | Caleb Cushing 1853 | James Campbell 1853 | James C. Dobbin 1853 | Robert McClelland 1853 |
| John B. Floyd 1857<br>Joseph Holt 1861 | J. S. Black 1857<br>Edw. M. Stanton 1860 | Aaron V. Brown 1857<br>Joseph Holt 1859 | Isaac Toucey 1857 | Jacob Thompson 1857 |
| S. Cameron 1861<br>E. M. Stanton 1862 | Edward Bates 1861<br>Titian J. Coffey 1863<br>James Speed 1864 | Horatio King 1861<br>M'tgomery Blair 1861<br>Wm. Dennison 1864 | Gideon Wells 1861 | Caleb B. Smith 1861<br>John P. Usher 1863 |
| E. M. Stanton 1865<br>U. S. Grant 1867<br>L. Thomas 1868<br>J. M. Schofield 1868 | James Speed 1865<br>Henry Stanbery 1866<br>Wm. M. Evarts 1868 | Wm. Dennison 1865<br>A. W. Randall 1866 | Gideon Wells 1865 | John P. Usher 1865<br>James Harlan 1865<br>O. H. Browning 1866 |
| J. A. Rawlins 1869<br>W. T. Sherman 1869<br>W. W. Belknap 1869<br>Alphonso Taft 1876<br>J. D. Cameron 1876 | E. R. Hoar 1869<br>A. T. Ackerman 1870<br>Geo. H. Williams 1871<br>Edw. Pierrepont 1875<br>Alphonso Taft 1876 | J. A. J. Creswell 1869<br>Jas. W. Marshall 1874<br>Marshall Jewell 1874<br>James N. Tyner 1876 | Adolph E. Borie 1869<br>Geo. M. Robeson 1869 | Jacob D. Cox 1869<br>C. Delano 1870<br>Zach. Chandler 1875 |
| G. W. McCrary 1877<br>Alex. Ramsey 1879 | Chas. Devens 1877 | David M. Key 1877<br>Horace Maynard 1880 | R. W. Thompson 1877<br>Nathan Goff, Jr. 1881 | Carl Schurz 1877 |

† Not in Cabinet until 1829.

## Presidential Elections, 1789–1876

| Year | Number of States | Candidates | Party | Popular vote | Electoral vote | Percentage of popular vote |
|------|------|------------|-------|--------------|----------------|----------------------------|
| 1789 | 11 | GEORGE WASHINGTON | No party designations | | 69 | |
| | | John Adams | | | 34 | |
| | | Other Candidates | | | 35 | |
| 1792 | 15 | GEORGE WASHINGTON | No party designations | | 132 | |
| | | John Adams | | | 77 | |
| | | George Clinton | | | 50 | |
| | | Other Candidates | | | 5 | |
| 1796 | 16 | JOHN ADAMS | Federalist | | 71 | |
| | | Thomas Jefferson | Democratic-Republican | | 68 | |
| | | Thomas Pinckney | Federalist | | 59 | |
| | | Aaron Burr | Democratic-Republican | | 30 | |
| | | Other Candidates | | | 48 | |
| 1800 | 16 | THOMAS JEFFERSON | Democratic-Republican | | 73 | |
| | | Aaron Burr | Democratic-Republican | | 73 | |
| | | John Adams | Federalist | | 65 | |
| | | Charles C. Pinckney | Federalist | | 64 | |
| | | John Jay | Federalist | | 1 | |
| 1804 | 17 | THOMAS JEFFERSON | Democratic-Republican | | 162 | |
| | | Charles C. Pinckney | Federalist | | 14 | |
| 1808 | 17 | JAMES MADISON | Democratic-Republican | | 122 | |
| | | Charles C. Pinckney | Federalist | | 47 | |
| | | George Clinton | Democratic-Republican | | 6 | |
| 1812 | 18 | JAMES MADISON | Democratic-Republican | | 128 | |
| | | DeWitt Clinton | Federalist | | 89 | |
| 1816 | 19 | JAMES MONROE | Democratic-Republican | | 183 | |
| | | Rufus King | Federalist | | 34 | |
| 1820 | 24 | JAMES MONROE | Democratic-Republican | | 231 | |
| | | John Quincy Adams | Independent Republican | | 1 | |
| 1824 | 24 | JOHN QUINCY ADAMS | Democratic-Republican | 108,740 | 84 | 30.5 |
| | | Andrew Jackson | Democratic-Republican | 153,544 | 99 | 43.1 |
| | | William H. Crawford | Democratic-Republican | 46,618 | 41 | 13.1 |
| | | Henry Clay | Democratic-Republican | 47,136 | 37 | 13.2 |
| 1828 | 24 | ANDREW JACKSON | Democrat | 647,286 | 178 | 56.0 |
| | | John Quincy Adams | National Republican | 508,064 | 83 | 44.0 |
| 1832 | 24 | ANDREW JACKSON | Democrat | 687,502 | 219 | 55.0 |
| | | Henry Clay | National Republican | 530,189 | 49 | 42.4 |
| | | William Wirt | Anti-Masonic | 33,108 | 7 | 2.6 |
| | | John Floyd | National Republican | | 11 | |
| 1836 | 26 | MARTIN VAN BUREN | Democrat | 765,483 | 170 | 50.9 |
| | | William H. Harrison | Whig | | 73 | |
| | | Hugh L. White | Whig | 739,795 | 26 | 49.1 |
| | | Daniel Webster | Whig | | 14 | |
| | | W. P. Mangum | Whig | | 11 | |
| 1840 | 26 | WILLIAM H. HARRISON | Whig | 1,274,624 | 234 | 53.1 |
| | | Martin Van Buren | Democrat | 1,127,781 | 60 | 46.9 |
| 1844 | 26 | JAMES K. POLK | Democrat | 1,338,464 | 170 | 49.6 |
| | | Henry Clay | Whig | 1,300,097 | 105 | 48.1 |
| | | James G. Birney | Liberty | 62,300 | | 2.3 |
| 1848 | 30 | ZACHARY TAYLOR | Whig | 1,360,967 | 163 | 47.4 |
| | | Lewis Cass | Democrat | 1,222,342 | 127 | 42.5 |
| | | Martin Van Buren | Free Soil | 291,263 | | 10.1 |
| 1852 | 31 | FRANKLIN PIERCE | Democrat | 1,601,117 | 254 | 50.9 |
| | | Winfield Scott | Whig | 1,385,453 | 42 | 44.1 |
| | | John P. Hale | Free Soil | 155,825 | | 5.0 |
| 1856 | 31 | JAMES BUCHANAN | Democrat | 1,832,955 | 174 | 45.3 |
| | | John C. Frémont | Republican | 1,339,932 | 114 | 33.1 |
| | | Millard Fillmore | American | 871,731 | 8 | 21.6 |
| 1860 | 33 | ABRAHAM LINCOLN | Republican | 1,865,593 | 180 | 39.8 |
| | | Stephen A. Douglas | Democrat | 1,382,713 | 12 | 29.5 |
| | | John C. Breckinridge | Democrat | 848,356 | 72 | 18.1 |
| | | John Bell | Constitutional Union | 592,906 | 39 | 12.6 |
| 1864 | 36 | ABRAHAM LINCOLN | Republican | 2,206,938 | 212 | 55.0 |
| | | George B. McClellan | Democrat | 1,803,787 | 21 | 45.0 |
| 1868 | 37 | ULYSSES S. GRANT | Republican | 3,013,421 | 214 | 52.7 |
| | | Horatio Seymour | Democrat | 2,706,829 | 80 | 47.3 |
| 1872 | 37 | ULYSSES S. GRANT | Republican | 3,596,745 | 286 | 55.6 |
| | | Horace Greeley | Democrat | 2,843,446 | * | 43.9 |
| 1876 | 38 | RUTHERFORD B. HAYES | Republican | 4,036,572 | 185 | 48.0 |
| | | Samuel J. Tilden | Democrat | 4,284,020 | 184 | 51.0 |

Percentage of popular vote given for any election year may not total 100 per cent because candidates receiving less than 1 per cent of the popular vote have been omitted.

Prior to the passage of the Twelfth Amendment in 1804, the electoral college voted for two presidential candidates; the runner-up became Vice-President. Data from *Historical Statistics of the United States, Colonial Times to 1957* (1961), pp. 682–683, and *The World Almanac.*

# INDEX

*Page numbers in italics refer to illustrations.*

701